THE HOME BOOK
OF
AMERICAN
QUOTATIONS

THE HOME BOOK
OF
AMERICAN
QUOTATIONS

SELECTED AND ARRANGED BY
BRUCE BOHLE

Gramercy Publishing Company
New York

This 1986 edition is published by Gramercy Publishing Company,
distributed by Crown Publishers, Inc., by arrangement with
Dodd, Mead & Company, Inc.

Printed and Bound in the United States of America

Library of Congress Cataloging-in-Publication Data

Home book of American quotations.

   Reprint. Originally published: New York : Dodd, Mead, 1967.
   Includes index.
   1. Quotations, American.   I. Bohle, Bruce.
PN6081.H634   1986   081   86-3119

ISBN: 0-517-60356-X
h g f e d c b a

PREFATORY NOTE

THE HOME BOOK OF AMERICAN QUOTATIONS is patterned on Stevenson's HOME BOOK OF QUOTATIONS, a classic reference work that draws its material from all times and nations. But though the two are similar in structure, this book, by being exclusively American, has an identity and character of its own. It is hard to define that character; perhaps Mark Twain came close to it when he wrote, "Some of those old American words do have a kind of bully swing to them." And some of the new ones, too.

Understandably, this collection gives prominence to topics that are distinctively American —for example, advertising and sports. It reflects, as well, a lively American interest in politics and humor. But along with this vein of colloquialism there is generous representation of the thoughts of Emerson, Thoreau, Franklin, Jefferson, Lincoln, Santayana, the Roosevelts, Woodrow Wilson, John F. Kennedy, Adlai Stevenson, and many others, together with selections from authors ranging from Longfellow to Robert Frost. The compiler, in short, has striven to include as many worthy sources as possible.

The sources are American (by birth, naturalization, or, in a very few cases, by adoption or long association), or they are non-American but deal specifically with America. The quotations are grouped according to subject matter and are presented alphabetically (or, in a few instances, chronologically) under each subject heading. There is one exception to this order of presentation within a topic heading: where two or more quotations are closely related and thus logically belong together, they are so presented, regardless of alphabetical order. In such cases only the first (main) quotation of the group is numbered. The numbers given to the individual quotations, and the numbers of the pages on which the quotations appear, are keyed to corresponding numbers in the concordance, an index of key words that will help the reader locate individual selections with which he is reasonably familiar (familiar, at least, to the extent of knowing a key word or words). The reader is advised, as well, to make use of the cross references supplied under many subject headings in the body of the book. Thus, under Ambition he will find a group of quotations, together with the suggestion that he "see also" related material at Aspiration and Fame.

Those who are familiar with anthologies of this sort realize that the books grow with succeeding editions. None of them contains all "the quotations," any more than a single edition of a dictionary contains all "the words." A book of quotations covering an appreciable span of time begins with certain classic sayings, of which "Taxation without representation is tyranny" is an example. A limited number of other quotations of this sort, from the writings and speeches of noted men of the past that have stood the test of time and frequent repetition, provide the foundation. But what of the vast body of new material, contemporary with the compiler, that history has not had the chance to judge fully? To fail to make good use of it would deprive the collection of a measure of significance for the compiler's own day and age. And perhaps for succeeding generations as well, since many quotations are not only born but made. So the compiler selects also new material that seems most likely to endure and that is most likely to serve his current readers.

Because an effort was made to present as many points of view as possible on controversial subjects, some quotations are in direct contradiction. On reflection, the reader will see that such conflict in itself is proof that the mere presentation of a statement in a book such as this does not constitute an endorsement of it. The compiler functions as an editor, not as a censor or advocate. To quote a man is not necessarily to subscribe to what he says.

BRUCE BOHLE

TABLE OF CONTENTS

D

E

F

T

U

V

W

Y

Z

A

ABSENCE

See also Parting

1

Distance only lends enchantment,
  Though the ocean waves divide;
Absence makes the heart grow fonder,
  Longing to be near your side.
  ARTHUR GILLESPIE, *Absence Makes the Heart Grow Fonder.*

2

Two evils, monstrous either one apart,
Possessed me, and were long and loath at
    going:
A cry of Absence, Absence, in the heart,
And in the wood the furious winter blowing.
  JOHN CROWE RANSOM, *Winter Remembered.*

3

Jest a-wearyin' fer you—
All the time a-feelin' blue.
  FRANK L. STANTON, *Wearyin' fer You.*

4

'Tis said that absence conquers love,
  But oh! believe it not;
I've tried, alas! its power to prove,
  But thou are not forgot.
  FREDERICK WILLIAM THOMAS, *Song.*

ACCIDENT, see Chance

ACT, ACTION

See also Deeds; Extremes; Fanaticism

5

We are taught by great actions that the universe is the property of every individual in
it.
  EMERSON, *Nature, Addresses, and Lectures: Beauty.*

6

Why should we be cowed by the name of
Action? . . . The rich mind lies in the sun
and sleeps, and is Nature. To think is to
act.
  EMERSON, *Essays, First Series: Spiritual Laws.*

7

Act, if you like,—but you do it at your peril.
Men's actions are too strong for them. Show
me a man who has acted and who has not
been the victim and slave of his action.
  EMERSON, *Representative Men: Goethe.*

8

I see how many firm acts have been done;
how many valiant *noes* have this day been

spoken, when others would have uttered ruinous *yeas.*
  EMERSON, *Essays, Second Series: Character.*

9

The frontier experience taught us the great
value of individual initiative and self-reliance . . . But the individualism of the frontier . . . has generated impatience with the
complex and tedious procedures of law and
glorified the virtues of direct individual action. It has instilled in us an easy familiarity
with violence and vigilante justice. In the
romanticized form in which it permeates the
television and other mass media, the mythology of the frontier conveys the message that
killing a man is not bad as long as you don't
shoot him in the back, that violence is only
reprehensible when its purpose is bad and
that in fact it is commendable and glorious
when it is perpetrated by good men for a
good purpose.
  J. W. FULBRIGHT, Address in Washington,
    D.C., 5 Dec., 1963.

10

In this era of nuclear weapons and cold war,
we live with constant crises and the continuing and immediate danger of incineration by
hydrogen bombs. We are a people who have
faced dangers before but we have always
been able to overcome them by direct and
immediate action. Now we are confronted
with dangers vastly greater than we or any
other nation has ever before known and we
see no end to them and no solutions to them.
Nor are there any solutions. There are only
possibilities, limited, intermittent, and ambiguous, to alleviate the dangers of our time.
For the rest, we have no choice but to try to
live with the unsolved problems of a revolutionary world.
  J. W. FULBRIGHT, Address in Washington,
    D.C., 5 Dec., 1963.

11

It is not book learning young men need, nor
instruction about this and that, but a stiffening of the vertebrae which will cause them to
be loyal to a trust, to act promptly, to concentrate their energies, do a thing—"carry a
message to Garcia."
  ELBERT HUBBARD, *A Message to Garcia,*
    first published in *The Philistine,* March,
    1900. Lieut. Andrew S. Rowan, Bureau
    of Military Intelligence, was the man

who carried the message to Garcia, 1 May, 1898.

1

Lyndon acts like there was never going to be a tomorrow.

> CLAUDIA TAYLOR (MRS. LYNDON B.) JOHNSON, referring to her husband. Quoted as an oft-spoken remark. (*New York Times Magazine*, 29 Nov., 1964, p. 28)

2

Let's get this thing airborne.

> LYNDON B. JOHNSON, Order, to subordinates aboard the presidential plane in Dallas, 22 Nov., 1963, a few minutes after he was sworn into office following the assassination of John F. Kennedy. The order directed a return to Washington, D.C. (H. A. ZEIGER, *Lyndon B. Johnson: Man and President,* p. 10)

3

Trust no Future, howe'er pleasant!
Let the dead Past bury its dead!
Act,—act in the living Present!
Heart within, and God o'erhead!

> H. W. LONGFELLOW, *A Psalm of Life.*

4

No action, whether foul or fair,
Is ever done, but it leaves somewhere
A record, written by fingers ghostly,
As a blessing or a curse, and mostly
In the greater weakness or greater strength
Of the acts which follow it.

> H. W. LONGFELLOW, *The Golden Legend,* Pt. ii.

5

Every man feels instinctively that all the beautiful sentiments in the world weigh less than a single lovely action.

> J. R. LOWELL, *Among My Books: Rousseau and the Sentimentalists.*

6

Actions speak louder than words.

> This maxim is part of the literature of all languages.

7

Fear God and Take Your Own Part.

> THEODORE ROOSEVELT, Title of book.

ACTING, ACTORS

See also Stage

8

An actor is a sculptor who carves in snow.

> LAWRENCE BARRETT (attributed to him by Wilton Lackaye).

9

For an actress to be a success she must have the face of Venus, the brains of Minerva, the grace of Terpsichore, the memory of Macaulay, the figure of Juno, and the hide of a rhinoceros.

> ETHEL BARRYMORE. (G. J. NATHAN, *The Theatre in the Fifties*)

10

You will realize, too, that to be an actor you also have to be a human being. You will have to seek education and culture, and you will have to develop a deep understanding and affection for human nature. I remember my beginnings very well. I also remember each heartache and obstacle. But someday, you may say, as I do, that it's worth it.

> RALPH BELLAMY, Foreword to *Opportunities in Acting,* by DICK MOORE. As president of Actors' Equity Association, the actors' union of the legitimate stage, Bellamy was addressing himself to stagestruck readers.

11

His life was what the marquees describe as a "continuous performance."

> JOHN MASON BROWN, writing of Alexander Woollcott in the introduction to *The Portable Woollcott.*

12

Then there are no more actors.

> RUFUS CHOATE, on hearing of the death of Junius Brutus Booth in 1852.

The Artist is a rare, rare breed. There were but two, forsooth,
In all me time (the stage's prime!) and The Other One was Booth.

> EDMUND VANCE COOKE, *The Other One Was Booth* (referring to Edwin Booth).

It's a great loss—there's damned few of us left.

> JOHN L. SULLIVAN, reacting to the death of Edwin Booth.

13

He played the King as though he expected someone to play the ace.

> EUGENE FIELD, commenting on the unsuccessful performance of a luckless actor in the title role of *King Lear.* This quip, which has become a classic of drama criticism, appeared in a review in the Denver *Post.*

14

Yes, films are a director's medium, not an actor's. . . . And on the stage, in contrast to films, if you're clicking, it's like rising in an emotional graph to the end. . . . it's like an airplane rising from sluggish water, balanced on the step under its belly. . . . That's the feeling you can get, with luck. You're sailing. You say to yourself, "Tonight you're gonna soar, baby."

> HENRY FONDA, Interview, New York *Times,* 26 Apr., 1964.

When you act in television you know you do not really mean much to your audience. You do not move your audience. Television is a built-in mediocrity because it is not drama.

It is just an adjunct of the advertising business.

> DANA ANDREWS, Interview with Murray Schumach, New York *Times*, 22 Dec., 1963, shortly after Andrews' election as president of the Screen Actors Guild.

1

An actress's life is so transitory—suddenly you're a building.

> HELEN HAYES, commenting in Nov., 1955, on the news that a New York theater was being renamed for her.

2

It worries me to beat the band
To hear folks say our life is grand;
Wish they'd try some one-night stand—
Ain't it awful, Mabel?

> JOHN EDWARD HAZZARD, *Ain't It Awful, Mabel?*

3

And on the last day when we leave those we love
And move in a mournful procession,
I hope we'll both play star engagements above,
For I'm sure they "admit the profession."

> JOSEPH JEFFERSON, Letter to Laurence Hutton.

4

Life has its heroes and its villains, its soubrettes and its ingenues, and all roles may be acted well.

> J. W. KRUTCH, *The Modern Temper*.

5

Too lined for Hamlet, on the whole;
For tragic Lear, too coarsely built,
Himself becomes his favorite role,
Played daily to the hilt.

> PHYLLIS MCGINLEY, *The Love Letters of Phyllis McGinley: The Old Actor*.

6

Actors and actresses revel in applause. They tingle to critical cheers. Save for these ecstasies, they're happiest when looking into a mirror.

> RICHARD MANEY, *Fanfare*, p. 216.

7

"Ham," a poor and generally fatuous performer, was originally "ham fatter," a neophyte in the minstrel ranks, forced to sing "Ham Fat," an old ditty of the George Christy days.

> EDWARD B. MARKS, *They All Sang*.

A little ham is an asset to the actor. It contributes to his color and charm. But an all-out ham can be as obnoxious as a drunk on a roller-coaster. Ham is not peculiar to actors. All the theatre's workers are infected.

> RICHARD MANEY, *Fanfare* (1957), p. 274.

8

My preoccupation with my career is minimal. Acting isn't really a creative profession. It's an interpretative one.

> PAUL NEWMAN, Interview with Hal Boyle of the Associated Press, 27 July, 1964.

9

Her name, cut clear upon this marble cross,
Shines, as it shone when she was still on earth;
While tenderly the mild, agreeable moss
Obscures the figures of her date of birth.

> DOROTHY PARKER, *The Actress*.

10

I think one of the deaths of Hollywood is that producers tried to make everybody normal. Nobody would be in this business if he were normal. When you think of the people you knew—all the Barrymores, Errol Flynn, Charles Laughton—they were eccentrics. I don't want to read about some of these actresses who are around today. They sound like my niece in Scarsdale. I love my niece in Scarsdale, but I won't buy tickets to see her act.

> VINCENT PRICE, Interview with Joseph Finnigan, United Press International, 28 Feb., 1964.

11

Actors are like politicians, and politicians are like actors. They both spend time each day contemplating their image. They both have a desire to be loved.

> GORE VIDAL, Interview, New York *Times*, 6 Oct., 1963.

12

Every now and then, when you're on stage, you hear the best sound a player can hear. . . . It is the sound of a wonderful, deep silence that means you've hit them where they live.

> SHELLEY WINTERS, *That Wonderful, Deep Silence; Theatre Arts*, June, 1956.

ADAM AND EVE

13

The fall of the first Adam was the end of the beginning; the rise of the second Adam was the beginning of the end.

> S. W. DUFFIELD, *Fragments*.

14

What you have told us is all very good. It is indeed bad to eat apples. It is better to make them all into cider.

> BENJAMIN FRANKLIN, *Remarks Concerning the Savages of North America*. (This remark was an Indian's response to a missionary's recital of the story of Adam and Eve.)

15

Adam
Had 'em.

> STRICKLAND GILLILAN, *Lines on the Antiquity of Microbes*.

Was the apple applesauce
Eve ate in the garden?
Aren't you all a total loss?
No? I beg your pardon!
> SAMUEL HOFFENSTEIN, *Poems in Praise of Practically Nothing.* No. 4.

1
Adam was but human—this explains it all. He did not want the apple for the apple's sake, he wanted it only because it was forbidden.
> MARK TWAIN, *Pudd'nhead Wilson's Calendar.*

2
Whoever has lived long enough to find out what life is, knows how deep a debt of gratitude we owe to Adam, the first great benefactor of our race. He brought death into the world.
> MARK TWAIN, *Pudd'nhead Wilson's Calendar.*

3
In Adam's fall We sinnèd all.
> UNKNOWN, *The New England Primer.*

ADAPTABILITY

4
Make yourself necessary to somebody.
> EMERSON, *Conduct of Life: Considerations by the Way.*

5
We must make the best of those ills which cannot be avoided.
> ALEXANDER HAMILTON, Letter to Mrs. Hamilton, 20 Feb., 1801.

6
I make the most of all that comes
And the least of all that goes.
> SARA TEASDALE, *The Philosopher.*

7
Mrs. Akemit was not only like St. Paul, "all things to all men," but she had gone a step beyond that excellent theologue. She could be all things to one man.
> HARRY LEON WILSON, *The Spenders.*

ADMIRATION

See also Affection, Love

8
I love Henry, but I cannot like him; and as for taking his arm, I should as soon think of taking the arm of an elm-tree.
> EMERSON, *Lectures and Biographical Sketches: Thoreau.* Quoting a friend of Henry D. Thoreau.

9
However incumbent it may be on most of us to do our duty, there is, in spite of a thousand narrow dogmatisms, nothing in the world that any one is under the least obligation to *like*—not even (one braces one's self to risk the declaration) a particular kind of writing.
> HENRY JAMES, *Flaubert.*

10
Assuredly nobody will care for him who cares for nobody.
> THOMAS JEFFERSON, *Letter to Maria Cosway* (1786).

ADVERSITY

See also Misfortune, Trouble

11
They seemed Like old companions in adversity.
> BRYANT, *A Winter Piece.*

12
You can't keep a good man down.
> M. F. CAREY, Title and refrain of song (1900).

13
Bad times have a scientific value. These are occasions a good learner would not miss.
> EMERSON, *Conduct of Life: Considerations by the Way.*

14
Strong men greet war, tempest, hard times. They wish, as Pindar said, "to tread the floors of hell, with necessities as hard as iron."
> EMERSON, *Letters and Social Aims: Progress of Culture.*

15
A nation is molded by the tests that its peoples meet and master.
> LYNDON B. JOHNSON, News Conference, Johnson City, Tex., 20 Mar., 1965.

16
The bravest sight in all this world is a man fighting against odds.
> FRANKLIN K. LANE, *The Unconquerable Soul.*

17
Let us be patient! These severe afflictions
  Not from the ground arise,
But oftentimes celestial benedictions
  Assume this dark disguise.
> LONGFELLOW, *Resignation.*

18
    Whom unmerciful disaster
Followed fast and followed faster.
> EDGAR ALLAN POE, *The Raven.*

ADVERTISING

See also Publicity

19
Good times, bad times, there will always be advertising. In good times, people want to advertise; in bad times, they have to.
> BRUCE BARTON. (*Town & Country,* Feb., 1955)

20
The first law in advertising is to avoid the concrete promise . . . and cultivate the delightfully vague.
> JOHN CROSBY, Column, New York *Herald Tribune,* 18 Aug., 1947. He was referring specifically to broadcasting commercials.

1

Commercials on television are similar to sex and taxes; the more talk there is about them, the less likely they are to be curbed.

> JACK GOULD, Column, New York *Times*, 20 Oct., 1963.

2

Who's kidding whom? What's the difference between Giant and Jumbo? Quart and *full* quart? Two-ounce and *big* two-ounce? What does Extra Long mean? What's a *tall* 24-inch? And what busy shopper can tell?

> MARYA MANNES. (*Life*, 12 June, 1964, p. 64)

3

I think that I shall never see
A billboard lovely as a tree.
Indeed, unless the billboards fall
I'll never see a tree at all.

> OGDEN NASH, *Song of the Open Road.*

4

You wouldn't tell lies to your own wife. Don't tell them to mine. Do as you would be done by. If you tell lies about a product, you will be found out—either by the Government, which will prosecute you, or by the consumer, who will punish you by not buying your product a second time.

> DAVID OGILVY, *Confessions of an Advertising Man,* ch. 5.

5

It is a mistake to use highfalutin language when you advertise to uneducated people. I once used the word *obsolete* in a headline, only to discover that 43 per cent of the housewives had no idea of what it meant. In another headline, I used the word *ineffable*, only to discover that I didn't know what it meant myself.

> DAVID OGILVY, *Confessions of an Advertising Man,* ch. 6, ii.

6

The Hidden Persuaders.

> VANCE PACKARD, Title of book (1955).

7

That "producer's economy," then beginning to prevail in America, which first creates articles and then attempts to create a demand for them; an economy that has flooded the country with breakfast foods, shaving soaps, poets, and professors of philosophy.

> GEORGE SANTAYANA, *Persons and Places.*

8

The walking-stick serves the purpose of an advertisement that the bearer's hands are employed otherwise than in useful effort, and it therefore has utility as an evidence of leisure.

> THORSTEIN VEBLEN, *The Theory of the Leisure Class.* Chapt. 10.

9

As far as I'm concerned, Pierre Salinger is a bar of soap, and we're going to sell him as effectively as we can.

> CHRISTY WALSH, JR., Statement to reporters, 20 May, 1964, describing his technique in publicizing Salinger during the latter's campaign for the Democratic senatorial nomination in California in 1964. Walsh, a former advertising executive, was referring to a "saturation technique" employing a series of "spot" television appearances by the candidate.

10

Half the money I spend on advertising is wasted, and the trouble is I don't know which half.

> JOHN WANAMAKER. Credited originally to the first Lord Leverhulme. (DAVID OGILVY, *Confessions of an Advertising Man,* ch. 3)

11

The codfish lays ten thousand eggs,
   The homely hen lays one.
The codfish never cackles
   To tell you what she's done.
And so we scorn the codfish,
   While the humble hen we prize,
Which only goes to show you
   That it pays to advertise.

> UNKNOWN, *It Pays to Advertise.*

Famous Slogans

12

Steinway: the instrument of the immortals.

> N. W. AYER AND SON (Philadelphia agency), 1928.

13

Eventually, why not now?

> Attributed to BENJAMIN S. BULL, 1907, for Gold Medal Flour. The slogan was acquired in 1928 by General Mills, Inc.

14

Kodak.

> GEORGE EASTMAN, Trade-mark (1888). Eastman declared, "I devised the name myself. A trade-mark should be short, vigorous, incapable of being misspelled to an extent that will destroy its identity, and—in order to satisfy trade-mark laws—it must mean nothing." (I. E. LAMBERT, *The Public Accepts.*)

15

At 2 a.m. a thousand babies need their bottles—your light company is still up and dressed.

> FULLER AND SMITH (Cleveland agency), 1928, for Westinghouse Electric Corp.

16

Before you invest—investigate.

> Attributed to S. P. HALLE, Cleveland Better Business Bureau, and later adopted by the National Better Business Bureau and its affiliates.

1

57 varieties.

Attributed to H. J. HEINZ of the company bearing his name. Adopted in 1896 and registered in 1907. The idea is said to have been inspired by an advertisement for shoes that enumerated varied styles. (I. E. LAMBERT, *The Public Accepts.*)

2

Nature in the raw is seldom mild.

GEORGE WASHINGTON HILL (Lucky Strike cigarettes).

Reach for a Lucky instead of a sweet.

GEORGE WASHINGTON HILL (Lucky Strike cigarettes). In 1964, just after publication of the Surgeon General's report linking cigarette smoking with serious diseases, some candy makers paraphrased the original slogan: "Reach for a sweet instead."

It's toasted.

ANONYMOUS (Lucky Strike cigarettes).

L-S-M-F-T. Lucky Strike means fine tobacco.

ANONYMOUS.

3

The watch that made the dollar famous.

Attributed to R. H. INGERSOLL. According to I. E. LAMBERT, in *The Public Accepts,* Ingersoll once discovered, at a social gathering, that his hostess could not recall his name but readily identified him with the inexpensive watch his company made.

4

Embarrassing moments: when you have been making funny remarks about the party—and find it's your hostess you are talking to—be nonchalant—light a Murad.

LENNEN AND MITCHELL (New York agency), 1928, for P. Lorillard Co. This was one of a series of advertisements that offered a variety of "embarrassing moments."

5

Obey that impulse.

THOMAS L. MASSON, Subscription Slogan (1895) for the old *Life*. Masson was its editor for many years.

6

MILD enough for anybody . . . and yet *they satisfy*.

NEWELL-EMMETT Co. (New York agency), 1928, for Liggett and Myers Tobacco Co. (Chesterfield cigarettes).

7

Say it with flowers.

PATRICK F. O'KEEFE, Slogan, Society of American Florists (1917).

8

Ask the man who owns one.

Attributed to JAMES WARD PACKARD, one of the pioneer builders of Packard automobiles. During the early years of the company, he is said to have been asked for descriptive material on its product; lacking such material, he is said to have advised the prospective customer to seek the word-of-mouth testimonial suggested by the slogan, which first appeared in 1903. (I. E. LAMBERT, *The Public Accepts.*)

9

Keep that schoolgirl complexion.

Attributed to CHARLES S. PEARCE, c. 1917, for the Palmolive Co., later Colgate-Palmolive Co.

10

From contented cows.

Attributed to HELEN SHAW THOMPSON, an advertising copywriter for the Carnation Co., by E. A. Stuart, a company officer. (I. E. LAMBERT, *The Public Accepts.*)

11

The skin you love to touch.

J. WALTER THOMPSON Co. (Cincinnati office), c. 1910, for Woodbury's facial soap.

12

The ham what am.

ANONYMOUS, c. 1900, for Armour and Co.

13

Hasn't scratched yet.

ANONYMOUS, for Bon Ami Co.

14

When better automobiles are built, Buick will build them.

ANONYMOUS.

15

I'd walk a mile for a Camel.

ANONYMOUS.

16

Sleep like a kitten.

ANONYMOUS, 1933, for Chesapeake and Ohio Railway Co.

17

The pause that refreshes.

ANONYMOUS (Coca-Cola).

18

The more you eat, the more you want.

ANONYMOUS (Cracker-Jack).

19

Banish tattletale gray.

ANONYMOUS (Fels-Naptha soap).

20

When it's time to re-tire, buy a Fisk.

ANONYMOUS. This slogan, with art work depicting a yawning child in a one-piece pajama suit with a tire slung over his shoulder, first appeared in 1907. The illustration was created by Burr Giffen for Fisk Rubber Co. and later used by the successor firm, United States Rubber Co. (I. E. LAMBERT, *The Public Accepts.*)

1
Children cry for it.
ANONYMOUS (Fletcher's Castoria).

2
Watch the Fords go by.
ANONYMOUS, c. 1908.

3
Good to the last drop.
ANONYMOUS (General Foods Corp., for Maxwell House Coffee). At least one source, I. E. LAMBERT in *The Public Accepts,* credits the slogan to Theodore Roosevelt. The latter is said to have coined it in 1907, in complimenting his host, Joel Cheek, who perfected this blend.

4
See America first.
ANONYMOUS. The popularity of this slogan is credited to Louis W. Hill, Sr., of St. Paul, who used it extensively in advertising the Great Northern Railway in 1914, at which time he was president of that line. He did not claim authorship, however. (I. E. LAMBERT, *The Public Accepts.*)

5
Even your best friends won't tell you.
ANONYMOUS (Listerine).

6
When it rains, it pours.
ANONYMOUS, 1911. (Morton Salt Co.)

7
Uneeda Biscuit.
ANONYMOUS (National Biscuit Co.). First used about 1899.

8
Not a cough in a carload.
ANONYMOUS (Old Gold cigarettes).

9
Call for Philip Morris.
ANONYMOUS.

10
99-44/100 per cent pure.
ANONYMOUS, 1883, for Procter and Gamble Co. (Ivory soap).

11
It floats.
ANONYMOUS (Procter and Gamble Co., Ivory soap).

12
His master's voice.
ANONYMOUS. The illustration for this famous slogan, a listening dog, was created by Francis Barraud for the Gramophone Co., Ltd. of London. The slogan and illustration eventually became the property of the Radio Corp. of America, successor to the Victor Talking Machine Co., which had succeeded the Gramophone Co. (I. E. LAMBERT, *The Public Accepts.*)

13
The beer that made Milwaukee famous.
ANONYMOUS, c. 1895, for Joseph Schlitz Brewing Co.

14
Motorists wise—Simoniz.
ANONYMOUS.

15
Ask dad—he knows.
ANONYMOUS (Sweet Caporal cigarettes).

16
No springs—honest weight.
ANONYMOUS (Toledo scales)

17
Don't write—telegraph.
ANONYMOUS, c. 1917. The slogan first appeared in Western Union window displays.

18
Breakfast of champions.
ANONYMOUS (Wheaties).

ADVICE

19
In June the air is full of advice. People are graduating and getting married and setting out on vacations, and it is the fate of these people to be battered with advice until they scream for mercy.
RUSSELL BAKER, "Observer" Column, New York *Times,* 8 June, 1965, p. 40.

20
Advice: the smallest current coin.
AMBROSE BIERCE, *The Devil's Dictionary.*

21
When you can, always advise people to do what you see they really want to do, so long as what they want to do isn't dangerously unlawful, stupidly unsocial or obviously impossible. Doing what they want to do, they may succeed; doing what they don't want to do, they won't.
JAMES GOULD COZZENS, *By Love Possessed.*

22
Good counsel failing men may give, for why?
He that's aground knows where the shoal doth lie. . . .
Thus, like a whetstone, many men are wont
To sharpen others while themselves are blunt.
BENJAMIN FRANKLIN, *Poor Richard,* 1734.

23
He that won't be counselled can't be helped.
BENJAMIN FRANKLIN, *Poor Richard,* 1747.

24
All my life, when I have been faced with a particular problem, I tried to find the man who knew more than anybody else about that problem. Then I have asked for his advice. After I get the best advice available to me, I try to follow it.
LYNDON B. JOHNSON. (BOOTH MOONEY, *The Lyndon Johnson Story*)

1
Consult the dead upon the things that were,
But the living only on things that are.
> LONGFELLOW, *The Golden Legend*, Pt. i.

2
I tell ye wut, my jedgment is you're pooty
    sure to fail,
Ez long 'z the head keeps turnin' back for
    counsel to the tail.
> J. R. LOWELL, *Biglow Papers*. Ser. ii, No.
> 3.

3
He had only one vanity, he thought he could
give advice better than any other person.
> MARK TWAIN, *The Man that Corrupted
> Hadleyburg*.

AFFECTATION, see Hypocrisy
AFFECTION
See also Love

4
What is so pleasant as these jets of affection
which make a young world for me again?
. . . The moment we indulge our affections,
the earth is metamorphosed; there is no winter and no night; all tragedies, all ennuis,
vanish,—all duties even.
> EMERSON, *Essays, First Series: Friend-
> ship*.

5
A woman's whole life is a history of the
affections.
> WASHINGTON IRVING, *The Sketch-Book:
> The Broken Heart*.

6
We are not enemies, but friends. We must
not be enemies. Though passion may have
strained, it must not break our bonds of
affection.
> ABRAHAM LINCOLN, First Inaugural Ad-
> dress, 4 Mar., 1861.

7
Talk not of wasted affection, affection never
    was wasted;
If it enrich not the heart of another, its wa-
    ters, returning
Back to their springs, like the rain, shall fill
    them full of refreshment.
> LONGFELLOW, *Evangeline*. Pt. ii, st. 1.

8
I never met a man I didn't like.
> WILL ROGERS, Speech, 1930. He repeated
> this remark many times during his pub-
> lic appearances.

9
The nation which indulges toward another an
habitual hatred or an habitual fondness is in
some degree a slave. It is a slave to its ani-
mosity or to its affection, either of which is
sufficient to lead it astray from its duty and
its interest.
> GEORGE WASHINGTON, Farewell Address,
> 17 Sept., 1796.

AFFLICTION, see Adversity

AGE
I—Age: Youth and Age
See also Youth

10
Youth is perennially, and naturally, in revolt
against age. Only by belittling the past can
one assure himself and the world of his importance. Nobody, at 20, is going to admit
the possibility that all the best poems may
have been written, the best pictures painted,
the best music composed. Even in the world
of business it is not true, as is sometimes
supposed, that to be a meek young yes-man
is the way to the top. A surer way is to
challenge authority with new ideas—and
prove you are right.
> BRUCE BLIVEN, *By 1966 Half of Us Will
> Be Under 25* (article, *New York Times
> Magazine*, 8 Dec. 1963).

11
Age, out of heart, impatient, sighed:—
"I ask what will the *Future* be?"
Youth laughed contentedly, and cried:—
"The future leave to me!"
> FLORENCE EARLE COATES, *Youth and Age*.

12
Youth is everywhere in place. Age, like
woman, requires fit surroundings.
> EMERSON, *Society and Solitude: Old Age*.

13
Nature is full of freaks, and now puts an old
head on young shoulders, and then a young
heart beating under fourscore winters.
> EMERSON, *Society and Solitude: Old Age*.

14
In youth we clothe ourselves with rainbows,
and go as brave as the zodiac. In age, we put
out another sort of perspiration,—gout,
fever, rheumatism, caprice, doubt, fretting,
avarice.
> EMERSON, *Conduct of Life: Fate*.

15
Young folks are smart, but all ain't good
    thet's new,
I guess the gran'thers they knowed sunthin',
    tu.
> J. R. LOWELL, *The Biglow Papers*: Ser. ii,
> *Mason and Slidell*.

16
The young man who has not wept is a savage, and the old man who will not laugh is a
fool.
> GEORGE SANTAYANA, *Dialogues in Limbo*.

17
Youth is the time for the adventures of the
body, but age for the triumphs of the mind.
> LOGAN PEARSALL SMITH, *On Reading
> Shakespeare*.

18
If within the old man there is not a young
man,—within the sophisticated, one unso-

phisticated,—then he is but one of the devil's angels.

H. D. THOREAU, *Journal,* 26 Oct., 1853.

1

The tears of the young who go their way,
Last a day;
But the grief is long of the old who stay.

J. T. TROWBRIDGE, *A Home Idyll,* pt. 15.

2

Youth, large, lusty, loving—youth full of grace, force, fascination,
Do you know that Old Age may come after you with equal grace, force, fascination?

WALT WHITMAN, *Youth, Day, Old Age and Night.*

II—Age: Middle Age

3

Once he sang of summer,
Nothing but the summer;
Now he sings of winter,
Of winter bleak and drear;
Just because there's fallen
A snowflake on his forehead
He must go and fancy
'Tis winter all the year!

THOMAS BAILEY ALDRICH, *A Snowflake.*

4

Since more than half my hopes came true
And more than half my fears
Are but the pleasant laughing-stock
Of these my middle years:— . . .
Shall I not bless the middle years?
Not I for youth repine
While warmly round me cluster lives
More dear to me than mine.

SARAH N. CLEGHORN, *Contented at Forty.*

5

Of middle age the best that can be said is that a middle-aged person has likely learned how to have a little fun in spite of his troubles.

DON MARQUIS, *The Almost Perfect State.*

6

Let us, then, love the perfect day,
The twelve o'clock of life, and stop
The two hands pointing to the top,
And hold them tightly while we may.

JOAQUIN MILLER, *The Sea of Fire.* Canto xxiii.

7

To be interested in the changing seasons is, in this middling zone, a happier state of mind than to be hopelessly in love with spring.

GEORGE SANTAYANA, *Little Essays.*

8

Among the peaceful harvest days,
An Indian Summer comes at last!

ADELINE D. T. WHITNEY, *Equinoctial.*

III—Age: Old Age

9

And there is healing in old trees,
Old streets a glamour hold;
Why may not I, as well as these,
Grow lovely, growing old?

KARLE WILSON BAKER, *Let Me Grow Lovely.*

10

Avarice is the vice of declining years.

GEORGE BANCROFT, *History of U.S.*

11

To me, old age is always fifteen years older than I am.

BERNARD M. BARUCH, upon observing his 85th birthday, in 1955.

12

Then welcome age, and fear not sorrow;
Today's no better than tomorrow. . . .
I know we grow more lovely
Growing wise.

ALICE CORBIN, *Two Voices.*

13

Age . . . is a matter of feeling, not of years.

GEORGE WILLIAM CURTIS, *Prue and I.*

14

The year grows rich as it groweth old,
And life's latest sands are its sands of gold!

JULIA C. R. DORR, *To the "Bouquet Club."*

15

I am long on ideas, but short on time. I expect to live to be only about a hundred.

THOMAS A. EDISON, *Golden Book,* April, 1931.

16

The older I get, the more wisdom I find in the ancient rule of taking first things first—a process which often reduces the most complex human problems to manageable proportions.

DWIGHT D. EISENHOWER, *Let's Be Honest with Ourselves; The Reader's Digest,* Dec., 1963.

17

I'm saving that rocker for the day when I feel as old as I really am.

DWIGHT D. EISENHOWER, Interview with United Press International, 13 Oct., 1965, the day before his 75th birthday.

18

We do not count a man's years, until he has nothing else to count.

EMERSON, *Society and Solitude: Old Age.*

19

The essence of age is intellect.

EMERSON, *Society and Solitude: Old Age.*

20

[Age] has weathered the perilous capes and shoals in the sea whereon we sail, and the chief evil of life is taken away in removing the grounds of fear. . . . At every stage we lose a foe. At fifty years, 'tis said, afflicted citizens lose their sick-headaches.

EMERSON, *Society and Solitude: Old Age.*

1

Few envy the consideration enjoyed by the oldest inhabitant.
    EMERSON, *Society and Solitude: Old Age.*

2

It is time to be old, To take in sail.
    EMERSON, *Terminus.*

3

Spring still makes spring in the mind
    When sixty years are told;
Love makes anew this throbbing heart,
    And we are never old.
Over the winter glaciers
    I see the summer glow,
And through the wild-piled snowdrift,
    The warm rosebuds below.
    EMERSON, *The World-Soul,* st. 14.

4

Our admiration of the antique is not admiration of the old, but of the natural.
    EMERSON, *Essays, First Series: History.*

5

Nature abhors the old.
    EMERSON, *Essays, First Series: Circles.*

6

Old age brings along with its ugliness the comfort that you will soon be out of it. . . . To be out of the war, out of debt, out of the drouth, out of the blues, out of the dentist's hands, out of the second thoughts, mortifications, and remorses that inflict such twinges and shooting pains,—out of the next winter, and the high prices!
    EMERSON, *Journals,* vol. 10.

7

I don't like the phrase "Older Americans." I don't like the phrase "Senior Citizen." But we had to give a name to a group of people that are being squeezed out of American life like a tube of toothpaste that's come to the end.
    JOHN E. FOGARTY, U.S. Representative from Rhode Island, sponsor of the Older Americans Act of 1965. (JULIUS HORWITZ, *This Is the Age of the Aged; New York Times Magazine,* 16 May, 1965, p. 25)

8

All would live long, but none would be old.
    BENJAMIN FRANKLIN, *Poor Richard,* 1749.

9

Many foxes grow gray, but few grow good.
    BENJAMIN FRANKLIN, *Poor Richard,* 1749.

10

Old boys have their playthings as well as young ones; the difference is only in the price.
    BENJAMIN FRANKLIN, *Poor Richard,* 1752.

11

"Gray temples at twenty?"—Yes! *white* if we please!

Where the snow-flakes fall thickest there's nothing can freeze!
    OLIVER WENDELL HOLMES, *The Boys.*

12

And if I should live to be
The last leaf upon the tree
    In the spring,
Let them smile, as I do now,
At the old forsaken bough
    Where I cling.
    OLIVER WENDELL HOLMES, *The Last Leaf.*

13

And a crook is in his back,
And a melancholy crack
    In his laugh.
    OLIVER WENDELL HOLMES, *The Last Leaf.*

14

Call him not old whose visionary brain
Holds o'er the past its undivided reign.
For him in vain the envious seasons roll
Who bears eternal summer in his soul.
    OLIVER WENDELL HOLMES, *The Old Player.*

15

To be seventy years young is sometimes far more cheerful and hopeful than to be forty years old.
    OLIVER WENDELL HOLMES, Letter to Julia Ward Howe, on her 70th birthday, 27 May, 1889.

16

Youth longs and manhood strives, but age remembers,
Sits by the raked-up ashes of the past,
Spreads its thin hand above the whitening embers
That warm its creeping life-blood till the last.
    OLIVER WENDELL HOLMES, *The Iron Gate.*

17

My aunt! my poor deluded aunt!
    Her hair is almost gray;
Why will she train that winter curl
    In such a spring-like way?
    OLIVER WENDELL HOLMES, *My Aunt.*

18

And bended Age, whose rusted sickle lies
In the scant harvest of remembered days.
    R. U. JOHNSON, *Youth and the Sea.*

19

It is too late! Ah, nothing is too late
Till the tired heart shall cease to palpitate.
Cato learned Greek at eighty; Sophocles
Wrote his grand Oedipus, and Simonides
Bore off the prize of verse from his compeers,
When each had numbered more than fourscore years, . . .
Chaucer, at Woodstock with the nightingales,
At sixty wrote the Canterbury Tales;
Goethe at Weimar, toiling to the last,

Completed Faust when eighty years were
    past.
These are indeed exceptions; but they show
How far the gulf-stream of our youth may
    flow
Into the arctic regions of our lives. . . .
For age is opportunity no less
Than youth itself, though in another dress,
And as the evening twilight fades away
The sky is filled with stars, invisible by day.
    LONGFELLOW, *Morituri Salutamus.*

1

Whatever poet, orator, or sage
May say of it, old age is still old age.
It is the waning, not the crescent moon;
The dusk of evening, not the blaze of noon;
It is not strength, but weakness; not desire,
But its surcease; not the fierce heat of fire,
The burning and consuming element,
But that of ashes and of embers spent.
    LONGFELLOW, *Morituri Salutamus.*

2

The course of my long life hath reached at
    last,
In fragile bark o'er a tempestuous sea,
The common harbor, where must rendered
    be,
Account of all the actions of the past.
    LONGFELLOW, *Old Age.*

3

You are beautiful and faded,
Like an old opera tune
Played upon a harpsichord.
    AMY LOWELL, *A Lady.*

4

Old loves, old aspirations, and old dreams,
More beautiful for being old and gone.
    J. R. LOWELL, *The Parting of the Ways.*

5

As life runs on, the road grows strange
    With faces new, and near the end
The milestones into headstones change,
    'Neath every one a friend.
    J. R. LOWELL, *Sixty-eighth Birthday.*

6

I promise to keep on living as though I expected to live forever. Nobody grows old by
merely living a number of years. People grow
old only by deserting their ideals. Years may
wrinkle the skin, but to give up interest
wrinkles the soul.
    GENERAL DOUGLAS MACARTHUR, Address
        at the dedication of the MacArthur
        Monument, Los Angeles, 26 Jan., 1955.

7

The older I grow the more I distrust the
familiar doctrine that age brings wisdom.
    H. L. MENCKEN, *Prejudices,* ser. iii.

8

We age inevitably:
    The old joys fade and are gone:
And at last comes equanimity and the flame
    burning clear.
    JAMES OPPENHEIM, *New Year's Eve.*

9

Generally money lies nearest them that are
nearest their graves.
    WILLIAM PENN, *Fruits of Solitude.*

10

Darling, I am growing old,
Silver threads among the gold
Shine upon my brow today;
Life is fading fast away.
    EBEN E. REXFORD, *Silver Threads Among
        the Gold.*

11

I'm growing fonder of my staff;
    I'm growing dimmer in the eyes;
I'm growing fainter in my laugh;
    I'm growing deeper in my sighs;
I'm growing careless of my dress;
    I'm growing frugal of my gold;
I'm growing wise, I'm growing—yes,
    I'm growing old.
    JOHN G. SAXE, *I'm Growing Old.*

12

We grow with years more fragile in body,
but morally stouter, and we can throw off the
chill of a bad conscience almost at once.
    LOGAN PEARSALL SMITH, *Afterthoughts.*

13

With years a richer life begins,
    The spirit mellows:
Ripe age gives tone to violins,
    Wine, and good fellows.
    JOHN TOWNSEND TROWBRIDGE, *Three
        Worlds.*

14

Pick the right grandparents, don't eat or
drink too much, be circumspect in all things,
and take a two-mile walk every morning before breakfast.
    HARRY S TRUMAN, Prescription for reach-
        ing the age of 80. He made the state-
        ment to reporters in Washington, 8
        May, 1964, on his own 80th birthday,
        and said he hoped to live to be 90, but
        only "if the old think-tank is working."

15

I shall grow old, but never lose life's zest,
Because the road's last turn will be the best.
    HENRY VAN DYKE, *The Zest of Life.*

16

Venerable men! you have come down to us
from a former generation. Heaven has boun-
teously lengthened out your lives, that you
might behold this joyous day
    DANIEL WEBSTER, Address, at laying the
        cornerstone of the Bunker Hill Monu-
        ment, 17 June, 1825.

17

A little more tired at close of day,
A little less anxious to have our way;
A little less ready to scold and blame;
A little more care of a brother's name;
And so we are nearing the journey's end,
Where time and eternity meet and blend.
    ROLLIN J. WELLS, *Growing Old.*

1
Women sit or move to and fro, some old,
    some young,
The young are beautiful—but the old are
    more beautiful than the young.
    WALT WHITMAN, *Beautiful Women.*

2
How strange it seems, with so much gone
Of life and love, to still live on!
    J. G. WHITTIER, *Snow-Bound.*

IV—Age: The Age

3
The riddle of the age has for each a private
solution.
    EMERSON, *Conduct of Life: Fate.*

4
Every Age, like every human body, has its
own distemper.
    EMERSON, *Nature, Addresses and Lec-
    tures: Lecture on the Times.*

5
The world always had the same bankrupt
look, to foregoing ages as to us,—as of a
failed world just re-collecting its old withered forces to begin again and try to do a
little business.
    EMERSON, *Papers from the Dial: Past and
    Present.*

6
What age was not dull? When was not the
majority wicked? or what progress was ever
made by society?
    EMERSON, *Journals,* vol. 4.

7
The golden age never was the present age.
    BENJAMIN FRANKLIN, *Poor Richard,*
    1750.

8
The illusion that times that were are better
than those that are, has probably pervaded
all ages.
    HORACE GREELEY, *The American Conflict.*

9
The lament for a golden age is only a lament
for golden men.
    H. D. THOREAU, *Journal,* 5 April, 1841.

10
And, cast in some diviner mould,
Let the new cycle shame the old!
    J. G. WHITTIER, *Centennial Hymn.*

AGRICULTURE, see Farming

AIM, see Purpose

ALE AND BEER
See also Drinking, Wine

11
Here with my beer I sit,
While golden moments flit:
Alas! they pass unheeded by:
And as they fly,
I, being dry, sit, idly sipping here
My beer.
    GEORGE ARNOLD, *Beer.*

12
God made yeast, as well as dough, and loves
fermentation just as dearly as he loves vege-
tation.
    EMERSON, *Essays, Second Series: New
    England Reformers.*

13
They who drink beer will think beer.
    WASHINGTON IRVING, *Sketch Book: Strat-
    ford.* Quoted.

14
The man who called it "near beer" was a bad
judge of distance.
    PHILANDER JOHNSON, *Shooting Stars.* Also
    attributed to Luke McLuke, columnist
    of the Cincinnati *Enquirer.*

15
While beer brings gladness, don't forget
That water only makes you wet.
    HARRY LEON WILSON, *The Spenders.*
    Quoted.

AMBITION
See also Aspiration, Fame

16
Ambition has its disappointments to sour us,
    but never the good fortune to satisfy
    us.
    BENJAMIN FRANKLIN, *On True Happiness.*

17
        What madness is ambition!
What is there in that little breath of men
Which they call Fame, that should induce
    the brave
To forfeit ease and that domestic bliss
Which is the lot of happy ignorance?
    PHILIP FRENEAU, *Columbus in Chains.*

18
Too many people have gone in for this senseless chasing of rainbows. How many rainbows does one need?
    FREDERICK LOEWE, announcing the end of
    a career during which he composed the
    music for *My Fair Lady, Brigadoon,*
    and *Camelot.* (Interview with Milton
    Esterow, New York *Times,* 1 Oct.,
    1964)

19
Most people would succeed in small things if
they were not troubled with great ambitions.
    LONGFELLOW, *Drift-Wood: Table-Talk.*

20
Keeping up with the Joneses.
    ARTHUR R. (POP) MONAND, Title of his
    American cartoon strip, which appeared
    from 1914 to 1938.

"Superior people," Stuart Chase said, "lord it
over their pecuniary inferiors by wasteful
expenditures, whereupon the inferiors move
heaven and earth to improve their status by
spending to the limit themselves." This is so

true that we have embodied it in an expression—keeping up with the Joneses.

STEWART H. HOLBROOK, *The Age of the Moguls.*

1
The Status Seekers.

VANCE PACKARD, Title of book (1959). This best-selling exploration of American class behavior helped to make the public conscious of the word "status" and of the expression "status symbol."

2
And this is the moral,—Stick to your sphere;
Or, if you insist, as you have the right,
On spreading your wings for a loftier flight,
The moral is,—Take care how you light.

J. T. TROWBRIDGE, *Darius Green.*

3
How like a mounting devil in the heart
Rules the unrein'd ambition!

N. P. WILLIS, *Parrhasius.*

4
Ambition has but one reward for all:
A little power, a little transient fame,
A grave to rest in, and a fading name!

WILLIAM WINTER, *The Queen's Domain.*

AMERICA
I—America: Songs of Praise

5
America! America!
  God shed His grace on thee
And crown thy good with brotherhood
  From sea to shining sea!

KATHARINE LEE BATES, *America the Beautiful.*

6
O, Columbia, the gem of the ocean,
  The home of the brave and the free,
The shrine of each patriot's devotion,
  A world offers homage to thee.

THOMAS À BECKET, *Columbia, the Gem of the Ocean.* Becket, an English actor, probably wrote it in 1843 for another English actor, David Taylor Shaw, though the exact circumstances are surrounded by controversy. It was first published by Shaw: "written, composed and sung by David T. Shaw, and arranged by T. à Becket, Esq." Then Becket published it as "written and composed by T. à Becket, and sung by D. T. Shaw."

7
God Bless America.

IRVING BERLIN, Title and refrain of song, first sung in public by Kate Smith on a radio broadcast on Armistice Day, 11 Nov., 1938.

8
Great Mother of a mighty race
All earth shall be thy dwelling-place;

Democracy, thy holy name
Shall set the continents aflame,
Shall thrill the islands of the sea,
And keep thy children ever free.

WILLIAM MILL BUTLER, *Democracy.*

9
The land of the free and the home of the brave.

FRANCIS SCOTT KEY, *The Star-Spangled Banner.*

10
Long as thine Art shall love true love,
Long as thy Science truth shall know,
Long as thine Eagle harms no Dove,
Long as thy law by law shall grow,
Long as thy God is God above,
Thy brother every man below,
So long, dear Land of all my love,
Thy name shall shine, thy fame shall grow!

SIDNEY LANIER, *The Centennial Meditation of Columbia.*

11
Thou, too, sail on, O Ship of State!
Sail on, O Union, strong and great!
Humanity with all its fears,
With all the hopes of future years,
Is hanging breathless on thy fate! . . .
Sail on, nor fear to breast the sea!
Our hearts, our hopes, are all with thee,
Our hearts, our hopes, our prayers, our tears,
Our faith triumphant o'er our fears,
Are all with thee,—are all with thee!

LONGFELLOW, *The Building of the Ship.*

12
My country, 'tis of thee,
Sweet land of liberty,
  Of thee I sing;
Land where my fathers died,
Land of the pilgrims' pride,
From every mountain side
  Let freedom ring.

SAMUEL FRANCIS SMITH, *America.*

13
So it's home again, and home again, America for me!
My heart is turning home again, and there I long to be
In the land of youth and freedom beyond the ocean bars,
Where the air is full of sunlight, and the flag is full of stars.

HENRY VAN DYKE, *America for Me.*

14
An angel's heart, an angel's mouth,
  Not Homer's, could alone for me
Hymn well the great Confederate South,
  Virginia first, and Lee.

PHILIP STANHOPE WORSLEY, *R. E. Lee.*

II—America: Ideals and Principles
See also Constitution

15
Driven from every other corner of the earth,

freedom of thought and the right of private judgment in matters of conscience direct their course to this happy country as their last asylum.

SAMUEL ADAMS, Speech, Philadelphia, 1 Aug., 1776.

1
Westward the course of empire takes its way;
The first four acts already past,
A fifth shall close the drama with the day;
Time's noblest offspring is the last.

BISHOP GEORGE BERKELEY, *On the Prospect of Planting Arts and Learning in America.* Inspired by the author's unfulfilled project to found a college in Bermuda where young Indians might be trained as missionaries. The first line is often misquoted as "Westward the star of empire takes its way . . ."

2
Here the free spirit of mankind, at length,
Throws its last fetters off; and who shall place
A limit to the giant's unchained strength,
Or curb his swiftness in the forward race?
W. C. BRYANT, *The Ages.*

3
Most Americans are born drunk. . . . They have a sort of permanent intoxication from within, a sort of invisible champagne. . . . Americans do not need to drink to inspire them to do anything.

G. K. CHESTERTON. (*New York Times Magazine,* 28 June, 1931)

4
Here [in America] individuals of all nations are melted into a new race of men.

MICHEL GUILLAUME JEAN DE CREVECOUR, *Letters from an American Farmer,* Let. 3 (1782).

5
I feel that you are justified in looking into the future with true assurance, because you have a mode of living in which we find the joy of life and the joy of work harmoniously combined. Added to this is the spirit of ambition which pervades your very being, and seems to make the day's work like a happy child at play.

ALBERT EINSTEIN, *New Year's Greeting,* 1931.

6
America means opportunity, freedom, power.

EMERSON, *Public and Private Education.*

7
While European genius is symbolized by some majestic Corinne crowned in the capitol at Rome, American genius finds its true type in the poor negro soldier lying in the trenches by the Potomac with his spelling

book in one hand and his musket in the other.

EMERSON, *Books.*

8
America is a country of young men.

EMERSON, *Society and Solitude: Old Age.*

The youth of America is their oldest tradition. It has been going on now for three hundred years.

OSCAR WILDE, *A Woman of No Importance.*

9
In America, the geography is sublime, but the men are not; the inventions are excellent, but the inventors one is sometimes ashamed of.

EMERSON, *Conduct of Life: Considerations by the Way.*

10
I esteem it a chief felicity of this country that it excels in women.

EMERSON, *Essays, Second Series: Manners.*

11
Bring me men to match my mountains;
Bring me men to match my plains,—
Men with empires in their purpose,
And new eras in their brains.

SAM WALTER FOSS, *The Coming American.*

12
I have often and often in the course of the Session, and the vicissitudes of my hopes and fears as to its issue, looked at that behind the President without being able to tell whether it was rising or setting. But now at length I have the happiness to know that it is a rising and not a setting Sun.

BENJAMIN FRANKLIN, Report of the Constitutional Convention, 17 Sept., 1787. Franklin was referring to the emblem —a sunburst—on the President's chair; as the last members of the convention signed the Constitution, he was sure of a "rising sun."

13
This was the basic heritage of America—a heritage of tolerance, moderation, and individual liberty that was implanted from the very beginnings of European settlement in the New World. America has quite rightly been called a nation that was "born free."

J. W. FULBRIGHT, Address in Washington, D.C., 5 December, 1963.

14
Our country has liberty without license and authority without despotism.

JAMES, CARDINAL GIBBONS, Address in Rome, 25 March, 1887.

15
Ours is the only country deliberately founded on a good idea.

JOHN GUNTHER, *Inside U.S.A.*

16
Power may justly be compared to a great

river which, while kept within its due bounds is both beautiful and useful; but when it overflows its banks, it is then too impetuous to be stemmed, it bears down all before it and brings destruction and desolation wherever it comes. If this then is the nature of power, let us at least do our duty, and like wise men use our utmost care to support liberty, the only bulwark against lawless power. . . . The question before the court and you gentlemen of the jury is not of small nor private concern; it is not the cause of the poor printer, nor of New York, alone; . . . It is the cause of liberty . . . the liberty both of exposing and opposing arbitrary power by speaking and writing Truth.

> ANDREW HAMILTON, arguing the case of John Peter Zenger, New York, 4 Aug., 1735. Zenger was on trial for criticizing William Cosby, colonial governor of New York, in Zenger's New York *Weekly Journal*. His acquittal, the first milestone in the fight for a free press in America, established truth, as well as the fact of publication, as a matter for jury determination in libel cases.

1
Emerson says that the Englishman of all men stands most firmly on his feet. But it is not the whole of man's mission to be found standing, even at the most important post. Let him take one step forward,—and in that advancing figure you have the American.

> T. W. HIGGINSON, *Americanism in Literature*.

2
We are the Romans of the modern world— the great assimilating people.

> OLIVER WENDELL HOLMES, *The Autocrat of the Breakfast Table* (1858).

3
America is the only place where man is full-grown!

> O. W. HOLMES, *The Professor at the Breakfast-Table*.

4
To embody human liberty in workable government, America was born.

> HERBERT HOOVER, Speech at Republican national convention, Cleveland, 10 June, 1936.

5
This will never be a civilized country until we expend more money for books than we do for chewing-gum.

> ELBERT HUBBARD, *The Philistine*, vol. xxv.

6
The almighty dollar, that great object of universal devotion throughout our land,

seems to have no genuine devotees in these peculiar villages.

> WASHINGTON IRVING, *The Creole Village*. (*Knickerbocker Magazine*, Nov., 1836)

It is true that America produces and consumes more cars, soap, and bathtubs than any other nation, but we live among these objects rather than by them. Americans build skyscrapers; Le Corbusier worships them. Ehrenburg, our Soviet critic, fell in love with the Check-O-Mat in American railway stations, writing home paragraphs of song to this gadget—while deploring American materialism. When an American heiress wants to buy a man, she at once crosses the Atlantic. The only really materialistic people I have ever met have been Europeans.

> MARY MCCARTHY, *Perspective* (1953).

7
My God! how little do my countrymen know what precious blessings they are in possession of, and which no other people on earth enjoy!

> THOMAS JEFFERSON, Letter to James Monroe, 17 June, 1785.

8
Equal and exact justice to all men, . . . freedom of religion, freedom of the press, freedom of person under the protection of the habeas corpus; and trial by juries impartially selected,—these principles form the bright constellation which has gone before us.

> THOMAS JEFFERSON, First Inaugural Address, 4 March, 1801.

9
I am a free man, an American, a United States Senator, and a Democrat, in that order.

I am also a liberal, a conservative, a Texan, a taxpayer, a rancher, a businessman, a consumer, a parent, a voter, and not as young as I used to be nor as old as I expect to be—and I am all these things in no fixed order.

I am unaware of any descriptive word in the second paragraph which qualifies, modifies, amends, or is related by hyphenation to the terms listed in the first paragraph. In consequence, I am not able—not even the least interested in trying—to define my political philosophy by the choice of a one-word or two-word label. This may be against the tide, but, if so, the choice is deliberate.

> LYNDON B. JOHNSON, *My Political Philosophy*, originally published in 1958 as a copyrighted article in *The Texas Quarterly* of the University of Texas.

10
First, I believe every American has something to say and, under our system, a right to an audience.

Second, I believe there is always a national answer to each national problem, and, believing this, I do not believe that there are necessarily two sides to every question.

Third, I regard achievement of the full potential of our resources—physical, human, and otherwise—to be the highest purpose of governmental policies next to the protection of those rights we regard as inalienable.

Fourth, I regard waste as the continuing enemy of our society and the prevention of waste—waste of resources, waste of lives, or waste of opportunity—to be the most dynamic of the responsibilities of our Government.

LYNDON B. JOHNSON, *My Political Philosophy,* originally published in 1958 as a copyrighted article in *The Texas Quarterly* of the University of Texas.

1
I am a yes man for everything that is American. I am a yes man for anything that will aid in the defense of this republic. I am a yes man to the Commander-in-Chief, as every good soldier should be in time of emergency.

LYNDON B. JOHNSON. (BOOTH MOONEY, *The Lyndon Johnson Story.*) The statement was made, during Johnson's unsuccessful campaign for the Democratic nomination for U.S. Senator from Texas in 1941, in reply to opponents' charges that he was a "yes man" to President Franklin D. Roosevelt.

2
In short, we must be constantly prepared for the worst and constantly acting for the best —strong enough to win a war and wise enough to prevent one.

LYNDON B. JOHNSON, State of the Union Message, 8 Jan., 1964.

3
My most fervent prayer is to be a President who can make it possible for every boy in this land to grow to manhood by loving his country—instead of dying for it.

LYNDON B. JOHNSON, Address in Washington, D.C., 24 Mar., 1964.

4
The Great Society asks not how much, but how good; not only how to create wealth but how to use it; not only how fast we are going, but where we are headed. It proposes as the first test for a nation: the quality of its people.

LYNDON B. JOHNSON, State of the Union message, 4 Jan., 1965. For the first use of "Great Society" by Johnson, see SOCIETY.

5
For this is what America is all about. It is the uncrossed desert and the unclimbed ridge. It is the star that is not reached and

the harvest that's sleeping in the unplowed ground.

LYNDON B. JOHNSON, Inaugural Address, 20 Jan., 1965.

6
The promise of America is a simple promise. Every person shall share in the blessings of this land. And they shall share on the basis of their merits as a person. They shall not be judged by their color or by their beliefs or by their religion or by where they were born or the neighborhood in which they live.

LYNDON B. JOHNSON, News Conference, Washington, D.C., 13 Mar., 1965.

7
And so, my fellow Americans: ask not what your country can do for you—ask what you can do for your country. My fellow citizens of the world: ask not what America will do for you, but what together we can do for the freedom of man.

JOHN F. KENNEDY, Inaugural Address, 20 Jan., 1961.

8
America is a tune. It must be sung together.

GERALD STANLEY LEE, *Crowds,* bk. v, iii, 12.

9
Intellectually I know that America is no better than any other country; emotionally I know she is better than every other country.

SINCLAIR LEWIS, Interview in Berlin, 29 Dec., 1930.

10
What constitutes the bulwark of our own liberty and independence? It is not our frowning battlements, our bristling sea coasts. . . . Our reliance is in the love of liberty which God has planted in us. Our defense is in the spirit which prized liberty as the heritage of all men, in all lands everywhere.

ABRAHAM LINCOLN, Speech in Edwardsville, Ill., 13 Sept., 1858.

11
America is the last abode of romance and other medieval phenomena.

ERIC LINKLATER, *Juan in America.*

12
The soil out of which such men as he are made is good to be born on, good to live on, good to die for and to be buried in.

J. R. LOWELL, *Among My Books: Second Series: Garfield.*

13
It is my earnest hope—indeed the hope of all mankind—that from this solemn occasion a better world shall emerge out of the blood and carnage of the past. A world founded upon faith and understanding, a world dedicated to the dignity of man and the fulfillment of his most cherished wish for freedom, tolerance and justice. . . . Let us pray that peace be now restored to the world and that

God will preserve it always. These proceedings are now closed.

> GENERAL DOUGLAS MACARTHUR, Statement on accepting the Japanese surrender aboard the U.S.S. Missouri, 2 Sept., 1945.

1
There are those, I know, who will say that the liberation of humanity, the freedom of man and mind, is nothing but a dream. They are right. It is. It is the American dream.

> ARCHIBALD MACLEISH. (*The Reader's Digest,* Feb., 1961)

2
You can not spill a drop of American blood without spilling the blood of the whole world. . . . We are not a nation, so much as a world.

> HERMAN MELVILLE, *Redburn.*

3
I believe in the United States of America as a government of the people, by the people, for the people; whose just powers are derived from the consent of the governed; a democracy in a republic; a sovereign nation of many sovereign states; a perfect union, one and inseparable; established upon those principles of freedom, equality, justice, and humanity for which American patriots sacrificed their lives and fortunes. I therefore believe it is my duty to my country to love it, to support its constitution, to obey its laws, to respect its flag, and to defend it against all enemies.

> WILLIAM TYLER PAGE, *The American's Creed.* (Accepted by the House of Representatives, 3 April, 1918.)

4
Looking forward beyond my stay on earth, I can see our country becoming richer and more powerful. But to make her prosperity more than superficial, her moral and intellectual development should keep pace with her material wealth.

> GEORGE PEABODY. Inscription beneath his bust, Hall of Fame, New York.

5
I see one-third of a nation ill-housed, ill-clad, and ill-nourished.

> FRANKLIN D. ROOSEVELT, Inaugural Address, 20 Jan., 1937. The phrase "one-third of a nation" became synonymous with American economic ills during the 1930's. It was the title of a noted "Living Newspaper" production of the Federal Theatre Project in 1938, which dramatized ills in housing.

Americans today enjoy the highest standard of living in the history of mankind. But for nearly a fifth of our fellow citizens, this is a hollow achievement. They often live without hope, below minimum standards of decency.

. . . We cannot and need not wait for the gradual growth of the economy to lift this forgotten fifth of our nation above the poverty line.

> LYNDON B. JOHNSON, Economic Report to Congress, 20 Jan., 1964.

6
Four freedoms . . . The first is freedom of speech and expression—everywhere in the world. The second is freedom of every person to worship God in his own way—everywhere in the world. The third is freedom from want . . . everywhere in the world. The fourth is freedom from fear . . . anywhere in the world.

> FRANKLIN D. ROOSEVELT, Message to Congress, 6 Jan., 1941, proposing the lend-lease program. The substance of these aims, termed essential to the post-war world, was included in the Atlantic Charter, Aug., 1941.

7
The first requisite of a good citizen in this republic of ours is that he shall be able and willing to pull his weight.

> THEODORE ROOSEVELT, Address in New York, 11 Nov., 1902.

8
There can be no fifty-fifty Americanism in this country. There is room here for only 100 per cent Americanism, only for those who are Americans and nothing else.

> THEODORE ROOSEVELT, Speech at Republican Convention, Saratoga, N.Y. Also in *Foes of Our Own Household.*

Some Americans need hyphens in their names because only part of them has come over.

> WOODROW WILSON, Address in Washington, D.C.. 16 May, 1914.

Hyphenated Americans.

> THEODORE ROOSEVELT, *Metropolitan Magazine,* Oct., 1915. Referring to divided allegiance.

9
Always the path of American destiny has been into the unknown. Always there arose enough of reserves of strength, balances of sanity, portions of wisdom to carry the nation through to a fresh start with ever-renewing vitality.

> CARL SANDBURG, commenting, 19 Nov., 1959, on the 96th anniversary of Lincoln's Gettysburg address.

10
In what sometimes looks like American greediness and jostling for the front place, all is love of achievement, nothing is unkindness; it is a fearless people, and free from malice, as you might see in their eyes and

gestures, even if their conduct did not prove it.

GEORGE SANTAYANA, *Character and Opinion in the U.S.*

1

America is a "happy-ending" nation.

DORE SCHARY, Address to the Harvard Club of Los Angeles. (Quoted as foreword in Louis Kronenberger, *Company Manners*)

2

The American people never carry an umbrella. They prepare to walk in eternal sunshine.

ALFRED E. SMITH, Article, 1931.

3

You must obey this, now, for a law—that "he that will not work shall not eat."

JOHN SMITH, *The Generall Historie of Virginia.*

4

In the United States there is more space where nobody is than where anybody is. This is what makes America what it is.

GERTRUDE STEIN, *The Geographical History of America.*

5

The reason American cities are prosperous is that there is no place to sit down.

ALFRED J. TALLEY, Interview following his return to the United States from Europe.

6

At once three outstanding characteristics of the American mind are apparent—equalitarianism, love of freedom, and bounding energy. But the most deep-seated, I am sure, is energy.

STEPHEN JAMES LAKE TAYLOR (BARON TAYLOR OF HARLOW), *Deep Analysis of the American Mind; New York Times Magazine*, 23 Feb., 1964.

7

Since many [Western Europeans who settled in America] were escaping from tyranny . . . it is not surprising that the Americans do not love the machinery of government. So they have deliberately created a system of government which will permit each of them to do what he likes to a degree unknown elsewhere in the world.

STEPHEN JAMES LAKE TAYLOR (BARON TAYLOR OF HARLOW), *Deep Analysis of the American Mind; New York Times Magazine*, 23 Feb., 1964.

8

To the impartial observer the Americans seem to enjoy themselves as much as any people on earth, and more than most. But they are the victims of insatiable curiosity. They like knowing what makes things tick, including themselves.

STEPHEN JAMES LAKE TAYLOR (BARON TAYLOR OF HARLOW), *Deep Analysis of the American Mind; New York Times Magazine*, 23 Feb., 1964.

9

The next Augustine Age will dawn on the other side of the Atlantic. There will perhaps be a Thucydides at Boston, a Xenophon at New York.

HORACE WALPOLE, Letter to Sir Horace Mann, 24 Nov., 1774.

10

Liberty has still a continent to live in.

HORACE WALPOLE, Letter, 17 Feb., 1779.

11

Let our object be, our country, our whole country, and nothing but our country. And, by the blessing of God, may that country itself become a vast and splendid monument, not of oppression and terror, but of wisdom, of peace, and of liberty, upon which the world may gaze with admiration forever.

DANIEL WEBSTER, Speech in Charlestown, Mass., 17 June, 1825, at laying of cornerstone of Bunker Hill Monument.

12

I shall know but one country. The ends I aim at shall be my country's, my God's, and Truth's. I was born an American; I live an American; I shall die an American.

DANIEL WEBSTER, Speech, 17 July, 1850.

13

O America because you build for mankind I build for you.

WALT WHITMAN, *By Blue Ontario's Shore.*

14

America lives in the heart of every man everywhere who wishes to find a region where he will be free to work out his destiny as he chooses.

WOODROW WILSON, Speech in Chicago, 6 April, 1912.

15

The interesting and inspiring thought about America is that she asks nothing for herself except what she has a right to ask for humanity itself.

WOODROW WILSON, Speech in New York, 17 May, 1915.

16

Just what is it that America stands for? If she stands for one thing more than another, it is for the sovereignty of self-governing people.

WOODROW WILSON, Speech in Pittsburgh, 29 Jan., 1916.

17

America is not anything if it consists of each of us. It is something only if it consists of all of us; and it can consist of all of us only as our spirits are banded together in a common enterprise. That common enterprise is the enterprise of liberty and justice and right.

WOODROW WILSON, Speech in Pittsburgh, 29 Jan., 1916.

1

Americanism consists in utterly believing in the principles of America.

> WOODROW WILSON, Address in West Point, 13 June, 1916.

2

The right is more precious than peace.

> WOODROW WILSON, Address to Congress, 2 Apr., 1917.

3

I tell you, fellow citizens, that the war was won by the American spirit. . . . You know what one of our American wits said, that it took only half as long to train an American army as any other, because you had only to train them to go one way.

> WOODROW WILSON, Speech in Kansas City, Mo., 6 Sept., 1919.

4

Sometime people call me an idealist. Well, that is the way I know I am an American. America is the only idealistic nation in the world.

> WOODROW WILSON, Speech in Sioux Falls, S. Dak., 8 Sept., 1919.

5

The fabulous country—the place where miracles not only happen, but where they happen all the time.

> THOMAS WOLFE, Of Time and the River.

The Melting Pot

6

America! half brother of the world!
With something good and bad of every land.

> P. J. BAILEY, Festus: The Surface.

7

There were human beings aboard the Mayflower,
Not merely ancestors.

> STEPHEN VINCENT BENÉT, Western Star, bk. i, p. 133.

8

Remember that when you say
"I will have none of this exile and this stranger
For his face is not like my face and his speech is strange,"
You have denied America with that word.

> STEPHEN VINCENT BENÉT, Western Star, bk. i, p. 180.

9

I was made by a Dago and presented to the American people on behalf of the French Government for the purpose of welcomin' Irish immigrants into the Dutch city of New York.

> O. HENRY, Sixes and Sevens: The Lady Higher Up, referring to the Statue of Liberty.

10

Not merely a nation but a nation of nations.

> LYNDON B. JOHNSON, Speech in Washington, D.C., 11 May, 1965, upon designat-ing Ellis Island, port of entry for millions of immigrants, as part of the Statue of Liberty National Monument in New York harbor.

11

A Nation of Immigrants.

> JOHN F. KENNEDY, Title of Book, published posthumously (1964).

12

Give me your tired, your poor,
Your huddled masses yearning to breathe free,
The wretched refuse of your teeming shore,
Send these, the homeless, tempest-tossed, to me:
I lift my lamp beside the golden door.

> EMMA LAZARUS, The New Colossus. These lines are inscribed on the Statue of Liberty.

13

She of the open soul and open door,
With room about her hearth for all mankind!

> J. R. LOWELL, Commemoration Ode.

14

Races didn't bother the Americans. They were something a lot better than any race. They were a People. They were the first self-constituted, self-declared, self-created People in the history of the world.

> ARCHIBALD MacLEISH, A Time to Act.

15

You who have been born in America, I wish I could make you understand what it is like not to be an American—not to have been an American all your life—and then suddenly, with the words of a man in flowing robes, to be one, for that moment, and forever after. . . . One moment, you belong with your fathers to a million dead yesterdays. The next, you belong with America to a million unborn tomorrows.

> GEORGE M. MARDIKIAN, Song of America (1956). The author, an Armenian immigrant, describes his feelings upon becoming a U.S. citizen.

16

America is God's Crucible, the great Melting Pot where all the races of Europe are melting and re-forming! . . . God is making the American.

> ISRAEL ZANGWILL, The Melting-Pot.

Supreme Court Decisions

17

To hold that a state cannot consistently with the First and Fourteenth Amendments utilize its public school system to aid any or all religious faiths or sects in the dissemination of their doctrines and ideals does not . . . manifest a governmental hostility to religion or religious teachings. A manifestation of such hostility would be at war with our national tradition as embodied in the First

Amendment's guaranty of the free exercise of religion. For the First Amendment rests upon the premise that both religion and government can best work to achieve their lofty aims if each is left free from the other within its respective sphere. Or . . . The First Amendment has erected a wall between Church and State which must be kept high and impregnable.

> Hugo L. Black, speaking for the majority in the U.S. Supreme Court decision, McCollum vs. Board of Education of School District No. 71, Champaign County, Ill., 8 March, 1948. This historic decision declared unconstitutional the use of released time in which churches teach religion in public schools.

1
Does segregation of children in public schools solely on the basis of race, even though the physical facilities and other "tangible" factors may be equal, deprive the children of the minority group of equal educational opportunities? We believe that it does.

> Chief Justice Earl Warren, Opinion in U.S. Supreme Court case, Brown vs. Board of Education of Topeka, Kan., 17 May, 1954. The unanimous decision in this historic case was the pioneer ruling in establishing the unconstitutionality of racial segregation in public schools (segregation based on "separate but equal" facilities).

2
While it may not be possible to draw Congressional districts with mathematical precision, that is no excuse for ignoring our Constitution's plain objective of making equal representation for equal numbers of people the fundamental goal for the House of Representatives.

> Hugo L. Black, speaking for the majority in a U.S. Supreme Court decision, 17 Feb., 1964. It held that the Constitution requires that Congressional districts within each state be substantially equal in population. The court in this case (Wesberry vs. Sanders) found the existing apportionment of Congressional districts in Georgia unfair to city voters. The case climaxed a growing controversy over alleged discrimination against urban areas in the apportionment of seats in the House of Representatives. This and the Supreme Court ruling of 15 June, 1964, ordering the apportionment of both houses of state legislatures on a basis of population only, are paraphrased: "One man, one vote."

3
Thus we consider this case against the background of a profound national commitment to the principle that debate on public issues should be uninhibited, robust, and wide-open, and that it may well include vehement, caustic, and sometimes unpleasantly sharp attacks on government and public officials. . . . Criticism of their official conduct does not lose its constitutional protection merely because it is effective criticism and hence diminishes their official reputations. . . . the pall of fear and timidity imposed upon those who would give voice to public criticism is an atmosphere in which the First Amendment freedoms cannot survive.

> William J. Brennan, Jr., speaking for the majority in a Supreme Court decision, 9 Mar., 1964. The court reversed an Alabama judgment against the New York *Times,* which was based on the contention of Alabama city and state officials that they had been libeled by publication of an advertisement criticizing the officials' conduct during racial unrest in 1960. The case marked the first occasion in which the Supreme Court had found an ordinary civil libel action in conflict with the guarantees of speech and press freedom in the Bill of Rights.

III—America: The Union

4
E Pluribus Unum. (One from many.)

> Motto for seal of the United States, proposed originally 10 Aug., 1776, by a committee made up of Benjamin Franklin, John Adams, and Thomas Jefferson, and adopted 20 June, 1782. This motto appeared on the title page of the *Gentleman's Journal* of Jan., 1692.

5
I never use the word "Nation" in speaking of the United States; I always use the word "Union," or "Confederacy." We are not a Nation, but a Union, a confederacy of equal and sovereign States.

> John C. Calhoun, Letter to Oliver Dyer, 1 Jan., 1849.

6
The Constitution, in all its provisions, looks to an indissoluble Union composed of indestructible States.

> Salmon P. Chase, Decision in Texas vs. White, 7 Wallace, 725.

7
We join ourselves to no party that does not carry the flag and keep step to the music of the Union.

> Rufus Choate, Letter to Whig Convention, Worcester, Mass., 1 Oct., 1855.

8
I have heard something said about allegiance to the South. I know no South, no North, no

East, no West, to which I owe any allegiance.

HENRY CLAY, Speech in U.S. Senate, 1848.

1

The gentleman speaks of Virginia being my country. The Union, sir, is my country.

HENRY CLAY, Speech in U.S. Senate, 1848.

2

They talk defensively of "states' rights" when they and we well know that there can be no such thing as a state's right to default on a national duty.

LEROY COLLINS, Address before Greater Columbia (S.C.) Chamber of Commerce, 3 Dec., 1963. Collins, himself a Southerner, was assailing in particular extremist Southern politicians.

3

The North! the South! the West! the East!
No one the most and none the least,
But each with its own heart and mind,
Each of its own distinctive kind,
Yet each a part and none the whole,
But all together form one soul;
That soul Our Country at its best,
No North, no South, no East, no West,
No yours, no mine, but always Ours,
Merged in one Power with lesser powers,
For no one's favor, great or small,
But all for Each and each for All.

EDMUND VANCE COOKE, *Each for All.*

4

Then join hand in hand, brave Americans all,—
By uniting we stand, by dividing we fall!

JOHN DICKINSON, *Liberty Song.* (First published in the Boston *Gazette*, 18 July, 1768.)

A song for our banner! The watchword recall
Which gave the Republic her station:
"United we stand, divided we fall!"
It made and preserves us a nation!
The union of lakes, the union of lands,
The union of States none can sever,
The union of hearts, the union of hands,
And the flag of our union forever!

GEORGE P. MORRIS, *The Flag of Our Union.*

5

This glorious Union shall not perish! Precious legacy of our fathers, it shall go down honored and cherished to our children. Generations unborn shall enjoy its privileges as we have done; and if we leave them poor in all besides, we will transmit to them the boundless wealth of its blessings!

EDWARD EVERETT, Speech at Union Meeting, Faneuil Hall, Boston.

6

Yes, we must, indeed, all hang together, or,

most assuredly, we shall all hang separately.

Attributed to BENJAMIN FRANKLIN, in replying to John Hancock. The latter, just before the signing of the Declaration of Independence, had addressed the Continental Congress as follows: "It is too late to pull different ways; the members of the Continental Congress must hang together."

7

I am not a Virginian, but an American.

PATRICK HENRY, Speech in the Continental Congress, 5 Sept., 1774.

8

One flag, one land, one heart, one hand,
One nation, evermore!

O. W. HOLMES, *Voyage of the Good Ship Union.*

9

Our federal Union, it must be preserved.

ANDREW JACKSON, Toast, offered at a banquet in Washington, D.C., 13 April, 1830, on Jefferson's birthday.

10

The cement of this Union is the heart blood of every American.

THOMAS JEFFERSON, *Writings,* vol. xiv.

11

When any one State in the American Union refuses obedience to the Confederation by which they have bound themselves, the rest have a natural right to compel obedience.

THOMAS JEFFERSON, *Writings,* vol. xvii.

12

These are the United States—a united people with a united purpose. Our American unity does not depend upon unanimity. We have differences but now, as in the past, we can derive from those differences strength, not weakness; wisdom, not despair.

LYNDON B. JOHNSON, Address to joint session of Congress, 27 Nov., 1963—his first major speech after his accession to the presidency.

13

This, then, is the state of the union: free and restless, growing and full of hope. So it was in the beginning. So it shall always be, while God is willing, and we are strong enough to keep the faith.

LYNDON B. JOHNSON, State of the Union message, 4 Jan., 1965.

14

Let us now join reason to faith, and action to experience, to transform our unity of interest into a unity of purpose. For the hour and the day and the time are here to achieve progress without strife, to achieve change without hatred; not without difference of opinion, but without the deep and abiding divisions which scar the Union for generations.

LYNDON B. JOHNSON, Inaugural Address, 20 Jan., 1965.

1
This government, with its institutions, belongs to the people who inhabit it. Whenever they shall grow weary of the existing government, they can exercise their constitutional right of amending it, or their revolutionary right to dismember or overthrow it.

> ABRAHAM LINCOLN, Speech at first Republican state convention in Illinois, 1856. Also quoted by Theodore Roosevelt at Ohio constitutional convention, 1912.

2
Liberty and Union, now and forever, one and inseparable!

> DANIEL WEBSTER, Speech, 26 Jan., 1830.

3
Let us then stand by the constitution as it is, and by our country as it is, one, united, and entire; let it be a truth engraven on our hearts; let it be borne on the flag under which we rally in every exigency, that we have one country, one constitution, one destiny.

> DANIEL WEBSTER, Speech in New York, 15 March, 1837.

4
It [the Civil War] created in this country what had never existed before—a national consciousness. It was not the salvation of the Union; it was the rebirth of the Union.

> WOODROW WILSON, Memorial Day Address, 1915.

5
Let us keep our eyes and our hearts steadily fixed upon the old flag of our fathers. . . . It has a star for every State. Let us resolve that there shall be a State for every star!

> ROBERT C. WINTHROP, Speech in Boston, 22 Aug., 1862.

IV—America: America and the World

6
America, in the assembly of nations, since her admission among them, has invariably, though often fruitlessly, held forth to them the hand of honest friendship, of equal freedom, of generous reciprocity. She has uniformly spoken among them, though often to heedless and often to disdainful ears, the language of equal liberty, equal justice, and equal rights.

> JOHN QUINCY ADAMS, Address, 4 July, 1821.

7
It is hardness and materialism, exaggeration and boastfulness; in a false smartness, a false audacity, a want of soul and delicacy.

> MATTHEW ARNOLD, Discourses on America, 1884.

8
Oh mother of a mighty race,
Yet lovely in thy youthful grace!
The elder dames, thy haughty peers,
Admire and hate thy blooming years.
With words of shame
And taunts of scorn they join thy name.

> BRYANT, Oh Mother of a Mighty Race.

9
A dirty chimney on fire.

> THOMAS CARLYLE, Letter, referring to the American Civil War.

He was probably fond of them, but he was always able to conceal it.

> MARK TWAIN, My First Lie. The reference is to Carlyle's expressed dislike of Americans.

10
The American never imitates the Englishman in simply taking for granted both his own patriotism and his own superiority.

> G. K. CHESTERTON, Generally Speaking.

11
The world is not a big Red sea in which this country is being scuttled, but a vast arena of political upheaval, in which the quest for freedom, ever stronger, has overthrown the colonial empires of the past. It isn't a tidy world, nor is it a secure one. But it is one for which the United States set the revolutionary example.

> FRANK CHURCH, Speech in the U.S. Senate, 12 Jan., 1965.

12
We recognize and accept our own deep involvement in the destiny of men everywhere.

> DWIGHT D. EISENHOWER, Second Inaugural Address, 21 Jan., 1957.

13
To be effective in the nation's rightful role as a Free World leader, our people and their government should always, in my view, display a spirit of firmness without truculence, conciliation without appeasement, confidence without arrogance.

> DWIGHT D. EISENHOWER, The White House Years: Mandate for Change 1953–1956.

14
The character and strength the United States brings to world councils can only reflect the inner courage, strength and wisdom we have developed as a nation. This is national morale, and it is my unshakable conviction that morale, even more than sheer power, is the deciding factor in the fate of a nation.

> DWIGHT D. EISENHOWER, Let's Be Honest with Ourselves; The Reader's Digest, Dec., 1963.

15
In dealing with the communists . . . I believe we should keep reminding ourselves that *the basic conflict between their system and ours is a moral one.* Our form of government is based on the deep-rooted spiritual values spelled out in the familiar phrases of the Declaration of Independence. . . . The

communists see our moral precepts as a direct threat to their ideology.

> DWIGHT D. EISENHOWER, *Let's Be Honest with Ourselves; The Reader's Digest,* Dec., 1963.

Here is our difference with the Communists —and our strength. They would use their skills to forge new chains of tyranny. We would use ours to free men from the bonds of the past.

> LYNDON B. JOHNSON, Message to Congress, 14 Jan., 1965. He was contrasting the systems' goal in foreign aid.

1
The less America looks abroad, the grander its promise.

> EMERSON, *Lectures: Character.*

2
That is the point which decides the welfare of a people; *which way does it look?* If to any other people, it is not well with them. If occupied with their own affairs and thoughts and men . . . they are sublime.

> EMERSON, *Letters and Social Aims: Social Aims.*

3
We are confronted with a complex and fluid world situation and we are not adapting ourselves to it. We are clinging to old myths in the face of new realities and we are seeking to escape the contradictions by narrowing the permissible bounds of public discussion, by relegating an increasing number of ideas and viewpoints to a growing category of "unthinkable thoughts."

> J. WILLIAM FULBRIGHT, Address in U.S. Senate, 25 Mar., 1964. In this controversial address, the chairman of the Senate Foreign Relations Committee called for a more flexible foreign policy. He cited as "old myths" U.S. policy toward the Communist bloc in general, and in particular with regard to Cuba, the war in Vietnam, and the controversy over U.S. rights in Panama.

4
I cannot conclude without mentioning how sensibly I feel the dismemberment of America from this empire, and that I should be miserable indeed if I did not feel that no blame on that account can be laid at my door, and did I not also know that knavery seems to be so much the striking feature of its inhabitants that it may not in the end be an evil that they will become aliens to this kingdom.

> GEORGE III OF ENGLAND, Letter to Shelburne, 10 Nov., 1782.

5
Note how perverse is the attitude of the weak toward their benefactors. They feel generosity as oppression; they want to retali-

ate. They say to their benefactors, "May the day come when you shall be weak and we will send bundles to America."

> ERIC HOFFER, *The Passionate State of Mind* (1954), p. 29.

6
Thou, O my country, hast thy foolish ways, Too apt to purr at every stranger's praise!

> O. W. HOLMES, *An After-Dinner Poem.*

7
The fact is that the Americans are not a thoughtful people; they are too busy to stop and question their values.

> DEAN W. R. INGE. (MARCHANT, *Wit and Wisdom of Dean Inge,* No. 217.)

8
I fought in Korea so I would not have to fight on Main Street in Wichita.

> MAJOR JAMES JABARA of Wichita, Kan., on returning home from combat. This statement by one of the heroes of the Korean war was quoted, not long after it was first spoken, by Eleanor Roosevelt in a speech before the Democratic national convention in Chicago, 23 July, 1952.

9
Europe, the great American sedative.

> HENRY JAMES, *The Wings of the Dove.*

10
Peace and friendship with all mankind is our wisest policy, and I wish we may be permitted to pursue it.

> THOMAS JEFFERSON, Letter to C. W. F. Dumas, 1786.

11
Peace, commerce, and honest friendship with all nations,—entangling alliances with none.

> THOMAS JEFFERSON, First Inaugural, 4 Mar., 1801.

12
We owe gratitude to France, justice to England, good will to all, and subservience to none.

> THOMAS JEFFERSON, *Writings,* vol. ix.

13
The less we have to do with the enmities of Europe the better. Not in our day, but at no distant one, we may shake a rod over the heads of all, which may make the stoutest tremble. But I hope our wisdom will grow with our power, and teach us that the less we use our power the greater it will be.

> THOMAS JEFFERSON, *Writings,* vol. xiv.

14
The day is not distant when we may formally require a meridian of partition through the ocean which separates the two hemispheres, on the hither side of which no European gun shall ever be heard, nor an American on the other.

> THOMAS JEFFERSON, *Writings,* vol. xv.

15
We must meet our duty and convince the

world that we are just friends and brave enemies.

THOMAS JEFFERSON, *Writings,* vol. xix.

1

Our first and fundamental maxim should be never to entangle ourselves in the broils of Europe. Our second, never to suffer Europe to intermeddle with cis-Atlantic affairs.

THOMAS JEFFERSON, Letter to James Monroe, 24 Oct., 1823. This letter was instrumental in the adoption of the Monroe Doctrine. See also Monroe in this section.

2

The people in this country have more blessed hopes than bitter victories. The people of this country and the world expect more from their leaders than just a show of brute force. And so our hope and our purpose is to employ reasoned agreement instead of ready aggression, to preserve our honor without a world in ruins, to substitute if we can understanding for retaliation.

LYNDON B. JOHNSON, Address in Washington, D.C., 24 Mar., 1964.

3

We have voted as many, but tonight we must face the world as one.

LYNDON B. JOHNSON, Speech in Austin, Tex., 4 Nov., 1964. This call for unity was sounded in the early-morning hours following election night, when tabulations showed him a winner by a landslide over Barry M. Goldwater in the contest for the presidency.

4

We aspire to nothing that belongs to others. We seek no dominion over our fellow man, but man's dominion over tyranny and misery.

LYNDON B. JOHNSON, Inaugural Address, 20 Jan., 1965.

5

I am willing to love all mankind, except an American.

SAMUEL JOHNSON. (Boswell, *Life,* iii, 290.)

6

In these circumstances it is clear that the main element of any United States policy toward the Soviet Union must be that of a long-term, patient but firm and vigilant containment of Russian expansive tendencies.

GEORGE KENNAN, *The Sources of Soviet Conduct,* in *Foreign Affairs,* July, 1947. This was the first use of "containment" as a label for the American policy pursued throughout the Truman administration—and thereafter under different names. Later in the article Kennan described "containment" more fully: "a policy of firm containment, designed to confront the Russians with unalterable

counter-force at every point where they show signs of encroaching upon the interests of a peaceful and stable world." The article was published anonymously, as written by "X." Subsequently the author acknowledged it as his work, and the editors of *Foreign Affairs* further confirmed the authorship in a letter to the compiler.

I would suggest that we have begun to move beyond the policy of containment; that the central trend of our times is the emergence of what, for lack of a better label, might be called a policy of cease-fire, and peaceful change. I would suggest, further, that we may be approaching something close to a world consensus on such a policy.

No analogy is ever perfect, but if the policy of containment stands for "limited war," then the policy of cease-fire perhaps stands for "limited peace." I believe this mutation is occurring simply because the H-bomb has made "limited" war too dangerous.

ADLAI E. STEVENSON, Dag Hammarskjöld Memorial Lecture, Princeton University, 23 Mar., 1964.

7

At what point then is the approach of danger to be expected? I answer if it ever reach us it must spring up amongst us; it cannot come from abroad. If destruction be our lot, we must ourselves be its author and finisher. As a nation of free men, we must live through all time or die by suicide.

ABRAHAM LINCOLN, *Perpetuation of Our Political Institutions.*

8

For some reason or other, the European has rarely been able to see America except in caricature. . . . We do not ask to be sprinkled with rosewater, but may perhaps fairly protest against being drenched with the rinsings of an unclean imagination.

J. R. LOWELL, *On a Certain Condescension in Foreigners.*

9

We owe it, therefore, to candor, and to the amicable relations existing between the United States and those [European] powers, to declare that we should consider any attempt on their part to extend their system to any portion of this hemisphere, as dangerous to our peace and safety.

JAMES MONROE, Message to Congress, 2 Dec., 1823, stating the Monroe Doctrine.

10

You cannot conquer America.

WILLIAM PITT, Address in the House of Commons, 18 Nov., 1777.

1
The desire for riches is their ruling passion.
  Duc de la Rochefoucault-Liancourt,
    *Travels Throughout the United States
    of North America,* 1798.

2
To rouse their [Americans'] eager interest,
their distinguished consideration and their
undying devotion, all that is necessary is to
hold them up to the ridicule of the rest of
the universe. Dickens won them to him forever by merciless projections of typical
Americans as windbags, swindlers and assas-
sins.
  Bernard Shaw, in reacting to the Nobel
    prize award to Sinclair Lewis, 1931.

3
Why is it, whenever a group of international-
ists get together, they always decide that
Uncle Sam must be the goat?
  Bertrand H. Snell, Interview, 7 May,
    1931.

4
President Johnson has directed me to affirm
to this Assembly that there will be no "Johnson policy" toward the United Nations—any
more than there was a "Kennedy policy."
There was—and is—only a United States
policy, and that . . . outlasts violence and
outlives men.
  Adlai E. Stevenson, Address to United
    Nations General Assembly, 26 Nov.,
    1963 (four days following the assassina-
    tion of President John F. Kennedy).

5
Gigantic daughter of the West
We drink to thee across the flood. . . .
For art not thou of English blood?
  Alfred Tennyson, *Hands All Round.*

6
The Soviet Union and the United States are
both unpopular today. In Western eyes, the
Soviet Union is aggressive and oppressive.
The United States, however, takes obvious
pains to avoid committing these sins—so
why is she unpopular, too? . . . The big,
strong and rich are always unpopular with
the small, weak and poor. . . . When a
smaller dog finds itself boxed up with a larger dog, the smaller dog is inclined to snarl
and bristle. This is not only dog nature, it is
human nature.
  Arnold J. Toynbee, *Again Nationalism
    Threatens; New York Times Magazine,*
    3 Nov., 1963.

7
'Tis our true policy to steer clear of permanent alliances, with any portion of the foreign world.
  George Washington, *Farewell Address,*
    17 Sept., 1796.

Against the insidious wiles of foreign influence, . . . the jealousy of a free people

ought to be constantly awake, since history
and experience prove that foreign influence is
one of the most baneful foes of republican
government.
  George Washington, *Farewell Address,*
    17 Sept., 1796.

Why forego the advantages of so peculiar a
situation? Why quit our own to stand upon
foreign ground? Why, by interweaving our
destiny with that of any part of Europe, entangle our peace and prosperity in the toils
of European ambition, rivalship, interest,
humor or caprice?
  George Washington, *Farewell Address,*
    17 Sept., 1796.

8
America can not be an ostrich with its head
in the sand.
  Woodrow Wilson, Address in Des
    Moines, Ia., 1 Feb., 1916.

Every time Europe looks across the Atlantic
to see the American eagle, it observes only
the rear end of an ostrich.
  H. G. Wells, *America.*

There is a small articulate minority in this
country which advocates changing our national symbol which is the eagle to that of
the ostrich and withdrawing from the UN.
  Eleanor Roosevelt, Speech before the
    Democratic national convention in Chi-
    cago, 23 July, 1952.

9
The best way to help mankind is to begin at
home and put our own house in order. . . .
Internationalism, as it is practised, is another
name for money juggling and the operations
of bankers. . . . I am ready and eager for
Uncle Sam to turn over the job of being
catspaw for the world to someone else.
  W. E. Woodward, *Money for Tomorrow.*

**V—America: Famous Historical
Sayings**

**See also Constitution, Democracy,
Politics, War**

10
All other sovereignties, united as one
strength, shall compel the submission and
performance of the sentence, with damages to
the suffering party, and charges to the
sovereignties that obliged their submission.
  William Penn, *Essay Towards the Pres-
    ent and Future Peace of Europe* (c.
    1670). This is a pioneer statement of the
    policy of collective security. It proposed
    an annual General Assembly of govern-
    mental delegates having the power to
    settle international disputes, by employ-
    ing collective force against aggression if
    necessary.

1
Taxation without representation is tyranny.
> JAMES OTIS, Argument on the illegality of the Writs of Assistance before the Superior Court of Massachusetts, Feb., 1761. Historians now contend that the exact wording of Otis' famous statement is uncertain; it existed originally only in some notes made by John Adams, and these were revised by Adams some fifty years after the speech was delivered. In a letter to William Tudor, biographer of Otis, dated 9 June, 1818, Adams recalled this key part of the famous speech as follows: "And here he gave reins to his genius, in declamation . . . against the tyranny of taxation without representation." On 1 Oct., 1963, British Foreign Secretary Lord Home (later Prime Minister Sir Alec Douglas-Home) made a new paraphrase: "no representation without taxation" in the United Nations. Addressing the U.N., he said it was intolerable for members to demand voting rights without paying assessed shares of U.N. costs.

2
Caesar had his Brutus; Charles the First, his Cromwell; and George the Third ["Treason!" cried the Speaker]—*may profit by their example*. If *this* be treason, make the most of it.
> PATRICK HENRY, Speech in the Virginia Convention, 29 May, 1765.

3
Is life so dear or peace so sweet as to be purchased at the price of chains and slavery? Forbid it, Almighty God! I know not what course others may take; but as for me, give me liberty, or give me death!
> PATRICK HENRY, Speech in the Virginia House of Delegates, 23 Mar., 1775.

4
Listen, my children, and you shall hear,
Of the midnight ride of Paul Revere,
On the eighteenth of April, in Seventy-five;
Hardly a man is now alive
Who remembers that famous day and year.
> LONGFELLOW, *Paul Revere's Ride.*

5
One if by land and two if by sea.
> LONGFELLOW, *Paul Revere's Ride.* This refers to the signals given to Revere by lantern from the tower of North Church, Boston, 18 Apr., 1775.

6
What a glorious morning is this!
> SAMUEL ADAMS, upon hearing the sound of gunfire in Boston, 19 Apr., 1775.

7
Stand your ground. Don't fire unless fired upon, but if they mean to have a war let it begin here.
> CAPTAIN JOHN PARKER, addressing his men on Lexington Green at the outset of the Revolutionary War, 19 Apr., 1775.

8
In the name of the Great Jehovah and the Continental Congress.
> ETHAN ALLEN, demanding the surrender of Fort Ticonderoga, 10 May, 1775. According to Allen's own account, he gave this reply to Captain de la Place, commander of the garrison there, when the latter asked in whose name Allen demanded the surrender.

9
Men, you are all marksmen—don't one of you fire until you see the white of their eyes.
> ISRAEL PUTNAM, at the Battle of Bunker Hill, 17 June, 1775. Frothingham's *History of the Siege of Boston* is among the authorities supporting Putnam's claim to the statement quoted, which is ascribed by others to Colonel William Prescott.

10
The Spirit of '76.
> ARCHIBALD M. WILLARD, Title of painting, first shown at the Centennial Exhibition, Philadelphia, 1876. The original title was "Yankee Doodle." The three familiar figures in the painting are an old man beating a drum, a soldier of the Continental army blowing a fife, and a boy in uniform, also drumming.

11
Don't give up the ship! You will beat them off!
> CAPTAIN JAMES MUGFORD, of the schooner *Franklin,* 19 May, 1776. These were his dying words during a British attack in Boston Harbor.

Keep the guns going! Fight her till she strikes or sinks! Don't give up the ship!
> CAPTAIN JAMES LAWRENCE, commander of the American frigate *Chesapeake,* 1 June, 1813. Lawrence is said to have repeated these words until his death, after being mortally wounded early in the action against the British *Shannon.* The quotation is attributed also to Benjamin Russell, editor of the Boston *Centinel;* some authorities claim that Russell coined it in his account of Lawrence's death.

Don't give up the ship!
> Signal floated at the masthead of Commodore Oliver Hazard Perry's flagship *Lawrence,* 10 Sept., 1813, during the battle of Lake Erie.

1

There, I guess King George will be able to read that.

> JOHN HANCOCK, on signing the Declaration of Independence, 4 July, 1776. He was referring to the boldness of his handwriting. The term "John Hancock" has become synonymous with "signature" from this.

2

Every kind of service, necessary to the public good, becomes honorable by being necessary.

> NATHAN HALE, 10 Sept., 1776. This statement was made to Hale's friend Captain William Hull, when the latter protested against Hale's entering the British lines as a spy.

3

I only regret that I have but one life to lose for my country.

> NATHAN HALE, spoken at the gallows in New York, 22 Sept., 1776, just before he was hanged by the British as a spy.

Witness to the world that I die like a man.

> MAJOR JOHN ANDRÉ, 2 Oct., 1780. The statement was made just before he was hanged as a spy.

4

Don't tread on me.

> Motto of the first flag of the American Revolution. The design was that of a pine tree with a rattlesnake coiled at its foot. The flag was flown from John Paul Jones's ship *Alfred* in 1776.

5

These are the times that try men's souls. The summer soldier and the sunshine patriot will, in this crisis, shrink from the service of their country; but he that stands it *now,* deserves the love and thanks of man and woman. Tyranny, like hell, is not easily conquered; yet we have this consolation with us, that the harder the conflict, the more glorious the triumph.

> THOMAS PAINE, *The Crisis* (intro., Dec., 1776).

6

It is the object only of war that makes it honorable. And if there was ever a just war since the world began, it is this in which America is now engaged. . . . We fight not to enslave, but to set a country free, and to make room upon the earth for honest men to live in.

> THOMAS PAINE, *The Crisis* (1776).

7

Put none but Americans on guard to-night.

> GEORGE WASHINGTON, derived from his circular letter to regimental commanders, dated 30 Apr., 1777, regarding recruits for his bodyguard: "You will therefore send me none but natives."

The order was prompted by an attempt by a deserter from the British army, Thomas Hickey, to poison Washington.

8

There, my boys, are your enemies, red-coats and Tories. You must beat them—or Molly Stark is a widow to-night.

> Attributed to COLONEL JOHN STARK, 16 Aug., 1777, at the battle of Bennington.

9

I have not yet begun to fight.

> JOHN PAUL JONES, 23 Sept., 1779, when his surrender was demanded by the opposing British, and when his ship *Bonhomme Richard* was sinking under him.

10

Put Watts into 'em, boys! Give 'em Watts!

> Attributed to REVEREND JAMES CALDWELL, 23 June, 1780. He is said to have shouted this while giving American troops hymnbooks to serve as wadding. The reference is to Isaac Watts (1674–1748), noted English hymn writer.

11

A National debt, if it is not excessive, will be to us a national blessing.

> ALEXANDER HAMILTON, Letter to Robert Morris, 30 Apr., 1781.

At the time we were funding our national debt, we heard much about "a public debt being a public blessing"; that the stock representing it was a creation of active capital for the aliment of commerce, manufactures, and agriculture.

> THOMAS JEFFERSON, Letter to John W. Epps, 6 Nov., 1813.

12

He defeated the Americans with great slaughter.

> UNKNOWN, Inscription on the tomb of Lord Cornwallis, Westminster Abbey. It was Cornwallis' own surrender at Yorktown, 17 Oct., 1781, that virtually ended the Revolutionary War.

13

The Government of the United States of America is not, in any sense, founded on the Christian religion.

> UNKNOWN, Treaty with Tripoli, 1796.

14

Millions for defense but not a cent for tribute.

> ROBERT GOODLOE HARPER, Toast, 18 June, 1798, at dinner in Philadelphia given by Congress in honor of John Marshall following his return from France. Harper was a member of Congress from South Carolina. Marshall's trip to France, as U.S. envoy, was aimed at stopping French attacks on U.S. shipping. By "tribute," Harper explained, he had in mind shipping losses through plunder,

not the payment of a bribe. (See below)

No, no; not a penny!

> CHARLES COTESWORTH PINCKNEY, 26 Oct., 1797. This was in reply to a demand made to Pinckney, in his role as American ambassador to France, for the payment of $250,000, the price necessary (it was said) to secure Pinckney and other U.S. envoys an audience with the French Directory in their effort to halt French attacks on American shipping. The demand was made by a secret agent named Hottenguer on behalf of Talleyrand, French foreign minister.

1

We give up the fort when there's not a man left to defend it.

> CAPTAIN GEORGE CROGHAN, 1 Aug., 1813. This was his reply to the British General Proctor at Fort Stephenson, Lower Sandusky, Ohio.

2

No ill luck stirring but what lights upon Uncle Sam's shoulders.

> UNKNOWN, Editorial, Troy (N.Y.) *Post,* 7 Sept., 1813. This is the first known use of the term "Uncle Sam."

3

Uncle Sam and John Bull.

> UNKNOWN, Editorial, *Columbian Centinel,* Dec., 1814.

4

We must consult Brother Jonathan.

> GEORGE WASHINGTON, referring to his Revolutionary War secretary and aide-de-camp, Col. Jonathan Trumbull. "Brother Jonathan" became synonymous with America.

5

Yankee Doodle, keep it up,
Yankee Doodle, dandy;
Mind the music and the step,
And with the girls be handy.

> EDWARD BANGS, *The Yankee's Return to Camp.* This is the chorus of the first version of the song, attributed to Bangs by Dr. Edward Everett Hale, though some authorities credit it to Dr. Richard Shuckburg, an officer in the British army during the French and Indian War. The music dates back at least to the reign of Charles II.

6

We have met the enemy and they are ours —two ships, two brigs, one schooner and one sloop.

> OLIVER HAZARD PERRY, Dispatch to General William Henry Harrison, 10 Sept., 1813, announcing Perry's victory in the battle of Lake Erie.

7

General Washington set the example of voluntary retirement after eight years. I shall follow it. And a few more precedents will oppose the obstacle of habit to any one who after a while shall endeavor to extend his term.

> THOMAS JEFFERSON, *Writings,* vol. xi.

8

Our country! in her intercourse with foreign nations may she always be in the right; but our country, right or wrong!

> STEPHEN DECATUR, Toast, Apr. 1816, at a dinner in his honor in Norfolk, Va. (MACKENZIE, *Life* of Decatur)

I hope to find my country in the right; however, I will stand by her, right or wrong.

> JOHN J. CRITTENDEN, Congressman from Kentucky, Speech in Congress, May, 1846. The statement was prompted by a message from President Polk relating to war with Mexico.

Our country, right or wrong! When right, to be kept right; when wrong, to be put right!

> CARL SCHURZ, Speech in U.S. Senate, 1872.

"My country, right or wrong," is a thing that no patriot would think of saying except in a desperate case. It is like saying, "My mother, drunk or sober."

> G. K. CHESTERTON, *The Defendant.*

9

The Era of Good Feelings.

> BENJAMIN RUSSELL, Title of article on Monroe's administration in the *Columbian Centinel,* Boston, 12 July, 1817.

10

This bill is an attempt to reduce the country south of Mason and Dixon's line to a state of worse than colonial bondage.

> JOHN RANDOLPH, of Roanoke, Va., Speech in Congress, 15 Apr., 1824, referring to the Missouri Compromise. The Mason-Dixon line, separating the free state of Pennsylvania and the then slave states of Maryland and Virginia, came to be regarded, by extension, as the boundary beyond which slavery should not be permitted.

11

Sink or swim, live or die, survive or perish, I give my heart and my hand to this vote.

> DANIEL WEBSTER, Eulogy on John Adams and Thomas Jefferson, 2 Aug., 1826. It introduced a speech supposedly made by Adams in favor of adoption of the Declaration of Independence. The phrase was derived from records of a conversation between Adams and Jonathan Sewall in 1774: "I answered that the die was now cast; I had passed the Rubicon. Sink or swim, live or die, survive or

perish with my country, was my unalterable determination."

1

I am in earnest—I will not equivocate—I will not excuse—I will not retreat a single inch AND I WILL BE HEARD.

> WILLIAM LLOYD GARRISON, *Salutatory, The Liberator.* Vol. i, No. 1, 1 Jan., 1831.

2

I will be as harsh as truth and as uncompromising as justice.

> WILLIAM LLOYD GARRISON. *The Liberator,* 1831.

3

He who dallies is a dastard; he who doubts is damned.

> Attributed to GEORGE MCDUFFIE, of South Carolina. It was quoted by Gov. James Hamilton of South Carolina in 1831, during the nullification period; by J. C. S. Blackburn, of Kentucky, in Congress, Feb., 1877, during the Hayes-Tilden controversy; and by Henry Watterson in his *Courier-Journal,* Louisville, in supporting Tilden.

4

Our manifest destiny to overspread the continent allotted by Providence for the free development of our yearly multiplying millions.

> JOHN L. O'SULLIVAN, *United States Magazine and Democratic Review,* vol. xvii, July–Aug., 1845. The quotation is from an editorial against opposition to the annexation of Texas. This was the first published use of the famous phrase "manifest destiny." (J. W. PRATT, *American Historical Review,* xxxii, 795)

It is our manifest destiny to lead and rule all other nations.

> JAMES GORDON BENNETT, Editorial. New York *Herald,* 3 Apr., 1865.

That word, "manifest destiny," which is profanely used, signifies the sense all men have of the prodigious energy and opportunity lying idle here.

> EMERSON, *Journals,* 1865.

5

If I were a Mexican, I would tell you, "Have you not enough room in your own country to bury your dead men? If you come into mine, I will greet you with bloody hands and welcome you to hospitable graves."

> THOMAS CORWIN, Speech, U.S. Senate, 11 Feb., 1846, delivered against entrance of the United States into the Mexican War, and in reply to Lewis Cass's assertion, "We want room."

6

Our country: whether bounded by the St. John's and the Sabine, or however otherwise bounded or described, and be the measurements more or less;—still our country, to be cherished in all our hearts, to be defended by all our hands!

> ROBERT C. WINTHROP, Toast, 4 July, 1846, at dinner in Faneuil Hall, Boston. He referred to the annexation of Texas.

7

A little more grape, Captain Bragg.

> Attributed to GENERAL ZACHARY TAYLOR, 22 Feb., 1847, at the battle of Buena Vista. The "Bragg" was Captain Braxton Bragg, of Taylor's command. This famous quotation has been denied by a number of authorities, including Ethan Allen Hitchcock, Inspector General of General Winfield Scott's army in Mexico.

8

Captain Bragg, it is better to lose a battery than a battle.

> Attributed to GENERAL ZACHARY TAYLOR, 22 Feb., 1847, at the battle of Buena Vista. This is said to have been his response to Captain Braxton Bragg, when the latter reported he would have to fall back or lose his battery.

9

General Taylor never surrenders.

> THOMAS L. CRITTENDEN, 22 Feb., 1847, battle of Buena Vista. This reply, on behalf of General Zachary Taylor, was in response to a demand for surrender, made by General Santa Ana, the Mexican commander. It became the slogan of Taylor's successful presidential campaign of 1848.

10

I shall defer my visit to Faneuil Hall, the cradle of American liberty, until its doors shall fly open upon golden hinges to lovers of Union as well as lovers of liberty.

> DANIEL WEBSTER, Letter, Apr., 1851, to friends who had invited him to speak in Boston, but who had been denied use of Faneuil Hall by the mayor and alderman, who presumably were reacting to a famous Webster speech of 7 March, 1851.

11

Go West, young man, go West!

> JOHN L. B. SOULE, Editorial, Terre Haute (Ind.) *Express,* 1851.

Go West, young man.

> HORACE GREELEY, Letter to W. H. Verity, 1854.

Go West, young man, and grow up with the country.

> HORACE GREELEY, *Hints Toward Reform.*

1

Cotton is King; or Slavery in the Light of Political Economy.

> DAVID CHRISTY, Title of book, 1855.

You dare not make war on cotton. Cotton is king.

> JAMES H. HAMMOND, Speech, March, 1858, U.S. Senate.

2

An irrepressible conflict between opposing and enduring forces.

> WILLIAM H. SEWARD, speech, 25 Oct., 1858. The forces were freedom and slavery.

3

Den I wish I was in Dixie! Horray! Hooray!
In Dixie's land we'll took our stand,
To lib an' die in Dixie!

> DANIEL DECATUR EMMETT, *Dixie* (1859).

To arms! To arms! To arms, in Dixie! . . .
For Dixie's land we take our stand,
And live or die for Dixie!

> ALBERT PIKE, *Dixie* (1861).

4

If any one attempts to haul down the American flag, shoot him on the spot.

> GENERAL JOHN A. DIX, Telegram, 29 Jan., 1861. Dix, Secretary of the Treasury, wired from Washington to William Hemphill Jones, a Treasury clerk who had been sent to New Orleans, ordering the arrest of Captain Breshwood, commander of the revenue cutter *McClennand*, when it was feared Breshwood would turn over the craft to Confederate authorities.

5

All we ask is to be let alone.

> JEFFERSON DAVIS, Inaugural Address, as President of the Confederate States of America, 18 Feb., 1861.

6

Say to the seceded States: "Wayward sisters, depart in peace!"

> WINFIELD SCOTT, Letter to W. H. Seward, 3 March, 1861.

7

I have been unable to make up my mind to raise my hand against my native state, my relatives, my children, and my home.

> ROBERT E. LEE, Statement upon resigning his commission in the U.S. Army at the time of Virginia's secession from the Union, Apr., 1861.

8

On to Richmond!

> FITZ-HENRY WARREN, Headline, New York *Tribune,* June, 1861.

9

A rich man's war and a poor man's fight.

> UNKNOWN, Slogan that appeared in the Confederacy in 1861, protesting against laws favoring wealthy slave owners.

10

All quiet along the Potomac to-night.

> ETHEL LYNN BEERS, *All Quiet along the Potomac.* The words were attributed to General George B. McClellan, commander of the Army of the Potomac, and undoubtedly helped to decrease his popularity in the North, which was impatient for progress in the war.

11

There is Jackson standing like a stone wall!

> BRIGADIER GENERAL BARNARD E. BEE, at the Battle of Bull Run, 21 July, 1861. He was referring to General Thomas Jonathan Jackson, thereafter known as "Stonewall," though Jackson himself said that Bee had signified Jackson's brigade by the remark.

12

Yell like furies when you charge!

> GENERAL THOMAS JONATHAN (STONEWALL) JACKSON, at the Battle of Bull Run, July, 1861.

13

No terms except an unconditional and immediate surrender can be accepted. I propose to move immediately upon your works.

> U. S. GRANT, 16 Feb., 1862, in reply to General Simon B. Buckner at Fort Donelson, Ky. (BADEAU, *Military History of U. S. Grant.*)

14

In times like the present, men should utter nothing for which they would not willingly be responsible through time and in eternity.

> ABRAHAM LINCOLN, Message to Congress, 1 Dec., 1862.

15

The Father of Waters again goes unvexed to the sea.

> ABRAHAM LINCOLN, Letter to James C. Conkling, 26 Aug., 1863. With the capture of Vicksburg, the Mississippi River had come entirely into the control of Union forces.

16

I propose to fight it out on this line if it takes all summer.

> U. S. GRANT, 11 May, 1864, to General Henry W. Halleck.

17

Damn the torpedoes!

> DAVID GLASGOW FARRAGUT, 5 Aug., 1864, at the battle of Mobile Bay.

18

Hold the fort, for I am coming!

> Attributed to GENERAL WILLIAM TECUMSEH SHERMAN, 5 Oct., 1864, as a message to General Corse, signaled from the top of Kenesaw Mountain, when Corse was attacked at Allatoona. Through constant usage, this has become the accepted version. The actual message was, "Hold out; relief is coming."

1
Now he belongs to the ages.
EDWIN M. STANTON, upon the death of Abraham Lincoln, 15 Apr., 1865.

2
Fellow-citizens: Clouds and darkness are around Him; His pavilion is dark waters and thick clouds; justice and judgment are the establishment of His throne; mercy and truth shall go before His face! God reigns and the Government at Washington lives.
JAMES A. GARFIELD, Address, Apr., 1865, from the balcony of the New York Custom House to a throng, following the assassination of President Lincoln.

America is the place where you cannot kill your government by killing the men who conduct it.
WOODROW WILSON, Address in Helena, Mont., 11 Sept., 1919. He was referring to the assassination of Lincoln; at the same time he cited James A. Garfield's address to the crowd in New York following the tragedy.

3
The way to resumption is to resume.
SALMON P. CHASE, Letter to Horace Greeley, 17 May, 1866.

4
The solid South.
GENERAL JOHN SINGLETON MOSBY, Letter, 1876, to a former Confederate comrade.

5
Waving the bloody shirt.
OLIVER P. MORTON, U.S. Senator from 1867 to 1879, is the man to whom this expression is attributed, as it applies to American politics. It was used to describe the Republicans' post-Civil War practice, in election campaigns, of citing their party's record in saving the Union and of denouncing the Democrats for bringing on the war.

It is a relief to remember that this phrase [waving the bloody shirt] is no invention of our politics. It dates back to Scotland three centuries ago. After a massacre in Glenfruin, not so savage as has stained our annals, two hundred and twenty widows rode on white palfreys to Stirling Tower, bearing each on a spear her husband's bloody shirt.
ROSCOE CONKLING, Speech in New York, 17 Sept., 1880. The phrase appears in English literature in the works of Sir Philip Sidney and Edward Gibbon.

6
I am thankful I have lived to see the day when the greenback can raise its right hand and declare "I know that my Redeemer liveth."
R. G. INGERSOLL, Speech, 1 Jan., 1879, from the sub-Treasury steps in Wall Street, upon resumption of specie payments.

7
Well, isn't this a billion dollar country?
Attributed to CHARLES FOSTER, Secretary of the Treasury under Harrison, in reply to the Democratic gibe about a "billion dollar Congress" [the 51st]. The quotation is also attributed to Thomas B. Reed, Speaker of the House of Representatives.

8
I have considered the pension list of the republic a roll of honor.
GROVER CLEVELAND, 5 July, 1888, in veto of Mary Ann Dougherty's pension.

9
We want no war of conquest. . . . War should never be entered upon until every agency of peace has failed.
WILLIAM MCKINLEY, Inaugural Address, 4 Mar., 1897.

10
Remember the Maine!
Slogan widely heard in the Spanish-American War. The U.S. battleship *Maine* was destroyed by a mine in the harbor of Havana, 15 Feb., 1898. The slogan was reminiscent of the rallying cry of the Texan war of independence from Mexico, "Remember the Alamo!," referring to the famous battle of the Alamo in Texas. And it was the pattern for the World War II slogan "Remember Pearl Harbor!," which referred to the Japanese attack on 7 Dec., 1941.

11
Please remain. You furnish the pictures and I'll furnish the war.
WILLIAM RANDOLPH HEARST, Telegram, March, 1898. (JOHN K. WINKLER, *W. R. Hearst.*) The message was sent to the artist Frederic Remington when the latter expressed a desire to return to the United States from Cuba, where he had been sent by Hearst to supply illustrations of the war with Spain for Hearst's newspapers. Remington complained that there was no war—and thus no material for him.

12
You may fire when you are ready, Gridley.
ADMIRAL GEORGE DEWEY, 1 May, 1898. Gridley was the captain of Dewey's flagship at the battle of Manila.

13
Don't cheer, boys; the poor devils are dying.
CAPTAIN JOHN WOODWARD PHILIP, 4 July, 1898. The skipper of the U.S. battleship *Texas* was referring to the burning Spanish ship *Vizcaya* at the battle of Santiago. (LODGE, *War with Spain.*)

1
The open door.
> JOHN HAY, 2 Jan., 1900. As Secretary of State, Hay was announcing the successful completion of negotiations designed to assure equality of trade with China for all nations. The phrase "open door" was used to describe the new policy.

2
I took Panama without consulting the Cabinet.
> THEODORE ROOSEVELT, *Memoirs*. The reference is to the revolution of 1 Nov., 1903, by which Panama became a republic.

3
We want Perdicaris alive or Raisuli dead.
> JOHN HAY, Cablegram, 22 June, 1904, to the American consul to Morocco. Ion H. Perdicaris, an American citizen, had been kidnapped by Raisuli, a Moroccan bandit, and held for ransom. The book *AP, The Story of the News* declares that the famous terse statement was suggested to Secretary of State Hay by Edwin M. Hood, an Associated Press reporter in Washington, for use in place of the lengthy dispatch Hay had prepared.

4
Remember, my son, that any man who is a bear on the future of this country will go broke.
> J. PIERPONT MORGAN, quoted by his son in a speech at the Chicago Club, 10 Dec., 1908. J. P. Morgan was paraphrasing his father, Junius Spencer Morgan.

5
We shall not, I believe, be obliged to alter our policy of watchful waiting.
> WOODROW WILSON, Message to Congress (relating to Mexico), 2 Dec., 1913.

6
We must be impartial in thought as well as in action. The United States must be neutral in fact as well as in name.
> WOODROW WILSON, Proclamation, 19 Aug., 1914.

7
Hold the Imperial German Government to strict accountability.
> WOODROW WILSON, Note to the German Government, 10 Feb., 1915.

8
Our whole duty, for the present, at any rate, is summed up in the motto: America first.
> WOODROW WILSON, Speech in New York, 20 Apr., 1915. In World War II, the expression "America first" became the rallying cry of non-interventionists.

9
There is such a thing as a man being too proud to fight.
> WOODROW WILSON, Speech in Philadelphia, 10 May, 1915. In his *Fighting Years*, Oswald Garrison Villard declares: "I supplied the President through Tumulty with a phrase which brought down upon him a storm of abuse and denunciation. The words 'too proud to fight' were mine."

10
Out of the trenches and back to their homes by Christmas.
> HENRY FORD, stating the purpose of his peace ship *Oscar II*, Dec., 1915. Ford abandoned this ill-fated project well before its completion.

11
Keep the home fires burning, while your hearts are yearning,
Tho' your lads are far away they dream of home.
> LENA GUILBERT FORD, *Keep the Home Fires Burning*. The theme was suggested by Ivor Novello, who set the words to music; the song was published in 1915.

12
You have laid upon me this double obligation: "We are relying upon you, Mr. President, to keep us out of war, but we are relying upon you, Mr. President, to keep the honor of the nation unstained."
> WOODROW WILSON, Address in Cleveland, 29 Jan., 1916.

He kept us out of war!
> MARTIN H. GLYNN, Keynote Speech, Democratic national convention, St. Louis, 15 June, 1916. This statement, referring to Woodrow Wilson, became the party's slogan in the ensuing campaign.

13
A little group of wilful men.
> WOODROW WILSON, Statement, 3 Mar., 1916. His reference was to eleven Senators who, by filibustering, had prevented the passage of a bill to authorize the President to arm U.S. merchantmen.

14
Wake up America.
> AUGUSTUS P. GARDNER, Speech, 16 Oct., 1916.

15
The world must be made safe for democracy.
> WOODROW WILSON, War Address to Congress, 2 Apr., 1917.

16
We have five hundred thousand and one lampposts in America, and that is where the German reservists will find themselves if they try any uprising.
> JAMES W. GERARD, U.S. ambassador to Germany, in reply to the German foreign minister, Zimmermann, who had predicted an uprising by 500,000 German reservists in America if the United

States entered World War I. (GERARD, *My Four Years in Germany*.)

1

Over there, over there, send the word, send the word over there!
That the Yanks are coming, the Yanks are coming,
The drums rum-tumming ev'rywhere:
So prepare, say a pray'r,
Send the word, send the word to beware!
We'll be over, we're coming over,
And we won't come back till it's over, over there.

> GEORGE M. COHAN, *Over There* (1917). This song, which became an official marching song of the U.S. Army, won for Cohan a public expression of thanks from President Woodrow Wilson.

2

Lafayette, we are here.

> COLONEL C. E. STANTON, Address, 4 July, 1917, at the grave of Lafayette in the Picpus Cemetery, Paris. This is often mistakenly attributed to General John J. Pershing, who himself cited Stanton as its author. (PERSHING, *My Experiences in the World War*.)

3

Come on, you sons of bitches! Do you want to live forever?

> GUNNERY SERGEANT DANIEL DALY, U.S. Marine Corps, 4 June, 1918, at Lucy-le-Bocage, on the fringe of Belleau Wood. Daly later declared his actual words were, "For Christ's sake, men, come on! Do you want to live forever?" The first version, however, is the one that has gained popular acceptance through repeated usage. A similar quotation is attributed to Frederick the Great at Kolin, 18 June, 1757.

4

The legend, "Heaven, Hell, or Hoboken by Christmas," on a tent near General Headquarters of our Expeditionary Force in France reflected the spirit of the whole American Army.

> GREGORY MASON, *How America Finished*, Paris, 7 Dec., 1918.

5

How'ya gonna keep 'em down on the farm,
After they've seen Paree?

> SAM M. LEWIS and JOE YOUNG, Title and refrain of song (1919) with music by Walter Donaldson.

6

America's present need is not heroics but healing; not nostrums but normalcy; not revolution but restoration; . . . not surgery but serenity.

> WARREN G. HARDING, Speech in Boston, May, 1920.

7

Profitless prosperity.

> A. W. SHAW, *The Underlying Trend of Business*. (*Magazine of Business,* Nov., 1927.)

8

Era of wonderful nonsense.

> WESTBROOK PEGLER, Newspaper Column. The reference was to the stock-market speculation of 1929, but the phrase was often used later to typify the 1920's in general.

9

Wall Street Lays An Egg.

> SIME SILVERMAN, Headline in *Variety,* referring to the stock-market crash of 1929.

10

Brother, can you spare a dime?

> E. Y. HARBURG, Song title and refrain (1932).

11

The only thing we have to fear is fear itself.

> FRANKLIN D. ROOSEVELT, First Inaugural Address, 4 Mar., 1933.

12

In the field of world policy, I would dedicate this nation to the policy of a good neighbor.

> FRANKLIN D. ROOSEVELT, First Inaugural Address, 4 Mar., 1933.

13

If I were asked to state the great objective which church and state are both demanding for the sake of every man and woman and child in this country, I would say that that great objective is a more abundant life.

> FRANKLIN D. ROOSEVELT, Address to the Federal Council of the Churches of Christ, 6 Dec., 1933. The phrase "a more abundant life" figured prominently in a number of subsequent Roosevelt speeches.

14

Every man a king.

> HUEY PIERCE LONG, Title of autobiography (1933). LONG also used this as the slogan of his share-the-wealth movement.

15

Share the wealth.

> HUEY PIERCE LONG, Name of the political movement launched by him in Louisiana in 1934. Long, nicknamed "the Kingfish," described its purpose as the elimination of poverty through the redistribution of wealth.

16

Okie use' to mean you was from Oklahoma. Now it means you're scum.

> JOHN STEINBECK, *The Grapes of Wrath*, referring to the great migration of the 1930's.

17

The former allies have blundered in the past by offering Germany too little, and offering even that too late, until finally Nazi Germany has become a menace to all mankind.

> ALLAN NEVINS, *Germany Disturbs the Peace. (Current History,* May, 1935.) David Lloyd George used the words "too late, or too little, or both . . . the road to disaster" in addressing the House of Commons in March, 1940, the day after Finland's fall.

1

It seems unfortunately true that the epidemic of world lawlessness is spreading. When an epidemic of physical disease starts to spread, the community . . . joins in a quarantine of the patients in order to protect the health of the community against the spread of the disease.

> FRANKLIN D. ROOSEVELT, Address in Chicago, 5 Oct., 1937. This famous "quarantine speech" called for, in effect, a quarantine of aggressors, or collective security.

2

South America becomes very quisling conscious.

> *Time,* 24 May, 1940. This pioneer use of "quisling" as synonymous with collaboration with the enemy derived from the case of Vidkun Quisling, leader of the Norwegian Nazi party, who headed the Nazi-sponsored government after the German invasion of Norway in April, 1940. He was executed as a traitor in 1945.

3

The hand that held the dagger has struck it into the back of its neighbor.

> FRANKLIN D. ROOSEVELT, Address, 10 June, 1940. The reference was to Italy's declaration of war on France.

4

And while I am talking to you mothers and fathers, I give you one more assurance. I have said this before, but I shall say it again and again and again. Your boys are not going to be sent into any foreign wars.

> FRANKLIN D. ROOSEVELT, Speech in Boston, 30 Oct., 1940. This was delivered just before his re-election to a third term. SAM ROSENMAN wrote, in his *Working With Roosevelt:* "Every time the President had made this statement before Boston—and every time thereafter —he added to it the words he himself had so carefully added to the foreign policy plank: 'Except in case of attack.' I suggested that he add the same words this time but he suddenly got stubborn about it—I could not understand why. 'It's not necessary,' he said. 'If we're attacked it's no longer a foreign war.' "

5

We must be the great arsenal of democracy.

> FRANKLIN D. ROOSEVELT, Radio Address, 29 Dec., 1940.

6

First, their countries seek no aggrandizement, territorial or otherwise. Second, they desire to see no territorial changes that do not accord with the freely expressed wishes of the people concerned.

> FRANKLIN D. ROOSEVELT and WINSTON CHURCHILL, *The Atlantic Charter,* formulated on the U.S.S. *Augusta,* 14 Aug., 1941.

7

Yesterday, December 7, 1941—a date that will live in infamy—the United States of America was suddenly and deliberately attacked by naval and air forces of the Empire of Japan.

> FRANKLIN D. ROOSEVELT, Message to Congress, 8 Dec., 1941, in which he asked for a declaration of war.

8

A bloody monument to divided responsibility.

> COLONEL HIGH J. KNERR, referring to the Japanese attack on Pearl Harbor, 7 Dec., 1941. (*American Mercury,* June, 1942.)

9

Praise the Lord and pass the ammunition.

> LIEUTENANT COMMANDER HOWELL FORGY, U.S. Navy Chaplain, to a chain of men passing ammunition aboard the cruiser *New Orleans,* Pearl Harbor, 7 Dec., 1941. This is also attributed to Fleet Chaplain William B. Maguire, who denied it. The quotation became the title of an inspirational song.

10

We are now in this war. We are in it—all the way. . . . We are going to win the war, and we are going to win the peace that follows.

> FRANKLIN D. ROOSEVELT, Radio Address, 9 Dec., 1941.

11

The militarists of Berlin and Tokyo started this war, but the massed angered forces of common humanity will finish it.

> FRANKLIN D. ROOSEVELT, Address before joint session of Congress, 6 Jan., 1942.

12

Sighted sub. Sank same.

> DONALD FRANCIS MASON, Radio Message to U.S. Navy Department, 26 Feb., 1942.

13

I shall return.

> GENERAL DOUGLAS MACARTHUR, to his fellow officers when he departed from the Philippine Islands for Australia, 11 Mar., 1942.

1

I shall keep a soldier's faith.

> GENERAL DOUGLAS MACARTHUR, upon his arrival in Melbourne, Australia, Mar., 1942. (CONSIDINE, *MacArthur the Magnificent.*)

2

Bataan has fallen, but the spirit that made it stand—a beacon to all the liberty-loving people of the world—cannot fall!

> LIEUTENANT NORMAN REYES, Radio Report, of the fall of Bataan, 9 Apr., 1942. This was sent from a tunnel in the fortress of Corregidor. (ROMULO, *I Saw the Fall of the Philippines*, p. 302.)

3

Scratch one flat-top.

> LIEUTENANT COMMANDER ROBERT E. DIXON, Radio Message to his aircraft carrier after sinking a Japanese carrier off Misima Island during the battle of the Coral Sea, 7 May, 1942. (JOHNSTON, *Queen of the Flat-Tops*, p. 181.)

4

I claim we got a hell of a beating. We got run out of Burma, and it is humiliating as hell. I think we should find out what caused it and go back and retake it.

> GENERAL JOSEPH W. STILWELL, Statement, May, 1942.

5

We shall attack and attack until we are exhausted, and then we shall attack again.

> MAJOR GENERAL GEORGE S. PATTON, JR., to his troops before they sailed for North Africa, 15 Nov., 1942.

6

Take her down.

> COMMANDER HOWARD W. GILMORE, Order to the crew of his submarine, *Growler*, during action against the Japanese in the South Pacific, Feb., 1943. He gave the order while lying on her deck, mortally wounded, knowing that the delay involved in getting him safely inside might mean the submarine's destruction.

7

America's Holy Grail lies on Corregidor.

> GENERAL DOUGLAS MACARTHUR, Statement, on the first anniversary of the surrender of the fortress, Manila Bay, 8 May, 1943.

8

Hell, we haven't started to fight. Our artillery hasn't been overrun yet.

> GENERAL TERRY ALLEN, at the invasion of Sicily, July, 1943.

9

The Grumlin does the same job of sabotage on the home front that the Gremlin does to the airplanes of our pilots fighting the Axis.

> SAM RAYBURN, Speech at East Texas State Teachers College, 5 Aug., 1943. The term "Gremlins" was applied to the perverse imps that caused unforseen, and often unexplainable, mechanical difficulties. The first one was supposed to have been born in a beer bottle in 1923. (See *Newsweek*, 7 Sept., 1942.)

10

God Is My Co-Pilot.

> ROBERT L. SCOTT, JR., Title of his book based on World War II action.

11

The Seabees are always happy to welcome the Marines.

> LIEUTENANT BOB RYAN, greeting Marines as they landed at Segi, New Georgia, Sept., 1943. Although the Seabees were supposed to land simultaneously with the Marines, or shortly thereafter, they had arrived first.

12

G. I. Joe.

> Name popularly used during World War II to identify American soldiers, especially infantrymen. The initials stand for "government issue."

13

Kilroy was here.

> UNKNOWN. There are many theories about the origin of this very popular saying, which was scrawled by American service men on walls and other surfaces wherever they penetrated during World War II. "Kilroy" became synonymous with each of them.

14

Hurry up and wait.

> UNKNOWN. This was an often-heard service men's lament about military practice as it affected their daily routine in World War II.

15

The difficult we do immediately. The impossible takes a little longer.

> Motto, U.S. Army Corps of Engineers. Other branches of the armed forces also employed this, paraphrasing slightly.

16

Suppose you're a sergeant machine-gunner, and your army is retreating and the enemy advancing. The captain takes you to a machine gun covering the road. "You're to stay here and hold this position," he tells you. "For how long?" you ask. "Never mind," he answers, "just hold it." Then you know you're expendable. In a war anything can be expendable—money or gasoline or equipment or most usually men. They are expending you and that machine gun to get time.

> W. L. WHITE, *They Were Expendable*, p. 3.

17

The eyes of the world are upon you. The

hopes and prayers of liberty-loving people everywhere march with you.

> GENERAL DWIGHT D. EISENHOWER, Message to his troops at the invasion of Normandy, 6 June, 1944.

1

People of the Philippines, I have returned.

> GENERAL DOUGLAS MACARTHUR, Radio Address, 20 Oct., 1944, upon landing on Leyte.

2

Nuts!

> GENERAL ANTHONY C. MCAULIFFE, Retort to a German demand for surrender at Bastogne, Belgium, 22 Dec., 1944. In a letter to the compiler, General McAuliffe reported:
>
> " 'Nuts' was the reply. I received a surrender demand addressed to 'The American Commander' and signed 'The German Commander.' It threatened heavy shelling and bombing and suggested that I consider the effects on the Belgian civilians in the town. After reading it, I commented 'Nuts' and went out to visit the troops. Upon my return to the C.P., I was told that the German envoys still remained at the 327th Infantry regimental C.P., were still blindfolded and were asking for an official reply to their official communication. My staff suggested that my first crack would be appropriate, so I said: 'Write it up.' They typed: 'To the German Commander. Nuts. (signed) The American Commander.' The English-speaking German officer did not understand. Our Colonel Harper said: 'It means the same as "Go to Hell." You understand that, don't you?' He did."

3

Expedience and justice frequently are not even on speaking terms.

> ARTHUR H. VANDENBERG, Speech in U.S. Senate, 8 Mar., 1945. He referred to the ceding of eastern Poland to the Soviet Union, as decided at the Yalta conference of Roosevelt, Churchill, and Stalin.

4

Sixteen hours ago an American airplane dropped one bomb on Hiroshima. . . . It is a harnessing of the basic power of the universe. The force from which the sun draws its powers has been loosed against those who brought war to the Far East.

> HARRY S TRUMAN, Statement on the first use of the atomic bomb in combat, 6 Aug., 1945.

5

A shadow has fallen upon the scenes so lately lighted by the Allied victory. From Stettin in the Baltic to Trieste in the Adriatic, an iron curtain has descended across the Continent.

> WINSTON CHURCHILL, Address at Westminster College, Fulton, Mo., 5 Mar., 1946. The use of "iron curtain" in this sense dates from Churchill's speech. An earlier use occurs in H. G. WELLS's *The Food of the Gods,* bk. iii, ch. 4, pt. 1 and pt. 3 (1904): "Redwood had still imperfectly apprehended the fact that an iron curtain had dropped between him and the outer world." The phrase was used in a sense closer to its present one in GEORGE M. CRILE's *A Mechanistic View of War and Peace,* ch. 4, p. 69 (1915): "Mexico . . . with a deep rooted grievance, and an iron curtain at its frontier."

6

We are here to make a choice between the quick and the dead.

> BERNARD M. BARUCH, Statement to the United Nations Atomic Energy Commission, 14 June, 1946.

7

Cold war.

> HERBERT BAYARD SWOPE. Mr. Swope, in a letter to Burton Stevenson, editor of *The Home Book of Quotations* and *The Home Book of Verse,* declared: "I have been using the phrase 'cold war,' as B. M. Baruch and others will confirm, since 1945, several months before the death of President Roosevelt. I put it in writing in one or two letters in 1946. . . . I put it in a speech that Baruch made to the South Carolina legislature . . . 16 April, 1947." The speech marked the first public use of the phrase.

Let us not be deceived—we are today in the midst of a cold war.

> BERNARD M. BARUCH, Speech before the South Carolina Legislature, 16 Apr., 1947.

In the interview, which was brief, Baruch said he was the first person to use the phrase "cold war." He said it was suggested to him by Herbert Bayard Swope, former editor of the defunct New York *World.*

> Interview with Bernard M. Baruch, Boston *Globe,* 1 Apr., 1949.

8

Our policy is directed not against any country or doctrine but against hunger, poverty, desperation and chaos. . . . At this critical point in history, we of the United States are deeply conscious of our responsibilities toward the world. We know that in this trying period, between a war that is over and a peace that is not yet secure, the destitute and oppressed of the earth look chiefly to us for sustenance and support until they can again face life with self-confidence and self-reliance.

GEORGE CATLETT MARSHALL, Address at Harvard University, 5 June, 1947, outlining the European Recovery Program, the system of postwar economic assistance that became known as the Marshall Plan.

I had referred to the idea [European Recovery Program] as the "Marshall Plan" when it was discussed in staff meetings because I wanted General Marshall to get full credit for his brilliant contributions to the measure which he helped formulate.

HARRY S TRUMAN, *The Truman Memoirs, Pt. II* (1956).

1
In the face of this victory of United Nations arms the Communists committed one of the most offensive acts of international lawlessness of historic record by moving without any notice of belligerency elements of alien Communist forces across the Yalu River into North Korea and massing a great concentration of possible reinforcing divisions with adequate supply behind the privileged sanctuary of the adjacent Manchurian border.

GENERAL DOUGLAS MACARTHUR, Communiqué No. 11, 6 Nov., 1950.

United Nations forces are now being attacked from the safety of a privileged sanctuary.

HARRY S TRUMAN, Statement, 15 Nov., 1950. (Quoted by FRAZIER HUNT in *The Untold Story of Douglas MacArthur*, p. 482. According to Hunt, "It was the first time that the phrase 'privileged sanctuary' had been used in a public document.")

2
Retreat, hell! We're just fighting in another direction.

GENERAL O. P. SMITH, U.S. Marine Corps, Retort at Changjin Reservoir, North Korea, 1950. *Retreat, Hell* became the title of a film based on the Korean War.

3
When I joined the army, even before the turn of the century, it was the fulfillment of all my boyish hopes and dreams. . . . I still remember the refrain of one of the most popular barracks ballads of that day, which proclaimed most proudly that old soldiers never die; they just fade away. And like the old soldier of that ballad, I now close my military career and just fade away.

GENERAL OF THE ARMY DOUGLAS MACARTHUR, Address before a joint session of the U.S. Congress, 19 Apr., 1951. The ballad referred to stemmed from a hymn, *Kind Words Can Never Die*, written about 1855 by "Sister" Abby Hutchinson and set to music by Horace Waters. When Miss Hutchinson's group of evangelists toured Civil War camps of the Union Army, the song was adapted for army use. British soldiers also sang a version of it in World War I.

4
In war there is no substitute for victory.

GENERAL DOUGLAS MACARTHUR, Address to joint session of Congress, 19 Apr., 1951.

5
It is fatal to enter any war without the will to win it.

GENERAL DOUGLAS MACARTHUR, Speech, Republican national convention, 7 July, 1952.

Of all the campaigns of my life, twenty major ones to be exact, the one I felt most sure of was the one I was deprived of waging. I could have won the war in Korea in a maximum of ten days, with considerably fewer casualties than were suffered during the so-called truce period, and it would have altered the course of history.

GENERAL DOUGLAS MACARTHUR. Quoted by Bob Considine of the Hearst newspapers in an interview granted 27 Jan., 1954, but not published until 8 Apr., 1964, three days after MacArthur's death, in keeping with his stipulation that it not be released during his lifetime.

6
Let's face it. Let's talk sense to the American people. Let's tell them the truth, that there are no gains without pains, that we are now on the eve of great decisions, not easy decisions, like resistance when you're attacked, but a long, patient, costly struggle which alone can assure triumph over the great enemies of man—war, poverty, and tyranny—and the assaults upon human dignity which are the most grievous consequences of each.

ADLAI E. STEVENSON, Acceptance Speech, Democratic national convention, 26 July, 1952.

7
When I was in Paris last week, I said that . . . the United States would have to undertake an agonizing reappraisal of basic foreign policy in relation to Europe. This statement, I thought, represented a self-evident truth.

JOHN FOSTER DULLES, Address to National Press Club, Washington, D.C., 22 Dec., 1953.

8
Local defense must be reinforced by the further deterrent of massive retaliatory power.

JOHN FOSTER DULLES, Speech before the

Council of Foreign Relations, 12 Jan., 1954. The instrument of this policy, aimed at deterring international aggression, became known popularly as "massive retaliation."

Our capacity to retaliate must be, and is, massive in order to deter all forms of aggression.
JOHN FOSTER DULLES, Speech in Chicago, 8 Dec., 1955.

1
You have to take chances for peace, just as you must take chances in war. Some say that we were brought to the verge of war. Of course we were brought to the verge of war. The ability to get to the verge without getting into the war is the necessary art. If you cannot master it, you inevitably get into war. If you try to run away from it, if you are scared to go to the brink, you are lost. We've had to look it square in the face—on the question of enlarging the Korean War, on the question of getting into the Indo-china war, on the question of Formosa. We walked to the brink and we looked it in the face. We took strong action.
JOHN FOSTER DULLES. Quoted by JAMES SHEPLEY, chief of the *Time-Life* Washington bureau, in *How Dulles Averted War, Life,* 16 Jan., 1956. This quotation was the key part of an article that aroused international controversy and caused Dulles' critics to coin the term "brinkmanship" in describing his policy as Secretary of State. On 17 Jan., 1956, at a news conference, Dulles verified the "substance" of the quotations "specifically attributed to me" in the article.

The art of diplomacy, especially in this atomic age, must lead to peace, not war or the brink of war.
ADLAI E. STEVENSON, Statement in Chicago, 14 Jan., 1956, referring to the "brink of war" statement by John Foster Dulles in the then-current issue of *Life.*

If we ever get suckered into World War III it will be because we appear to be weak. . . . I believe that the Eisenhower-Dulles program of what we call brinkmanship, the retaliation effect in the maintaining of a strong military, is essential in keeping peace in the world today.
BARRY M. GOLDWATER, U.S. Senator from Arizona, Radio Address to a Franklin Square, N.Y., high-school history class, broadcast from his home in Washington, 8 Nov., 1963, via his own amateur transmitter.

After all, brinkmanship is absolutely neces-

sary in this troubled world of ours to keep the peace. But it must be used intelligently and not recklessly.
DWIGHT D. EISENHOWER, Statement during filmed television program, *Conversation at Gettysburg,* made by Eisenhower and Barry M. Goldwater at Gettysburg, Pa., and shown nationally 22 Sept., 1964, during the presidential campaign.

2
With all deliberate speed.
U.S. Supreme Court Decision, 31 May, 1955. This historic ruling made unconstitutional "separate but equal schools" for Negroes, and directed integrated schooling "with all deliberate speed."

There has been entirely too much deliberation and not enough speed. The time for mere "deliberate speed" has run out and that phrase can no longer justify denying these Prince Edward children their constitutional rights to an education equal to that afforded by the public schools in the other parts of Virginia.
HUGO L. BLACK, Majority Opinion, U.S. Supreme Court, 25 May, 1964. On this date the court ordered reopening, on an integrated basis, of the schools in Prince Edward County, Va. In 1959, faced with an order to integrate at once, the county (alone among all those in the state and throughout the rest of the nation) had shut down its public schools rather than operate them on an integrated basis.

3
Whenever normal agencies prove inadequate to the task and it becomes necessary for the Executive Branch of the Federal Government to use its powers and authority to uphold Federal Courts, the President's responsibility is inescapable.

In accordance with that responsibility I have today issued an Executive Order directing the use of troops under Federal authority to aid in the execution of Federal law at Little Rock, Arkansas.
DWIGHT D. EISENHOWER, Address to the nation, 24 Sept., 1957, explaining the dispatch of troops under the command of Major General Edwin A. Walker, to enforce integration of the races at Central High School.

4
Let the word go forth from this time and place, to friend and foe alike, that the torch has been passed to a new generation of Americans—born in this century, tempered by war, disciplined by a hard and bitter peace, proud of our ancient heritage—and unwilling to witness or permit the slow undoing of those human rights to which this nation has always been committed, and to

which we are committed today at home and around the world.

    JOHN F. KENNEDY, Inaugural Address, 20 Jan., 1961.

1

To our sister republics south of our border, we offer a special pledge—to convert our good words into good deeds—in a new alliance for progress—to assist free men and free governments in casting off the chains of poverty.

    JOHN F. KENNEDY, Inaugural Address, 20 Jan., 1961.

2

We intend to bury no one—and we do not intend to be buried.

    LYNDON B. JOHNSON, State of the Union Message, 8 Jan., 1964. The reference is to the highly controversial statement by Nikita Khrushchev: "We will bury you."

Whether you like it or not, history is on our side. We will bury you.

    NIKITA S. KHRUSHCHEV, Statement at Kremlin diplomatic reception, Moscow, 18 Nov., 1956.

Our firm conviction is that sooner or later capitalism will give way to socialism. No one can halt man's forward movement, just as no one can prevent day following night.

    NIKITA S. KHRUSHCHEV, Statement in Leipzig, 9 Aug., 1957. (In *Conquest Without War*, an anthology of speeches by Khrushchev, compiled and edited by N. H. Mager and Jacques Katel, p. 49.)

My life would be too short to bury every one of you if this were to occur to me. . . . I said that in the course of historical progress and in the historical sense, capitalism would be buried and communism would come to replace capitalism.

    NIKITA S. KHRUSHCHEV, Statement in Tatabanya, Hungary. Reported in *Pravda*, 9 Apr., 1958. (In *Conquest Without War*, an anthology of the speeches of Khrushchev, compiled and edited by N. H. Mager and Jacques Katel, p. 49.)

Capitalism is a worn-out old mare while socialism is new, young, and full of teeming energy.

    NIKITA S. KHRUSHCHEV, Statement in Tatabanya, Hungary. Reported in *Pravda*, 9 Apr., 1958. (In *Conquest Without War*, p. 49.)

The words "We will bury capitalism" should not be taken literally as indicating what is done by ordinary gravediggers who carry a spade and dig graves and bury the dead. What I had in mind was the outlook for the development of human society. Socialism will inevitably succeed capitalism.

    NIKITA S. KHRUSHCHEV, Statement to civic authorities, Los Angeles, 19 Sept., 1959. (In *Conquest Without War*, p. 49.)

The revisionists are producing their own opposites and will be buried by them. This is an inexorable law.

    UNKNOWN, from a lengthy polemic transmitted by the official New China News Agency, broadcast by Peking radio and reproduced in *People's Daily* and the Chinese theoretical journal *Red Flag*, 3 Feb., 1964. (Reported in the New York *Herald Tribune*, 4 Feb., 1964.) The polemic was typical of the Communist Chinese attacks on the Soviet Union during this period, which invariably blamed Moscow "revisionists," notably Nikita S. Khrushchev, for the prevailing split in international Communist ranks. In this case the Soviet leadership in general was described as "the greatest splitters of our time."

We face in Communist hostility and expansionism a formidable force, whether Mr. Khrushchev and Mr. Mao Tse-tung pull together or apart. They disagree so far only on whether capitalism should be peacefully or violently buried. They are both for the funeral.

    ADLAI E. STEVENSON, *The Hard Kind of Patriotism; Harper's Magazine*, July, 1963.

3

This Administration here and now declares unconditional war on poverty in America.

    LYNDON B. JOHNSON, State of the Union Message, 8 Jan., 1964.

ANCESTRY

See also Posterity

4

Three generations from shirtsleeves to shirtsleeves.

    Attributed to ANDREW CARNEGIE. A verifiable quotation from his published work is the following, contained in a letter: "Even in Yorkshire the proverb is, 'Three generations from clogs to clogs.'" (HENDRICK, *Life*, vol. ii)

5

The pride of ancestry increases in the ratio of distance.

    GEORGE WILLIAM CURTIS, *Prue and I*, ch. 6.

6

The pedigree of honey
Does not concern the bee;

A clover, any time, to him
Is aristocracy.
    EMILY DICKINSON, *Poems*, Pt. ii, No. 56.

1
How shall a man escape from his ancestors
or draw off from his veins the black drop
which he drew from his father's or his mother's life? It often appears in a family, as if
all the qualities of the progenitors were pot-
ted in several jars—some ruling quality in
each son or daughter of the house,—and
sometimes the unmixed temperament, the
rank unmitigated elixir, the family vice, is
drawn off in a separate individual, and the
others are proportionally relieved.
    EMERSON, *Conduct of Life: Fate.*

2
What can I do against the influence of Race,
in my history? What can I do against hered-
ity and constitutional habits; against scrofu-
la, lymph, impotence?
    EMERSON, *Representative Men: Mon-
    taigne.*

3
Noblesse oblige; or, superior advantages bind
you to larger generosity.
    EMERSON, *Letters and Social Aims: Prog-
    ress of Culture.*

4
Men resemble their contemporaries even
more than their progenitors.
    EMERSON, *Representative Men: Uses of
    Great Men.*

5
This body in which we journey across the
isthmus between the two oceans is not a private carriage, but an omnibus.
    OLIVER WENDELL HOLMES, *The Guardian
    Angel.*

6
No, my friends, I go (always other things
being equal) for the man who inherits family
traditions and the cumulative humanities of
at least four or five generations.
    OLIVER WENDELL HOLMES, *The Autocrat
    of the Breakfast-Table.*

7
O Damsel Dorothy! Dorothy Q.!
Strange is the gift that I owe to you; . . .
What if, a hundred years ago,
Those close-shut lips had answered No,
When forth the tremulous question came
That cost the maiden her Norman name,
And under the folds that look so still
The bodice swelled with the bosom's thrill?
Should I be I, or would it be
One-tenth another, to nine-tenths me?
    OLIVER WENDELL HOLMES, *Dorothy Q.*

8
I don't know who my grandfather was; I am
much more concerned to know what his
grandson will be.
    ABRAHAM LINCOLN. (GROSS, *Lincoln's
    Own Stories*)

9
The stairway of time ever echoes with the
wooden shoe going up and the polished boot
coming down.
    JACK LONDON, *What Life Means to Me,
    Cosmopolitan Magazine*, March, 1906.

10
Somehow I've always had a sort of sneakin'
  Idee that peddygrees is purty much
Like monkeys' tails—so long they're apt to
  weaken
    The yap that drags 'em round.
    ROBERTUS LOVE, *The Boy from Hodgens-
    ville.*

11
They talk about their Pilgrim blood,
    Their birthright high and holy!
A mountain-stream that ends in mud
    Methinks is melancholy.
    JAMES RUSSELL LOWELL, *An Interview
    with Miles Standish.*

12
Sence I've ben here, I've hired a chap to
  look about for me
To git me a transplantable an' thrifty fem'ly-
  tree.
    JAMES RUSSELL LOWELL, *Biglow Papers,*
    Ser. ii, No. 3.

13
Of a very old stock a most eminent
  scion,— . . .
Whose pedigree, traced to earth's earliest
  years,
Is longer than anything else but their ears.
    JAMES RUSSELL LOWELL, *A Fable for Crit-
    ics.*

14
i have often noticed that
ancestors never boast
of the descendants who boast
of ancestors i would
rather start a family than
finish one blood will tell but often
it tells too much.
    DON MARQUIS, *a roach of the taverns.*

15
Aristocracy is always cruel.
    WENDELL PHILLIPS, *Speeches: Toussaint
    L'Ouverture.*

16
Those transparent swindles—transmissible
nobility and kingship.
    MARK TWAIN, *A Connecticut Yankee at
    King Arthur's Court.*

17
The stream is brightest at its spring,
    And blood is not like wine;
Nor honored less than he who heirs
    Is he who founds a line.
    JOHN GREENLEAF WHITTIER, *Amy Went-
    worth.*

ANGELS

18
I know that they are happy

With their angel-plumage on.
PARK BENJAMIN, *The Departed*.

1
We trust, in plumed procession,
For such the angels go,
Rank after rank, with even feet
And uniforms of snow.
EMILY DICKINSON, *Poems*, Pt. i, No. 16.

2
Was there no star that could be sent,
No watcher in the firmament,
No angel from the countless host
That loiters round the crystal coast,
Could stoop to heal that only child?
EMERSON, *Threnody*.

3
How did he get thar? Angels.
  He could never have walked in that
    storm.
They jest scooped down and toted him
  To whar it was safe and warm.
And I think that saving a little child,
  And fotching him to his own,
Is a derned sight better business
  Than loafing around the Throne.
JOHN HAY, *Little Breeches*.

4
Writ in the climate of heaven, in the lan-
  guage spoken by angels.
LONGFELLOW, *The Children of the Lord's
  Supper*.

5
There are two angels, that attend unseen
Each one of us, and in great books record
Our good and evil deeds. He who writes
  down
The good ones, after every action closes
His volume, and ascends with it to God.
The other keeps his dreadful day-book open
Till sunset, that we may repent; which do-
  ing,
The record of the action fades away,
And leaves a line of white across the page.
LONGFELLOW, *Christus:* pt. ii, *The School
  of Salerno*.

6
An angel stood and met my gaze,
  Through the low doorway of my tent;
The tent is struck, the vision stays;—
  I only know she came and went.
JAMES RUSSELL LOWELL, *She Came and
  Went*.

7
But all God's angels come to us disguised:
Sorrow and sickness, poverty and death,
One after other lift their frowning masks,
And we behold the Seraph's face beneath,
All radiant with the glory and the calm
Of having looked upon the front of God.
JAMES RUSSELL LOWELL, *On the Death of
  a Friend's Child*.

8
Around our pillows golden ladders rise,
And up and down the skies,

With winged sandals shod,
The angels come, and go, the Messengers of
  God!
R. H. STODDARD, *Hymn to the Beautiful*.

9
Sweet souls around us watch us still,
Press nearer to our side;
Into our thoughts, into our prayers,
With gentle helpings glide.
HARRIET BEECHER STOWE, *The Other
  World*.

10
When I see angels in pettycoats I'm always
sorry they hain't got wings so they kin quietly fly off whare they will be appreshiated.
ARTEMUS WARD, *Piccolomini*.

11
Like the patriarch's angel hold it fast
  Till it gives its blessing.
WHITTIER, *My Soul and I*.

12
With silence only as their benediction,
  God's angels come
Where, in the shadow of a great affliction,
  The soul sits dumb!
WHITTIER, *To My Friend on the Death of
  His Sister*.

ANGER
See also Hatred, Passion

13
Never forget what a man says to you when
he is angry.
HENRY WARD BEECHER, *Life Thoughts*.

14
Anger is an expensive luxury in which only
men of a certain income can indulge.
GEORGE WILLIAM CURTIS, *Prue and I*.

15
A man should study ever to keep cool. He
makes his inferiors his superiors by heat.
EMERSON, *Social Aims*.

16
Our temperatures differ in capacity of heat,
or, we boil at different degrees.
EMERSON, *Society and Solitude: Eloquence*.

17
Anger and folly walk cheek by jole;
repentance treads on both their heels.
BENJAMIN FRANKLIN, *Poor Richard*,
  1741.

18
A man in a passion rides a mad horse.
BENJAMIN FRANKLIN, *Poor Richard*,
  1749.

19
Thar ain't no sense in gittin' riled.
BRET HARTE, *Jim*.

20
When angry, count ten before you speak; if
very angry, an hundred.
THOMAS JEFFERSON, *Writings*, vol. xvi.

When angry, count four; when very angry, swear.
> MARK TWAIN, *Pudd'nhead Wilson's Calendar.*

1
Says he, "I reckon I'm a ding-dang fool
For gettin' het up when I might stay cool:
If you are a hoss—then I'm a mule,"
Under the Joshua tree.
> HENRY H. KNIBBS, *Under the Joshua Tree.*

2
Sensitive, swift to resent, but as swift in atoning for error.
> HENRY WADSWORTH LONGFELLOW, *The Courtship of Miles Standish:* pt. ix, *The Wedding Day,* st. 3.

3
The one that fust gits mad's most ollers wrong.
> JAMES RUSSELL LOWELL, *Biglow Papers.* Ser. ii, *Mason and Slidell.*

4
Every normal man must be tempted, at times, to spit on his hands, hoist the black flag, and begin slitting throats.
> H. L. MENCKEN, *Prejudices,* ser. i.

5
Every stroke our fury strikes is sure to hit ourselves at last.
> WILLIAM PENN, *Fruits of Solitude.*

ANXIETY, see Fear, Worry

APOLOGY, see Excuse

APPEARANCE

6
Black Tragedy lets slip her grim disguise
And shows you laughing lips and roguish eyes;
But when, unmasked, gay Comedy appears,
How wan her cheeks are, and what heavy tears!
> THOMAS BAILEY ALDRICH, *Masks.*

7
There's less in this than meets the eye.
> TALLULAH BANKHEAD, Remark to Alexander Woollcott during a performance of Maeterlinck's *The Burgomaster of Stilemonde* at the Belmont Theatre, New York, 24 Mar., 1919. This classic one-line critique was traced to its source with the help of Richard Maney, theatrical press agent and long-time associate of Miss Bankhead. He recalled, "The mot received wide circulation when Woollcott quoted it in his review in the [New York] *Times* of March 25, crediting it to 'the beautiful young woman who accompanied me.' This was shortly after Tallulah stormed up from Huntsville, Ala., to besiege Broadway and lay waste the Algonquin Hotel."

8
Always scorn appearances and you always may.
> EMERSON, *Essays, First Series: Self-Reliance.*

9
Don't judge by appearances, but by his actions more,
You never know when you may drive a good man from your door;
Clothes don't make the man, you know, some wise person wrote,
For many an honest heart may beat beneath a ragged coat.
> HAWLEY FRANCK, *Many an Honest Heart May Beat Beneath a Ragged Coat* (song, 1901, with music by Arthur Trevelyan).

10
After all, you can't expect men not to judge by appearances.
> ELLEN GLASGOW, *The Sheltered Life.*

11
Hit look lak sparrer-grass, hit feel like sparrer-grass, hit tas'e lak sparrer-grass, en I bless ef 'taint sparrer-grass.
> JOEL CHANDLER HARRIS, *Nights with Uncle Remus.*

When I see a bird that walks like a duck and swims like a duck and quacks like a duck, I call that bird a duck.
> RICHARD CARDINAL CUSHING, commenting on the propriety of calling Fidel Castro a Communist. (New York *Times,* 1 March, 1964.)

12
The outward forms the inward man reveal,—
We guess the pulp before we cut the peel.
> OLIVER WENDELL HOLMES, *A Rhymed Lesson.*

13
I remember that it was once reported of General Marshall, when he first entered V.M.I., that he landed in the awkward squad. And he stayed there, on and on. He could not drill. He could not march. All he could do was swear, look uncomfortable, and be embarrassed whenever he was spoken to. So, cheer up, gentlemen, and be courteous to each of your classmates. No matter how unpromising he might look today, remember he may be your Chief of Staff one day.
> LYNDON B. JOHNSON, Address at the dedication of the George C. Marshall Research Library, Virginia Military Institute, Lexington, Va., 23 May, 1964.

14
And things are not what they seem.
> HENRY WADSWORTH LONGFELLOW, *A Psalm of Life.*

15
Of the terrible doubt of appearances,

Of the uncertainty after all, that we may be
    deluded,
That may-be reliance and hope are but spec-
    ulations after all,
That may-be identity beyond the grave is a
    beautiful fable only,
May-be the things I perceive, the animals,
    plants, men, hills, shining and flowing
    waters,
The skies of day and night, colors, densities,
    forms, may-be these are (as doubtless
    they are) only apparitions, and the real
    something has yet to be known.
    WALT WHITMAN, *Of the Terrible Doubt
    of Appearances.*

1
Ain't he the damnedest simulacrum!
    WALT WHITMAN, referring to Algernon
    Charles Swinburne, after the latter had
    turned against him.

APPETITE, see Eating

APPLAUSE, see Praise

APPLE

2
But I, when I undress me
    Each night, upon my knees
Will ask the Lord to bless me
    With apple pie and cheese!
    EUGENE FIELD, *Apple Pie and Cheese.*

3
What is more melancholy than the old apple-
trees that linger about the spot where once
stood a homestead, but where there is now
only a ruined chimney rising out of a grassy
and weed-grown cellar? They offer their fruit
to every wayfarer—apples that are bitter-
sweet with the moral of time's vicissitude.
    NATHANIEL HAWTHORNE, *Mosses from an
    Old Manse: The Old Manse.*

4
There's plenty of boys that will come
hankering and gruvvelling around when
you've got an apple, and beg the core off
you; but when *they've* got one, and you beg
for the core, and remind them how you give
them a core one time, they make a mouth at
you, and say thank you 'most to death, but
there ain't a-going to *be* no core.
    MARK TWAIN, *Tom Sawyer Abroad.*

APRIL

See also Spring

5
Make me over, Mother April,
When the sap begins to stir!
Make me man or make me woman,
Make me oaf or ape or human,
Cup of flower or cone of fir;
Make me anything but neuter
When the sap begins to stir!
    BLISS CARMAN, *Spring Song.*

6
Once more in misted April
    The world is growing green,
Along the winding river
    The plumey willows lean.
    BLISS CARMAN, *An April Morning.*

7
April's amazing meaning doubtless lies
    In tall, hoarse boys and slips
Of slender girls with suddenly wider eyes
    And parted lips.
    GEORGE DILLON, *April's Amazing Mean-
    ing.*

8
April's rare capricious loveliness.
    JULIA C. R. DORR, *November.*

9
April is the cruellest month, breeding
Lilacs out of the dead land, mixing
Memory and desire, stirring
Dull roots with spring rain.
    T. S. ELIOT, *The Waste Land: The Burial
    of the Dead.*

10
And April winds are magical,
    And thrill our tuneful frames;
The garden-walks are passional
    To bachelors and dames.
    EMERSON, *April.*

11
Oh, the lovely fickleness of an April day!
    W. H. GIBSON, *Pastoral Days: Spring.*

12
Sweet April! many a thought
Is wedded unto thee, as hearts are wed.
    LONGFELLOW, *An April Day.*

13
When April rain had laughed the land
    Out of its wintry way,
And coaxed all growing things to greet
    With gracious garb the May.
    SHAEMAS O'SHEEL, *While April Rain
    Went By.*

14
Oh, hush, my heart, and take thine ease
    For here is April weather!
The daffodils beneath the trees
    Are all a-row together.
    LIZETTE WOODWORTH REESE, *April
    Weather.*

15
The lyric sound of laughter
    Fills all the April hills,
The joy-song of the crocus,
    The mirth of daffodils.
    CLINTON SCOLLARD, *April Music.*

16
A gush of bird-song, a patter of dew,
    A cloud, and a rainbow's warning,
Suddenly sunshine and perfect blue—
    An April day in the morning.
    HARRIET PRESCOTT SPOFFORD, *April.*

17
O sweet wild April came over the hills,

He skipped with the winds and he tripped
　　with the rills;
His raiment was all of daffodils.
Sing hi, sing hey, sing ho!
　　WILLIAM FORCE STEAD, *Sweet Wild April.*

ARCHITECTURE

1

Architecture is preëminently the art of significant forms in space—that is, forms significant of their functions.
　　CLAUDE BRAGDON, *Wake Up and Dream.*
　　(*Outlook,* 27 May, 1931)

Architecture is the art of how to waste space.
　　PHILIP JOHNSON. (New York *Times,*
　　"Ideas and Men," 27 Dec., 1964, p.
　　9E)

2

The Gothic cathedral is a blossoming in stone subdued by the insatiable demand of harmony in man. The mountain of granite blooms into an eternal flower.
　　EMERSON, *Essays, First Series: History.*

3

Earth proudly wears the Parthenon,
As the best gem upon her zone,
And Morning opes with haste her lids
To gaze upon the Pyramids;
O'er England's abbeys bends the sky,
As on its friends, with kindred eye;
For out of Thought's interior sphere
These wonders rose to upper air;
And Nature gladly gave them place,
Adopted them into her race,
And granted them an equal date
With Andes and with Ararat.
　　EMERSON, *The Problem.*

4

In dim cathedrals, dark with vaulted gloom,
What holy awe invests the saintly tomb!
　　OLIVER WENDELL HOLMES, *A Rhymed
　　Lesson.*

5

　　　Ah, to build, to build!
That is the noblest art of all the arts.
Painting and sculpture are but images,
Are merely shadows cast by outward things
On stone or canvas, having in themselves
No separate existence. Architecture,
Existing in itself, and not in seeming
A something it is not, surpasses them
As substance shadow.
　　LONGFELLOW, *Michael Angelo,* pt. i, sec.
　　2.

6

　　　The architect
Built his great heart into these sculptured
　　stones,
And with him toiled his children, and their
　　lives
Were builded, with his own, into the walls,

As offerings unto God.
　　LONGFELLOW, *The Golden Legend:* pt. iii,
　　In the Cathedral.

7

In the elder days of Art,
　　Builders wrought with greatest care
Each minute and unseen part;
　　For the Gods see everywhere.
　　LONGFELLOW, *The Builders.*

8

　　　Giotto's tower,
The lily of Florence blossoming in stone.
　　LONGFELLOW, *Giotto's Tower.*

9

In the greenest of our valleys
　　By good angels tenanted,
Once a fair and stately palace
　　(Radiant palace) reared its head.
In the monarch Thought's dominion
　　It stood there!
Never seraph spread a pinion
　　Over fabric half so fair.
　　POE, *The Haunted Palace.* From *The Fall
　　of the House of Usher.*

10

As if the story of a house
Were told, or ever could be.
　　EDWIN ARLINGTON ROBINSON, *Eros Tu-
　　rannos.*

11

Everything betrays us as a bunch of catchpenny materialists devoted to a blatant, screeching insistence on commercialism. If you look around you, and you give a damn, it makes you want to commit suicide.
　　EDWARD DURELL STONE, Interview with
　　William Borders, New York *Times,* 26
　　Aug., 1964, just before the former re-
　　ceived an award from the Building
　　Stone Institute as "architect of the
　　year." He was referring specifically to
　　American architecture. (New York
　　Times, 27 Aug., 1964)

ARGUMENT

12

We arg'ed the thing at breakfast, we arg'ed
　　the thing at tea,
And the more we arg'ed the question, the
　　more we didn't agree.
　　WILL CARLETON, *Betsy and I Are Out.*

13

Slow to argue, but quick to act.
　　BRET HARTE, *John Burns of Gettysburg.*

14

Anything that argues me into his idea of perfect social and political equality with the Negro is but a specious and fantastic arrangement of words, by which a man can prove a horse-chestnut to be a chestnut horse.
　　ABRAHAM LINCOLN, Speech in Ottawa, Ill.,
　　21 Aug., 1858.

1

There is no good in arguing with the inevitable. The only argument available with an east wind is to put on your overcoat.

> J. R. LOWELL, *Democracy and Other Addresses: Democracy.*

2

Con was a thorn to brother Pro—
  On Pro we often sicked him:
Whatever Pro would claim to know
  Old Con would contradict him!

> CHRISTOPHER MORLEY, *The Twins.*

3

It were endless to dispute upon everything that is disputable.

> WILLIAM PENN, *Fruits of Solitude.*

4

I am not arguing with you—I am telling you.

> J. McNEILL WHISTLER, *The Gentle Art of Making Enemies.* Quoted.

ARISTOCRACY, see Ancestry

ART AND ARTISTS

See also Architecture, Painting, Sculpture

5

But he is dust; we may not know
  His happy or unhappy story:
Nameless, and dead these centuries,
  His work outlives him,—there's his glory!

> THOMAS BAILEY ALDRICH, *On an Intaglio Head of Minerva.*

6

Every artist dips his brush in his own soul, and paints his own nature into his pictures.

> HENRY WARD BEECHER, *Proverbs from Plymouth Pulpit.*

7

Art strives for form, and hopes for beauty.

> GEORGE BELLOWS. (STANLEY WALKER, *City Editor*)

8

Work thou for pleasure! Sing or paint or carve
The thing thou lovest, though the body starve.
Who works for glory misses oft the goal;
Who works for money coins his very soul.
Work for the work's sake, then, and it may be
That these things shall be added unto thee.

> KENYON COX, *The Gospel of Art.* (*Century Magazine*, Feb., 1895.)

9

Living is a form of not being sure, not knowing what next or how. The moment you know how, you begin to die a little. The artist never entirely knows. We guess. We may be wrong, but we take leap after leap in the dark.

> AGNES DE MILLE. (Quoted by JANE HOWARD, in *The Grande Dame of Dance, Life,* 15 Nov., 1963.)

10

Is adversity in the arts ennobling? I doubt it. I struggled 15 years before I made any success. It didn't make me a better person, it just made me hungry. Whatever moral character you're ever going to have you pretty well have by the time you're 20. Repeated failures don't help.

> AGNES DE MILLE. (Quoted by JANE HOWARD in *The Grande Dame of Dance, Life,* 15 Nov., 1963.)

11

What is the public's responsibility to the arts? You have to learn to distinguish good from bad, support the good and write your congressman. He may not be able to read your letters, but he can count them.

> AGNES DE MILLE. (Quoted by JANE HOWARD in *The Grande Dame of Dance, Life,* 15 Nov., 1963.)

12

To my mind the old masters are not art; their value is in their scarcity.

> THOMAS A. EDISON. (*Golden Book,* April, 1931)

13

The conscious utterance of thought, by speech or action, to any end, is Art. . . . From its first to its last works, Art is the spirit's voluntary use and combination of things to serve its end.

> EMERSON, *Society and Solitude: Art.*

14

Painting was called "silent poetry," and poetry "speaking painting." The laws of each art are convertible into the laws of any other.

> EMERSON, *Society and Solitude: Art.*

15

The torpid artist seeks inspiration at any cost, by virtue or by vice, by friend or by fiend, by prayer or by wine.

> EMERSON, *Conduct of Life: Power.*

16

You cannot hide any secret. If the artist succor his flagging spirits by opium or wine, his work will characterize itself as the effect of opium or wine.

> EMERSON, *Conduct of Life: Worship.*

17

There is no way to success in art but to take off your coat, grind paint, and work like a digger on the railroad, all day and every day.

> EMERSON, *Conduct of Life: Power.*

18

Perpetual modernness is the measure of merit in every work of art.

> EMERSON, *Representative Men: Plato.*

19

The true artist has the planet for his pedestal; the adventurer, after years of strife, has nothing broader than his shoes.

> EMERSON, *Representative Men: Uses of Great Men.*

1

Artists must be sacrificed to their art. Like bees, they must put their lives into the sting they give.

> EMERSON, *Letters and Social Aims: Inspiration.*

2

Every artist was first an amateur.

> EMERSON, *Letters and Social Aims: Progress of Culture.*

3

'Tis the privilege of Art
Thus to play its cheerful part,
Man on earth to acclimate
And bend the exile to his fate.

> EMERSON, *Essays, First Series: Art.*

4

New arts destroy the old.

> EMERSON, *Essays, First Series: Circles.*

5

The arts and inventions of each period are only its costumes, and do not invigorate men.

> EMERSON, *Essays, First Series: Self-Reliance.*

6

Art is the path of the creator to his work.

> EMERSON, *Essays, Second Series: The Poet.*

7

These temples grew as grows the grass;
Art might obey, but not surpass.

> EMERSON, *The Problem.*

8

And in their vaunted works of Art,
The master-stroke is still her part.

> EMERSON, *Nature,* pt. ii.

9

Life too near paralyses art.

> EMERSON, *Journals,* vol. v.

10

Classic art was the art of necessity: modern romantic art bears the stamp of caprice and chance.

> EMERSON, *Journals,* 1856.

11

Art is a jealous mistress, and if a man have a genius for painting, poetry, music, architecture, or philosophy, he makes a bad husband and an ill provider.

> EMERSON, *Conduct of Life: Wealth.*

Art is an absolute mistress; she will not be coquetted with or slighted; she requires the most entire self-devotion, and she repays with grand triumphs.

> CHARLOTTE CUSHMAN. (*American Actors*)

12

Nature paints the best part of the picture, carves the best part of the statue, builds the best part of the house, speaks the best part of the oration.

> EMERSON, *Essays, First Series: Art.*

Art is the child of Nature.

> LONGFELLOW, *Kéramos.*

He is the greatest artist, then,
Whether of pencil or of pen,
Who follows Nature.

> LONGFELLOW, *Kéramos.*

Nature is usually wrong.

> J. McNEILL WHISTLER, *"Ten O'Clock."*

Nature contains the elements, in colour and form, of all pictures, as the keyboard contains the notes of all music. But the artist is born to pick, and choose, and group with science, these elements, that the result may be beautiful.

> J. McNEILL WHISTLER. Inscription beneath his bust in the Hall of Fame.

13

To me nature is everything that man is born to, and art is the difference he makes in it.

> JOHN ERSKINE, *Gentle Reader,* Dec. 1931.

14

Bohemia is nothing more than the little country in which you do not live.

> O. HENRY, *The Trimmed Lamp: The Country of Elusion.*

One of those queer artistic dives
Where funny people had their fling.
Artists, and writers, and their wives—
Poets, all that sort of thing.

> OLIVER HERFORD, *The Women of the Better Class.*

Bohème is not down on the map because it is not a money-order office.

> ELBERT HUBBARD, *The Philistine,* vol. xi.

I'd rather live in Bohemia than in any other land.

> JOHN BOYLE O'REILLY, *Bohemia.*

15

The temple of art is built of words. Painting and sculpture and music are but the blazon of its windows, borrowing all their significance from the light, and suggestive only of the temple's uses.

> J. G. HOLLAND, *Plain Talks on Familiar Subjects: Art and Life.*

16

And I thought, like Dr. Faustus, of the emptiness of art,
How we take a fragment for the whole, and call the whole a part.

> OLIVER WENDELL HOLMES, *Nux Postcoenatica.*

17

Art is not a thing: it is a way.

> ELBERT HUBBARD, *Epigrams.*

18

The artist needs no religion beyond his work.

> ELBERT HUBBARD, *The Philistine,* vol. xi.

1
Build your art horse-high, pig-tight and bull-strong.
> ELBERT HUBBARD, *Epigrams*. "Horse-high, pig-tight and bull-strong" is the definition of a legal boundary fence.

2
Scratch an artist and you surprise a child.
> JAMES G. HUNEKER, *Chopin*.

3
Great art is an instant arrested in eternity.
> JAMES G. HUNEKER, *Pathos of Distance*.

4
An art is a handicraft in flower.
> GEORGE ILES, *Jottings*.

5
Art is nothing more than the shadow of humanity.
> HENRY JAMES, *Lectures: University in Arts*.

6
In art economy is always beauty.
> HENRY JAMES, *The Altar of the Dead*.

7
America has not always been kind to its artists and scholars. Somehow the scientists always seem to get the penthouse while the arts and humanities get the basement.
> LYNDON B. JOHNSON, Speech, upon signing the Arts and Humanities Act of 1965, 29 Sept., 1965.

8
We must never forget that art is not a form of propaganda, it is a form of truth. And as Mr. [Archibald] MacLeish once remarked of poets, "There is nothing worse for our trade than to be in style." In free society art is not a weapon and it does not belong to the sphere of polemics and ideology. Artists are not engineers of the soul.
> JOHN F. KENNEDY, Address at Amherst College, Amherst, Mass., 26 Oct., 1963.

9
I look forward to an America which will reward achievement in the arts as we reward achievement in business or statecraft.
> JOHN F. KENNEDY, Address at Amherst College, Amherst, Mass., 26 Oct., 1963.

I see little of more importance to the future of our country and our civilization than full recognition of the place of the artist. If art is to nourish the roots of our culture, society must set the artist free to follow his vision wherever it takes him.
> JOHN F. KENNEDY, Address at Amherst College, Amherst, Mass., 26 Oct., 1963.

10
For art establishes the basic human truths which must serve as the touchstones of our judgment.
> JOHN F. KENNEDY, Address at Amherst College, Amherst, Mass., 26 Oct., 1963.

11
It may be different elsewhere. But democratic society—in it—the highest duty of the writer, the composer, the artist is to remain true to himself and to let the chips fall where they may. In serving his vision of the truth the artist best serves his nation. And the nation which disdains the mission of art invites the fate of Robert Frost's hired man—"the fate of having nothing to look backward to with pride and nothing to look forward to with hope."
> JOHN F. KENNEDY, Address at Amherst College, Amherst, Mass., 26 Oct., 1963.

The artist, however faithful to his personal vision of reality, becomes the last champion of the individual mind and sensibility against an intrusive society and an officious state. The great artist is thus a solitary figure. He has, as [Robert] Frost said, "a lover's quarrel with the world." In pursuing his perceptions of reality he must often sail against the currents of his time. This is not a popular role.
> JOHN F. KENNEDY, Address at Amherst College, Amherst, Mass., 26 Oct., 1963.

12
If sometimes our great artists have been the most critical of our society it is because their sensitivity and their concern for justice, which must motivate any true artist, makes him aware that our nation falls short of its highest potential.
> JOHN F. KENNEDY, Address at Amherst College, Amherst, Mass., 26 Oct., 1963.

13
To draw a moral, to preach a doctrine, is like shouting at the north star. Life is a vast and awful business. The great artist sets down his vision of it and is silent.
> LUDWIG LEWISOHN, *Modern Drama*.

14
Art is power.
> LONGFELLOW, *Hyperion*, bk. iii.

15
Nature is a revelation of God;
Art a revelation of man.
> LONGFELLOW, *Hyperion*, bk. iii.

16
Art is long, and Time is fleeting.
> LONGFELLOW, *A Psalm of Life*.

17
Art is the gift of God, and must be used
Unto His glory.
> LONGFELLOW, *Michael Angelo*, pt. i, sec. 2.

18
Emigravit is the inscription on the tombstone where he lies;
Dead he is not, but departed,—for the artist never dies.
> LONGFELLOW, *Nuremberg*.

19
Art is the desire of a man to express himself,

to record the reactions of his personality to the world he lives in.

> AMY LOWELL, *Tendencies in Modern American Poetry*.

1

The arts are always in trouble. It is their nature to be in trouble.

> ARCHIBALD MACLEISH, Statement marking the 50th anniversary of the American Society of Composers, Authors and Publishers (ASCAP); New York *Times*, 16 Feb., 1964.

2

Artists don't see the world the way it wants to be seen and the world reciprocates.

> ARCHIBALD MACLEISH, Statement marking the 50th anniversary of the American Society of Composers, Authors and Publishers; New York *Times*, 16 Feb., 1964.

3

At one time a famous state undertook to resolve the problem of the arts by getting along without them. The venture did not succeed. Sparta is today an undistinguished valley visited by tourists who remember something about a boy with a fox in his shirt. At other times and in other places governments have gone at the trouble the other way around: they have attempted to domesticate the arts by supporting the artists. This method has sometimes worked as, for example, in Florence during the years when the Princes were artists themselves, and in France when the French were Parisians. Elsewhere its success has been dubious. In Russia, where artists are rewarded with the best apartments and the prettiest dachas, works of art are rare.

> ARCHIBALD MACLEISH, Statement marking the 50th anniversary of the American Society of Composers, Authors and Publishers (ASCAP); New York *Times*, 16 Feb., 1964.

4

The artist of today says to the public: If you don't understand this you are dumb. I maintain that you are not. If you have to go the whole way to meet the artist, it's his fault.

> MARYA MANNES. (*Life*, 12 June, 1964, p. 64)

5

Nothing can come out of an artist that is not in the man.

> H. L. MENCKEN, *Prejudices*, ser. v.

6

And now too late, we see these things are one:
That art is sacrifice and self-control,
And who loves beauty must be stern of soul.

> ALICE DUER MILLER, *An American to France*.

7

Art is a reaching out into the ugliness of the world for vagrant beauty and the imprisoning of it in a tangible dream.

> GEORGE JEAN NATHAN, *Critic and the Drama*.

8

Great art is as irrational as great music. It is mad with its own loveliness.

> GEORGE JEAN NATHAN, *House of Satan*.

9

The artist and censor differ in this wise: that the first is a decent mind in an indecent body and that the second is an indecent mind in a decent body.

> GEORGE JEAN NATHAN, *The Autobiography of an Attitude*.

10

Art is a form of catharsis.

> DOROTHY PARKER, *Art*.

11

Authors and actors and artists and such
Never know nothing and never know much . . .
Playwrights and poets and such horses' necks
Start off from anywhere, end up at sex.
Diarists, critics, and similar roe
Never say nothing, and never say no.
People Who Do Things exceed my endurance:
God, for a man that solicits insurance!

> DOROTHY PARKER, *Bohemia*.

12

All loved Art in a seemly way
With an earnest soul and a capital A.

> JAMES JEFFREY ROCHE, *The V-a-s-e*.

13

The question no longer is whether there should be government support of the arts. The question is the extent of that support.

> NELSON A. ROCKEFELLER. (New York *Times*, "Ideas and Men," 30 May, 1965, p. 11-E)

14

The artist is a dreamer consenting to dream of the actual world.

> GEORGE SANTAYANA, *The Life of Reason*.

15

Nothing is so poor and melancholy as art that is interested in itself and not in its subject.

> GEORGE SANTAYANA, *The Life of Reason*.

16

Fashion is a potency in art, making it hard to judge between the temporary and the lasting.

> E. C. STEDMAN, *Poets of America*.

17

All arts are one,—all branches on one tree;
All fingers, as it were, upon one hand.

> W. W. STORY, *A Contemporary Criticism*.

18

This thing which you would almost bet
Portrays a Spanish omelette,

Depicts instead, with wondrous skill,
A horse and cart upon a hill.

Now, Mr. Dove has too much art
To show the horse or show the cart;
Instead, he paints the *creak* and *strain*.
Get it? No pike is half as plain.
BERT LESTON TAYLOR, *Post-Impressionism.*

1
I do not want Michael Angelo for breakfast
—for luncheon—for dinner—for tea—for
supper—for between meals.
MARK TWAIN, *Innocents Abroad.*

2
A great artist can paint a great picture on a
small canvas.
CHARLES DUDLEY WARNER, *Washington
Irving.*

3
Art happens—no hovel is safe from it, no
Prince may depend upon it, the vastest intel-
ligence cannot bring it about.
J. McNEILL WHISTLER, *"Ten O'Clock."*

4
Art has been maligned. . . . She is a goddess
of dainty thought—reticent of habit, abjur-
ing all obtrusiveness, purposing in no way to
better others.
J. MC NEILL WHISTLER, *"Ten O'Clock."*

5
Listen! There never was an artistic period.
There never was an Art-loving nation.
J. McNEILL WHISTLER, *"Ten O'Clock."*

6
Art is upon the Town!—to be chucked under
the chin by the passing gallant.
J. McNEILL WHISTLER, *"Ten O'Clock."*

7
A life passed among pictures makes not a
painter—else the policeman in the National
Gallery might assert himself. As well allege
that he who lives in a library must needs die
a poet.
J. McNEILL WHISTLER, *The Gentle Art of
Making Enemies.*

ASPIRATION

See also Ambition, Purpose

8
Make no little plans: they have no magic to
stir men's blood. . . . Make big plans, aim
high in hope and work.
DANIEL H. BURNHAM, Article, *Christian
Science Monitor,* 18 Jan., 1927. BURN-
HAM, an architect, was referring to his
plans for work in Chicago.

9
Hitch your wagon to a star. Let us not fag in
paltry works which serve our pot and bag
alone. Let us not lie and steal. No god will
help. We shall find all their teams going the
other way: every god will leave us. Work
rather for those interests which the divinities
honor and promote,—justice, love, freedom,
knowledge, utility.
EMERSON, *Society and Solitude: Civilization.*

10
Everything good in man leans on what is
higher. All our strength and success in the
work of our hands depend on our borrowing
the aid of the elements. . . . Now that is the
wisdom of a man, in every instance of his
labor, to hitch his wagon to a star, and see
his chore done by the gods themselves.
EMERSON, *Society and Solitude: Civilization.*

11
God, give me hills to climb,
And strength for climbing!
ARTHUR GUITERMAN, *Hills.*

12
Heaven is not reached at a single bound;
But we build the ladder by which we rise
From the lowly earth to the vaulted skies,
And we mount to its summit round by
round.
JOSIAH GILBERT HOLLAND, *Gradatim.*

13
The shades of night were falling fast,
As through an Alpine village passed
A youth, who bore, 'mid snow and ice,
A banner with the strange device,
Excelsior!
LONGFELLOW, *Excelsior.*

14
My . . . aspirations are my only friends.
LONGFELLOW, *Masque of Pandora,* pt. iii.

15
I see, but cannot reach, the height
That lies forever in the light,
And yet forever and forever,
When seeming just within my grasp,
I feel my feeble hands unclasp,
And sink discouraged into night!
LONGFELLOW, *The Golden Legend: A Vil-
lage Church.*

16
The thing we long for, that we are
For one transcendent moment.
JAMES RUSSELL LOWELL, *Longing.*

17
A fierce unrest seethes at the core
Of all existing things:
It was the eager wish to soar
That gave the gods their wings. . . .
There throbs through all the worlds that are
This heart-beat hot and strong,
And shaken systems, star by star,
Awake and glow in song.
DON MARQUIS, *Unrest.*

18
Why thus longing, thus forever sighing
For the far-off, unattain'd, and dim.
While the beautiful all round thee lying
Offers up its low, perpetual hymn?
HARRIET W. SEWALL, *Why Thus Longing?*

1

Sky, be my depth;
Wind, be my width and my height;
World, my heart's span:
Loneliness, wings for my flight!
    LEONORA SPEYER, *Measure Me, Sky.*

2

Ye skies, drop gently round my breast
    And be my corselet blue;
Ye earth, receive my lance in rest,
    My faithful charger you.
    H. D. THOREAU, *The Great Adventure.*

3

All great ideas, the races' aspirations,
All heroisms, deeds of rapt enthusiasts,
Be ye my Gods.
    WALT WHITMAN, *Gods.*

4

Better with naked nerve to bear
The needles of this goading air,
Than, in the lap of sensual ease, forego
The godlike power to do, the godlike aim to
    know.
    JOHN GREENLEAF WHITTIER, *Last Walk in
    Autumn.*

5

Let the thick curtain fall;
I better know than all
How little I have gained,
How vast the unattained.
    JOHN GREENLEAF WHITTIER, *My Tri-
    umph.*

6

The self which desires a thing is not the self
which at last possesses that thing. As one
approaches any goal, it seems more and more
reasonable that one should reach it, and desire commences to look beyond.
    RICHARD P. WILBUR, Commencement Ad-
    dress, Washington University, St. Louis,
    1964. Published in *Washington Univer-
    sity Magazine,* Summer, 1964, p. 47.

7

Press on!—"for in the grave there is no
    work
And no device"—Press on! while yet ye
    may!
    N. P. WILLIS, *Press On!* Poem delivered
    at the departure of the senior class of
    Yale College, 1827.

ASS

8

The mule is haf hoss and haf jackass, and
then kums a full stop, natur discovering her
mistake.
    JOSH BILLINGS, *On Mules.*

9

Until the Donkey tried to clear
The Fence, he thought himself a Deer.
    ARTHUR GUITERMAN, *A Poet's Proverbs.*

10

Because a Donkey takes a whim

To Bray at You, why Bray at Him?
    ARTHUR GUITERMAN, *A Poet's Proverbs.*

11

Better an ass that carries us than a horse
that throws us.
    JOSIAH GILBERT HOLLAND, *Gold-Foil: The
    Infallible.*

12

When a jackass brays, no one pays any attention to him, not even other jackasses. But
when a lion brays like a jackass, even the
lions in the neighborhood may be pardoned
for exhibiting a little surprise.
    GEORGE JEAN NATHAN, *Testament of a
    Critic.*

13

To the great he is great; to the fool he's a
    fool:
In the world's dreary desert a crystalline
    pool,
Where a lion looks in and a lion appears;
But an ass will see only his own ass's ears.
    J. T. TROWBRIDGE, *On Amos Bronson Al-
    cott.*

ATHEISM

See also Doubt, Heresy

14

Who seeks perfection in the art
Of driving well an ass and cart,
Or painting mountains in a mist,
Seeks God although an Atheist.
    FRANCIS CARLIN, *Perfection.*

15

    There is no unbelief;
Whoever plants a seed beneath the sod
And waits to see it push away the clod,
    He trusts in God.
    LIZZIE YORK CASE, *There Is No Unbelief.*

16

There are no atheists in the fox-holes.
    REVEREND WILLIAM THOMAS CUMMINGS,
    Sermon on Bataan, Philippine Islands,
    March, 1942. Father Cummings was an
    Army chaplain. The quotation is some-
    times attributed to Colonel W. J.
    Clear.

17

The infidels of one age have been the aure-
oled saints of the next. The destroyers of the
old are the creators of the new.
    ROBERT GREEN INGERSOLL, *The Great In-
    fidels.*

18

God is not dumb, that He should speak no
    more;
If thou hast wanderings in the wilderness
And find'st not Sinai, 'tis thy soul is poor.
    JAMES RUSSELL LOWELL, *Bibliolatres.*

19

Infidelity does not consist in believing or in
disbelieving: it consists in professing to believe what one does not believe.
    THOMAS PAINE, *Age of Reason,* pt. i.

1

My atheism, like that of Spinoza, is true piety towards the universe and denies only gods fashioned by men in their own image, to be servants of their human interests.

GEORGE SANTAYANA, *Soliloquies in England: On My Friendly Critics.*

2

An atheist is a man who has no invisible means of support.

FULTON J. SHEEN. (*Look,* 14 Dec., 1955)

3

What behaved well in the past or behaves well to-day is not such a wonder,
The wonder is always and always how there can be a mean man or an infidel.

WALT WHITMAN, *Song of Myself,* pt. xxii.

AUTHORS, see Writing

AUTUMN

4

The melancholy days are come, the saddest of the year,
Of wailing winds, and naked woods, and meadows brown and sear.

WILLIAM CULLEN BRYANT, *The Death of the Flowers.*

5

There is something in the autumn that is native to my blood—
Touch of manner, hint of mood;
And my heart is like a rhyme,
With the yellow and the purple and the crimson keeping time.

BLISS CARMAN, *A Vagabond Song.*

6

The scarlet of the maples can shake me like a cry
Of bugles going by.
And my lonely spirit thrills
To see the frosty asters like a smoke upon the hills.

BLISS CARMAN, *A Vagabond Song.*

7

A haze on the far horizon,
The infinite, tender sky,
The ripe, rich tint of the cornfields,
And the wild geese sailing high,—
And all over upland and lowland
The charm of the goldenrod,—
Some of us call it Autumn,
And others call it God.

WILLIAM HERBERT CARRUTH, *Each in His Own Tongue.*

8

A breath, whence no man knows,
Swaying the grating weeds, it blows;
It comes, it grieves, it goes.
Once it rocked the summer rose.

JOHN VANCE CHENEY, *Passing of Autumn.*

9

The red upon the hill
Taketh away my will;

If anybody sneer,
Take care, for God is here,
That's all.

EMILY DICKINSON, *Mysteries.*

10

These are the days when skies put on
The old, old sophistries of June,—
A blue and gold mistake.

EMILY DICKINSON, *Indian Summer.*

11

The morns are meeker than they were.

EMILY DICKINSON, *Autumn.*

12

My sorrow when she's here with me,
Thinks these dark days of autumn rain
Are beautiful as days can be;
She loves the bare, the withered tree;
She walks the sodden pasture lane.

ROBERT FROST, *My November Guest.*

13

The world puts on its robes of glory now;
The very flowers are tinged with deeper dyes;
The waves are bluer, and the angels pitch
Their shining tents along the sunset skies.

ALLBERT LAIGHTON, *Autumn.*

14

It was Autumn, and incessant
Piped the quails from shocks and sheaves,
And, like living coals, the apples
Burned among the withering leaves.

H. W. LONGFELLOW, *Pegasus in Pound.*

15

What visionary tints the year puts on,
When falling leaves falter through motionless air
Or numbly cling and shiver to be gone!
How shimmer the low flats and pastures bare,
As with her nectar Hebe Autumn fills
The bowl between me and those distant hills,
And smiles and shakes abroad her misty, tremulous hair!

JAMES RUSSELL LOWELL, *An Indian Summer Reverie.*

16

Sorrow and the scarlet leaf,
Sad thoughts and sunny weather;
Ah me! this glory and this grief
Agree not well together!

T. W. PARSONS, *A Song for September.*

17

O, it sets my heart a clickin' like the tickin' of a clock,
When the frost is on the punkin and the fodder's in the shock.

JAMES WHITCOMB RILEY, *When the Frost Is on the Punkin.*

18

The tints of autumn—a mighty flower garden

blossoming under the spell of the enchanter,
Frost.
    JOHN GREENLEAF WHITTIER, *Patucket
       Falls.*

1
We lack but open eye and ear
To find the Orient's marvels here;
The still small voice in autumn's hush,
Yon maple wood the burning bush.
    JOHN GREENLEAF WHITTIER, *The Chapel
       of the Hermits.*

AVARICE
See also Money

2
Avarice and happiness never saw each other,
how then should they become acquainted?
    BENJAMIN FRANKLIN, *Poor Richard,*
       1734.

3
If I knew a miser, who gave up every kind
of comfortable living, all the pleasure of doing good to others, all the esteem of his fellow-citizens, and the joys of benevolent
friendship, for the sake of accumulating
wealth, Poor man, said I, you pay too much
for your whistle.
    BENJAMIN FRANKLIN, *The Whistle.*

4
Punishment of a miser,—to pay the drafts of
his heir in his tomb.
    NATHANIEL HAWTHORNE, *American Note-
      Books,* 10 July, 1838.

5
One of the weaknesses of our age is our apparent inability to distinguish our needs
from our greeds.
    DON ROBINSON, *Phi Delta Kappan,* May,
      1963. Reprinted in *The Reader's Digest,*
      Dec., 1963.

B

BABY
See also Birth

6
Babies are bits of star-dust blown from the
hand of God. Lucky the woman who knows
the pangs of birth for she has held a star.
    LARRY BARRETTO, *The Indiscreet Years.*

7
Oh, mother! laugh your merry note,
  Be gay and glad, but don't forget
From baby's eyes look out a soul
  That claims a home in Eden yet.
    ETHEL LYNN BEERS, *Weighing the Baby.*

8
There came to port last Sunday night
  The queerest little craft,
Without an inch of rigging on;
  I looked and looked—and laughed.
It seemed so curious that she
  Should cross the unknown water,
And moor herself within my room—
  My daughter! O my daughter!
    GEORGE W. CABLE, *The New Arrival.*

9
Now from the coasts of morning pale
Comes safe to port thy tiny sail.
Now have we seen by early sun
Thy miracle of life begun.
    GRACE HAZARD CONKLING, *To a New-Born
      Baby Girl.*

10
He is so little to be so large!
Why, a train of cars, or a whale-back barge
Couldn't carry the freight of the monstrous
    weight
Of all his qualities, good and great.
    EDMUND VANCE COOKE, *The Intruder.*

11
Which is the way to Baby-land?

Any one can tell;
Up one flight,
To your right;
Please to ring the bell.
    GEORGE COOPER, *Babyland.*

12
His flesh is angels' flesh, all alive.
    EMERSON, *Society and Solitude: Domestic
      Life.*

13
  When you fold your hands, Baby Lou-
    ise, . . .
Are you trying to think of some angel-taught
    prayer
  You learned above, Baby Louise?
    MARGARET EYTINGE, *Baby Louise.*

14
What is the little one thinking about?
Very wonderful things, no doubt! . . .
Who can tell what a baby thinks?
Who can follow the gossamer links
  By which the mannikin feels his way
Out from the shore of the great unknown,
Blind, and wailing, and alone,
  Into the light of day?
    J. G. HOLLAND, *Bitter-Sweet,* pt. i.

15
God one morning, glad of heaven,
  Laughed—and that was you!
    BRIAN HOOKER, *A Little Person.*

16
About the only thing we have left that actually discriminates in favor o' the plain people
is the stork.
    KIN HUBBARD, *Sayings.*

17
O child! O new-born denizen
Of life's great city! on thy head
The glory of the morn is shed,

Like a celestial benison.
> HENRY WADSWORTH LONGFELLOW, *To a Child*.

1
The greatest poem ever known
Is one all poets have outgrown:
The poetry, innate, untold,
Of being only four years old.
> CHRISTOPHER MORLEY, *To a Child*.

2
Something to live for came to the place,
  Something to die for maybe,
Something to give even sorrow a grace,
  And yet it was only a baby!
> HARRIET PRESCOTT SPOFFORD, *Only*.

3
Sweetest li'l' feller, everybody knows;
Dunno what to call him, but he's mighty lak'
  a rose.
> FRANK L. STANTON, *Mighty Lak' a Rose*.

4
A baby is an inestimable blessing and bother.
> MARK TWAIN, Letter, 1876.

5
The most wonderful sound our ears can hear
is the sound of a new-born baby.
> UNKNOWN, Inscription in the room where
> Lyndon B. Johnson was born, in a house
> near Johnson City, Tex. The inscription
> was placed there by his mother, Mrs.
> Rebekah Baines Johnson, and was often
> pointed out to visitors after Johnson be-
> came President.

BACHELOR

6
Swift and sure go the lonely feet,
  And the single eye sees cold and true,
And the road that has room and to spare for
  one
May be sorely narrow for two.
> AMELIA JOSEPHINE BURR, *To Lovers*.

7
Space is ample, east and west,
But two cannot go abreast.
> EMERSON, *The Over-Soul*.

8
The happy marrid man dies in good stile at
home, surrounded by his weeping wife and
children. The old bachelor don't die at all—
he sort of rots away, like a pollywog's tail.
> ARTEMUS WARD, *The Draft in Baldins-
> ville*.

9
Who travels alone, without lover or friend,
But hurries from nothing, to nought at the
  end.
> ELLA WHEELER WILCOX, *Reply to Rud-
> yard Kipling's Poem*. The Kipling poem
> referred to, *The Winners*, has these
> lines:
> Down to Gehenna or up to the Throne,
> He travels the fastest who travels alone.

BANK, BANKER, see Finance

BEAUTY

10
What is lovely never dies,
But passes into other loveliness,
Star-dust, or sea-foam, flower or wingèd air.
> THOMAS BAILEY ALDRICH, *A Shadow of
> the Night*.

11
Too bright, too beautiful to last.
> WILLIAM CULLEN BRYANT, *The Rivulet*.

12
Beauty is like the surf that never ceases,
Beauty is like the night that never dies,
Beauty is like a forest pool where peace is
And a recurrent waning planet lies.
> STRUTHERS BURT, *I Know a Lovely Lady
> Who Is Dead*.

13
When death hath poured oblivion through
  my veins,
  And brought me home, as all are brought,
    to lie
In that vast house, common to serfs and
  thanes,—
  I shall not die, I shall not utterly die,
For beauty born of beauty—*that* remains.
> MADISON CAWEIN, *Beauty*.

14
Beauty has no relation to price, rarity, or
age.
> JOHN COTTON DANA, *Libraries*.

15
Beauty is not caused, It is.
> EMILY DICKINSON, *Further Poems*, No.
> 49.

16
Beauty crowds me till I die,
Beauty, mercy have on me!
Yet if I expire to-day
Let it be in sight of thee!
> EMILY DICKINSON, *Poems*, Pt. v, No. 43.

17
Things that are lovely
  Can tear my heart in two—
Moonlight on still pools,
  You.
> DOROTHY DOW, *Things*.

18
Beauty, what is that? There are phalanxes of
beauty in every comic show. Beauty neither
buys food nor keeps up a home.
> MAXINE ELLIOT, Newspaper Interview,
> 1908.

19
Beauty's the thing that counts
In women; red lips
And black eyes are better than brains.
> MARY J. ELMENDORF, *Beauty's the Thing*.

20
Beauty is the virtue of the body, as virtue is
the beauty of the soul.
> EMERSON, *Natural History of Intellect:
> Michael Angelo*.

1

Beauty is the mark God sets upon virtue.
EMERSON, *Nature, Addresses, and Lectures: Beauty.*

The ancients called beauty the flowering of virtue.
EMERSON, *Essays, First Series: Love.*

Chant the beauty of the good.
EMERSON, *Society and Solitude: Success.*

2

Beauty rests on necessities. The line of beauty is the line of perfect economy.
EMERSON, *Conduct of Life: Beauty.*

The beautiful rests on the foundations of the necessary.
EMERSON, *Essays, Second Series: The Poet.*

3

We ascribe beauty to that which is simple; which has no superfluous parts; which exactly answers its end.
EMERSON, *Conduct of Life: Beauty.*

4

Beauty without grace is the hook without the bait. Beauty, without expression, tires.
EMERSON, *Conduct of Life: Beauty.*

5

A beautiful woman is a practical poet, taming her savage mate, planting tenderness, hope, and eloquence in all whom she approaches.
EMERSON, *Conduct of Life: Beauty.*

6

Any extraordinary degree of beauty in man or woman involves a moral charm.
EMERSON, *Conduct of Life: Worship.*

7

Beauty brings its own fancy price, for all that a man hath will he give for his love.
EMERSON, *Social Aims.*

8

He thought it happier to be dead.
To die for Beauty, than live for bread.
EMERSON, *Beauty.*

9

Rhodora! if the sages ask thee why
This charm is wasted on the earth and sky,
Tell them, dear, that if eyes were made for seeing,
Then Beauty is its own excuse for being.
EMERSON, *The Rhodora.*

Art's perfect forms no moral need,
And beauty is its own excuse.
JOHN GREENLEAF WHITTIER, *Songs of Labor: Dedication.*

10

Beauty—what is it? A perfume without name:
A sudden hush where clamor was before:
Across the darkness a faint ghost of flame:
A far sail, seen from a deserted shore.
ARTHUR D. FICKE, *Epitaph for the Poet V.*

11

Nothing in human life, least of all in religion, is ever right until it is beautiful.
HARRY EMERSON FOSDICK, *As I See Religion.*

12

Beauty and folly are old companions.
BENJAMIN FRANKLIN, *Poor Richard,* 1734.

13

A ship under sail and a big-bellied woman
Are the handsomest two things that can be seen common.
BENJAMIN FRANKLIN, *Poor Richard,* 1735.

14

Who walks with beauty holds inviolate
The guarded secrets of the years to come,
Sees unborn Aprils crowding at the gate
Of living gardens white with petaled plum.
DANIEL WHITEHEAD HICKY, *Who Walks with Beauty.*

15

Wisdom is the abstract of the past, but beauty is the promise of the future.
OLIVER WENDELL HOLMES, *The Professor at the Breakfast Table.*

16

Beauty is the index of a larger fact than wisdom.
OLIVER WENDELL HOLMES, *The Professor at the Breakfast Table.*

17

Ugliness creates bitterness. Ugliness is an eroding force on the people of our land.
CLAUDIA T. (MRS. LYNDON B.) JOHNSON, Speech opening the White House Conference on Natural Beauty, 24 May, 1965.

18

Beauty, the smile of God, Music, His voice.
ROBERT UNDERWOOD JOHNSON, *Goethals of Panama.*

19

I'm tired of all this nonsense about beauty being only skin-deep. That's deep enough. What do you want—an adorable pancreas?
JEAN KERR, *The Snake Has All the Lines: Mirror, Mirror, on the Wall, I Don't Want to Hear One Word Out of You,* p. 158.

20

Beautiful in form and feature,
Lovely as the day,
Can there be so fair a creature
Formed of common clay?
H. W. LONGFELLOW, *The Masque of Pandora,* pt. i.

21

Not ten yoke of oxen
Have the power to draw us
Like a woman's hair!
H. W. LONGFELLOW, *The Saga of King Olaf,* pt. xvi.

1

    She was not fair,
Nor beautiful;—those words express her
not.
But, oh, her looks had something excellent,
That wants a name!
    H. W. LONGFELLOW, *Hyperion,* bk. iii.

2

Christian endeavor is notoriously hard on female pulchritude.
    H. L. MENCKEN, *The Aesthetic Recoil;
    American Mercury,* July, 1931.

3

    Euclid alone
Has looked on Beauty bare. Fortunate they
Who, though once only and then but far
    away,
Have heard her massive sandal set on stone.
    EDNA ST. VINCENT MILLAY, *Sonnets.*

4

Praised be the gods that made my spirit
    mad;
Kept me aflame and raw to beauty's touch.
    ANGELA MORGAN, *June Rapture.*

5

Who walks with Beauty has no need to
    fear;
The sun and moon and stars keep pace with
    him,
Invisible hands restore the ruined year,
And time, itself, grows beautifully dim.
    DAVID MORTON, *Who Walks with Beauty.*

6

Beauty makes idiots sad and wise men merry.
    GEORGE JEAN NATHAN, *House of Satan.*

7

Beauty is ever to the lonely mind
A shadow fleeting; she is never plain.
She is a visitor who leaves behind
The gift of grief, the souvenir of pain.
    ROBERT NATHAN, *Beauty Is Ever.*

8

Goodness is a special kind of truth and beauty. It is truth and beauty in human behavior.
    HARRY ALLEN OVERSTREET, *The Enduring
    Quest.*

9

Helen, thy beauty is to me
    Like those Nicaean barks of yore,
That gently, o'er a perfumed sea,
    The weary, wayworn wanderer bore
    To his own native shore.
    EDGAR ALLAN POE, *To Helen.*

10

On desperate seas long wont to roam,
    Thy hyacinth hair, thy classic face,
Thy naiad airs have brought me home
    To the glory that was Greece
    And the grandeur that was Rome.
    EDGAR ALLAN POE, *To Helen.*

11

There is nothing in the laws of nature or the
nature of man to require that a state which
is big and vital and productive must also be
mundane and dirty and ugly.
    NELSON A. ROCKEFELLER, in announcing,
        as governor of New York, a program of
        state awards for "the enhancement of
        material and man-made beauty," 9 May,
        1965.

12

It is in rare and scattered instants that beauty smiles even on her adorers, who are reduced for habitual comfort to remembering
her past favours.
    GEORGE SANTAYANA, *Little Essays.*

13

All things of beauty are not theirs alone
    Who hold the fee; but unto him no less
Who can enjoy, than unto them who own,
    Are sweetest uses given to possess.
    JOHN G. SAXE, *The Beautiful.*

14

Beauty vanishes like a vapor,
Preach the men of musty morals.
    HARRIET PRESCOTT SPOFFORD, *Evanes-
    cence.*

15

Beauty is momentary in the mind—
The fitful tracing of a portal;
But in the flesh it is immortal.
    WALLACE STEVENS, *Peter Quince at the
    Clavier.*

16

Beauty is not immortal. In a day
Blossom and June and rapture pass away.
    ARTHUR STRINGER, *A Fragile Thing Is
    Beauty.*

17

O beauty, are you not enough?
Why am I crying after love?
    SARA TEASDALE, *Spring Night.*

18

Beauty remains, but we are transitory.
    CHARLES HANSON TOWNE, *Enigma.*

19

Beauty is altogether in the eye of the be-
holder.
    LEW WALLACE, *The Prince of India,* bk.
    iii.

20

O Beauty, old yet ever new!
Eternal Voice and Inward Word.
    JOHN GREENLEAF WHITTIER, *The Shadow
    and the Light.*

21

Beauty seen is never lost.
    JOHN GREENLEAF WHITTIER, *Sunset on
    the Bearcamp.*

22

The Beauty which old Greece or Rome
Sung, painted, wrought, lies close at home.
    JOHN GREENLEAF WHITTIER, *To ——.*

23

Beauty abides, nor suffers mortal change,
Eternal refuge of the orphaned mind.
    G. E. WOODBERRY, *The North Shore
    Watch.*

1
Say not of Beauty she is good,
Or aught but beautiful.
ELINOR WYLIE, *Beauty*.

BEE

2
How many cups the bee partakes,—
    The debauchee of dews!
EMILY DICKINSON, *Poems*, Pt. ii, No. 39.

3
The murmur of a bee
A witchcraft yieldeth me.
If any ask me why,
'Twere easier to die
Than tell.
EMILY DICKINSON, *Poems*, Pt. ii, No. 54.

4
Oh, for a bee's experience
Of clovers and of noon!
EMILY DICKINSON, *Poems*, Pt. ii, No. 65.

5
Burly, dozing humble-bee,
Where thou art is clime for me.
EMERSON, *The Humble-Bee*.

6
Wiser far than human seer,
Yellow-breeched philosopher!
Seeing only what is fair,
Sipping only what is sweet,
Thou dost mock at fate and care,
Leave the chaff, and take the wheat.
EMERSON, *The Humble-Bee*.

7
No matter how you seem to fatten on a
crime, that can never be good for the bee
which is bad for the hive.
EMERSON, *Lectures and Biographical Studies: the Sovereignty of Ethics*.

8
Honey is sweet, but the bee stings.
BENJAMIN FRANKLIN, *Poor Richard*, 1758.

9
While Honey lies in Every Flower, no
    doubt,
It takes a Bee to get the Honey out.
ARTHUR GUITERMAN, *A Poet's Proverbs*.

10
From Beavers, Bees should learn to mend
    their ways;
A Bee just Works; a Beaver Works and
    Plays.
ARTHUR GUITERMAN, *A Poet's Proverbs*.

11
No good sensible working bee listens to the
advice of a bedbug on the subject of business.
ELBERT HUBBARD, *Epigrams*.

BEER, see Ale and Beer
BEGINNING

12
I'd like to get away from earth awhile
And then come back to it and begin over.

May no fate willfully misunderstand me
And half grant what I wish and snatch me
    away
Not to return. Earth's the right place for
    love:
I don't know where it's likely to go better.
ROBERT FROST, *Birches*.

13
Great is the art of beginning, but greater the
    art is of ending;
Many a poem is marred by a superfluous
    verse.
HENRY WADSWORTH LONGFELLOW, *Elegiac Verse*, st. 14.

14
Anybody can start something.
JOHN A. SHEDD, *Salt from My Attic*.

15
All glory comes from daring to begin.
EUGENE F. WARE, *John Brown*.

16
Others shall sing the song,
Others shall right the wrong,—
Finish what I begin,
And all I fail of win.
JOHN GREENLEAF WHITTIER, *My Triumph*, st. 10.

BEHAVIOR
See also Golden Rule, Manners

17
Make yourself necessary to somebody. Do
not make life hard to any.
EMERSON, *Conduct of Life: Considerations by the Way*.

18
If thou wouldst not be known to do anything, never do it.
EMERSON, *Essays, First Series: Spiritual Laws*.

19
A beautiful form is better than a beautiful
face; a beautiful behavior is better than a
beautiful form: . . . it is the finest of the
fine arts.
EMERSON, *Essays, Second Series: Manners*.

20
The laws of behavior yield to the energy of
the individual.
EMERSON, *Essays, Second Series: Manners*.

21
Be civil to all; sociable to many; familiar
with few; friend to one; enemy to none.
BENJAMIN FRANKLIN, *Poor Richard*, 1756.

22
Four precepts: to break off customs; to
shake off spirits ill-disposed; to meditate on
youth; to do nothing against one's genius.
NATHANIEL HAWTHORNE, *American Note-Books*, 25 Oct., 1836.

23
Let what will be said or done, preserve your

sang-froid immovable, and to every obstacle oppose patience, perseverance and soothing language.

THOMAS JEFFERSON, *Writings*, vol. viii.

1

Never suffer a thought to be harbored in your mind which you would not avow openly. When tempted to do anything in secret, ask yourself if you would do it in public. If you would not, be sure it is wrong.

THOMAS JEFFERSON, *Writings*, vol. xix.

2

My code of life and conduct is simply this: work hard; play to the allowable limit; disregard equally the good and bad opinion of others; never do a friend a dirty trick; . . . never grow indignant over anything; . . . live the moment to the utmost of its possibilities, . . . and be satisfied with life always, but never with oneself.

GEORGE JEAN NATHAN, *Testament of a Critic.*

3

Four things a man must learn to do
If he would make his record true:
To think without confusion clearly;
To love his fellow-men sincerely;
To act from honest motives purely;
To trust in God and Heaven securely.

HENRY VAN DYKE, *Four Things.*

4

As a rule, there is no surer way to the dislike of men than to behave well where they have behaved badly.

LEW WALLACE, *Ben Hur,* bk. iv.

5

Heed how thou livest. Do no act by day
Which from the night shall drive thy peace away.

JOHN GREENLEAF WHITTIER, *Conduct.*

BELIEF

See also Creeds, Faith, Trust

6

We are born believing. A man bears beliefs, as a tree bears apples.

EMERSON, *Conduct of Life: Worship.*

7

Belief consists in accepting the affirmations of the soul; unbelief, in denying them.

EMERSON, *Representative Men: Montaigne.*

8

For, dear me, why abandon a belief
Merely because it ceases to be true?
Cling to it long enough, and not a doubt
It will turn true again, for so it goes.
Most of the change we think we see in life
Is due to truths being in and out of favour.

ROBERT FROST, *The Black Cottage.*

9

Fields are won by those who believe in the winning.

T. W. HIGGINSON. *Americanism in Literature.*

10

Ignorance is preferable to error; and he is less remote from truth who believes nothing, than he who believes what is wrong.

THOMAS JEFFERSON, *Writings,* vol. ii.

11

For we are a nation of believers. Underneath the clamor of building and the rush of our day's pursuits, we are believers in justice and liberty and union, and in our own Union. We believe that every man must some day be free. And we believe in ourselves.

LYNDON B. JOHNSON, Inaugural Address, 20 Jan., 1965.

He is an incorrigible believer. He believes in everything that works.

JAMES RESTON, *What's He Like? And How Will He Do?; New York Times Magazine,* 17 Jan., 1965, p. 8. The reference is to Lyndon B. Johnson.

12

They believed—faith, I'm puzzled—I think I may call
Their belief a believing in nothing at all,
Or something of that sort; I know they all went
For a general union of total dissent.

JAMES RUSSELL LOWELL, *A Fable for Critics.*

13

O thou, whose days are yet all spring,
Faith, blighted once, is past retrieving;
Experience is a dumb, dead thing;
The victory's in believing.

JAMES RUSSELL LOWELL, *To---.*

14

It is easier to believe than to doubt.

EVERETT DEAN MARTIN, *The Meaning of a Liberal Education.*

15

The brute necessity of believing something so long as life lasts does not justify any belief in particular.

GEORGE SANTAYANA, *Scepticism.*

BELLS

16

The Bell calls others to Church, but itself never minds the Sermon.

BENJAMIN FRANKLIN, *Poor Richard,* 1754.

17

For bells are the voice of the church;
They have tones that touch and search
The hearts of young and old.

LONGFELLOW, *The Bells of San Blas.*

1
These bells have been anointed.
  LONGFELLOW, *The Golden Legend: Prologue.*

2
The bells themselves are the best of preachers,
Their brazen lips are learned teachers,
From their pulpits of stone, in the upper air,
Sounding aloft, without crack or flaw,
Shriller than trumpets under the Law.
Now a sermon and now a prayer.
  LONGFELLOW, *The Golden Legend,* pt. iii.

3
Keeping time, time, time
  In a sort of Runic rhyme
To the tintinnabulation that so musically wells
  From the bells, bells, bells.
  EDGAR ALLAN POE, *The Bells.*

4
Hear the mellow wedding bells, Golden bells!
What a world of happiness their harmony foretells.
  EDGAR ALLAN POE, *The Bells.*

5
And she breathed the husky whisper:—
"Curfew must not ring to-night."
  ROSE HARTWICK THORPE, *Curfew Must Not Ring To-night.* Later, in signed quotations from this poem, the author changed "must" to "shall."

BELLY

6
I can reason down or deny everything except this perpetual belly: feed he must and will, and I cannot make him respectable.
  EMERSON, *Representative Men: Montaigne.*

7
A full Belly is the Mother of all Evil.
  BENJAMIN FRANKLIN, *Poor Richard,* 1744.

8
A full belly makes a dull brain.
  BENJAMIN FRANKLIN, *Poor Richard,* 1758.

9
He had a broad face and a little round belly,
That shook, when he laughed, like a bowlful of jelly.
  CLEMENT CLARKE MOORE, *A Visit from St. Nicholas.*

BENEFITS
See also Gifts, Kindness

10
The favor of the great is no inheritance.
  BENJAMIN FRANKLIN, *Poor Richard,* 1733.

11
When befriended, remember it; when you befriend, forget it.
  BENJAMIN FRANKLIN, *Poor Richard,* 1740.

12
Write injuries in dust, benefits in marble.
  BENJAMIN FRANKLIN, *Poor Richard,* 1747.

13
He that has once done you a kindness will be more ready to do you another, than he whom you yourself have obliged.
  BENJAMIN FRANKLIN, *Autobiography.* Quoted as a maxim.

14
Though we may think we are specially blest,
We are certain to pay for the favors we get!
  JOHN G. SAXE, *The Gifts of the Gods.*

BIBLE

15
The Bible is like an old Cremona; it has been played upon by the devotion of thousands of years until every word and particle is public and tunable.
  EMERSON, *Letters and Social Aims: Quotation and Originality.*

16
Out from the heart of nature rolled
The burdens of the Bible old.
  EMERSON, *The Problem.*

17
The word unto the prophet spoken
Was writ on tables yet unbroken:
The word by seers or sibyls told,
In groves of oak, or fanes of gold,
Still floats upon the morning wind,
Still whispers to the willing mind.
  EMERSON, *The Problem.*

18
I'm looking for loopholes.
  Attributed to W. C. FIELDS, explaining why he was reading the Bible shortly before his death. (Quoted by Ben Hecht, originally in *Playboy,* subsequently in *The Reader's Digest,* Mar., 1961.

19
As long as woman regards the Bible as the charter of her rights, she will be the slave of man. The Bible was not written by a woman. Within its lids there is nothing but humiliation and shame for her.
  R. G. INGERSOLL, *The Liberty of Man, Woman and Child.*

20
So *we're* all right, an' I, fer one,
  Don't think our cause'll lose in vally
By rammin' Scriptur' in our gun,
  An' gittin' Natur' fer an ally.
  JAMES RUSSELL LOWELL, *The Biglow Papers,* Ser. ii, No. vii.

1

The Old Testament is tribal in its provinciality; its god is a local god, and its village police and sanitary regulations are erected into eternal laws.

JOHN MACY, *The Spirit of American Literature.*

2

What is a home without a Bible?
'Tis a home where daily bread
For the *body* is provided,
But the *soul* is never fed.

CHARLES D. MEIGS, *Home Without a Bible.*

3

The Bible is a book of faith, and a book of doctrine, and a book of morals, and a book of religion, of special revelation from God; but it is also a book which teaches man his own individual responsibility, his own dignity, and his equality with his fellow-man.

DANIEL WEBSTER, Speech at Bunker Hill Monument, 17 June, 1843.

4

O Bible! say I, "What follies and monstrous barbarities are defended in *thy* name."

WALT WHITMAN, paraphrasing Madame Roland. (*Uncollected Prose,* Vol. i)

5

We search the world for truth; we cull
The good, the pure, the beautiful,
From graven stone and written scroll,
From all old flower-fields of the soul;
And, weary seekers of the best,
We come back laden from our quest,
To find that all the sages said
Is in the Book our mothers read.

JOHN GREENLEAF WHITTIER, *Miriam.*

BIRDS

6

Strange, beautiful, unquiet thing,
Lone flute of God.

JOSEPH AUSLANDER, *A Blackbird Suddenly.*

7

No voice awoke. Dwelling sedate, apart,
Only the thrush, the thrush that never spoke,
Sang from her bursting heart.

LAURA BENÉT, *The Thrush.*

8

You alone can lose yourself
Within a sky, and rob it of its blue!

MAXWELL BODENHEIM, *Advice to a Blue-Bird.*

9

Vainly the fowler's eye
Might mark thy distant flight to do thee wrong,
As, darkly painted on the crimson sky,
Thy figure floats along.

WILLIAM CULLEN BRYANT, *To a Waterfowl.*

10

Merrily swinging on brier and weed,
Near to the nest of his little dame,
Over the mountain-side or mead,
Robert of Lincoln is telling his name:
Bob-o'-link, bob-o'-link,
Spink, spank, spink;
Snug and safe is this nest of ours,
Hidden among the summer flowers.
Chee, chee, chee.

WILLIAM CULLEN BRYANT, *Robert of Lincoln.*

11

I wonder if it *is* a bird
That sings within the hidden tree,
Or some shy angel calling me
To follow far away.

GRACE HAZARD CONKLING, *Nightingales.*

12

The robin is the one
That speechless from her nest
Submits that home and certainty
And sanctity are best.

EMILY DICKINSON, *Poems,* Pt. ii, No. 6.

13

Sweet Robin, I have heard them say
That thou wert there upon the day
The Christ was crowned in cruel scorn,
And bore away one bleeding thorn;
And so the blush upon thy breast,
In shameful sorrow, was impressed;
And thence thy genial sympathy
With our redeemed humanity.

GEORGE WASHINGTON DOANE, *Robin Redbreast.*

14

Jay-bird don't rob his own nes'.

JOEL CHANDLER HARRIS, *Plantation Proverbs.*

15

Listen to the mocking bird, listen to the mocking bird,
Still singing where the weeping willows wave.

ALICE HAWTHORNE, *Listen to the Mocking Bird* (song, 1870).

16

God gives every bird its food, but does not throw it into the nest.

JOSIAH G. HOLLAND, *Gold Foil: Providence.*

17

The crack-brained bobolink courts his crazy mate,
Poised on a bulrush tipsy with his weight.

OLIVER WENDELL HOLMES, *Spring.*

18

Why art thou but a nest of gloom
While the bobolinks are singing?

WILLIAM DEAN HOWELLS, *The Bobolinks Are Singing.*

19

The Wings of the Dove.

HENRY JAMES, Title of novel.

1
Seagulls . . . slim yachts of the element.
ROBINSON JEFFERS, *Pelicans.*

2
And all it lends to the eye is this—
A sunbeam giving the air a kiss.
HARRY KEMP, *The Hummingbird.*

3
I had a silvery name, I had a silvery name,
I had a silvery name—do you remember
The name you cried beside the tumbling
    sea?
"Darling . . . darling . . . darling . . .
    darling . . ."
Said the Chinese nightingale.
VACHEL LINDSAY, *The Chinese Nightin-
    gale.*

4
Do you ne'er think what wondrous beings
    these?
  Do you ne'er think who made them, and
    who taught
The dialect they speak, where melodies
  Alone are the interpreters of thought?
Whose household words are songs in many
    keys,
  Sweeter than instrument of man e'er
    caught!
LONGFELLOW, *The Birds of Killingworth.*

5
Even the blackest of them all, the crow,
Renders good service as your man-at-arms,
Crushing the beetle in his coat of mail,
And crying havoc on the slug and snail.
LONGFELLOW, *Birds of Killingworth.*

6
Enjoy the Spring of Love and Youth,
  To some good angel leave the rest;
For Time will teach thee soon the truth,
  There are no birds in last year's nest!
LONGFELLOW, *It Is Not Always May.*

7
Then from the neighboring thicket the mock-
    ing-bird, wildest of singers,
Swinging aloft on a willow spray that hung
    o'er the water,
Shook from his little throat such floods of
    delirious music,
That the whole air and the woods and the
    waves seemed silent to listen.
LONGFELLOW, *Evangeline,* pt. ii, sec. 2.

8
To the red rising moon, and loud and deep
The nightingale is singing from the steep.
LONGFELLOW, *Keats.*

9
The swallow is come! The swallow is come!
  O, fair are the seasons, and light
Are the days that she brings with her dusky
    wings,
  And her bosom snowy white!
LONGFELLOW, *Hyperion,* bk. ii.

10
  June's bridesman, poet o' the year,

10 *(cont.)*
Gladness on wings, the bobolink, is here;
Half-hid in tip-top apple-blooms he swings,
Or climbs against the breeze with quiverin'
    wings,
Or, givin' way to 't in a mock despair,
Runs down, a brook o' laughter, thru the
    air.
JAMES RUSSELL LOWELL, *Biglow Papers,*
    Ser. ii. No. 6.

11
A wonderful bird is the pelican!
His bill will hold more than his belican.
  He can take in his beak
  Food enough for a week
But I'm darned if I see how the helican.
DIXON L. MERRITT, *The Pelican.*

12
Bird of the broad and sweeping wing,
  Thy home is high in heaven,
Where wide the storms their banners fling,
  And the tempest clouds are driven.
JAMES GATES PERCIVAL, *To the Eagle.*

13
O, far, far, far,
As any spire or star,
Beyond the cloistered wall!
O, high, high, high,
A heart-throb in the sky—
Then not at all!
LIZETTE WOODWORTH REESE, *The Lark.*

14
And the humming-bird that hung
  Like a jewel up among
The tilted honeysuckle horns.
JAMES WHITCOMB RILEY, *The South Wind
    and the Sun.*

15
Hush! With sudden gush
As from a fountain sings in yonder bush
The Hermit Thrush.
JOHN BANISTER TABB, *Overflow.*

16
The bluebird carries the sky on his back.
THOREAU, *Journal.* (EMERSON, *Thoreau*)

17
The birds know when the friend they love is
    nigh,
For I am known to them, both great and
    small.
JONES VERY, *Nature.*

BIRTH

See also Ancestry, Baby

18
When each comes forth from his mother's
womb, the gate of gifts closes behind him.
EMERSON, *Conduct of Life: Fate.*

19
A man is not completely born until he be
dead.
BENJAMIN FRANKLIN, *Letters: To Miss
    Hubbard.*

20
Where'er a single slave doth pine,

Where'er one man may help another,—
Thank God for such a birthright, brother,—
That spot of earth is thine and mine!
There is the true man's birthplace grand,
His is a world-wide fatherland!
  JAMES RUSSELL LOWELL, *The Fatherland.*

1
Lest, selling that noble inheritance for a poor
mess of pottage, you never enter into his
eternal rest.
  WILLIAM PENN, *No Cross, No Crown*, pt.
  ii.

Shall we sell our birthrite for a mess of pot-
ash?
  ARTEMUS WARD, Lecture.

2
Infinitely more important than any other
question in this country—that is the question
of race suicide, complete or partial.
  THEODORE ROOSEVELT, Letter to Bessie
  Van Vorst, 18 Oct., 1902. It was reprint-
  ed as a preface to her *The Woman Who
  Toils.*

3
I 'spect I growed. Don't think nobody never
made me.
  HARRIET BEECHER STOWE, *Uncle Tom's
  Cabin.*

4
Why is it that we rejoice at a birth and
grieve at a funeral? It is because we are not
the person involved.
  MARK TWAIN, *Pudd'nhead Wilson's Calendar.*

5
My father got me strong and straight and
    slim
  And I give thanks to him.
My mother bore me glad and sound and
    sweet,
  I kiss her feet!
  MARGUERITE WILKINSON, *The End.*

6
Born of a Monday, fair in the face,
Born of a Tuesday, full of God's grace.
Born of a Wednesday, merry and glad,
Born of a Thursday, sour and sad,
Born of a Friday, Godly given,
Born of a Saturday, work for your living,
Born of a Sunday, ne'er shall you want,
So ends the week, and there's an end on't.
  UNKNOWN. (BRAND, *Popular Antiquities.
  Notes and Queries*, ser. v, vii, 424)

Monday's child is fair of face,
Tuesday's child is full of grace,
Wednesday's child is full of woe,
Thursday's child has far to go,
Friday's child is loving and giving,
Saturday's child works hard for its living,
And a child that's born on the Sabbath day

Is fair and wise and good and gay.
  UNKNOWN. (BRAY, *Traditions of Devon,*
  ii, 288)

Birthstones

7
January
By her who in this month is born,
No gems save *Garnets* should be worn;
They will insure her constancy,
True friendship and fidelity.

February
The February born will find
Sincerity and peace of mind;
Freedom from passion and from care,
If they the *Pearl* will always wear.

March
Who in this world of ours their eyes
In March first open shall be wise;
In days of peril firm and brave,
And wear a *Bloodstone* to their grave.

April
She who from April dates her years,
Diamonds should wear, lest bitter tears
For vain repentance flow; this stone,
Emblem of innocence is known.

May
Who first beholds the light of day
In Spring's sweet flowery month of May
And wears an *Emerald* all her life,
Shall be a loved and happy wife.

June
Who comes with Summer to this earth
And owes to June her day of birth,
With ring of *Agate* on her hand,
Can health, wealth, and long life command.

July
The glowing *Ruby* should adorn
Those who in warm July are born,
Then will they be exempt and free
From love's doubt and anxiety.

August
Wear a *Sardonyx* or for thee
No conjugal felicity.
The August-born without this stone
'Tis said must live unloved and lone.

September
A maiden born when Autumn leaves
Are rustling in September's breeze,
A *Sapphire* on her brow should bind.
'Twill cure diseases of the mind.

October
October's child is born for woe,
And life's vicissitudes must know;
But lay an *Opal* on her breast,
And hope will lull those woes to rest.

November
Who first comes to this world below
With drear November's fog and snow
Should prize the *Topaz'* amber hue—
Emblem of friends and lovers true.

December
If cold December gave you birth,
The month of snow and ice and mirth,
Place on your hand a *Turquoise* blue,
Success will bless whate'er you do.
> UNKNOWN. (*Notes and Queries*, 11 May, 1889, p. 371.)

BIRTHDAY
See also Age

1
Fifty years spent, and what do they bring me?
Now I can buy the meadow and hill:
Where is the heart of the boy to sing thee?
Where is the life for thy living to fill?
> STRUTHERS BURT, *Fifty Years Spent.*

2
I'm going to call up my mother and congratulate her.
> HUBERT H. HUMPHREY, to reporters at a White House reception, 26 May, 1965, the day before his fifty-fourth birthday.

3
Past my next milestone waits my seventieth year.
I mount no longer when the trumpets call;
My battle-harness idles on the wall,
The spider's castle, camping-ground of dust,
Not without dints, and all in front, I trust.
> JAMES RUSSELL LOWELL, *Epistle to George William Curtis: Postscript, 1887.*

4
Old Age, on tiptoe, lays her jewelled hand
Lightly in mine.
> GEORGE SANTAYANA, *A Minuet on Reaching the Age of Fifty.*

5
I keep some portion of my early dream;
  Brokenly light, like moonbeams on a river,
It lights my life, a far elusive gleam,
  Moves as I move, and leads me on forever.
> J. T. TROWBRIDGE, *Twoscore and Ten.*

BLESSING

6
Bless the four corners of this little house,
  And be the lintel blest;
And bless the hearth, and bless the board,
  And bless each place of rest.
> ARTHUR GUITERMAN, *House Blessing.*

7
God bless us every one, prayed Tiny Tim,
  Crippled and dwarfed of body, yet so tall

Of soul, we tiptoe earth to look on him,
  High towering over all.
> JAMES WHITCOMB RILEY, *God Bless Us Every One.*

8
You bless us, please sah, eben ef we's doin' wrong tonight,
Kase den we'll need de blessin' more'n ef we's doin' right;
An' let de blessin' stay wid us untel we comes to die
An' goes to keep our Christmas wid dem sheriffs in de sky.
> IRWIN RUSSELL, *Christmas Night in the Quarters.*

9
He who blesses most is blest:
  And God and man shall own his worth
Who toils to leave as his bequest
  An added beauty to the earth.
> JOHN GREENLEAF WHITTIER, *Lines for the Agricultural Exhibition at Amesbury.*

BOAT, see Ship
BODY

10
I built a house of sticks and mud,
And God built one of flesh and blood.
How queer that was, how strange that is,
That my poor house should shelter His.

And yet my house of sticks and clay
Is standing sturdy still today;
While God's house in a narrow pit
Is rotting where men buried it.
> N. D. ANDERSON, *The Two Houses.*

11
The human body is a magazine of inventions, the patent office, where are the models from which every hint is taken. All the tools and engines on earth are only extensions of its limbs and senses.
> EMERSON, *Society and Solitude: Works and Days.*

What a plastic little creature he is! so shifty, so adaptive! his body a chest of tools.
> EMERSON, *Letters and Social Aims: Resources.*

12
The body of man is the type after which a dwelling house is built.
> EMERSON, *Representative Men: Montaigne.*

13
Since the body is a pipe through which we tap all the succors and virtues of the material world, it is certain that a sound body must be at the root of any excellence in manners and actions.
> EMERSON, *Lectures and Biographical Studies: Aristocracy.*

14
It is the soundness of the bones that ulti-

mates itself in the peach-bloom complexion.
EMERSON, *Conduct of Life: Beauty.*

1
Our bodies do not fit us, but caricature and satirize us. Man is physically as well as metaphysically a thing of shreds and patches, borrowed unequally from good and bad ancestors and a misfit from the start.
EMERSON, *Conduct of Life: Beauty.*

2
The body borrows the elements of its blood from the whole world, and the mind its belief.
EMERSON, *Journals,* 1864.

3
For the body at best
Is a bundle of aches,
Longing for rest;
It cries when it wakes.
EDNA ST. VINCENT MILLAY, *Moriturus.*

4
She whose body's young and cool
Has no need of dancing-school.
DOROTHY PARKER, *Salome's Dancing Lesson.*

5
Pocahontas' body, lovely as a poplar, sweet as a red haw in November or a pawpaw in May, did she wonder? does she remember? . . . in the dust, in the cool tombs?
CARL SANDBURG, *Cool Tombs.*

6
If anything is sacred the human body is sacred.
WALT WHITMAN, *I Sing the Body Electric,* sec. 6.

7
Have you ever loved the body of a woman?
Have you ever loved the body of a man?
Do you not see that these are exactly the same to all in all nations and times all over the earth?
WALT WHITMAN, *I Sing the Body Electric,* sec. 6.

BOLDNESS

8
There are periods when the principles of experience need to be modified, . . . when in truth to *dare* is the highest wisdom.
WILLIAM ELLERY CHANNING, *Works,* p. 641.

9
Finite to fail, but infinite to venture.
EMILY DICKINSON, *Poems.*

10
One would say he had read the inscription on the gates of Busyrane,—"Be bold;" and on the second gate,—"Be bold, be bold, and evermore be bold;" and then again had paused well at the third gate,—"Be not too bold."
EMERSON, *Representative Men: Plato.*

Write on your doors the saying wise and old,

"Be bold! be bold!" and everywhere, "Be bold;
Be not too bold!" Yet better the excess
Than the defect; better the more than less;
Better like Hector in the field to die,
Than like a perfumed Paris turn and fly.
LONGFELLOW, *Morituri Salutamus.*

BOOKS
See also Fiction, Library, Reading, Writing

11
Books are the most mannerly of companions, accessible at all times, in all moods, frankly declaring the author's mind, without offence.
AMOS BRONSON ALCOTT, *Concord Days.*

12
That is a good book which is opened with expectation and closed with profit.
AMOS BRONSON ALCOTT, *Table Talk:* bk. i, *Learning-Books.*

13
Books are the compasses and telescopes and sextants and charts which other men have prepared to help us navigate the dangerous seas of human life.
JESSE LEE BENNETT, *Books as Guides*

14
Books we must have though we lack bread.
ALICE WILLIAMS BROTHERTON, *Ballade of Poor Bookworms.*

15
As a writer, I hold uncut pages to be comment on an owner and an insult to an author. A book for me is something to be read, not kept under glass or in a safe. I want to dog-ear it, to underline it, to annotate it, and mark my favorite passages, and make my own index on the blank pages at the back.
JOHN MASON BROWN, "Seeing Things," *The Saturday Review,* 22 Sept., 1951. Reprinted in *As They Appear,* p. 6—a collection of Brown's essays.

16
It is chiefly through books that we enjoy intercourse with superior minds. . . . In the best books, great men talk to us, give us their most precious thoughts, and pour their souls into ours.
WILLIAM ELLERY CHANNING, *On Self-Culture.*

17
Books are the true levellers. They give to all, who will faithfully use them, the society, the spiritual presence, of the best and greatest of our race.
WILLIAM ELLERY CHANNING, *On Self-Culture.*

18
Old Books are best! With what delight
Does "Faithorne fecit" greet our sight.
BEVERLY CHEW, *Old Books Are Best.*

19
Wouldst thou find my ashes? Look

In the pages of my book;
And, as these thy hands doth turn,
Know here is my funeral urn.
> ADELAIDE CRAPSEY, *The Immortal Residue.*

1
He ate and drank the precious words,
  His spirit grew robust;
He knew no more that he was poor,
  Nor that his frame was dust.
He danced along the dingy days,
  And this bequest of wings
Was but a book. What liberty
  A loosened spirit brings!
> EMILY DICKINSON, *Poems*, Pt. i, No. 21.

2
There is no frigate like a book
  To take us lands away,
Nor any coursers like a page
  Of prancing poetry.
> EMILY DICKINSON, *Poems*, Pt. i, No. 99.

3
Books are the quietest and most constant of friends; they are the most accessible and wisest of counsellors, and the most patient of teachers.
> CHARLES W. ELIOT, *The Happy Life.*

4
In the highest civilization, the book is still the highest delight. He who has once known its satisfactions is provided with a resource against calamity.
> EMERSON, *Letters and Social Aims: Quotation and Originality.*

5
We prize books, and they prize them most who are themselves wise.
> EMERSON, *Letters and Social Aims: Quotation and Originality.*

6
There are books . . . which take rank in our life with parents and lovers and passionate experiences.
> EMERSON, *Society and Solitude: Books.*

7
The colleges, whilst they provide us with libraries, furnish no professor of books; and I think no chair is so much wanted.
> EMERSON, *Society and Solitude: Books.*

8
A man's library is a sort of harem, and tender readers have a great pudency in showing their books to a stranger.
> EMERSON, *Society and Solitude: Books.*

9
The virtue of books is to be readable.
> EMERSON, *Society and Solitude: Eloquence.*

10
Books are the best things, well used: abused, among the worst.
> EMERSON, *Nature, Addresses and Lectures: The American Scholar.*

11
Books are for the scholar's idle times. When he can read God directly, the hour is too precious to be wasted in other men's transcripts of their reading.
> EMERSON, *Nature, Addresses and Lectures: The American Scholar.*

12
When the mind wakes, books are set aside as impertinent.
> EMERSON, *Books.*

13
Some books leave us free and some books make us free.
> EMERSON, *Journals*, 22 Dec., 1839.

14
One master could so easily be conceived as writing all the books of the world. They are all alike.
> EMERSON, *Journals,* vol. vii.

15
Women are by nature fickle, and so are men. . . . Not so with books, for books cannot change. A thousand years hence they are what you find them today, speaking the same words, holding forth the same comfort.
> EUGENE FIELD, *Love Affairs of a Bibliomaniac.*

16
Old books, as you well know, are books of the world's youth, and new books are fruits of its age.
> OLIVER WENDELL HOLMES, *The Professor at the Breakfast-Table*, ch. 9.

17
The foolishest book is a kind of leaky boat on a sea of wisdom; some of the wisdom will get in anyhow.
> OLIVER WENDELL HOLMES, *The Poet at the Breakfast-Table.*

18
No book is of much importance, the vital thing is, What do you yourself think?
> ELBERT HUBBARD, *Philistine*, vol. xviii.

19
Dear little child, this little book
  Is less a primer than a key
To sunder gates where wonder waits
  Your "Open Sesame!"
> RUPERT HUGHES, *With a First Reader.*

20
Books and ideas are the most effective weapons against intolerance and ignorance.
> LYNDON B. JOHNSON, commenting as he signed into law a bill providing increased Federal aid for library services, 11 Feb., 1964.

21
The love of learning, the sequestered nooks,
And all the sweet serenity of books.
> LONGFELLOW, *Morituri Salutamus.*

22
The pleasant books, that silently among
  Our household treasures take familiar places,
And are to us as if a living tongue

Spake from the printed leaves or pictured
   faces!
   LONGFELLOW, *The Seaside and the Fireside: Dedication.*

1
Books are sepulchres of thought;
The dead laurels of the dead.
   LONGFELLOW, *Wind Over the Chimney.*

2
Many readers judge of the power of a book
by the shock it gives their feelings.
   LONGFELLOW, *Kavanagh.*

3
For books are more than books, they are the
   life
The very heart and core of ages past,
The reason why men lived and worked and
   died,
The essence and quintessence of their lives.
   AMY LOWELL, *The Boston Athenaeum.*

4
All books are either dreams or swords,
You can cut, or you can drug, with words.
   AMY LOWELL, *Sword Blades and Poppy
   Seed.*

5
If I were asked what book is better than a
cheap book, I should answer that there is one
book better than a cheap book, and that is a
book honestly come by.
   JAMES RUSSELL LOWELL, speaking before
   the U.S. Senate Committee on Patents,
   29 Jan., 1886.

6
And the loved books that younger grow with
years.
   JAMES RUSSELL LOWELL, *Epistle to
   George William Curtis: Postscript,
   1887.*

7
What a sense of security in an old book
   which
Time has criticised for us!
   JAMES RUSSELL LOWELL, *My Study Win-
   dows: Library of Old Authors.*

8
He fed his spirit with the bread of books,
And slaked his thirst at the wells of thought.
   EDWIN MARKHAM, *Young Lincoln.*

9
The books which help you most are those
which make you think the most.
   THEODORE PARKER, *World of Matter and
   World of Men.*

10
Wear the old coat and buy the new book.
   AUSTIN PHELPS, *The Theory of Preach-
   ing.*

11
The peace of great books be for you,
Stains of pressed clover leaves on pages,
Bleach of the light of years held in leather.
   CARL SANDBURG, *For You.*

12
Books are the treasured wealth of the world,

the fit inheritance of generations and nations.
   HENRY DAVID THOREAU, *Walden: Reading.*

13
Good books are the most precious of blessings to a people; bad books are among the
worst of curses.
   EDWIN PERCY WHIPPLE, *Essays: Romance
   of Rascality.*

14
Then falter not, O book, fulfil your destiny,
You not a reminiscence of the land alone,
You too as a lone bark cleaving the ether,
   purpos'd
I know not whither, yet ever full of faith.
   WALT WHITMAN, *In Cabin'd Ships at Sea.*

15
Camerado, this is no book,
Who touches this touches a man, . . .
It is I you hold and who holds you,
I spring from the pages into your arms.
   WALT WHITMAN, *So Long.*

16
What holy cities are to nomadic tribes—a
symbol of race and a bond of union—great
books are to the wandering souls of men:
they are the Meccas of the mind.
   G. E. WOODBERRY, *Torch.*

BORES

17
I have not had my hearing aid open to that
man for years.
   BERNARD M. BARUCH, on how to handle a
   bore. (New York *Times* obituary of Baruch, 21 June, 1965, p. 16)

18
Bore: a person who talks when you wish him
to listen.
   AMBROSE BIERCE, *The Devil's Dictionary.*

19
To inflict anyone with a compulsory interview of more than ten minutes indicates a
crude state of civilization.
   EMERSON, *Social Aims.*

20
All men are bores, except when we want
them.
   OLIVER WENDELL HOLMES, *The Autocrat
   of the Breakfast-Table,* ch. 1.

21
Every one of us is interested in interesting
people. That is to say, we don't feel responsible for the rehabilitation of bores. In life,
we avoid them. We feel no compunction
about cutting them dead. If we have misgiv-
ings about our lack of charity, we contribute
to a charity.
   WALTER KERR, *How Not to Write a Play:
   In General.*

22
And so dull that the men who retailed them
   out-doors

Got the ill name of augurs, because they
    were bores.
    JAMES RUSSELL LOWELL, *A Fable for Crit-
    ics*, 1. 54.

1
There was one feudal custom worth keeping,
    at least,
Roasted bores made a part of each well-or-
    dered feast.
    JAMES RUSSELL LOWELL, *A Fable for Crit-
    ics*, 1. 1226.

2
Again I hear that creaking step!—
    He's rapping at the door!
Too well I know the boding sound
    That ushers in a bore.
    J. G. SAXE, *My Familiar*.

3
I do not tremble when I meet
    The stoutest of my foes,
But Heaven defend me from the friend
    Who comes—but never goes!
    J. G. SAXE, *My Familiar*.

He says a thousand pleasant things,—
    But never says "Adieu."
    J. G. SAXE, *My Familiar*.

4
A bore is a man who, when you ask him how
he is, tells you.
    BERT LESTON TAYLOR, *The So-Called Hu-
    man Race*.

BORROWING AND LENDING
See also Debt

5
The borrower runs in his own debt.
    EMERSON, *Essays, First Series: Compensa-
    tion*.

6
Lend money to an enemy, and thou'lt gain
him; to a friend, and thou'lt lose him.
    BENJAMIN FRANKLIN, *Poor Richard*,
    1740.

7
He that goes a-borrowing, goes a-sorrowing.
    BENJAMIN FRANKLIN, *Poor Richard*,
    1758.

8
Creditors have better memories than debt-
ors.
    BENJAMIN FRANKLIN, *Poor Richard*,
    1758.

9
The holy passion of Friendship is of so sweet
and steady and loyal and enduring a nature
that it will last through a whole lifetime, if
not asked to lend money.
    MARK TWAIN. *Pudd'nhead Wilson's Cal-
    endar*.

10
Let us all be happy, and live within our
means, even if we have to borrow the money
to do it.
    ARTEMUS WARD, *Natural History*.

11
God bless pawnbrokers!
They are quiet men.
    MARGUERITE WILKINSON, *Pawnbrokers*.

BOSTON

12
A Boston man is the east wind made flesh.
    Attributed to THOMAS APPLETON.

13
And this is the good old Boston,
    The home of the bean and the cod,
Where the Lowells talk to the Cabots,
    And the Cabots talk only to God.
    J. C. BOSSIDY, *On the Aristocracy of Har-
    vard*.

Then here's to the City of Boston,
    The town of the cries and the groans,
Where the Cabots can't see the Kabot-
    schniks
    And the Lowells won't speak to the
    Cohns.
    FRANKLIN P. ADAMS, *Revised*.

Here's to the town of New Haven,
    The home of the Truth and the Light,
Where God talks to Jones in the very same
    tones
    That He uses with Hadley and Dwight.
    F. S. JONES, *On the Democracy of Yale*.

14
Boston's a hole, the herring-pond is wide,
V-notes are something, liberty still more.
    ROBERT BROWNING, *Mr. Sludge "The Me-
    dium."*

15
The rocky nook with hill-tops three
    Looked eastward from the farms,
And twice each day the flowing sea
    Took Boston in its arms.
    EMERSON, *Boston*.

16
The sea returning day by day
    Restores the world-wide mart;
So let each dweller on the Bay
    Fold Boston in his heart,
Till these echoes be choked with snows,
Or over the town blue ocean flows.
    EMERSON, *Boston*.

17
We say the cows laid out Boston. Well, there
are worse surveyors.
    EMERSON, *Conduct of Life: Wealth*.

18
Full of crooked little streets; but I tell you
Boston has opened, and kept open, more
turnpikes that lead straight to free thought
and free speech and free deeds than any other city of live men or dead men.
    OLIVER WENDELL HOLMES, *The Professor
    at the Breakfast-Table*, ch. 1.

19
That's all I claim for Boston,—that it is the

thinking center of the continent, and therefore of the planet.
> OLIVER WENDELL HOLMES, *The Professor at the Breakfast-Table*, ch. 4.

1
The heart of the world beats under the three hills of Boston.
> OLIVER WENDELL HOLMES, *The Professor at the Breakfast-Table*, ch. 12.

2
Boston State-house is the hub of the solar system. You couldn't pry that out of a Boston man if you had the tire of all creation straightened out for a crow-bar.
> OLIVER WENDELL HOLMES, *The Autocrat of the Breakfast-Table*, ch. 6.

Massachusetts has been the wheel within New England, and Boston the wheel within Massachusetts. Boston therefore is often called the "hub of the world," since it has been the source and fountain of the ideas that have reared and made America.
> REV. F. B. ZINCKLE, *Last Winter in the United States* (1868).

3
Boston is a moral and intellectual nursery always busy applying first principles to trifles.
> GEORGE SANTAYANA. (*Santayana: The Later Years,* ed. by Daniel Cory)

4
Boston is a state of mind.
> Attributed to MARK TWAIN. Sometimes also credited to Emerson and Thomas G. Appleton.

5
Solid men of Boston, make no long orations;
Solid men of Boston, drink no long potations;
Solid men of Boston, go to bed at sundown;
Never lose your way like the loggerheads of London.
> ANONYMOUS, *Billy Pitt and the Farmer.* (DEBRETT, *Asylum for Fugitive Pieces,* 1786) The first two lines were quoted in a letter from Daniel Webster to the Rev. C. B. Haddock, 9 Mar., 1849; Webster added, "I take them to myself."

Solid men of Boston, banish long potations!
Solid men of Boston, make no long orations!
> CHARLES MORRIS, *Pitt and Dundas's Return to London from Wimbledon.* (*Lyra Urbanica,* 1840) The quotation refers to Boston, Lincolnshire, England; it is often applied also to Boston, Mass.

A solid man of Boston;
A comfortable man with dividends,
And the first salmon and the first green peas.
> LONGFELLOW, *John Endicott,* act 4.

BOY, BOYHOOD
See also Childhood, Children, Youth

6
God bless all little boys who look like Puck,
  With wide eyes, wider mouths and stick-out ears,
Rash little boys who stay alive by luck
  And heaven's favor in this world of tears.
> ARTHUR GUITERMAN, *Blessing on Little Boys.*

7
Has there any old fellow got mixed with the boys?
If there has, take him out, without making a noise.
> OLIVER WENDELL HOLMES, *The Boys.*

8
Then here's to our boyhood, its gold and its gray!
The stars of its winter, the dews of its May!
> OLIVER WENDELL HOLMES, *The Boys.*

9
O for one hour of youthful joy!
Give back my twentieth spring!
I'd rather laugh, a bright-haired boy,
Than reign, a gray-beard king.
> OLIVER WENDELL HOLMES, *The Old Man Dreams.*

10
A boy has two jobs. One is just being a boy.
The other is growing up to be a man.
> HERBERT HOOVER, Speech, 21 May, 1956, marking the fiftieth anniversary of the Boys' Clubs of America.

11
I remember the gleams and glooms that dart
  Across the school-boy's brain;
The song and the silence in the heart,
That in part are prophecies, and in part
  Are longings wild and vain.
    And the voice of that fitful song
    Sings on, and is never still:
"A boy's will is the wind's will,
And the thoughts of youth are long, long thoughts."
> LONGFELLOW, *My Lost Youth,* st. 7.

12
Perhaps there lives some dreamy boy, untaught
In schools, some graduate of the field or street,
Who shall become a master of the art,
An admiral sailing the high seas of thought.
> LONGFELLOW, *Possibilities.*

13
When I was a beggarly boy
  And lived in a cellar damp,
I had not a friend nor a toy,
  But I had Aladdin's lamp.
> JAMES RUSSELL LOWELL, *Aladdin.*

14
One of the best things in the world to be is a

boy; it requires no experience, but needs some practice to be a good one.
> CHARLES DUDLEY WARNER, *Being a Boy*, ch. 1.

1
Blessings on thee, little man,
Barefoot boy, with cheek of tan!
With thy turned-up pantaloons,
And thy merry whistled tunes.
> JOHN GREENLEAF WHITTIER, *The Barefoot Boy*.

2
Oh, for boyhood's time of June,
Crowding years in one brief moon.
> JOHN GREENLEAF WHITTIER, *The Barefoot Boy*.

3
The sweetest roamer is a boy's young heart.
> GEORGE E. WOODBERRY, *Agathon*.

BRAIN, see Mind
BRAVERY, see Courage
BREAD

4
Man does not live by bread alone, but by faith, by admiration, by sympathy.
> EMERSON, *Lectures, and Biographical Studies: The Sovereignty of Ethics*.

5
Will it bake bread?
> EMERSON, *Essays, First Series: Prudence*. In full: "A prudence which asks but one question of any project,—Will it bake bread?"

6
When you came, you were like red wine and honey,
And the taste of you burnt my mouth with its sweetness.
Now you are like morning bread,
Smooth and pleasant.
I hardly taste you at all, for I know your savor;
But I am completely nourished.
> AMY LOWELL, *A Decade*.

7
Corn, which is the staff of life.
> EDWARD WINSLOW, *Good Newes from New England* (1624).

BREVITY

8
For brief as water falling will be death,
and brief as flower falling, or a leaf,
brief as the taking, and the giving, breath;
thus natural, thus brief, my love, is grief.
> CONRAD AIKEN, *And in the Human Heart*, sonnet 18.

9
Bilin' down his repoort, wuz Finnigin!
An' he writed this here: "Musther Flannigan:
Off agin, on agin,

Gone agin.—Finnigin."
> STRICKLAND GILLILAN, *Finnigin to Flannigan*.

10
Hubert, to be eternal you don't have to be endless.
> MURIEL HUMPHREY (MRS. HUBERT H. HUMPHREY), to her husband, in commenting on the length of one of his speeches. (*Democrats' Wives Hit the Campaign Trail*, by OLIVIA SKINNER; St. Louis *Post-Dispatch*, 2 Oct., 1964, p. 3D)

11
As man is now constituted, to be brief is almost a condition of being inspired.
> GEORGE SANTAYANA, *Little Essays*.

12
Not that the story need be long, but it will take a long while to make it short.
> HENRY DAVID THOREAU, Letter to a friend.

BRIBERY

13
There is no luck in literary reputation. They who make up the final verdict upon every book are not the partial and noisy readers of the hour when it appears; but a court as of angels, a public not to be bribed, not to be entreated, and not to be overawed, decides upon every man's title to fame.
> EMERSON, *Essays, First Series: Spiritual Laws*.

14
Few men have virtue to withstand the highest bidder.
> GEORGE WASHINGTON, *Moral Maxims: Virtue and Vice*.

BROTHER, BROTHERHOOD

15
The idea that there are national, or European, or North American interests which can be safely pursued in disregard of a common interest belongs to that past which has brought us all such loss and suffering.
> DEAN ACHESON, *Withdrawal from Europe? 'An Illusion'*; New York Times Magazine, 15 Dec., 1963.

16
While there is a lower class I am in it. While there is a criminal class I am of it. While there is a soul in prison I am not free.
> EUGENE V. DEBS, *Labor and Freedom*.

17
To live is good. To live vividly is better. To live vividly together is best.
> MAX EASTMAN. (*The Reader's Digest*, Dec., 1963.)

18
Yes, you'd know him for a heathen
If you judged him by the hide,
But bless you, he's my brother,

For he's just like me inside.
ROBERT FREEMAN, *The Heathen.*

1
"Men work together," I told him from the heart,
"Whether they work together or apart."
ROBERT FROST, *The Tuft of Flowers.*

2
To-day, old friend, remember still
That I am Joe and you are Bill.
OLIVER WENDELL HOLMES, *Bill and Joe.*

3
Down in their hearts, wise men know this truth: the only way to help yourself is to help others.
ELBERT HUBBARD, *The Philistine*, vol. 18.

4
The world has narrowed to a neighborhood before it has broadened to brotherhood.
LYNDON B. JOHNSON, Response to a toast proposed by Adlai E. Stevenson at a luncheon given by the latter in honor of Johnson and the leadership of the United Nations, New York City, 17 Dec., 1963. Johnson recalled at the time that he had first used substantially the same words in an address at the high-school graduation of his daughter Lynda Bird.

5
In the final analysis, our most basic common link is that we all inhabit this small planet. We all breathe the same air. We all cherish our children's future. And we are all mortal.
JOHN F. KENNEDY, Address at American University, Washington, D.C., 10 June, 1963.

6
We must learn to live together as brothers or perish together as fools.
REV. MARTIN LUTHER KING, JR., Address in St. Louis, 23 Mar., 1964. He was referring specifically to the need for true racial integration in the United States.

7
The crest and crowning of all good,
Life's final star, is Brotherhood.
EDWIN MARKHAM, *Brotherhood.*

8
There is a destiny which makes us brothers;
None goes his way alone.
EDWIN MARKHAM, *A Creed.*

9
The brotherhood of man under the fatherhood of God.
NELSON A. ROCKEFELLER. This expression was used by him repeatedly during his campaign for the 1964 Republican presidential nomination, notably in the primary elections beginning in February of that year. Reporters covering his campaign helped to make this a familiar quotation by referring to it by a shorthand title: Bomfog.

10
We can truly begin to perceive the meaning of our great propositions—of liberty and equality—if we see them as part of the patrimony of all men. We shall not love our corner of the planet less for loving the planet too, and resisting with all our skill and passion the dangers that would reduce it to smoldering ashes.
ADLAI E. STEVENSON, *The Hard Kind of Patriotism; Harper's Magazine*, July, 1963.

11
For, on this shrunken globe, men can no longer live as strangers. Men can war against each other as hostile neighbors, as we are determined not to do; or they can coexist in frigid isolation, as we are doing. But our prayer is that men everywhere will learn, finally, to live as brothers.
ADLAI E. STEVENSON, *The Hard Kind of Patriotism; Harper's Magazine*, July, 1963.

12
The little brown brother.
WILLIAM HOWARD TAFT (1900). The reference was to the Filipinos.

13
Throw out the life-line across the dark wave,
There is a brother whom someone must save.
EDWARD SMITH UFFORD, *Throw Out the Life-Line.*

14
Whoever degrades another degrades me,
And whatever is done or said returns at last to me.
WALT WHITMAN, *Song of Myself*, sec. 24.

15
Not till the sun excludes you do I exclude you,
Not till the waters refuse to glisten for you and the leaves to rustle for you, do my words refuse to glisten and rustle for you.
WALT WHITMAN, *To a Common Prostitute.*

BROWN, JOHN

16
I am fully persuaded that I am worth inconceivably more to hang than for any other purpose.
JOHN BROWN, Speech at his trial, 2 Nov., 1859.

17
I, John Brown, am now quite certain that the crimes of this guilty land will never be purged away but with Blood.
JOHN BROWN, Statement, in writing, 2 Dec., 1859, the date of his execution.

1

John Brown's body lies a-mouldering in the grave,
　His soul is marching on!
　　CHARLES SPRAGUE HALL, *John Brown's Body*. This is sometimes attributed to Frank E. Jerome.

2

The death of Brown is more than Cain killing Abel: it is Washington slaying Spartacus.
　　VICTOR HUGO, *A Word Concerning John Brown to Virginia*, 2 Dec., 1859.

3

John Brown died on the scaffold for the slave;
Dark was the hour when we dug his hallowed grave;
Now God avenges the life he gladly gave,
　Freedom reigns to-day!
　　EDNA DEAN PROCTOR, *John Brown*.

4

But, Virginians, don't do it! for I tell you that the flagon,
　Filled with blood of Old Brown's offspring, was first poured by Southern hands;
And each drop from Old Brown's life-veins, like the red gore of the dragon,
　May spring up a vengeful Fury, hissing through your slave-worn lands:
And Old Brown, Osawatomie Brown,
May trouble you more than ever, when you've nailed his coffin down!
　　E. C. STEDMAN, *How Old Brown Took Harper's Ferry* (Nov., 1859, during Brown's trial).

5

John Brown of Ossawatomie, they led him out to die;
And lo! a poor slave-mother with her little child pressed nigh.
Then the bold, blue eye grew tender, and the old harsh face grew mild,
As he stooped between the jeering ranks and kissed the negro's child!
The shadows of his stormy life that moment fell apart;
And they who blamed the bloody hand forgave the loving heart.
That kiss from all its guilty means redeemed the good intent,
And round the grisly fighter's hair the martyr's aureole bent!
　　JOHN GREENLEAF WHITTIER, *Brown of Ossawatomie*.

BURDEN

See also Care

6

Oh, there are moments for us here, when seeing
　Life's inequalities, and woe, and care,
The burdens laid upon our mortal being

Seem heavier than the human heart can bear.
　　WILLIS G. CLARK, *A Song of May*.

7

In the final choice a soldier's pack is not so heavy a burden as a prisoner's chains.
　　DWIGHT D. EISENHOWER, Inaugural Address, 20 Jan., 1953.

8

But wilt thou measure all thy road,
See thou lift the lightest load.
　　EMERSON, *Conduct of Life: Considerations by the Way*.

9

I would rather have a big burden and a strong back, than a weak back and a caddy to carry life's luggage.
　　ELBERT HUBBARD, *The Philistine*, vol. xx.

10

Bowed by the weight of centuries he leans
Upon his hoe and gazes on the ground,
The emptiness of ages in his face,
And on his back the burden of the world.
　　EDWIN MARKHAM, *The Man with the Hoe*, st. 1.

BUSINESS

See also Commerce, Corporations, Finance

11

Don't speculate unless you can make it a full-time job. Beware of barbers, beauticians, waiters—of anyone—bringing gifts of "inside" information or "tips." . . . Don't try to buy at the bottom and sell at the top. This can't be done—except by liars.
　　BERNARD M. BARUCH, *Baruch: My Own Story*, ch. 19.

12

"Business is business," the Little Man said,
"A battle where 'everything goes,'
Where the only gospel is 'get ahead,'
　And never spare friends or foes."
　　BERTON BRALEY, *Business Is Business*.

13

Mr. Morgan buys his partners: I grow my own.
　　ANDREW CARNEGIE. (HENDRICK, *Life*)

14

Steel is Prince or Pauper.
　　ANDREW CARNEGIE. (HENDRICK, *Life*)

15

The business of America is business.
　　CALVIN COOLIDGE, Address before the American Society of Newspaper Editors, Washington, D.C., 17 Jan., 1925.

When a President said that "the business of America is business," he told us something about the degree to which a standard of living can do stand-in duty for a way of life.
　　ADLAI E. STEVENSON, *The Hard Kind of Patriotism; Harper's Magazine*, July, 1963.

1

I have always recognized that the object of business is to make money in an honorable manner. I have endeavored to remember that the object of life is to do good.

> PETER COOPER, Speech at a reception in his honor, 1874. (*Dictionary of American Biography*, iv)

2

We must hold a man amenable to reason for the choice of his daily craft or profession. It is not an excuse any longer for his deeds that they are the custom of his trade. What business has he with an evil trade? Has he not a *calling* in his character?

> EMERSON, *Essays, First Series: Spiritual Laws.*

3

The ways of trade are grown selfish to the borders of theft, and supple to the borders (if not beyond the borders) of fraud.

> EMERSON, *Nature Addresses and Essays: Man the Reformer.*

4

Drive thy business or it will drive thee.

> BENJAMIN FRANKLIN, *Poor Richard*, 1758.

5

Lord Stafford mines for coal and salt,
The Duke of Norfolk deals in malt,
The Douglas in red herrings.

> FITZ-GREENE HALLECK, *Alnwick Castle.*

6

Never fear the want of business. A man who qualifies himself well for his calling, never fails of employment.

> THOMAS JEFFERSON, *Writings*, vol. viii, p. 385.

7

We haven't done anything for business this week—but it is only Monday morning.

> LYNDON B. JOHNSON, Speech at the annual meeting of the U.S. Chamber of Commerce, Washington, D.C., 27 Apr., 1964.

8

My father always told me that all businessmen were sons-of-bitches, but I never believed it till now!

> Attributed to JOHN F. KENNEDY, supposedly his off-the-record reaction, as President, to United States Steel Corporation's announcement of a price rise for steel, 10 Apr., 1962. For several weeks controversy was stirred by publication of this quotation. At a press conference, 9 May, 1962, Kennedy termed the quotation "innacurate." He said that the elder Kennedy had not referred to all businessmen: "He confined it, and I would confine it." The President added that he and the steel companies were working in harmony; by then U.S. Steel

and the five other firms that followed its lead had rescinded the price rise. Kennedy's strong personal influence in bringing this about resulted in charges of anti-business bias against his administration, however. A statement by the joint House-Senate Republican leadership, 19 Apr., 1962, called the administration intervention in steel pricing a "display of naked political power never seen before in this nation."

The steel industry is giving President Eisenhower its award as the man who did the most for the steel industry this year. I got the award last year, and the steel men came down to Washington to present it to me—but the Secret Service men wouldn't let them in.

> JOHN F. KENNEDY, Speech at a Democratic fund-raising dinner in New York, 23 May, 1963. The first, and serious, reference was to an American Iron and Steel Institute tribute to Eisenhower in May, 1963.

9

This administration is pro-the-public-interest. Nor do I say that all these policies could please all American businessmen all of the time. So long as the interests and views of businessmen frequently clash with each other, no President could possibly please them all.

> JOHN F. KENNEDY, Address to the Florida Chamber of Commerce in Tampa, 18 Nov., 1963.

10

Business today consists in persuading crowds.

> GERALD STANLEY LEE, *Crowds*, bk. ii, ch. 5.

11

A man's success in business today turns upon his power of getting people to believe he has something that they want.

> GERALD STANLEY LEE, *Crowds*, bk. ii, ch. 9.

12

There is no better ballast for keeping the mind steady on its keel, and saving it from all risk of *crankiness*, than business.

> JAMES RUSSELL LOWELL, *Among My Books: New England Two Centuries Ago.*

13

When I see a merchant over-polite to his customers, begging them to taste a little brandy and throwing half his goods on the counter—thinks I, that man has an axe to grind.

> CHARLES MINER, *Essays from the Desk of Poor Robert the Scribe: Who'll Turn the Grindstones?*

1

We demand that big business give people a square deal.

> THEODORE ROOSEVELT, Letter, written at the time of the suit to dissolve the Steel Trust.

We demand that big business give the people a square deal; in return we must insist that when any one engaged in big business honestly endeavors to do right he shall himself be given a square deal.

> THEODORE ROOSEVELT, *Autobiography.*

2

Homestead, Braddock, Birmingham, they make their steel with men.
Smoke and blood is the mix of steel.

> CARL SANDBURG, *Smoke and Steel.*

3

The Jungle.

> UPTON SINCLAIR, Title of novel (1906) dealing with the Chicago stockyards. It led to an investigation of the packing industry, which in turn led to passage of the Pure Food and Drug Act of 1906.

4

Businessmen don't elect Presidents anyway. The common people elect them. I proved that back in 1948.

> HARRY S TRUMAN, Statement at press conference in New York, 9 Jan., 1964.

5

. . . for many years I thought what was good for our country was good for General Motors, and vice versa.

> CHARLES ERWIN WILSON, in testimony before the U.S. Senate Armed Services Committee, Jan., 1953. As a former high officer of General Motors Corp. and then still a heavy stockholder in the company, Wilson appeared before the committee just after his nomination to be Secretary of Defense in the original Eisenhower cabinet. He was asked whether, if the situation arose, he could make a decision in the interests of the country but "extremely adverse" to General Motors. He replied in full: "I could. I cannot conceive of one because for many years I thought what was good for our country was good for General Motors, and vice versa." His nomination was not approved by the committee until 23 Jan., 1953, however—after he promised to dispose of all his G.M. stock.
>
> A printed transcript of the committee hearings (which were closed) eventually established this quotation. Release of the transcript was prompted by a widely quoted version of his remark, at odds with the foregoing and extremely controversial at the time. Wilson was supposed to have said: "What's good for General Motors is good for the country."

6

Business is the lone God of our Congress.

> PHILIP WYLIE, *Opus 21.*

C

CAMEL

7

With strength and patience all his grievous loads are borne,
And from the world's rose-bed he only asks a thorn.

> W. R. ALGER, *Mussud's Praise of the Camel.*

8

The Black Camel.

> EARL DERR BIGGERS, Title of novel. The original use of "black camel," referring to death, is credited to the 19th-century Algerian chief Abd-el-Kader.

9

A Camel's all lumpy And bumpy and humpy—
Any shape does for me!

> C. E. CARRYL, *The Plaint of the Camel.*

10

There's never a question About *my* digestion,
Anything does for me!

> C. E. CARRYL, *The Plaint of the Camel.*

CANDLE

11

The smallest candle fills a mile with its rays, and the papillae of a man runs out to every star.

> EMERSON, *Conduct of Life: Fate.*

12

My candle burns at both ends;
　It will not last the night;
But ah, my foes, and oh, my friends—
　It gives a lovely light!

> EDNA ST. VINCENT MILLAY, *A Few Figs from Thistles: First Fig.*

13

It is better to light one candle than to curse the darkness.

> UNKNOWN, Motto of the Christophers.

She would rather light a candle than curse the darkness, and her glow has warmed the world.

> ADLAI E. STEVENSON, Tribute to Eleanor Roosevelt, upon her death in Nov., 1962. This was used as a motto by the

Eleanor Roosevelt Memorial Foundation.

CANDOR
See also Sincerity

1
Gracious to all, to none subservient,
Without offence he spake the word he
  meant.
THOMAS BAILEY ALDRICH, *The Sisters'
Tragedy.*

2
I don't complain of Betsy or any of her acts
Exceptin' when we've quarreled and told
  each other facts.
WILL CARLETON, *Betsy and I Are Out.*

3
Candor, my tepid Friend,
Come not to play with me!
The Myrrhs and Mochas of the Mind
Are its Iniquity.
EMILY DICKINSON, *Poems,* pt. v, No.
  109.

4
Nothing astonishes men so much as common
sense and plain dealing.
EMERSON, *Essays, First Series: Art.*

5
Frankness invites frankness.
EMERSON, *Essays, First Series: Prudence.*

6
        You know I say
Just what I think, and nothing more nor
  less, . . .
I cannot say one thing and mean another.
HENRY WADSWORTH LONGFELLOW, *Giles
Corey,* act ii, sc. 3.

7
There's a brave fellow! There's a man of
  pluck!
A man who's not afraid to say his say,
Though a whole town's against him.
H. W. LONGFELLOW, *John Endicott,* act ii,
sc. 2.

8
I blurt ungrateful truths, if so they be,
That none may need to say them after me.
JAMES RUSSELL LOWELL, *Epistle to
George William Curtis.*

CARE
See also Burden, Trouble, Worry

9
And the night shall be filled with music
  And the cares, that infest the day,
Shall fold their tents, like the Arabs,
  And as silently steal away.
HENRY WADSWORTH LONGFELLOW, *The
Day Is Done.*

10
Black Care rarely sits behind a rider whose
pace is fast enough.
THEODORE ROOSEVELT, *Ranch Life.*

11
Old Care has a mortgage on every estate,
And that's what you pay for the wealth that
  you get.
JOHN G. SAXE, *Gifts of the Gods.*

CASTLE

12
I find the gayest castles in the air that were
ever piled, far better for comfort and for use,
than the dungeons in the air that are daily
dug and caverned out by grumbling, discontented people.
EMERSON, *Conduct of Life: Considerations by the Way.*

13
When I could not sleep for cold,
  I had fire enough in my brain,
And builded, with roofs of gold,
  My beautiful castles in Spain.
JAMES RUSSELL LOWELL, *Aladdin.*

14
If one advances confidently in the direction
of his dreams, and endeavors to live the life
which he has imagined, he will meet with a
success unexpected in common hours. . . .
If you have built castles in the air, your
work need not be lost; that is where they
should be. Now put the foundations under
them.
HENRY DAVID THOREAU, *Walden,* ch. 18.

CAT

15
The Cat in Gloves catches no Mice.
BENJAMIN FRANKLIN, *Poor Richard,*
1754.

The Cat that always wears Silk Mittens
Will catch no Mice to feed her Kittens.
ARTHUR GUITERMAN, *A Poet's Proverbs.*

16
The Cat on your hearthstone to this day pre-
  sages,
By solemnly sneezing, the coming of rain!
ARTHUR GUITERMAN, *The First Cat.*

17
Cats and monkeys, monkeys and cats—all
human life is there.
HENRY JAMES, *The Madonna of the Future.*

18
        the great open spaces
where cats are cats
DON MARQUIS, *mehitabel has an adventure.*

19
I cannot agree that it should be the declared
public policy of Illinois that a cat visiting a
neighbor's yard or crossing the highway is a
public nuisance. It is in the nature of cats to
do a certain amount of unescorted roaming
. . . to escort a cat abroad on a leash is

against the nature of the owner. Moreover, cats perform useful service, particularly in the rural areas. The problem of the cat vs. the bird is as old as time. If we attempt to resolve it by legislation, who knows but what we may be called upon to take sides as well in the age-old problems of dog vs. cat, bird vs. bird, or even bird vs. worm. In my opinion, the State of Illinois and its local governing bodies already have enough to do without trying to control feline delinquency.

ADLAI E. STEVENSON, Message to Illinois Senate, 23 Apr., 1949, accompanying his veto of a bill that would have punished owners of cats who permitted the animals to roam at large without leashes. Stevenson was governor of the state when he wrote this, one of his most widely quoted passages.

1
We should be careful to get out of an experience only the wisdom that is in it—and stop there; lest we be like the cat that sits down on a hot stove-lid. She will never sit down on a hot stove-lid again—and that is well; but also she will never sit down on a cold one anymore.

MARK TWAIN, *Pudd'nhead Wilson's New Calendar.*

CAUSE

2
The humblest citizen of all the land, when clad in the armor of a righteous cause, is stronger than all the hosts of Error.

WILLIAM JENNINGS BRYAN, Speech at the Democratic national convention, Chicago, 1896.

3
Our cause is just, our union is perfect.

JOHN DICKINSON, *Declaration on Taking Up Arms* (1775). This has been mistakenly attributed to Thomas Jefferson.

4
Great causes are never tried on their merits.

EMERSON, *Essays, Second Series: Nature.*

5
Then conquer we must, for our cause it is just,—
And this be our motto,—"In God is our trust!"

FRANCIS SCOTT KEY, *The Star-Spangled Banner.*

6
That cause is strong which has not a multitude, but one strong man behind it.

JAMES RUSSELL LOWELL, *Democracy: Books and Libraries.*

7
Pledged to the glory of a mighty cause.

ANGELA MORGAN, *Conquerors.*

8
A bad cause will ever be supported by bad means and bad men.

THOMAS PAINE, *The Crisis*, No. ii.

9
It is not a field of a few acres of ground, but a cause, that we are defending, and whether we defeat the enemy in one battle, or by degrees, the consequences will be the same.

THOMAS PAINE, *The Crisis*, No. iv.

CAUSE AND EFFECT

10
Jesus of Nazareth was the most scientific man that ever trod the globe. He plunged beneath the material surface of things, and found the spiritual cause.

MARY BAKER EDDY, *Science and Health with Key to the Scriptures.*

11
Behind the coarse effect is a fine cause. . . . Cause and effect are two sides of one fact.

EMERSON, *Essays, First Series: Circles.*

12
Cause and effect, means and ends, seed and fruit, cannot be severed; for the effect already blooms in the cause, the end pre-exists in the means, the fruit in the seed.

EMERSON, *Essays, First Series: Compensation.*

13
Do not clutch at sensual sweetness until it is ripe on the slow tree of cause and effect.

EMERSON, *Essays, First Series: Prudence.*

14
Cause and effect, the chancellors of God.

EMERSON, *Essays, First Series: Self-Reliance.*

15
Everything is the cause of itself.

EMERSON, *Journals*, 1856.

CAUTION, see Prudence
CERTAINTY

16
To be positive: to be mistaken at the top of one's voice.

AMBROSE BIERCE, *The Devil's Dictionary.*

17
In this world, nothing is certain but death and taxes.

BENJAMIN FRANKLIN, *Letter to M. Leroy*, 1789.

18
How shall I hedge myself with certainties?

HELEN FRAZEE-BOWER, *Certainties.*

19
Certitude is not the test of certainty.

JUSTICE OLIVER WENDELL HOLMES, *Natural Law.*

20
The public . . . demands certainties . . . But there *are* no certainties.

H. L. MENCKEN, *Prejudices, First Series*, ch. 3.

CHANCE

See also Cause and Effect, Fortune, Gambling, Luck

1
Work and acquire, and thou hast chained the wheel of Chance.
EMERSON, *Essays, First Series: Self-Reliance.*

2
The ancients . . . exalted Chance into a divinity.
EMERSON, *Essays, Second Series: Experience.*

3
Chance cannot touch me! Time cannot hush me!
MARGARET WITTER FULLER, *Dryad Song.*

4
Things do not happen in this world—they are brought about.
WILL H. HAYS, Speech during campaign of 1918. (New York *American,* 10 Dec., 1922)

5
At first laying down, as a fact fundamental,
That nothing with God can be accidental.
LONGFELLOW, *The Golden Legend,* pt. vi.

6
I shot an arrow into the air
It fell to earth, I knew not where;
For, so swiftly it flew, the sight
Could not follow it in its flight.
LONGFELLOW, *The Arrow and the Song.*

I shot a rocket in the air,
It fell to earth, I knew not where
Until next day, with rage profound,
The man it fell on came around.
TOM MASON, *Enough.*

7
A pinch of probably is worth a pound of perhaps.
JAMES THURBER, *Lanterns and Lances.*

CHANGE

See also Consistency

8
Weep not that the world changes—did it keep
A stable, changeless state, 'twere cause indeed to weep.
WILLIAM CULLEN BRYANT, *Mutation.*

9
We do not fear this world of change.
DWIGHT D. EISENHOWER, Second Inaugural Address, 21 Jan., 1957.

10
The least change in our point of view gives the whole world a pictorial air.
EMERSON, *Nature, Addresses: Idealism.*

11
There is danger in reckless change; but greater danger in blind conservatism.
HENRY GEORGE, *Social Problems.*

12
There is a certain relief in change, even though it be from bad to worse; as I have found in travelling in a stage-coach, that it is often a comfort to shift one's position and be bruised in a new place.
WASHINGTON IRVING, *Tales of a Traveller: Preface.*

13
We must change to master change.
LYNDON B. JOHNSON, State of the Union Message, 12 Jan., 1966.

14
It is impossible to rock a boat resting at the bottom of an ocean. The thing to do is get it back to the top.
JOHN V. LINDSAY, Speech to the Women's National Press Club, Washington, D.C., 15 Dec., 1964. This was shortly after he had won re-election to the U.S. House of Representatives, as a Republican from New York, in the face of a strong Democratic trend nationally. It was his reply to those in his party who claimed that change in the top structure of the G.O.P. amounted to rocking the boat.

15
To something new, to something strange.
LONGFELLOW, *Kéramos,* l. 32.

16
O visionary world, condition strange,
Where naught abiding is but only change.
JAMES RUSSELL LOWELL, *Commemoration Ode.*

17
To some will come a time when change
Itself is beauty, if not heaven.
EDWIN ARLINGTON ROBINSON, *Llewellyn and the Tree.*

18
Change means the unknown. . . . It means, too many people cry, insecurity. Nonsense! No one from the beginning of time has had security.
ELEANOR ROOSEVELT. (ARCHIBALD MAC-LEISH, *Tribute to a 'Great American Lady'; New York Times Magazine,* 3 Nov., 1963)

19
We emphasize that we believe in change because we were born of it, we have lived by it, we prospered and grew great by it. So the status quo has never been our god, and we ask no one else to bow down before it.
CARL T. ROWAN, Speech in Belgrade, Nov., 1964. This was delivered in Rowan's capacity as director of the U.S. Information Agency.

20
Fallow and change we need, nor constant toil,
Not always the same crop on the same soil.
W. W. STORY, *A Contemporary Criticism.*

21
Things do not change; we change.
HENRY DAVID THOREAU, *Walden: Conclusion.*

CHARACTER

1
Happiness is not the end of life: character is.
  HENRY WARD BEECHER, *Life Thoughts.*

2
A character is like an acrostic—read it forward, backward, or across, it still spells the same thing.
  EMERSON, *Essays, First Series: Self-Reliance.*

3
We pass for what we are. Character teaches above our wills.
  EMERSON, *Essays, First Series: Self-Reliance.*

4
The force of character is cumulative.
  EMERSON, *Essays, First Series: Self-Reliance.*

5
Human character evermore publishes itself. The most fugitive deed and word, the intimated purpose, expresses character.
  EMERSON, *Essays, First Series: Spiritual Laws.*

6
Character,—a reserved force which acts directly by presence and without means.
  EMERSON, *Essays, Second Series: Character.*

7
Character is centrality, the impossibility of being displaced or overset.
  EMERSON, *Essays, Second Series: Character.*

8
No change of circumstances can repair a defect of character.
  EMERSON, *Essays, Second Series: Character.*

9
Character gives splendor to youth and awe to wrinkled skin and gray hairs.
  EMERSON, *Conduct of Life: Beauty.*

10
Use what language you will, you can never say anything but what you are.
  EMERSON, *Conduct of Life: Worship.*

Don't *say* things. What you *are* stands over you the while, and thunders so that I cannot hear what you say to the contrary.
  EMERSON, *Letters and Social Aims: Social Aims.*

11
Character is higher than intellect. . . . A great soul will be strong to live, as well as to think.
  EMERSON, *Nature, Addresses, and Lectures: The American Scholar.*

12
Character, that sublime health which values one moment as another, and makes us great in all conditions.
  EMERSON, *Society and Solitude: Works and Days.*

13
Character is that which can do without success.
  EMERSON, *Uncollected Lectures: Character.*

14
A great character . . . is a dispensation of Providence, designed to have not merely an immediate, but a continuous, progressive, and never-ending agency. It survives the man who possessed it; survives his age,—perhaps his country, his language.
  EDWARD EVERETT, Speech, 4 July, 1835.

15
The Porcupine, whom one must Handle, gloved,
May be respected, but is never Loved.
  ARTHUR GUITERMAN, *A Poet's Proverbs.*

16
Time could not chill him, fortune sway,
Nor toil with all its burdens tire.
  OLIVER WENDELL HOLMES, *F.W.C.*

17
We must have a weak spot or two in a character before we can love it much. People that do not laugh or cry, or take more of anything than is good for them, or use anything but dictionary-words, are admirable subjects for biographies. But we don't always care most for those flat pattern-flowers that press best in the herbarium.
  OLIVER WENDELL HOLMES, *The Professor at the Breakfast-Table,* ch. 3.

18
Character is like a tree and reputation like its shadow. The shadow is what we think of it; the tree is the real thing.
  ABRAHAM LINCOLN. (GROSS, *Lincoln's Own Stories,* p. 109)

19
The wisest man could ask no more of Fate
Than to be simple, modest, manly, true,
Safe from the Many, honored by the Few;
To count as naught in World, or Church, or State,
But inwardly in secret to be great.
  JAMES RUSSELL LOWELL, *Sonnet: Jeffries Wyman.*

20
It's not what you were, it's what you are to-day.
  DAVID MARION, Title of song (1898).

21
Character is what you are in the dark.
  DWIGHT L. MOODY, *Sermons: Character.*

22
Character is much easier kept than recovered.
  THOMAS PAINE, *The Crisis,* No. xv.

1

Character is the governing element of life, and is above genius.
> FREDERICK SAUNDERS, *Stray Leaves: Life's Little Day.*

2

Fame is what you have taken,
Character's what you give;
When to this truth you waken,
Then you begin to live.
> BAYARD TAYLOR, *Improvisations*, sec. 11.

3

How can we expect a harvest of thought who have not had a seed-time of character?
> HENRY DAVID THOREAU, *Journal.* (EMERSON, *Thoreau*)

4

What does Africa,—what does the West stand for? Is not our own interior white on the chart? black though it may prove, like the coast, when discovered.
> HENRY DAVID THOREAU, *Walden: Conclusion.*

5

I would be true, for there are those who trust me;
I would be pure, for there are those that care.
I would be strong, for there is much to suffer,
I would be brave, for there is much to dare.
I would be friend to all—the foe, the friendless;
I would be giving, and forget the gift.
I would be humble, for I know my weakness;
I would look up—and laugh—and love—and lift.
> HOWARD ARNOLD WALTER, *My Creed.*

6

I am as bad as the worst, but thank God I am as good as the best.
> WALT WHITMAN.

7

Character is a by-product; it is produced in the great manufacture of daily duty.
> WOOODROW WILSON, Address at Arlington, Va., 31 May, 1915.

CHARITY

See also Gifts, Giving; Philanthropy

8

In charity to all mankind, bearing no malice or ill-will to any human being.
> JOHN QUINCY ADAMS, Letter to A. Bronson, 30 July, 1838.

9

The living need charity more than the dead.
> GEORGE ARNOLD, *The Jolly Old Pedagogue.*

10

No rich man's largesse may suffice his soul,
Nor are the plundered succored by a dole.
> EDMUND VANCE COOKE, *From the Book of Extenuations.*

11

The worst of charity is, that the lives you are asked to preserve are not worth preserving.
> EMERSON, *Conduct of Life: Considerations by the Way.*

12

Give no bounties: make equal laws: secure life and prosperity and you need not give alms.
> EMERSON, *Conduct of Life: Wealth.*

13

Pity, and Self-sacrifice, and Charity.
> THEODOSIA GARRISON, *These Shall Prevail.*

14

Charity is indeed a noble and beautiful virtue, grateful to man, and approved by God. But charity must be built on justice. It cannot supersede justice.
> HENRY GEORGE, *The Condition of Labor.*

15

Let welfare be a private concern.
> BARRY M. GOLDWATER, *The Conscience of a Conservative* (1961).

16

I have no great confidence in organized charities. Money is left and buildings are erected and sinecures provided for a good many worthless people. Those in immediate control are almost, or when they were appointed were almost, in want themselves, and they naturally hate other beggars.
> ROBERT G. INGERSOLL, *Organized Charities.*

17

The best form of charity is extravagance. . . . The prodigality of the rich is the providence of the poor.
> ROBERT G. INGERSOLL, *Hard Times and the Way Out.*

18

I deem it the duty of every man to devote a certain portion of his income for charitable purposes; and that it is his further duty to see it so applied as to do the most good of which it is capable. This I believe to be best insured by keeping within the circle of his own inquiry and information the subjects of distress to whose relief his contributions should be applied.
> THOMAS JEFFERSON, *Writings,* vol. xi, p. 92.

19

With malice toward none; with charity for all.
> ABRAHAM LINCOLN, Second Inaugural Address, 4 Mar., 1865.

20

In this cold world where Charity lies bleating
Under a thorn, and none to give him greeting.
> EDNA ST. VINCENT MILLAY, *Love Sonnet.*

21

The organized charity, scrimped and iced,

In the name of a cautious, statistical Christ.
    JOHN BOYLE O'REILLY, *In Bohemia*.

1
God's servants making a snug living
By guiding Mammon in smug giving.
    KEITH PRESTON, *Professional Welfare Workers*.

2
To be supported by the charity of friends or a government pension is to go into the almshouse.
    HENRY D. THOREAU, *Journal*, 13 Mar., 1853.

3
All hearts confess the saints elect
    Who, twain in faith, in love agree,
And melt not in an acid sect
    The Christian pearl of charity!
    JOHN GREENLEAF WHITTIER, *Snow-Bound*, 1. 670.

CHASTITY

4
Chastity, they admit, is very well—but then think of Mirabeau's passion and temperament!
    EMERSON, *Letters and Social Aims: Poetry and Imagination*.

5
Not lightly be thy citadel subdued;
    Not ignobly, not untimely,
Take praise in solemn mood;
    Take love sublimely.
    RICHARD WATSON GILDER, *Ah, Be Not False*.

6
A woman's chastity consists, like an onion, of a series of coats.
    NATHANIEL HAWTHORNE, *Journals*, 16 Mar., 1854.

7
Men are virtuous because women are; women are virtuous from necessity.
    EDGAR WATSON HOWE, *A Letter from Mr. Biggs*.

CHEATING

8
Don't steal; thou'lt never thus compete
Successfully in business. Cheat.
    AMBROSE BIERCE, *The Devil's Dictionary: The Decalogue Revised*.

9
It is as impossible for a man to be cheated by any one but himself, as for a thing to be, and not to be, at the same time.
    EMERSON, *Essays, First Series: Compensation*.

10
Three things are men most likely to be cheated in, a horse, a wig, and a wife.
    BENJAMIN FRANKLIN, *Poor Richard*, 1736.

11
We know that there are chiselers. At the bottom of every case of criticism and obstruction we have found some selfish interest, some private axe to grind.
    FRANKLIN D. ROOSEVELT, Radio Address, 22 Oct., 1933, referring to employers not fulfilling their pledges under the National Recovery Administration. This was the pioneer official use of a slang word, deriving from the French *"ciseler"* (to cut or trim), that was widely revived during the NRA era. It was used in America, in other connections, as early as 1848.

12
It is almost always worth while to be cheated; people's little frauds have an interest which more than repays what they cost us.
    LOGAN PEARSALL SMITH, *Afterthoughts*.

CHEERFULNESS
See also Optimism

13
Health is the condition of wisdom, and the sign is cheerfulness,—an open and noble temper.
    EMERSON, *Society and Solitude: Success*.

14
How often it seems the chief good to be born with a cheerful temper . . . Like Alfred, "good fortune accompanies him like a gift of God."
    EMERSON, *Society and Solitude: Success*.

15
So of cheerfulness, or a good temper, the more it is spent, the more of it remains.
    EMERSON, *Conduct of Life: Considerations by the Way*.

16
That which befits us is cheerfulness and courage.
    EMERSON, *Essays, Second Series: New England Reformers*.

17
Cheerfulness, without which no man can be a poet—for beauty is his aim.
    EMERSON, *Representative Men: Shakespeare*.

18
Cheer up! the worst is yet to come!
    PHILANDER JOHNSON, *Shooting Stars; Everybody's Magazine*, May, 1920.

19
Cheerfulness in most cheerful people, is the rich and satisfying result of strenuous discipline.
    EDWIN PERCY WHIPPLE, *Success and Its Conditions: Cheerfulness*.

CHICAGO

20
Chicago: City on the Make.
    NELSON ALGREN, Title of prose-poem (1951).

1
Chicago, That Toddling Town.
　　FRED FISHER, Title of song (1922), with
　　words and music by Fisher, that became
　　a perennial favorite.

2
Queen of the West! by some enchanter
　　taught
To lift the glory of Aladdin's court.
　　BRET HARTE, *Chicago*.

3
The Second City.
　　A. J. LIEBLING, Title of book, *Chicago:
　　The Second City* (1952). Earlier its
　　content appeared as a three-part profile
　　in *The New Yorker*, Jan. 12, 19, and 26,
　　1952. In the first part Liebling wrote:
　　"The census of 1890 showed that it
　　[Chicago] had displaced Philadelphia as
　　the second city of the United States,
　　and it was preparing to go right through
　　the roof." The term Second City also
　　became well known in the 1960s as the
　　name of a Chicago cabaret and as the
　　title of its revue.

4
Sputter, city! Bead with fire
Every ragged roof and spire; . . .
Burst to bloom, you proud, white flower,
But—remember that hot hour
When the shadow of your brand
Laps the last cool grain of sand—
You will still be just a scar
On a little, lonesome star.
　　MILDRED PLEW MERRYMAN, *To Chicago at
　　Night*.

5
　　　　Gigantic, wilful, young,
Chicago sitteth at the northwest gates,
　　With restless violent hands and casual
　　tongue
Moulding her mighty fates.
　　WILLIAM VAUGHN MOODY, *An Ode in
　　Time of Hesitation*.

6
Old Loopy.
　　CHRISTOPHER MORLEY, Title of essay
　　(1935) subtitled "A Love Letter for
　　Chicago."

7
O great city of visions, waging the war of the
　　free,
Beautiful, strong and alert, a goddess in pur-
　　pose and mien.
　　WALLACE RICE, *Chicago*.

8
Hog-Butcher for the World,
Tool-maker, Stacker of Wheat,
Player with Railroads and the Nation's
　　Freight-handler;
Stormy, husky, brawling,
City of the Big Shoulders.
　　CARL SANDBURG, *Chicago*.

9
There is no use trying to be neutral about
Chicago.
　　EDWARD WAGENKNECHT, *Chicago* (1964).

10
Then lift once more thy towers on high,
And fret with spires the western sky,
To tell that God is yet with us,
And love is still miraculous.
　　JOHN GREENLEAF WHITTIER, *Chicago*, re-
　　ferring to the celebrated fire of 1871.

11
The people of Germany are just as responsible for Hitler as the people of Chicago are
for the Chicago *Tribune*.
　　ALEXANDER WOOLLCOTT, Remark on radio
　　program "People's Platform," 23 Jan.,
　　1943. These were Woollcott's last words;
　　he died a few hours after speaking them
　　and after collapsing at the microphone.
　　The subject of the forum was "Is Ger-
　　many Incurable?".

12
The windy city.
　　UNKNOWN.

CHILDHOOD

*See also Boy, Boyhood; Children; Girl;
Youth*

13
"My children," said an old man to his boys,
scared by a figure in the dark entry, "my
children, you will never see anything worse
than yourselves."
　　EMERSON, *Essays, First Series: Spiritual
　　Laws*.

14
The greatest poem ever known
Is one all poets have outgrown:
The poetry, innate, untold,
Of being only four years old.
　　CHRISTOPHER MORLEY, *To a Child*.

15
Our days, our deeds, all we achieve or are,
Lay folded in our infancy; the things
Of good or ill we choose while yet unborn.
　　JOHN TOWNSEND TROWBRIDGE, *Sonnet:
　　Nativity*.

16
The hills are dearest which our childish feet
Have climbed the earliest; and the streams
　　most sweet
Are ever those at which our young lips
　　drank.
　　JOHN GREENLEAF WHITTIER, *The Bridal
　　of Pennacook*: pt. vi, *At Pennacook*.

17
How dear to this heart are the scenes of my
　　childhood,
　　When fond recollection recalls them to
　　view;
The orchard, the meadow, the deep-tangled
　　wildwood,

And every loved spot which my infancy knew.
SAMUEL WOODWORTH, *The Old Oaken Bucket.* (Originally in *The Post-Chaise Annual,* Baltimore, 1819)

CHILDREN

See also Boy, Boyhood; Childhood; Girl; Youth

1
Eat no green apples or you'll droop,
Be careful not to get the croup,
Avoid the chicken-pox and such,
And don't fall out of windows much.
EDWARD ANTHONY, *Advice to Small Children.*

2
In silence I must take my seat, . . .
I must not speak a useless word,
For children must be seen, not heard.
B. W. BELLAMY, *Open Sesame,* vol. 1, p. 167. (Quoted as from *Table Rules for Little Folks*)

3
It is a great pity that men and women forget that they have been children. Parents are apt to be foreigners to their sons and daughters.
GEORGE WILLIAM CURTIS, *Prue and I,* ch. 7.

4
Better to be driven out from among men than to be disliked of children.
RICHARD HENRY DANA, *The Idle Man: Domestic Life.*

5
Respect the child. Be not too much his parent. Trespass not on his solitude.
EMERSON, *Lectures and Biographical Sketches: Education.*

6
Let thy child's first lesson be obedience, and the second will be what thou wilt.
BENJAMIN FRANKLIN, *Poor Richard.*

7
Teach your child to hold his tongue; he'll learn fast enough to speak.
BENJAMIN FRANKLIN, *Poor Richard,* 1734.

8
"Late children," says the Spanish proverb, "are early orphans."
BENJAMIN FRANKLIN, *Letter to John Alleyn.*

9
You are the bows from which your children as living arrows are sent forth.
KAHLIL GIBRAN, *The Prophet: On Children.*

10
Children are our most valuable natural resource.
HERBERT HOOVER. A remark he made on numerous occasions. (New York *Times* obituary of Hoover, 21 Oct., 1964, p. 42)

11
One laugh of a child will make the holiest day more sacred still.
ROBERT G. INGERSOLL, *The Liberty of Man, Woman and Child.*

12
Across the fields of yesterday
He sometimes comes to me,
A little lad just back from play—
The lad I used to be.

And yet he smiles so wistfully
Once he has crept within,
I wonder if he hopes to see
The man I might have been.
THOMAS S. JONES, JR., *Sometimes.*

13
Between the dark and the daylight,
When the night is beginning to lower,
Comes a pause in the day's occupations,
That is known as the Children's Hour.
LONGFELLOW, *The Children's Hour,* st. 1.

14
The patter of little feet.
LONGFELLOW. *The Children's Hour,* st. 2.

15
Ah! what would the world be to us
If the children were no more?
We should dread the desert behind us
Worse than the dark before.
LONGFELLOW, *Children,* st. 4.

16
Ye are better than all the ballads
That ever were sung or said;
For ye are living poems,
And all the rest are dead.
LONGFELLOW, *Children,* st. 9.

17
Where is the promise of my years,
Once written on my brow?
Ere errors, agonies, and fears
Brought with them all that speaks in tears,
Ere I had sunk beneath my peers;
Where sleeps that promise now?
ADAH ISAACS MENKEN, *Infelix.*

18
Who knows the thoughts of a child?
NORA PERRY, *Who Knows?*

19
How pleasant is Saturday night,
When I've tried all the week to be good,
Not spoken a word that is bad,
And obliged every one that I could.
NANCY DENNIS SPROAT, *How Pleasant Is Saturday Night.*

20
Children are the keys of Paradise.
RICHARD HENRY STODDARD, *The Children's Prayer.*

21
If there is anything that will endure
The eye of God, because it still is pure,
It is the spirit of a little child.

Fresh from his hand, and therefore unde-
filed.
> RICHARD HENRY STODDARD, *The Children's
> Prayer.*

1
But still I dream that somewhere there must
be
The spir't of a child hat waits for me.
> BAYARD TAYLOR, *The Poet's Journal:
> Third Even'ng.*

2
I called the boy to my knee one day,
  And I said. 'You're just past four;
Will you laugh in the same lighthearted way
  When you've turned, say, thirty more?"
Then I thought of a past I'd fain erase—
  More clouded skies than blue—
And I anxiously peered in his upturned face
  For it seemed to say. "Did you?'
> CARL WERNER, *The Questioner*

3
We need love's tender lessons taught
  As only weakness can;
God hath His small interpreters;
  The child must teach the man.
> JOHN GREENLEAF WHITTIER, *Child-Songs*

CHRIST

4
Christ preached the greatness of man. We
preach the greatness of Christ. The first is
affirmative; the last negative
> EMERSON, *Journals,* 1867.

5
Jesus, whose name is not so much written as
ploughed into the history of this world.
> EMERSON, *Nature, Addresses, and Lec-
> tures· Address.*

6
Jesus was Jesus because he refused to listen
to another and listened at home.
> EMERSON, *Uncollected Lectures: Natural
> Religion;* also *The Sove eignty of Eth-
> ics.*

7
An era in human history is the life of Jesus,
and its immense influence for good leaves all
the perversion and superstition that has accrued almost harmless
> EMERSON, *Uncol ected Lectures: Natural
> Religion*

8
Shepherd of mortals here behold
A little flock, a ways'de fold
That w 't thy presence to be blest—
O Man of Naza eth, be our guest.
> DANIEL HENDERSON, *Hymn for a House-
> hold*

9
Mine eyes have seen the glory of the coming
  of the Lord;
He is trampling out he vintage where the
  grapes of wrath are stored;

He hath loosed the fateful lightning of His
  terrible swift sword;
    His truth is marching on.
> JULIA WARD HOWE, *Battle-Hymn of the
> Republic.*

10
But Thee, but Thee, O sovereign Seer of
  time,
But Thee, O poets' Poet, Wisdom's Tongue,
But Thee, O man's best Man, O love s best
  Love,
O perfect life in perfect labor writ,
O all men's Comrade, Servant King, or
  Priest,— . .
Oh, what amiss may I forgive in Thee,
Jesus, good Paragon, thou Crystal Christ?
> SIDNEY LANIER, *The Crystal.*

11
The hands of Christ seem very frail,
For they were broken by a nail.
But only they reach Heaven at last
Whom these frail, broken hands hold fast.
> JOHN RICHARD MORELAND, *His Hands.*

12
Love cannot die, nor truth betray;
Christ rose upon an April day.
> JOHN RICHARD MORELAND, *Resurgam.*

CHRISTIANITY
See also Religion

13
I hold that the Christian religion is the best
yet promulgated, but do not thence infer
that it is not susceptible of improvement;
nor do I wish to confound its doctrines with
its founder, and to worsh p one of my fellow-
beings.
> AMOS BRONSON ALCOTT, *Diary.*

14
If a man cannot be a Christian in the place
where he is, he cannot be a Christian anywhere.
> HENRY WARD BEECHER, *Life Thoughts.*

15
Chris ians and camels receive their burdens
kneeh g.
> AMBROSE BIERCE, *The Devil's Dictionary.*

16
A Christian is one who rejoices in the superiority of a ival.
> EDWIN BOOTH. (W. L. PHELPS, *Jealousy)*

17
A pagan heart, a Christian soul had he.
  He followed Christ, yet for dead Pan he
  sighed.
As if Theocritus in Sicily
  Had come upon the Figure crucified.
> MAURICE FRANCIS EGAN, *Maurice de Guë-
> rin.*

18
Two inestimable advantages Christianity
has given us; first the Sabbath, the jubilee of

the whole world; . . . and secondly, the institution of preaching.
> EMERSON, *Nature, Addresses, and Lectures: Address.*

1
Every Stoic was a Stoic; but in Christendom, where is the Christian?
> EMERSON, *Essays, First Series: Self-Reliance.*

2
He who shall introduce into public affairs the principles of primitive Christianity will change the face of the world.
> BENJAMIN FRANKLIN, Letter to the French ministry, Mar., 1778.

3
Millions of innocent men, women and children, since the introduction of Christianity, have been burned, tortured, fined and imprisoned, yet we have not advanced one inch toward uniformity. What has been the effect of coercion? To make one-half of the world fools and the other half hypocrites.
> THOMAS JEFFERSON, *Notes on Virginia.*

4
To the corruptions of Christianity I am, indeed, opposed; but not to the genuine precepts of Jesus himself. I am a Christian in the only sense in which he wished any one to be; sincerely attached to his doctrines in preference to all others; ascribing to himself every human excellence; and believing he never claimed any other.
> THOMAS JEFFERSON, *Writings,* vol. x., p. 379.

5
Of all the systems of morality, ancient or modern, which have come under my observation, none appear to me so pure as that of Jesus.
> THOMAS JEFFERSON, *Writings,* vol. xiii, p. 377.

6
In extracting the pure principles which [Jesus] taught, we should have to strip off the artificial vestments in which they have been muffled by priests, who have travestied them into various forms, as instruments of riches and power to themselves . . . there will be found remaining the most sublime and benevolent code of morals which has ever been offered to man.
> THOMAS JEFFERSON, *Writings,* vol. xiii, p. 389.

7
The doctrines which flowed from the lips of Jesus himself are within the comprehension of a child; but thousands of volumes have not yet explained the Platonisms engrafted on them.
> THOMAS JEFFERSON, *Writings,* vol. xiv, p. 149.

8
What was invented two thousand years ago was the spirit of Christianity.
> GERALD STANLEY LEE, *Crowds,* bk. ii, ch. 18.

9
Silence the voice of Christianity, and the world is well-nigh dumb, for gone is that sweet music which kept in order the rulers of the people, which cheers the poor widow in her lonely toil, and comes like light through the windows of morning, to men who sit stooping and feeble, with failing eyes and a hungering heart.
> THEODORE PARKER, *Critical and Miscellaneous Writings: A Discourse of the Transient and Permanent in Christianity.*

10
No pain, no palm; no thorns, no throne; no gall, no glory; no cross, no crown.
> WILLIAM PENN, *No Cross, No Crown.*

11
Christianity is the world's monumental fraud if there be no future life.
> MARTIN J. SCOTT, *Religion and Commonsense,* p. 120.

12
Whatever makes men good Christians, makes them good citizens.
> DANIEL WEBSTER, Speech in Plymouth, Mass., 22 Dec., 1820.

CHRISTMAS

13
Oh, the Shepherds in Judea!—
Do you think the Shepherds know
How the whole round world is brightened
In the ruddy Christmas glow?
> MARY AUSTIN, *The Shepherds in Judea.*

14
O little town of Bethlehem,
How still we see thee lie!
Above thy deep and dreamless sleep
The silent stars go by.
> PHILLIPS BROOKS, *O Little Town of Bethlehem.*

15
Glory to God, this wondrous morn,
On earth the Saviour Christ is born.
> BLISS CARMAN, *Bethlehem.*

16
Not believe in Santa Claus! You might as well not believe in fairies. . . . Nobody sees Santa Claus, but that is no sign there is no Santa Claus. The most real things in the world are those which neither children nor men can see. No Santa Claus! Thank God! he lives and he lives forever.
> FRANCIS P. CHURCH, *Is There a Santa Claus?*. This famous editorial, which originally appeared in the New York *Sun,* 21 Sept., 1897, was in reply to a child, Virginia O'Hanlon, whose faith

had been shaken by skeptical play-
mates.

Yes, Virginia, there is a Santa Claus. He exists as certainly as love and generosity and
devotion exist.

> FRANCIS P. CHURCH, *Is There a Santa
> Claus?; New York Sun,* 21 Sept., 1897.

1

'Most all the time, the whole year round,
    there ain't no flies on me,
But jest 'fore Christmas I'm as good as I kin
    be!

> EUGENE FIELD, *Jest 'fore Christmas.*

2

What babe new born is this that in a manger
    cries?
Near on her lowly bed his happy mother
    lies.
Oh, see the air is shaken with white and
    heavenly wings—
This is the Lord of all the earth, this is the
    King of Kings.

> RICHARD WATSON GILDER, *A Christmas
> Hymn.*

3

Fra Lippo, we have learned from thee
A lesson of humanity:
To every mother's heart forlorn,
In every house the Christ is born.

> RICHARD WATSON GILDER, *A Madonna of
> Fra Lippo Lippi.*

4

There's a song in the air!
    There's a star in the sky!
There's a mother's deep prayer
    And a Baby's low cry!
And the star rains its fire where the Beauti-
    ful sing,
For the manger of Bethlehem cradles a
    King.

> JOSIAH G. HOLLAND, *A Christmas Carol.*

5

On Christmas day in the morning.

> WASHINGTON IRVING, *Sketch Book: The
> Sunny Bank* (quoted from an old Eng-
> lish carol).

6

I heard the bells on Christmas Day
Their old, familiar carols play,
    And wild and sweet
    The words repeat,
Of peace on earth,
    good-will to men!

> HENRY WADSWORTH LONGFELLOW, *Christ-
> mas Bells.*

7

Hail to the King of Bethlehem,
Who weareth in his diadem
The yellow crocus for the gem
Of his authority!

> HENRY WADSWORTH LONGFELLOW, *The
> Golden Legend: The Nativity,* pt. ix.

8

"What means this glory round our feet,"
    The Magi mused, "more bright than
        morn?"
And voices chanted clear and sweet,
    "To-day the Prince of Peace is born!"

> JAMES RUSSELL LOWELL, *A Christmas
> Carol.*

9

While rich men sigh and poor men fret,
Dear me! we can't spare Christmas yet!

> EDWARD S. MARTIN, *Christmas, 1898.*

10

'Twas the night before Christmas, when all
    through the house
Not a creature was stirring, not even a
    mouse.

> CLEMENT CLARKE MOORE, *A Visit from St.
> Nicholas.* Often erroneously attributed
> to Henry Livingston.

11

Have you seen God's Christmas tree in the
    sky,
With its trillions of tapers blazing high?

> ANGELA MORGAN, *Christmas Tree of An-
> gels.*

12

It came upon the midnight clear,
    That glorious song of old.

> EDMUND HAMILTON SEARS, *Christmas
> Carols.*

13

The real meaning of Christmas has been
overlaid by sentimental varnish and com-
mercial dust.

> REV. MYRON J. TAYLOR, Sermon preached
> at Central Church of Christ, Ports-
> mouth, Ohio, 22 Dec., 1963. This sermon
> received nationwide attention because it
> was part of a program designed to show
> a "typical American family" and a "typ-
> ical American city" at Christmastime to
> a visiting Russian family, that of Victor
> Pozdneyev, a Moscow automotive engi-
> neer. The Russians' visit was sponsored
> by the Portsmouth Junior Chamber of
> Commerce.

14

Blow, bugles of battle, the marches of
    peace;
East, west, north, and south let the long
    quarrel cease;
Sing the song of great joy that the angels
    began,
Sing the glory of God and of good-will to
    man!

> JOHN GREENLEAF WHITTIER, *A Christmas
> Carmen.*

CHURCHES

See also Religion

15

The world is weary of the church that keeps
silent on the issues of life.

> REV. DR. EDWIN T. DAHLBERG, Address in

Lincoln, Neb., to pastors of the Church of the Brethren, 23 June, 1964. The occasion was a retreat opening the annual world conference of this church.

1
Accepts the village church as part of the sky.
> EMERSON, *Journals*, 1867.

2
If I should go out of church whenever I hear a false sentiment I could never stay there five minutes. But why come out? The street is as false as the church.
> EMERSON, *Essays, Second Series: New England Reformers.*

3
The multitude of false churches accredits the true religion.
> EMERSON, *Essays, Second Series: Nature.*

4
Bless all the churches, and blessed be God, who, in this our great trial, giveth us the churches.
> Attributed to ABRAHAM LINCOLN, Statement to a Methodist delegation, 14 May, 1864.

5
>   You have made
> The cement of your churches out of tears
> And ashes, and the fabric will not stand.
>> EDWIN ARLINGTON ROBINSON, *Captain Craig.*

6
> The peace of great churches be for you,
> Where the players of lofty pipe organs
> Practice old lovely fragments, alone.
>> CARL SANDBURG, *For You.*

7
There warn't anybody at the church, except maybe a hog or two, . . . If you notice, most folks don't go to church only when they've got to; but a hog is different.
> MARK TWAIN, *Adventures of Huckleberry Finn*, ch. 18.

CIRCUMSTANCE

See also Chance, Destiny, Fate, Providence

8
Tyrannical Circumstance!
> EMERSON, *Conduct of Life: Fate.*

9
Under all this running sea of circumstance, whose waters ebb and flow with perfect balance, lies the aboriginal abyss of real Being.
> EMERSON, *Essays, First Series: Compensation.*

10
You think me the child of my circumstances: I make my circumstance.
> EMERSON, *Nature, Addresses, and Lectures: The Transcendentalist.*

11
This fearful concatenation of circumstances.
> DANIEL WEBSTER, Argument, on the mur-

der of Captain White, 1830. (*Works*, vi, 88)

CITIES

12
All cities are superb at night because their hideous corners are devoured in darkness.
> BROOKS ATKINSON Column, New York *Times*, 17 Mar., 1964.

13
The Bible shows how the world progresses. It begins with a garden, but ends with a holy city.
> PHILLIPS BROOKS. (ALLEN, *Life and Letters*)

14
> How fast the flitting figures come!
>   The mild, the fierce, the stony face;
> Some bright with thoughtless smiles and some
>   Where secret tears have left their trace.

> These struggling tides of life hat seem
>   In wayward, aimless course to tend,
> Are eddies of the m'ghty stream
>   That rolls to its appointed end.
>> WILLIAM CULLEN BRYANT, *The Crowded Street.*

15
The city is recruited from the country.
> EMERSON, *Essays, Second Series: Manners.*

16
Cities give not the human senses room enough.
> EMERSON, *Essays, Second Series: Nature.*

17
Cities force growth and make men talkative and entertaining, but they make them artificial.
> EMERSON, *Society and Solitude: Farming.*

18
The zenith city of the unsalted seas.
> THOMAS FOSTER, Speech, referring to Duluth, Minn., 4 July, 1868. This is often attributed to Proctor Knott, who quoted it in the House of Representatives, 27 Jan., 1871.

19
> Farmer Jake Bentley talks some o' movin' to the city so he kin keep a son
>> KIN HUBBARD, *Abe Martin's Broadcast.*

20
I view great cities as penitential to the morals, the health, and the liberties of man.
> THOMAS JEFFERSON, Letter to Benjamin Rush. 23 Sept., 1800.

21
The mobs of great cities add just so much to the support of pure government as sores do to the strength of the human body
> THOMAS JEFFERSON, *Writings*, vol. ii, p. 229.

22
Who's ground the grist of trodden ways—

The gray dust and the brown—
May love red tiling two miles off,
    But cannot love a town.
    LESLIE NELSON JENNINGS, *Highways.*

1
Golden towns where golden houses are.
    JOYCE KILMER, *Roofs.*

2
Even cities have their graves!
    HENRY WADSWORTH LONGFELLOW, *Amalfi.*

3
Go down into the city. Mingle with the details; . . . your elation and your illusion vanish like ingenuous snowflakes that have kissed a hot dog sandwich on its fiery brow.
    DON MARQUIS, *The Almost Perfect State.*

4
For students of the troubled heart
Cities are perfect works of art.
    CHRISTOPHER MORLEY, *John Mistletoe*, p. 27.

5
O praise me not the country—
The meadows green and cool,
The solemn glow of sunsets, the hidden silver
    pool!
    The city for my craving,
    Her lordship and her slaving,
    The hot stones of her paving
        For me, a city fool!
    CHRISTOPHER MORLEY *O Praise Me Not the Country.*

6
All cities are mad: but the madness is gallant. All cities are beautiful: but the beauty is grim.
    CHRISTOPHER MORLEY *Where the Blue Begins*, p. 55.

7
America is now an overdeveloped urban nation with an underdeveloped system for dealing with its city problems.
    JAMES RESTON Washington Column, New York *Times*, 9 Jan., 1966.

8
As for these communities, I think I had rather keep bachelor's hall in hell than go to board in heaven.
    HENRY DAVID THOREAU, *Journal*, 3 Mar., 1841.

9
City-building is just a privilege of citizenship.
    ROBERT L. THORNTON, SR. (Quoted in New York *Times* obituary of Thornton, 16 Feb., 1964). Thornton, mayor of Dallas, 1953–61, was noted for his role in building that city.

10
For the earth that breeds the trees
Breeds cities, too, and symphonies.
    JOHN HALL WHEELOCK, *Earth.*

11
A great city is that which has the greatest
    men and women,
If it be a few ragged huts it is still the
    greatest city in the whole world.
    WALT WHITMAN, *Song of the Broad-Axe*, sec. 4.

CIVILIZATION

12
Civilization degrades the many to exalt the few.
    AMOS BRONSON ALCOTT, *Table-Talk: Pursuits.*

13
Wealth may not produce civilization, but civilization produces money.
    HENRY WARD BEECHER, *Proverbs from Plymouth Pulpit.*

14
Every prison is the exclamation point and every asylum is the question mark in the sentences of civilization.
    SAMUEL A. W. DUFFIELD, *Essays: Righteousness.*

15
Civilization exists by geological consent, subject to change without notice.
    WILL DURANT, *What Is Civilization?*

16
Is civilization only a higher form of idolatry, that man should bow down to a flesh-brush, to flannels, to baths, diet, exercise, and air?
    MARY BAKER EDDY, *Science and Health*, p. 174.

17
The true test of civilization is, not the census, nor the size of cities, nor the crops,—no, but the kind of man the country turns out.
    EMERSON, *Society and Solitude: Civilization.*

18
The highest civility has never loved the hot zones. Wherever snow falls there is usually civil freedom. Where the banana grows, man is sensual and cruel.
    EMERSON, *Society and Solitude: Civilization.*

19
As long as our civilization is essentially one of property, of fences, of exclusiveness, it will be mocked by delusions.
    EMERSON, *Representative Men: Napoleon.*

20
The test of civilization is the power of drawing the most benefit out of cities.
    EMERSON, *Journals*, 1864.

21
What is civilization? I answer, the power of good women.
    EMERSON, *Miscellanies: Woman.*

1
The civilized man has built a coach, but has lost the use of his feet.
EMERSON, *Essays, First Series: Self-Reliance.*

2
Comfort, opportunity, number, and size are not synonymous with civilization.
ABRAHAM FLEXNER, *Universities,* p. 40.

3
The true civilization is where every man gives to every other every right that he claims for himself.
ROBERT G. INGERSOLL, Interview, Washington *Post,* 14 Nov., 1880.

4
The history of civilization is the history of the slow and painful enfranchisement of the human race.
ROBERT G. INGERSOLL, *The Declaration of Independence.*

5
Civilization was thrust into the brain of Europe on the point of a Moorish lance.
ROBERT G. INGERSOLL, Address, New York, 24 Jan., 1888.

6
Civilization begins at home.
HENRY JAMES, *Siege of London,* ch. 5.

7
The ancient world, we may remind ourselves, was not destroyed because the traditions were false. They were submerged, neglected, lost. For the men adhering to them had become a dwindling minority who were overthrown and displaced by men who were alien to the traditions, having never been initiated and adopted into them. May it not be that while the historical circumstances are obviously so different, something like that is happening again?
WALTER LIPPMANN, *The Public Philosophy* (1955), ch. viii, sec. 3.

8
This nation, the Soviet Union and the world are destined to live for a long time with feet dangling over the grave that beckons to the human civilization which is our common heritage. Against that immense void of darkness, this treaty is a feeble candle. It is a flicker of light where there had been no light.
MIKE MANSFIELD, commenting on the nuclear test-ban treaty of 1963.

9
Human beings do not carry civilization in their genes. All that we do carry in our genes are certain capacities—the capacity to learn to walk upright, to use our brains, to speak, to relate to our fellow men, to construct and use tools, to explore the universe, and to express that exploration in religion, in art, in science, in philosophy.
MARGARET MEAD, *Human Nature Will Flower, If--; New York Times Magazine,* 19 Apr., 1964.

10
Does the thoughtful man suppose that . . . the present experiment in civilization is the last the world will see?
GEORGE SANTAYANA, *The Life of Reason,* vol. ii, p. 127.

11
Civilization—the art and practice of living equably in the community—is merely a few thousand years old.
THORNTON WILDER. (FLORA LEWIS, *Thornton Wilder at 65; New York Times Magazine,* 15 Apr., 1962)

12
Civilization in itself is a long hard *fight* to maintain and advance.
THORNTON WILDER. (FLORA LEWIS, *Thornton Wilder at 65; New York Times Magazine,* 15 Apr., 1962)

CLOUDS

13
There's a silver lining
Through the dark cloud shining,
Turn the dark cloud inside out,
  Till the boys come home.
LENA GUILBERT FORD, *Keep the Home Fires Burning* (music by Ivor Novello).

every cloud
has its silver
lining but it is
sometimes a little
difficult to get it to
the mint
DON MARQUIS, *certain maxims of archy.*

14
Be still, sad heart! and cease repining;
Behind the clouds is the sun still shining.
HENRY WADSWORTH LONGFELLOW, *The Rainy Day.*

15
The sun is set; and in his latest beams
Yon little cloud of ashen gray and gold,
Slowly upon the amber air unrolled,
The falling mantle of the Prophet seems.
HENRY WADSWORTH LONGFELLOW, *A Summer Day by the Sea.*

16
Nature is always kind enough to give even her clouds a humorous lining.
JAMES RUSSELL LOWELL, *My Study Windows: Thoreau.*

17
Becalmed along the azure sky,
The argosies of cloudland lie,
Whose shores, with many a shining rift,
Far off their pearl-white peaks uplift.
J. T. TROWBRIDGE, *Midsummer.*

18
Behind the cloud the starlight lurks,
  Through showers the sunbeams fall;

For God, who loveth all His works,
Has left His hope with all!
JOHN GREENLEAF WHITTIER, *A Dream of Summer.*

1
Wait till the clouds roll by, Jenny,
Wait till the clouds roll by;
Jenny, my own true loved one,
Wait till the clouds roll by.
J. T. WOOD, *Wait Till the Clouds Roll By.*

COLLEGES

2
Universities where individualism is dreaded as nothing else, wherein manufactories of patent drama, business schools and courses for the propagation of fine embroidery are established on the order of the monied.
THOMAS BEER, *The Mauve Decade,* p. 207.

3
Ye can lade a man up to th' university, but ye can't make him think.
FINLEY PETER DUNNE, *Mr. Carnegie's Gift.*

4
One of the benefits of a college education is to show the boy its little avail.
EMERSON, *Conduct of Life: Culture.*

5
Colleges hate geniuses, just as convents hate saints.
EMERSON, *Public and Private Education.*

6
A university—an institution consciously devoted to the pursuit of knowledge, the solution of problems, the ciritcal appreciation of achievement, and the training of men at a really high level.
ABRAHAM FLEXNER, *Universities,* p. 42.

7
Don't join too many gangs . . .
Join the United States and join the family—
But not much in between unless a college.
ROBERT FROST, *Build Soil.*

8
A pine bench, with Mark Hopkins at one end of it and me at the other, is a good enough college for me!
JAMES A. GARFIELD, Address at a Williams College alumni dinner, New York, 28 Dec., 1871. (WASHINGTON GLADDEN, *Recollections,* p. 73.) Garfield was commenting unfavorably on a movement designed to provide new buildings for the college, where he had been a student under Mark Hopkins. In Garfield's view, the faculty was much more important than physical property. His words are often quoted: "A university is a student on one end of a log and Mark Hopkins on the other."

9
Learn to give
Money to colleges while you live.
OLIVER WENDELL HOLMES, *Parson Turell's Legacy.*

10
A college degree does not lessen the length of your ears: it only conceals it.
ELBERT HUBBARD, *Epigrams.*

11
Colleges are places where pebbles are polished and diamonds are dimmed.
ROBERT G. INGERSOLL, *Abraham Lincoln.*

12
It is . . . a small college, and yet there are those that love it.
DANIEL WEBSTER, Argument, in presenting the Dartmouth College case to the Supreme Court. This was quoted by Chauncey A. Goodrich in a letter to Rufus Choate. (QUINT, *Story of Dartmouth*)

13
We have let the idea of freedom under self-respect go to seed in our colleges and are turning out too many hard-boiled, hard-hearted, hard-headed dumb-bells.
WILLIAM ALLEN WHITE, Editorial, Emporia *Gazette.*

COLUMBUS, CHRISTOPHER

14
Columbus! Other title needs he none.
FLORENCE EARLE COATES, *Columbus.*

15
Every ship that comes to America got its chart from Columbus.
EMERSON, *Representative Men: Uses of Great Men.*

16
Columbus discovered no isle or key so lonely as himself.
EMERSON, *Society and Solitude.*

17
Would that we had the fortunes of Columbus.
Sailing his caravels a trackless way,
He found a Universe—he sought Cathay.
God give such dawns as when, his venture o'er,
The Sailor looked upon San Salvador.
God lead us past the setting of the sun
To wizard islands, of august surprise;
God make our blunders wise.
VACHEL LINDSAY, *Litany of the Heroes.*

18
He gained a world; he gave that world
Its grandest lesson: "On! sail on!"
JOAQUIN MILLER, *Columbus.*

19
Into Thy hands, O Lord,
Into Thy hands I give my soul.
EDNA DEAN PROCTOR, *Columbus Dying.*
Based on Columbus' last words: "In

manus tuas, Domine, commendo spiritum meum."

1
Columbus found a world, and had no chart,
Save one that faith deciphered in the skies;
To trust the soul's invincible surmise
Was all his science and his only art.
    GEORGE SANTAYANA, *O World.*

COMFORT

2
The lust for comfort, that stealthy thing that enters the house as a guest, and then becomes a host, and then a master.
    KAHLIL GIBRAN, *The Prophet: On Houses.*

3
Is there, is there balm in Gilead?
    EDGAR ALLAN POE, *The Raven*, st. 15.

4
Most of the luxuries and many of the so-called comforts of life are not only not indispensable, but positive hindrances to the elevation of mankind.
    HENRY DAVID THOREAU, *Walden: Economy.*

5
I believe in status symbols as a means of identification. . . . On the street or in the office, there are symbols that show a man's position—the private secretary, the personal barber, the big black limousine, the executive washroom. People need symbols in proportion to their status. Even the street sweeper likes a new broom. . . . How would we know a man is a king if he didn't wear a crown?
    DR. ROBERT TURFBOER, Interview (reported by Associated Press), 16 Dec., 1963. He based his observations on his work at Yale University School of Medicine and as psychiatric consultant to major business concerns.

COMMERCE
See also Business

6
Protection and patriotism are reciprocal. This is the road that all great nations have trod.
    JOHN C. CALHOUN, Speech in U.S. House of Representatives, 12 Dec., 1811, referring to tariffs.

7
God is making commerce his missionary.
    JOSEPH COOK, *Boston Monday Lectures: Conscience*

8
And where they went on trade intent
    They did what freeman can,
Their dauntless ways did all men praise,
    The merchant was a man.
The world was made for honest trade—
To plant and eat be none afraid.
    EMERSON, *Boston.*

9
The most advanced nations are always those who navigate the most.
    EMERSON, *Society and Solitude: Civilization.*

10
The greatest meliorator of the world is selfish, huckstering trade.
    EMERSON, *Society and Solitude: Works and Days.*

11
Trade, that pride and darling of our ocean, that educator of nations, that benefactor in spite of itself, ends in shameful defaulting, bubble, and bankruptcy, all over the world.
    EMERSON, *Society and Solitude: Works and Days.*

12
Commerce is of trivial import; love, faith, truth of character the aspiration of man, these are sacred.
    EMERSON, *Essays, First Series: Circles.*

13
There are geniuses in trade, as well as in war, or the State, or letters . . Nature seems to authorize trade, as soon as you see a natural merchant, who appears not so much a private agent as her factor and Minister of Commerce.
    EMERSON, *Essays, Second Series: Character.*

14
The craft of the merchant is this bringing a thing from where it abounds to where it is costly.
    EMERSON, *Conduct of Life: Wealth.*

15
Free-trade, they concede, is very well as a principle, but it is never quite time for its adoption.
    EMERSON, *Letters and Social Aims: Poetry and Imagination.*

16
No nation was ever ruined by trade.
    BENJAMIN FRANKLIN, *Thoughts on Commercial Subjects.*

17
What is more incongruous than the administering of custom-house oaths and the searching of trunks and hand-bags under the shadow of "Liberty Enlightening the World'?
    HENRY GEORGE *Protection or Free Trade,* ch. 9.

18
The grass will grow in the streets of a hundred cities, a thousand towns· the weeds will overrun millions of farms if that protection is taken away.
    HERBERT HOOVER, Speech in New York City, 31 Oct., 1932, during the presidential campaign. Referring to protective tariffs.

1

Commerce is the great civilizer. We exchange ideas when we exchange fabrics.

   ROBERT G. INGERSOLL, *Reply to the Indianapolis Clergy.*

2

Our interest will be to throw open the doors of commerce, and to knock off all its shackles, giving perfect freedom to all persons for the vent of whatever they may choose to bring into our ports, and asking the same in theirs.

   THOMAS JEFFERSON, *Writings,* vol. ii, p. 240.

3

The merchant has no country.

   THOMAS JEFFERSON, *Writings,* vol. xiv, p. 119.

4

I do not mean to say that it may not be for the general interest to foster for awhile certain infant manufactures, until they are strong enough to stand against foreign rivals, but when evident that they will never be so, it is against right to make the other branches of industry support them.

   THOMAS JEFFERSON, *Writings,* vol. xv, p. 432.

5

It accorded well with two favorite ideas of mine, of leaving commerce free, and never keeping an unnecessary soldier.

   THOMAS JEFFERSON, *Writings,* vol. xvii, p. 330.

6

I have come to a resolution myself, as I hope every good citizen will, never again to purchase any article of foreign manufacture which can be had of American make, be the difference of price what it may.

   THOMAS JEFFERSON, *Writings,* vol. xix, p. 223.

7

The tariff is the Gulf Stream of politics. It flows through both parties, and each is trying to catch the other in bathing and steal his clothes.

   PATRICK FRANCIS MURPHY, Speech at the Manhattan Club.

COMPANIONS, COMPANIONSHIP

8

Accident counts for much in companionship as in marriage.

   HENRY BROOKS ADAMS, *The Education of Henry Adams,* ch. 4.

9

Evil communications corrupt good mutton.

   GEORGE WILLIAM CURTIS, *Nile Notes of a Howadji.* ch. 3. Much earlier, Menander put it: "Evil communications corrupt good character." In the *New Testament, I Corinthians,* xv, 33, the parallel passage is: "Evil communications corrupt good manners."

10

Go with mean people and you think life is mean.

   EMERSON, *Representative Men: Plutarch.*

11

Men who know the same things are not long the best company for each other.

   EMERSON, *Representative Men: Uses of Great Men.*

12

Hail! Hail! the gang's all here,—
What the hell do we care,
What the hell do we care?
Hail! Hail! we're full of cheer,—
What the hell do we care, Bill!

   D. A. ESTROM, *Hail! Hail! the Gang's All Here* (song, 1897, sung to an air from the Gilbert-Sullivan *Pirates of Penzance*). It was first popular during the war with Spain.

13

Ez soshubble ez a baskit er kittens.

   JOEL CHANDLER HARRIS, *Legends of the Old Plantation,* ch. 3.

14

A man's mind is known by the company it keeps.

   JAMES RUSSELL LOWELL, *My Study Windows: Pope.*

"A man is known by the company he keeps"—it is the motto of a prig. Little men with foot rules six inches long, applied their measuring sticks in this way to One who lived nineteen centuries ago. "He sit at meat with publicans and sinners," they tauntingly said, assuming that his character was smirched thereby.

   ELBERT HUBBARD, *The Philistine,* vol. xii, p. 62.

A man is known by the paper he pays for.

   JOHN A. SHEDD, *Salt from My Attic.*

15

We are for the most part more lonely when we go abroad among men than when we stay in our chambers. A man thinking or working is always alone, let him be where he will.

   HENRY DAVID THOREAU, *Walden: Solitude.*

16

When a university course convinces like a slumbering woman and child convince,
When the minted gold in the vault smiles like the night-watchman's daughter,
When warrantee deeds loafe in chairs opposite and are my friendly companions,
I intend to reach them my hand, and make as much of them as I do of men and women like you.

   WALT WHITMAN, *A Song for Occupations,* sec. 6.

COMPENSATION

1
There is a day of sunny rest
  For every dark and troubled night:
And grief may bide an evening guest.
  But joy shall come with early light.
    WILLIAM CULLEN BRYANT, *Blessed Are
    They That Mourn.*

2
 The fiercest agonies have shortest reign.
    WILLIAM CULLEN BRYANT, *Mutation.*

3
Each loss has its compensation;
  There is healing for every pain;
But the bird with the broken pinion
  Never soars so high again.
    HEZEKIAH BUTTERWORTH, *The Broken
    Pinion.*

4
Every excess causes a defect; every defect
an excess. Every sweet hath its sour; every
evil its good. . . . For every grain of wit
there is a grain of folly. For everything you
have missed, you have gained something
else; and for everything you gain, you lose
something.
    EMERSON, *Essays, First Series: Compensa-
    tion.*

5
Evermore in the world is this marvellous
balance of beauty and disgust, magnificence
and rats.
    EMERSON, *Conduct of Life: Considera-
    tions by the Way.*

6
Forever and ever it takes a pound to lift a
pound.
    EMERSON, *Lectures and Biographical Stud-
    ies: Aristocracy.*

7
It is a comfort that the medal has two sides.
There is much vice and misery in the world,
I know; but more virtue and happiness, I
believe.
    THOMAS JEFFERSON, *Writings*, vol. xii, p.
    379.

8
But the nearer the dawn the darker the
    night,
And by going wrong all things come right;
Things have been mended that were worse,
And the worse, the nearer they are to mend.
    HENRY WADSWORTH LONGFELLOW, *Tales
    of a Wayside Inn: The Baron of St.
    Castine*, 1. 265.

9
Merciful Father, I will not complain,
I know that the sunshine shall follow the
    rain.
    JOAQUIN MILLER, *For Princess Maud.*

10
Them ez wants, must choose.
Them ez hez, must lose.

Them ez knows, won't blab.
Them ez guesses, will gab.
Them ez borrows, sorrows.
Them ez lends, spends.
Them ez gives, lives.
Them ez keeps dark, is deep.
Them ez kin earn, kin keep.
Them ez aims, hits.
Them ez hez, gits.
Them ez waits, win.
Them ez *will, kin.*
    EDWARD ROWLAND SILL, *A Baker's Duzzen
    uv Wize Sawz.*

11
"The cross, if rightly borne, shall be
No burden, but support to thee;"
So, moved of old time for our sake,
The holy monk of Kempen spake.
    JOHN GREENLEAF WHITTIER, *The Cross.*
    Referring to Thomas à Kempis.

12
God's ways seem dark, but, soon or late,
  They touch the shining hills of day.
    JOHN GREENLEAF WHITTIER, *For Right-
    eousness' Sake.*

COMPROMISE

13
What are facts but compromises? A fact
merely marks the point where we have
agreed to let investigation cease.
    BLISS CARMAN, Article, *Atlantic Monthly,*
    May, 1906.

14
People talk about the middle of the road as
though it were unacceptable. Actually, all
human problems, excepting morals, come
into the gray areas. Things are not all black
and white. There have to be compromises.
The middle of the road is all of the usable
surface. The extremes, right and left, are in
the gutters.
    DWIGHT D. EISENHOWER. (New York
    Times, "Ideas and Men," 10 Nov.,
    1963)

15
Everything yields. The very glaciers are viscous, or regelate into conformity, and the
stiffest patriots falter and compromise.
    EMERSON, *Miscellanies: The Fortune of
    the Republic.*

16
Every compromise was surrender and invited
new demands.
    EMERSON, *Miscellanies: American Civili-
    zation.*

17
Compromise is never anything but an ignoble
truce between the duty of a man and the
terror of a coward.
    REGINALD WRIGHT KAUFFMAN, *The Way
    of Peace.*

1

There are two kinds of weakness, that which breaks and that which bends.

 JAMES RUSSELL LOWELL, *Among My Books: Shakespeare Once More.*

2

Soft-heartedness, in times like these,
Shows sof'ness in the upper story!

 JAMES RUSSELL LOWELL, *The Biglow Papers*, Ser. ii, No. 7.

3

From compromise and things half done,
 Keep me with stern and stubborn pride;
And when at last the fight is won,
 God, keep me still unsatisfied.

 LOUIS UNTERMEYER, *Prayer.*

CONCEIT

See also Egotism, Self-Love, Vanity

4

Conceit is God's gift to little men.

 BRUCE BARTON, *Conceit.*

5

Conceit is the most incurable disease that is known to the human soul.

 HENRY WARD BEECHER, *Proverbs from Plymouth Pulpit.*

6

The world tolerates conceit from those who are successful, but not from anybody else.

 JOHN BLAKE, *Uncommon Sense.*

7

I laugh at the lore and the pride of man,
At the sophist schools, and the learned clan;
For what are they all, in their high conceit,
When man in the bush with God may meet?

 EMERSON, *Good-Bye.*

8

Conceit, which destroys almost all the fine wits.

 EMERSON, *Letters and Social Aims: Social Aims.*

CONDUCT, see Behavior, Manners

CONFIDENCE

See also Trust

9

Underlying the whole scheme of civilization is the confidence men have in each other, confidence in their integrity, confidence in their honesty, confidence in their future.

 W. BOURKE COCKRAN, Speech in New York City, 18 Aug., 1896, in reply to William Jennings Bryan and other free-silver advocates.

10

Nor fate, nor chance, nor any star commands
Success and failure—naught but your own hands.

 SAMUEL VALENTINE COLE, *Works and Days.*

11

Self-trust is the essence of heroism.

 EMERSON, *Essays, First Series: Heroism.*

12

Trust thyself: every heart vibrates to that iron string.

 EMERSON, *Essays, First Series: Self-Reliance.*

13

They can conquer who believe they can. It is he who has done the deed once who does not shrink from attempting it again.

 EMERSON, *Society and Solitude: Courage.*

14

Self-trust is the first secret of success.

 EMERSON, *Society and Solitude: Success.*

15

You are uneasy; you never sailed with *me* before, I see.

 ANDREW JACKSON, to an elderly man during a trip down Chesapeake Bay in an old steamboat. (PARTON, *Life of Jackson*, vol. iii, p. 493)

When lightning struck Lady Bird's plane, a lot of good came out of it. She's willing to start riding with me again.

 LYNDON B. JOHNSON, Interpolated Remark in Speech at the annual meeting of the U.S. Chamber of Commerce, Washington, D.C., 27 Apr., 1964. The remark followed shortly after Mrs. Johnson experienced a stormy airplane trip and not long after there had been much comment about Johnson's speeding on Texas highways during an Easter vacation from Washington.

16

The way you overcome shyness is to become so wrapped up in something that you forget to be afraid. Lyndon expects a lot of me, and so I've learned not to be afraid any more.

 CLAUDIA TAYLOR JOHNSON (MRS. LYNDON B. JOHNSON). (MARJORIE HUNTER, *Public Servant Without Pay: New York Times Magazine*, 15 Dec., 1963)

17

If you once forfeit the confidence of your fellow citizens, you can never regain their respect and esteem.

 ABRAHAM LINCOLN. (A. K. McCLURE, *Lincoln's Yarns and Stories*, p. 124)

18

You must do the thing you think you cannot do.

 ELEANOR ROOSEVELT, *You Learn by Living.*

19

A noble person confers no such gift as his whole confidence: none so exalts the giver and the receiver; it produces the truest gratitude.

 HENRY D. THOREAU, Letter to Emerson, 12 Feb., 1843.

1
Confidence is a thing not to be produced by compulsion. Men cannot be forced into trust.
> DANIEL WEBSTER, Speech, U.S. Senate, 1833.

CONSCIENCE

2
When Conscience wakens who can with her strive?
Terrors and troubles from a sick soul drive?
Naught so unpitying as the ire of sin,
The inappeas'ble Nemesis within.
> ABRAHAM COLES, *The Light of the World.*

3
Conscience emphasizes the word "ought."
> JOSEPH COOK, *Boston Monday Lectures: Conscience.*

4
Our secret thoughts are rarely heard except in secret. No man knows what conscience is until he understands what solitude can teach him concerning it.
> JOSEPH COOK, *Boston Monday Lectures: Conscience.*

5
We must not harbor disconsolate consciences, borrowed too from the consciences of other nations. We must set up the strong present tense against all the rumors of wrath, past or to come.
> EMERSON, *Essays, Second Series: Experience.*

6
The prosperous and beautiful
To me seem not to wear
The yoke of conscience masterful,
Which galls me everywhere.
> EMERSON, *The Park.*

7
Evil societies always try to kill their consciences.
> JAMES FARMER, Address at the funeral service for Michael Schwerner, a murdered civil-rights worker, Aug., 1964. Schwerner met his death in Mississippi; Farmer addressed the funeral gathering in his post as national director of the Congress of Racial Equality (CORE).

8
Keep conscience clear, then never fear.
> BENJAMIN FRANKLIN, *Poor Richard*, 1749.

9
A good conscience is a continual Christmas.
> BENJAMIN FRANKLIN, *Poor Richard*, 1749.

10
Sell not your conscience; thus are fetters wrought.
What is a Slave but One who can be Bought?
> ARTHUR GUITERMAN, *A Poet's Proverbs.*

11
I ever understood an impartial liberty of conscience to be the natural rights of all men. . . . Liberty of conscience is the first step to having a religion.
> WILLIAM PENN, *The People's Ancient and Just Liberties Asserted* (1673).

12
Passion is here a soilure of the wits,
We're told, and Love a cross for them to bear;
Joy shivers in the corner where she knits
And Conscience always has the rocking-chair,
Cheerful as when she tortured into fits
The first cat that was ever killed by Care.
> EDWIN ARLINGTON ROBINSON, *New England.*

13
Conscience is instinct bred in the house,
Feeling and Thinking propagate the sin
By an unnatural breeding in and in.
> HENRY DAVID THOREAU, *Conscience.* (*A Week on the Concord and Merrimack Rivers*)

14
A conscience worth keeping,
Laughing not weeping;
A conscience wise and steady,
And forever ready;
Not changing with events,
Dealing in compliments;
A conscience exercised about
Large things that one *may* doubt.
> HENRY DAVID THOREAU, *Conscience.* (*A Week on the Concord and Merrimack Rivers*)

15
Labor to keep alive in your breast that little spark of celestial fire, called Conscience.
> GEORGE WASHINGTON, *Moral Maxims: Conscience.*

CONSEQUENCES

16
The event is the print of your form. It fits you like your skin.
> EMERSON, *Conduct of Life: Fate.*

17
What we call results are beginnings.
> EMERSON, *Representative Men: Plato.*

18
A Foregone Conclusion.
> WILLIAM DEAN HOWELLS, Title of novel.

19
There are in nature neither rewards nor punishments—there are consequences.
> ROBERT G. INGERSOLL, *Some Reasons Why.*

20
The old pitcher went to the well once too often, but I'm glad the championship remains in America.
> JOHN L. SULLIVAN, Comment, just after

his defeat in the ring by James J. Corbett, 7 Sept., 1892. The first part of this quotation is a variant of a maxim that dates back at least to the Middle Ages.

CONSERVATISM
See also Politics

1
The current political movement that describes itself as conservative is not conservative but by every test reactionary. The reactionary-conservative thinks primarily in terms of the past, of a world in which the problems confronting him were fewer and simpler, of conditions which will never return. The liberal understands that factors exist today which were not present yesterday and knows that neither wishful thinking nor meaningless oratory will remove them. Unlike the reactionary-conservative, the liberal seeks to deal with the world as it is today.

> HARRY J. CARMAN, Letter to the Editor, St. Louis *Post-Dispatch,* published 10 Aug., 1964. The writer was chairman of the American Liberal Association at the time.

2
All conservatives are such from personal defects. They have been effeminated by position or nature, born halt and blind, through luxury of their parents, and can only, like invalids, act on the defensive.

> EMERSON, *Conduct of Life: Fate.*

3
Men are conservative when they are least vigorous, or when they are most luxurious. They are conservatives after dinner.

> EMERSON, *Essays, Second Series: New England Reformers.*

4
Conservatism . . . believes in a negative fate; . . . it distrusts nature.

> EMERSON, *Nature, Addresses, and Lectures: The Conservative.*

5
There is always a certain meanness in the argument of conservatism, joined with a certain superiority in its fact.

> EMERSON, *Nature, Addresses, and Lectures: The Conservative.*

6
I never dared be radical when young
For fear it would make me conservative when old.

> ROBERT FROST, *Precaution.*

7
A conservative, briefly, has a philosophy based upon the proven values of the past. When we seek answers for the problems of today we look to the past to see if those problems existed. Generally, they have. So

we ask: What was the answer? Did it work? If it did, let us try it again.

> BARRY M. GOLDWATER, *Goldwater Defines 'Conservatism'; New York Times Magazine,* 24 Nov., 1963.

8
I know of several liberals I'd like to give transfusions.

> BARRY M. GOLDWATER, Comment on donating blood to the American Red Cross in Washington, D.C., 15 Jan., 1964. The comment, quoted by United Press International, was in reply to a reporter's query about whether Goldwater's blood would make a recipient conservative.

9
My idea of a conservative is one who desires to retain the wisdom and the experience of the past and who is prepared to apply the best of that wisdom and experience to meet the changes which are inevitable in every new generation. The term "liberal" came to the United States in its political sense from England during the nineteenth century. As defined by them at that time, a liberal would be the conservative of today. . . . The conservative is the true liberal.

> HERBERT HOOVER, 1962. (*Herbert Hoover in His Own Words; New York Times Magazine,* 9 Aug., 1964)

10
A conservative is a man who is too cowardly to fight and too fat to run.

> ELBERT HUBBARD, *One Thousand and One Epigrams.*

11
What is conservatism? Is it not adherence to the old and tried, against the new and untried?

> ABRAHAM LINCOLN, Address, Cooper Institute, New York, 27 Feb., 1860.

12
To be a conservative in the 18th century in most of Europe was to believe in keeping things as they were, opposing change. In the American republic, however . . . the opposite was true: To be a conservative in America was to believe in the conservation of the American revolution, which meant, necessarily, the conservation of that freedom of change by which, and by which alone, revolutionary principles can be realized. Men do not achieve the unalienable right to life, liberty and the pursuit of happiness—to say nothing of the equality of opportunity which is fundamental to everything else—by keeping things the way they were.

> ARCHIBALD MacLEISH, *Tribute to a 'Great American Lady'; New York Times Magazine,* 3 Nov., 1963.

13
Indeed, what passes for political conservatism in our day is very largely . . . fear [of

the future], with anti-Communism replacing belief in freedom as a national cause and a whole list of hatreds and rejections and denials as ultimate objectives.

> ARCHIBALD MACLEISH, *Tribute to a 'Great American Lady'; New York Times Magazine,* 3 Nov., 1963.

1

We *are* in one sense a very conservative people—for no nation in history has had so much to conserve. Suggestions that everything is not perfect and that things must be changed *do* arouse the suspicion that something *I* cherish and *I* value may be modified.

> ADLAI E. STEVENSON, *The Hard Kind of Patriotism; Harper's Magazine,* July, 1963.

2

To defend every abuse, every self-interest, every encrusted position of privilege in the name of love of country—when in fact it is only love of the status quo—that indeed is the lie in the soul to which any conservative society is prone.

> ADLAI E. STEVENSON, *The Hard Kind of Patriotism; Harper's Magazine,* July, 1963.

3

Generally young men are regarded as radicals. This is a popular misconception. The most conservative persons I ever met are college undergraduates.

> WOODROW WILSON, Address in New York, 19 Nov., 1905.

CONSISTENCY, INCONSISTENCY

4

True consistency, that of the prudent and the wise, is to act in conformity with circumstances, and not to act always the same way under a change of circumstances.

> JOHN C. CALHOUN, Speech, 16 Mar., 1848.

5

A foolish consistency is the hobgoblin of little minds, adored by little statesmen and philosophers and divines.

> EMERSON, *Essays, First Series: Self-Reliance.*

6

With consistency a great soul has simply nothing to do. . . . Speak what you think today in words as hard as cannon balls, and tomorrow speak what to-morrow thinks in hard words again, although it contradict everything you said to-day.

> EMERSON, *Essays, First Series: Self-Reliance.*

7

I think you will find that people who honestly mean to be true really contradict themselves much more rarely than those who try to be "consistent."

> OLIVER WENDELL HOLMES, *The Professor at the Breakfast-Table,* ch. 2.

8

Gineral C. is a dreffle smart man;
  He's ben on all sides thet give places or pelf;
But consistency still wuz a part of his plan,—
  He's been true to *one* party,—an' thet is himself.

> JAMES RUSSELL LOWELL, *Biglow Papers,* Ser. i, No. 3. The reference is to Caleb Cushing.

9

Do I contradict myself?
Very well then I contradict myself.
(I am large, I contain multitudes.)

> WALT WHITMAN, *Song of Myself,* sec. 51.

CONSTITUTION

10

No person . . . shall be compelled in any criminal case to be a witness against himself.

> Bill of Rights, Article v. (25 Sept., 1789). This section had particular reference to post-World War II events. From it has come the expressions "to take the Fifth" and, in cases of alleged subversive activity, "Fifth Amendment Communist."

11

Whenever the Constitution comes between men and the virtue of the white women of South Carolina, I say—to hell with the Constitution.

> COLE L. BLEASE, Public Statement, 1911, while he was governor of South Carolina.

12

What's the Constitution between friends?

> TIMOTHY J. CAMPBELL, Comment to President Cleveland, about 1885, when the latter refused to sign a bill on the ground that it was unconstitutional. The quotation is attributed to Campbell, a Tammany member of the U.S. House of Representatives, on the authority of William Tyler Page.

13

In essence, the Constitution is not a literary composition but a way of ordering society, adequate for imaginative statesmanship, if judges have imagination for statesmanship.

> FELIX FRANKFURTER.

14

As the British Constitution is the most subtile organism which has proceeded from the womb and the long gestation of progressive history, so the American Constitution is, so far as I can see, the most wonderful work ever struck off at a given time by the brain and purpose of man.

WILLIAM E. GLADSTONE, *Kin beyond Sea.* (*North American Review,* Sept., 1878)

1

Reassertion of the fundamental character of the Constitution, not as a treaty between the States, but rather as a charter emanating directly from the people, is ever necessary in the face of assertions, made even to this day, that the States, or rather their legislatures, are to be the final judges of their own powers and those of the national government . . . These echoes of nullification are denied by the Constitution itself and by our national experience. They have no place in our day when our unity as a people is indispensable for survival.

ARTHUR GOLDBERG, Address at the annual convention, American Bar Association, Chicago, Aug., 1963.

2

These decisions give support to a current mistaken view of the Constitution and the constitutional function of this Court. This view, in a nutshell, is that every major social ill in this country can find its cure in some constitutional "principle," and that this Court should "take the lead" in promoting reform when other branches of government fail to act. The Constitution is not a panacea for every blot upon the public welfare, nor should this Court, ordained as a judicial body, be thought of as a general haven for reform movements. This Court, limited in function, does not serve its high purpose when it exceeds its authority, even to satisfy justified impatience with the slow workings of the political process.

JOHN MARSHALL HARLAN, Associate Justice, U.S. Supreme Court, in dissenting in the legislative-apportionment cases during the 1963–64 term of the court.

3

The Constitution is what the judges say it is.

CHARLES EVANS HUGHES, Speech in Elmira, N.Y., 3 May, 1907.

4

Some men look at Constitutions with sanctimonious reverence, and deem them like the ark of the covenant, too sacred to be touched. They ascribe to the men of the preceding age a wisdom more than human, and suppose what they did to be beyond amendment. . . . Laws and institutions must go hand in hand with the progress of the human mind. . . . We might as well require a man to wear the coat that fitted him as a boy, as civilized society to remain ever under the regime of their ancestors.

THOMAS JEFFERSON, *Writings,* vol. xv, p. 40.

5

Our basic law—the Constitution—is distinctive among the basic law of all nations, even the free nations of the West, in that it prescribes no national dogma: economic, social, or religious.

LYNDON B. JOHNSON, *My Political Philosophy,* originally published as a copyrighted article in 1958 by *The Texas Quarterly* of the University of Texas.

6

It is the genius of our Constitution that under its shelter of enduring institutions and rooted principles there is ample room for the rich fertility of American political invention.

LYNDON B. JOHNSON, State of the Union Message, 12 Jan., 1966.

7

It's got so it is as easy to amend the Constitution of the United States as it used to be to draw a cork.

THOMAS RILEY MARSHALL. (*Literary Digest,* 20 June, 1925, p. 45)

8

All that is valuable in the United States Constitution is one thousand years old.

WENDELL PHILLIPS, Speech in Boston, 17 Feb., 1861.

9

We hold that the Constitution follows the flag, and denounce the doctrine that an Executive or Congress deriving their existence and their powers from the Constitution can exercise lawful authority beyond it, or in violation of it. We assert that no nation can long endure half republic and half empire, and we warn the American people that imperialism abroad will lead quickly and inevitably to despotism at home.

Platform of the Democratic Party, adopted at the national convention in Kansas City, Mo., 5 July, 1900. This is the first known record of "Constitution follows the flag"; the authorship is credited to the platform committee.

No matther whether th' Constitution follows th' flag or not, th' Supreme Coort follows th' iliction returns.

FINLEY PETER DUNNE, *Mr. Dooley's Opinions: The Supreme Court's Decisions* (1900).

10

Our Constitution is so simple and practical that it is possible always to meet extraordinary needs by changes in emphasis and arrangement without loss of essential form.

FRANKLIN D. ROOSEVELT, First Inaugural Address, 4 Mar., 1933.

11

There is a higher law than the Constitution.

WILLIAM H. SEWARD, Speech in the U.S. Senate, Mar., 1850. He was condemning

Daniel Webster for support of the Fugitive Slave Law.

1
I have never been more struck by the good sense and the practical judgment of the Americans than in the manner in which they elude the numberless difficulties resulting from their Federal Constitution.
> ALEXIS DE TOCQUEVILLE, *Democracy in America*, pt. i, ch. 8.

2
The John Birch Society is determined to uphold the Constitution.
> ROBERT WELCH, Statement at press conference in St. Louis, 13 May, 1964. Welch, founder and leader of the strongly conservative organization, had often emphasized adherence to the Constitution as the keystone of the society's beliefs; the motto "return to the Constitution" was frequently heard from conservative groups and candidates during the 1950's and 1960's. During this press conference Welch discussed the Birch campaign to impeach Chief Justice Earl Warren for "tearing down the Constitution."

3
The Constitution does not provide for first and second class citizens.
> WENDELL L. WILLKIE, *An American Program*.

CONTEMPLATION

4
All civil mankind have agreed in leaving one day for contemplation against six for practice.
> EMERSON, *Lectures and Biographical Studies: The Preacher*.

5
If I were to compare action of a much higher strain with a life of contemplation, I should not venture to pronounce with much confidence in favor of the former.
> EMERSON, *Representative Men: Goethe*.

CONTENTMENT

See also Happiness; Moderation; Want, Wants

6
A good man is contented.
> EMERSON, *Essays, First Series: Spiritual Laws*.

7
Content is the Philosopher's Stone, that turns all it touches into gold.
> BENJAMIN FRANKLIN, *Poor Richard*, 1758.

8
He that's content hath enough.
> BENJAMIN FRANKLIN, *Poor Richard*, 1758.

9
I do not own an inch of land,
But all I see is mine.
> LUCY LARCOM, *A Strip of Blue*.

10
A flower more sacred than far-seen success
　Perfumes my solitary path; I find
Sweet compensation in my humbleness,
　And reap the harvest of a quiet mind.
> J. T. TROWBRIDGE, *Twoscore and Ten*, st. 28.

CONVERSATION

See also Speech

11
Debate is masculine; conversation is feminine.
> AMOS BRONSON ALCOTT, *Concord Days: May*.

12
Many can argue, not many converse.
> AMOS BRONSON ALCOTT, *Concord Days: May*.

13
Conversation is an art in which a man has all mankind for his competitors, for it is that which all are practising every day while they live.
> EMERSON, *Conduct of Life: Considerations by the Way*.

14
The best of life is conversation.
> EMERSON, *Conduct of Life: Behavior*.

15
You may talk of all subjects save one, namely, your maladies.
> EMERSON, *Conduct of Life: Behavior*.

There is one topic peremptorily forbidden to all rational mortals, namely, their distempers. If you have not slept, or if you have slept, or if you have headache, or sciatica, or leprosy, or thunder-stroke, I beseech you, by all angels, to hold your peace, and not pollute the morning by corruption and groans.
> EMERSON, *Conduct of Life: Behavior*.

Never name sickness; and, above all, beware of unmuzzling the valetudinarian.
> EMERSON, *Table-Talk*.

16
Conversation is a game of circles.
> EMERSON, *Essays, First Series: Circles*.

17
In good conversation parties don't speak to the words, but to the meanings of each other.
> EMERSON, *Letters and Social Aims: Social Aims*.

18
Wise, cultivated, genial conversation is the last flower of civilization. . . . Conversation is our account of ourselves.
> EMERSON, *Miscellanies: Woman*.

1
The conversation of men is a mixture of regrets and apprehensions.

EMERSON, *Natural History of Intellect: The Tragic.*

2
Conversation is the vent of character as well as of thought.

EMERSON, *Society and Solitude: Clubs.*

3
Conversation is the laboratory and workshop of the student.

EMERSON, *Society and Solitude: Clubs.*

4
Inject a few raisins of conversation into the tasteless dough of existence.

O. HENRY, *Complete Life of John Hopkins.*

5
Talking is like playing on the harp; there is as much in laying the hands on the strings to stop their vibration as in twanging them to bring out the music.

OLIVER WENDELL HOLMES, *The Autocrat of the Breakfast-Table,* ch. 1.

6
The man that often speaks, but never talks.

OLIVER WENDELL HOLMES, *The Banker's Secret.*

7
Conversation seems to always tire me.

GEORGE W. LEDERER, *I'm Tired* (1901).

8
A single conversation across the table with a wise man is better than ten years' study of books.

HENRY WADSWORTH LONGFELLOW, *Hyperion,* ch. 7. This is quoted from the Chinese.

9
He speaketh not; and yet their lies
A conversation in his eyes.

HENRY WADSWORTH LONGFELLOW, *The Hanging of the Crane,* sec. 3.

10
Be humble and gentle in your conversation; and of few words, I charge you; but always pertinent when you speak.

WILLIAM PENN, *Letters to His Wife and Children.*

CORPORATIONS

11
I see in the near future a crisis approaching that unnerves me and causes me to tremble for the safety of my country. As a result of the war, corporations have been enthroned, and an era of corruption in high places will follow. . . . I feel at this moment more anxiety for the safety of my country than ever before, even in the midst of war.

Attributed to ABRAHAM LINCOLN. This is not found in his works, however, and is probably apocryphal.

12
The biggest corporation, like the humblest private citizen, must be held to strict compliance with the will of the people.

THEODORE ROOSEVELT, Speech in Cincinnati, 1902.

13
There are persons who . . . complain of oppression, speculation, and pernicious influence of wealth. They cry out loudly against all banks and corporations, and a means by which small capitalists become united in order to produce important and beneficial results. They carry on mad hostility against all established institutions. They would choke the fountain of industry and dry all streams.

DANIEL WEBSTER, Speech in U.S. Senate, March, 1838.

COSMOPOLITANISM

14
Go where he will, the wise man is at home,
His hearth the earth, his hall her azure dome.

EMERSON, *Woodnotes,* pt. i, sec. 3.

15
The truth is that Mr. James's cosmopolitanism is, after all, limited; to be really cosmopolitan, a man must be at home even in his own country.

THOMAS W. HIGGINSON, *Short Studies of American Authors: Henry James, Jr.*

16
Home is anywhere for me
On this purple-tented sea.

JOHN G. NEIHARDT, *Outward.*

17
My country is the world, and my religion is to do good.

THOMAS PAINE, *Rights of Man,* pt. ii, ch. 5.

Our country is the world—our countrymen are all mankind.

WILLIAM LLOYD GARRISON, Motto of *The Liberator.*

18
O gentle hands that soothed the soldier's brow
And knew no service save of Christ's the Lord!
Thy country now is all humanity.

G. E. WOODBERRY, *Edith Cavell.*

COURAGE

See also Boldness, Valor

19
We have hard work to do, and loads to lift;
Shun not the struggle—face it; 'tis God's gift.

MALTBIE BABCOCK, *Be Strong.*

20
And though hard be the task,

"Keep a stiff upper lip."
  PHOEBE CARY, *Keep a Stiff Upper Lip.*

1
To fight aloud is very brave,
But gallanter, I know,
Who charge within the bosom
The cavalry of woe.
  EMILY DICKINSON, *Poems,* Pt. i, No. 16.

2
I think even lying on my bed I can still do
something.
  DOROTHEA LYNDE DIX, Remark, a few
    days before her death, 17 July, 1887.

3
Courage consists in equality to the problem
before us.
  EMERSON, *Society and Solitude: Courage.*

4
A great part of courage is the courage of
having done the thing before.
  EMERSON, *Society and Solitude: Courage.*

5
Have the courage not to adopt another's
courage.
  EMERSON, *Society and Solitude: Courage.*

6
What a new face courage puts on every-
thing!
  EMERSON, *Letters and Social Aims: Re-
    sources.*

7
Here comes Courage! that seized the lion
absent, and ran away from the present
mouse.
  BENJAMIN FRANKLIN, *Poor Richard's Al-
    manac,* 1775.

8
The greatest test of courage on earth is to
bear defeat without losing heart.
  ROBERT G. INGERSOLL, *The Declaration of
    Independence.*

9
I'd rather give my life than be afraid to give
it.
  LYNDON B. JOHNSON, Reply to U.S. Secret
    Service agents, 25 Nov., 1963, as he
    joined the group walking in the proces-
    sion at the funeral of John F. Kennedy
    in Washington, D.C. The agents had ar-
    gued that a safer course would be for
    him to ride to St. Matthew's Cathedral
    in an automobile. (Quoted in the New
    York *Herald Tribune* and St. Louis *Post-
    Dispatch,* 26 Nov., 1963; and by Doug-
    las B. Cornell in an Associated Press
    dispatch datelined 17 Apr., 1964.)

10
The courage of life is often a less dramatic
spectacle than the courage of a final moment; but it is no less than a magnificent
mixture of triumph and tragedy. A man does
what he must—in spite of personal consequences, in spite of obstacles and dangers
and pressures—and that is the basis of all
human morality.
  JOHN F. KENNEDY, *Profiles in Courage.*

11
Only those are fit to live who are not afraid
to die.
  GENERAL DOUGLAS MACARTHUR, Address
    to the Filipino air force, 31 July, 1941.
    (CONSIDINE, *MacArthur the Magnifi-
    cent,* p. 9)

12
Last, but by no means least, courage—moral
courage, the courage of one's convictions, the
courage to see things through. The world is
in a constant conspiracy against the brave.
It's the age-old struggle—the roar of the
crowd on one side and the voice of your
conscience on the other.
  GENERAL DOUGLAS MACARTHUR, Public
    Statement in New York, 26 Jan., 1964
    (his 84th and last birthday). He was
    enumerating the "many things, some of
    them not within the covers of books
    written by any man," that were taught
    him at the U.S. Military Academy.

13
This is another day! Are its eyes blurred
With maudlin grief for any wasted past?
A thousand thousand failures shall not
    daunt!
Let dust clasp dust, death, death; I am
    alive!
  DON MARQUIS, *This Is Another Day.*

14
Courage is the most common and vulgar of
the virtues.
  HERMAN MELVILLE. (COURNOS, *Modern
    Plutarch,* p. 86)

15
Give me the serenity to accept what cannot
    be changed.
Give me the courage to change what can be
    changed.
The wisdom to know one from the other.
  REINHOLD NIEBUHR. (In *The Way of
    Light: A Manual of Praise, Prayer and
    Meditation*)

God grant me the courage to change the
things I can change, the serenity to accept
those I cannot change, the wisdom to know
the difference—but God grant me the courage not to give up what I think is right even
though I think it is hopeless.
  Attributed to ADMIRAL CHESTER W. NIM-
    ITZ, in *The Armed Forces Prayer
    Book* (1951).

16
I heard of a high British officer who went
over the battlefield just after the action was
over. American boys were still lying dead in
their foxholes, their rifles still grasped in firing position in their dead hands. And the
veteran English soldier remarked time and

again, in a sort of hushed eulogy spoken only to himself, "Brave men. Brave men!"

ERNIE PYLE, *Here Is Your War*. Used as the foreword to Pyle's *Brave Men*.

1
Courage is doing what you're afraid to do. There can be no courage unless you're scared.

EDWARD V. (EDDIE) RICKENBACKER. (PEGGY STREIT, *What Is Courage?; New York Times Magazine*, 24 Nov., 1963)

2
Where there is a brave man there is the thickest of the fight, there the post of honor.

HENRY D. THOREAU, *Journal*, 2 Dec., 1839.

3
Courage is resistance to fear, mastery of fear—not absence of fear.

MARK TWAIN, *Pudd'nhead Wilson's Calendar*.

COURTESY

See also Manners

4
Life is short, but there is always time for courtesy.

EMERSON, *Uncollected Lectures: Social Aims*.

5
The whole of heraldry and of chivalry is in courtesy.

EMERSON, *Essays, First Series: History*.

6
What boots it, thy virtue,
  What profit thy parts,
While one thing thou lackest—
  The art of all arts,
The only credentials,
  Passport to success,
Opens castle and parlor,
  Address, man, address?

EMERSON, *Tact*.

7
Politeness is artificial good humor; it covers the natural want of it, and ends by rendering habitual a substitute nearly equivalent to the real virtue.

THOMAS JEFFERSON, *Writings*, vol. xii, p. 198.

8
Intelligence and courtesy not always are combined;
Often in a wooden house a golden room we find.

HENRY WADSWORTH LONGFELLOW, *Art and Tact*.

9
Politeness is the art of choosing among one's real thoughts.

ABEL STEVENS, *Life of Mme. de Staël*, ch. 4.

COURTSHIP

10
For this is a sort of engagement, you see,
Which is binding on you but not binding on me.

WILLIAM ALLEN BUTLER, *Nothing to Wear*.

11
Pursued man loves to think himself pursuer.

EDMUND VANCE COOKE, *From the Book of Extenuations: Ruth*.

A man always chases a woman until she catches him.

UNKNOWN. (Columnist in the El Paso Times.)

12
It's better to change your attitude an' pay some heart balm than to be dug up later an' analyzed.

KIN HUBBARD, *Abe Martin's Broadcast*, p. 85.

13
I can march up to a fortress and summon the place to surrender,
But march up to a woman with such a proposal, I dare not.
I'm not afraid of bullets, nor shot from the mouth of a cannon,
But of a thundering "No!" point-blank from the mouth of a woman,
That I confess I'm afraid of, nor am I ashamed to confess it!

LONGFELLOW, *The Courtship of Miles Standish*, pt. ii.

14
If I am not worth the wooing, I surely am not worth the winning.

HENRY WADSWORTH LONGFELLOW, *The Courtship of Miles Standish*, pt. iii.

15
Archly the maiden smiled, and, with eyes overrunning with laughter,
Said, in a tremulous voice, "Why don't you speak for yourself, John?"

LONGFELLOW, *The Courtship of Miles Standish*, pt. iii.

16
He stood a spell on one foot fust,
  Then stood a spell on t'other,
An' on which one he felt the wust
  He couldn't ha' told ye nuther.

JAMES RUSSELL LOWELL, *The Courtin'*, st. 19.

COW

17
I never saw a PURPLE COW,
  I never HOPE to see one;
But I can tell you, anyhow,
  I'd rather SEE than BE one.

GELETT BURGESS, *The Purple Cow*.

1

The cross cow holds up her milk.
  EMERSON, *Society and Solitude: Clubs.*

2

God's jolly cafeteria
With four legs and a tail.
  E. M. ROOT, *The Cow.*

COWARDICE

3

God Almighty hates a quitter.
  SAMUEL FESSENDEN, of Connecticut, at
    the Republican national convention in
    St. Louis, June, 1896. He was referring
    to Joseph Manley. (ROBINSON, *Life of
    Reed*)

4

Cowardice, as distinguished from panic, is
almost always simply a lack of ability to
suspend the functioning of the imagination.
  ERNEST HEMINGWAY, *Men at War:* Intro-
    duction.

5

Then to side with Truth is noble when we
    share her wretched crust,
Ere her cause bring fame and profit, and 'tis
    prosperous to be just;
Then it is the brave man chooses, while the
    coward stands aside,
Doubting in his abject spirit, till his Lord is
    crucified.
  JAMES RUSSELL LOWELL, *The Present Cri-
    sis*, st. 11.

6

Only the cowards are sinners,
  Fighting the fight is all.
  JOHN G. NEIHARDT, *Battle Cry.*

7

There are several good protections against
temptations, but the surest is cowardice.
  MARK TWAIN, *Pudd'nhead Wilson's New
    Calendar.*

8

The blues of mental and physical wear and
tear are not as devastating as the yellows of
the quitter.
  JAMES J. WALKER, Interview. 20 Sept.,
    1931.

CREDIT

9

Every innocent man has in his countenance a
promise to pay, and hence credit.
  EMERSON, *Letters and Social Aims: Social
    Aims.*

10

Creditors are a superstitious set, great observers of set days and times.
  BENJAMIN FRANKLIN, *Poor Richard.*

11

The only road, the sure road, to unquestioned credit and a sound financial condition
is the exact and punctual fulfilment of every
pecuniary obligation, public and private, according to its letter and spirit.
  RUTHERFORD B. HAYES, Speech in Brook-
    lyn, N.Y., 21 Dec., 1880.

12

He smote the rock of the national resources,
and abundant streams of revenue gushed
forth. He touched the dead corpse of public
credit, and it sprang upon its feet.
  DANIEL WEBSTER, Eulogy on Alexander
    Hamilton, 10 Mar., 1831.

CREEDS
See also Religion

13

As men's prayers are a disease of the will, so
are their creeds a disease of the intellect.
  EMERSON, *Essays, First Series: Self-Reli-
    ance.*

14

Orthodoxy is a corpse that does not know it
is dead.
  ELBERT HUBBARD, *Epigrams.*

15

My creed is this:
  Happiness is the only good.
  The place to be happy is here.
  The time to be happy is now.
  The way to be happy is to help make oth-
    ers so.
  ROBERT G. INGERSOLL, Motto on the title
    page of Vol. xii, *Works* (Farrell, ed.).

16

I belong to the Great Church which holds
the world within its starlit aisles; that claims
the great and good of every race and clime;
that finds with joy the grain of gold in every
creed, and floods with light and love the
germs of good in every soul.
  ROBERT G. INGERSOLL, Declaration, in dis-
    cussion with Rev. Henry M. Field on
    Faith and Agnosticism. (Farrell, *Life*,
    vol. vi)

17

As the forehead of Man grows broader, so do
    his creeds; . . .
For no form of a god, and no fashion
Man has made in his desperate passion,
But is worthy some worship of mine;—
Not too hot with a gross belief,
  Nor yet too cold with pride,
I will bow me down where my brothers
    bow,
  Humble, but open eyed.
  DON MARQUIS, *The God-Maker, Man.*

18

I believe in one God and no more, and I
hope for happiness beyond this life. I believe
in the equality of man; and I believe that
religious duties consist in doing justice, loving
mercy, and in endeavoring to make our fel-
low-creatures happy.
  THOMAS PAINE, *The Age of Reason*, ch.
    1.

1

Men have dulled their eyes with sin,
　And dimmed the light of heaven with
　　doubt,
And built their temple-walls to shut thee in,
　And framed their iron creeds to shut thee
　　out.
　　HENRY VAN DYKE, *God of the Open Air.*

CRIME

2

Public Enemy Number One.
　　HENRY BARRETT CHAMBERLIN. This term
　　was coined when he was director of the
　　Chicago Crime Commission, and was
　　first applied to Al Capone. In the 1930s
　　Municipal Judge John H. Lyle of Chi-
　　cago drafted a register of "public ene-
　　mies." In 1950 the Federal Bureau of
　　Investigation issued its first list of "Ten
　　Most Wanted Fugitives." (CHARLES
　　and BONNIE REMSBERG, *Roll of Dishon-
　　or; New York Times Magazine,* 26 Jan.,
　　1964.)

3

The reason of idleness and crime is the de-
ferring of our hopes. Whilst we are waiting
we beguile the time with jokes, with sleep,
with eating, and with crimes.
　　EMERSON, *Essays, Second Series: Nomi-
　　nalist and Realist.*

4

Men never speak of crime as lightly as they
think.
　　EMERSON, *Essays, Second Series: Experi-
　　ence.*

5

"It is worse than a crime, it is a blunder,"
said Napoleon, speaking the language of the
intellect.
　　EMERSON, *Essays, Second Series: Experi-
　　ence.*

6

Whenever a man commits a crime, God finds
a witness. . . . Every secret crime has its
reporter.
　　EMERSON, *Uncollected Lectures: Natural
　　Religion.*

7

The battle against crime is greater than we
realize because we're facing a new type of
criminal today who kills for kicks. People
who are bored with life and have no discipline from within—and it's unfashionable to
discipline from without—go along for kicks,
until they must try the supreme kick, to kill
another human being. . . . Sometimes I
think that the archcriminal was the man who
invented the safety razor and eliminated the
razor strop that used to hang by the sink.
　　ERLE STANLEY GARDNER, Address to the
　　Bar Association of St. Louis, 1 Oct.,
　　1963.

8

Every crime destroys more Edens than our
own.
　　NATHANIEL HAWTHORNE, *The Marble
　　Faun,* vol. i, ch. 23.

9

It could probably be shown by facts and
figures that there is no distinctly native
American criminal class except Congress.
　　MARK TWAIN, *Pudd'nhead Wilson's New
　　Calendar,* ch. 8.

CRITICISM

I—Criticism: General

10

Blame is safer than praise.
　　EMERSON, *Essays, First Series: Compensa-
　　tion.*

11

Criticism should not be querulous and wasting, all knife and root-puller, but guiding,
instructive, inspiring, a south wind, not an
east wind.
　　EMERSON, *Journals.*

12

The greatest corrective known to man is criticism with good will. We have lost the art of
cross criticism in the daily media. It was
better in the days when publishers went out
and horsewhipped each other when they
differed on important issues.
　　MORRIS ERNST, Speech in St. Louis, 16
　　July, 1964.

13

Blame-all and praise-all are two blockheads.
　　BENJAMIN FRANKLIN, *Poor Richard,*
　　1734.

14

The sting of a reproach is the Truth of it.
　　BENJAMIN FRANKLIN, *Poor Richard,*
　　1746.

15

It is through criticism . . . that the race has
managed to come out of the woods and lead
a civilized life. The first man who objected
to the general nakedness, and advised his fellows to put on clothes, was the first critic.
　　E. L. GODKIN, *Problems of Modern De-
　　mocracy.*

16

The Stones that Critics hurl with Harsh In-
　　tent
A Man may use to build his Monument.
　　ARTHUR GUITERMAN, *A Poet's Proverbs.*

17

Criticism is no doubt good for the soul but
we must beware that it does not upset our
confidence in ourselves.
　　HERBERT HOOVER, Statement on his nineti-
　　eth birthday, New York City, 10 Aug.,
　　1964.

18

A critic is a man who expects miracles.
　　JAMES G. HUNEKER, *Iconoclasts,* p. 139.

1
No critic has ever settled anything.
> JAMES G. HUNEKER, *Pathos of Distance,*
> p. 281.

2
I find the pain of a little censure, even when it is unfounded, is more acute than the pleasure of much praise.
> THOMAS JEFFERSON, *Writings,* vol. vii, p.
> 299.

3
The men who create power make an indispensable contribution to the nation's greatness. But the men who question power make a contribution just as indispensable, especially when that questioning is disinterested.
> JOHN F. KENNEDY, Speech at Amherst
> College, Amherst, Mass., 26 Oct., 1963.

4
There will always be dissident voices heard in the land, expressing opposition without alternatives, finding fault but never favor, perceiving gloom on every side and seeking influence without responsibility. Those voices are inevitable.
> JOHN F. KENNEDY, Speech prepared for
> delivery in Dallas, 22 Nov., 1963, the
> day of his assassination.

5
A wise scepticism is the first attribute of a good critic.
> JAMES RUSSELL LOWELL, *Among My*
> *Books: Shakespeare Once More.*

6
We, who look on with critic eyes
Exempt from action's crucial test,
Human ourselves, at least are wise
In honoring one who did his best.
> JAMES RUSSELL LOWELL, Verses sent to
> Grover Cleveland, 10 Dec., 1889, to-
> gether with an expression of regret for
> non-attendance at a meeting in Boston
> that Cleveland addressed.

7
From Juvenal to Voltaire and from Swift to H. L. Mencken, critics have weighed their own lands in the balance and found reasons for denouncing a generation of vipers. Americans have been especially open to castigation because they had a golden opportunity to create a bright new society in an unpolluted continent.
> ALLAN NEVINS, *What Has Happened to*
> *Our Morality?; New York Times Mag-*
> *azine,* 10 June, 1962.

8
You won't have Nixon to kick around any more.
> RICHARD M. NIXON, Statement to the
> press, 7 Nov., 1962, the day after the
> California election in which he unsuc-
> cessfully tried to unseat Governor Ed-

mund G. (Pat) Brown. Nixon angrily assailed elements of the press that he called hostile to him, during this press conference, which he called "my last." On 17 Nov., 1962, in telegrams to several newspapers, he described the governorship race as "my last campaign for public office." On 25 Apr., 1964, Nixon referred to this celebrated blast at the press, in off-the-record remarks at the annual stag dinner of the Gridiron Club in Washington. Betty Beale, columnist of the Washington *Star,* quoted him thus: "My friends of the press—if I have any. If I haven't any, maybe it is more my fault than theirs. I hope that a man can lose his temper once in sixteen years and be forgiven for it." Miss Beale also quoted Nixon: "If this party is supposed to be dedicated to love, what better evidence is there than for Harry Truman to take a drink from Dick Nixon without asking someone else to taste it first?"

9
A critic is a legless man who teaches running.
> CHANNING POLLOCK, *The Green Book.*

10
Any jackass can kick down a barn, but it takes a good carpenter to build one.
> Attributed to SAM RAYBURN, and quoted
> by Lyndon B. Johnson in 1952, in re-
> sponse to Texas' swing to Dwight D.
> Eisenhower in the presidential election
> of that year. (HENRY A. ZEIGER, *Lyndon*
> *B. Johnson: Man and President,* p. 47)

11
The men with the muck-rake are often indispensable to the well-being of society, but only if they know when to stop raking the muck.
> THEODORE ROOSEVELT, Address at a Grid-
> iron Club dinner, Washington, 14 Apr.,
> 1906.

12
Criticism . . . is a serious and public function: it shows the race assimilating the individual, dividing the immortal from the mortal part of a soul.
> GEORGE SANTAYANA, *The Life of Reason,*
> iv, 151.

13
Our society can stand a large dose of constructive criticism just because it is so solid and has so much to conserve. It is only if keen and lively minds constantly compare the ideal and the reality and see the shadow —the shadow of self-righteousness, of suburban sprawl, of racial discrimination, of interminable strikes—it is only then that the shadow can be dispelled and the unique

brightness of our national experiment can be seen and loved.

> ADLAI E. STEVENSON, *The Hard Kind of Patriotism; Harper's Magazine,* July, 1963.

1
Self-criticism is a mark of social maturity.

> GORE VIDAL, *Primary Vote for a 'Best Man'; New York Times,* 5 Apr., 1964.

2
I fancy that it is just as hard to do your duty when men are sneering at you as when they are shooting at you.

> WOODROW WILSON, Speech at the Brooklyn Navy Yard, 11 May, 1914.

II—Criticism: The Arts

See also Stage

3
This is the kind of thing that comes to you when you've outlived your critics.

> THOMAS HART BENTON, Remark at a dinner in his honor, in Kansas City, Mo., on his 75th birthday, 15 Apr., 1964.

4
His entrances down the aisles of New York theaters were more dramatic than most of the shows he reviewed.

> JOHN MASON BROWN, Introduction to *The Portable Woollcott.* The reference is to Alexander Woollcott.

5
We actors are in business. No one hit us over the head and forced us. So you've got to stick your neck out. If you can't take it, get out and be an insurance salesman.

> KIRK DOUGLAS. (Quoted by William Glover in an Associated Press dispatch datelined New York, 11 Nov., 1963)

6
The female knee is a joint and not an entertainment.

> PERCY HAMMOND, Review, in the Chicago *Tribune,* of a Shubert musical show with a "preponderance of leg."

7
What a blessed thing it is that Nature, when she invented, manufactured, and patented her authors, contrived to make critics out of the chips that were left!

> OLIVER WENDELL HOLMES, *The Professor at the Breakfast-Table,* ch. 1.

8
The practice of "reviewing" . . . has nothing in common with the art of criticism.

> HENRY JAMES, *Criticism.*

9
Once upon a time, Oppenheimer told me he liked or disliked a play. Now he tells me he likes or dislikes a play because. . . .

> ARTHUR KOBER, commenting on George Oppenheimer, after the latter became drama critic of *Newsday* in 1955. (*The Passionate Playgoer,* p. 4)

10
He could gauge the old books by the old set of rules,
And his very old nothings pleased very old fools;
But give him a new book, fresh out of the heart,
And you put him at sea without compass or chart.

> JAMES RUSSELL LOWELL, *A Fable for Critics,* l. 205.

11
It is impossible to think of a man of any actual force and originality . . . who spent his whole life appraising and describing the work of other men.

> H. L. MENCKEN, *Prejudices,* ser. iii, p. 87.

12
Criticism is the art of appraising others at one's own value.

> GEORGE JEAN NATHAN, *The World in Falseface.*

13
Criticism is the art wherewith a critic tries to guess himself into a share of the artist's fame.

> GEORGE JEAN NATHAN, *The House of Satan,* p. 98.

14
There are two kinds of dramatic critics: destructive and constructive. I am a destructive. There are two kinds of guns: Krupp and pop.

> GEORGE JEAN NATHAN, *The World in Falseface.*

15
The dramatic critic who is without prejudice is on the plane with the general who does not believe in taking human life.

> GEORGE JEAN NATHAN, *Comedians All.*

16
No chronically happy man is a trustworthy critic.

> GEORGE JEAN NATHAN, *The Theatre in the Fifties.*

17
A man of such infinite wisdom and flawless taste that any opinion he may utter is to be accepted immediately and without question —unless you happen to disagree with him.

> GEORGE OPPENHEIMER, defining a critic. (*The Passionate Playgoer,* ed. by George Oppenheimer, p. 3)

18
When they praise me, it bores me; when they pan me, it annoys me.

> ARTUR RUBINSTEIN, on critics. (*Rubinstein Speaking; New York Times Magazine,* 26 Jan., 1964)

19
I will tell you when he has written some.

> IGOR STRAVINSKY, Comment upon being asked to evaluate the music of a promi-

nent colleague among composers. (*New York Times Magazine,* 10 June, 1962, p. 24)

1

I have just read your lousy review buried in the back pages. You sound like a frustrated old man who never made a success, an eight-ulcer man on a four-ulcer job, and all four ulcers working. I have never met you, but if I do you'll need a new nose and plenty of beefsteak and perhaps a supporter below. Westbrook Pegler, a guttersnipe, is a gentleman compared to you. You can take that as more of an insult than as a reflection on your ancestry.

HARRY S TRUMAN, Note to Paul Hume, music critic of the Washington *Post,* 6 Dec., 1950, in reply to Hume's unfavorable review of Margaret Truman's concert in the capital on 5 Dec., 1950. This famous example of criticism of a critic was signed "HST," but the White House acknowledged its authorship. Hume had granted Miss Truman's attractiveness on stage, but added: "Yet Miss Truman cannot sing very well. She is flat a good deal of the time. . . . She communicates almost nothing of the music she presents . . ."

It is a great tragedy that in this awful hour the people of the United States must accept in lieu of leadership the nasty malice of a president whom Bernard Baruch in a similar incident called a rude, uncouth, ignorant man. Let us pray.

WESTBROOK PEGLER, Public Statement, New York, 9 Dec., 1950. This was Pegler's reaction to Harry Truman's reaction to Paul Hume's review.

2

The trade of critic, in literature, music, and the drama, is the most degraded of all trades.

MARK TWAIN, *Autobiography,* vol. ii, p. 69.

3

You should not say it is not good. You should say you do not like it; and then, you know, you're perfectly safe.

J. MCNEILL WHISTLER. (DON SEITZ, *Whistler Stories*)

4

A certain columnist has been barred from all Shubert openings. Now he can wait three days and go to their closings.

WALTER WINCHELL, writing of himself. (SAMUEL HOPKINS ADAMS, *A. Woollcott, His Life and World,* ch. 6)

5

Unbridled enthusiasm, incredible elasticity, and tumultuous overpraise are distinguishing marks of the whole platoon. The dramatic

critics of New York, ranging as they do from the late twenties to the early eighties, and extraordinarily varied in their origins, education, intelligence, and personal beauty, are alike in one respect. They are all be-trousered Pollyannas.

ALEXANDER WOOLLCOTT, *Shouts and Murmurs* (1923).

CULTURE

6

The acquiring of culture is the developing of an avid hunger for knowledge and beauty.

JESSE LEE BENNETT, *On Culture.*

7

Culture is one thing, and varnish another.

EMERSON, *Journals,* 1868.

8

Culture with us . . . ends in a headache. . . . Do not craze yourself with thinking, but go about your business anywhere. Life is not intellectual or critical; but sturdy.

EMERSON, *Essays, Second Series: Experience.*

9

Culture implies all that which gives the mind possession of its own powers; as languages to the critic, telescope to the astronomer.

EMERSON, *Letters and Social Aims: Progress of Culture.*

10

The triumph of culture is to overpower nationality.

EMERSON, *Uncollected Lectures: Table-Talk.*

11

The essence of a self-reliant and autonomous culture is an unshakable egoism.

H. L. MENCKEN, *Prejudices,* ser. ii.

12

Culture is on the horns of this dilemma: if profound and noble it must remain rare, if common it must become mean.

GEORGE SANTAYANA, *The Life of Reason,* ii, 111.

13

The longing to be primitive is a disease of culture.

GEORGE SANTAYANA, *Little Essays,* p. 163.

14

Culture is the habit of being pleased with the best and knowing why.

HENRY VAN DYKE.

15

There's the long race to develop our culture. The whole story of thousands of years, Greece, Palestine, Magna Charta, the French Revolution, it's the story of a boy growing up, learning to straighten his shoulders. But we haven't learned enough yet to live side by side.

THORNTON WILDER. (FLORA LEWIS, *Thornton Wilder at 65; New York Times Magazine,* 15 Apr., 1962)

CUSTOM

See also Habit

1
The interrogation of custom at all points is an inevitable stage in the growth of every superior mind.

EMERSON, *Representative Men: Montaigne.*

2
Custom meets us at the cradle and leaves us only at the tomb.

ROBERT G. INGERSOLL, *Individuality.*

3
Custom has furnished the only basis which ethics have ever had.

JOSEPH WOOD KRUTCH, *The Modern Temper,* p. 13.

4
The custom of the country.

MARK TWAIN, *Innocents at Home,* ch. 10.

5
Old customs, habits, superstitions, fears,
All that lies buried under fifty years.

JOHN GREENLEAF WHITTIER, *The Countess.*

CYNICISM

6
A cynic can chill and dishearten with a single word.

EMERSON, *Society and Solitude: Success.*

7
Life is too short to waste
In critic peep or cynic bark,
Quarrel or reprimand:

'Twill soon be dark;
Up! mind thine own aim, and
God speed the mark!

EMERSON, *To J.W.*

8
Then why should I sit in the scorner's seat,
Or hurl the cynic's ban?
Let me live in my house by the side of the road
And be a friend of man.

SAM WALTER FOSS, *The House by the Side of the Road,* st. 5.

9
Cynicism is the intellectual cripple's substitute for intelligence. It is the dishonest businessman's substitute for conscience. It is the communicator's substitute, whether he is advertising man or editor or writer, for self-respect.

RUSSELL LYNES, Address: *How High Is the American Brow?,* 25 Apr., 1963.

10
When the twentieth century opened we Americans fooled ourselves by believing our world was better than it was. But now two generations later may we not be fooling ourselves by believing our world worse than it is?

REV. RALPH W. SOCKMAN, Commencement Address, New York University, 7 June, 1964.

11
The only deadly sin I know is cynicism.

HENRY L. STIMSON, *On Active Service in Peace and War:* Introduction.

D

DANCE

12
Waltz me around again, Willie, around and around and around,
The music is dreamy, it's peaches and creamy,
Oh! don't let my feet touch the ground!

WILL D. COBB, *Waltz Me Around Again, Willie* (1906).

13
Dancing as a career can represent freedom from sex. It can be a complete, though unconscious, substitute for physical love. Dance is the one physical performance for women that frees them from either moral responsibility or physical hazard.

AGNES DE MILLE. (JANE HOWARD, *The Grande Dame of Dance; Life,* 15 Nov., 1963)

14
Dancing is such a despised and dishonored trade that if you tell a doctor or a lawyer you do choreography he'll look at you as if you were a hummingbird. Dancers don't get invited to visit people. It is assumed a boy dancer will run off with the spoons and a girl with the head of the house.

AGNES DE MILLE. (JANE HOWARD, *The Grande Dame of Dance; Life,* 15 Nov., 1963)

15
Sometimes dancing and music can describe a true image of the customs of a country better than words in a newspaper.

GENE KELLY. (JOYCE BRINKLEY, *On a Culture Safari;* New York *Times,* 26 Jan., 1964)

16
When I was very young, I danced all day and sometimes all night. But the dancer is like the boxer . . . he has to have the discipline of constant training.

GENE KELLY. (JOYCE BRINKLEY, *On a Culture Safari;* New York *Times,* 26 Jan., 1964)

17
Merrily, merrily whirled the wheels of the dizzying dances

Under the orchard-trees and down the path
    to the meadows.
    HENRY WADSWORTH LONGFELLOW, *Evangeline*, pt. i, sec. 4.

1

o i should worry and fret
death and i will coquette
there's a dance in the old dame yet
toujours gai toujours gai
    DON MARQUIS, *archy and mehitabel*.

2

dance mehitabel dance
caper and shake a leg
what little blood is left
will fizz like wine in a keg
    DON MARQUIS, *archy and mehitabel*.

3

Dancing is wonderful training for girls, it's
the first way you learn to guess what a man
is going to do before he does it.
    CHRISTOPHER MORLEY, *Kitty Foyle*, ch. 11.

4

Casey would waltz with a strawberry
    blonde,
    And the band played on.
    JOHN F. PALMER, *The Band Played On* (set to music with lasting success in 1894 by Charles B. Ward).

DANGER

5

As soon as there is life there is danger.
    EMERSON, *Public and Private Education*.

6

All tools are in one sense edge-tools, and are
dangerous.
    EMERSON, *Society and Solitude: Works and Days*.

7

Young man, you are standing on the brink of
an abscess.
    ANDREW FREEDMAN, owner of the New York Giants baseball team, in 1898, to Charley Dryden, a sports writer who had offended him. (STANLEY WALKER, *City Editor*, p. 118)

8

I saw a delicate flower had grown up two
feet high between the horses' feet and the
wheel track. An inch more to the right or left
had sealed its fate, or an inch higher. Yet it
lived to flourish, and never knew the danger
it incurred. It did not borrow trouble, nor
invite an evil fate by apprehending it.
    HENRY D. THOREAU, *Journal*, Sept., 1850.

9

The most dangerous situation that humanity
has ever faced in all history.
    HAROLD C. UREY, *One World or None*, ch. 2.

DARKNESS

10

Come, blessed Darkness, come and bring thy
    balm
    For eyes grown weary of the garish day!
    JULIA C. R. DORR, *Darkness*.

11

The Dark at the Top of the Stairs.
    WILLIAM INGE, Title of play (1957).

12

Darkness of slumber and death, forever sinking and sinking.
    LONGFELLOW, *Evangeline*, pt. ii, sec. 5, 1. 108.

13

Lo! darkness bends down like a mother of
    grief
On the limitless plain, and the fall of her
    hair
It has mantled a world.
    JOAQUIN MILLER, *From Sea to Sea*, st. 4.

14

Darkness there, and nothing more.
    EDGAR ALLAN POE, *The Raven*, st. 4.

DAUGHTER

15

You appear to me so superior, so elevated
above other men; I contemplate you with
such strange mixture of humility, admiration,
reverence, love and pride, that very little
superstition would be necessary to make me
worship you as a superior being . . . I had
rather not live than not be the daughter of
such a man.
    THEODOSIA BURR, Letter to her father, Aaron Burr. (PARTON, *Life and Times of Aaron Burr*, ii, 188)

16

An undutiful Daughter will prove an unmanageable Wife.
    BENJAMIN FRANKLIN, *Poor Richard*, 1752.

17

Then farewell, my dear; my loved daughter,
    adieu;
The last pang of life is in parting from you.
    THOMAS JEFFERSON, *A Deathbed Advice from T.J. to M.R.*

18

If I had a daughter, I would bring her up as
a clinging vine.
    MARY LATHROP, first woman member of the American Bar Association.

DAWN
See also Day

19

Oh, say can you see by the dawn's early
    light,
What so proudly we hailed at the twilight's
    last gleaming?
    FRANCIS SCOTT KEY, *The Star-Spangled Banner*, st. 1.

1

Oft when the white, still dawn
Lifted the skies and pushed the hills apart,
I've felt it like a glory in my heart.
  EDWIN MARKHAM, *Joy of the Morning.*

2

Out of the scabbard of the night,
  By God's hand drawn,
Flashes his shining sword of light,
  And lo,—the dawn!
  FRANK DEMPSTER SHERMAN, *Dawn.*

3

What humbugs we are, who pretend to live
for Beauty, and never see the Dawn!
  LOGAN PEARSALL SMITH, *Afterthoughts.*

4

Day's sweetest moments are at dawn.
  ELLA WHEELER WILCOX, *Dawn.*

5

For what human ill does not dawn seem to
be an alleviation?
  THORNTON WILDER, *The Bridge of San
    Luis Rey.*

DAY

See also Dawn

6

Well, this is the end of a perfect day,
  Near the end of a journey, too;
But it leaves a thought that is big and
    strong,
  With a wish that is kind and true.
For mem'ry has painted this perfect day
  With colors that never fade,
And we find at the end of a perfect day,
  The soul of a friend we've made.
  CARRIE JACOBS BOND, *A Perfect Day.*

7

He is only rich who owns the day. There is
no king, rich man, fairy, or demon who possesses such power as that. . . . The days are
made on a loom whereof the warp and woof
are past and future time.
  EMERSON, *Society and Solitude: Works
    and Days.*

8

Write it on your heart that every day is the
best day in the year. No man has learned
anything rightly until he knows that every
day is Doomsday.
  EMERSON, *Society and Solitude: Works
    and Days.*

9

A day is a miniature eternity.
  EMERSON, *Journals,* vol. iv, p. 26.

10

This is my busy day.
  EUGENE FIELD, Notice above his desk at
    the Denver *Tribune,* 1882.

11

Out of the shadows of night
The world rolls into light;
  It is daybreak everywhere.
  HENRY WADSWORTH LONGFELLOW, *Bells of
    San Blas.*

12

One day, with life and heart,
Is more than time enough to find a world.
  JAMES RUSSELL LOWELL, *Columbus.*

13

This is another day! And flushed Hope
    walks
Adown the sunward slopes with golden
    shoon.
  DON MARQUIS, *This Is Another Day.*

14

Only that day dawns to which we are awake.
There is more day to dawn. The sun is but a
morning star.
  HENRY D. THOREAU, *Walden:* Conclu-
    sion.

15

Count that day lost whose low descending
    sun
Views from thy hand no worthy action
    done.
  UNKNOWN. (STANIFORD, *Art of Reading,*
    p. 27; Boston, 1803) This is a variant of
    a maxim whose first known use was in
    England in the late 17th century.

DEATH

See also Grave

16

When a pious visitor inquired sweetly,
"Henry, have you made your peace with
God?" he replied, "We have never quar-
relled."
  J. BROOKS ATKINSON, *Henry Thoreau, the
    Cosmic Yankee,* p. 29.

17

Why be afraid of death
As though your life were breath?
  MALTBIE D. BABCOCK, *Emancipation.*

18

I died in my boots like a pioneer
With the whole wide sky above me.
  STEPHEN VINCENT BENÉT, *The Ballad of
    William Sycamore.*

19

He cannot read his tombstone when he's
dead.
  BERTON BRALEY, *Do It Now.*

20

    All that tread
The globe are but a handful to the tribes
That slumber in its bosom.
  WILLIAM CULLEN BRYANT, *Thanatopsis.*

21

Loveliest of lovely things are they
On earth that soonest pass away.
  WILLIAM CULLEN BRYANT, *A Scene on the
    Banks of the Hudson.*

22

Raise then, the hymn to Death. Deliverer!
God hath anointed thee to free the op-
    pressed
And crush the oppressor.
  WILLIAM CULLEN BRYANT, *Hymn to
    Death,* 1. 33.

1

In death I desire that no one shall look upon my face and once more I charge my family, as already and repeatedly I have done, that they shall put on none of the bogus habiliments of so-called mourning. Folds of black crepe never ministered to the memory of the departed; they only made the wearers unhappy and self-conscious.

> IRVIN S. COBB, Letter written late in 1943, shortly before his death, to the editor of the Paducah (Ky.) *Sun-Democrat*, with instructions that it be sealed until his death.

2

How can I speak into a grave? How can I battle with a shroud? Silence is a duty and a doom.

> ROSCOE CONKLING, spoken after the assassination of Garfield. (STODDARD, *As I Knew Them*, p. 114)

3

So he died for his faith. That is fine—
More than most of us do.
But say, can you add to that line
That he lived for it, too?

> ERNEST CROSBY, *Life and Death*.

4

This quiet Dust was Gentlemen and Ladies,
And Lads and Girls;
Was laughter and ability and sighing,
And frocks and curls.

> EMILY DICKINSON, *This Quiet Dust*.

5

The world feels dusty
When we stop to die;
We want the dew then,
Honors taste dry.

> EMILY DICKINSON, *Poems*, p. 331.

6

The little toy dog is covered with dust,
But sturdy and stanch he stands;
And the little toy soldier is red with rust,
And his musket moulds in his hands.
Time was when the little toy dog was new,
And the soldier was passing fair;
And that was the time when our Little Boy Blue
Kissed them and put them there.

> EUGENE FIELD, *Little Boy Blue*.

7

When death puts out the flame, the snuff will tell
If we are wax or tallow, by the smell.

> BENJAMIN FRANKLIN, *Poor Richard*, 1739.

8

Why fear death? It is the most beautiful adventure in life.

> CHARLES FROHMAN, final words before going down with the *Lusitania*, 7 May, 1915. (Reported by Rita Jolivet)

9

A craven fear of death is entering the American consciousness; so much so that many recently felt that honoring the chief despot himself was the price we had to pay to avoid nuclear destruction.

> BARRY M. GOLDWATER, *The Conscience of a Conservative* (Macfadden ed., 1961; p. 90).

10

At my door the Pale Horse stands
To carry me to unknown lands.

> JOHN HAY, *The Stirrup Cup*.

11

Oh, nobody knows when de Lord is goin ter call, *Roll dem bones*.
It may be in de Winter time, and maybe in de Fall, *Roll dem bones*.
But yer got ter leabe yer baby and yer home an all—*So roll dem bones*.

> DUBOSE HEYWARD, *Gamesters All*.

12

Behold—not him we knew!
This was the prison which his soul looked through.

> OLIVER WENDELL HOLMES, *The Last Look*.

13

Whom the gods love die young no matter how long they live.

> ELBERT HUBBARD, *Philistine*, vol. xxiv, cover.

The good die young, so men have sadly sung
Who do not know the happier reason why
Is never that they die while they are young,
But that the good are young until they die.

> ARTHUR GUITERMAN, *Thus Spake Theodore Roosevelt*.

14

When death comes, he respects neither age nor merit. He sweeps from this earthly existence the sick and the strong, the rich and the poor, and should teach us to live to be prepared for death.

> ANDREW JACKSON, Letter: "My Dear E.," 12 Dec., 1824.

15

We are but tenants, and . . . shortly the great Landlord will give us notice that our lease has expired.

> JOSEPH JEFFERSON, Inscription on his monument at Sandwich, Cape Cod, Mass.

16

The problem is not the death of one man—the problem is the life of this organization.

> JOHN F. KENNEDY, Statement on the death of Dag Hammarskjöld, United Nations Secretary General. Upon Kennedy's death, these words were applied to the event by Adlai E. Stevenson in addressing the UN, 26 Nov., 1963.

1
To die with honor when one can no longer
live with honor.
> JOHN LUTHER LONG, *Madame Butterfly.*
> From an inscription on a samurai
> sword.

2
And, as she looked around, she saw how
    Death the consoler,
Laying his hand upon many a heart, had
    healed it forever.
> HENRY WADSWORTH LONGFELLOW, *Evangeline*, pt. ii, sec. v, 1. 88.

3
The young may die, but the old must!
> HENRY WADSWORTH LONGFELLOW, *The
> Golden Legend:* pt. iv, *The Cloisters.*

4
There is no confessor like unto Death!
    Thou canst not see him, but he is near:
Thou needst not whisper above thy breath,
    And he will hear.
> HENRY WADSWORTH LONGFELLOW, *The
> Golden Legend,* pt. v.

5
"O Caesar, we who are about to die
Salute you!" was the gladiators' cry
In the arena, standing face to face
With death and with the Roman populace.
> HENRY WADSWORTH LONGFELLOW, *Morituri Salutamus,* l. 1.

6
So Nature deals with us, and takes away
    Our playthings one by one, and by the
        hand
    Leads us to rest so gently, that we go
Scarce knowing if we wish to go or stay,
    Being too full of sleep to understand
        How far the unknown transcends the
            what we know.
> HENRY WADSWORTH LONGFELLOW, *Nature,*
> l. 9.

7
There is a Reaper, whose name is Death,
    And, with his sickle keen,
He reaps the bearded grain at a breath,
    And the flowers that grow between.
> HENRY WADSWORTH LONGFELLOW, *The
> Reaper and the Flowers.*

8
There is no Death! What seems so is transition;
    This life of mortal breath
Is but a suburb of the life elysian,
    Whose portal we call Death.
> HENRY WADSWORTH LONGFELLOW, *Resignation.*

9
As a former comrade in arms, his death kills
something within me.
> GENERAL DOUGLAS MACARTHUR, Public
> Statement on the assassination of John
> F. Kennedy, 22 Nov., 1963.

10
A piece of each of us died at that moment.
> MIKE MANSFIELD, Public Statement on
> the assassination of John F. Kennedy,
> 24 Nov., 1963.

11
A flame kindled of human decency, courage,
and dedication does not die.
> MIKE MANSFIELD, Eulogy on John F.
> Kennedy. Spoken in the Senate, 11
> Dec., 1963.

12
They are not dead; life's flag is never
    furled:
They passed from world to world.
> EDWIN MARKHAM, *Our Dead, Overseas.*

13
Death, however, Is a spongy wall,
Is a sticky river, Is nothing at all.
> EDNA ST. VINCENT MILLAY, *Moriturus.*

14
Death is but a name, a date,
A milestone by the stormy road,
Where you may lay aside your load
And bow your face and rest and wait,
Defying fear, defying fate.
> JOAQUIN MILLER, *A Song of Creation,*
> canto iv, st. 12.

15
O death where is thy sting? O grave where is
thy victory? Where, indeed? Many a badly
stung survivor, faced with the aftermath of
some relative's funeral, has ruefully conceded that the victory has been won hands down
by a funeral establishment—in disastrously
unequal battle.
> JESSICA MITFORD, *The American Way of
> Death.*

16
All victory ends in the defeat of death.
That's sure. But does defeat end in the victory of death? That's what I wonder!
> EUGENE O'NEILL, *Mourning Becomes
> Electra: Homecoming,* act iii.

17
Death is the scion Of the house of hope.
> DOROTHY PARKER, *Death.*

18
Life's race well run,
Life's work well done,
Life's victory won,
    Now cometh rest.
> Attributed to Dr. EDWARD HAZEN PARKER
> (by his brother), *Funeral Ode on President Garfield,* 1881. (*Notes and Queries,*
> vol. vii, p. 406) Also claimed for John
> Mills, an English banker of the same period.

19
Death is but crossing the world, as friends do
the sea; they live in one another still.
> WILLIAM PENN, *Fruits of Solitude.*

20
They that love *beyond* the *world,* cannot be
separated. Death cannot kill what *never* dies.

Nor can Spirits ever be divided that love and live in the *same* Divine Principle; the Root and Record of their *Friendship*.
> WILLIAM PENN, *Fruits of Solitude*, pt. ii.

1

And the fever called "Living"
Is conquered at last.
> EDGAR ALLAN POE, *For Annie*.

2

It's all a world where bugs and emperors
Go singularly back to the same dust.
> EDWIN ARLINGTON ROBINSON, *Ben Jonson Entertains a Man from Stratford*.

3

For a man who has done his natural duty, death is as natural and welcome as sleep.
> GEORGE SANTAYANA. (*Greatest Thoughts on Immortality,* p. 115)

4

Yes, all men are dust, but some are gold-dust.
> JOHN A. SHEDD, *Salt from My Attic*, p. 45.

5

Death is the mother of beauty; hence from her
Alone shall come fulfillment to our dreams.
> WALLACE STEVENS, *Sunday Morning*.

6

The report of my death was an exaggeration.
> MARK TWAIN, Cablegram from London to a New York newspaper, 2 June, 1897.

My attention has been directed to the footnote on page 312 of the fourth edition of *American Democracy in Theory and Practice,* which states that I died in 1962. This information is not in accord with the latest edition of the Congressional Directory, which indicates that I was re-elected in 1962 to be a Senator from Arizona for a term of six years.

P.S.: I have not as yet determined whether I will be a candidate for re-election to the United States Senate for a term beginning in January, 1969.
> CARL HAYDEN, Letter to the authors of the textbook cited, Marver H. Bernstein and Walter F. Murphy, 2 Apr., 1965. Senator Hayden was 87 at the time.

Thank you for your spirited letter informing us of our grave error in reporting your demise. Actually we caught the mistake just a shade after the book was published in 1963, and by exorcising it from later printings we hoped to shroud your eyes from our mistake. Clearly, however, our oversight has returned to haunt us, and we have had a pall over our lives knowing that we were unsuccessful in burying our error. On the other hand, we are delighted that the news of your death was greatly exaggerated, and we wish you the best of luck in your next campaign. It's obvious to us, at least, that your opponent won't stand a ghost of a chance.
> WALTER F. MURPHY and MARVER H. BERNSTEIN, Letter to Senator Carl Hayden, 6 May, 1965.

7

Each person is born to one possession which outvalues all the others—his last breath.
> MARK TWAIN, *Pudd'nhead Wilson's Calendar*.

8

All say, "How hard it is that we have to die"—a strange complaint to come from the mouths of people who have had to live.
> MARK TWAIN, *Pudd'nhead Wilson's Calendar*.

9

Death, the only immortal who treats us all alike, whose pity and whose peace and whose refuge are for all—the soiled and the pure, the rich and the poor, the loved and the unloved.
> MARK TWAIN, Memorandum written on his deathbed. (*Unpublished Diaries of Mark Twain*)

10

Joy, shipmate, joy!
(Pleas'd to my soul at death I cry,)
Our life is closed, our life begins,
The long, long anchorage we leave,
The ship is clear at last, she leaps!
She swiftly courses from the shore,
Joy, shipmate, joy!
> WALT WHITMAN, *Joy, Shipmate, Joy!*

11

Come lovely and soothing death,
Undulate round the world, serenely arriving, arriving,
In the day, in the night, to all, to each,
Sooner or later, delicate death.
> WALT WHITMAN, *Memories of President Lincoln*, sec. 14.

12

All goes onward and outward, nothing collapses,
And to die is different from what any one supposed, and luckier.
Has any one supposed it lucky to be born?
I hasten to inform him or her it is just as lucky to die, and I know it.
> WALT WHITMAN, *Song of Myself*, sec. 6–7.

13

My foothold is tenon'd and mortis'd in granite,
I laugh at what you call dissolution,
And I know the amplitude of time.
> WALT WHITMAN, *Song of Myself*, sec. 20.

14

Death softens all resentments, and the consciousness of a common inheritance of frailty and weakness modifies the severity of judgment.

JOHN GREENLEAF WHITTIER, *Ichabod:* Note.

1
'Tis infamy to die and not be missed.

CARLOS WILCOX, *The Religion of Taste.*

2
I think of death as some delightful journey
That I shall take when all my tasks are done.

ELLA WHEELER WILCOX, *The Journey.*

Death: Last Words

3
This is the last of earth! I am content.

JOHN QUINCY ADAMS, last words. (JOSIAH QUINCY, *Life of John Quincy Adams*)

4
Now comes the mystery.

HENRY WARD BEECHER, last words.

5
Tell mother—tell mother—I died for my country.

JOHN WILKES BOOTH, last words. (*Dictionary of American Biography*)

6
The South, the poor South.

JOHN C. CALHOUN, last words. (*Dictionary of American Biography*)

7
Remember, we meet again to celebrate the victory.

JOSEPH H. CHOATE, to Arthur Balfour, 13 May, 1917, the day before Choate's death; spoken at the close of exercises at the Cathedral of St. John the Divine. (MARTIN, *Life of Joseph Hodges Choate,* iii, 391)

8
A dying man can do nothing easy.

BENJAMIN FRANKLIN, last words, in reply to a suggestion by his daughter that he change his position in bed, so that he might breathe more easily.

9
Turn up the lights. I don't want to go home in the dark.

O. HENRY, last words. (C. A. SMITH, *O. Henry,* p. 250. The final part of the quotation is said to be based on a popular song of the period, 1910: "I'm Afraid to Go Home in the Dark.") A nurse who attended the dying author quoted him thus: "Put up the shades. I don't want to go home in the dark."

10
I strike my flag.

ISAAC HULL, last words.

11
I must arrange my pillows for another weary night.

WASHINGTON IRVING, last words.

12
Let us cross the river and rest in the shade.

GENERAL THOMAS JONATHAN (STONEWALL) JACKSON, last words.

13
I resign my spirit to God, my daughter to my country.

THOMAS JEFFERSON, last words.

14
Let the tent be struck.

GENERAL ROBERT E. LEE, last words.

15
It is God's way. His will, not ours, be done.

WILLIAM MCKINLEY, last words. (*Dictionary of American Biography*)

16
I always talk better lying down.

JAMES MADISON, last words.

17
Put out the light.

THEODORE ROOSEVELT, last words.

18
I leave this world without a regret.

HENRY DAVID THOREAU, last words.

19
It is well. I die hard, but am not afraid to go.

GEORGE WASHINGTON, last words.

20
I have known thee all the time.

JOHN GREENLEAF WHITTIER, last words, to his niece.

DEBT

See also Borrowing and Lending

21
Nothing (except having a baby) makes a woman feel more important than paying bills.

HAL BOYLE, Column, Associated Press, datelined New York, 21 Oct., 1964.

22
A man in debt is so far a slave.

EMERSON, *Conduct of Life: Wealth.*

23
One man thinks justice consists in paying debts. . . . But that second man . . . asks himself, Which debt must I pay first, the debt to the rich, or the debt to the poor? the debt of money, or the debt of thought to mankind?

EMERSON, *Essays, First Series: Circles.*

24
Always pay; for first or last you must pay your entire debt.

EMERSON, *Essays, First Series: Compensation.*

25
Wilt thou seal up the avenue of ill?
Pay every debt as if God wrote the bill!

EMERSON, *Suum Cuique.*

26
Rather go to bed supperless than rise in debt.

BENJAMIN FRANKLIN, *Poor Richard,* 1758.

1
The second vice is lying; the first is running in debt.
> BENJAMIN FRANKLIN, *The Way to Wealth*, i, 449.

2
A National debt, if it is not excessive, will be to us a national blessing.
> ALEXANDER HAMILTON, Letter to Robert Morris, 30 Apr., 1781.

At the time we were funding our national debt, we heard much about "a public debt being a public blessing"; that the stock representing it was a creation of active capital for the aliment of commerce, manufactures, and agriculture.
> THOMAS JEFFERSON, Letter to John W. Epps, 6 Nov., 1813.

The gentleman has not seen how to reply to this, otherwise than by supposing me to have advanced the doctrine that a national debt is a national blessing.
> DANIEL WEBSTER, Second Speech on Foote's Resolution, 26 Jan., 1830. (*Works*, iii, 303)

3
A mortgage casts a shadow on the sunniest field.
> ROBERT G. INGERSOLL, *About Farming in Illinois*.

4
Never spend your money before you have it.
> THOMAS JEFFERSON, *Writings*, vol. xvi, p. 111.

5
And looks the whole world in the face,
> For he owes not any man.
> HENRY WADSWORTH LONGFELLOW, *The Village Blacksmith*.

6
The Lord giveth and the landlord taketh away.
> JOHN W. RAPER, *Giving and Taking*.

DECEIT
See also Cheating; Hypocrisy; Lies and Lying

7
If Life's a lie, and Love's a cheat,
> As I have heard men say,
Then here's a health to fond deceit—
> God bless you, dear, today!
> JOHN BENNETT, *God Bless You, Dear, To-day*

8
Who hath deceived thee so often as thyself?
> BENJAMIN FRANKLIN, *Poor Richard*, 1738.

9
Which I wish to remark—
> And my language is plain,—
That for ways that are dark
> And for tricks that are vain,

The heathen Chinee is peculiar.
> BRET HARTE, *Plain Language from Truthful James*.

10
To be deceived in your true heart's desire
Was bitterer than a thousand years of fire!
> JOHN HAY, *A Woman's Love*.

11
Masters of Deceit.
> J. EDGAR HOOVER, Title of book (1958) on Communism in the United States and how to fight it.

12
You can fool some of the people all of the time, and all of the people some of the time, but you cannot fool all of the people all the time.
> ABRAHAM LINCOLN, Speech in Bloomington, Ill., 29 May, 1856. William P. Kellogg is the authority for this. Other students of Lincoln are in fundamental agreement about the substance of the quotation, but differ on the date and place of delivery. The quotation has also been attributed, much less frequently, to P. T. Barnum.

13
The lintel low enough to keep out pomp and pride:
The threshold high enough to turn deceit aside.
> HENRY VAN DYKE, *For the Friends at Hurstmont: The Door*.

DECEMBER
14
Ah, distinctly I remember it was in the bleak December.
> EDGAR ALLAN POE, *The Raven*.

15
The sun that brief December day
Rose cheerless over hills of gray,
And, darkly circled, gave at noon
A sadder light than waning moon.
> JOHN GREENLEAF WHITTIER, *Snow-Bound*.

DECISION, DETERMINATION
16
I answered that the die was now cast; I had passed the Rubicon. Sink or swim, live or die, survive or perish with my country was my unalterable determination.
> JOHN ADAMS, Conversation with Jonathan Sewall, 1774. (ADAMS, *Works*, vol. iv, p. 8)

17
He only is a well-made man who has a good determination.
> EMERSON, *Conduct of Life: Culture*.

18
I like the sayers of No better than the sayers of Yes.
> EMERSON, *Journals*.

1

How do you exert leadership over a business organization? You do not do it by sitting on a top floor behind a desk. Nor can you be expected to know everybody. But you understand the problems, and when you are confronted with one that requires a decision it is not put off and put off and put off. . . . My experience in business has been that and my experience here in the Senate has been that. One of [Robert A.] Taft's great attributes was that he made decisions. You never had to say, "Well, what are we going to do tomorrow?" He told you. That, to me, is leadership.

> BARRY M. GOLDWATER, *Goldwater Defines 'Conservatism'; New York Times Magazine*, 24 Nov., 1963.

2

He will not dither. He will decide. He will not agonize, he will act.

> HUBERT HUMPHREY, Speech to the annual convention of the National Association for the Advancement of Colored People, Washington, D.C., 23 June, 1964. He referred to Lyndon B. Johnson and the latter's role in pressing for civil-rights legislation.

3

Alibi Ike.

> RING LARDNER, Title of story.

4

Decide not rashly. The decision made Can never be recalled.

> HENRY WADSWORTH LONGFELLOW, *Masque of Pandora: Tower of Prometheus on Mount Caucasus.*

5

Once to every man and nation comes the
  moment to decide,
In the strife of Truth with Falsehood, for the
  good and evil side;
Some great cause, God's new Messiah, offering each the bloom or blight,
Parts the goats upon the left hand, and the
  sheep upon the right,
And the choice goes by forever 'twixt that
  darkness and that light.

> JAMES RUSSELL LOWELL, *The Present Crisis*, st. 5.

6

The greatest part of the President's job is to make decisions . . . He can't pass the buck to anybody.

> HARRY S TRUMAN, Address broadcast nationally from Washington, D.C., 15 Jan., 1953.

7

The buck stops here.

> UNKNOWN, Motto mounted on the desk of Harry S Truman while he was President, as a reminder of the ultimate responsibility inherent in that post. (*American Heritage*, Aug., 1964, p. 49)

DEEDS

See also Act, Action

8

The manly part is to do with might and main what you can do.

> EMERSON, *Conduct of Life: Wealth.*

9

As we are, so we do; and as we do, so is it done to us.

> EMERSON, *Conduct of Life: Worship.*

10

Do the thing and you have still the power; but they who do not the thing have not the power.

> EMERSON, *Essays, First Series: Compensation.*

11

Counsel that I once heard given to a young person, "Always do what you are afraid to do."

> EMERSON, *Essays, First Series: Heroism.*

12

We know better than we do.

> EMERSON, *Essays, First Series: The Over-Soul.*

13

Go put your creed into the deed,
Nor speak with double tongue.

> EMERSON, *Ode: Concord.*

14

While you do that which no other man can do, every man is a willing spectator.

> EMERSON, *Public and Private Education.*

15

Well done is better than well said.

> BENJAMIN FRANKLIN, *Poor Richard's Almanac*, 1737.

16

If you'd have it done, Go: if not, Send.

> BENJAMIN FRANKLIN, *Poor Richard's Almanac*, 1743.

17

Saying and doing have quarrelled and parted.

> BENJAMIN FRANKLIN, *Poor Richard's Almanac*, 1756.

18

I count this thing to be grandly true:
That a noble deed is a step toward God.

> JOSIAH G. HOLLAND, *Gradatim.*

19

The reward for a good deed is to have done it.

> ELBERT HUBBARD, *Philistine*, vol. xx, p. 139.

20

I strive for the best and I do the possible.

> LYNDON B. JOHNSON, a statement that appeared frequently in his speeches and conversations. (HENRY A. ZEIGER, *Lyndon B. Johnson: Man and President.* p 116)

1

I will do my best. That is all I can do. I ask
for your help and God's.
> LYNDON B. JOHNSON, conclusion of his
> first public statement as President, 22
> Nov., 1963. This was issued at Andrews
> Air Force Base, near Washington, D.C.,
> following his arrival from Dallas, the
> scene of the assassination of John F.
> Kennedy.

2

He who does something at the head of one
regiment will eclipse him who does nothing
at the head of a hundred.
> ABRAHAM LINCOLN, Letter to General
> Hunter.

3

Every guilty deed
Holds in itself the seed
Of retribution and undying pain.
> HENRY WADSWORTH LONGFELLOW, *The
> Masque of Pandora,* pt. viii.

4

But the good deed, through the ages
Living in historic pages,
Brighter grows and gleams immortal,
Unconsumed by moth or rust.
> HENRY WADSWORTH LONGFELLOW, *The
> Norman Baron.*

5

Whene'er a noble deed is wrought,
Whene'er is spoken a noble thought,
Our hearts, in glad surprise,
To higher levels rise.
> HENRY WADSWORTH LONGFELLOW, *Santa
> Filomena.*

6

Deeds are better things than words are,
Actions mightier than boastings.
> HENRY WADSWORTH LONGFELLOW, *The
> Song of Hiawatha,* pt. ix.

7

Thinking the deed, and not the creed,
Would help us in our utmost need.
> HENRY WADSWORTH LONGFELLOW, *Tales
> of a Wayside Inn: prelude,* l. 221.

8

Something attempted, something done,
Has earned a night's repose.
> HENRY WADSWORTH LONGFELLOW, *The
> Village Blacksmith.*

9

And what they dare to dream of, dare to
do.
> JAMES RUSSELL LOWELL, *Commemoration
> Ode.*

10

There's a man in the world who is never
turned down, wherever he chances to stray;
he gets the glad hand in the populous town,
out where the farmers make hay; he's greet-
ed with pleasure on deserts of sand, and deep
in the aisles of the woods; wherever he goes
there's the welcoming hand—he's the Man
Who Delivers the Goods.
> WALT MASON, *The Man Who Delivers the
> Goods.*

11

The dreaming doer is the master poet—
And lo, the perfect lyric is a deed!
> JOHN G. NEIHARDT, *The Lyric Deed.*

12

Space is as nothing to spirit, the deed is
outdone by the doing.
> RICHARD REALF, *Indirection.*

13

Your dad will never be reckoned among the
great. But you can be sure he did his level
best and gave all he had to his country.
There is an epitaph in Boothill Cemetery in
Tombstone, Arizona, which reads, "Here lies
Jack Williams; he done his damndest." What
more can a person do?
> HARRY S TRUMAN, Note to his daughter
> Margaret, written shortly before his sec-
> ond term as President expired early in
> 1953. (ALFRED STEINBERG, *The Man
> from Missouri,* p. 418)

14

A slender acquaintance with the world must
convince every man that actions, not words,
are the true criterion.
> GEORGE WASHINGTON, *Social Maxims:
> Friendship.*

15

Each crisis brings its word and deed.
> JOHN GREENLEAF WHITTIER, *The Lost
> Occasion,* l. 58.

16

Forget the poet, but his warning heed,
And shame his poor word with your nobler
deed.
> JOHN GREENLEAF WHITTIER, *The Panora-
> ma,* conclusion.

DEFEAT, see Failure
DELAY

See also Lateness, Procrastination

17

Delay is preferable to error.
> THOMAS JEFFERSON, *Writings,* vol. viii, p.
> 338.

18

Do not delay,
Do not delay: the golden moments fly!
> HENRY WADSWORTH LONGFELLOW, *The
> Masque of Pandora,* pt. vii.

19

Hurry up and wait.
> UNKNOWN, a familiar saying among en-
> listed personnel in the armed forces dur-
> ing World War II.

DEMOCRACY

See also Government, Voting

20

As the happiness of the people is the sole end

of government, so the consent of the people
is the only foundation of it, in reason, morality, and the natural fitness of things.

> JOHN ADAMS, Proclamation adopted by
> the Council of Massachusetts Bay,
> 1774.

1

The manners of women are the surest criterion by which to determine whether a republican government is practicable in a nation or
not.

> JOHN ADAMS, Diary, 2 June, 1778. (C. F.
> Adams, *Life of Adams*. Vol. iii, p. 171)

2

The declaration that our People are hostile
to a government made by themselves, for
themselves, and conducted by themselves, is
an insult.

> JOHN ADAMS, Address to the citizens of
> Westmoreland Co., Va., 1798.

3

Will anybody deny now that the Government at Washington, as regards its own people, is the strongest government in the world
at this hour? And for this simple reason, that
it is based on the will, and the good will, of
an instructed people.

> JOHN BRIGHT, Speech in Rochdale, Eng-
> land, 24 Nov., 1863.

4

The Ship of Democracy, which has weathered all storms, may sink through the mutiny
of those on board.

> GROVER CLEVELAND, Letter to Wilson S.
> Bissell, 15 Feb., 1894.

5

A monarchy is like a man-of-war,—bad shots
between wind and water hurt it exceedingly;
there is danger of capsizing. But democracy
is a raft. You cannot easily overturn it. It is
a wet place, but it is a pretty safe one.

> JOSEPH COOK, *Boston Monday Lectures:
> Labor.*

Fisher Ames expressed the popular security
more wisely, when he compared a monarchy
and a republic, saying that a monarchy is a
merchantman, which sails well, but will
sometimes strike on a rock and go to the
bottom; whilst a republic is a raft, which
would never sink, but then your feet are
always in the water.

> EMERSON, *Essays, Second Series: Politics.*

6

The governments of the past could fairly be
characterized as devices for maintaining in
perpetuity the place and position of certain
privileged classes. . . . The Government of
the United States is a device for maintaining
in perpetuity the rights of the people, with
the ultimate extinction of all privileged
classes.

> CALVIN COOLIDGE, Speech in Philadelphia,
> 25 Sept., 1924.

7

The government is a government of the people and for the people.

> THOMAS COOPER, *Some Information Re-
> specting America* (London, 1795).

8

One of the most difficult decisions the individual in a democracy faces is whether or
not he should forgo an immediate personal
gain or advantage for the good of his country.

> DWIGHT D. EISENHOWER, *Let's Be Honest
> with Ourselves; The Reader's Digest,*
> Dec., 1963.

9

Our democratic system rests on the premise
that the mass of democratic citizens will
make right decisions most of the time in response to critical issues—and that a device
exists by which the majority can reverse
wrong decisions.

> MILTON S. EISENHOWER, *The Need for a
> New American; The Educational Rec-
> ord,* Oct., 1963.

10

Most citizens have neither the knowledge
nor the wisdom to decide . . . issues wisely,
yet the burden of decision in a democracy is
inescapably ours. Nor is it an answer to say
we elect representatives to deal with such
problems, for often we know less about them
than we know about the issues; and they are
not inherently or invariably wise. Indeed,
they often must rely on specialists who disagree with each other and often cannot even
communicate with one another.

> MILTON S. EISENHOWER, *The Need for a
> New American; The Educational Rec-
> ord,* Oct., 1963.

11

The democrat is a young conservative; the
conservative is an old democrat. The aristocrat is the democrat ripe and gone to seed.

> EMERSON, *Representative Men: Napoleon.*

12

Democracy becomes a government of bullies
tempered by editors.

> EMERSON, *Journals,* vol. vii, p. 193.

13

Humanity is singing everywhere
All men are equal. Dupes of democracy!

> DONALD EVANS, *Bonfire of Kings.*

14

Democracy is based upon the conviction that
there are extraordinary possibilities in ordinary people.

> HARRY EMERSON FOSDICK, *Democracy.*

15

You cannot possibly have a broader basis for
any government than that which includes all
the people, with all their rights in their

hands, and with an equal power to maintain their rights.

> WILLIAM LLOYD GARRISON, *Life*, vol. iv, p. 224.

1

I don't object to a dictatorship as violently as some people do because I realize that not all people in this world are ready for democratic processes. . . . If they have to have a dictator in order to keep Communism out, then I don't think we can object to that.

> BARRY GOLDWATER, Statement on television program *Issues and Answers*, American Broadcasting Co., 7 Apr., 1963.

2

Would shake hands with a king upon his throne,
And think it kindness to his majesty.

> FITZ-GREENE HALLECK, *Connecticut*.

3

A representative democracy, where the right of election is well secured and regulated, and the exercise of the legislative, executive, and judiciary authorities is vested in select persons, chosen really and not nominally by the people, will, in my opinion, be most likely to be happy, regular, and durable.

> ALEXANDER HAMILTON, *Works*, vol. ix, p. 72.

4

Democracy—the ballot box—has few worshippers any longer except in America.

> DEAN W. R. INGE. (MARCHANT, *Wit and Wisdom of Dean Inge*. No. 216)

5

The republican is the only form of government which is not eternally at open or secret war with the rights of mankind.

> THOMAS JEFFERSON, Reply to Address, 1790.

6

I know no safe depository of the ultimate powers of society but the people themselves; and if we think them not enlightened enough to exercise their control with a wholesome discretion, the remedy is not to take it from them, but to inform their discretion by education.

> THOMAS JEFFERSON, Letter to W. C. Jarvis, 28 Sept., 1820.

7

Governments are republican only in proportion as they embody the will of the people, and execute it.

> THOMAS JEFFERSON, *Writings*, vol. xv, p. 33.

8

No government can continue good but under the control of the people.

> THOMAS JEFFERSON, *Writings*, vol. xv, p. 234.

9

The qualifications of self-government in society are not innate. They are the result of habit and long training, and for these they will require time and probably much suffering.

> THOMAS JEFFERSON, *Writings*, vol. xvi, p. 22.

10

Men, by their constitutions, are naturally divided into two parties: 1. Those who fear and distrust the people, and wish to draw all powers from them into the hands of the higher classes. 2. Those who identify themselves with the people, have confidence in them, cherish and consider them as the most honest and safe, although not the most wise, depository of the public interests. . . . In every country these two parties exist. . . . The appellation of Aristocrats and Democrats is the true one, expressing the essence of all.

> THOMAS JEFFERSON, *Writings*, vol. xvi, p. 73.

11

It is an axiom in my mind that our liberty can never be safe but in the hands of the people themselves.

> THOMAS JEFFERSON, *Writings*, vol. xix, p. 24.

12

I may not be a great President, but as long as I am here, I am going to try to be a good President and do my dead level best to see this system preserved, because when the final chips are down, it is not going to be the number of people we have or the number of acres or the number of resources that win; the thing that is going to make us win is our system of government.

> LYNDON B. JOHNSON, Interview televised nationally from Washington, D.C., 15 Mar., 1964. These were his concluding words.

13

In a democracy, the people have to want to do what must be done.

> LYNDON B. JOHNSON, Speech at graduation exercises of the National Cathedral School for Girls, Washington, D.C., 1 June, 1965.

14

Democracy which began by liberating man politically has developed a dangerous tendency to enslave him through the tyranny of majorities and the deadly power of their opinion.

> LUDWIG LEWISOHN, *The Modern Drama*, p. 17.

15

It is very easy to talk about being against communism. It is equally important to believe those things which provide a satisfying and effective alternative. Democracy is that satisfying, affirmative alternative.

> DAVID E. LILIENTHAL, Testimony before the joint Congressional Committee on Atomic Energy, 3 Feb., 1947.

1

The world will little note nor long remember what we say here, but it can never forget what they did here. . . . It is rather for us to be here dedicated to the great task remaining before us—that from these honored dead we take increased devotion to that cause for which they gave the last full measure of devotion; that we here highly resolve that these dead shall not have died in vain; that this nation, under God, shall have a new birth of freedom; and that government of the people, by the people, for the people, shall not perish from the earth.

> ABRAHAM LINCOLN, Address at Gettysburg National Cemetery, 19 Nov., 1863.

2

The Western liberal democracies are a declining power in human affairs. I argue that this is due to a derangement of the functions of their governments which disables them in coping with the mounting disorder. I do not say, indeed it is impossible to know surely, whether the malady can be cured or whether it must run its course. But I do say that if it cannot be cured, it will continue to erode the safeguards against despotism, and the failure of the West may be such that freedom will be lost and will not be restored again except by another revolution.

> WALTER LIPPMANN, The Public Philosophy (1955), ch. iii, sec. 2.

3

In the light of this monstrous crime, we can see that in a free country, which we are and intend to be, unrestrained speech and thought are inherently subversive. Democracy can be made to work only when the bonds of the community are inviolate, and stronger than all the parties and factions and interests and sects.

> WALTER LIPPMANN, Column, New York Herald Tribune, 26 Nov., 1963. The opening reference is to the assassination of John F. Kennedy.

4

Envy, the vice of republics.

> HENRY WADSWORTH LONGFELLOW, Evangeline, pt i, l. 35.

5

President Lincoln defined democracy to be "the government of the people, by the people, for the people." This is a sufficiently compact statement of it as a political arrangement. Theodore Parker said that "Democracy meant not 'I'm as good as you are,' but 'You're as good as I am.'" And this is

the ethical conception of it, necessary as a complement of the other.

> JAMES RUSSELL LOWELL, Essays: Democracy.

6

Democ'acy gives every man
The right to be his own oppressor.

> JAMES RUSSELL LOWELL, The Biglow Papers, Ser. ii. No. 7.

7

The government of the Union, then, is emphatically and truly a government of the people. In form and in substance it emanates from them. Its powers are granted by them, and are to be exercised directly on them and for their benefit.

> JOHN MARSHALL, Opinion in case of McCulloch vs. Maryland, 1819.

8

The most popular man under a democracy is not the most democratic man, but the most despotic man. The common folk delight in the exactions of such a man. They like him to boss them. Their natural gait is the goose-step.

> H. L. MENCKEN, Prejudices, ser. ii, p. 221.

9

The problem of democracy is not the problem of getting rid of kings. It is the problem of clothing the whole people with the elements of kingship. To make kings and queens out of a hundred million people: that is the Problem of American democracy.

> F. C. MOREHOUSE, The Problem of Democracy.

10

There is what I call the American idea. . . . This idea demands . . . a democracy,—that is, a government of all the people, by all the people, for all the people.

> THEODORE PARKER, Speech at Anti-Slavery Convention, Boston, 29 May, 1850.

For there is the democratic idea: that all men are endowed by their creator with certain natural rights; . . . that they are equal as men; . . . and therefore government is to be of all the people, by all the people, and for all the people.

> THEODORE PARKER, Address to the Anti-Slavery Society, Boston, 13 May, 1854.

Democracy is direct self-government, over all the people, for all the people, by all the people.

> THEODORE PARKER, Sermon at Music Hall, Boston, 4 July, 1858, later published as a pamphlet titled On the Effect of Slavery on the American People. Herndon, in his Life of Lincoln, relates that he gave a copy of the pamphlet to Lincoln and that the latter marked the passage quoted here.

1

The estate goes before the steward; the foundation before the house, people before their representatives, and the creation before the creator. The steward lives by preserving the estate; the house stands by reason of its foundation; the representative depends upon the people, as the creature subsists by the power of its creator.

WILLIAM PENN, *England's Present Interest Considered* (1674), p. 392.

2

We have sometimes been tempted to define democracy as an institution in which the whole is equal to the scum of all the parts.

KEITH PRESTON, *Pot Shots from Pegasus,* p. 138.

3

The whole thing is gloriously unpredictable, occasionally tragic, often frustrating and sometimes uproariously funny. How democracy works nobody quite knows. It is the worst system of government in the world, says Winston Churchill, "except all those other systems."

JAMES RESTON, Washington Column, New York *Times,* 20 Jan., 1964.

4

We must be the great arsenal of democracy.

FRANKLIN D. ROOSEVELT, Radio Address, 29 Dec., 1940.

5

Democracies are prone to war, and war consumes them.

W. H. SEWARD, *Eulogy on John Quincy Adams.*

6

In a government like ours, founded by the people, managed by the people.

JOSEPH STORY, *On the Constitution,* sec. 304.

7

He who would save liberty must put his trust in democracy.

NORMAN THOMAS. (*Saturday Review of Literature,* 7 June, 1930)

8

The people's government made for the people, made by the people, and answerable to the people.

DANIEL WEBSTER, Second Speech on Foote's Resolution, 26 Jan., 1830.

9

Thunder on! Stride on! Democracy. Strike with vengeful stroke!

WALT WHITMAN, *Rise O Days,* sec. 3.

10

I speak the pass-word primeval, I give the sign of democracy,

By God! I will accept nothing which all cannot have their counterpart of on the same terms.

WALT WHITMAN, *Song of Myself,* sec. 24.

11

In a self-governed country there is one rule for everybody, and that is the common interest. Everything must be squared by that. We can square it only by knowing its exact shape and movement.

WOODROW WILSON, Speech in Trenton, N.J., accepting the Democratic nomination for the governorship of New Jersey, 15 Sept., 1910.

12

I believe in Democracy because it releases the energies of every human being.

WOODROW WILSON, Address in New York, 4 Sept., 1912.

13

The beauty of a Democracy is that you never can tell when a youngster is born what he is going to do with you, and that, no matter how humbly he is born . . . he has got a chance to master the minds and lead the imaginations of the whole country.

WOODROW WILSON, Address in Columbus, Ohio, 10 Dec., 1915.

14

The world must be made safe for democracy.

WOODROW WILSON, War Address to Congress, 2 Apr., 1917.

The world that is safe for democracy and is safely democratic is shrunken. It is still shrinking.

WALTER LIPPMANN, *The Public Philosophy* (1955), ch. vi, sec. 2.

DESPAIR

15

Me too thy nobleness has taught
To master my despair;
The fountains of my hidden life
Are through thy friendship fair.

EMERSON, *Friendship.*

16

Despair ruins some, Presumption many.

BENJAMIN FRANKLIN, *Poor Richard,* 1747.

17

The mass of men lead lives of quiet desperation. What is called resignation is confirmed desperation. . . . A stereotyped but unconscious despair is concealed even under what are called the games and amusements of mankind.

HENRY D. THOREAU, *Walden,* ch. 1.

DESTINY

See also Circumstance, Fate, Fortune, Providence

18

Alas! that one is born in blight,
Victim of perpetual slight, . . .
And another is born
To make the sun forgotten.

EMERSON, *Destiny.*

1

The bitterest tragic element in life is the belief in a brute Fate or Destiny.

> EMERSON, *Natural History of Intellect: The Tragic.*

2

Art and power will go on as they have done, —will make day out of night, time out of space, and space out of time.

> EMERSON, *Society and Solitude: Works and Days.*

3

Earth loves to gibber o'er her dross,
  Her golden souls, to waste;
The cup she fills for her god-men
  Is a bitter cup to taste.

> DON MARQUIS, *Wages.*

4

Our manifest destiny to overspread the continent allotted by Providence for the free development of our yearly multiplying millions.

> JOHN L. O'SULLIVAN, *United States Magazine and Democratic Review,* vol. xvii, pp. 5–10, July-Aug., 1845. This first known published use of the familiar term "manifest destiny" appeared in an editorial by O'Sullivan, denouncing opposition to the annexation of Texas. The term became a stock phrase of advocates of American expansionism.

5

This generation of Americans has a rendezvous with destiny.

> FRANKLIN D. ROOSEVELT, Speech upon accepting renomination for a second presidential term, 27 June, 1936.

6

Allons! through struggle and wars!
The goal that was named cannot be countermanded.

> WALT WHITMAN, *Song of the Open Road,* Sec. 14.

7

The day we fashion Destiny, our web of Fate we spin.

> JOHN GREENLEAF WHITTIER, *The Crisis,* st. 10.

DIGNITY

8

We have exchanged the Washingtonian dignity for the Jeffersonian simplicity, which was in truth only another name for the Jacksonian vulgarity.

> BISHOP HENRY C. POTTER, Washington Centennial Service Address, New York, 30 Apr., 1889.

9

Our dignity is not in what we do, but what we understand.

> GEORGE SANTAYANA, *Little Essays,* p. 202.

10

Perhaps the only true dignity of man is his capacity to despise himself.

> GEORGE SANTAYANA, *Little Essays,* p. 230.

11

No race can prosper till it learns that there is as much dignity in tilling a field as in writing a poem.

> BOOKER T. WASHINGTON, *Up from Slavery.*

DIPLOMACY

12

Unhappily, amity is not the inevitable result of close relations between either people or peoples. Marriage and war lock both into close embrace. Sometimes the parties live happily ever after; sometimes they don't. So it is with allies.

> DEAN ACHESON, *Withdrawal from Europe? 'An Illusion'; New York Times Magazine,* 15 Dec., 1963.

13

International arbitration may be defined as the substitution of many burning questions for a smouldering one.

> AMBROSE BIERCE, *The Devil's Dictionary.*

14

In dealing with the Communists, remember that in their mind what is secret is serious, and what is public is merely propaganda.

> CHARLES E. BOHLEN, commenting from long experience in the Foreign Service. (James Reston, Washington Column, New York *Times,* 2 Jan., 1966)

15

United States foreign policy is going through its most difficult phase. Not only are we having trouble convincing our Western allies and our Latin American friends that we are doing the right thing, but we're having a heck of a time persuading our own university students and professors.

> ART BUCHWALD, Syndicated Column, 20 May, 1965. This was during the height of university-directed criticism of U.S. foreign policy in the Vietnamese and Dominican civil strife.

16

American diplomacy is easy on the brain but hell on the feet.

> CHARLES G. DAWES, American ambassador to Great Britain, Speech in Washington, 2 June, 1931.

It depends on which you use.

> HENRY PRATHER FLETCHER, commenting on Dawes's observation. The speaker was himself an American diplomat.

17

When I was in Paris last week, I said that . . . the United States would have to undertake an agonizing reappraisal of basic foreign policy in relation to Europe. This statement, I thought, represented a self-evident truth.

> JOHN FOSTER DULLES, Address to National Press Club, Washington, D.C., 22 Dec., 1953.

1

You have to take chances for peace, just as you must take chances in war. Some say that we were brought to the verge of war. Of course we were brought to the verge of war. The ability to get to the verge without getting into the war is the necessary art. If you cannot master it, you inevitably get into war. If you try to run away from it, if you are scared to go to the brink, you are lost. We've had to look it square in the face—on the question of enlarging the Korean War, on the question of getting into the Indochina war, on the question of Formosa. We walked to the brink and we looked it in the face. We took strong action.

> JOHN FOSTER DULLES. Quoted by JAMES SHEPLEY in *How Dulles Averted War. Life,* 16 Jan., 1956. This controversial enunciation of Dulles' policies as Secretary of State caused his critics to coin the term "brinkmanship" in describing them.

The art of diplomacy, especially in this atomic age, must lead to peace, not war or the brink of war.

> ADLAI E. STEVENSON, Statement in Chicago, 14 Jan., 1956, referring to the "brink of war" statement by John Foster Dulles.

2

Diplomacy is to do and say
The nastiest thing in the nicest way.

> ISAAC GOLDBERG, *The Reflex.*

3

The only summit meeting that can succeed is one that does not take place.

> BARRY M. GOLDWATER, *Why Not Victory?* (Macfadden ed., 1963, p. 45). Winston Churchill first used "summit," with reference to present-day diplomacy, in 1954, a year before the first such meeting.

4

You young men, you don't know how fortunate you are. All you have to do to get into the Foreign Service is to answer a few questions. I had to shoot a tiger.

> JOSEPH C. GREW, speaking to Foreign Service aspirants, and recalling his own first assignment, as clerk in the U.S. consulate in Cairo, in 1905. Grew had shot a tiger in China during a grand tour, a feat that impressed President Theodore Roosevelt and led to the appointment. (New York *Times* obituary of Grew, 27 May, 1965, p. 37)

5

Until points of gravest import yielded slowly
  one by one,
And by Love was consummated what Diplomacy begun.

> BRET HARTE, *Concepción de Arguello.*

6

There are three species of creatures who
  when they seem coming are going,
When they seem going they come: Diplomats, women, and crabs.

> JOHN HAY, *Distichs.*

7

I wish there were some giant economy-size aspirin tablet that would work on international headaches. But there isn't. The only cure is patience with reason mixed in.

> LYNDON B. JOHNSON, Speech in Belleville, Ill., during the presidential campaign, 21 Oct., 1964.

8

Let us never negotiate out of fear. But let us never fear to negotiate.

> JOHN F. KENNEDY, Inaugural Address, 20 Jan., 1961.

9

It is never too early to try; it is never too late to talk; and it is high time that many disputes on the agenda of this Assembly were taken off the debating schedule and placed on the negotiating table.

> JOHN F. KENNEDY, Address to General Assembly of the United Nations, 20 Sept., 1963.

10

European Councils, where artful and refined plausibility is forever called in to aid the most pernicious designs.

> RICHARD HENRY LEE, Speech in the House of Representatives.

11

Any results I may have obtained were not by diplomacy, sleight of hand, eloquence or charity.

> ROBERT MOSES, long a prominent—and controversial—figure in New York City affairs. (New York Times News Service dispatch, 1 Sept., 1965)

12

This is the devilish thing about foreign affairs: they are foreign and will not always conform to our whims.

> JAMES RESTON, Washington Column, New York *Times,* 16 Dec., 1964, p. 42.

13

The world is a very complicated place. I am skeptical of dealing with complicated situations in easy and dramatic phrases. Policy is not a matter of rhetoric but of right and wise conduct. When I write a sentence, I ask myself: "Is this really so?"

> DEAN RUSK. (E. W. KENWORTHY, *Evolution of Our No. 1 Diplomat; New York Times Magazine,* 18 Mar., 1962)

1

After four years at the United Nations, I sometimes yearn for the peace and tranquillity of a political convention.

ADLAI E. STEVENSON. (New York *Times, Ideas and Men,* 16 Aug., 1964)

2

A diplomat's life is made up of three ingredients: protocol, Geritol and alcohol.

ADLAI E. STEVENSON. (*New York Times Magazine,* 7 Feb., 1965, p. 22)

3

This Administration, we are told, has revised the traditional concept that a diplomat is someone sent to lie abroad for his country and believes he is sent abroad to drink for his country. "Think American" has for years been our envoys' instruction code. Now it's "Drink American."

C. L. SULZBERGER, Column, New York *Times,* 26 May, 1965, p. 46. The reference was to President Lyndon B. Johnson's urging that American wines be given preference at diplomatic functions at home and abroad. Sir Henry Wotton of England coined the maxim, "An ambassador is an honest man sent to lie abroad for the commonwealth" (1651).

4

'Tis our true policy to steer clear of permanent alliances, with any portion of the foreign world.

GEORGE WASHINGTON, Farewell Address, 17 Sept., 1796.

5

Why quit our own to stand upon foreign ground? Why, by interweaving our destiny with that of any part of Europe, entangle our peace and prosperity in the toils of European ambition, rivalship, interest, humor or caprice?

GEORGE WASHINGTON, Farewell Address, 17 Sept., 1796.

DISCONTENT

6

Discontent is the want of self-reliance: it is infirmity of will.

EMERSON, *Essays, First Series: Self-Reliance.*

7

The more discontent the better we like it.

EMERSON, *Papers from the Dial: A Letter.*

8

Man is not so far lost but that he suffers ever the great Discontent which is the elegy of his loss and the prediction of his recovery.

EMERSON, *Papers from the Dial: Thoughts on Modern Literature.*

9

The discontented Man finds no easy Chair.

BENJAMIN FRANKLIN, *Poor Richard,* 1753.

10

Let thy discontents be thy secrets.

BENJAMIN FRANKLIN, *Poor Richard,* 1758.

11

The splendid discontent of God
With Chaos, made the world;
And from the discontent of man
The world's best progress springs.

ELLA WHEELER WILCOX, *Discontent*

DISEASE

See also Doctors, Medicine

12

There are no such things as incurables; there are only things for which man has not found a cure.

BERNARD M. BARUCH, Address to the President's Committee on Employment of the Physically Handicapped, 30 Apr, 1954.

13

Like any other major experience, illness actually changes us. How? Well, for one thing we are temporarily relieved from the pressure of meeting the world head-on. . . . We enter a realm of introspection and self-analysis. We think soberly, perhaps for the first time, about our past and future. . . . Illness gives us that rarest thing in the world—a *second chance,* not only at health but at life itself!

DR. LOUIS E. BISCH, *Turn Your Sickness into an Asset; The Reader's Digest,* Nov., 1937, and reprinted Dec., 1963.

14

Illness knocks a lot of nonsense out of us; it induces humility, cuts us down to size. . . . When we are a bit scared the salutary effect of sickness is particularly marked. For only when the . . . gate grows narrow do some people discover their soul, their God, their life work.

DR. LOUIS E. BISCH, *Turn Your Sickness into an Asset; The Reader's Digest,* Nov., 1937, and reprinted Dec., 1963.

15

He seems a little under the weather, somehow; and yet he's not sick.

WILLIAM DUNLAP, *The Memoirs of a Water Drinker* (1836), i, 80.

16

Disease can carry its ill-effects no farther than mortal mind maps out the way. . . . Disease is an image of thought externalized. . . . We classify disease as error, which nothing but Truth or Mind can heal. . . . Disease is an experience of so-called mortal mind. It is fear made manifest on the body.

MARY BAKER EDDY, *Science and Health,* pp. 176, 411, 483, 493.

17

Sickness, sin, and death, being inharmonious, do not originate in God nor belong to His government. His law, rightly understood, destroys them.

MARY BAKER EDDY, *Science and Health*, p. 472.

1

It is dainty to be sick, if you have leisure and convenience for it.

EMERSON, *Journals*, vol. v, p. 162.

2

We er sorter po'ly, Sis Tempy, I'm blige ter you. You know w'at de jay-bird say ter der squinch-owls, "I'm sickly but sassy."

JOEL CHANDLER HARRIS, *Nights with Uncle Remus*, ch. 50.

3

A bodily disease which we look upon as whole and entire within itself, may, after all, be but a symptom of some ailment in the spiritual part.

NATHANIEL HAWTHORNE, *The Scarlet Letter*, ch. 10.

4

Some maladies are rich and precious and only to be acquired by the right of inheritance or purchased with gold.

NATHANIEL HAWTHORNE, *Mosses from an Old Manse: The Procession of Life*.

5

The higher you go in age the more humble you are and the better you're likely to be as a patient.

LIEUTENANT GENERAL LEONARD D. HEATON, U.S. Army Surgeon General, Interview reported by Associated Press, 7 Mar., 1964. He was commenting on Douglas MacArthur, then 84, on whom Heaton had just performed a major operation. He rated both MacArthur and Dwight D. Eisenhower, on whom he operated in 1956 for an intestinal obstruction caused by ileitis, "excellent patients."

6

If you feed a cold, as is often done, you frequently have to starve a fever.

BERNARR MACFADDEN, *When a Cold Is Needed; Physical Culture*, Feb., 1934.

7

Did you ever have the measles, and if so, how many?

ARTEMUS WARD, *The Census*.

8

A person's age is not dependent upon the number of years that have passed over his head, but upon the number of colds that have passed through it.

DR. SHIRLEY W. WYNNE, quoting Dr. Woods Hutchinson.

DOCTORS

See also Medicine

9

In the hands of the discoverer, medicine becomes a heroic art. . . . Wherever life is dear he is a demigod.

EMERSON, *Resources*.

10

Good is a good doctor, but Bad is sometimes a better.

EMERSON, *Conduct of Life: Considerations by the Way*.

11

When one's all right, he's prone to spite
The doctor's peaceful mission;
But when he's sick, it's loud and quick
He bawls for a physician.

EUGENE FIELD, *Doctors*.

12

He's the best physician that knows the worthlessness of the most medicines.

BENJAMIN FRANKLIN, *Poor Richard*, 1733.

13

He's a fool that makes his doctor his heir.

BENJAMIN FRANKLIN, *Poor Richard*, 1733.

14

Beware of the young doctor and the old barber.

BENJAMIN FRANKLIN, *Poor Richard*, 1733.

15

God heals, and the Doctor takes the Fee.

BENJAMIN FRANKLIN, *Poor Richard*, 1744.

16

If you must listen to his doubtful chest,
Catch the essentials and ignore the rest.
. . .
So of your questions: don't, in mercy, try
To pump your patient absolutely dry;
He's not a mollusk squirming in a dish,
You're not Agassiz, and he's not a fish.

OLIVER WENDELL HOLMES, *The Morning Visit*.

17

Talk of your science! after all is said
There's nothing like a bare and shiny head;
Age lends the graces that are sure to please;
Folks want their doctors mouldy, like their cheese.

OLIVER WENDELL HOLMES, *Rip Van Winkle, M.D.*, pt. ii.

18

A country doctor needs more brains to do his work passably than the fifty greatest industrialists in the world require.

WALTER B. PITKIN, *The Twilight of the American Mind*, p. 118.

19

The alienist is not a joke;
He finds you cracked and leaves you broke.

KEITH PRESTON, *The Alienist*.

20

Medicine men have always flourished. A good medicine man has the best of everything and, best of all, he doesn't have to work.

JOHN B. WATSON, *Behaviorism*, p. 4.

DOCTRINE

1
Doctrine is nothing but the skin of truth set up and stuffed.
> HENRY WARD BEECHER, *Life Thoughts*.

2
Any doctrine that will not bear investigation is not a fit tenant for the mind of an honest man.
> ROBERT G. INGERSOLL, *Intellectual Development*.

3
No doctrine, however high, however true, can make men happy until it is translated into life.
> HENRY VAN DYKE, *Joy and Power*.

4
Better heresy of doctrine, than heresy of heart.
> JOHN GREENLEAF WHITTIER, *Mary Garvin*.

DOGS

5
Old dog Tray's ever faithful,
  Grief cannot drive him away;
He's gentle, he is kind; I'll never, never find
  A better friend than old dog Tray.
> STEPHEN COLLINS FOSTER, *Old Dog Tray*.

6
It's good for him. And if you've ever followed dogs, you like to hear them yelp.
> LYNDON B. JOHNSON, Remark at press conference, Washington, D.C., 27 Apr., 1964, explaining why he had lifted one of his pet beagles by the ears. This was one of several instances of dogs figuring in controversial political news. Photographs of the dog, standing on its hind legs and with its ears in the President's hands, brought charges of mistreatment from veterinarians and many dog owners.

7
Killing the dog does not cure the bite.
> ABRAHAM LINCOLN.

8
Her new bark is worse than ten times her old bite.
> JAMES RUSSELL LOWELL, *A Fable for Critics*, l. 28.

9
The censure of a dog is something no man can stand.
> CHRISTOPHER MORLEY, *The Haunted Bookshop*, p. 193.

10
The dog is man's best friend.
He has a tail on one end.
Up in front he has teeth.
And four legs underneath.
> OGDEN NASH, *An Introduction to Dogs*.

11
One other thing I probably should tell you, because if I don't they'll probably be saying this about me too: We did get something—a gift—after the election. A man down in Texas heard Pat on the radio mention the fact that our two youngsters would like to have a dog. And, believe it or not, the day before we left on this campaign trip we got a message from Union Station in Baltimore saying they had a package for us. We went down to get it. You know what it was? It was a little cocker spaniel dog in a crate that had been sent all the way from Texas. Black and white spotted. And our little girl—Trisha, the six-year-old—named it Checkers. And you know the kids love the dog, and I just want to say this right now, that regardless of what they say about it, we're going to keep it.
> RICHARD M. NIXON, Speech broadcast nationally from Los Angeles, 23 Sept., 1952. After the disclosure that Nixon had received a special $18,235 "expense fund" from political supporters over a two-year period, his position as Vice Presidential candidate on the Republican ticket was challenged. In this speech, one of the high points of the 1952 campaign, he defended the contributions. The mention of the dog became one of the most memorable aspects of the controversial address, which is often referred to as the "Checkers speech."

12
These Republican leaders have not been content with attacks on me, on my wife, or on my sons. No, not content with that, they now include my little dog, Fala.
> FRANKLIN D. ROOSEVELT, Speech at Teamsters' dinner, Washington, D.C., 23 Sept., 1944. This was in reply to the charge that the President had sent a destroyer to the Aleutian Islands to fetch his Scotty, a dog famous in political history, at great expense to taxpayers.

13
No man who hates dogs or babies can be all bad.
> LEO ROSTEN, Remark at a Friars Club testimonial banquet for W. C. Fields, Hollywood, 1938. This is often incorrectly attributed to Fields himself. In a letter to the compiler, Rosten said, "I *think* the remark was entirely spontaneous, and one of those happy *ad libs* God sends you. I didn't have the faintest inkling that I would be called upon to make any remarks, and those I made were uttered in an almost total daze."

14
If you pick up a starving dog and make him prosperous, he will not bite you. That is the

principal difference between a dog and a man.

> MARK TWAIN, *Pudd'nhead Wilson's Calendar.*

1

Gentlemen of the Jury: The one absolutely unselfish friend that man can have in this selfish world, the one that never deserts him. the one that never proves ungrateful or treacherous, is his dog.

> GEORGE GRAHAM VEST, *Eulogy on the Dog.*

2

A reasonable amount o' fleas is good fer a dog—keeps him from broodin' over *bein'* a dog.

> EDWARD NOYES WESTCOTT, *David Harum,* p. 284.

3

My little old dog:
A heart-beat At my feet.

> EDITH WHARTON, *A Lyrical Epigram.*

4

I've got a lot of sympathy for people where a sudden change catches 'em—but I've always liked bird dogs better than kennel-fed dogs . . . one who'll get out and hunt for food rather than sit on his fanny and yell.

> CHARLES ERWIN WILSON, Remark at press conference, Detroit, 11 Oct., 1954. Wilson, then Secretary of Defense, was commenting on unemployment as a result of cutbacks in defense production. The comparison of men and dogs caused spirited controversy, which both President Eisenhower and Vice President Nixon attempted to assuage. Two days after the press conference, Wilson apologized for "inept remarks," at a dinner in Chicago. Earlier that day, in Detroit, after undergoing a physical checkup, Wilson jokingly told reporters that some of his colleagues "seem to think I have foot-in-mouth disease."

DOLLAR, THE

5

"The American nation in the Sixth Ward is a fine peopl " he says. "They love th' eagle," he says, "on the back iv a dollar."

> FINLEY PETER DUNNE, *Mr. Dooley in Peace and War: Oratory on Politics.*

6

The Americans have little faith. They rely on the power of the dollar.

> EMERSON, *Nature, Addresses and Lectures: Man the Reformer.*

7

You know a dollar would go much farther in those days.

> W. M. EVARTS, Remark to Lord Coleridge, at Mount Vernon. This was in response to the latter's observation that he had

heard that Washington was able to throw a dollar across the Potomac. (LUCY, *Diary of Two Parliaments*) Later, Evarts was quoted thus: "But I met a journalist just afterwards who said, 'Oh, Mr. Evarts, you should have said that it was a small matter to throw a dollar across the Potomac for a man who had chucked a Sovereign across the Atlantic.'" (*Collections and Recollections,* p. 181)

8

The almighty dollar, that great object of universal devotion throughout our land, seems to have no genuine devotees in these peculiar villages.

> WASHINGTON IRVING, *Wolfert's Roost: The Creole Village.* This first appeared in the *Knickerbocker Magazine,* Nov., 1836.

"The Almighty Dollar" is the only object of worship.

> UNKNOWN, Editorial, *Philadelphia Public Ledger,* 2 Dec., 1836.

9

Dollar Diplomacy.

> UNKNOWN. This term, dating from 1910, was applied to the policy of Secretary of State Philander Knox, whereby the interests of America were promoted through the investment of capital abroad. (*Harper's Weekly,* 23 Apr., 1910, p. 8)

DOUBT

See also Atheism, Heresy

10

There are minutes that fix the fate
　Of battles and of nations,
　(Christening the generations,)
When valor were all too late,
　If a moment's doubt be harbored.

> HENRY HOWARD BROWNELL, *The Bay Fight.*

11

I am the doubter and the doubt.

> EMERSON, *Brahma.*

12

Scepticism is unbelief in cause and effect.

> EMERSON, *Conduct of Life: Worship.*

13

Scepticism is slow suicide.

> EMERSON, *Essays, First Series: Self-Reliance.*

14

Doubt is the beginning, not the end, of wisdom.

> GEORGE ILES, *Jottings.*

15

Too much doubt is better than too much credulity.

> ROBERT G. INGERSOLL, *How to Reform Mankind.*

1
An honest man can never surrender an honest doubt.
 WALTER MALONE, *The Agnostic's Creed.*

2
   But the gods are dead—
Ay, Zeus is dead, and all the gods but Doubt,
And doubt is brother devil to Despair!
 JOHN BOYLE O'REILLY, *Prometheus: Christ.*

3
Four be the things I'd been better without:
Love, curiosity, freckles, and doubt.
 DOROTHY PARKER, *Inventory.*

4
The only limit to our realization of tomorrow will be our doubts of today. Let us move forward with strong and active faith.
 FRANKLIN D. ROOSEVELT, Address originally intended for national broadcast, 13 Apr., 1945 (the day following his death).

5
When in doubt tell the truth.
 MARK TWAIN, *Pudd'nhead Wilson's New Calendar.*

6
Ever insurgent let me be,
Make me more daring than devout;
From sleek contentment keep me free,
And fill me with a buoyant doubt.
 LOUIS UNTERMEYER, *Prayer.*

7
Doubt makes the mountain which faith can move.
 UNKNOWN, Toledo *Blade,* Jan., 1931.

DREAMS

8
Don't tell me what you dream'd last night, for I've been reading Freud.
 FRANKLIN P. ADAMS, *Don't Tell Me What You Dream'd Last Night* (music by Brian Hooker).

9
Let us go in and dance once more
On the dream's glimmering floor, . . .
 CONRAD AIKEN, *Nocturne of Remembered Spring.*

10
Back of the Job—the Dreamer
 Who's making the dream come true.
 BERTON BRALEY, *The Thinker.*

11
Ah, how the years exile us into dreams.
 JAMES CASSIDY, *Fire Island.*

12
I walked beside the evening sea
And dreamed a dream that could not be;
The waves that plunged along the shore
Said only: "Dreamer, dream no more!"
 GEORGE WILLIAM CURTIS, *Ebb and Flow.*

13
A crooked street goes past my door, entwining
 love of every land;
It wanders, singing, round the world, to Ashkelon and Samarkand.
To roam it is an ecstasy, each mile the easier it seems,
And yet the longest street on earth is this—the Street of Dreams.
 CHARLES DIVINE, *The Crooked Street of Dreams.*

14
Beautiful dreamer, wake unto me,
Starlight and dewdrop are waiting for thee;
Sounds of the rude world heard in the day,
Lulled by the moonlight have all passed away.
 STEPHEN C. FOSTER, *Beautiful Dreamer,* st. 1.

15
I dream of Jeanie with the light brown hair,
Borne like a vapor on the summer air;
I see her tripping where the bright streams play,
Happy as the daisies that dance on her way.
 STEPHEN C. FOSTER, *Jeanie with the Light Brown Hair.*

16
All men of action are dreamers.
 JAMES G. HUNEKER, *Pathos of Distance,* p. 111.

17
Reality rarely matches dream, but only dreams give nobility to purpose.
 LYNDON B. JOHNSON, Labor Day Address in Detroit, 7 Sept., 1964.

18
There's a long, long trail a-winding
 Into the land of my dreams,
Where the nightingales are singing,
 And a white moon beams.
There's a long, long night of waiting
 Until my dreams all come true,
Till the day when I'll be going down
 That long, long trail with you.
 STODDARD KING, *There's a Long, Long Trail* (music by Alonzo Elliott).

19
Is this a dream? Oh, if it be a dream,
Let me sleep on, and do not wake me yet!
 HENRY WADSWORTH LONGFELLOW, *The Spanish Student,* act iii, sc. 5.

20
Yet to have greatly dreamed precludes low ends.
 JAMES RUSSELL LOWELL, *Columbus.*

21
A house of dreams untold,
It looks out over the treetops,
And faces the setting sun.
 EDWARD MacDOWELL, *From a Log Cabin:* Heading. The lines are inscribed on a memorial tablet at his grave.

1

The more a man dreams, the less he believes.

H. L. MENCKEN, *Prejudices,* ser. ii, p. 101.

2

But that a dream can die will be a thrust
Between my ribs forever of hot pain.

EDNA ST. VINCENT MILLAY, *Here Is a Wound.*

3

A salesman is got to dream, boy. It comes with the territory.

ARTHUR MILLER, *Death of a Salesman:* requiem.

4

For a dreamer lives forever,
And a toiler dies in a day.

JOHN BOYLE O'REILLY, *The Cry of the Dreamer.*

5

He whom a dream hath possessed knoweth
no more of doubting.

SHAEMAS O'SHEEL, *He Whom a Dream Hath Possessed.*

6

That holy dream—that holy dream,
While all the world were chiding,
Hath cheered me as a lovely beam
A lonely spirit guiding.

EDGAR ALLAN POE, *A Dream.*

7

All that we see or seem
Is but a dream within a dream.

EDGAR ALLAN POE, *A Dream Within a Dream.*

8

Deep into that darkness peering, long I stood
there, wondering, fearing,
Doubting, dreaming dreams no mortal ever
dared to dream before.

EDGAR ALLAN POE, *The Raven.*

9

Meet me in Dreamland, sweet dreamy
Dreamland,
There let my dreams come true.

BETH SLATER WHITSON, *Meet Me Tonight in Dreamland.*

DRESS

See also Fashion

10

Bloomers.

The name derives from Mrs. Amelia Jenks Bloomer, American dress reformer, who first wore them in 1851. A knee-length skirt covered the bloomers (trousers cut full and gathered at the ankles).

11

Rags are royal raiment when worn for virtue's sake.

BARTLEY T. CAMPBELL, *The White Slave,* act 3.

12

Let him wear brand-new garments still,
Who has a threadbare soul, I say.

BLISS CARMAN, *The Mendicants.*

13

A petticoat is no great shakes after all, when
it hangs fluttering on a clothes line.

LORENZO DOW, *Potent Sermons,* iii, 133.

14

It is only when mind and character slumber
that the dress can be seen.

EMERSON, *Letters and Social Aims: Social Aims.*

15

The sense of being perfectly well-dressed gives a feeling of inward tranquillity which religion is powerless to bestow.

EMERSON, *Letters and Social Aims: Social Aims.* Emerson was quoting a woman of his acquaintance, said to have been Mrs. Helen Bell.

16

The least mistake in sentiment takes all the
beauty out of your clothes.

EMERSON, *Journal,* 1860.

17

There is one other reason for dressing well, namely that dogs respect it, and will not attack you in good clothes.

EMERSON, *Journal,* 1870.

18

They [the English] think him the best dressed man, whose dress is so fit for his use that you cannot notice or remember to describe it.

EMERSON, *English Traits,* p. 89.

19

The Frenchman invented the ruffle, the Englishman added the shirt.

EMERSON, *English Traits,* p. 89.

20

Many a one, for the sake of finery on the back, has gone with a hungry belly, and half-starved their families. "Silks and satins, scarlets and velvets, put out the kitchen fire," as Poor Richard says.

BENJAMIN FRANKLIN, *The Way to Wealth.*

21

Fond pride of dress is sure a very curse;
Ere fancy you consult, consult your purse.

BENJAMIN FRANKLIN, *The Way to Wealth.*

22

Eat to please thyself, but dress to please others.

BENJAMIN FRANKLIN, *Poor Richard,* 1738.

23

If you wear your cambric ruffles as I do, and take care not to mend the holes, they will come in time to be lace; and feathers, my dear girl, may be had in America from every cock's tail.

BENJAMIN FRANKLIN, Letter to his daughter, 3 June, 1779.

1

The things named "pants" in certain documents,
A word not made for gentlemen, but "gents."
> OLIVER WENDELL HOLMES, *A Rhymed Lesson*, l. 422.

2

Be sure your tailor is a man of sense;
But add a little care, a decent pride,
And always err upon the sober side.
> OLIVER WENDELL HOLMES, *A Rhymed Lesson*, l. 425.

3

A man made by God and not by a tailor.
> ANDREW JACKSON, referring to Sam Houston. (MCELROY, *Grover Cleveland*, ii, 258)

4

Tell him to go ahead with the blue suit. We can use that no matter what happens.
> LYNDON B. JOHNSON, Reply, to a query from a tailor from whom Johnson had ordered two suits shortly before the latter was stricken with a severe heart attack in July, 1955. While Johnson was in a Washington hospital, the tailor called to inquire whether he should proceed with the order. (HENRY A. ZEIGER, *Lyndon B. Johnson: Man and President*, p. 59)

5

It's not the skirt that breaks papa, it's the chiffon ruffles.
> F. M. KNOWLES, *A Cheerful Year Book.*

6

Well, that's about it. That's what we have and that's what we owe. It isn't very much, but Pat and I have the satisfaction that every dime that we've got is honestly ours. I should say this—that Pat doesn't have a mink coat. But she does have a respectable Republican cloth coat. And I always tell her that she'd look good in anything.
> RICHARD M. NIXON, Speech broadcast nationally from Los Angeles, 23 Sept., 1952. This was the famous talk in which Nixon, then the Republican vice-presidential candidate, gave an accounting of his financial affairs, after it was disclosed that he had received a special expense fund of $18,235 from California supporters during a two-year period in the early 1950's. "Pat" is Nixon's wife. Mink coats became synonymous with corruption in the Truman administration, then coming to a close. The term "Republican cloth coat" was later used derisively by the Democrats during the succeeding Republican administration.

7

Where did you get that hat?
Where did you get that tile?
Isn't it a nobby one,
And just the proper style?
> JOSEPH J. SULLIVAN, *Where Did You Get That Hat?*, a popular song, written in 1888.

8

As for Clothing, . . . perhaps we are led oftener by the love of novelty and a regard for the opinions of men, in procuring it, than by a true utility.
> HENRY D. THOREAU, *Walden*, ch. 1.

9

I say, beware of all enterprises that require new clothes, and not rather a new wearer of clothes.
> HENRY D. THOREAU, *Walden*, ch. 1.

10

No man ever stood the lower in my estimation for having a patch in his clothes; yet I am sure that there is a greater anxiety, commonly, to have fashionable, or at least clean and unpatched clothes, than to have a sound conscience.
> HENRY D. THOREAU, *Walden*, ch. 1.

11

Clothes introduced sewing, a kind of work which you may call endless; a woman's dress, at least, is never done.
> HENRY D. THOREAU, *Walden*, ch. 1.

12

Costume is not dress.
> J. MCNEILL WHISTLER, *"Ten O'Clock."*

DRINKING

See also Ale and Beer, Drunkenness, Wine

13

Fill up the goblet and reach to me some!
Drinking makes wise, but dry fasting makes glum.
> W. R. ALGER, *Oriental Poetry: Wine Song of Kaitmas.*

14

I am willing to taste any drink once.
> JAMES BRANCH CABELL, *Jurgen*, p. 6.

15

For though within this bright seductive place
My dollars go not far,
I never more shall see them face to face,
When they have crossed the bar!
> BLISS CARMAN, *Crossing the Bar.*

16

He seldom went up to town without coming down "three sheets in the wind."
> R. H. DANA, *Two Years Before the Mast*, ch. 20.

17

Among the Indians of the extreme north . . . there is a liquor made which . . . is called hoochinoo. The ingredients . . . are simple and innocent, being only yeast, flour, and either sugar or molasses.
> EDWARD R. EMERSON, *Beverages, Past and Present.* In a more highly developed civilization this became "hooch."

1
The peculiar charm of alcohol lies in the sense of careless well-being and bodily and mental comfort which it creates. It unburdens the individual of his cares and his fears. . . . Under such conditions it is easy to laugh or to weep, to love or to hate, not wisely but too well.
DR. HAVEN EMERSON, *Alcohol and Man.*

2
Many estates are spent in the getting,
Since women for tea forsook spinning and
knitting,
And men for punch forsook hewing and
splitting.
BENJAMIN FRANKLIN, *The Way to Wealth,* vol. i, p. 446.

3
Some say three fingers, some sav two;
I'll leave the choice to you.
JOHN HAY, *The Mystery of Gilgal,* st. 5.

4
I saved shoe-leather by keeping one foot on the foot-rest.
O. HENRY, *The Four Million: Memoirs of a Yellow Dog.*

5
Drink always rubbed him the right way.
O. HENRY, *The Rubaiyat of a Scotch Highball.*

6
If wine tells truth,—and so have said the
wise,—
It makes me laugh to think how brandy lies!
OLIVER WENDELL HOLMES, *The Banker's Secret,* l. 161.

7
The warm, champagny, old-particular, brandy-punchy feeling.
OLIVER WENDELL HOLMES, *Nux Postcoenatica.*

8
For it's always fair weather
When good fellows get together,
With a stein on the table and a good song
ringing clear.
RICHARD HOVEY, *Spring.*

9
The Elixir of Perpetual Youth,
Called Alcohol.
HENRY WADSWORTH LONGFELLOW, *The Golden Legend,* pt. i.

10
Touch the goblet no more!
It will make thy heart sore
To its very core!
HENRY WADSWORTH LONGFELLOW, *The Golden Legend,* pt. i.

11
I've made it a rule never to drink by daylight and never to refuse a drink after dark.
H. L. MENCKEN.

12
What makes the cider blow its cork
With such a merry din?

What makes those little bubbles rise
And dance like harlequin?
It is the fatal apple, boys,
The fruit of human sin.
CHRISTOPHER MORLEY, *A Glee Upon Cider.*

13
Candy Is dandy
But liquor Is quicker.
OGDEN NASH, *Reflection on Ice-Breaking.*

14
The great
Should be as large in liquor as in love.
EDWIN ARLINGTON ROBINSON, *Ben Jonson Entertains a Man from Stratford.*

15
At the punch-bowl's brink,
Let the thirsty think
What they say in Japan:
"First the man takes a drink,
Then the drink takes a drink,
Then the drink takes the man!"
E. R. SILL, *An Adage from the Orient.*

16
The vials of summer never made a man sick, but those which he stored in his cellar. Drink the wines, not of your bottling, but Nature's bottling; not kept in goat-skins or pig-skins, but the skins of a myriad fair berries.
HENRY D. THOREAU, *Journal,* 23 Aug., 1853.

17
They drink with impunity, or anybody who invites them.
ARTEMUS WARD, *Moses the Sassy: Programme.*

18
It is rarely seldum that I seek consolation in the Flowin Bole.
ARTEMUS WARD, *On "Forts."*

19
Said Aristotle unto Plato,
"Have another sweet potato?"
Said Plato unto Aristotle,
"Thank you, I prefer the bottle."
OWEN WISTER, *Philosophy 4.* Quoted.

20
Father, dear father, come home with me
now!
The clock in the steeple strikes one.
HENRY CLAY WORK, *Come Home, Father.*
Published in 1862, this soon became a
classic temperance song. In the second
verse, the clock strikes two, and in the
third it strikes three; meanwhile the
baby has died.

21
The Lips That Touch Liquor Must Never Touch Mine.
GEORGE W. YOUNG, Title and refrain of song (c. 1870).

22
The great utility of rum has given it the medical name of an antifogmatic. The quan-

tity taken every morning is in exact proportion to the thickness of the fog.

UNKNOWN, *Massachusetts Spy*, 12 Nov., 1789.

1

It's a long time between drinks.

UNKNOWN. According to tradition this remark, which antedates the Civil War, was made during a conference between the governors of the Carolinas. Nothing in historical record substantiates that, though there are many accounts that attribute the remark to individual governors of the two states.

DRUNKENNESS

2

Boy, us for plain myrtle, while under this fertile
Old grapevine myself I seclude,
For you and bibacious young Quintus Horatius—
Stewed.

FRANKLIN P. ADAMS, *Persicos Odi*.

3

A dark brown taste, a burning thirst,
A head that's ready to split and burst.

GEORGE ADE, *Remorse*, from *The Sultan of Sulu*.

4

The water-wagon is the place for me!
Last night my feelings were immense;
Today I feel like thirty cents!
No time for mirth, no time for laughter—
The cold gray dawn of the morning after.

GEORGE ADE, *Remorse*, from *The Sultan of Sulu*.

5

The best audience is one that is intelligent, well-educated—and a little drunk.

ALBEN W. BARKLEY, quoted by Adlai E. Stevenson. (New York *Times*, 15 Feb., 1965, p. 15)

6

One evening in October,
When I was far from sober,
And dragging home a load with manly pride,
My feet began to stutter,
So I laid down in the gutter,
And a pig came up and parked right by my side.
Then I warbled, "It 's fair weather
When good fellows get together,"
Till a lady passing by was heard to say:
"You can tell a man who boozes
By the company he chooses."
Then the pig got up and slowly walked away.

BENJAMIN H. BURT. (DE WOLF HOPPER, *Once a Clown, Always a Clown*, p. 237)

7

People can't tell us apart, we stagger so much alike.

FINLEY PETER DUNNE, *Cross-Examinations*.

8

The secret of drunkenness is that it insulates us in thought, whilst it unites us in feeling.

EMERSON, *Journal*, 1857. This is quoted from a letter from a man identified as "George R---, of Madison, Wis."

9

There is this to be said in favor of drinking, that it takes the drunkard first out of society, then out of the world.

EMERSON, *Journal*, 1866.

10

How gracious those dews of solace that over my senses fall
At the clink of the ice in the pitcher the boy brings up the hall.

EUGENE FIELD, *The Clink of the Ice*.

11

Since the creation of the world there has been no tyrant like Intemperance, and no slaves so cruelly treated as his.

WILLIAM LLOYD GARRISON, *Life*, vol. i, p. 268.

12

Licker talks mighty loud w'en it git loose from de jug.

JOEL CHANDLER HARRIS, *Plantation Proverbs*.

13

Alcoholic psychosis is nothin' more or less'n ole D.T.'s in a dinner suit.

KIN HUBBARD, *Abe Martin's Broadcast*, p. 20.

14

Every man that had any respect for himself would have got drunk, as was the custom of the country on all occasions of public moment.

MARK TWAIN, *Innocents at Home*, ch. 10.

DUTY

15

He who is false to present duty breaks a thread in the loom, and will find the flaw when he may have forgotten its cause.

HENRY WARD BEECHER, *Life Thoughts*.

16

God has never failed to make known to me the path of duty.

GROVER CLEVELAND, Letter, 18 Mar., 1906.

17

What I must do is all that concerns me, not what the people think.

EMERSON, *Essays, First Series: Self-Reliance*.

18

So nigh is grandeur to our dust,
So near is God to man,

When Duty whispers low, *Thou must*,
The youth replies, *I can*.
  EMERSON, *Voluntaries*, st. iii, l. 13.

1
He were n't no saint,—but at jedgment
  I'd run my chance with Jim,
'Longside of some pious gentlemen
  That wouldn't shook hands with him.
He seen his duty, a dead-sure thing,—
  And went for it thar and then;
And Christ ain't a-going to be too hard
  On a man that died for men.
  JOHN HAY, *Jim Bludso*.

2
No one will consider the day as ended, until
the duties it brings have been discharged.
  GENERAL JOSEPH HOOKER, Order, upon
    taking command of the Dept. of the
    Northwest, 1865.

3
I slept, and dreamed that life was Beauty;
I woke, and found that life was Duty.
  ELLEN STURGIS HOOPER, *Beauty and Duty*.

4
The straightest path perhaps which may be
    sought,
Lies through the great highway men call "I
    ought."
  ELLEN STURGIS HOOPER, *The Straight
    Road*.

5
Duty then is the sublimest word in our language. Do your duty in all things. You cannot do more. You should never wish to do
less.
  ROBERT E. LEE. This is inscribed beneath
    his bust in the Hall of Fame.

6
For the day never comes when it'll du
To kick off Dooty like a worn-out shoe.
  JAMES RUSSELL LOWELL, *Biglow Papers*,
    ser. ii, No. 11.

7
Duty—honor—country. Those three hallowed words reverently dictate what you
ought to be, what you can be, what you will
be. They are your rallying points: to build
courage when courage seems to fail; to regain faith when there seems to be little cause
for faith; to create hope when hope becomes
forlorn.
  GENERAL DOUGLAS MACARTHUR, Address
    to cadets and graduates, U.S. Military
    Academy, West Point, 12 May, 1962
    (his final visit there). The academy's

coat of arms bears the motto "Duty,
Honor, Country."

8
Duty determines destiny.
  WILLIAM MCKINLEY, Speech in Chicago,
    19 Oct., 1898.

9
When Duty comes a-knocking at your gate,
Welcome him in; for if you bid him wait,
He will depart only to come once more
And bring seven other duties to your door.
  EDWIN MARKHAM, *Duty*.

10
If a sense of duty tortures a man, it also
enables him to achieve prodigies.
  H. L. MENCKEN, *Prejudices*, ser. i, p. 64.

11
A categorical imperative crying in the wilderness, a duty which nobody need listen to,
or suffer from disregarding, seemed rather a
forlorn authority.
  GEORGE SANTAYANA, *Essays: Kant*.

12
It is my belief that every freedom, every
right, every privilege, has its price, its corresponding duty, without which it cannot be
enjoyed.
  HENRY A. WALLACE, Address to Free
    World Association, New York City, 8
    May, 1942.

13
A sense of duty pursues us ever. It is omnipresent, like the Deity. If we take to ourselves the wings of the morning, and dwell in
the uttermost parts of the sea, duty performed or duty violated is still with us, for
our happiness or our misery. If we say the
darkness shall cover us, in the darkness as in
the light our obligations are yet with us.
  DANIEL WEBSTER, Argument on the Mur-
    der of Captain White.

14
Simple duty hath no place for fear.
  JOHN GREENLEAF WHITTIER, *Abraham
    Davenport* (last line).

15
There's life alone in duty done,
  And rest alone in striving.
  JOHN GREENLEAF WHITTIER, *The Drovers*.

16
There is no question what the roll of honor
in America is. The roll of honor consists of
the names of men who have squared their
conduct by ideals of duty.
  WOODROW WILSON, Speech in Washington,
    27 Feb., 1916.

E

EARS

17
The hearing ear is always found close to the
speaking tongue.
  EMERSON, *English Traits*, ch. 4.

18
The ear is the only true writer and the only
true reader. I have known people who could
read without hearing the sentence sounds and
they were the fastest readers. Eye readers we

call them. They can get the meaning by glances. But they are bad readers because they miss the best part of what a good writer puts into his work.

ROBERT FROST. (MARGARET BARTLETT ANDERSON, *Robert Frost and John Bartlett*, 1963)

1
Calm on the listening ear of night
    Come Heaven's melodious strains,
Where wild Judea stretches far
    Her silver-mantled plains.
    EDMUND HAMILTON SEARS, *Christmas Song.*

EARTH
See also World

2
Earth is but the frozen echo of the silent voice of God.
    SAMUEL M. HAGEMAN, *Silence.*

3
In great matters and small, we must move forward together. There is no other way for us all on this small planet.
    LYNDON B. JOHNSON, Address at White House to 113 diplomats representing foreign lands, 13 Dec., 1963.

4
O maternal earth which rocks the fallen leaf to sleep!
    EDGAR LEE MASTERS, *The Spoon River Anthology: Washington McNeely.*

5
Man makes a great fuss
About this planet
Which is only a ball-bearing
In the hub of the universe.
    CHRISTOPHER MORLEY, *The Hubbub of the Universe.*

6
Visit to a Small Planet.
    GORE VIDAL, Title of play (1957), a satiric comedy about a man from outer space who visits the earth.

7
Christ's love and Homer's art
Are but the workings of her heart.
    JOHN HALL WHEELOCK, *Earth.*

8
Yea, the quiet and cool sod
Bears in her breast the dream of God.
    JOHN HALL WHEELOCK, *Earth.*

9
The earth, that is sufficient,
I do not want the constellations any nearer,
I know they are very well where they are,
I know they suffice for those who belong to them.
    WALT WHITMAN, *Leaves of Grass: Song of the Open Road.*

10
In this broad earth of ours,
Amid the measureless grossness and the slag,

Enclosed and safe within its central heart,
Nestles the seed perfection.
    WALT WHITMAN, *Leaves of Grass: Song of the Universal.*

11
The green earth sends her incense up
    From many a mountain shrine;
From folded leaf and dewy cup
    She pours her sacred wine.
    JOHN GREENLEAF WHITTIER, *The Worship of Nature*, st. 5.

EASTER

12
Tomb, thou shalt not hold Him longer;
Death is strong, but Life is stronger;
Stronger than the dark, the light;
Stronger than the wrong, the right;
Faith and Hope triumphant say
Christ will rise on Easter Day.
    PHILLIPS BROOKS, *An Easter Carol.*

13
'Twas Easter Sunday. The full blossomed trees
Filled all the air with fragrance and with joy.
    HENRY WADSWORTH LONGFELLOW, *The Spanish Student*, act i, sc. 3.

14
O chime of sweet Saint Charity,
    Peal soon that Eastern morn
When Christ for all shall risen be,
    And in all hearts new-born!
    JAMES RUSSELL LOWELL, *Godminster Chimes*, st. 7.

15
Lift your glad voices in triumph on high,
For Jesus hath risen, and man cannot die.
    HENRY WARE, JR., *Lift Your Glad Voices.*

EATING

16
All people are made alike.
They are made of bones, flesh and dinners.
Only the dinners are different.
    GERTRUDE LOUISE CHENEY, *People.* Written in 1927 when the author was aged nine.

17
Not for renewal, but for eating's sake,
They stuff their bellies with to-morrow's ache.
    EDMUND VANCE COOKE, *From the Book of Extenuations: Lazarus.*

18
My dinners have never interfered with my business. They have been my recreation. . . . A public banquet, if eaten with thought and care, is no more of a strain than a dinner at home.
    CHAUNCEY DEPEW, Interview, on his 80th birthday.

19
Taking food and drink is a great enjoyment for healthy people, and those who do not

enjoy eating seldom have much capacity for enjoyment or usefulness of any sort.

CHARLES W. ELIOT, *The Happy Life.*

1

Let the stoics say what they please, we do not eat for the good of living, but because the meat is savory and the appetite is keen.

EMERSON, *Essays, Second Series: Nature.*

2

Men are . . . conservatives after dinner.

EMERSON, *Essays, Second Series: New England Reformers.*

3

The way to a man's heart is through his stomach.

FANNY FERN, *Willis Parton.*

4

When I demanded of my friend what viands he preferred,
He quoth: "A large cold bottle, and a small hot bird!"

EUGENE FIELD, *The Bottle and the Bird.*

5

Eat to live, and not live to eat.

BENJAMIN FRANKLIN, *Poor Richard,* 1733.

6

A fat kitchen, a lean will.

BENJAMIN FRANKLIN, *Poor Richard,* 1733.

7

To lengthen thy life, lessen thy meals.

BENJAMIN FRANKLIN, *Poor Richard,* 1733.

8

What one relishes, nourishes.

BENJAMIN FRANKLIN, *Poor Richard,* 1734.

9

Bad commentators spoil the best of books,
So God sends meat, (they say,) the devil cooks.

BENJAMIN FRANKLIN, *Poor Richard,* 1735.

10

I saw few die of hunger; of eating, a hundred thousand.

BENJAMIN FRANKLIN, *Poor Richard,* 1736.

11

Who dainties love, shall Beggars prove.

BENJAMIN FRANKLIN, *Poor Richard,* 1749.

12

If, after exercise, we feed sparingly, the digestion will be easy and good, the body lightsome, the temper cheerful, and all the animal functions performed agreeably.

BENJAMIN FRANKLIN, *The Art of Procuring Pleasant Dreams.*

13

Lazy fokes' stummucks don't git tired.

JOEL CHANDLER HARRIS, *Plantation Proverbs.*

14

Among the great whom Heaven has made to shine,
How few have learned the art of arts,—to dine!
Nature, indulgent to our daily need,
Kind-hearted mother! taught us all to feed;
But the chief art,—how rarely Nature flings
This choicest gift among her social kings!

OLIVER WENDELL HOLMES, *The Banker's Secret,* l. 31.

15

The true essentials of a feast are only fun and feed.

OLIVER WENDELL HOLMES, *Nux Postcoenatica,* st. 11.

16

In order to know whether a human being is young or old, offer it food of different kinds at short intervals. If young, it will eat anything at any hour of the day or night. If old, it observes stated periods.

OLIVER WENDELL HOLMES, *The Professor at the Breakfast-Table,* ch. 3.

17

We never repent of having eaten too little.

THOMAS JEFFERSON, *Writings,* vol. xvi, p. 111.

18

Ticker tape ain't spaghetti.

FIORELLO H. LA GUARDIA, Speech to the United Nations Relief and Rehabilitation Commission, 29 Mar., 1946.

19

Your supper is like the hidalgo's dinner, very little meat, and a great deal of tablecloth.

HENRY WADSWORTH LONGFELLOW, *The Spanish Student,* act i, sc. 4.

20

Timid roach, why be so shy?
We are brothers, thou and I.
In the midnight, like thyself,
I explore the pantry shelf!

CHRISTOPHER MORLEY, *Nursery Rhymes for the Tender-Hearted.*

21

Drink and dance and laugh and lie,
Love, the reeling midnight through,
For tomorrow we shall die!
(But, alas, we never do.)

DOROTHY PARKER, *The Flaw in Paganism.*

22

If thou rise with an appetite, thou art sure never to sit down without one.

WILLIAM PENN, *Fruits of Solitude.*

23

The Receipts of Cookery are swelled to a Volume, but a good Stomach excels them all.

WILLIAM PENN, *Fruits of Solitude.*

24

A very man—not one of nature's clods—
With human failings, whether saint or sinner:
Endowed perhaps with genius from the gods

But apt to take his temper from his dinner.
J. G. SAXE, *About Husbands.*

1
They take their pride in making their dinner
cost much; I take my pride in making my
dinner cost little.
HENRY D. THOREAU. (EMERSON, *Thoreau*)

2
The nearest.
HENRY D. THOREAU, Reply, upon being
asked, while eating, which dish he preferred. (EMERSON, *Thoreau*)

3
Seeing is deceiving. It's eating that's believ-
ing.
JAMES THURBER, *Further Fables for Our
Time.*

4
The frightful manner of feeding with their
knives, till the whole blade seemed to enter
into the mouth; and the still more frightful
manner of cleaning the teeth afterwards with
a pocket-knife.
FRANCES TROLLOPE, *Domestic Manners of
the Americans,* ch. 3.

5
There is no spectacle on earth more appealing than that of a beautiful woman in the act
of cooking dinner for someone she loves.
THOMAS WOLFE, *The Web and the Rock,*
ch. 28.

ECONOMY

See also Thrift

6
A penny saved is two pence clear,
A pin a day's a groat a year.
BENJAMIN FRANKLIN, *Necessary Hints to
Those that Would Be Rich.*

7
A shilling spent idly by a fool, may be
picked up by a wiser person.
BENJAMIN FRANKLIN, Letter to Benjamin
Vaughan, 26 July, 1784.

8
Spare and have is better than spend and
crave.
BENJAMIN FRANKLIN, *Poor Richard,*
1758.

9
For age and want save while you may,
No morning sun lasts a whole day.
BENJAMIN FRANKLIN, *The Way to
Wealth.*

10
We now have a President who tries to save
money by turning off lights in the White
House, even as he heads toward a staggering
addition to the national debt. "L.B.J."
should stand for Light Bulb Johnson.
BARRY M. GOLDWATER, Speech in Chicago,
10 Apr., 1964. The Senator from Arizona, then campaigning for the Republi-

can presidential nomination, was commenting on the economy drive in the
early days of the Johnson Administration—in particular, the order directing
the turning off of unneeded lights.

I am not in favor of turning out the lights at
City Hall. We operate enough in the dark as
it is.
THEODORE R. KUPFERMAN, commenting as
a New York City Councilman. (New
York *Times,* 31 May, 1964)

11
I mean business on economy. Of course I
have some trouble in my own Administration. My Cabinet consists of nine salesmen
and one credit manager.
LYNDON B. JOHNSON, Remark during a
meeting of the Business Council (officials of major U.S. corporations) and
Cabinet members of the Johnson Administration at the White House, Dec.,
1963. The President humorously implied
that all but Secretary of the Treasury C.
Douglas Dillon (the "credit manager")
were trying to "sell" him on outlays for
their own departments. (New York
Times News Service, 30 Dec., 1963)

12
Controlling waste is like bailing a boat—you
have to keep at it.
LYNDON B. JOHNSON, Speech at ceremonies honoring U.S. government employ-
ees cited for making suggestions for cutting the cost of government; Washington, D.C., 4 Dec., 1964.

13
I have said that I believe in the tight fist and
the open mind—a tight fist with money and
an open mind to the needs of America.
LYNDON B. JOHNSON, Speech, Washington,
D.C., 4 Dec., 1964.

14
The man who saves the pennies is a dandy
and a duck—if he always has a quarter for
the guy that's out of luck.
WALT MASON, *The Penny Saved.*

15
Frugality is good, if liberality be joined with
it. The first is leaving off superfluous ex-
penses; the last bestowing them to the benefit of others that need. The first without the
last begets covetousness; the last without
the first begets prodigality.
WILLIAM PENN, *Fruits of Solitude.*

ECONOMY, THE

16
What this country needs is a good five-cent
nickel.
FRANKLIN P. ADAMS, *The Sun Dial*
(1932).

1

The limit on what our economy can stand is what we are willing to discipline and organize ourselves to do. It may not be possible to have the defenses we need and everything else we crave. But we have the resources for as large an effort as may be necessary, provided we are willing to curb the fancied wants which conflict with that effort.

> BERNARD M. BARUCH, *Baruch: My Own Story*, ch. 22 (1957).

2

I have never believed in abandoning our economy to the ruthless workings of the marketplace regardless of the human suffering that might be caused.

> BERNARD M. BARUCH. (New York *Times* obituary of Baruch, 21 June, 1965, p. 16)

3

Inflation is the most important economic fact of our time—the single greatest peril to our economic health.

> BERNARD M. BARUCH. (New York *Times* obituary of Baruch, 21 June, 1965, p. 16)

4

If our history teaches us anything, it is this lesson: So far as the economic potential of our nation is concerned, the believers in the future of America have always been the realists. I count myself as one of this company.

> DWIGHT D. EISENHOWER, State of the Union message, 9 Jan., 1958.

5

Emphatically, our economy is not the Federal Reserve System, or the Treasury, or the Congress, or the White House. This nation of 43,000,000 families, 174,000,000 people, is what we all think and what we do; that is our economy. Our economy is the result of millions of decisions we all make every day about producing, earning, saving, investing, and spending.

> DWIGHT D. EISENHOWER, Speech to the American Management Association conference on economic mobilization. 20 May, 1958.

6

As much wisdom may be expended on a private economy as on an empire, and as much wisdom may be drawn from it.

> EMERSON, *Essays, First Series: Prudence.*

A creative economy is the fuel of magnificence.

> EMERSON, *Lectures and Biographical Sketches: Aristocracy.*

7

We think that where a capitalist can put up a dollar, he can get a return on it. A manager can get up early to work, and with money and men he can build a better mousetrap. A laborer who is worthy of his hire stands a chance of getting attention, and maybe a little profit-sharing system, and the highest minimum wages of any nation in the world. Those three together combine to give us the end product that we call free enterprise.

> LYNDON B. JOHNSON, Speech to 35 state governors, White House, 25 Nov., 1963, his third full day as President.

I have often said that this free-enterprise system is made up of three parts—the man who has to invest the money, buy the machinery; the man who manages the men that work; and the men that work. All three of them have been pulling pretty good together.

> LYNDON B. JOHNSON, Press Conference, Washington, D.C., 19 Apr., 1964.

8

No one can bury us or bluff us or beat us so long as our economy remains strong.

> LYNDON B. JOHNSON, Speech, Washington, D.C., 26 Feb., 1964, marking the signing into law of tax-reduction legislation.

9

The economy was never stronger in your lifetime. But statistics must not be sedatives. Economic power is important only as it is put to human use.

> LYNDON B. JOHNSON, Speech at United Automobile Workers' convention, Atlantic City, N.J., 23 Mar., 1964.

10

The mere absence of war is not peace. The mere absence of recession is not growth.

> JOHN F. KENNEDY, State of the Union message. 14 Jan., 1963.

11

These unhappy times call for the building of plans that rest upon the forgotten, the unorganized but indispensable units of economic power, for plans like those of 1917 that build from the bottom up and not from the top down, that put their faith once more in the forgotten man at the bottom of the economic pyramid.

> FRANKLIN D. ROOSEVELT, Radio Address, 7 Apr., 1932.

The Forgotten Man works and votes—generally he prays—but his chief business in life is to pay.

> WILLIAM GRAHAM SUMNER, *The Forgotten Man*. (In *The Forgotten Man and Other Essays*, 1883)

The State cannot get a cent for any man without taking it from some other man, and this latter must be a man who has produced and saved it. The latter is the Forgotten Man.

> WILLIAM GRAHAM SUMNER, *What Social Classes Owe to Each Other.*

The Forgotten Man was never more completely forgotten than he is now. Congress does not know that he exists. The President [Warren G. Harding] suspects that there is such a person, who may turn up at the polls in November, but he is not quite sure.

> FRANK I. COBB, Editorial, New York *World*, Sept., 1922.

The Forgotten Man is a myth.

> ALFRED E. SMITH. (Editorial, *The New Outlook*, Oct., 1932)

1

If I were asked to state the great objective which church and state are both demanding for the sake of every man and woman and child in this country, I would say that the great objective is a more abundant life.

> FRANKLIN D. ROOSEVELT, Address before the Federal Council of the Churches of Christ, 6 Dec., 1933. The phrase "more abundant life" was used by him on several subsequent occasions.

2

In 1776 we sought freedom from the tyranny of a political autocracy—from the eighteenth-century royalists who held special privileges from the crown. . . . Since that struggle, however, man's inventive genius released new forces in our land which reordered the lives of our people. . . . Out of this modern civilization economic royalists carved new dynasties. . . . The royalists of the economic order have conceded that political freedom was the business of the Government, but they have maintained that economic slavery was nobody's business. . . . These economic royalists complain that we seek to overthrow the institutions of America.

> FRANKLIN D. ROOSEVELT, Address upon accepting the second nomination for the presidency, Democratic National Convention, Philadelphia, 27 June, 1936. "Economic royalists" became a widely discussed term during the Roosevelt years.

3

We have always known that heedless self-interest was bad morals; we know now that it is bad economics.

> FRANKLIN D. ROOSEVELT, Inaugural Address, 20 Jan., 1937.

4

A program whose basic thesis is not that the system of free private enterprise for profit has failed in this generation, but that it has not yet been tried.

> FRANKLIN D. ROOSEVELT, Economic Message, 29 Apr., 1938.

EDUCATION

See also Colleges, Teaching

5

The chief wonder of education is that it does not ruin everybody concerned in it, teachers and taught.

> HENRY ADAMS, *The Education of Henry Adams*, p. 55.

6

Observation more than books, experience rather than persons, are the prime educators.

> AMOS BRONSON ALCOTT, *Table Talk*, pt. ii.

7

Higher education is no longer a luxury but a necessity.

> ANTHONY J. CELEBREZZE, Testimony before a subcommittee on education, U.S. House of Representatives, 1 Feb., 1965. As Secretary of Health, Education, and Welfare, he was urging approval of legislation calling for federal aid to education.

8

School-days, school-days, dear old golden rule days,
Readin' and 'ritin' and 'rithmetic,
Taught to the tune of a hick'ry stick;
You were my queen in calico,
I was your bashful barefoot beau,
And you wrote on my slate, I love you, Joe,
When we were a couple of kids.

> WILL D. COBB, *School-Days* (song, 1907, with music by Gus Edwards).

9

When eras die, their legacies
  Are left to strange police;
Professors in New England guard
  The glory that was Greece.

> CLARENCE DAY, *Thoughts Without Words*.

10

Higher education must abandon the comfortable haven of objectivity, the sterile pinnacle of moral neutrality. In our perilous world, we cannot avoid moral judgments; that is a privilege only of the uninvolved.

> MILTON S. EISENHOWER, *The Need for a New American; The Educational Record*, Oct., 1963.

11

The best university that can be recommended to a man of ideas is the gauntlet of the mob.

> EMERSON, *Essays: Society and Solitude*.

12

The Roman rule was to teach a boy nothing that he could not learn standing.

> EMERSON, *Essays, Second Series: New England Reformers*.

13

We are students of words: we are shut up in schools and colleges and recitation-rooms for ten or fifteen years, and come out at last with a bag of wind, a memory of words, and do not know a thing.

> EMERSON, *Essays, Second Series: New England Reformers*.

1

In alluding just now to our system of education, I spoke of the deadness of its details. . . . It is a system of despair.

EMERSON, *Essays, Second Series: New England Reformers.*

2

The secret of education lies in respecting the pupil.

EMERSON, *Lectures and Biographical Sketches: Education.*

3

With universal cheap education, we have stringent theology, but religion is low.

EMERSON, *Lectures and Biographical Sketches: The Man of Letters.*

4

Most Americans do value education as a business asset, but not as the entrance into the joy of intellectual experience or acquaintance with the best that has been said and done in the past. They value it not as an experience, but as a tool.

W. H. P. FAUNCE, Letter to Abraham Flexner, 16 Jan., 1928. (FLEXNER, *Universities*)

5

The prevailing philosophy of education tends to discredit hard work.

ABRAHAM FLEXNER, *Universities*, p. 47.

6

Can a girl's trained intelligence be trusted to learn how to wash, feed, or clothe a baby? Certainly not: there is apparently no fund of experience upon which an educated person may draw! The girl's education may therefore be interrupted, suspended, or confused, in order that under artificial conditions she may be taught such things, probably by spinsters. Can the trained intelligence of a young man be trusted to learn salesmanship, marketing or advertising? Certainly not: the educational process has once more to be interrupted, suspended or confused, in order that he may learn the "principles" of salesmanship from a Ph.D. who has never sold anything, or the "principles" of marketing from a Ph.D. who has never marketed anything.

ABRAHAM FLEXNER, *Universities*, p. 71.

7

Without ideals, without effort, without scholarship, without philosophical continuity, there is no such thing as education.

ABRAHAM FLEXNER, *Universities*, p. 97.

8

Nations have recently been led to borrow billions for war; no nation has ever borrowed largely for education. Probably no nation is rich enough to pay for both war and civilization. We must make our choice; we cannot have both.

ABRAHAM FLEXNER, *Universities*, p. 302.

9

A learned blockhead is a greater blockhead than an ignorant one.

BENJAMIN FRANKLIN, *Poor Richard*, 1734.

10

Next in importance to freedom and justice is popular education, without which neither freedom nor justice can be permanently maintained.

JAMES A. GARFIELD, Letter, accepting nomination for presidency, 12 July, 1880.

11

The most significant fact in this world today is, that in nearly every village under the American flag, the school-house is larger than the church.

ROBERT G. INGERSOLL, Speech at Thirteen Club Dinner, 13 Dec., 1886.

12

Enlighten the people generally and tyranny and oppressions of both mind and body will vanish like evil spirits at the dawn of day.

THOMAS JEFFERSON, Letter to Du Pont de Nemours, 1816. (*Works,* xiv, 491)

13

By far the most important bill in our whole code, is that for the diffusion of knowledge among the people. No other sure foundation can be devised for the preservation of freedom and happiness. If anybody thinks that kings, nobles, priests are good conservators of the public happiness, send him here [to Europe].

THOMAS JEFFERSON, *Writings*, vol. v, p. 394.

14

They [academies] commit their pupils to the theatre of the world, with just taste enough of learning to be alienated from industrious pursuits, and not enough to do service in the ranks of science.

THOMAS JEFFERSON, *Writings*, vol. xiv, p. 150.

15

At the desk where I sit, I have learned one great truth. The answer for all our national problems—the answer for all the problems of the world—comes down to a single word. That word is "education."

LYNDON B. JOHNSON, Address before the 200th anniversary convocation, Brown University, Providence, R.I., 28 Sept., 1964.

16

The three R's of our school system must be supported by the three T's—teachers who are superior, techniques of instruction that are modern, and thinking about education which places it first in all our plans and hopes.

LYNDON B. JOHNSON, Message to Congress, 12 Jan., 1965.

1

We think of schools as places where youth learns, but our schools also need to learn.

LYNDON B. JOHNSON, Message to Congress, 12 Jan., 1965.

2

A child miseducated is a child lost.

JOHN F. KENNEDY, State of the Union Address, 11 Jan., 1962.

3

It might be said now that I have the best of both worlds: a Harvard education and a Yale degree.

JOHN F. KENNEDY, upon getting an honorary degree from Yale University, June, 1962.

4

I desire to see the time when education, and by its means, morality, sobriety, enterprise and industry, shall become much more general than at present.

ABRAHAM LINCOLN, Communication to Sangamon *Journal*, 1832.

5

The idea that going to college is one of the inherent rights of man seems to have obtained a baseless foothold in the minds of many of our people.

A. LAWRENCE LOWELL, Address at Haverford College, 17 Apr., 1931.

6

But it was in making education not only common to all, but in some sense compulsory on all, that the destiny of the free republics of America was practically settled.

JAMES RUSSELL LOWELL, *Among My Books: New England Two Centuries Ago.*

7

The better part of every man's education is that which he gives himself.

JAMES RUSSELL LOWELL, *My Study Windows: Lincoln.*

The only really educated men are self-educated.

JESSE LEE BENNETT, *Culture and a Liberal Education.*

Self-education is fine when the pupil is a born educator.

JOHN A. SHEDD, *Salt from My Attic,* p. 28.

8

The Common School is the greatest discovery ever made by man.

HORACE MANN, Inscription beneath his bust in the Hall of Fame.

9

Finally, education alone can conduct us to that enjoyment which is, at once, best in quality and infinite in quantity.

HORACE MANN, *Lectures and Reports on Education,* lecture 1.

10

In our country and in our times no man is worthy the honored name of statesman who does not include the highest practicable education of the people in all his plans of administration.

HORACE MANN, *Lectures on Education,* lecture 3.

11

A highbrow is a person educated beyond his intelligence.

BRANDER MATTHEWS, Epigram.

12

That's what education means—to be able to do what you've never done before.

GEORGE HERBERT PALMER, *Life of Alice Freeman Palmer.* The author was quoting an exclamation of the Palmers' cook when Mrs. Palmer baked a loaf of bread, without previous experience.

13

Education is the only interest worthy the deep, controlling anxiety of the thoughtful man.

WENDELL PHILLIPS, *Speeches: Idols.*

14

There is nothing so stupid as an educated man, if you get off the thing that he was educated in.

WILL ROGERS. (DURANT, *On the Meaning of Life,* p. 61)

15

True education makes for inequality; the inequality of individuality, the inequality of success; the glorious inequality of talent, of genius; for inequality, not mediocrity, individual superiority, not standardization, is the measure of the progress of the world.

FELIX E. SCHELLING, *Pedagogically Speaking.*

16

Wisdom is ever a blessing; education is sometimes a curse.

JOHN A. SHEDD, *Salt from My Attic,* p. 29.

17

Learn to live, and live to learn,
Ignorance like a fire doth burn,
Little tasks make large return.

BAYARD TAYLOR, *To My Daughter.*

18

What does education often do? It makes a straight-cut ditch of a free, meandering brook.

HENRY D. THOREAU, *Journal,* Oct., 1850.

19

The specialist who is trained but uneducated, technically skilled but culturally incompetent, is a menace.

DAVID B. TRUMAN, Address in Chicago to Columbia University alumni, 15 Apr., 1964.

20

An overeducated s.o.b.

HARRY S TRUMAN, referring to Senator J.

W. Fulbright. This description followed the release, 5 Feb., 1951, of a report by a Senate committee, headed by Fulbright, that charged irregularities in the functioning of the Reconstruction Finance Corporation, and connected them to "an influence ring with White House contacts."

1

Soap and education are not as sudden as a massacre, but they are more deadly in the long run.

> MARK TWAIN, *The Facts Concerning My Recent Resignation.*

2

Intelligence appears to be the thing that enables a man to get along without education. Education appears to be the thing that enables a man to get along without the use of his intelligence.

> ALBERT EDWARD WIGGAM, *The New Decalogue of Science.*

3

We must believe the things we teach our children.

> WOODROW WILSON. (COHN, *The Fabulous Democrats*)

4

Slavery is but half abolished, emancipation is but half completed, while millions of freemen with votes in their hands are left without education. Justice to them, the welfare of the States in which they live, the safety of the whole Republic, the dignity of the elective franchise,—all alike demand that the still remaining bonds of ignorance shall be unloosed and broken, and the minds as well as the bodies of the emancipated go free.

> ROBERT C. WINTHROP, Yorktown Oration, 19 Oct., 1881.

EGGS

5

All the goodness of a good egg cannot make up for the badness of a bad one.

> CHARLES A. DANA, *The Making of a Newspaper Man,* maxim 5.

6

There is always a best way of doing everything, if it be to boil an egg.

> EMERSON, *Conduct of Life: Behavior.*

7

No wonder, Child, we prize the Hen,
Whose Egg is mightier than the Pen.

> OLIVER HERFORD, *The Hen.*

8

Can you unscramble eggs?

> J. PIERPONT MORGAN.

9

Put all your eggs in one basket, and—watch the basket.

> MARK TWAIN, *Pudd'nhead Wilson's Calendar.*

EGOTISM

See also Conceit, Self-Love, Vanity

10

The pest of society is egotists.

> EMERSON, *Conduct of Life: Culture.*

11

It is an amiable illusion, which the shape of our planet prompts, that every man is at the top of the world.

> EMERSON, *Table-Talk.*

12

E is the Egotist dread
Who, as some one has wittily said,
    Will talk till he's blue
    About Himself when you
Want to talk about Yourself instead.

> OLIVER HERFORD, *The Egotist.*

13

When a man tries himself, the verdict is usually in his favor.

> EDGAR WATSON HOWE. (*New American Literature,* p. 490)

14

Intolerance itself is a form of egoism, and to condemn egoism intolerantly is to share it.

> GEORGE SANTAYANA, *Words of Doctrine,* p. 151.

15

When I'm playful, I use the meridians of longitude and parallels of latitude for a seine, and drag the Atlantic ocean for whales. I scratch my head with the lightning and purr myself to sleep with the thunder.

> MARK TWAIN, *Life on the Mississippi.*

ENDURANCE

16

Behold, we live through all things,—famine, thirst,
Bereavement, pain; all grief and misery,
All woe and sorrow; life inflicts its worst
On soul and body,—but we can not die,
Though we be sick and tired and faint and worn,—
Lo, all things can be borne!

> ELIZABETH AKERS ALLEN, *Endurance.*

17

The victory of endurance born.

> WILLIAM CULLEN BRYANT, *The Battle-Field,* st. 8.

18

All this will not be finished in the first 100 days. Nor will it be finished in the first 1,000 days, nor in the life of this Administration, nor even perhaps in our lifetime on this planet. But let us begin.

> JOHN F. KENNEDY, Inaugural Address, 20 Jan., 1961, after summarizing his goals.

19

I don't understand why we're suddenly so fatigued. The struggle won't be over in this century.

> JOHN F. KENNEDY, Statement at press conference, Washington, D.C., 14 Nov.

1963. He was referring to Congressional reluctance to accept his foreign-aid program. He added, "I feel certain that whoever succeeds me as President of the United States will continue it." Eight days later he was succeeded by Lyndon B. Johnson.

1

Sorrow and silence are strong, and patient endurance is godlike.

> HENRY WADSWORTH LONGFELLOW, *Evangeline,* pt. ii, sec. 1, l. 60.

2

Endurance is the crowning quality,
And patience all the passion of great hearts.

> JAMES RUSSELL LOWELL, *Columbus.*

ENEMY

3

They love him, gentlemen, and they respect him, not only for himself, but for his character, for his integrity and judgment and iron will; but they love him most for the enemies he has made.

> GOVERNOR EDWARD S. BRAGG of Wisconsin, Speech, seconding the nomination of Grover Cleveland for the presidency at the Democratic National Convention in Chicago, 9 July, 1884. "They" referred to the young men of Wisconsin; "enemies," to Tammany Hall, which opposed the nomination.

4

The truly civilized man has no enemies.

> CHARLES F. DOLE, *The Smoke and the Flame.*

5

The assailant makes the strength of the defense. Therefore, we ought to pray, give us a good enemy.

> EMERSON, *Journal,* 1865.

6

Do good to thy friend to keep him, to thy enemy to gain him.

> BENJAMIN FRANKLIN, *Poor Richard's Almanac.*

7

Love your Enemies, for they tell you your Faults.

> BENJAMIN FRANKLIN, *Poor Richard,* 1756.

8

You and I were long friends; you are now my enemy, and I am

> Yours, Benjamin Franklin.

> BENJAMIN FRANKLIN, Letter to William Strahan, 5 July, 1775.

9

Nobuddy ever fergits where he buried a hatchet.

> KIN HUBBARD, *Abe Martin's Broadcast.*

10

We are not enemies, but friends. We must not be enemies. Though passion may have strained, it must not break, our bonds of affection.

> ABRAHAM LINCOLN, Inaugural Address, 4 Mar., 1861.

11

If we could read the secret history of our enemies, we should find in each man's life sorrow and suffering enough to disarm all hostility.

> HENRY WADSWORTH LONGFELLOW, *Driftwood.*

12

None but yourself, who are your greatest foe.

> HENRY WADSWORTH LONGFELLOW, *Michael Angelo,* pt. ii, sec. 3.

13

The man who has no enemies has no following.

> DONN PIATT, *Memories of the Men Who Saved the Union:* Preface.

14

A man's greatness can be measured by his enemy.

> DONN PIATT, *Memories of Men Who Saved the Union:* Appendix.

15

It takes your enemy and your friend, working together, to hurt you to the heart: the one to slander you and the other to get the news to you.

> MARK TWAIN, *Pudd'nhead Wilson's Calendar.*

16

I'm lonesome. They are all dying. I have hardly a warm personal enemy left.

> J. A. McNEILL WHISTLER. (SEITZ, *Whistler Stories*)

17

I no doubt deserved my enemies, but I don't believe I deserved my friends.

> WALT WHITMAN. (BRADFORD, *Biography and the Human Heart,* p. 75)

ENGLAND AND THE ENGLISH

18

A nation of shopkeepers.

> SAMUEL ADAMS, Oration said to have been given in the State House, Philadelphia, 1 Aug., 1776. There is doubt as to whether the oration was actually delivered; no American edition is known, though copies of a professed English reprint exist. Adam Smith used the phrase in *Wealth of Nations,* vol. ii, bk. iv, ch. 7 (1775).

Governments of nations of shopkeepers must keep shop also.

> EMERSON, *Journal,* 1862.

19

The English are not an inventive people; they don't eat enough pie.

> THOMAS A. EDISON. (*Golden Book,* Apr., 1931)

1
The sea which, according to Virgil's famous line, divided the poor Britons utterly from the world, proved to be the ring of marriage with all nations.
> EMERSON, *English Traits*, p. 47.

2
I find the Englishman to be him of all men who stands firmest in his shoes.
> EMERSON, *English Traits*, p. 106.

3
Every one of these islanders is an island himself, safe, tranquil, incommunicable.
> EMERSON, *English Traits*, p. 109.

4
The stability of England is the security of the modern world.
> EMERSON, *English Traits*, p. 143.

5
England has no higher worship than Fate. She lives in the low plane of the winds and waves, watches like a wolf a chance for plunder; . . . never a lofty sentiment, never a duty to civilization, never a generosity, a moral self-restraint.
> EMERSON, *Journal*, 1862.

6
An Englishman has firm manners. He rests secure on the reputation of his country, on his family, and his expectations at home. There is in his manners a suspicion of insolence. If his belief in the Thirty-nine Articles does not bind him much, his belief in the fortieth does:—namely, that he shall not find his superiors elsewhere.
> EMERSON, *Journal*, 1868.

7
England is my wife—America, my mistress. It is very good sometimes to get away from one's wife.
> SIR CEDRIC HARDWICKE. (Associated Press obituary of Sir Cedric, datelined New York City, 6 Aug., 1964)

8
Englishmen are not made of polishable substance.
> NATHANIEL HAWTHORNE, *Journals*, 13 Feb., 1854.

9
His home!—the Western giant smiles,
And twirls the spotty globe to find it;—
This little speck the British Isles?
'Tis but a freckle,—never mind it!
> OLIVER WENDELL HOLMES, *A Good Time Going*.

10
He [the Englishman] is like a stout ship, which will weather the roughest storm uninjured, but roll its masts overboard in the succeeding calm.
> WASHINGTON IRVING, *Sketch Book: John Bull*.

11
His very faults smack of the raciness of his good qualities.
> WASHINGTON IRVING, *Sketch Book: John Bull*.

12
An Englishman is never so natural as when he's holding his tongue.
> HENRY JAMES, *The Portrait of a Lady*, ch. 10.

13
This is the true character of the English Government, and it presents the singular phenomenon of a nation, the individuals of which are as faithful to their private engagements and duties, as honorable, as worthy as those of any Nation on earth, and yet whose government is the most unprincipled at this day known.
> THOMAS JEFFERSON, *Writings*, vol. xii, p. 376.

14
The real power and property of the government is in the great aristocratical families of the nation. The nest of office being too small for all of them to cuddle into it at once, the contest is eternal which shall crowd the other out. For this purpose they are divided into two parties, the INS and the OUTS.
> THOMAS JEFFERSON, *Writings*, vol. xii, p. 376.

15
Of all the sarse thet I can call to mind,
England *doos* make the most onpleasant kind:
It's you're the sinner ollers, she's the saint;
Wut's good's all English, all thet is n't ain't;
Wut profits her is ollers right an' just,
An' ef you don't read Scriptur so, you must;
She's praised herself ontil she fairly thinks
There ain't no light in Natur when she winks; . . .
She's all thet's honest, honnable, an' fair,
An' when the vartoos died they made her heir.
> JAMES RUSSELL LOWELL. *The Biglow Papers: Mason and Slidell*.

16
Not a Bull of them all but is persuaded he bears Europa upon his back.
> JAMES RUSSELL LOWELL, *On a Certain Condescension in Foreigners*.

17
The New World's Sons, from England's breasts we drew
Such milk as bids remember whence we came;
Proud of her Past, wherefrom our Present grew,
This window we inscribe with Raleigh's name.
> JAMES RUSSELL LOWELL, Inscription on

the Raleigh window in St. Margaret's, Westminster.

1
I have loved England, dearly and deeply,
Since that first morning, shining and pure,
The white cliffs of Dover I saw rising steeply
Out of the sea that once made her secure.

I had no thought then of husband or lover,
I was a traveler, the guest of a week,
Yet when they pointed 'the white cliffs of Dover,"
Startled I found there were tears on my cheek.
> ALICE DUER MILLER, *The White Cliffs of Dover*, stanzas i, ii This first appeared in *Life*, 31 Mar., 1944.

2
The expression "as right as rain" must have been invented by an Englishman.
> WILLIAM LYON PHELPS, *The Country or the City*.

3
    And broad-based under all
Is planted England's oaken-hearted mood,
    As rich in fortitude
As e'er went worldward from the island-wall.
> BAYARD TAYLOR, *America*.

4
The English are mentioned in the Bible: Blessed are the meek, for they shall inherit the earth.
> MARK TWAIN, *Pudd'nhead Wilson's New Calendar*.

5
A power which has dotted over the surface of the whole globe with her possessions and military posts, whose morning drum-beat, following the sun, and keeping company with the hours, circles the earth with one continuous and unbroken strain of the martial airs of England.
> DANIEL WEBSTER, Speech, 7 May, 1834. (*Works*, vol. iv, p. 110)

6
O Englishmen!—in hope and creed,
    In blood and tongue our brothers!
We too are heirs of Runnymede;
    And Shakespeare's fame and Cromwell's deed
Are not alone our mother's.
> JOHN GREENLEAF WHITTIER, *To Englishmen*.

ENTHUSIASM

7
He too serves a certain purpose who only stands and cheers.
> HENRY ADAMS, *The Education of Henry Adams*, ch. 24.

8
Nothing great was ever achieved without enthusiasm.
> EMERSON, *Essays, First Series: Circles*.

9
Enthusiasm is the leaping lightning, not to be measured by the horse-power of the understanding.
> EMERSON, *Letters and Social Aims: Progress of Culture*.

10
Every great and commanding moment in the annals of the world is the triumph of some enthusiasm.
> EMERSON, *Nature, Addresses, and Lectures: Man the Reformer*.

11
Two dry Sticks will burn a green One.
> BENJAMIN FRANKLIN, *Poor Richard*, 1755.

12
A little ginger 'neath the tail
Will oft for lack of brains avail.
> T. F. MACMANUS, *Cave Sedem*.

13
An ounce of enterprise is worth a pound of privilege.
> FREDERIC R. MARVIN, *The Companionship of Books*, p. 318.

14
I don't think I've come to it yet.
> BRANCH RICKEY, Reply to an interviewer when, at 77, Rickey was asked to name his greatest thrill in baseball.

ENVY

15
There is a time in every man's education when he arrives at the conviction that envy is ignorance.
> EMERSON, *Essays, First Series: Self-Reliance*.

16
Things we haven't got we disparage.
> ELBERT HUBBARD, *The Philistine*, vol. xxvii, p. 42.

17
Men always hate most what they envy most.
> H. L. MENCKEN, *Prejudices*, ser. iv, p. 130.

18
Pity is for the living, envy is for the dead.
> MARK TWAIN, *Pudd'nhead Wilson's New Calendar*.

EQUALITY

19
Every denial of freedom, every denial of equal opportunity for a livelihood, for an education, for the right to participate in representative government diminishes me. There, is the moral basis for our cause.
> EVERETT M. DIRKSEN, paraphrasing John Donne, in commenting on the civil-

rights bill passed in 1964. Dirksen, as Senate minority leader, played a major role in its enactment.

1

Equal opportunity and mutual respect are matters not only of law, but also of the human heart and spirit, and the latter are not always amenable to law.

DWIGHT D. EISENHOWER, Article, New York *Herald Tribune,* 25 May, 1964. This was an attempt to set forth broad guidelines for the selection of a Republican presidential candidate for the election of that year.

2

As a man is equal to the Church and equal to the State, so he is equal to every other man.

EMERSON, *Essays, Second Series: New England Reformers.*

3

The Spartan principle of "calling that which is just, equal; not that which is equal, just."

EMERSON, *Essays, Second Series: Politics.*

4

There is a little formula, couched in pure Saxon, which you may hear in the corners of streets and in the yard of the dame's school, from very little republicans: "I'm as good as you be," which contains the essence of the Massachusetts Bill of Rights and of the American Declaration of Independence.

EMERSON, *Natural History of Intellect: Boston.*

5

Inequality is as dear to the American heart as liberty itself.

W. D. HOWELLS, *Impressions and Experiences: New York Streets,* p. 202.

6

We hold these truths to be self-evident, that all men are created equal.

THOMAS JEFFERSON, *Declaration of Independence.*

7

We have talked long enough in this country about equal rights. We have talked for a hundred years or more. It is time now to write the next chapter, and to write it in the books of law.

LYNDON B. JOHNSON, Address to joint session of Congress, 27 Nov., 1963, his first major speech as President.

8

I only hope that we recognize that it's been a hundred years since Abraham Lincoln freed the slaves of their chains. But he has not freed all the people of the bigotry that exists. And it's been a hundred years since President Lincoln signed the Emancipation Proclamation, but a great many people do not have equal rights as of now. And while emancipation may be a proclamation, it is not a fact until education is blind to color, until employment is unaware of race.

LYNDON B. JOHNSON, Statement at press conference, Washington, D.C., 16 Apr., 1964.

9

Finally, it should be clear by now that a nation can be no stronger abroad than she is at home. Only America which practices what it preaches about equal rights and social justice will be respected by those whose choice affects our future.

JOHN F. KENNEDY, Address prepared for delivery in Dallas, 22 Nov., 1963. This speech was to have been given at a luncheon meeting at the Trade Mart. Shortly before the scheduled meeting, Kennedy met death by assassination.

10

Equality in society beats inequality, whether the latter be of the British-aristocratic sort or of the domestic-slavery sort.

ABRAHAM LINCOLN, Speech in Peoria, Ill., 16 Oct., 1854.

11

I leave you, hoping that the lamp of liberty will burn in your bosoms, until there shall no longer be a doubt that all men are created free and equal.

ABRAHAM LINCOLN, Speech in Chicago, 10 July, 1858.

12

Fourscore and seven years ago, our fathers brought forth on this continent a new nation, conceived in liberty, and dedicated to the proposition that all men are created equal.

ABRAHAM LINCOLN, Gettysburg Address, 19 Nov., 1863.

13

I am an aristocrat. I love liberty; I hate equality.

JOHN RANDOLPH OF ROANOKE. (BRUCE, *Randolph of Roanoke,* vol. ii, p. 203)

14

Be the inferior of no man, nor of any man be the superior. Remember that every man is a variation of yourself. No man's guilt is not yours, nor is any man's innocence a thing apart.

WILLIAM SAROYAN, *The Time of Your Life,* act i.

15

Equality—the greatest of all doctrines and the most difficult to understand.

MARK VAN DOREN, at a gathering of his former students, New York, 16 Apr., 1964. The comment was an effort to sum up the theme of one of his poems.

16

I say that the century on which we are entering—the century which will come of this war—can be and must be the century of the common man.

HENRY A. WALLACE, Address to Free

World Association, New York City, 8 May, 1942.

1

I celebrate myself, and sing myself,
And what I assume you shall assume,
For every atom belonging to me as good as
  belongs to you.
WALT WHITMAN, *Song of Myself*, line 1.

ERROR

2

If frequently I fret and fume,
  And absolutely will not smile,
I err in company with Hume,
  Old Socrates and T. Carlyle.
FRANKLIN P. ADAMS, *Erring in Company*.

3

I have known men who could see through the motivations of others with the skill of a clairvoyant, only to prove blind to their own mistakes. I have been one of those men.
BERNARD M. BARUCH. (New York *Times* obituary of Baruch, 21 June, 1965, p. 16)

4

Error is the discipline through which we advance.
WILLIAM ELLERY CHANNING, *The Present Age*.

5

Yesterday's errors let yesterday cover.
SUSAN COOLIDGE, *New Every Morning*.

6

Truth is immortal; error is mortal.
MARY BAKER EDDY, *Science and Health*, p. 466.

7

Had she not been mistaken, she would have accomplished less. (Si non errasset, fecerit illa minus.)
EMERSON, *Journal*, 1857, referring to DELIA BACON and her *Philosophy of Shakespeare's Plays Unfolded*.

8

An error cannot be believed sincerely enough to make it a truth.
ROBERT G. INGERSOLL, *The Great Infidels*.

9

Error of opinion may be tolerated where reason is left free to combat it.
THOMAS JEFFERSON, First Inaugural Address.

10

I shall try to correct errors when shown to be errors, and I shall adopt new views so fast as they shall appear to be new views.
ABRAHAM LINCOLN, Letter to Horace Greeley, 22 Aug., 1862.

11

Sometimes we may learn more from a man's errors than from his virtues.
HENRY WADSWORTH LONGFELLOW, *Hyperion*, bk. iv, ch. 3.

12

Nine times out of ten, in the arts as in life, there is actually no truth to be discovered; there is only error to be exposed.
H. L. MENCKEN, *Prejudices*, ser. iii, p. 93.

13

A man whose errors take ten years to correct is quite a man.
J. ROBERT OPPENHEIMER, commenting on errors in the early scientific work of Albert Einstein, which delayed for ten years the publication of Einstein's collected works. Dr. Oppenheimer's remark was made during a symposium on Einstein in Paris, 13 Dec., 1965.

14

If I have erred, I err in company with Abraham Lincoln.
THEODORE ROOSEVELT, Speech during the presidential election campaign of 1912.

15

If you find a mistake in this paper, please consider that it was there for a purpose. We publish something for everyone, including those who are always looking for mistakes.
UNKNOWN, Weekly Bulletin of the First Congregational Church, San Diego. (Reported by Associated Press in dispatch datelined San Diego, 16 Oct., 1963)

EVIL

See also Goodness

16

Evil is here in the world, not because God wants it or uses it here, but because he knows not how at the moment to remove it. . . . Evil, therefore, is a fact not to be explained away, but to be accepted; and accepted not to be endured, but to be conquered. It is a challenge neither to our reason nor to our patience, but to our courage.
JOHN HAYNES HOLMES. (NEWTON, *My Idea of God*, p. 119)

17

Evil is only good perverted.
HENRY WADSWORTH LONGFELLOW, *The Golden Legend*, pt. ii.

18

Evil springs up, and flowers, and bears no seed,
And feeds the green earth with its swift decay,
Leaving it richer for the growth of truth.
JAMES RUSSELL LOWELL, *Prometheus*, l. 263.

19

Dirty work at the crossroads!
WALTER MELVILLE, *No Wedding Bells for Him*.

20

No man is justified in doing evil on the ground of expediency.
THEODORE ROOSEVELT, *The Strenuous Life*.

1
The world is round. Only one-third of the human beings are asleep at one time, and the other two-thirds are awake and up to some mischief somewhere.

DEAN RUSK, Comment to a Congressional committee, 26 Jan., 1966.

2
For by excess of evil, evil dies.

GEORGE SANTAYANA, *Sorrow*.

3
Despise evil and ungodliness, but not men of ungodliness or evil. These, understand.

WILLIAM SAROYAN, *The Time of Your Life*, act i.

4
Perish with him the folly that seeks through evil good.

JOHN GREENLEAF WHITTIER, *Brown of Ossawatomie*.

EVOLUTION

5
A fire-mist and a planet,
    A crystal and a cell,
A jellyfish and a saurian
    And caves where the cavemen dwell;
Then a sense of law and beauty,
    And a face turned from the clod—
Some call it Evolution,
    And others call it God.

W. H. CARRUTH, *Each in His Own Tongue*.

6
"The unfit die—the fit both live and thrive."
Alas, who says so? They who do survive.

SARAH N. CLEGHORN, *The Survival of the Fittest*.

7
Each animal or vegetable form remembers the next inferior and predicts the next higher.

EMERSON, *Poetry and Imagination*.

8
How far off yet is the trilobite! how far the quadruped! how inconceivably remote is man! All duly arrive, and then race after race of men. It is a long way from granite to the oyster; farther yet to Plato and the preaching of the immortality of the soul.

EMERSON, *Essays, Second Series: Nature*.

9
Recall from Time's abysmal chasm
That piece of primal protoplasm
The First Amoeba, strangely splendid,
From whom we're all of us descended.

ARTHUR GUITERMAN, *Ode to the Amoeba*.

10
Children, behold the Chimpanzee;
He sits on the ancestral tree
From which we sprang in ages gone.
I'm glad we sprang: had we held on,
We might, for aught that I can say,
Be horrid Chimpanzees to-day.

OLIVER HERFORD, *The Chimpanzee*.

11
From what flat wastes of cosmic slime,
    And stung by what quick fire,
Sunward the restless races climb!—
    Men risen out of mire!

DON MARQUIS, *Unrest*.

12
A man sat on a rock and sought
    Refreshment from his thumb;
A dinotherium wandered by
    And scared him some.
His name was Smith. The kind of rock
    He sat upon was shale.
One feature quite distinguished him:
    He had a tail.

DAVID LAW PROUDFIT, *Prehistoric Smith*.

13
I am proud of those bright-eyed, furry, four-footed or feathered progenitors, and not at all ashamed of my cousins, the Tigers and Apes and Peacocks.

LOGAN PEARSALL SMITH, *Trivia: Desires*.

EXAMPLE

14
I have ever deemed it more honorable and more profitable, too, to set a good example than to follow a bad one.

THOMAS JEFFERSON, *Writings*, vol. xiv, p. 222.

15
So, when a great man dies,
For years beyond our ken,
The light he leaves behind him lies
Upon the paths of men.

HENRY WADSWORTH LONGFELLOW, *Charles Sumner*.

16
Lives of great men all remind us
    We can make our lives sublime,
And, departing, leave behind us
    Footprints on the sands of time.

HENRY WADSWORTH LONGFELLOW, *A Psalm of Life*.

17
Few things are harder to put up with than the annoyance of a good example.

MARK TWAIN, *Pudd'nhead Wilson's Calendar*.

18
I tread in the footsteps of illustrious men . . . in receiving from the people the sacred trust confided to my illustrious predecessor.

MARTIN VAN BUREN, Inaugural Address, 4 Mar., 1837. The reference was to Andrew Jackson.

EXCUSE

19
Stoop not then to poor excuse.

EMERSON, *Sursum Corda*.

1
Let us never bow and apologize more.
> EMERSON, *Essays, First Series: Self-Reliance.*

2
Apologizing—a very desperate habit—one that is rarely cured. Apology is only egotism wrong side out.
> OLIVER WENDELL HOLMES, *The Professor at the Breakfast-Table,* ch. 6.

3
The great liability of the engineer compared to men of other professions is that his works are out in the open where all can see them. . . . If his works do not work, he is damned.
> HERBERT HOOVER, 1916. (*Herbert Hoover in His Own Words; New York Times Magazine,* 9 Aug., 1964)

4
Don't make excuses—make good.
> ELBERT HUBBARD, *Epigrams.*

5
Explanations explanatory of things explained.
> ABRAHAM LINCOLN, referring to Stephen A. Douglas in the Lincoln-Douglas debates.

6
I do not trouble my spirit to vindicate itself or be understood,
I see that the elementary laws never apologize.
> WALT WHITMAN, *Song of Myself,* sec. 20.

7
That's like blaming the Johnstown flood on a leaky toilet in Altoona, Pennsylvania.
> STANLEY WOODWARD, commenting acidly on the reason given by the Army football coach, Earl (Red) Blaik, for the Cadets' loss to the University of Michigan. Blaik had seemed to put the blame for the rout on a single Army player's inadequacy.

EXPERIENCE

8
All experience is an arch, to build upon.
> HENRY ADAMS, *The Education of Henry Adams,* p. 87.

9
It takes longer to hard-boil a man or a woman than an egg.
> FREDERICK LEWIS ALLEN, *Only Yesterday,* p. 118.

10
An expert is one who knows more and more about less and less.
> NICHOLAS MURRAY BUTLER, Commencement Address, Columbia University.

11
This gave me that precarious gait
Some call experience.
> EMILY DICKINSON, *Poems,* Pt. i. No. 136.

12
Only so much do I know, as I have lived.
> EMERSON, *Nature Addresses: The American Scholar.*

13
Experience keeps a dear school, yet Fools will learn in no other.
> BENJAMIN FRANKLIN, *Poor Richard,* 1743.

14
I have but one lamp by which my feet are guided, and that is the lamp of experience.
> PATRICK HENRY, Speech in the Virginia House of Delegates, 23 Mar., 1775. Arranged by William Wirt, 1818.

15
Nor deem the irrevocable Past,
  As wholly wasted, wholly vain,
If, rising on its wrecks, at last
  To something nobler we attain.
> HENRY WADSWORTH LONGFELLOW, *Ladder of St. Augustine,* st. 12.

16
One thorn of experience is worth a whole wilderness of warning.
> JAMES RUSSELL LOWELL, *Among My Books: Shakespeare Once More.*

17
Who heeds not experience, trust him not.
> JOHN BOYLE O'REILLY, *Rules of the Road.*

18
What man would be wise, let him drink of the river
  That bears on its bosom the record of time;
A message to him every wave can deliver
  To teach him to creep till he knows how to climb.
> JOHN BOYLE O'REILLY, *Rules of the Road.*

19
The main point is getting some experience. The experienced people are better than the inexperienced. Think how it is in that tennis game or in that race or whatever it is. When the whistle blows you have only a limited amount of time to do what you have to do. You either do it then or you don't do it at all.
> BYRON R. WHITE, an outstanding athlete before he entered government service and rose to a place on the Supreme Court. (ALFRED WRIGHT, *A Modest All-America Who Sits on the Highest Bench. Sports Illustrated,* 10 Dec., 1962)

EXTREMES

See also Act, Action; Fanaticism; Politics

20
Extremes meet, and there is no better example than the haughtiness of humility.
> EMERSON, *Letters and Social Aims: Greatness.*

1

The one thing in common to all extremist groups is their inflexible conviction that they are right and their opponents are evil. Acting on this principle, they are no longer open to reason, no longer willing to respect the wishes of the majority. . . . They are fundamentally destructive of the democratic process itself.

> MAX FREEDMAN, Syndicated Column, 30 July, 1965.

2

I would remind you that extremism in the defense of liberty is no vice. And let me remind you also that moderation in the pursuit of justice is no virtue!

> BARRY M. GOLDWATER, Speech, accepting the Republican nomination for the presidency, at the party's national convention in San Francisco, 16 July, 1964.

To extol extremism whether "in defense of liberty" or "in pursuit of justice" is dangerous, irresponsible and frightening. Any sanction of lawlessness, of the vigilante and of the unruly mob can only be deplored. . . . I shall continue to fight extremism within the Republican party. It has no place in the party. It has no place in America.

> NELSON ROCKEFELLER, Public Statement issued 17 July, 1964, in San Francisco, in direct reply to Barry Goldwater's controversial statement about extremism and moderation.

The essence of the matter is that to be an extremist is to encourage and condone the taking of the law into unauthorized private hands. It is in truth shocking that the Republican candidate for President is unconscious of this sovereign truth. For the distinction between private violence and public force is the central principle of a civilized society.

> WALTER LIPPMANN, Syndicated Newspaper Column, 21 July, 1964, referring to Barry Goldwater's acceptance speech at the Republican national convention.

If I were to paraphrase the two sentences in question in the context in which I uttered them I would do it by saying that wholehearted devotion to liberty is unassailable and that half-hearted devotion to justice is indefensible.

> BARRY M. GOLDWATER, Letter to Richard M. Nixon, released for publication 9 Aug., 1964. Nixon, among others, had sought clarification of the controversial statements about extremism, as set forth in Goldwater's acceptance speech at the Republican national convention, after Goldwater's critics construed them as a blanket endorsement of extremism.

Extremism in the pursuit of the Presidency is an unpardonable vice. Moderation in the affairs of the nation is the highest virtue.

> LYNDON B. JOHNSON, Speech in New York City, 31 Oct., 1964, during the presidential campaign. A paraphrase of Barry Goldwater's statement on extremism and moderation.

We condemn extremism, whether from the right or left, including the extreme tactics of such organizations as the Communist party, the Ku Klux Klan and the John Birch Society. We know what violence and hate can do. We have seen the tragic consequences of misguided zeal and twisted logic.

> Democratic National Platform, 1964.

3

The question is not whether we will be extremist but what kind of extremist will we be. Will we be extremists for hate or will we be extremists for love? Will we be extremists for the preservation of injustice—or will we be extremists for the cause of justice?

> REV. MARTIN LUTHER KING, JR., Letter, written Apr., 1963, while he was in City Jail, Birmingham, Ala. Addressed to "My Dear Fellow Clergymen," the letter was his answer to a public statement by white clergymen who criticized him for "unwise and untimely" demonstrations. (*Time*, 3 Jan., 1964)

4

In that dramatic scene on Calvary's hill, three men were crucified for the same crime—the crime of extremism. Two were extremists for immorality, and thus fell below their environment. The other, Jesus Christ, was an extremist for love, truth and goodness, and thereby rose above his environment. So, after all, maybe the South, the nation and the world are in dire need of creative extremists.

> REV. MARTIN LUTHER KING, JR., Letter written Apr., 1963, while he was in City Jail, Birmingham, Ala. (*Time*, 3 Jan., 1964)

5

While the people retain their virtue and vigilance, no administration, by any extreme of wickedness or folly, can very seriously injure the government in the short space of four years.

> ABRAHAM LINCOLN, Inaugural Address, 4 Mar., 1861.

6

In the world of the extremists there can be no solution of important issues by conciliation and consent. There must always be a winner and a loser. The conflict must always end in unconditional surrender. There is no such thing as the harmonizing of interests.

> WALTER LIPPMANN, Syndicated Column, 12 Nov., 1964.

EYES

1

A gray eye is a sly eye,
  And roguish is a brown one;
Turn full upon me thy eye,—
  Ah, how its wavelets drown one!
A blue eye is a true eye;
  Mysterious is a dark one,
Which flashes like a spark-sun!
  A black eye is the best one.
  W. R. ALGER, *Poetry of the Orient: Mirtsa Schaffy on Eyes.*

2

Thine eyes are springs, in whose serene
And silent waters heaven is seen;
Their lashes are the herbs that look
On their young figures in the brook.
  WILLIAM CULLEN BRYANT, *Oh, Fairest of the Rural Maids.*

3

It does not hurt weak eyes to look into beautiful eyes never so long.
  EMERSON, *Conduct of Life: Beauty.*

4

How many furtive inclinations are avowed by the eye, though dissembled by the lips!
  EMERSON, *Conduct of Life: Behavior.*

5

Eyes are bold as lions,—roving, running, leaping, here and there, far and near. They speak all languages. . . . What inundation of life and thought is discharged from one soul into another through them!
  EMERSON, *Conduct of Life: Behavior.*

6

There are asking eyes, asserting eyes, prowling eyes; and eyes full of fate,—some of good. and some of sinister omen.
  EMERSON, *Conduct of Life: Behavior.*

7

An eye can threaten like a loaded and levelled gun, or can insult like hissing or kicking; or, in its altered mood, by beams of kindness, it can make the heart dance with joy.
  EMERSON, *Conduct of Life: Behavior.*

8

The eyes of other people are the eyes that ruin us. If all but myself were blind, I should want neither fine clothes, fine houses, nor fine furniture.
  BENJAMIN FRANKLIN, Letter to Benjamin Vaughan.

9

Men of cold passions have quick eyes.
  NATHANIEL HAWTHORNE, *Journals,* 1837.

10

There are eyes of blue,
There are eyes of brown, too;
  There are eyes of every size,
And eyes of every hue.
  But I surmise, that if you are wise,
  You'll be careful of the maiden with the dreamy eyes.
  JAMES WELDON JOHNSON, *The Maiden with the Dreamy Eyes.*

11

As President, I have no eyes but constitutional eyes; I cannot see you.
  ABRAHAM LINCOLN, to the Confederate Commissioners from South Carolina.

12

And thy deep eyes, amid the gloom,
Shine like jewels in a shroud.
  HENRY WADSWORTH LONGFELLOW, *The Golden Legend,* pt. iv.

13

I dislike an eye that twinkles like a star. Those only are beautiful which, like the planets, have a steady, lambent light,—are luminous, but not sparkling.
  HENRY WADSWORTH LONGFELLOW, *Hyperion,* bk. iii, ch. 4.

14

O lovely eyes of azure,
Clear as the waters of a brook that run
Limpid and laughing in the summer sun.
  HENRY WADSWORTH LONGFELLOW, *The Masque of Pandora,* pt. i.

15

What the eye views not, the heart craves not, as well as rues not.
  WILLIAM PENN, *No Cross, No Crown,* pt. i, ch. 5, sec. 11.

16

Somebody loves me, how do I know?
Somebody's eyes have told me so!
  HATTIE STARR, *Somebody Loves Me.*

F

FACE

17

Beautiful faces are those that wear
Whole-souled honesty printed there.
  ELLEN P. ALLERTON, *Beautiful Things.*

18

I will not lend my countenance to the enterprise.
  GROVER CLEVELAND, Reply to John Finley, who urged him to have his portrait painted. (NEVINS, *Grover Cleveland,* p. 762)

19

"Say, boys! if you give me just another
  whiskey I'll be glad,
And I'll draw right here a picture of the face
  that drove me mad.
Give me that piece of chalk with which you
  mark the baseball score,

You shall see the lovely Madeleine upon the
    barroom floor."
    H. ANTOINE D'ARCY, *The Face Upon the
    Floor.*

1
I have always considered my face a convenience rather than an ornament.
    OLIVER WENDELL HOLMES, *Life and Let-
    ters,* vol. ii, p. 103.

2
The human face is the masterpiece of God.
The eyes reveal the soul, the mouth the
    flesh.
The chin stands for purpose, the nose means
    will.
    ELBERT HUBBARD, *Little Journeys: Leon-
    ardo.*

3
In my poor, lean, lank face nobody has ever
seen that any cabbages were sprouting.
    ABRAHAM LINCOLN, Speech during the
    Lincoln-Douglas debates.

4
A face that had a story to tell. How different
faces are in this particular! Some of them
speak not. They are books in which not a
line is written, save perhaps a date.
    HENRY WADSWORTH LONGFELLOW, *Hype-
    rion,* bk. i, ch. 4.

5
       The light upon her face
Shines from the windows of another world.
Saints only have such faces.
    HENRY WADSWORTH LONGFELLOW, *Mi-
    chael Angelo,* pt. ii, sec. 6.

6
In this sea of upturned faces there is something which excites me strangely, deeply, before I even begin to speak.
    DANIEL WEBSTER, Speech in Faneuil Hall,
    Boston, 30 Sept., 1842.

7
In the faces of men and women I see God.
    WALT WHITMAN, *Song of Myself,* st. 48.

FACTS

8
Facts, when combined with ideas, constitute
the greatest force in the world. They are
greater than armaments, greater than finance,
greater than science, business and law because they are the common denominator of
all of them.
    CARL W. ACKERMAN, Address, 26 Sept.,
    1931.

9
If you get all the facts, your judgment can
be right; if you don't get all the facts, it
can't be right.
    BERNARD M. BARUCH. (St. Louis *Post-
    Dispatch,* 21 June, 1965, p. 5A)

10
No facts to me are sacred; none are profane.
    EMERSON, *Essays, First Series: Circles.*

11
Time dissipates to shining ether the solid
angularity of facts. No anchor, no cable, no
fences avail to keep a fact a fact.
    EMERSON, *Essays, First Series: History.*

12
I distrust the facts and the inferences.
    EMERSON, *Essays, Second Series: Experi-
    ence.*

13
Why covet a knowledge of new facts? Day
and night, house and garden, a few books, a
few actions, serve us as well as would all
trades and spectacles.
    EMERSON, *Essays, Second Series: The
    Poet.*

14
A concept is stronger than a fact.
    CHARLOTTE P. GILMAN, *Human Work.*

15
I believe that in ninety-nine cases out of a
hundred, the American people will make the
right decision—if and when they are in possession of the essential facts about any given
issue.
    ADLAI E. STEVENSON, Speech in Fairfield,
    Ill., June, 1950.

16
Facts, or what a man believes to be facts, are
delightful. . . . Get your facts first, and
then you can distort them as much as you
please.
    MARK TWAIN. (Kipling, *From Sea to Sea.*
    Letter 37)

17
Dr. Facts.
    WOODROW WILSON, his sobriquet for Ber-
    nard M. Baruch, who served Wilson and
    impressed the President as a man with a
    devotion to fact.

FAILURE

18
They fail, and they alone, who have not
    striven.
    THOMAS BAILEY ALDRICH, *Enamored Ar-
    chitect of Airy Rhyme.*

19
The fight is lost—and he knows it is lost—
    and yet he is fighting still!
    E. J. APPLETON, *The Fighting Failure.*

20
And if I should lose, let me stand by the
    road
And cheer as the winners go by!
    BERTON BRALEY, *Prayer of a Sportsman.*

21
It might be easier
    To fail with land in sight,
Than gain my blue peninsula
    To perish of delight.
    EMILY DICKINSON, *Poems,* Pt. i, No. 132.

22
And nothing to look backward to with pride

And nothing to look forward to with hope.
ROBERT FROST, *The Death of the Hired Man.*

1
To flounder is the precondition of all art, and the crying shame in the theater is only that it costs so much.
WILLIAM GIBSON, Letter to Drama Editor, New York *Times,* 31 May, 1964.

2
In two words: im-possible.
SAMUEL GOLDWYN. (ALVA JOHNSON, *The Great Goldwyn*)

3
Who would not rather founder in the fight
Than not have known the glory of the fray?
RICHARD HOVEY, *Two and Fate.*

4
A failure is a man who has blundered, but is not able to cash in the experience.
ELBERT HUBBARD, *Epigrams.*

5
Treating her handsomely buttered no parsnips.
HENRY JAMES, *The Ambassadors,* p. 315.

6
The probability that we may fail in the struggle ought not to deter us from the support of a cause we believe to be just.
ABRAHAM LINCOLN, Speech in Springfield, Ill., Dec., 1839.

7
To fail at all is to fail utterly.
JAMES RUSSELL LOWELL, *Among My Books: Dryden.*

8
"All honor to him who shall win the prize,"
The world has cried for a thousand years;
But to him who tries and fails and dies,
I give great honor and glory and tears.
JOAQUIN MILLER, *For Those Who Fail.*

9
Post-mortems on defeats are never very useful unless they say something about the future.
JAMES RESTON, Column, New York *Times,* 15 July, 1964. Referring to the defeat of the liberal forces of the Republican party at the party's national convention then taking place in San Francisco.

10
One of the advantages of defeat in life—maybe the main advantage—is that it provides an excuse for change. Defeat in love —one of our more popular institutions—in business, or especially in sport, invariably leads to new adventures, new products, new presidents of the company, and new managers or coaches of the team. But not in politics—at least on Capitol Hill. There defeat entrenches the defeated.
JAMES RESTON, Washington Column, New York *Times,* 18 Dec., 1964.

11
America celebrates success, but occasionally it pauses to regret the men who didn't quite make it—the also-rans, the good men who arrived near the top at the wrong time, the rejected and the disappointed.
JAMES RESTON, Article, New York *Times,* 15 July, 1965, p. 1, evaluating the career of Adlai E. Stevenson.

12
Never mind;
If some of us were not so far behind,
The rest of us were not so far ahead.
EDWIN ARLINGTON ROBINSON, *Inferential.*

13
And the last sleeping-place of Nebuchadnezzar—
When I arrive there I shall tell the wind:
"You ate grass; I have eaten crow—
Who is better off now or next year?"
CARL SANDBURG, *Losers.*

14
I cannot give you the formula for success, but I can give you the formula for failure—which is: Try to please everybody.
HERBERT BAYARD SWOPE, Address at dinner in his honor given by Interfaith in Action, 20 Dec., 1950.

15
God, though this life is but a wraith,
Although we know not what we use.
Although we grope with little faith,
Give me the heart to fight—and lose.
LOUIS UNTERMEYER, *Prayer.*

16
Have you heard that it was good to gain the day?
I also say it is good to fall, battles are lost in the same spirit in which they are won.
WALT WHITMAN, *Song of Myself,* sec. 18.

17
To those who've fail'd, in aspiration vast,
To unnam'd soldiers fallen in front on the lead,
To calm, devoted engineers—to over-ardent travellers—to pilots on their ships,
To many a lofty song and picture without recognition—I'd rear a laurel-cover'd monument.
WALT WHITMAN, *To Those Who've Fail'd.*

18
Sweeter than any sung
My songs that found no tongue;
Nobler than any fact
My wish that failed to act.

Others shall sing the song,
Others shall right the wrong,—
Finish what I begin,
And all I fail of win.
JOHN GREENLEAF WHITTIER, *My Triumph,* stanzas 9, 10.

FAITH
See also Belief

19
He who, from zone to zone,

Guides through the boundless sky thy certain
flight,
In the long way that I must tread alone,
  Will lead my steps aright.
> WILLIAM CULLEN BRYANT, *To a Water-
> fowl.*

1
Faith is love taking the form of aspiration.
> WILLIAM ELLERY CHANNING, *Note-Books:
> Faith.*

2
Faith is a fine invention
For gentlemen who see;
But microscopes are prudent
In an emergency!
> EMILY DICKINSON, *Poems*, Pt. i, No. 56.

3
Man is not born and does not die collective-
ly. He enters this world and leaves it—alone.
And through most of life's most meaningful
experiences he is alone. Fortunate he is, in
my judgment, whose aloneness is enveloped
in a Faith that is abiding, satisfying, and
inspiring.
> MILTON S. EISENHOWER, *The Need for a
> New American; The Educational Rec-
> ord,* Oct., 1963.

4
The faith that stands on authority is not
faith. The reliance on authority measures the
decline of religion.
> EMERSON, *Essays, First Series: The Over-
> Soul.*

5
The disease with which the human mind now
labors is want of faith.
> EMERSON, *Essays, Second Series: New
> England Reformers.*

6
In the affairs of this World, Men are saved,
not by Faith, but by the Want of it.
> BENJAMIN FRANKLIN, *Poor Richard,*
> 1754.

7
The way to see by Faith is to shut the Eye
of Reason.
> BENJAMIN FRANKLIN, *Poor Richard,*
> 1758.

8
God reigneth. All is well!
> OLIVER WENDELL HOLMES, *Hymn at the
> Funeral Services of Charles Sumner.*

9
Faith, as an intellectual state, is self-reliance.
> OLIVER WENDELL HOLMES, *The Professor
> at the Breakfast-Table,* ch. 4.

10
Faith always implies the disbelief of a lesser
fact in favor of a greater. A little mind often
sees the unbelief, without seeing the belief of
large ones.
> OLIVER WENDELL HOLMES, *The Professor
> at the Breakfast-Table,* ch. 5.

11
Surely investigation is better than unthinking faith. Surely reason is a better guide than
fear.
> ROBERT G. INGERSOLL, *The Liberty of
> Man, Woman and Child.*

12
Faith is often the boast of the man who is
too lazy to investigate.
> F. M. KNOWLES, *A Cheerful Year Book.*

13
Our faith triumphant o'er our fears.
> HENRY WADSWORTH LONGFELLOW, *The
> Building of the Ship.*

14
Ye whose hearts are fresh and simple,
Who have faith in God and nature.
> HENRY WADSWORTH LONGFELLOW, *Hiawa-
> tha:* Introduction.

15
The only faith that wears well and holds its
color in all weathers, is that which is woven
of conviction and set with the sharp mordant
of experience.
> JAMES RUSSELL LOWELL, *My Study Win-
> dows: Abraham Lincoln.*

16
Faith may be defined briefly as an illogical
belief in the occurrence of the improbable.
> H. L. MENCKEN, *Prejudices*, ser. iii, p.
> 267.

17
But give me, Lord, eyes to behold the
    truth;
A seeing sense that knows the eternal right;
A heart with pity filled, and gentlest ruth;
A manly faith that makes all darkness light.
> THEODORE PARKER, *The Higher Good.*

18
Faith is a kind of winged intellect. The great
workmen of history have been men who believed like giants.
> DR. CHARLES H. PARKHURST, *Sermons:
> Walking by Faith.*

19
I know no deeper doubt to make me mad,
I need no brighter love to keep me pure.
To me the faiths of old are daily bread;
I bless their hope, I bless their will to save.
> GEORGE SANTAYANA, *What Riches Have
> You.*

20
Reason is the triumph of the intellect, faith
of the heart.
> JAMES SCHOULER, *History of the United
> States,* vol. ii.

21
One by one, like leaves from a tree,
All my faiths have forsaken me.
> SARA TEASDALE, *Leaves.*

22
The mason asks but a narrow shelf to spring
his brick from; man requires only an infi-

nitely narrower one to spring his arch of
faith from.
>   HENRY D. THOREAU, *Journal,* 31 Jan.,
>   1852.

1

Through the dark and stormy night
Faith beholds a feeble light
Up the blackness streaking;
Knowing God's own time is best,
In a patient hope I rest.
    For the full day-breaking!
>   JOHN GREENLEAF WHITTIER, *Barclay of
>   Ury,* st. 16.

2

We live by Faith; but Faith is not the slave
Of text and legend. Reason's voice and
    God's,
Nature's and Duty's, never are at odds.
>   JOHN GREENLEAF WHITTIER, *Require-
>   ment.*

FAME

See also Success

3

A celebrity is a person who works hard all
his life to become well known, then wears
dark glasses to avoid being recognized.
>   FRED ALLEN, *Treadmill to Oblivion.*

4

Distinction is the consequence, never the object, of a great mind.
>   WASHINGTON ALLSTON, Aphorism, written
>   on the wall of his studio.

5

Fame always brings loneliness. Success is as
ice cold and lonely as the north pole.
>   VICKI BAUM, *Grand Hotel,* p. 134.

6

My advice to a young man seeking deathless
fame would be to espouse an unpopular
cause and devote his life to it.
>   GEORGE WILLIAM CURTIS, *Wendell Phil-
>   lips.*

7

Fame is a fickle food
Upon a shifting plate.
>   EMILY DICKINSON, *Poems,* Pt. v, No. 4.

8

If a man can write a better book, preach a
better sermon, or make a better mouse-trap,
than his neighbor, though he builds his house
in the woods, the world will make a beaten
path to his door.
>   Attributed to RALPH WALDO EMERSON,
>   and almost certainly spoken by him in a
>   lecture either in San Francisco or Oak-
>   land in April or May, 1871. This ver-
>   sion, credited to Emerson, appears on
>   page 38 of an anthology, *Borrowings,*
>   "Compiled by Ladies of the First Uni-
>   tarian Church of Oakland, California,"
>   and published in December, 1889. Mrs.
>   Sarah S. B. Yule, who contributed the

quotation to the anthology, asserted in
The Docket of Feb., 1912 that "to the
best of my knowledge and belief, I copied it in my handbook from an address
delivered long years ago, it being my
custom to write everything there that I
thought particularly good, if expressed
in concise form; and when we were
compiling *Borrowings,* I drew from this
old handbook freely."

I trust a good deal to common fame, as we
all must. If a man has good corn, or wood, or
boards, or pigs, to sell, or can make better
chairs or knives, crucibles, or church organs,
than anybody else, you will find a broad,
hard-beaten road to his house, though it be
in the woods.
>   EMERSON, *Journals: Common Fame,* 1855,
>   vol. viii, p. 528. In the *Journals of
>   Ralph Waldo Emerson,* the editors, Ed-
>   ward Waldo Emerson and Waldo Emer-
>   son Forbes, used this footnote: "There
>   has been much inquiry in the newspa-
>   pers, recently [1911], as to whether Mr.
>   Emerson wrote a sentence very like the
>   above, which has been attributed to him
>   in print. The Editors do not find the
>   latter in his works; but there can be
>   little doubt that it was a memory-quota-
>   tion by some hearer, or, quite probably,
>   correctly reported from one of his lec-
>   tures, the same image in differing
>   words."

If a man knows the law, people find it out,
tho' he live in a pine shanty, and resort to
him. And if a man can pipe or sing, so as to
wrap the prisoned soul in an elysium; or can
paint landscape, and convey into oils and
ochres all enchantments of Spring and Autumn; or can liberate and intoxicate all people who hear him with delicious songs and
verses; it is certain that the secret cannot be
kept: the first witness tells it to a second,
and men go by fives and tens and fifties to
his door.
>   EMERSON, *Journals: Common Fame,* 1855,
>   vol. viii, p. 528.

If a man write a better book, preach a better
sermon, or build a better mouse-trap than his
neighbor, though he build his house in the
woods, the world will make a beaten path to
his door.
>   ELBERT HUBBARD, *A Thousand and One
>   Epigrams* (1911), p. 166. Earlier Hub-
>   bard used the same quotation, in slightly
>   different form, in *The Philistine* and
>   credited it to Emerson. Subsequently
>   Hubbard claimed authorship. But since
>   the first number of *The Philistine* did
>   not appear until 1895, and the quotation

appeared in *Borrowings* in 1889, Hubbard's claim appears groundless.

A man can't be hid. He may be a peddler in the mountains, but the world will find him out to make him a king of finance. He may be carrying cabbages from Long Island, when the world will demand that he run the railways of a continent. He may be a groceryman on a canal, when the country shall come to him and put him in his career of usefulness. So that there comes a time finally when all the green barrels of petroleum in the land suggest but two names and one great company.

> DR. JOHN RANDOLPH PAXTON, Sermon, *He Could Not Be Hid,* 25 Aug., 1889. (Reported in the New York *Sun,* 26 Aug., 1889.) Dr. Paxton has also been credited with the "mouse-trap" quotation. More likely the foregoing is an adaptation from Emerson.

1
The longest wave is quickly lost in the sea.
> EMERSON, *Representative Men: Plato.*

2
He pays too high a price
  For knowledge and for fame
Who sells his sinews to be wise,
  His teeth and bones to buy a name,
And crawls through life a paralytic
To earn the praise of bard and critic.
> EMERSON, *Fame.*

3
Fame is proof that the people are gullible.
> EMERSON.

4
Fame usually comes to those who are thinking about something else,—very rarely to those who say to themselves, "Go to, now, let us be a celebrated individual!" The struggle for fame, as such, commonly ends in notoriety;—that ladder is easy to climb, but it leads to the pillory which is crowded with fools who could not hold their tongues and rogues who could not hide their tricks.
> OLIVER WENDELL HOLMES, *The Autocrat of the Breakfast-Table,* ch 12.

5
Ah, pensive scholar, what is fame?
A fitful tongue of leaping flame;
A giddy whirlwind's fickle gust,
That lifts a pinch of mortal dust;
A few swift years, and who can show
Which dust was Bill, and which was Joe?
> OLIVER WENDELL HOLMES, *Bill and Joe,* st. 7.

6
Fame is delightful, but as collateral it does not rank high.
> ELBERT HUBBARD, *Epigrams.*

7
I must have introduced more than a thousand notables, all of 'em supposed to be important. Hell, there aren't that many important people in the world.
> CLARENCE BUDINGTON KELLAND, describing his activities as toastmaster of the Dutch Treat Club in New York City in the 1930's. (New York *Herald Tribune* obituary of Mr. Kelland, 20 Feb., 1964)

8
Sleep on, O brave-hearted, O wise man that kindled the flame—
To live in mankind is far more than to live in a name.
> VACHEL LINDSAY, *The Eagle That Is Forgotten.*

9
Fame comes only when deserved, and then is as inevitable as destiny, for it is destiny.
> HENRY WADSWORTH LONGFELLOW, *Hyperion,* bk. i, ch. 8.

10
His fame was great in all the land.
> HENRY WADSWORTH LONGFELLOW, *Tales of a Wayside Inn: The Student's Tale: Emma and Eginhard,* l. 50.

11
Death is not an automatic confirmer of fame: more often than not it opens questions that life had seemed to close, dissolving indestructible reputations in its ironic silence. Only rarely does a great name grow greater when its owner leaves it, as Eleanor Roosevelt's unquestionably has.
> ARCHIBALD MACLEISH, *Tribute to a 'Great American Lady'; New York Times Magazine,* 3 Nov., 1963. The opening sentences.

12
Fame lulls the fever of the soul, and makes
Us feel that we have grasp'd an immortality.
> JOAQUIN MILLER, *Ina,* sc. 4, l. 273.

13
As he rose like a rocket, he fell like a stick.
> THOMAS PAINE, *Letter to His Addressers.* The reference is to Edmund Burke.

14
We toil for fame
  We live on crusts,
We make a name,
  Then we are busts.
> L. H. ROBBINS, *Lines,* intended for delivery at the unveiling of Hall of Fame memorials to James Monroe, Matthew Maury, Walt Whitman, and J. A. McNeill Whistler.

15
No true and permanent Fame can be founded except in labors which promote the happiness of mankind.
> CHARLES SUMNER, Address, *Fame and Glory,* delivered at Amherst College, 11 Aug., 1847.

1
Fame is but a slow decay—
Even this shall pass away.

> THEODORE TILTON, *Even This Shall Pass Away.*

FAMILY

See also Home

2
A "good" family, it seems, is one that used to be better.

> CLEVELAND AMORY, *Who Killed Society?*

3
The security and elevation of the family and of family life are the prime objects of civilization, and the ultimate ends of all industry.

> CHARLES W. ELIOT, *The Happy Life.*

4
Happy will that house be in which the relations are formed from character.

> EMERSON, *Society and Solitude: Domestic Life.*

5
Most of the persons whom I see in my own house I see across a gulf.

> EMERSON, *Journals,* vol. v, p. 324.

6
I believe in the fireside. I believe in the democracy of home. I believe in the republicanism of the family.

> ROBERT G. INGERSOLL, *The Liberty of Man, Woman and Child.*

7
A holy family, that make
Each meal a Supper of the Lord.

> HENRY WADSWORTH LONGFELLOW, *The Golden Legend,* pt. i.

8
God gives us relatives; thank God, we can choose our friends.

> ADDISON MIZNER, *The Cynics' Calendar,* p. 1.

9
The family is one of nature's masterpieces.

> GEORGE SANTAYANA, *The Life of Reason,* vol. ii, p. 35.

FANATICISM

See also Extremes; Politics; Reform, Reformers

10
There is no strong performance without a little fanaticism in the performer.

> EMERSON, *Journals,* vol. ix, p. 203.

11
This, I believe, is the core of the democratic spirit. When we acknowledge our own fallibility, tolerance and compromise become possible and fanaticism becomes absurd.

> J. W. FULBRIGHT, Address at Rockefeller Public Service Awards luncheon, Washington, D.C., 5 Dec., 1963.

12
Fanaticism is not a characteristic of mature societies but of unstable and politically primitive societies. Nor is it an expression of strength and self-confidence.

> J. W. FULBRIGHT, Address, Sept., 1964, during the presidential campaign.

13
The irresponsibles win elections—but always for the other party.

> LYNDON B. JOHNSON, commenting on his role as Senate majority leader during the Eisenhower Administration, when he was frequently criticized by fellow Democrats for not following a more aggressively partisan course. (HENRY A. ZEIGER, *Lyndon B. Johnson: Man and President,* p. 61)

14
What we have to realize is that, though speech and gossip and rumor are free, the safety of the Republic is at stake when extremists go unrestrained. Extremists may profess any ideology. But what they all have in common is that they treat opponents as enemies, outside the laws and the community of their fellow men. . . . An extremist is an outsider. For him the government in Washington is a hated foreign power and the President in Washington is an invading conqueror. There is no limit, therefore, to his hatred, which feeds upon the venom of malice, slander and hallucination.

> WALTER LIPPMANN, Syndicated Column commenting on the assassination of John F. Kennedy. (New York *Herald Tribune,* 26 Nov., 1963)

15
The fanatics of today are the outgrowth of yesterday's false preachments. No longer can those in positions of responsibility merely abhor violence, yet preach the dark doctrines which inspire violence.

> CARL E. SANDERS, Speech in Augusta, Ga., 25 Nov., 1963. The governor of Georgia was addressing an audience at a memorial service for John F. Kennedy.

16
Fanaticism consists in redoubling your effort when you have forgotten your aim.

> GEORGE SANTAYANA, *The Life of Reason,* vol. i, p. 13.

17
What a price we pay for this fanaticism!

> EARL WARREN, Eulogy to John F. Kennedy, 24 Nov., 1963.

FARMING

18
You come to us and tell us that the great cities are in favor of the gold standard; we reply that the great cities rest upon our broad and fertile prairies. Burn down your cities and leave our farms, and your cities will spring up again as if by magic; but de-

stroy our farms and the grass will grow in the streets of every city in the country.

> WILLIAM JENNINGS BRYAN, Speech at Democratic national convention, Chicago, 8 July, 1896.

1

Far back in the ages,
   The plough with wreaths was crowned;
The hands of kings and sages
   Entwined the chaplet round.

> WILLIAM CULLEN BRYANT, *Ode for an Agricultural Celebration.*

2

The first farmer was the first man, and all historic nobility rests on possession and use of land.

> EMERSON, *Society and Solitude: Farming.*

3

The glory of the farmer is that, in the division of labors, it is his part to create. All trade rests at last on his primitive activity.

> EMERSON, *Society and Solitude: Farming.*

4

The farmer is covetous of his dollar, and with reason.

> EMERSON, *Conduct of Life: Wealth.*

5

Drop a grain of California gold into the ground, and there it will lie unchanged until the end of time; . . . drop a grain of our blessed gold into the ground and lo! a mystery.

> EDWARD EVERETT, Address on Agriculture, Boston, Oct., 1855. The reference is to wheat.

6

A Plowman on his legs is higher than a Gentleman on his Knees.

> BENJAMIN FRANKLIN, *Poor Richard,* 1746.

7

He that by the Plough would thrive,
Himself must either hold or drive.

> BENJAMIN FRANKLIN, *Poor Richard,* 1747.

8

Plough deep while sluggards sleep.

> BENJAMIN FRANKLIN, *Poor Richard,* 1758.

9

A man's soul may be buried and perish under a dungheap or in a furrow of the field, just as well as under a pile of money.

> NATHANIEL HAWTHORNE, *Journals,* 1 June, 1841.

10

To plow is to pray—to plant is to prophesy, and the harvest answers and fulfills.

> ROBERT G. INGERSOLL, *About Farming in Illinois.*

11

Those who labor in the earth are the chosen people of God, if He ever had a chosen people, whose breasts He has made His peculiar deposit for substantial and genuine virtue.

> THOMAS JEFFERSON, *Writings,* vol. ii, p. 229.

12

Whenever there are in any country uncultivated lands and unemployed poor it is clear that the laws of property have been so far extended as to violate natural right. The earth is given as a common stock for men to labor and live on. . . . The small landowners are the most precious part of the State.

> THOMAS JEFFERSON, *Writings,* vol. xix, p. 17.

13

The best fertilizer for a piece of land is the footprints of its owner.

> LYNDON B. JOHNSON, Remark, made during an inspection of his Texas ranch during the Christmas holidays, 1963. (JAMES RESTON, Washington Column, New York *Times,* 8 Jan., 1964)

14

No one hates his job so heartily as a farmer.

> H. L. MENCKEN, *What Is Going on in the World; American Mercury,* Nov., 1933.

15

The farmer is endeavoring to solve the problem of a livelihood by a formula more complicated than the problem itself. To get his shoestrings he speculates in herds of cattle. With consummate skill he has set his trap with a hair springe to catch comfort and independence, and then, as he turned away, got his own leg into it. This is the reason he is poor.

> HENRY D. THOREAU, *Walden,* ch. 1.

16

He was a very inferior farmer when he first began, . . . and he is now fast rising from affluence to poverty.

> MARK TWAIN, *Rev. Henry Ward Beecher's Farm.*

17

Blessed be agriculture! if one does not have too much of it.

> CHARLES DUDLEY WARNER, *My Summer in a Garden:* Preliminary.

18

Let us never forget that the cultivation of the earth is the most important labor of man.

> DANIEL WEBSTER, Remarks on agriculture, Boston, 13 Jan., 1840.

19

When tillage begins, other arts follow. The farmers, therefore, are the founders of human civilization.

> DANIEL WEBSTER, Remarks on agriculture, Boston, 13 Jan., 1840.

20

Heap high the farmer's wintry hoard!
Heap high the golden corn!

No richer gift has Autumn poured
    From out her lavish horn!
    JOHN GREENLEAF WHITTIER, *The Corn-
        Song.*

1
Give fools their gold, and knaves their pow-
    er;
Let fortune's bubbles rise and fall;
Who sows a field, or trains a flower,
Or plants a tree, is more than all.
    JOHN GREENLEAF WHITTIER, *A Song of
        Harvest.*

2
Farming is not really a business; it is an
occupation.
    W. E. WOODWARD, *Money for Tomorrow,*
        p. 177.

3
Ten acres and a mule.
    UNKNOWN, a phrase that originated in the
        United States in 1862 and indicated
        what a slave expected to get upon eman-
        cipation.

FASHION
See also Dress

4
To live content with small means; to seek
elegance rather than luxury, and refinement
rather than fashion.
    WILLIAM HENRY CHANNING, *My Sym-
        phony.*

5
By and large the fashion industry has made
it a misdemeanor to be a Woman; an affront
against a society in which the ideal and only
permissible figure is that of a girl of twenty
in a size 8.
    MARYA MANNES, *Juno in Limbo; Harper's
        Magazine,* July, 1964, p. 38.

6
You cannot be both fashionable and first-
rate.
    LOGAN PEARSALL SMITH, *Afterthoughts.*

7
Every generation laughs at the old fashions,
but follows religiously the new.
    HENRY D. THOREAU, *Walden,* ch. 1.

8
Give feminine fashions time enough and they
will starve all the moths to death.
    UNKNOWN. (Detroit *Free Press,* June,
        1925)

FATE
See also Destiny, Fortune, Providence

9
The bow is bent, the arrow flies,
The wingèd shaft of fate.
    IRA ALDRIDGE, *On William Tell,* st. 12.

10
Whatever limits us, we call Fate. . . . The
limitations refine as the soul purifies, but the
ring of necessity is always perched at the
top.
    EMERSON, *Conduct of Life: Fate.*

11
'Tis weak and vicious people who cast the
blame on Fate.
    EMERSON, *Conduct of Life: Fate.*

12
Fate is nothing but the deeds committed in a
prior state of existence.
    EMERSON, *Conduct of Life: Fate.* Quoted
        as a Hindu proverb.

13
Fate, then, is a name for facts not yet passed
under the fire of thought. . . . Fate is un-
penetrated causes.
    EMERSON, *Conduct of Life: Fate.*

14
If we are related we shall meet.
    EMERSON, *Essays, Second Series: Charac-
        ter.*

15
Be the proud captain still of thine own fate.
    JAMES B. KENYON, *The Black Camel.*

16
All are architects of Fate,
    Working in these walls of Time;
Some with massive deeds and great,
    Some with ornaments of rhyme.
    HENRY WADSWORTH LONGFELLOW, *The
        Builders,* st. 1.

17
For some must follow, and some command
Though all are made of clay!
    HENRY WADSWORTH LONGFELLOW, *Kera-
        mos,* l. 6.

18
Let us, then, be up and doing,
    With a heart for any fate.
    HENRY WADSWORTH LONGFELLOW, *A
        Psalm of Life.*

19
Fate is the gunman that all gunmen dread;
    Fate stings the Stinger for his roll of
        green;
    Fate, Strong-arm Worker, on the bean
Of strong-arm workers bumps his pipe of
    lead.
    DON MARQUIS, *Proverbs.*

20
The outward wayward life we see,
    The hidden springs we may not know.
        . . .
It is not ours to separate
The tangled skein of will and fate.
    JOHN GREENLEAF WHITTIER, *Snow-Bound,*
        l. 565.

FATHER

21
We admire our fathers quite too much. It
shows that we have no energy in ourselves,
when we rate it so prodigiously high. Rather

let us shame the fathers by superior virtue in the sons.

EMERSON, *Journal*, 1861.

1

While we criticise the fathers for being narrow, we should not forget that they were also deep. We are inclined to be so broad that people can see through us most any place.

WILLIAM HIRAM FOULKES, Sermon.

2

The commonest axiom of history is that every generation revolts against its fathers and makes friends with its grandfathers.

LEWIS MUMFORD, *The Brown Decades*.

3

No man is responsible for his father. That is entirely his mother's affair.

MARGARET TURNBULL, *Alabaster Lamps*, p. 300.

FATNESS

4

When a 220-pound man laughs, there is twice as much of him having a good time as when a 110-pound man laughs. This is one of the advantages of being fat.

HAL BOYLE, Column, Associated Press, datelined 1 Oct., 1964.

5

The next time you see a fat man plodding by, restrain that impulse to laugh. Give the matter a second thought. Isn't the real reason you want to poke fun at him the fact that you're secretly jealous of him? After all, you know—and he knows, too—that any fool can be skinny if he wants to. All he has to do is quit eating.

HAL BOYLE, Column, Associated Press datelined 1 Oct., 1964.

6

W'at good eesa wife eef she don'ta be fat?

THOMAS A. DALY, *Da Styleesha Wife*.

7

Nobody loves a fat man.

EDMUND DAY, *The Round-Up*. This line was made famous by the actor Maclyn Arbuckle, as Sheriff "Slim" Hoover.

The reason everybody loves a fat man is that everyone feels superior to him; if you give a fellow a reason to feel superior to you he can't help liking you.

HAL BOYLE, Column, Associated Press, datelined 14 Oct., 1965.

8

Who ever hears of fat men heading a riot, or herding together in turbulent mobs?—no— no, 'tis your lean, hungry men who are continually worrying society, and setting the whole community by the ears.

WASHINGTON IRVING, *Knickerbocker's History of New York*, book iii, ch. 2.

9

There are few brains that would not be bet-

ter for living on their own fat a little while.

JAMES RUSSELL LOWELL, *A Moosehead Journal*.

10

No gentleman ever weighs more than two hundred pounds.

THOMAS B. REED, Reply, when someone questioned Reed's statement that his own weight was 199 pounds. (ROBINSON, *Life of Reed*.)

11

I find no sweeter fat than sticks to my own bones.

WALT WHITMAN, *Song of Myself*.

FAULTS

12

Every man in his lifetime needs to thank his faults. . . . Has he a defect of temper that unfits him to live in society? Thereby he is driven to entertain himself alone and acquire habits of self-help; and thus, like the wounded oyster, he mends his shell with pearl.

EMERSON, *Essays, First Series: Compensation*.

13

A benevolent man should allow a few faults in himself, to keep his friends in countenance.

BENJAMIN FRANKLIN, *Autobiography*, ch. 1.

14

Let me be a little kinder,
Let me be a little blinder
To the faults of those around me,
Let me praise a little more.

EDGAR A. GUEST, *A Creed*.

15

His very faults smack of the raciness of his good qualities.

WASHINGTON IRVING, *Sketch Book: John Bull*. Concerning the Englishman.

16

Mistakes remember'd are not faults forgot.

R. H. NEWELL, *The Orpheus C. Kerr Papers: Columbia's Agony*, st. 9.

17

With all her faults I love her still.

MONROE H. ROSENFELD, Title and refrain of popular song (1888).

18

It is no one's fault, but everyone's problem.

ROBERT F. WAGNER, JR. commenting in July, 1965, on the acrimonious debate over the water shortage that threatened New York City during the final months of his last term as mayor.

19

But, by all thy nature's weakness,
Hidden faults and follies known,
Be thou, in rebuking evil,
Conscious of thine own.

JOHN GREENLEAF WHITTIER, *What the Voice Said*, st. 15.

FAVOR
See Benefits, Gifts, Kindness

FEAR

1
It's flopsweat down your back, enough to rot the timbers of the stage.
> DAVID BURNS, referring to stage fright. (LEWIS FUNKE, *Always in the Wings—the Shakes; New York Times Magazine,* 17 May, 1964)

2
O praise not him who fears his God
But show me him who knows not fear!
> JAMES FENIMORE COOPER, *Fate.*

3
The first and great commandment is, Don't let them scare you.
> ELMER DAVIS, *But We Were Born Free.*

4
Fear is an instructor of great sagacity, and the herald of all revolutions.
> EMERSON, *Essays, First Series: Compensation.*

5
All infractions of love and equity in our social relations are speedily punished. They are punished by fear.
> EMERSON, *Essays, First Series: Compensation.*

6
If I quake, what matters it what I quake at?
> EMERSON, *Essays, Second Series: Character.*

7
Fear always springs from ignorance.
> EMERSON, *Nature, Addresses, and Lectures: The American Scholar.*

8
He has not learned the lesson of life who does not every day surmount a fear.
> EMERSON, *Society and Solitude: Courage.*

9
Our tragedy today is a general and universal physical fear so long sustained by now that we can even bear it. There are no longer problems of the spirit. There is only the question: when will I be blown up?
> WILLIAM FAULKNER, Address in Stockholm, 10 Dec., 1950, upon accepting the Nobel Prize in literature.

10
There is the fear that we shan't prove worthy in the eyes of someone who knows us at least as well as we know ourselves. That is the fear of God. And there is the fear of Man—fear that men won't understand us and we shall be cut off from them.
> ROBERT FROST. (*Newsweek,* 11 Feb., 1963)

11
A good scare is worth more to a man than good advice.
> E. W. HOWE, *Howe's Monthly.*

12
The thing we fear we bring to pass.
> ELBERT HUBBARD, *The Philistine,* vol. xxv, p. 143.

13
There is no panic on our agenda.
> LYNDON B. JOHNSON, Speech in Los Angeles, 21 Feb., 1964.

14
The one permanent emotion of the inferior man is fear—fear of the unknown, the complex, the inexplicable. What he wants beyond everything else is safety.
> H. L. MENCKEN, *Prejudices,* ser. ii, p. 75.

15
Nerves provide me with energy. They work for me. It's when I don't have them, when I feel at ease, that I get worried.
> MIKE NICHOLS. (Lewis Funke, *Always in the Wings—the Shakes; New York Times Magazine,* 17 May, 1964)

16
You gain strength, courage and confidence by every experience in which you really stop to look fear in the face.
> ELEANOR ROOSEVELT, *You Learn by Living.*

17
Nothing is so much to be feared as fear.
> HENRY D. THOREAU, quoted as from Thoreau's unpublished manuscripts by Ralph Waldo Emerson in the latter's address at Thoreau's funeral, 8 May, 1862. Later included in EMERSON's *Lectures and Biographical Sketches.*

The only thing we have to fear is fear itself.
> FRANKLIN D. ROOSEVELT, First Inaugural Address, 4 Mar., 1933.

18
Fear is the father of courage and the mother of safety.
> HENRY H. TWEEDY, Sermon in Princeton University chapel.

FEELING

19
Thought is deeper than all speech,
Feeling deeper than all thought.
> CHRISTOPHER PEARSE CRANCH, *Thought.*

20
There are moments in life, when the heart is so full of emotion,
That if by chance it be shaken, or into its depths like a pebble
Drops some careless word, it overflows, and its secret,
Spilt on the ground like water, can never be gathered together.
> HENRY WADSWORTH LONGFELLOW, *The Courtship of Miles Standish,* pt. vi, l. 12.

21
Sentiment is intellectualized emotion, emo-

tion precipitated, as it were, in pretty crystals by the fancy.

> JAMES RUSSELL LOWELL, *Among My Books: Rousseau and the Sentimentalists.*

1

I have no feelings except a few which I reserve for Mrs. Marshall.

> GEORGE C. MARSHALL, to Dean Acheson, when Marshall assumed his duties as secretary of state and announced that he wanted his colleagues to be completely truthful to the point of bluntness, if necessary. (H. S. TRUMAN, *Memoirs,* 1956)

2

The wealth of rich feelings—the deep—the pure;
With strength to meet sorrow, and faith to endure.

> FRANCES S. OSGOOD, *To F. D. Maurice.*

FICTION

3

Novelists, whatever else they may be besides, are also children talking to children—in the dark.

> BERNARD DE VOTO, *The World of Fiction.*

4

Novels are as useful as Bibles, if they teach you the secret that the best of life is conversation, and the greatest success is confidence.

> EMERSON, *Conduct of Life: Behavior.*

5

How far off from life and manners and motives the novel still is! Life lies about. us dumb; the day, as we know it, has not yet found a tongue.

> EMERSON, *Society and Solitude: Books.*

6

Great is the poverty of their [novelists'] inventions. She was beautiful and he fell in love.

> EMERSON, *Society and Solitude: Books.*

7

We have seen an American woman write a novel of which a million copies were sold in all languages, and which had one merit, of speaking to the universal heart, and was read with equal interest to three audiences, namely, in the parlor, in the kitchen, and in the nursery of every house.

> EMERSON, *Society and Solitude: Success.* Referring to Harriet Beecher Stowe and *Uncle Tom's Cabin.*

8

When writing a novel a writer should create living people; people not characters.

> ERNEST HEMINGWAY, *Death in the Afternoon,* ch. 16.

9

History is bright and fiction dull with homely men who have charmed women.

> O. HENRY, *Roads of Destiny.*

10

The only reason for the existence of a novel is that it does attempt to represent life.

> HENRY JAMES, *The Art of Fiction.*

11

The only obligation to which in advance we may hold a novel, without incurring the accusation of being arbitrary, is that it be interesting.

> HENRY JAMES, *The Art of Fiction.*

12

A little attention to the nature of the human mind evinces that the entertainments of fiction are useful as well as pleasant. . . . Everything is useful which contributes to fix the principles and practices of virtue.

> THOMAS JEFFERSON, *Writings,* vol. iv, p. 237.

13

Character in decay is the theme of the great bulk of superior fiction.

> H. L. MENCKEN, *Prejudices,* ser. i, p. 41.

14

I was taught that the only place worth writing about is the human heart. The description of that bleak and wonderful terrain is the principal responsibility of the novelist, and those writings tend to live which best detail what happens there.

> JAMES A. MICHENER, *How Much People, How Much Place?; Authors Guild Bulletin,* Apr., 1964, p. 1.

FIDELITY

15

Whatever the outcome of the appeal, I do not intend to turn my back on Alger Hiss.

> DEAN ACHESON, upon being informed of the conviction of Hiss for perjury early in 1950. Hiss, who had been a State Department associate of Acheson, was one of the central figures in a celebrated case involving charges of the transmitting of secret U.S. documents to the Soviet Union.

16

This thing Allegiance, as I suppose,
Is a ring fitted in the subject's nose,
Whereby that organ is kept rightly pointed
To smell the sweetness of the Lord's anointed.

> AMBROSE BIERCE, *The Devil's Dictionary,* p. 22.

17

Many free countries have lost their liberty, and ours may lose hers: but if she shall, be it my proudest plume, not that I was the last to desert, but that I never deserted her.

> ABRAHAM LINCOLN, Speech in Springfield, Ill., Dec., 1839.

18

There is something in the unselfish and self-sacrificing love of a brute, which goes directly to the heart of him who has had frequent occasion to test the paltry friendship and gossamer fidelity of mere Man.

EDGAR ALLAN POE, *The Black Cat.*

1
Always True to You (in My Fashion).

COLE PORTER, Title and refrain of song from the musical comedy *Kiss Me, Kate* (1948). Fidelity, in this case, is a highly elastic quality.

2
It is better to be faithful than famous.

THEODORE ROOSEVELT. (RIIS, *Theodore Roosevelt, the Citizen,* p. 403)

3
The secret of a good life is to have the right loyalties and to hold them in the right scale of values.

NORMAN THOMAS, *Great Dissenters.*

4
It is easier for a man to be loyal to his club than to his planet; the by-laws are shorter, and he is personally acquainted with the other members.

E. B. WHITE, *One Man's Meat.*

5
Semper fidelis. (Ever faithful.)

UNKNOWN, a Latin maxim that is the motto of the U.S. Marine Corps.

FIGHTING

See also War

6
"Oh, the fighting races don't die out,
If they seldom die in bed."

J. I. C. CLARK, *The Fighting Race,* st. 5.

7
I, too, am fighting my campaign.

EMERSON, *Journal,* 1864.

8
I propose to fight it out on this line if it takes all summer.

U. S. GRANT, Dispatch to General Henry W. Halleck, 11 May, 1864.

9
Life's sovereign moment is a battle won.

OLIVER WENDELL HOLMES, *The Banker's Secret.*

10
I have not yet begun to fight.

JOHN PAUL JONES, Reply to an ultimatum to surrender, as his *Bonhomme Richard* was sinking under him during an engagement with the British *Serapis,* 23 Sept., 1779.

11
Ef you want peace, the thing you've gut tu du
Is jes' to show you're up to fightin', tu.

JAMES RUSSELL LOWELL, *The Biglow Papers,* Ser. ii, No. 2.

12
You who are old,
And have fought the fight,
And have won or lost or left the fight,
Weight us not down

With fears of the world, as we run!

CALE YOUNG RICE, *The Young to the Old.*

13
We're eyeball to eyeball, and the other fellow just blinked.

DEAN RUSK, Comment, Oct., 1962, during the tense period that followed U.S. demands for the removal of Soviet missiles from Cuba. Rusk had just been informed that some Soviet ships, bound for Cuba with more missiles, had suddenly turned tail during the voyage.

14
To fight is a radical instinct; if men have nothing else to fight over they will fight over words, fancies, or women, or they will fight because they dislike each other's looks, or because they have met walking in opposite directions. To knock a thing down, especially if it is cocked at an arrogant angle, is a deep delight to the blood.

GEORGE SANTAYANA, *Soliloquies in England: On War.*

15
For it is often easier to fight for principles than to live up to them.

ADLAI E. STEVENSON, Speech in New York City, 27 Aug., 1952, during the presidential campaign.

16
The joy of life is a fighting chance.

NORMAN THOMAS, Televison documentary, *Norman Thomas: Years of Protest,* 1 Mar., 1966, WNDT, New York City.

17
Not to the swift, the race:
Not to the strong, the fight:
Not to the righteous, perfect grace:
Not to the wise, the light.

HENRY VAN DYKE, *Reliance.*

18
By a sudden and adroit movement I placed my left eye agin the Secesher's fist. . . . The ground flew up and hit me in the hed.

ARTEMUS WARD, *Thrilling Scenes in Dixie.*

19
There is such a thing as a man being too proud to fight.

WOODROW WILSON, Address in Philadelphia, 10 May, 1915.

FINANCE

See also Business, Money

20
It is a curious fact that capital is generally most fearful when prices of commodities and securities are low and safe, and boldest at the heights when there is danger.

BERNARD M. BARUCH. (New York *Times* obituary of Baruch, 21 June, 1965, p. 16)

21
Repeatedly in my market operations I have sold a stock while it was rising—and that has

been one reason why I have held on to my fortune.

> BERNARD M. BARUCH. (New York *Times* obituary of Baruch, 21 June, 1965, p. 16)

1

Trusts are largely private affairs.

> JAMES G. BLAINE, Speech in Portland, Me., during the presidential campaign of 1888.

2

A power has risen up in the government greater than the people themselves, consisting of many and various and powerful interests . . . held together by the cohesive power of the vast surplus in the banks.

> JOHN C. CALHOUN, Speech in U. S. Senate, 27 May, 1836.

Cohesive power of public plunder.

> GROVER CLEVELAND, paraphrasing Calhoun.

3

They throw cats and dogs together and call them elephants.

> ANDREW CARNEGIE, Interview, referring to industrial promoters.

4

The communism of combined wealth and capital, the outgrowth of overweening cupidity and selfishness which assiduously undermines the justice and integrity of free institutions, is not less dangerous than the communism of oppressed poverty and toil which, exasperated by injustice and discontent, attacks with wild disorder the citadel of misrule.

> GROVER CLEVELAND, Annual Message, 1888.

5

Trust.

> SAMUEL C. T. DODD introduced this word, in its financial sense, in 1882, while acting as attorney for John D. Rockefeller.

This is the original trust.

> UNKNOWN, Report of Committee, New York State Senate, following investigation of the Standard Oil Company, 1888.

6

What good, honest, generous men at home will be wolves and foxes on change!

> EMERSON, *Conduct of Life: Fate.*

7

This bank-note world.

> FITZ-GREENE HALLECK, *Alnwick Castle.*

8

Earnest attention should be given to those combinations of capital commonly called Trusts.

> BENJAMIN HARRISON, Message to Congress, 3 Dec., 1889.

9

He [Daniel Drew] seems never to have denied his most celebrated piece of knavery, which he used in his cattle business for many years. As a big herd of anywhere from six hundred to a thousand head of Ohio beef approached New York City, Drew had his drovers salt them well, then, just before reaching the market place, he let them drink their fill. Cattle were sold live-weight. Drew's processing with salt and water added many tons to the average herd. "Watered stock" soon became a term in Wall Street.

> STEWART H. HOLBROOK, *The Age of the Moguls*, p. 21.

10

I sincerely believe that banking establishments are more dangerous than standing armies, and that the principle of spending money to be paid by posterity, under the name of funding, is but swindling futurity on a large scale.

> THOMAS JEFFERSON, Letter to Elbridge Gerry, 26 Jan., 1799.

11

Special privilege.

> ROBERT M. LA FOLLETTE, Speech in U.S. Senate, referring to trusts.

12

Monopolies are odious, contrary to the spirit of free government and the principles of commerce and ought not to be suffered.

> Maryland Declaration of 1776. The reference is to grants of monopoly by royal decree.

13

What are fantastically termed securities.

> S. WEIR MITCHELL, *Characteristics*, ch. 2.

14

Undigested securities.

> J. PIERPONT MORGAN, Interview, New York *Times*, 30 Mar., 1903. The reference is to securities issued to inflate and water the capitalization of trusts and combinations, promoted and floated in 1901.

15

Bankers Are Just Like Anybody Else, Except Richer.

> OGDEN NASH, Title of poem from the collection *I'm a Stranger Here Myself.*

16

He has subjugated Wall street.

> JOSEPH PULITZER, in the New York *World*, referring to Theodore Roosevelt.

17

An indefinable something is to be done, in a way nobody knows how, at a time nobody knows when, that will accomplish nobody knows what. That, as I understand it, is the program against the trusts.

> THOMAS B. REED. (W. A. ROBINSON, *Life of Reed*)

1
One-third of the people in the United States promote, while the other two-thirds provide.
> WILL ROGERS, *The Illiterate Digest*, p. 121.

2
The money-changers have fled from their high seats in the temple of our civilization. We may now restore that temple to the ancient truths.
> FRANKLIN D. ROOSEVELT, First Inaugural Address, 4 Mar., 1933.

3
Malefactors of great wealth.
> THEODORE ROOSEVELT, Speech in Provincetown, Mass., 20 Aug., 1907.

4
The System.
> LINCOLN STEFFENS. The term described the supercommunity of interests that existed between trusts.

The Octopus.
> FRANK NORRIS, Title of novel based on "the system."

5
Banks are failing all over the country, but not the sand banks, solid and warm and streaked with bloody blackberry vines. You may run on them as much as you please, even as the crickets do, and find their account in it. They are the stockholders in these banks, and I hear them creaking their content. In these banks, too, and such as these, are my funds deposited, funds of health and enjoyment. Invest in these country banks. Let your capital be simplicity and contentment.
> HENRY D. THOREAU, *Journal*, 14 Oct., 1859.

6
Where are the c-c-c-customers' yachts?
> WILLIAM R. TRAVERS, on being shown a squadron of brokers' yachts in New York harbor. (HENRY CLEWS, *Fifty Years in Wall Street*, p. 416)

7
The way to stop financial joy-riding is to arrest the chauffeur, not the automobile.
> WOODROW WILSON. (LINTHICUM, *Wit and Wisdom of Woodrow Wilson*)

8
The mother of trusts.
> WOODROW WILSON, 1898. The reference is to New Jersey, whose laws authorized the creation of "holding-corporations."

I made the first speech in favor of organizing industrial consolidations in the eighties. Later the Chicago newspapers gave me the title of "Father of Trusts."
> CHARLES R. FLINT, *Memories of an Active Life*.

9
The Seven Sisters.
> UNKNOWN. This term applied to seven laws, drawn up by Woodrow Wilson when he was governor of New Jersey, designed to end the state's statutory benevolence toward trusts.

FLAG

10
Uncover when the flag goes by, boys,
'Tis freedom's starry banner that you greet,
  Flag famed in song and story
  Long may it wave, Old Glory
The flag that has never known defeat.
> CHARLES L. BENJAMIN AND GEORGE SUTTON, *The Flag That Has Never Known Defeat*.

11
Hats off!
Along the street there comes
A blare of bugles, a ruffle of drums.
A flash of color beneath the sky:
Hats off!
The flag is passing by.
> H. H. BENNETT, *The Flag Goes By*.

12
Your banner's constellation types
  White freedom with its stars,
But what's the meaning of the stripes?
  They mean your negroes' scars.
> THOMAS CAMPBELL, *To the United States of North America* (1838).

England! Whence came each glowing hue
That tints your flag of meteor light,—
The streaming red, the deeper blue,
Crossed with the moonbeams' pearly white?
The blood, the bruise—the blue, the red—
Let Asia's groaning millions speak;
The white it tells of colour fled
From starving Erin's pallid cheek.
> GEORGE LUNT, *Answer to Thomas Campbell*. (Published in the Newburyport, Mass., *News*)

13
You're a Grand Old Flag.
> GEORGE M. COHAN, Title and refrain of an enduring song (1906), with words and music by Cohan.

14
Here's to the red of it,
There's not a thread of it,
No, not a shred of it,
In all the spread of it,
  From foot to head,
But heroes bled for it,
Faced steel and lead for it,
Precious blood shed for it,
  Bathing in red.
> JOHN DALY, *A Toast to the Flag*.

15
When Freedom from her mountain height
  Unfurled her standard to the air,

She tore the azure robe of night,
    And set the stars of glory there.
She mingled with its gorgeous dyes
The milky baldric of the skies,
And striped its pure celestial white
With streakings of the morning light.
Then from his mansion in the sun
She called her eagle bearer down,
And gave into his mighty hand
The symbol of her chosen land.
    JOSEPH RODMAN DRAKE, *The American Flag.*

1
There it is—Old Glory!
    CAPTAIN WILLIAM DRIVER, when an American flag was raised on a new ship of which he had just been named master, at Salem, Mass., Dec., 1831. This is considered the most likely of many claims to the origin of "Old Glory."

2
See the power of national emblems. Some stars, lilies, leopards, a crescent, a lion, an eagle, or other figure which came into credit God knows how, on an old rag of bunting, blowing in the wind on a fort at the ends of the earth, shall make the blood tingle under the rudest or the most conventional exterior.
    EMERSON, *Essays, Second Series: The Poet.*

3
I have seen the glories of art and architecture, and mountain and river; I have seen the sunset on the Jungfrau, and the full moon rise over Mont Blanc; but the fairest vision on which these eyes ever looked was the flag of my country in a foreign land. Beautiful as a flower to those who love it, terrible as a meteor to those who hate it, it is the symbol of the power and glory, and the honor, of fifty millions of Americans.
    GEORGE FRISBIE HOAR, Speech, 1878.

4
Nail to the mast her holy flag.
    OLIVER WENDELL HOLMES, *Old Ironsides.*

5
Ay, tear her tattered ensign down!
    Long has it waved on high,
And many an eye has danced to see
    That banner in the sky.
    OLIVER WENDELL HOLMES, *Old Ironsides.*

6
The flag of our stately battles, not struggles
    of wrath and greed,
Its stripes were a holy lesson, its spangles a
    deathless creed:
'T was red with the blood of freemen and
    white with the fear of the foe;
And the stars that fight in their courses
    'gainst tyrants its symbols know.
    JULIA WARD HOWE, *The Flag.*

7
The simple stone of Betsy Ross
Is covered now with mold and moss,
But still her deathless banner flies,
And keeps the color of the skies.
A nation thrills, a nation bleeds,
A nation follows where it leads,
And every man is proud to yield
His life upon a crimson field
    For Betsy's battle flag!
    MINNA IRVING, *Betsy's Battle Flag.*

8
Oh, say can you see by the dawn's early
    light,
What so proudly we hailed at the twilight's
    last gleaming?
Whose broad stripes and bright stars, thro'
    the perilous fight,
O'er the ramparts we watched were so gallantly streaming?
And the rockets' red glare, the bombs bursting in air,
Gave proof thro' the night that our flag was
    still there.
Oh, say does that star-spangled banner yet
    wave
O'er the land of the free and the home of the
    brave?
    FRANCIS SCOTT KEY, *The Star-Spangled Banner*, st. 1. Originally titled *Defence of Fort M'Henry*, it first was published in *The Baltimore Patriot*, 20 Sept., 1814. It gained official status as the American national anthem by an act of Congress in 1931.

9
Oh! thus be it ever, when freemen shall
    stand
Between their loved homes and the war's
    desolation!
Blest with victory and peace, may the heaven-rescued land
Praise the Power that hath made and preserved us a nation.
Then conquer we must, for our cause it is
    just,
And this be our motto: "In God is our
    trust."
And the star-spangled banner in triumph
    shall wave
O'er the land of the free and the home of the
    brave.
    FRANCIS SCOTT KEY, *The Star-Spangled Banner*, st. 4.

10
I am not the flag; not at all. I am but its shadow. I am whatever you make me, nothing more. I am your belief in yourself, your dream of what a People may become. . . . I am the day's work of the weakest man, and the largest dream of the most daring. . . . I am the clutch of an idea, and the reasoned purpose of resolution. I am no more than

you believe me to be and I am all that you
believe I can be. I am whatever you make
me, nothing more.
  FRANKLIN K. LANE, *Makers of the Flag.*

1

The cross, the flag are the embodiment of
our ideals and teach us not only how to live
but how to die.
  GENERAL DOUGLAS MACARTHUR, Statement made on Bataan peninsula, Philip-
  pine Islands, Feb., 1942, upon accepting
  chairmanship of the United States Flag
  Foundation.

2

  Where bastard Freedom waves
Her fustian flag in mockery over slaves.
  THOMAS MOORE, *To the Lord Viscount
  Forbes,* l. 153. Written from the City of
  Washington.

3

Your flag and my flag,
  And how it flies today
In your land and my land
  And half a world away!
Rose-red and blood-red
  The stripes forever gleam;
Snow-white and soul-white—
  The good forefathers' dream;
Sky-blue and true-blue,
  With stars to gleam aright—
The gloried guidon of the day,
  A shelter through the night.
  WILBUR D. NESBIT, *Your Flag and My
  Flag.*

4

What shall I say to you, Old Flag?
You are so grand in every fold,
So linked with mighty deeds of old,
So steeped in blood where heroes fell,
So torn and pierced by shot and shell,
So calm, so still, so firm, so true,
My throat swells at the sight of you,
  Old Flag!
  HUBBARD PARKER, *Old Flag.*

5

My name is as old as the glory of God,
So I came by the name of Old Glory.
  JAMES WHITCOMB RILEY, *The Name of
  Old Glory.*

6

Yes, we'll rally round the flag, boys, we'll
  rally once again,
Shouting the battle-cry of Freedom,
We will rally from the hill-side, we'll gather
  from the plain,
Shouting the battle-cry of Freedom.
  GEORGE F. ROOT, *The Battle-Cry of Free-
  dom.*

7

She's up there—Old Glory—where lightnings
  are sped,
She dazzles the nations with ripples of red,

And she'll wave for us living, or droop o'er
  us dead—
  The flag of our country forever.
  F. L. STANTON, *Our Flag Forever.*

8

I pledge allegiance to the flag of the United
States and to the Republic for which it
stands, one nation, indivisible, with liberty
and justice for all.
  JAMES B. UPHAM AND FRANCIS BELLAMY,
  Pledge to the Flag. This first appeared
  in *The Youth's Companion,* 8 Sept.,
  1892. Impetus for the pledge was provided by the proclamation of President
  Benjamin Harrison, setting aside 31
  Oct., 1892 for observance of the 400th
  anniversary of the discovery of America; part of the observance included
  suitable exercises in the schools.

9

"Shoot, if you must, this old gray head,
But spare your country's flag," she said.

  . . .

"Who touches a hair of yon gray head
Dies like a dog! March on!" he said.
  JOHN GREENLEAF WHITTIER, *Barbara
  Frietchie.*

10

When I think of the flag, . . . I see alternate strips of parchment upon which are
written the rights of liberty and justice, and
stripes of blood to vindicate those rights, and
then, in the corner, a prediction of the blue
serene into which every nation may swim
which stands for these great things.
  WOODROW WILSON, Address in New York
  City, 17 May, 1915.

The lines of red are lines of blood, nobly and
unselfishly shed by men who loved the liberty of their fellowmen more than they loved
their own lives and fortunes. God forbid that
we should have to use the blood of America
to freshen the color of the flag. But if it
should ever be necessary, that flag will be
colored once more, and in being colored will
be glorified and purified.
  WOODROW WILSON, Address in New York
  City, 17 May, 1915.

11

The flag is the embodiment, not of sentiment
but of history. It represents the experiences
made by men and women, the experiences of
those who do and live under that flag.
  WOODROW WILSON, Address, 14 June,
  1915.

12

Its red for love, and its white for law;
And its blue for the hope that our fathers
  saw,
  Of a larger liberty.
  UNKNOWN, *The American Flag.*

FLATTERY

1
Flattery is like Kolone water, tew be smelt of, not swallowed.
JOSH BILLINGS, *Philosophy*.

2
We love flattery even though we are not deceived by it, because it shows that we are of importance enough to be courted.
EMERSON, *Essays, Second Series: Gifts*.

3
Strive not to hew your path through life—it really doesn't pay;
Be sure the salve of flattery soaps all you do and say;
Herein the only royal road to fame and fortune lies:
Put not your trust in vinegar—molasses catches flies!
EUGENE FIELD, *Uncle Eph*, st. 4.

4
Let those flatter who fear; it is not an American art.
THOMAS JEFFERSON, *Writings,* vol. i, p. 185.

5
When my friend, Judge Douglas, came to Chicago, . . . he complimented me as being a "kind, amiable and intelligent gentleman." . . . I was not very much accustomed to flattery, and it came the sweeter to me. I was rather like the Hoosier with the gingerbread, when he said he reckoned he loved it better than any other man, and got less of it.
ABRAHAM LINCOLN, Speech in Ottawa, Ill., replying to Stephen A. Douglas, 31 July, 1858. (STERN, *Life and Writings of Abraham Lincoln*, p. 468)

6
We flatter those we scarcely know,
We please the fleeting guest,
And deal full many a thoughtless blow
To those who love us best.
ELLA WHEELER WILCOX, *Life's Scars*, st. 3.

FLOWERS

7
Flowers are the sweetest things God ever made and forgot to put a soul into.
HENRY WARD BEECHER, *Life Thoughts*.

8
Flowers have an expression of countenance as much as men or animals. Some seem to smile; some have a sad expression; some are pensive and diffident; others again are plain, honest and upright, like the broad-faced sunflower and the hollyhock.
HENRY WARD BEECHER, *Star Papers: A Discourse of Flowers*.

9
Flowers are Love's truest language; they betray,
Like the divining rods of Magi old,
Where precious wealth lies buried, not of gold,
But love—strong love, that never can decay!
PARK BENJAMIN, *Sonnet*.

10
The south wind searches for the flowers whose fragrance late he bore,
And sighs to find them in the wood and by the stream no more.
WILLIAM CULLEN BRYANT, *The Death of the Flowers*.

11
Loveliest of lovely things are they
On earth that soonest pass away.
The rose that lives its little hour
Is prized beyond the sculptured flower.
WILLIAM CULLEN BRYANT, *A Scene on the Banks of the Hudson*.

12
Earth laughs in flowers.
EMERSON, *Hamatreya*.

13
The Amen! of Nature is always a flower.
OLIVER WENDELL HOLMES, *The Autocrat of the Breakfast-Table*, ch. 10.

14
Yellow japanned buttercups and star-disked dandelions,—just as we see them lying in the grass, like sparks that have leaped from the kindling sun of summer.
OLIVER WENDELL HOLMES, *The Professor at the Breakfast-Table*, ch. 10.

15
Only the flower sanctifies the vase.
ROBERT UNDERWOOD JOHNSON, *The Temple*.

16
Spake full well, in language quaint and olden,
One who dwelleth by the castled Rhine,
When he called the flowers, so blue and golden,
Stars, that in earth's firmament do shine.
HENRY WADSWORTH LONGFELLOW, *Flowers*, st. 1. The reference is to the poet Frederick Wilhelm Carové.

17
Violet! sweet violet!
Thine eyes are full of tears;
Are they wet
Even yet
With the thought of other years?
Or with gladness are they full,
For the night so beautiful?
JAMES RUSSELL LOWELL, *Song*.

18
You are brief, and frail, and blue—
Little sisters, I am, too.
You are heaven's masterpieces—
Little loves, the likeness ceases.
DOROTHY PARKER, *Sweet Violets*.

1

Rose is a rose is a rose is a rose.
> GERTRUDE STEIN, *Geography and Plays: Sacred Emily.*

Speaking of the device of rose is a rose is a rose is a rose, it was I who found it in one of Gertrude Stein's manuscripts and insisted upon putting it as a device on the letter paper, on the table linen and anywhere that she would permit that I would put it.
> GERTRUDE STEIN, *The Autobiography of Alice B. Toklas,* p. 169.

2

One of the attractive things about the flowers is their beautiful reserve.
> HENRY D. THOREAU, *Journal,* 17 June, 1853.

3

A morning-glory at my window satisfies me more than the metaphysics of books.
> WALT WHITMAN, *Song of Myself,* sec. 24.

4

When lilacs last in the dooryard bloom'd,
And the great star early droop'd in the western sky in the night,
I mourn'd, and yet shall mourn with ever-returning spring.
> WALT WHITMAN, *When Lilacs Last in the Dooryard Bloom'd,* st. 1.

FOOL

5

There's a sucker born every minute.
> Attributed to P. T. BARNUM.

6

The wise through excess of wisdom is made a fool.
> EMERSON, *Essays, Second Series: Experience.*

7

The wise man draws more advantage from his enemies, than the fool from his friends.
> BENJAMIN FRANKLIN, *Poor Richard,* 1749.

8

Wise men learn by others' harms, fools scarcely by their own.
> BENJAMIN FRANKLIN, *Poor Richard,* 1758.

9

Hello, sucker!
> TEXAS GUINAN. This greeting to patrons of night clubs where she was hostess became her trademark.

10

He dares to be a fool, and that is the first step in the direction of wisdom.
> JAMES G. HUNEKER, *Pathos of Distance,* p. 257.

11

The right to be a cussed fool
Is safe from all devices human,
It's common (ez a gin'l rule)

To every critter born o' woman.
> JAMES RUSSELL LOWELL, *The Biglow Papers,* ser. ii, No. 7.

12

The strong fool breasts the flood and dies,
The weak fool turns his back and flies.
> JOAQUIN MILLER, *A Song of Creation,* canto v, st. 2.

13

Men never turn rogues without turning fools.
> THOMAS PAINE, *The Crisis,* No. 3.

14

A way foolishness has of revenging itself is to excommunicate the world.
> GEORGE SANTAYANA, *Little Essays,* p. 112.

15

Hain't we got all the fools in town on our side? And ain't that a big enough majority in any town?
> MARK TWAIN, *The Adventures of Huckleberry Finn,* ch. 26.

16

Let us be thankful for the fools. But for them the rest of us could not succeed.
> MARK TWAIN, *Pudd'nhead Wilson's New Calendar.*

17

The best way to silence any friend of yours whom you know to be a fool is to induce him to hire a hall.
> WOODROW WILSON, Speech in New York, 27 Jan., 1916.

FORCE

See also Might, Power, Strength

18

I hope we are learning that force is not always the answer to Communism but even can become its greatest incubator.
> LEROY COLLINS, Speech in San Juan, P.R., 25 May, 1965.

19

Communists only respect force. You remember the remark attributed to Stalin at the Yalta Conference when he was told of the importance of the views of Pope Pius XII. "How many divisions does Pope Pius command?" Stalin asked at the time. That shows us the Communist mentality clearly.
> DWIGHT D. EISENHOWER, Interview with a New York *Times* reporter, 9 May, 1965. (New York *Times,* 10 May, 1965)

20

Once you decide to use force, you had better make sure you have plenty of it. If you need a battalion to do a job, it's much better to have the strength of a division. You probably won't suffer any casualties at all in that way.
> DWIGHT D. EISENHOWER, Interview with a New York *Times* reporter, 9 May,

1965. (New York *Times,* 10 May, 1965)

1
We love force and we care very little how it is exhibited.
EMERSON, *Journal,* vol. v, p. 262.

2
Democracy will never solve its problems at the end of a billy club.
LYNDON B. JOHNSON, Speech in Washington, D.C., 28 July, 1964, referring to a "deep discontent" centering around racial unrest in the United States.

3
In your statement you asserted that our actions, even though peaceful, must be condemned because they precipitate violence. Isn't this like condemning the robbed man because his possession of money precipitated the evil act of robbery? Isn't this like condemning Socrates because his unswerving commitment to truth and his philosophical delvings precipitated the misguided popular mind to make him drink the hemlock? Isn't this like condemning Jesus because his unique God-consciousness and never-ceasing devotion to God's will precipitated the evil act of the Crucifixion?
REV. MARTIN LUTHER KING, JR., Letter, addressed to "My Dear Fellow Clergymen," and written in Apr., 1963, while Dr. King was in the Birmingham, Ala., city jail as a result of leading Negroes' civil-rights demonstrations. The letter was a reply to a public statement by white clergymen, criticizing him for "unwise and untimely" demonstrations. (*Time,* 3 Jan., 1964)

4
Some of you have knives, and I ask you to put them up. Some of you may have arms, and I ask you to put them up. Get the weapon of nonviolence, the breastplate of righteousness, the armor of truth, and just keep marching.
REV. MARTIN LUTHER KING, JR., addressing Negro civil-rights workers in Gadsden, Ala., late in 1963. (*Time,* 3 Jan., 1964)

5
All of the nations of the world, for realistic as well as spiritual reasons, must come to the abandonment of the use of force.
FRANKLIN D. ROOSEVELT AND WINSTON CHURCHILL, *The Atlantic Charter,* proclaimed 14 Aug., 1941.

FORTUNE

See also Chance, Destiny, Luck, Providence

6
Incapable of compromises,
Unable to forgive or spare,
The strange awarding of the prizes
He had no fortitude to bear.
WILLA CATHER, *A Likeness.*

7
Nature magically suits a man to his fortunes, by making them the fruit of his character.
EMERSON, *Conduct of Life: Fate.*

8
He that waits upon fortune, is never sure of a dinner.
BENJAMIN FRANKLIN, *Poor Richard,* 1734.

9
A change of fortune hurts a wise man no more than a change of the moon.
BENJAMIN FRANKLIN, *Poor Richard,* 1756.

10
Fortune comes well to all that comes not late.
HENRY WADSWORTH LONGFELLOW, *The Spanish Student,* act iii, sc. 5, l. 281.

11
The wheel goes round and round,
And some are up and some are on the down,
And still the wheel goes round.
JOSEPHINE POLLARD, *The Wheel of Fortune.*

12
A man is never so on trial as in the moment of excessive good-fortune.
LEW WALLACE, *Ben Hur,* bk. v, ch. 7.

FRANCE AND THE FRENCH

13
The French woman says, "I am a woman and a Parisienne, and nothing foreign to me appears altogether human."
EMERSON, *Uncollected Lectures: Table-Talk.*

14
Liberty, equality, fraternity (*Liberté, égalité, fraternité*).
Attributed to BENJAMIN FRANKLIN, who is said to have suggested it. This became the watchword of the French Revolution and is still widely used as a motto in France.

15
That will go, that will last (*Ça ira, ça tiendra*).
BENJAMIN FRANKLIN, according to CASSAGNAC (*History of the Girondists,* i, 373), who states that the *Ça Ira,* the revolutionary song of France, was composed by an itinerant musician who took the refrain from this observation by Franklin on the revolution

16
If a sparrow cannot fall without God's knowledge, how can an empire rise without His aid?
BENJAMIN FRANKLIN, in proposing that the sessions of the Constitutional Con-

vention (May, 1787) be opened with prayer.

1

Fifty million Frenchmen can't be wrong.
> Attributed to TEXAS GUINAN. (New York *World-Telegram,* 21 Mar., 1931)

2

The last time I saw Paris.
> OSCAR HAMMERSTEIN II, Title of lyric from the film *Lady Be Good* (1940). This was also the title of a memoir (1942) by Elliot Paul.

3

These things are managed so well in France.
> BRET HARTE, *The Tale of a Pony.*

4

Something of the monkey aspect inseparable from a little Frenchman.
> NATHANIEL HAWTHORNE, *Journals,* 5 July, 1837.

5

Everything is on such a clear financial basis in France. It is the simplest country to live in. No one makes things complicated by becoming your friend for any obscure reason. If you want people to like you, you have only to spend a little money.
> ERNEST HEMINGWAY, *The Sun Also Rises.*

6

In a comparison of this with other countries we have the proof of primacy which was given to Themistocles after the battle of Salamis. Every general voted himself the first reward of valor, and the second to Themistocles. So, ask the travelled inhabitant of any nation, in what country on earth you would rather live? Certainly in my own. . . . which would be your second choice? France.
> THOMAS JEFFERSON, *Writings,* vol. i, p. 159.

7

Never was there a country where the practice of governing too much had taken deeper root and done more mischief.
> THOMAS JEFFERSON, *Writings,* vol. vii, p. 445.

8

How'ya gonna keep 'em down on the farm, After they've seen Paree?
> SAM M. LEWIS AND JOE YOUNG, Title and Refrain of song (1919) with music by Walter Donaldson. This was one of the most enduring songs inspired by World War I.

9

The Frenchman feels an easy mastery in speaking his mother tongue, and attributes it to some native superiority of parts that lifts him high above us barbarians of the West.
> JAMES RUSSELL LOWELL, *On a Certain Condescension in Foreigners.*

10

Half artist and half anchorite,
Part siren and part Socrates.
> PERCY MACKAYE, *France.*

11

The cross of the Legion of Honor has been conferred upon me. However, few escape that distinction.
> MARK TWAIN, *A Tramp Abroad,* ch. 8.

FRANKNESS, see Candor

FRAUD, see Deceit

FREEDOM
See also Liberty

12

I for one will never concede that we cannot do as much in defense of our freedoms as any enemy may be doing to destroy them.
> BERNARD M. BARUCH. (New York *Times* obituary of Baruch, 21 June, 1965, p. 16)

13

"Freedom!" their battle-cry,—
"Freedom! or leave to die!"
> G. H. BOKER, *The Black Regiment.*

14

O Freedom! thou art not, as poets dream,
A fair young girl, with light and delicate limbs,
And wavy tresses. . . . A bearded man,
Armed to the teeth, art thou; one mailèd hand
Grasps the broad shield, and one the sword; thy brow
Glorious in beauty though it be, is scarred
With tokens of old wars; thy massive limbs
Are strong with struggling.
> WILLIAM CULLEN BRYANT, *The Antiquity of Freedom.*

15

Freedom comes from human beings, rather than from laws and institutions.
> CLARENCE DARROW, in his defense of Henry Sweet, 19 May, 1926. Sweet was on trial in Detroit as a result of a civil disorder that came about when, with a group of fellow Negroes, he moved into a district of Detroit populated, up to that time, exclusively by whites.

16

But we were born free.
> ELMER DAVIS, Title of book (1954).

17

We must be ready to dare all for our country. For history does not long entrust the care of freedom to the weak or the timid.
> DWIGHT D. EISENHOWER, First Inaugural Address, 20 Jan., 1953.

18

May the light of freedom, coming to all darkened lands, flame brightly—until at last the darkness is no more.
> DWIGHT D. EISENHOWER, Second Inaugural Address, 21 Jan., 1957.

1

Only our individual faith in freedom can keep us free.

> DWIGHT D. EISENHOWER, *Let's Be Honest with Ourselves; The Reader's Digest*, Dec., 1963.

2

For what avail the plough or sail,
Or land or life, if freedom fail?

> EMERSON, *Boston*.

3

Wherever snow falls, man is free. Where the orange blooms, man is the foe of man.

> EMERSON, *Journals*, 1862.

4

When "freedom" is worshipped as a sublime and mystical state rather than as simply a necessary condition for human fulfillment, the faith in freedom itself ceases to express the democratic spirit and becomes something quite different; it ceases to express the conscience of a conservative and becomes instead the faith of a fanatic.

> J. W. FULBRIGHT, Address, Sept., 1964, during the presidential campaign. The reference is to the Republican nominee, Barry Goldwater.

5

Why read ye not the changeless truth,
The free can conquer but to save?

> JOHN HAY, *Northward*. This was quoted by President McKinley in a message on the Philippines.

6

If we wish to be free—if we mean to preserve inviolate those inestimable privileges for which we have been so long contending —if we mean not basely to abandon the noble struggle in which we have been so long engaged, and which we have pledged ourselves never to abandon until the glorious object of our contest shall be obtained—we must fight! I repeat it, sir, we must fight!

> PATRICK HENRY, Address to Virginia convention of delegates to the Continental Congress, 23 Mar., 1775.

7

Freedom is the open window through which pours the sunlight of the human spirit and of human dignity. With the preservation of these moral and spiritual qualities and with God's grace will come further greatness for our country.

> HERBERT HOOVER, Statement on his ninetieth birthday, New York City, 10 Aug., 1964.

8

We are not free; it was not intended we should be. A book of rules is placed in our cradle, and we never get rid of it until we reach our graves. Then we are free, and only then.

> EDGAR WATSON HOWE, *Howe's Monthly*.

9

In the beauty of the lilies Christ was born across the sea,
With a glory in his bosom that transfigures you and me;
As he died to make men holy, let us die to make men free,
While God is marching on.

> JULIA WARD HOWE, *Battle Hymn of the Republic*.

10

There is no freedom on earth or in any star for those who deny freedom to others.

> ELBERT HUBBARD, *A Thousand and One Epigrams*.

11

We Americans know that freedom, like peace, is indivisible.

> HAROLD L. ICKES, Speech in New York City, 18 May, 1941.

Freedom is an indivisible word. If we want to enjoy it, and fight for it, we must be prepared to extend it to everyone, whether they are rich or poor, whether they agree with us or not, no matter what their race or the color of their skin.

> WENDELL L. WILLKIE, *One World*, ch. 13.

12

The only struggle worthy of man's unceasing sacrifice—the struggle to be free.

> LYNDON B. JOHNSON, Address in New York City, 23 Feb., 1966, upon accepting the national freedom award of Freedom House. The concluding words.

13

In the long history of the world, only a few generations have been granted the role of defending freedom in its hour of maximum danger. I do not shrink from this responsibility—I welcome it. I do not believe that any of us would exchange places with any other people or any other generation. The energy, the faith, the devotion which we bring to this endeavor will light our country and all who serve it—and the glow from that fire can truly light the world.

> JOHN F. KENNEDY, Inaugural Address, 20 Jan., 1961.

14

My fellow citizens of the world: ask not what America will do for you, but what together we can do for the freedom of man.

> JOHN F. KENNEDY, Inaugural Address, 20 Jan., 1961.

15

All free men, wherever they may live, are citizens of Berlin. And therefore, as a free man, I take pride in the words *Ich bin ein Berliner*.

> JOHN F. KENNEDY, Address in West Berlin, 26 June, 1963.

16

In today's world, freedom can be lost without a shot being fired, by ballots as well as bullets. The success of our leadership is dependent upon respect for our mission in the world as well as our missiles—on a clearer recognition of the virtues of freedom as well as the evils of tyranny.

> JOHN F. KENNEDY, Speech prepared for delivery in Dallas, Tex., Nov. 22, 1963, the day of his assassination.

1

The masses that Hitler was planning to dominate are the modern men who find in freedom from the constraints of the ancestral order an intolerable loss of guidance and of support. With Gide they are finding that the burden of freedom is too great an anxiety.

> WALTER LIPPMANN, *The Public Philosophy*, bk. ii, ch. 8.

2

What we are suffering from in modern times is the failure of the primitive liberals to see that freedom does not begin when tyranny is overthrown. Freedom is a way of life which requires authority, discipline, and government of its own kind.

> WALTER LIPPMANN, Syndicated Newspaper Column, 4 Aug., 1964.

3

Freedom is re-created year by year,
In hearts wide open on the Godward side.

> JAMES RUSSELL LOWELL, *Freedom*, 1. 21.

4

No! true freedom is to share
All the chains our brothers wear.

> JAMES RUSSELL LOWELL, *Stanzas on Freedom*.

5

Our present and future danger may lie in our failure to recognize that if we were to achieve freedom from responsibility, all our freedoms would be lost. All the freedom mankind has achieved to date has been achieved only because individuals accepted responsibility.

> ARTHUR H. MOTLEY, Speech in St. Louis, 28 Jan., 1965.

6

Free men set themselves free.

> JAMES OPPENHEIM, *The Slave*.

7

Tyranny, like hell, is not easily conquered, yet we have this consolation within us, that the harder the conflict, the more glorious the triumph. What we obtain too cheap, we esteem too lightly. . . . It would be strange indeed if so celestial an article as freedom should not be highly rated.

> THOMAS PAINE, *The Crisis:* Introduction.

8

Those who expect to reap the blessings of freedom, must, like men, undergo the fatigue of supporting it.

> THOMAS PAINE, *The Crisis*, No. iv.

9

The first is freedom of speech and expression—everywhere in the world. The second is freedom of every person to worship God in his own way—everywhere in the world. The third is freedom from want . . . everywhere in the world. The fourth is freedom from fear . . . anywhere in the world.

> FRANKLIN D. ROOSEVELT, Message to Congress, 6 Jan., 1941. These "essential human freedoms," upon which the world of "future days" was to be founded, became famous as the "four freedoms."

10

We cannot save freedom with pitchforks and muskets alone after a dictator combination has gained control of the rest of the world.

> FRANKLIN D. ROOSEVELT, Address by radio, 4 July, 1941.

11

If freedom had been the happy, simple, relaxed state of ordinary humanity, man would have everywhere been free—whereas through most of time and space he has been in chains. Do not let us make any mistake about this. The natural government of man is servitude. Tyranny is the normal pattern of government.

> ADLAI E. STEVENSON, A. Powell Davies Memorial Address, Washington, D.C., 18 Jan., 1959. (*Contemporary Forum*, ed. by Ernest J. Wrage and Barnet Baskerville, p. 360)

12

We have confused the free with the free and easy.

> ADLAI E. STEVENSON, *Putting First Things First: A Democratic View*.

13

What other liberty is there worth having, if we have not freedom and peace in our minds,—if our inmost and most private man is but a sour and turbid pool?

> HENRY D. THOREAU, *Journal*, 26 Oct., 1853.

14

That man is free who is protected from injury.

> DANIEL WEBSTER, Address to the Charlestown Bar, 10 May, 1847.

15

Freedom exists only where the people take care of the government.

> WOODROW WILSON, Speech in New York City, 4 Sept., 1912.

16

Only free peoples can hold their purpose and their honor steady to a common end, and prefer the interests of mankind to any narrow interest of their own.

> WOODROW WILSON, War Address to Congress, 2 Apr., 1917.

FRIEND, FRIENDSHIP

1
One friend in a lifetime is much; two are many; three are hardly possible.
> HENRY ADAMS, *The Education of Henry Adams,* p. 312.

2
Until harsh experience taught him the folly of it, he was always willing to endorse a friend's note, and surely greater love hath no man than this: laying down one's life is nothing in comparison.
> GAMALIEL BRADFORD, *As God Made Them: Henry Clay,* p. 63.

3
There is nothing final between friends.
> WILLIAM JENNINGS BRYAN, Reply, as Secretary of State, to Viscount Chinda, the Japanese Ambassador, 23 May, 1914. Bryan had been asked whether the decision of the United States to support a law just passed by the California legislature, which excluded Japanese from holding title to real estate in California, was final.

4
Love is only chatter,
Friends are all that matter.
> GELETT BURGESS, *Willy and the Lady.*

5
How to Win Friends and Influence People.
> DALE CARNEGIE, Title of book (1938).

6
Friends should not be chosen to flatter. The quality we should prize is that rectitude which will shrink from no truth. Intimacies which increase vanity destroy friendship.
> WILLIAM ELLERY CHANNING, *Note-Book: Friendship.*

7
What is a Friend? I will tell you. It is a person with whom you dare to be yourself.
> FRANK CRANE, *A Definition of Friendship.*

8
Friendship should be surrounded with ceremonies and respects, and not crushed into corners. Friendship requires more time than poor, busy men can usually command.
> EMERSON, *Conduct of Life: Behavior.*

9
'Tis a French definition of friendship, *rien que s'entendre,* good understanding.
> EMERSON, *Conduct of Life: Behavior.*

10
A day for toil, an hour for sport,
But for a friend is life too short.
> EMERSON, *Conduct of Life: Considerations by the Way.*

11
We take care of our health; we lay up money; we make our roof tight, and our clothing sufficient; but who provides wisely that he shall not be wanting in the best property of all,—friends?
> EMERSON, *Conduct of Life: Considerations by the Way.*

12
A man's friends are his magnetisms.
> EMERSON, *Conduct of Life: Fate.*

13
A friend is a person with whom I may be sincere.
> EMERSON, *Essays, First Series: Friendship.*

14
A friend may well be reckoned the masterpiece of Nature.
> EMERSON, *Essays, First Series: Friendship.*

15
The only way to have a friend is to be one.
> EMERSON, *Essays, First Series: Friendship.*

16
Better be a nettle in the side of your friend than his echo.
> EMERSON, *Essays, First Series: Friendship.*

17
A divine person is the prophecy of the mind; a friend is the hope of the heart.
> EMERSON, *Essays, Second Series: Character.*

18
Three things are known only in three places: Valour, which knows itself only in war; Wisdom, only in anger; and Friendship, only in need.
> EMERSON, *Journal,* 1863. Quoted as a Persian maxim.

19
Friends are fictions founded on some single momentary experience.
> EMERSON, *Journals,* vol. x, p. 11.

20
Keep your friendships in repair.
> EMERSON, *Table-Talk.*

21
Be slow in choosing a friend, slower in changing.
> BENJAMIN FRANKLIN, *Poor Richard.*

22
There are three faithful friends—an old wife, an old dog, and ready money.
> BENJAMIN FRANKLIN, *Poor Richard,* 1738.

23
A Father's a Treasure; a Brother's a Comfort; a Friend is both.
> BENJAMIN FRANKLIN, *Poor Richard,* 1747.

24
There's a freedom to associate, and there's a freedom not to associate.
> BARRY M. GOLDWATER, Speech in Washington, D.C., to Republican campaign workers during the presidential campaign, 19 Oct., 1964. He was referring to racial integration, a major campaign issue.

1
I have no trouble with my enemies. But my Goddam friends, White, they are the ones that keep me walking the floor nights.
> WARREN G. HARDING, to William Allen White, 1923. (COHN, *The Fabulous Democrats*, p. 127)

2
I find friendship to be like wine, raw when new, ripened with age, the true old man's milk and restorative cordial.
> THOMAS JEFFERSON, *Writings*, vol. xiii, p. 77.

3
I see no comfort in outliving one's friends and remaining a mere monument of the times which are past.
> THOMAS JEFFERSON, *Writings*, vol. xviii, p. 297.

4
Thrice blessed are our friends:
They come, they stay—
And presently go away.
> RICHARD R. KIRK, *Thrice Blessed*.

5
No beggar ever felt him condescend,
No prince presume; for still himself he bare
At manhood's simple level, and where'er
He met a stranger, there he left a friend.
> JAMES RUSSELL LOWELL, *Agassiz*, pt. ii, sec. 2.

6
The more people are reached by mass communication, the less they communicate with each other. The proliferation of one-way messages, whether in print or on air, seems to have increased rather than lessened the alienation of the individual. Friendly, gregarious America is full of intensely lonely people for whom radio and television provide the illusory solace of company.
> MARYA MANNES, *But Will It Sell?*

7
Friendship is a union of spirits, a marriage of hearts, and the bond thereof virtue.
> WILLIAM PENN, *Fruits of Solitude*.

8
There can be no Friendship where there is no *Freedom*. Friendship loves a *Free* Air, and will not be fenced up in straight and narrow Enclosures.
> WILLIAM PENN, *Fruits of Solitude*.

9
This is the comfort of friends, that though they may be said to die, yet their friendship and society are, in the best sense, ever present, because immortal.
> WILLIAM PENN, *Fruits of Solitude*.

10
A true friend unbosoms freely, advises justly, assists readily, adventures boldly, takes all patiently, defends courageously, and continues a friend unchangeably.
> WILLIAM PENN, *Fruits of Solitude*.

11
The friendship between me and you I will not compare to a chain; for that the rains might rust, or the falling tree might break.
> WILLIAM PENN, Treaty with the Indians. (BANCROFT, *History of the United States*)

12
Friendship is the greatest enrichment that I have found.
> ADLAI E. STEVENSON, at the funeral of Lloyd Lewis in Libertyville, Ill., 1949.

13
Friends will be much apart. They will respect more each other's privacy than their communion.
> HENRY D. THOREAU, *Journal*, 22 Feb., 1841.

14
Nothing makes the earth seem so spacious as to have friends at a distance; they make the latitudes and longitudes.
> HENRY D. THOREAU, Letter to Mrs. E. Castleton, 22 May, 1843.

15
A man cannot be said to succeed in this life who does not satisfy one friend.
> HENRY D. THOREAU, *Winter: Journal*, 19 Feb., 1857.

16
There is an old time toast which is golden for its beauty. "When you ascend the hill of prosperity may you not meet a friend."
> MARK TWAIN, *Pudd'nhead Wilson's New Calendar*.

17
A slender acquaintance with the world must convince every man, that actions, not words, are the true criterion of the attachment of friends; and that the most liberal professions of good-will are very far from being the surest marks of it.
> GEORGE WASHINGTON, *Social Maxims: Friendship*.

18
Be courteous to all, but intimate with few, and let those few be well tried before you give them your confidence. True friendship is a plant of slow growth, and must undergo and withstand the shocks of adversity before it is entitled to the appellation.
> GEORGE WASHINGTON, Letter, Newburgh, N.Y., 15 Jan., 1783.

19
To the rare few, who, early in life, have rid themselves of the friendship of the many.
> J. McNEILL WHISTLER, *The Gentle Art of Making Enemies:* Dedication.

20
Feast, and your halls are crowded;
Fast, and the world goes by.
> ELLA WHEELER WILCOX, *Solitude*.

21
True friendship is of royal lineage. It is of the same kith and breeding as loyalty and

self-forgetting devotion and proceeds upon a higher principle even than they. For loyalty may be blind, and friendship must not be; devotion may sacrifice principles of right choice which friendship must guard with an excellent and watchful care. . . . The object of love is to serve, not to win.

> WOODROW WILSON, Baccalaureate Sermon, Princeton University, 9 May, 1907.

FUTURE

1
I never think of the future. It comes soon enough.

> ALBERT EINSTEIN, Interview, Dec., 1930.

2
All these tidal gatherings, growth and decay,
Shining and darkening, are forever
Renewed; and the whole cycle impenitently
Revolves, and all the past is future.

> ROBINSON JEFFERS, *Practical People.*

3
We should all be concerned about the future because we will have to spend the rest of our lives there.

> CHARLES F. KETTERING, *Seed for Thought.*

4
Trust no Future, howe'er pleasant!

> HENRY WADSWORTH LONGFELLOW, *A Psalm of Life*, st. 6.

5
Tomorrow is the ambushed walk avoided by the circumspect. Tomorrow is the fatal rock on which a million ships are wrecked.

> WALT MASON, *Tomorrow.*

6
The woman named Tomorrow
sits with a hairpin in her teeth
and takes her time
and does her hair the way she wants it.

> CARL SANDBURG, *Four Preludes.*

G

GAMBLING

7
And remember, dearie, never give a sucker an even break.

> Attributed to W. C. FIELDS, though the line is from Act II of *Poppy,* by DOROTHY DONNELLY. The line is so closely identified with Fields that many think he contributed it to this stage work. *Never Give a Sucker an Even Break* was the title of a later film in which Fields starred.

8
I come down dah wid my hat caved in,
Doodah! doodah!
I go back home wid a pocket full of tin,
Oh! doodah day!
Gwine to run all night!
Gwine to run all day!
I'll bet my money on de bobtail nag—
Somebody bet on de bay.

> STEPHEN C. FOSTER, *Camptown Races.*

9
Keep flax from fire, youth from gaming.

> BENJAMIN FRANKLIN, *Poor Richard.*

10
The strength of Monaco is the weakness of the world.

> H. A. GIBBONS, *Riviera Towns: Monte Carlo.*

11
Why they call a feller that keeps losin' all the time a good sport gits me.

> KIN HUBBARD, *Abe Martin's Broadcast,* p. 28.

12
I never gamble.

> J. P. MORGAN, the elder, upon terminating a business conversation with Bernard M. Baruch in 1909. The two were considering a joint venture in sulfur mining; Baruch was deputized to inspect a site in Texas, and returned with a fairly optimistic report but an unfortunate choice of language. He told Morgan he would be willing to "gamble" half the price necessary to buy the site, from his own funds. Morgan dismissed the younger man abruptly with these words. (BARUCH, *Baruch: My Own Story,* ch. 18)

13
If there were two birds sitting on a fence, he would bet you which one would fly first.

> MARK TWAIN, *The Jumping Frog.*

14
There are two times in a man's life when he should not speculate: when he can't afford it, and when he can.

> MARK TWAIN, *Pudd'nhead Wilson's New Calendar.*

15
It [gambling] is the child of avarice, the brother of iniquity, and the father of mischief.

> GEORGE WASHINGTON, Letter to Bushrod Washington, 15 Jan., 1783.

GARDEN

16
Who loves a garden still his Eden keeps,
Perennial pleasures plants, and wholesome harvests reaps.

> AMOS BRONSON ALCOTT, *Tablets: The Garden,* bk. i, *Antiquity.*

17
My tent stands in a garden

Of aster and golden-rod,
Tilled by the rain and the sunshine,
And sown by the hand of God.
　　Bliss Carman, *An Autumn Garden.*

1
A garden is like those pernicious machineries
which catch a man's coat-skirt or his hand,
and draw in his arm, his leg and his whole
body to irresistible destruction.
　　Emerson, *Conduct of Life: Wealth.*

2
What makes a garden
And why do gardens grow?
Love lives in gardens—
God and lovers know!
　　Caroline Giltinan, *The Garden.*

3
He who makes a garden
Works hand in hand with God.
　　Douglas Malloch, *Who Makes a Garden.*

4
My garden will never make me famous,
I'm a horticultural ignoramus,
I can't tell a stringbean from a soybean,
Or even a girl bean from a boy bean.
　　Ogden Nash, *Versus: He Digs, He Dug, He Has Dug.*

GENEROSITY, see Gifts, Giving
GENIUS

5
As diamond cuts diamond, and one hone
smoothes a second, all the parts of intellect
are whetstones to each other; and genius,
which is but the result of their mutual
sharpening, is character too.
　　C. A. Bartol, *Radical Problems: Individualism.*

6
Men ov genius are like eagles, tha live on
what tha kill, while men ov talents is like
crows, tha live on what has been killed for
them.
　　Josh Billings, *Talent and Genius.*

7
Genius is one per cent inspiration and ninety-
nine per cent perspiration.
　　Thomas A. Edison, Newspaper Interview.
(*Golden Book,* Apr., 1931)

8
Genius is religious. It is a larger imbibing of
the common heart.
　　Emerson, *Essays, First Series: The Over-Soul.*

9
We call partial half-lights, by courtesy, genius; talent which converts itself into money;
talent which glitters to-day that it may dine
and sleep well tomorrow.
　　Emerson, *Essays, First Series: Prudence.*

10
To believe your own thought, to believe that
what is true for you in your private heart is
true for all men—that is genius.
　　Emerson, *Essays, First Series: Self-Reliance.*

11
That necessity of isolation which genius
feels. Each must stand on his glass tripod if
he would keep his electricity.
　　Emerson, *Essays: Society and Solitude.*

12
When the will is absolutely surrendered to
the moral sentiment, that is virtue; when the
wit is surrendered to intellectual truth, that
is genius. Talent for talent's sake is a bauble
and a show. Talent working with joy in the
cause of universal truth lifts the possessor to
a new power.
　　Emerson, *Letters and Social Aims: Progress of Culture.*

13
The miracles of genius always rest on profound convictions which refuse to be analyzed.
　　Emerson, *Letters and Social Aims: Progress of Culture.*

14
When Nature has work to be done, she cre-
ates a genius to do it.
　　Emerson, *Nature Addresses and Lectures: The Method of Nature.*

15
Great geniuses have the shortest biographies.
Their cousins can tell you nothing about
them. They lived in their writings, and so
their house and street life was trivial and
commonplace.
　　Emerson, *Representative Men: Plato.*

16
In all great works of art . . . the Genius
draws up the ladder after him.
　　Emerson, *Representative Men: Shakespeare.*

17
Genius even, as it is the greatest good, is the
greatest harm.
　　Emerson, *Society and Solitude: Farming.*

18
We owe to genius always the same debt, of
lifting the curtain from the common, and
showing us that divinities are sitting disguised in the seeming gang of gypsies and
peddlers.
　　Emerson, *Society and Solitude: Works and Days.*

19
Genius without education is like silver in the
mine.
　　Benjamin Franklin, *Poor Richard,*
1750.

20
Perhaps, moreover, he whose genius appears
deepest and truest excels his fellows in nothing save the knack of expression; he throws
out occasionally a lucky hint at truths of

which every human soul is profoundly though unutterably conscious.

> NATHANIEL HAWTHORNE, *Mosses from an Old Manse: The Procession of Life.*

1
Genius is lonely without the surrounding presence of people to inspire it.

> T. W. HIGGINSON, *Atlantic Essays: A Plea for Culture.*

2
Nature is the master of talents; genius is the master of nature.

> J. G. HOLLAND, *Plain Talk on Familiar Subjects: Art and Life.*

3
Genius is always impatient of its harness; its wild blood makes it hard to train.

> OLIVER WENDELL HOLMES, *The Professor at the Breakfast-Table,* ch. 10.

4
A person of genius should marry a person of character. Genius does not herd with genius.

> OLIVER WENDELL HOLMES, *The Professor at the Breakfast-Table,* ch. 12.

5
Genius is the capacity of evading hard work.

> ELBERT HUBBARD, *The Philistine,* vol. xi, p. 114.

6
Genius is the ability to act rightly without precedent—the power to do the right thing the first time.

> ELBERT HUBBARD, *A Thousand and One Epigrams,* p. 39.

7
Genius never drops from the skies.

> JAMES G. HUNEKER, *Pathos of Distance,* p. 103.

8
In the republic of mediocrity genius is dangerous.

> ROBERT G. INGERSOLL, *Liberty in Literature.*

9
There is the same difference between talent and genius that there is between a stone mason and a sculptor.

> ROBERT G. INGERSOLL, *Shakespeare.*

10
Whatever question there may be of his talent, there can be none, I think, of his genius. It was a slim and crooked one, but it was eminently personal. He was unperfect, unfinished, inartistic; he was worse than provincial—he was parochial.

> HENRY JAMES, *Hawthorne,* ch. iv, p. 94.
> He was referring to Henry D. Thoreau.

11
Genius, in truth, means little more than the faculty of perceiving in an unhabitual way.

> WILLIAM JAMES, *The Principles of Psychology,* ch. 20.

12
Men of genius are often dull and inert in society, as the blazing meteor when it descends to the earth is only a stone.

> HENRY WADSWORTH LONGFELLOW, *Kavanagh,* ch. 13.

13
Many have genius, but, wanting art, are forever dumb.

> HENRY WADSWORTH LONGFELLOW, *Kavanagh,* ch. 20.

14
    All the means of action—
The shapeless masses, the materials—
Lie everywhere about us. What we need
Is the celestial fire to change the flint
Into transparent crystal, bright and clear.
That fire is genius!

> HENRY WADSWORTH LONGFELLOW, *The Spanish Student,* act i, sc. 5.

15
Talent is that which is in a man's power; genius is that in whose power a man is.

> JAMES RUSSELL LOWELL, *Among My Books: Rousseau and the Sentimentalists.*

16
There is no work of genius which has not been the delight of mankind, no word of genius to which the human heart and soul have not, sooner or later, responded.

> JAMES RUSSELL LOWELL, *Among My Books: Rousseau and the Sentimentalists.*

17
It is the privilege of genius that to it life never grows commonplace as to the rest of us.

> JAMES RUSSELL LOWELL, *Democracy and Other Addresses: On Unveiling the Bust of Fielding.*

18
I think it may as well be admitted that the disease of the endocrine glands called genius simply does not appear among women as frequently as it does among men. If one can find consolation in the thought, neither does idiocy.

> ELSIE McCORMICK, in the New York *World.*

19
Genius, cried the commuter,
As he ran for the 8:13,
Consists of an infinite capacity
For catching trains.

> CHRISTOPHER MORLEY, *An Ejaculation.*

20
The heart and soul of genius may be mad, but the mind of true genius is ever as clear as the heavens seen through pine trees.

> GEORGE JEAN NATHAN, *Materia Critica.*

21
Genius is the father of a heavenly line; but the mortal mother, that is industry.

> THEODORE PARKER, *Ten Sermons on Reli-*

gion: Of the Culture of the Religious Powers.

1
Originality and genius must be largely fed and raised on the shoulders of some old tradition.

GEORGE SANTAYANA, *The Life of Reason,* vol. ii, p. 101.

2
Eccentricity is not a proof of genius, and even an artist should remember that originality consists not only in doing things differently, but also in "doing things better."

E. C. STEDMAN, *Victorian Poets,* ch. 9.

3
Hunger is the handmaid of genius.

MARK TWAIN, *Pudd'nhead Wilson's New Calendar.*

4
Of the three requisites of genius, the first is soul, and the second, soul, and the third, soul.

E. P. WHIPPLE, *Literature and Life: Genius.*

5
Talent repeats; Genius creates. Talent is a cistern; Genius a fountain.

E. P. WHIPPLE, *Literature and Life: Genius.*

GENTLEMAN

6
The character of gentleman . . . is frequent in England, rare in France, and found, where it is found, in age or the latest period of manhood; while in Germany the character is almost unknown. But the proper antipode of a gentleman is to be sought for among the Anglo-American democrats.

SAMUEL TAYLOR COLERIDGE, *Biographia Literaria: Satyrane's Letters,* No. 2.

7
What fact more conspicuous in modern history than the creation of the gentleman?

EMERSON, *Essays, Second Series: Manners.*

8
Living blood and a passion of kindness does at last distinguish God's gentleman from Fashion's.

EMERSON, *Essays, Second Series: Manners.*

9
The flowering of civilization is the finished man, the man of sense, of grace, of accomplishment, of social power—the gentleman.

EMERSON, *Miscellanies: Fortune of the Republic.*

10
According to my mild way of thinking, it is not essential that a gentleman should be bright.

CORRA HARRIS, who authenticated the quotation, but was unable to recall where in her output it came.

11
Old Crestien rightly says no language can Express the worth of a true Gentleman.

JAMES RUSSELL LOWELL, *An Epistle to George William Curtis.*

12
It don't cost nothin' to be a gentleman.

JOHN L. SULLIVAN, Admonition to a rowdy.

13
Conspicuous consumption of valuable goods is a means of reputability to the gentleman of leisure.

THORSTEIN VEBLEN, *The Theory of the Leisure Class,* ch. 4.

GIFTS, GIVING

14
Wives like to open packages more than they care what's inside them. So bring her home many inexpensive presents each year, but only one that really strains your pocketbook. The big one is for her to show to her friends, the others just for her to know that you thought of her often.

HAL BOYLE, Column, Associated Press, datelined New York, 21 Oct., 1964.

15
It is not the weight of jewel or plate,
   Or the fondle of silk or fur;
'Tis the spirit in which the gift is rich,
   As the gifts of the Wise Ones were,
And we are not told whose gift was gold,
   Or whose was the gift of myrrh.

EDMUND VANCE COOKE, *The Spirit of the Gift.*

16
The great gifts are not got by analysis. . . . Nature hates calculators.

EMERSON, *Essays, Second Series: Experience.*

17
The gift, to be true, must be the flowing of the giver unto me, correspondent to my flowing unto him.

EMERSON, *Essays, Second Series: Gifts.*

18
Rings and jewels are not gifts, but apologies for gifts. The only gift is a portion of thyself. . . . Therefore the poet brings his poem; the shepherd, his lamb; the farmer, corn; the miner, a gem; the sailor, coral and shells; the painter, his picture; the girl, a handkerchief of her own sewing.

EMERSON, *Essays, Second Series: Gifts.*

19
It is always so pleasant to be generous, though very vexatious to pay debts.

EMERSON, *Essays, Second Series: Gifts.*

20
We do not quite forgive a giver. The hand that feeds us is in some danger of being bitten.

EMERSON, *Essays, Second Series: Gifts.*

1

A man being sometimes more generous when he has but a little money than when he has plenty, perhaps through fear of being thought to have but little.

BENJAMIN FRANKLIN, *Autobiography*, ch. 1.

2

The only things we ever keep
Are what we give away.

LOUIS GINSBERG, *Song*.

3

Generosity is the flower of justice.

NATHANIEL HAWTHORNE, *American Note-Books*, 19 Dec., 1850.

4

I had rather be a beggar and spend my last dollar like a king, than be a king and spend my money like a beggar.

ROBERT G. INGERSOLL, *The Liberty of Man, Woman and Child*.

5

The greatest grace of a gift, perhaps, is that it anticipates and admits of no return.

HENRY WADSWORTH LONGFELLOW, *Journals and Letters*, 28 Feb., 1871.

6

Give what you have. To some one, it may be better than you dare to think.

HENRY WADSWORTH LONGFELLOW, *Kavanagh*, ch. 30.

7

That is no true alms which the hand can hold;
He gives only the worthless gold
 Who gives from a sense of duty.

JAMES RUSSELL LOWELL, *The Vision of Sir Launfal*, pt. i, st. 6.

8

Not what we give, but what we share,
For the gift without the giver is bare;
Who gives himself with his alms feeds three,
Himself, his hungering neighbor, and me.

JAMES RUSSELL LOWELL, *The Vision of Sir Launfal*, pt. ii, st. 8.

9

For all you can hold in your cold, dead hand
Is what you have given away.

JOAQUIN MILLER, *Peter Cooper*. Quoting an ancient Sanskrit proverb.

10

Take gifts with a sigh: most men give to be paid.

JOHN BOYLE O'REILLY, *Rules of the Road*.

11

Back of the sound broods the silence, back of the gift stands the giving;
Back of the hand that receives thrill the sensitive nerves of receiving.

RICHARD REALF, *Indirection*.

12

Nobody shoots at Santa Claus.

ALFRED E. SMITH, Speech, 1936, attacking New Deal spending.

13

I have always been deeply impressed by an old Jewish proverb which says, "What you give for the cause of charity in health is gold; what you give in sickness is silver; what you give after death is lead."

NATHAN STRAUS, Will (first paragraph).

14

The richest gifts we can bestow are the least marketable.

HENRY D. THOREAU, Letter to Emerson, 12 Feb., 1843.

15

Only he can be trusted with gifts who can present a face of bronze to expectations.

HENRY D. THOREAU, *Journal*. (EMERSON, *Thoreau*)

16

Behold, I do not give lectures or a little charity,
When I give I give myself.

WALT WHITMAN, *Song of Myself*, sec. 40.

GIRL

17

There is Nothing Like a Dame.

OSCAR HAMMERSTEIN II, Title of song from the musical play *South Pacific*, with music by Richard Rodgers.

18

I Enjoy Being a Girl.

OSCAR HAMMERSTEIN II, Title of song from the musical comedy *Flower Drum Song*, with music by Richard Rodgers.

19

Defiant love sonnets
demanding nude joys
lure girls to be naughty
and live like the boys.

ALFRED KREYMBORG, *E.S.V.M.—Authors in Epigram*.

20

There was a little girl
Who had a little curl
 Right in the middle of her forehead,
And when she was good
She was very, very good,
 But when she was bad she was horrid.

Attributed to HENRY WADSWORTH LONGFELLOW. The poet's son (ERNEST W. LONGFELLOW, *Random Memories*, p. 15) declared that these familiar lines were composed while the elder Longfellow was walking in his garden, carrying his second daughter, "Edith with the golden hair." Another version of their background, which also credits Longfellow with authorship, is in *The Home Life of Longfellow*, by BLANCHE R. TUCKER-MACHETTA, p. 90.

21

I know a maiden fair to see,
 Take care!
She can both false and friendly be,

Beware! Beware!
Trust her not, She is fooling thee!
>HENRY WADSWORTH LONGFELLOW, *Beware! (Hüt du Dich!)*

1

Gentlemen Prefer Blondes.
>ANITA LOOS, Title of story (1925).

2

A girl never really looks as well as she does on board a steamship, or even a yacht.
>ANITA LOOS, *Gentlemen Prefer Blondes,* ch. 1.

3

Men seldom make passes
At girls who wear glasses.
>DOROTHY PARKER, *News Item.*

4

The rare and radiant maiden, whom the angels name Lenore—
Nameless here for evermore.
>EDGAR ALLAN POE, *The Raven.*

5

There! little girl, don't cry!
>JAMES WHITCOMB RILEY, *A Life-Lesson.*

6

You may tempt the upper classes
With your villainous demi-tasses,
But Heaven will protect the working-girl!
>EDGAR SMITH, *Heaven Will Protect the Working-Girl.* The song was sung with great success by Marie Dressler in *Tillie's Nightmare* (1909).

7

See the three skirts in the back? That's the Missus and the two squabs. Young one's only a flapper.
>HARRY LEON WILSON, *Bunker Bean* (1912). The term "flapper" was further popularized by F. Scott Fitzgerald in the 1920's.

If there's anything in a beauty nap most o' the flappers I see must suffer from insomnia.
>KIN HUBBARD, *Abe Martin's Broadcast,* p. 119.

If a davenport is a sheik's workbench, a rumble seat is a flapper's showcase.
>G. E. SAMS. (*Pathfinder,* No. 1866)

GOD

See also Religion

8

I sometimes wish that God were back
In this dark world and wide;
For though some virtues he might lack,
He had his pleasant side.
>GAMALIEL BRADFORD, *Exit God.*

9

I would rather walk with God in the dark than go alone in the light.
>MARY GARDINER BRAINARD, *Not Knowing.*

10

A picket frozen on duty—
A mother starved for her brood—

Socrates drinking the hemlock,
And Jesus on the rood;
And millions who, humble and nameless,
The straight, hard pathway trod—
Some call it Consecration,
And others call it God.
>W. H. CARRUTH, *Each in His Own Tongue.*

11

God is to me that creative Force, behind and in the universe, who manifests Himself as energy, as life, as order, as beauty, as thought, as conscience, as love.
>HENRY SLOANE COFFIN. (NEWTON, *My Idea of God,* p. 125)

12

Every law of matter or the body, supposed to govern man, is rendered null and void by the law of Life, God.
>MARY BAKER EDDY, *Science and Health,* p. 380.

13

God is incorporeal, divine, supreme, infinite Mind, Spirit, Soul, Principle, Life, Truth, Love.
>MARY BAKER EDDY, *Science and Health,* p. 465.

14

A true love to God must begin with a delight in his holiness, and not with a delight in any other attribute; for no other attribute is truly lovely without this.
>JONATHAN EDWARDS, *A Treatise Concerning Religious Affections: Works,* vol. v, p. 143.

15

God is clever, but not dishonest.
>DR. ALBERT EINSTEIN. This maxim is engraved over a fireplace in Fine Hall, Princeton, N.J.

16

Fear God, and where you go men will think they walk in hallowed cathedrals.
>EMERSON, *Conduct of Life: Worship.*

17

God enters by a private door into every individual.
>EMERSON, *Essays, First Series: Intellect.*

18

To Be is to live with God.
>EMERSON, *Journals,* 1865.

19

As the bird alights on the bough, then plunges into the air again, so the thoughts of God pause but for a moment in any form.
>EMERSON, *Letters and Social Aims: Poetry and Imagination.*

20

As thus we sat in darkness,
Each one busy in his prayers,—
"We are lost!" the captain shouted,
As he staggered down the stairs.

But his little daughter whispered,
As she took his icy hand,

"Isn't God upon the ocean,
  Just the same as on the land?"
    JAMES T. FIELDS, *Ballad of the Tempest.*

1
God is not a cosmic bell-boy for whom we
can press a button to get things.
    HARRY EMERSON FOSDICK, *Prayer.*

2
I believe in God the Father Almighty because wherever I have looked, through all
that I see around me, I see the trace of an
intelligent mind, and because in natural laws,
and especially in the laws which govern the
social relations of men, I see, not merely the
proofs of intelligence, but the proofs of be-
neficence.
    HENRY GEORGE, Speech in New York,
      1887.

3
I just want to lobby for God.
    REV. WILLIAM FRANKLIN (BILLY) GRA-
      HAM, Comment, 12 Dec., 1955, upon
      opening a national headquarters for
      his organization in Washington, D.C.

4
The great soul that sits on the throne of the
universe is not, never was, and never will be,
in a hurry.
    J. G. HOLLAND, *Gold-Foil: Patience.*

5
One unquestioned text we read,
All doubt beyond, all fear above;
Nor crackling pile nor cursing creed
Can burn or blot it: *God Is Love.*
    OLIVER WENDELL HOLMES, *What We All
      Think.*

6
An honest God is the noblest work of man.
    ROBERT G. INGERSOLL, *The Gods.*

7
The God of many men is little more than
their court of appeal against the damnatory
judgment passed on their failures by the
opinion of the world.
    WILLIAM JAMES, *Varieties of Religious
      Experience,* p. 138.

8
God, to be God, must transcend what is. He
must be the maker of what ought to be.
    RUFUS M. JONES. (NEWTON, *My Idea of
      God,* p. 63)

9
I claim not to have controlled events, but
confess plainly that events have controlled
me.
    ABRAHAM LINCOLN, Speech, 1864.

10
Let nothing disturb thee,
Let nothing affright thee,
All things are passing,
God changeth never.
    HENRY WADSWORTH LONGFELLOW, *Santa
      Teresa's Bookmark* (after Santa Teresa
      de Avila).

11
An' you've gut to git up airly
  Ef you want to take in God.
    JAMES RUSSELL LOWELL, *The Biglow Pa-
      pers,* Sec. i, No. 1.

12
Whom the heart of man shuts out,
Sometimes the heart of God takes in.
    JAMES RUSSELL LOWELL, *The Forlorn.*

13
Darkness is strong, and so is Sin,
But surely God endures forever!
    JAMES RUSSELL LOWELL, *Villa Franca*
      (conclusion).

14
Whoever falls from God's right hand
  Is caught into his left.
    EDWIN MARKHAM, *The Divine Strategy.*

15
I see little evidence in this world of the so-
called goodness of God. On the contrary, it
seems to me that, on the strength of His
daily acts, He must be set down a most stupid, cruel and villainous fellow.
    H. L. MENCKEN. (DURANT, *On the Mean-
      ing of Life,* p. 34)

16
God, I can push the grass apart
And lay my finger on Thy heart!
    EDNA ST. VINCENT MILLAY, *Renascence.*

17
In God we trust.
    Motto of the United States, adopted offi-
      cially by Congress in 1956 for use on
      coins and one-dollar bills. The words
      were first used on U.S. coins in 1864,
      however, when Salmon P. Chase was
      Secretary of the Treasury in Lincoln's
      cabinet. A slightly different wording of
      this sentiment is contained in the fourth
      stanza of FRANCIS SCOTT KEY's *The
      Star-Spangled Banner:* "And this be
      our motto: 'In God is our trust.'"

18
Only God is permanently interesting. Other
things we may fathom, but he out-tops our
thought and can neither be demonstrated nor
argued down.
    J. F. NEWTON, *My Idea of God,* p. 5.

19
God be with you, till we meet again,
  By his counsels guide, uphold you,
  With his sheep securely fold you;
God be with you, till we meet again.
    JEREMIAH EAMES RANKIN, *Mizpah.*

20
Pardon, not wrath, is God's best attribute.
    BAYARD TAYLOR, *The Temptation of Has-
      san Ben Khaled,* st. 11.

21
Whate'er we leave to God, God does
And blesses us.
    HENRY D. THOREAU, *Inspiration.*

22
A dear Companion here abides;

Close to my thrilling heart He hides;
The holy silence is His Voice:
I lie and listen, and rejoice.
  J. T. TROWBRIDGE, *Midsummer.*

1
When the universe began
God, they say, created man.
Later, with a mocking nod,
Man annihilated God.
  MIRIAM VEDDER, *Warning.*

2
In the faces of men and women I see God.
  WALT WHITMAN, *Song of Myself*, sec. 48.

3
And I say to mankind, Be not curious about
    God,
For I who am curious about each am not
    curious about God,
(No array of terms can say how much I am
    at peace about God and about death.)
  WALT WHITMAN, *Song of Myself*, sec. 48.

4
Our fathers' God! From out whose hand
The centuries fall like grains of sand,
We meet to-day, united, free,
And loyal to our land and Thee,
To thank Thee for the era done,
And trust Thee for the opening one.
  JOHN GREENLEAF WHITTIER, *Centennial
    Hymn.*

5
Yet, in the maddening maze of things,
    And tossed by storm and flood,
To one fixed trust my spirit clings;
    I know that God is good!
  JOHN GREENLEAF WHITTIER, *The Eternal
    Goodness.*

6
Who fathoms the Eternal Thought?
    Who talks of scheme and plan?
The Lord is God! He needeth not
    The poor device of man.
  JOHN GREENLEAF WHITTIER, *The Eternal
    Goodness.*

GOLDEN RULE, THE
7
The Golden Rule works like gravitation.
  C. F. DOLE, *Cleveland Address.*

8
Every man takes care that his neighbor does
not cheat him. But a day comes when he
begins to care that he do not cheat his neighbor. Then all goes well.
  EMERSON, *Conduct of Life: Worship.*

9
In our dealings with each other we should be
guided by the Golden Rule.
  WILLIAM DEAN HOWELLS, *The Rise of Si-
    las Lapham*, vol. ii, p. 26.

10
Do unto the other feller the way he'd like to
do unto you, an' do it fust.
  EDWARD NOYES WESTCOTT, *David Harum.*

11
His statecraft was the Golden Rule,
    His right of vote a sacred trust;
Clear, over threat and ridicule,
    All heard his challenge: "Is it just?"
  JOHN GREENLEAF WHITTIER, *Sumner.*

12
Deal with another as you'd have
    Another deal with you;
What you're unwilling to receive,
    Be sure you never do.
  UNKNOWN, *The New England Primer.*

GOODNESS
See also Nobility, Virtue
13
Who soweth good seed shall surely reap.
  JULIA C. R. DORR, *To the "Bouquet
    Club."*

14
That is good which commends to me my
country, my climate, my means and materials, my associates.
  EMERSON, *Society and Solitude: Works
    and Days.*

15
How wicked we are, and how good they were
then.
  OLIVER WENDELL HOLMES, *The Poet at
    the Breakfast-Table: Aunt Tabitha.*

16
The good, as I conceive it, is happiness, happiness for each man after his own heart, and
for each hour according to its inspiration.
  GEORGE SANTAYANA, *Soliloquies in Eng-
    land.*

17
Be good (if you can't be good, be careful).
  HARRINGTON TATE, Refrain of popular
    song (1907).

18
The greater part of what my neighbors call
good I believe in my soul to be bad, and if I
repent of anything, it is very likely to be my
good behavior.
  HENRY D. THOREAU, *Walden*, ch. 1.

19
As for doing good, that is one of the profes-
sions that are full.
  HENRY D. THOREAU, *Walden: Economy.*

20
If not good, why then evil,
If not good god, good devil.
Goodness!—you hypocrite, come out of that,
Live your life, do your work, then take your
    hat.
  HENRY D. THOREAU, *A Week on the Con-
    cord and Merrimack Rivers.*

21
Goodness Had Nothing to Do With It.
  MAE WEST, Title of autobiography (1959).
    This was originally a line from her play
    Diamond Lil (1928).

22
Roaming in thought over the Universe, I saw

the little that is Good steadily hastening
toward immortality,
And the vast all that is call'd Evil I saw
hastening to merge itself and become
lost and dead.
    WALT WHITMAN, *Roaming in Thought.*

1
His daily prayer, far better understood
In acts than words, was simply doing good.
    JOHN GREENLEAF WHITTIER, *Daniel Neall.*

2
The evil cannot brook delay,
The good can well afford to wait.
Give ermined knaves their hour of crime;
Ye have the future grand and great,
The safe appeal of Truth to time!
    JOHN GREENLEAF WHITTIER, *For Right-
    eousness' Sake.*

3
There are two kinds of people on earth to-
day,
Just two kinds of people, no more, I say.
Not the good and the bad, for 'tis well un-
derstood
That the good are half bad and the bad are
half good. . . .
No! the two kinds of people on earth I
mean
Are the people who lift and the people who
lean.
    ELLA WHEELER WILCOX, *Lifting and Lean-
    ing.*

GOSSIP, see Scandal
GOVERNMENT
See also Constitution, Democracy, Politics

4
A government of laws and not of men.
    JOHN ADAMS, Constitution of Massachu-
    setts: Declaration of Rights, Art. 30
    (1780). See *American Bar Association
    Journal,* Dec., 1929, p. 747.

5
The essence of a free government consists in
an effectual control of rivalries.
    JOHN ADAMS, *Discourses on Davila.*

6
You talk about capitalism and communism
and all that sort of thing, but the important
thing is the struggle everybody is engaged in
to get better living conditions, and they are
not interested too much in the form of government.
    BERNARD BARUCH, Press Conference in
    New York City, 18 Aug., 1964, on the
    eve of his 94th birthday.

7
Law represents the effort of men to organize
society; government, the efforts of selfishness to overthrow liberty.
    HENRY WARD BEECHER, *Proverbs from
    Plymouth Pulpit.*

8
I believe every citizen should support the
government when final action is taken,
whether he approves of the action or not.
    WILLIAM JENNINGS BRYAN. (New York
    Times, 2 June, 1898)

9
While the people should patriotically and
cheerfully support their Government its
functions do not include the support of the
people.
    GROVER CLEVELAND, Message upon vetoing
    the Texas Seed Bill, 16 Feb., 1887.

10
The principal business of government is to
further and promote human strivings.
    WILBUR L. CROSS. (New York *Times,* 29
    Mar., 1931)

11
Of all the tasks of government, the most
basic is to protect its citizens against violence.
    JOHN FOSTER DULLES, Speech at the Asso-
    ciated Press annual luncheon, 22 Apr.,
    1957.

12
We Republicans believe in limited government, but also in effective and humane government. We believe in keeping government
as close to the people as possible—in letting
each citizen do for himself what he can do
for himself, then making any call for government assistance first on the local government, then on the state government, and
only in the final resort on the Federal Government. But we do not shrink from a recognition that there are national problems that
require national solutions. When they arise,
we act.
    DWIGHT D. EISENHOWER, Article written
    for the New York *Herald Tribune,* 25
    May, 1964.

13
Our best protection against bigger government in Washington is better government in
the states.
    DWIGHT D. EISENHOWER, Address before
    National Governors' Conference, Cleve-
    land, 8 June, 1964.

14
An institution is the lengthened shadow of
one man.
    EMERSON, *Essays, First Series: Self-Reli-
    ance.*

15
No institution will be better than the institu-
tor.
    EMERSON, *Essays, Second Series: Charac-
    ter.*

16
If you would rule the world quietly, you
must keep it amused.
    EMERSON, *Essays, Second Series: New*

England Reformers. Quoted as the maxim of a tyrant.

1
Every actual State is corrupt.

EMERSON, *Essays, Second Series: Politics.*

2
The teaching of politics is that the Government, which was set for protection and comfort of all good citizens, becomes the principal obstruction and nuisance with which we have to contend. . . . The cheat and bully and malefactor we meet everywhere is the Government.

EMERSON, *Journal,* 1860.

3
Government has been a fossil: it should be a plant.

EMERSON, *Miscellanies: To the Mercantile Library Association.*

4
I fear Washington and centralized government more than I do Moscow.

BARRY M. GOLDWATER, Speech in Spartanburg, S.C., 15 Sept., 1960.

5
It is my chore to ask you to consider the toughest proposition ever faced by believers in the free-enterprise system: the need for a frontal attack against Santa Claus—not the Santa Claus of the holiday season, of course, but the Santa Claus of the free lunch, the government handout, the Santa Claus of something-for-nothing and something-for-everyone.

BARRY M. GOLDWATER, Address before the Economic Club of New York City, 15 Jan., 1964.

6
A government that is big enough to give you all you want is big enough to take it all away.

BARRY M. GOLDWATER, Speech in West Chester, Pa., during the presidential campaign, 21 Oct., 1964.

7
It's political Daddyism, and it's as old as demagogues and despotism.

BARRY M. GOLDWATER, Speech in New York City during the presidential campaign, 26 Oct., 1964. He was referring to the paternalism of the "everlastingly growing Federal government."

8
A welfare state is one that guarantees a broad series of economic protections that any citizen can claim when he is no longer able to provide for himself. In a welfare state, the benefits an individual receives are political rights, not charity, and there should be no occasion for apology or embarrassment in applying for them. Moreover, the services made available by a welfare state will parallel in quality and coverage those open to individuals who are able to draw on private resources.

ANDREW HACKER, *Again the Issue of 'The Welfare State'; New York Times Magazine,* 22 Mar., 1964, p. 9.

9
There can be no truer principle than this— that every individual of the community at large has an equal right to the protection of government.

ALEXANDER HAMILTON, Address at Constitutional Convention, 29 June, 1787.

10
The very basis of representative government is a two-party system. It is one of the essential checks and balances against inefficiency, dishonesty, and tyranny.

HERBERT HOOVER, 1951. (*Herbert Hoover in His Own Words,* compiled by LOUIS P. LOCHNER; *New York Times Magazine,* 9 Aug., 1964, p. 15)

11
An organized, effective opposition which insists upon disclosure of the facts and submits them to the anvil of debate is the one safety representative government has. Moreover, the people must have alternative programs of action upon which they may decide at the ballot box. Beyond this, any party in power accumulates barnacles and deadwood which can only be rid by a change in administration.

HERBERT HOOVER, 1951. (*Herbert Hoover in His Own Words,* compiled by LOUIS P. LOCHNER; *New York Times Magazine,* 9 Aug., 1964, p. 15)

12
The essence of our self-government lies in self-government outside of political government. The fabric of American life is woven around our tens of thousands of voluntary associations, the churches, the private schools and colleges, the research institutions, the professional societies, women's organizations, business, labor, and farmers' associations. And by no means the least, our charitable institutions. . . . If these voluntary activities were to be absorbed by government agencies, this civilization would be over. Something neither free nor noble would take its place.

HERBERT HOOVER, 1954. (*Herbert Hoover in His Own Words,* compiled by LOUIS P. LOCHNER; *New York Times Magazine,* 9 Aug., 1964, p. 15)

13
I am convinced that those societies (as the Indians) which live without government, enjoy in their general mass an infinitely greater degree of happiness than those who live under the European governments. Among the former, public opinion is in the place of law, and restrains morals as powerfully as laws

ever did anywhere. Among the latter, under pretense of governing, they have divided their nations into two classes, wolves and sheep.

THOMAS JEFFERSON, Letter, Paris, 16 Jan., 1787.

1

It is error alone which needs support of government. Truth can stand by itself.

THOMAS JEFFERSON, Letter to Tyler, 1804.

2

Were we directed from Washington when to sow and when to reap, we should soon want bread.

THOMAS JEFFERSON, *Papers,* vol. i, p. 66.

3

It is really more questionable than may at first be thought, whether Bonaparte's dumb legislature, which said nothing and did much, may not be preferable to one which talks much and does nothing.

THOMAS JEFFERSON, *Writings,* vol. i, p. 86.

The notorious "do-nothing" Republican 80th Congress.

HARRY S TRUMAN, Speech in Dexter, Ia., 18 Sept., 1948.

At the turn of the century that cynical American observer, Ambrose Bierce, defined Congress as: "A body of men who meet to repeal laws." At this time cynical Washington observers could shorten the definition to: "A body of men who meet."

Editorial, New York *Times,* 1 Jan., 1964, commenting on the lack of productivity of the 88th Congress.

4

A wise and frugal government, which shall restrain men from injuring one another, which shall leave them otherwise free to regulate their own pursuits of industry and improvement, and shall not take from the mouth of labor the bread it has earned—this is the sum of good government.

THOMAS JEFFERSON, *Writings,* vol. iii, p. 320.

5

The whole of government consists in the art of being honest.

THOMAS JEFFERSON, *Writings,* vol. vi, p. 186.

6

The only orthodox object of the institution of government is to secure the greatest degree of happiness possible to the general mass of those associated under it.

THOMAS JEFFERSON, *Writings,* vol. xviii, p. 135.

7

The care of human life and happiness, and not their destruction, is the first and only legitimate object of good government.

THOMAS JEFFERSON, *Notes on Virginia: Writings,* vol. iii, p. 263.

8

After all, government is just a device to protect man so that he may earn his bread in the sweat of his labor.

HUGH S. JOHNSON, *Where Do We Go from Here?* (*The American,* July, 1935, p. 90)

9

Aside from being strong and aside from being solvent, this Government must always be compassionate. We must bear in mind that, as I said before, we are the servants of the people.

LYNDON B. JOHNSON, Speech before field officials of the Internal Revenue Service, Washington, D.C., 11 Feb., 1964.

10

The truth is, far from crushing the individual, government at its best liberates him from the enslaving forces of his environment.

LYNDON B. JOHNSON, Commencement Address, Swarthmore College, Swarthmore, Pa., 8 June, 1964.

11

Government exists to protect freedom and enlarge the opportunities of every citizen. The American Government is not to be feared and attacked. It is to be helped as long as it serves its country well and changed when it neglects its duty.

LYNDON B. JOHNSON, Address before annual Boy Scout jamboree, Valley Forge, Pa., 24 July, 1964.

12

Government is an Irish boy from Boston who grew up to be President. Government is the son of a German immigrant from Pekin, Ill., who became a leader of the American Senate. Government is a rancher from Montana, a banker from New York, an automobile maker from Detroit; government is the son of a tenant farmer from Texas who is speaking to you tonight.

LYNDON B. JOHNSON, Address before annual Boy Scout jamboree, Valley Forge, Pa., 24 July, 1964. He was referring, respectively, to John F. Kennedy, Everett M. Dirksen, Mike Mansfield, C. Douglas Dillon (then Secretary of the Treasury), Robert S. McNamara (then Secretary of Defense), and himself.

13

When a white man governs himself, that is self-government; but when he governs himself and also governs another man, that is despotism. . . . No man is good enough to govern another man without that other's consent.

ABRAHAM LINCOLN, Speech in Peoria, Ill.,

16 Oct., 1854, during the Lincoln-Douglas debates.

1

This country, with its institutions, belongs to the people who inhabit it. Whenever they shall grow weary of the existing government, they can exercise their constitutional right of amending it, or their revolutionary right to dismember or overthrow it.

ABRAHAM LINCOLN, First Inaugural Address, 4 Mar., 1861.

2

It is possible to govern a state without giving the masses of the people full representation. But it is not possible to go on for long without a government which can and does in fact govern. If, therefore, the people find that they must choose whether they will be represented in an assembly which is incompetent to govern, or whether they will be governed without being represented, there is no doubt at all as to how the issue will be decided. They will choose authority, which promises to be paternal, in preference to freedom which threatens to be fratricidal. For large communities cannot do without being governed.

WALTER LIPPMANN, *The Public Philosophy*. Book I, ch. 6.

3

The vanity and presumption of governing beyond the grave is the most ridiculous and insolent of all tyrannies. Man has no property in the generations which are to follow.

THOMAS PAINE, Reply to Burke, 1791.

4

Government, even in its best state, is but a necessary evil; in its worst state, an intolerable one.

THOMAS PAINE, *Common Sense*, ch. 1.

There are no necessary evils in government. Its evils exist only in its abuses.

ANDREW JACKSON, Message accompanying his veto of the Bank Bill, 10 July, 1832.

5

Government arrogates to itself that it alone forms men. . . . Everybody knows that government never began anything. It is the whole world that thinks and governs.

WENDELL PHILLIPS, Lecture: *Idols*, Boston, 4 Oct., 1859.

6

One of the greatest delusions in the world is the hope that the evils of this world can be cured by legislation. I am happy in the belief that the solution of the great difficulties of life and government are in better hands even than that of this body.

THOMAS B. REED. (W. A. ROBINSON, *Life*)

7

It's just a red herring to get the minds of the voters off the sins of the 80th Congress.

HARRY S TRUMAN, Statement, 17 Sept., 1948, rejecting the Communists-in-government charge as an issue in the presidential election of that year. During that campaign he coined and made famous the term "do-nothing Congress."

8

The very idea of the power and the right of the People to establish Government, presupposes the duty of every individual to obey the established Government.

GEORGE WASHINGTON, Farewell Address, 1796.

9

The aggregate happiness of society, which is best promoted by the practice of a virtuous policy, is, or ought to be, the end of all government.

GEORGE WASHINGTON, *Political Maxims*.

10

Influence is not government.

GEORGE WASHINGTON, *Political Maxims*.

11

We have been taught to regard a representative of the people as a sentinel on the watchtower of liberty.

DANIEL WEBSTER, Speech in U.S. Senate, 7 May, 1834.

12

My reading of history convinces me that most bad government has grown out of too much government.

JOHN SHARP WILLIAMS, *Thomas Jefferson*, p. 49.

13

Government is not a warfare of interests. We shall not gain our ends by heat and bitterness, which make it impossible to think either calmly or fairly. Government is a matter of common counsel, and everyone must come into the consultation with the purpose to yield to the general view, which seems most nearly to correspond with the common interest. If any decline frank conference, keep out, hold off, they must take the consequences and blame only themselves if they are in the end badly served.

WOODROW WILSON, Speech upon accepting the Democratic nomination for governor of New Jersey, 15 Sept., 1910, Trenton, N.J.

14

No man ever saw a government. I live in the midst of the Government of the United States, but I never saw the Government of the United States.

WOODROW WILSON, Speech in Pittsburgh, Pa., 29 Jan., 1916.

15

The world is governed too much.

UNKNOWN, Motto of the Boston *Globe*.

I confess the motto of the *Globe* newspaper is so attractive to me that I can seldom find much appetite to read what is below it in its columns.

> EMERSON, *Essays, Second Series: New England Reformers*.

GRAMMAR

1
The grammar has a rule absurd
Which I would call an outworn myth:
"A preposition is a word
You mustn't end a sentence with!"

> BERTON BRALEY, *No Rule to Be Afraid Of*.

2
You can be a little ungrammatical if you come from the right part of the country.

> ROBERT FROST. (*The Atlantic*, Jan., 1962)

3
When a thought takes one's breath away, a lesson on grammar seems an impertinence.

> T. W. HIGGINSON, Preface to *Poems* (1890) by EMILY DICKINSON.

4
Grammar is the grave of letters.

> ELBERT HUBBARD, *A Thousand and One Epigrams*, p. 114.

5
When I read some of the rules for speaking and writing the English language correctly, . . . I think—
Any fool can make a rule
And every fool will mind it.

> HENRY D. THOREAU, *Journal*, 3 Feb., 1860.

6
Why care for grammar as long as we are good?

> ARTEMUS WARD, *Natural History*, pt. v.

GRASS

7
Grass grows at last above all graves.

> JULIA C. R. DORR, *Grass-Grown*.

8
The green grass floweth like a stream
Into the ocean's blue.

> JAMES RUSSELL LOWELL, *The Sirens*, l. 87.

9
The murmur that springs
From the growing of grass.

> EDGAR ALLAN POE, *Al Aaraaf*, pt. ii, l. 124.

10
Pile the bodies high at Austerlitz and Waterloo.
Shovel them under and let me work—
I am the grass; I cover all.

> CARL SANDBURG, *Grass*.

11
A child said *What is the grass?* fetching it to me with full hands;

How could I answer the child? I do not know what it is any more than he.
I guess it must be the flag of my disposition, out of hopeful green stuff woven.
Or I guess it is the handkerchief of the Lord,
A scented gift and remembrancer designedly dropt. . . .
And now it seems to me the beautiful uncut hair of graves.

> WALT WHITMAN, *Song of Myself*, sec. 6.

GRATITUDE

12
Next to ingratitude, the most painful thing to bear is gratitude.

> HENRY WARD BEECHER, *Proverbs from Plymouth Pulpit*.

13
Be thankful f'r what ye have not, Hinnissy —'tis the on'y safe rule.

> FINLEY PETER DUNNE, *Thanksgiving*.

14
I sincerely wish ingratitude was not so natural to the human heart as it is.

> ALEXANDER HAMILTON, Letter to George Washington, 25 Mar., 1783.

15
Lord, for the erring thought
Not into evil wrought:
Lord, for the wicked will
Betrayed and baffled still:
For the heart from itself kept,
Our thanksgiving accept.

> WILLIAM DEAN HOWELLS, *Thanksgiving*.

16
One can never pay in gratitude; one can only pay "in kind" somewhere else in life.

> ANNE MORROW LINDBERGH, *"Listen! the Wind"*, ch. 19.

17
Gratitude is a nice touch of beauty added last of all to the countenance, giving a classic beauty, an angelic loveliness, to the character.

> THEODORE PARKER, Sermon: *Of Moral Dangers Incident to Prosperity*.

18
No longer forward nor behind
I look in hope or fear;
But, grateful, take the good I find,
The best of now and here.

> JOHN GREENLEAF WHITTIER, *My Psalm*, st. 3.

GRAVE

19
Done with the work of breathing; done
With all the world; the mad race run
Through to the end; the golden goal
Attained and found to be a hole!

> AMBROSE BIERCE, *The Devil's Dictionary*, p. 63.

1

Earth laughs in flowers, to see her boastful
        boys
Earth-proud, proud of the earth which is not
        theirs;
Who steer the plough, but can not steer their
        feet
Clear of the grave.
        EMERSON, *Hamatreya.*

2

And now he has no single plot of ground,
Excepting that in which he sleeps so sound!
        HENRY HARRISON, *Epitaph for a Real-Es-
        tate Dealer.*

3

Oh, the grave!—the grave!—It buries every
error—covers every defect—extinguishes every resentment! From its peaceful bosom
spring none but fond regrets and tender recollections. Who can look down upon the
grave even of an enemy and not feel a com-
punctious throb, that he should ever have
warred with the poor handful of earth that
lies mouldering before him?
        WASHINGTON IRVING, *The Sketch-book:
        Rural Funerals.*

4

The grave itself is but a covered bridge,
Leading from light to light, through a brief
        darkness!
        HENRY WADSWORTH LONGFELLOW, *The
        Golden Legend,* pt. v.

5

He spake well who said that graves are the
        footprints of angels.
        HENRY WADSWORTH LONGFELLOW, *Hype-
        rion,* bk. iv, ch. 5.

6

Our hearts, though stout and brave,
        Still, like muffled drums, are beating
Funeral marches to the grave.
        HENRY WADSWORTH LONGFELLOW, *A
        Psalm of Life.*

7

Both, heirs to some six feet of sod,
        Are equal in the earth at last.
        JAMES RUSSELL LOWELL, *The Heritage.*

8

For rain it hath a friendly sound
To one who's six feet underground;
And scarce the friendly voice or face:
A grave is such a quiet place.
        EDNA ST. VINCENT MILLAY, *Renascence.*

9

Now limb doth mingle with dissolvèd limb
In nature's busy old democracy.
        WILLIAM VAUGHN MOODY, *An Ode in
        Time of Hesitation.*

10

A grave seems only six feet deep
        And three feet wide,
Viewed with the calculating eye
        Of one outside.

But when fast bound in the chill loam
        For that strange sleep,
Who knows how wide its realm may be?
        Its depths, how deep?
        JOHN RICHARD MORELAND, *A Grave.*

11

        The low green tent
Whose curtain never outward swings.
        JOHN GREENLEAF WHITTIER, *Snow-Bound,*
        st. 13.

GRAVEYARD

12

I could never understand why a gravestone
should carry mention of the only two events
[birth and death] in the career of the de-
ceased with which he had absolutely nothing
to do—unless he committed suicide.
        IRVIN S. COBB, Letter written late in 1943
        to the editor of the Paducah (Ky.) *Sun-
        Democrat.*

13

I like that ancient Saxon phrase, which calls
        The burial-ground God's-Acre! It is just;
It consecrates each grave within its walls,
        And breathes a benison o'er the sleeping
        dust.
        HENRY WADSWORTH LONGFELLOW, *God's-
        Acre.*

14

This is the field and Acre of our God,
This is the place where human harvests
        grow.
        HENRY WADSWORTH LONGFELLOW, *God's-
        Acre.*

15

There are slave-drivers quietly whipped un-
        derground,
There bookbinders, done up in boards, are
        fast bound,
There card-players wait till the last trump be
        played,
There all the choice spirits get finally laid,
There the babe that's unborn is supplied
        with a berth,
There men without legs get their six feet of
        earth,
There lawyers repose, each wrapped up in his
        case,
There seekers of office are sure of a place,
There defendant and plaintiff get equally
        cast,
There shoemakers quietly stick to the last.
        JAMES RUSSELL LOWELL, *A Fable for
        Critics,* l. 1656.

16

The country home I need is a cemetery.
        MARK TWAIN. (PAINE, *Mark Twain*)

GREATNESS

17

The fellow that does his job every day. The
mother who has children and gets up and

gets the breakfast and keeps them clean and sends them off to school. The fellow who keeps the streets clean—without him we wouldn't have any sanitation. The Unknown Soldier. Millions of men.

BERNARD M. BARUCH, Press Conference, New York City, 18 Aug., 1964, on the eve of his 94th birthday. This was his reply to a question: who was the greatest man of Baruch's time?

1

Greatness, after all, in spite of its name, appears to be not so much a certain size as a certain quality in human lives. It may be present in lives whose range is very small.

PHILLIPS BROOKS, Sermons: Purpose and Use of Comfort.

2

How dreary to be somebody!
How public, like a frog
To tell your name the livelong day
To an admiring bog!

EMILY DICKINSON, Poems, Pt. i, No. 27.

3

The measure of a master is his success in bringing all men round to his opinion twenty years later.

EMERSON, Conduct of Life: Culture.

4

Great men, great nations, have not been boasters and buffoons, but perceivers of the terror of life, and have manned themselves to face it.

EMERSON, Conduct of Life: Fate.

5

He is great who confers the most benefits.

EMERSON, Essays, First Series: Compensation.

6

The essence of greatness is the perception that virtue is enough.

EMERSON, Essays, First Series: Heroism.

7

It is easy in the world to live after the world's opinion; it is easy in solitude after our own; but the great man is he who in the midst of the crowd keeps with perfect sweetness the independence of solitude.

EMERSON, Essays, First Series: Self-Reliance.

8

Every great man is a unique. The Scipionism of Scipio is precisely that part he could not borrow. Shakespeare will never be made by the study of Shakespeare. Do that which is assigned to you, and you cannot hope too much or dare too much.

EMERSON, Essays, First Series: Self-Reliance.

9

To be great is to be misunderstood.

EMERSON, Essays, First Series: Self-Reliance.

10

If I cannot carry forests on my back
Neither can you crack a nut.

EMERSON, Fable. This is what the squirrel replied to the mountain, which had called it "Little Prig."

11

The great man makes the great thing. Wherever Macdonald sits, there is the head of the table.

EMERSON, Nature Addresses and Lectures: The American Scholar. The second sentence paraphrases a Scottish saying.

12

It is as easy to be great as to be small.

EMERSON, Representative Men: Plato.

13

I count him a great man who inhabits a higher sphere of thought, into which other men rise with labor and difficulty.

EMERSON, Representative Men: Uses of Great Men.

14

He is great who is what he is from nature, and who never reminds us of others.

EMERSON, Representative Men: Uses of Great Men.

15

The bigger they come the harder they fall.

BOB FITZSIMMONS, spoken just before his bout with Jim Jeffries, which the latter won, 25 July, 1902, in San Francisco.

16

There was never yet a truly great man that was not at the same time truly virtuous.

BENJAMIN FRANKLIN, The Busy-body, No. 3.

17

Great lives never go out. They go on.

BENJAMIN HARRISON, Address at the cottage at Mt. McGregor where Grant died.

18

Great men are the gifts of kind Heaven to our poor world; instruments by which the Highest One works out his designs; light-radiators to give guidance and blessing to the travelers of time.

MOSES HARVEY, Columbus.

19

Great men are rarely isolated mountain-peaks; they are the summits of ranges.

T. W. HIGGINSON, Atlantic Essays: Plea for Culture.

20

Our grandeur lies in our illusions.

SAMUEL HOFFENSTEIN, Grandeur.

21

The Great Man is a man who lives a long way off.

ELBERT HUBBARD, The Philistine, xii, 36.

22

We lived in the shadow of greatness.

OTTO KERNER, Governor of Illinois, speaking for the people of his state at the bier of Adlai E. Stevenson in the capitol, Springfield, Ill., 16 July, 1965.

1
So when a great man dies,
  For years beyond our ken,
The light he leaves behind him lies
  Upon the paths of men.
    HENRY WADSWORTH LONGFELLOW, *Charles Sumner.*

2
Great men stand like solitary towers in the city of God.
    HENRY WADSWORTH LONGFELLOW, *Kavanagh,* ch. 1.

3
The heights by great men reached and kept
  Were not attained by sudden flight,
But they, while their companions slept,
  Were toiling upward in the night.
    HENRY WADSWORTH LONGFELLOW, *The Ladder of St. Augustine.* This is inscribed beneath Longfellow's bust in the Hall of Fame.

4
A great man is made up of qualities that meet or make great occasions.
    JAMES RUSSELL LOWELL, *My Study Windows: Garfield.*

5
That man is great who can use the brains of others to carry on his work.
    DONN PIATT, *Memories of Men Who Saved the Union: W. H. Seward.*

6
Far better it is to dare mighty things, to win glorious triumphs, even though checkered by failure, than to take rank with those poor spirits who neither enjoy much nor suffer much because they live in the gray twilight that knows neither victory nor defeat.
    THEODORE ROOSEVELT, Speech before the Hamilton Club, Chicago, 10 Apr., 1899.

7
Call to Greatness.
    ADLAI E. STEVENSON, Title of book (1954).

8
Life is good in America, but the good life still eludes us. Our standard of living is admittedly high, but measured by those things that truly distinguish a civilization, our living standards are hardly high at all. We

have, I fear, confused power with greatness.
    STEWART L. UDALL, Commencement Address, Dartmouth College, Hanover, N.H., 13 June, 1965.

GREED, see Avarice
GRIEF
See also Sorrow

9
Why should I sorrow for what was pain?
A cherished grief is an iron chain.
    STEPHEN VINCENT BENÉT, *King David.*

10
The only thing grief has taught me is to know how shallow it is.
    EMERSON, *Essays, Second Series: Experience.*

11
Some men are above grief and some below it.
    EMERSON, *Natural History of Intellect: The Tragic.*

12
Oh, well has it been said, that there is no grief like the grief which does not speak!
    HENRY WADSWORTH LONGFELLOW, *Hyperion,* bk. ii, ch. 2.

GUILT

13
    God hath yoked to guilt
Her pale tormenter, misery.
    WILLIAM CULLEN BRYANT, *Inscription for the Entrance to a Wood.*

14
Let no guilty man escape.
    ULYSSES S. GRANT, Indorsement of a letter concerning the Whiskey Ring, 29 July, 1875.

15
The legal terms of guilt and innocence strike me as silly. We've all contributed to that error long enough, and it's a mistake to go along with it. If we could be any help after the jury has made up its mind, that would be a different matter.
    DR. KARL A. MENNINGER, in rejecting a defense request that he testify at the murder trial of Jack Ruby, killer of Lee Harvey Oswald, early in 1964. (Quoted in New York *Times,* "Ideas and Men," 1 Mar., 1964)

H

HABIT

16
Habit is the approximation of the animal system to the organic. It is a confession of failure in the highest function of being,

which involves a perpetual self-determination, in full view of all existing circumstances.
    OLIVER WENDELL HOLMES, *The Autocrat of the Breakfast-Table,* ch. 7.

1

Cultivate only the habits that you are willing should master you.

> ELBERT HUBBARD, *The Philistine,* vol. xxv, p. 62.

2

Habit is the enormous fly-wheel of society, its most precious conservative agent.

> WILLIAM JAMES, *Psychology,* vol. i, p. 121.

3

For the ordinary business of life, an ounce of habit is worth a pound of intellect.

> THOMAS B. REED. (W. A. ROBINSON, *Life*)

4

Habit is habit, and not to be flung out of the window by any man, but coaxed downstairs a step at a time.

> MARK TWAIN, *Pudd'nhead Wilson's Calendar.*

5

Nothing so needs reforming as other people's habits.

> MARK TWAIN, *Pudd'nhead Wilson's Calendar.*

HAND

6

There is a hand that has no heart in it, there is a claw or paw, a flipper or fin, a bit of wet cloth to take hold of, a piece of unbaked dough on the cook's trencher, a cold clammy thing we recoil from, or greedy clutch with the heat of sin, which we drop as a burning coal. What a scale from the talon to the horn of plenty, is this human palm-leaf! Sometimes it is like a knife-shaped, thin-bladed tool we dare not grasp, or like a poisonous thing we shake off, or unclean member, which, white as it may look, we feel polluted by!

> C. A. BARTOL, *The Rising Faith: Training.*

7

Let him value his hands and feet, he has but one pair.

> EMERSON, *Conduct of Life: Fate.*

8

Help, Hands, for I have no Lands.

> BENJAMIN FRANKLIN, *Poor Richard,* 1758.

9

Hands of invisible spirits touch the strings
Of that mysterious instrument, the soul,
And play the prelude of our fate.

> HENRY WADSWORTH LONGFELLOW, *The Spanish Student,* act i, sc. 3.

10

And blessed are the horny hands of toil.

> JAMES RUSSELL LOWELL, *A Glance Behind the Curtain,* l. 204.

11

No man can feel himself alone
The while he bravely stands
Between the best friends ever known

His two good, honest hands.

> NIXON WATERMAN, *Interludes.*

HAPPINESS

See also Joy, Pleasure

12

Real happiness is cheap enough, yet how dearly we pay for its counterfeit.

> HOSEA BALLOU, *MS. Sermons.*

13

The happiest heart that ever beat
Was in some quiet breast
That found the common daylight sweet,
And left to Heaven the rest.

> JOHN VANCE CHENEY, *The Happiest Heart.*

14

The best way to secure future happiness is to be as happy as is rightfully possible to-day.

> CHARLES W. ELIOT, *The Happy Life.*

15

To fill the hour—that is happiness; to fill the hour, and leave no crevice for a repentance or an approval.

> EMERSON, *Essays, Second Series: Experience.*

16

Human felicity is produced not so much by great pieces of good fortune that seldom happen, as by little advantages that occur every day.

> BENJAMIN FRANKLIN, *Autobiography,* ch. 1.

17

Happiness Makes Up in Height for What It Lacks in Length.

> ROBERT FROST, Title of poem (1942).

18

Most of the disappointments of later life could be lightened immeasurably if we could learn—and truly believe—early in life that what we confusedly call "happiness" is a direction and not a place.

> SYDNEY J. HARRIS, Publishers Newspaper Syndicate. (*The Reader's Digest,* Dec., 1963, p. 205)

19

Happiness in this world, when it comes, comes incidentally. Make it the object of pursuit, and it leads us a wild-goose chase, and is never attained.

> NATHANIEL HAWTHORNE, *Journals,* 21 Oct., 1852.

20

Happiness is a habit—cultivate it.

> ELBERT HUBBARD, *Epigrams.*

21

It's pretty hard to tell what does bring happiness. Poverty an' wealth have both failed.

> KIN HUBBARD, *Abe Martin's Broadcast,* p. 191.

22

Happiness is not a reward—it is a consequence. Suffering is not a punishment—it is a result.

> ROBERT G. INGERSOLL, *The Christian Religion*.

1

Happiness is the legal tender of the soul.

> ROBERT G. INGERSOLL, *The Liberty of Man, Woman and Child*.

2

Happiness is the only good, reason the only torch, justice the only worship, humanity the only religion, and love the only priest.

> ROBERT G. INGERSOLL, *A Tribute to Eben Ingersoll*.

3

How to gain, how to keep, how to recover happiness is in fact for most men at all times the secret motive of all they do, and of all they are willing to endure.

> WILLIAM JAMES, *Varieties of Religious Experience*, p. 78.

4

As far as the job as President goes, it's rewarding, and I've given before this group the definition of happiness of the Greeks. I'll define it again: the full use of your powers along lines of excellence. I find that, therefore, the Presidency provides some happiness.

> JOHN F. KENNEDY, Press Conference, 31 Oct., 1963.

5

To be strong Is to be happy!

> HENRY WADSWORTH LONGFELLOW, *The Golden Legend*, pt. ii, l. 731.

6

The rays of happiness, like those of light, are colorless when unbroken.

> HENRY WADSWORTH LONGFELLOW, *Kavanagh*, ch. 13.

7

Now the heart is so full that a drop overfills it,
We are happy now because God wills it.

> JAMES RUSSELL LOWELL, *The Vision of Sir Launfal:* Prelude.

8

Happiness puts on as many shapes as discontent, and there is nothing odder than the satisfactions of one's neighbor.

> PHYLLIS McGINLEY, *The Province of the Heart: Pipeline and Sinker*, p. 79.

9

Happiness is the goal of every normal human being. As it is given to few men to die happy, the best that man can hope and strive and pray for is momentary happiness during life, repeated as frequently as the cards allow.

> GEORGE JEAN NATHAN, *Testament of a Critic*, p. 6.

10

The foolish man seeks happiness in the distance;

The wise grows it under his feet.

> JAMES OPPENHEIM, *The Wise*.

11

Happiness is a by-product of an effort to make some one else happy.

> GRETTA PALMER, *Permanent Marriage*.

12

Happiness is a way-station between too little and too much.

> CHANNING POLLOCK, *Mr. Moneypenny*.

13

It is wrong to assume that men of immense wealth are always happy.

> JOHN D. ROCKEFELLER, Remark to his Sunday-school class. (HOLBROOK, *The Age of the Moguls*, p. 134)

14

Happiness is the only sanction of life; where happiness fails, existence remains a mad and lamentable experiment.

> GEORGE SANTAYANA, *Little Essays*, p. 251.

15

Happiness is a wine of the rarest vintage, and seems insipid to the vulgar taste.

> LOGAN PEARSALL SMITH, *Afterthoughts*.

16

So long as we can lose any happiness, we possess some.

> BOOTH TARKINGTON, *Looking Forward*, p. 172.

17

Man is the artificer of his own happiness.

> HENRY D. THOREAU, *Journal*, 21 Jan., 1838.

18

What wisdom, what warning can prevail against gladness? There is no law so strong which a little gladness may not transgress.

> HENRY D. THOREAU, *Journal*, 3 Jan., 1853.

19

Happy days are here again,
The skies above are clear again.
Let us sing a song of cheer again,
Happy days are here again!

> JACK YELLEN, *Happy Days Are Here Again*. Originally heard in the musical comedy *Chasing Rainbows* (1929), the song became a sort of unofficial anthem of the Democratic party, beginning with the national convention of 1936.

HASTE

20

Never lose your presence of mind, and never get hurried.

> EMERSON, *Books*.

21

Nothing is more vulgar than haste.

> EMERSON, *Conduct of Life: Behavior*.

22

Let us leave hurry to slaves.

> EMERSON, *Essays, Second Series: Manners*.

1
Excuse my dust.
DOROTHY PARKER, Epitaph for herself.

HAT

2
Here's your hat, what's your hurry?
BARTLEY C. COSTELLO, Title and Refrain
of popular song (1904).

3
The hat is the *ultimatum moriens* of respectability.
OLIVER WENDELL HOLMES, *The Autocrat
of the Breakfast-Table*, ch. 8.

Virtue may flourish in an old cravat,
But man and nature scorn the shocking hat.
OLIVER WENDELL HOLMES, *A Rhymed
Lesson*, l. 452.

4
         bumped
off the running board of existence
to furnish plumage
for a lady's hat
DON MARQUIS, *unjust*.

5
A woman's hat, when worn indoors, serves no
utilitarian purpose, and its virtue as a protection against the elements went out with
the sunbonnet. It is purely an article of
adornment, worn to attract attention, to en-
hance the appearance of the wearer and earn
admiration. However, the artistic creation
that would add to the beauty of a garden
party would be, in most cases, entirely out of
place in a courtroom.
JUSTICE CLEMENT L. SHINN, Opinion in
The People of the State of California vs.
Herbert Rainey, District Court of Appeal, Los Angeles, 14 Jan., 1964. In the
first hearing of this case, the presiding
judge of a lower court asked one of the
rival attorneys, a woman, to remove her
hat in the courtroom. She refused, and
contended that the judge's request was
prejudicial. Justice Shinn's appellate-
court opinion made note of this controversy before proceeding to a review of
the case proper.

6
Where did you get that hat?
JOSEPH J. SULLIVAN, Title and Refrain of
popular song (1888).

HATRED

7
You lose a lot of time hating people.
MARIAN ANDERSON, commenting on why
she forgave the Daughters of the American Revolution, after the D.A.R. refused the use of Constitution Hall for
Miss Anderson's memorable Easter Sunday concert in Washington, D.C., in
1939. (Quoted by Joan Barthel, Interview, New York *Times*, 18 Apr., 1965,
p. 13X)

8
Hatred is self-punishment.
HOSEA BALLOU, *MS. Sermons*.

9
I do not believe in the law of hate.
CLARENCE DARROW, in his defense of Henry Sweet, Detroit, 19 May, 1926. Sweet
was on trial as a consequence of a civil
disorder that resulted when, with a
group of fellow Negroes, he moved into
a Detroit district populated exclusively
by whites up to that time.

10
Hate at first sight.
EMERSON, *Society and Solitude: Works
and Days*.

11
Hating people is like burning down your own
house to get rid of a rat.
HARRY EMERSON FOSDICK, *The Wages of
Hate*.

12
Hatred—ah yes, but what are little hates
But little deaths that wander on and on.
WALTER GREENOUGH, *The Vision*.

13
I want to urge all men and women in this
land of ours to resist with all their dedication
the spiritual cancer of hate. If we hate others, we not only sin against them in the eyes
of the Almighty God, but we undermine and
eventually destroy our own integrity. By hating, we indicate and express that poverty of
the spirit which is far more dangerous to the
nation's future than the economic poverty
that we are making war on and that we have
announced as our objective to eliminate.
LYNDON B. JOHNSON, Press Conference,
Washington, D.C., 5 Sept., 1964.

14
The only solace for the nation's shame and
grief can come from a purge, or at least the
reduction of, the hatred and venom which lie
so close to the surface of our national life.
We have allowed the community of the
American people to be rent with enmity.
Only if and as we can find our way back into
the American community will we find our
way back to confidence in the American destiny. We must stop the flow of the poison
that when men differ, say about taxes or civil
rights or Russia, they cannot be reconciled
by persuasion and debate, and that those
who take the other view are implacable enemies.
WALTER LIPPMANN, Syndicated Column
commenting on the assassination of
John F. Kennedy. (New York *Herald
Tribune*, 26 Nov., 1963)

1
Folks never understand the folks they hate.
  JAMES RUSSELL LOWELL, *Biglow Papers*,
    ser. ii, *Mason and Slidell*.

2
For him who fain would teach the world
  The world holds hate in fee—
For Socrates, the hemlock cup;
  For Christ, Gethsemane.
  DON MARQUIS, *Wages*.

3
A little murder now and then,
A little bit of burglarizing,
Won't earn the hate of fellow-men
As much as being patronizing.
  R. T. WOMBAT, *Quatrains*.

HEALTH

See also Medicine

4
Happiness lies, first of all, in health.
  GEORGE WILLIAM CURTIS, *Lotus-Eating:
    Trenton*.

5
Health is not a condition of matter, but of
Mind; nor can the material senses bear reli-
able testimony on the subject of health.
  MARY BAKER EDDY, *Science and Health*, p.
    120.

6
The first wealth is health. Sickness is poor-
spirited, and cannot serve any one; it must
husband its resources to live. But health or
fulness answers its own ends, and has to
spare, runs over, and inundates the neighbor-
hoods and creeks of other men's necessities.
  EMERSON, *Conduct of Life: Power*.

7
Health is the first muse.
  EMERSON, *Letters and Social Aims: Inspi-
    ration*.

8
Give me health and a day, and I will make
the pomp of emperors ridiculous.
  EMERSON, *Nature, Addresses, and Lec-
    tures: Beauty*.

9
Early to bed and early to rise,
Makes a man healthy, wealthy, and wise.
  BENJAMIN FRANKLIN, *Poor Richard*,
    1758.

10
And each imbibes his rations from a Hygien-
  ic Cup—
The Bunny and the Baby and the Prophylac-
  tic Pup.
  ARTHUR GUITERMAN, *Strictly Germ-Proof*.

11
Oh, powerful bacillus,
With wonder how you fill us,
    Every day!
While medical detectives,
With powerful objectives,
    Watch your play.
  W. T. HELMUTH, *Ode to the Bacillus*.

12
The most uninformed mind with a healthy
body is happier than the wisest valetudinarian.
  THOMAS JEFFERSON, *Writings,* vol. vi, p.
    167.

13
Joy and Temperance and Repose
Slam the door on the doctor's nose.
  HENRY WADSWORTH LONGFELLOW, *The
    Best Medicines*.

14
The doctor is sure that my health is poor, he
says that I waste away; so bring me a can of
the shredded bran, and a bale of the toasted
hay.
  WALT MASON, *Health Food*.

15
He had had much experience of physicians,
and said, "The only way to keep your health
is to eat what you don't want, drink what
you don't like, and do what you'd druther
not."
  MARK TWAIN, *Pudd'nhead Wilson's New
    Calendar*.

16
Say you are well, or all is well with you.
And God shall hear your words and make
    them true.
  ELLA WHEELER WILCOX, *Speech*.

HEART

17
In each human heart are a tiger, a pig, an ass
and a nightingale. Diversity of character is
due to their unequal activity.
  AMBROSE BIERCE, *The Devil's Dictionary*.

18
In the desert
I saw a creature, naked, bestial,
Who, squatting upon the ground,
Held his heart in his hand
And ate of it.
I said, "Is it good, friend?"
"It is bitter-bitter," he answered;
"But I like it
Because it is bitter,
And because it is my heart."
  STEPHEN CRANE, *The Heart*.

19
The heart asks pleasure first,
And then, excuse from pain;
And then, those little anodynes
That deaden suffering.
And then, to go to sleep;
And then, if it should be
The will of its Inquisitor,
The liberty to die.
  EMILY DICKINSON, *Poems*. Pt. i. No. 9.

20
Futile the winds To a heart in port.
  EMILY DICKINSON, *Poems*, p. 141.

1

The heart has arguments with which the understanding is not acquainted.
> EMERSON, *Conduct of Life: Worship.* Quoted.

2

His heart was as great as the world, but there was no room in it to hold the memory of a wrong.
> EMERSON, *Letters and Social Aims: Greatness.* Referring to Lincoln.

3

The heart of the fool is in his mouth, but the mouth of the wise man is in his heart.
> BENJAMIN FRANKLIN, *Poor Richard,* 1733.

4

There is an evening twilight of the heart,
When its wild passion-waves are lulled to rest.
> FITZ-GREENE HALLECK, *Twilight.*

5

The great conservative is the heart.
> NATHANIEL HAWTHORNE, *Journals,* 6 Jan., 1854.

6

The heart is wiser than the intellect.
> JOSIAH G. HOLLAND, *Kathrina,* p. ii, st. 9.

7

Whatever comes from the brain carries the hue of the place it came from, and whatever comes from the heart carries the heat and color of its birthplace.
> OLIVER WENDELL HOLMES, *The Professor at the Breakfast-Table,* ch. 6.

8

'Tis the heart's current lends the cup its glow,
Whate'er the fountain whence the draught may flow.
> OLIVER WENDELL HOLMES, *A Sentiment.*

9

O hearts that break and give no sign
Save whitening lips and fading tresses.
> OLIVER WENDELL HOLMES, *The Voiceless.*

10

My heart is a kicking horse
Shod with Kentucky steel!
> VACHEL LINDSAY, *My Fathers Came from Kentucky.*

11

For his heart was in his work, and the heart
Giveth grace unto every Art.
> HENRY WADSWORTH LONGFELLOW, *The Building of the Ship,* l. 7.

12

It is the heart, and not the brain,
That to the highest doth attain.
> HENRY WADSWORTH LONGFELLOW, *The Building of the Ship,* l. 124.

13

The heart hath its own memory, like the mind,
  And in it are enshrined

The precious keepsakes, into which is wrought
  The giver's loving thought.
> HENRY WADSWORTH LONGFELLOW, *From My Arm-Chair,* st. 12.

14

Ye whose hearts are fresh and simple,
Who have faith in God and nature.
> HENRY WADSWORTH LONGFELLOW, *Hiawatha:* Introduction.

15

Every human heart is human.
> HENRY WADSWORTH LONGFELLOW, *Hiawatha:* Introduction, l. 91.

16

For his heart was hot within him,
Like a living coal his heart was.
> HENRY WADSWORTH LONGFELLOW, *Hiawatha,* pt. iv.

17

With a heart for any fate.
> HENRY WADSWORTH LONGFELLOW, *A Psalm of Life.*

18

Glorious fountain! Let my heart be
Fresh, changeful, constant, Upward, like thee!
> JAMES RUSSELL LOWELL, *The Fountain.*

19

All that hath been majestical
  In life or death, since time began,
Is native in the simple heart of all,
  The angel heart of man.
> JAMES RUSSELL LOWELL, *An Incident in a Railroad Car.*

20

There's a girl in the heart of Maryland
With a heart that belongs to me.
> BALLARD MACDONALD, *There's a Girl in the Heart of Maryland* (1913).

21

The heart has eyes that the brain knows nothing of.
> CHARLES H. PARKHURST, *Sermons: Coming to the Truth.*

22

My heart belongs to daddy.
> COLE PORTER, Title and refrain of song from the musical comedy *Leave It to Me* (1938). A newcomer to Broadway, Mary Martin, stopped the show with this number.

HEAVEN

23

        To appreciate heaven well
'Tis good for a man to have some fifteen minutes of hell.
> WILL CARLETON, *Gone with a Handsomer Man.*

24

And so upon this wise I prayed—
  Great Spirit, give to me
A heaven not so large as yours,

But large enough for me.
EMILY DICKINSON, *Poems*, Pt. i, No. 39.

1
Who has not found the heaven below
  Will fail of it above.
    EMILY DICKINSON, *Poems*, Pt. i, No. 100.

2
I never spoke with God,
Nor visited in heaven;
Yet certain am I of the spot
As if the chart were given.
    EMILY DICKINSON, *Poems*, Pt. iv, No. 17.

3
Hello, Central! give me heaven,
For my mama's there.
    CHARLES K. HARRIS, *Hello, Central! Give Me Heaven* (1901).

4
Heaven is largely a matter of digestion, and digestion is mostly a matter of mind.
    ELBERT HUBBARD, *A Thousand and One Epigrams*, p. 34.

5
    When Christ ascended
Triumphantly, from star to star,
He left the gates of heaven ajar.
    HENRY WADSWORTH LONGFELLOW, *The Golden Legend*, pt. ii, sc. 2.

6
We see but dimly through the mists and vapors;
  Amid these earthly damps
What seem to us but sad, funereal tapers
  May be heaven's distant lamps.
    HENRY WADSWORTH LONGFELLOW, *Resignation*, st. 4.

7
He sat upon the deck,
  The Book was in his hand;
"Do not fear! Heaven is as near,"
  He said, "by water as by land!"
    HENRY WADSWORTH LONGFELLOW, *Sir Humphrey Gilbert*.

8
For a cap and bells our lives we pay,
  Bubbles we buy with a whole soul's tasking:
'Tis heaven alone that is given away,
  'Tis only God may be had for the asking.
    JAMES RUSSELL LOWELL, *The Vision of Sir Launfal:* prelude.

9
Not only around our infancy
Doth heaven with all its spendors lie;
Daily, with souls that cringe and plot,
We Sinais climb and know it not.
    JAMES RUSSELL LOWELL, *The Vision of Sir Launfal*, pt. i, prelude. Wordsworth had written earlier, "Heaven lies about us in our infancy."

10
No man can resolve himself into Heaven.
    DWIGHT L. MOODY, *Heaven*.

11
How vast is heaven? lo it will fit

In any space you give to it. . . .
So broad—it takes in all things true;
So narrow—it can hold but you.
    JOHN RICHARD MORELAND, *How Vast Is Heaven*.

12
Men have fiendishly conceived a heaven only to find it insipid, and a hell to find it ridiculous.
    GEORGE SANTAYANA, *Little Essays*, p. 278.

13
    Could we but know
The land that ends our dark, uncertain travel.
    E. C. STEDMAN, *The Undiscovered Country*.

14
As much of heaven is visible as we have eyes to see.
    WILLIAM WINTER, Address: *The Actor and His Duty*, 4 June, 1889.

HELL

15
Hell is paved with great granite blocks hewn from the hearts of those who said, "I can do no other."
    HEYWOOD BROUN, Syndicated Column, 20 Jan., 1934.

16
Hell may have a worse climate [than heaven] but undoubtedly the company is sprightlier.
    IRVIN S. COBB, Letter written late in 1943 to the editor of the Paducah (Ky.) *Sun-Democrat*.

17
Hell Maria!
    CHARLES GATES DAWES, at a Congressional Committee hearing, 2 Feb., 1921. The expression is said to be of Ohio origin. STANLEY FROST elaborated on it in *Hell an' Maria—Revised* (*The Outlook*, 27 Aug., 1924): "Some meticulous but soulless editor tried to make sense by writing in the 'and.' Thus Dawes got his nickname and the great Dawes myth its start."

18
Satan the envious said with a sigh:
Christians know more about their hell than I.
    ALFRED KREYMBORG, *Envious Satan*.

19
What you Kansas farmers ought to do is to raise less corn and raise more hell.
    MRS. MARY ELIZABETH CLYENS LEASE, Speech, during campaign against J. J. Ingalls, 1890.

What's the matter with Kansas? . . . We have decided to send three or four harpies out lecturing, telling the people that Kansas is raising hell and letting the corn go to weeds.

> WILLIAM ALLEN WHITE, Editorial, Emporia *Gazette,* 15 Aug., 1896.

1
Hell is when you're dumb. Hell is when you're a slave. Hell is when you don't have freedom and when you don't have justice. And when you don't have equality, that's hell. . . . And the devil is the one who deprives you of justice . . . equality . . . civil rights. The devil is the one who robs you of your right to be a human being. I don't have to tell you who the devil is. You know who the devil is.

> MALCOLM X, when a leading spokesman for the Black Muslim sect, most militant of the civil-rights advocates. (*Life,* 31 May, 1963, p. 30)

2
Hell is both sides of the tomb, and a devil may be respectable and wear good clothes.

> CHARLES H. PARKHURST, *Sermons: The Pharisee's Prayer.*

3
If I owned Texas and Hell, I would rent out Texas and live in Hell.

> GENERAL PHILIP H. SHERIDAN, Remark at the officers' mess, Fort Clark, Tex., 1855. (On the authority of Judge Richard B. Levy of Texarkana.)

4
It doesn't matter what they preach,
  Of high or low degree;
The old Hell of the Bible
  Is Hell enough for me.

> FRANK L. STANTON, *Hell.*

5
Hell itself may be contained within the compass of a spark.

> HENRY D. THOREAU, *Journal,* 19 Dec., 1838.

6
Hell is given up *so* reluctantly by those who don't expect to go there.

> HARRY LEON WILSON, *The Spenders,* p. 241.

7
I would send them to hell across lots if they meddled with me.

> BRIGHAM YOUNG, Speech, 1857.

HERESY

See also Atheism, Doubt

8
Only heretics grow old gracefully.

> ELBERT HUBBARD, *The Philistine,* xi, 89.

9
Heresy is what the minority believe; it is the name given by the powerful to the doctrine of the weak.

> ROBERT G. INGERSOLL, *Heretics and Heresies.*

10
In the history of the world, the man who is ahead has always been called a heretic.

> ROBERT G. INGERSOLL, *The Liberty of Man, Woman and Child.*

11
Better heresy of doctrine than heresy of heart.

> JOHN GREENLEAF WHITTIER, *Mary Garvin.*

HERO, HEROISM

12
There is no king nor sovereign state
That can fix a hero's rate.

> EMERSON, *Astraea.*

13
The characteristic of genuine heroism is its persistency. All men have wandering impulses, fits and starts of generosity. But when you have resolved to be great, abide by yourself, and do not weakly try to reconcile yourself with the world. The heroic cannot be the common, nor the common the heroic.

> EMERSON, *Essays, First Series: Heroism.*

14
Heroism feels and never reasons and therefore is always right.

> EMERSON, *Essays, First Series: Heroism.*

15
The hero is not fed on sweets,
Daily his own heart he eats;
Chambers of the great are jails,
And head-winds right for royal sails.

> EMERSON, *Heroism.*

16
Each man is a hero and an oracle to somebody.

> EMERSON, *Letters and Social Aims: Quotation and Originality.*

17
Every hero becomes a bore at last.

> EMERSON, *Representative Men: Uses of Great Men.*

18
The greatest obstacle to being heroic is the doubt whether one may not be going to prove one's self a fool; the truest heroism is to resist the doubt, and the profoundest wisdom to know when it ought to be resisted, and when to be obeyed.

> NATHANIEL HAWTHORNE, *The Blithedale Romance,* ch. 2.

19
A hero cannot be a hero unless in an heroic world.

> NATHANIEL HAWTHORNE, *Journals,* 7 May, 1850.

20
In a truly heroic life there is no peradventure. It is always either doing or dying.

> ROSWELL D. HITCHCOCK, *Eternal Atonement: Life Through Death.*

21
The idol of to-day pushes the hero of yester-

day out of our recollection; and will, in turn, be supplanted by his successor of to-morrow.

> WASHINGTON IRVING, *The Sketch Book: Westminster Abbey.*

1

You are one of the authentic American heroes of this century.

> LYNDON B. JOHNSON, Telegram to General Douglas MacArthur, 26 Jan., 1964, MacArthur's 84th birthday.

2

It was absolutely involuntary. They sank my boat.

> JOHN F. KENNEDY, replying to a question posed by a small boy during a trip to the West Coast by Kennedy: "Mr. President, how did you become a war hero?" (*The Kennedy Wit,* ed. by Bill Adler: sec. ii, *The Presidency*)

3

Crowds speak in heroes.

> GERALD STANLEY LEE, *Crowds,* bk. iv, ch. 3.

4

Dost thou know what a hero is? Why, a hero is as much as one should say,—a hero.

> HENRY WADSWORTH LONGFELLOW, *Hyperion,* bk. i, ch. 1.

5

In the world's broad field of battle,
  In the bivouac of Life,
Be not like dumb, driven cattle!
  Be a hero in the strife!

> HENRY WADSWORTH LONGFELLOW, *A Psalm of Life.*

6

Nor deem that acts heroic wait on chance,
Or easy were as in a boy's romance;
The man's whole life precludes the single
    deed
That shall decide if his inheritance
Be with the sifted few of matchless breed,
Our race's sap and sustenance,
Or with the unmotivated herd that only sleep
    and feed.

> JAMES RUSSELL LOWELL, *Under the Old Elm.*

7

To be negative is just the other side of having a very clear idea of gallantry and beauty. I would like to see the return of the hero—I mean the man who really stands up and is counted, ethically, morally and humanly, and so becomes larger than himself.

> MARYA MANNES. (*New Bites by a Girl Gadfly; Life,* 12 June, 1964, p. 59)

8

It is possible to keep all of the people in a heroic mood part of the time, as in war; it is possible to keep part of the people in a heroic mood all of the time, as with the best

policeman, social workers and scientists; but it is not possible to keep all the people in a heroic mood all the time.

> ALLAN NEVINS, *What Has Happened to Our Morality?; New York Times Magazine,* 10 June, 1962, p. 12.

9

'Tis sweet to hear of heroes dead,
  To know them still alive;
But sweeter if we earn their bread,
  And in us they survive.

> HENRY D. THOREAU, *The Great Adventure.*

10

What a hero one can be without moving a finger!

> HENRY D. THOREAU, *Journal,* 13 July, 1838.

11

One brave deed makes no hero.

> JOHN GREENLEAF WHITTIER, *The Hero.*

HISTORY

12

History shows you prospects by starlight, or, at best, by the waning moon.

> RUFUS CHOATE, *New England History.*

13

While we read history we make history.

> GEORGE WILLIAM CURTIS, *The Call of Freedom.*

14

Every great crisis of human history is a pass of Thermopylae, and there is always a Leonidas and his three hundred to die in it, if they can not conquer.

> GEORGE WILLIAM CURTIS, *The Call of Freedom.*

15

There is properly no history, only biography.

> EMERSON, *Essays, First Series: History.*

16

All history resolves itself very easily into the biography of a few stout and earnest persons.

> EMERSON, *Essays, First Series: Self-Reliance.*

17

In analysing history do not be too profound, for often the causes are quite superficial.

> EMERSON, *Journals,* vol. iv, p. 160.

18

The use of history is to give value to the present hour and its duty.

> EMERSON, *Society and Solitude: Works and Days.*

19

History is bunk.

> HENRY FORD, Statement on the witness stand, Mt. Clemens, Mich., in his libel suit against the Chicago *Tribune,* July, 1919.

1

Historians relate, not so much what is done, as what they would have believed.

    Benjamin Franklin, *Poor Richard*, 1739.

2

History is but the unrolled scroll of prophecy.

    James A. Garfield, *The Province of History*.

3

History fades into fable; fact becomes clouded with doubt and controversy; the inscription moulders from the tablet: the statue falls from the pedestal. Columns, arches, pyramids, what are they but heaps of sand; and their epitaphs, but characters written in the dust?

    Washington Irving, *The Sketch-Book: Westminster Abbey*.

4

History, by apprising [men] of the past, will enable them to judge of the future.

    Thomas Jefferson, *Writings*, vol. i, p. 207.

5

History, in general, only informs us what bad government is.

    Thomas Jefferson, *Writings*, vol. xi, p. 223.

6

He is happiest of whom the world says least, good or bad.

    Thomas Jefferson, Letter to John Adams, 1786.

7

Blest is that Nation whose silent course of happiness furnishes nothing for history to say.

    Thomas Jefferson, *Writings*, vol. xi, p. 180.

It is a base untruth to say that happy is the nation that has no history. Thrice happy is the nation that has a glorious history.

    Theodore Roosevelt, Speech before the Hamilton Club, Chicago, 10 Apr., 1899.

8

For history is more than the record of man's conflict with nature and himself. It is the knowledge which gives dimension to the present, direction to the future, and humility to the leaders of men. A nation, like a person, not conscious of its own past is adrift without purpose or protection against the contending forces of dissolution.

    Lyndon B. Johnson, Proclamation, setting 22 Nov., 1964 (the first anniversary of the assassination of John F. Kennedy) as "a day of national rededication."

9

History casts its shadow far into the land of song.

    Henry Wadsworth Longfellow, *Outre-Mer: Ancient Spanish Ballads*.

10

Old events have modern meanings; only that survives

Of past history which finds kindred in all hearts and lives.

    James Russell Lowell, *Mahmood*, l. 1.

11

The course of life is like the sea;

Men come and go; tides rise and fall;

And that is all of history.

    Joaquin Miller, *The Sea of Fire*, canto iv.

12

I am always amazed that the people who attack me never ask the first question that a historian would ask: Is it true?

    Arthur Schlesinger, Jr., commenting on criticism of his book on John F. Kennedy, *A Thousand Days,* published in 1965. (William V. Shannon, *Controversial Historian of the Age of Kennedy; New York Times Magazine,* 21 Nov., 1965)

13

The history of the world is the record of a man in quest of his daily bread and butter.

    H. W. van Loon, *The Story of Mankind*.

14

It has been said that the only thing we learn from history is that we do not learn. But surely we can learn if we have the will to do so. Surely there is a lesson to be learned from this tragic event.

    Earl Warren, Eulogy to John F. Kennedy, 24 Nov., 1963.

HOME

See also Cosmopolitanism, House

15

As much as I converse with sages and heroes, they have very little of my love and admiration. I long for rural and domestic scenes, for the warbling of birds and the prattling of my children.

    John Adams, Letter to his wife, 16 Mar., 1777.

16

'Member dat rainy eve dat I drove you out

    Wid nothing but a fine tooth comb?

I knows I'se to blame; well, ain't dat a shame?

    Bill Bailey, won't you please come home?

    Hughie Cannon, *Bill Bailey, Won't You Please Come Home* (song, 1902). It was introduced by John Queen in the farce comedy *Town Topics* in Newburgh, N.Y.

17

Fare you well, old house! you're naught that can feel or see,

But you seem like a human bein'—a dear old friend to me;

And we never will have a better home, if *my* opinion stands,

Until we commence a-keepin' house in the house not made with hands.
>Will Carleton, *Out of the Old House, Nancy.*

1

Wherever smoke wreaths Heavenward curl—
Cave of a hermit, Hovel of churl,
Mansion of merchant, princely dome—
　Out of the dreariness
　Into its cheeriness,
　Come we in weariness
　　Home.
>Stephen Chalmers, *Home.*

2

Home,—the nursery of the infinite.
>William Ellery Channing, *Note-Book: Children.*

3

Cleave to thine acre; the round year
Will fetch all fruits and virtues here.
Fool and foe may harmless roam,
Loved and lovers bide at home.
>Emerson, *Conduct of Life: Considerations by the Way.*

4

My idea of a home is a house in which each member of the family can on the instant kindle a fire in his or her private room.
>Emerson, *Journals.*

5

Stay at home. The way to have large occasional views is to have large habitual views.
>Emerson, *Table-Talk.*

6

Way down upon de Swanee ribber
　Far, far away,
Dere's wha my heart is turning ebber,
　Dere's wha de old folks stay.
All up and down de whole creation,
　Sadly I roam,
Still longing for de old plantation,
　And for de old folks at home.
>Stephen Collins Foster, *Old Folks at Home.*

7

Home is the place where, when you have to go there,
They have to take you in.
>Robert Frost, *The Death of the Hired Man.*

8

It takes a heap o' livin' in a house t' make it home.
>Edgar A. Guest, *Home.*

But meanwhile I ask you to believe that
It takes a heap of other things besides
A heap o' livin' to make a home out of a house.
To begin with, it takes a heap o' payin'.
>Ogden Nash, *A Heap o' Livin'.*

9

Home, in one form or another, is the great object of life.
>Josiah G. Holland, *Gold Foil: Home.*

10

A man is always nearest to his good when at home, and farthest from it when away.
>Josiah G. Holland, *Gold Foil: Home.*

11

　Where we love is home,
Home that our feet may leave, but not our hearts.
>Oliver Wendell Holmes, *Homesick in Heaven*, st. 5.

12

Home is where the heart is.
>Elbert Hubbard, *A Thousand and One Epigrams*, p. 73. This is much more widely attributed to Pliny the Elder.

13

Goethe once said, "He is happiest, king or peasant, who finds his happiness at home." And Goethe knew—because he never found it.
>Elbert Hubbard, *Epigrams.*

14

The happiness of the domestic fireside is the first boon of mankind; and it is well it is so, since it is that which is the lot of the mass of mankind.
>Thomas Jefferson, *Writings*, vol. xiii, p. 220.

15

Any old place I can hang my hat is home, sweet home to me.
>William Jerome and Jean Schwartz, Title of popular song (1901).

16

Lyndon, I want to go home to the hill country. That's the part of the world where people know when you're sick, miss you when you die, and love you while you live.
>Samuel Ealy Johnson, to his son, Lyndon B. Johnson, 1937, while the elder Johnson was slowly dying in a hospital in Temple, Tex. "The hill country" refers to central Texas, birthplace of father and son. (New York *Times*, 20 Apr., 1964)

17

There's no place like home, and many a man is glad of it.
>F. M. Knowles, *A Cheerful Year Book.*

18

Stay, stay at home, my heart, and rest;
Home-keeping hearts are happiest,
For those that wander they know not where
Are full of trouble and full of care;
　To stay at home is best.
>Henry Wadsworth Longfellow *Song*, st. 1.

19

The many make the household,
But only one the home.
>James Russell Lowell, *The Dead House*, st. 9.

20

Joy dwells beneath a humble roof;
Heaven is not built of country seats

But little queer suburban streets.
  CHRISTOPHER MORLEY, *To The Little House.*

1
Round the hearth-stone of home, in the land of our birth,
The holiest spot on the face of the earth.
  GEORGE POPE MORRIS, *Land Ho!*

2
Home is heaven and orgies are vile,
But I like an orgy, once in a while.
  OGDEN NASH, *Home, 99 44/100% Sweet Home.*

3
Home interprets heaven. Home is heaven for beginners.
  CHARLES PARKHURST, *Sermons: The Perfect Peace.*

4
'Mid pleasures and palaces though we may roam,
Be it ever so humble, there's no place like home.
  JOHN HOWARD PAYNE, *Home, Sweet Home,* from the first act of his opera *Clari, the Maid of Milan,* produced at Covent Garden, London, 8 May, 1823.

5
I read within a poet's book
  A word that starred the page,
"Stone walls do not a prison make,
  Nor iron bars a cage."

Yes, that is true, and something more:
  You'll find, where'er you roam,
That marble floors and gilded walls
  Can never make a home.

But every house where Love abides
  And Friendship is a guest,
Is surely home, and home, sweet home;
  For there the heart can rest.
  HENRY VAN DYKE, *Home Song.*

HONESTY

6
Honesty rare as a man without self-pity,
Kindness as large and plain as a prairie wind.
  STEPHEN VINCENT BENÉT, *John Brown's Body:* Invocation.

7
He never flunked, and he never lied,—
I reckon he never knowed how.
  JOHN HAY, *Jim Bludso.*

8
No public man can be just a little crooked.
  HERBERT HOOVER, 1951. (*Herbert Hoover in His Own Words,* compiled by LOUIS P. LOCHNER; *New York Times Magazine,* 9 Aug., 1964, p. 15)

9
If parents want honest children they should be honest themselves.
  ROBERT G. INGERSOLL, *How to Reform Mankind.*

10
Every honest man will suppose honest acts to flow from honest principles.
  THOMAS JEFFERSON, *Writings,* vol. x, p. 304.

11
Barring that natural expression of villainy which we all have, the man looked honest enough.
  MARK TWAIN, *A Mysterious Visit.*

12
I hope I shall always possess firmness and virtue enough to maintain what I consider the most enviable of all titles, the character of an "Honest Man."
  GEORGE WASHINGTON, *Moral Maxims.*

13
Such was our friend. Formed on the good old plan,
A true and brave and downright honest man!
  JOHN GREENLEAF WHITTIER, *Daniel Neall.*

HONOR

14
All honor's wounds are self-inflicted.
  ANDREW CARNEGIE. (HENDRICK, *Life*)

15
Some things the honorable man cannot do, never does. He never wrongs or degrades a woman. He never oppresses or cheats a person weaker or poorer than himself. He never betrays a trust. He is honest, sincere, candid and generous.
  CHARLES W. ELIOT, *The Durable Satisfactions of Life,* p. 6.

16
The louder he talked of his honor, the faster we counted our spoons.
  EMERSON, *Conduct of Life: Worship.*

17
Posts of honor are evermore posts of danger and of care.
  JOSIAH G. HOLLAND, *Gold-Foil: Every Man Has His Place.*

18
When there is a lack of honor in government, the morals of the whole people are poisoned.
  HERBERT HOOVER, 1951. (*Herbert Hoover in His Own Words,* compiled by LOUIS P. LOCHNER; *New York Times Magazine,* 9 Aug., 1964, p. 15)

19
A Century of Dishonor.
  HELEN HUNT JACKSON, Title of report (1881) on the treatment of the American Indians by the government and people of the United States.

1
Nobody can acquire honor by doing what is wrong.
> THOMAS JEFFERSON, *Writings,* vol. xvi, p. 444.

2
A nation reveals itself not only by the men it produces but also by the men it honors, the men it remembers.
> JOHN F. KENNEDY, Address at Amherst College, Amherst, Mass., 26 Oct., 1963.

3
When honor comes to you be ready to take it;
> But reach not to seize it before it is near.
> JOHN BOYLE O'REILLY, *Rules of the Road.*

4
A Quixotic sense of the honorable—of the chivalrous.
> EDGAR ALLAN POE, Letter to Mrs. Whitman, 18 Oct., 1848.

5
To repay honor with dishonor.
> ADLAI E. STEVENSON, Public Statement broadcast nationally in July, 1952, just after the Democratic party nominated him for the presidency in Chicago. He said in full: "I did not seek it [the nomination]. I did not want it. I am, however, persuaded that to shirk it, to evade it, would be to repay honor with dishonor."

6
If somebody throws a brick at me I can catch it and throw it back. But when somebody awards a decoration to me, I am out of words.
> HARRY S TRUMAN, on receiving the Gold Grand Cross of Merit, Austria's highest decoration, in Washington, D.C., 7 May, 1964, the day before his 80th birthday.

7
When faith is lost, when honor dies,
> The man is dead!
> JOHN GREENLEAF WHITTIER, *Ichabod,* st. 8.

HOPE
See also Optimism

8
Hope is the parent of faith.
> C. A. BARTOL, *Radical Problems: Hope.*

9
Hope is the thing with feathers
That perches in the soul.
> EMILY DICKINSON, *Poems.* Pt. i, No. 32.

10
He that lives upon hope will die fasting.
> BENJAMIN FRANKLIN, *Poor Richard,* 1758.

11
It is natural to man to indulge in the illusions of hope. We are apt to shut our eyes against a painful truth, and listen to the song of that siren, till she transforms us into beasts.
> PATRICK HENRY, Speech in the Virginia House of Delegates, 23 Mar., 1775. (Arranged by William Wirt, 1818)

12
I suppose it can be truthfully said that Hope is the only universal liar who never loses his reputation for veracity.
> ROBERT G. INGERSOLL, Address, Manhattan Liberal Club, at the celebration of the 155th Paine anniversary. (*Truth-Seeker,* 28 Feb., 1892)

13
Hope—that star of life's tremulous ocean.
> PAUL MOON JAMES, *The Beacon.*

14
'Tis hope supports each noble flame,
'Tis hope inspires poetic lays;
Our heroes fight in hopes of fame,
And poets write in hopes of praise.
> THOMAS JEFFERSON, *To Ellen.* In his *Lit-* 1734.

18
Hope, the patent medicine
For disease, disaster, sin.
> WALLACE RICE, *Hope.*

HORSE, HORSEMANSHIP

19
Such horses are
The jewels of the horseman's hands and thighs,
They go by the word and hardly need the rein.
> STEPHEN VINCENT BENÉT, *John Brown's Body,* bk. iv.

20
If you ride a horse, sit close and tight,
If you ride a man, sit easy and light.
> BENJAMIN FRANKLIN, *Poor Richard,* erary Bible.

15
Let those of us who are well-fed, well-clothed, and well-housed never forget and never overlook those who live on the outskirts of hope.
> LYNDON B. JOHNSON, Message to the Plasterers' Union, marking its hundredth anniversary, 31 Aug., 1964.

16
We have discovered that every child who learns, and every man who finds work, and every sick body that's made whole—like a candle added to an altar—brightens the hope of all the faithful.
> LYNDON B. JOHNSON, Inaugural Address, 20 Jan., 1965.

17
The setting of a great hope is like the setting of the sun. The brightness of our life is gone.
> HENRY WADSWORTH LONGFELLOW, *Hyperion,* bk. i, ch. 1.

1

For the want of a nail the shoe was lost,
For the want of a shoe the horse was lost,
For the want of a horse the rider was lost,
For the want of a rider the battle was lost,
For the want of a battle the kingdom was
    lost—
And all for want of a horseshoe-nail.
> BENJAMIN FRANKLIN, *Poor Richard,* 1758.
> An elaboration of lines from GEORGE
> HERBERT'S *Jacula Prudentum.*

2

Saddle-leather is in some respects even preferable to sole-leather. . . . One's hepar, or,
in vulgar language, liver, . . . goes up and
down like the dasher of a churn in the midst
of the other vital arrangements, at every step
of a trotting horse. The brains also are shak-
en up like coppers in a money-box.
> OLIVER WENDELL HOLMES, *The Autocrat
> of the Breakfast-Table,* ch. 7, p. 166.

3

It makes men imperious to sit a horse.
> OLIVER WENDELL HOLMES, *Elsie Venner.*

4

I do not allow myself to suppose that either
the convention or the League have concluded
to decide that I am either the greatest or
best man in America, but rather they have
concluded it is not best to swap horses while
crossing the river, and have further concluded that I am not so poor a horse that they
might not make a botch of it in trying to
swap.
> ABRAHAM LINCOLN, Address to a delega-
> tion of the National Union League,
> which had called to congratulate him on
> his renomination as Republican presi-
> dential candidate, 9 June, 1864.

5

Hurrah, hurrah for Sheridan!
Hurrah, hurrah for horse and man!
And when their statues are placed on high,
Under the dome of the Union sky,—
The American soldier's Temple of Fame,—
There with the glorious General's name
Be it said in letters both bold and bright:
"Here is the steed that saved the day
By carrying Sheridan into the fight,
From Winchester,—twenty miles away!"
> THOMAS BUCHANAN READ, *Sheridan's
> Ride.*

HOSPITALITY

6

Stay is a charming word in a friend's vocabulary.
> AMOS BRONSON ALCOTT, *Concord Days:
> June.*

7

When friends are at your hearthside met,
Sweet courtesy has done its most
If you have made each guest forget

That he himself is not the host.
> THOMAS BAILEY ALDRICH, *Hospitality.*

8

Come right in. The doors are closed only in
the interest of efficient air-conditioning.
> GEORGE DOCKING, Sign on his office door
> during his two terms as governor of
> Kansas, 1957–60. (New York *Times*
> obituary of Docking, 21 Jan., 1964)

9

Hospitality consists in a little fire, a little
food, and an immense quiet.
> EMERSON, *Journal,* 1856.

10

Hail Guest! We ask not what thou art:
If Friend, we greet thee, hand and heart;
If Stranger, such no longer be;
If Foe, our love shall conquer thee.
> ARTHUR GUITERMAN, *Old Welsh Door
> Verse.*

11

For it's always fair weather
When good fellows get together,
With a stein on the table and a good song
    ringing clear.
> RICHARD HOVEY, *A Stein Song.*

12

Welcome to your house.
> LYNDON B. JOHNSON, Greeting to White
> House visitors and tourists. (JAMES
> RESTON, Washington column, New York
> *Times,* 24 Apr., 1964)

13

The lintel low enough to keep out pomp and
    pride;
The threshold high enough to turn deceit
    aside;
The doorband strong enough from robbers to
    defend;
This door will open at a touch to welcome
    every friend.
> HENRY VAN DYKE, *Inscription for a
> Friend's House.*

HOUSE

See also Home

14

A House Is Not a Home.
> POLLY ADLER, Title of memoir.

15

Every spirit makes its house, but afterwards
the house confines the spirit.
> EMERSON, *Conduct of Life: Fate.*

16

A man builds a fine house; and now he has a
master, and a task for life: he is to furnish,
watch, show it, and keep it in repair, the rest
of his days.
> EMERSON, *Society and Solitude: Works
> and Days.*

17

The house is a castle which the King cannot
enter.
> EMERSON, *English Traits: Wealth.*

1
Is not a small house best? Put a woman into a small house, and after five years she comes out large and healthy.
EMERSON, *Journals,* vol. vii, p. 47.

2
It is very difficult to understand anybody without visiting his home. Houses reveal character.
GILBERT HIGHET, *Talents and Geniuses: The House High on the Hill,* p. 151.

3
A house, we like to believe, can be a noble consort to man and the trees. The house should have repose and such texture as will quiet the whole and make it graciously one with external nature.
FRANK LLOYD WRIGHT, *The Natural House.*

HUMANITY, see Man

HUMILITY

4
It behooves all of us—whether in government, in the academic world or in the press—to avoid that most dangerous disease, infectious omniscience.
GEORGE W. BALL, Commencement Address at Miami University, Oxford, Ohio, June, 1965.

5
Humility must always be the portion of any man who receives acclaim earned in the blood of his followers and the sacrifices of his friends.
GENERAL DWIGHT D. EISENHOWER, Address in London, 12 June, 1945.

6
Humility is the most difficult of all virtues to achieve; nothing dies harder than the desire to think well of oneself.
T. S. ELIOT, *Shakespeare and the Stoicism of Seneca.*

7
None shall rule but the humble,
 And none but Toil shall have.
EMERSON, *Boston Hymn.*

8
Why is there such a lack of grace today? There can only be one answer. The people have gotten away from humility. We must recognize it and face it. May God help us to be a humble people.
REV. WILLIAM FRANKLIN (BILLY) GRAHAM, *America's Hour of Decision.*

9
Let me be a little meeker
With the brother that is weaker,
Let me think more of my neighbor
And a little less of me.
EDGAR A. GUEST, *A Creed.*

10
Wisdom has taught us to be calm and meek,
To take one blow, and turn the other cheek;

It is not written what a man shall do,
If the rude caitiff smite the other too!
OLIVER WENDELL HOLMES, *Non-Resistance.*

11
In the Middle Ages it was the fashion to wear hair shirts to remind one's self of trouble and sin. Many years ago I concluded that a few hair shirts were part of the mental wardrobe of every man. The President differs only from other men in that he has a more extensive wardrobe.
HERBERT HOOVER, 1929. (*Herbert Hoover in His Own Words,* compiled by LOUIS P. LOCHNER; *New York Times Magazine,* 9 Aug., 1964, p. 15)

12
Turning the other cheek is a kind of moral jiu-jitsu.
GERALD STANLEY LEE, *Crowds,* bk. iv, ch. 9.

13
A man who has humility will have acquired in the last reaches of his beliefs the saving doubt of his own certainty. Though he produces wealth and uses it, and though he resists evil, he will have little acquisitiveness and posessiveness, he will have no final attachment to things, he will have no strong lust for power or for vengeance. He cannot and he will not be perfect. But in some measure he will be pulled toward perfection.
WALTER LIPPMANN, *The Public Philosophy,* bk. II, ch. 10.

14
No more lessen or dissemble thy merit, than overrate it; for though humility be a virtue, an affected one is not.
WILLIAM PENN, *Fruits of Solitude.*

15
Now there will be a lot of self-serving people, special interests, who are around here and can't afford to wait for an appointment. Then when they're summoned, they'll come sliding in here on their vests and tell you over and over that the President is a smart man, smarter than anyone else. Now, Harry, you and I know he ain't.
SAM RAYBURN, giving advice to Harry S Truman in 1945, just after the swearing in of Truman as President. Quoted by Lyndon B. Johnson shortly after he succeeded John F. Kennedy as President in 1963. (HENRY A. ZEIGER, *Lyndon B. Johnson: Man and President,* pp. 112–13)

16
Humility like darkness reveals the heavenly lights.
HENRY D. THOREAU, *Walden:* Conclusion.

1
Some editors ate crow and left the feathers
on.
> HARRY S TRUMAN, commenting on the
> friendly tone of newspaper editorials
> just after he returned to private life ear-
> ly in 1953—in marked contrast to the
> widespread criticism of his administra-
> tion. (ALFRED STEINBERG, *The Man
> from Missouri,* p. 420)

2
Early in life I had to choose between honest
arrogance and hypocritical humility. I chose
honest arrogance, and have seen no occasion
to change.
> FRANK LLOYD WRIGHT.

HUMOR
3
i am sorry that i cannot accept your kind
offer to prepare an article on the humor of
1950. the assorted problems that attend the
preparation of my television show leave me
no time for comments on humor. if i remain
in television too long i will probably forget
what humor is.
> FRED ALLEN, Letter to Walter Yust, editor
> of the *Encyclopaedia Britannica,* 11
> Nov., 1950, replying to an invitation to
> write an article for the *Britannica* annu-
> al for that year.

4
I think funny.
> ABE BURROWS. (LEWIS FUNKE, drama-
> news column, New York *Times,* 29
> Mar., 1964)

5
Guess his humor ain't refined
Quite enough to suit my mind.
> ELLIS PARKER BUTLER, *Jabed Meeker,
> Humorist.* The reference is to Mark
> Twain.

6
Men will confess to treason, murder, arson,
false teeth, or a wig. How many of them will
own up to a lack of humor?
> FRANK MOORE COLBY, *Essays,* vol. i.

7
Beware of jokes; . . . we go away hollow
and ashamed.
> EMERSON, *Letters and Social Aims: Social
> Aims.*

8
I never dare to write As funny as I can.
> OLIVER WENDELL HOLMES, *The Height of
> the Ridiculous.*

9
Humor's the true democracy.
> ROBERT U. JOHNSON, *Divided Honors.*

10
The saddest ones are those that wear
  The jester's motley garb.
> DON MARQUIS, *The Tavern of Despair.*

11
It [a sense of humor] always withers in the
presence of the messianic delusion, like justice and truth in front of patriotic passion.
> H. L. MENCKEN, *Prejudices,* ser. i, p. 32.

12
He must not laugh at his own wheeze:
A snuff-box has no right to sneeze.
> KEITH PRESTON, *The Humorist.*

13
Everything is funny as long as it is happening to somebody else.
> WILL ROGERS, *The Illiterate Digest,* p.
> 131.

14
Humor is emotional chaos remembered in
tranquillity.
> JAMES THURBER. (MAX EASTMAN, *The
> Enjoyment of Laughter*)

15
Guides cannot master the subtleties of the
American joke.
> MARK TWAIN, *Innocents Abroad,* ch. 27.

16
Everything human is pathetic. The secret
source of Humor itself is not joy but sorrow.
There is no humor in heaven.
> MARK TWAIN, *Pudd'nhead Wilson's New
> Calendar.*

HUNGER
17
I've never known a country to be starved
into democracy.
> GEORGE D. AIKEN, commenting to report-
> ers, 27 Mar., 1964, in support of a con-
> troversial position just taken by a fellow
> U.S. Senator, J. William Fulbright, who
> had urged an end to the U.S.-sponsored
> economic boycott of Cuba.

We had a fat Germany that gave us a very
hard time.
> WALT W. ROSTOW, Address in London, 10
> Mar., 1964, before British businessmen.
> In his capacity as State Department pol-
> icy-planning counselor, Rostow was
> seeking to discourage British trade with
> Cuba. The remark quoted was in reply
> to British Prime Minister Sir Alec
> Douglas-Home's defense of such trade
> on the ground that "a well-fed Commu-
> nist is less dangerous than a hungry
> one."

18
An empty stomach is not a good political
adviser.
> ALBERT EINSTEIN, *Cosmic Religion,* p.
> 107.

19
Hunger is the best Pickle.
> BENJAMIN FRANKLIN, *Poor Richard,*
> 1750.

1

Hungry rooster don't cackle w'en he fine a
wum.

> JOEL CHANDLER HARRIS, *Plantation Prov-
> erbs.*

2

Who ever hears of fat men heading a riot, or
herding together in turbulent mobs?—no—
no, 'tis your lean, hungry men who are continually worrying society, and setting the
whole community by the ears.

> WASHINGTON IRVING, *Knickerbocker's
> History of New York,* bk. iii, ch. 2.

3

Somewhere—the place it matters not—some-
where
I saw a child, hungry and thin of face—
Eyes in whose pools life's joys no longer
stirred,
Lips that were dead to laughter's eager kiss,
Yet parted fiercely to a crust of bread.

> CARDINAL FRANCIS JOSEPH SPELLMAN,
> *Prayer for Children.*

4

A hungry man is not a free man.

> ADLAI E. STEVENSON, Speech in Kasson,
> Minn., 6 Sept., 1952, during the presi-
> dential campaign of that year.

HURRY, see Haste
HUSBAND
See also Marriage, Wife

5

Fat tends to make a man a better husband.
His wife is generally happy in the knowledge
she is not married to a woman chaser. Few
fat men chase girls, because they get winded
too easily.

> HAL BOYLE, Column, Associated Press, 1
> Oct., 1964.

6

Some husbands are born optimists. They go
through life believing that somehow, somewhere, they eventually will arrive someplace
on time—with their wife. It never happens.

> HAL BOYLE, Column, Associated Press, 16
> June, 1964.

7

Art is a jealous mistress, and if a man have a
genius for painting, poetry, music, architecture, or philosophy, he makes a bad husband
and an ill provider.

> EMERSON, *Conduct of Life: Wealth.*

8

I should like to see any kind of a man, dis-
tinguishable from a gorilla, that some good
and even pretty woman could not shape a
husband out of.

> OLIVER WENDELL HOLMES, *The Professor
> at the Breakfast-Table,* ch. 7.

9

Enjoy your husband, but never think you
know him thoroughly.

> CLAUDIA TAYLOR (MRS. LYNDON B.) JOHN-
> SON. (OLIVIA SKINNER, *Democrats'
> Wives Hit the Campaign Trail;* St.
> Louis *Post-Dispatch,* 2 Oct., 1964, p. 3-
> D)

10

Husbands never become good; they merely
become proficient.

> H. L. MENCKEN, *A Mencken Chrestoma-
> thy.*

11

He tells you when you've got on too much
lipstick,
And helps you with your girdle when your
hips stick.

> OGDEN NASH, *Versus: The Perfect Hus-
> band.*

HYPOCRISY
See also Deceit

12

Great King of Cant!

> AMBROSE BIERCE, *An Imposter.* The refer-
> ence is to Andrew Carnegie.

13

It is with a pious fraud as with a bad action;
it begets a calamitous necessity of going on.

> THOMAS PAINE, *Age of Reason,* pt. i.

14

He knows how much of what men paint
themselves
Would blister in the light of what they are.

> EDWIN ARLINGTON ROBINSON, *Ben Jonson
> Entertains a Man from Stratford.*

15

Making the world safe for hypocrisy.

> THOMAS WOLFE, *Look Homeward, Angel!,*
> pt. iii.

I

IDEALS

16

Our ideals are our better selves.

> AMOS BRONSON ALCOTT, *Table Talk:
> Habits.*

17

An idealist is a person who helps other people to be prosperous.

> HENRY FORD, testifying in Mt. Clemens,
> Mich., in his libel suit against the Chi-
> cago *Tribune,* July, 1919.

18

An idealist without illusions.

> JOHN F. KENNEDY, describing himself.
> (Quoted by Arthur M. Schlesinger, Jr.,
> Interview: *Meet the Press,* NBC-TV, 28
> Nov., 1965)

19

Every man has at times in his mind the ideal

of what he should be, but is not. . . . Man never falls so low that he can see nothing higher than himself.

THEODORE PARKER, *A Lesson for the Day.*

1

Ideals are like stars; you will not succeed in touching them with your hands. But like the seafaring man on the desert of waters, you choose them as your guides, and following them you will reach your destiny.

CARL SCHURZ, Speech, Apr., 1859.

2

When they come downstairs from their Ivory Towers, Idealists are apt to walk straight into the gutter.

LOGAN PEARSALL SMITH, *Afterthoughts.*

3

We have two lives about us,
Two worlds in which we dwell,
Within us and without us,
Alternate Heaven and Hell:—
Without, the somber Real,
Within, our heart of hearts,
The beautiful Ideal.

R. H. STODDARD, *The Castle in the Air.*

4

Our bitterest wine is always drained from crushed ideals.

ARTHUR STRINGER, *The Devastator.*

IDEAS

See also Mind, Thought

5

If the ancients left us ideas, to our credit be it spoken that we moderns are building houses for them.

AMOS BRONSON ALCOTT, *Table Talk: Enterprise.*

6

God screens us evermore from premature ideas.

EMERSON, *Essays, First Series: Spiritual Laws.*

7

The party of virility rules the hour, the party of ideas and sentiments rules the age.

EMERSON, *Journal,* 1864.

8

Ideas must work through the brains and the arms of good and brave men, or they are no better than dreams.

EMERSON, *Miscellanies: American Civilization.*

9

It is a lesson which all history teaches wise men to put trust in ideas, and not in circumstances.

EMERSON, *Miscellanies: War.*

10

When we are exalted by ideas, we do not owe this to Plato, but to the idea, to which also Plato was debtor.

EMERSON, *Representative Men: Uses of Great Men.*

11

Ideas are, in truth, forces. Infinite, too, is the power of personality. A union of the two always makes history.

HENRY JAMES, *Charles W. Eliot,* i, 235.

12

An idea, to be suggestive, must come to the individual with the force of a revelation.

WILLIAM JAMES, *Varieties of Religious Experience,* p. 113.

13

He who receives an idea from me, receives instruction himself without lessening mine; as he who lights his taper at mine receives light without darkening me.

THOMAS JEFFERSON, *Writings,* vol. xiii, p. 334.

14

To die for an idea: it is unquestionably noble. But how much nobler it would be if men died for ideas that were true!

H. L. MENCKEN, *Prejudices,* ser. v, p. 283.

15

There is no squabbling so violent as that between people who accepted an idea yesterday and those who will accept the same idea tomorrow.

CHRISTOPHER MORLEY, *Religio Journalistici.*

16

For an idea ever to be fashionable is ominous, since it must afterwards be always old-fashioned.

GEORGE SANTAYANA, *Words of Doctrine,* 55.

17

Through thy idea, lo, the immortal reality!
Through thy reality, lo, the immortal idea!

WALT WHITMAN, *Thou Mother with Thy Equal Brood,* sec. ii.

IDLENESS

18

Sloth is the tempter that beguiles, and expels from paradise.

AMOS BRONSON ALCOTT, *Table Talk: Pursuits.*

19

Every once in a while it is important to do nothing. . . . Nothing is harder to do. Some puritan perversity in the American character makes us hate the nothing-doers of the world. A man quietly doing nothing is a challenge to the American system. He must be cajoled, badgered and, if necessary, blackguarded into purposeful living.

RUSSELL BAKER, "Observer" Column, New York *Times,* 29 June, 1965, p. 34.

20

Idleness is emptiness; the tree in which the sap is stagnant, remains fruitless.

HOSEA BALLOU, *MS. Sermons.*

1
Self-indulgence includes failure to fulfill the recognized responsibilities of citizenship. It is the worst form of laziness and leads, inevitably, to centralization of power.

DWIGHT D. EISENHOWER, Address before the National Governors' Conference, Cleveland, 8 June, 1964.

2
That man is idle who can do something better.

EMERSON.

3
All things are easy to industry, all things difficult to sloth.

BENJAMIN FRANKLIN, *Poor Richard*, 1734.

4
Sloth, like rust, consumes faster than labor wears.

BENJAMIN FRANKLIN, *Poor Richard*, 1744.

5
Trouble springs from idleness, and grievous toil from needless ease.

BENJAMIN FRANKLIN, *Poor Richard*, 1758.

6
Idleness and pride tax with a heavier hand than kings and parliaments.

BENJAMIN FRANKLIN, *Letter on the Stamp Act*, 11 July, 1765.

7
Laziness travels so slowly that poverty soon overtakes him.

BENJAMIN FRANKLIN, *Way to Wealth*, pt. i.

8
Idleness is the sepulchre of a living man.

JOSIAH G. HOLLAND, *Gold-Foil: Indolence*.

9
To do nothing is the way to be nothing.

NATHANIEL HOWE, *A Chapter of Proverbs*.

10
Idleness is the evil that lies behind juvenile delinquency. It is the most damnable thing that can happen to a kid—to have nothing to do.

BRANCH RICKEY.

11
The more characteristic American hero in the earlier day, and the more beloved type at all times, was not the hustler but the whittler.

MARK SULLIVAN, *Our Times*, vol. iii, p. 297.

12
I am happiest when I am idle. I could live for months without performing any kind of labour, and at the expiration of that time I should feel fresh and vigorous enough to go right on in the same way for numerous more months.

ARTEMUS WARD, *Natural History*, ch. 3.

13
I loafe and invite my soul,

I lean and loafe at my ease observing a spear of summer grass.

WALT WHITMAN, *Song of Myself*, sec. i.

The American poet Whitman
Did little to assist the razor industry,
But he erected a plausible philosophy
Of indolence,
Which, without soft concealments,
He called *Loafing*.

CHRISTOPHER MORLEY, *A Happy Life*.

14
The lazy man gets round the sun
As quickly as the busy one.

R. T. WOMBAT, *Quatrains*.

IGNORANCE

15
To be ignorant of one's ignorance is the malady of the ignorant.

AMOS BRONSON ALCOTT, *Table Talk: Discourse*.

16
I honestly believe it iz better tew know nothing than tew know what ain't so.

JOSH BILLINGS, *Encyclopedia of Proverbial Philosophy*, p. 286.

17
Ignorance and superstition ever bear a close, and even a mathematical, relation to each other.

JAMES FENIMORE COOPER, *Jack Tier*, ch. 13.

18
An experiment in ignorance.

ARCHIBALD COX, in describing a program of segregated education in Prince Edward County, Va. The U.S. Solicitor General referred to the local officials' efforts to evade the 1954 Supreme Court ruling against segregation in public schools, by closing public schools and setting up a system of "private" schools, for white children, financed largely by state and local aid, in 1959. In May, 1964, the Supreme Court held Prince Edward's course unconstitutional. (New York *Times*, 3 May, 1964)

19
The recipe for perpetual ignorance is: be satisfied with your opinions and content with your knowledge.

ELBERT HUBBARD, *The Philistine*, vol. v, p. 23.

20
There is no slavery but ignorance.

ROBERT G. INGERSOLL, *The Liberty of Man, Woman and Child*.

21
If a nation expects to be ignorant and free, it expects what never was and never will be.

THOMAS JEFFERSON, *Writings*, vol. xiv, p. 382.

22
Thomas Jefferson said no nation can be both

ignorant and free. Today no nation can be both ignorant and great.

> LYNDON B. JOHNSON, State of the Union message, 4 Jan., 1965.

1

A man must have a certain amount of intelligent ignorance to get anywhere.

> CHARLES F. KETTERING, Remark on his 70th birthday, 29 Aug., 1946.

2

The tragedy of ignorance is its complacency.

> ROBERT QUILLEN, Syndicated Editorial, 1932.

3

You know, Percy, everybody is ignorant, only on different subjects.

> WILL ROGERS, The Illiterate Digest, p. 64.

4

Miraculously ignorant.

> MARK TWAIN, The Innocents at Home, ch. 1.

ILLNESS, see Disease
ILLUSION

5

Death only grasps; to live is to pursue,—
Dream on! there's nothing but illusion true!

> OLIVER WENDELL HOLMES, The Old Player.

6

Certainty generally is illusion, and repose is not the destiny of man.

> JUSTICE OLIVER WENDELL HOLMES, The Path of the Law.

7

Therefore trust to thy heart, and to what the world calls illusions.

> HENRY WADSWORTH LONGFELLOW, Evangeline, pt. ii, sec. 2, l. 112.

8

Better a dish of illusion and a hearty appetite for life, than a feast of reality and indigestion therewith.

> H. A. OVERSTREET, The Enduring Quest, p. 197.

9

Don't part with your illusions. When they are gone, you may still exist, but you have ceased to live.

> MARK TWAIN, Pudd'nhead Wilson's Calendar.

IMAGINATION

10

Imagination is as good as many voyages— and how much cheaper.

> GEORGE WILLIAM CURTIS, Prue and I: Preface.

11

To make a prairie it takes a clover and one bee,—
And revery.
The revery alone will do

If bees are few.

> EMILY DICKINSON, Poems, Pt. ii. No. 97.

12

Imagination is more important than knowledge.

> ALBERT EINSTEIN, On Science.

13

Imagination is not a talent of some men but is the health of every man.

> EMERSON, Letters and Social Aims: Poetry and Imagination.

14

The body travels more easily than the mind, and until we have limbered up our imagination we continue to think as though we had stayed home. We have not really budged a step until we take up residence in someone else's point of view.

> JOHN ERSKINE, The Complete Life, ch. 8.

15

Solitude is as needful to the imagination as society is wholesome for the character.

> JAMES RUSSELL LOWELL, Dryden.

IMITATION
See also Plagiarism, Quotation

16

Imitation is suicide.

> EMERSON, Essays, First Series: Self-Reliance.

17

There is a difference between imitating a good man and counterfeiting him.

> BENJAMIN FRANKLIN, Poor Richard, 1738.

18

The imitator is a poor kind of creature. If the man who paints only the tree, or flower, or other surface he sees before him were an artist, the king of artists would be the photographer.

> J. A. McNEILL WHISTLER, The Gentle Art of Making Enemies.

IMMORALITY, see Morality
IMMORTALITY
See also Death

19

As to immortality, my conviction stands thus: If there be anything in me that is of permanent worth and service to the universe, the universe will know how to preserve it. Whatsoever in me is not of permanent worth and service, neither can nor should be preserved.

> HORACE JAMES BRIDGES. (NEWTON, My Idea of God, p. 176)

20

Whitman once said to me that he would as soon hope to argue a man into good health as to argue him into a belief in immortality. He said he knew it was so without proof; but I never could light my candle at his great torch.

JOHN BURROUGHS. (BARRUS, *Life and Letters of John Burroughs*)

1

Immortality is the glorious discovery of Christianity.

WILLIAM ELLERY CHANNING, *Immortality*.

2

The origin of the absurd idea of immortal life is easy to discover; it is kept alive by hope and fear, by childish faith, and by cowardice.

CLARENCE DARROW. (*Greatest Thoughts on Immortality*, p. 111)

3

Human society may most wisely seek justice and right in this world without depending on any other world to redress the wrongs of this.

CHARLES W. ELIOT. (*Greatest Thoughts on Immortality*, p. 108)

4

Other world! There is no other world! Here or nowhere is the whole fact.

EMERSON, *Natural Religion*.

5

I believe in immortality fundamentally, not because I vehemently crave it for myself as an individual, but because its denial seems to me to land the entire race in a hopeless situation and to reduce philosophy to a counsel of despair.

HARRY EMERSON FOSDICK. (*Greatest Thoughts on Immortality*, p. 12)

6

Here is my Creed. I believe in one God, Creator of the Universe. That he governs it by his Providence. That he ought to be worshipped. That the most acceptable service we render him is doing good to his other children. That the soul of Man is immortal, and will be treated with justice in another life respecting its conduct in this.

BENJAMIN FRANKLIN, Letter to Ezra Stiles, 9 Mar., 1790.

7

Work for immortality if you will; then wait for it.

JOSIAH G. HOLLAND, *Gold-Foil: Patience*.

8

Is there beyond the silent night
    An endless day?
Is death a door that leads to light?
    We cannot say.

ROBERT G. INGERSOLL, *Declaration of the Free*.

9

The idea of immortality . . . will continue to ebb and flow beneath the mists and clouds of doubt and darkness as long as love kisses the lips of death. It is the rainbow—Hope, shining upon the tears of grief.

ROBERT G. INGERSOLL, *The Ghosts*.

10

Let us not be uneasy then about the different roads we may pursue, as believing them the shortest, to that our last abode, but following the guidance of a good conscience, let us be happy in the hope that by these different paths we shall all meet in the end.

THOMAS JEFFERSON, *Writings*, vol. xiv, p. 198.

11

Dust thou art, to dust returnest,
    Was not spoken of the soul.

HENRY WADSWORTH LONGFELLOW, *A Psalm of Life*.

12

There is no more mystery or miracle or supernaturalness . . . in the wholly unproved fact of immortality than there is in the wholly unexplainable fact of life or in the unimaginable fact of the universe.

HOWARD LEE MCBAIN, Address, Columbia University, New York City, 7 Jan., 1934.

13

The few little years we spend on earth are only the first scene in a Divine Drama that extends on into Eternity.

EDWIN MARKHAM, Address at the Funeral of Adam Willis Wagnalls.

14

I do not believe in immortality and have no desire for it. The belief in it issues from the puerile egos of inferior men.

H. L. MENCKEN. (DURANT, *On the Meaning of Life*, p. 35)

15

Life is pleasant and I have enjoyed it, but I have no yearning to clutter up the Universe after it is over.

H. L. MENCKEN. (*Greatest Thoughts on Immortality*, p. 114)

16

The universe is a stairway leading nowhere unless man is immortal.

E. Y. MULLINS. (NEWTON, *My Idea of God*, p. 199)

17

All men desire to be immortal.

THEODORE PARKER, *Sermon on the Immortal Life*, 20 Sept., 1846.

18

The cry of the human for a life beyond the grave comes from that which is noblest in the soul of man.

HENRY VAN DYKE. (*Greatest Thoughts on Immortality*, p. 68)

19

I swear I think there is nothing but immortality.

WALT WHITMAN, *To Think of Time*.

20

I swear I think now that everything without exception has an eternal soul!

WALT WHITMAN, *To Think of Time*.

1
Alas for him who never sees
The stars shine through his cypress-trees!
Who, hopeless, lays his dead away,
Nor looks to see the breaking day
Across the mournful marbles play!
Who hath not learned, in hours of faith,
    The truth to flesh and sense unknown,
That Life is ever lord of Death,
    And Love can never lose its own!
> JOHN GREENLEAF WHITTIER, *Snow-Bound*,
> l. 203.

INDECISION

2
On the Plains of Hesitation bleach the bones
of countless millions who, at the Dawn of
Victory, sat down to wait—and waiting,
died.
> GEORGE W. CECIL, Advertisement, *Ameri-can Magazine*, Mar., 1923, p. 87. This
> advertisement, titled "The Warning of
> the Desert," written for the Internation-
> al Correspondence Schools, was signed
> "William A. Lawrence," Cecil's pen
> name. The lines were enclosed in quota-
> tion marks.

On the Plains of Hesitation bleach the bones
of countless thousands who, on the eve of
Victory, rested—and resting, died.
> ADLAI E. STEVENSON, Speech in Chicago, 3
> Nov., 1952, paraphrasing Cecil's lines.

3
There is no more miserable human being
than one in whom nothing is habitual but
indecision.
> WILLIAM JAMES, *The Principles of Psy-chology*, ch. 10.

4
I mean a kin' o' hangin' roun' an' settin' on a
fence.
> JAMES RUSSELL LOWELL, *The Biglow Pa-pers*. Ser. ii, No. 3.

INDEPENDENCE

5
Whoso would be a man, must be a Non-con-
formist.
> EMERSON, *Essays, First Series: Self-Reli-ance.*

6
For years I have been known for saying "Include me out."
> SAMUEL GOLDWYN, Address to students of
> Balliol College, Oxford, 1 Mar., 1945.

7
It *was* certainly better to suffer as a sheep
than as a lamb. One might as well perish by
the sword as by famine.
> HENRY JAMES, *The Ambassadors*, p. 211.

8
We've a war, an' a debt, an' a flag; an' ef
this
Ain't to be inderpendunt, why, wut on airth
    is?
> JAMES RUSSELL LOWELL, *Biglow Papers*,
> Ser. ii, No. 4.

9
I would rather sit on a pumpkin and have it
all to myself than be crowded on a velvet
cushion.
> HENRY D. THOREAU, *Walden*, ch. 1.

10
Voyager upon life's sea,
    To yourself be true,
And whate'er your lot may be,
    Paddle your own canoe.
> UNKNOWN, *Paddle Your Own Canoe*, pub-
> lished anonymously in the "Editor's
> Drawer" of *Harper's Monthly*, May,
> 1854. A prefatory note explained that
> the poem was written by a "lady of In-
> diana."

11
So live that you can look any man in the eye
and tell him to go to hell.
> UNKNOWN. This was first given currency
> by one of the engineers of the Panama
> Canal. (MENCKEN, *The American Lan-guage*, p. 434) Also used by John D.
> Rockefeller, Jr. in an address at Dart-
> mouth College, June, 1930.

INDEPENDENCE DAY

12
Yesterday the greatest question was decided
which ever was debated in America; and a
greater perhaps never was, nor will be, decided among men. A resolution was passed
without one dissenting colony, that those
United Colonies are, and of right ought to
be, free and independent States.
> JOHN ADAMS, Letter to Mrs. Adams, 3
> July, 1776.

13
The second day of July, 1776, will be the
most memorable epoch in the history of
America. I am apt to believe that it will be
celebrated by succeeding generations as the
great anniversary festival. It ought to be
commemorated as the day of deliverance, by
solemn acts of devotion to God Almighty. It
ought to be solemnized with pomp and parade, with shows, games, sports, guns, bells,
bonfires, and illuminations, from one end of
this continent to the other, from this time
forward forevermore.
> JOHN ADAMS, Letter to Mrs. Adams, 3
> July, 1776.

14
Independence forever!
> JOHN ADAMS. He murmured these words
> on the morning of the day he died, 4
> July, 1826, upon being aroused by the

discharge of cannon and upon being told that the blast signalled Independence Day. Four days earlier he had used the same words, upon being asked for a toast to be offered in his name on the holiday.

It is my living sentiment, and by the blessing of God it shall be my dying sentiment,—Independence now and Independence forever!
> DANIEL WEBSTER, Eulogy in memory of John Adams and Thomas Jefferson, 2 Aug., 1826. These were the closing words of an imaginary speech attributed to Adams, which was part of the eulogy.

1
The United States is the only country with a known birthday.
> JAMES G. BLAINE, *America's Natal Day.*

2
That which distinguishes this day from all others is that then both orators and artillerymen shoot blank cartridges.
> JOHN BURROUGHS, *Journal,* 4 July, 1859.

3
While Gen'l Howe with a Large Armament is advancing towards N. York, our Congress resolved to Declare the United Colonies Free and Independent States. A Declaration for this Purpose, I expect, will this day pass Congress. . . . It is gone so far that we must now be a free independent State, or a Conquered Country.
> ABRAHAM CLARK, Letter to Elias Dayton, Philadelphia, 4 July, 1776. Clark was a member of the Continental Congress from New Jersey.

4
The flippant mistaking for freedom of some paper preamble like a "Declaration of Independence."
> EMERSON, *Conduct of Life: Fate.*

Declarations of Independence make nobody really independent.
> GEORGE SANTAYANA. (INGE, *Wit and Wisdom*)

5
Let independence be our boast,
Ever mindful what it cost;
Ever grateful for the prize,
Let its altar reach the skies!
> JOSEPH HOPKINSON, *Hail, Columbia!*

6
When in the course of human events, it becomes necessary for one people to dissolve the political bonds which have connected them with another, and to assume among the powers of the earth the separate and equal station to which the laws of nature and of nature's God entitle them, a decent respect to the opinons of mankind requires that they should declare the causes which impel them to the separation.
> THOMAS JEFFERSON, Declaration of Independence: Preamble.

7
We hold these truths to be self-evident, that all men are created equal, that they are endowed by their Creator with certain unalienable Rights, that among these are Life, Liberty and the pursuit of Happiness. That to secure these rights, Governments are instituted among Men, deriving their just powers from the consent of the governed. That whenever any Form of Government becomes destructive of these ends, it is the Right of the People to alter or to abolish it, and to institute new Government, laying its foundation on such principles and organizing its powers in such form, as to them shall seem most likely to effect their Safety and Happiness. . . . We, therefore, . . . do . . . solemnly publish and declare, That these United Colonies are, and of Right ought to be free and independent States. . . . And for the support of this Declaration, with a firm reliance on the protection of Divine Providence, We mutually pledge to each other our Lives, our Fortunes, and our sacred Honor.
> THOMAS JEFFERSON, Declaration of Independence, as adopted by the Continental Congress, Philadelphia, 4 July, 1776.

8
To-day her thanks shall fly on every wind,
Unstinted, unrebuked, from shore to shore,
One love, one hope, and not a doubt behind!
Cannon to cannon shall repeat her praise,
Banner to banner flap it forth in flame;
Her children shall rise up to bless her name,
And wish her harmless length of days,
The mighty mother of a mighty brood,
Blessed in all tongues and dear to every blood,
The beautiful, the strong, and, best of all, the good.
> JAMES RUSSELL LOWELL, *Ode for the Fourth of July, 1876,* l. 43.

9
A safe and sane Fourth.
> TOM MASSON, Editorial, *Life* (1896).

10
Day of glory! Welcome day!
Freedom's banners greet thy ray.
> JOHN PIERPONT, *The Fourth of July.*

11
Jefferson's Declaration of Independence is a practical document for the use of practical men. It is not a thesis for philosophers, but a whip for tyrants; it is not a theory of government, but a program of action.
> WOODROW WILSON, Speech in Indianapolis, 13 Apr., 1911.

INDIAN

1
Two distinct and equally false images of the Indian have persisted in literature: one of the ignorant and brutal savage, the other of the guileless child of nature, first conceived by Rousseau. He was neither. He belonged to a race in process of growth, with probably a higher spiritual endowment and potential than any other primitive people.

> J. DONALD ADAMS, "Speaking of Books," *New York Times Book Review,* 9 Aug., 1964, p. 2.

2
All that we deprived the Negro of besides his freedom, we took from the Indian also—adequate opportunity, equal rights as a citizen and more besides. We overran the land that had been his for centuries, and without adequate recompense; we broke, and still break, treaty after treaty solemnly made; in many cases we broke his morale as well.

> J. DONALD ADAMS, "Speaking of Books," *New York Times Book Review,* 9 Aug., 1964, p. 2.

3
His erect and perfect form, though disclosing some irregular virtues, was found joined to a dwindled soul. Master of all sorts of woodcraft, he seemed a part of the forest and the lake, and the secret of his amazing skill seemed to be that he partook of the nature and fierce instincts of the beasts he slew. . . . Thomas Hooker anticipated the opinion of Humboldt, and called them "the ruins of mankind."

> EMERSON, *Miscellanies: Historical Discourse.*

4
The interest of the Puritans in the natives was heightened by a suspicion at that time prevailing that these were the lost ten tribes of Israel.

> EMERSON, *Miscellanies: Historical Discourse.*

5
Savages we call them, because their manners differ from ours.

> BENJAMIN FRANKLIN, *Remarks Concerning the Savages of North America.*

6
A Century of Dishonor.

> HELEN HUNT JACKSON, Report (1881) on the treatment of the Indians by the U.S. government and people.

7
For a subject worked and reworked so often in novels, motion pictures, and television, American Indians remain probably the least understood and most misunderstood Americans of us all. . . . When we forget great contributors to our American history—when we neglect the heroic past of the American Indian—we thereby weaken our own heritage.

> JOHN F. KENNEDY, *The American Heritage Book of Indians:* Introduction (1961).

8
Ever since the white men first fell upon them, the Indians of what is now the United States have been hidden from white men's view by a number of conflicting myths. The oldest of these is the myth of the Noble Red Man or the Child of Nature, who is credited either with a habit of flowery oratory or implacable dullness or else with an imbecilic inability to converse in anything more than grunts and monosyllables. The first myth was inconvenient. White men soon found their purposes better served by the myth of ruthless, faithless savages, and later, when the "savages" had been broken, of drunken, lazy good-for-nothings.

> OLIVER LA FARGE, *Myths That Hide the American Indian; American Heritage,* Oct., 1956, p. 5.

9
Lo, the poor Indian! whose untutor'd mind
Sees God in clouds, or hears him in the wind;
His soul proud Science never taught to stray
Far as the solar walk or milky way;
Yet simple nature to his hope has giv'n,
Behind the cloud-topt hill, an humbler Heav'n; . . .
To be, contents his natural desire;
He asks no Angel's wing, no Seraph's fire;
But thinks, admitted to that equal sky,
His faithful dog shall bear him company.

> ALEXANDER POPE, *Essay on Man;* Epis. i, l. 99.

10
The only good Indian is a dead Indian.

> GENERAL PHILIP H. SHERIDAN. According to Edward M. Ellis, who asserted he was present at the time, Sheridan made the remark at old Fort Cobb, Indian Territory, in Jan., 1869, when an Indian chief was presented to Sheridan as a "good Indian."

11
You can make an Injun of a white man but you can never make a white man of an Injun.

> GENERAL WILLIAM T. SHERMAN.

12
Ye say they all have passed away,
    That noble race and brave;
That their light canoes have vanished
    From off the crested wave;
That mid the forests where they roamed
    There rings no hunter's shout;
But their name is on your waters;

Ye may not wash it out.
LYDIA HUNTLY SIGOURNEY, *Indian Names.*

INDIVIDUALITY
See also Character, Personality

1
You and I know that there is a correlation between the creative and the screwball. So we must suffer the screwball gladly.
KINGMAN BREWSTER, JR., Speech in Hartford, Conn., 29 Oct., 1964.

2
Conform and be dull.
J. FRANK DOBIE, *The Voice of the Coyote:* Introduction.

3
Everything that tends to insulate the individual . . . tends to true union as well as greatness.
EMERSON, *The American Scholar.*

4
The individual is always mistaken.
EMERSON, *Essays, Second Series: Experience.*

5
Each man . . . is justified in his individuality, as his nature is found to be immense.
EMERSON, *Essays, Second Series: Nominalist and Realist.*

6
The universal does not attract us until housed in an individual.
EMERSON, *Nature, Addresses, and Lectures: The Method of Nature.*

7
To clap copyright on the world: this is the ambition of individualism.
EMERSON, *Representative Men: Plato.*

8
The American system of rugged individualism.
HERBERT HOOVER, Speech in New York City, 22 Oct., 1928; also *The New Day* (1934), p. 154.

While I can make no claim for having introduced the term "rugged individualism," I should be proud to have invented it.
HERBERT HOOVER, *The Challenge to Liberty* (1934), ch. 5.

9
We will have differences. Men of different ancestries, men of different tongues, men of different colors, men of different environments, men of different geographies do not see everything alike. Even in our own country we do not see everything alike. If we did we would all want the same wife—and that would be a problem, wouldn't it!
LYNDON B. JOHNSON, Speech to field officials of the Internal Revenue Service, Washington, D.C., 11 Feb., 1964.

10
We cannot expect that all nations will adopt like systems, for conformity is the jailer of freedom and the enemy of growth.
JOHN F. KENNEDY, Address to the United Nations General Assembly, 25 Sept., 1961.

11
Paradoxically, the strong American tendency to conform may have been fostered by our very variety of cultural backgrounds. A nation like ours, made up of diverse racial strains, each with its own mores and sanctions, must have found "assimilation" and "conformity" almost exact synonyms.
LOUIS KRONENBERGER, *Company Manners,* p. 173.

12
I'll be damned if I'll be a public utility.
HENRY R. LUCE, Reply to a friend who had said that *Time* should never say anything not in accord with popular opinion or taste, because the magazine's standing caused people to look on it as a sort of public utility. (New York *Times* résumé of Luce's career, by John M. Lee, 17 Apr., 1964)

13
If a man does not keep pace with his companions, perhaps it is because he hears a different drummer. Let him step to the music which he hears, however measured or far away.
HENRY D. THOREAU, *Walden.*

14
Individualism is a fatal poison. But individuality is the salt of common life. You may have to live in a crowd, but you do not have to live like it, nor subsist on its food. You may have your own orchard. You may drink at a hidden spring. Be yourself if you would serve others.
HENRY VAN DYKE, *The School of Life,* p. 33.

15
Underneath all, individuals,
I swear nothing is good to me now that ignores individuals. . . .
The only government is that which makes minute of individuals,
The whole theory of the universe is directed unerringly to one single individual—namely to You.
WALT WHITMAN, *By Blue Ontario's Shore,* sec. 15.

16
I wear my hat as I please indoors or out.
Why should I pray? Why should I venerate and be ceremonious?
Having pried through the strata, analyzed to a hair, counsel'd with doctors and calculated close,
I find no sweeter fat than sticks to my own bones.
WALT WHITMAN, *Song of Myself,* sec. 20.

INDUSTRY
See also Idleness, Labor, Work

1
In the ordinary business of life, industry can do anything which genius can do, and very many things which it cannot.
> HENRY WARD BEECHER, *Proverbs from Plymouth Pulpit.*

2
My constant attendance, I never making a St. Monday, recommended me to the master.
> BENJAMIN FRANKLIN, *Autobiography*, ch. 1. That is, never making Monday a holiday necessitated by week-end carousing.

3
The sound of your hammer at five in the morning, or nine at night, heard by a creditor, makes him easy six months longer.
> BENJAMIN FRANKLIN, *Letter to My Friend, A.B.*

4
Diligence is the mother of good luck.
> BENJAMIN FRANKLIN, *Poor Richard's Almanack,* 1736.

5
At the working man's house hunger looks in, but dares not enter.
> BENJAMIN FRANKLIN, *Poor Richard,* 1737.

6
Industry need not wish.
> BENJAMIN FRANKLIN, *Poor Richard,* 1739.

7
The used key is always bright.
> BENJAMIN FRANKLIN, *Poor Richard,* 1744.

8
The sleeping fox catches no poultry.
> BENJAMIN FRANKLIN, *Poor Richard,* 1758.

9
Have you ever told a coal miner in West Virginia or Kentucky that what he needs is individual initiative to go out and get a job when there isn't any?
> ROBERT F. KENNEDY, Testimony during a House of Representatives subcommittee hearing on the 1964 anti-poverty bill, Apr., 1964.

10
Let us, then, be up and doing.
> HENRY WADSWORTH LONGFELLOW, *A Psalm of Life.*

11
I've got a lot of sympathy for people where a sudden change catches 'em—but I've always liked bird dogs better than kennel-fed dogs . . . one who'll get out and hunt for food rather than sit on his fanny and yell.
> CHARLES ERWIN WILSON, Remark at press conference, Detroit, 11 Oct., 1954. Wil-

son, then Secretary of Defense, was commenting on unemployment as a result of cutbacks in defense production. The comparison of men and dogs caused spirited controversy, which both President Eisenhower and Vice President Nixon attempted to assuage. Two days after the press conference, Wilson apologized for "inept remarks," at a dinner in Chicago.

INTELLIGENCE
See also Mind

12
Humanity i love you because
when you're hard up you pawn your
intelligence to buy a drink.
> E. E. CUMMINGS, *Humanity i love you.*

13
The intelligent have a right over the ignorant; namely, the right of instructing them.
> EMERSON, *Representative Men: Plato: New Readings.*

14
The Moral Obligation to Be Intelligent.
> JOHN ERSKINE, Title of Book (1915).

15
Ennui, felt on proper occasions, is a sign of intelligence.
> CLIFTON FADIMAN, *Reading I've Liked.*

16
The test of a first-rate intelligence is the ability to hold two opposed ideas in the mind at the same time, and still retain the ability to function.
> F. SCOTT FITZGERALD, *The Crack-up.*

17
It is not the insurrections of ignorance that are dangerous, but the revolts of intelligence.
> JAMES RUSSELL LOWELL, *Democracy.*

18
The [U.S.] Military Academy taught me many things, some of them not within the covers of books written by any man. . . . The third is intelligence, rather than sentiment or emotion. Sentimentality has muddled many problems and settled none. Intellect is man's only hope for improvement over his present state.
> GENERAL DOUGLAS MACARTHUR, Public Statement, 26 Jan., 1964, on his 84th birthday.

INTEMPERANCE, see Drinking, Drunkenness
INTENTION
See also Purpose

19
A good intention clothes itself with sudden power.
> EMERSON, *Conduct of Life: Fate.*

1

With mere good intentions, hell is proverbially paved.

> WILLIAM JAMES, *The Principles of Psychology*, ch. 10.

2

For there's nothing we read of in torture's inventions,
Like a well-meaning dunce, with the best of intentions.

> JAMES RUSSELL LOWELL, *A Fable for Critics*, l. 250.

INTOLERANCE, see Tolerance

INVENTION

3

A tool is but the extension of a man's hand, and a machine is but a complex tool. And he that invents a machine augments the power of a man and the well-being of mankind.

> HENRY WARD BEECHER, *Proverbs from Plymouth Pulpit: Business*.

4

'Tis frivolous to fix pedantically the date of particular inventions. They have all been invented over and over fifty times. Man is the arch machine, of which all these shifts drawn from himself are toy models.

> EMERSON, *Conduct of Life: Fate*.

5

Only an inventor knows how to borrow, and every man is or should be an inventor.

> EMERSON, *Letters and Social Aims: Quotation and Originality*.

6

Invention breeds invention.

> EMERSON, *Society and Solitude: Works and Days*.

IRELAND AND THE IRISH

7

A Little Bit of Heaven, Sure They Call It Ireland.

> J. KEIRN BRENNAN, Title of song (1914), with music by Ernest R. Ball.

8

The Irish are the cry-babies of the Western world.

> HEYWOOD BROUN, *It Seems to Me*.

9

"Well, here's thank God for the race and the sod!"
Said Kelly and Burke and Shea.

> J. I. C. CLARKE, *The Fighting Race*.

10

"Oh, the fighting races don't die out,
If they seldom die in bed,
For love is first in their hearts, no doubt,"
Said Burke.

> J. I. C. CLARKE, *The Fighting Race*.

11

My lips are sealed, and that is a pretty hard position to put an Irishman in.

> MATTHEW J. CULLIGAN, Reply to inquiring reporters just after he had been removed from his post as president of the Curtis Publishing Company at a meeting of the firm's board of directors in Philadelphia, 19 Oct., 1964. He explained that he was bound by an agreement not to discuss proceedings of the meeting.

12

There is no doubt in my mind that nothing could have been started until the Irish invented politics.

> LYNDON B. JOHNSON, Speech in New York City, at a dinner-meeting of the Friendly Sons of St. Patrick, 17 Mar., 1964.

13

I am an Irishman by osmosis.

> LYNDON B. JOHNSON, Speech in New York City, at a dinner-meeting of the Friendly Sons of St. Patrick, 17 Mar., 1964.

14

"Throw him down, McCloskey," was to be the battle cry,—
"Throw him down, McCloskey, you can lick him if you try."

> JOHN W. KELLY, *Throw Him Down, McCloskey*. A song made famous by Maggie Cline in 1890.

15

Ireland Must Be Heaven, for My Mother Came from There.

> JOE MCCARTHY, HOWARD JOHNSON, FRED FISHER, Title of song (1916), with words and music by this trio.

16

Has anybody here seen Kelly?
Kelly from the Emerald Isle?

> WILLIAM J. MCKENNA, *Has Anybody Here Seen Kelly?* Sung by Nora Bayes in *The Jolly Bachelors* (1908).

17

The Irish say your trouble is their trouble and your
joy their joy? I wish
I could believe it;
I am troubled, I'm dissatisfied, I'm Irish.

> MARIANNE MOORE, *Spenser's Ireland*.

18

My Wild Irish Rose.

> CHAUNCEY OLCOTT, Title of song (1899), with words and music by Olcott.

19

When Irish Eyes Are Smiling.

> CHAUNCEY OLCOTT AND GEORGE GRAFF, JR., Title of song (1912), with music by Ernest R. Ball.

20

Where the dear old Shannon's flowing,
Where the three-leaved Shamrock grows,
Where my heart is I am going,
To my little Irish rose.
And the moment that I meet her
With a hug and kiss I'll greet her,
For there's not a colleen sweeter
Where the River Shannon flows.

> JAMES J. RUSSELL, *Where the River Shannon Flows* (song, 1905, with music also by Russell).

1
Give an Irishman lager for a month, and he's a dead man. An Irishman is lined with copper, and the beer corrodes it. But whiskey polishes the copper and is the saving of him.
> MARK TWAIN, *Life on the Mississippi*, ch. 23.

2
May the enemies of Ireland never eat bread nor drink whisky, but be tormented with itching without benefit of scratching.
> UNKNOWN, Toast traditionally offered during the celebration of St. Patrick's Day

about the time of George Washington. (Associated Press feature story on St. Patrick's Day, by Hugh A. Mulligan, datelined New York, 16 Mar., 1964)

IRONY

3
Irony is jesting hidden behind gravity.
> JOHAN WEISS, *Wit, Humor and Shakespeare.*

4
Irony is an insult conveyed in the form of a compliment.
> E. P. WHIPPLE, *Literature and Life: Wit.*

J

JACKSON, ANDREW

5
In answer to our shouting, fire lit his eye of gray;
Erect, but thin and pallid, he passed upon his bay. . . .
But spite of fever and fasting, and hours of sleepless care,
The soul of Andrew Jackson shone forth in glory there.
> THOMAS DUNN ENGLISH, *The Battle of New Orleans.*

6
Old turkey-cock on a forest rock,
Old faithful heart who could boast and strut;
I will think of you when the woods are cut—
Old, old Andrew Jackson. . . .
He broke the bones of all cattle who horned him,
He broke the bones of all who scorned him,— . . .
The finest hope from the Cave of Adullam,
Since Davis ascended the throne;—
Old Andrew Jackson, the old, old raven, lean as a bone!
> VACHEL LINDSAY, *Old Old Old Andrew Jackson.*

7
This is the day that we honor "Old Hickory,"
Honor him, aye, for the name that he bore!
Fierce as a fighter, and yet above trickery,
Virile and valiant and leal to the core!
> CLINTON SCOLLARD, *Old Hickory.*

JEFFERSON, THOMAS

8
Thomas Jefferson still lives.
> JOHN ADAMS. These last words of Adams, spoken 4 July, 1826, were not strictly true, since Jefferson had died on the

morning of that day. But they were highly prophetic words in another sense.

9
He had a steadfast and abiding faith in justice, righteousness and liberty as the prevailing and abiding forces in the conduct of States, and that justice and righteousness were sure to prevail where any people bear rule in perfect liberty.
> GEORGE F. HOAR, *Thomas Jefferson.*

10
Here was buried Thomas Jefferson, author of the Declaration of American Independence, of the statute of Virginia for religious freedom, and father of the University of Virginia.
> THOMAS JEFFERSON, Epitaph, written for himself.

11
I have the consolation to reflect that during the period of my administration not a drop of the blood of a single fellow citizen was shed by the sword of war or of the law.
> THOMAS JEFFERSON, *Writings*, vol. xix, p. 256.

12
I think this is the most extraordinary collection of talent, of human knowledge, that has ever been gathered together at the White House—with the possible exception of when Thomas Jefferson dined alone.
> JOHN F. KENNEDY, Greeting to guests at a White House dinner honoring Nobel Prize winners, 29 Apr., 1962.

13
Since the days when Jefferson expounded his code of political philosophy, the whole world has become his pupil.
> MICHAEL MACWHITE, Address at the University of Virginia, 13 Apr., 1931.

14
A gentleman of thirty-two who could calculate an eclipse, survey an estate, tie an artery, plan an edifice, try a cause, break a horse, dance a minuet and play the violin.
> JAMES PARTON, *Life of Jefferson*, p. 164.

1
The immortality of Thomas Jefferson does not lie in any one of his achievements, but in his attitude toward mankind.
WOODROW WILSON, Speech in Washington, D.C., 13 Apr., 1916.

JESUS CHRIST, see Christ

JEW

2
To be a Jew is a destiny.
VICKI BAUM, *And Life Goes On,* p. 193.

3
The gentleman will please remember that when his half-civilized ancestors were hunting the wild boar in Silesia, mine were princes of the earth.
JUDAH BENJAMIN, Reply to a taunt by a Senator of German descent. (MOORE, *Reminiscences of Sixty Years in the National Metropolis*)

4
If my theory of relativity is proven successful, Germany will claim me as a German and France will declare that I am a citizen of the world. Should my theory prove untrue, France will say that I am a German and Germany will declare that I am a Jew.
ALBERT EINSTEIN, Address, Sorbonne, Paris.

5
The sufferance, which is the badge of the Jew, has made him, in these days, the ruler of the rulers of the earth.
EMERSON, *Conduct of Life: Fate.*

6
His cup is gall, his meat is tears,
His passion lasts a thousand years.
EMMA LAZARUS, *Crowing of the Red Cock.*

7
Still on Israel's head forlorn,
Every nation heaps its scorn.
EMMA LAZARUS, *The World's Justice.*

8
I do not believe that being a Jew has either helped or harmed me in my public life. . . . You ask whether I have a comment to make to my fellow Jews who may want some day to become publicly known and feel that Judaism may hold them back because of either discrimination or prejudice. My answer is that I think any man, who is seeking public office and allows his ambition to affect his religious affiliation, is not worthy of the confidence of his fellow citizens. I know of very few instances in which a man was looked down upon because he was a Jew. On the other hand I know of many instances where a man sought to hide his religion [and] lost the respect of his fellow citizens.
HERBERT H. LEHMAN, Letter to a young Jewish boy who had written Lehman to inquire whether being a Jew had proved a personal handicap. This reply was written several years before Lehman's death, and was read at his funeral service in New York City, 8 Dec., 1963.

9
My advice in a word is: Never be ashamed of being a Jew. Never try to hide it. Never try to compromise with your convictions because they may not agree with those of the group in which you find yourself.
HERBERT H. LEHMAN, Letter to a young Jewish boy, read at Lehman's funeral service in New York City, 8 Dec., 1963.

JOY

See also Happiness, Pleasure

10
To-day, whatever may annoy,
The word for me is Joy, just simple Joy.
JOHN KENDRICK BANGS, *The Word.*

11
The joy late coming late departs.
LEWIS J. BATES, *Some Sweet Day.*

12
Is bliss, then, such abyss
I must not put my foot amiss
For fear I spoil my shoe?
EMILY DICKINSON, *Poems,* Pt. i, No. 135.

13
All human joys are swift of wing,
For heaven doth so allot it,
That when you get an easy thing,
You find you haven't got it.
EUGENE FIELD, *Ways of Life.*

14
Joy comes, grief goes, we know not how.
JAMES RUSSELL LOWELL, *The Vision of Sir Launfal:* Pt. i, Prelude.

15
I found more joy in sorrow
Than you could find in joy.
SARA TEASDALE, *The Answer.*

16
Grief can take care of itself, but to get the full value from joy you must have somebody to divide it with.
MARK TWAIN, *Pudd'nhead Wilson's New Calendar.*

17
The sweetest joys a heart can hold
Grow up between its crosses.
NIXON WATERMAN, *Recompense.*

18
Joy is a fruit that Americans eat green.
AMANDO ZEGRI. (*Golden Book,* May, 1931)

JUDGE

19
The judge weighs the arguments, and puts a brave face on the matter, and, since there

must be a decision, decides as he can, and hopes he has done justice.

> EMERSON, *Conduct of Life: Considerations by the Way.*

1

When the judges shall be obliged to go armed, it will be time for the courts to be closed.

> JUDGE S. J. FIELD, of California, in 1889, upon being advised to arm himself.

2

A judge should be compounded of the faculties that are demanded of the historian and the philosopher and the prophet. The last demand upon him—to make some forecast of the consequences of his action—is perhaps the heaviest. To pierce the curtain of the future, to give shape and visage to mysteries still in the womb of time, is the gift of imagination.

> FELIX FRANKFURTER.

3

Judges are apt to be naif, simple-minded men, and they need something of Mephistopheles.

> JUSTICE OLIVER WENDELL HOLMES, *Law and the Court.*

JUDGMENT

4

I bear no enmity to any human being; but, alas! as Mrs. Placid said to her friend, by which of thy good works wouldst thou be willing to be judged?

> ABIGAIL ADAMS, *Letters,* p. 411.

5

If I was as bad as they say I am,
    And you were as good as you look,
I wonder which one would feel the worse
    If each for the other was took?

> GEORGE BARR BAKER, *Good and Bad.*

6

Cruel and cold is the judgment of man,
    Cruel as winter, and cold as the snow;
But by-and-by will the deed and the plan
    Be judged by the motive that lieth below.

> LEWIS J. BATES, *By-and-By.*

7

E'er you remark another's sin,
Bid your own conscience look within.

> BENJAMIN FRANKLIN, *Poor Richard,* 1741.

8

It is therefore that the older I grow, the more apt I am to doubt my own judgment, and to pay more respect to the judgment of others.

> BENJAMIN FRANKLIN, Speech prepared for the American Constitutional Convention in Philadelphia, 17 Sept., 1787, and read for the aged Franklin by a representative.

9

We judge ourselves by what we feel capable of doing, while others judge us by what we have already done.

> HENRY WADSWORTH LONGFELLOW, *Kavanagh,* ch. 1.

10

In men whom men condemn as ill
I find so much of goodness still,
In men whom men pronounce divine
I find so much of sin and blot,
I do not dare to draw a line
Between the two, where God has not.

> JOAQUIN MILLER, *Byron.*

11

They have a right to censure, that have a heart to help.

> WILLIAM PENN, *Fruits of Solitude,* p. 15.

12

We must stand afar off to judge St. Peter's.

> WENDELL PHILLIPS, Speech, 17 Feb., 1861.

13

It's the bad that's in the best of us
Leaves the saint so like the rest of us!
It's the good in the darkest-curst of us
Redeems and saves the worst of us!
It's the muddle of hope and madness;
It's the tangle of good and badness;
It's the lunacy linked with sanity
Makes up, and mocks, humanity!

> ARTHUR STRINGER, *Humanity.*

14

One cool judgment is worth a thousand hasty councils.

> WOODROW WILSON, Speech in Pittsburgh, 29 Jan., 1916.

15

There is so much good in the worst of us,
And so much bad in the best of us,
That it hardly becomes any of us
To talk about the rest of us.

> UNKNOWN, *Good and Bad.* First printed in the Marion, Kan., *Record.*

JUNE

16

Flame-flowered, yellow-petalled June.

> DON BLANDING, *Hawaiian June.*

17

June Is Bustin' Out All Over.

> OSCAR HAMMERSTEIN II, Title of song, from the musical play *Carousel* (1945), with music by Richard Rodgers.

18

And what is so rare as a day in June?
    Then, if ever, come perfect days;
Then Heaven tries the earth if it be in tune,
    And over it softly her warm ear lays.

> JAMES RUSSELL LOWELL, *The Vision of Sir Launfal:* Pt. i. Prelude.

19

No price is set on the lavish summer;
June may be had by the poorest comer.

> JAMES RUSSELL LOWELL, *The Vision of Sir Launfal:* Pt. i. Prelude.

1

Tell you what I like the best—
'Long about knee-deep in June,
'Bout the time strawberries melts
On the vine,—some afternoon
Like to jes' git out and rest,
And not work at nothin' else!

> JAMES WHITCOMB RILEY, *Knee-Deep in
> June.*

JURY

2

Whin the case is all over, the jury'll pitch th'
tistimony out iv the window, an' consider
three questions: "Did Lootgert look as
though he'd kill his wife? Did his wife look
as though she ought to be kilt? Isn't it time
we wint to supper?"

> FINLEY PETER DUNNE, *On Expert Testi-
> mony.*

3

Trial by juries impartially selected.

> THOMAS JEFFERSON, First Inaugural Ad-
> dress, 4 Mar., 1801. One of the princi-
> ples, he declared, that "should be the
> creed of our political faith."

JUSTICE

4

I always felt from the beginning that you
had to defend people you disliked and feared
as well as those you admired.

> ROGER BALDWIN. (WILLIE MORRIS, *Barely
> Winded at Eighty; The New Republic,*
> 25 Jan., 1964)

5

What seems just at one time in a man's life
may come to seem unjust at other times. I
grew up in a segregated society. It never
occurred to me that this was unjust.

> LEROY COLLINS, Television Interview,
> *Face the Nation,* 20 Dec., 1964. Speak-
> ing as director of the Community Rela-
> tions Service, conciliation agency cre-
> ated by the 1964 Civil Rights Law, Col-
> lins added that he had since changed his
> view on the injustice of segregation.

6

Justice is blind. Blind she is, an' deef an'
dumb an' has a wooden leg.

> FINLEY PETER DUNNE, *Cross-Examina-
> tions.*

7

One man's justice is another's injustice; one
man's beauty another's ugliness; one man's
wisdom another's folly.

> EMERSON, *Essays, First Series: Circles.*

8

It is better to suffer injustice than to do it.

> EMERSON, *Representative Men: Plato.*

9

All that is needed to remedy the evils of our
time is to do justice and give freedom.

> HENRY GEORGE, *The Condition of Labor.*

10

That which is unjust can really profit no
one; that which is just can really harm no
one.

> HENRY GEORGE, *The Land Question,* ch.
> 14.

11

That justice is the highest quality in the
moral hierarchy I do not say, but that it is
the first. That which is above justice must be
based on justice, and include justice, and be
reached through justice.

> HENRY GEORGE, *Social Problems,* ch. 9.

12

He reminds me of the man who murdered
both his parents, and then, when sentence
was about to be pronounced, pleaded for
mercy on the grounds that he was an or-
phan.

> ABRAHAM LINCOLN. (GROSS, *Lincoln's
> Own Stories,* p. 179)

13

Man is unjust, but God is just; and finally
justice Triumphs.

> HENRY WADSWORTH LONGFELLOW, *Evan-
> geline,* pt. i, sec. 3, l. 34.

14

Exact justice is commonly more merciful in
the long run than pity, for it tends to foster
in men those stronger qualities which make
them good citizens.

> JAMES RUSSELL LOWELL, *Among My
> Books: Dante.*

15

Injustice is relatively easy to bear; what
stings is justice.

> H. L. MENCKEN, *Prejudices,* ser. iii, p.
> 101.

16

If elected, I shall see to it that every man
has a square deal, no less and no more.

> THEODORE ROOSEVELT, Address, 4 Nov.,
> 1904.

17

Communism is the corruption of a dream of
justice.

> ADLAI E. STEVENSON, Speech in Urbana,
> Ill., 1951.

18

"Thrice is he armed that hath his quarrel
just"—
And four times he who gets his fist in fust.

> ARTEMUS WARD, *Shakespeare Up-to-Date.*

19

The administration of justice is the firmest
pillar of government.

> GEORGE WASHINGTON, Letter to Edmund
> Randolph, 27 Sept., 1789.

20

Justice, sir, is the great interest of man on
earth.

> DANIEL WEBSTER, *On Mr. Justice Story.*

21

Every unpunished murder takes away some-

thing from the security of every man's life.
> DANIEL WEBSTER, *Argument, Murder of Captain Joseph White, Salem, Mass.,* 3 Aug., 1830.

1

The hope of all who suffer,
The dread of all who wrong.
> JOHN GREENLEAF WHITTIER, *Mantle of St. John De Matha,* st. 21.

2

The laws of changeless justice bind
  Oppressor and oppressed;
And, close as sin and suffering joined,
  We march to Fate abreast.
> JOHN GREENLEAF WHITTIER, *Song of the Negro Boatmen.* This was quoted by Booker T. Washington in a famous speech in Atlanta in 1895.

3

You stand here convicted of seeking to corrupt the administration of justice. You stand here convicted of having tampered, really, with the very soul of this nation.
> FRANK W. WILSON, U.S. District Judge, in passing sentence on James R. Hoffa, head of the Teamsters Union, for attempting to rig a Federal jury; Chattanooga, Tenn., 12 Mar., 1964.

4

When you reflect on it, the only thing that allowed the human race to stop living as animals and to start living as human beings was by adopting a set of rules—a system of justice. Maintaining a system of justice in an orderly society is essential to whatever else people accomplish.
> FRANK W. WILSON, U.S. District Judge, in commenting on the eight-year prison term to which he sentenced Teamster leader James R. Hoffa; Chattanooga, Tenn., 12 Mar., 1964.

5

Justice has nothing to do with expediency. Justice has nothing to do with any temporary standard whatever. It is rooted and grounded in the fundamental instincts of humanity.
> WOODROW WILSON, Speech in Washington, D.C., 26 Feb., 1916.

Expedience and justice frequently are not even on speaking terms.
> ARTHUR H. VANDENBERG, Speech in U.S. Senate, 8 Mar., 1945, in protest against the Yalta agreement that ceded Polish territory to the Soviet Union.

K

KINDNESS

6

Little deeds of kindness,
  Little words of love,
Help to make earth happy
  Like the Heaven above.
> JULIA FLETCHER CARNEY, *Little Things.*

7

If I can stop one heart from breaking,
  I shall not live in vain;
If I can ease one life the aching,
  Or cool one pain,
Or help one fainting robin
  Unto his nest again
I shall not live in vain.
> EMILY DICKINSON, *Poems,* Pt. i, No. 6.

8

Good Will is the mightiest practical force in the universe.
> C. F. DOLE, *Cleveland Address.*

9

Let me be a little kinder,
Let me be a little blinder
To the faults of those around me.
> EDGAR A. GUEST, *A Creed.*

10

Kindness is the sunshine in which virtue grows.
> ROBERT G. INGERSOLL, *A Lay Sermon.*

11

Though he was rough, he was kindly.
> HENRY WADSWORTH LONGFELLOW, *The Courtship of Miles Standish,* pt. iii.

12

The kindness I have longest remembered has been of this sort,—the sort unsaid; so far behind the speaker's lips that almost it already lay in my heart. It did not have far to go to be communicated.
> HENRY D. THOREAU, Letter to Emerson, 12 Feb., 1843.

13

We hate the kindness which we understand.
> HENRY D. THOREAU, Letter to Emerson, 12 Feb., 1843.

14

So many gods, so many creeds,
  So many paths that wind and wind,
While just the art of being kind
Is all the sad world needs.
> ELLA WHEELER WILCOX, *The World's Need.*

KINGS

15

If the king is in the palace, nobody looks at the walls.
> EMERSON, *Essays, Second Series: Nature.*

16

They are not kings who sit on thrones, but they who know how to govern.
> EMERSON, *Society and Solitude: Eloquence.*

17

There is not a single crowned head in Europe

whose talents or merits would entitle him to be elected a vestryman by the people of any parish in America.

> THOMAS JEFFERSON, Letter to George Washington, 2 May, 1788.

1
If any of our countrymen wish for a king, give them Aesop's fable of the frogs who asked a King; if this does not cure them, send them to Europe. They will go back republicans.

> THOMAS JEFFERSON, *Writings*, vol. vi, p. 225.

2
There is no king who has not had a slave among his ancestors, and no slave who has not had a king among his.

> HELEN KELLER, *Story of My Life*, p. 4.

3
Ah! vainest of all things
Is the gratitude of kings

> HENRY WADSWORTH LONGFELLOW, *Belisarius*, st. 8.

4
Scratch a king and find a fool.

> DOROTHY PARKER, *Salome's Dancing Lesson*.

5
All kings is mostly rapscallions.

> MARK TWAIN, *Huckleberry Finn*, ch. 23.

KISS, KISSING

6
I wonder who's kissing her now?

> FRANK R. ADAMS AND WILL M. HOUGH, Title and refrain of song (1912), with music by Joseph E. Howard.

7
Isn't it strange how one man's kiss can grow
To be like any other's . . . or a woman's
To be like any woman's?

> MAXWELL ANDERSON, *Elizabeth the Queen*, act i.

8
A paroxysmal kiss.

> HENRY WARD BEECHER, his description of the kiss he had given Mrs. Henry C. Bowen. It was widely quoted in the 1870's. (*Tilton vs. Beecher*, vol. i, p. 66)

9
Something made of nothing, tasting very sweet,
A most delicious compound, with ingredients complete;
But if, as on occasion, the heart and mind are sour,
It has no great significance, and loses half its power.

> MARY E. BUELL, *The Kiss*.

10
An old Spanish saying is that "a kiss without a mustache is like an egg without salt."

> MADISON CAWEIN, *Nature-Notes*.

11
Kisses kept are wasted;
Love is to be tasted.

> EDMUND VANCE COOKE, *Kisses Kept Are Wasted*.

12
The anatomical juxtaposition of two orbicularis oris muscles in a state of contraction.

> DR. HENRY GIBBONS, Definition of a kiss.

13
Never a lip is curved with pain
That can't be kissed into smiles again.

> BRET HARTE, *The Lost Galleon*.

14
The sound of a kiss is not so loud as that of a cannon, but its echo lasts a great deal longer.

> OLIVER WENDELL HOLMES, *The Professor at the Breakfast-Table*, ch. 11.

15
I never thought I'd be kissing the president of a company—on the lips.

> BOB HOPE, in describing what it was like to work in television opposite Lucille Ball, president of the producing firm Desilu. (LARRY GLENN, *Bob Hope Bounces a Ball Named Lucy*, drama section, New York *Times*, 19 Apr., 1964)

16
The kiss of death.

> ALFRED E. SMITH, Speech, in describing William Randolph Hearst's support of Ogden Mills, 1926.

KNOWLEDGE
See also Wisdom

17
They know enough who know how to learn.

> HENRY ADAMS, *Education of Henry Adams*, p. 314.

18
Men are called fools in one age for not knowing what they were called fools for averring in the age before.

> HENRY WARD BEECHER, *Life Thoughts*.

19
It is better to know nothing than to know what ain't so.

> JOSH BILLINGS, *Josh Billings's Encyclopedia of Wit and Wisdom*, p. 286. This appeared in 1874; subsequently he paraphrased the saying on several occasions without varying the basic sense.

20
There's lots of people—this town wouldn't hold them—
Who don't know much excepting what's told them.

> WILL CARLETON, *City Ballads*, p. 143.

21
Knowledge is the only instrument of production that is not subject to diminishing returns.

> J. M. CLARK, *Overhead Costs in Modern Industry*. (*Jour. Pol. Econ.*, Oct., 1927)

1

We don't know one millionth of one per cent about anything.

THOMAS A. EDISON. (*Golden Book*, Apr., 1931)

2

All our progress is an unfolding, like the vegetable bud. You have first an instinct, then an opinion, then a knowledge.

EMERSON, *Essays, First Series: Intellect.*

3

We know nothing rightly, for want of perspective.

EMERSON, *Essays, Second Series: Nature.*

4

Knowledge is the only elegance.

EMERSON, *Journal*, 1856.

5

Knowledge is the knowing that we cannot know.

EMERSON, *Representative Men: Montaigne.*

6

Knowledge is the antidote to fear,—Knowledge, Use and Reason, with its higher aids.

EMERSON, *Society and Solitude: Courage.*

7

There is no knowledge that is not power.

EMERSON, *Society and Solitude: Old Age.*

Every addition to true knowledge is an addition to human power.

HORACE MANN, *Lectures on Education,* No. 1.

If materialistic knowledge is power, it is not wisdom. It is but a blind force.

MARY BAKER EDDY, *Science and Health*, p. 196.

8

An investment in knowledge pays the best interest.

BENJAMIN FRANKLIN, *Poor Richard.*

9

A man of vast and varied misinformation.

WILLIAM GAYNOR, while mayor of New York, in describing Rabbi Stephen S. Wise.

10

Ole man Know-All died las' year.

JOEL CHANDLER HARRIS, *Plantation Proverbs.*

11

Knowledge and timber shouldn't be much used till they are seasoned.

OLIVER WENDELL HOLMES, *The Autocrat of the Breakfast-Table*, ch. 6.

12

It is the province of knowledge to speak, and it is the privilege of wisdom to listen.

OLIVER WENDELL HOLMES, *The Poet at the Breakfast-Table*, ch. 10.

13

The tree of knowledge in your garden grows, Not single, but at every humble door.

OLIVER WENDELL HOLMES, *Wind-Clouds and Star-Drifts:* pt. viii, *Manhood,* l. 46.

14

Banish me from Eden when you will, but first let me eat of the fruit of the tree of knowledge.

ROBERT G. INGERSOLL, *The Gods.*

15

What man knows is everywhere at war with what he wants.

JOSEPH WOOD KRUTCH, *The Modern Temper*, p. 14.

16

Metaphysics may be, after all, only the art of being sure of something that is not so, and logic only the art of going wrong with confidence.

JOSEPH WOOD KRUTCH, *The Modern Temper*, p. 228.

17

Simple as it seems, it was a great discovery that the key of knowledge could turn both ways, that it could open, as well as lock, the door of power to the many.

JAMES RUSSELL LOWELL, *Among My Books: New England Two Centuries Ago.*

18

All I know is what I read in the papers.

WILL ROGERS, a recurrent line in his stage and radio routines and lectures.

19

An artist may visit a museum, but only a pedant can live there.

GEORGE SANTAYANA, *The Life of Reason,* vol. iv, p. 129.

20

To know that we know what we know, and that we do not know what we do not know, that is true knowledge.

HENRY D. THOREAU, *Walden,* ch. 1. A paraphrase of Confucius.

21

Any piece of knowledge I acquire today has a value at this moment exactly proportioned to my skill to deal with it. Tomorrow, when I know more, I recall that piece of knowledge and use it better.

MARK VAN DOREN, *Liberal Education.*

22

Knowledge, in truth, is the great sun in the firmament. Life and power are scattered with all its beams.

DANIEL WEBSTER, Address at the laying of the cornerstone of Bunker Hill Monument, 1825.

23

Knowledge is the only fountain, both of the love and the principles of human liberty.

DANIEL WEBSTER, Address at the dedication of Bunker Hill Monument, 17 June, 1843.

24

He who binds

His soul to knowledge, steals the key of heaven.

NATHANIEL P. WILLIS, *The Scholar of Thibét Ben Khorat*, pt. ii, l. 6 fr. end.

L

LABOR

See also Industry, Work

1
Labor is discovered to be the grand conqueror, enriching and building up nations more surely than the proudest battles.
WILLIAM ELLERY CHANNING, *War.*

2
Honor lies in honest toil.
GROVER CLEVELAND, Letter, accepting the presidential nomination, 18 Aug., 1884. (STODDARD, *Life of Cleveland*, ch. 15)

3
American labor, which is the capital of our workingmen.
GROVER CLEVELAND, First Annual Message, Dec., 1885.

4
There can be no distress, there can be no hard times, when labor is well paid. The man who raises his hand against the progress of the workingman raises his hand against prosperity.
W. BOURKE COCKRAN, Speech in New York City, 18 Aug., 1896.

5
There is no right to strike against the public safety by anybody, anywhere, any time.
CALVIN COOLIDGE, Telegram to Samuel Gompers, 14 Sept., 1919, referring to a strike by Boston police. This famous message was composed when Coolidge was governor of Massachusetts; it and his forthright handling of the strike brought him national prominence.

6
The American workman who strikes ten blows with his hammer, while the foreign workman only strikes one, is really vanquishing that foreigner, as if the blows were aimed at and told on his person.
EMERSON, *Conduct of Life: Worship.*

7
The path that leads to a loaf of bread
  Winds through the swamps of toil,
And the path that leads to a suit of clothes
  Goes through a flowerless soil,
And the paths that lead to the loaf of bread
And the suit of clothes are hard to tread.
SAM WALTER FOSS, *Paths.*

8
He that hath a trade hath an estate; he that hath a calling hath an office of profit and honor.
BENJAMIN FRANKLIN, *Poor Richard,* 1758.

9
For as labor cannot produce without the use of land, the denial of the equal right to the use of land is necessarily the denial of the right of labor to its own produce.
HENRY GEORGE, *Progress and Poverty,* bk. vii, ch. 1.

10
Labor is the curse of the world, and nobody can meddle with it without becoming proportionately brutified.
NATHANIEL HAWTHORNE, *American Note-Books,* 12 Aug., 1841.

11
All eyes are opened or opening to the rights of man. The general spread of the light of science has already laid open to every view the palpable truth that the mass of mankind has not been born with saddles on their backs nor a few favored few booted and spurred, ready to ride them legitimately, by the grace of God.
THOMAS JEFFERSON, Letter to Roger Weightman, 24 June, 1826.

12
Horny-handed sons of toil.
DENIS KEARNEY (BIG DENNY), Speech in San Francisco, c. 1878.

And blessed are the horny hands of toil.
JAMES RUSSELL LOWELL, *A Glance Behind the Curtain,* l. 205.

13
Labor, like Israel, has many sorrows.
JOHN L. LEWIS, Speech broadcast from Washington, D.C., 3 Sept., 1937.

14
By some it is assumed that labor is available only in connection with capital—that nobody labors unless somebody else owning capital, somehow, by the use of it, induces him to do it. . . . But another class of reasoners . . . hold that labor is prior to, and independent of, capital; that, in fact, capital is the fruit of labor, and could never have existed if labor had not first existed.
ABRAHAM LINCOLN, Address in Milwaukee, 30 Sept., 1859.

15
I hold that if the Almighty had ever made a set of men that should do all the eating and none of the work, He would have made them with mouths only and no hands; and if He had ever made another class that He intended should do all the work and no eating, He would have made them with hands only and no mouths.
ABRAHAM LINCOLN, *Mud-sill Theory of Labor.*

16
One half of the world must sweat and groan that the other half may dream.
HENRY WADSWORTH LONGFELLOW, *Hyperion,* bk. i, ch. 4.

1
The nobility of labor—the long pedigree of toil.
> HENRY WADSWORTH LONGFELLOW, *Nuremberg*.

2
From labor there shall come forth rest.
> HENRY WADSWORTH LONGFELLOW, *To a Child*, l. 162.

3
His brow is wet with honest sweat,
  He earns whate'er he can,
And looks the whole world in the face,
  For he owes not any man.
> HENRY WADSWORTH LONGFELLOW, *The Village Blacksmith*.

4
Toiling—rejoicing—sorrowing,
  Onward through life he goes;
Each morning sees some task begin,
  Each evening sees it close;
Something attempted, something done,
  Has earned a night's repose.
> HENRY WADSWORTH LONGFELLOW, *The Village Blacksmith*.

5
Labor is the handmaid of religion.
> C. H. PARKHURST, *Sermons: Pattern in Mount*.

6
No man needs sympathy because he has to work. . . . Far and away the best prize that life offers is the chance to work hard at work worth doing.
> THEODORE ROOSEVELT, Address in Syracuse, N.Y., Labor Day, 1903.

7
The test of a vocation is the love of the drudgery it involves.
> LOGAN PEARSALL SMITH, *Afterthoughts*.

8
Labor is the law of happiness.
> ABEL STEVENS, *Life of Mme. de Staël*, ch. 16.

9
The workingmen of the world would find their best friend in the carpenter of Nazareth.
> REV. MYRON J. TAYLOR, Sermon at Central Church of Christ, Portsmouth, Ohio, 22 Dec., 1963. This service gained national attention when it was attended by a visiting Russian Communist, Victor Pozdneyev, his wife, and their two children, who spent the Christmas holidays with a Portsmouth family at the invitation of that city's Junior Chamber of Commerce, to observe Christmas in the home of a typical American family.

10
Great thoughts hallow any labor.
> HENRY D. THOREAU, *Journal*, 20 Apr., 1841.

11
The callous palms of the laborer are conversant with finer tissues of self-respect and heroism, whose touch thrills the heart, than the languid fingers of idleness.
> HENRY D. THOREAU, *Walking*.

12
Heaven is blessed with perfect rest but the blessing of earth is toil.
> HENRY VAN DYKE, *The Toiling of Felix*.

13
No race can prosper till it learns that there is as much dignity in tilling a field as in writing a poem.
> BOOKER T. WASHINGTON, *Up from Slavery*.

14
Labor in this country is independent and proud. It has not to ask the patronage of capital, but capital solicits the aid of labor.
> DANIEL WEBSTER, Speech, Apr., 1824.

LANGUAGE

See also Grammar, Speech, Words

15
We cannot call a man educated who does not know how to use the language, including the language of science, mathematics. But our specialized men today all too often speak in strangely fractionated jargons and do not understand even the words—let alone the rationale—of other eminent specialists. To make communication more meaningful, to make possible wiser judgments on modern complex problems, the ivory tower of Babel must come down.
> MILTON S. EISENHOWER, *The Need for a New American; The Educational Record*, Oct., 1963, p. 306.

16
Language is the archives of history. . . .
Language is fossil poetry.
> EMERSON, *Essays, Second Series: The Poet*.

17
The language of the street is always strong.
> EMERSON, *Journals*, 1840.

18
Language is a city to the building of which every human being brought a stone.
> EMERSON, *Letters and Social Aims: Quotation and Originality*.

19
I like to be beholden to the great metropolitan English speech, the sea which receives tributaries from every region under heaven.
> EMERSON, *Society and Solitude: Books*.

20
Language,—human language,—after all is but little better than the croak and cackle of fowls, and other utterances of brute nature, —sometimes not so adequate.
> NATHANIEL HAWTHORNE, *American Note-Books*, 14 July, 1850.

1
Every language is a temple, in which the soul of those who speak it is enshrined.
> OLIVER WENDELL HOLMES, *The Professor at the Breakfast-Table,* ch. 2.

2
Language is the picture and counterpart of thought.
> MARK HOPKINS, Address, 1 Dec., 1841.

3
Today the cost of failure to communicate is not silence or serenity but destruction and disillusion.
> LYNDON B. JOHNSON, Address at Georgetown University, marking the 175th anniversary of that school; Washington, D.C., 3 Dec., 1964.

4
The American language differs from English in that it seeks the top of expression while English seeks its lowly valleys.
> SALVADOR DE MADARIAGA, *Americans Are Boys.*

5
Language, as well as the faculty of speech, was the immediate gift of God.
> NOAH WEBSTER, Preface to his Dictionary.

6
Language is the expression of ideas, and if the people of one country cannot preserve an identity of ideas they cannot retain an identity of language.
> NOAH WEBSTER, Preface to his Dictionary.

LATENESS

See also Delay

7
Ah! nothing is too late
Till the tired heart shall cease to palpitate.
> HENRY WADSWORTH LONGFELLOW, *Morituri Salutamus,* st. 24.

8
Better late than never, as Noah remarked to the Zebra, which had understood that passengers arrived in alphabetical order.
> BERT LESTON TAYLOR, *The So-Called Human Race,* p. 265.

9
If you're there before it's over, you're on time.
> JAMES J. WALKER, Remark to reporters, on arriving late at a dinner, Oct., 1931.

LAUGHTER

10
In the language of screen comedians four of the main grades of laugh are the titter, the yowl, the belly laugh and the boffo. The titter is just a titter. The yowl is a runaway titter. Anyone who has ever had the pleasure knows all about a belly laugh. The boffo is the laugh that kills.
> JAMES AGEE, *Comedy's Greatest Era; Life,* 5 Sept., 1949.

11
Laffing iz the sensation ov pheeling good all over, and showing it principally in one spot.
> JOSH BILLINGS, *Laffing.*

12
Laughter's never an end, it's a by-product.
> STRUTHERS BURT, *Festival,* ch. 13.

13
Always Leave Them Laughing When You Say Good-bye.
> GEORGE M. COHAN, Title of song.

14
Beware you don't laugh, for then you show all your faults.
> EMERSON, *Conduct of Life: Behavior.*

15
To see the Kaiser's epitaph
Would make a weeping willow laugh.
> OLIVER HERFORD, *The Laughing Willow.* Sometimes paraphrased to include figures from more recent history.

16
Laughter and tears are meant to turn the wheels of the same sensibility; one is windpower and the other water-power, that is all.
> OLIVER WENDELL HOLMES, *The Autocrat of the Breakfast-Table,* ch. 4.

17
I'd rather laugh, a bright-haired boy,
Than reign, a gray-beard king.
> OLIVER WENDELL HOLMES, *The Old Man Dreams.*

18
When laughter is humble, when it is not based on self-esteem, it is wiser than tears.
> GEORGE SANTAYANA, *Soliloquies in England.*

19
If life were always merry,
  Our souls would seek relief
And rest from weary laughter
  In the quiet arms of grief.
> HENRY VAN DYKE, *If All the Skies Were Sunshine.*

20
The laughter of man is the contentment of God.
> JOHAN WEISS, *Wit, Humor, and Shakespeare.*

21
Laugh and the world laughs with you
  Weep and you weep alone,
For the sad old earth must borrow its mirth,
  But has trouble enough of its own.
> ELLA WHEELER WILCOX, *Solitude.* This first appeared in the New York *Sun,* 25 Feb., 1883.

LAW

1

Laws are not masters but servants, and he rules them who obeys them.

> HENRY WARD BEECHER, *Proverbs from Plymouth Pulpit: Political.*

2

Laws and institutions are constantly tending to gravitate. Like clocks, they must be occasionally cleansed, and wound up, and set to true time.

> HENRY WARD BEECHER, *Life Thoughts.*

3

Law is whatever is boldly asserted and plausibly maintained.

> AARON BURR. (PARTON, *Life and Times of Aaron Burr,* vol. i, p. 149)

4

The absolute justice of the State, enlightened by the perfect reason of the State: that is law.

> RUFUS CHOATE, *Conservative Force of the American Bar.*

5

No man has ever yet been hanged for breaking the spirit of a law.

> GROVER CLEVELAND. (RHODES, *History of the United States,* vol. viii, p. 403; HIBBEN, *Peerless Leader,* p. 155)

6

Let a man keep the law,—any law,—and his way will be strewn with satisfactions.

> EMERSON, *Essays, First Series: Prudence.*

7

No law can be sacred to me but that of my nature. Good and bad are but names very readily transferable to that or this; the only right is what is after my own constitution; the only wrong what is against it.

> EMERSON, *Essays, First Series: Self-Reliance.*

8

Good men must not obey the laws too well.

> EMERSON, *Essays, Second Series: Politics.*

9

The wise know that foolish legislation is a rope of sand which perishes in the twisting.

> EMERSON, *Essays, Second Series: Politics.*

10

Any laws but those we make for ourselves are laughable.

> EMERSON, *Essays, Second Series: Politics.*

11

Things have their laws as well as men, and things refuse to be trifled with.

> EMERSON, *Essays, Second Series: Politics.*

12

Laws like to cobwebs, catch small flies,
Great ones break them before your eyes.

> BENJAMIN FRANKLIN, *Poor Richard,* 1734.

13

Laws too gentle are seldom obeyed; too severe, seldom executed.

> BENJAMIN FRANKLIN, *Poor Richard,* 1756.

14

I know no method to secure the repeal of bad or obnoxious laws so effective as their stringent execution.

> U. S. GRANT, Inaugural Address, 4 Mar., 1869.

15

One of the current notions that holds subtle capacity for serious mischief is a view of the judicial function that seems increasingly coming into vogue. This is that all deficiencies in our society which have failed of correction by other means should find a cure in the courts . . . Some well-meaning people apparently believe that the judicial, rather than the political, process is more likely to breed better solutions of pressing or thorny problems. This is a compliment to the judiciary, but untrue to democratic principle.

> JOHN MARSHALL HARLAN, Address at the annual convention, American Bar Association, Chicago, Aug., 1963. (*Time,* 23 Aug., 1963, p. 17)

16

It is only rogues who feel the restraint of law.

> JOSIAH G. HOLLAND, *Gold-Foil: Perfect Liberty.*

17

Laws that do not embody public opinion can never be enforced.

> ELBERT HUBBARD, *Epigrams.*

For law is meaningless if there is no public will to observe it. And this public will, in turn, can exist only when the law is just and deserving of honor. . . . There are not enough jails, not enough policemen, not enough courts to enforce a law not supported by the people.

> HUBERT H. HUMPHREY, Address in Williamsburg, Va., 1 May, 1965.

18

We cannot expect to breed respect for law and order among people who do not share the fruits of our freedom.

> HUBERT H. HUMPHREY, Address in Williamsburg, Va., 1 May, 1965.

19

Laws spring from the instinct of self-preservation.

> ROBERT G. INGERSOLL, *Some Mistakes of Moses.*

20

Were it made a question whether no law, as among the savage Americans, or too much law, as among the civilized Europeans, submits man to the greatest evil, one who has seen both conditions of existence would pronounce it to be the last; and that the sheep are happier of themselves, than under the care of wolves.

> THOMAS JEFFERSON, *Writings,* vol. ii, p. 128.

1

A strict observance of the written laws is doubtless one of the high virtues of a good citizen, but it is not the highest. The laws of necessity, of self-preservation, of saving our country when in danger, are of higher obligation.

> THOMAS JEFFERSON, *Writings,* vol. xii, p. 418.

2

I did not become President to preside over mounting violence and deepening disorder.

> LYNDON B. JOHNSON, Speech to 264 leading U.S. business executives at the White House, 23 July, 1964. He referred to outbreaks of racial violence in Mississippi, Georgia, and New York City during the summer of that year. The statement is a paraphrase of Winston Churchill: "I have not become the King's First Minister in order to preside over the liquidation of the British Empire."

3

There is no greater wrong, in our democracy, than violent, willful disregard of law.

> LYNDON B. JOHNSON, Public Statement, 15 Aug., 1965, referring to rioting in Los Angeles at that time.

4

We prefer world law, in the age of self-determination, to world war in the age of mass extermination.

> JOHN F. KENNEDY, Address to the United Nations General Assembly, 25 Sept., 1961.

5

Despotism and anarchy prevail when a constitutional order does not exist. Both are lawless and arbitrary. Indeed, despotism may be defined as the anarchy of lawless rulers, and anarchy as the despotism of lawless crowds.

> WALTER LIPPMANN, *The Public Philosophy* (1955), bk. ii, ch. 11.

6

The best use of good laws is to teach men to trample bad laws under their feet.

> WENDELL PHILLIPS, Speech, 12 Apr., 1852.

7

No man is above the law and no man is below it; nor do we ask any man's permission when we require him to obey it.

> THEODORE ROOSEVELT, Message, Jan., 1904.

8

It is a form of anarchy to say that a person need not comply with a particular statute with which he disagrees. Ours is a government of laws, not of men, and our system cannot tolerate the philosophy that obedience to law rests upon the personal likes or dislikes of any individual citizen, whether he supports or opposes the statute in question.

> RICHARD RUSSELL, Speech in Rome, Ga.,

15 July, 1964. He was specifically urging compliance with the recently enacted 1964 civil rights act, against which he had led the Southerners' unsuccessful fight in the Senate.

9

I will not say with Lord Hale, that "The law will admit of no rival," . . . but I will say that it is a jealous mistress, and requires a long and constant courtship. It is not to be won by trifling favors, but by lavish homage.

> JOSEPH STORY, *The Value and Importance of Legal Studies.* (*Miscellaneous Writings,* p. 523)

10

The Law: It has honored us, may we honor it.

> DANIEL WEBSTER, Toast at the Charleston Bar dinner, 10 May, 1847.

11

Law is the crystallization of the habit and thought of society.

> WOODROW WILSON, Lecture at Princeton University, 1893.

12

What we seek is the reign of law, based upon the consent of the governed and sustained by the organized opinion of mankind.

> WOODROW WILSON, Speech at Mount Vernon, 4 July, 1918. The reference was to the League of Nations.

13

No person shall be . . . deprived of life, liberty, or property, without due process of law.

> Bill of Rights, Article v (25 Sept., 1789). Submitted by the First Congress at its first session. The Bill of Rights was adopted 15 Dec., 1791, as the first ten amendments of the U.S. Constitution.

14

No state shall make or enforce any law which shall abridge the privileges or immunities of the citizens of the United States; nor shall any state deprive any person of life, liberty or property without due process of law, nor deny to any person within its jurisdiction the equal protection of the laws.

> Constitution of the United States, 14th Amendment (28 July, 1868)

LAWYERS

15

No use pounding on the log. The coon's out.

> SILAS BRYAN, to lawyers who pleaded their cases before him. (HIBBEN, *The Peerless Leader,* p. 6)

16

The good lawyer is not the man who has an eye to every side and angle of contingency, and qualifies all his qualifications, but who throws himself on your part so heartily, that he can get you out of a scrape.

> EMERSON. *Conduct of Life: Power.*

1

God works wonders now and then;
Behold! a lawyer, an honest man.
>   BENJAMIN FRANKLIN, *Poor Richard*,
>   1733.

2

Necessity has no law; I know some attorneys
of the same.
>   BENJAMIN FRANKLIN, *Poor Richard*,
>   1734.

3

A good lawyer, a bad neighbor.
>   BENJAMIN FRANKLIN, *Poor Richard*, 1737,
>   quoting the French: *"Bon avocat, mau-*
>   *vais voisin."*

4

When lawyers take what they would give
And doctors give what they would take.
>   OLIVER WENDELL HOLMES, *Latter-Day*
>   *Warnings.*

5

That one hundred and fifty lawyers should
do business together is not to be expected.
>   THOMAS JEFFERSON, *Writings*, vol. i, p. 86.
>   He was referring to lawyers, "whose
>   trade is talking," as members of Con-
>   gress.

6

The study of the law is useful in a variety of
points of view. It qualifies a man to be useful to himself, to his neighbors and to the
public. It is the most certain stepping-stone
in a political line.
>   THOMAS JEFFERSON, *Writings,* vol. viii, p.
>   17.

7

Discourage litigation. Persuade your neighbors to compromise whenever you can. . . .
As a peace-maker the lawyer has a superior
opportunity of being a good man. There will
still be business enough.
>   ABRAHAM LINCOLN, Notes for Law Lec-
>   ture, 1 July, 1850. (STERN, *Writings of*
>   *Lincoln,* p. 328)

8

Why is there always a secret singing
When a lawyer cashes in?
Why does a hearse horse snicker
Hauling a lawyer away?
>   CARL SANDBURG, *The Lawyers Know Too*
>   *Much.*

9

Most good lawyers live well, work hard and
die poor.
>   DANIEL WEBSTER, Speech in Charleston,
>   S.C., 10 May, 1847.

10

The New England folks have a saying that
three Philadelphia lawyers are a match for
the very devil himself.
>   UNKNOWN, Salem *Observer,* 13 Mar.,
>   1824.

We have an expression in New York, when
we meet a very difficult problem—"You will
have to get a Philadelphia lawyer to solve
that." Few people know that there is a basis
of truth in the expression, for in 1735, when
no New York lawyer could be obtained to
defend John Peter Zenger, accused of criminal libel, because his two lawyers, James Alexander and William Smith, having chal-
lenged the jurisdiction of the court, had already been disbarred, the friends of Zenger
came to Philadelphia and obtained the services of Andrew Hamilton, then eighty years
of age, to go to New York without fee, and
defend the action in the face of a hostile
court.
>   HARRY WEINBERGER, Address: *The Lib-*
>   *erty of the Press,* Independence Hall,
>   Philadelphia, 9 Mar., 1934.

LEADER

11

A leader is best
When people barely know that he exists.
>   WITTER BYNNER, *The Way of Life Ac-*
>   *cording to Laotzu.*

12

The greatest leader of our time has been
struck down by the foulest deed of our
time.
>   LYNDON B. JOHNSON, to joint session of
>   Congress, 27 Nov., 1963, five days after
>   the assassination of John F. Kennedy.

13

The final test of a leader is that he leaves
behind him in other men the conviction and
the will to carry on.
>   WALTER LIPPMANN, Column, in tribute to
>   Franklin D. Roosevelt, 14 Apr., 1945.

14

As I stand aloof and look there is to me
something profoundly affecting in large
masses of men following the lead of
those who do not believe in men.
>   WALT WHITMAN, *Thought.*

LEISURE
See also Idleness, Sport

15

Leisure pastime in this country has become
so complicated that it is now hard work.
. . . We are not far from the time when a
man after a hard weekend of leisure will go
thankfully off to his job to unwind.
>   RUSSELL BAKER, "Observer" Column, New
>   York *Times,* 28 July, 1964.

16

Viewed in the long perspective, it is ironic, if
not fantastic, that easing the burden of toil
should be viewed as a problem and not as a
blessing. Since time immemorial, men's lives
have been constricted by the need for exhausting labor, as they still are in many parts

of the world. We should rejoice that technology is now freeing us from that burden.

> BRUCE BLIVEN, *Using Our Leisure Is No Easy Job; New York Times Magazine*, 26 Apr., 1964, p. 115.

1

I feel like a locomotive hitched to a boy's express wagon.

> GROVER CLEVELAND, in 1897, upon being asked how it felt to have no official responsibility. (McELROY, *Grover Cleveland*, ii, 269)

2

Is there no road now to Leisurely Lane? We traveled it long ago!
A place for the lagging of leisurely steps, sweet and shady and slow.

> VIRGINIA WOODWARD CLOUD, *Leisurely Lane*.

3

Sweet is the pleasure itself cannot spoil.
Is not true leisure one with true toil?

> JOHN S. DWIGHT, *True Rest*.

4

A life of leisure and a life of laziness are two things.

> BENJAMIN FRANKLIN, *Poor Richard*, 1746.

5

Employ thy time well if thou meanest to gain leisure.

> BENJAMIN FRANKLIN, *Poor Richard*, 1758.

6

Leisure is the time for doing something useful.

> NATHANIEL HOWE, *A Chapter of Proverbs*.

7

He enjoys true leisure who has time to improve his soul's estate.

> HENRY D. THOREAU, *Journal*, 11 Feb., 1840.

8

A broad margin of leisure is as beautiful in a man's life as in a book.

> HENRY D. THOREAU, *Journal*, 28 Dec., 1852.

LENDING, see Borrowing

LETTERS

9

Not even a formal autobiography is quite so revealing as the relaxed, informal words a man sets down at a particular place and time for the eyes of a friend.

> CARLOS BAKER, *A Search for the Man As He Really Was; New York Times Book Review*, 26 July, 1964, p. 4.

10

Carrier of news and knowledge,
Instrument of trade and industry,
Promoter of mutual acquaintance,
Of peace and good-will
Among men and nations.

> CHARLES W. ELIOT, Inscription on south-

east corner of post office, Washington, D.C.

11

Messenger of sympathy and love,
Servant of parted friends,
Consoler of the lonely,
Bond of the scattered family,
Enlarger of the common life.

> CHARLES W. ELIOT, Inscription on southwest corner of post office, Washington, D.C.

12

The tongue is prone to lose the way,
Not so the pen, for in a letter
We have not better things to say,
But surely say them better.

> EMERSON, *Life*.

13

For my part, I could easily do without the post-office. . . . I never received more than one or two letters in my life that were worth the postage.

> HENRY D. THOREAU, *Walden*, ch. 2.

LIBERTY

See also Freedom

14

The broad goal of our foreign policy is to enable the people of the United States to enjoy in peace the blessings of liberty.

> JOHN FOSTER DULLES, Address before the Foreign Policy Association, New York City, 16 Feb., 1955.

15

Liberty is always dangerous, but it is the safest thing we have.

> HARRY EMERSON FOSDICK, *Liberty*.

16

Those, who would give up essential liberty to purchase a little temporary safety, deserve neither liberty nor safety.

> Attributed to BENJAMIN FRANKLIN. In *Historical Review of Pennsylvania* (1759), and often heard during the Revolutionary period.

17

Only in fetters is liberty:
Without its banks could a river be?

> LOUIS GINSBERG, *Fetters*.

18

Is life so dear or peace so sweet as to be purchased at the price of chains and slavery? Forbid it, Almighty God! I know not what course others may take; but as for me, give me liberty, or give me death!

> PATRICK HENRY, Speech in Virginia House of Delegates, 23 Mar., 1775.

19

Sir, we are not weak if we make a proper use of those means which the God of nature hath placed in our power. Three millions of people, armed in the holy cause of liberty, and in such a country as that which we possess, are invincible by any force which our enemy can send against us.

> PATRICK HENRY, Speech in Virginia House of Delegates, 23 Mar., 1775.

1

Liberty is the breath of progress.

> ROBERT G. INGERSOLL, *How to Reform Mankind.*

2

The tree of liberty must be refreshed from time to time with the blood of patriots and tyrants. It is its natural manure.

> THOMAS JEFFERSON, Letter to William S. Smith, Paris, 13 Nov., 1787. (*Writings,* iv, 467)

3

The God who gave us life, gave us liberty at the same time.

> THOMAS JEFFERSON, *Summary View of the Rights of British America.*

4

The ground of liberty must be gained by inches.

> THOMAS JEFFERSON, *Writings,* vol. viii, p. 3.

5

We are not to expect to be translated from despotism to liberty in a feather bed.

> THOMAS JEFFERSON, *Writings,* vol. viii, p. 13.

6

The boisterous sea of liberty is never without a wave.

> THOMAS JEFFERSON, *Writings,* vol. xv, p. 283.

7

The purpose of liberty is not merely to allow error but to discover truth, not only to restrict the powers of the government but to enrich the judgment of the nation.

> LYNDON B. JOHNSON, Speech at graduation exercises of the National Cathedral School for Girls, Washington, D.C., 1 June, 1965.

8

The deadliest foe of democracy is not autocracy but liberty frenzied. Liberty is not foolproof. For its beneficent working it demands self-restraint.

> OTTO KAHN, Speech at the University of Wisconsin, Madison, 14 Jan., 1918.

9

Let every nation know, whether it wishes us well or ill, that we shall pay any price, bear any burden, meet any hardship, support any friend, oppose any foe to assure the survival and the success of liberty.

> JOHN F. KENNEDY, Inaugural Address, 20 Jan., 1961.

10

The world has never had a good definition of the word liberty, and the American people, just now, are much in want of one. We all declare for liberty; but in using the same word we do not all mean the same thing. With some the word liberty may mean for each man to do as he pleases with himself, and the product of his labor; while with others the same word may mean for some men to do as they please with other men, and the product of other men's labor. Here are two, not only different, but incompatible things, called by the same name, liberty. And it follows that each of the things is, by the respective parties, called by two different and incompatible names—liberty and tyranny.

> ABRAHAM LINCOLN, Address in Baltimore, 18 Apr., 1864.

11

My hope is that both liberty and democracy can be preserved before the one destroys the other. Whether this can be done is the question of our time, what with more than half the world denying and despairing of it.

> WALTER LIPPMANN, *The Public Philosophy,* bk. i, ch. 1 (1955).

12

The inescapable price of liberty is an ability to preserve it from destruction.

> GENERAL DOUGLAS MACARTHUR, to President Quezon of the Philippine Islands. (MILLER, *MacArthur,* p. 192)

13

The history of the world shows that republics and democracies have generally lost their liberties by way of passing from civilian to quasi-military status. Nothing is more conducive to arbitrary rule than the military junta.

> GENERAL DOUGLAS MACARTHUR. (*General's Words Live On;* New York *Herald Tribune,* 6 Apr., 1964, p. 15)

14

He that would make his own liberty secure must guard even his enemy from oppression.

> THOMAS PAINE, *Dissertation on First Principles of Government,* p. 242.

15

Eternal vigilance is the price of liberty.

> WENDELL PHILLIPS, Address: *Public Opinion,* before the Massachusetts Antislavery Society, 28 Jan., 1852. When it was said that Phillips was quoting Thomas Jefferson, he challenged one and all to find this famous statement in the works of Jefferson or anyone else. The statement has also been attributed to Patrick Henry. A close approximation of it appears in a speech by the Irish judge John Philpot Curran, 10 July, 1790.

16

The manna of popular liberty must be gathered each day, or it is rotten. . . . Only by uninterrupted agitation can a people be kept sufficiently awake to principle not to let liberty be smothered by material prosperity.

Republics exist only on tenure of being agitated.

> WENDELL PHILLIPS, Address: *Public Opinion,* Boston, 28 Jan., 1852.

1

Liberty, when it begins to take root, is a plant of rapid growth.

> GEORGE WASHINGTON, Letter to James Madison, 2 Mar., 1788.

2

If the true spark of religious and civil liberty be kindled, it will burn. Human agency cannot extinguish it.

> DANIEL WEBSTER, Address at Bunker Hill Monument, 17 June, 1825.

3

God grants liberty only to those who love it, and are always ready to guard and defend it.

> DANIEL WEBSTER, Speech in U.S. Senate, 3 June, 1834.

4

Liberty exists in proportion to wholesome restraint; the more restraint on others to keep off from us, the more liberty we have.

> DANIEL WEBSTER, Speech, 10 May, 1847.

5

Liberty has never come from the government. Liberty has always come from the subjects of it. The history of liberty is a history of resistance. The history of liberty is a history of limitations of governmental power, not the increase of it.

> WOODROW WILSON, Speech before New York Press Club, 9 Sept., 1912.

6

I would rather belong to a poor nation that was free than to a rich nation that had ceased to be in love with liberty. We shall not be poor if we love liberty.

> WOODROW WILSON, Speech in Mobile, Ala., 27 Oct., 1912.

7

Liberty does not consist in mere general declarations of the rights of men. It consists in the translation of those declarations into definite action.

> WOODROW WILSON, Address in Independence Hall, Philadelphia, 4 July, 1914.

8

A liberty to do that only which is good, just, and honest.

> JOHN WINTHROP, *Life and Letters*, ii, 341.

9

The thing they forget is that liberty and freedom and democracy are so very precious that you do not fight to win them once and stop.

> SERGEANT ALVIN C. YORK. Quoted by Franklin D. Roosevelt in an Armistice Day speech, 11 Nov., 1941, as a reply to those who were then saying that

World War I had been a futile struggle.

LIBRARY
See also Books, Reading

10

The richest minds need not large libraries.

> AMOS BRONSON ALCOTT, *Table Talk: Learning-Books.*

11

A library is but the soul's burial-ground. It is the land of shadows.

> HENRY WARD BEECHER, *Star Papers: Oxford, The Bodleian Library.*

12

Libries niver encouraged lithrachoor anny more thin tombstones encourage livin'. No wan iver wrote annythin' because he was tol' that a hundherd years fr'm now his books might be taken down fr'm a shelf in a granite sepulcher an' some wan wud write "Good" or "This man is crazy" in th' margin. What lithrachoor needs is fillin' food.

> FINLEY PETER DUNNE, *Dissertations by Mr. Dooley: The Carnegie Libraries.*

13

Consider what you have in the smallest chosen library. A company of the wisest and wittiest men that could be picked out of all civil countries, in a thousand years, have set in best order the results of their learning and wisdom. The men themselves were hid and inaccessible, solitary, impatient of interruption, fenced by etiquette; but the thought which they did not uncover to their bosom friend is here written out in transparent words to us, the strangers of another age.

> EMERSON, *Society and Solitude: Books.*

14

Meek young men grow up in libraries.

> EMERSON, *Nature, Addresses and Lectures: The American Scholar.*

15

Every library should try to be complete on something, if it were only the history of pinheads.

> OLIVER WENDELL HOLMES, *The Poet at the Breakfast-Table*, ch. 8.

16

I have often thought that nothing would do more extensive good at small expense than the establishment of a small circulating library in every county, to consist of a few well-chosen books, to be lent to the people of the county, under such regulations as would secure their safe return in due time.

> THOMAS JEFFERSON, *Writings*, vol. xii, p. 282.

17

Libraries can be of indispensable service in lifting the dead weight of poverty and ignorance.

> FRANCIS KEPPEL, Address at opening session of annual American Library Associ-

ation conference, St. Louis, 28 June, 1964. He was speaking as U.S. Commissioner of Education.

LIES AND LYING
See also Deceit, Truth

1
McCarthy is the only major politician in the country who can be labeled "liar" without fear of libel.

> JOSEPH AND STEWART ALSOP, Syndicated Column, 3 Dec., 1953. Referring to the late Senator from Wisconsin. (RICHARD H. ROVERE, *Senator Joe McCarthy*, p. 52)

2
A little inaccuracy saves a world of explanation.

> C. E. AYRES, *Science, the False Messiah*.

3
In all matters which concern my daughter I would have you lie like a gentleman.

> JAMES BRANCH CABELL, *Jurgen*, p. 64.

4
Every violation of truth is not only a sort of suicide in the liar, but is a stab at the health of human society.

> EMERSON, *Essays, First Series: Prudence*.

5
Figures won't lie, but liars will figure.

> GENERAL CHARLES H. GROSVENOR, who, as a Representative from Ohio, was famous for his predictions of presidential elections.

6
Sin has many tools, but a lie is the handle which fits them all.

> OLIVER WENDELL HOLMES, *The Autocrat of the Breakfast-Table*, ch. 6.

7
A good lie for its own sake is ever pleasing to honest men, but a patched up record never.

> ELBERT HUBBARD, *The Philistine*, vol. i, p. 88.

8
It is better to be lied about than to lie.

> ELBERT HUBBARD, *The Philistine*, vol. xi, p. 48.

9
There is no vice so mean, so pitiful, so contemptible; and he who permits himself to tell a lie once, finds it much easier to do it a second and third time, till at length it becomes habitual.

> THOMAS JEFFERSON, *Writings*, vol. v, p. 83.

10
Men cannot live with a lie and not be stained by it.

> LYNDON B. JOHNSON, Address upon signing the voting-rights law of 1965, 6 Aug., 1965. He was referring to earlier denial of such a right, specifically to Negroes, in the face of a profession of equal rights for all.

11
There is nothing so pathetic as a forgetful liar.

> F. M. KNOWLES, *A Cheerful Year Book*.

12
Statistics are like alienists—they will testify for either side.

> F. H. LA GUARDIA, *The Banking Investigations; Liberty*, 13 May, 1933.

13
> The nimble lie
> Is like the second-hand upon a clock;
> We see it fly, while the hour-hand of truth
> Seems to stand still, and yet it moves unseen,
> And wins at last, for the clock will not strike
> Till it has reached the goal.

> HENRY WADSWORTH LONGFELLOW, *Michael Angelo*, pt. iii, sec. 5.

14
Men lie, who lack courage to tell truth.

> JOAQUIN MILLER, *Ina*, sc. iii.

15
> But a lie, whatever the guise it wears,
> Is a lie, as it was of yore.
> And a truth that has lasted a million years
> Is good for a million more!

> TED OLSON, *Things That Endure*.

16
Equivocation is half-way to lying, as lying the whole way to hell.

> WILLIAM PENN, *Fruits of Solitude*, p. 36.

17
The only thing that ever came back from the grave that we know of was a lie.

> MARILLA M. RICKER, *The Philistine*, vol. 25, p. 101.

18
I have no use for liars, national, international, or those found in private life.

> THEODORE ROOSEVELT, Speech at Arlington Cemetery.

19
If the Republicans stop telling lies about us, we will stop telling the truth about them.

> ADLAI E. STEVENSON, Speech in Bakersfield, Calif., during the 1952 presidential campaign.

20
Figures often beguile me, particularly when I have the arranging of them myself; in which case the remark attributed to Disraeli would often apply with justice and force: "There are three kinds of lies: lies, damned lies, and statistics."

> MARK TWAIN, *Autobiography*, vol. i, p. 246.

21
An experienced, industrious, ambitious, and often quite picturesque liar.

> MARK TWAIN, *My Military Campaign*.

1
One of the striking differences between a cat and a lie is that a cat has only nine lives.

MARK TWAIN, *Pudd'nhead Wilson's Calendar.*

2
There are 869 different forms of lying, but only one of them has been squarely forbidden. Thou shalt not bear false witness against thy neighbor.

MARK TWAIN, *Pudd'nhead Wilson's New Calendar.*

3
Ananias Club.

UNKNOWN, Name given by the press to an imaginary association composed of those whom Theodore Roosevelt had termed liars, beginning with Senator Tillman in 1906.

LIFE

4
Gosh! I feel like a real good cry!
Life, he says, is a cheat, a fake.
Well, I agree with the grouchy guy—
The best you get is an even break.

FRANKLIN P. ADAMS, *Ballade of Schopenhauer's Philosophy.*

5
The less of routine, the more of life.

A. B. ALCOTT, *Table Talk: Habits.*

6
One must have lived greatly whose record would bear the full light of day from beginning to its close.

A. B. ALCOTT, *Table Talk: Learning.*

7
God asks no man whether he will accept life. That is not the choice. You *must* take it. The only choice is *how.*

HENRY WARD BEECHER, *Life Thoughts.*

8
There is an eternity behind and an eternity before, and this little speck in the center, however long, is comparatively but a minute.

JOHN BROWN, after his arrest at Harper's Ferry, Oct., 1859.

9
Life is just a bowl of cherries.

LEW BROWN AND RAY HENDERSON, Title and opening line of song (1931), from *George White's Scandals,* 11th ed. Words and music by Brown and Henderson.

10
So live, that when thy summons comes to join
The innumerable caravan, which moves
To that mysterious realm, where each shall take
His chamber in the silent halls of death,
Thou go not, like the quarry-slave at night,
Scourged to his dungeon, but, sustained and soothed
By an unfaltering trust, approach thy grave
Like one who wraps the drapery of his couch
About him, and lies down to pleasant dreams.

WILLIAM CULLEN BRYANT, *Thanatopsis.*

11
Life is a fragment, a moment between two eternities, influenced by all that has preceded, and to influence all that follows. The only way to illumine it is by extent of view.

WILLIAM ELLERY CHANNING, *Note-book: Life.*

12
To live content with small means; to seek elegance rather than luxury, and refinement rather than fashion; to be worthy, not respectable, and wealthy, not rich; to study hard, think quietly, talk frankly; to listen to stars and birds, to babes and sages, with open heart; to bear all cheerfully, do all bravely, await occasion, hurry never; in a word, to let the spiritual, unbidden and unconscious, grow up through the common: this is to be my symphony.

WILLIAM HENRY CHANNING, *My Symphony.*

13
Life's a very funny proposition you can bet,
And no one's solved the problem properly as yet;
Young for a day, then old and gray, . . .
Life's a very funny proposition after all.

GEORGE M. COHAN, *Life's a Funny Proposition* (from *Little Johnny Jones,* 1907).

14
I took one draught of life,
I'll tell you what I paid,
Precisely an existence—
The market-price, they said.

EMILY DICKINSON, *Further Poems,* CXX.

15
Life is a mystery as deep as ever death can be;
Yet oh, how dear it is to us, this life we live and see!

MARY MAPES DODGE, *The Two Mysteries.*

16
If ye live enough befure thirty ye won't care to live at all afther fifty.

FINLEY PETER DUNNE, *Mr. Dooley's Philosophy: Casual Observations.*

17
Only a life lived for others is a life worth while.

ALBERT EINSTEIN. (*Youth,* June, 1932)

18
Science, rapidly giving us the means to build a new world, does not tell us what kind of world it should be or how we as individuals and citizens can live in it. Perhaps it is . . .

that the more able we are to control life, the less able we are to live it.

> MILTON S. EISENHOWER, *The Need for a New American; The Educational Record,* Oct., 1963, p. 304.

1

Life is a boundless privilege, and when you pay for your ticket, and get into the car, you have no guess what good company you will find there.

> EMERSON, *Conduct of Life: Considerations by the Way.*

2

Life is an ecstasy.

> EMERSON, *Conduct of Life: Fate.*

3

The life of man is the true romance, which, when it is valiantly conducted, will yield the imagination a higher joy than any fiction.

> EMERSON, *Essays, First Series: New England Reformers.*

4

Life is a series of surprises, and would not be worth taking or keeping if it were not.

> EMERSON, *Essays, Second Series: Experience.*

5

We are always getting ready to live, but never living.

> EMERSON, *Journals,* vol. iii, p. 276.

6

All life is an experiment. The more experiments you make the better.

> EMERSON, *Journals.*

7

Life's well enough, but we shall be glad to get out of it, and they will all be glad to have us.

> EMERSON, *Representative Men: Montaigne.*

8

No power of genius has ever yet had the smallest success in explaining existence. The perfect enigma remains.

> EMERSON, *Representative Men: Plato.*

9

Fill my hour, ye gods, so that I may not say, whilst I have done this, "Behold, also, an hour of my life is gone,"—but rather, "I have lived an hour."

> EMERSON, *Society and Solitude: Works and Days.*

10

Life is too short to waste
  In critic peep or cynic bark,
Quarrel or reprimand;
  'Twill soon be dark;
Up! mind thine own aim and
  God save the mark!

> EMERSON, *To J. W.*

11

Though we sometimes speak of a primrose path, we all know that a bad life is just as difficult, just as full of obstacles and hardships, as a good one. . . . The only choice is

in the kind of life one would care to spend one's efforts on.

> JOHN ERSKINE. (DURANT, *On the Meaning of Life,* p. 41)

12

I should have no objection to a repetition of the same life from its beginning, only asking the advantages authors have in a second edition to correct some faults of the first.

> BENJAMIN FRANKLIN, *Autobiography,* ch. 1.

13

This is rather an embryo state, a preparation for living.

> BENJAMIN FRANKLIN, Letter to Miss Hubbard, 23 Feb., 1756. Referring to life as a preparation for a finer afterlife.

14

Wish not so much to live long as to live well.

> BENJAMIN FRANKLIN, *Poor Richard,* 1738.

15

He was integrated into life,
He was a member of life,
He was harmonized, orchestrated, identified
  with the program of being.

> ZONA GALE, *Walt Whitman.*

16

A noble life, crowned with heroic death, rises above and outlives the pride and pomp and glory of the mightiest empire of the earth.

> JAMES A. GARFIELD, Speech in the House of Representatives, 9 Dec., 1858.

17

Not whence, but why and whither are the vital questions.

> A. W. GREELY, *Reminiscences,* p. 338.

18

Life is made up of sobs, sniffles, and smiles, with sniffles predominating.

> O. HENRY, *Gifts of the Magi.*

19

It is my business to stay alive!

> FANNY DIXWELL HOLMES, wife of Justice Oliver Wendell Holmes. This was spoken in reply to her maid, when Mrs. Holmes was 88 and in failing health; the maid had said, "You will die if you don't eat." (CATHERINE DRINKER BOWEN, *Yankee from Olympus,* p. 400)

20

Life is a fatal complaint, and an eminently contagious one.

> OLIVER WENDELL HOLMES, *The Poet at the Breakfast-Table,* ch. 12.

21

Life is a great bundle of little things.

> OLIVER WENDELL HOLMES, *The Professor at the Breakfast-Table,* ch. 1.

22

Life is an end in itself, and the only question

as to whether it is worth living is whether you have had enough of it.

> JUSTICE OLIVER WENDELL HOLMES, Supreme Court decision.

1

Life seems to me like a Japanese picture which our imagination does not allow to end with the margin.

> JUSTICE OLIVER WENDELL HOLMES, Message to the Federal Bar Association, 1932.

2

Life is a preparation for the future; and the best preparation for the future is to live as if there were none.

> ELBERT HUBBARD, *The Philistine*, vol. xx, p. 46.

3

Life is just one damned thing after another.

> Claimed by ELBERT HUBBARD, *A Thousand and One Epigrams* (1911). Also attributed to Frank Ward O'Malley.

It is not true that life is one damn thing after another—it's one damn thing over and over.

> EDNA ST. VINCENT MILLAY. (*Letters of Edna St. Vincent Millay*, ed. by Allen R. Macdougall)

4

Live all you can; it's a mistake not to. It doesn't so much matter what you do in particular so long as you have your life.

> HENRY JAMES, *The Ambassadors*, p. 149.

5

The earth belongs to the living, not the dead.

> THOMAS JEFFERSON, *Writings*, vol. xiii, p. 269.

6

Life is a loom, weaving illusion.

> VACHEL LINDSAY, *The Chinese Nightingale*.

7

The good life in the good society, though attainable, is never attained and possessed once and for all. So what has been attained will again be lost if the wisdom of the good life in a good society is not transmitted.

> WALTER LIPPMANN, *The Public Philosophy*, bk. ii, ch. 8.

8

And in the wreck of noble lives
Something immortal still survives.

> HENRY WADSWORTH LONGFELLOW, *Building of the Ship*, l. 375.

9

Tell me not, in mournful numbers,
Life is but an empty dream!

> HENRY WADSWORTH LONGFELLOW, *A Psalm of Life*.

10

Life is real! Life is earnest!
And the grave is not its goal.

> HENRY WADSWORTH LONGFELLOW, *A Psalm of Life*.

11

Thus at the flaming forge of life
Our fortunes must be wrought;
Thus on its sounding anvil shaped
Each burning deed and thought.

> HENRY WADSWORTH LONGFELLOW, *The Village Blacksmith*, st. 8.

12

Most men make the voyage of life as if they carried sealed orders which they were not to open till they were fairly in mid-ocean.

> JAMES RUSSELL LOWELL, *Among My Books: Dante*.

13

The finest art, the most difficult to learn, is the art of living.

> JOHN MACY, *About Women*, p. 122.

14

We come back inevitably to the fundamental questions: What are people for? What is living for? If the answer is a life of dignity, decency and opportunity, then every increase in population means a decrease in all three. The crowd is a threat to each single being.

> MARYA MANNES. (*New Bites by a Girl Gadfly; Life*, 12 June, 1964, p. 62)

15

Life is like a scrambled egg.

> DON MARQUIS, *Frustration*.

16

A little work, a little sweating, a few brief, flying years; a little joy, a little fretting, some smiles and then some tears; a little resting in the shadow, a struggle to the height, a futile search for El Dorado, and then we say Good Night.

> WALT MASON, *The Journey*.

17

Degenerate sons and daughters,
Life is too strong for you—
It takes life to love Life.

> EDGAR LEE MASTERS, *Lucinda Matlock*.

18

Life's a voyage that's homeward bound.

> HERMAN MELVILLE. (COURNOS, *Modern Plutarch*, p. 87)

19

The basic fact about human existence is not that it is a tragedy, but that it is a bore.

> H. L. MENCKEN, *Prejudices*.

20

Our lives are merely strange dark interludes in the electrical display of God the Father!

> EUGENE O'NEILL, *Strange Interlude*.

21

Avoid running at all times. Don't look back. Someone might be gaining on you.

> LEROY (SATCHEL) PAIGE, *How to Stay Young; Collier's*, 13 June, 1953, p. 55.

22

Razors pain you;
Rivers are damp;

Acids stain you;
And drugs cause cramp.
Guns aren't lawful;
Nooses give;
Gas smells awful;
You might as well live.
> DOROTHY PARKER, *Résumé.*

1
How the Other Half Lives.
> JACOB A. RIIS, Title of book.

2
Is life worth living?
Aye, with the best of us—
Heights of us, depths of us—
Life is the test of us!
> CORINNE ROOSEVELT ROBINSON, *Life, a Question.*

3
Life was meant to be lived, and curiosity must be kept alive. One must never, for whatever reason, turn his back on life.
> ELEANOR ROOSEVELT, *The Autobiography of Eleanor Roosevelt.*

4
I wish to preach, not the doctrine of ignoble ease, but the doctrine of the strenuous life.
> THEODORE ROOSEVELT, Speech to the Hamilton Club, Chicago, 10 Apr., 1899.

5
In life as in a football game, the principle to follow is: Hit the line hard.
> THEODORE ROOSEVELT, *The Strenuous Life: The American Boy.*

6
The poorest way to face life is to face it with a sneer.
> THEODORE ROOSEVELT, Speech at the University of Paris.

7
What good are vitamins? Eat a lobster, eat a pound of caviar—live! If you are in love with a beautiful blonde with an empty face and no brains at all, don't be afraid. Marry her! Live!
> ARTUR RUBINSTEIN. (*Rubinstein Speaking; New York Times Magazine,* 26 Jan., 1964)

8
Life is not a spectacle or a feast; it is a predicament.
> GEORGE SANTAYANA, *Articles and Essays.*

9
Nothing can be meaner than the anxiety to live on, to live on anyhow and in any shape; a spirit with any honour is not willing to live except in its own way, and a spirit with any wisdom is not over-eager to live at all.
> GEORGE SANTAYANA, *Little Essays,* p. 164.

10
There is no cure for birth and death save to enjoy the interval.
> GEORGE SANTAYANA, *Soliloquies in England.*

11
The Time of Your Life.
> WILLIAM SAROYAN, Title of play (1939).

12
In the time of your life, live—so that in that good time there shall be no ugliness or death for yourself or for any life your life touches. . . . In the time of your life, live—so that in that wondrous time you shall not add to the misery and sorrow of the world, but shall smile to the infinite delight and mystery of it.
> WILLIAM SAROYAN, *The Time of Your Life,* act i.

13
There are two things to aim at in life: first, to get what you want; and, after that, to enjoy it. Only the wisest of mankind achieve the second.
> LOGAN PEARSALL SMITH, *Afterthoughts.*

14
Not what we would but what we must
Makes up the sum of living;
Heaven is both more and less than just
In taking and in giving.
> R. H. STODDARD, *The Country Life.*

15
Our life is scarce the twinkle of a star
In God's eternal day.
> BAYARD TAYLOR, *Autumnal Vespers.*

16
I know I am—that simplest bliss
That millions of my brothers miss.
> BAYARD TAYLOR, *Prince Deukalion,* act 4.

17
I love a life whose plot is simple,
And does not thicken with every pimple.
> HENRY D. THOREAU, *Conscience.*

18
My life is like a stroll upon the beach,
As near the ocean's edge as I can go.
> HENRY D. THOREAU, *The Fisher's Boy.*

19
The art of life, of a poet's life, is, not having anything to do, to do something.
> HENRY D. THOREAU, *Journal,* 29 Apr., 1852.

20
Keep breathing.
> SOPHIE TUCKER, on the secret of achieving a long life. Spoken 13 Jan., 1964, her 80th birthday anniversary.

21
All say, "How hard it is to die"—a strange complaint from people who have had to live. Pity is for the living, envy for the dead.
> MARK TWAIN, *Pudd'nhead Wilson's Calendar.*

22
Many people are so afraid to die that they never begin to live.
> HENRY VAN DYKE, *Counsels by the Way: Courage.*

23
O I see now that life cannot exhibit all to me, as day cannot,

I see that I am to wait for what will be
exhibited by death.
WALT WHITMAN, *Night on the Prairies*.

1
Our lives are albums written through
With good or ill, with false or true;
And as the blessed angels turn
The pages of our years,
God grant they read the good with smiles,
And blot the ill with tears!
JOHN GREENLEAF WHITTIER, *Written in a
Lady's Album*.

LIGHT
See also Candle
2
Light is the first of painters. There is no
object so foul that intense light will not
make it beautiful.
EMERSON, *Nature*, ch. 3.

3
The great world of light, that lies
Behind all human destinies.
HENRY WADSWORTH LONGFELLOW, *To a
Child*.

4
Medicinal as light.
JAMES RUSSELL LOWELL, *Commemoration
Ode*.

5
The thing to do is to supply light and not
heat.
WOODROW WILSON, Speech in Pittsburgh,
29 Jan., 1916.

LINCOLN, ABRAHAM
6
No king this man, by grace of God's intent;
No, something better, freeman,—President!
A nature, modeled on a higher plan,
Lord of himself, an inborn gentleman.
GEORGE HENRY BOKER, *Our Heroic
Themes*. This early tribute was read be-
fore members of Phi Beta Kappa at
Harvard, 20 July, 1865.

7
Oh, slow to smite and swift to spare,
Gentle and merciful and just!
Who, in the fear of God, didst bear
The sword of power, a nation's trust!
WILLIAM CULLEN BRYANT, *Abraham Lin-
coln*.

8
O Uncommon Commoner! may your name
Forever lead like a living flame!
Unschooled scholar! how did you learn
The wisdom a lifetime may not earn?
EDMUND VANCE COOKE, *The Uncommon
Commoner*.

9
Hail, Lincoln! As the swift years lengthen
Still more majestic grows thy fame;
The ties that bind us to thee strengthen;

Starlike-immortal shines thy name.
NATHAN HASKELL DOLE, *Lincoln's Birthday*.

10
His heart was as great as the world, but there
was no room in it to hold the memory of a
wrong.
EMERSON, *Letters and Social Aims: Greatness*.

11
A martyr to the cause of man
His blood is freedom's eucharist,
And in the world's great hero list
His name shall lead the van.
CHARLES G. HALPIN, *The Death of Lin-
coln*.

12
Lincoln had faith in time, and time has justified his faith.
BENJAMIN HARRISON, Lincoln Day Address, Chicago, 1898.

13
Strange mingling of mirth and tears, of the
tragic and grotesque, of cap and crown, of
Socrates and Rabelais, of Aesop and Marcus
Aurelius—Lincoln, the gentlest memory of
the world.
ROBERT G. INGERSOLL, *Lincoln*.

14
Lincoln was not a type. He stands alone—no
ancestors, no fellows, no successors.
ROBERT G. INGERSOLL, *Lincoln*.

15
Lincoln's words have become the common
covenant of our public life. Let us now get
on with his work.
LYNDON B. JOHNSON, Address at Lincoln
Memorial, Washington, D.C., 12 Feb.,
1964.

16
If the good people in their wisdom shall see
fit to keep me in the background, I have
been too familiar with disappointment to be
much chagrined.
ABRAHAM LINCOLN, Communication, Sangamon *Journal*, when he was first a
candidate for the Illinois legislature
in 1832.

17
I have now come to the conclusion never
again to think of marrying, and for this reason: I can never be satisfied with anyone
who would be blockhead enough to have
me.
ABRAHAM LINCOLN, Letter to Mrs. Brown-
ing, 1 Apr., 1838, after he was rejected
by Mary Owens.

Mr. Lincoln was deficient in those little links
which make up the path of a woman's happiness.
MARY OWENS, in explaining why she refused to marry Lincoln.

1

Nobody ever expected me to be President. In my poor, lean, lank face nobody has ever seen that any cabbages were sprouting.

ABRAHAM LINCOLN, Speech against Douglas, in the campaign of 1860.

2

They have seen in his [Douglas's] round, jolly, fruitful face, post-offices, land-offices, marshal-ships and cabinet-appointments, chargé-ships and foreign missions, bursting out in wonderful exuberance.

ABRAHAM LINCOLN, Speech against Douglas, in the campaign of 1860.

3

His head is bowed. He thinks of men and kings.
Yea, when the sick world cries, how can he sleep?
Too many peasants fight, they know not why;
Too many homesteads in black terror weep.

VACHEL LINDSAY, *Abraham Lincoln Walks at Midnight.*

4

That nation has not lived in vain which has given the world Washington and Lincoln, the best great men and the greatest good men whom history can show.

HENRY CABOT LODGE, Address: *Lincoln,* given before the Massachusetts legislature, 12 Feb., 1909.

5

Here was a man to hold against the world,
A man to match the mountains and the sea.

EDWIN MARKHAM, *Lincoln, The Man of the People.*

6

One fire was on his spirit, one resolve—
To send the keen axe to the root of wrong,
Clearing a free way for the feet of God,
The eyes of conscience testing every stroke.

EDWIN MARKHAM, *Lincoln, The Man of the People.*

7

So came the Captain with the mighty heart;
And when the judgment thunders split the house,
Wrenching the rafters from their ancient rest,
He held the ridgepole up, and spiked again
The rafters of the house.

EDWIN MARKHAM, *Lincoln, The Man of the People.*

8

His grave a nation's heart shall be,
His monument a people free!

CAROLINE ATHERTON MASON, *President Lincoln's Grave.*

9

I am Ann Rutledge who sleeps beneath these weeds,
Beloved of Abraham Lincoln,
Wedded to him, not through union,
But through separation.
Bloom forever, O Republic,
From the dust of my bosom.

EDGAR LEE MASTERS, *Ann Rutledge.* The lines are on her tombstone in Petersburg, Ill.

10

When Abraham Lincoln was shoveled into the tombs, he forgot the copperheads and the assassin . . . in the dust, in the cool tombs.

CARL SANDBURG, *Cool Tombs.*

11

I will make a prophecy which will perhaps sound strange at the moment. In fifty years, perhaps much sooner, Lincoln's name will stand written upon the honor roll of the American Republic next to that of Washington, and there it will remain for all time.

CARL SCHURZ, Letter to Theodore Petrasch, 12 Oct., 1864.

12

There is Lincoln on the other side of the street. Just look at Old Abe.

LESLIE SMITH, at River and Harbor Convention, July, 1847—the first known use of the nickname. (WASHBURNE, *Reminiscences of Lincoln,* p. 16)

13

Now he belongs to the ages.

EDWIN M. STANTON, at the death of Lincoln, 15 Apr., 1865.

14

One of the people! born to be
Their curious epitome;
To share yet rise above
Their shifting hate and love.

R. H. STODDARD, *Abraham Lincoln.*

15

You lay a wreath on murdered Lincoln's bier,
You, who with mocking pencil wont to trace,
Broad for the self-complacent British sneer,
His length of shambling limb, his furrowed face.

TOM TAYLOR, *Abraham Lincoln; Punch,* 6 May, 1865. The lines appeared with a full-page cartoon, "Britannia Sympathises with Columbia," which represented *Punch* among the mourners at Lincoln's bier. Thus *Punch* sought to atone for its earlier abusive treatment of Lincoln.

16

His love shone as impartial as the sun.

MAURICE THOMPSON, *At Lincoln's Grave.*

17

Heroic soul, in homely garb half-hid,
Sincere, sagacious, melancholy, quaint;
What he endured, no less than what he did,
Has reared his monument, and crowned him saint.

J. T. TROWBRIDGE, *Lincoln.*

1

O Captain! my Captain! our fearful trip is
  done,
The ship has weather'd every rack, the prize
  we sought is won,
The port is near, the bells I hear, the people
  all exulting,
While follow eyes the steady keel, the vessel
  grim and daring;
    But O heart! heart! heart!
      O the bleeding drops of red,
        Where on the deck my Captain lies,
        Fallen cold and dead.
WALT WHITMAN, *O Captain! My Captain!*

2

The ship is anchor'd safe and sound, its voyage closed and done.
From fearful trip the victor ship comes in
  with object won;
    Exult, O shores, and ring, O bells!
      But I with mournful tread,
        Walk the deck my Captain lies,
        Fallen cold and dead.
WALT WHITMAN, *O Captain! My Captain!*

3

He leaves for America's history and biography, so far, not only its most dramatic reminiscence—he leaves, in my opinion, the
greatest, best, most characteristic, artistic,
moral personality.
WALT WHITMAN, *Specimen Days: Death
  of President Lincoln.*

4

This dust was once the man,
Gentle, plain, just and resolute, under whose
  cautious hand,
Against the foulest crime in history known in
  any land or age,
Was saved the Union of these States.
WALT WHITMAN, *This Dust Was Once the
  Man.*

5

Lincoln was a very normal man with very
normal gifts, but all upon a great scale, all
knit together in loose and natural form, like
the great frame in which he moved and
dwelt.
WOODROW WILSON, Speech in Chicago, 12
  Feb., 1909.

LITERATURE

6

Only the more rugged mortals should attempt to keep up with current literature.
GEORGE ADE, *Fables in Slang: Didn't Care
  for Story-books.*

7

Life comes before literature, as the material
always comes before the work. The hills are
full of marble before the world blooms with
statues.
PHILLIPS BROOKS, *Literature and Life.*

8

Literature is an investment of genius which
pays dividends to all subsequent times.
JOHN BURROUGHS, *Literary Fame.*

9

Literature . . . is an art, a science, a profession, a trade, and an accident. The literature
that is of lasting value is an accident. It is
something that happens.
SAMUEL McC. CROTHERS, *Free Trade vs.
  Protection in Literature.*

10

Our high respect for a well-read man is
praise enough of literature.
EMERSON, *Letters and Social Aims: Quotation.*

11

Literature is the effort of man to indemnify
himself for the wrongs of his condition.
EMERSON, *Natural History of Intellect:
  Landor.*

12

All modern American literature comes from
one book by Mark Twain called *Huckleberry
Finn.*
ERNEST HEMINGWAY, *The Green Hills of
  Africa,* ch. 1.

13

It takes a great deal of history to produce a
little literature.
HENRY JAMES, *Hawthorne,* ch. 1.

14

Literature is my Utopia. Here I am not dis-
franchised. No barrier of the senses shuts me
out from the sweet, gracious discourse of my
book-friends.
HELEN KELLER, *The Story of My Life.*

15

By American literature in the proper sense
we ought to mean literature written in an
American way, with an American turn of
language and an American cast of thought.
The test is that it couldn't have been written
anywhere else.
STEPHEN LEACOCK, *Mark Twain as a National Asset.*

16

Our American professors like their literature
clear and cold and pure and very dead.
SINCLAIR LEWIS, Address: *The American
  Fear of Literature,* Stockholm, 12 Dec.,
  1930. This was delivered upon accepting
  the Nobel Prize in literature.

17

I think literature is on the verge of becoming
public property instead of the preserve of
the relative few.
ARTHUR MILLER, Address to a congress of
  P.E.N., the international association of
  writers, in Bled, Yugoslavia, 5 July,
  1965. (Associated Press dispatch datelined Bled, 5 July, 1965)

18

Great literature is simply language charged

with meaning to the utmost possible degree.
Ezra Pound, *How to Read,* pt. 2.

1
To turn events into ideas is the function of literature.
George Santayana, *Little Essays,* p. 138.

2
"Classic." A book which people praise and don't read.
Mark Twain, *Pudd'nhead Wilson's New Calendar,* ch. 25.

3
In the civilization of to-day it is undeniable that, over all the arts, literature dominates, serves beyond all.
Walt Whitman, *Democratic Vistas.*

4
Literature is the orchestration of platitudes.
Thornton Wilder, *Literature.*

LOSS
See also Failure

5
And if I should lose, let me stand by the road
And cheer as the winners go by!
Berton Braley, *Prayer of a Sportsman.*

6
For every thing you have missed, you have gained something else; and for every thing you gain, you lose something.
Emerson, *Essays, First Series: Compensation.*

7
The cheerful loser is a winner.
Elbert Hubbard, *One Thousand and One Epigrams.*

LOVE

8
Romance cannot be put into quantity production—the moment love becomes casual, it becomes commonplace.
Frederick Lewis Allen, *Only Yesterday,* p. 239.

9
If two stand shoulder to shoulder against the gods,
Happy together, the gods themselves are helpless
Against them, while they stand so.
Maxwell Anderson, *Elizabeth the Queen.*

10
Dawn love is silver,
Wait for the west:
Old love is gold love—
Old love is best.
Katharine Lee Bates, *For a Golden Wedding.*

11
Love is the coldest of critics.
George William Curtis, *Prue and I,* ch. 7.

12
Nobody wants to kiss when they are hungry.
Dorothy Dix.

13
To infinite, ever present Love, all is Love, and there is no error, no sin, sickness, nor death.
Mary Baker Eddy, *Science and Health,* p. 567.

14
In the last analysis, love is only the reflection of a man's own worthiness from other men.
Emerson, *Essays, First Series: Friendship.*

15
Thou art to me a delicious torment.
Emerson, *Essays, First Series: Friendship.*

16
All mankind love a lover.
Emerson, *Essays, First Series: Of Love.*

17
Lovers should guard their strangeness.
Emerson, *Essays, Second Series: Manners.*

18
The accepted and betrothed lover has lost the wildest charm of his maiden in her acceptance of him.
Emerson, *Essays, Second Series: Nature.*

19
I love Henry, but I cannot like him; and as for taking his arm, I should as soon think of taking the arm of an elm-tree.
Emerson, *Lectures and Biographical Sketches: Thoreau.* Quoting a friend of Thoreau.

20
And as in the Dark all Cats are grey, the Pleasure of Corporal Enjoyment with an old Woman is at least equal and frequently superior; every Knack being by Practice capable of improvement.
Benjamin Franklin, Letter to an unidentified young friend, 25 June, 1745. Franklin's fifth stated reason for preferring older women to young ones.

21
If Jack's in love, he's no judge of Jill's Beauty.
Benjamin Ffanklin, *Poor Richard,* 1748.

22
If you would be loved, love and be lovable.
Benjamin Franklin, *Poor Richard,* 1755.

23
Earth's the right place for love:
I don't know where it's likely to go better.
Robert Frost, *Birches.*

24
Perhaps true love can best be recognized by the fact that it thrives under circumstances

which would blast anything else into small pieces.

ERNEST HAVEMANN, *Men, Women, and Marriage*, p. 215.

1

Wisely a woman prefers to a lover a man
    who neglects her.
This one may love her some day, some day
    the lover will not.

JOHN HAY, *Distichs*.

2

To love is to know the sacrifices which eternity exacts from life.

JOHN OLIVER HOBBES, *School for Saints*, ch. 25.

3

Love is sparingly soluble in the words of men, therefore they speak much of it; but one syllable of a woman's speech can dissolve more of it than a man's heart can hold.

OLIVER WENDELL HOLMES, *The Autocrat of the Breakfast-Table*, ch. 11.

4

No love so true as love that dies untold.

OLIVER WENDELL HOLMES, *The Mysterious Illness*.

5

To a man the disappointment of love may occasion some bitter pangs: it wounds some feelings of tenderness—it blasts some prospects of felicity; but he is an active being —he may dissipate his thoughts in the whirl of varied occupation. . . . But a woman's is comparatively a fixed, a secluded, and meditative life. . . . Her lot is to be wooed and won; and if unhappy in her love, her heart is like some fortress that has been captured, and sacked, and abandoned, and left desolate.

WASHINGTON IRVING, *The Sketch Book: The Broken Heart*.

6

We are a nation of lovers, and not a nation of haters.

LYNDON B. JOHNSON, Speech in Harrisburg, Pa., 10 Sept., 1964.

7

Archly the maiden smiled, and, with eyes
    overrunning with laughter,
Said, in a tremulous voice, "Why don't you
    speak for yourself, John?"

HENRY WADSWORTH LONGFELLOW, *The Courtship of Miles Standish*, pt. iii.

8

Love, that of every woman's heart
Will have the whole, and not a part,
That is to her, in Nature's plan,
More than ambition is to man,
Her light, her life, her very breath,
With no alternative but death.

HENRY WADSWORTH LONGFELLOW, *The Golden Legend*, pt. iv, sec. 7.

9

Love keeps the cold out better than a cloak.
It serves for food and raiment.

HENRY WADSWORTH LONGFELLOW, *The Spanish Student*, act i, sc. 5, l. 52.

10

There's nothing in this world so sweet as
    love,
And next to love the sweetest thing is hate.

HENRY WADSWORTH LONGFELLOW, *The Spanish Student*, act ii, sc. 5.

11

True Love is but a humble, low-born thing,
And hath its food served up in earthen
    ware;
It is a thing to walk with, hand in hand,
Through the everydayness of this workday
    world.

JAMES RUSSELL LOWELL, *Love*.

12

I Love my Wife, But Oh You Kid!

JIMMY LUCAS, Title and Refrain of song (1909).

13

Europeans used to say Americans were puritanical. Then they discovered that we were not puritans. So now they say that we are obsessed with sex.

MARY McCARTHY. (*Lady with a Switchblade; Life*, 20 Sept., 1963, p. 62)

14

There seems to be a cult of love in America. Perhaps this is so because today there are so few human contacts left except that one. Actually, only one person in a thousand ever really falls in love.

MARY McCARTHY. (*Lady with a Switchblade; Life*, 20 Sept., 1963, p. 64)

15

In an age where the lowered eyelid is just a sign of fatigue, the delicate game of love is pining away. Freud and flirtation are poor companions.

MARYA MANNES. (*New Bites by a Girl Gadfly; Life*, 12 June, 1964, p. 60)

16

The art of flirtation is dying. A man and woman are either in love these days or just friends. In the realm of love, reticence and sophistication should go hand in hand, for one of the joys of life is discovery. Nowadays, instead of progressing from *vous* to *tu*, from Mister to Jim, it's "darling" and "come to my place" in the first hour.

MARYA MANNES. (*New Bites by a Girl Gadfly; Life*, 12 June, 1964, p. 62)

17

A caress is better than a career.

ELISABETH MARBURY, Interview, on careers for women.

18

He drew a circle that shut me out—
Heretic, rebel, a thing to flout.
But Love and I had the wit to win:

We drew a circle that took him in!
EDWIN MARKHAM, *Outwitted*.

1

To be in love is merely to be in a state of
perceptual anaesthesia—to mistake an ordinary young man for a Greek god or an ordinary young woman for a goddess.
H. L. MENCKEN, *Prejudices*, ser. i.

2

Love is based upon a view of woman that is
impossible to any man who has had any experience of them
H. L. MENCKEN, *Prejudices*, ser. iv.

3

This have I known always: Love is no more
Than the wide blossom which the wind as-
sails,
Than the great tide that treads the shifting
shore,
Strewing fresh wreckage gathered in the
gales;
Pity me that the heart is slow to learn
What the swift mind beholds at every turn.
EDNA ST. VINCENT MILLAY, *Sonnets*, No.
6. (*The Harp-Weaver and Other
Poems*)

4

Any kiddie in school can love like a fool,
But hating, my boy, is an art.
OGDEN NASH, *Plea for Less Malice To-
ward None*.

5

Romantic love is the privilege of emperors,
kings, soldiers and artists; it is the butt of
democrats, traveling salesmen, magazine
poets and the writers of American novels.
GEORGE JEAN NATHAN, *Testament of a
Critic*, p. 14.

6

Hell's afloat in lovers' tears.
DOROTHY PARKER.

7

They that love beyond the world cannot be
separated by it. Death cannot kill what never
dies.
WILLIAM PENN, *Fruits of Solitude*.

8

She was a child and I was a child,
In this kingdom by the sea,
But we loved with a love that was more than
love,—
I and my Annabel Lee;
With a love that the winged seraphs of heav-
en
Coveted her and me.
EDGAR ALLAN POE, *Annabel Lee*.

9

As one who cons at evening o'er an album all
alone,
And muses on the faces of the friends that
he has known,
So I turn the leaves of Fancy till, in shadowy design,

I find the smiling features of an old sweet-
heart of mine.
JAMES WHITCOMB RILEY, *An Old Sweet-
heart of Mine*.

10

The hours I spent with thee, dear heart,—
Are as a string of pearls to me;
I count them over, every one apart,
My rosary, my rosary.
ROBERT CAMERON ROGERS, *My Rosary*.

11

Take back your gold, for gold can never buy
me,
Take back your bribe, and promise you'll
be true;
Give me the love, the love that you'd deny
me;
Make me your wife, that's all I ask of
you.
MONROE H. ROSENFELD, *Take Back Your
Gold* (1897).

12

Even the inconstant flame may burn brightly, if the soul is naturally combustible.
GEORGE SANTAYANA, *Life of Reason*, vol.
ii, p. 25.

13

Lust is the oldest lion of them all.
MARJORIE ALLEN SEIFFERT, *An Italian
Chest*.

14

Love better is than Fame.
BAYARD TAYLOR, *To J. L. G.*

15

Everywhere I look I see—
Fact or fiction, life or play,
Still the little game of Three:
B and C in love with A.
BERT LESTON TAYLOR, *Old Stuff*.

16

There is no remedy for love but to love
more.
HENRY D. THOREAU, *Journal*, 25 July,
1839.

17

I lose my respect for the man who can make
the mystery of sex the subject of a coarse
jest, yet, when you speak earnestly and seriously on the subject, is silent.
HENRY D. THOREAU, *Journal*, 12 Apr.,
1852.

18

You must get your living by loving.
HENRY D. THOREAU, *Journal*, 13 Mar.,
1853.

19

All that a man has to say or do that can
possibly concern mankind, is in some shape
or other to tell the story of his love,—to
sing, and, if he is fortunate and keeps alive,
he will be forever in love.
HENRY D. THOREAU, *Journal*, 6 May,
1854.

1

Love is the strange bewilderment which overtakes one person on account of another person.

JAMES THURBER AND E. B. WHITE, *Is Sex Necessary?*

2

We love the things we love in spite
Of what they are.

LOUIS UNTERMEYER, *Love.*

3

Love is not getting, but giving; not a wild dream of pleasure, and a madness of desire —oh, no, love is not that—it is goodness, and honor, and peace and pure living.

HENRY VAN DYKE, *Little Rivers: A Handful of Heather.*

4

Will you love me in December as you do in
    May,
Will you love me in the good old fashioned
    way?
When my hair has all turned gray,
Will you kiss me then and say,
That you love me in December as you do in
    May?

JAMES J. WALKER, *Will You Love Me in December As You Do in May?* Set to music by Ernest R. Ball, 1905.

5

Come up and see me sometime.

MAE WEST, *Diamond Lil.*

6

Love scarce is love that never knows
    The sweetness of forgiving.

JOHN GREENLEAF WHITTIER, *Among the Hills*, st. 77.

7

Oh, rank is good, and gold is fair,
    And high and low mate ill;
But love has never known a law
    Beyond its own sweet will!

JOHN GREENLEAF WHITTIER, *Amy Wentworth.*

8

Love lights more fire than hate extinguishes,
And men grow better as the world grows
    old.

ELLA WHEELER WILCOX, *Optimism.*

9

They may talk of love in a cottage,
    And bowers of trellised vine—
Of nature bewitchingly simple,
    And milkmaids half divine, . . .
But give me a sly flirtation,
    By the light of a chandelier—
With music to play in the pauses,
    And nobody very near.

N. P. WILLIS, *Love in a Cottage.*

10

The Italian attitude is the important thing. "You're a woman and therefore worthy of admiration" is so charmingly un-American.

UNKNOWN, Article (unsigned), *A Pinch of Romance,* in the newspaper of the American Women's Club of Rome. The writer was defending Italian sidewalk Romeos, noted for their expressions of appreciation of feminine beauty. (Associated Press dispatch datelined Rome, 14 May, 1964)

LOYALTY, see Fidelity

LUCK

See also Chance, Fortune

11

Shallow men believe in luck. . . . Strong men believe in cause and effect.

EMERSON, *Conduct of Life: Worship.*

12

Dish yer rabbit foot'll gin you good luck.

JOEL CHANDLER HARRIS, *Brother Rabbit and His Famous Foot.*

13

True luck consists not in holding the best of
    the cards at the table:
Luckiest he who knows just when to rise and
    go home.

JOHN HAY, *Distichs,* 15.

14

One leaf is for hope, and one is for faith,
And one is for love, you know,
And God put another in for luck.

ELLA HIGGINSON, *Four-Leaf Clover.*

15

Happy art thou, as if every day thou hadst
    picked up a horseshoe.

HENRY WADSWORTH LONGFELLOW, *Evangeline*, pt. i, st. 2.

LULLABY, see Sleep

LUXURY

16

The pomp of the Persian I hold in Aversion,
I loathe all those gingerbread tricks.

FRANKLIN P. ADAMS, *Persicos Odi.*

17

You can only drink thirty or forty glasses of beer a day, no matter how rich you are.

ADOLPHUS BUSCH, Newspaper Interview.

18

Too much plenty makes mouth dainty.

BENJAMIN FRANKLIN, *Poor Richard,* 1749.

19

Silks and satins, scarlets and velvets, put out the kitchen fire.

BENJAMIN FRANKLIN, *Poor Richard,* 1758.

20

There is a limit to luxury.

ELBERT HUBBARD, *The Philistine*, vol. xx, p. 186.

21

Most of the luxuries, and many of the so-called comforts of life, are not only not indispensable, but positive hindrances to the elevation of mankind.

> HENRY DAVID THOREAU, *Walden*, ch. 1.

1
Give me the luxuries of life and I will willingly do without the necessities.

> FRANK LLOYD WRIGHT.

M

MACHINES

2
Things are in the saddle and ride mankind.

> EMERSON, *Ode*.

3
Armed with his machinery man can dive, can fly, can see atoms like a gnat; he can peer into Uranus with his telescope, or knock down cities with his fists of gunpowder.

> EMERSON, *Resources*.

4
The machine unmakes the man. Now that the machine is so perfect, the engineer is nobody.

> EMERSON, *Society and Solitude: Works and Days*.

5
One machine can do the work of fifty ordinary men. No machine can do the work of one extraordinary man.

> ELBERT HUBBARD, *The Philistine*, vol. xviii, p. 26.

6
Don't throw a monkey-wrench into the machinery.

> PHILANDER JOHNSON. (*Everybody's Magazine,* May, 1920, p. 36)

7
It is never the machines that are dead. It is only the mechanically-minded men that are dead.

> GERALD STANLEY LEE, *Crowds,* pt. ii, ch. 5.

8
Machinery is the sub-conscious mind of the world.

> GERALD STANLEY LEE, *Crowds,* pt. ii, ch. 8.

9
The image of the automation engineer may not excite the imagination as does the image of the astronaut, but the fate of mankind in the foreseeable future will depend more on what we do manipulating machines here on earth than on how we do hurtling them through the heavens.

> ADLAI E. STEVENSON, Address at the 30th-anniversary dinner of the graduate faculty of the New School for Social Research, New York City, Apr., 1964.

MADNESS

10
That's the first lunatic I've had for an engineer. He probably ought to be shot at sunrise, but I guess we'll let him off, because nobody was hurt.

> THOMAS E. DEWEY, during a whistle-stop speech in Beaucoup, Ill., 12 Oct., 1948, in the midst of the presidential campaign. His speech was suddenly interrupted when the railroad observation coach, from the back platform of which he was talking, lurched backward in the direction of the audience gathered along the tracks. The totally unexpected movement of the train in reverse prompted Dewey to make his impromptu and very unflattering comment about the engineer. It received national circulation over a period of several days, very likely to Dewey's disadvantage.

11
Much madness is divinest sense
  To a discerning eye;
Much sense the starkest madness.
  'Tis the majority
In this, as all, prevails.
  Assent, and you are sane;
Demur,—you're straightway dangerous,
  And handled with a chain.

> EMILY DICKINSON, *Poems*, Pt. i, No. 11.

12
The present state of insane persons, confined within this commonwealth, in cages, closets, cellars, stalls, pens! Chained, naked, beaten with rods, and lashed into obedience.

> DOROTHEA LYNDE DIX, Memorial to the Legislature of Massachusetts, 1843, p. 4.

13
I myself have seen more than nine thousand idiots, epileptics and insane in the United States . . . bound with galling chains, bowed beneath fetters, lacerated with ropes, scourged with rods.

> DOROTHEA LYNDE DIX, first petition to Congress. (Senate Misc. Doc., No. 150, 30 Cong., 1st Sess.)

14
Sanity consists in not being subdued by your means.

> EMERSON, *Conduct of Life: Considerations by the Way*.

15
Whom the Gods would destroy they first make mad.

> HENRY WADSWORTH LONGFELLOW, *Masque of Pandora*, pt. vi, l. 58.

1
My dear Sir, take any road, you can't go amiss. The whole state is one vast insane asylum.

> JAMES L. PETIGRU, in 1860, upon being asked directions for reaching the insane asylum in Charleston, S.C. The state was then preparing to secede from the Union.

2
Sanity is a madness put to good uses.

> GEORGE SANTAYANA, *Little Essays*, p. 146.

3
Am placing your letter temporarily in my crackpot file, and later shall consign it to the wastebasket.

> STEPHEN M. YOUNG, Letter to a constituent, in reply to an insulting letter sent to Young when the latter was Senator from Ohio during the 1960's. Senator Young explained the unusual action by declaring, "Every man has a right to answer back when being bullied." (New York Times News Service dispatch, datelined Columbus, O., 5 Nov., 1964)

MAJORITY AND MINORITY

4
When great changes occur in history, when great principles are involved, as a rule the majority are wrong.

> EUGENE V. DEBS, Speech during trial, Cleveland, 12 Sept., 1918.

5
Any time we deny any citizen the full exercise of his Constitutional rights, we are weakening our own claim to them.

> DWIGHT D. EISENHOWER, *Let's Be Honest with Ourselves; The Reader's Digest*, Dec., 1963.

6
Shall we judge a country by the majority, or by the minority? By the minority, surely.

> EMERSON, *Conduct of Life: Considerations by the Way.*

7
All history is a record of the power of minorities, and of minorities of one.

> EMERSON, *Letters and Social Aims: Progress of Culture.*

8
If by the mere force of numbers a majority should deprive a minority of any clearly written constitutional right, it might, in a moral point of view, justify revolution—certainly would if such a right were a vital one.

> ABRAHAM LINCOLN, First Inaugural Address, 4 Mar., 1861.

9
That cause is strong which has not a multitude, but one strong man behind it.

> JAMES RUSSELL LOWELL, Address in Chelsea, Mass., 22 Dec., 1885.

10
One, of God's side, is a majority.

> WENDELL PHILLIPS, Speech on John Brown, at Harpers Ferry, W. Va., 1 Nov., 1859.

One, with God, is always a majority, but many a martyr has been burned at the stake while the votes were being counted.

> THOMAS B. REED. (W. A. ROBINSON, *Life of Reed*)

11
Governments exist to protect the rights of minorities. The loved and the rich need no protection,—they have many friends and few enemies.

> WENDELL PHILLIPS, Address in Boston, 21 Dec., 1860.

12
When you get too big a majority, you're immediately in trouble.

> SAM RAYBURN. This became known as Rayburn's law, and developed out of his own difficulties, as majority leader in the House of Representatives, during the second term of Franklin Roosevelt's administration, which began with a lopsided Democratic majority. Rayburn contended that such majorities tended always to produce splinter groups created along ethnic and sectional lines. (Quoted by Charles Halleck, House Republican leader, and Lewis Deschler, House parliamentarian, Interview with the Associated Press, datelined Washington, D.C., 19 Nov., 1964)

13
How a minority,
Reaching majority,
Seizing authority,
Hates a minority!

> LEONARD H. ROBBINS, *Minorities.*

14
The mainstream of American political thought and action.

> NELSON A. ROCKEFELLER, an expression used by him repeatedly during the 1964 campaign for the Republican presidential nomination, to characterize the position of himself and other candidates of the party's liberal and moderate wings. He termed the eventual winner of the nomination, Barry M. Goldwater, as the candidate of a minority outside the mainstream.

15
The only tyrannies from which men, women and children are suffering in real life are the tyrannies of minorities.

> THEODORE ROOSEVELT, Speech in New York City, 20 Mar., 1912.

16
The great mass of the people are in more danger of having their rights invaded and

their liberties destroyed by the overweening influence of organized minorities, who have fanatical or selfish interests to serve, than by the force of an unthinking or cruel majority.

> OSCAR W. UNDERWOOD, *Drifting Sands of Party Politics*, p. 6.

MALICE

See also Slander

1
In charity to all, bearing no malice or ill-will to any human being.

> JOHN QUINCY ADAMS, Letter to A. Bronson, 30 July, 1838.

2
With malice toward none, with charity for all, with firmness in the right, as God gives us to see the right.

> ABRAHAM LINCOLN, Second Inaugural Address, 4 Mar., 1865.

3
I have endured a great deal of ridicule without much malice; and have received a great deal of kindness, not quite free from ridicule.

> ABRAHAM LINCOLN, Letter to James H. Hackett, 2 Nov., 1863.

4
I'm just an amiable, kindly old thing, as I've always been. I was born a kindly old thing. If anyone takes that seriously, hah! My specialty is detached malevolence.

> ALICE ROOSEVELT LONGWORTH, on her 80th birthday, 12 Feb., 1964. (*Newsweek*, 24 Feb., 1964)

5
Malice . . . the basest of all instincts, passions, vices—the most hateful.

> MARK TWAIN, *The Character of Man*.

MAN

See also Evolution

6
It needs a man to perceive a man.

> AMOS BRONSON ALCOTT, *Table Talk: Creeds*.

7
I come to speak to you in defense of a cause as holy as the cause of liberty—the cause of humanity.

> WILLIAM JENNINGS BRYAN, Address, Democratic national convention, Chicago, 8 July, 1896.

8
A man said to the universe:
"Sir, I exist!"
"However," replied the universe,
"The fact has not created in me
A sense of obligation."

> STEPHEN CRANE, *War Is Kind*, pt. 4.

9
Man is not order of nature, sack and sack, belly and members, link in a chain, nor any

ignominious baggage, but a stupendous antagonism, a dragging together of the poles of the Universe.

> EMERSON, *Conduct of Life: Fate*.

10
A man ought to compare advantageously with a river, an oak, a mountain.

> EMERSON, *Conduct of Life: Fate*.

11
I have seen human nature in all its forms; it is everywhere the same, but the wilder it is, the more virtuous.

> EMERSON, *Conduct of Life: Worship*. Quoting a traveler.

12
Most men and most women are merely one couple more.

> EMERSON, *Conduct of Life: Fate*.

13
A man is the whole encyclopedia of facts.

> EMERSON, *Essays, First Series: History*.

14
Nature never rhymes her children, nor makes two men alike.

> EMERSON, *Essays, Second Series: Character*.

15
Every man is an impossibility until he is born.

> EMERSON, *Essays, Second Series: Experience*.

16
Too good for banning, and too bad for blessing.

> EMERSON, *Essays, Second Series: Manners*.

17
Men in all ways are better than they seem.

> EMERSON, *Essays, Second Series: New England Reformers*.

18
Man's conclusions are reached by toil.
Woman arrives at the same by sympathy.

> EMERSON, *Journal*, 1866.

19
Man is the will, and woman the sentiment. In this ship of humanity, Will is the rudder, and Sentiment the sail; when woman affects to steer, the rudder is only a masked sail.

> EMERSON, *Miscellanies: Woman*.

20
Men are all inventors sailing forth on a voyage of discovery.

> EMERSON, *Resources*.

21
I decline to accept the end of man.

> WILLIAM FAULKNER, Address in Stockholm, 10 Dec., 1950, upon accepting the Nobel Prize in literature.

22
I believe that man will not merely endure: he will prevail. He is immortal, not because he alone among creatures has an inexhaustible voice, but because he has a soul, a spirit

capable of compassion and sacrifice and endurance.

> WILLIAM FAULKNER, Address in Stockholm, 10 Dec., 1950, upon accepting the Nobel Prize in literature.

1

Every person is a bundle of possibilities and he is worth what life may get out of him before it is through.

> HARRY EMERSON FOSDICK, *The Rebirth of Self.*

2

He was close on to six feet tall, of military bearing, and of such extraordinary vitality that young ladies asserted they could feel him ten feet away.

> C. HARTLEY GRATTAN, *Bitter Bierce,* p. 39.
> The reference is to Ambrose Bierce.

3

Married men laugh at
Single men. Single men laugh
At the married men.
Wan Lo tells me that women
Laugh up their sleeves at both.

> HENRY HARRISON, *Wan Lo Tanka.*

4

Breathes there a man with hide so tough
Who says two sexes aren't enough?

> SAMUEL HOFFENSTEIN, *The Sexes.*

5

Of course everybody likes and respects self-made men. It is a great deal better to be made in that way than not to be made at all.

> OLIVER WENDELL HOLMES, *The Autocrat of the Breakfast-Table,* ch. 1.

6

It is a curious fact that when we get sick we want an uncommon doctor. If we have a construction job, we want an uncommon engineer. When we get into a war, we dreadfully want an uncommon admiral and an uncommon general. Only when we get into politics are we content with the common man.

> HERBERT HOOVER, advocating the uncommon man. (New York *Times* obituary of Hoover, 21 Oct., 1964, p. 40)

7

A man is as good as he has to be, and a woman as bad as she dares.

> ELBERT HUBBARD, *Epigrams.*

8

Behind every successful man stands a surprised mother-in-law.

> HUBERT HUMPHREY, Speech during the 1964 presidential campaign. (New York *Times,* "Ideas and Men," 11 Oct., 1964, p. 13E)

9

Man is a machine into which we put what we call food and produce what we call thought.

> ROBERT G. INGERSOLL, *The Gods.*

10

Man passes away; his name perishes from record and recollection; his history is as a tale that is told, and his very monument becomes a ruin.

> WASHINGTON IRVING, *The Sketch Book: Westminster Abbey,* conclusion.

11

A man in trouble *must* be possessed, somehow, of a woman.

> HENRY JAMES, *The Ambassadors,* p. 211.

12

Man, biologically considered, . . . is the most formidable of all the beasts of prey, and, indeed, the only one that preys systematically on its own species.

> WILLIAM JAMES, *Memories and Studies,* p. 301.

13

The mass of men are neither wise nor good.

> JOHN JAY, Letter to Washington, 27 June, 1786.

14

Man is an imitative animal. This quality is the germ of all education in him. From his cradle to his grave he is learning to do what he sees others do.

> THOMAS JEFFERSON, *Writings,* vol. ii, p. 225.

15

John Kennedy believed so strongly that one's aim should not just be the most comfortable life possible but that we should all do something to right the wrongs we see and not just complain about them. We owe that to our country, and our country will suffer if we don't serve her. He believed that one man can make a difference, and that every man should try.

> JACQUELINE KENNEDY, Television Broadcast in memory of her husband, John F. Kennedy, 29 May, 1964.

16

So now he is a legend when he would have preferred to be a man.

> JACQUELINE KENNEDY, Article (untitled) in *Look,* 17 Nov., 1964, p. 36. The reference is to her husband, John F. Kennedy.

17

I accept this award today with an abiding faith in America and an audacious faith in the future of mankind. I refuse to accept the idea that the "isness" of man's present nature makes him morally incapable of reaching up for the eternal "oughtness" that forever confronts him.

> REV. MARTIN LUTHER KING, JR., Address in Oslo, 10 Dec., 1964, upon receiving the Nobel Peace Prize.

18

Man is a torch, then ashes soon,
May and June, then dead December,
Dead December, then again June.

> VACHEL LINDSAY, *The Chinese Nightingale.*

1

As unto the bow the cord is,
So unto the man is woman;
Though she bends him, she obeys him,
Though she draws him, yet she follows;
Useless each without the other!

> HENRY WADSWORTH LONGFELLOW, *Hiawatha*, pt. x.

2

In this world a man must either be anvil or hammer.

> HENRY WADSWORTH LONGFELLOW, *Hyperion*, bk. iv, ch. 7.

3

A man of mark.

> HENRY WADSWORTH LONGFELLOW, *Tales of a Wayside Inn: The Saga of King Olaf*, pt. ix, st. 2.

4

The surest plan to make a Man
Is, think him so.

> JAMES RUSSELL LOWELL, *Jonathan to John*, st. 9.

5

Before Man made us citizens, great Nature made us men.

> JAMES RUSSELL LOWELL, *On the Capture of Certain Fugitive Slaves Near Washington.*

6

He is a dull man who is always sure, and a sure man who is always dull.

> H. L. MENCKEN, *Prejudices,* ser. ii, ch. 1.

7

God made man merely to hear some praise
Of what He'd done on those Five Days.

> CHRISTOPHER MORLEY, *Fons et Origo.*

8

An ingenious assembly of portable plumbing.

> CHRISTOPHER MORLEY.

9

Down with your pride of birth
And your golden gods of trade!
A man is worth to his mother, Earth,
All that a man has made!

> JOHN G. NEIHARDT, *Cry of the People.*

10

Man never falls so low that he can see nothing higher than himself.

> THEODORE PARKER, *A Lesson for the Day.*

11

Men are made stronger on realization that the helping hand they need is at the end of their own right arm.

> SIDNEY J. PHILLIPS, Address at the dedication of the Booker T. Washington Memorial Highway, Virginia, July, 1953.

12

Our self-made men are the glory of our institutions.

> WENDELL PHILLIPS, Speech in Boston, 21 Dec., 1860.

13

The first time a young man goes to the ticket window of a burlesque house, he is taking a long step into the world of being his own man, a considerably longer one than he takes when he lights up a cigarette at home for the first time.

> JACK RICE, Column, St. Louis *Post-Dispatch*, 11 June, 1964.

14

When a man fronts catastrophe on the road, he looks in his purse—but a woman looks in her mirror.

> MARGARET TURNBULL, *The Left Lady,* p. 44.

15

Of all created creatures man is the most detestable. Of the entire brood he is the only one . . . that possesses malice. . . . Also . . . he is the only creature that has a nasty mind.

> MARK TWAIN, *The Character of Man.*

16

All I care to know is that a man is a human being—that is enough for me; he can't be any worse.

> MARK TWAIN, *Concerning the Jews.*

17

Man is the only animal that blushes. Or needs to.

> MARK TWAIN, *Pudd'nhead Wilson's New Calendar.*

18

A round man cannot be expected to fit a square hole right away. He must have time to modify his shape.

> MARK TWAIN, *More Tramps Abroad,* ch. 71.

19

Mankind, when left to themselves, are unfit for their own government.

> GEORGE WASHINGTON, Letter to Lee, 31 Oct., 1786.

20

Each of us inevitable;
Each of us limitless—each of us with his or her right upon the earth.

> WALT WHITMAN, *Salut au Monde,* sec. 11.

21

I am an acme of things accomplished, and I am encloser of things to be.

> WALT WHITMAN, *Song of Myself,* sec. 44.

22

I am as bad as the worst, but thank God I am as good as the best.

> WALT WHITMAN.

23

A man to match his mountains.

> JOHN GREENLEAF WHITTIER, *Among the Hills.*

24

In thy lone and long night-watches, sky above and sea below,
Thou didst learn a higher wisdom than the babbling schoolmen know;

God's stars and silence taught thee, as His
    angels only can,
That the one sole sacred thing beneath the
    cope of heaven is Man!
    JOHN GREENLEAF WHITTIER, *The Branded
        Hand,* st. 9.

1

And step by step, since time began,
I see the steady gain of man.
    JOHN GREENLEAF WHITTIER, *The Chapel
        of the Hermits.*

MANNERS

See also Behavior, Courtesy

2

Manners are the happy ways of doing
things. . . . If they are superficial, so are
the dew-drops which give such a depth to the
morning meadows.
    EMERSON, *Conduct of Life: Behavior.*

3

Manners have been somewhat cynically defined to be a contrivance of wise men to keep
fools at a distance.
    EMERSON, *Conduct of Life: Behavior.*

4

Fine manners need the support of fine manners in others.
    EMERSON, *Conduct of Life: Behavior.*

5

God may forgive sins, he said, but awkward-
ness has no forgiveness in heaven or earth.
    EMERSON, *Essays: Society and Solitude.*

6

Good manners are made up of petty sacrifices.
    EMERSON, *Letters and Social Aims: Social
        Aims.*

7

Manners are greater than laws; by their delicate nature they fortify themselves with an
impassible wall of defence.
    EMERSON, *Public and Private Education.*

8

Perhaps, if we could examine the manners of
different nations with impartiality, we should
find no people so rude, as to be without any
rules of politeness; nor any so polite, as not
to have some remains of rudeness.
    BENJAMIN FRANKLIN, *Remarks Concern-
        ing the Savages of North America.*

9

More tears have been shed over men's lack
of manners than their lack of morals.
    HELEN HATHAWAY, *Manners for Men.*

10

I don't recall your name, but your manners
are familiar.
    OLIVER HERFORD, in acknowledging the
        greeting of a back-slapping man when
        the latter descended on Herford at The
        Players, New York club, with a confi-
        dent "You remember me?"

11

Rudeness is the weak man's imitation of
strength.
    ERIC HOFFER, *The Passionate State of
        Mind,* p. 138.

12

Self-respect is at the bottom of all good
manners. They are the expression of discipline, of good-will, of respect for other people's rights and comforts and feelings.
    EDWARD S. MARTIN, *A Father to His
        Freshman Son.*

13

Good manners are the technic of expressing
consideration for the feelings of others.
    ALICE DUER MILLER, *I Like American
        Manners; Saturday Evening Post,* 13
        Aug., 1932.

14

The most delightful of companions is he who
combines the mind of a gentleman with the
emotions of a bum. . . . Toward men, ever
an aristocrat; toward women, ever a commoner—that way lies success.
    GEORGE JEAN NATHAN, *The Autobiogra-
        phy of an Attitude.*

15

Training is everything. The peach was once a
bitter almond; cauliflower is nothing but
cabbage with a college education.
    MARK TWAIN, *Pudd'nhead Wilson's Cal-
        endar.*

16

Good breeding consists in concealing how
much we think of ourselves and how little we
think of the other person.
    MARK TWAIN, Unpublished Diaries.

17

Breakfast is the one meal at which it is perfectly good manners to read the paper.
    AMY VANDERBILT, *Amy Vanderbilt's Com-
        plete Book of Etiquette.*

18

Manners,—the final and perfect flower of
noble character.
    WILLIAM WINTER, *The Actor and His
        Duty.*

MARCH

19

The stormy March has come at last,
    With winds and clouds and changing
        skies;
I hear the rushing of the blast
    That through the snowy valley flies.
    WILLIAM CULLEN BRYANT, *March.*

20

March comes, a kind of interregnum, winter's sovereignty relaxing, spring not yet in
control. But the pattern is now established.
    Editorial, New York *Times,* 1 Mar., 1964.

21

Ah, March! we know thou art
Kind-hearted, 'spite of ugly looks and
    threats,

And, out of sight, art nursing April's violets!
    HELEN HUNT JACKSON, *March*.

1

With rushing winds and gloomy skies,
The dark and stubborn Winter dies:
Far-off, unseen, Spring faintly cries,
Bidding her earliest child arise: March!
    BAYARD TAYLOR, *March*.

2

Up from the sea the wild north wind is blow-
    ing
    Under the sky's gray arch;
Smiling, I watch the shaken elm boughs,
    knowing
    It is the wind of March.
    JOHN GREENLEAF WHITTIER, *March*.

MARRIAGE

3

Relations between the sexes are so complicated that the only way you can tell if members of the set are "going together" is if
they're married. Then, almost certainly, they
are not.
    CLEVELAND AMORY, *Who Killed Society?*

4

Marriage always demands the greatest understanding of the art of insincerity possible
between two human beings.
    VICKI BAUM, *And Life Goes On,* p. 141.

5

Well-married, a man is winged: ill-matched,
he is shackled.
    HENRY WARD BEECHER, *Proverbs from
    Plymouth Pulpit*.

6

They stood before the altar and supplied
The fire themselves in which their fat was
    fried.
    AMBROSE BIERCE, *The Devil's Dictionary*,
    p. 23.

7

Marriage: The state or condition of a community consisting of a master, a mistress,
and two slaves, making in all, two.
    AMBROSE BIERCE, *The Devil's Dictionary*,
    p. 213.

8

His wife not only edited his works but edited
him.
    VAN WYCK BROOKS, *The Ordeal of Mark
    Twain*, ch. 5.

9

Won 1880. One 1884.
    WILLIAM JENNINGS BRYAN, Inscription on
    wedding ring presented to his wife.
    (PAXTON HIBBEN, *Life of Bryan*)

10

People marry through a variety of other reasons, and with varying results; but to marry
for love is to invite inevitable tragedy.
    JAMES BRANCH CABELL, *The Cream of the
    Jest*, p. 235.

11

I shall marry in haste and repeat at leisure.
    JAMES BRANCH CABELL, *Jurgen*, ch. 38.

12

The reason that husbands and wives do not
understand each other is because they belong
to different sexes.
    DOROTHY DIX, Syndicated Column.

13

It is not marriage that fails; it is people that
fail. All that marriage does is to show people
up.
    HARRY EMERSON FOSDICK, *Marriage*.

14

Wedlock, as old men note, hath likened
    been
Unto a public crowd or common rout;
Where those that are without would fain get
    in,
And those that are within would fain get
    out.
    BENJAMIN FRANKLIN, *Poor Richard*,
    1734.

15

Where there's marriage without love, there
will be love without marriage.
    BENJAMIN FRANKLIN, *Poor Richard*,
    1734.

16

You cannot pluck roses without fear of
    thorns,
Nor enjoy a fair wife without danger of
    horns.
    BENJAMIN FRANKLIN, *Poor Richard*,
    1734.

17

Keep thy eyes wide open before marriage,
and half shut afterwards.
    BENJAMIN FRANKLIN, *Poor Richard*,
    1738.

18

Marriage is the proper remedy. It is the most
natural state of man, and therefore the state
in which you will find solid happiness.
    BENJAMIN FRANKLIN, Letter to an uni-
    dentified young man, 25 June, 1745.

19

It is the man and woman united that makes
the complete human being. Separate she
wants his force of body and strength of reason; he her softness, sensibility and acute
discernment. Together they are most likely
to succeed in the world. A single man has not
nearly the value he would have in that state
of union. He is an incomplete animal. He
resembles the odd half of a pair of scissors.
    BENJAMIN FRANKLIN, Letter to an uni-
    dentified young man, 25 June, 1745.

20

If you get a prudent, healthy wife, your industry in your profession, with her good
economy, will be fortune sufficient.
    BENJAMIN FRANKLIN, Letter to an uni-
    dentified young man, 25 June, 1745.

1

Women marry because they don't want to work.

> MARY GARDEN, Newspaper Interview.

2

How to Be Happy Though Married.

> REV. E. J. HARDY, Title of Book (1910).

3

All happily married people have managed to accept the fact that marriage is no better and no worse than any other human institution. Also, perhaps even more important, *they have learned to accept themselves and each other for what they really and honestly are.*

> ERNEST HAVEMANN, *Men, Women, and Marriage,* p. 104.

4

Residents of the East like to point out that people in the West fall in love and then get married, whereas Orientals get married and then fall in love. The Eastern order of things seems to have worked better than most Westerners realize.

> ERNEST HAVEMANN, *Men, Women, and Marriage,* p. 189.

5

Men in single state should tarry,
While women, I suggest, should marry.

> SAMUEL HOFFENSTEIN, *Advice on Marriage.*

6

Husband and wife come to look alike at last.

> OLIVER WENDELL HOLMES, *The Professor at the Breakfast-Table,* ch. 7.

7

The torment of one, the felicity of two, the strife and enmity of three.

> WASHINGTON IRVING.

8

To Have and to Hold.

> MARY JOHNSTON, Title of novel.

9

Now I think that I should have known that he was magic all along. I did know it—but I should have guessed it could not last. I should have known that it was asking too much to dream that I might have grown old with him and see our children grow up together.

> JACQUELINE KENNEDY, writing of her husband, John F. Kennedy. Article (untitled), *Look,* 17 Nov., 1964, p. 36.

10

Marrying a man is like buying something you've been admiring for a long time in a shop window. You may love it when you get it home, but it doesn't always go with everything else in the house.

> JEAN KERR, *The Snake Has All the Lines: The Ten Worst Things About a Man,* p. 121.

11

Marriage is a lottery, but you can't tear up your ticket if you lose.

> F. M. KNOWLES, *A Cheerful Year Book.*

12

Matrimony is something that the bachelor misses and the widower escapes.

> F. M. KNOWLES, *A Cheerful Year Book.*

13

'Tis sad when you think of her wasted life,
  For youth cannot mate with age,
And her beauty was sold for an old man's gold—
  She's a bird in a gilded cage.

> ARTHUR J. LAMB, *A Bird in a Gilded Cage.* Set to music, 1900, by Harry von Tilzer.

14

There was I, waiting at the church,
  Waiting at the church, waiting at the church,
When I found he'd left me in the lurch,
  Lor, how it did upset me!
All at once he sent me round a note
Here's the very note, This is what he wrote,
Can't get away to marry you today—
  My wife won't let me.

> FRED W. LEIGH, *Waiting at the Church* (song, 1906, with music by Henry E. Pether). This was long associated with the name of the popular singer Vesta Victoria.

15

Marriage is a lot of things—an alliance, a sacrament, a comedy, or a mistake; but it is definitely not a partnership because that implies equal gain. And every right-thinking woman knows the profit in matrimony is by all odds hers.

> PHYLLIS McGINLEY, *The Province of the Heart: How to Get Along with Men,* p. 73.

16

Who are happy in marriage? Those with so little imagination that they cannot picture a better state, and those so shrewd that they prefer quiet slavery to a hopeless rebellion.

> H. L. MENCKEN, *Prejudices,* ser. ii, p. 245.

17

Marriage, as everyone knows, is chiefly an economic matter. But too often it is assumed that its economy concerns only the wife's hats; it also concerns, and perhaps more importantly, the husband's cigars. No man is genuinely happy, married, who has to drink worse whiskey than he used to drink when he was single.

> H. L. MENCKEN, *Prejudices,* ser. iv.

18

Was it for this I uttered prayers,
And sobbed and cursed and kicked the stairs,
That now, domestic as a plate,

I should retire at half-past eight?
  EDNA ST. VINCENT MILLAY, *Grown-Up.*

1
Accursed from their birth they be
Who seek to find monogamy,
Pursuing it from bed to bed—
I think they would be better dead.
  DOROTHY PARKER, *Monogamy.*

2
It takes patience to appreciate domestic
bliss; volatile spirits prefer unhappiness.
  GEORGE SANTAYANA, *The Life of Reason,*
    vol. ii, p. 4.

3
Domestic squalls that sometimes reach cy-
clonic proportions may be expected when an
old man plunges into the matrimonial pool
with a young woman. The old man lives in
the past; the young woman lives in the future. She chews gum while he smokes a pipe.
At the table she calls for calories and vitamins, while he calls for hog and hominy. She
likes ragtime while he prefers *In the Sweet
By and By.* She can dance all night, but
nature drives him in with the swallows.
  JUSTICE GLENN TERRELL, Florida Supreme
    Court, Opinion. (Quoted in Associated
    Press dispatch reporting his death, date-
    lined Tallahassee, Fla., 13 Jan., 1964)

4
If you mean gettin' hitched, I'm in!
  ARTEMUS WARD, *Artemus Ward, His
    Book: The Showman's Courtship.*

5
Alas, she married another. They frequently
do. I hope she is happy—because I am.
  ARTEMUS WARD, Lecture.

6
He is dreadfully married. He's the most mar-
ried man I ever saw in my life.
  ARTEMUS WARD, *A Mormon Romance.*

7
Marriage is a status of antagonistic co-operation. In such a status, necessarily, centripetal
and centrifugal forces are continuously at
work, and the measure of its success obviously depends on the extent to which the centripetal forces are predominant.
  FEDERAL JUDGE JOHN M. WOOLSEY, Deci-
    sion rendered 6 Apr., 1931, in which he
    held that Marie Stopes's *Married Love*
    was not obscene.

MARTYR AND MARTYRDOM

8
The martyr cannot be dishonored.
  EMERSON, *Essays, First Series: Compensa-
    tion.*

9
Pain is superficial and therefore fear is. The
torments of martyrdom are probably most
keenly felt by the bystanders.
  EMERSON, *Society and Solitude: Courage.*

10
Tortured for the republic. (*Strangulatus pro
republica.*)
  JAMES A. GARFIELD, Last Words, written
    as he was dying, 17 July, 1882.

11
Perhaps there is no happiness in life so per-
fect as the martyr's.
  O. HENRY, *The Trimmed Lamp: The
    Country of Elusion.*

12
The dungeon oped its hungry door
To give the truth one martyr more.
  JAMES RUSSELL LOWELL, *On the Death of
    C. R. Torrey.*

13
Every step of progress the world has made
has been from scaffold to scaffold, and from
stake to stake.
  WENDELL PHILLIPS, *Woman's Rights.*

14
There have been quite as many martyrs for
bad causes as for good ones.
  HENDRIK WILLEM VAN LOON, *America.*

MASTER

15
The measure of a master is his success in
bringing all men round to his opinion twenty
years later.
  EMERSON, *Conduct of Life: Culture.*

16
Down in de cornfield,
  Hear dat mournful sound:
All de darkies am a-weeping,
  Massa's in de cold, cold ground.
  STEPHEN C. FOSTER, *Massa's in de Cold
    Ground.*

17
The eye of a master will do more work than
both his hands.
  BENJAMIN FRANKLIN, *Poor Richard,*
    1758.

18
The man who gives me employment, which I
must have or suffer, that man is my master,
let me call him what I will.
  HENRY GEORGE, *Social Problems,* ch. 5.

MAY

19
By great good fortune May does follow April
and redeems many promises that April has
forfeited.
  BROOKS ATKINSON, "Critic at Large" Col-
    umn, New York *Times,* 30 Apr., 1965.

20
Here's to the day when it is May
  And care as light as a feather,
When your little shoes and my big boots
  Go tramping over the heather.
  BLISS CARMAN, *A Toast.*

21
What potent blood hath modest May!
  EMERSON, *May-Day.*

1
The voice of one who goes before, to make
The paths of June more beautiful, is thine
Sweet May!
> HELEN HUNT JACKSON, *May.*

2
May is a pious fraud of the almanac.
> JAMES RUSSELL LOWELL, *Under the Willows.*

3
The hawthorne-scented dusks of May.
> DON MARQUIS, *An Open Fire.*

MEDICINE

See also Disease, Doctors, Health

4
Though I have patches on me pantaloons,
I've ne'er a wan on me intestines.
> FINLEY PETER DUNNE, *Thanksgiving.*

5
Then comes the question, how do drugs, hygiene and animal magnetism heal? It may be affirmed that they do not heal, but only relieve suffering temporarily, exchanging one disease for another.
> MARY BAKER EDDY, *Science and Health*, p. 483.

6
Dr. Bigelow's formula was, that fevers are self-limiting; afterwards that all disease is so; therefore no use in treatment. Dr. Holmes said, No use in drugs. Dr. Samuel Jackson said, Rest, absolute rest, is the panacea.
> EMERSON, *Journal*, 1860.

7
Many dishes, many diseases. Many medicines, few cures.
> BENJAMIN FRANKLIN, *Poor Richard*, 1734.

8
I firmly believe that if the whole *materia medica* could be sunk to the bottom of the sea, it would be all the better for mankind and all the worse for the fishes.
> OLIVER WENDELL HOLMES, Lecture at Harvard Medical School.

9
The worst about medicine is that one kind makes another necessary.
> ELBERT HUBBARD, *The Philistine*, vol. xxvii, p. 61.

10
I believe we may safely affirm that the inexperienced and presumptuous band of medical tyros let loose upon the world destroys more of human life in one year than all the Robin Hoods, Cartouches, and MacHeaths do in a century.
> THOMAS JEFFERSON, Letter to Jasper Wistar, 21 June, 1807.

11
It is the sick who need medicine and not the well.
> THOMAS JEFFERSON, *Writings*, vol. x, p. 103.

MEEKNESS

12
Wisdom has taught us to be calm and meek,
To take one blow, and turn the other cheek.
> OLIVER WENDELL HOLMES, *Non-Resistance.*

13
It's goin' t' be fun t' watch an' see how long th' meek kin keep the earth after they inherit it.
> KIN HUBBARD, *Sayings.*

14
The meek, the terrible meek, the fierce agonizing meek, are about to enter into their inheritance.
> CHARLES RANN KENNEDY, *The Terrible Meek.*

15
Let the meek inherit the earth—they have it coming to them.
> JAMES THURBER. (*Life*, 14 Mar., 1960)

MEETING

16
Between cultivated minds the first interview is the best.
> EMERSON, *Journals*, vol. iii, p. 496.

17
As vessels starting from ports thousands of miles apart pass close to each other in the naked breadth of the ocean, nay, sometimes even touch in the dark.
> OLIVER WENDELL HOLMES, *The Professor at the Breakfast-Table*, ch. 3.

18
No one ever won an interview.
> GARSON KANIN. (RICHARD MANEY, *Fanfare*, p. 195)

19
The joy of meeting not unmixed with pain.
> HENRY WADSWORTH LONGFELLOW, *Morituri Salutamus*, l. 113.

20
Ships that pass in the night, and speak each
    other in passing,
Only a signal shown and a distant voice in
    the darkness;
So on the ocean of life, we pass and speak
    one another,
Only a look and a voice, then darkness again
    and a silence.
> HENRY WADSWORTH LONGFELLOW, *Tales of a Wayside Inn: The Theologian's Tale.*

21
Say good-bye er howdy-do—
What's the odds betwixt the two?
Comin'—goin'—every day—
Best friends first to go away—
Grasp of hands you'd ruther hold
Than their weight in solid gold,
Slips their grip while greetin' you,—
Say good-bye er howdy-do?
> JAMES WHITCOMB RILEY, *Good-Bye er Howdy-Do.*

MEMORIAL DAY, see Soldier

MEMORY

See also Past

1

If only those old walls could talk, how boring they would be!

ROBERT BENCHLEY, *If These Old Walls Could Talk!* Inspired by the wrecking of the old Waldorf-Astoria Hotel in New York City, where, as a young reporter, Benchley had covered many an uninspiring banquet and meeting.

2

Ah, we fondly cherish
  Faded things
That had better perish.
  Memory clings
To each leaf it saves.
    J. H. BONER, *Gather Leaves and Grasses.*

3

O Genevieve, sweet Genevieve,
  The days may come, the days may go,
But still the hands of mem'ry weave
  The blissful dreams of long ago.
    GEORGE COOPER, *Sweet Genevieve.* Set to music about 1877 by Henry Tucker.

4

    I am with you,
Wandering through Memory Lane.
    B. G. DE SYLVA, *Memory Lane.* Set to music in 1924 by Larry Spier and Con Conrad.

5

Where is the heart that doth not keep,
  Within its inmost core,
Some fond remembrance hidden deep,
  Of days that are no more?
    ELLEN CLEMENTINE HOWARTH, *'Tis But a Little Faded Flower.*

6

A retentive memory is a good thing, but the ability to forget is the true token of greatness.
    ELBERT HUBBARD, *Epigrams.*

7

The leaves of memory seemed to make
A mournful rustling in the dark.
    HENRY WADSWORTH LONGFELLOW, *The Fire of Driftwood.*

8

This memory brightens o'er the past,
  As when the sun, concealed
Behind some cloud that near us hangs,
  Shines on a distant field.
    HENRY WADSWORTH LONGFELLOW, *A Gleam of Sunshine,* st. 14.

9

There comes to me out of the Past
A voice, whose tones are sweet and wild,
Singing a song almost divine,
And with a tear in every line.
    HENRY WADSWORTH LONGFELLOW, *Tales of a Wayside Inn,* Pt. iii: Interlude.

10

Nothing now is left But a majestic memory.
    HENRY WADSWORTH LONGFELLOW, *Three Friends of Mine,* l. 10.

11

Memory performs the impossible for man; holds together past and present, gives continuity and dignity to human life. This is the companion, this the tutor, the poet, the library, with which you travel.
    MARK VAN DOREN, *Liberal Education.*

MIGHT

See also Force, Power, Strength

12

Let us have faith that right makes might, and in that faith let us to the end dare to do our duty as we understand it.
    ABRAHAM LINCOLN, Address at Cooper Institute, New York City, 27 Feb., 1860.

It has been said of the world's history hitherto that might makes right. It is for us and for our time to reverse the maxim, and to say that right makes might.
    ABRAHAM LINCOLN.

13

Crowns of roses fade—crowns of thorns endure. Calvaries and crucifixions take deepest hold of humanity—the triumphs of might are transient—they pass and are forgotten—the sufferings of right are graven deepest on the chronicle of nations.
    ABRAM J. RYAN, *A Land Without Ruins: Foreword.*

14

But let the free-winged angel Truth their guarded passes scale,
To teach that right is more than might, and justice more than mail!
    JOHN GREENLEAF WHITTIER, *Brown of Ossawatomie.*

MIND

See also Intelligence, Thought

15

I wanted school to save me from Harlem. I knew I was black, of course, but I also knew I was smart. I didn't know how I would use my mind or even if I could. But that was the only thing I had to use. And I was going to get whatever I wanted that way and I was going to get my revenge that way.
    JAMES BALDWIN, Television Program, recalling his childhood; WNEW-TV, New York City, 1 June, 1964.

16

Some men are like pyramids, which are very broad where they touch the ground, but grow narrow as they reach the sky.
    HENRY WARD BEECHER, *Life Thoughts.*

17

here is little Effie's head
whose brains are made of gingerbread

when the judgment day comes
God will find six crumbs.
    E. E. CUMMINGS, *Portrait*.

1
Life is not a static thing. The only people
who do not change their minds are incompe-
tents in asylums, who can't, and those in
cemeteries.
    EVERETT M. DIRKSEN, News Conference,
    Washington, D.C., 1 Jan., 1965.

2
God is Mind, and God is infinite; hence all
is Mind.
    MARY BAKER EDDY, *Science and Health*,
    p. 492.

3
Intellect annuls Fate. So far as a man thinks
he is free.
    EMERSON, *Conduct of Life: Fate*.

4
A great mind is a good sailor, as a great heart
is.
    EMERSON, *English Traits*, ch. 2.

5
The growth of the intellect is spontaneous in
every expansion.
    EMERSON, *Essays, First Series: Intellect*.

6
Nothing is at last sacred but the integrity of
your own mind.
    EMERSON, *Essays, First Series: Self-Reli-
    ance*.

7
Nothing is old but the mind.
    EMERSON, *Letters and Social Aims: Prog-
    ress of Culture*.

8
The mind does not create what it perceives,
any more than the eye creates the rose.
    EMERSON, *Representative Men: Plato,
    New Readings*.

9
Sampson with his strong Body, had a weak
Head, or he would not have laid it in a Har-
lot's lap.
    BENJAMIN FRANKLIN, *Poor Richard*,
    1756.

10
The mind need never stop growing. Indeed,
one of the few experiences which never pall
is the experience of watching one's own
mind, and observing how it produces new
interests, responds to new stimuli, and develops new thoughts, apparently without effort
and almost independently of one's own conscious control.
    GILBERT HIGHET, *Talents and Geniuses*, p.
    308.

11
Our brains are seventy-year clocks. The Angel of Life winds them up once for all, then
closes the case, and gives the key into the
hand of the Angel of the Resurrection.
    OLIVER WENDELL HOLMES, *The Autocrat
    of the Breakfast-Table*, ch. 8.

12
One-story intellects, two-story intellects,
three-story intellects with skylights. All fact-
collectors . . . are one-story men. Two-
story men compare, reason, generalize. . . .
Three-story men idealize, imagine, predict;
their best illumination comes from above,
through the skylight.
    OLIVER WENDELL HOLMES, *The Poet at
    the Breakfast-Table*, ch. 2.

13
Little minds are interested in the extraordinary; great minds in the commonplace.
    ELBERT HUBBARD, *Epigrams*.

14
He who endeavors to control the mind by
force is a tyrant, and he who submits is a
slave.
    ROBERT G. INGERSOLL, *Some Mistakes of
    Moses*.

15
I don't care anything about reasons, but I
know what I like.
    HENRY JAMES, *The Portrait of a Lady*, ch.
    24.

16
A strong body makes the mind strong.
    THOMAS JEFFERSON, *Writings*, vol. v, p.
    83.

17
The human mind is our fundamental resource.
    JOHN F. KENNEDY, Message to Congress,
    on education, 20 Feb., 1961.

18
Most brains reflect but the crown of a hat.
    JAMES RUSSELL LOWELL, *A Fable for Crit-
    ics*, l. 704.

19
Housewives deserve well-furnished minds.
They have to live in them such a lot of the
time.
    PHYLLIS McGINLEY.

20
The perversion of the mind is only possible
when those who should be heard in its defense are silent.
    ARCHIBALD MacLEISH, *The Irresponsibles*.

21
Too clever is dumb.
    OGDEN NASH, *When the Moon Shines*.

22
Let's face it: Intellectual achievement and
the intellectual elite are alien to the main
stream of American society. They are off to
the side in a sub-section of esoteric isolation
labeled "odd-ball," "high brow," "egghead,"
"double-dome."
    ELMO ROPER, *Roadblocks to Bookbuying;
    Publishers' Weekly*, 16 June, 1958.

23
An improper mind is a perpetual feast.
    LOGAN PEARSALL SMITH, *Afterthoughts*.

24
Those who corrupt the public mind are just

as evil as those who steal from the public purse.

>ADLAI E. STEVENSON, Speech in Albuquerque, N. Mex., 12 Sept., 1952.

1

Eggheads, unite! You have nothing to lose but your yolks.

>ADLAI E. STEVENSON, Remark, during the 1952 presidential campaign, in reply to the Republican taunt of "egghead."

2

I have found that no exertion of the legs can bring two minds much nearer to one another.

>HENRY D. THOREAU.

3

Let Your Mind Alone.

>JAMES THURBER, Title of book (1937).

4

Mind is the great lever of all things.

>DANIEL WEBSTER, Address at the cornerstone laying of Bunker Hill Monument.

5

If we work upon marble, it will perish. If we work upon brass, time will efface it. If we rear temples, they will crumble to dust. But if we work upon men's immortal minds, if we imbue them with high principles, with the just fear of God and love of their fellow men, we engrave on those tablets something which no time can efface, and which will brighten and brighten to all eternity.

>DANIEL WEBSTER, Speech in Faneuil Hall, 1852.

6

I have a single-track mind.

>WOODROW WILSON, Speech before the National Press Club, Washington, D.C.

7

He has a bungalow mind.

>WOODROW WILSON, speaking of President Harding. (THOMPSON, *Presidents I've Known*, p. 334)

MINORITY, see Majority
MIRACLE

8

We must not sit down, and look for miracles. Up, and be doing, and the Lord will be with thee. Prayer and pains, through faith in Christ Jesus, will do anything.

>JOHN ELIOT, *Indian Grammar Begun: Postscript.*

9

Miracles exist as ancient history merely; they are not in the belief, nor in the aspiration of society.

>EMERSON, *Nature, Addresses, and Lectures: Address.*

10

To aim to convert a man by miracles is a profanation of the soul.

>EMERSON, *Nature, Addresses, and Lectures: Address.*

11

The question before the human race is, whether the God of Nature shall govern the world by His own laws, or whether priests and kings shall rule it by fictitious miracles.

>THOMAS JEFFERSON, Letter to John Adams, 1815.

12

To me every hour of the light and dark is a miracle,
Every cubic inch of space is a miracle.

>WALT WHITMAN, *Miracles,* l. 17.

MISFORTUNE
See also Adversity, Trouble

13

A person seldom falls sick, but the bystanders are animated with the faint hope that he will die.

>EMERSON, *Conduct of Life: Considerations by the Way.*

14

To bear other people's afflictions, every one has courage and enough to spare.

>BENJAMIN FRANKLIN, *Poor Richard,* 1740.

15

There are a good many real miseries in life that we cannot help smiling at, but they are the smiles that make wrinkles and not dimples.

>OLIVER WENDELL HOLMES, *The Poet at the Breakfast-Table,* ch. 3.

16

Little minds are tamed and subdued by misfortune, but great minds rise above it.

>WASHINGTON IRVING, *Sketch Book: Philip of Pokanoket.*

17

Misfortune makes strange bedfellows.

>HENRY JAMES, *The Portrait of a Lady,* ch. 5.

18

The misfortunes hardest to bear are those which never come.

>JAMES RUSSELL LOWELL, Address: *Democracy,* Birmingham, 6 Oct., 1884.

19

If misery loves company, misery has company enough.

>HENRY D. THOREAU, *Journal,* 1 Sept., 1851.

20

Anyone can stand his own misfortunes; but when I read in the papers all about the rascalities and outrages going on I realize what a creature the human animal is.

>MARK TWAIN. (PAINE, *Mark Twain*)

MODERATION
See also Temperance

21

Moderation in the pursuit of justice is no virtue!

>BARRY M. GOLDWATER, Speech, 16 July,

1964, upon accepting the presidential nomination, Republican national convention, San Francisco.

1

I, who preached moderation to everyone else, never practiced it myself. I didn't have ulcers; I gave them to the people who worked for me. I didn't tolerate inefficiency or ineptitude. I blew my top over trifles. I'd spend hours on the phone haranguing for votes. My breakfast was black coffee and four cigarettes. Late at night, after a sixteen-hour day, I'd wolf down a chicken-fried steak, fried potatoes and half a dozen slices of bread.

> LYNDON B. JOHNSON, commenting on his recovery from a heart attack suffered 2 July, 1955. (HENRY A. ZEIGER, *Lyndon B. Johnson: Man and President*, p. 59–60)

2

What we lack is a popularity of moderation.

> STANLEY MARCUS, commenting on his city, Dallas, shortly after the assassination of President Kennedy there. (Interview with Tom Yarbrough, St. Louis *Post-Dispatch*, 18 Dec., 1963)

3

Christmas is coming. I would ask Santa for these presents: quality to balance our quantity, restraint to balance our excesses, and humility to balance our pride. . . . I would say our next objective is balance. We must not lose the precious quality of individualism, but unthinking individualism is either arrogance or selfishness.

> CHARLES A. MEYER, Statement before the Dallas Chamber of Commerce, 3 Dec., 1963. He was speaking as a director of that body, less than two weeks after the assassination of John F. Kennedy in Dallas.

MODESTY

See also Humility

4

I do not think it entirely inappropriate to introduce myself to this audience. I am the man who accompanied Jacqueline Kennedy to Paris, and I have enjoyed it.

> JOHN F. KENNEDY, Statement at SHAPE Headquarters, Paris, 2 June, 1961. (*The Kennedy Wit: The Family*, ed. by Bill Adler)

5

Modesty antedates clothes and will be resumed when clothes are no more. Modesty died when clothes were born. Modesty died when false modesty was born.

> MARK TWAIN. (PAINE, *Mark Twain*, vol. iii, p. 1513)

6

Modesty in a man is a crime. Don't be modest. It is a woman's virtue.

> FREDERICK WARDE, Interview on his 80th birthday, 23 Feb., 1931.

7

Vanity as an impulse has without doubt been of far more benefit to civilization than modesty has ever been.

> WILLIAM E. WOODWARD, *George Washington*, ch. 5.

MONEY

See also Avarice, Dollar, Riches

8

You shall not press down upon the brow of labor this crown of thorns; you shall not crucify mankind upon a cross of gold.

> WILLIAM JENNINGS BRYAN, Speech at the Democratic national convention, Chicago, 10 July, 1896.

9

Nothing is more common than the mistake that money and property are identical. They are not. A redundancy of money does not prove any prosperity. There may be a very large amount of circulating medium and very great poverty. . . . It is not the volume of money but the activity of money that counts.

> W. BOURKE COCKRAN, Speech in New York City, 18 Aug., 1896, replying to William Jennings Bryan and other advocates of free silver.

10

Money never can circulate freely and actively unless there be absolute confidence in its value. If a man doubt whether the money in his pocket will be as valuable tomorrow as it is today, he will decline to exchange his commodity against it.

> W. BOURKE COCKRAN, Speech in New York City, 18 Aug., 1896.

11

They hired the money, didn't they?

> CALVIN COOLIDGE, 1925, referring to the money borrowed during World War I by France and other allies.

12

My neighbor, a jolly farmer, in the tavern barroom, thinks that the use of money is sure and speedy spending. For his part, he says, he puts his down his neck and gets the good of it.

> EMERSON, *Representative Men: Montaigne*.

13

Money is like an arm or a leg—use it or lose it.

> HENRY FORD, Interview, New York *Times*, 8 Nov., 1931.

1

The use of money is all the advantage there is in having money.

BENJAMIN FRANKLIN, *Hints to Those That Would Be Rich.*

2

Remember that money is of a prolific generating nature. Money can beget money, and its offspring can beget more.

BENJAMIN FRANKLIN, *Letters: To My Friend, A. B.,* 1748.

3

If you would know the value of money, go and try to borrow some.

BENJAMIN FRANKLIN, *Poor Richard,* 1758.

4

Money is the commonest of our talents.

WILLIAM GIBSON, Letter to Drama Editor, New York *Times,* 31 May, 1964.

5

This bank-note world.

FITZ-GREENE HALLECK, *Alnwick Castle.*

6

Money is an essential ingredient to happiness in this world.

ALEXANDER HAMILTON, Letter to John Laurens, Dec., 1779.

Money is the symbol of nearly everything that is necessary for man's well-being and happiness. . . . Money means freedom, independence, liberty.

EDWARD E. BEALS, *The Law of Financial Success.*

7

You Can't Take It with You.

MOSS HART AND GEORGE S. KAUFMAN, Title of comedy (1937).

8

Put not your trust in money, but put your money in trust.

OLIVER WENDELL HOLMES, *The Autocrat of the Breakfast-Table,* ch. 2.

9

Gold is the money of monarchs; kings covet it; the exchanges of the nations are effected by it. . . . It is the instrument of gamblers and speculators, and the idol of the miser and the thief. . . . No people in a great emergency ever found a faithful ally in gold. It is the most cowardly and treacherous of all metals. It makes no treaty that it does not break. It has no friend whom it does not sooner or later betray.

JOHN J. INGALLS, Speech on the coinage of silver dollars, U.S. Senate, 15 Feb., 1878.

10

The plainest print cannot be read through a gold eagle.

ABRAHAM LINCOLN, Speech in Springfield, Ill., 26 June, 1857.

11

In the race for money some men may come first, but man comes last.

MARYA MANNES. (*New Bites by a Girl Gadfly; Life,* 12 June, 1964, p. 62)

12

Do you know the only thing that gives me pleasure? It's to see my dividends coming in.

JOHN D. ROCKEFELLER. (WINKLER, *John D.*)

13

Happiness lies not in the mere possession of money; it lies in the joy of achievement, in the thrill of creative effort.

FRANKLIN D. ROOSEVELT, First Inaugural Address, 4 Mar., 1933.

14

It isn't the sum you get, it's how much you can buy with it that's the important thing; and it's that that tells whether your wages are high in fact or only high in name.

MARK TWAIN, *A Connecticut Yankee at King Arthur's Court,* p. 292.

15

It's harder to give away money than it is to make it. After all, you want it to be useful.

MAXWELL M. UPSON, upon pledging $9,000,000 in stock as a bequest to Cornell University, 10 Oct., 1964.

16

It is not a custom with me to keep money to look at.

GEORGE WASHINGTON, Letter to J. P. Custis, Jan., 1780.

17

Whenever you git holt of a ten-dollar note you want to git it *into you* or *onto ye* jest 's quick 's you kin. We're here today an' gone tomorrer, and the' ain't no pocket in a shroud.

EDWARD NOYES WESTCOTT, *David Harum,* p. 204.

MONUMENT

18

The marble keeps merely a cold and sad memory of a man who would else be forgotten. No man who needs a monument ever ought to have one.

NATHANIEL HAWTHORNE, *English Note-Books:* 12 Nov., 1857, *Westminster Abbey.*

19

Let it rise! Let it rise, till it meet the sun in his coming; let the earliest light of the morning gild it, and the parting day linger and play on its summit.

DANIEL WEBSTER, Address upon laying the cornerstone of Bunker Hill Monument.

MOON, THE

20

The moon is distant from the sea,
And yet with amber hands

She leads him, docile as a boy,
Along appointed sands.
> EMILY DICKINSON, *Poems*, Pt. iii, No. 31.

1
The man who has seen the rising moon break out of the clouds at midnight, has been present like an archangel at the creation of light and of the world.
> EMERSON, *Essays, First Series: History.*

2
A sweet little Venus we'll fondle between us,
When I wed my old man in the moon.
> JAMES THORNTON, *My Sweetheart's the Man in the Moon* (1892).

3
Everyone is a moon, and has a dark side which he never shows to anybody.
> MARK TWAIN, *Pudd'nhead Wilson's New Calendar.*

4
But tenderly Above the sea
Hangs, white and calm, the hunter's moon.
> JOHN GREENLEAF WHITTIER, *The Eve of Election*, st. 1.

MORALITY

5
Morality is a private and costly luxury.
> HENRY ADAMS, *The Education of Henry Adams*, ch. 22.

6
Morality, said Jesus, is kindness to the weak; morality, said Nietzsche, is the bravery of the strong; morality, said Plato, is the effective harmony of the whole. Probably all three doctrines must be combined to find a perfect ethic; but can we doubt which of the elements is fundamental?
> WILL DURANT, *The Story of Philosophy.*

7
Men talk of "mere Morality," which is much as if one should say "Poor God, with nobody to help him."
> EMERSON, *Conduct of Life: Worship.*

8
He who wears his morality but as his best garment were better naked.
> KAHLIL GIBRAN, *The Prophet: On Religion.*

9
So far, about morals, I know only that what is moral is what you feel good after and what is immoral is what you feel bad after.
> ERNEST HEMINGWAY, *Death in the Afternoon*, ch. 1.

10
We are doomed to be moral and cannot help ourselves.
> JOHN HAYNES HOLMES, *Morality.*

11
Friendly cynics and fierce enemies alike often underestimate or ignore the strong thread of moral purpose which runs through the fabric of American history.
> LYNDON B. JOHNSON, Speech at American Bar Association meeting, Aug., 1964.

12
Rhetoric takes no real account of the art in literature, and morality takes no account of the art in life.
> JOSEPH WOOD KRUTCH, *The Modern Temper*, p. 154.

13
Morality without religion is only a kind of dead reckoning,—an endeavor to find our place on a cloudy sea.
> HENRY WADSWORTH LONGFELLOW, *Kavanagh*, ch. 13.

14
To denounce moralizing out of hand is to pronounce a moral judgment.
> H. L. MENCKEN, *Prejudices*, ser. i, p. 19.

15
The difference between a moral man and a man of honor is that the latter regrets a discreditable act even when it has worked.
> H. L. MENCKEN, *Prejudices*, ser. iv, p. 206.

16
These Republican gentlemen can't have it both ways—they can't be for morality on Tuesday and Thursday, and then be for special interests for their clients on Monday, Wednesday and Friday.
> HARRY S TRUMAN, Speech, 29 Mar., 1952, lashing back at Republican attacks on corruption in his administration. (ALFRED STEINBERG, *The Man from Missouri*, p. 407)

17
There is no such thing as morality; it is not immoral for the tiger to eat the wolf, or the wolf the cat, or the cat the bird, and so on down; that is their business. . . . It is not immoral to create the human species—with or without ceremony; nature intended exactly these things.
> MARK TWAIN. (PAINE, *Mark Twain*)

MOTHER, MOTHERHOOD

18
Don't aim to be an earthly Saint, with eyes fixed on a star,
Just try to be the fellow that your Mother thinks you are.
> WILL S. ADKIN, *Just Try to Be the Fellow.*

19
Where there is a mother in the house, matters speed well.
> AMOS BRONSON ALCOTT, *Table Talk: Nurture.*

20
The mother's heart is the child's schoolroom.
> HENRY WARD BEECHER, *Life Thoughts.*

1

She's somebody's mother, boys, you know,
For all she's aged, and poor, and slow.
> MARY D. BRINE, *Somebody's Mother*, first
> published in *Harper's Weekly*, 2 Mar.,
> 1878.

2

The sweetest sounds to mortals given
Are heard in Mother, Home, and Heaven.
> WILLIAM GOLDSMITH BROWN, *Mother,
> Home, Heaven.*

3

Men are what their mothers made them.
> EMERSON, *Conduct of Life: Fate.*

All that I am my mother made me.
> JOHN QUINCY ADAMS.

All that I am or hope to be, I owe to my
angel mother.
> Attributed to ABRAHAM LINCOLN.

4

A mother is not a person to lean on but a
person to make leaning unnecessary.
> DOROTHY CANFIELD FISHER, *Her Son's
> Wife.*

5

You may have tangible wealth untold;
Caskets of jewels and coffers of gold.
Richer than I you can never be—
I had a mother who read to me.
> STRICKLAND GILLILAN, *The Reading
> Mother.*

6

What Is Home Without a Mother?
> ALICE HAWTHORNE, Title of Poem.

7

Youth fades; love droops; the leaves of
friendship fall:
A mother's secret love outlives them all.
> OLIVER WENDELL HOLMES, *The Mother's
> Secret.*

8

Put them all together, they spell "Mother,"
A word that means the world to me.
> HOWARD JOHNSON, *Mother* (1915).

9

This is a moment I deeply wish my parents
could have lived to share. In the first place
my father would have enjoyed what you
have so generously said of me—and my
mother would have believed it.
> LYNDON B. JOHNSON, Commencement Ad-
> dress at Baylor University, Waco, Tex.,
> 28 May, 1965. These were his opening
> words.

10

I pray that our Heavenly Father may assuage the anguish of your bereavement and
leave you only the cherished memory of the
loved and lost, and the solemn pride that
must be yours to have laid so costly a sacrifice upon the altar of freedom.
> ABRAHAM LINCOLN, Letter, 21 Nov., 1864,
> to Mrs. Bixby of Boston, who lost five
> sons in the Civil War. This famous let-

ter is said to have been drafted by John
Hay, Lincoln's secretary.

11

>   A woman's love
Is mighty, but a mother's heart is weak,
And by its weakness overcomes.
> JAMES RUSSELL LOWELL, *A Legend of
> Brittany,* pt. ii, st. 43.

12

My mother was a lady, like yours you will
allow.
> EDWARD B. MARKS, *My Mother Was a
> Lady.* Made famous by Lottie Gilson in
> 1896.

13

The bravest battle that ever was fought;
Shall I tell you where and when?
On the maps of the world you will find it
not;
It was fought by the mothers of men.
> JOAQUIN MILLER, *The Bravest Battle.*

14

One moment makes a father, but a mother
Is made by endless moments, load on load.
> JOHN G. NEIHARDT, *Eight Hundred
> Rubles.*

15

They say that man is mighty,
He governs land and sea,
He wields a mighty scepter
O'er lesser powers that be;
But a mightier power and stronger
Man from his throne has hurled,
For the hand that rocks the cradle
Is the hand that rules the world.
> WILLIAM ROSS WALLACE, *What Rules the
> World.*

"The hand that rocks the cradle"—but today
there's no such hand.
It is bad to rock the baby, they would have
us understand;
So the cradle's but a relic of the former foolish days,
When mothers reared their children in unsci-
entific ways;
When they jounced them and they bounced
them, those poor dwarfs of long ago—
The Washingtons and Jeffersons and Ad-
amses, you know.
> Attributed to BISHOP WILLIAM CROSWELL
> DOANE, *What Might Have Been.*

MURDER

16

What a cruel, foul, and most unnatural murder!
> SEAN O'CASEY, Letter to Rose Russell of
> New York City, addressed from Tor-
> quay, Devonshire, England, 23 Nov.,
> 1963. He was referring to the assassina-
> tion of John F. Kennedy.

17

Lizzie Borden took an axe

And gave her Mother forty whacks;
When she saw what she had done,
She gave her Father forty-one.

> UNKNOWN, *Lizzie Borden*, on the murder
> of Lizzie Borden's father and stepmoth-
> er in Fall River, Mass., 4 Aug., 1892.

There's no evidence of guilt,
    Lizzie Borden,
That should make your spirit wilt,
    Lizzie Borden;
Many do not think that you
Chopped your father's head in two,
It's so hard a thing to do,
    Lizzie Borden.

> A. L. BIXBY, *To Lizzie*.

1

Jesse James had a wife,
She's a mourner all her life;
    His children they were brave;
Oh, the dirty little coward
That shot Mr. Howard,
    Has laid poor Jesse in his grave.

> UNKNOWN, *Jesse James*, a song on the
> murder of Jesse James (who had been
> living under the name of Thomas How-
> ard) by Robert Ford in St. Joseph, Mo.,
> 3 Apr., 1882.

MUSIC

2

There's only two ways to sum up music:
either it's good or it's bad. If it's good you
don't mess about it; you just enjoy it.

> LOUIS ARMSTRONG, on the difficulty of de-
> fining jazz.

3

He could fiddle all the bugs off a sweet-pota-
to-vine.

> STEPHEN VINCENT BENÉT, *The Mountain
> Whippoorwill*.

4

Come on and hear, come on and hear, Alexander's Ragtime Band.

> IRVING BERLIN, *Alexander's Ragtime Band*
> (1911).

5

The Fiddle: An instrument to tickle human
ears by friction of a horse's tail on the en-
trails of a cat.

> AMBROSE BIERCE, *The Devil's Dictionary*.

6

Composers tend to assume that everyone
loves music. Surprisingly enough, everyone
doesn't.

> AARON COPLAND, *ASCAP and the Sym-
> phonic Composer; New York Times
> Magazine*, 16 Feb., 1964.

7

It is safe to say that no man ever went
wrong, morally or mentally, while listening
to a symphony.

> JUSTICE JOHN J. DILLON, New York State
> Supreme Court, Decision, 31 Dec., 1964,

granting tax exemption on a Bedford,
N.Y., estate, Caramoor, used for public
concerts.

8

Music is the poor man's Parnassus.

> EMERSON, *Letters and Social Aims: Poetry
> and Imagination*.

9

The composer is always in danger of becoming the forgotten man. The painter, the
sculptor, the poet can each speak for himself.
Only the composer must have an interpreter,
a translator, who sometimes communicates
faithfully and sometimes comes between the
creator and his audience.

> HOWARD HANSON, *ASCAP and the Forgot-
> ten Man; New York Times Magazine*,
> 16 Feb., 1964.

10

Music was a thing of the soul—a rose-lipped
shell that murmured of the eternal sea—a
strange bird singing the songs of another
shore.

> JOSIAH G. HOLLAND, *Plain Talks on Famil-
> iar Subjects: Art and Life*.

11

Music is the only one of the arts that can
not be prostituted to a base use.

> ELBERT HUBBARD, *A Thousand and One
> Epigrams*, p. 39.

12

Music remains the only art, the last sanctuary, wherein originality may reveal itself in
the face of fools and not pierce their mental
opacity.

> JAMES G. HUNEKER, *Iconoclasts*, p. 142.

13

Last year, more Americans went to symphonies than went to baseball games. This may
be viewed as an alarming statistic, but I
think that both baseball and the country will
endure.

> JOHN F. KENNEDY, at a White House
> Youth Concert, 6 Aug., 1962. (*The
> Kennedy Wit*, ed. by Bill Adler: *The
> Presidency*)

14

The public of today must pay its debt to the
great composers of the past by supporting
the living creators of the present.

> SERGE KOUSSEVITZKY. (HOWARD HANSON,
> *ASCAP and the Forgotten Man; New
> York Times Magazine*, 16 Feb., 1964)

15

Yea, music is the Prophet's art
Among the gifts that God hath sent,
One of the most magnificent!

> HENRY WADSWORTH LONGFELLOW, *Chris-
> tus*, pt. iii, interlude 2

16

He is the best of all musicians,
He the sweetest of all singers.

> HENRY WADSWORTH LONGFELLOW, *Hiawa-
> tha*, pt. vi, l. 20.

1

He is dead, the sweet musician!
He has gone from us forever,
He has moved a little nearer
To the Master of all music.
> HENRY WADSWORTH LONGFELLOW, *Hiawatha*, pt. xv, l. 56.

2

Music is the universal language of mankind.
> HENRY WADSWORTH LONGFELLOW, *Outre-Mer: Spanish Ballads*.

3

Wagner's music is better than it sounds.
> BILL NYE.

4

Don't tell Mr. Hurok, but I love playing the piano so much I would do it for nothing.
> ARTUR RUBINSTEIN. (*Rubinstein Speaking; New York Times Magazine*, 26 Jan., 1964) "Mr. Hurok" is Sol Hurok, the noted impresario.

5

What most people relish is hardly music; it is rather a drowsy reverie relieved by nervous thrills.
> GEORGE SANTAYANA, *The Life of Reason*, iv, 51.

6

Music is essentially useless, as life is.
> GEORGE SANTAYANA, *Little Essays*, p. 130.

7

Music is feeling, then, not sound.
> WALLACE STEVENS, *Peter Quince at the Clavier*.

8

The trouble with music appreciation in general is that people are taught to have too much respect for music; they should be taught to love it instead.
> IGOR STRAVINSKY. (*New York Times Magazine*, 27 Sept., 1964)

9

I love music more than my own convenience.

Actually, I love it more than myself—but it is vastly more lovable than I.
> GEORGE SZELL. (*Newsweek*, 28 Jan., 1963)

10

Polyphony, flatted fifths, half tones—they don't mean a thing. I just pick up my horn and play what I feel.
> JACK TEAGARDEN. (New York *Times* obituary of the famous jazzman, 16 Jan., 1964)

11

Music hath caught a higher pace than any virtue that I know. It is the arch-reformer; it hastens the sun to its setting; it invites him to his rising; it is the sweetest reproach, a measured satire.
> HENRY D. THOREAU, *Winter: Journal*, 8 Jan., 1842.

12

All music is what awakes from you when you are reminded by the instruments,
It is not the violins and the cornets, it is not the oboe nor the beating drums, nor the score of the baritone singer singing his sweet romanza, nor that of the men's chorus, nor that of the women's chorus.
It is nearer and farther than they.
> WALT WHITMAN, *A Song for Occupations*, pt. 4.

13

Over the piano was printed a notice: "Please do not shoot the pianist. He is doing his best."
> OSCAR WILDE, *Impressions of America: Leadville*.

14

Servant and master am I: servant of those dead, and master of those living. Through my spirit immortals speak the message that makes the world weep and laugh, and wonder and worship. . . . For I am the instrument of God. I am Music.
> UNKNOWN, *Music*. (*International Musician*, July, 1928) Recited by Walter Damrosch.

N

NAME

See also Reputation

15

We must have your name. There will be more efficacy in it than in many an army.
> JOHN ADAMS, Letter to George Washington, 1798, when war with France threatened.

16

> Strong towers decay,
But a great name shall never pass away.
> PARK BENJAMIN, *A Great Name*.

17

No orator can measure in effect with him who can give good nicknames.
> EMERSON, *Representative Men: Plato*.

18

Navies nor armies can exalt the state, . . .
But one great name can make a country great.
> RICHARD WATSON GILDER, *To James Russell Lowell*.

19

Alone I walked on the ocean strand,

A pearly shell was in my hand;
I stopped, and wrote upon the sand
  My name, the year, the day.
As onward from the spot I passed,
One lingering look behind I cast,
A wave came rolling high and fast,
  And washed my lines away.
    HANNAH FLAGG GOULD, *A Name in the
    Sand.*

1
I long ago made my peace with the nickname.
    CLAUDIA TAYLOR JOHNSON (MRS. LYNDON
    B. JOHNSON), referring to "Lady Bird."
    (MARJORIE HUNTER, *Public Servant
    Without Pay: The First Lady; New
    York Times Magazine,* 15 Dec., 1963, p.
    73)

2
Ah, with what lofty hope we came!
But we forget it, dream of fame,
And scrawl, as I do here, a name.
    JAMES RUSSELL LOWELL, *For an Auto-
    graph,* st. 6.

3
Let us speak plain: there is more force in
names
Than most men dream of; and a lie may
keep
Its throne a whole age longer if it skulk
Behind the shield of some fair-seeming
name.
    JAMES RUSSELL LOWELL, *A Glance Behind
    the Curtain,* l. 251.

4
Call Me Mister.
    Title of revue (1946) with sketches by
    ARNOLD AUERBACH and ARNOLD HOR-
    WITT, music by HAROLD ROME. The
    theme was soldiers' return to civilian
    life.

5
Some American Sobriquets:
The Old Man Eloquent: John Quincy Ad-
ams
The American Cato: Samuel Adams
The Mill-Boy of the Slashes: Henry Clay
The Nestor of the Press: Charles A. Dana
The Little Giant: Stephen A. Douglas
Ike: Dwight D. Eisenhower
The Pathfinder: John Charles Frémont
Unconditional Surrender: U. S. Grant
The Cincinnatus of the West, Old Tippeca-
noe: William Henry Harrison
Papa: Ernest Hemingway
Old Hickory: Andrew Jackson
Stonewall: Thomas Jonathan Jackson
The Sage of Monticello: Thomas Jefferson
The Little Flower: Fiorello H. LaGuardia
Light-Horse Harry: Henry Lee
Iron Pants: Curtis E. LeMay

Father Abraham, Old Abe, Honest Abe, The
Rail-Splitter: Abraham Lincoln
The Swamp-Fox: Francis Marion
Old Blood and Guts: George S. Patton
Black Jack: John J. Pershing
Old Fuss and Feathers: Winfield Scott
The Happy Warrior: Alfred E. Smith
Vinegar Joe: Joseph W. Stilwell
Old Rough and Ready: Zachary Taylor
Father of His Country: George Washington
The Schoolmaster of the Republic: Noah
Webster

NATION

6
A treaty is the promise of a nation.
    FISHER AMES, Speech on treaty with
    Great Britain, 28 Apr., 1796.

7
I am firm in my conviction that . . . there
is no calamity which a great nation can invite which equals that which follows from a
supine submission to wrong and injustice,
and the consequent loss of national self-respect and honor, beneath which are shielded
and defended a people's safety and greatness.
    GROVER CLEVELAND, Message to Congress,
    on the Venezuelan question, 17 Dec.,
    1895. Based on a draft by Richard Ol-
    ney, Secretary of State. For contrasted
    texts see NEVINS, *Grover Cleveland,* p.
    640.

8
How much more are men than nations!
    EMERSON, *Letters and Social Aims: Prog-
    ress of Culture.*

9
A nation never falls but by suicide.
    EMERSON, *Journal,* 1861.

10
Justice is as strictly due between neighbor
nations as between neighbor citizens. A high-
wayman is as much a robber when he plun-
ders in a gang as when single; and a nation
that makes an unjust war is only a *great
gang.*
    BENJAMIN FRANKLIN, Letter, 14 Mar.,
    1785.

11
A nation is a thing that lives and acts like a
man, and men are the particles of which it is
composed.
    JOSIAH G. HOLLAND, *Plain Talks: The Na-
    tional Heart.*

12
Until nations are generous they will never be
wise; true policy is generous policy; all bitterness, selfishness, etc., may gain small ends,
but lose great ones.
    WASHINGTON IRVING, Letter, March,
    1823.

1

If a nation expects to be ignorant and free, it expects what never was and never will be.

THOMAS JEFFERSON, *Writings,* vol. xiv, p. 382.

2

No nation is permitted to live in ignorance with impunity.

THOMAS JEFFERSON, *Writings,* vol. xix, p. 407.

3

I know of no existing nation that deserves to live, and I know of very few individuals.

H. L. MENCKEN, *Prejudices,* ser. iv, p. 208.

4

The true greatness of nations is in those qualities which constitute the greatness of the individual.

CHARLES SUMNER, *Oration on the True Grandeur of Nations.*

5

There was never a nation great until it came to the knowledge that it had nowhere in the world to go for help.

CHARLES DUDLEY WARNER, *Studies: Comments on Canada,* ch. 3.

6

No nation is fit to sit in judgment upon any other nation.

WOODROW WILSON, Address in New York City, 20 Apr., 1915.

7

The nation's honor is dearer than the nation's comfort; yes, than the nation's life itself.

WOODROW WILSON, Speech, 29 Jan., 1916.

NATURE

8

The most unhappy thing about conservation is that it is never permanent. Save a priceless woodland or an irreplaceable mountain today, and tomorrow it is threatened from another quarter. Man, our most ingenious predator, sometimes seems determined to destroy the precious treasures of his own environment.

HAL BORLAND, *New York Times Book Review,* 23 Feb., 1964, p. 7.

9

Because of the true man's totality and centrality, he has the almost divine function of guardianship over the world of nature. Once this role is ignored or misused, he is in danger of being shown ultimately by nature who, in reality, is the conqueror, and who the conquered.

JOSEPH EPES BROWN, *The Spiritual Legacy of the American Indian.*

10

It could also be said, under another perspective, that in the past man had to protect himself from the forces of nature, whereas today it is nature that must be protected from man.

JOSEPH EPES BROWN, *The Spiritual Legacy of the American Indian.*

11

To him who in the love of Nature holds
Communion with her visible forms, she speaks
A various language; for his gayer hours
She has a voice of gladness, and a smile
And eloquence of beauty, and she glides
Into his darker musings, with a mild
And healing sympathy, that steals away
Their sharpness, ere he is aware.

WILLIAM CULLEN BRYANT, *Thanatopsis*

12

Go forth under the open sky, and list
To Nature's teachings.

WILLIAM CULLEN BRYANT, *Thanatopsis.*

13

Nature reads not our labels, "great" and "small";
Accepts she one and all.

JOHN VANCE CHENEY, *The Man with the Hoe: A Reply.*

14

At home with Nature, and at one with God!

FLORENCE EARLE COATES, *The Angelus.*

15

Inebriate of air am I,
And debauchee of dew,
Reeling, through endless summer days,
From inns of molten blue.

EMILY DICKINSON, *Poems.* Pt. i, No. 20.

16

Nature is a rag-merchant, who works up every shred and ort and end into new creations; like a good chemist whom I found, the other day, in his laboratory, converting his old shirts into pure white sugar.

EMERSON, *Conduct of Life: Considerations by the Way.*

17

Nature is what you may do. . . . Nature is the tyrannous circumstance, the thick skull, the sheathed snake, the ponderous rock-like jaw; necessitated activity, violent direction.

EMERSON, *Conduct of Life: Fate.*

18

Nature is no spendthrift, but takes the shortest way to her ends.

EMERSON, *Conduct of Life: Fate.*

19

Nature is a mutable cloud which is always and never the same.

EMERSON, *Essays, First Series: History.*

20

Nature, as we know her, is no saint. . . . She comes eating, drinking and sinning.

EMERSON, *Essays, Second Series: Experience.*

21

Nature hates calculators.

EMERSON, *Essays, Second Series: Experience.*

1

There is nothing so wonderful in any particular landscape as the necessity of being beautiful under which every landscape lies.

EMERSON, *Essays, Second Series: Nature.*

2

He who knows what sweets and virtues are in the ground, the waters, the plants, the heavens, and how to come at these enchantments, is the rich and royal man.

EMERSON, *Essays, Second Series: Nature.*

3

How cunningly nature hides every wrinkle of her inconceivable antiquity under roses and violets and morning dew!

EMERSON, *Letters and Social Aims: Progress of Culture.*

4

Nature pardons no mistakes. Her yea is yea, and her nay, nay.

EMERSON, *Nature, Addresses and Lectures: Discipline.*

5

Miller owns this field, Locke that, and Manning the woodland beyond. But none of them owns the landscape. There is a property in the horizon which no man has but he whose eye can integrate all the parts, that is, the poet. This is the best part of these men's farms, yet to this their warranty-deeds give no title.

EMERSON, *Nature, Addresses and Lectures: Nature.*

6

Nature works on a method of all for each and each for all.

EMERSON, *Society and Solitude: Farming.*

7

Nature is a volume of which God is the author.

MOSES HARVEY, *Science and Religion.*

8

Nature is religious only as it manifests God.

MARK HOPKINS, Sermon, 30 May, 1843.

9

Nature, in thy largess, grant
I may be thy confidant!

FREDERICK L. KNOWLES, *To Mother Nature.*

10

The natural alone is permanent.

HENRY WADSWORTH LONGFELLOW, *Kavanagh,* ch. 13.

11

Every formula which expresses a law of nature is a hymn of praise to God.

MARIA MITCHELL, Inscription beneath her bust in the Hall of Fame.

12

I was blood-sister to the clod,
Blood-brother to the stone.

WILLIAM VAUGHN MOODY, *The Fire-Bringer.*

13

Laws of Nature are God's thoughts thinking themselves out in the orbits and the tides.

CHARLES H. PARKHURST, *Sermons: Pattern in Mount.*

14

The modern "nature-faker" is of course an object of derision to every . . . true nature-lover.

THEODORE ROOSEVELT, *Everybody's Magazine,* Sept., 1907.

15

Nature will bear the closest inspection. She invites us to lay our eye level with her smallest leaf, and take an insect view of its plain.

HENRY D. THOREAU, *Journal,* 22 Oct., 1839.

16

It is the marriage of the soul with Nature that makes the intellect fruitful, and gives birth to imagination.

HENRY D. THOREAU, *Journal,* 21 Aug., 1851.

17

"Nature" is but another name for health, and the seasons are but different states of health.

HENRY D. THOREAU, *Journal,* 23 Aug., 1853.

18

For I'd rather be thy child
And pupil, in the forest wild,
Than be the king of men elsewhere,
And most sovereign slave of care;
To have one moment of thy dawn,
Than share the city's year forlorn.

HENRY D. THOREAU, *Nature.*

19

The sun-swept spaces which the good God made.

CHARLES HANSON TOWNE, *City Children.*

20

Nature is rarely allowed to enter the sacred portals of civilized society.

HENDRIK WILLEM VAN LOON, *Multiple Man.*

21

I believe a leaf of grass is no less than the
        journey-work of the stars,
And the pismire is equally perfect, and a
        grain of sand, and the egg of the wren,
And the tree-toad is a chef-d'oeuvre for the
        highest,
And the running blackberry would adorn the
        parlors of heaven,
And the narrowest hinge in my hand puts to
        scorn all machinery,
And the cow crunching with depress'd head
        surpasses any statue,
And a mouse is miracle enough to stagger
        sextillions of infidels.

WALT WHITMAN, *Song of Myself,* sec. 31.

1

Nature speaks in symbols and in signs.

JOHN GREENLEAF WHITTIER, *To Charles Sumner.*

2

I have no patience with people who say they love nature and go out to look at a field on Sunday afternoon. Our families, the way we live with our fellowmen, are a part of nature, too.

THORNTON WILDER. (FLORA LEWIS, *Thornton Wilder at 65; New York Times Magazine,* 15 Apr., 1962, p. 28)

3

Man is not content to take nature as he finds her. He insists on making her over.

F. J. E. WOODBRIDGE, *Contrasts in Education,* p. 17.

NECESSITY

4

We do what we must, and call it by the best names.

EMERSON, *Conduct of Life: Considerations by the Way.*

5

Let us build altars to the Beautiful Necessity, which secures that all is made of one piece.

EMERSON, *Conduct of Life: Fate.*

6

No man can quite exclude the element of necessity from his labor.

EMERSON, *Essays, First Series: Art.*

7

Necessity does everything well.

EMERSON, *Essays, Second Series: Gifts.*

8

Necessity never made a good bargain.

BENJAMIN FRANKLIN, *Poor Richard,* 1735.

NEGRO

See also Brown, John; Equality; Slavery

9

I think if God is good and we don't lose our nerve, we may turn this into a country instead of a European outpost, a European outpost culturally and spiritually. The whole doctrine of white supremacy comes from Europe.

JAMES BALDWIN, Statement to the New York *Times,* 15 June, 1964—part of a survey of the Negro in the theater.

10

Segregation in the South is a way of life. It is a precious and sacred custom. It is one of our dearest and most treasured possessions. It is the means whereby we live in social peace, order and security.

JUDGE THOMAS P. BRADY, Address before the Commonwealth Club of California, San Francisco, 4 Oct., 1957. (*Contemporary Forum,* ed. by ERNEST J. WRAGE AND BARNET BASKERVILLE, p. 334)

11

The passage of the Civil Rights bill of August 29, 1957, marks the beginning of another Reconstruction Era in the South. It is as dark a day as was May 17, 1954, the date of the illegal, unconstitutional and Communistic Black Monday decision.

JUDGE THOMAS P. BRADY, Address before the Commonwealth Club of California, San Francisco, 4 Oct., 1957. (*Contemporary Forum,* ed. by ERNEST J. WRAGE AND BARNET BASKERVILLE, p. 339). The decision was the Supreme Court ban on "separate but equal" public education.

12

Wherever the Negro goes in the United States, it is certain that discrimination will be his constant companion, now and for a long time ahead. . . . Leave the Negro in the South or move him away altogether and the shadow will still be there, and no one knows this better than the Negro who goes and the Negro who stays.

HODDING CARTER, *If All the Negroes Quit the South; New York Times Magazine,* 27 May, 1962, p. 52.

13

I would like to see a time when man loves his fellow man and forgets his color or his creed. We will never be civilized until that time comes. I know the Negro race has a long road to go. I believe that the life of the Negro race has been a life of tragedy, of injustice, of oppression. The law has made him equal, but man has not.

CLARENCE DARROW, in his defense of Henry Sweet, 19 May, 1926, in Detroit. Sweet was on trial as the result of a civil disorder that ocurred when he and other Negroes moved into a district in Detroit that had been occupied exclusively by whites.

14

If the race that we belong to owes anything to any human being, or to any power in the universe, they owe it to these black men. Above all other men, they owe an obligation and a duty to these black men that can never be repaid.

CLARENCE DARROW, in his defense of Henry Sweet, 19 May, 1926, in Detroit.

15

Together they gave to the nation and world undying proof that Americans of African descent possess the pride, courage, and devotion of the patriot soldier.

CHARLES WILLIAM ELIOT, Inscription on the Robert Gould Shaw Monument in Boston. The full inscription is a tribute to the "white officers" and "black rank and file" of the 54th Regiment of Massachusetts Infantry during the Civil War.

1

While European genius is symbolized by some majestic Corinne crowned in the capitol at Rome, American genius finds its true type in the poor negro soldier lying in the trenches by the Potomac with his spelling book in one hand and his musket in the other.

> EMERSON, Lecture: *Books.*

2

The Negro, thanks to his temperament, appears to make the greatest amount of happiness out of the smallest capital.

> EMERSON, *Journal,* vol. x, p. 176.

3

We may yet find a rose-water that will wash the negro white.

> EMERSON, *Society and Solitude: Works and Days.*

4

I'm coming, I'm coming, for my head is bending low:
I hear those gentle voices calling, "Old Black Joe."

> STEPHEN C. FOSTER, *Old Black Joe* (1860).

5

Forced integration is just as wrong as forced segregation.

> BARRY M. GOLDWATER, Speech in Chicago, 16 Oct., 1964, during the presidential campaign.

6

The Negro revolution is a fraud. It has no faith in the character and potentialities of the Negro masses. It has no taste for real enemies, real battlegrounds and desperate situations. It wants cheap victories and the easy way.

> ERIC HOFFER, *The Negro Is Prejudiced Against Himself; New York Times Magazine,* 29 Nov., 1964, p. 102.

7

We Shall Overcome.

> ZILPHIA HORTON, PETE SEEGER, FRANK HAMILTON, AND GUY CARAWAN, Title and refrain of song that emerged as the anthem of the civil rights movement in the 1960's. The song grew in the tradition of folk music. The basic tune is credited to Mrs. Horton, who conducted a folk school in Tennessee in the 1940's and there taught the song to hundreds of students and associates. Later three folk singers—Seeger, Hamilton, and Carawan—contributed new material, including verses. The product of this joint effort was first published in 1962.

8

In this hour, it is not our respective races which are at stake—it is our nation. Let those who care for their country come forward, North and South, white and Negro, to lead the way through this moment of challenge and decision. The Negro says, "Now." Others say, "Never." The voice of responsible Americans—the voice of those who died here and of the great man who spoke here—their voices say, "Together." There is no other way.

> LYNDON B. JOHNSON, Memorial Day Address, Gettysburg, Pa., 30 May, 1963.

9

Let us close the springs of racial poison. Let us pray for wise and understanding hearts. Let us lay aside irrelevant differences and make our nation whole.

> LYNDON B. JOHNSON, Public Statement, 2 July, 1964, upon signing the Civil Rights Bill of that year.

10

Our problem with frontlash is to hold it where it is. For every backlash the Democrats lose, we pick up three frontlash.

> LYNDON B. JOHNSON, Speech in Atlantic City, N.J., 28 Aug., 1964. "Backlash," or "white backlash," was a widely used term during the 1964 presidential campaign, signifying white reaction against Negro gains in civil rights, and consequent defection from Johnson, who supported civil rights. "Frontlash" meant the defection of moderate Republicans from their party's candidate, Barry M. Goldwater, because of his conservative views on civil rights. The election returns largely justified Johnson's prediction.

11

The real hero of this struggle is the American Negro. His actions and protests, his courage to risk safety, and even to risk his life, have awakened the conscience of this nation. His demonstrations have been designed to call attention to injustice; designed to provoke change; designed to stir reform. He has called upon us to make good the promise of America.

> LYNDON B. JOHNSON, Address to a joint session of Congress, on voting rights, 15 Mar., 1965.

12

Freedom is not enough. You do not take a person who for years has been hobbled by chains and liberate him, bring him up to the starting line, and then say, you're free to compete with all the others, and still justly believe that you have been completely fair.

> LYNDON B. JOHNSON, Commencement Address at Howard University, Washington, D.C., 4 June, 1965.

13

When pioneers subdued a continent to the need of man they did not tame it for the Negro. When the Liberty Bell rang out in Philadelphia it did not toll for the Negro. When Andrew Jackson threw open the doors of democracy they did not open for the Negro. It was only at Appomattox a century ago that an American victory was also a Negro victory.

> LYNDON B. JOHNSON, Speech, upon signing the voting-rights bill of 1965, Washington, D.C., 6 Aug., 1965.

1

A rioter with a Molotov cocktail in his hands is not fighting for civil rights any more than a Klansman with a sheet on his back and mask on his face

> LYNDON B. JOHNSON, Speech in Washington, D.C., 20 Aug., 1965, shortly after the riots in the Negro section of Los Angeles.

2

We are confronted primarily with a moral issue. It is as old as the Scriptures and is as clear as the American Constitution.

> JOHN F. KENNEDY, Address delivered on television, June, 1963, dealing with civil rights.

3

I ask you to look into your hearts—not in search of charity, for the Negro neither wants nor needs condescension—but for the one plain, proud and priceless quality that unites us all as Americans: a sense of justice.

> JOHN F. KENNEDY, Message to Congress on civil rights, 19 June, 1963.

4

We are not fighting for the right to be like you. We respect ourselves too much for that. When we fight for freedom, we mean freedom for us to be black, or brown, and you to be white and yet live together in a free and equal society. This is the only way that integration can mean dignity for both of us.

> JOHN OLIVER KILLENS, Explanation of the 'Black Psyche'; New York Times Magazine, 7 June, 1964.

5

Before the Pilgrims landed at Plymouth, we were here. Before the pen of Jefferson etched across the pages of history the majestic words of the Declaration of Independence, we were here. For more than two centuries, our foreparents labored in this country without wages; they made cotton "king," and they built the homes of their masters in the midst of brutal injustice and shameful humiliation—and yet out of a bottomless vitality, they continued to thrive and develop. If the inexpressible cruelties of slavery could not stop us, the opposition we now face will surely fail. We will win our freedom because the sacred heritage of our nation and the eternal will of God are embodied in our echoing demands.

> REV. MARTIN LUTHER KING, JR., Letter, written Apr., 1963, while he was in city

jail in Birmingham, Ala., following his participation in civil rights demonstrations in that city. This famous letter was his reply to a group of white clergymen who had criticized his part in the demonstrations.

6

I have a dream. . . . It is a dream deeply rooted in the American dream. . . . I have a dream that one day in the red hills of Georgia, sons of former slaves and the sons of former slave-owners will be able to sit down together at the table of brotherhood.

> REV. MARTIN LUTHER KING, JR., Address delivered at the foot of Lincoln Memorial, Washington, D.C., 28 Aug., 1963—the high point of the civil rights "march" on the capital and one of the best-remembered documents on civil rights.

7

Yes, our souls have been tried in the cold and bitter Valley Forges of the Deep South, and black and white together, we have met the test. We shall overcome.

> REV. MARTIN LUTHER KING, JR., Speech in New York City, 17 Dec., 1964, upon accepting the city's medallion of honor.

8

Segregation is on its deathbed—the question now is, how costly will the segregationists make the funeral?

> REV. MARTIN LUTHER KING, JR., Address to students at Villanova University, Villanova, Pa., 20 Jan., 1965.

9

All I ask for the Negro is that if you do not like him, let him alone. If God gave him but little, that little let him enjoy.

> ABRAHAM LINCOLN, Speech in Springfield, Ill., 17 July, 1858.

10

In this and like communities, public sentiment is everything. With public sentiment, nothing can fail; without it, nothing can succeed. Consequently he who molds public sentiment goes deeper than he who enacts statutes or pronounces decisions.

> ABRAHAM LINCOLN, Speech in Ottawa, Ill., 31 July, 1858. He was referring to slavery. The substance of this quotation was repeated many times beginning in the 1950's, with specific reference to public sentiment's part in securing equality for the Negro.

11

Anything that argues me into his idea of perfect social and political equality with the Negro is but a specious and fantastic arrangement of words, by which a man can prove a horse-chestnut to be a chestnut horse.

> ABRAHAM LINCOLN, Speech in Ottawa, Ill., 21 Aug., 1858.

1

In the right to eat the bread . . . which his own hand earns, he [the Negro] *is my equal and the equal of Judge Douglas, and the equal of every living man.*

> ABRAHAM LINCOLN, Lincoln-Douglas Debates; first joint debate, Ottawa, Ill., 21 Aug., 1858.

2

The black man in this country has been sitting on the hot stove for nearly 400 years. And no matter how fast the brainwashers and the brainwashed think they are helping him advance, it's still too slow for the man whose behind is burning on that hot stove!

> MALCOLM X. (GORDON PARKS, *What Their Cry Means to Me; Life,* 31 May, 1963, p. 31)

3

The black man has died under the flag. His women have been raped under it. He has been oppressed, starved and beaten under it—and still after what happened in Mississippi they'll ask him to fight their enemies under it. I'll do my fighting right here at home, where the enemy looks me in the eye every day of my life. I'm not talking against the flag. I'm talking *about* it!

> MALCOLM X. (GORDON PARKS, *What Their Cry Means to Me; Life,* 31 May, 1963, p. 31)

4

The Negro problem is not only America's greatest failure but also America's great opportunity for the future. If America should follow its own deepest convictions, its well-being at home would be increased directly. At the same time America's prestige and power abroad would rise.

> GUNNAR MYRDAL, *An American Dilemma* (1944).

5

Some doubt the courage of the negro. Go to Haiti and stand on those fifty thousand graves of the best soldiers France ever had, and ask them what they think of the negro's sword.

> WENDELL PHILLIPS, *Toussaint L'Ouverture.*

6

On the tenth anniversary of the Supreme Court's public school integration decision, the paradox and the tragedy of the American Negro are fairly clear. He is gaining legally but falling behind economically. He is slowly getting the rights but not the skills of a modern computerized society.

> JAMES RESTON, Washington Column, New York *Times,* 15 May, 1964.

7

Wheel about, turn about,
   Do jis so,
An' ebery time I wheel about

I jump Jim Crow.

> THOMAS D. (DADDY) RICE, *Jump Jim Crow.* This was part of Rice's repertoire of song and dance, based on his impressions of Negro entertainers, that developed into the minstrel show about 1830. By the end of the century "Jim Crow" —like "Uncle Tom" later—took on a radically different meaning; it was applied expressly to segregation and rigid stratification of the races.

8

For more than a century before the Declaration of Independence, the negroes had been regarded as beings of an inferior order . . . so far inferior that they had no rights which a white man was bound to respect.

> ROGER BROOKE TANEY, Chief Justice of the U.S. Supreme Court, Decision in the Dred Scott case, 1857. (*Howard's Reports,* vol. xix, p. 407)

9

I believe in the brotherhood of man, not merely the brotherhood of white men but the brotherhood of all men before law.

> HARRY S TRUMAN, Speech at a political rally in Sedalia, Mo., 1940. (JONATHAN DANIELS, *The Man of Independence,* p. 339)

10

I wish to make it clear that I am not appealing for social equality of the Negro. The Negro himself knows better than that, and the highest type of Negro leaders say quite frankly they prefer the society of their own people. Negroes want justice, not social relations.

> HARRY S TRUMAN, Speech to an audience of Negroes in Chicago, July, 1940. (JONATHAN DANIELS, *The Man of Independence,* p. 338)

11

The top dog in a world which is over half colored ought to clean his own house.

> HARRY S TRUMAN. (JONATHAN DANIELS, *The Man of Independence,* 1950, p. 336)

12

Law and order are the Negro's best friend— make no mistake about that. The opposite of law and order is mob rule, and that is the way of the Ku Klux Klan and the night riders and the lynch mobs.

> ROBERT F. WAGNER, Address in New York City, 22 July, 1964, broadcast as an appeal to halt racial rioting in his city. Wagner was mayor at the time.

13

The Afrikan may be Our Brother . . . But the Afrikan isn't our sister & our wife & our uncle. He isn't sevral of our brothers & all our fust wife's relashuns. He isn't our grandfather and our grate grandfather, & our Aunt in the country.

> ARTEMUS WARD, *The Crisis.*

1

In all things that are purely social we can be as separate as the fingers, yet one as the hand in all things essential to mutual progress.

> BOOKER T. WASHINGTON, Address in Atlanta, 18 Sept., 1895.

2

The wisest among my race understand that the agitation of questions of social equality is the extremest folly, and that progress in the enjoyment of all the privileges that will come to us must be the result of severe and constant struggle rather than of artificial forcing.

> BOOKER T. WASHINGTON, Address in Atlanta, 18 Sept., 1895.

3

There is no defense or security for any of us except in the highest intelligence and development of all. If anywhere there are efforts tending to curtail the fullest growth of the Negro, let these efforts be turned into stimulating, encouraging, and making him the most useful and intelligent citizen. Effort or means so invested will pay a thousand per cent interest. These efforts will be twice blessed—blessing him that gives and him that takes.

> BOOKER T. WASHINGTON, Address in Atlanta, 18 Sept., 1895.

4

The Negro American has been waiting upon voluntary action since 1876. He has found what other Americans have discovered: voluntary action has to be sparked by something stronger than prayers, patience and lamentations. If the thirteen colonies had waited for voluntary action by England, this land today would be a part of the British Commonwealth.

> ROY WILKINS, Testimony before the Senate Commerce Committee, July, 1963. As executive secretary of the National Association for the Advancement of Colored People, he was a witness during hearings on the Civil Rights Act that became law a year later.

5

The Negro may wind up with a mouthful of civil rights, but an empty stomach and living in a hovel.

> WHITNEY M. YOUNG, JR., Address in St. Louis, 15 Dec., 1963—speaking as executive director, National Urban League.

6

Uncle Tom: a subservient Negro (or lately, one who warns against violence in civil rights demonstrations).

> Time, 2 Aug., 1963, p. 14. The term derives from the exemplary hero of HARRIET BEECHER STOWE'S novel, Uncle Tom's Cabin (1852). By the 1950's the term had undergone radical transformation in Negro parlance, as indicated by this definition.

Uncle Tom: A Negro accused by another of comporting himself among white people in a manner which the accuser interprets as servile or cowardly; or a Negro who other Negroes feel has betrayed, or sullied, in any way, a dignified, militant, forthright Negro image. "Tomming" is the verb form.

> ALEX HALEY, In 'Uncle Tom' Are Our Guilt and Hope; New York Times Magazine, 1 Mar., 1964.

7

All persons born or naturalized in the United States, and subject to the jurisdiction thereof, are citizens of the United States and of the State wherein they reside. No State shall make or enforce any law which shall abridge the privileges or immunities of citizens of the United States; nor shall any State deprive any person of life, liberty, or property, without due process of law; nor deny to any person within its jurisdiction the equal protection of the laws.

> Fourteenth Amendment, U.S. Constitution, adopted 28 July, 1868.

8

The right of citizens of the United States to vote shall not be denied or abridged by the United States or by any State on account of race, color, or previous condition of servitude.

> Fifteenth Amendment, U.S. Constitution, adopted 30 Mar., 1870.

9

Separate but equal.

> U.S. Supreme Court Decision, 1896, in Plessy vs. Ferguson. In this historic case the court, by upholding the constitutionality of a Louisiana statute requiring racial segregation on common carriers, affirmed a doctrine that became the basis for Negro-white relationships in public accommodations, education, and other areas in many parts of the United States. The opinion noted: "We cannot say that a law [establishing separate but equal railway accommodations] which authorizes or even requires the separation of the two races in public conveyances is unreasonable."

We conclude that in the field of public education the doctrine of "separate but equal" has no place. Separate educational facilities are inherently unequal.

> EARL WARREN, Supreme Court Decision, 17 May, 1954. This was the most famous in a series of opinions that gradually reversed the doctrine of "separate but equal." It dealt specifically with five cases in public education.

1

With all deliberate speed.
> U.S. Supreme Court Decision, 31 May,
> 1955—a directive ordering desegregation
> in public schools.

NEIGHBOR

2

It is other folks' dogs and children that make
most of the bad feelin's between neighbors.
> ELLIS PARKER BUTLER, *The Confessions of
> a Daddy,* ch. 1.

3

Sometimes a neighbor whom we have disliked a lifetime for his arrogance and conceit
lets fall a single commonplace remark that
shows us another side, another man, really; a
man uncertain, and puzzled, and in the dark
like ourselves.
> WILLA CATHER, *Shadows on the Rock:*
> Epilogue.

4

There is a heaven, for ever, day by day,
The upward longing of my soul doth tell me
so.
There is a hell, I'm quite as sure; for pray,
If there were not, where would my neighbors
go?
> PAUL LAURENCE DUNBAR, *Theology.*

5

My apple trees will never get across
And eat the cones under his pines, I tell
him.
He only says, "Good fences make good
neighbors."
> ROBERT FROST, *Mending Wall.*

6

The impersonal hand of government can
never replace the helping hand of a neighbor.
> HUBERT H. HUMPHREY, Address in Wash-
> ington, D.C., 10 Feb., 1965.

7

In the field of world policy, I would dedicate
this nation to the policy of a good neighbor.
> FRANKLIN D. ROOSEVELT, First Inaugural
> Address, 4 Mar., 1933.

8

I am as desirous of being a good neighbor as
I am of being a bad subject.
> HENRY DAVID THOREAU, *Civil Disobedi-
> ence.*

NEW YORK CITY

9

If 1,668,172 people (out of New York's total
population of 7,710,346) are to be set down
in one narrow strip of land between two quiet rivers, you can hardly improve on this
solid mass of buildings and the teeming organism of human life that streams through
them. For better or worse, this is real.
> BROOKS ATKINSON, "Critic at Large" Col-
> umn, New York *Times,* 17 Mar., 1964.

10

All the beauties of Manhattan are man-
made.
> BROOKS ATKINSON, "Critic at Large" Col-
> umn, New York *Times,* 17 Mar., 1964.

11

My life had begun . . . in the invincible
and indescribable squalor of Harlem. Here in
this ghetto I was born. And here it was intended by my countrymen that I should live
and perish. And in that ghetto I was tormented. I felt caged, like an animal. I wanted to escape. I felt if I did not get out I
would slowly strangle.
> JAMES BALDWIN, Television Narrative
> based on his life, WNEW-TV, New
> York City, 1 June, 1964.

12

No king, no clown, to rule this town!
> WILLIAM O. BARTLETT, in the New York
> *Sun,* about 1870. He referred to William
> Marcy (Boss) Tweed and the latter's
> associate in the Tweed ring, Peter B.
> Sweeney.

13

The Sidewalks of New York.
> JAMES BLAKE AND CHARLES LAWLOR, Title
> and refrain of song (1894), later identi-
> fied with Alfred E. Smith.

14

Give my regards to Broadway.
> GEORGE M. COHAN, Title and refrain of
> song (1904).

15

New York is a sucked orange.
> EMERSON, *Conduct of Life: Culture.*

16

Stream of the living world
  Where dash the billows of strife!—
One plunge in the mighty torrent
  Is a year of tamer life!
City of glorious days,
  Of hope, and labor and mirth,
With room and to spare, on thy splendid
  bays,
  For the ships of all the earth.
> RICHARD WATSON GILDER, *The City.*

17

The lusts of the flesh can be gratified anywhere; it is not this sort of license that distinguishes New York. It is, rather, a lust of
the total ego for recognition, even for emi-
nence. More than elsewhere, everybody here
wants to be Somebody.
> SYDNEY J. HARRIS, *Strictly Personal.*

18

If there ever was an aviary overstocked with
jays it is that Yaptown-on-the-Hudson,
called New York. . . . "Little old New
York's good enough for us"—that's what
they sing.
> O. HENRY, *Gentle Grafter: A Tempered
> Wind.*

19

What else can you expect from a town that's

shut off from the world by the ocean on one side and New Jersey on the other?

   O. HENRY, *Gentle Grafter: A Tempered Wind.*

1

Well, little old Noisyville-on-the-Subway is good enough for me.

   O. HENRY, *Strictly Business: The Duel.*

2

Far below and around lay the city like a ragged purple dream, the wonderful, cruel, enchanting, bewildering, fatal, great city.

   O. HENRY, *Strictly Business: The Duel.*

3

In dress, habits, manners, provincialism, routine and narrowness, he acquired that charming insolence, that irritating completeness, that sophisticated crassness, that overbalanced poise that makes the Manhattan gentleman so delightfully small in his greatness.

   O. HENRY, *Voice of the City: Defeat of the City.*

4

It's a city where everyone mutinies but no one deserts.

   HARRY HERSHFIELD, Interview, New York *Times,* 5 Dec., 1965.

5

The Bow'ry, the Bow'ry!
They say such things, and they do strange things
On the Bow'ry, the Bow'ry!
I'll never go there any more!

   CHARLES H. HOYT, *The Bowery* (song, 1891, with music by Percy Gaunt). It was introduced in *A Trip to Chinatown* at the Madison Square Theatre, New York City.

6

The renowned and ancient city of Gotham.

   WASHINGTON IRVING, *Salmagundi,* No. xvi, Wednesday, 11 Nov., 1807, ch. 109 (chapter heading). This is the earliest reference to New York City as Gotham.

7

There is no greenery; it is enough to make a stone sad.

   NIKITA S. KHRUSHCHEV, during a visit to New York City, Oct., 1960.

8

No other city in the United States can divest the visitor of so much money with so little enthusiasm. In Dallas, they take away with gusto; in New Orleans, with a bow; in San Francisco, with a wink and a grin. In New York, you're lucky if you get a grunt.

   FLETCHER KNEBEL, *But It's a Tough Place to Visit; Look,* 26 Mar., 1963.

9

Harlem has a black belt where darkies dwell in a heaven where white men seek a little hell.

   ALFRED KREYMBORG, *Harlem.* Referring to the Harlem of the jazz age.

10

Manhattan's a hell where culture rarely grew;
But it lets two lives do all they care to do.

   ALFRED KREYMBORG, *Two Lives and Six Million.*

11

Not like the brazen giant of Greek fame,
With conquering limbs astride from land to land;
Here at our sea-washed, sunset gates shall stand
A mighty woman with a torch, whose flame
Is the imprisoned lightning, and her name
Mother of exiles.

   EMMA LAZARUS, *The New Colossus.*

12

Some day this old Broadway shall climb to the skies,
As a ribbon of cloud on a soul-wind shall rise,
And we shall be lifted, rejoicing by night,
Till we join with the planets who choir their delight.
The signs in the streets and the signs in the skies
Shall make a new Zodiac, guiding the wise,
And Broadway make one with that marvelous stair
That is climbed by the rainbow-clad spirits of prayer.

   VACHEL LINDSAY, *A Rhyme About an Electrical Advertising Sign.*

13

New York attracts the most talented people in the world in the arts and professions. It also attracts them in other fields. Even the bums are talented.

   EDMUND LOVE, *Subways Are for Sleeping,* introduction.

14

New York is truly the City of Man. It is humanity in microcosm, reflecting the infinite variety as well as the infinite capacity for good or evil of the human race.

   DIOSDADO MACAPAGAL, in 1964, when he visited the United States as President of the Philippines.

15

New York, the nation's thyroid gland.

   CHRISTOPHER MORLEY, *Shore Leave.*

16

The Bronx?
No thonx.

   ODGEN NASH. These lines originally appeared in *The New Yorker* in 1931.

I wrote those lines, "The Bronx? No thonx";
I shudder to confess them.
Now I'm an older, wiser man
I cry, "The Bronx? God bless them!"

   OGDEN NASH. Written for the Bronx golden jubilee, 1964. (New York *Times,* 27 May, 1964)

1
Vulgar of manner, overfed,
Overdressed and underbred;
Heartless, Godless, hell's delight,
Rude by day and lewd by night;
Bedwarfed the man, o'ergrown the brute,
Ruled by Jew and prostitute;
Purple-robed and pauper-clad,
Raving, rotting, money-mad;
A squirming herd in Mammon's mesh,
A wilderness of human flesh;
Crazed with avarice, lust and rum,
New York, thy name's Delirium.
    BYRON R. NEWTON, *Owed to New York*
    (1906).

2
Up in the heights of the evening skies I see
    my City of Cities float
In sunset's golden and crimson dyes:
    I look and a great joy clutches my
        throat!
Plateau of roofs by canyons crossed: win-
    dows by thousands fire-furled—
O gazing, how the heart is lost in the Deepest
    City in the World.
    JAMES OPPENHEIM, *New York from a
    Skyscraper.*

3
Who that has known thee but shall burn
    In exile till he come again
To do thy bitter will, O stern
    Moon of the tides of men!
    JOHN REED, *Proud New York.*

4
Just where the Treasury's marble front
    Looks over Wall Street's mingled nations,
Where Jews and Gentiles most are wont
    To throng for trade and last quotations;
Where, hour by hour, the rates of gold
    Outrival, in the ears of people,
The quarter-chimes, serenely tolled
    From Trinity's undaunted steeple.
    E. C. STEDMAN, *Pan in Wall Street.*

5
It can destroy an individual, or it can fulfill
him, depending a good deal on luck. No one
should come to New York to live unless he is
willing to be lucky.
    E. B. WHITE, *Here Is New York.*

6
City of hurried and sparkling waters! city of
    spires and masts!
City nested in bays! my city!
    WALT WHITMAN, *Mannahatta.*

7
A little strip of an island with a row of well-
fed folks up and down the middle, and a lot
of hungry folks on each side.
    HARRY LEON WILSON, *The Spenders,* ch.
    8.

8
We plant a tub and call it Paradise. . . .
New York is the great stone desert.
    ISRAEL ZANGWILL, *The Melting-Pot,* act
    ii.

NEWS
See also Press

9
Tell those guys out there to get the smell of
warm blood into their copy.
    HUGH BAILLIE, Instruction to United
    Press war correspondents during World
    War II, while he was president of that
    news agency.

10
When a dog bites a man that is not news, but
when a man bites a dog that is news.
    JOHN B. BOGART, about 1880, when he was
    city editor of the New York *Sun.* F. M.
    MOTT, in *American Journalism,* and
    Frank M. O'Brien, a later editor of the
    Sun, are authorities for this attribution,
    though the classic definition is also cred-
    ited to Charles A. Dana, most famous of
    Sun editors; and STANLEY WALKER, in
    City Editor, attributes it to a Dana as-
    sistant, Amos Cummings.

11
News is almost by definition bad news.
    MARQUIS W. CHILDS, Political Column, St.
    Louis *Post-Dispatch,* 25 Aug., 1964, p. 1-
    C.

12
Journalists have always been our most old-
fashioned class, being too busy with the news
of the day to lay aside the mental habits of
fifty years before.
    FRANK MOORE COLBY, *Constrained Atti-
    tudes.*

13
All the news that's fit to print.
    ADOLPH S. OCHS, Motto of the New York
    Times, of which he was publisher,
    1896–1935.

14
News is as hard to hold as quicksilver, and it
fades more rapidly than any morning-glory.
    STANLEY WALKER, *City Editor,* p. 20.

15
Women, wampum and wrongdoing are always news.
    STANLEY WALKER, *City Editor,* p. 44.

16
The atmosphere of events.
    WOODROW WILSON, his definition of news.

NIGHT

17
Night is a stealthy, evil Raven,
Wrapt to the eyes in his black wings.
    THOMAS BAILEY ALDRICH, *Day and Night.*

18
The day is great and final. The night is for
the day, but the day is not for the night.
    EMERSON, *Society and Solitude: Success.*

19
The Night walked down the sky
With the moon in her hand.
    FREDERICK L. KNOWLES, *A Memory.*

1

I stood on the bridge at midnight,
  As the clocks were striking the hour,
And the moon rose o'er the city,
  Behind the dark church-tower.
  HENRY WADSWORTH LONGFELLOW, *The Bridge.*

2

The day is done, and the darkness
  Falls from the wings of Night,
As a feather is wafted downward
  From an eagle in his flight.
  HENRY WADSWORTH LONGFELLOW, *The Day Is Done.*

3

The shades of night were falling fast.
  HENRY WADSWORTH LONGFELLOW, *Excelsior.*

4

I felt her presence, by its spell of might,
  Stoop o'er me from above;
The calm, majestic presence of the Night,
  As of the one I love.
  HENRY WADSWORTH LONGFELLOW, *Hymn to the Night.*

5

O holy Night! from thee I learn to bear
  What man has borne before!
Thou layest thy finger on the lips of Care,
  And they complain no more.
  HENRY WADSWORTH LONGFELLOW, *Hymn to the Night.*

6

Midnight! the outpost of advancing day!
The frontier town and citadel of night!
  HENRY WADSWORTH LONGFELLOW, *The Two Rivers,* pt. i.

7

God makes sech nights, all white an' still
  Fur 'z you can look or listen,
Moonshine an' snow on field an' hill,
  All silence an' all glisten.
  JAMES RUSSELL LOWELL, *The Courtin'.*

8

O wild and wondrous midnight,
  There is a might in thee
To make the charmèd body
  Almost like spirit be,
And give it some faint glimpses
  Of immortality!
  JAMES RUSSELL LOWELL, *Midnight.*

9

Once upon a midnight dreary, while I pondered, weak and weary.
  EDGAR ALLAN POE, *The Raven.*

10

Come, drink the mystic wine of Night,
Brimming with silence and the stars;
While earth, bathed in this holy light,
Is seen without its scars.
  LOUIS UNTERMEYER, *The Wine of Night.*

11

Press close, bare-bosom'd night—press close,
  magnetic nourishing night!

Night of south winds—night of the large few
  stars!
Still nodding night—mad naked summer
  night.
  WALT WHITMAN, *Song of Myself,* sec. 21.

12

Day full blown and splendid—day of the
  immense sun, action, ambition, laughter,
The Night follows close with millions of
  suns, and sleep and restoring darkness.
  WALT WHITMAN, *Youth, Day, Old Age and Night.*

NIGHTINGALE

13

I wonder if it *is* a bird
That sings within the hidden tree,
Or some shy angel calling me
To follow far away?
  GRACE HAZARD CONKLING, *Nightingales.*

14

I had a silvery name, I had a silvery name,
I had a silvery name—do you remember
The name you cried beside the tumbling
  sea?
"Darling . . . darling . . . darling . . .
  darling . . ."
Said the Chinese nightingale.
  VACHEL LINDSAY, *The Chinese Nightingale.*

15

To the red rising moon, and loud and deep
The nightingale is singing from the steep.
  HENRY WADSWORTH LONGFELLOW, *Keats.*

NOBILITY

16

No one can build his security upon the nobleness of another person.
  WILLA CATHER, *Alexander's Bridge,* ch. 8.

17

There is a natural aristocracy among men.
The grounds of this are virtue and talents.
  THOMAS JEFFERSON, *Writings,* vol. xiii, p. 396.

18

    Be noble in every thought
And in every deed!
  HENRY WADSWORTH LONGFELLOW, *The Golden Legend,* pt. ii.

19

Noble by birth, yet nobler by great deeds.
  HENRY WADSWORTH LONGFELLOW, *Tales of a Wayside Inn: Emma and Eginhard,* l. 82.

20

Be noble! and the nobleness that lies
In other men, sleeping, but never dead,
Will rise in majesty to meet thine own.
  JAMES RUSSELL LOWELL, *Sonnets,* No. 4.

21

Jacqueline Kennedy has given the American

people from this day on one thing they have always lacked—majesty.

UNKNOWN, Dispatch, London *Evening Standard*, 25 Nov., 1963. This front-page story, filed from Washington and

headlined "The heroic dignity of Jackie Kennedy," paid tribute to her bearing at the funeral of her husband, John F. Kennedy.

O

OBEDIENCE

1
I'll go where you want me to go, dear Lord,
  O'er mountain or plain or sea;
I'll say what you want me to say, dear
  Lord,
  I'll be what you want me to be.
  MARY BROWN, *I'll Go Where You Want Me to Go* (hymn).

2
By contenting ourselves with obedience we become divine.
  EMERSON, *Essays, First Series: Spiritual Laws.*

3
Obedience alone gives the right to command.
  EMERSON, *Lectures and Sketches: Perpetual Forces.*

4
I profess . . . so much of the Roman principle as to deem it honorable for the general of yesterday to act as a corporal today, if his services can be useful to his country.
  THOMAS JEFFERSON, *Writings*, vol. xiii, p. 186.

OCEAN, see Sea

OCTOBER

5
And suns grow meek, and the meek suns grow brief,
And the year smiles as it draws near its death.
  WILLIAM CULLEN BRYANT, *October: A Sonnet.*

6
The sweet calm sunshine of October, now
  Warms the low spot; upon its grassy mould
The purple oak-leaf falls; the birchen bough
  Drops its bright spoil like arrow-heads of gold.
  WILLIAM CULLEN BRYANT, *October, 1866.*

7
There is something in October sets the gypsy blood astir:
We must rise and follow her,
When from every hill of flame
She calls, and calls each vagabond by name.
  BLISS CARMAN, *Vagabond Song.*

8
There is no season when such pleasant and sunny spots may be lighted on, and produce

so pleasant an effect on the feelings, as now in October.
  NATHANIEL HAWTHORNE, *American Note-Books*, 7 Oct., 1841.

9
The skies they were ashen and sober;
  The leaves they were crispèd and sere—
  The leaves they were withering and sere;
It was night in the lonesome October
  Of my most immemorial year.
  EDGAR ALLAN POE, *Ulalume.*

10
October in New England,
  And I not there to see
The glamour of the goldenrod,
  The flame of the maple tree!
  ODELL SHEPARD, *Home Thoughts.*

11
And close at hand, the basket stood
With nuts from brown October's wood.
  JOHN GREENLEAF WHITTIER, *Snow-Bound.*

OPINION

12
Ultimate objectives must be paramount; immediate reactions are less important.
  DWIGHT D. EISENHOWER, *The White House Years: Mandate for Change 1953–1956.* Referring specifically to "ultimate objectives" of U.S. policy and "immediate reactions" of other nations.

13
Every opinion reacts on him who utters it.
  EMERSON, *Essays, First Series: Compensation.*

14
When private men shall act with original views, the lustre will be transferred from the actions of kings to those of gentlemen.
  EMERSON, *Essays, First Series: Self-Reliance.*

15
Stay at home in your mind. Don't recite other people's opinions.
  EMERSON, *Letters and Social Aims: Social Aims.*

16
The bloated vanity called public opinion.
  EMERSON, *Miscellanies: War.*

17
The only sin which we never forgive in each other is difference of opinion.
  EMERSON, *Society and Solitude: Clubs.*

18
Singularity in the right hath ruined many:

happy those who are convinced of the general opinion.

> BENJAMIN FRANKLIN, *Poor Richard*, 1757.

1

Insofar as it represents a genuine reconciliation of differences, a consensus is a fine thing; insofar as it represents the concealment of differences, it is a miscarriage of democratic procedure. I think we Americans tend to put too high a value on unanimity . . . as if there were something dangerous and illegitimate about honest differences of opinion honestly expressed by honest men.

> J. W. FULBRIGHT, Speech, U.S. Senate, 22 Oct., 1965.

2

It is not often that an opinion is worth expressing which cannot take care of itself.

> OLIVER WENDELL HOLMES, *Medical Essays*, p. 211.

3

A man's opinions, look you, are generally of much more value than his arguments.

> OLIVER WENDELL HOLMES, *The Professor at the Breakfast-Table*, ch. 5.

4

With effervescing opinions, as with the not yet forgotten champagne, the quickest way to let them get flat is to let them get exposed to the air.

> JUSTICE OLIVER WENDELL HOLMES, Opinion, U.S. Supreme Court, 1920.

5

The average man believes a thing first, and then searches for proof to bolster his opinion.

> ELBERT HUBBARD, *The Philistine*, vol. xi, p. 36.

6

For the most part, we inherit our opinions.

> ROBERT G. INGERSOLL, *Why I Am an Agnostic*.

7

Error of opinion may be tolerated where reason is left free to combat it.

> THOMAS JEFFERSON, First Inaugural Address, 4 Mar., 1801.

8

I never had an opinion in politics or religion which I was afraid to own.

> THOMAS JEFFERSON, *Writings*, vol. vii, p. 299.

9

I very much suspect that if thinking men would have the courage to think for themselves, and to speak what they think, it would be found they do not differ in . . . opinions as much as is supposed.

> THOMAS JEFFERSON, *Writings*, vol. xiii, p. 349.

10

The good opinion of mankind, like the lever of Archimedes, with the given fulcrum, moves the world.

> THOMAS JEFFERSON, *Writings*, vol. xiv, p. 222.

11

One man's Mede is another man's Persian.

> GEORGE S. KAUFMAN.

12

Too often we . . . enjoy the comfort of opinion without the discomfort of thought.

> JOHN F. KENNEDY, Speech at Yale University, 1962.

13

The foolish and the dead alone never change their opinion.

> JAMES RUSSELL LOWELL, *My Study Windows: Abraham Lincoln*.

14

The pressure of public opinion is like the pressure of the atmosphere; you can't see it—but, all the same, it is sixteen pounds to the square inch.

> JAMES RUSSELL LOWELL, Interview with Julian Hawthorne. (BRANDER MATTHEWS, New York *Times*, 2 Apr., 1922)

15

Truth is one forever absolute, but opinion is truth filtered through the moods, the blood, the disposition of the spectator.

> WENDELL PHILLIPS, *Idols*.

16

It were not best that we should all think alike; it is difference of opinion that makes horse-races.

> MARK TWAIN, *Pudd'nhead Wilson's Calendar*.

17

Loyalty to petrified opinion never yet broke a chain or freed a human soul.

> MARK TWAIN, Inscription beneath his bust in the Hall of Fame.

18

Public opinion is stronger than the legislature, and nearly as strong as the ten commandments.

> CHARLES DUDLEY WARNER, *My Summer in a Garden: 16th Week*.

19

Inconsistencies of opinion, arising from changes of circumstances, are often justifiable.

> DANIEL WEBSTER, Speech in U.S. Senate, 25 July, 1846.

20

Opinion ultimately governs the world.

> WOODROW WILSON, Speech, 20 Apr., 1915.

OPPORTUNITY

21

As th' pote says, Opporchunity knocks at ivry man's dure wanst. On some men's dures it hammers till it breaks down th' dure an' thin it goes in an' wakes him up if he's asleep, an' iver afterward it wurruks f'r him as a night-watchman. On other men's dures it knocks an' runs away, an' on th' dures iv some men it knocks an' whin they come out it hits thim over th' head with an axe. But ivrywan has an opporchunity.

FINLEY PETER DUNNE, *Mr. Carnegie's Gift.*

1

No great man ever complains of want of opportunity.

EMERSON, *Journals*, vol. v, p. 534.

2

Seek not for fresher founts afar,
Just drop your bucket where you are.

SAM WALTER FOSS, *Opportunity.*

Let down your buckets where you are.

BOOKER T. WASHINGTON, Address, Atlanta Exposition, 1895.

3

Opportunity is the great bawd.

BENJAMIN FRANKLIN, *Poor Richard,* 1735.

4

Keep thou from the Opportunity, and God will keep thee from the Sin.

BENJAMIN FRANKLIN, *Poor Richard,* 1744.

5

We sail, at sunrise, daily, "outward bound."

HELEN HUNT JACKSON, *Outward Bound.*

6

We must open the doors of opportunity. But we must also equip our people to walk through those doors.

LYNDON B. JOHNSON, Address to delegates to a National Urban League conference, Washington, D.C., 10 Dec., 1964.

7

Never before has man had such capacity to control his own environment—to end thirst and hunger—to conquer poverty and disease—to banish illiteracy and massive human misery. We have the power to make this the best generation of mankind in the history of the world—or to make it the last.

JOHN F. KENNEDY, Address to the General Assembly of the United Nations, 20 Sept., 1963.

8

I happen, temporarily, to occupy this White House. I am a living witness that any one of your children may look to come here as my father's child has.

ABRAHAM LINCOLN, Address to Ohio soldiers, 22 Aug., 1864.

9

          The Gods implore not,
Plead not, solicit not; they only offer
Choice and occasion, which being once passed
Return no more.

HENRY WADSWORTH LONGFELLOW, *Masque of Pandora: Tower of Prometheus on Mount Caucasus.*

10

There is no security on this earth; there is only opportunity.

GENERAL DOUGLAS MACARTHUR. (COURT-

NEY WHITNEY, *MacArthur: His Rendezvous with History*)

11

They do me wrong who say I come no more
  When once I knock and fail to find you in;
For every day I stand outside your door
  And bid you wake, and rise to fight and win.

WALTER MALONE, *Opportunity.*

12

Opportunities are seldom labeled.

JOHN A. SHEDD, *Salt from My Attic,* p. 14.

OPTIMISM

See also Pessimism

13

I hate the Pollyanna pest
Who says that All Is for the Best.

FRANKLIN P. ADAMS, *Thoughts on the Cosmos.*

14

Some day Love shall claim his own
Some day Right ascend his throne,
Some day hidden Truth be known;
  Some day—some sweet day.

LEWIS J. BATES, *Some Sweet Day.*

15

Optimist: A proponent of the doctrine that black is white.

AMBROSE BIERCE, *Devil's Dictionary,* p. 239.

16

The optimist proclaims that we live in the best of all possible worlds; and the pessimist fears this is true.

JAMES BRANCH CABELL, *The Silver Stallion,* p. 112.

17

O Light divine! we need no fuller test
  That all is ordered well;
We know enough to trust that all is best
  Where Love and Wisdom dwell.

C. P. CRANCH, *Oh Love Supreme.*

18

God! I will not be an owl,
But sun me in the Capitol.

EMERSON, *Mithridates.*

19

Yet spake yon purple mountain,
Yet said yon ancient wood,
That Night or Day, that Love or Crime,
Leads all souls to the Good.

EMERSON, *The Park.*

20

Over the winter glaciers
I see the summer glow,
And through the wild-piled snowdrift,
The warm rosebuds below.

EMERSON, *The World-Soul.*

21

To look up and not down,
To look forward and not back,

To look out and not in,—
and
To lend a hand.
>   EDWARD EVERETT HALE, *Ten Times One Is Ten.*

1
Optimism is a kind of heart stimulant—the digitalis of failure.
>   ELBERT HUBBARD, *A Thousand and One Epigrams,* p. 80.

2
A health unto the happy,
A fig for him who frets!
It is not raining rain to me,
  It's raining violets.
>   ROBERT LOVEMAN, *April Rain.*

3
        It is good.
To lengthen to the last a sunny mood.
>   JAMES RUSSELL LOWELL, *A Legend of Brittany,* pt. i, st. 6.

4
There's just as much bunk among the busters as among the boosters.
>   KEITH PRESTON, *Pot Shots from Pegasus,* p. 145.

5
Somewhere above us, in elusive ether,
  Waits the fulfillment of our dearest dreams.
>   BAYARD TAYLOR, *Ad Amicos.*

6
Then, like an old-time orator
  Impressively he rose;
"I make the most of all that comes
And the least of all that goes."
>   SARA TEASDALE, *The Philosopher.*

7
What will be will be well, for what is is well.
>   WALT WHITMAN, *To Think of Time.*

8
I know that the soul is aided
  Sometimes by the heart's unrest,
And to grow means often to suffer—
  But whatever is—is best.
>   ELLA WHEELER WILCOX, *Whatever Is, Is Best.*

9
'Twixt optimist and pessimist
  The difference is droll;
The optimist sees the doughnut,
  The pessimist, the hole.
>   McLANDBURGH WILSON, *Optimist and Pessimist.*

10
Two knights contended in the list—
An optimist, a pessimist;
But each by mist was blinded so
That neither struck a single blow.
>   R. T. WOMBAT, *Quatrains.*

ORATOR AND ORATORY
See also Speech

11
An orator is a man who says what he thinks and feels what he says.
>   WILLIAM JENNINGS BRYAN. (HIBBEN, *The Peerless Leader,* p. 118)

12
Glittering and sounding generalities.
>   RUFUS CHOATE, Letter to the Maine Whig Committee, 1856, referring to the Declaration of Independence.

13
There is no inspiration in evil and . . . no man ever made a great speech on a mean subject.
>   EUGENE V. DEBS, *Efficient Expression.*

14
Ye could waltz to it.
>   FINLEY PETER DUNNE, referring to the oratory of Senator Albert J. Beveridge.

15
There is no true orator who is not a hero.
>   EMERSON, *Letters and Social Aims: Eloquence.*

16
WHEREAS, it has become obvious that three minutes is ample time for any member to speak to the record to impress the Folks Back Home, and
WHEREAS, it is equally obvious that no member of this House can speak for longer than three minutes without repeating himself,
ORDERED, that any member who speaks at any one time for longer than three minutes shall, at the sole discretion of the Speaker, be shot, stuffed and displayed in a glass case in the State Museum—bearing around his neck the legend—
  Here am I, for E'er enshrined,
  My mouth is open, teeth are shined;
  My colleagues' treatment less than kind,
  I talked them all deaf, dumb and blind.
>   JAMES S. ERWIN of the Maine House of Representatives, Legislative Order proposed in that assembly, 19 May, 1965. It was read and "indefinitely postponed." The order and poem, both original, were inspired by one of Rep. Erwin's long-winded colleagues.

17
You'd scarce expect one of my age
To speak in public on the stage;
And if I chance to fall below
Demosthenes or Cicero,
Don't view me with a critic's eye,
But pass my imperfections by.
Large streams from little fountains flow,

Tall oaks from little acorns grow.
> DAVID EVERETT, *Lines Written for a School Declamation by a Little Boy of Seven.* (*Columbian Orator*, Boston, 1797)

1

Amplification is the vice of the modern orator. . . . Speeches measured by the hour die with the hour.
> THOMAS JEFFERSON, *Writings*, vol. xvi, p. 30.

2

Come on down to the speakin' tonight!
> LYNDON B. JOHNSON, his familiar greeting to street crowds, shouted through a bullhorn, during the 1964 presidential campaign. (TOM WICKER, *Lyndon Johnson is 10 Feet Tall; New York Times Magazine,* 23 May, 1965, p. 92)

3

Hot air has thawed out many a cold reception.
> F. M. KNOWLES, *A Cheerful Year Book.*

4

Nut while the two-legged gab-machine's so plenty.
> JAMES RUSSELL LOWELL, *The Biglow Papers,* Ser. ii, No. 11.

5

The capital of the orator is in the bank of the highest sentimentalities and the purest enthusiasms.
> EDWARD G. PARKER, *The Golden Age of American Oratory,* ch. 1.

6

There is Truth and Beauty in Rhetoric; but it oftener serves ill turns than good ones.
> WILLIAM PENN, *Fruits of Solitude.*

7

I sometimes marvel at the extraordinary docility with which Americans submit to speeches.
> ADLAI E. STEVENSON, Speech to the American Legion, Chicago, 1950.

8

When I was a boy I never had much sympathy for a holiday speaker. He was just a kind of interruption between the hot dogs, a fly in the lemonade.
> ADLAI E. STEVENSON, Speech in Flint, Mich., 1952.

ORDER

9

Chaos often breeds life, when order breeds habit.
> HENRY ADAMS, *The Education of Henry Adams,* p. 249.

10

Order is a lovely thing;
On disarray it lays its wing,
Teaching simplicity to sing.
It has a meek and lowly grace,
Quiet as a nun's face.
> ANNA HEMPSTEAD BRANCH, *The Monk in the Kitchen.*

11

For the world was built in order
  And the atoms march in tune;
Rhyme the pipe, and Time the warder,
  The sun obeys them, and the moon.
> EMERSON, *Monadnock,* st. 12.

ORIGINALITY

See also Imitation, Plagiarism

12

No bird has ever uttered note
That was not in some first bird's throat;
Since Eden's freshness and man's fall
No rose has been original.
> THOMAS BAILEY ALDRICH, *Originality.*

13

What is originality? It is being one's self, and reporting accurately what we see and are.
> EMERSON, *Letters and Social Aims: Quotation and Originality.*

14

A thought is often original, though you have uttered it a hundred times.
> OLIVER WENDELL HOLMES, *The Autocrat of the Breakfast-Table,* ch. 1.

15

You shall no longer take things at second or
    third hand, nor look through the eyes of
    the dead, nor feed on the spectres in
    books.
> WALT WHITMAN, *Song of Myself,* sec. 2.

P

PAIN

See also Suffering

16

The fiercest agonies have shortest reign.
> WILLIAM CULLEN BRYANT, *Mutation,* l. 4.

17

Iron, left in the rain
  And fog and dew,
With rust is covered.—Pain

Rusts into beauty too.
> MARY CAROLYN DAVIES, *Rust.*

18

Oh, what a bellyache!
> DWIGHT D. EISENHOWER, at the time he underwent surgery, in 1956, for removal of an intestinal obstruction.

19

He has seen but half the universe who never

has been shewn the house of Pain.
> EMERSON, *Natural History of Intellect:
> The Tragic.*

1
Under pain, pleasure,—
Under pleasure, pain lies.
> EMERSON, *The Sphinx.*

2
The tree will be there long after the discomfort is gone.
> JOHN F. KENNEDY, Note to Prime Minister Diefenbaker of Canada, 9 June, 1961. Diefenbaker had just written to Kennedy, expressing regret that Kennedy had sprained his back during a tree-planting ceremony in Canada a short time earlier. (*The Kennedy Wit*, ed. by Bill Adler: *The Presidency*)

3
Pain makes man think. Thought makes man wise. Wisdom makes life endurable.
> JOHN PATRICK, *The Teahouse of the August Moon.*

4
No pain, no palm; no thorn, no throne.
> WILLIAM PENN, *No Cross, No Crown.*

5
Pain is no longer pain when it is past.
> MARGARET JUNKIN PRESTON, *Nature's Lesson.*

6
Let's tell them [the American people] the truth, that there are no gains without pains.
> ADLAI E. STEVENSON, Speech of acceptance at the Democratic national convention that nominated him for the presidency, Chicago, 26 July, 1952.

7
It changed the soul of one to sour
  And passionate regret;
To one it gave unselfish power
  To love and to forget.
> SELDEN L. WHITCOMB, *Pain.*

8
But, soon or late, the fact grows plain
  To all through sorrow's test:
The only folks who give us pain
  Are those we love the best.
> ELLA WHEELER WILCOX, *Cupid Wounds.*

PAINTING
See also Art and Artists

9
The love of gain never made a painter, but it has marred many.
> WASHINGTON ALLSTON, *Lectures on Art: Aphorisms.*

10
Pictures must not be too picturesque.
> EMERSON, *Essays, First Series: Art.*

11
How strongly I have felt of pictures that when you have seen one well, you must take

your leave of it; you shall never see it again.
> EMERSON, *Essays, Second Series: Experience.*

12
One picture in ten thousand, perhaps, ought to live in the applause of mankind, from generation to generation until the colors fade and blacken out of sight or the canvas rot entirely away.
> NATHANIEL HAWTHORNE, *The Marble Faun*, bk. ii, ch. 12.

13
The picture that approaches sculpture nearest
Is the best picture.
> HENRY WADSWORTH LONGFELLOW, *Michael Angelo*, pt. ii, sec. 4.

14
I believe in paintings like I believe in God.
> SAM SALZ, Interview with Milton Esterow, New York *Times*, 15 Feb., 1964, p. 25. Describing his feeling for his role as one of the world's leading art dealers.

15
A picture is not wrought
By hands alone, good Padre, but by thought.
> WILLIAM W. STORY, *Padre Bandelli Proses.*

16
A tortoise-shell cat having a fit in a platter of tomatoes.
> MARK TWAIN, Description of Turner's "The Slave Ship."

17
A kiss from my mother made me a painter.
> BENJAMIN WEST.

18
The Attorney-General: The labour of two days, then, is that for which you ask two hundred guineas!
Mr. Whistler: No—I ask it for the knowledge of a lifetime.
> J. McNEILL WHISTLER, *The Gentle Art of Making Enemies*, p. 5. Whistler under cross-examination during his suit against Ruskin.

19
A life passed among pictures makes not a painter—else the policeman in the National Gallery might assert himself. As well allege that he who lives in a library must needs be a poet.
> J. McNEILL WHISTLER, *The Gentle Art of Making Enemies*, p. 26.

PARTING

20
Parting is all we know of heaven,
And all we need of hell.
> EMILY DICKINSON, *Poems*, Pt. i, No. 96.

21
The day goes by like a shadow o'er the heart,

With sorrow where all was delight:
The time has come when the darkies have to part,
    Then my old Kentucky Home, good-night!
    STEPHEN COLLINS FOSTER, *My Old Kentucky Home.*

1
Say "au revoir" but not "good-bye,"
Though past is dead, Love cannot die.
    HARRY KENNEDY, *Say "Au Revoir" but Not "Good-bye"* (1893).

2
No one, not in my situation, can appreciate my feeling of sadness at this parting. To this place, and the kindness of these people, I owe everything. . . . Trusting in Him who can go with me, and remain with you, and be everywhere for good, let us confidently hope that all will yet be well.
    ABRAHAM LINCOLN, Address in Springfield, Ill., 11 Feb., 1861, bidding farewell before taking up the burdens of the presidency.

3
    They who go
Feel not the pain of parting; it is they
Who stay behind that suffer.
    HENRY WADSWORTH LONGFELLOW, *Michael Angelo*, pt. i, prologue.

4
There's something in the parting hour
    Will chill the warmest heart,
Yet kindred, comrades, lovers, friends,
    Are fated all to part.
    EDWARD POLLOCK, *The Parting Hour.*

5
I now bid you a welcome adoo.
    ARTEMUS WARD, *The Shakers.*

PASSION
See also Anger, Love
6
Passion, though a bad regulator, is a powerful spring.
    EMERSON, *Conduct of Life: Considerations by the Way.*

7
Bee to the blossom, moth to the flame;
Each to his passion; what's in a name?
    HELEN HUNT JACKSON, *Vanity of Vanities.*

8
        Passion is power,
And, kindly tempered, saves. All things declare
Struggle hath deeper peace than sleep can bring.
    WILLIAM VAUGHN MOODY, *The Masque of Judgment*, act iii, sc. 2.

9
It may be called the Master Passion, the hunger for self-approval.
    MARK TWAIN, *What Is Man?*, ch. 6.

10
She parried Time's malicious dart,
    And kept the years at bay,
Till passion entered in her heart
    And aged her in a day!
    ELLA WHEELER WILCOX, *The Destroyer.*

PAST
See also Memory, Time
11
Thou unrelenting past.
    WILLIAM CULLEN BRYANT, *To the Past.*

12
Why should we grope among the dry bones of the past, or put the living generation into masquerade out of its faded wardrobe?
    EMERSON, *Essays, Second Series: Lecture.*

13
I know of no way of judging the future but by the past.
    PATRICK HENRY, Speech, Virginia Convention, March, 1775.

14
Cheerful Yesterdays.
    THOMAS W. HIGGINSON, Title of autobiography.

15
No past is dead for us, but only sleeping, Love.
    HELEN HUNT JACKSON, *At Last.*

16
The dogmas of the quiet past are inadequate to the stormy present.
    ABRAHAM LINCOLN, Second Annual Message to Congress, 1862.

17
Look not mournfully into the Past. It comes not back again. Wisely improve the Present. It is thine. Go forth to meet the shadowy Future, without fear, and with a manly heart.
    HENRY WADSWORTH LONGFELLOW, *Hyperion*, bk. i, motto.

18
Nor deem the irrevocable Past
    As wholly wasted, wholly vain,
If, rising on its wrecks, at last
    To something nobler we attain.
    HENRY WADSWORTH LONGFELLOW, *The Ladder of St. Augustine.*

19
Let the dead Past bury its dead!
    HENRY WADSWORTH LONGFELLOW, *A Psalm of Life.*

20
Safe in the hallowed quiets of the past.
    JAMES RUSSELL LOWELL, *The Cathedral*, l. 235.

21
The past has been completely destroyed—how can anybody sane be a reactionary? In fact, reactionaries never do care about the past. They only imagine they do.
    MARY MCCARTHY. (*Lady with a Switchblade; Life*, 20 Sept., 1963, p. 64)

1
The Past is a bucket of ashes.
  CARL SANDBURG, *Prairie.*

2
Those who cannot remember the past are condemned to repeat it.
  GEORGE SANTAYANA, *The Life of Reason,* p. 284.

3
The past at least is secure.
  DANIEL WEBSTER, Speech on Foote's Resolution, U.S. Senate, 26 Jan., 1830.

PATIENCE
See also Endurance

4
Serene I fold my hands and wait.
  JOHN BURROUGHS, *Waiting.*

5
Perhaps the wife of a patient man must have her quota of patience, too!
  EDMUND VANCE COOKE, *From the Book of Extenuations: Job.*

6
There was a time when Patience ceased to be a virtue. It was long ago.
  CHARLOTTE PERKINS GILMAN, *The Forerunner.*

7
Who longest waits of all most surely wins.
  HELEN HUNT JACKSON, *The Victory of Patience.*

8
Patience and fortitude.
  FIORELLO H. LA GUARDIA, Saying that became closely identified with him, largely through his radio broadcasts on the New York City municipal station, WNYC, during World War II.

9
Rule by patience, Laughing Water!
  HENRY WADSWORTH LONGFELLOW, *Hiawatha,* pt. x.

10
Learn to labor and to wait.
  HENRY WADSWORTH LONGFELLOW, *A Psalm of Life.*

11
All things come round to him who will but wait.
  HENRY WADSWORTH LONGFELLOW, *Tales of a Wayside Inn: The Student's Tale,* last line (quoted).

Everything comes to him who hustles while he waits.
  THOMAS A. EDISON. (*Golden Book,* Apr., 1931)

Alas! all things come too late for those who wait.
  JAMES G. HUNEKER, *Chopin,* p. 77.

12
That's the advantage of having lived 65 years. You don't feel the need to be impatient any longer.
  THORNTON WILDER. (FLORA LEWIS, *Thornton Wilder at 65; New York Times Magazine,* 15 Apr., 1962, p. 28)

PATRIOTISM
See also America, Flag, Independence Day

13
The die was now cast; I had passed the Rubicon. Swim or sink, live or die, survive or perish with my country was my unalterable determination.
  JOHN ADAMS, *Works,* vol. iv, p. 8. (In a conversation with Jonathan Sewell, 1774.)

14
No man can be a patriot on an empty stomach.
  WILLIAM C. BRANN, *The Iconoclast: Old Glory.*

15
And they who for their country die
  Shall fill an honored grave,
For glory lights the soldier's tomb,
  And beauty weeps the brave.
  JOSEPH RODMAN DRAKE, *To the Defenders of New Orleans.*

16
Patriotism means equipped forces and a prepared citizenry.
  DWIGHT D. EISENHOWER, First Inaugural Address, 20 Jan., 1953.

17
Patriotism has its roots deep in the instincts and the affections. Love of country is the expansion of filial love.
  DAVID D. FIELD, *Speeches: A Memorial Address.*

18
How can a man be said to have a country when he has no right to a square inch of soil?
  HENRY GEORGE, *Social Problems,* ch. 2.

19
I only regret that I have but one life to lose for my country.
  NATHAN HALE, Last Words, 22 Sept., 1776.

20
They love their land because it is their own,
And scorn to give aught other reason why.
  FITZ-GREENE HALLECK, *Connecticut.*

21
He loves his country best who strives to make it best.
  ROBERT G. INGERSOLL, Decoration Day Oration, 1882.

22
I think patriotism is like charity—it begins at home.
  HENRY JAMES, *The Portrait of a Lady,* ch. 10.

1

Indeed, I tremble for my country when I reflect that God is just.

> THOMAS JEFFERSON, *Notes on Virginia: Manners.*

2

And so, my fellow Americans: ask not what your country can do for you—ask what you can do for your country.

> JOHN F. KENNEDY, Inaugural Address, 20 Jan., 1961.

3

Patriotism is often an arbitrary veneration of real estate above principles.

> GEORGE JEAN NATHAN, *Testament of a Critic*, p. 16.

4

A man who is good enough to shed his blood for his country is good enough to be given a square deal afterwards.

> THEODORE ROOSEVELT, *Life of Benton.*

5

Don't spread patriotism too thin.

> THEODORE ROOSEVELT. (*Metropolitan Magazine*, July, 1918)

6

The patriots are those who love America enough to wish to see her as a model to mankind.

> ADLAI E. STEVENSON, *The Hard Kind of Patriotism; Harper's Magazine*, July, 1963.

7

Do not . . . regard the critics as questionable patriots. What were Washington and Jefferson and Adams but profound critics of the colonial status quo?

> ADLAI E. STEVENSON, *The Hard Kind of Patriotism; Harper's Magazine*, July, 1963.

8

There are misguided patriots who feel we pay too much attention to other nations, that we are somehow enfeebled by respecting world opinion. . . . The founding fathers did not think it was "soft" or "un-American" to respect the opinions of others, and today for a man to love his country truly, he must also know how to love mankind.

> ADLAI E. STEVENSON, *The Hard Kind of Patriotism; Harper's Magazine*, July, 1963.

9

No patriots so defaced America as those who, in the name of Americanism, launched a witch-hunt which became a byword around the world. We have survived it. We shall survive John Birchism and all the rest of the superpatriots—but only at the price of perpetual and truly patriotic vigilance.

> ADLAI E. STEVENSON, *The Hard Kind of Patriotism; Harper's Magazine*, July, 1963.

10

Patriotism knows neither latitude nor longitude. It is not climatic.

> E. A. STORRS, *Political Oratory*, ch. 2.

11

A great and lasting war can never be supported on this principle [patriotism] alone. It must be aided by a prospect of interest, or some reward.

> GEORGE WASHINGTON, Letter to John Banister, Valley Forge, 21 Apr., 1778.

12

Let our object be, our country, our whole country, and nothing but our country.

> DANIEL WEBSTER, Address at the laying of the cornerstone of Bunker Hill Monument, 17 June, 1825.

13

If it be the pleasure of heaven that my country shall require the poor offering of my life, the victim shall be ready at the appointed hour of sacrifice, come when that hour may.

> DANIEL WEBSTER, Supposed Speech of John Adams.

14

Patriotism has become a mere national self-assertion, a sentimentality of flag-cheering with no constructive duties.

> H. G. WELLS, *The Future in America.*

15

They went where duty seemed to call,
   They scarcely asked the reason why;
   They only knew they could but die,
And death was not the worst of all!

> JOHN GREENLEAF WHITTIER, *Lexington.*

16

There are no points of the compass on the chart of true patriotism.

> ROBERT C. WINTHROP, Letter to Boston Commercial Club, 12 June, 1879.

17

Our land is the dearer for our sacrifices. The blood of our martyrs sanctifies and enriches it. Their spirit passes into thousands of hearts. How costly is the progress of the race. It is only by the giving of life that we can have life.

> REV. E. J. YOUNG, *Lesson of the Hour; Monthly Religious Magazine*, May, 1865.

PEACE

See also War

18

Peace is never long preserved by weight of metal or by an armament race. Peace can be made tranquil and secure only by understanding and agreement fortified by sanctions. We must embrace international cooperation or international disintegration.

> BERNARD M. BARUCH, Address to the United Nations Atomic Energy Commission, 14 June, 1946.

19

There is no more dangerous misconception

than this which misconstrues the arms race as the cause rather than a symptom of the tensions and divisions which threaten nuclear war. If the history of the past fifty years teaches us anything, it is that peace does not follow disarmament—disarmament follows peace.

> BERNARD M. BARUCH, Memorandum composed for U.S. Government officials, 6 Jan., 1961, but first made public almost three years later. (Quoted by ARTHUR KROCK, "In the Nation" Column; New York *Times,* 26 Dec., 1963)

1

As I read this to-day what a change! The world convulsed by war as never before. Men slaying each other like wild beasts.

> ANDREW CARNEGIE, *Autobiography,* conclusion.

2

Modern war could now destroy much of the life on this planet. But also it may be possible that craven purchase of peace at the expense of principle can result in destroying much of the human spirit on this planet. Peace, under certain conditions, could lead to a degradation of the human race and to subjecting human beings to a form of mental decay which obliterates the capacity for moral and intellectual judgment.

> JOHN FOSTER DULLES, Address in Washington, D.C., 11 Apr., 1955.

3

'Tis startin' a polis foorce to prevint war. . . . How'll they be ar-med? What a foolish question. They'll be ar-med with love, if coorse.

> FINLEY PETER DUNNE, *On Making a Will.* The reference is to William Jennings Bryan's speech on the League of Nations in 1920.

4

Peace cannot be kept by force. It can only be achieved by understanding.

> ALBERT EINSTEIN, *Notes on Pacifism.*

5

We seek peace, knowing that peace is the climate of freedom.

> DWIGHT D. EISENHOWER, Second Inaugural Address, 21 Jan., 1957.

6

Peace and justice are two sides of the same coin.

> DWIGHT D. EISENHOWER, News Conference, 6 Feb., 1957.

7

Peace is a blessing, and like most blessings, it must be earned.

> DWIGHT D. EISENHOWER, *Let's Be Honest with Ourselves; The Reader's Digest,* Dec., 1963.

8

The god of Victory is said to be one-handed, but Peace gives victory to both sides.

> EMERSON, *Journal,* 1867.

9

I have no illusions that peace can be achieved rapidly, but I have every confidence that it is going to be possible to inch toward it, inch by agonizing inch.

> ARTHUR J. GOLDBERG, Address at the ceremony marking his inauguration as U.S. ambassador to the United Nations, 26 July, 1965.

10

Nor is there such a thing as peaceful coexistence.

> BARRY M. GOLDWATER. (*New York Times Magazine,* 17 Sept., 1961) Though poles apart from Lenin, Goldwater thus recalls the Russian's famous statement: "International imperialism disposing of the might of capital cannot coexist with the Soviet Republic. Conflict is unavoidable."

But I would say to the leaders of the Soviet Union, and to their people, that if either of our countries is to be fully secure, we need a much better weapon than the H-bomb, a weapon better than ballistic missiles or nuclear submarines, and that better weapon is peaceful co-operation.

> JOHN F. KENNEDY, Address to the General Assembly of the United Nations, 20 Sept., 1963.

We cannot be unaware that there is afoot in the land a militant minority protest. . . . And if it can be thought of as a policy, it can be thought of only as a policy of conversion or extinction. And nowadays that means co-extinction.

> ADLAI E. STEVENSON, Address to the World Affairs Council, Philadelphia, 24 Sept., 1964. In defense of coexistence.

11

Let us have peace!

> U. S. GRANT, Letter, accepting the nomination to the presidency, 29 May, 1868.

12

An association of men who will not quarrel with one another is a thing which never yet existed, from the greatest confederacy of nations down to a town-meeting or a vestry.

> THOMAS JEFFERSON, Letter to John Taylor, 1798.

13

In this age where there can be no losers in peace and no victors in war, we must recognize the obligation to match national strength with national restraint—we must be prepared at one and the same time for both the confrontation of power and the limitation of power—we must be ready to defend the national interest and to negotiate the common interest.

> LYNDON B. JOHNSON, Address to a joint session of Congress, 27 Nov., 1963—his first major statement of policy after he became President.

1

Our understanding of how to live—live with one another—is still far behind our knowledge of how to destroy one another.

> LYNDON B. JOHNSON, Address to the General Assembly of the United Nations, 17 Dec., 1963.

2

There is only one item on the agenda of this conference—it is the leading item on the agenda of mankind—and that one item is peace.

> LYNDON B. JOHNSON, Message to the disarmament conference in Geneva, 21 Jan., 1964.

3

The best way to begin disarming is to begin —and the United States is ready to conclude firm agreements in these areas and to consider any other reasonable proposal.

> LYNDON B. JOHNSON, Message to the disarmament conference in Geneva, 21 Jan., 1964.

4

For America today, as in Jefferson's time, peace must be our passion. It is not enough for America to be a sentinel on the frontiers of freedom. America must also be on the watchtower seeking out the horizons of peace.

> LYNDON B. JOHNSON, Address at the University of California, Los Angeles, 21 Feb., 1964.

5

In other words, our guard is up but our hand is out.

> LYNDON B. JOHNSON, Speech at annual luncheon of the Associated Press, New York City, 20 Apr., 1964.

6

Peace was his message to the world.

> LYNDON B. JOHNSON, referring to Jawaharlal Nehru, in letter of condolence to President Sarvepalli Radhakrishnan of India, 27 May, 1964, the day of Nehru's death.

7

Peace is more than the absence of aggression. It is the creation of a world community in which every nation can follow its own course without fear of its neighbors.

> LYNDON B. JOHNSON, Labor Day Address, 7 Sept., 1964, in Detroit.

8

If we are to live together in peace, we must come to know each other better.

> LYNDON B. JOHNSON, State of the Union message, 4 Jan., 1965.

9

The cost of freedom is always high, but Americans have always paid it. And one path we shall never choose, and that is the path of surrender, or submission.

> JOHN F. KENNEDY, Address broadcast nationally, 22 Oct., 1962, dealing with the Cuban missile crisis of that year.

10

The mere absence of war is not peace.

> JOHN F. KENNEDY, State of the Union message, 14 Jan., 1963.

11

Peace is a daily, a weekly, a monthly process, gradually changing opinions, slowly eroding old barriers, quietly building new structures. And however undramatic the pursuit of peace, that pursuit must go on.

> JOHN F. KENNEDY, Address to the General Assembly of the United Nations, 20 Sept., 1963.

12

Peace does not rest in charters and covenants alone. It lies in the hearts and minds of the people. And if it is cast out there, then no act, no pact, no treaty or organization can ever hope to preserve it. So let us not rest all our hopes for peace on parchment and paper—let us strive also to build peace in the hearts and minds of our people.

> JOHN F. KENNEDY, Address to the General Assembly of the United Nations, 20 Sept., 1963.

13

Today we may have reached a pause in the cold war—but that is not a lasting peace. A test-ban treaty is a milestone—but that is not the millennium. We have not been released from our obligations—we have been given an opportunity. And if we fail to make the most of this moment . . . then the shaming indictment of posterity will rightly point its finger at us all.

> JOHN F. KENNEDY, Address to the General Assembly of the United Nations, 20 Sept., 1963.

President Kennedy, I am sure, would regard as his best memorial the fact that in his three years as President the world became a little safer and the way ahead became a little brighter.

> LYNDON B. JOHNSON, Address to the General Assembly of the United Nations, 17 Dec., 1963.

Peace who was becoming bright-eyed, now sits in the shadows of death; her handsome champion has been killed as he walked by her very side. Her gallant boy is dead.

> SEAN O'CASEY, Letter to Mrs. Rose Russell, a leader of the New York City Teachers Union, 23 Nov., 1963. Referring to the death of John F. Kennedy.

1

Buried was the bloody hatchet;
Buried was the dreadful war-club;
Buried were all warlike weapons,
And the war-cry was forgotten.
Then was peace among the nations.
 HENRY WADSWORTH LONGFELLOW, *Hiawatha,* pt. xiii, l. 7.

2

If man does find the solution for world peace it will be the most revolutionary reversal of his record we have ever known.
 GEORGE C. MARSHALL, Report of Chief of Staff, U.S. Army, 1 Sept., 1945.

3

If I must choose between peace and righteousness, I choose righteousness.
 THEODORE ROOSEVELT, *Unwise Peace Treaties.*

4

Professional pacifists, the peace-at-any-price, non-resistance, universal arbitration people, are seeking to Chinafy this country.
 THEODORE ROOSEVELT, Speech in San Francisco.

5

For lo! the days are hastening on,
 By prophet-bards foretold,
When with the ever-circling years,
 Comes round the age of gold;
When Peace shall over all the earth
 Its ancient splendors fling
And the whole world sends back the song
 Which now the angels sing.
 EDMUND HAMILTON SEARS, *The Angels' Song.*

6

The will to peace cannot be legislated. It must be developed, and can only be developed by organized, patient effort. The laws and institutions of international co-operation have to evolve out of a combination of the common aspirations and experience of the peoples of the world.
 ADLAI E. STEVENSON, Speech in London, 1945.

7

The focus of the problem does not lie in the atom; it resides in the hearts of men.
 HENRY L. STIMSON, *The Bomb and the Opportunity; Harper's Magazine,* Mar., 1946.

There is no evil in the atom; only in men's souls.
 ADLAI E. STEVENSON, Speech in Hartford, Conn., 18 Sept., 1952.

8

The battlefield as a place of settlement of disputes is gradually yielding to arbitral courts of justice.
 WILLIAM HOWARD TAFT, *Dawn of World Peace; U.S. Bureau of Education Bulletin,* No. 8.

9

Peace is always beautiful.
 WALT WHITMAN, *The Sleepers.*

10

When Earth, as if on evil dreams,
 Looks back upon her wars,
And the white light of Christ outstreams
 From the red disk of Mars,

His fame who led the stormy van
 Of battle well may cease;
But never that which crowns the man
 Whose victory was Peace.
 JOHN GREENLEAF WHITTIER, *William Francis Bartlett.*

11

Peace is the healing and elevating influence of the world.
 WOODROW WILSON, Address in Philadelphia, 10 May, 1915.

12

There is a price which is too great to pay for peace, and that price can be put in one word. One cannot pay the price of self-respect.
 WOODROW WILSON, Speech in Des Moines, Ia., 1 Feb., 1916.

13

It must be a peace without victory.
 WOODROW WILSON, Address to U.S. Senate, 22 Jan., 1917.

14

Only a peace between equals can last.
 WOODROW WILSON, Address to U.S. Senate, 22 Jan., 1917.

15

A steadfast concert for peace can never be maintained except by a partnership of democratic nations. . . . It must be a league of honor, a partnership of opinion.
 WOODROW WILSON, Address to Congress, asking for a declaration of war against Germany, 2 Apr., 1917.

16

Open covenants of peace openly arrived at. . . . Absolute freedom of navigation upon the seas outside territorial waters alike in peace and in war. . . . The removal, so far as possible, of all economic barriers and the establishment of an equality of trade conditions among all nations. . . . Adequate guarantees given and taken that national armaments will be reduced to the lowest point consistent with domestic safety.
 WOODROW WILSON, Address to Congress, 8 Jan., 1918. First four of the Fourteen Points.

17

There is one thing that the American people always rise to and extend their hand to, and that is the truth of justice and of liberty and of peace. We have accepted that truth and we are going to be led by it, and it is going to lead us, and through us the world, out into pastures of quietness and peace such as the world never dreamed of before.

WOODROW WILSON, Speech in Pueblo, Colo., 25 Sept., 1919, urging acceptance of the League of Nations.

PEACE OF MIND

1
To insure Peace of Mind ignore the Rules and Regulations.

GEORGE ADE, *Forty Modern Fables: The Crustacean.*

2
After dreams of horror, comes again
The welcome morning with its rays of peace.

WILLIAM CULLEN BRYANT, *Mutation,* l. 5.

3
Nothing can bring you peace but yourself.

EMERSON, *Essays: Of Self-Reliance.*

4
Heaven is to be at peace with things.

GEORGE SANTAYANA, *Sonnet 49.*

5
To be glad of life because it gives you the chance to love and to work and to play and to look up at the stars, to be satisfied with your possessions but not contented with yourself until you have made the best of them, to despise nothing in the world except falsehood and meanness and to fear nothing except cowardice, to be governed by your admirations rather than by your disgusts, to covet nothing that is your neighbor's except his kindness of heart and gentleness of manners, to think seldom of your enemies, often of your friends, and every day of Christ, and to spend as much time as you can, with body and with spirit, in God's out-of-doors, these are little guideposts on the footpath to peace.

HENRY VAN DYKE, *The Footpath to Peace.*

6
Peace! It's wonderful!

UNKNOWN, Motto of the disciples of Father Divine.

PEOPLE, THE

7
Nothing is more uncertain than a dependence upon public bodies. They are moved like the wind, but rather more uncertain.

ABRAHAM CLARK, Letter to James Caldwell, 7 Mar., 1777.

8
Government is a trust, and the officers of the government are trustees; and both the trust and the trustees are created for the benefit of the people.

HENRY CLAY, Address in Ashland, Ky., 1829.

9
He did not lead the people—he rather followed the wisest and best thought of the people, and his successors will do likewise.

CHARLES W. ELIOT, Letter to his mother, written in 1865, from Rome. The reference is to Lincoln—Eliot's reaction upon getting word of Lincoln's death.

10
Leave this hypocritical prating about the masses. Masses are rude, lame, unmade, pernicious in their demands and influence, and need not to be flattered, but to be schooled. . . . The mass are animal, in pupilage, and near chimpanzee. But the units, whereof the mass is composed, are neuters, every one of which may be grown to a queen-bee.

EMERSON, *Conduct of Life: Considerations by the Way.*

11
March without the people, and you march into night; their instincts are a finger-pointing of Providence, always turned toward real benefit.

EMERSON, *Conduct of Life: Power.* Quoted as said by "a French deputy from the tribune."

12
The man in the street does not know a star in the sky.

EMERSON, *Conduct of Life: Worship.*

13
A mob is a society of bodies voluntarily bereaving themselves of reason. . . . A mob is man voluntarily descending to the nature of the beast.

EMERSON, *Essays, First Series: Compensation.*

14
The people are to be taken in very small doses. If solitude is proud, so is society vulgar.

EMERSON, *Essays: Society and Solitude.*

15
No one should ever give the people what they want. What if the president of a college would say, "Give the students what they want"? He would be laughed out of existence.

MORRIS ERNST, Address in St. Louis, 16 July, 1964. He was specifically deriding the television network owners who answer criticism of programming by saying they give the public what it wants.

16
A Mob's a Monster; Heads enough, but no Brains.

BENJAMIN FRANKLIN, *Poor Richard,* 1747.

17
I shall on all subjects have a policy to recommend, but none to enforce against the will of the people.

U. S. GRANT, First Inaugural Address, 4 Mar., 1869.

18
He was like a daddy to me always: he al-

ways talked to me just that way. He was the one person I ever knew—anywhere—who was never afraid. Whatever you talked to him about, whatever you asked him for, like projects for your district, there was just one way to figure it with him. I know some of them called it demagoguery; they can call it anything they want, but you could be damn sure that the only test he had was this: Was it good for the folks?

> LYNDON B. JOHNSON, on Franklin D. Roosevelt. (HENRY A. ZEIGER, *Lyndon B. Johnson: Man and President,* p. 36)

1
These programs will take hold and succeed only when we become determined that nothing is to take priority over people.

> LYNDON B. JOHNSON, Annual Manpower Report to Congress, 9 Mar., 1964, in which he called for a broad range of legislation to create jobs and train workers for them.

2
There is in any large-scale dispute a question of the public interest. This interest must always be overriding. But we must never delude ourselves that we are serving the public interest if at any time we suppress the legitimate rights of the conflicting parties.

> LYNDON B. JOHNSON, News Conference, Washington, D.C., 11 Apr., 1964.

3
As long as I am President, this Government will not set one group against another—but will build a creative partnership between business and labor, farm areas and urban centers, consumer and producer. This is what I mean when I choose to be a President of all the people.

> LYNDON B. JOHNSON, Speech in Minneapolis, 27 June, 1964. Thereafter he repeated the phrase "President of all the people" on numerous occasions, and his Administration was often referred to as "government by consensus."

4
You can fool some of the people all of the time, and all of the people some of the time, but you cannot fool all of the people all the time.

> ABRAHAM LINCOLN, Speech in Bloomington, Ill., 29 May, 1856. On the authority of William P. Kellogg. (See also under Deceit.)

5
The Lord prefers common-looking people. That is the reason He makes so many of them.

> ABRAHAM LINCOLN. (JAMES MORGAN, *Our Presidents,* vi; C. T. WETTSTEIN, *Was Lincoln an Infidel?,* p. 84)

6
This country, with its institutions, belongs to the people who inhabit it.

> ABRAHAM LINCOLN, First Inaugural Address, 4 Mar., 1861.

7
Why should there not be a patient confidence in the ultimate justice of the people? Is there any better or equal hope in the world?

> ABRAHAM LINCOLN, First Inaugural Address, 4 Mar., 1861.

8
People Are Funny.

> ART LINKLETTER, Title of book (1953). Earlier the title of his radio and television shows.

9
The public, with its mob yearning to be instructed, edified and pulled by the nose, demands certainties; . . . but there are no certainties.

> H. L. MENCKEN, *Prejudices,* ser. i, p. 46.

10
Common sense, in so far as it exists, is all for the bourgeoisie. Nonsense is the privilege of the aristocracy. The worries of the world are for the common people.

> GEORGE JEAN NATHAN, *Autobiography of an Attitude.*

11
The Mob destroys spiritual values by accepting them; it destroys great men by adopting their principles.

> FRANK K. NOTCH, *King Mob,* p. 63.

12
Let the people think they govern and they will be governed.

> WILLIAM PENN, *Some Fruits of Solitude,* l. 67.

13
There is no tyranny so despotic as that of public opinion among a free people.

> DONN PIATT, *Memories of the Men Who Saved the Union: Lincoln.*

14
It is an ancient axiom of statecraft that you can always give the public anything but you can never take away what you once have given, without enormous trouble.

> WALTER B. PITKIN, *Twilight of the American Mind,* p. 222.

15
Let a man proclaim a new principle. Public sentiment will surely be on the other side.

> THOMAS B. REED. (W. A. ROBINSON, *Life of Reed*)

16
The object of government is the welfare of the people.

> THEODORE ROOSEVELT, *The New Nationalism.*

17
He is the people personified; that is the secret of his popularity. His government is the

most representative that has ever existed in world history.

> CARL SCHURZ, Letter to Theodore Petrasch, 12 Oct., 1864. The reference is to Lincoln.

1

Better we lose the election than mislead the people; and better we lose than misgovern the people.

> ADLAI E. STEVENSON, Speech, accepting the presidential nomination, Democratic national convention, 26 July, 1952.

2

The people are wise—wiser than the Republicans think.

> ADLAI E. STEVENSON, Speech, accepting the presidential nomination, Democratic national convention, 26 July, 1952.

3

Government . . . cannot be wiser than the people.

> ADLAI E. STEVENSON, Speech in Chicago, 29 Sept., 1952.

4

As citizens of this democracy, you are the rulers and the ruled, the law-givers and the law-abiding, the beginning and the end.

> ADLAI E. STEVENSON, Speech in Chicago, 29 Sept., 1952.

5

Folks are better than angels.

> EDWARD THOMPSON TAYLOR, minister of the Seamen's Bethel, North Square, Boston. This remark was in reply to friends who sought to comfort him, as he lay dying in 1871, by assuring him that he would soon be among the angels.

6

The mass never comes up to the standard of its best member, but on the contrary degrades itself to a level with the lowest.

> HENRY D. THOREAU, *Journal*, 14 Mar., 1838.

7

The public be damned.

> WILLIAM H. VANDERBILT, Reply to Clarence Dresser, a reporter for the Chicago *Tribune*, 1883. Vanderbilt had been asked whether the public had been consulted about the proposed discontinuance of a fast mail train to Chicago over the New York Central Railroad. When Vanderbilt explained that the run was not profitable, the reporter asked, "Are you working for the public or for your stockholders?" Vanderbilt replied: "The public be damned! I'm working for my stockholders." Henry Clews is authority for this version of the incident. (See letters in the New York *Times*, 25 Aug., 1918; New York *Herald*, 1 Oct., 1918; 28 Oct., 1918)

My grandfather, William H. Vanderbilt, had, considering his numerous philanthropic gifts, an unmerited reputation for indifference to the welfare of others. It was, as is often the case, founded on a remark shorn of its context. This is the version of the "public be damned" story that was given me by a friend of the family. Mr. Vanderbilt was on a business trip and, after a long and arduous day, had gone to his private car for a rest. A swarm of reporters arrived asking to come on board for an interview. Mr. Vanderbilt sent word that he was too tired and did not wish to give an interview, but would receive one representative of the press for a few minutes. A young man arrived saying, "Mr. Vanderbilt, *your* public *demands* an interview." This made Mr. Vanderbilt laugh, and he answered, "Oh, *my* public be damned!" In due course the young man left and next morning his article appeared in the paper with a large headline reading, "Vanderbilt Says 'The Public be Damned.' "

> CONSUELO VANDERBILT BALSAN, *The Glitter and the Gold* (1952), p. 3.

PERSEVERANCE
See also Resolution

8

Even the woodpecker owes his success to the fact that he uses his head and keeps pecking away until he finishes the job he starts.

> COLEMAN COX, *Perseverance.*

9

A pretty good firm is "Watch & Waite,"
And another is "Attit, Early & Layte;"
And still another is "Doo & Dairet;"
But the best is probably "Grinn & Barrett."

> WALTER G. DOTY, *The Best Firm.*

10

They did not strike twelve the first time.

> EMERSON, *English Traits*, ch. 19.

11

Hold on with a bulldog grip, and chew and choke as much as possible.

> ABRAHAM LINCOLN, Telegram to General Grant during the siege of Petersburg, 17 Aug., 1864.

12

"Brave admiral, say but one good word:
What shall we do when hope is gone?"
The words leapt like a leaping sword:
"Sail on! sail on! sail on! and on!"

> JOAQUIN MILLER, *Columbus.*

13

And the saying grew, as sayings will grow
    From hard endeavor and bangs and bumps:
"He got in a mighty hard row of stumps;
But he tried, and died trying to hoe his row."

> JOAQUIN MILLER, *A Hard Row of Stumps.*

14

'Tain't no use to sit and whine
'Cause the fish ain't on your line;

Bait your hook an' keep on tryin',
  Keep a-goin'!
FRANK L. STANTON, *Keep A-goin'*.

PERSONALITY

See also Character, Individuality

1
Men with a passion for anonymity.
LOUIS BROWNLOW, Report of President's
  Committee on Administrative Manage-
  ment, during the second term of the
  New Deal. Brownlow was chairman of
  the committee; the reference was to
  Franklin D. Roosevelt's assistants, nota-
  bly Harry Hopkins.

2
I am the owner of the sphere,
Of the seven stars and the solar year,
Of Caesar's hand, and Plato's brain,
Of Lord Christ's heart, and Shakespeare's
  strain.
EMERSON, *Essays, First Series: History*,
  Motto.

3
Bashfulness and apathy are a tough husk
in which a delicate organization is protected
from premature ripening.
EMERSON, *Essays, First Series: Friendship*.

4
As I am, so I see.
EMERSON, *Essays, Second Series: Experi-
  ence*.

5
There are three Johns: 1, the real John,
known only to his Maker; 2, John's ideal
John, never the real one, and often very unlike him; 3, Thomas's ideal John, never the
real John, nor John's John, but often very
unlike either.
OLIVER WENDELL HOLMES, *The Autocrat
  of the Breakfast-Table*, ch. 3.

6
I am four monkeys.
One hangs from a limb,
tail-wise,
chattering at the earth;
another is cramming his belly with cocoa-
  nut;
the third is up in the top branches,
quizzing the sky;
and the fourth—
he's chasing another monkey.
How many monkeys are you?
ALFRED KREYMBORG, *The Tree*.

7
I am bigger than anything that can happen
to me. All these things, sorrow, misfortune
and suffering, are outside my door. I am in
the house and I have a key.
CHARLES F. LUMMIS.

8
Absent he is a character understood, but
present he is a force respected.
GEORGE SANTAYANA, *Interpretations of
  Poetry and Religion*, p. 273.

9
Personality is to a man what perfume is to a
flower.
CHARLES M. SCHWAB, *Ten Commandments of Success*.

10
For an impenetrable shield, stand inside
yourself.
HENRY D. THOREAU, *Journal*, 27 June,
  1840.

11
It is native personality, and that alone, that
endows a man to stand before presidents or
generals, or in any distinguish'd collection,
with *aplomb*—and *not* culture, or any
knowledge or intellect whatever.
WALT WHITMAN, *Democratic Vistas*.

12
Nothing endures but personal qualities.
WALT WHITMAN, *Song of the Broad-Axe*,
  sec. 4.

13
What is commonest, cheapest, nearest, easi-
  est, is Me.
WALT WHITMAN, *Song of Myself*, sec. 14.

PESSIMISM

See also Optimism

14
Just because there's fallen
A snowflake on his forehead
He must go and fancy
'Tis winter all the year.
THOMAS BAILEY ALDRICH, *A Snowflake*.

15
I know those miserable fellows, and I hate
them, who see a black star always riding
through the light and colored clouds in the
sky overhead.
EMERSON, *Conduct of Life: Considerations by the Way*.

16
There are people who have an appetite for
grief, pleasure is not strong enough and they
crave pain, mithridatic stomachs which must
be fed on poisoned bread, natures so doomed
that no prosperity can sooth their ragged
and dishevelled desolation.
EMERSON, *Natural History of Intellect:
  The Tragic*.

17
A pessimist is one who has been intimately
acquainted with an optimist.
ELBERT HUBBARD, *A Thousand and One
  Epigrams*, p. 121.

18
My granddad, viewing earth's worn cogs,
Said things were going to the dogs;
His granddad in his house of logs
Swore things were going to the dogs;

His granddad in the Flemish bogs
Vowed things were going to the dogs;
His granddad in his old skin togs
Said things were going to the dogs.
Well, there's one thing I have to state:
Those dogs have had a good long wait.
    UNKNOWN, *Going to the Dogs.*

PHILADELPHIA

1
On the whole, I'd rather be in Philadelphia.
    W. C. FIELDS, proposed as his epitaph.

2
They say that the lady from Philadelphia,
who is staying in town, is very wise. Suppose
I go and ask her what is best to be done?
    LUCRETIA P. HALE, *Peterkin Papers,* ch.
    1.

3
Philadelphia is the most pecksniffian of
American cities, and thus probably leads the
world.
    H. L. MENCKEN, *The American Language.*

4
In Boston they ask, How much does he
know? In New York, How much is he
worth? In Philadelphia, Who were his parents?
    MARK TWAIN, *What Paul Bourget Thinks
    of Us.*

5
City of Brotherly Love.
    From the Greek *philadelphia:* brotherly
    love (*philia:* love, and *adelphos:* broth-
    er).

(For Philadelphia lawyers, see LAWYERS.)

PHILANTHROPY

**See also Brother, Brotherhood; Charity;
Gifts, Giving**

6
There is no beautifier of complexion, or
form, or behavior, like the wish to scatter
joy and not pain around us.
    EMERSON, *Conduct of Life: Behavior.*

7
I tell thee, thou foolish philanthropist, that I
grudge the dollar, the dime, the cent I give
to such men as do not belong to me and to
whom I do not belong.
    EMERSON, *Essays, First Series: Self-Reli-
    ance.*

8
It is easy to live for others; everybody
does.
    EMERSON, *Journals,* vol. vii, p. 46.

9
Take egotism out, and you would castrate
the benefactors.
    EMERSON, *Journals,* vol. ix, p. 519.

10
We owe to man higher succors than food and
fire. We owe to man man.
    EMERSON, *Society and Solitude: Domestic
    Life.*

11
Let me live in my house by the side of the
    road
And be a friend of man.
    SAM WALTER FOSS, *The House by the Side
    of the Road.*

12
W'en you see a man in woe,
Walk right up and say "hullo."
Say "hullo" and "how d'ye do,"
"How's the world a-usin' you?"
    SAM WALTER FOSS, *Hullo.*

13
The most acceptable service of God is doing
good to man.
    BENJAMIN FRANKLIN, *Autobiography,* ch.
    l.

14
I expect to pass through this world but once.
Any good therefore that I can do, or any
kindness that I can show to any fellow creature, let me do it now. Let me not defer or
neglect it, for I shall not pass this way
again.
    Attributed to STEPHEN GRELLET, an
    American Quaker of French birth, but
    not found in his writings. It has also
    been credited, with less authority, to
    Emerson, Edward Courtenay, John Wes-
    ley, William Penn, Thomas Carlyle, and
    others.

15
The hands that help are holier than the lips
that pray.
    ROBERT G. INGERSOLL, *The Children of the
    Stage.*

16
We rise by raising others—and he who
stoops above the fallen, stands erect.
    ROBERT G. INGERSOLL, *Tribute to Roscoe
    Conkling.*

17
He's true to God who's true to man; wherev-
    er wrong is done
To the humblest and the weakest, 'neath the
    all-beholding sun.
    JAMES RUSSELL LOWELL, *On the Capture
    of Fugitive Slaves Near Washington,* st.
    7.

18
To pity distress is but human; to relieve it is
Godlike.
    HORACE MANN, *Lectures on Education,*
    lecture 6.

19
If you give to a thief he cannot steal from
you, and he is then no longer a thief.
    WILLIAM SAROYAN, *The Human Comedy,*
    ch. 4.

20
He saw the goodness, not the taint,
    In many a poor, do-nothing creature,
And gave to sinner and to saint,
    But kept his faith in human nature.
    E. C. STEDMAN, *Horace Greeley.*

1
As for doing good, that is one of the professions that are full.
    HENRY D. THOREAU, *Walden: Economy.*

2
The poor must be wisely visited and liberally cared for, so that mendicity shall not be tempted into mendacity, nor want exasperated into crime.
    ROBERT C. WINTHROP, Yorktown Oration, 1881.

PHILOSOPHY

3
Unintelligible answers to insoluble problems.
    HENRY ADAMS, defining philosophy. (BERT LESTON TAYLOR, *The So-Called Human Race*, p. 154)

4
    To take things as they be—
    That's my philosophy.
No use to holler, mope, or cuss—
If they was changed they might be wuss.
    JOHN KENDRICK BANGS, *A Philosopher.*

5
Philosophy is common-sense in a dress suit.
    OLIVER S. BRASTON, *Philosophy.*

6
Philosophy—the thoughts of men about human thinking, reasoning and imagining, and the real values in human existence.
    CHARLES W. ELIOT, Inscription on public library, Warren, Pa.

7
Philosophy is the account which the mind gives to itself of the constitution of the world.
    EMERSON, *Representative Men: Plato.*

8
The Arabians say that Abul Khain, the mystic, and Abu Ali Seena, the philosopher, conferred together; and, on parting, the philosopher said, "All that he sees I know"; and the mystic said, "All that he knows I see."
    EMERSON, *Representative Men: Swedenborg.*

9
The society which scorns excellence in plumbing because plumbing is a humble activity and tolerates shoddiness in philosophy because it is an exalted activity will have neither good plumbing nor good philosophy. Neither its pipes nor its theories will hold water.
    JOHN W. GARDNER, *Excellence: Can We Be Equal and Excellent Too?* When Gardner was named Secretary of Health, Education and Welfare in the cabinet of Lyndon B. Johnson, 27 July, 1965, Mr. Johnson quoted this passage at the White House ceremony.

10
A modest confession of ignorance is the ripest and last attainment of philosophy.
    ROSWELL D. HITCHCOCK, *Eternal Atonement: Secret Things of God.*

11
God made no man so simple or his life so sterile that such experience can be summarized in an adjective. Yet we seem bent today on reducing every man's philosophy to a mere vital statistic.
    LYNDON B. JOHNSON, *My Political Philosophy; Texas Quarterly* of the University of Texas, 1958.

12
There are philosophies which are unendurable not because men are cowards, but because they are men.
    LUDWIG LEWISOHN, *Modern Drama*, p. 222.

13
There is no record in human history of a happy philosopher.
    H. L. MENCKEN, *Prejudices.*

14
Philosophy drips gently from his tongue
Who hath three meals a day in guarantee.
    CHRISTOPHER MORLEY, *So This Is Arden.*

15
Say, Not so, and you will outcircle the philosophers.
    HENRY D. THOREAU, *Journal*, 26 June, 1840.

16
To be a philosopher is not merely to have subtle thoughts, nor even to found a school, but so to love wisdom as to live according to its dictates, a life of simplicity, independence, magnanimity, and trust.
    HENRY D. THOREAU, *Walden*, ch. 1.

17
How can a man be a philosopher and not maintain his vital heat by better methods than other men?
    HENRY D. THOREAU, *Walden*, ch. 1.

PILGRIM FATHERS

See also Puritans

18
Wild was the day; the wintry sea
    Moaned sadly on New England's strand,
When first the thoughtful and the free,
    Our fathers, trod the desert land.
    WILLIAM CULLEN BRYANT, *The Twenty-Second of December.*

19
They fell upon an ungenial climate . . . that called out the best energies of the men, and of the women too, to get a mere subsistence out of the soil. In their efforts to do that, they cultivated industry and frugality at the same time—which is the real foundation of the greatness of the Pilgrims.
    ULYSSES S. GRANT, Speech at New England Society dinner, 22 Dec., 1880.

1

What sought they thus afar?
  Bright jewels of the mine?
The wealth of seas, the spoils of war?
  —They sought a faith's pure shrine!
    FELICIA DOROTHEA HEMANS, *The Landing
      of the Pilgrim Fathers.*

2

Ay, call it holy ground,
  The soil where first they trod!
They have left unstained what there they
    found—
  Freedom to worship God!
    FELICIA DOROTHEA HEMANS, *The Landing
      of the Pilgrim Fathers.*

3

O Exile of the wrath of kings!
  O Pilgrim Ark of Liberty!
The refuge of divinest things,
  Their record must abide in thee!
    JULIA WARD HOWE, *Our Country.*

4

Down to the Plymouth Rock, that had been
  to their feet a doorstep
Into a world unknown,—the corner-stone of
  a nation.
    HENRY WADSWORTH LONGFELLOW, *The
      Courtship of Miles Standish,* pt. v, st. 2.

5

Our Pilgrim stock wuz pithed with hardi-
  hood.
    JAMES RUSSELL LOWELL, *The Biglow Pa-
      pers,* Ser. ii, No. 6.

6

They talk about their Pilgrim blood,
  Their birthright high and holy!
A mountain-stream that ends in mud
  Methinks is melancholy.
    JAMES RUSSELL LOWELL, *Interview with
      Miles Standish.*

7

Give it only the fulcrum of Plymouth Rock,
an idea will upheave the continent.
    WENDELL PHILLIPS, Speech in New York
      City, 21 Jan., 1863.

8

Neither do I acknowledge the right of Plymouth to the whole rock. No, the rock under-
lies all America: it only crops out here.
    WENDELL PHILLIPS, Speech at dinner of
      the Pilgrim Society, Plymouth, Mass.,
      21 Dec., 1855.

9

The Pilgrim spirit has not fled:
  It walks in noon's broad light;
And it watches the bed of the glorious dead,
  With the holy stars by night.
    JOHN PIERPONT, *The Pilgrim Fathers.*

10

The Pilgrims rose, at this, God's word,
  And sailed the wintry seas:
With their own flesh nor blood conferred,
  Nor thought of wealth or ease.

They left the towers of Leyden town,

They left the Zuyder Zee;
And where they cast their anchor down,
  Rose Freedom's realm to be.
    JEREMIAH EAMES RANKIN, *The Word of
      God to Leyden Came.*

PIONEER

11

I died in my boots like a pioneer
With the whole wide sky above me.
    STEPHEN VINCENT BENÉT, *The Ballad of
      William Sycamore.*

12

Pioneering does not pay.
    ANDREW CARNEGIE. (HENDRICK, *Life of
      Carnegie*)

13

There are pioneer souls that blaze their
    paths
  Where highways never ran.
    SAM WALTER FOSS, *The House by the Side
      of the Road.*

14

Shall I tell you who he is, this key figure in
the arch of our enterprise? That slender,
dauntless, plodding, modest figure is the
American pioneer. . . . His is this one
glory—he found the way.
    FRANKLIN K. LANE, *The American Pio-
      neer.*

15

Humble the lot, yet his the race,
  When Liberty sent forth her cry,
Who thronged in conflict's deadliest place,
  To fight—to bleed—to die!
    ALFRED B. STREET, *The Settler.*

16

Their fame shrinks not to names and dates
  On votive stone, the prey of time;—
Behold where monumental States
  Immortalize their lives sublime.
    WILLIAM H. VENABLE, *The Founders of
      Ohio.*

17

Conquering, holding, daring, venturing as we
  go the unknown ways,
    Pioneers! O pioneers!
    WALT WHITMAN, *Pioneers! O Pioneers!*

O Pioneers!
    WILLA CATHER, Title of novel.

18

The paths to the house I seek to make,
But leave to those to come the house itself.
    WALT WHITMAN, *Thou Mother with Thy
      Equal Brood.*

PITY

19

Pity is the deadliest feeling that can be
offered to a woman.
    VICKI BAUM, *And Life Goes On,* p. 201.

1
Compassion will cure more sins than condemnation.
> HENRY WARD BEECHER, *Proverbs from Plymouth Pulpit.*

2
Give plenty of what is given to you,
  Listen to pity's call;
Don't think the little you give is great,
  And the much you get is small.
> PHOEBE CARY, *A Legend of the Northland.*

3
To blame him were absurd; to pity were profane.
> CHARLES TOWNSEND COPELAND, *Copeland Reader:* Introduction.

4
She knows as well as anyone
That Pity, having played, soon tires.
> EDWIN ARLINGTON ROBINSON, *The Poor Relation.*

5
O brother man! fold to thy heart thy brother.
Where pity dwells, the peace of God is
  there.
> JOHN GREENLEAF WHITTIER, *Worship,* st. 13.

PLACE

6
Accept the place the divine providence has found for you.
> EMERSON, *Essays, First Series: Self-Reliance.*

7
A place for everything, and everything in its place.
> EMERSON, *Journal,* 2 Aug., 1857. Quoted.

8
The place does not make the man, nor the sceptre the king. Greatness is from within.
> ROBERT G. INGERSOLL, *Voltaire.*

9
Nothing useless is, or low;
  Each thing in its place is best;
And what seems but idle show
  Strengthens and supports the rest.
> HENRY WADSWORTH LONGFELLOW, *The Builders,* st. 2.

PLAGIARISM

See also Imitation, Quotation

10
It is as difficult to appropriate the thoughts of others as it is to invent.
> EMERSON, *Letters and Social Aims: Quotation and Originality.*

11
It has come to be practically a sort of rule in literature, that a man, having once shown himself capable of original writing, is entitled thenceforth to steal from the writings of others at discretion. Thought is the property of him who can entertain it, and of him who can adequately place it.
> EMERSON, *Representative Men: Shakespeare.*

12
Every man is a borrower and a mimic, life is theatrical and literature a quotation.
> EMERSON, *Society and Solitude: Success.*

13
Though old the thought and oft exprest,
'Tis his at last who says it best.
> JAMES RUSSELL LOWELL, *For an Autograph,* st. 1.

14
Every generation has the privilege of standing on the shoulders of the generation that went before; but it has no right to pick the pockets of the first-comer.
> BRANDER MATTHEWS, *Recreations of an Anthologist,* p. 20.

15
Take the whole range of imaginative literature, and we are all wholesale borrowers. In every matter that relates to invention, to use, or beauty or form, we are borrowers.
> WENDELL PHILLIPS, Lecture: *The Lost Arts.*

PLEASURE

See also Happiness, Joy

16
The rule of my life is to make business a pleasure, and pleasure my business.
> AARON BURR, Letter to Pichon.

17
Pleasure may perfect us as truly as prayer.
> WILLIAM ELLERY CHANNING, *Note-Book: Joy.*

18
Whenever you are sincerely pleased, you are nourished.
> EMERSON, *Conduct of Life: Considerations by the Way.*

19
The pleasure of life is according to the man that lives it, and not according to the work or place.
> EMERSON, *Conduct of Life: Fate.*

20
Pleasure is far sweeter as a recreation, than a business.
> ROSWELL D. HITCHCOCK, *Eternal Atonement,* viii.

21
Pleasure-seekers never find theirs.
> ELBERT HUBBARD, *Epigrams.*

22
It is said of me that when I was young I divided my time impartially among wine, women and song. I deny this categorically. Ninety per cent of my interests were women.
> ARTUR RUBINSTEIN. (*Rubinstein Speaking; New York Times Magazine,* 26 Jan., 1964)

1
A life of pleasure requires an aristocratic setting to make it interesting.

> GEORGE SANTAYANA, *Life of Reason*, vol. ii, p. 135.

2
That man is the richest whose pleasures are the cheapest.

> HENRY D. THOREAU, *Journal*, 11 Mar., 1856.

3
Pleasure comes, but not to stay;
Even this shall pass away.

> THEODORE TILTON, *All Things Shall Pass Away*.

POETRY

4
Poetry is the worst mask in the world behind which folly and stupidity could attempt to hide their features.

> WILLIAM CULLEN BRYANT, *Lectures on Poetry: The Nature of Poetry*.

5
Poetry is not a turning loose of emotion, but an escape from emotion; it is not the expression of personality, but an escape from personality. But, of course, only those who have personality and emotions know what it means to want to escape from these things.

> T. S. ELIOT, *Tradition and the Individual Talent*.

6
There is a great deal, in the writing of poetry, which must be conscious and deliberate.

> T. S. ELIOT, *Tradition and the Individual Talent*.

7
Good poetry could not have been otherwise written than it is. The first time you hear it, it sounds rather as if copied out of some invisible tablet in the Eternal mind, than as if arbitrarily composed by the poet. The feeling of all great poets has accorded with this. They found the verse, not made it. The muse brought it to them.

> EMERSON, *Essays, First Series: Art*.

8
The true poem is the poet's mind.

> EMERSON, *Essays, First Series: Of History*.

9
It is not metres, but a metre-making argument that makes a poem.

> EMERSON, *Essays, Second Series: The Poet*.

10
It does not need that a poem should be long. Every word was once a poem.

> EMERSON, *Essays, Second Series: The Poet*.

11
Only that is poetry which cleanses and mans me.

> EMERSON, *Letters and Social Aims: Inspiration*.

12
Poetry is faith. To the poet the world is virgin soil; all is practicable; the men are ready for virtue; it is always time to do right.

> EMERSON, *Letters and Social Aims: Poetry and Imagination*.

13
Poetry is the only verity—the expression of a sound mind speaking after the ideal, not after the apparent.

> EMERSON, *Letters and Social Aims: Poetry and Imagination*.

14
Test of the poet is knowledge of love,
For Eros is older than Saturn or Jove.

> EMERSON, *Quatrains: Casella*.

15
The finest poetry was first experience.

> EMERSON, *Representative Men: Shakespeare*.

16
Matches are made in heaven, and for every thought its proper melody and rhyme exists, though the odds are immense against our finding it, and only genius can rightly say the banns.

> EMERSON, *Social Aims: Poetry and Imagination*.

17
The poet is never the poorer for his song.

> EMERSON, *Society and Solitude: Works and Days*.

18
Writing free verse is like playing tennis with the net down.

> ROBERT FROST, Address at Milton Academy, Milton, Mass., 17 May, 1935.

19
Poetry is a way of taking life by the throat.

> ROBERT FROST. (*Vogue*, 15 Mar., 1963)

20
Poets, Being poor,
Must use words with economy.

> WILLIAM GRIFFITH, *Laconic*.

21
I would rather risk for future fame upon one lyric than upon ten volumes.

> OLIVER WENDELL HOLMES.

22
There is no mere earthly immortality that I envy so much as the poet's. If your name is to live at all, it is so much better to have it live in people's hearts than only in their brains.

> OLIVER WENDELL HOLMES, *The Poet at the Breakfast-Table*, ch. 4.

23
Poetry is the bill and coo of sex.

> ELBERT HUBBARD, *Epigrams*.

24
When power leads man toward arrogance, poetry reminds him of his limitations. When power narrows the areas of man's concern, poetry reminds him of the richness and di-

versity of his existence. When power corrupts, poetry cleanses.
     JOHN F. KENNEDY, Address at Amherst
       College, Amherst, Mass., 26 Oct., 1963.

1
          The bards sublime,
Whose distant footsteps echo
Through the corridors of time.
     HENRY WADSWORTH LONGFELLOW, *The
       Day Is Done*.

2
God sent his Singers upon earth
With songs of sadness and of mirth,
That they might touch the hearts of men,
And bring them back to heaven again.
     HENRY WADSWORTH LONGFELLOW, *The
       Singers*.

3
Finally, most of us believe that concentration is the very essence of poetry.
     AMY LOWELL, *Imagist Poetry*.

4
Never did Poesy appear
   So full of heaven to me, as when
I saw how it would pierce through pride and
     fear
   To the lives of coarsest men.
     JAMES RUSSELL LOWELL, *Incident in a
       Railroad Car*, st. 18.

5
A poem should not mean But be.
     ARCHIBALD MACLEISH, *Ars Poetica*.

6
gods i am pent in a cockroach
i with the soul of a dante
am mate and companion of fleas
i with the gift of a homer
must smile when a mouse calls me pal
tumble bugs are my familiars
this is the punishment meted
because i have written vers libre
     DON MARQUIS, *the wail of archy*.

7
Poetry is a comforting piece of fiction set to
more or less lascivious music.
     H. L. MENCKEN, *Prejudices*, ser iii, p.
       150.

8
Poetry has done enough when it charms, but
prose must also convince.
     H. L. MENCKEN, *Prejudices*, ser. iii, p.
       166.

9
Blake, Homer, Job, and you,
Have made old wine-skins new.
Your energies have wrought
Stout continents of thought.
     MARIANNE MOORE, *That Harp You Play
       So Well*.

10
Truth is enough for prose:
Calmly it goes
To tell just what it knows.

For verse, skill will suffice—

Delicate, nice
Casting of verbal dice.

Poetry, men attain
By subtler pain
More flagrant in the brain—

An honesty unfeigned,
A heart unchained.
A madness well restrained.
     CHRISTOPHER MORLEY, *At the Mermaid
       Cafeteria*.

11
The pearl Is a disease of the oyster.
A poem Is a disease of the spirit
Caused by the irritation
Of a granule of Truth
Fallen into that soft gray bivalve
We call the mind.
     CHRISTOPHER MORLEY, *Bivalves*.

12
I would define, in brief, the Poetry of words
as the Rhythmical Creation of Beauty. Its
sole arbiter is Taste.
     EDGAR ALLAN POE, *The Poetic Principle*.

13
Poetry is still the supremely inclusive speech
which escapes, as if unaware of them, the
strictures and reductions of the systematic
logical understanding.
     JOHN CROWE RANSOM, *Selected Poems*
       (1963).

14
It is difficult to write the proper poem nowadays because after many ages of hard prose
we have come far from the primitive and
natural speech of poetry.
     JOHN CROWE RANSOM, *Selected Poems*
       (1963).

15
Poetry is a language that tells us, through a
more or less emotional reaction, something
that cannot be said.
     EDWIN ARLINGTON ROBINSON, Newspaper
       Interview.

16
Poetry is the journal of a sea animal living
on land, wanting to fly in the air. Poetry is a
search for syllables to shoot at the barriers of
the unknown and the unknowable. Poetry is
a phantom script telling how rainbows are
made and why they go away.
     CARL SANDBURG, *Poetry Considered; Atlantic Monthly*, Mar., 1923.

17
Poetry is an art, and chief of the fine arts:
the easiest to dabble in, the hardest in which
to reach true excellence.
     E. C. STEDMAN, *Victorian Poets*, ch. 5.

18
          The Poet in his Art
Must intimate the whole, and say the smallest part.
     WILLIAM WETMORE STORY, *The Unexpressed*.

1

Poetry is nothing but healthy speech.

HENRY D. THOREAU, *Journal*, 4 Sept., 1841.

2

Poetry implies the whole truth, philosophy expresses a particle of it.

HENRY D. THOREAU, *Journal*, 26 June, 1852.

3

The messages of great poems to each man and woman are, Come to us on equal terms, only then can you understand us. We are no better than you, what we inclose you inclose, what we enjoy you may enjoy.

WALT WHITMAN, *Leaves of Grass:* Preface.

POETS

4

I agree with one of your reputable critics that a taste for drawing-rooms has spoiled more poets than ever did a taste for gutters.

THOMAS BEER, *The Mauve Decade*, p. 235.

5

All great poets have been men of great knowledge.

WILLIAM CULLEN BRYANT, *Lectures on Poetry: Relation of Poetry to Time and Place.*

6

Most joyful let the Poet be;
It is through him that all men see.

WILLIAM ELLERY CHANNING THE YOUNGER, *The Poet of the Old and New Times.*

7

I reckon, when I count at all,
First Poets—then the Sun—
Then Summer—then the Heaven of God—
And then the list is done.
But looking back—the first so seems
To comprehend the whole—
The others look a needless show,
So I write Poets—All.

EMILY DICKINSON, *Poems*, Pt. vi, No. 9.

8

Poets should be law-givers; that is, the boldest lyric inspiration should not chide and insult, but should announce and lead the civil code, and the day's work.

EMERSON, *Essays, First Series: Of Prudence.*

9

The sign and credentials of the poet are that he announces that which no man has foretold.

EMERSON, *Essays, Second Series: The Poet.*

10

The experience of each new age requires a new confession, and the world seems always waiting for its poet.

EMERSON, *Essays, Second Series: The Poet.*

11

Do not judge the poet's life to be sad because of his plaintive verses and confessions of despair. Because he was able to cast off his sorrows into these writings, therefore went he onward free and serene to new experiences.

EMERSON, *Journals,* vol. v, p. 520.

12

Let the poet, of all men, stop with his inspiration. The inexorable rule in the muse's court, *either inspiration or silence,* compels the bard to report only his supreme moments.

EMERSON, *Letters and Social Aims: Poetry and Imagination.*

13

All men are poets at heart.

EMERSON, *Nature, Addresses, and Lectures: Literary Ethics.*

14

There was never poet who had not the heart in the right place.

EMERSON, *Society and Solitude: Success.*

15

The poet's voice need not merely be the record of man; it can be one of the props, the pillars, to help him endure and prevail.

WILLIAM FAULKNER, Address in Stockholm, 10 Dec., 1950, upon accepting the Nobel Prize in literature.

16

What are our poets, take them as they fall,
Good, bad, rich, poor, much read, not read at all?
Them and their works in the same class you'll find—
They are the mere wastepaper of mankind.

BENJAMIN FRANKLIN, *Paper.*

17

I don't call myself a poet yet. It's for the world to say whether you're a poet or not. I'm one-half teacher, one-half poet, and one-half farmer. That's three halves.

ROBERT FROST, commenting on his 80th birthday, in Mar., 1954.

18

It is not the statesman, the warrior, or the monarch that survives, but the despised poet, whom they may have fed with their crumbs, and to whom they owe all that they now are or have—a name.

NATHANIEL HAWTHORNE, *Our Old Home: Up the Thames.*

19

Next to being a great poet, is the power of understanding one.

HENRY WADSWORTH LONGFELLOW, *Hyperion*, bk. ii, ch. 3.

20

All that is best in the great poets of all countries is not what is national in them, but what is universal.

HENRY WADSWORTH LONGFELLOW, *Kavanagh*, ch. 20.

1

Nothing is more certain than that great poets are no sudden prodigies but slow results.

> JAMES RUSSELL LOWELL, *My Study Windows: Chaucer.*

2

Nine-tenths of the best poetry of the world has been written by poets less than thirty years old; a great deal more than half of it has been written by poets under twenty-five.

> H. L. MENCKEN, *Prejudices,* ser. iii, p. 147.

3

The degree in which a poet's imagination dominates reality is, in the end, the exact measure of his importance and dignity.

> GEORGE SANTAYANA, *The Life of Reason,* vol. iv, p. 114.

4

Every man will be a poet if he can; otherwise a philosopher or man of science. This proves the superiority of the poet.

> HENRY D. THOREAU, *Journal,* 11 Apr., 1852.

POLITENESS, see Courtesy, Manners

POLITICS

See also America; Conservatism; Constitution; Democracy; Extremes; Fanaticism; Flag; Government; Independence Day; Majority and Minority; Orator and Oratory; Patriotism; People, The; Power; Reform and Reformers; Statesman; Treason; Vote and Voting

I—Definitions

5

Practical politics consists in ignoring facts.

> HENRY ADAMS, *The Education of Henry Adams,* ch. 24.

6

Modern politics is, at bottom, a struggle not of men but of forces.

> HENRY ADAMS, *The Education of Henry Adams,* ch. 28.

7

Di-plomacy has become a philanthropic pursoot like shop-keepin', but politics, me lords, is still th' same ol' spoort iv highway rob-b'ry.

> FINLEY PETER DUNNE, *Observations by Mr. Dooley: International Amenities.*

8

Politics is a profession; a serious, complicated, and in its true sense a noble one.

> DWIGHT D. EISENHOWER, Letter to Leonard V. Finder, publisher of the Manchester (N.H.) *Evening Leader,* 1948, in which he also said: "my decision to remove myself completely from the political scene is definite and positive."

9

A good deal of our politics is physiological.

> EMERSON, *Conduct of Life: Fate.*

10

Politics is the science of how who gets what, when and why.

> SIDNEY HILLMAN, *Political Primer* (1944).

11

Being a politician is a poor profession. Being a public servant is a noble one.

> HERBERT HOOVER. (RICHARD M. KETCHUM, *Faces from the Past; American Heritage,* Dec., 1964, p. 31)

12

He proved that a man can be both decent and political.

> HUBERT H. HUMPHREY, of Adlai E. Stevenson; memorial telecast on Stevenson, Columbia Broadcasting System, 19 July, 1965.

13

Politics, like religion, hold up torches of martyrdom to the reformers of error.

> THOMAS JEFFERSON, *Writings,* vol. xiii, p. 69.

14

What President Kennedy stood for is making politics an honorable profession.

> ROBERT F. KENNEDY, Press Conference, New York City, 25 May, 1964, in connection with the opening of an exhibit of the belongings of his brother, John F. Kennedy.

15

Politics is the science of exigencies.

> THEODORE PARKER, *Ten Sermons: Of Truth.*

16

He sees politics as an exercise in adapting oneself to all sorts of people and situations, of discussing and bargaining with legitimate groups in search of a consensus.

> JAMES RESTON, *What's He Like? And How Will He Do?; New York Times Magazine,* 17 Jan., 1965, p. 8. Referring to Lyndon B. Johnson.

17

I tell you Folks, all Politics is Apple Sauce.

> WILL ROGERS, *The Illiterate Digest,* p. 30.

18

Politics . . . are but the cigar-smoke of a man.

> HENRY D. THOREAU, *Walking.* (See also Harry M. Daugherty on "a smoke-filled room" in this section.)

19

Politics I conceive to be nothing more than the science of the ordered progress of society along the lines of greatest usefulness and convenience to itself.

> WOODROW WILSON, Address at Pan-American Scientific Congress, Washington, D.C., 6 Jan., 1916.

II—Maxims

1
Knowledge of human nature is the beginning and end of political education.

> HENRY ADAMS, *The Education of Henry Adams*, ch. 12.

2
Vote for the man who promises least; he'll be the least disappointing.

> BERNARD M. BARUCH. (*Meyer Berger's New York*)

3
I go for honorable compromise wherever it can be made. Life itself is but a compromise between death and life, the struggle continuing throughout our whole existence until the great destroyer finally triumphs. . . . Let no one who is not above the frailties of our common nature disdain compromise.

> HENRY CLAY, Speech, 8 Apr., 1850. (*Works*, vol. vi, p. 412) Clay gained fame as the "Great Compromiser" for his part in effecting the Missouri Compromise of 1820 and the compromise tariff of 1833.

4
The attempt to turn a complex problem of the head into a simple moral question for the heart to answer, is of course a necessary part of all political discussions.

> FRANK MOORE COLBY, *The Colby Essays*, vol. 2.

5
I seldom think of politics more than eighteen hours a day.

> LYNDON B. JOHNSON, Speech to a Texas audience, 1958. (HENRY A. ZEIGER, *Lyndon B. Johnson: Man and President*, p. 68)

6
My daddy told me that if I didn't want to get shot at, I should stay off the firing lines. This is politics.

> LYNDON B. JOHNSON. (HENRY A. ZEIGER, *Lyndon B. Johnson: Man and President*, p. 65)

7
If you're in politics and you can't tell when you walk into a room who's for you and who's against you, then you're in the wrong line of work.

> LYNDON B. JOHNSON. (BOOTH MOONEY, *The Lyndon Johnson Story*, 1963)

8
Politics is like football. If you see daylight, go through the hole.

> JOHN F. KENNEDY, on the authority of Pierre Salinger, Kennedy's press secretary. (JOSEPH ALSOP, Syndicated Column, New York *Herald Tribune*, 3 Apr., 1964)

9
We trust a man with making constitutions on less proof of competence than we should demand before we gave him our shoe to patch.

> JAMES RUSSELL LOWELL, *On a Certain Condescension in Foreigners*.

10
In a political campaign, the most important thing is the ability to turn lemons into lemonade—to make the potentially damaging issues work for you, not against you.

> DEBS MYERS. (New York *Times*, 3 Feb., 1965, p. 24)

11
There is no Canaan in politics.

> WENDELL PHILLIPS, Speech: *Public Opinion*, 28 Jan., 1852.

12
Civilization dwarfs political machinery.

> WENDELL PHILLIPS, Speech on the election of Lincoln, 7 Nov., 1860.

13
In politics you've got to have a sense of humor. If you don't have humor you'll end up in a nuthouse with a lot of paper dolls.

> MICHAEL PRENDERGAST, speaking from a background of long experience as chairman of the Democratic party in New York, State. (New York *Times*, 17 May, 1964)

14
In politics, as in love, timing and luck are fundamental.

> JAMES RESTON, Washington Column, New York *Times*, 3 Jan., 1964.

15
This element of fate or accident is what makes politics such a ridiculously intriguing business. It is supposed to be governed by rigid rules, but somebody or something is always intervening to change the game, and even the normal reactions to human conduct somehow fail to apply to presidential candidates.

> JAMES RESTON, Washington Column, New York *Times*, 20 Jan., 1964.

16
This is one enduring principle of American politics: Outside interference, even by popular—let alone unpopular—figures, defeats its own end.

> JAMES RESTON, Washington Column, New York *Times*, 24 July, 1964.

17
Politics has got so expensive that it takes lots of money to even get beat with.

> WILL ROGERS, Newspaper Column, 28 June, 1931.

18
Our policy is "Nothing is no good."

> WILL ROGERS, *The Illiterate Digest*.

19
Don't hit at all if it is honorably possible to avoid hitting; but *never* hit soft.

> THEODORE ROOSEVELT. (J. B. BISHOP, *Theodore Roosevelt*, vol. ii, p. 437)

20
I could tell you that I have succumbed to

the urging of my many friends. But the truth is that this candidacy is a genuine draft—a draft inspired by the candidate himself.

> PIERRE SALINGER, announcing his candidacy for the Democratic nomination for Senator from California, 21 Mar., 1964. He won the nomination but lost to his Republican opponent, George Murphy, in the November election.

1

The cut of the clothes may change, but that's it. If you look at a cage of monkeys today, or ten years from today, they'll act the same. They never change. Believe me, that's the way human beings are.

> LOUIS SAXE, Interview with Bernard Weinraub, New York *Times,* 26 Oct., 1964, p. 27. Saxe, a prominent New York lawyer and lifelong Republican, was commenting, at age 91, on the similarity of politicians through the years.

2

You can't beat somebody with nobody.

> MARK SULLIVAN, *Our Times,* vol. iii, p. 289. Often attributed to "Uncle Joe" Cannon, speaker of the House of Representatives for many years.

3

Partisan politics should stop at the boundaries of the United States. I'm extremely sorry you have allowed a bunch of screwballs to come between us.

> HARRY S TRUMAN, Letter to Dwight D. Eisenhower, 16 Aug., 1952. In his *Memoirs,* Truman explains that he had offered both Eisenhower and the latter's opponent in the 1952 campaign, Adlai E. Stevenson, weekly briefings on the world situation. Eisenhower replied that he wanted it understood that the "possession of these reports will in no other way limit my freedom to discuss and analyze foreign programs." Truman then answered with this letter, convinced that "the politicians had already begun to mishandle him."

I never had any falling out with him. The only trouble was, he had a lot of damn fool Republicans around him. He's a good man.

> HARRY S TRUMAN, on Dwight D. Eisenhower. (New York *Times,* "Ideas and Men," 29 Dec., 1963)

I took the position that politics stopped at the water's edge. We had but one President and commander-in-chief.

> LYNDON B. JOHNSON, Speech to Federal revenue agents, Washington, D.C., 11 Feb., 1964. He was replying to Republican critics of his foreign policy by citing his former role as Senate majority leader during the Eisenhower administration.

4

If you don't like the heat, get out of the kitchen.

> HARRY S TRUMAN, on the rigors of practical politics; also attributed to Major General Harry Vaughan, Truman's military aide. (Truman's "give 'em hell" remark is included in this section among famous political phrases.)

5

There never was a non-partisan in politics. A man cannot be a non-partisan and be effective in a political party. When he's in any party he's partisan—he's got to be. The only way a man can act as a non-partisan is when he is in office, either as President or head of a state or county or city.

> HARRY S TRUMAN, *Mr. Citizen* (1960), p. 166.

6

If you want to get on the front page of a newspaper you should attack someone, especially when you're in politics.

> HARRY S TRUMAN, News Conference in New York City, 9 Jan., 1964.

7

Carry the battle to them. Don't let them bring it to you. Put them on the defensive. And don't ever apologize for anything.

> HARRY S TRUMAN, to Hubert H. Humphrey during the 1964 campaign, when Humphrey ran, successfully, for Vice President. (New York *Times,* 20 Sept., 1964)

8

I am not a politician, and my other habits are good.

> ARTEMUS WARD, *Fourth of July Oration.*

9

Politics make strange bedfellows.

> CHARLES DUDLEY WARNER, *My Summer in a Garden,* ch. 15 (1871).

10

Things have come to a helluva pass
When a man can't cudgel his own jackass.

> HENRY WATTERSON, Reply to critics who charged him with undue criticism of the Governor of Kentucky.

III—The Seamy Side

11

Partisanship should only be a method of patriotism. He who is a partisan merely for the sake of spoils is a buccaneer. He who is a partisan merely for the sake of a party name is a ghost of the past among living events. He who is merely the partisan of an ordinary organization is only a pebble in the sling of a boss. But he who is the partisan of principle is a prince of citizenship.

> ALBERT J. BEVERIDGE, Address in Boston, 27 Apr., 1898.

12

What a vicious practice is this of our politicians at Washington pairing off! as if one man who votes wrong, going away, could excuse you, who mean to vote right, for going away; or as if your presence did not tell in more ways than in your vote. Suppose the three hundred heroes at Thermopylae had paired off with three hundred Persians: would it have been all the same to Greece, and to history?

> EMERSON, *Conduct of Life: Considerations by the Way.*

1
Politics is a deleterious profession, like some poisonous handicrafts.

> EMERSON, *Conduct of Life: Power.*

2
In politics and in trade, bruisers and pirates are of better promise than talkers and clerks.

> EMERSON, *Essays, Second Series: Manners.*

3
There is a certain satisfaction in coming down to the lowest ground of politics, for we get rid of cant and hyprocrisy.

> EMERSON, *Representative Men: Napoleon.*

4
Priests are no more necessary to religion than politicians to patriotism.

> JOHN HAYNES HOLMES, *The Sensible Man's View of Religion.*

5
You can't adopt politics as a profession and remain honest.

> LOUIS McHENRY HOWE, Address, Columbia University School of Journalism, 17 Jan., 1933.

6
I am against government by crony.

> HAROLD L. ICKES, upon resigning as Secretary of the Interior, Feb., 1946. President Truman was the target of this barb.

7
The purification of politics is an iridescent dream. Government is force. . . . The Decalogue and the Golden Rule have no place in a political campaign. . . . The commander who lost the battle through the activity of his moral nature would be the derision and jest of history.

> JOHN J. INGALLS, Article, New York *World,* 1890.

8
I know, sir, that it is the habit of some gentlemen to speak with censure or reproach of the politics of New York. . . . It may be, sir, that the politicians of New York are not as fastidious as some gentlemen are as to disclosing the principles on which they act. They boldly preach what they practice. When they are not contending for victory, they avow their intention of enjoying the fruits of it. . . . They see nothing wrong in the rule that to the victor belong the spoils of the enemy.

> WILLIAM L. MARCY, Speech in 1832, during a debate on the confirmation of Martin Van Buren as Minister to England. Marcy, U.S. Senator from New York, was defending Van Buren from the attack of Henry Clay.

9
"Vote early and vote often," the advice openly displayed on the election banners in one of our northern cities.

> W. P. MILES, of South Carolina, Speech in U.S. House of Representatives, 31 Mar., 1858.

10
O ye who lead, Take heed!
Blindness we may forgive, but baseness we will smite.

> WILLIAM VAUGHN MOODY, *An Ode in Time of Hesitation.*

11
What this country needs, in addition to that 5-cent cigar, is not a means of protecting the country against the misleading statements of advertisers so much as a means of protecting it against the more false and dangerous statements of politicians. . . . More harm is done by swallowing political baloney in this country than by swallowing arsenic or smoking reefers. It's not what's up front in the tobacco of North Carolina that counts, but what's out back in the politics of Washington.

> JAMES RESTON, Washington Column, New York *Times,* 26 June, 1964.

12
Elections almost always emphasize the worst. They exaggerate everything, including our national weakness for overstatement, and in the process they distort what they are supposed to clarify.

> JAMES RESTON, Washington Column, New York *Times,* 25 Oct., 1964.

13
Political campaigns are designedly made into emotional orgies which endeavor to distract attention from the real issues involved, and they actually paralyze what slight powers of cerebration man can normally muster.

> JAMES H. ROBINSON, *The Human Comedy.* ch. 9.

14
Even more important than winning the election is governing the nation. That is the test of a political party—the acid, final test.

> ADLAI E. STEVENSON, Speech upon accepting the presidential nomination, Democratic national convention, Chicago, 26 July, 1952.

15
I would like most to be remembered as hav-

ing contributed to a higher level of political dialogue in the United States.

> ADLAI E. STEVENSON, on a London television program in July, 1959, in reply to a query about the quality he would emphasize if he were able to write his own epitaph. (*Contemporary Forum,* ed. by ERNEST J. WRAGE AND BARNET BASKERVILLE, p. 354)

1

The demagogue is the curse of the modern world; and of all the demagogues, the worst are those financed by well-meaning wealthy men who sincerely believe that their wealth is likely to be safer if they can hire men with political "it" to change the signposts and lure the people back into slavery of the most degraded kind.

> HENRY A. WALLACE, Address to Free World Association, New York City, 8 May, 1942.

2

Tin-horn politicians.

> WILLIAM ALLEN WHITE, Editorial, Emporia (Kan.) *Gazette,* 25 Oct., 1901.

IV—Parties

3

This party comes from the grass roots. It has grown from the soil of the people's hard necessities.

> ALBERT J. BEVERIDGE, Address at Bull Moose Convention in Chicago, 5 Aug., 1912.

4

Stalwart Republicans.

> JAMES G. BLAINE, in 1877, in describing the Congressional group who fought to sustain the privileges of the Republicans in the South.

5

Any well-established village in New England or the northern Middle West could afford a town drunkard, a town atheist, and a few Democrats.

> D. W. BROGAN, *The American Character.*

6

Party honesty is party expediency.

> GROVER CLEVELAND, Interview, New York *Commercial Advertiser,* 19 Sept., 1889.

7

"I don't like a rayformer," said Mr. Hennessy.

"Or anny other raypublican," said Mr. Dooley.

> FINLEY PETER DUNNE, *Observations by Mr. Dooley: Reform Administration.*

8

The party should be a knight in shining armor on a white charger.

> DWIGHT D. EISENHOWER, Interview, New York *Times,* 13 Sept., 1965, p. 29. Referring to the Republican party.

9

The vice of our leading parties in this country is that they do not plant themselves on the deep and necessary grounds to which they are respectively entitled, but lash themselves to fury in the carrying of some local and momentary measure, nowise useful to the commonwealth. Of the two great parties which at this hour almost share the nation between them, I should say that one has the best cause, and the other contains the best men.

> EMERSON, *Essays, Second Series: Politics.*

10

The Democratic party is the party of the Poor marshalled against the Rich. . . . But they are always officered by a few self-seeking deserters from the Rich or Whig party.

> EMERSON, *Journals,* 1857.

11

All free governments are party governments.

> JAMES A. GARFIELD, Remarks on the death of Oliver H. P. Morton, U.S. House of Representatives, 18 Jan., 1878.

12

You cannot in this game of politics fight your own party. It just doesn't work.

> BARRY M. GOLDWATER, News Conference, Scottsdale, Ariz., 4 Nov., 1964, at which he conceded defeat in the presidential contest. He was obviously unhappy about lukewarm support given by some Republicans during the campaign.

13

He serves his party best who serves the country best.

> RUTHERFORD B. HAYES, Inaugural Address, 5 Mar., 1877.

14

Yes, I am a Democrat still—very still.

> DAVID B. HILL, reaffirming his party affiliation rather faintly after the nomination of William Jennings Bryan in 1896.

15

If I could not go to heaven but with a party, I would not go there at all.

> THOMAS JEFFERSON, Letter to Francis Hopkinson, 1789.

16

I think that it is very important that we have a two-party country. I am a fellow that likes small parties, and the Republican party is about the size I like.

> LYNDON B. JOHNSON, Press Conference, Washington, D.C., 21 Apr., 1964.

17

There is no Republican way or Democratic way to clean the streets.

> FIORELLO H. LA GUARDIA, while mayor of New York City. Quoted by John V. Lindsay during his campaign for the same post in 1965.

18

Is there a distinct and coherent political

movement, . . . a political philosophy with a clear set of principles, which one might perhaps call the New Republicanism?

> Arthur Larson, *A Republican Looks at His Party,* ch. 1 (1956). President Eisenhower and his supporters used the term New Republicanism on numerous occasions thereafter.

1

He was earnest about these objects. They were of eternal importance, like baseball or the Republican Party.

> Sinclair Lewis, *Babbitt,* ch. 1.

2

A headless torso that must find a central nervous system.

> John V. Lindsay, defining the Republican party after its decisive defeat in the 1964 presidential election, in a speech to the Women's National Press Club, Washington, D.C., 15 Dec., 1964.

3

Our differences are policies, our agreements principles.

> William McKinley, Speech in Des Moines, Ia., 1901.

4

There is always some basic principle that will ultimately get the Republican party together. If my observations are worth anything, that basic principle is the cohesive power of public plunder.

> A. J. McLaurin, Speech in U.S. Senate, May, 1906.

5

My father was a Democrat; my mother was a Republican; I am an Episcopalian.

> George C. Marshall, on his stand in the 1952 presidential election.

6

Any party which takes credit for the rain must not be surprised if its opponents blame it for the drought.

> Dwight W. Morrow, Speech, Oct., 1930.

7

A good party is better than the best man that ever lived.

> Thomas B. Reed. (W. A. Robinson, *Life of Reed*)

8

The Democratic party is like a man riding backward in a railroad car; it never sees anything until it has got past it.

> Thomas B. Reed. (W. A. Robinson, *Life of Reed*)

9

The Republicans have their splits right after election and Democrats have theirs just before an election.

> Will Rogers, Syndicated Column, 29 Dec., 1930.

10

I am not a member of any organized political party. I am a Democrat.

> Attributed to Will Rogers.

11

The Democratic party is like a mule—without pride of ancestry or hope of posterity.

> Emory Storrs, Speech during the campaign of 1888. Also attributed to William C. Linton, Ignatius Donnelly, and Judge Gay Gordon.

12

They are sort of like Nixon Democrats.

> Harry S Truman, Reply upon being asked to define a "Truman Republican," 15 Mar., 1964.

13

Now is the time for all good men to come to the aid of the party.

> Charles E. Weller, Sentence devised to test the practicability of the first typewriter, constructed in Milwaukee by Christopher Latham Sholes in 1867. Weller was a court reporter and friend of Sholes. The sentence, which covers a wide range of the keyboard, was inspired by a political campaign then in progress. It is still widely used.

V—Liberals, Conservatives, and Others

See also Conservatism

14

A liberal is a man who cultivates the skills that make freedom operational. He is always a man on special assignment.

> Max Ascoli, *The Reporter,* 30 Jan., 1964.

15

The true liberal is liberal in human relations and conservative in his economics. He seeks to conserve a capitalistic system characterized by free enterprise and the profit motive because it is essential to liberty.

> Harry J. Carman, Letter to the Editor, St. Louis *Post-Dispatch,* 10 Aug., 1964. Carman was speaking as chairman of the American Liberal Association.

16

For all the partisan uses to which the term has been put lately, the "mainstream" does stand for something real. It is a shorthand description of the American political mind or, more accurately, the minds of tens of millions of voters and citizens who form the broad base of our political system.

> Andrew Hacker, *What's the Mainstream?; New York Times Magazine,* 6 Sept., 1964, p. 5.

17

One of the greatest tragedies would be to have two political parties made up just of the right and the left.

> Albertis Harrison, Jr., speaking as Governor of Virginia. (New York *Times,* 30 Aug., 1964, p. 11E, "Ideas and Men.")

18

He's a working liberal and not a talking liberal.

> Lyndon B. Johnson, speaking admiringly

of a member of his staff. (MARQUIS W. CHILDS, Column, St. Louis *Post-Dispatch,* 31 Mar., 1964)

1

I want to be progressive without getting both feet off the ground at the same time. . . . If I had to place a label on myself, I would want to be a progressive who is prudent.

LYNDON B. JOHNSON, Interview televised nationally from Washington, D.C., 15 Mar., 1964.

Everybody is in doubt about whether President Johnson is a conservative progressive or a progressive conservative, and he is in clover.

JAMES RESTON, Washington Column, New York *Times,* 20 Jan., 1964.

2

Some of the radicals of the '30s are still radicals, like me. But they are so as individuals, they don't belong to any group. And all of us are richer now. It is harder to remain radical when richer because you have to face up, at least in theory, to giving up what you've got.

MARY McCARTHY. (*Lady with a Switchblade; Life,* 20 Sept., 1963, p. 64)

3

Socialism is simply the degenerate capitalism of bankrupt capitalists. Its one genuine object is to get more money for its professors.

H. L. MENCKEN, *Prejudices,* ser. iii, p. 109.

4

We in America—having given extremism, as it were, a constitutional right to exist—have been able to afford the active presence of a far Left and a far Right because we have been overwhelmingly a nation of moderates.

HARRY AND BONARO OVERSTREET, *The Strange Tactics of Extremism* (1964).

5

I'm as conservative as the Constitution, as liberal as Lincoln, and as progressive as Theodore Roosevelt.

GEORGE ROMNEY, News Conference, Hartford, Conn., 23 Feb., 1965.

6

The liberal party is a party which believes that, as new conditions and problems arise beyond the power of men and women to meet as individuals, it becomes the duty of the Government itself to find new remedies with which to meet them.

FRANKLIN D. ROOSEVELT, *Public Papers and Addresses, 1938:* Introduction.

7

The Democratic party will live and continue to receive the support of the majority of Americans just so long as it remains a liberal party.

FRANKLIN D. ROOSEVELT, Address in Denton, Md., 5 Sept., 1938.

8

I am reminded of four definitions: A radical is a man with both feet firmly planted—in the air; a conservative is a man with two perfectly good legs who, however, has never learned to walk; a reactionary is a somnambulist walking backwards; a liberal is a man who uses his legs and his hands at the behest of his head.

FRANKLIN D. ROOSEVELT, Radio Address, 26 Oct., 1939.

9

Every reform movement has a lunatic fringe.

THEODORE ROOSEVELT, speaking of the Progressive party in 1913. The quotation is paraphrased in his *Autobiography,* ch. 7.

10

Parlor bolshevism.

THEODORE ROOSEVELT. (*Metropolitan Magazine,* June, 1918)

11

The radical Right.

TELFORD TAYLOR, *Grand Inquest* (1954): Foreword, p. 16.

The Radical Right.

Title of a collection of essays, ed. by DANIEL BELL (1963). This was an updated expansion of an earlier volume, *The New American Right* (1955), in which "radical Right" appeared, though not as a title.

In conservative periods, the radical Right is characteristically disorganized and dormant. . . . But the election of a progressive administration has a galvanizing effect. The radical Right grows desperate. It feels that the nation is in mortal danger, that there is only a short time left to save the American way of life, that it is five minutes before midnight, that it must rally and resist before it is too late.

ARTHUR SCHLESINGER, JR., *The 'Threat' of the Radical Right; New York Times Magazine,* 17 June, 1962, p. 10.

A radical Right and a radical Left we shall always have with us. But in a strong and stable country they are dangerous only when they infect considerable sections of the moderate center.

WALTER LIPPMANN, Syndicated Column, 3 Mar., 1964.

Unlike the true conservative, the radical Right denies patriotism to those whose vision of America differs from its own, and continually raises the specter of communism to becloud issues.

AARON GOLDMAN, Address, National Community Relations Advisory Council plenary session, St. Louis, 28 June, 1964.

The radical Right is not so much the enemy of Communism as it is the enemy of freedom.

> FRANK CHURCH, Speech, U.S. Senate, 12 Jan., 1965.

1

But as much as any public man in this century [Lyndon B. Johnson] has, without ever formulating his purposes in large, philosophic phrases, exemplified and promoted the moderate way in American public life. To win the game? Yes, by all means. To have his way to the last possible point to which he could have his way? Certainly yes. But to have his way, and his party's way, *in such a manner as to leave the fewest possible scars and frustrations, so that what has at length been agreed upon in strife and struggle may, at least, be operable.*

> WILLIAM S. WHITE, *The Professional: Lyndon B. Johnson.*

2

By "radical" I understand one who goes too far; by "conservative" one who does not go far enough; by "reactionary" one who won't go at all. I suppose I must be a "progressive," which I take to be one who insists on recognizing new facts, adjusting policies to facts and circumstances as they arise.

> WOODROW WILSON, Speech in New York City, 29 Jan., 1911.

3

By a progressive I do not mean a man who is ready to move, but a man who knows where he is going when he moves.

> WOODROW WILSON, Speech in St. Paul, Minn., 9 Sept., 1919.

4

The principal candidate against him [Bryan] was Colonel S. F. Norton, of Chicago, . . . originator of the phrase so important to the Populist politics, "Middle of the road."

> UNKNOWN, Report on the Democratic national convention of 1896, Chicago *Inter-Ocean*, 26 July, 1896, p. 1. In this context, "middle of the roaders" were referred to as a splinter group—almost as a third party.

The middle of the road is where the white line is—and that's the worst place to drive.

> ROBERT FROST, Interview, *Collier's*, 27 Apr., 1956, p. 42. The Eisenhower administration of that period was frequently described as "middle of the road."

VI—The Politician in Profile

5

As we look over the list of the early leaders of the republic, Washington, John Adams, Hamilton, and others, we discern that they were all men who insisted upon being themselves and who refused to truckle to the people. With each succeeding generation, the growing demand of the people that its elective officials shall not lead but merely register the popular will has steadily undermined the independence of those who derive their power from popular election.

> JAMES TRUSLOW ADAMS, *The Adams Family*, p. 95.

6

A political leader must keep looking over his shoulder all the time to see if the boys are still there. If they aren't still there, he's no longer a political leader.

> BERNARD M. BARUCH. (New York *Times* obituary of Baruch, 21 June, 1965, p. 16)

7

An honest politician is one who, when he is bought, will stay bought.

> SIMON CAMERON, Republican boss of Pennsylvania, about 1860. On the authority of Thomas B. Reed.

8

The only promise I ever made was to say: "Boys, I'll do the best I can." If you are honest and intelligent, that is the only platform you need to have.

> JOHN NANCE GARNER, Interview with Carlton Wilson, United Press International, datelined Uvalde, Tex., 18 Nov., 1963.

9

We cannot safely leave politics to politicians, or political economy to college professors.

> HENRY GEORGE, *Social Problems*, p. 9.

10

There are two courses open to a minority party. It can indulge in the politics of partisanship, or it can remain true to the politics of responsibility. The first course is tempting to the weak, but ultimately would be rejected by the American people. The second course is difficult but is the road upon which we can offer leadership to the American people that will be accepted.

> LYNDON B. JOHNSON, Speech at Jefferson-Jackson Dinner, New York City, 1953, shortly after he became Senate minority leader.

11

When we got into office, the thing that surprised me most was to find that things were just as bad as we'd been saying they were.

> JOHN F. KENNEDY, Speech at a dinner marking his birthday, Washington, D.C., 27 May, 1961.

12

"Pol" is to politician what cop is to policeman.

> FLETCHER KNEBEL, *The Unknown JFK; Look*, 17 Nov., 1964, p. 46.

13

The most political animal to occupy the

White House since Andrew Jackson, if not since the creation of the Federal Government, has just completed the first six months of his Presidency.

> ARTHUR KROCK, Washington Column, New York *Times*, 24 May, 1964. Referring to Lyndon B. Johnson.

1

With exceptions so rare that they are regarded as miracles and freaks of nature, successful democratic politicians are insecure and intimidated men. They advance politically only as they placate, appease, bribe, seduce, bamboozle, or otherwise manage to manipulate the demanding and threatening elements in their constituencies.

> WALTER LIPPMANN, *The Public Philosophy*, bk. i, ch. 2.

2

To the people they're ollers ez slick ez molasses,
An' butter their bread on both sides with
    The Masses.

> JAMES RUSSELL LOWELL, *The Biglow Papers*, Ser. i, No. 4. Referring to politicians.

3

A marciful Providunce fashioned us holler,
O' purpose thet we might our princerples
    swaller.

> JAMES RUSSELL LOWELL, *The Biglow Papers*, Ser. i, No. 4.

4

Ez to my princerples, I glory
    In hevin' nothin' o' the sort;
I aint a Whig, I aint a Tory,
    I'm jest a canderdate, in short.

> JAMES RUSSELL LOWELL, *The Biglow Papers*, Ser. i, No. 7.

5

Skilled to pull wires, he baffles Nature's
    hope,
Who sure intended him to stretch a rope.

> JAMES RUSSELL LOWELL, *The Boss*. Probably referring to Boss Tweed of New York.

6

Overnominated and underelected.

> RICHARD M. NIXON, describing his plight to a dinner audience in Washington, D.C., in 1965. (ROBERT J. DONOVAN, Article, *New York Times Magazine*, 25 Apr., 1965, p. 14)

7

There lies beneath this mossy stone
    A politician who
Touched a live issue without gloves,
    And never did come to.

> KEITH PRESTON, *Epitaph*.

8

When the water reaches the upper deck, follow the rats.

> CLAUDE SWANSON, on the authority of Joseph Alsop: Column, New York *Herald Tribune*, 5 Feb., 1964. Quoted as "one of the basic rules of American politics."

9

My pollertics, like my religion, bein of a exceedin accommodatin character.

> ARTEMUS WARD, *The Crisis*.

10

Things get very lonely in Washington sometimes. The real voice of the great people of America sometimes sounds faint and distant in that strange city. You hear politics until you wish that both parties were smothered in their own gas.

> WOODROW WILSON, Speech in St. Louis, 5 Sept., 1919.

Things always look so much better away from Washington

> JOHN F. KENNEDY, on the authority of Hale Boggs, of the U.S. House of Representatives. Boggs quoted Kennedy on the floor of the House, 5 Dec., 1963, during a memorial session dedicated to the slain President. These words were spoken to Boggs just before Kennedy's fateful trip to Texas.

VII—The Presidency

11

I would rather be right than be President.

> HENRY CLAY, Speech, 1850. This was his reply to those who said that his advocacy of the Missouri Compromise measures of 1850 would injure his chances for the presidency.

The gentleman need not worry. He will never be either.

> THOMAS B. REED, Reply to Congressman Springer when the latter quoted Clay's preference for being right. (W. A. ROBINSON, *Thomas B. Reed*)

12

While it is wise for the President to get all the competent advice possible, final judgments are necessarily his own. No one can share with him the responsibility for them. No one can make his decisions for him. . . . His decisions are final and usually irreparable. This constitutes the appalling burden of his office.

> CALVIN COOLIDGE, *Autobiography*.

13

The Presidency is more than an administrative office. It must be the symbol of American ideals. The high and the lowly must be seen with the same eyes, met in the same spirit. It must be the instrument by which national conscience is livened and it must under the guidance of the Almighty interpret and follow that conscience.

> HERBERT HOOVER, 1928. (*Herbert Hoover in His Own Words*, compiled by Louis P. Lochner; *New York Times Magazine*, 9 Aug., 1964, p. 15)

1

In the Middle Ages it was the fashion to wear hair shirts to remind one's self of trouble and sin. Many years ago I concluded that a few hair shirts were part of the mental wardrobe of every man. The President differs only from other men in that he has a more extensive wardrobe.

HERBERT HOOVER, Speech in Washington, D.C., 14 Dec., 1929.

2

No man can be President without looking back upon the effort given to the country by the thirty Presidents who in my case have preceded me. No man of imagination can be President without thinking of what shall be the course of his country under the thirty more Presidents who will follow him. He must think of himself as a link in the long chain of his country's destiny, past and future.

HERBERT HOOVER, during his administration. (RICHARD M. KETCHUM, *Faces from the Past; American Heritage,* Dec., 1964, p. 31)

3

I shall often go wrong through defect of judgment. When right, I shall often be thought wrong by those whose positions will not command a view of the whole ground. I ask your indulgence for my own errors, which will never be intentional, and your support against the errors of others, who may condemn what they would not if seen in all its parts.

THOMAS JEFFERSON, First Inaugural Address, 4 March, 1801.

4

In a government like ours, it is the duty of the Chief Magistrate . . . to endeavor, by all honorable means, to unite in himself the confidence of the whole people.

THOMAS JEFFERSON, Letter to J. Garland Jefferson, 25 Jan., 1810.

5

The Presidency is no place for a timid soul or a torpid spirit. It is the one place where a petty temper and a narrow view cannot reside. For the Presidency is both a legacy from the past and a profusion of hope for the future.

LYNDON B. JOHNSON, Speech in Miami Beach, Fla., 27 Feb., 1964.

6

A President's hardest task is not to do what is right, but to know what is right.

LYNDON B. JOHNSON, State of the Union Message, 4 Jan., 1965.

7

It's not the kind of place you would pick to live in; it's a place you go to after work. . . . I feel like I am in the middle of an air raid. Then at 8 a.m. when I am trying to read a report from a general, all the tourists are going by right under your bed. And when you're trying to take a nap, Lady Bird [Mrs. Johnson] is in the next room with Laurance Rockefeller and eighty ladies talking about the daffodils on Pennsylvania avenue.

LYNDON B. JOHNSON, on life in the White House. (New York Times News Service dispatch, datelined Washington, D.C., 6 May, 1965)

8

It is pre-eminently a place of moral leadership. All of our great Presidents were leaders of thought at times when certain historic ideas in the life of the nation had to be clarified.

FRANKLIN D. ROOSEVELT, on the presidency. (New York *Times,* 13 Nov., 1932)

9

I declined to adopt the view that what was imperatively necessary for the Nation could not be done by the President unless he could find some specific authorization to do it.

THEODORE ROOSEVELT, *An Autobiography.*

10

The true view of the executive function is . . . that the President can exercise no powers which cannot be fairly and reasonably traced to some specific grant of power or justly implied and included within such express grant as proper and necessary to its exercise. Such specific grant must be either in the Federal Constitution or in an act of Congress passed in pursuance thereof. There is no undefined residuum of power which he can exercise because it seems to him to be in the public interest.

WILLIAM HOWARD TAFT, *Our Chief Magistrate and His Powers.*

11

To be President of the United States is to be lonely, very lonely at times of great decisions.

HARRY S TRUMAN, *Memoirs: Years of Decisions.*

12

My movements to the chair of Government will be accompanied by feelings not unlike those of a culprit who is going to the place of his execution.

GEORGE WASHINGTON, Letter to Henry Knox, 1 Apr., 1789.

13

The President is at liberty, both in law and conscience, to be as big a man as he can. His capacity will set the limit; and if Congress be overborne by him, it will be no fault of the makers of the Constitution—it will be from no lack of constitutional powers on its part, but only because the President has the nation behind him, and Congress has not.

WOODROW WILSON, *Constitutional Government in the United States.*

VIII—The Vice-Presidency

1

The most insignificant that ever . . . man contrived.

 JOHN ADAMS, on the vice-presidency.

2

Th' prisidincy is th' highest office in th' gift iv th' people. Th' vice-prisidincy is th' next highest an' th' lowest. It isn't a crime exactly. Ye can't be sint to jail f'r it, but it's a kind iv a disgrace. It's like writin' anonymous letters.

 FINLEY PETER DUNNE, *Dissertations by Mr. Dooley: The Vice-President.*

3

Worst damfool mistake I ever made was letting myself be elected Vice-President of the United States. Should have stuck with my old chores as Speaker of the House. I gave up the second most important job in the Government for one that didn't amount to a hill of beans. I spent eight long years as Mr. Roosevelt's spare tire. I might still be Speaker if I hadn't let them elect me Vice-President.

 JOHN NANCE GARNER. (FRANK X. TOLBERT, *What Is Cactus Jack Up to Now?; Saturday Evening Post*, 2 Nov., 1963)

4

Alexander Throttlebottom.

 GEORGE S. KAUFMAN AND MORRIE RYSKIND, *Of Thee I Sing* (1931). In this satiric musical comedy, Throttlebottom was the forgotten fellow and amiable nonentity who became Vice President. His name became part of the political language, a symbol of public indifference to, and mild contempt for, a post once regarded as superfluous.

5

Once there were two brothers. One ran away to sea, the other was elected Vice-President, and nothing was ever heard of either of them again.

 THOMAS R. MARSHALL, *Recollections.*

6

The Vice-President of the United States is like a man in a cataleptic state: he cannot speak; he cannot move; he suffers no pain; and yet he is perfectly conscious of everything that is going on about him.

 THOMAS R. MARSHALL, Statement to the press.

7

Take it to the Vice-President; he needs something to keep him awake.

 THEODORE ROOSEVELT, to a White House butler who was puzzled about the best procedure for disposing of a chandelier in the Treaty Room of the White House. In the era before air conditioning, breeze through the open windows caused the chandelier to tinkle at night,

and so disturb the President's sleep until Roosevelt ordered its removal. Lyndon B. Johnson quoted these words, and recalled the background of the story, during a tour of the White House, 22 Jan., 1964.

IX—Office Holding

8

No man who ever held the office of President would congratulate a friend on obtaining it. He will make one man ungrateful, and a hundred men his enemies, for every office he can bestow.

 JOHN ADAMS, on the election of his son, John Quincy Adams, to the presidency. (QUINCY, *Figures of the Past*, p. 74)

9

I'm glad to sit in the back row. I would rather be a servant in the house of the Lord than to sit in the seats of the mighty.

 ALBEN W. BARKLEY, Speech at Washington & Lee University, Lexington, Va., 30 Apr., 1956. Barkley, at the time, was serving as junior Senator from Kentucky, after a long and distinguished career as Senator and then as Vice-President. These were among his last words; moments later he collapsed to the floor, dead of a heart attack.

10

Can you let me know what positions you have at your disposal with which to reward deserving Democrats?

 WILLIAM JENNINGS BRYAN, Letter to Walter W. Vick, Receiver General, 20 Aug., 1913.

11

I am glad to have the public know that I appreciate the services of those who work in politics and feel an interest in seeing them rewarded.

 WILLIAM JENNINGS BRYAN, Interview, New York *Times*, 16 Jan., 1915.

12

This office-seeking is a disease. It is even catching.

 GROVER CLEVELAND, Interview in 1885. (NEVINS, *Grover Cleveland*, p. 235)

13

Take from the United States the appointment of postmasters and let the towns elect them, and you deprive the Federal Government of half a million defenders.

 EMERSON, *Journals*, 1860.

14

What are we here for, except the offices?

 WEBSTER FLANAGAN, leader of the Republican party in Texas, at the Republican national convention of 1880. (*Dictionary of American Biography*, vol. vi, p. 453; *The Nation*, 10 June, 1880)

1

I shall never *ask*, never *refuse,* nor ever *resign* an office.

> BENJAMIN FRANKLIN, *Autobiography.*

2

Public office in this country has few attractions. The pecuniary emolument is so inconsiderable as to amount to a sacrifice to any man who can employ his time with advantage in any liberal profession.

> ALEXANDER HAMILTON, Autobiographic Letter, 2 May, 1797.

3

A garden, you know, is a very useful refuge of a disappointed politician. Accordingly, I have purchased a few acres about nine miles from town, have built a house, and am cultivating a garden.

> ALEXANDER HAMILTON, Letter to Charles Cotesworth Pinckney, 29 Dec., 1802.

4

Whenever a man has cast a longing eye on offices, a rottenness begins in his conduct.

> THOMAS JEFFERSON, Letter to T. Coxe, 1799.

5

If a due participation of office is a matter of right, how are vacancies to be obtained? Those by death are few: by resignation, none. [*often given in paraphrased form:*] Few die and none resign.

> THOMAS JEFFERSON, Letter to a committee of merchants of New Haven, 12 July, 1801.

6

Of the various executive duties, no one excited more anxious concern than that of placing the interest of our fellow citizens in the hands of honest men, with understanding sufficient for their stations. No duty is at the same time more difficult to fulfil.

> THOMAS JEFFERSON, Letter to Elias Shipman, 12 July, 1801.

7

No duty the Executive has to perform is so trying as to put the right man in the right place.

> THOMAS JEFFERSON. (J. B. MCMASTER, *History of the People of the United States,* vol. ii, p. 586)

8

There's not a particle of doubt
We've turned a bunch of rascals out,
And put a nice clean aggregation
In very serious temptation.

> KEITH PRESTON, *Post-election Misgivings.*

9

Every man who takes office in Washington either grows or swells, and when I give a man an office, I watch him carefully to see whether he is swelling or growing.

> WOODROW WILSON, Address in Washington, 15 May, 1916.

10

No religious test shall ever be required as a qualification to any office or public trust under the United States.

> Constitution of the United States, art. vi, sec. 3.

When a man assumes a public trust, he should consider himself as public property.

> THOMAS JEFFERSON, in a conversation with Baron Humboldt. (RAYNER, *Life of Jefferson,* p. 356)

The very essence of a free government consists in considering offices as public trusts, bestowed for the good of the country, and not for the benefit of an individual or a party.

> JOHN C. CALHOUN, Speech, 13 Feb., 1835.

An' in convartin' public trusts
To very privit uses.

> JAMES RUSSELL LOWELL, *The Biglow Papers,* Ser. i, No. 6.

The phrase, "public office is a public trust," has of late become common property.

> CHARLES SUMNER, Speech in U. S. Senate, 31 May, 1872.

Public officials are the trustees of the people.

> GROVER CLEVELAND, Letter upon accepting nomination for mayor of Buffalo, 1881.

X—Machinery of Politics

11

This day the caucus club meets . . . in the garret of Tom Dawes, the adjutant of the Boston regiment.

> JOHN ADAMS, *Diary,* Feb., 1753; vol. ii, p. 164. The first known appearance of "caucus" in print.

12

Esthetically speaking, Presidential Inaugurations have begun to go the way of the Hollywood biblical epic. Both are afflicted by the national passion for overproducing the simplest of dramas.

> RUSSELL BAKER, Article, New York *Times,* 21 Jan., 1965, p. 16.

13

In several ways, the [political] convention is a peculiar institution. Like an impatient Brigadoon, it comes to life every four years; it is master of its own rules, and its decisions are as irrevocable as a haircut. Yet, the convention isn't even mentioned in the Constitution or in any law ever passed by Congress. In this sense, it might be described as the most unofficial official (or most official unofficial) gathering in politics.

> DAVID BRINKLEY, *The Way It's Been;* New York *Times,* 12 July, 1964, sec. 11, p. 3.

1

In my opinion it is high time for the principle of full consideration but majority action to replace the current provision for minority rule through the filibuster and the threat of the filibuster.

> PAUL H. DOUGLAS, Testimony, in support of a new cloture rule before the Subcommittee on Standing Rules of the U.S. Senate, 1965.

2

Most campaigns are rough campaigns. I'm an old campaigner. . . . One of the first things I learned: the people are not much interested in my personal opinion of my opponent.

> LYNDON B. JOHNSON, News Conference, Washington, D.C., 24 July, 1964.

3

The convention is the voice, the bone and the sinews of a political party—and sometimes it even nominates an Abraham Lincoln.

> FLETCHER KNEBEL, *One Vote for the Convention System; New York Times Magazine*, 23 Aug., 1964.

4

The right to filibuster is, I have always believed, a precious usage, invaluable to the preservation of freedom. For it can prevent any sudden dictation by a scant majority in a moment of public hysteria. To close down on a filibuster is, therefore, something to be done only very rarely and only after there is convincing proof that a bill has been thoroughly considered and debated, and that to delay any longer would do much harm to the country.

> WALTER LIPPMANN, Syndicated Column, 11 June, 1964.

5

The filibuster is not the exclusive weapon of any philosophy, party or section; distinguished Senators of both parties, representing every shade of political thought and every area of the country, have taken part on occasion in extended debates in support of a minority position.

> RICHARD B. RUSSELL, *Russell Defends the Filibuster; New York Times Magazine*, 15 Mar., 1964. At the time of this writing, Senator Russell was leading Southern opposition to civil-rights legislation.

6

I am about to leave you on a long journey, and the route, by the way, won't be a military or political secret. I intend to cover as much ground as time and strength and our resources permit.

> ADLAI E. STEVENSON, Speech of farewell at the Illinois State Fair, Springfield, 14 Aug., 1952, just before embarking on his first presidential campaign.

7

A campaign addressed not to men's minds and to their best instincts, but to their passions, emotions and prejudices, is unworthy at best. Now, with the fate of the nation at stake, it is unbearable.

> ADLAI E. STEVENSON, Speech in Chicago during the 1952 presidential campaign.

8

Talking for Buncombe.

> FELIX WALKER, Speech, on the Missouri Bill, U.S. House of Representatives, 25 Feb., 1820. Toward the close of lengthy debate on this bill, Walker, whose home district included Buncombe County, N.C., arose to speak. Several colleagues in the House urged him not to, knowing his talent for long speeches, and in the interest of putting the bill to a vote; but he refused, stating that he was bound "to make a speech for Buncombe." From this derives the word "buncombe" or "bunkum."

"Talking to Bunkum!" This is an old and common saying at Washington, when a member of Congress is making one of those humdrum and unlistened-to "long talks" which have lately become so fashionable—not with the hope of being heard in the House, but to afford an enlightened representative a pretence for sending a copy of his speech to his constituents.

> UNKNOWN, *Niles Weekly Register*, 27 Sept., 1828; Vol. xxxv, No. 889, p. 66.

9

The presidential campaign speech is, like jazz, one of the few truly American art forms. It is not, of course, unknown in other democratic countries, but nowhere else has it achieved the same degree of virtuosity; nowhere else is it so accurate a reflection of national character: by turns solemn or witty, pompous or deeply moving, full of sense or full of wind.

> ANONYMOUS, *American Heritage*, Aug., 1964, p. 88.

XI—Famous Phrases

10

I placed it where it would do the most good.

> OAKES AMES, Letter to Henry S. McComb, referring to Crédit Mobilier stock distributed to members of Congress in 1872.

11

You shall not press down upon the brow of labor this crown of thorns; you shall not crucify mankind upon a cross of gold.

> WILLIAM JENNINGS BRYAN, Speech at the Democratic national convention, Chicago, 10 July, 1896. These concluding words of one of the most electrifying political speeches of all time were almost identical with a passage from one

of his speeches in the House of Representatives, given 22 Dec., 1894.

1

The enemy's country.

> WILLIAM JENNINGS BRYAN, during the 1896 campaign, in describing the East —specifically New York.

2

The burning issue of imperialism growing out of the Spanish War involves the very existence of the Republic and the destruction of our free institutions. We regard it as the paramount issue of the campaign.

> WILLIAM JENNINGS BRYAN, Platform, adopted by the Democratic national convention, 5 July, 1900.

3

We are Republicans, and we don't propose to leave our party and identify ourselves with the party whose antecedents have been rum, Romanism, and rebellion.

> REV. SAMUEL DICKINSON BURCHARD, Speech of congratulation to James G. Blaine at the Fifth Avenue Hotel, New York City, 29 Oct., 1884. Burchard was spokesman for clergymen supporting the Republican presidential candidate. But Blaine's failure to repudiate promptly the highly controversial "rum, Romanism, and rebellion" remark probably cost him the election in a close race.

4

I never said, "Great is Tammany and Croker is its prophet." Bryan did.

> CHAMP CLARK, *Memories.*

5

The other side can have a monopoly of all the dirt in this campaign.

> GROVER CLEVELAND, during the campaign of 1884, upon destroying a packet of "evidence" relating to the private life of his opponent, James G. Blaine. (NEVINS, *Grover Cleveland,* p. 169)

6

The boy orator of the Platte.

> W. J. CONNELL in describing—derisively —William Jennings Bryan during the Congressional campaign of 1890.

7

I do not choose to run for President in 1928.

> CALVIN COOLIDGE, Statement to press in 1927.

8

Perhaps one of the most important accomplishments of my administration has been minding my own business.

> CALVIN COOLIDGE, News Conference, 1 Mar., 1929.

I should like to be known as a former President who tries to mind his own business.

> CALVIN COOLIDGE. (*Cosmopolitan Magazine,* May, 1930)

9

Power politics is the diplomatic name for the law of the jungle.

> ELY CULBERTSON, *Must We Fight Russia?*

10

The convention will be deadlocked, and after the other candidates have gone their limit, some twelve or fifteen men, worn out and bleary-eyed for lack of sleep, will sit down, about two o'clock in the morning, around a table in a smoke-filled room in some hotel, and decide the nomination. When that time comes, Harding will be selected.

> HARRY M. DAUGHERTY, campaign manager for Warren G. Harding, predicting with great accuracy the method of Harding's nomination for the presidency at the Republican national convention in Chicago in 1920. The "smoke-filled room" was that of Col. George Harvey at the Blackstone Hotel; the meeting occurred about 2 a.m. on June 12, and it broke a deadlock involving Gen. Leonard Wood and Gov. Frank O. Lowden. Harding emerged as the compromise candidate, and Daugherty's phrase became an enduring one in American politics—synonymous with practical politics.

11

That's why it's time for a change.

> THOMAS E. DEWEY, Speech in San Francisco, 21 Sept., 1944. The slogan was even more prominent in the campaign of 1952, however.

The Republicans have pegged their campaign largely on one theme—that it's time for a change because of the "top to bottom mess in Washington." In developing this theme they have pounded relentlessly at two charges—that the [Truman] Administration has been "riddled" with corruption, and that it has been "slow" in weeding Communists out of Government.

> New York *Times,* 21 Sept., 1952.

12

I could travel from Boston to Chicago by the light of my own effigies.

> STEPHEN A. DOUGLAS, in 1854, after passage of the Kansas-Nebraska bill, which he had supported. (RHODES, *History of the United States,* vol. i, p. 496)

13

I shall go to Korea.

> DWIGHT D. EISENHOWER, Campaign Speech in Detroit, 24 Oct., 1952. In this memorable speech Eisenhower listed two pledges: "to bring the Korean War to an early and honorable end," and to make a personal visit to the combat area as a means of bringing about peace. He made the trip late in November, following his election.

The Independence will be at your disposal if you still desire to go to Korea.

>   HARRY S TRUMAN, the final sentence of a Congratulatory Message to Dwight D. Eisenhower just after the 1952 election returns were in. Truman made no secret of his feeling that the promise to go to Korea was a politically motivated gesture.

1

Water flowed like wine.

>   WILLIAM M. EVARTS, describing a dinner at the White House in 1877 during the administration of Rutherford B. Hayes, whose wife was a prohibitionist.

2

What's the use of wasting dynamite when insect-powder will do?

>   CARTER GLASS, in an unpublished speech, Democratic caucus, 1913.

3

I will offer a choice, not an echo. This will not be an engagement of personalities. It will be an engagement of principles.

>   BARRY M. GOLDWATER, Speech in Phoenix, Ariz., 3 Jan., 1964, in which he announced formally that he would seek the Republican presidential nomination that year.

I have come here to offer our party a choice. I reject the echo we have thus far been handed . . . the echo of fear, or reaction . . . the echo from the Never Never Land that puts our nation backward to a lesser place in the world of free men.

>   WILLIAM W. SCRANTON, Speech at the Republican state convention, Baltimore, Md., 12 June, 1964, in which he announced his candidacy for the presidential nomination. The target of his remarks was Barry M. Goldwater, who eventually won the nomination.

4

Here comes another of the spellbinders!

>   WILLIAM CASSIUS GOODLOE, referring to the widely publicized Republican stump-speakers in the campaign of 1888.

5

I can't remember a time when a President had prosperity and poverty going for him at the same time.

>   LEONARD HALL, commenting, as former chairman of the Republican National Committee, on Lyndon B. Johnson's "war on poverty" during a time of general prosperity. (*Time*, 15 May, 1964, p. 31)

6

We'll stand pat!

>   MARK HANNA, replying to a reporter when asked to state the issue of the 1900 campaign to re-elect McKinley.

7

We drew a pair of deuces and filled.

>   WARREN G. HARDING, describing his nomination for the presidency in 1920 to a group of reporters just after he was selected. He was employing poker terms: to "fill" is to get a "full house," a pair and three of a kind.

8

One thing, if no more, I have gained by my custom-house experience—to know a politician. It is a knowledge which no previous thought, or power of sympathy, could have taught me, because the animal, or the machine rather, is not in nature.

>   NATHANIEL HAWTHORNE, *Note-Books*, 15 Mar., 1840. This is said to be the origin of the term "machine politics."

9

Ours is a land . . . filled with millions of happy homes, blessed with comfort and opportunity. . . . In no nation are the fruits of accomplishment more secure. . . . I have no fears for the future of our country. It is bright with hope.

>   HERBERT HOOVER, Inaugural Address, 4 Mar., 1929.

10

They are playing politics at the expense of human misery.

>   HERBERT HOOVER, Statement to press, 9 Dec., 1930, after members of Congress introduced bills for unemployment relief.

11

Like an armed warrior, like a plumed knight, James G. Blaine marched down the halls of the American Congress and threw his shining lance full and fair against the brazen forehead of every traitor to his country and every maligner of his fair reputation.

>   ROBERT G. INGERSOLL, Speech, nominating James G. Blaine for President, Republican national convention, Cincinnati, 15 June, 1876.

12

John Marshall has made his decision: now let him enforce it!

>   ANDREW JACKSON, as President, referring to the Supreme Court decision in Worcester vs. Georgia, 3 Mar., 1832, which upheld the right of the Cherokee Indians to retain possession of land from which the state was trying to evict them. (GREELEY, *The American Conflict*, vol. i, p. 106)

13

We are swinging round the circle.

>   ANDREW JOHNSON, Speech on the presidential Reconstruction tour, Aug., 1866.

14

Good-by, Culpeper. God bless you, Culpeper! What did Dick Nixon ever do for Culpeper?

> LYNDON B. JOHNSON, Speech (conclusion) in Culpeper, Va., during the 1960 campaign. This is the best-remembered example of Johnson's whistle-stop technique during an intensive tour of the South in behalf of the Kennedy-Johnson ticket.

1

I have noted with interest your suggestion as to where those who vote for my opponent should go. While I understand and sympathize with your deep motivation. I think it is important that our side try to refrain from raising the religious issue.

> JOHN F. KENNEDY, Address in New York City, 19 Oct., 1960, quoting his own humorous telegram to Harry S Truman. The latter, campaigning for Kennedy during the 1960 race, had stirred Republican ire by suggesting to a San Antonio audience that any Texan who voted for Kennedy's opponent should "go to hell."

2

The brains trust.

> JAMES M. KIERAN, of the New York Times, in a conversation with Franklin D. Roosevelt at Hyde Park, N.Y., Aug., 1932—referring to the group of Columbia University professors who were then advising F.D.R. during his campaign. This durable phrase later became "brain trust," and was used in much the same sense.

3

He looks as if he had been weaned on a pickle.

> ALICE ROOSEVELT LONGWORTH, describing Calvin Coolidge by quoting her physician. (*Crowded Hours,* p. 337)

4

Much of what Mr. [Henry] Wallace calls his global thinking is, no matter how you slice it, still Globaloney.

> CLARE BOOTHE LUCE, Speech in the House of Representatives, 9 Feb., 1943.

5

While I cannot take the time to name all of the men in the State Department who have been named as members of the Communist party and members of a spy ring, I have here in my hand a list of 205 that were known to the Secretary of State as being members of the Communist party and who nevertheless are still working and shaping the policy of the State Department.

> JOSEPH R. MCCARTHY, Speech in Wheeling, W. Va., 9 Feb., 1950. This was the speech that first brought national attention to the Senator from Wisconsin. Subsequently he changed the figure

many times, and even denied having specified 205 originally. (He kept no notes of the speech, and spoke from no prepared text.) The speech was unheralded, and did not attract national attention for several days, but its eventual impact was tremendous. The version quoted here is from the Wheeling *Intelligencer,* which covered the speech; it is the version quoted by RICHARD H. ROVERE in his *Senator Joe McCarthy,* p. 125, and by ALFRED STEINBERG, *The Man from Missouri,* p. 371.

6

The Democratic label is now the property of men and women who have been unwilling to recognize evil or who bent to whispered pleas from the lips of traitors . . . men and women who wear the political label stitched with the idiocy of a Truman, rotted by the deceit of an [Dean] Acheson, corrupted by the Red slime of a [Harry Dexter] White.

> JOSEPH R. MCCARTHY, Speech, 1950.

7

The issue between the Republicans and Democrats is clearly drawn. It has been deliberately drawn by those who have been in charge of twenty years of treason.

> JOSEPH R. MCCARTHY, Speech in Charleston, W. Va., 4 Feb., 1954. He gave the title "Twenty Years of Treason" to a series of nine speeches delivered on a nine-day tour arranged by the Republican national committee.

Point of Order!

> Title of Film (1964) based on the Army-McCarthy hearings of 1954—a documentary produced by Emile de Antonio and Daniel Talbot. The title quotes a parliamentary expression identified with McCarthy.

McCarthyism.

> HERBERT BLOCK, Political Cartoon signed "Herblock," Washington *Post,* 1950. The term was crudely lettered on a barrel of mud, depicted in the cartoon as supported precariously on a tower composed of buckets of mud. The cartoon is included in *The Herblock Book* (1952), p. 145, and introduced "McCarthyism" to the language.

We have seen the technique of the "Big 'Lie,' " elsewhere employed by the totalitarian dictators with devastating success, utilized here for the first time on a sustained basis in our history.

> Senate Foreign Relations Committee, Report, adopted by a vote of nine to two, 18 July, 1950. Referring to the tactics of Senator Joseph R. McCarthy.

I don't want to see the Republican party ride to political victory on the four horsemen of calumny—fear, ignorance, bigotry, and smear.

> MARGARET CHASE SMITH, Speech in U.S. Senate, 1 June, 1950. Senator Smith's anti-McCarthyism manifesto, which was widely quoted, became known as her "declaration of conscience."

Were the junior Senator from Wisconsin in the pay of the Communists, he could not have done a better job for them.

> RALPH E. FLANDERS, Speech in U.S. Senate, 1 June, 1954. This was one of the strongest anti-McCarthy speeches ever delivered. Late in 1954 the Senate, as a body, voted censure of McCarthy.

1

The steam-roller was first heard of in American politics in June, 1908, when it was applied by Oswald F. Schuette, of the Chicago *Inter-Ocean,* to the methods employed by the Roosevelt-Taft majority in the Republican National Committee in over-riding the protests against seating Taft delegates from Alabama and Arkansas.

> H. L. MENCKEN, *The American Language,* p. 372.

2

Mournfully I prophesy that the program of these sons of the wild jackass who now control the Senate will probably go forward to complete consummation.

> GEORGE H. MOSES, Speech in Washington, D.C., 7 Nov., 1929, referring to insurgent (liberal) Republicans in the U.S. Senate—Borah, Brookhart, Johnson, La Follette, Norris, Nye, Shipstead, and Wheeler. Senator Moses, an orthodox Republican, was lamenting the difficulty of getting legislation for higher tariffs through the Senate because of the alliance of this group with Democrats. He afterwards stated that he drew his inspiration for this phrase from the *Old Testament: Jeremiah,* xiv, 6: "And the wild asses did stand in the high places, they snuffed up the wind like dragons."

3

One other thing I probably should tell you, because if I don't they'll probably be saying this about me too: We did get something—a gift—after the election. A man down in Texas heard Pat on the radio mention the fact that our two youngsters would like to have a dog. And, believe it or not, the day before we left on this campaign trip we got a message from Union Station in Baltimore saying they had a package for us. We went down to get it. You know what it was? It was a little cocker spaniel dog in a crate that had been sent all the way from Texas. Black and white

spotted. And our little girl—Trisha, the six-year-old—named it Checkers. And you know the kids love the dog, and I just want to say this right now, that regardless of what they say about it, we're going to keep it.

> RICHARD M. NIXON, Speech broadcast nationally from Los Angeles, 23 Sept., 1952. After the disclosure that Nixon had received a special $18,235 "expense fund" from political supporters over a two-year period, his position as Vice-Presidential candidate on the Republican ticket was challenged. In this famous "Checkers speech," he defended the contributions.

4

I should say this—that Pat [Mrs. Nixon] doesn't have a mink coat. But she does have a respectable Republican cloth coat.

> RICHARD M. NIXON, Speech from Los Angeles, 23 Sept., 1952, explaining his controversial expense fund. In defending his financial affairs, Nixon struck at the mink coat as a symbol of corruption within the Truman administration.

5

How can they tell?

> Attributed to DOROTHY PARKER, as her reaction to the news that Calvin Coolidge had died.

6

The Nine Old Men.

> DREW PEARSON AND ROBERT S. ALLEN, Title of book (1936) dealing with the Supreme Court. During the early years of the New Deal the court was under fire on the ground that it obstructed social legislation; early in 1937 F.D.R. made his unsuccessful attempt to have it reorganized.

7

The Happy Warrior of the political battlefield.

> FRANKLIN D. ROOSEVELT, Speech of Nomination, Democratic national convention, 26 June, 1924—referring to Alfred E. Smith.

8

If we can boondoggle our way out of the depression, that word is going to be enshrined in the hearts of the American people for years to come.

> FRANKLIN D. ROOSEVELT, Speech in Newark, N.J., 18 Jan., 1936. The word "boondoggle" (noun), said to have been coined about 1926 by Robert H. Link, a Rochester, N.Y. Scoutmaster, originally was applied to leather neckwear made and worn by Boy Scouts. When it was disclosed that New Deal work-relief projects in New York included a class in making boondoggles, critics soon used

the word in the general sense of any wasteful and useless project.

1

That great historic trio: Martin, Barton and Fish.

> FRANKLIN D. ROOSEVELT, Speech in Boston, 30 Oct., 1940, during the presidential campaign. He was speaking derisively of the influential anti-Roosevelt trio of Joseph Martin, Bruce Barton, and Hamilton Fish.

2

Clear everything with Sidney.

> Attributed to FRANKLIN D. ROOSEVELT, but never acknowledged by him, though the remark, supposedly made at the Democratic national convention of 1944 in Chicago, which nominated F.D.R. for a fourth term, was used widely by anti-Roosevelt forces. This was said to be Roosevelt's instructions to Robert Hannegan, chairman of the Democratic national committee, to clear details of the convention, especially the choice of a running mate, with Sidney Hillman of the Congress of Industrial Organizations (C.I.O.), a powerful labor ally of the Democrats.

3

These Republican leaders have not been content with attacks on me, on my wife, or on my sons. No, not content with that, they now include my little dog, Fala.

> FRANKLIN D. ROOSEVELT, Speech at Teamsters' dinner, Washington, D.C., 23 Sept., 1944. This was in reply to the charge that the President had sent a destroyer back to the Aleutian Islands to fetch his Scotty, a dog famous in political history, at great expense to taxpayers.

4

The first twelve years are the hardest.

> FRANKLIN D. ROOSEVELT, News Conference in Washington, D.C., 19 Jan., 1945.

5

I am as strong as a bull moose and you can use me to the limit.

> THEODORE ROOSEVELT, Letter to Mark Hanna, at the opening of the campaign of 1900. (BISHOP, *Theodore Roosevelt and His Times*, vol. i, p. 139)

It takes more than that to kill a Bull Moose.

> THEODORE ROOSEVELT, Speech in Milwaukee, Wis., on the night of the attempt to assassinate him, 14 Oct., 1912.

6

There is a homely adage which runs, "Speak softly and carry a big stick; you will go far." If the American nation will speak softly and yet build and keep at a pitch of the highest training a thoroughly efficient Navy, the Monroe Doctrine will go far.

> THEODORE ROOSEVELT, Speech, Minnesota State Fair, 2 Sept., 1901.

7

My hat's in the ring. The fight is on and I'm stripped to the buff.

> THEODORE ROOSEVELT, Newspaper Interview in Cleveland, 21 Feb., 1912, while on his way to Columbus to address the State Constitutional Convention.

I never wear a hat, so it must always be in the ring.

> RICHARD M. NIXON, Radio Interview in New York City, 20 Jan., 1964.

8

We fight in honorable fashion for the good of mankind; fearless of the future, unheeding of our individual fates, with unflinching hearts and undimmed eyes; we stand at Armageddon, and we battle for the Lord.

> THEODORE ROOSEVELT, Speech in Chicago, 17 June, 1912, on the eve of the Republican national convention, which renominated Taft.

9

The system they call "invisible government."

> ELIHU ROOT, referring to boss rule, specifically to Thomas C. Platt of New York.

10

Salamander? Call it Gerrymander?

> Attributed to BENJAMIN RUSSELL—his retort to the painter Gilbert Stuart, in 1811. Russell, editor of the Massachusetts *Centinel,* had hung on the wall of his office a map showing the proposed redistricting of Essex County, which the Democratic legislature was putting through in order to gain control of the district. Stuart, looking at the map, with the new district blocked off in color, remarked that it resembled a monstrous animal. He added claws, sketching with a pencil; then he said: "There, that will do for a salamander." Then Russell is said to have made his famous retort, which gave the language an enduring term for sinuous political redistricting. Russell had in mind the name of the Governor of Massachusetts, Elbridge Gerry, though it later developed that Gerry was opposed to the proposal. (BUCKINGHAM, *Specimens of Newspaper Writing,* vol. ii, p. 91; *Dictionary of American Biography,* vol. xvi. p. 238.) The origin of "gerrymander" is also credited, in other sources, to Richard Alsop and James Ogilvie.

11

I have come home to look after my fences.

> JOHN SHERMAN, Speech to his neighbors

in Mansfield, Ohio, referring to the fences around his farm. This is said to be the origin of the political expression, "to mend one's fences." (STODDARD, *As I Knew Them,* p. 161)

1

I will not accept if nominated, and will not serve if elected.

> WILLIAM TECUMSEH SHERMAN, Telegram to General Henderson of Missouri, 5 June, 1884. This was in final reply to Henderson, who was at the Republican national convention in Chicago, urging Sherman to accept the nomination for President.

2

Let's look at the record.

> ALFRED E. SMITH, during the campaign of 1928 and thereafter.

3

Hello, my old potato.

> ALFRED E. SMITH, to Franklin D. Roosevelt, at the Democratic State Convention, Albany, 4 Oct., 1932. It was the first meeting of the pair after Roosevelt defeated Smith for the presidential nomination at the Democratic national convention in Chicago, 1 July, 1932 in a bitter contest. Smith later verified the quotation, after it had been denied that he spoke the words.

4

Let's talk sense to the American people.

> ADLAI E. STEVENSON, Speech upon accepting the nomination for the presidency, Democratic national convention in Chicago, 26 July, 1952.

5

Someone asked . . . how I felt, and I was reminded of a story that a fellow townsman of ours used to tell—Abraham Lincoln. They asked him how he felt once after an unsuccessful election. He said he felt like a little boy who has stubbed his toe in the dark. He said that he was too old to cry, but it hurt too much to laugh.

> ADLAI E. STEVENSON, Speech on election night, 5 Nov., 1952. The unsuccessful election about which Lincoln commented was that of 1862, when the Democrats made gains in Congress and captured important governorships.

6

Congressmen? In Washington they hitch horses to them.

> TIMOTHY D. (BIG TIM) SULLIVAN, of New York City, upon announcing his decision to retire from the House of Representatives and return to the New York State Senate.

7

I'm going to give 'em hell.

> HARRY S TRUMAN, just before embarking on his first major whistle-stop tour in Sept., 1948.

It was in 1948, and we were holding an enthusiastic meeting [in Seattle] when some man with a great big voice cried from the galleries, "Give 'em hell, Harry!" I told him at that time, and I have been repeating it ever since, that I have never deliberately given anybody hell. I just tell the truth on the opposition—and they think it's hell.

> HARRY S TRUMAN, *Mr. Citizen* (1960), p. 149.

H.S.T. "gave 'em hell" then [1948], but L.B.J. has turned it around. He's now giving them heaven.

> JAMES RESTON, Washington Column, New York *Times,* 9 Sept., 1964. Contrasting Harry S Truman's aggressive campaign tactics with the "Great Society" approach of Lyndon B. Johnson in the campaign of 1964.

8

Kitchen cabinet.

> HARRY S TRUMAN, who organized this mythical group composed of, among others, a Secretary for Inflation, Secretary of Reaction, Secretary for Columnists, and Secretary of Semantics ("to furnish me with 40- to 50-dollar words").

9

Polls are like sleeping pills designed to lull the voters into sleeping on election day. You might call them "sleeping polls."

> HARRY S TRUMAN, Speech in Cleveland, 26 Oct., 1948, during the presidential campaign. On election day Truman upset the pollsters' predictions by defeating Thomas E. Dewey.

Mr. Truman would love us if we could show him out in front. Nobody wants to be shown behind.

> GEORGE GALLUP, head of the American Institute of Public Opinion, replying to Harry S Truman in a statement issued in Princeton, N.J., 27 Oct., 1948.

10

I don't like Nixon and I never will. I don't want to even discuss him. He called me a traitor, and if I'm a traitor the United States is in a helluva shape.

> HARRY S TRUMAN, during the Congressional campaign of 1954, when Vice-President Nixon campaigned widely on the "soft on Communism" issue—though he denied having called Truman a traitor. (ALFRED STEINBERG, *The Man from Missouri,* p. 425)

1
They are trying to make an elder statesman of me but they will never succeed.
> HARRY S TRUMAN, *Mr. Citizen*, p. 181—in response to someone who wanted to know if Mr. Truman was in the process of mellowing in the 1960s.

2
To nominate Grover Cleveland would be to march through a slaughter house into an open grave.
> HENRY WATTERSON, Editorial, Louisville *Courier-Journal*, on the campaign of 1892.

3
Pitiless publicity.
> WOODROW WILSON, on how to cure the ills of government. (SULLIVAN, *Our Times*, vol. iv, p. 119)

4
The Copperhead Bright Convention meets in Indianapolis today.
> UNKNOWN, Cincinnati *Gazette*, 30 July, 1862. Referring to the Indiana Democratic convention—the first use, in print, of "copperhead" in a political sense.

5
The Whigs, whether on the Lexington platform or some other non-committal platform, will be and must be at once known as the party that opposed their country in her just and generous war.
> UNKNOWN, *Resolutions of the Democratic National Convention*, 30 May, 1844. This is the first known recorded use of "platform" in a political sense in America. (See New York *Herald*, 6 May, 1848)

6
Mugwump.
> Indianapolis *Sentinel*, 1872. This is thought to be the first use of the word in a political sense. "Mugwump" is of Algonquin Indian origin, and means "Big Chief."

A mugwump is a person educated beyond his intellect.
> HORACE PORTER, Speech in 1884, during the Cleveland-Blaine campaign. At that time the word signified a bolter from the Republican party; now it is applied to political independents in general.

A mugwump is one of those boys who always has his mug on one side of the political fence and his wump on the other.
> ALBERT J. ENGEL, Speech in the House of Representatives, 23 Apr., 1936. Also credited to Harold W. Dodds.

7
Mulligan letters.
> Letters supposed to show corruption on the part of JAMES G. BLAINE in railroad and land deals in 1869. They were used against him with telling effect in his campaign for the presidency against Cleveland.

XII—Campaign Slogans
(Arranged Chronologically)

8
Tippecanoe and Tyler too.
> Republican campaign slogan for the Harrison-Tyler Ticket of 1840, sometimes attributed to ORSON E. WOODBURY. "Tippecanoe" was William Henry Harrison, whose indecisive victory over the Indians in 1811 occurred at the place where Tippecanoe Creek empties into the Wabash.

9
Fifty-four forty, or fight!
> WILLIAM ALLEN, Speech in U.S. Senate, 1844. This was adopted as the slogan of the war party in the campaign of that year, when open conflict with England seemed imminent. The Democratic convention of 1844 demanded reoccupation of all of Oregon up to 54° 40′, by means of force, if necessary. However, James K. Polk, the newly elected President, reached a compromise settlement based on the forty-ninth parallel.

10
We stand for free soil.
> LEONARD BACON, Motto of the *Independent*, which he helped found in 1848, and which he edited.

11
Young America!
> Slogan of an important group of the Democratic party in the campaign of 1852. Origin of the phrase probably traces to an address by EDWIN DE LEON of Charleston, S.C., in 1845, advocating political power in the hands of young people.

12
Free soil, free men, free speech, Frémont.
> Republican slogan, campaign of 1856.

13
Peace at any price; peace and union.
> Slogan in the Fillmore campaign, 1856.

14
Turn the rascals out!
> CHARLES A. DANA, New York *Sun*. Used thereafter as the slogan of Greeley's campaign against Grant in 1872.

15
The crime of '76.
> Democratic description of the election of Rutherford B. Hayes. He was the victor, by one vote in the electoral college, over Samuel J. Tilden. The Democrats claimed fraud.

16
Hurrah for Maria,
Hurrah for the kid

I voted for Grover
And am damn glad I did.

> UNKNOWN, Campaign Song during the Cleveland-Blaine campaign of 1884. The reference was to Maria Halpin of Buffalo; according to campaign rumor, her child had been fathered by Cleveland, a bachelor.

1

Ma! ma! where's my Pa?
Up in the White House, darling,
Making the laws, working the cause,
Up in the White House, dear.

> H. R. MONROE, *Ma! Ma! Where's My Pa?* This ditty of 1884 dealt with the charge that Cleveland was the father of an illegitimate child. The Republicans adapted it in the form of a jingle: "Ma! Ma! Where's my pa? Gone to the White House. Ha! Ha! Ha!"

2

Blaine, Blaine, Blaine,
The continental liar from the State of Maine,
Burn this letter!

> UNKNOWN, Campaign Jingle used by the Democrats during the campaign of 1884. Blaine had written a letter to a business associate, Warren G. Fisher, and had endorsed on the back, "Burn this letter." The endorsement was taken as evidence that Blaine, the Republican candidate, had profited personally through a business transaction.

3

I do not engage in criminal practice.

> GEORGE WILLIAM CURTIS, when asked why he did not speak for Blaine during the campaign of 1884. (NEVINS, *Grover Cleveland*, p. 178) This statement also has been attributed to Roscoe Conkling, by Muzzy in his biography of Blaine (p. 307).

4

He's all right!

> Slogan of the Prohibitionists and their presidential candidate, John P. St. John, in 1884. He had been a Republican party leader. During the campaign the Republicans started the cry, "What's the matter with St. John?"; the reply, intended to be taken ironically, was "Oh, he's all right!" The Prohibitionists soon adopted it for their own purposes. The slogan has also been credited to Tony Pastor, who is said to have originated it in the New York mayoralty campaign of 1884.

5

As Maine goes, so goes the nation.

> UNKNOWN, political saying that gained currency after Benjamin Harrison's victory in 1888.

As Maine goes, so goes Vermont.

> JAMES A. FARLEY, Interview, 4 Nov., 1936, after the 46 other states had just landed in the Democratic column in the re-election of Franklin D. Roosevelt.

6

The crime of 1873.

> WILLIAM JENNINGS BRYAN, Speech in the U.S. House of Representatives, 12 Aug., 1892, referring to the adoption of the gold standard by the United States. Bryan was an advocate of the free and unlimited coinage of silver at a fixed ratio to gold.

7

Elect McKinley, the Advance Agent of Prosperity!

> Republican campaign slogan, 1896

8

If the American people want me for this high office, I shall be only too willing to serve them. . . . Since studying this subject I am convinced that the office of President is not such a very difficult one to fill.

> ADMIRAL GEORGE DEWEY, announcing his candidacy, 4 Apr., 1900.

9

The full dinner pail.

> Republican campaign slogan, 1900.

10

If elected, I shall see to it that every man has a square deal, no less and no more.

> THEODORE ROOSEVELT, Address, 4 Nov., 1904.

11

If it is reorganization, a new deal and a change you are seeking, it is Hobson's choice. I am sorry for you, but it is really vote for me or not vote at all.

> WOODROW WILSON, Address in Camden, N.J., 24 Oct., 1910—the first known use of "new deal" in a political address by a candidate for office.

12

The New Freedom.

> WOODROW WILSON, Slogan of his first presidential campaign. Grover Cleveland said of it: "Sounds fine—I wonder what it means."

13

He kept us out of war!

> MARTIN H. GLYNN, Keynote Speech, Democratic national convention, St. Louis, 15 June, 1916. The reference was to Woodrow Wilson, and the claim became the Democratic campaign slogan of that year's election.

14

Keep cool with Coolidge.

> Republican campaign slogan of 1924, inspired by Calvin Coolidge's unruffled demeanor.

1
A chicken in every pot, a car in every garage.

> Republican campaign slogan, 1928. Coined by the Republican national committee.

2
I pledge you, I pledge myself, to a new deal for the American people.

> FRANKLIN D. ROOSEVELT, Speech to the Democratic national convention, which had just nominated him as its presidential candidate, 3 June, 1932.

3
Dixiecrats.

> Name popularly applied to the Southern faction that seceded from the regular Democratic party in the 1948 campaign, in protest against the civil-rights plank in the regular Democratic platform. As the Dixiecrat, or States' Rights, party, it carried five Southern states in the election of that year.

4
Every segment of our population and every individual have a right to expect from our Government a fair deal.

> HARRY S TRUMAN, State of the Union Message, 5 Jan., 1949.

5
The Great Crusade.

> DWIGHT D. EISENHOWER, a phrase that became his campaign slogan in the election of 1952.

6
We stand today on the edge of a new frontier—the frontier of the 1960's—a frontier of unknown opportunities and perils—a frontier of unfulfilled hopes and threats.

> JOHN F. KENNEDY, Speech upon accepting the Democratic presidential nomination, 16 July, 1960.

7
The great society is not a safe harbor . . . The great society is a place where men are more concerned with the quality of their goals than the quantity of their goods.

> LYNDON B. JOHNSON, Speech at the University of Michigan, Ann Arbor, Mich., 22 May, 1964—his first use of "great society" as an identifying symbol of his administration.

This nation, this generation, in this hour has man's first chance to build the Great Society—a place where the meaning of man's life matches the marvels of man's labor.

> LYNDON B. JOHNSON, Speech upon accepting the Democratic presidential nomination, Atlantic City, N.J., 27 Aug., 1964.

POSSESSION

8
See how possession always cheapens the thing that was precious.

> WILLIAM DEAN HOWELLS, *Pordenone.*

9
Aspiration sees only one side of every question; possession, many.

> JAMES RUSSELL LOWELL, *Among My Books: New England Two Centuries Ago.*

10
No one worth possessing
Can be quite possessed.

> SARA TEASDALE, *Advice to a Girl.*

POSSESSIONS

See also Property, Riches

11
By right or wrong,
Lands and goods go to the strong,
Property will brutely draw
Still to the proprietor;
Silver to silver creep and wind,
And kind to kind.

> EMERSON, *The Celestial Love.*

12
Much will have more.

> EMERSON, *Society and Solitude: Works and Days.*

13
This, and this alone, I contend for—that he who makes should have; that he who saves should enjoy.

> HENRY GEORGE, *Social Problems,* ch. 9.

14
You give but little when you give of your possessions. It is when you give of yourself that you truly give.

> KAHLIL GIBRAN, *The Prophet: On Giving.*

15
I like to walk about amidst the beautiful things that adorn the world; but private wealth I should decline, or any sort of personal possessions, because they would take away my liberty.

> GEORGE SANTAYANA, *Soliloquies in England: The Irony of Liberalism.*

16
I am amused to see from my window here how busily man has divided and staked off his domain. God must smile at his puny fences running hither and thither everywhere over the land.

> HENRY D. THOREAU, *Journal,* 20 Feb., 1842.

17
Each person is born to one possession which outvalues all his others—his last breath.

> MARK TWAIN, *Following the Equator,* vol. ii, ch. 6.

POSTERITY

18
Think of your forefathers! Think of your posterity!

> JOHN QUINCY ADAMS, Speech in Plymouth, Mass., 22 Dec., 1802.

1
Yes, and you seem resolved to speak until the arrival of your audience.

HENRY CLAY, Reply to a Congressman who had just admonished Clay with these words: "You . . . speak for the present generation; but I speak for posterity." (EPES SARGENT, *Life of Henry Clay*)

2
The love of posterity is the consequence of the necessity of death. If a man were sure of living forever here, he would not care about his offspring.

NATHANIEL HAWTHORNE, *American Note Books.*

3
The most glorious hero that ever desolated nations might have mouldered into oblivion among the rubbish of his own monument, did not some historian take him into favor, and benevolently transmit his name to posterity.

WASHINGTON IRVING, *Knickerbocker's History of New York,* bk. v, ch. 1.

4
Few can be induced to labor exclusively for posterity. Posterity has done nothing for us.

ABRAHAM LINCOLN, Speech, 22 Feb., 1842.

5
When we are planning for posterity, we ought to remember that virtue is not hereditary.

THOMAS PAINE, *Common Sense,* ch. 4.

POVERTY

See also Want

6
There is no man so poor but what he can afford to keep one dog. And I have seen them so poor that they could afford to keep three.

JOSH BILLINGS, *On Poverty.*

7
Squeamishness was never yet bred in an empty pocket.

JAMES BRANCH CABELL, *The Cream of the Jest,* p. 86.

8
Over the hill to the poor-house I'm trudgin' my weary way.

WILL CARLETON, *Over the Hill to the Poorhouse.*

9
They who have nothing have little to fear, Nothing to lose or to gain.

MADISON CAWEIN, *The Bellman.*

10
Rich men never whistle, poor men always do.

STEPHEN B. ELKINS, Speech, 1906.

11
Poverty demoralizes.

EMERSON, *Conduct of Life: Wealth.*

12
Poverty consists in feeling poor.

EMERSON, *Society and Solitude: Domestic Life.*

I've never been poor, only broke. Being poor is a frame of mind. Being broke is only a temporary situation.

MICHAEL TODD. (*Newsweek,* 31 Mar., 1958)

13
The greatest man in history was the poorest.

EMERSON, *Society and Solitude: Domestic Life.*

14
Light purse, heavy heart.

BENJAMIN FRANKLIN, *Poor Richard,* 1733.

15
For one poor Man there are an hundred indigent.

BENJAMIN FRANKLIN, *Poor Richard,* 1746.

16
We in America today are nearer to the final triumph over poverty than ever before in the history of any land. The poorhouse is vanishing from among us.

HERBERT HOOVER, Speech, 11 Aug., 1928, upon accepting the Republican nomination for the presidency.

17
A child born in poverty is likely to become a slow learner, possibly illiterate, a school dropout, a delinquent, perhaps a criminal. He is likely to live miserably and die young, leaving no legacy but offspring destined for the same fate.

HUBERT H. HUMPHREY, Speech in Washington, D.C., 10 Feb., 1965.

18
The prevalent fear of poverty among the educated classes is the worst moral disease from which our civilization suffers.

WILLIAM JAMES, *Varieties of Religious Experience,* p. 370.

19
This Administration here and now declares unconditional war on poverty in America.

LYNDON B. JOHNSON, State of the Union Message, 8 Jan., 1964.

20
Let us, above all, open wide the exits from poverty to the children of the poor.

LYNDON B. JOHNSON, Economic Report to Congress, 20 Jan., 1964.

21
I think we must have not just a war on poverty but we must have a war on waste.

LYNDON B. JOHNSON, Speech to Internal Revenue Service field officials, 11 Feb., 1964, Washington, D.C.

22
The wall between rich and poor is a wall of glass through which all can see.

LYNDON B. JOHNSON, Speech at Associated

Press luncheon, New York City, 20 Apr., 1964.

1

Poverty has many roots but the tap root is ignorance.

LYNDON B. JOHNSON, Message to Congress, on education, 12 Jan., 1965.

2

If a free society cannot help the many who are poor, it cannot save the few who are rich.

JOHN F. KENNEDY, Inaugural Address, 20 Jan., 1961.

3

There is inherited wealth in this country and also inherited poverty.

JOHN F. KENNEDY, Address at Amherst College, Amherst, Mass., 26 Oct., 1963.

4

There is nothing perfectly secure but poverty.

HENRY WADSWORTH LONGFELLOW, *Final Memorials:* Letter, 13 Nov., 1872.

5

The Little Sister of the Poor . . .
The Poor, and their concerns, she has
Monopolized, because of which
It falls to me to labor as
A Little Brother of the Rich.

E. S. MARTIN, *A Little Brother of the Rich.*

6

Poverty is a soft pedal upon all branches of human activity, not excepting the spiritual.

H. L. MENCKEN, *A Book of Prefaces,* ch. 4.

7

Poverty may be an unescapable misfortune, but that no more makes it honorable than a cocked eye is made honorable by the same cause.

H. L. MENCKEN, *Prejudices,* ser. iii, p. 17.

8

We shall never solve the paradox of want in the midst of plenty by doing away with plenty.

OGDEN MILLS, Speech in New York City, 21 Mar., 1934.

9

Wealth is conspicuous, but poverty hides.

JAMES RESTON, Column, New York *Times,* 8 May, 1964.

10

I see one-third of a nation ill-housed, ill-clad, and ill-nourished.

FRANKLIN D. ROOSEVELT, Inaugural Address, 20 Jan., 1937.

11

The awful phantom of the hungry poor.

HARRIET PRESCOTT SPOFFORD, *A Winter's Night.*

12

America's noblest destiny is not empire. It is to demonstrate the possibility of conquering poverty and keeping freedom in a land at peace.

NORMAN THOMAS, Speech broadcast nationally from New York City, 29 June, 1941.

13

Cultivate poverty like a garden herb, sage.

HENRY D. THOREAU, *Walden:* conclusion.

14

The town's poor seem to me often to live the most independent lives of any.

HENRY D. THOREAU, *Walden:* conclusion.

15

He is now fast rising from affluence to poverty.

MARK TWAIN, *Henry Ward Beecher's Farm.*

16

Happy must be the State
Whose ruler heedeth more
The murmurs of the poor
Than flatteries of the great.

JOHN GREENLEAF WHITTIER, *King Solomon and the Ants.*

17

I know how to be rich and still enjoy all the little comforts of poverty.

HARRY LEON WILSON, *The Spenders,* p. 24.

POWER

18

I am more and more convinced that man is a dangerous creature; and that power, whether vested in many or a few, is ever grasping, and like the grave, cries "Give, give!"

ABIGAIL ADAMS, Letter to her husband, John Adams, 27 Nov., 1775.

19

Power is poison.

HENRY ADAMS, *The Education of Henry Adams,* ch. 28.

20

Those who seek education in the paths of duty are always deceived by the illusion that power in the hands of friends is an advantage to them.

HENRY ADAMS, *The Education of Henry Adams,* ch. 28.

21

There is always room for a man of force, and he makes room for many.

EMERSON, *Conduct of Life: Power.*

22

You shall have joy, or you shall have power, said God; you shall not have both.

EMERSON, *Journals,* vol. vi, p. 282.

23

The love of power may be as dominant in the heart of a peasant as of a prince.

J. T. HEADLEY, *Miscellanies: Alison's History of Europe.*

24

Power flows to the man who knows how.

ELBERT HUBBARD, *The Philistine,* vol. xi, p. 50.

1

I have never been able to conceive how any rational being could propose happiness to himself from the exercise of power over others.

THOMAS JEFFERSON, *Writings,* vol. xiii, p. 18.

2

Power is where power goes.

LYNDON B. JOHNSON, in 1960, after he had lost the Democratic presidential nomination to John F. Kennedy, and was considering whether to accept second place on the ticket if such an offer was made. This was said to be his reply to an adviser who remarked that, as Vice-President, Johnson would have less power than he wielded as Senate majority leader. (HENRY A. ZEIGER, *Lyndon B. Johnson: Man and President,* p. 87)

3

All that I have I would have given gladly not to be standing here today.

LYNDON B. JOHNSON, Speech before a joint session of Congress, 27 Nov., 1963. These were the opening words of his first major speech as President, delivered five days after the assassination of John F. Kennedy.

4

We often say how impressive power is. But I do not find it impressive at all. The guns and the bombs, the rockets and the warships, are all symbols of human failure. They are necessary symbols. They protect what we cherish. But they are witness to human folly.

LYNDON B. JOHNSON, Address at Johns Hopkins University, Baltimore, 7 Apr., 1965.

5

The Robber Barons.

MATHEW JOSEPHSON, Title of book, dealing with the Rockefellers, Morgans, Vanderbilts, and the like.

6

In the past, those who foolishly sought power by riding the back of the tiger ended up inside.

JOHN F. KENNEDY, Inaugural Address, 20 Jan., 1961.

7

The first principle of a civilized state is that power is legitimate only when it is under contract. Then it is, as we say, duly constituted.

WALTER LIPPMANN, *The Public Philosophy,* bk. ii, ch. 11.

8

He who is firmly seated in authority soon learns to think security, and not progress, the highest lesson of statecraft.

JAMES RUSSELL LOWELL, *Among My Books: New England Two Centuries Ago.*

9

From the summit of power men no longer turn their eyes upward, but begin to look about them.

JAMES RUSSELL LOWELL, *Among My Books: New England Two Centuries Ago.*

10

Power is ever stealing from the many to the few.

WENDELL PHILLIPS, Address: *Public Opinion,* Boston, 28 Jan., 1852.

11

You know there will be some people around you who will try to build a wall around you. They have never been so close to the seat of power and they'll want this position for themselves.

SAM RAYBURN, to Harry S Truman, shortly after the ceremony by which Truman was sworn in as President in 1945. Quoted by Lyndon B. Johnson in a discussion with a group of Senators shortly after Johnson became President. (HENRY A. ZEIGER, *Lyndon B. Johnson: Man and President,* p. 112)

12

The Presidency is mysterious because it is formidable; mystery is inherent in power.

RICHARD H. ROVERE, *The Loneliest Place in the World; American Heritage,* Aug., 1964.

13

Boys, if you ever pray, pray for me now. I don't know whether you fellows ever had a load of hay fall on you, but when they told me yesterday what had happened, I felt like the moon, the stars, and all the planets had fallen on me.

HARRY S TRUMAN, on his first full day in office as President, during a conversation with newspapermen.

14

There must be, not a balance of power, but a community of power; not organized rivalries, but an organized common peace.

WOODROW WILSON, Address to U.S. Senate, 22 Jan., 1917.

PRAISE

See also Flattery

15

History will hold his finest eulogy.

GEORGE D. AIKEN, Speech in U.S. Senate, 11 Dec., 1963—one of a series of tributes to John F. Kennedy.

16

Be quick to praise. People like to praise those who praise them.

BERNARD M. BARUCH. (St. Louis *Post-Dispatch,* 21 June, 1965, p. 5A)

17

Applause: the echo of a platitude.

AMBROSE BIERCE, *The Devil's Dictionary,* p. 25.

1

We thirst for approbation, yet cannot forgive the approver.

EMERSON, *Essays, First Series: Circles.*

2

The silence that accepts merit as the most natural thing in the world, is the highest applause.

EMERSON, *Nature, Addresses, and Lectures:* Address, 15 July, 1838.

3

Let me praise a little more.

EDGAR A. GUEST, *A Creed.*

4

Don't strew me with roses after I'm dead.
When Death claims the light of my brow,
No flowers of life will cheer me: instead
You may give me my roses now!

THOMAS F. HEALEY, *Give Me My Roses Now.*

A rose to the living is more
Than sumptuous wreaths to the dead.

NIXON WATERMAN, *A Rose to the Living.*

5

Sweet is the scene where genial friendship plays
The pleasing game of interchanging praise.

OLIVER WENDELL HOLMES, *An After Dinner Poem.*

6

We are apt to love praise, but not to deserve it. But if we would deserve it, we must love virtue more than that.

WILLIAM PENN, *Fruits of Solitude.*

7

And so I charge ye, by the thorny crown,
And by the cross on which the Saviour bled,
And by your own soul's hope of fair renown,
Let something good be said.

JAMES WHITCOMB RILEY, *Let Something Good Be Said.*

8

I can live for two months on a good compliment.

MARK TWAIN. (PAINE, *Mark Twain*)

PRAYER

See also Sleep

9

Comin' In on a Wing and a Prayer.

HAROLD ADAMSON, Title of song (1943) popular during World War II.

10

O, do not pray for easy lives. Pray to be stronger men. Do not pray for tasks equal to your powers. Pray for powers equal to your tasks.

PHILLIPS BROOKS, *Going Up to Jerusalem.* (*Visions and Tasks,* p. 330)

11

Prayer is the little implement
Through which men reach

Where presence is denied them.

EMILY DICKINSON, *Poems,* Pt. i, No. 80.

12

The highest prayer is not one of faith merely; it is demonstration. Such prayer heals sickness, and must destroy sin and death.

MARY BAKER EDDY, *Science and Health,* p. 16.

13

What we seek we shall find; what we flee from flees from us; . . . and hence the high caution, that, since we are sure of having what we wish, we beware to ask only for high things.

EMERSON, *Conduct of Life: Fate.*

14

Prayer that craves a particular commodity, anything less than all good, is vicious. . . . Prayer as a means to a private end is meanness and theft.

EMERSON, *Essays, First Series: Self-Reliance.*

15

The prayer of the farmer kneeling in his field to weed it, the prayer of the rower kneeling with the stroke of his oar, are true prayers heard throughout nature.

EMERSON, *Essays, First Series: Self-Reliance.*

16

No man ever prayed heartily without learning something.

EMERSON, *Miscellanies: Nature.*

17

You pray in your distress and in your need: would that you might pray also in the fullness of your joy and in your days of abundance.

KAHLIL GIBRAN, *The Prophet: On Prayer*

18

And, when I pray, my heart is in my prayer.

HENRY WADSWORTH LONGFELLOW, *Giles Corey,* act ii, sc. 3.

19

Let our unceasing, earnest prayer
Be, too, for light,—for strength to bear
Our portion of the weight of care,
That crushes into dumb despair
One half the human race.

HENRY WADSWORTH LONGFELLOW, *The Goblet of Life,* st. 10.

20

Lord, help me live from day to day
In such a self-forgetful way,
That even when I kneel to pray,
My prayer shall be for—*others*.

CHARLES D. MEIGS, *Others.*

21

Making their lives a prayer.

JOHN GREENLEAF WHITTIER, *To A.K. on Receiving a Basket of Sea Mosses.*

22

Though smooth be the heartless prayer, no ear in heaven will mind it;

And the finest phrase falls dead, if there is
   no feeling behind it.
   ELLA WHEELER WILCOX, *Art and Heart.*

PREACHER AND PREACHING

1
God preaches,—a noted clergyman,—
   And the sermon is never long;
So instead of getting to heaven at last,
   I'm going all along!
   EMILY DICKINSON, *Poems,* Pt. ii, No. 57.

2
Alas for the unhappy man that is called to
stand in the pulpit, and *not* give the bread of
life.
   EMERSON, Address to the Senior Class,
      Divinity College, Cambridge, 15 July,
      1838.

3
I like the silent church before the service
begins, better than any preaching.
   EMERSON, *Essays, First Series: Self-Reli-*
      ance.

4
Great sermons lead the people to praise the
preacher. Good preaching leads the people to
praise the Saviour.
   CHARLES G. FINNEY, *Autobiography,* p.
      72.

5
None preaches better than the ant, and she
says nothing.
   BENJAMIN FRANKLIN, *Poor Richard,*
      1736.

6
When knaves fall out, honest men get their
goods; when priests dispute, we come at the
truth.
   BENJAMIN FRANKLIN, *Poor Richard,*
      1742.

7
A good example is the best sermon.
   BENJAMIN FRANKLIN, *Poor Richard,*
      1747.

8
The best of all the preachers are the men
   who live their creeds.
   EDGAR A. GUEST, *Sermons We See.*

9
In every country and in every age, the priest
has been hostile to liberty. He is always in
alliance with the despot, abetting his abuses
in return for protection to his own.
   THOMAS JEFFERSON, *Writings,* vol. xiv, p.
      119.

10
As pleasant songs, at morning sung,
The words that dropped from his sweet
   tongue
Strengthened our hearts; or, heard at night,
Made all our slumbers soft and light.
   HENRY WADSWORTH LONGFELLOW, *The*
      Golden Legend, pt. i.

11
Skilful alike with tongue and pen,

He preached to all men everywhere
The Gospel of the Golden Rule,
The New Commandment given to men,
Thinking the deed, and not the creed,
Would help us in our utmost need.
   HENRY WADSWORTH LONGFELLOW, *Tales*
      of a Wayside Inn: Prelude, l. 217.

12
Only the sinner has a right to preach.
   CHRISTOPHER MORLEY, *Tolerance,* p. 863.

13
Parson's coming up the hill,
   Meaning mighty well:
Thinks he's preached the doubters down.
   And old men never tell.
   JOHN CROWE RANSOM, *Under the Locusts.*

14
God's true priest is always free;
Free, the needed truth to speak,
Right the wronged, and raise the weak.
   JOHN GREENLEAF WHITTIER, *The Curse of*
      the Charter-Breakers.

PREJUDICE

15
A prejudice is a vagrant opinion without vis-
ible means of support.
   AMBROSE BIERCE, *The Devil's Dictionary.*

16
A system-grinder hates the truth.
   EMERSON, *Journals,* vol. iii, p. 523.

17
How many a useless stone we find
Swallowed in that capacious blind
Faith-swollen gullet, our ancestral mind.
   CHARLOTTE PERKINS GILMAN, *Forerunner.*

18
Prejudice, which sees what it pleases, cannot
see what is plain.
   NICHOLAS DEB. KATZENBACH, Address to
      the Federal Bar Association, Washing-
      ton, D.C., 18 Sept., 1964.

19
One may no more live in the world without
picking up the moral prejudices of the world
than one will be able to go to hell without
perspiring.
   H. L. MENCKEN, *Prejudices,* ser. ii, p.
      174.

20
There is nothing stronger than human preju-
dice.
   WENDELL PHILLIPS, Speech, 28 Jan.,
      1852.

21
Ignorance is stubborn and prejudice dies
hard.
   ADLAI E. STEVENSON, Address at the Unit-
      ed Nations, 1 Oct., 1963. This was a
      major U.S. policy statement on progress
      in eliminating racial discrimination.

22
It is never too late to give up our preju-
dices.
   HENRY D. THOREAU, *Walden,* ch. 1.

PREPAREDNESS

See also America, Peace, War

1
Before a country is ready to relinquish any winning weapon, it must have more than words to reassure it.

> BERNARD M. BARUCH. (New York *Times* obituary of Baruch, 21 June, 1965, p. 16)

2
No nation ever had an army large enough to guarantee it against attack in time of peace or insure it victory in time of war.

> CALVIN COOLIDGE, Address, 6 Oct., 1925.

3
Look at the hand. Each finger is not of itself a very good instrument for either defense or offense. But close it in a fist and it can become a very formidable weapon to defense.

> DWIGHT D. EISENHOWER, Address to North Atlantic Council, 2 Apr., 1959.

4
Forewarned, forearmed.

> BENJAMIN FRANKLIN, *Poor Richard,* 1736, paraphrasing CERVANTES in *Don Quixote.*

5
The good sense of the people will always be found to be the best army.

> THOMAS JEFFERSON, *Writings,* vol. vi, p. 55.

6
To aim at such a navy as the greater European nations possess would be a foolish and wicked waste of the energies of our countrymen. It would be to pull on our own heads that load of military expense which makes the European laborer go supperless to bed.

> THOMAS JEFFERSON, *Writings,* vol. vii, p. 241.

7
I have spent my life getting ready for this moment.

> LYNDON B. JOHNSON, to his hill country neighbors in Texas, 2 Nov., 1964, while he was home, awaiting the outcome of the presidential election, held the following day.

8
We have learned at a terrible and brutal cost that retreat does not bring safety and weakness does not bring peace.

> LYNDON B. JOHNSON, Press Conference in Washington, D.C., 28 July, 1965.

9
Ef you want peace, the thing you've gut to du
Is jes' to show you're up to fightin', tu.

> JAMES RUSSELL LOWELL, *The Biglow Papers,* Ser. ii, No. 2.

10
God, give us Peace! not such as lulls to sleep,
But sword on thigh and brow with purpose knit!

And let our Ship of State to harbor sweep,
Her ports all up, her battle-lanterns lit,
And her leashed thunders gathering for their leap.

> JAMES RUSSELL LOWELL, *The Washers of the Shroud.*

11
For all your days prepare,
And meet them all alike:
When you are the anvil, bear—
When you are the hammer, strike.

> EDWIN MARKHAM, *Preparedness.*

12
There is no record in history of a nation that ever gained anything valuable by being unable to defend itself.

> H. L. MENCKEN, *Prejudices,* ser. v. p. 33.

13
There is a homely adage which runs, "Speak softly and carry a big stick; you will go far."

> THEODORE ROOSEVELT, Speech, Minnesota State Fair, 2 Sept., 1901. The origin of the adage he quoted is uncertain.

14
Broomstick preparedness.

> THEODORE ROOSEVELT, *The Great Adventure.*

15
Peace the offspring is of Power.

> BAYARD TAYLOR, *A Thousand Years.*

16
"Thrice is he armed that hath his quarrel just"—
And four times he who gets his fist in fust.

> ARTEMUS WARD, *Shakespeare Up-to-Date.*

17
To be prepared for war is one of the most effectual means of preserving peace.

> GEORGE WASHINGTON, Address to Congress, 8 Jan., 1790. Theodore Roosevelt later misquoted Washington in an address at the University of Pennsylvania: "To be prepared for war is the most effective means to promote peace."

PRESENT, THE

See also Life, Past, Time

18
It isn't the experience of today that drives men mad. It is the remorse for something that happened yesterday, and the dread of what tomorrow may disclose.

> ROBERT J. BURDETTE, *The Golden Day.*

19
To those leaning on the sustaining infinite, today is big with blessings.

> MARY BAKER EDDY, *Science and Health:* Preface, p. vii.

20
Those who live to the future must always appear selfish to those who live to the present.

> EMERSON, *Essays, Second Series: Character.*

1
This passing moment is an edifice
Which the Omnipotent cannot rebuild.
    EMERSON, *Life.*

2
An everlasting Now reigns in nature, which
hangs the same roses on our bushes which
charmed the Roman and the Chaldean in
their hanging gardens.
    EMERSON, *Society and Solitude: Works
    and Days.*

3
One to-day is worth two to-morrows.
    BENJAMIN FRANKLIN, *Poor Richard,*
    1758.

4
The present is the necessary product of all
the past, the necessary cause of all the future.
    ROBERT G. INGERSOLL, *What Is Religion?*

5
Our to-days and yesterdays
Are the blocks with which we build.
    HENRY WADSWORTH LONGFELLOW, *The
    Builders,* st. 3.

6
Build to-day, then, strong and sure,
    With a firm and ample base;
And ascending and secure
    Shall to-morrow find its place.
    HENRY WADSWORTH LONGFELLOW, *The
    Builders,* st. 8.

7
Trust no Future, howe'er pleasant!
    Let the dead Past bury its dead!
Act,—act in the living Present!
    Heart within, and God o'erhead!
    HENRY WADSWORTH LONGFELLOW, *A
    Psalm of Life.*

8
We're curus critters: Now ain't jes' the min-
    ute
Thet ever fits us easy while we're in it;
    Long ez 'twus futur', 'twould be perfect
    bliss—
Soon ez it's past, *thet* time's wuth ten o'
    this;
An' yit there ain't a man thet need be told
Thet Now's the only bird lays eggs o' gold.
    JAMES RUSSELL LOWELL, *The Biglow Pa-
    pers,* Ser. ii, No. 6.

9
The future works out geat men's purposes;
The present is enough for common souls,
Who, never looking forward, are indeed
Mere clay, wherein the footprints of their
    age
Are petrified forever.
    JAMES RUSSELL LOWELL, *A Glance Behind
    the Curtain,* st. 6.

10
The Present, the Present is all thou hast
    For thy sure possessing;
Like the patriarch's angel hold it fast

Till it gives its blessing.
    JOHN GREENLEAF WHITTIER, *My Soul and
    I,* st. 34.

PRESS, THE
See also News

11
Newspapers are the schoolmasters of the
common people. That endless book, the
newspaper, is our national glory.
    HENRY WARD BEECHER, *Proverbs from
    Plymouth Pulpit: The Press.*

12
Harmony seldom makes a headline.
    SILAS BENT, *Strange Bedfellows,* p. 179.

13
Whatever else one may say about the newspaper business, self-examination is one of its
virtues. Searching questions about right conduct or wrong conduct are put whenever
journalists gather.
    MARQUIS W. CHILDS, Article, St. Louis
    Post-Dispatch, 25 May, 1965, p. 1-B.

14
Old, old man, it is the wisdom of the age.
    STEPHEN CRANE, *The Black Riders,* No.
    xi.

15
What is the newspaper but a sponge or invention for oblivion?
    EMERSON, *Natural History of Intellect:
    Memory.*

16
The newspaper, which does its best to make
every square acre of land and sea give an
account of itself at your breakfast-table.
    EMERSON, *Society and Solitude: Works
    and Days.*

17
I won't say that the papers misquote me, but
I sometimes wonder where Christianity
would be today if some of those reporters
had been Matthew, Mark, Luke and John.
    BARRY M. GOLDWATER, Speech in Wash-
    ington, D.C., 10 Aug., 1964. During the
    presidential campaign of that year, it
    was the Republican candidate, Goldwa-
    ter, who charged hostile press treat-
    ment; during the F. D. Roosevelt, Tru-
    man, and Eisenhower administrations,
    the Democrats frequently complained of
    a "one-party press"—that is, a pro-Re-
    publican press. (See the Stevenson quo-
    tation in this section.)

The Senator might remember that the evangelists had a more inspiring subject.
    WALTER LIPPMANN, Syndicated Column,
    13 Aug., 1964, replying to Barry M. Gold-
    water's speech attacking the press.

18
Then hail to the Press! chosen guardian of
    freedom!

Strong sword-arm of justice! bright sunbeam
  of truth!
  HORACE GREELEY, *The Press.*

1

Were it left to me to decide whether we
should have a government without newspapers, or newspapers without a government, I
should not hesitate a moment to prefer the
latter.
  THOMAS JEFFERSON, *Writings,* vol. vi, p.
    55.

2

No government ought to be without censors;
and where the press is free none ever will.
  THOMAS JEFFERSON, *Writings,* vol. viii, p.
    406.

3

The man who never looks into a newspaper
is better informed than he who reads them,
inasmuch as he who knows nothing is nearer
the truth than he whose mind is filled with
falsehoods and errors.
  THOMAS JEFFERSON, *Writings,* vol. xi, p.
    224.

4

Perhaps an editor might . . . divide his paper into four chapters, heading the first,
Truths; 2d, Probabilities; 3d, Possibilities;
4, Lies.
  THOMAS JEFFERSON, *Writings,* vol. xi, p.
    224.

5

When the press is free and every man able to
read, all is safe.
  THOMAS JEFFERSON, *Writings,* vol. xiv, p.
    382.

6

The Wayward Press.
  A. J. LIEBLING, Title of a series of articles,
    dealing with the shortcomings of Ameri-
    can newspapers (and especially those of
    New York City), which appeared regu-
    larly in *The New Yorker* during the
    years after World War II. A book by
    Liebling, *The Wayward Pressman,* de-
    voted to the same subject, was pub-
    lished in 1947.

7

People everywhere confuse
What they read in newspapers with news.
  A. J. LIEBLING, *A Talkative Something or
    Other; The New Yorker,* 7 Apr., 1956,
    p. 154.

8

A press monopoly is incompatible with a free
press; and one can proceed with this principle: if there is a monopoly of the means of
communications—of radio, television, magazines, books, public meetings—it follows that
this society is by definition and in fact deprived of freedom.
  WALTER LIPPMANN, Syndicated Column,
    27 May, 1965 (part of an address to the
    International Press Institute in London
    on that date).

9

A free press is not a privilege but an organic
necessity in a great society. Without criticism and reliable and intelligent reporting,
the government cannot govern. For there is
no adequate way in which it can keep itself
informed about what the people of the country are thinking and doing and wanting.
  WALTER LIPPMANN, Syndicated Column,
    27 May, 1965 (part of an address to the
    International Press Institute in London
    on that date).

10

The paramount point is whether, like a sci-
entist or a scholar, the journalist puts truth
in the first place or in the second. If he puts
it in the second place, he is a worshiper of
the bitch goddess Success. Or he is a conceit-
ed man trying to win an argument. Insofar as
he puts truth in the first place, he rises toward—I will not say into, but toward—the
company of those who taste and enjoy the
best things in life.
  WALTER LIPPMAN, Syndicated Column, 27
    May, 1965 (part of an address to the
    International Press Institute on that
    date).

11

Behold the whole huge earth sent to me heb-
domadally in a brown-paper wrapper!
  JAMES RUSSELL LOWELL, *The Biglow Pa-
    pers,* Ser. i, No. 6.

12

All successful newspapers are ceaselessly
querulous and bellicose. They never defend
anyone or anything if they can help it; if the
job is forced upon them, they tackle it by
denouncing someone or something else.
  H. L. MENCKEN, *Prejudices,* ser. i, ch. 13.

13

I have always thought that I would like to
be a newspaperman myself, because I love
the classics and I love good literature.
  JOHN P. O'BRIEN, Speech to a group of
    journalists, in 1933, when he was mayor
    of New York City.

14

We live under a government of men and
morning newspapers.
  WENDELL PHILLIPS, Address: *The Press.*

15

I know that . . . it will always fight for
progress and reform, never tolerate injustice
or corruption, always fight demagogues of all
parties, never belong to any party, always
oppose privileged classes and public plunder-
ers, never lack sympathy with the poor, always remain devoted to the public welfare,
never be satisfied with merely printing news,
always be drastically independent, never be

afraid to attack wrong, whether by predatory plutocracy or predatory poverty.

> JOSEPH PULITZER, Statement, 10 Apr., 1907—the platform of the St. Louis *Post-Dispatch.*

1

News value.

> JULIAN RALPH, Phrase coined in 1892, in a talk to students of Brander Matthews' class in English at Columbia University. (THOMAS BEER, *The Mauve Decade*)

2

All I know is what I read in the papers.

> WILL ROGERS, Remark that occurred often in his humorous lectures and stage monologues.

3

[I am] considerably concerned when I see the extent to which we are developing a one-party press in a two-party country.

> ADLAI E. STEVENSON, Speech in Portland, Ore., during the 1952 presidential campaign.

4

Here shall the Press the People's right maintain,
Unawed by influence and unbribed by gain;
Here patriot Truth her glorious precepts draw,
Pledged to Religion, Liberty, and Law.

> JOSEPH STORY, Motto of the Salem *Register*, adopted in 1802. (STORY, *Life of Joseph Story*, vol. i, ch. 6)

5

We tell the public which way the cat is jumping. The public will take care of the cat.

> ARTHUR HAYS SULZBERGER, of the New York *Times*. (*Time*, 8 May, 1950)

6

Blessed are they who never read a newspaper, for they shall see Nature, and, through her, God.

> HENRY D. THOREAU, *Essays and Other Writings*, p. 254.

7

This "Present" book, indeed, is blue, but the hue of its thought is yellow.

> HENRY D. THOREAU, *Familiar Letters.*

8

It is time for scientists, alienists, and psychological investigators to make a careful study of the Yellow literary atmosphere.

> CHARLES DUDLEY WARNER, *The Yellows in Literature; Harper's Magazine*, vol. xc, p. 481.

9

"Yellow journalism" traces its origin to these comics of the Hearst and Pulitzer newspapers, a phrase credited to Ervin Wardman, who, before he died in January, 1923, was publisher of Munsey's *Herald.*

> JOHN K. WINKLER, *W. R. Hearst*, p. 110.

Dick Outcault, the cartoonist of the *New York World,* evolved his "Yellow Kid" cartoons, and the urchin in the yellow gabardine, purchased by the Hearst interests, had taken New York's fancy. *The Press,* in duty bound, was whanging away at the Hearst sensationalism and vulgarity, when one dull day it occurred to me that our shopworn tag of "The New Journalism" could be improved upon, and I put all the vitriol of my nature into an editorial which I captioned "Yellow Kid Journalism." When the galleys came up from the pressroom the caption proved to be two letters too long for the column, and having no time to frame another, I struck out the middle word. Thus by sheer accident was created the phrase "Yellow Journalism."

> POST WHEELER, *Dome of Many-Coloured Glass*, p. 97 (2 Feb., 1896).

10

For forty years he has carried out, rather literally, the dictum of Mr. Dooley that the mission of a modern newspaper is to "comfort the afflicted and afflict the comfortable."

> JOHN K. WINKLER, *W. R. Hearst*, p. 12.

PRICE
See also Worth

11

You cannot make a cheap palace.

> EMERSON, *Journals*, 1857.

12

Wisdom is never dear, provided the article be genuine.

> HORACE GREELEY, Address in Houston, 23 May, 1871.

13

Never buy what you do not want because it is cheap; it will be dear to you.

> THOMAS JEFFERSON, *Writings,* vol. xvi, p. 111.

14

Earth gets its price for what Earth gives us.

> JAMES RUSSELL LOWELL, *The Vision of Sir Launfal:* pt. i. prelude.

15

What we obtain too cheaply we esteem too lightly; it is dearness only which gives everything its value.

> THOMAS PAINE, *The Crisis:* introduction.

PRIDE
See also Self-Respect, Vanity

16

Pride is handsome, economical; pride eradicates so many vices, letting none subsist but itself, that it seems as if it were a great gain to exchange vanity for pride. . . . Only one drawback: proud people are intolerably selfish, and the vain are gentle and giving.

> EMERSON, *Essays: Conduct of Life.*

1
Pride breakfasted with Plenty, dined with Poverty, supped with Infamy.
> BENJAMIN FRANKLIN, *Poor Richard,* 1757.

2
There is no pride on earth like the pride of intellect and science.
> ROSWELL D. HITCHCOCK, *Eternal Atonement: Secret Things of God.*

3
Wounded vanity knows when it is mortally hurt; and limps off the field, piteous, all disguises thrown away. But pride carries its banner to the last.
> HELEN HUNT JACKSON, *Ramona,* ch. 13.

4
Pride costs us more than hunger, thirst, and cold.
> THOMAS JEFFERSON, *Writings,* vol. xvi, p. 111.

5
If the President gets out of his car and talks to a colored boy in New Orleans, or a widow woman in Kentucky, or a banker in New England, they feel pretty important. It's good for their morale, and this is an important part of democracy.
> LYNDON B. JOHNSON, to Jack Dempsey, in Reno, Nev., 12 Oct., 1964, during the presidential campaign. Dempsey expressed concern about the President's practice of mingling with street crowds; Johnson gave this explanation.

6
Pride goeth forth on horseback grand and gay,
But cometh back on foot, and begs its way.
> HENRY WADSWORTH LONGFELLOW, *The Bell of Atri,* st. 6.

7
The passions grafted on wounded pride are the most inveterate; they are green and vigorous in old age.
> GEORGE SANTAYANA, *Little Essays,* p. 22.

8
Your true pilot cares nothing about anything on earth but the river, and his pride in his occupation surpasses the pride of kings.
> MARK TWAIN, *Life on the Mississippi,* ch. 7.

PRINCIPLE

9
We must be willing, individually and as a nation, to accept whatever sacrifices may be required of us. A people that values its privileges above its principles soon loses both.
> DWIGHT D. EISENHOWER, First Inaugural Address, 20 Jan., 1953.

10
We may be personally defeated, but our principles never.
> WILLIAM LLOYD GARRISON. (W. P. GAR-

RISON AND F. J. T. GARRISON, *William Lloyd Garrison,* vol. i)

11
When a fellow says it hain't the money but the principle o' the thing, it's th' money.
> KIN HUBBARD, *Hoss Sense and Nonsense.*

12
Every difference of opinion is not a difference of principle.
> THOMAS JEFFERSON, First Inaugural Address, 4 Mar., 1801.

13
Important principles may and must be inflexible.
> ABRAHAM LINCOLN, Address in Washington, D.C., 11 Apr., 1865.

14
I *don't* believe in princerple,
But, oh, I *du* in interest!
> JAMES RUSSELL LOWELL, *The Biglow Papers,* Ser. i, No. 6.

15
Ez to my princerples, I glory
In hevin' nothin' o' the sort.
> JAMES RUSSELL LOWELL, *The Biglow Papers,* Ser. i, No. 7.

16
It is often easier to fight for principles than to live up to them.
> ADLAI E. STEVENSON, Speech in New York City, 27 Aug., 1952.

PRIVACY, see Solitude
PROCRASTINATION
See also Delay

17
Stay with the Procession or you will Never Catch up.
> GEORGE ADE, *Forty Modern Fables: The Old-Time Pedagogue.*

18
Never leave that till to-morrow which you can do to-day.
> BENJAMIN FRANKLIN, *Poor Richard,* 1757.

There is a maxim, "Never put off till to-morrow what you can do to-day." It is a maxim for sluggards. A better reading of it is, "Never do to-day what you can as well do to-morrow," because something may occur to make you regret your premature action.
> AARON BURR. (PARTON, *Life of Aaron Burr,* p. 150)

Never put off until Tomorrow what should have been Done early in the Seventies.
> GEORGE ADE, *Forty Modern Fables: The Third and Last Call.*

19
procrastination is the
art of keeping
up with yesterday
> DON MARQUIS, *certain maxims of archy.*

PROGRESS

1

It is the darling delusion of mankind that the world is progressive in religion, toleration, freedom, as it is progressive in machinery.

    MONCURE D. CONWAY, *Dogma and Science.*

2

So long as all the increased wealth which modern progress brings, goes but to build up great fortunes, to increase luxury, and make sharper the contest between the House of Have and the House of Want, progress is not real and cannot be permanent.

    HENRY GEORGE, *Progress and Poverty:* Introductory.

3

Social progress makes the well-being of all more and more the business of each; it binds all closer and closer together in bonds from which none can escape.

    HENRY GEORGE, *Social Problems.*

4

All progress begins with a crime.

    ELBERT HUBBARD, *A Thousand and One Epigrams,* p. 109.

5

Change, movement, progress—so long as they are material or mechanical—we are always panting to embrace. So great, indeed, is the obloquy in America of being a stick-in-the-mud that, if you just give us new mud, or mud of a new color, or best of all mud under a new, high-sounding name, we are the greatest stick-in-the-muds on earth.

    LOUIS KRONENBERGER, *The Cart and the Horse.*

6

Not enjoyment, and not sorrow,
  Is our destined end or way;
But to act, that each to-morrow
  Find us farther than to-day.

    HENRY WADSWORTH LONGFELLOW, *A Psalm of Life.*

7

From lower to the higher next,
Not to the top, is Nature's text;
And embryo Good, to reach full stature,
Absorbs the Evil in its nature.

    JAMES RUSSELL LOWELL, *Festina Lente:* Moral.

8

New times demand new measures and new men;
The world advances, and in time outgrows
The laws that in our fathers' day were best;
And, doubtless, after us, some purer scheme
Will be shaped out by wiser men than we.

    JAMES RUSSELL LOWELL, *A Glance Behind the Curtain.*

9

New occasions teach new duties, time makes
  ancient good uncouth;

They must upward still and onward, who
  would keep abreast of truth.

    JAMES RUSSELL LOWELL, *The Present Crisis.*

10

Every step of progress the world has made has been from scaffold to scaffold and from stake to stake.

    WENDELL PHILLIPS, Speech for women's rights, 15 Oct., 1851.

11

The test of our progress is not whether we add more to the abundance of those who have much; it is whether we provide enough for those who have too little.

    FRANKLIN D. ROOSEVELT, Second Inaugural Address, 20 Jan., 1937.

12

The material progress and prosperity of a nation are desirable chiefly so far as they lead to the moral and material welfare of all good citizens.

    THEODORE ROOSEVELT, *The New Nationalism.*

13

Life means progress, and progress means suffering.

    HENDRIK WILLEM VAN LOON, *Tolerance,* p. 89.

14

And step by step, since time began,
I see the steady gain of man.

    JOHN GREENLEAF WHITTIER, *The Chapel of the Hermits.*

PROHIBITION

See also Temperance

15

Prohibition has made nothing but trouble.

    ALPHONSE (AL) CAPONE, Newspaper Interview.

16

Forbidden fruit a flavor has
  That lawful orchards mocks;
How luscious lies the pea within
  The pod that Duty locks!

    EMILY DICKINSON, *Poems,* Pt. i, No. 87.

17

Vicious actions are not hurtful because they are forbidden, but forbidden because they are hurtful.

    BENJAMIN FRANKLIN, *Autobiography,* ch. 1.

18

There are conditions relating to its [prohibition's] enforcement which savor of a nationwide scandal. It is the most demoralizing factor in our public life.

    WARREN G. HARDING, Message to Congress, 8 Dec., 1922.

19

The law of Maine will hardly take effect while the law of fermentation stands unre-

pealed on the pages of heaven's statute
book.
> OLIVER WENDELL HOLMES, Address before
> the New England Society in New York,
> Dec., 1865, referring to the Maine pro-
> hibition law.

1
A law made to be habitually and openly violated is a frightful demoralizer of society.
> OLIVER WENDELL HOLMES, Address before
> the New England Society in New York,
> Dec., 1885, referring to the Maine pro-
> hibition law.

2
Our country has deliberately undertaken a
great social and economic experiment, noble
in motive and far-reaching in purpose.
> HERBERT HOOVER, Letter to Senator Wil-
> liam E. Borah, 28 Feb., 1928, and re-
> peated in his address accepting the Re-
> publican nomination for the presidency.
> Later he was taunted with having called
> prohibition "a noble experiment." Hoo-
> ver took note of this in his memoirs:
> "This phrase, 'a great social experiment,
> noble in motive' was distorted into a
> 'noble experiment,' which of course was
> not at all what I had said or intended to
> say."

3
The Commission, by a large majority, does
not favor the repeal of the Eighteenth
Amendment. I am in accord with this view.
> HERBERT HOOVER, Letter of Transmissal,
> accompanying the Wickersham Report,
> Jan., 1931.

4
Whether or not the world would be vastly
benefited by a total banishment from it of all
intoxicating drinks seems not now an open
question. Three-fourths of mankind confess
the affirmative with their tongues, and I believe all the rest acknowledge it in their
hearts.
> ABRAHAM LINCOLN, Address before The
> Washington Society of Springfield, Ill.,
> 22 Feb., 1842.

5
Of old, all invitations ended
  With the well-known *R.S.V.P.*,
But now our laws have been amended
  The hostess writes *B.Y.O.B.*
> CHRISTOPHER MORLEY, *Thoughts on Being
> Invited to Dinner*. "B.Y.O.B." meant
> "Bring your own booze."

6
The prohibition law, written for weaklings
and derelicts, has divided the nation, like
Gaul, into three parts—wets, drys, and hypocrites.
> MRS. CHARLES H. SABIN, Address, 9 Feb.,
> 1931.

7
Good-bye, John. You were God's worst enemy. You were Hell's best friend. I hate you
with a perfect hatred.
> BILLY SUNDAY, Funeral Oration over John
> Barleycorn, Norfolk, Va., 16 Jan., 1920.

8
He found out a new thing—namely, that to
promise not to do a thing is the surest way in
the world to make a body want to go and do
that very thing.
> MARK TWAIN, *The Adventures of Tom
> Sawyer*, ch. 22.

9
Temperance is moderation in the things that
are good and total abstinence from the things
that are bad.
> FRANCES E. WILLARD, the definition ac-
> cepted by the Women's Christian Tem-
> perance Union (WCTU) from its found-
> ing.

10
In all matters having to do with the personal
habits and customs of large numbers of our
people, we must be certain that the established processes of legal change are followed.
> WOODROW WILSON, Veto Message on the
> Volstead Act, 27 Oct., 1919.

11
It is here at last—dry America's first birthday. At one minute past twelve to-morrow
morning a new nation will be born. . . . To-
night John Barleycorn makes his last will
and testament. Now for an era of clear thinking and clean living.
> UNKNOWN, Anti-Saloon League Mani-
> festo, 15 Jan., 1920.

PROMISE

12
Vote for the man who promises least; he'll
be the least disappointing.
> BERNARD M. BARUCH. (*Meyer Berger's
> New York*)

13
A promise must never be broken.
> ALEXANDER HAMILTON, Letter to his son
> Philip, aged ten, 5 Dec., 1791.

14
Promise is a promise, dough you make it in
de dark er de moon.
> JOEL CHANDLER HARRIS, *Nights with Un-
> cle Remus*, ch. 39.

15
And they all had trust in his cussedness,
And knowed he would keep his word.
> JOHN HAY, *Jim Bludso*.

16
Half the promises people say were never
kept were never made.
> E. W. HOWE, *Howe's Montly*.

17
You ain't heard nothin' yet, folks.
> AL JOLSON, Line interpolated in *The Jazz
> Singer* (1927), the film that broke the
> sound barrier.

1
He is too experienced a parent ever to make positive promises.
    CHRISTOPHER MORLEY, *Thunder on the Left*, ch. 5.

2
I don't believe irresponsible promises are good politics. Promise-peddling and double talk may be expedient and catch some votes from the unwary and innocent, but promises also have a way of coming home to roost.
    ADLAI E. STEVENSON, Speech in Peru, Ill., in 1948, during his successful campaign for the governorship of that state.

PROPERTY
See also Possessions

3
Property is in its nature timid and seeks protection, and nothing is more gratifying to government than to become a protector.
    JOHN C. CALHOUN, Speech, 21 Mar., 1834.

4
If a man owns land, the land owns him.
    EMERSON, *Conduct of Life: Wealth.*

5
My cow milks me.
    EMERSON, *Journals*, vol. v, p. 406.

6
What we call real estate—the solid ground to build a house on—is the broad foundation on which nearly all the guilt of this world rests.
    NATHANIEL HAWTHORNE, *The House of the Seven Gables: The Flight of the Two Owls.*

7
It was in the medieval doctrine that to kings belongs authority, but to private persons, property, that the way was discovered to limit the authority of the king and to promote the liberties of the subject. Private property was the original source of freedom. It is still its main bulwark. . . . When men have yielded without serious resistance to the tyranny of . . . dictators, it is because they have lacked property.
    WALTER LIPPMANN, *The Method of Freedom.*

8
The personal right to acquire property, which is a natural right, gives to property, when acquired, a right to protection, as a social right.
    JAMES MADISON, *Writings*, vol. iv, p. 51.

9
Every man holds his property subject to the general right of the community to regulate its use to whatever degree the public welfare may require it.
    THEODORE ROOSEVELT, Speech in Osawatomie, Kan., 31 Aug., 1910.

PROSPERITY

10
Prosperity is only an instrument to be used, not a deity to be worshipped.
    CALVIN COOLIDGE, Speech, 11 June, 1928.

11
Reverse cannot befall that fine Prosperity
Whose sources are interior.
    EMILY DICKINSON, *Poems*, Pt. v, No. 8.

12
We had to meet the severest test that can come to a people, the test of prosperity.
    JOHN FOSTER DULLES, Address in Washington, D.C., 11 Apr., 1955, referring to America's growth into a world power.

13
The days of palmy prosperity are not those most favorable to the display of public virtue or the influence of wise and good men.
    EDWARD EVERETT, *Mount Vernon Papers*, No. 14.

14
Prosperity cannot be restored by raids upon the public treasury.
    HERBERT HOOVER, Statement to press, 9 Dec., 1930.

15
I'll say this fer adversity—people seem to be able to stand it, an' that's more'n I kin say fer prosperity.
    KIN HUBBARD, *Abe Martin's Broadcast*, p. 79.

16
Agriculture, manufactures, commerce and navigation, the four pillars of our prosperity, are the most thriving when left most free to individual enterprise.
    THOMAS JEFFERSON, *Writings*, vol. iii, p. 337.

17
If the period of prosperity could be expressed in a single word, that word would be confidence; and if the period of adversity, as we call it, could be expressed in a single word, that word would be distrust.
    THOMAS B. REED. (W. A. ROBINSON, *Life of Reed*)

18
Let me see no other conflict but with prosperity. If my path run on before me level and smooth, it is all a mirage; in reality it is steep and arduous as a chamois pass.
    HENRY D. THOREAU, *Journal*, 25 June, 1840.

19
Prosperity is just around the corner.
    UNKNOWN, Campaign Slogan employed by the Republicans in the national election of 1932.

20
Prosperity would seem more soundly shored if, by a saving grace, more of us had the grace to save.
    ANONYMOUS, Editorial: *Is Thrift Un-American?; Life*, 7 May, 1956.

PROVERBS AND FAMILIAR SAYINGS

The familiar sayings that follow the first five general quotations on proverbs are those that do not fit naturally under other subject headings in this book.

1
Proverbs, like the sacred books of each nation, are the sanctuary of the intuitions.
EMERSON, *Essays, First Series: Compensation.*

2
Never utter the truism, but live it among men.
EMERSON, *Journals,* vol. iii, p. 455.

3
Much of the wisdom of the world is not wisdom.
EMERSON, *Works,* vol. i, p. 155.

4
Almost every wise saying has an opposite one, no less wise, to balance it.
GEORGE SANTAYANA, *Little Essays,* p. 237.

5
It is more trouble to make a maxim than it is to do right.
MARK TWAIN, *Pudd'nhead Wilson's New Calendar.*

6
The practice for which W. E. Woodward, in a novel [*Bunk*] published in 1923, invented the word "debunking."
FREDERICK LEWIS ALLEN, *Only Yesterday,* p. 236.

7
What Price Glory?
MAXWELL ANDERSON AND LAURENCE STALLINGS, Title of play (1924).

8
Are You a Bromide?
GELETT BURGESS, Title of essay, *Smart Set,* Apr., 1906. "Bromide" is now applied both to commonplace people and to their ideas and statements.

9
Pigs Is Pigs.
ELLIS PARKER BUTLER, Title of story dealing with guinea pigs.

10
Out where the handclasp's a little stronger,
Out where the smile dwells a little longer,
    That's where the West begins.
ARTHUR CHAPMAN, *Out Where the West Begins.*

11
The marines have landed, and the situation is well in hand.
RICHARD HARDING DAVIS, Cable from Panama, 1885.

12
We may well call it [coal] black diamonds. Every basket is power and civilization. For coal is a portable climate. It carries the heat of the tropics to Labrador and the polar circle; and it is the means of transporting itself whither-soever it is wanted.
EMERSON, *Conduct of Life: Wealth.*

13
Here Skugg lies snug As a bug in a rug.
BENJAMIN FRANKLIN, Letter to Miss Georgiana Shipley, 26 Sept., 1772.

14
A big butter-and-egg man.
TEXAS GUINAN, in introducing from the floor of her night club a generous stranger, in New York City in 1924. The man, who refused to reveal his name, paid all the checks in the house and distributed $50 bills to the entertainers. He said only that he was in the dairy produce business.

15
Nifty! [short for *magnificat*]
BRET HARTE, *The Tale of a Pony.*

16
An' all us other children, when the supper things is done,
We set around the kitchen fire an' has the mostest fun
A-list'nin' to the witch tales 'at Annie tells about
An' the gobble-uns 'at gits you
Ef you Don't Watch Out!
JAMES WHITCOMB RILEY, *Little Orphant Annie.*

17
Who's afraid of the big bad wolf?
ANN RONELL, Title and refrain of song used in the WALT DISNEY film *The Three Little Pigs* (1933).

18
Mollycoddles instead of vigorous men.
THEODORE ROOSEVELT, Speech in Cambridge, Mass., 23 Feb., 1907.

19
Nothing doing. That's just baloney. Everybody knows I can't lay bricks.
ALFRED E. SMITH, when governor of New York. He was laying the cornerstone of the New York State Office Building, when asked to permit the taking of a motion picture showing him actually laying the brick.

No matter how thin you slice it, it's still baloney.
ALFRED E. SMITH, Speech, 1936.

20
Stuffed shirt.
Attributed to FAY TEMPLETON, who is said to have applied it to a plunger named John Gates.

21
Curfew shall not ring to-night!
ROSE HARTWICK THORPE, *Curfew Must Not Ring To-night.*

22
Stop—Look—Listen!
RALPH R. UPTON, Slogan coined in 1912,

principally for signs at railroad crossings, when he was a lecturer on safety for the Puget Sound Power Company, Seattle.

1

I'm from Missouri; you've got to show me.
> WILLARD D. VANDIVER, Speech at a naval banquet in Philadelphia, 1899, while he was a Representative from Missouri.

2

All dressed up and nowhere to go.
> WILLIAM ALLEN WHITE, Remark, referring to the Progressive Party after the retirement of Theodore Roosevelt in 1916.

3

I acknowledge the corn.
> CHARLES A. WICKLIFFE, of Kentucky, during debate in the House of Representatives, 1828. (DE VERE, *Americanisms*)

4

O.K.
> UNKNOWN. It is now believed that this expression traces to a vogue for acronyms that became manifest in Boston about 1838. In *The American Language*, H. L. MENCKEN cites the appearance of "O.K." in the Boston *Morning Post* of 23 Mar., 1839 as the first known printed use of the term, and bases his conclusion on the authority of Allen Walker Read, who has made a long study of the term's etymology. "O.K." first gained wide currency during the national election of 1840, when Martin Van Buren was supported by the O.K. Club, which derived its name from Old Kinderhook, N.Y., Van Buren's birthplace. Supporters of his opponent, William Henry Harrison, are said to have displayed a banner, "The People Is Oll Korrect," at a Harrison-Tyler meeting in Urbana, Ohio, 15 Sept., 1840, during the same campaign. For many years it was believed that "O.K." was first used in the record of a financial transaction involving Andrew Jackson, dated 6 Oct., 1790. Authorities on the subject later concluded that the wording on this document was not "O.K." but "O.R" (for "order received"). Woodrow Wilson was among those who believed the term derived from the Choctaw "Okeh," meaning "it is so."

5

Nineteen suburbs in search of a metropolis.
> UNKNOWN, referring to Los Angeles.

PROVIDENCE

See also Destiny, Fate

6

Providence labors with quaint instruments, dilapidating Troy by means of a wooden rocking-horse, and loosing sin into the universe through a half-eaten apple.
> JAMES BRANCH CABELL, *Cream of the Jest*, p. 87.

7

Providence has a wild, rough, incalculable road to its end, and it is of no use to try to whitewash its huge, mixed instrumentalities, or to dress up that terrific benefactor in a clean shirt and white neckcloth of a student in divinity.
> EMERSON, *Conduct of Life: Fate.*

8

What is the operation we call Providence? There lies the unspoken thing, present, omnipresent. Every time we converse we translate it into speech.
> EMERSON, *Essays, Second Series: New England Reformers.*

9

> Behind the dim unknown,
> Standeth God within the shadow, keeping
> watch above his own.
> JAMES RUSSELL LOWELL, *The Present Crisis*, st. 8.

10

There are many scapegoats for our sins, but the most popular is providence.
> MARK TWAIN, *More Tramps Abroad.*

11

So, darkness in the pathway of Man's life
Is but the shadow of God's providence,
By the great Sun of Wisdom cast thereon;
And what is dark below is light in Heaven.
> JOHN GREENLEAF WHITTIER, *Tauler*, l. 79.

PRUDENCE

12

Prudence is God taking thought for oxen.
> EMERSON, *Essays, First Series: Prudence.*

13

To do the contradictory is a tough problem; namely with might and main to try to prevent from coming to pass the very situation in relation to which you're making preparations. That's what we have to do in life so much. You build a fireproof house and nevertheless take out fire insurance.
> FELIX FRANKFURTER.

14

Don't throw stones at your neighbors, if your own windows are glass.
> BENJAMIN FRANKLIN, *Poor Richard*, 1736.

15

He that scatters thorns, let him not go barefoot.
> BENJAMIN FRANKLIN, *Poor Richard*, 1736.

16

Speak with contempt of none, from slave to king;

The meanest bee hath, and will use, a sting.
> BENJAMIN FRANKLIN, *Poor Richard*, 1743.

1

Great Estates may venture more,
But little Boats must keep near Shore.
> BENJAMIN FRANKLIN, *Poor Richard*, 1751.

2

The Boldest Farmer heeds the Cautious Rule
To stand Behind the Bull, Before the Mule.
> ARTHUR GUITERMAN, *A Poet's Proverbs*, p. 106.

3

Take things always by their smooth handle.
> THOMAS JEFFERSON, *Writings*, vol. xvi, p. 111.

4

When you have got an elephant by the hind leg, and he is trying to run away, it's best to let him run.
> ABRAHAM LINCOLN, Remark, to Charles A. Dana, 14 Apr., 1865, just before his death. Lincoln had been urged to arrest Jacob Thompson, a Confederate commissioner who was trying to flee to Europe. (WILSON, *Life of Charles A. Dana*, p. 358; MITCHELL, *Memoirs of an Editor*, p. 35)

5

A whirlwind of caution.
> JAMES RESTON, Washington Column, New York *Times*, 16 Dec., 1964, p. 42. Referring to Lyndon B. Johnson.

6

It is by the goodness of God that in our country we have those three unspeakably precious things: freedom of speech, freedom of conscience, and the prudence never to practice either.
> MARK TWAIN, *Pudd'nhead Wilson's Calendar*.

7

Whatever satisfies souls is true;
Prudence entirely satisfies the craving and glut of souls.
> WALT WHITMAN, *Song of Prudence*, l. 40.

8

Who never wins can rarely lose,
Who never climbs as rarely falls.
> JOHN GREENLEAF WHITTIER, *To James T. Fields*, st. 13.

PUBLIC, THE, see People, The
PUBLICITY

9

The effect of power and publicity on all men is the aggravation of self, a sort of tumor that ends by killing the victim's sympathies.
> HENRY ADAMS, *The Education of Henry Adams*, ch. 10.

10

As gaslight is found to be the best nocturnal police, so the universe protects itself by pitiless publicity.
> EMERSON, *Conduct of Life: Worship*.

Pitiless publicity.
> WOODROW WILSON, his prescription, from Emerson, for curing the ills of government. (SULLIVAN, *Our Times*, vol. iv, p. 119)

11

In every field of human endeavor, he that is first must perpetually live in the white light of publicity.
> THEODORE F. MACMANUS, *The Penalty of Leadership; Saturday Evening Post*, 2 Jan., 1915.

12

The best public relations comes from doing good things and by not doing bad things.
> STANLEY MARCUS, Statement titled "What's Right with Dallas?," Dallas *Times Herald*, 1 Jan., 1964. This was a leading Dallas citizen's frank analysis of his city in the days shortly after John F. Kennedy met his death there.

13

Do the right thing and nine times out of ten it turns out to be the right thing politically. To paraphrase Mark Twain, the difference between doing the right thing and almost the right thing is the difference between lightning and the lightning bug.
> DEBS MYERS, speaking as an expert on political public relations. (New York *Times* profile, 3 Feb., 1965, p. 24)

14

That essential American strategy: publicity.
> RICHARD H. ROVERE, *Senator Joe McCarthy*, p. 10.

15

They have a propaganda machine that is almost equal to Stalin's.
> HARRY S TRUMAN, Letter to Representative Gordon L. McDonough of California, 29 Aug., 1950, referring to the Marine Corps. This was one of the most famous of President Truman's characteristically blunt remarks, and it aroused such a protest that he apologized in short order. McDonough had written to Truman, suggesting that the Marines receive direct representation on the Joint Chiefs of Staff, equivalent to that of the Army, Navy, and Air Force. Truman replied, in part: "For your information the Marine Corps is the Navy's police force and as long as I am President that is what it will remain. They have a propaganda machine that is almost equal to Stalin's." On 6 Sept., 1950, Truman wrote to General Clifton B. Cates, Marine Corps Commandant: "I sincerely regret the unfortunate choice of language which I used in my letter of

Aug. 29 to Congressman McDonough concerning the Marine Corps."

PUNISHMENT

See also Retribution

1
Crime and punishment grow out of one stem. Punishment is a fruit that unsuspected ripens within the flower of the pleasure which concealed it.

EMERSON, *Essays, First Series: Compensation.*

2
There is no den in the wide world to hide a rogue. Commit a crime, and the earth is made of glass.

EMERSON, *Essays, First Series: Compensation.*

3
The world does not grow better by force or by the policeman's club.

WILLIAM J. GAYNOR, *Letters and Speeches,* p. 314.

4
The best of us being unfit to die, what an inexpressible absurdity to put the worst to death!

NATHANIEL HAWTHORNE, *Journals,* 13 Oct., 1851.

5
The greatest punishment is to be despised by your neighbors, the world, and members of your family.

E. W. HOWE, *Howe's Monthly.*

6
No more fiendish punishment could be devised, were such a thing physically possible, than that one should be turned loose in society and remain absolutely unnoticed by all the members thereof.

WILLIAM JAMES, *The Principles of Psychology,* ch. 12.

7
The object of punishment is, prevention from evil; it never can be made impulsive to good.

HORACE MANN, *Lectures and Reports on Education,* lecture 7.

8
The soul itself its awful witness is.
Say not in evil doing, "No one sees."

JOHN GREENLEAF WHITTIER, *The Inward Judge.*

9
Poor Floyd Ireson, for his hard heart,
Tarred and feathered and carried in a cart
By the women of Marblehead!

JOHN GREENLEAF WHITTIER, *Skipper Ireson's Ride.*

PURITANS

See also Pilgrim Fathers

10
The Puritan has been made a popular scape-goat, and the word has become a catch-basin for undeserved reproaches.

SILAS BENT, *Justice O. W. Holmes,* p. 54.

11
It never frightened a Puritan when you bade him stand still and listen to the speech of God. His closet and his church were full of the reverberations of the awful, gracious, beautiful voice for which he listened.

PHILLIPS BROOKS, *Sermons: The Seriousness of Life.*

12
There was a State without kings or nobles; there was a church without a bishop; there was a people governed by grave magistrates which it had elected, and equal laws which it had framed.

RUFUS CHOATE, Speech before the New England Society, 22 Dec., 1843.

13
'Twas founded be th' Puritans to give thanks f'r bein' presarved fr'm the Indyans, an' we keep it to give thanks we are presarved fr'm th' Puritans.

FINLEY PETER DUNNE, *Thanksgiving.*

14
Coexisting uneasily with our English heritage of tolerance and moderation, the Puritan way of thinking has injected an absolutist strand into American thought—a strand of stern moralism in our public policy and in our standards of personal behavior.

J. WILLIAM FULBRIGHT, Address in Washington, D.C., 5 Dec., 1963.

15
My Fathers and Brethren, this is never to be forgotten that New England is originally a plantation of religion, not a plantation of trade.

JOHN HIGGINSON, Election Sermon, 27 May, 1663.

16
Puritanism, believing itself quick with the seed of religious liberty, laid, without knowing it, the egg of democracy.

JAMES RUSSELL LOWELL, *Among My Books: New England Two Centuries Ago.*

17
He had stiff knees, the Puritan,
That were not good at bending.

JAMES RUSSELL LOWELL, *An Interview with Miles Standish,* st. 12.

18
What the Puritans gave the world was not thought, but action.

WENDELL PHILLIPS, Speech, 21 Dec., 1855.

19
The Puritan was not a man of speculation. He originated nothing. . . . The distinction between his case and that of others was simply that he practised what he believed.

WENDELL PHILLIPS, *The Puritan Principle.*

PURPOSE

1
The one prudence in life is concentration; the one evil is dissipation: and it makes no difference whether our dissipations are coarse or fine. . . . Everything is good which takes away one plaything and delusion more, and drives us home to add one stroke of faithful work.
EMERSON, *Conduct of Life: Power.*

2
We aim above the mark to hit the mark. Every act hath some falsehood or exaggeration in it.
EMERSON, *Essays, Second Series: Nature.*

3
In the name of noble purposes men have committed unspeakable acts of cruelty against one another.
J. WILLIAM FULBRIGHT, Address in Washington, D.C., 5 Dec., 1963.

4
Every night before I turn out the lights to sleep, I ask myself this question: Have I done everything that I can do to unite this country? Have I done everything I can to help unite the world, to try to bring peace and hope to all the peoples of the world? Have I done enough?
LYNDON B. JOHNSON, Address at Johns Hopkins University, Baltimore, 7 Apr., 1965.

5
A man must have goals. There is not sufficient time, even in two terms, to achieve these goals. Almost all Presidents leave office feeling that their work is unfinished. I have a lot to do, and so little time in which to do it.
JOHN F. KENNEDY, quoted by Jim Bishop

in a syndicated newspaper article, 25 Nov., 1963. Mr. Kennedy spoke prophetically; the article was based on an interview granted three weeks before his death.

6
The Almighty has his own purposes.
ABRAHAM LINCOLN, Second Inaugural Address, 4 Mar., 1865.

7
Men are not flattered by being shown that there has been a difference of purpose between the Almighty and them.
ABRAHAM LINCOLN, Letter to Thurlow Weed, 14 Mar., 1865.

8
Greatly begin! Though thou have time
But for a line, be that sublime—
Not failure, but low aim is crime.
JAMES RUSSELL LOWELL, *For an Autograph.*

9
Purpose clean as light from every taint.
JAMES RUSSELL LOWELL, *Under the Old Elm.*

10
Purpose is what gives life a meaning.
C. H. PARKHURST, *Sermons: Pattern in the Mount.*

11
'Tis the motive exalts the action;
'Tis the doing, and not the deed.
MARGARET JUNKIN PRESTON, *The First Proclamation of Miles Standish.*

12
A day of unselfish purpose is always a day of confident hope.
WOODROW WILSON, Speech, upon accepting the Democratic nomination for governor of New Jersey, 15 Sept., 1910, Trenton, N.J.

Q

QUARRELING

13
When we quarrel, how we wish we had been blameless!
EMERSON, *Journals,* vol. ix, p. 497.

14
And were an epitaph to be my story
I'd have a short one ready for my own.
I would have written of me on my stone:
I had a lover's quarrel with the world.
ROBERT FROST, *The Lesson for Today.*

15
i have noticed that when chickens quit quarreling over their food they often find that there is enough for all of them i wonder if it might not be the same way with the human race
DON MARQUIS, *archy's life of mehitabel.*

16
Difference of religion breeds more quarrels than difference of politics.
WENDELL PHILLIPS, Address, 7 Nov., 1860.

17
For souls in growth, great quarrels are great emancipations.
LOGAN PEARSALL SMITH, *Afterthoughts.*

QUOTATION

See also Plagiarism

18
One must be a wise reader to quote wisely and well.
AMOS BRONSON ALCOTT, *Table Talk: Quotation.*

1

The adventitious beauty of poetry may be felt in the greater delight which a verse gives in happy quotation than in the poem.
    EMERSON, *Essays, First Series: Art.*

2

Next to the originator of a good sentence is the first quoter of it.
    EMERSON, *Letters and Social Aims: Quotation and Originality.*

3

We are as much informed of a writer's genius by what he selects as by what he originates.
    EMERSON, *Letters and Social Aims: Quotation and Originality.*

4

A great man quotes bravely, and will not draw on his invention when his memory serves him with a word as good.
    EMERSON, *Letters and Social Aims: Quotation and Originality.*

5

By necessity, by proclivity, and by delight, we all quote. We quote not only books and proverbs, but arts, sciences, religion, customs, and laws; nay, we quote temples and houses, tables and chairs by imitation.
    EMERSON, *Letters and Social Aims: Quotation and Originality.*

6

Quotation confesses inferiority.
    EMERSON, *Letters and Social Aims: Quotation and Originality.*

7

Every book is a quotation; and every house is a quotation out of all forests and mines and stone quarries.
    EMERSON, *Representative Men: Plato.*

8

Nothing gives an author so much pleasure as to find his works respectfully quoted by other learned authors.
    BENJAMIN FRANKLIN, *Pennsylvania Almanach.*

9

Famous remarks are seldom quoted correctly.
    SIMEON STRUNSKY, *No Mean City,* ch. 38.

R

READING

See also Books, Library

10

You think your pain and your heartbreak are unprecedented in the history of the world, but then you read. It was books that taught me that the things that tormented me most were the very things that connected me with all the people who were alive, or who had ever been alive.
    JAMES BALDWIN, Television Narrative about his life, WNEW-TV, New York City, 1 June, 1964.

11

I wish only to read that book it would have been a disaster to omit.
    EMERSON, *Books; Journals,* vol. ix, p. 429.

12

If I do not read, nobody will.
    EMERSON, *Journals,* vol. iii, p. 460.

13

We read often with as much talent as we write.
    EMERSON, *Journals,* vol. x, p. 67.

14

It is a tie between men to have read the same book.
    EMERSON, *Journals,* 1864.

15

If we encountered a man of rare intellect, we should ask him what books he read.
    EMERSON, *Letters and Social Aims: Quotation and Originality.*

16

Our high respect for a well-read man is praise enough of literature.
    EMERSON, *Letters and Social Aims: Quotation and Originality.*

17

One must be a great inventor to read well.
    EMERSON, *Nature, Addresses, and Lectures: The American Scholar.*

18

Every book is worth reading which sets the reader in a working mood.
    EMERSON, *Resources.*

19

The three practical rules, then, which I have to offer, are,—1. Never read any book that is not a year old. 2. Never read any but famed books. 3. Never read any but what you like.
    EMERSON, *Society and Solitude: Books.*

20

'Tis the good reader that makes the good book.
    EMERSON, *Society and Solitude: Success.*

21

All good and true book-lovers practise the pleasing and improving avocation of reading in bed.
    EUGENE FIELD, *Love Affairs of a Bibliomaniac,* p. 31.

22

Reading makes a full man—meditation a profound man—discourse a clear man.
    BENJAMIN FRANKLIN, *Poor Richard,* 1738.

1
Read much, but not many books.
> BENJAMIN FRANKLIN, *Poor Richard,* 1738.
> The sentiment was expressed originally
> by Pliny the Younger.

2
To read between the lines was easier than to
follow the text.
> HENRY JAMES, *The Portrait of a Lady,* ch.
> 13.

3
I'm reading more and enjoying it less.
> JOHN F. KENNEDY, News Conference,
> Washington, D.C., 9 May, 1962. This
> was his reaction to a question about
> press treatment of his administration.
> Kennedy humorously paraphrased a cur-
> rent cigarette advertisement that prom-
> ised much to those who were "smoking
> more now and enjoying it less."

4
Have you ever rightly considered what the
mere ability to read means? That it is the
key which admits us to the whole world of
thought and fancy and imagination? to the
company of saint and sage, of the wisest and
the wittiest at their wisest and wittiest moment? That it enables us to see with the
keenest eyes, hear with the finest ears, and
listen to the sweetest voices of all time?
> JAMES RUSSELL LOWELL, *Democracy and
> Other Addresses: Books and Libraries.*

5
More true knowledge comes by meditation
than by reading; for much reading is an oppression of the mind, and extinguishes the
natural candle, which is the reason of so
many senseless scholars in the world.
> WILLIAM PENN, *Advice to His Children.*

6
No man can read with profit that which he
cannot learn to read with pleasure.
> NOAH PORTER, *Books and Reading,* ch.
> 1.

7
People say that life is the thing, but I prefer
reading.
> LOGAN PEARSALL SMITH, *Afterthoughts.*

8
To read well, that is, to read true books in a
true spirit, is a noble exercise.
> HENRY D. THOREAU, *Walden: Reading.*

9
Books must be read as deliberately and re-
servedly as they were written.
> HENRY D. THOREAU, *Walden: Reading.*

10
The works of the great poets have never yet
been read by mankind, for only great poets
can read them. . . . Most men have learned
to read to serve a paltry convenience, . . .
but of reading as a noble intellectual exercise
they know little or nothing.
> HENRY D. THOREAU, *Walden: Reading.*

11
For what are the classics but the noblest
recorded thoughts of man? They are the only
oracles which are not decayed.
> HENRY D. THOREAU, *Walden: Reading.*

12
Nothing is worth reading that does not require an alert mind.
> CHARLES DUDLEY WARNER, *Backlog Stud-
> ies,* No. 1.

REASON

13
Reason, Justice and Equity never had weight
enough on the face of the earth to govern the
councils of men.
> THOMAS A. EDISON. (*Golden Book,* Apr.,
> 1931)

14
If you will not hear Reason, she will surely
rap your knuckles.
> BENJAMIN FRANKLIN, *Poor Richard,*
> 1758.

15
Ah, when to the heart of man
  Seemed it ever less than a treason
To go with the drift of things,
  To yield with a grace to reason
And bow and accept the end
  Of a love, or a season?
> ROBERT FROST, *Reluctance.*

16
Why and Wherefore set out one day,
  To hunt for a wild Negation.
They agreed to meet at a cool retreat
  On the Point of Interrogation.
> OLIVER HERFORD, *Metaphysics.*

17
Your own reason is the only oracle given you
by heaven, and you are answerable for, not
the rightness, but the uprightness of the decision.
> THOMAS JEFFERSON, *Writings,* vol. x, p.
> 178.

18
The people of the world, I think, prefer reasoned agreement to ready attack. And that is
why we must follow the Prophet Isaiah
many times before we send the Marines, and
say, "Come now, and let us reason together."
> LYNDON B. JOHNSON, Speech in Washing-
> ton, D.C., 24 Mar., 1964. The quotation
> from *Isaiah,* ch. i, 19, was a particular
> favorite of Mr. Johnson.

19
I would rather win a convert than an argument.
> LYNDON B. JOHNSON. (HENRY A. ZEIGER,
> *Lyndon B. Johnson: Man and Presi-
> dent,* p. 65)

20
Some folks dey would 'a' beat him:
Now, dat would only heat him;

I know jes' how to treat him:
  You mus' *reason* wid a mule.
  IRWIN RUSSELL, *Nebuchadnezzar.*

1
All the tools with which mankind works
upon its fate are dull, but the sharpest
among them is the reason.
  CARL VAN DOREN, *Many Minds*, p. 209.

2
Reason never has failed men. Only force and
oppression have made the wrecks in the
world.
  WILLIAM ALLEN WHITE, Emporia *Gazette*,
    1922.

REBELLION
See also Revolution
3
A little rebellion now and then is a good
thing, and as necessary in the political world
as storms in the physical.
  THOMAS JEFFERSON, *Writings*, vol. vi, p.
    64. The reference is to Shays's rebellion.

4
What country before ever existed a century
and a half without a rebellion?
  THOMAS JEFFERSON, Letter to William
    Stevens Smith, 13 Nov., 1787.

5
No doubt but it is safe to dwell
  Where ordered duties are;
No doubt the cherubs earn their wage
  Who wind each ticking star;
No doubt the system is quite right!—
  Sane, ordered, regular;
But how the rebel fires the soul
  Who dares the strong gods' ire.
  DON MARQUIS, *The Rebel.*

6
It doesn't take a majority to make a rebellion; it takes only a few determined leaders
and a sound cause.
  H. L. MENCKEN, *Prejudices*, ser. v, p. 141.

7
The marvelous rebellion of man at all signs
  reading "Keep Off."
  CARL SANDBURG, *Who Am I?*

REFORM, REFORMERS
8
Pride isn't one of my attributes. Either pride
or disappointment or failure doesn't enter
my calculations. I don't do something just
because I think I'll win. It's the reformer's
instinct, I suppose. It has nothing to do with
doing people good. I just try to put things to
rights. I tackle the things that arouse me—
injustice, cruelty, unfairness.
  ROGER BALDWIN. (WILLIE MORRIS, *Barely
    Winded at Eighty; The New Republic*,
    25 Jan., 1964)

9
A man that'd expict to thrain lobsters to fly
in a year is called a loonytic; but a man that
thinks men can be tu-rrned into angels be an
iliction is called a rayformer an' remains at
large.
  FINLEY PETER DUNNE, *Mr. Dooley's Phi-
    losophy.*

10
Every project in the history of reform, no
matter how violent and surprising, is good
when it is the dictate of a man's genius and
constitution, but very dull and suspicious
when adopted from another.
  EMERSON, *Essays, Second Series: New
    England Reformers.*

11
When we see a special reformer, we feel like
asking him, What right have you, sir, to your
one virtue?
  EMERSON, *Essays, Second Series: New
    England Reformers.*

12
The Reformer believes that there is no evil
coming from Change which a deeper thought
cannot correct.
  EMERSON, *Journals*, 1864.

13
Every reform is only a mask under cover of
which a more terrible reform, which dares
not yet name itself, advances.
  EMERSON, *Journals*, vol. vii, p. 205.

14
Reform is affirmative, conservatism negative; conservatism goes for comfort, reform
for truth. . . . Conservatism makes no poetry, breathes no prayer, has no invention; it
is all memory. Reform has no gratitude, no
prudence, no husbandry.
  EMERSON, *Nature, Addresses, and Lec-
    tures: The Conservative.*

15
Reform kicks with hoofs; it runs to egotism
and bloated self-conceit.
  EMERSON, *Nature, Addresses, and Lec-
    tures: The Conservative.*

16
No man's person I hate, though his conduct I
    blame;
I can censure a vice, without stabbing a
    name.
To amend—not reproach—is the bent of my
    mind;
A reproof is half lost when ill nature is
    joined.
Where merit appears, though in rags, I re-
    spect it,
And plead virtue's cause, should the whole
    world reject it.
  BENJAMIN FRANKLIN, *Poor Richard*,
    1734.

17
Absolutist movements are usually crusading
movements. Free as they are from any element of doubt as to their own truth and
virtue, they conceive themselves to have a
mission of spreading the truth and destroying

evil. They consider it to be their duty to regenerate mankind, however little it may wish to be regenerated.

> J. WILLIAM FULBRIGHT, Address in Washington, D.C., 5 Dec., 1963.

1

Reform must come from within, not from without. You cannot legislate for virtue.

> CARDINAL GIBBONS, Address in Baltimore, 13 Sept., 1909.

2

No True Reform has ever come to pass
Unchallenged by a Lion and an Ass.

> ARTHUR GUITERMAN, *A Poet's Proverbs*, p. 9.

3

Both claim the legal right to the pursuit of other people's happiness.

> ELBERT HUBBARD, *The Philistine*, vol. xxv, p. 52.

4

A single zealot may become persecutor, and better men be his victims.

> THOMAS JEFFERSON, *Notes on Virginia*.

5

When we reflect how difficult it is to move or deflect the great machine of society, how impossible to advance the notions of a whole people suddenly to ideal right, we see the wisdom of Solon's remark, that no more good must be attempted than the nation can bear.

> THOMAS JEFFERSON, *Writings*, vol. x, p. 255.

6

Any essential reform must, like charity, begin at home.

> JOHN MACY, *About Women*, p. 126.

7

For him who fain would teach the world
  The world holds hate in fee—
For Socrates, the hemlock cup;
  For Christ, Gethsemane.

> DON MARQUIS, *The Wages*.

8

When A annoys or injures B on the pretense of improving B, A is a scoundrel.

> H. L. MENCKEN, *Newspaper Days: 1899–1906*.

9

The race could save one-half its wasted labor
Would each reform himself and spare his neighbor.

> FRANK PUTNAM, *Reform*.

10

Every reform movement has a lunatic fringe.

> THEODORE ROOSEVELT, speaking of the Progressive party, in 1913.

11

We are told by Moralists with the plainest faces that immorality will spoil our looks.

> LOGAN PEARSALL SMITH, *Afterthoughts*.

12

No reforms come easy; even the most obvious will have its entrenched enemies. Each one is carried to us on the bent and the weary backs of patient, dedicated men and women.

> ADLAI E. STEVENSON, A. Powell Davies Memorial Address, Washington, D.C., 18 Jan., 1959. (*Contemporary Forum*, ed. by ERNEST J. WRAGE AND BARNET BASKERVILLE, p. 365)

13

God did not make man a hound-dog to scent out evil.

> JOHN TIMOTHY STONE, *Everyday Religion*.

14

One of the never solved enigmas of life is the number of people that bear a commission from no one, who, as a rule, are least informed on the principles of government, but who insist on exercising the power of government to make their neighbors live the lives they desire to prescribe for them.

> OSCAR W. UNDERWOOD, *Drifting Sands of Party Politics*, p. 365.

15

A reformer is a guy who rides through a sewer in a glass-bottomed boat.

> JAMES J. WALKER, Newspaper interview.

16

It is easy to condemn wrong and to fulminate against wrongdoers in effective rhetorical phrases; but that does not bring either reform or ease of mind. Reform will come only when we have done some careful thinking as to exactly what the things are that are being done in contravention of the public interest and as to the most simple, direct, and effective way of getting at the men who do them.

> WOODROW WILSON, Speech upon accepting the Democratic nomination for governor of New Jersey, 15 Sept., 1910, Trenton, N.J.

REGRET

See also Repentance

17

Familiar as an old mistake
And futile as regret.

> EDWIN ARLINGTON ROBINSON, *Bewick Finzer*.

18

Make the most of your regrets. . . . To regret deeply is to live afresh.

> HENRY D. THOREAU, *Journal*, 13 Nov., 1839.

19

For of all sad words of tongue or pen,
The saddest are these: "It might have been!"

> JOHN GREENLEAF WHITTIER, *Maud Muller*, l. 105.

If, of all sad words of tongue or pen,
The saddest are, "It might have been,"
More sad are these we daily see,
"It is, but it hadn't ought to be."
> BRET HARTE, *Mrs. Judge Jenkins.*

I plowed "perhaps," I planted "If" therein,
And sadly harvested "It Might Have Been."
> ARTHUR GUITERMAN, *A Poet's Proverbs,*
> p. 65.

And of all glad words of prose or rhyme,
The gladdest are, "Act while there yet is
time."
> FRANKLIN P. ADAMS, *Maud Muller Muta-*
> *tur.*

RELIGION
See also Angel, Atheism, Christianity, Creeds

1
Religion tends to speak the language of the
heart, which is the language of friends, lovers, children, and parents.
> E. S. AMES, (NEWTON, *My Idea of God,*
> p. 246)

2
Religion—a daughter of Hope and Fear, explaining to Ignorance the nature of the Unknowable.
> AMBROSE BIERCE, *The Devil's Dictionary.*

3
Impiety—your irreverence toward my deity.
> AMBROSE BIERCE, *The Devil's Dictionary.*

4
Religion is life, philosophy is thought; religion looks up, friendship looks in. We need
both thought and life, and we need that the
two shall be in harmony.
> JAMES FREEMAN CLARKE, *Ten Great Reli-*
> *gions,* pt. i, ch. 7, sec. 9.

5
I would no more quarrel with a man because
of his religion than I would because of his
art.
> MARY BAKER EDDY, *Miscellany,* p. 270.

6
We know too much, and are convinced of too
little. Our literature is a substitute for religion, and so is our religion.
> T. S. ELIOT, *A Dialogue on Dramatic Po-*
> *etry.*

7
The religion of one age is ever the poetry of
the next.
> EMERSON, *Character.*

8
A complete nation does not import its religion.
> EMERSON, *Character.*

9
Religion must always be a crab fruit; it cannot be grafted and keep its wild beauty.
> EMERSON, *Conduct of Life: Worship.*

10
What is called religion effeminates and demoralizes.
> EMERSON, *Conduct of Life: Worship.*

11
We believe that holiness confers a certain
insight, because not by private, but by our
public force can we share and know the nature of things.
> EMERSON, *Conduct of Life: Worship.*

12
God builds his temple in the heart on the
ruins of churches and religions.
> EMERSON, *Conduct of Life: Worship.*

13
Begin where we will, we are pretty sure in a
short space to be mumbling our ten commandments.
> EMERSON, *Essays, First Series: Prudence.*

14
I knew a witty physician who . . . used to
affirm that if there was disease in the liver,
the man became a Calvinist, and if that organ was sound, he became a Unitarian.
> EMERSON, *Essays, Second Series: Experi-*
> *ence.*

15
Religion is the relation of the soul to God,
and therefore the progress of sectarianism
marks the decline of religion. Religion is as
effectually destroyed by bigotry as by indifference.
> EMERSON, *Journals.*

16
Sects are stoves, but fire keeps its old prop-
erties through them all.
> EMERSON, *Journals,* 1861.

17
The religions we call false were once true.
> EMERSON, *Lectures and Biographical*
> *Sketches: Character.*

18
I see that sensible men and conscientious
men all over the world were of one religion,
—the religion of well-doing and daring.
> EMERSON, *Lectures and Biographical*
> *Sketches: The Preacher.*

19
We measure all religions by their civilizing
power.
> EMERSON, *Natural Religion.*

20
And what greater calamity can fall upon a
nation than the loss of worship.
> EMERSON, *Nature, Addresses, and Lec-*
> *tures: An Address at Cambridge,* 15
> July, 1838.

21
The religion which allies itself with injustice
to preach down the natural aspirations of the
masses is worse than atheism.
> HENRY GEORGE, *The Land Question,* p.
> 96.

22
Leave the matter of religion to the family
altar, the church, and the private school,

supported entirely by private contributions. Keep the church and the State for ever separate.

> U. S. GRANT, Speech in Des Moines, Ia., 1875.

1

I confidently expect that in the future even more than in the past, faith in an order, which is the basis of science, will not be dissevered from faith in an Ordainer, which is the basis of religion.

> ASA GRAY, Inscription beneath his bust in the Hall of Fame.

2

No priestcraft can longer make man content with misery here in the hope of compensation hereafter.

> G. STANLEY HALL, *Senescence*, p. 483.

3

We do ourselves wrong, and too meanly estimate the holiness above us, when we deem that any act or enjoyment good in itself, is not good to do religiously.

> NATHANIEL HAWTHORNE, *The Marble Faun*, bk. ii, ch. 7.

4

I would not do for a Methodist preacher, for I am a poor horseman. I would not suit the Baptists, for I dislike water. I would fail as an Episcopalian, for I am no ladies' man.

> JOHN HAY, Letter. (THAYER, *Life and Letters of John Hay*)

5

Religion is not a dogma, nor an emotion, but a service.

> ROSWELL D. HITCHCOCK, *Eternal Atonement.*

6

Priests are no more necessary to religion than politicians to patriotism.

> JOHN HAYNES HOLMES, *The Sensible Man's View of Religion.*

7

The enduring value of religion is in its challenge to aspiration and hope in the mind of man.

> ERNEST M. HOPKINS. (DURANT, *On the Meaning of Life*, p. 75)

8

Formal religion was organized for slaves: it offered them consolation which earth did not provide.

> ELBERT HUBBARD, *The Philistine*, vol. xxv, p. 89.

9

Religion has reduced Spain to a guitar, Italy to a hand-organ, and Ireland to exile.

> ROBERT G. INGERSOLL, *Gov. Rollin's Fast Day Proclamation.*

10

The day that this country ceases to be free for irreligion, it will cease to be free for religion.

> ROBERT H. JACKSON, Opinion, Zorach v. Clausor, 1952.

11

The highest flights of charity, devotion, trust, patience, bravery, to which the wings of human nature have spread themselves have been flown for religious ideals.

> WILLIAM JAMES, *Varieties of Religious Experience*, p. 259.

12

I must ever believe that religion substantially good which produces an honest life, and we have been authorized by one whom you and I equally respect, to judge of the tree by its fruit.

> THOMAS JEFFERSON, *Writings*, vol. xiv, p. 197.

13

I never told my own religion, nor scrutinized that of another. I never attempted to make a convert, nor wished to change another's creed. I have ever judged of others' religion by their lives . . . for it is from our lives and not from our words, that our religion must be read.

> THOMAS JEFFERSON, *Writings*, vol. xv, p. 60.

14

I believe that all religions play a useful and very necessary part in people's lives and I respect all religions that teach belief and faith in God.

> HERBERT H. LEHMAN, Letter to an unidentified Jewish youth who had written Lehman, asking whether the latter's Jewish faith had proved a handicap. Portions of the letter were read at Lehman's funeral service, 8 Dec., 1963. (New York *Times*, 9 Dec., 1963)

15

It is, I think, an error to believe that there is any need of religion to make life seem worth living.

> SINCLAIR LEWIS. (DURANT, *On the Meaning of Life*, p. 37)

16

The best that is possible in the human condition, and in the world as it is, is that the state and the churches should each be too strong to be conquered, not strong enough to have unlimited dominion.

> WALTER LIPPMANN, *The Public Philosophy*, bk. ii, ch. 10.

17

I propose that God should be openly and audibly invoked at the United Nations in accordance with any one of the religious faiths which are represented here. I do so in the conviction that we cannot make the United Nations into a successful instrument of God's peace without God's help—and that with His help we cannot fail.

> HENRY CABOT LODGE, JR., Letter to delegates of member states of the UN, 30 Dec., 1955. At the time Lodge was the chief U.S. delegate to the UN.

1
And learn there may be worship without
    words!
    JAMES RUSSELL LOWELL, *My Cathedral.*

2
Religion without mystery ceases to be religion.
    BISHOP WILLIAM THOMAS MANNING, Ser-
    mon, 2 Feb., 1930.

3
Religion is an attempt, a noble attempt, to
suggest in human terms more-than-human realities.
    CHRISTOPHER MORLEY, *Religio Journalis-
    tici.*

4
My own mind is my own church.
    THOMAS PAINE, *The Age of Reason,* ch.
    1.

5
My country is the world, and my religion is
to do good.
    THOMAS PAINE, *Rights of Man,* pt. ii, ch.
    5.

6
Every religion is good that teaches man to be
good.
    THOMAS PAINE, *Rights of Man,* pt. ii, ch.
    5.

7
Religion without joy,—it is no religion.
    THEODORE PARKER, *Of Conscious Reli-
    gion.*

8
The humble, meek, merciful, just, pious and
devout souls are everywhere of one religion
and when death has taken off the mask, they
will know one another, though the diverse
liveries they wore here make them strangers.
    WILLIAM PENN, *Fruits of Solitude.*

9
To be furious in religion is to be irreligiously
religious.
    WILLIAM PENN, *Fruits of Solitude.*

10
Difference of religion breeds more quarrels
than difference of politics.
    WENDELL PHILLIPS, Address, 7 Nov.,
    1860.

11
I got a religion that wants to take heaven out
of the clouds and plant it right here on the
earth where most of us can get a slice of
it.
    IRWIN SHAW, *Bury the Dead.*

12
The poor creatures . . . seated themselves
on the "anxious benches."
    FRANCES M. TROLLOPE, *Domestic Manners
    of the Americans,* ch. 8 (1832).

In front of the pulpit there was a space
railed off and strewn with straw, which I was
told was the anxious seat, and on which sat

those who were touched by their consciences.
    FREDERICK MARRYAT, *Diary in America*
    (1839).

13
Folks got up . . . and worked their way
. . . to the mourners' bench, with the tears
running down their faces.
    MARK TWAIN. (*Century Magazine,* Feb.,
    1885)

14
The race of men, while sheep in credulity,
are wolves for conformity.
    CARL VAN DOREN, *Why I Am an Unbe-
    liever.*

15
The Puritans nobly fled from a land of despotism to a land of freedim, where they
could not only enjoy their own religion, but
could prevent everybody else from enjoyin'
his.
    ARTEMUS WARD, *The London Punch Let-
    ters,* 5.

16
Each is not for its own sake,
I say the whole earth and all the stars in the
    sky are for religion's sake.
I say no man has ever yet been half devout
    enough,
None has ever yet adored or worship'd half
    enough,
None has begun to think how divine he him-
    self is, and how certain the future is.
I say that the real and permanent grandeur
    of these States must be their religion.
    WALT WHITMAN, *Starting from Paumanok,*
    sec. 7.

17
They who differ pole-wide serve
    Perchance the common Master,
And other sheep He hath than they
    Who graze one narrow pasture!
    JOHN GREENLEAF WHITTIER, *A Spiritual
    Manifestation.*

18
To all things clergic
I am allergic.
    ALEXANDER WOOLLCOTT. (SAMUEL HOP-
    KINS ADAMS, *A. Woollcott, His Life and
    His World*)

19
Congress shall make no law respecting an
establishment of religion, or prohibiting the
free exercise thereof.
    U.S. Constitution, First Amendment.

REPENTANCE
See also Conscience, Guilt

20
His soul smelt pleasant as rain-wet clover.
"I have sinned and repented and that's all
    over.
In his dealings with heathen, the Lord is
    hard,

But the humble soul is his spikenard."
STEPHEN VINCENT BENÉT, *King David.*

1

Remorse is memory awake.
EMILY DICKINSON, *Poems,* Pt. i, No. 69.

2

When prodigals return great things are done.
A. A. DOWTY, *The Siliad.* (BEETON, *Christmas Annual,* 1873)

3

The true physician does not preach repentance, he offers absolution.
H. L. MENCKEN, *Prejudices,* ser. iii, p. 269.

4

Repentance must be something more than mere remorse for sins: it comprehends a change of nature befitting heaven.
LEW WALLACE, *Ben Hur,* bk. vi, ch. 2.

5

A Christian is a man who feels
Repentance on a Sunday
For what he did on Saturday
And is going to do on Monday.
T. R. YBARRA, *The Christian.*

REPUTATION

See also Name

6

The solar system has no anxiety about its reputation.
EMERSON, *Conduct of Life: Worship.*

7

No book was ever written down by any but itself.
EMERSON, *Essays, First Series: Spiritual Laws.*

8

All reputations each age revises. Very few immutable men has history to show.
EMERSON, *Journals,* vol. v, p. 312.

9

A man has a reputation, and is no longer free, but must respect it.
EMERSON, *Society and Solitude: Works and Days.*

10

Glass, China, and Reputation, are easily crack'd and never well mended.
BENJAMIN FRANKLIN, *Poor Richard,* 1750.

11

How many people live on the reputation of the reputation they might have made!
OLIVER WENDELL HOLMES, *The Autocrat of the Breakfast-Table,* ch. 3.

12

Many a man's reputation would not know his character if they met on the street.
ELBERT HUBBARD, *The Philistine,* vol. iv, p. 82.

13

One man lies in his words and gets a bad reputation; another in his manners, and enjoys a good one.
HENRY D. THOREAU, *Journal,* 25 June, 1852.

14

There was worlds of reputation in it, but no money.
MARK TWAIN, *A Yankee at the Court of King Arthur,* ch. 9.

15

Associate yourself with men of good quality if you esteem your own reputation; for 'tis better to be alone than in bad company.
GEORGE WASHINGTON, *Rules of Civility,* No. 56.

RESOLUTION

See also Perseverance, Purpose

16

I am in earnest—I will not equivocate—I will not excuse—I will not retreat a single inch AND I WILL BE HEARD.
WILLIAM LLOYD GARRISON, Salutatory of the *Liberator,* Vol. i, No. 1, 1 Jan., 1831.

17

There is no such thing in man's nature as a settled and full resolve either for good or evil, except at the very moment of execution.
NATHANIEL HAWTHORNE, *Twice-Told Tales: Fancy's Show Box.*

18

Be firm! One constant element in luck
Is genuine solid old Teutonic pluck.
OLIVER WENDELL HOLMES, *A Rhymed Lesson,* l. 282.

19

He who breaks a resolution is a weakling;
He who makes one is a fool.
F. M. KNOWLES, *A Cheerful Year Book.*

20

Resolve, and thou art free.
HENRY WADSWORTH LONGFELLOW, *The Masque of Pandora,* pt. 6.

21

Let us, then, be up and doing,
With a heart for any fate;
Still achieving, still pursuing,
Learn to labor and to wait.
HENRY WADSWORTH LONGFELLOW, *A Psalm of Life.*

22

In life's small things be resolute and great
To keep thy muscle trained: know'st thou when Fate
Thy measure takes, or when she'll say to thee,
"I find thee worthy; do this deed for me"?
JAMES RUSSELL LOWELL, *Sayings,* No. 1.

RESPECTABILITY

1
To be worthy, not respectable.
WILLIAM HENRY CHANNING, *My Symphony.*

2
Men are respectable only as they respect.
EMERSON, *Lectures and Sketches: Sovereignty of Ethics.*

3
The only man to me who is not respectable is the man who consumes more than he produces.
ELBERT HUBBARD, *The Philistine*, vol. xx, p. 36.

4
Respectability is the dickey on the bosom of civilization.
ELBERT HUBBARD, *A Thousand and One Epigrams.*

5
The great artists of the world are never Puritans, and seldom even ordinarily respectable.
H. L. MENCKEN, *Prejudices*, ser. i, ch. 16.

RETRIBUTION

See also Justice, Punishment

6
God's mills grind slow,
But they grind woe.
WILLIAM R. ALGER, *Poetry of the Orient: Delayed Retribution.*

7
Nemesis is that recoil of Nature, not to be guarded against, which ever surprises the most wary transgressor.
EMERSON, *Journals*, 1364.

8
Nothing which we don't invite.
EMERSON, *Natural Religion.*

9
Whatever any one desires from another, the same returns upon himself.
EMERSON, *Natural Religion.*

10
       To be left alone
And face to face with my own crime, had been
Just retribution.
HENRY WADSWORTH LONGFELLOW. *The Masque of Pandora*, pt. 8.

11
The Fates are just; they give us but our own;
Nemesis ripens what our hands have sown.
JOHN GREENLEAF WHITTIER, *To a Southern Statesman.* Addressed to John C. Calhoun in 1846.

REVOLUTION

See also Rebellion

12
An oppressed people are authorized, whenever they can, to rise and break their fetters.
HENRY CLAY, Speech in the House of Representatives, 24 Mar., 1818.

13
I hope we are learning that not everyone who struggles for change is an instrument of Communism and that fundamental change does not necessarily mean Communism, just as not everyone who opposes Communism is a supporter of human freedom.
LEROY COLLINS, Speech in San Juan, P.R., 25 May, 1965.

14
Every revolution was first a thought in one man's mind.
EMERSON, *Essays, First Series: History.*

15
Every man carries a revolution in his waistcoat pocket.
EMERSON, referring to the inhabitants of Boston.

16
In every movement of protest, whether it takes the form of a struggle for political independence or for the removal of ancient grievances, there is always a tendency for the movement to grow more violent and extreme. Revolutions devour their children, and they usually begin with the leaders.
MAX FREEDMAN, Syndicated Column, 3 Aug., 1964.

17
A revolution, or anything that interrupts social order, may afford opportunities for the individual display of eminent virtues; but its effects are pernicious to general morality.
NATHANIEL HAWTHORNE, *The Snow Image*, ch. 3.

18
We welcome changes which advance the welfare of our people. Our system always needs repairs. The remedies in America are not revolution. They are, except for peace and war, mostly jobs of marginal repairs around a sound philosophy and a stout heart.
HERBERT HOOVER, 1954. (*Herbert Hoover in His Own Words*, compiled by LOUIS P. LOCHNER; *New York Times Magazine*, 9 Aug., 1964, p. 15)

19
Our "permanent revolution" is dedicated to broadening—for all Americans—the material and spiritual benefits of the democratic heritage.
LYNDON B. JOHNSON, Speech in Los Angeles, 21 Feb., 1964.

20
If by the mere force of numbers a majority should deprive a minority of any clearly written constitutional right, it might, in a moral point of view, justify revolution—

certainly would if such a right were a vital one.

> ABRAHAM LINCOLN, First Inaugural Address, 4 Mar., 1861.

1

The effect of every revolt is merely to make the bonds galling.

> H. L. MENCKEN, *Prejudices*, ser. ii, p. 245.

2

Revolutions are not made: they come. A revolution is as natural a growth as an oak. It comes out of the past. Its foundations are laid far back.

> WENDELL PHILLIPS, Speech before the Anti-Slavery Society, Boston, 28 Jan., 1852.

3

Insurrection of thought always precedes insurrection of arms.

> WENDELL PHILLIPS, Speech, 1 Nov., 1859.

4

Remember, remember always that all of us, and you and I especially, are descended from immigrants and revolutionists.

> FRANKLIN D. ROOSEVELT, Speech before the Daughters of the American Revolution, 21 Apr., 1938.

5

I know and all the world knows, that revolutions never go backwards.

> WILLIAM HENRY SEWARD, Speech: *The Irrepressible Conflict*, Oct., 1858.

6

The time to stop a revolution is at the beginning, not the end.

> ADLAI E. STEVENSON, Speech in San Francisco during the presidential campaign, 9 Sept., 1952.

7

The release of atomic energy constitutes a new force too revolutionary to consider in the framework of old ideas.

> HARRY S TRUMAN, Message to Congress, 3 Oct., 1945.

8

No people in the world ever did achieve their freedom by goody-goody talk and moral suasion: it being the immutable law that all revolutions that will succeed must *begin* in blood.

> MARK TWAIN, *A Connecticut Yankee at King Arthur's Court*, p. 164.

9

Repression is the seed of revolution.

> DANIEL WEBSTER, Speech, 1845.

REWARD

10

Perhaps the reward of the spirit who tries
Is not the goal but the exercise.

> EDMUND VANCE COOKE, *Prayer*.

11

What is vulgar, and the essence of all vulgar-

ity, but the avarice of reward? 'Tis the difference of artisan and artist, of talent and genius, of sinner and saint. The man whose eyes are nailed, not on the nature of his act, but on the wages, whether it be money, or office, or fame, is almost equally low.

> EMERSON, *Conduct of Life: Worship*.

12

The only reward of virtue is virtue.

> EMERSON, *Essays, First Series: Friendship*.

13

The reward of a thing well done is to have done it.

> EMERSON, *Essays: New England Reformers*.

14

Learning to the Studious; Riches to the Careful; Power to the Bold; Heaven to the Virtuous.

> BENJAMIN FRANKLIN, *Poor Richard*, 1754.

15

Not in rewards, but in the strength to strive,
The blessing lies.

> J. T. TROWBRIDGE, *Twoscore and Ten*.

RICHES

See also Money, Possessions

16

He frivols through the livelong day,
  He knows not Poverty, her pinch.
His lot seems light, his heart seems gay;
  He has a cinch.

> FRANKLIN P. ADAMS, *The Rich Man*.

17

Surplus wealth is a sacred trust which its possessor is bound to administer in his lifetime for the good of the community.

> ANDREW CARNEGIE, *The Gospel of Wealth*.

18

The man who dies rich dies disgraced.

> ANDREW CARNEGIE, *The Gospel of Wealth*.

19

The amassing of wealth is one of the worst species of idolatry, no idol more debasing.

> ANDREW CARNEGIE, Memorandum, dating from 1868 and found among his papers following his death.

20

Communism is a hateful thing. . . . But the communism of combined wealth and capital . . . is not less dangerous than the communism of oppressed poverty and toil.

> GROVER CLEVELAND, Annual Message, 1888.

21

'Tis as hard f'r a rich man to enther th' kingdom iv Hiven as it is f'r a poor man to get out iv Purgatory.

> FINLEY PETER DUNNE, *Mr. Dooley's Philosophy*.

22

If a man is wise, he gets rich, an' if he gets

rich, he gets foolish, or his wife does. That's what keeps the money movin' around.
>FINLEY PETER DUNNE, *Observations by Mr. Dooley.*

1
Wealth is an application of mind to nature; and the art of getting rich consists not in industry, much less in saving, but in a better order, a timeliness, in being at the right spot.
>EMERSON, *Conduct of Life: Wealth.*

2
Without a rich heart, wealth is an ugly beggar.
>EMERSON, *Essays, Second Series: Manners.*

3
Wealth is not his who has it, but his who enjoys it.
>BENJAMIN FRANKLIN, *Poor Richard,* 1736.

4
Now I have a sheep and cow, everybody bids me good-morrow.
>BENJAMIN FRANKLIN, *Poor Richard,* 1736.

5
He who multiplies Riches multiplies Cares.
>BENJAMIN FRANKLIN, *Poor Richard,* 1744.

6
If your riches are yours, why don't you take them with you to t'other world?
>BENJAMIN FRANKLIN, *Poor Richard,* 1751.

You Can't Take It With You.
>GEORGE S. KAUFMAN AND MOSS HART, Title of play (1937).

7
The Affluent Society.
>J. KENNETH GALBRAITH, Title of book (1958).

8
There are only three ways by which any individual can get wealth—by work, by gift, or by theft. And, clearly, the reason why the workers get so little is that the beggars and thieves get so much.
>HENRY GEORGE, *Social Problems.*

9
The ideal social state is not that in which each gets an equal amount of wealth, but in which each gets in proportion to his contribution to the general stock.
>HENRY GEORGE, *Social Problems.*

10
Great wealth always supports the party in power, no matter how corrupt it may be. It never exerts itself for reform, for it instinctively fears change.
>HENRY GEORGE, *Social Problems.*

11
It is almost as difficult to reconcile the principles of republican society with the existence of billionaires as of dukes.
>THOMAS WENTWORTH HIGGINSON.

12
The most prosperous, the best housed, the best fed, the best read, the most intelligent and the most secure generation in our history, or all history, is discontent.
>LYNDON B. JOHNSON, Speech in Washington, D.C., 28 July, 1964.

13
Wealth may be an excellent thing, for it means power, it means leisure, it means liberty.
>JAMES RUSSELL LOWELL, Speech for Harvard anniversary.

14
The most valuable of all human possessions, next to a superior and disdainful air, is the reputation of being well to do.
>H. L. MENCKEN, *Prejudices,* ser. iii, p. 310.

15
They'll make no pocket in my shroud.
>JOAQUIN MILLER, *The Dead Millionaire.*

16
Malefactors of great wealth.
>THEODORE ROOSEVELT, Speech in Provincetown, Mass., 20 Aug., 1907.

17
Those who set out to serve both God and Mammon soon discover that there is no God.
>LOGAN PEARSALL SMITH, *Afterthoughts.*

18
It is the wretchedness of being rich that you have to live with rich people.
>LOGAN PEARSALL SMITH, *Afterthoughts.*

19
To inherit property is not to be born—is to be still-born, rather.
>HENRY D. THOREAU, *Journal,* 13 Mar., 1853.

20
A man is rich in proportion to the number of things which he can afford to let alone.
>HENRY D. THOREAU, *Walden: Where I Lived, and What I Lived For.*

21
Superfluous wealth can buy superfluities only. Money is not required to buy one necessary of the soul.
>HENRY D. THOREAU, *Walden:* Conclusion.

22
Love your life, poor as it is. You may perhaps have some pleasant, thrilling, glorious hours, even in a poorhouse. The setting sun is reflected from the windows of the almshouse as brightly as from the rich man's abode.
>HENRY D. THOREAU, *Walden:* Conclusion.

1
The' ain't nothin' truer in the Bible 'n that sayin' thet them that has gits.
EDWARD NOYES WESTCOTT, *David Harum.*

2
A rich person ought to have a strong stomach.
WALT WHITMAN.

3
The people of this country are not jealous of fortunes, however great, which have been built up by the honest development of great enterprises, which have been actually earned by business energy and sagacity; they are jealous only of speculative wealth, of the wealth which has been piled up by no effort at all, but only by shrewd wits playing on the credulity of others. . . . This is "predatory wealth," and is found in stock markets.
WOODROW WILSON, Address in New York City, 13 Apr., 1908.

RIGHT
See also Might

4
I would rather be right than be President.
HENRY CLAY, Reply to Preston, of Kentucky, when told that Clay's advocacy of the Missouri Compromise of 1850 would injure his chances for the presidency.

5
I have tried so hard to do right.
GROVER CLEVELAND, last words. (McELROY, *Grover Cleveland,* vol. ii, p. 385)

6
Be sure you are right, then go ahead.
DAVID CROCKETT, Motto during War of 1812.

7
The last temptation is the greatest treason:
To do the right deed for the wrong reason.
T. S. ELIOT, *Murder in the Cathedral,* pt. 1.

8
Good and bad are but names very readily transferable to that or this; the only right is what is after my constitution; the only wrong what is against it.
EMERSON, *Essays, First Series: Self-Reliance.*

9
The axioms of geometry translate the laws of ethics.
EMERSON, *Natural Religion.*

10
Not always right in all men's eyes,
But faithful to the light within.
OLIVER WENDELL HOLMES, *A Birthday Tribute.*

11
My principle is to do whatever is right, and leave consequences to him who has the disposal of them.
THOMAS JEFFERSON, *Writings,* vol. xiii, p. 387.

He will hew to the line of right, let the chips fly where they may.
ROSCOE CONKLING, Speech at the Republican national convention, Chicago, 1880, referring to General Grant.

12
A President's hardest task is not to do what is right, but to know what is right.
LYNDON B. JOHNSON, State of the Union Message, 4 Jan., 1965.

13
They say that if you do this you will be standing with the Abolitionists. I say stand with anybody that stands right. Stand with him while he is right and part with him when he goes wrong.
ABRAHAM LINCOLN, Speech in Peoria, Ill., 16 Oct., 1854.

14
Let us have faith that right makes might, and in that faith let us to the end dare to do our duty as we understand it.
ABRAHAM LINCOLN, Address at Cooper Institute, New York City, 27 Feb., 1860.

15
It has been said of the world's history hitherto that might makes right. It is for us and for our time to reverse the maxim, and to say that right makes might.
ABRAHAM LINCOLN.

16
With malice toward none; with charity for all; with firmness in the right, as God gives us to see the right.
ABRAHAM LINCOLN, Second Inaugural Address, 4 Mar., 1865.

17
Wrong ever builds on quicksands, but the Right
To the firm center lays its moveless base.
JAMES RUSSELL LOWELL, *Prometheus,* l. 116.

18
They are slaves who dare not be
In the right with two or three.
JAMES RUSSELL LOWELL, *Stanzas on Freedom.*

19
Women would rather be right than reasonable.
OGDEN NASH, *Good Intentions: Frailty, Thy Name Is a Misnomer.*

20
Right as rain.
WILLIAM RAYMOND, *Love and Quiet Life,* p. 108.

1

Any man more right than his neighbors constitutes a majority of one.

HENRY DAVID THOREAU, *Civil Disobedience*.

2

Our allies are the millions who hunger and thirst after righteousness.

HARRY S TRUMAN, Inaugural Address, 20 Jan., 1949.

3

Always do right. This will gratify some people, and astonish the rest.

MARK TWAIN.

4

None of us has a patent on being right.

MILLARD E. TYDINGS, Speech in U.S. Senate.

5

The greatest right in the world is the right to be wrong.

HARRY WEINBERGER, *The First Casualties in War;* New York *Evening Post,* 10 Apr., 1917.

6

Democracy is the recurrent suspicion that more than half of the people are right more than half of the time.

E. B. WHITE, *World Government and Peace*.

7

No question is ever settled
Until it is settled right.

ELLA WHEELER WILCOX, *Settle the Question Right*. The same statement, as prose, has been attributed to Lincoln.

8

The right is more precious than peace.

WOODROW WILSON, War Message to Congress, 2 Apr., 1917.

RIGHTS

(The following treat the subject generally. See also America, Freedom, Liberty, Majority and Minority.)

9

The true Republic: men, their rights and nothing more; women, their rights and nothing less.

SUSAN B. ANTHONY, Motto of her paper *Revolution* (1868).

10

Rights can exist only under law, not independent of it.

TOM C. CLARK, Address in St. Louis, 9 Feb., 1965.

11

We don't believe in the God-given right of a Senator to talk as long as he wants to if it interferes with more basic human rights.

JAMES FARMER, Address in Baltimore, 23 Feb., 1964. Speaking as national director of the Congress of Racial Equality, he was referring to the possibility of a filibuster on the civil-rights bill of that year, on which Congressional action was about to begin.

12

You can not possibly have a broader basis for any government than that which includes all the people, with all their rights in their hands, and with an equal power to maintain their rights.

WILLIAM LLOYD GARRISON. (W. P. AND F. J. T. GARRISON, *William Lloyd Garrison,* vol. iv, p. 224)

13

Wherever there is a human being, I see God-given rights inherent in that being, whatever may be the sex or complexion.

WILLIAM LLOYD GARRISON. (W. P. AND F. J. T. GARRISON, *William Lloyd Garrison,* vol. iii, p. 390)

14

The equal right of all men to the use of land is as clear as their equal right to breathe the air—it is a right proclaimed by the fact of their existence. For we cannot suppose that some men have a right to be in this world, and others no right.

HENRY GEORGE, *Progress and Poverty,* bk. vii, ch. 1.

15

The sacred rights of mankind are not to be rummaged from among old parchments or musty records. They are written, as with a sunbeam, in the whole volume of human nature, by the hand of the divinity itself; and can never be erased or obscured by mortal power.

ALEXANDER HAMILTON, *The Farmer Refuted,* 5 Feb., 1775. This pamphlet, defending American liberty, was written while he was a college student.

16

Civil wrongs do not bring civil rights. Civil disobedience does not bring equal protection under the laws. Disorder does not bring law and order.

HUBERT H. HUMPHREY AND THOMAS H. KUCHEL, Joint Statement, April, 1964, during Congressional debate on the civil-rights bill of that year. Humphrey (Senate majority whip) and Kuchel (Senate minority whip) were referring to demonstrations designed to secure passage of a strong bill.

17

I am the inferior of any man whose rights I trample under foot.

ROBERT G. INGERSOLL, *Liberty*.

18

We hold these truths to be self-evident, that all men are created equal, that they are endowed by their Creator with certain unalienable Rights, that among these are Life, Liberty and the pursuit of Happiness.

THOMAS JEFFERSON, *Declaration of Independence*.

The Declaration of Independence speaks of certain unalienable rights given to Man by God—the rights to life, liberty, and the pursuit of happiness. Yet nothing is clearer than that these rights are far from unalienable. They can be taken from a man by other men; they can be surrendered by a whole people to the state; if they are to be preserved at all, the state, presumably, must secure them.

> MARY MCCARTHY, *On the Contrary: The Contagion of Ideas,* p. 43. Originally a speech to a group of teachers, delivered in 1952.

1

And yet the same revolutionary beliefs for which our forebears fought are still at issue around the globe—the belief that the rights of man come not from the generosity of the state but from the hand of God.

> JOHN F. KENNEDY, Inaugural Address, 20 Jan., 1961.

2

The right to interfere with the rights of others is no part of academic freedom.

> GRAYSON KIRK. (New York *Times,* "Ideas and Men," 6 June, 1965, p. 11E)

3

I believe that every right implies a responsibility; every opportunity, an obligation; every possession, a duty.

> JOHN D. ROCKEFELLER, JR., Address in New York City, 8 July, 1941.

4

Let's put the record straight. Our concern is not for some abstract concept of "states' rights." States have no rights—only people have rights. States have responsibilities.

> GEORGE ROMNEY, Testimony before the Republican platform committee, 8 July, 1964, during the party's national convention in San Francisco.

5

Government laws are needed to give us civil rights, and God is needed to make us civil.

> REV. RALPH W. SOCKMAN, Sermon at Riverside Church, New York City, 13 Dec., 1964.

RISING

6

Oh! how I hate to get up in the morning,
Oh! how I'd love to remain in bed;
  For the hardest blow of all
  Is to hear the bugler call,
"You've got to get up, you've got to get up,
You've got to get up this morning!"

> IRVING BERLIN, *Oh! How I Hate to Get Up in the Morning.*

7

Early to bed and early to rise,

Makes a man healthy, wealthy, and wise.

> BENJAMIN FRANKLIN, *Poor Richard,* 1758.

Early to rise and early to bed makes a male healthy and wealthy and dead.

> JAMES THURBER, *Fables for Our Time: The Shrike and the Chipmunks.*

8

Who riseth late must trot all the day.

> BENJAMIN FRANKLIN, *The Way to Wealth.*

9

Prone on my back I greet arriving day,
  A day no different than the one just o'er;
When I will be, to practically say,
  Considerable like I have been before.
Why then get up? Why wash, why eat, why pray?
  —Oh, leave me lay!

> ELEANOR PRESCOTT HAMMOND, *Oh, Leave Me Lay.* Originally published anonymously in the *Atlantic Monthly,* Aug., 1922.

10

The early tire gits the roofin' tack.

> KIN HUBBARD, *Abe Martin's Broadcast,* p. 118.

11

Many a good man has caught his death of cold getting up in the middle of the night to go home.

> LUKE MCLUKE, Epigram.

12

Yes; bless the man who first invented sleep,

  . . .

But blast the man with curses loud and deep, . . .

Who first invented, and went round advertising,

That artificial cut-off—Early Rising.

> JOHN GODFREY SAXE, *Early Rising.*

RIVER

13

It fills me full of joie de viver
To look across the Hudson River.

> FRANKLIN P. ADAMS, *Diary of Our Own Samuel Pepys,* 22 Mar., 1924.

14

Or lose thyself in the continuous woods
Where rolls the Oregon, and hears no sound,
Save his own dashings.

> WILLIAM CULLEN BRYANT, *Thanatopsis.*

15

A river is the cosiest of friends. You must love it and live with it before you can know it.

> GEORGE WILLIAM CURTIS, *Lotus-Eating: Hudson and Rhine.*

16

River, Stay 'Way from My Door.

> MORT DIXON, Title of song (1931), with music by Harry Woods.

1
Oh the moonlight's fair to-night along the
    Wabash,
  From the fields there comes the breath of
    new-mown hay;
Thro' the sycamores the candle lights are
    gleaming,
  On the banks of the Wabash far away.
    PAUL DRESSER, *On the Banks of the Wa-
    bash.*

2
Way down upon de Swanee ribber,
  Far, far away,
Dere's wha my heart is turning ebber,
  Dat's wha de old folks stay.
    STEPHEN COLLINS FOSTER, *Old Folks at
    Home.*

3
From the heart of the mighty mountains
    strong-souled for my fate I came,
My far-drawn track to a nameless sea
    through a land without a name; . . .
I stayed not, I could not linger; patient, re-
    sistless, alone,
I hewed the trail of my destiny deep in the
    hindering stone.
    SHARLOT M. HALL, *Song of the Colorado.*

4
Ol' man river, dat ol' man river,
He must know sumpin', but don't say nothin',
He just keeps rollin', he keeps on rollin'
    along.
    OSCAR HAMMERSTEIN II, *Ol' Man River,*
    referring to the Mississippi.

5
And Potomac flowed calmly, scarce heaving
    her breast,
With her low-lying billows all bright in the
    west,
For a charm as from God lulled the waters to
    rest
Of the fair-rolling river.
    PAUL HAMILTON HAYNE, *Beyond the Po-
    tomac.*

6
Out of the hills of Habersham,
  Down the valleys of Hall,
I hurry amain to reach the plain;
  Run the rapid and leap the fall,
Split at the rock, and together again
  Accept my bed, or narrow or wide,
  And flee from folly on every side
With a lover's pain to attain the plain,
  Far from the hills of Habersham,
  Far from the valleys of Hall.
    SIDNEY LANIER, *The Song of the Chatta-
    hoochee.*

7
Rivers perhaps are the only physical features
of the world that are at their best from the
air.
    ANNE MORROW LINDBERGH, *North to the
    Orient,* ch. 17.

8
        Two ways the rivers
Leap down to different seas, and as they roll
Grow deep and still, and their majestic pres-
    ence
Becomes a benefaction to the towns
They visit.
    HENRY WADSWORTH LONGFELLOW, *The
    Golden Legend,* pt. 5.

9
If it's your Mississippi in dry time,
If it's yours, Uncle Sam, when it's wet,
If it's your Mississippi in fly time,
In flood time it's your Mississippi yet.
    DOUGLAS MALLOCH, *Uncle Sam's River.*

10
Alone by the Schuylkill a wanderer rov'd,
  And bright were its flowery banks to his
    eye;
But far, very far, were the friends that he
    lov'd,
  And he gaz'd on its flowery banks with a
    sigh.
    THOMAS MOORE, *Lines Written on Leav-
    ing Philadelphia.*

11
        I like rivers
Better than oceans, for we see both sides.
    EDWIN ARLINGTON ROBINSON, *Roman
    Bartholow,* pt. 3.

12
The French who found the Ohio River
    named it
La Belle Rivière, meaning a woman easy to
    look at.
    CARL SANDBURG, *Whiffs of the Ohio River
    at Cincinnati.*

13
A monstrous big river.
    MARK TWAIN, *The Adventures of Huckle-
    berry Finn,* ch. 19.

14
It is the longest river in the world—four
thousand three hundred miles. . . . It is also
the crookedest river in the world, since in
one part of its journey it uses up one thousand and three hundred miles to cover the
same ground that the crow would fly over in
six hundred and seventy-five.
    MARK TWAIN, *Life on the Mississippi,* ch.
    1.

15
Your true pilot cares nothing about anything
on earth but the river, and his pride in his
occupation surpasses the pride of kings.
    MARK TWAIN, *Life on the Mississippi,* ch.
    7.

16
It is with rivers as it is with people: the
greatest are not always the most agreeable
nor the best to live with.
    HENRY VAN DYKE, *Little Rivers,* ch. 2.

17
The main social, political spine-character of
the States will probably run along the Ohio,

Missouri and Mississippi rivers, and west and north of them, including Canada.
WALT WHITMAN, *Democratic Vistas.*

1
The Father of Waters.

The Mississippi, which in turn comes from the Algonquin words for "great water" or "great river." Samuel Johnson, in *Rasselas*, refers to "the Father of Waters," meaning the Nile.

But what words shall describe the Mississippi, great father of waters, who (praise be to Heaven) has no young children like him!
CHARLES DICKENS, *American Notes.*

The Father of Waters again goes unvexed to the sea.
ABRAHAM LINCOLN, Letter to James C. Conkling, 26 Aug., 1863. Lincoln referred to Union control of the full length of the river.

Rolling, rolling from Arkansas, Kansas, Iowa,
Rolling from Ohio, Wisconsin, Illinois,
Rolling and shouting:
Till, at last, it is Mississippi,
The Father of Waters.
STEPHEN VINCENT BENÉT, *Ode to Walt Whitman.*

2
Oh, Shenandoah, I long to hear you,
Away, you rolling river,
Oh, Shenandoah, I love to hear you.

Away, I'm bound away
'Cross the wide Missouri.
UNKNOWN, *Shenandoah.*

ROMANCE

3
In love, one first deceives oneself and then others—and that is what is called romance.
JOHN L. BALDERSTON, *Berkeley Square*, p. 63.

4
Romance, like a ghost, eludes touching. It is always where you were, not where you are.
GEORGE WILLIAM CURTIS, *Lotus-Eating: Saratoga.*

5
Every form of human life is romantic.
T. W. HIGGINSON, *A Plea for Culture.*

6
He loved the twilight that surrounds
The borderland of old romance.
HENRY WADSWORTH LONGFELLOW, *Tales of a Wayside Inn:* Prelude.

7
To romance we owe the spirit of adventure, the code of honour, both masculine and feminine.
GEORGE SANTAYANA, *The Genteel Tradition at Bay.*

8
Tradition wears a snowy beard. Romance is always young.
JOHN GREENLEAF WHITTIER, *Mary Garvin*, l. 16.

S

SABBATH

9
There are many people who think that Sunday is a sponge to wipe out all the sins of the week.
HENRY WARD BEECHER, *Life Thoughts.*

10
Some keep the Sabbath going to church;
I keep it staying at home,
With a bobolink for a chorister,
And an orchard for a dome.
EMILY DICKINSON, *Poems*, Pt. ii, No. 57.

11
Yes, child of suffering, thou may'st well be sure
He who ordained the Sabbath loves the poor!
OLIVER WENDELL HOLMES, *Urania*, l. 325.

12
Day of the Lord, as all our days should be!
HENRY WADSWORTH LONGFELLOW, *John Endicott*, act ii, sc. 2.

13
Take the Sunday with you through the week,

And sweeten with it all the other days.
HENRY WADSWORTH LONGFELLOW, *Michael Angelo*, pt. i, st. 5.

14
He has taught me to abhor and detest the Sabbath day and hunt up new and troublesome ways to dishonor it.
MARK TWAIN, Letter to William Dean Howells, 27 Feb., 1885. "He" refers to the novelist George Washington Cable.

SAFETY

15
There is always safety in valor.
EMERSON, *English Traits: The Times.*

16
In skating over thin ice our safety is in our speed.
EMERSON, *Essays, First Series: Prudence.*

17
Though love repine, and reason chafe,
There came a voice without reply,—
" 'Tis man's perdition to be safe,
When for the truth he ought to die."
EMERSON, *Quatrains: Sacrifice.*

1
He that's secure is not safe.
    BENJAMIN FRANKLIN, *Poor Richard*,
        1748.

2
A ship in harbor is safe, but that is not what
ships are built for.
    JOHN A. SHEDD, *Salt from My Attic*, p.
        20.

SAILOR, see Sea, The
SAINT

3
Saint: a dead sinner revised and edited.
    AMBROSE BIERCE, *The Devil's Dictionary*.

4
A saint is a sceptic once in every twenty-four
hours.
    EMERSON, *Journals*, 1864.

5
Every saint, as every man, comes one day to
be superfluous.
    EMERSON, *Journals*, 1864.

6
The greatest saint may be a sinner that never
got down to "hard pan."
    OLIVER WENDELL HOLMES, *The Guardian
        Angel*, ch. 30.

7
The way of this world is to praise dead saints
and persecute living ones.
    NATHANIEL HOWE, Sermon.

8
It is easier to make a saint out of a libertine
than out of a prig.
    GEORGE SANTAYANA, *Little Essays*, p. 253.

SATIRE

9
True satire is not the sneering substance that
we know, but satire that includes the
satirist.
    FRANK MOORE COLBY, *The Colby Essays*,
        vol. i.

10
Satire is a lonely and introspective occupation, for nobody can describe a fool to the
life without much patient self-inspection.
    FRANK MOORE COLBY, *Simple Simon*.

11
Strange! that a Man who has wit enough to
write a Satire should have folly enough to
publish it.
    BENJAMIN FRANKLIN, *Poor Richard*,
        1742.

12
When there's more Malice shown than Mat-
ter,
On the Writer falls the Satyr.
    BENJAMIN FRANKLIN, *Poor Richard*,
        1747.

13
The arrows of sarcasm are barbed with con-

tempt. . . . It is the sneer of the satire, the
ridicule, that galls and wounds.
    WASHINGTON GLADDEN, *Things Old and
        New: Taming the Tongue*.

14
And I must twist my little gift of words
Into a scourge of rough and knotted cords
Unmusical, that whistle as they swing
To leave on shameless backs their purple
    sting.
    JAMES RUSSELL LOWELL, *Epistle to
        George William Curtis*.

15
The American public highly overrates its
sense of humor. We're great belly laughers
and prat fallers, but we never really did have
a real sense of humor. Not satire anyway.
We're a fat-headed, cotton-picking society.
When we realize finally that we aren't God's
given children, we'll understand satire.
    BILL MAULDIN. (*Time*, 21 July, 1961)

16
N.B.—This is rote Sarcastikul.
    ARTEMUS WARD, *A Visit to Brigham
        Young*.

17
Satire is what closes on Saturday night.
    UNKNOWN, a familiar saying in the the-
        ater. (Quoted by Groucho Marx in in-
        terview with Vernon Scott, United Press
        International, datelined Hollywood, 1
        Apr., 1964)

SAVING, see Thrift
SCANDAL
See also Slander

18
Everybody says it, and what everybody says
must be true.
    JAMES FENIMORE COOPER, *Miles Walling-
        ford*, ch. 30.

19
Do not be so impatient to set the town right
concerning the unfounded pretensions and
the false reputation of certain men of standing. They are laboring harder to set the town
right concerning themselves, and will certainly succeed.
    EMERSON, *Essays, Second Series: New
        England Reformers*.

20
In a contempt for the gabble of today's opinions the secret of the world is to be learned.
    EMERSON, *Nature, Studies and Addresses:
        Literary Ethics*.

21
Her mouth is a honey-blossom,
    No doubt, as the poet sings;
But within her lips, the petals,
    Lurks a cruel bee that stings.
    WILLIAM DEAN HOWELLS, *The Sarcastic
        Fair*.

1
Gossip is vice enjoyed vicariously.
ELBERT HUBBARD, *The Philistine,* vol. xix,
p. 104.

2
Nut while the two-legged gab-machine's so
plenty.
JAMES RUSSELL LOWELL, *The Biglow Papers,* Ser. ii, No. 11.

3
No mud can soil us but the mud we throw.
JAMES RUSSELL LOWELL, *Epistle to
George William Curtis.*

4
Gossips are people who have only one relative in common, but that relative the highest
possible; namely God.
CHRISTOPHER MORLEY, *Religio Journalistici.*

5
There are two kinds of people who blow
through life like a breeze,
And one kind is gossipers, and the other kind
is gossipees.
OGDEN NASH, *I'm a Stranger Here Myself: I Have It on Good Authority.*

6
Another good thing about gossip is that it is
within everybody's reach,
And it is much more interesting than any
other form of speech.
OGDEN NASH, *I'm a Stranger Here Myself: I Have It on Good Authority.*

7
How awful to reflect that what people say of
us is true.
LOGAN PEARSALL SMITH, *Afterthoughts.*

8
I had become one of the notorieties of the
metropolis of the world. . . . You could not
take up a newspaper, English, Scotch, or
Irish, without finding in it one or more references to the "vest-pocket million pounder"
and his latest doings and sayings. At first, in
these mentions, I was at the bottom of the
personal-gossip column; next, I was listed
above the knights, next above the barons,
and so on, . . . until I reached the highest
altitude possible, and there I remained, taking precedence of all dukes not royal, and of
all ecclesiastics except the Primate of all
England.
MARK TWAIN, *The Million Pound Bank-
note* (1893). Probably the first use of
"gossip column."

9
Have you heard of the terrible family They,
And the dreadful venemous things They
say?
Why, half the gossip under the sun,
If you trace it back, you will find begun
In that wretched House of They.
ELLA WHEELER WILCOX, *"They Say."*

SCHOLAR

10
It does not necessarily follow that a scholar
in the humanities is also a humanist—but it
should. For what does it avail a man to be
the greatest expert on John Donne if he cannot hear the bell tolling?
MILTON S. EISENHOWER, *The Need for a
New American; The Educational Record,* Oct., 1963, p. 306.

11
I offer perpetual congratulation to the schol-
ar; he has drawn the white lot in life.
EMERSON, *Lectures and Biographical
Sketches: The Man of Letters.*

12
Every man is a scholar potentially, and does
not need any one good so much as this of
right thought.
EMERSON, *Lectures and Biographical
Sketches: The Man of Letters.*

13
I cannot forgive a scholar his homeless
despondency.
EMERSON, *Lectures and Biographical
Sketches: The Man of Letters.*

14
Shall I tell you the secret of the true scholar? It is this: Every man I meet is my master in some point, and in that I learn of
him.
EMERSON, *Letters and Social Aims: Greatness.*

15
The office of the scholar is to cheer, to raise,
and to guide men by showing them facts
amidst appearances.
EMERSON, *Nature, Addresses, and Lectures: The American Scholar.*

16
The scholar is the student of the world; and
of what worth the world is, and with what
emphasis it accosts the soul of man, such is
the worth, such the call of the scholar.
EMERSON, *Nature, Addresses, and Lectures: Literary Ethics.*

17
He must be a solitary, laborious, modest, and
charitable soul. He must embrace solitude as
a bride.
EMERSON, *Nature, Addresses, and Lectures: Literary Ethics.*

18
The studious class are their own victims;
they are thin and pale, their feet are cold,
their heads are hot, the night is without
sleep, the day a fear of interruption,—pallor,
squalor, hunger, and egotism.
EMERSON, *Representative Men: Montaigne.*

19
Who learns by Finding Out has sevenfold

The Skill of him who learned by Being Told.
> ARTHUR GUITERMAN, *A Poet's Proverbs*, p. 73.

1

The world's great men have not commonly been great scholars, nor its great scholars great men.
> OLIVER WENDELL HOLMES, *The Autocrat of the Breakfast-Table*, ch. 6.

2

As turning the logs will make a dull fire burn, so changes of studies a dull brain.
> HENRY WADSWORTH LONGFELLOW, *Drift-Wood: Table Talk*.

3

The scholar digs his ivory cellar in the ruins of the past and lets the present sicken as it will.
> ARCHIBALD MACLEISH, *The Irresponsibles*.

4

The learned are seldom pretty fellows, and in many cases their appearance tends to discourage a love of study in the young.
> H. L. MENCKEN, *New Webster International Dictionary* (1934).

SCHOOL, see Education
SCIENCE

5

Science has taught us how to put the atom to work. But to make it work for good instead of for evil lies in the domain dealing with the principles of human duty. We are now facing a problem more of ethics than physics.
> BERNARD M. BARUCH, Address to United Nations Atomic Energy Commission, UN headquarters, New York City, 14 June, 1946.

Nature is neutral. Man has wrested from nature the power to make the world a desert or to make the deserts bloom. There is no evil in the atom; only in men's souls.
> ADLAI E. STEVENSON, Speech in Hartford, Conn., 18 Sept., 1952.

6

Putting on the spectacles of science in expectation of finding the answer to everything looked at signifies inner blindness.
> J. FRANK DOBIE, *The Voice of the Coyote*: Introduction.

7

Jesus of Nazareth was the most scientific man that ever trod the globe. He plunged beneath the material surface of things, and found the spiritual cause.
> MARY BAKER EDDY, *Science and Health*, p. 313.

8

Why does this magnificent applied science which saves work and makes life easier bring us so little happiness? The simple answer runs: Because we have not yet learned to make sensible use of it.
> ALBERT EINSTEIN, Address at California Institute of Technology, Feb., 1931.

9

Since I do not foresee that atomic energy is to be a great boon for a long time, I have to say that for the present it is a menace. Perhaps it is well that it should be. It may intimidate the human race into bringing order into its international affairs, which, without the pressure of fear, it would not do.
> ALBERT EINSTEIN, *Atlantic Monthly*, Nov., 1945.

10

Science is a little bit like the air you breathe—it is everywhere.
> DWIGHT D. EISENHOWER, upon rejecting the suggestion that a governmental department of science be established, 18 June, 1958.

11

Modern man worships at the temple of science, but science tells him only what is possible, not what is right.
> MILTON S. EISENHOWER, *The Need for a New American; The Educational Record*, Oct., 1963, p. 305.

12

And all their botany is Latin names.
> EMERSON, *Blight*, l. 22.

I pull a flower from the woods,—
A monster with a glass
Computes the stamens in a breath,
And has her in a class.
> EMILY DICKINSON, *Poems*, Pt. ii, No. 20.

13

'Tis a short sight to limit our faith in laws to those of gravity, of chemistry, of botany, and so forth.
> EMERSON, *Conduct of Life: Worship*.

14

Men love to wonder, and that is the seed of our science.
> EMERSON, *Society and Solitude: Works and Days*.

15

Science is the topography of ignorance.
> OLIVER WENDELL HOLMES, *Medical Essays*, p. 211.

16

Science is a first-rate piece of furniture for a man's upper-chamber, if he has common-sense on the ground floor.
> OLIVER WENDELL HOLMES, *The Poet at the Breakfast-Table*, ch. 5.

17

There is the fascination of watching a figment of the imagination emerge through the aid of science to a plan on paper. Then it moves to realization in stone or metal or energy. Then it brings jobs and homes to men. Then it elevates the standards of living and adds to the comforts of life. That is the engineer's high privilege.

> HERBERT HOOVER, 1916. (*Herbert Hoover in His Own Words,* compiled by LOUIS P. LOCHNER; *New York Times Magazine,* 9 Aug., 1964, p. 15)

1
Equipped with his five senses, man explores the universe around him and calls the adventure Science.

> EDWIN POWELL HUBBLE, *Science.*

2
Every science has been an outcast.

> ROBERT G. INGERSOLL, *The Liberty of Man, Woman and Child.*

3
No national sovereignty rules in outer space. Those who venture there go as envoys of the entire human race. Their quest, therefore, must be for all mankind, and what they find should belong to all mankind.

> LYNDON B. JOHNSON, News Conference, Johnson City, Tex., 29 Aug., 1965.

4
As man increases his knowledge of the heavens, why should he fear the unknown on earth? As man draws nearer to the stars, why should he not also draw nearer to his neighbor? As we push ever more deeply into the universe, probing its secrets, discovering its way, we must also constantly try to learn to co-operate across the frontiers that really divide earth's surface.

> LYNDON B. JOHNSON, News Conference, Johnson City, Tex., 29 Aug., 1965.

5
Let both sides seek to invoke the wonders of science instead of its terrors. Together let us explore the stars, conquer the deserts, eradicate disease, tap the ocean depths and encourage the arts and commerce.

> JOHN F. KENNEDY, Inaugural Address, 20 Jan., 1961. "Both sides" refers to the United States and its allies, on one hand, and to "those nations who would make themselves our adversary."

6
I think one of the things which warmed us most during this flight was the realization that however extraordinary computers may be, we are still ahead of them, and that man is still the most extraordinary computer of all.

> JOHN F. KENNEDY, Speech in Washington, D.C., 21 May, 1963, welcoming the astronaut Gordon Cooper after the latter's successful flight. Kennedy was referring to Cooper's taking over the controls of the space ship to achieve his landing.

7
Science contributes to our culture in many ways, as a creative intellectual activity in its own right, as the light which has served to illuminate man's place in the universe, and as the source of understanding of man's own nature.

> JOHN F. KENNEDY, Address to the National Academy of Sciences, Washington, D.C., 22 Oct., 1963.

8
In the years since man unlocked the power stored up within the atom, the world has made progress, halting but effective, toward bringing that power under human control. The challenge may be our salvation. As we begin to master the destructive potentialities of modern science, we move toward a new era in which science can fulfill its creative promise and help bring into existence the happiest society the world has ever known.

> JOHN F. KENNEDY, Address to the National Academy of Sciences, Washington, D.C., 22 Oct., 1963.

9
The language of science is universal, and perhaps scientists have been the most international of all professions in their outlook. . . . Every time you scientists make a major invention, we politicians have to invent a new institution to cope with it—and almost invariably, these days, it must be an international institution.

> JOHN F. KENNEDY, Address to the National Academy of Sciences, Washington, D.C., 22 Oct., 1963.

10
In a world that sits not on a powder keg but on a hydrogen bomb, one begins to suspect that the technician who rules our world is not the master magician he thinks he is but only a sorcerer's apprentice who does not know how to turn off what he has turned on—or even how to avoid blowing himself up.

> JOSEPH WOOD KRUTCH, *Wilderness as a Tonic; The Saturday Review,* 8 June, 1963, p. 15.

11
Science is a great game. It is inspiring and refreshing. The playing field is the universe itself.

> ISIDOR I. RABI. (New York *Times* profile of Dr. Rabi, 28 Oct., 1964, p. 38)

12
Columbus found a world, and had no chart,
Save one that faith deciphered in the skies;
To trust the soul's invincible surmise
Was all his science and his only art.

> GEORGE SANTAYANA, *O World.*

13
People must understand that science is inherently neither a potential for good or for evil. It is a potential to be harnessed by man to do his bidding. Man will determine its direction and its effects. Man, therefore,

must understand science if he is to harness it, to live with it, to grow with it.

> GLENN T. SEABORG. (Interview with Alton Blakeslee of the Associated Press, datelined Washington, D.C., 29 Sept., 1964)

1

Mystics always hope that science will some day overtake them.

> BOOTH TARKINGTON, *Looking Forward*, p. 112.

2

It will free man from his remaining chains, the chains of gravity which still tie him to this planet. It will open to him the gates of heaven.

> WERNHER VON BRAUN, referring to travel in outer space. (*Time*, 10 Feb., 1958)

3

If we continue at this leisurely pace, we will have to pass Russian customs when we land on the moon.

> WERNHER VON BRAUN. (United Press International compilation of outstanding quotations of 1959, datelined London, 29 Dec., 1959; in New York *Times* of 30 Dec., 1959)

4

To define it rudely but not inaptly, engineering is the art of doing that well with one dollar which any bungler can do with two after a fashion.

> ARTHUR M. WELLINGTON, *The Economic Theory of Railway Location:* Introduction.

5

Then there is technology, the excesses of scientists who learn how to make things much faster than we can learn what to do with them.

> THORNTON WILDER. (FLORA LEWIS, *Thornton Wilder at 65; New York Times Magazine,* 15 Apr., 1962, p. 28)

6

Science can give us only the tools in a box, mechanical miracles that it has already given us. But of what use to us are miraculous tools until we have mastered the human, cultural use of them? We do not want to live in a world where the machine has mastered the man; we want to live in a world where man has mastered the machine.

> FRANK LLOYD WRIGHT, Lecture in London, May, 1939.

7

The higher we soar on the wings of science, the worse our feet seem to get entangled in the wires.

> UNKNOWN, *The New Yorker*, 7 Feb., 1931.

SCULPTURE
See also Art and Artists

8

> A sculptor wields
> The chisel, and the stricken marble grows
> To beauty.
>> WILLIAM CULLEN BRYANT, *The Flood of Years*, l. 42.

9

The trouble is, the more it resembles me, the worse it looks.

> EMERSON, to Daniel Chester French, who was making a bust of him. (CABOT, *A Memoir of Ralph Waldo Emerson,* p. 679)

10

The statue is then beautiful when it begins to be incomprehensible.

> EMERSON, *Essays, First Series: Compensation.*

11

> Not from a vain or shallow thought
> His awful Jove young Phidias brought.
>> EMERSON, *The Problem.*

12

Every young sculptor seems to think that he must give the world some specimen of indecorous womanhood, and call it Eve, Venus, a Nymph, or any name that may apologize for a lack of decent clothing.

> NATHANIEL HAWTHORNE, *The Marble Faun,* ch. 14.

13

> Sculpture is more divine, and more like Nature,
> That fashions all her works in high relief,
> And that is sculpture. This vast ball, the Earth,
> Was moulded out of clay, and baked in fire;
> Men, women, and all animals that breathe
> Are statues and not paintings.
>> HENRY WADSWORTH LONGFELLOW, *Michael Angelo,* pt. iii, sec. 5.

14

> Sculpture is more than painting. It is greater
> To raise the dead to life than to create
> Phantoms that seem to live.
>> HENRY WADSWORTH LONGFELLOW, *Michael Angelo,* pt. iii, sec. 5.

15

The tendency to make the capital a catch-all for a variety of monuments to honor the immortals, the no-so-immortals, the greats, the near-greats, and the no-so-greats must stop. We must be on our guard lest the nation's capital come to resemble an unplanned cemetery.

> HUGH SCOTT, Senator from Pennsylvania, commenting on Washington, D.C., 10 Sept., 1960.

SEA, THE
See also Ship

1
For me, my craft is sailing on,
Through mists to-day, clear seas anon.
Whate'er the final harbor be,
'Tis good to sail upon the sea!
    JOHN KENDRICK BANGS, *The Voyage.*

2
Ocean, wherein the whale
    Swims minnow-small.
    WILLIAM ROSE BENÉT, *Whale,* st. 1.

3
Old ocean's gray and melancholy waste.
    WILLIAM CULLEN BRYANT, *Thanatopsis,* l.
        44.

4
The glad indomitable sea.
    BLISS CARMAN, *A Sea Child.*

5
To me, the sea is like a person—like a child
that I've known a long time. It sounds crazy,
I know, but when I swim in the sea I talk to
it. I never feel alone when I'm out there.
    GERTRUDE EDERLE, on the thirtieth anni-
        versary of her feat of swimming the
        English Channel. (New York *Post,* 5
        Sept., 1956)

6
I wiped away the weeds and foam,
I fetched my sea-born treasures home;
But the poor, unsightly, noisome things
Had left their beauty on the shore,
With the sun and the sand and the wild
    uproar.
    EMERSON, *Each and All,* referring to sea
    shells.

7
The wonder is always new that any sane man
can be a sailor.
    EMERSON, *English Traits,* p. 36.

8
Under every deep a lower deep opens.
    EMERSON, *Essays, First Series: Circles.*

9
And bid the broad Atlantic roll
A ferry of the free.
    EMERSON, *Ode,* Concord, 4 July, 1857.

10
Sea full of food, the nourisher of kinds,
Purger of earth, and medicine of men;
Creating a sweet climate by my breath,
Washing out harms and griefs from mem-
    ory,
And, in my mathematic ebb and flow,
Giving a hint of that which changes not.
    EMERSON, *Sea-Shore.*

11
The most advanced nations are always those
who navigate the most.
    EMERSON, *Society and Solitude: Civiliza-
    tion.*

12
Old soldiers, I know not why, seem to be
more accostable than old sailors.
    NATHANIEL HAWTHORNE, *Our Old Home:
    Up the Thames.*

13
From thy dead lips a clearer note is born
Than ever Triton blew from wreathèd horn.
    OLIVER WENDELL HOLMES, *The Cham-
    bered Nautilus.*

14
Of all the husbands on the earth,
The sailor has the finest berth,
For in 'is cabin he can sit
And sail and sail—and let 'er knit.
    WALLACE IRWIN, *A Grain of Salt.*

15
That the persons of our citizens shall be safe
in freely traversing the ocean, that the trans-
portation of our own produce, in our own
vessels, to the markets of our own choice,
and the return to us of the articles we want
for our own use, shall be unmolested, I hold
to be fundamental, and the gauntlet that
must be forever hurled at him who questions
it.
    THOMAS JEFFERSON, *Writings,* vol. xiv, p.
    301.

16
God bless them all who die at sea!
If they must sleep in restless waves,
God make them dream they are ashore,
With grass above their graves.
    SARAH ORNE JEWETT, *The Gloucester
    Mother,* st. 3.

17
The seas are but a highway between the
doorways of the nations.
    FRANKLIN K. LANE, *The American Pio-
    neer.*

18
The land is dearer for the sea,
The ocean for the shore.
    LUCY LARCOM, *On the Beach,* st. 11.

19
He who loves the ocean
And the ways of ships
May taste beside a mountain pool
Brine on his lips.
    MARY SINTON LEITCH, *He Who Loves the
    Ocean.*

20
The dim, dark sea, so like unto Death,
That divides and yet unites mankind!
    HENRY WADSWORTH LONGFELLOW, *The
    Building of the Ship,* l. 166.

21
Spanish sailors with bearded lips,
And the beauty and mystery of the ships,
    And the magic of the sea.
    HENRY WADSWORTH LONGFELLOW, *My
    Lost Youth,* st. 3.

22
My soul is full of longing
    For the secret of the sea,

And the heart of the great ocean
  Sends a thrilling pulse through me.
    HENRY WADSWORTH LONGFELLOW, *The
    Secret of the Sea.*

1
"Wouldst thou,"—so the helmsman an-
    swered,
  "Learn the secret of the sea?
Only those who brave its dangers
  Comprehend its mystery!"
    HENRY WADSWORTH LONGFELLOW, *The
    Secret of the Sea.*

2
And like the wings of sea-birds
Flash the white caps of the sea.
    HENRY WADSWORTH LONGFELLOW, *Twi-
    light.*

3
Come hither! come hither! my little daugh-
    tèr,
  And do not tremble so;
For I can weather the roughest gale
  That ever wind did blow.
    HENRY WADSWORTH LONGFELLOW, *The
    Wreck of the Hesperus.*

4
There is nothing so desperately monotonous
as the sea, and I no longer wonder at the
cruelty of pirates.
    JAMES RUSSELL LOWELL, *Fireside Travels:
    At Sea.*

5
For the Sea is Woman, the Sea is Wonder—
  Her other name is Fate!
    EDWIN MARKHAM, *Virgilia.*

6
Now small fowls flew screaming over the yet
yawning gulf; a sullen white surf beat
against its steep sides; then all collapsed, and
the great shroud of the sea rolled on as it
rolled five thousand years ago.
    HERMAN MELVILLE, *Moby Dick,* ch. 135.

7
Dat ole davil, sea.
    EUGENE O'NEILL, *Anna Christie,* act i.

8
The old, old sea, as one in tears,
  Comes murmuring with foamy lips,
And knocking at the vacant piers,
  Calls for its long lost multitude of ships.
    THOMAS BUCHANAN READ, *Come, Gentle
    Trembler.* This is quoted, incorrectly, in
    MARK TWAIN'S *Life on the Mississippi,*
    ch. 22.

9
The great naked sea shouldering a load of
salt.
    CARL SANDBURG, *Adelaide Crapsey.*

10
A life on the ocean wave,
  A home on the rolling deep,
Where the scattered waters rave,
  And the winds their revels keep!
    EPES SARGENT, *A Life on the Ocean Wave.*

11
Strike up the band, here comes a sailor,
Cash in his hand, just off a whaler;
Stand in a row, don't let him go;
Jack's a cinch, but every inch a sailor.
    ANDREW B. STERLING, *Strike Up the Band*
    (1900).

12
When winds are raging o'er the upper ocean
  And billows wild contend with angry oar,
'Tis said, far down beneath the wild commo-
    tion
That peaceful stillness reigneth evermore.
    HARRIET BEECHER STOWE, *Hymn.*

13
They scorn the strand who sail upon the
    sea.
    HENRY D. THOREAU, *The Fisher's Boy.*

14
We all like to see people sea-sick when we
are not ourselves.
    MARK TWAIN, *The Innocents Abroad,* ch
    3.

15
Of Christian souls more have been wrecked
    on shore
  Than ever were lost at sea.
    CHARLES H. WEBB, *With a Nantucket
    Shell.*

16
I send thee a shell from the ocean-beach;
But listen thou well, for my shell hath
    speech.
Hold to thine ear And plain thou'lt hear
Tales of ships.
    CHARLES H. WEBB, *With a Nantucket
    Shell.*

17
To me the sea is a continual miracle,
The fishes that swim—the rocks—the motion
    of the waves—the ships with men in
    them,
What stranger miracles are there?
    WALT WHITMAN, *Miracles.*

18
Thou sea that pickest and cullest the race in
    time, and unitest nations,
Suckled by thee, old husky nurse, embody-
    ing thee,
Indomitable, untamed as thee.
    WALT WHITMAN, *Song for All Seas, All
    Ships.*

19
Rocked in the cradle of the deep
I lay me down in peace to sleep;
Secure I rest upon the wave,
For Thou, O Lord! hast power to save.
    EMMA HART WILLARD, *Rocked in the Cra-
    dle of the Deep.* Written at sea, 14 July,
    1831.

20
Absolute freedom of navigation upon the
seas.
    WOODROW WILSON, Address to Congress,
    outlining the "Fourteen Points," 8 Jan.,

1918. This was the second of the four-teen.

1
Six days shalt thou labor and do all thou art able,
And on the seventh—holystone the decks and scrape the cable.
UNKNOWN, *The Philadelphia Catechism*, referring to the life of a sailor. (DANA, *Two Years Before the Mast*, ch. 3)

SECRET

2
The parties in both cases Enjoining secre-cy,—
Inviolable compact To notoriety.
EMILY DICKINSON, *Poems*, Pt. ii, No. 32.

3
You can take better care of your secret than another can.
EMERSON, *Journals*, 1863.

4
The secrets of life are not shown except to sympathy and likeness.
EMERSON, *Representative Men: Montaigne*.

5
Three may keep a secret if two of them are dead.
BENJAMIN FRANKLIN, *Poor Richard*, 1735.

SELF-CONTROL

6
No man is such a conqueror as the man who has defeated himself.
HENRY WARD BEECHER, *Proverbs from Plymouth Pulpit*.

7
Coolness and absence of heat and haste indi-cate fine qualities.
EMERSON, *Essays, Second Series: Manners*.

8
Nothing gives one person so much advantage over another as to remain always cool and unruffled under all circumstances.
THOMAS JEFFERSON, *Writings*, vol. xix, p. 241.

9
It is by presence of mind in untried emer-gencies that the native metal of a man is tested.
JAMES RUSSELL LOWELL, *My Study Windows: Lincoln*.

10
Such power there is in clear-eyed self-re-straint.
JAMES RUSSELL LOWELL, *Under the Old Elm*.

SELF-KNOWLEDGE

11
Just stand aside and watch yourself go by,

Think of yourself as "he" instead of "I."
STRICKLAND GILLILAN, *Watch Yourself Go By*.

12
I have to live with myself, and so
I want to be fit for myself to know;
I want to be able as days go by,
Always to look myself straight in the eye.
I don't want to stand with the setting sun
And hate myself for the things I've done.
EDGAR A. GUEST, *Myself*.

13
Nothing requires a rarer intellectual heroism than willingness to see one's equation written out.
GEORGE SANTAYANA, *Little Essays*, p. 37.

14
To understand oneself is the classic form of consolation; to elude oneself is the roman-tic.
GEORGE SANTAYANA, *Words of Doctrine*, p. 200.

15
Not on the outer world
For inward joy depend;
Enjoy the luxury of thought,
Make thine own self friend;
Not with the restless throng,
In search of solace roam,
But with an independent zeal
Be intimate at home.
LYDIA H. SIGOURNEY, *Know Thyself*.

16
Great God, I ask thee for no meaner pelf
Than that I may not disappoint myself.
HENRY D. THOREAU, *My Prayer*.

17
We can secure the people's approval, if we do right and try hard; but our own is worth a hundred of it, and no way has been found out of securing that.
MARK TWAIN, *Pudd'nhead Wilson's New Calendar*.

SELF-LOVE

See also Selfishness, Vanity

18
He that falls in love with himself, will have no rivals.
BENJAMIN FRANKLIN, *Poor Richard*, 1739.

19
Would you hurt a man keenest, strike at his self-love.
LEW WALLACE, *Ben Hur*, bk. vi, ch. 2.

20
Rule No. Six: Don't take yourself so damn seriously.
UNKNOWN. Originated in the Allied Mari-time Transport Council, 1917—on the authority of Dwight Morrow. (*Raleigh News and Observer*, 25 May, 1933)

SELF-RESPECT
See also Pride

1
I desire so to conduct the affairs of this administration that if at the end, when I come to lay down the reins of power, I have lost every other friend on earth, I shall at least have one friend left, and that friend shall be down inside of me.
> ABRAHAM LINCOLN, Reply to Missouri Committee of Seventy, 1864.

2
He that respects himself is safe from others;
He wears a coat of mail that none can pierce.
> HENRY WADSWORTH LONGFELLOW, *Michael Angelo,* pt. ii, sec. 3.

3
It is necessary to the happiness of man that he be mentally faithful to himself.
> THOMAS PAINE, *The Age of Reason,* ch. 1.

4
When an American says that he loves his country, he means not only that he loves the New England hills, the prairies glistening in the sun, the wide and rising plains, the great mountains, and the sea. He means that he loves an inner air, and inner light in which freedom lives and in which a man can draw the breath of self-respect.
> ADLAI E. STEVENSON, Speech in New York City, 27 Aug., 1952, during the presidential campaign.

SELF-SACRIFICE

5
Self-sacrifice which denies common sense is not a virtue. It's a spiritual dissipation.
> MARGARET DELAND.

6
Self-sacrifice is the real miracle out of which all the reported miracles grew.
> EMERSON, *Society and Solitude: Courage.*

7
There is something in the unselfish and self-sacrificing love of a brute, which goes directly to the heart of him who has had frequent occasion to test the paltry friendship and gossamer fidelity of mere Man.
> EDGAR ALLAN POE, *The Black Cat.*

8
The awful beauty of self-sacrifice.
> JOHN GREENLEAF WHITTIER, *Amy Wentworth,* l. 16.

SELFISHNESS
See also Self-Love

9
You mayn't be changed to a bird though you live
As selfishly as you can;
But you will be changed to a smaller thing—
A mean and selfish man.
> PHOEBE CARY, *A Legend of the Northland.*

10
All sensible people are selfish.
> EMERSON, *Conduct of Life: Considerations by the Way.*

11
Self-preservation is the first principle of our nature.
> ALEXANDER HAMILTON, *Full Vindication,* 15 Dec., 1774.

12
It is to the credit of human nature, that, except where its selfishness is brought into play, it loves more readily than it hates.
> NATHANIEL HAWTHORNE, *The Scarlet Letter,* ch. 13.

13
It is to be regretted that the rich and powerful too often bend the acts of government to their selfish purposes.
> ANDREW JACKSON, Message accompanying his veto of the Bank Bill, 10 July, 1832.

14
John Adams . . . said . . . Reason, Justice and Equity never had weight enough on the face of the earth to govern the councils of men. It is interest alone which does it.
> THOMAS JEFFERSON, *Writings,* vol. i, p. 49.

15
But somehow, when the dogs hed gut asleep,
Their love o' mutton beat their love o' sheep.
> JAMES RUSSELL LOWELL, *The Biglow Papers,* Ser. ii, No. 11.

16
Not a deed would he do, nor a word would he utter,
Till he'd weighed its relations to plain bread and butter.
> JAMES RUSSELL LOWELL, *A Fable for Critics,* l. 186.

17
I have yet to find a man worth his salt in any direction who did not think of himself first and foremost. . . . The man who thinks of others before he thinks of himself may become a Grand Master of the Elks, a Socialist of parts, or the star guest of honor at public banquets, but he will never become a great or successful artist, statesman, or even clergyman.
> GEORGE JEAN NATHAN, *Testament of a Critic,* p. 6.

18
I should like to have it said of my first administration that in it the forces of selfishness and of lust for power met their match. I should like to have it said of my second administration that in it these forces met their master.
> FRANKLIN D. ROOSEVELT, Speech in New York City, 31 Oct., 1936.

1
We have always known that heedless self-interest was bad morals; we know now that it is bad economics.
FRANKLIN D. ROOSEVELT, Second Inaugural Address, 20 Jan., 1937.

2
With the exception of the instinct of self-preservation, the propensity for emulation is probably the strongest and most alert and persistent of the economic motives proper.
THORSTEIN VEBLEN, *The Theory of the Leisure Class*, ch. 5.

SENSE

3
Much madness is divinest sense
  To a discerning eye;
Much sense the starkest madness.
EMILY DICKINSON, *Poems*, Pt. i, No. 11.

4
This dictate of common sense.
JONATHAN EDWARDS, *The Freedom of the Will*.

5
Nothing astonishes men so much as common sense and plain dealing.
EMERSON, *Essays, First Series: Art*.

6
Moral qualities rule the world, but at short distances the senses are despotic.
EMERSON, *Essays, Second Series: Manners*.

7
Common sense, which, one would say, means the shortest line between two points.
EMERSON, *Journals*, Mar., 1866.

8
Persons of good sense, I have since observed, seldom fall into disputation, except lawyers, university men, and men of all sorts that have been bred at Edinburgh.
BENJAMIN FRANKLIN, *Autobiography*, ch. 1.

9
One of the wisest things my daddy ever told me was that "so-and-so is a damned smart man, but the fool's got no sense."
LYNDON B. JOHNSON. (HENRY A. ZEIGER, *Lyndon B. Johnson: Man and President*, p. 65)

10
Common sense, in so far as it exists, is all for the bourgeoisie. Nonsense is the privilege of the aristocracy. The worries of the world are for the common people.
GEORGE JEAN NATHAN, *Autobiography of an Attitude*.

11
His motives are unquestionable, and he possesses to a remarkable degree the characteristic, God-given trait of this people, sound common sense.
CARL SCHURZ, Letter to Theodore Petrasch, 12 Oct., 1864. Referring to Abraham Lincoln.

12
Let's face it. Let's talk sense to the American people. Let's tell them the truth, that there are no gains without pains, that we are now on the eve of great decisions, not easy decisions, like resistance when you're attacked, but a long, patient, costly struggle which alone can assure triumph over the great enemies of man—war, poverty, and tyranny—and the assaults upon human dignity which are the most grievous consequences of each.
ADLAI E. STEVENSON, Speech, upon accepting the presidential nomination, Democratic national convention in Chicago, 26 July, 1952.

13
Why level downward to our dullest perception always, and praise that as common sense? The commonest sense is the sense of men asleep, which they express by snoring.
HENRY D. THOREAU, *Walden: Conclusion*.

SENTIMENTALISM

14
Society is infested by persons who, seeing that the sentiments please, counterfeit the expression of them. These we call sentimentalists,—talkers who mistake the description for the thing, saying for having.
EMERSON, *Letters and Social Aims: Social Aims*.

15
Sentimentalism is an irrational desire to be helpful to one's fellow-men. It sometimes appears as an ingratiating and even a redeeming quality in those who cannot or will not think. But the sentimentalist is really a dangerous character. He distrusts the intellect, because it might show him he was wrong. He believes in the primacy of the will, and this is what makes him dangerous.
ROBERT M. HUTCHINS, Address in Washington, D.C., 7 May, 1938. (*Contemporary Forum*, ed. by ERNEST J. WRAGE AND BARNET BASKERVILLE, p. 224)

16
The capital of the orator is in the bank of the highest sentimentalities and the purest enthusiasms.
EDWARD G. PARKER, *The Golden Age of American Oratory*, ch. 1.

SERENITY

17
Serene I fold my hands and wait,
  Nor care for wind nor tide nor sea;
I rave no more 'gainst time or fate,
  For lo! my own shall come to me.
JOHN BURROUGHS, *Waiting*.

1

Keep cool: it will be all one a hundred years hence.
> EMERSON, *Representative Men: Montaigne.*

2

America's present need is not heroics but healing; not nostrums but normalcy; not revolutions but restoration; . . . not surgery but serenity.
> WARREN G. HARDING, Speech in Boston, May, 1920.

3

Learn the sweet magic of a cheerful face;
Not always smiling, but at least serene.
> OLIVER WENDELL HOLMES, *The Morning Visit.*

4

In the midst of battles, in the roar of conflict, they found the serenity of death.
> ROBERT G. INGERSOLL, *Memorial Day Vision.*

5

The star of the unconquered will,
  He rises in my breast,
Serene, and resolute, and still,
  And calm and self-possessed.
> HENRY WADSWORTH LONGFELLOW, *The Light of Stars,* st. 7.

6

And all the sweet serenity of books.
> HENRY WADSWORTH LONGFELLOW, *Morituri Salutamus,* l. 232.

SHIP

See also Sea

7

Gray sail against the sky,
Gray butterfly!
Have you a dream for going,
Or are you only the blind wind's blowing?
> DANA BURNET, *A Sail at Twilight.*

8

A capital ship for an ocean trip
  Was "The Walloping Window-blind";
No gale that blew dismayed her crew
  Or troubled the captain's mind.
> CHARLES EDWARD CARRYL, *The Walloping Window-blind.* (From *Davy and the Goblin,* p. 89)

9

Like a true ship, committed to her element once for all at her Launching, she perished at sea.
> R. H. DANA, *Two Years Before the Mast.*

10

Everything was 'ship-shape and Bristol fashion.'
> R. H. DANA, *Two Years Before the Mast.*

11

The true ship is the ship builder.
> EMERSON, *Essays, First Series: Of History.*

12

This is the ship of pearl, which, poets feign,

Sails the unshadowed main,—
The venturous bark that flings
On the sweet summer wind its purpled wings.
> OLIVER WENDELL HOLMES, *The Chambered Nautilus.*

13

Ships, young ships,
I do not wonder men see you as women—
You in the white length of your loveliness
Reclining on the sea!
> SALLY BRUCE KINSOLVING, *Ships.*

14

Build me straight, O worthy Master!
  Stanch and strong, a goodly vessel
That shall laugh at all disaster,
  And with wave and whirlwind wrestle!
> HENRY WADSWORTH LONGFELLOW, *The Building of the Ship,* l. 1.

15

There's not a ship that sails the ocean,
But every climate, every soil,
Must bring its tribute, great or small,
And help to build the wooden wall!
> HENRY WADSWORTH LONGFELLOW, *The Building of the Ship,* l. 66.

16

She starts,—she moves,—she seems to feel
The thrill of life along her keel!
> HENRY WADSWORTH LONGFELLOW, *The Building of the Ship,* l. 349.

17

And the wind plays on those great sonorous harps, the shrouds and masts of ships.
> HENRY WADSWORTH LONGFELLOW, *Hyperion,* bk. i, ch. 7.

18

Ships that pass in the night, and speak each other in passing,
Only a signal shown and a distant voice in the darkness.
> HENRY WADSWORTH LONGFELLOW, *Tales of a Wayside Inn: The Theologian's Tale: Elizabeth,* pt. 4.

19

Never a ship sails out of the bay
But carries my heart as a stowaway.
> ROSELLE MERCER MONTGOMERY, *The Stowaway.*

20

Never, in these United States, has the brain of man conceived, or the hand of man fashioned, so perfect a thing as the clipper ship.
> SAMUEL ELIOT MORISON, *Maritime History of Massachusetts,* ch. 23.

21

Don't give up the ship. You will beat them off!
> CAPTAIN JAMES MUGFORD, of the schooner Franklin, 19 May, 1776. These were his last words during a British attack in Boston Harbor.

22

A ship is always referred to as "she" because

it costs so much to keep one in paint and powder.

> ADMIRAL CHESTER W. NIMITZ, Address before the Society of Sponsors of the U.S. Navy, 13 Feb., 1940.

1

Women are jealous of ships. They always suspect the sea. They know they're three of a kind when it comes to a man.

> EUGENE O'NEILL, *Mourning Becomes Electra*, act i.

2

It would have been as though he were in a boat of stone with masts of steel, sails of lead, ropes of iron, the devil at the helm, the wrath of God for a breeze, and hell for his destination.

> EMERY A. STORRS, Speech in Chicago, 1866, referring to President Andrew Johnson, who had threatened to use troops to force Congress to adjourn.

3

The ship is anchor'd safe and sound, its voyage closed and done,
From fearful trip the victor ship comes in with object won.

> WALT WHITMAN, *O Captain! My Captain!*

4

Whoever you are, motion and reflection are especially for you,
The divine ship sails the divine sea for you.

> WALT WHITMAN, *Song of the Rolling Earth.*

5

If all the ships I have at sea
Should come a-sailing home to me,
    Ah, well! the harbor would not hold
So many ships as there would be
If all my ships came home from sea.

> ELLA WHEELER WILCOX, *My Ships.*

SHIPWRECK

6

"We are lost!" the captain shouted,
    As he staggered down the stairs.

> JAMES THOMAS FIELDS, *Ballad of the Tempest.*

7

And fast through the midnight dark and drear,
    Through the whistling sleet and snow,
Like a sheeted ghost, the vessel swept
    Tow'rds the reef of Norman's Woe.

> HENRY WADSWORTH LONGFELLOW, *The Wreck of the Hesperus.*

8

No dust have I to cover me,
    My grave no man may show;
My tomb is this unending sea,
    And I lie far below.
My fate, O stranger, was to drown;

And where it was the ship went down
    Is what the sea-birds know.

> EDWIN ARLINGTON ROBINSON, *Inscription by the Sea.* (From the *Greek Anthology*)

SHOE

9

An open hand, an easy shoe,
And a hope to make the day go through.

> BLISS CARMAN, *The Joys of the Road.*

10

'Tis the same to him who wears a shoe, as if the whole earth were covered with leather.

> EMERSON, *Conduct of Life: Wealth.* Quoted as a Persian proverb.

11

The shoemaker makes a good shoe because he makes nothing else.

> EMERSON, *Letters and Social Aims: Greatness.*

12

Wynken, Blynken, and Nod one night
    Sailed off in a wooden shoe—
Sailed on a river of crystal light
    Into a sea of dew.

> EUGENE FIELD, *Wynken, Blynken, and Nod,* st. 1.

13

Oh, her heart's adrift with one
On an endless voyage gone!
    Night and morning
Hannah's at the window binding shoes.

> LUCY LARCOM, *Hannah Binding Shoes.*

14

The stairway of time ever echoes with the wooden shoe going up and the polished boot coming down.

> JACK LONDON, *What Life Means to Me; Cosmopolitan Magazine,* Mar., 1906. A restatement of a familiar saying.

15

There shoemakers quietly stick to the last.

> JAMES RUSSELL LOWELL, *A Fable for Critics.* Referring to the grave.

16

When boots and shoes are torn up to the lefts,
Cobblers must thrust their awls up to the hefts.

> NATHANIEL WARD, *The Simple Cobbler of Aggawam in America,* title page.

17

We shall walk in velvet shoes:
    Wherever we go
Silence will fall like dews
    On white silence below.

> ELINOR HOYT WYLIE, *Velvet Shoes,* st. 4.

SILENCE

18

There be
Three silent things:
The falling snow . . . the hour

Before the dawn . . . the mouth of one
Just dead.
ADELAIDE CRAPSEY, *Triad*.

1
The splendor of Silence,—of snow-jeweled
hills and of ice.
INGRAM CROCKETT, *Orion*.

2
O golden Silence, bid our souls be still,
And on the foolish fretting of our care
Lay thy soft touch of healing unaware!
JULIA CAROLINE RIPLEY DORR, *Silence*.

3
Remember what peace there may be in si-
lence.
MAX EHRMANN, *Desiderata*.

4
Persons in public positions—including me—
miss too many chances to keep their mouths
shut. I'm not passing up my chance tonight.
DWIGHT D. EISENHOWER, in refusing to
state publicly his preference for the Republican presidential nomination in advance of the 1964 national convention.
This comment was made at the commencement exercises of George Washington University, Washington, D.C., 7
June, 1964.

5
The silent organ loudest chants
The master's requiem.
EMERSON, *Dirge*, last lines.

6
The ancient sentence said, Let us be silent
for so are the gods. Silence is a solvent that
destroys personality, and gives us leave to be
great and universal.
EMERSON, *Essays, First Series: Intellect*.

7
And silence, like a poultice, comes
To heal the blows of sound.
OLIVER WENDELL HOLMES, *The Music-
Grinders*, st. 10.

8
Not much talk—a great, sweet silence.
HENRY JAMES, *A Bundle of Letters*, letter
4.

9
We often repent of what we have said, but
never, never, of that which we have not.
THOMAS JEFFERSON, *Writings*, vol. xiv, p.
117.

10
Eleanor Roosevelt taught us that sometimes
silence is the greatest sin.
CLAUDIA T. (MRS. LYNDON B.) JOHNSON,
Speech at first anniversary luncheon of
the Eleanor Roosevelt Memorial Foundation, New York City, 9 Apr., 1964.
She was referring to Mrs. Roosevelt's
courage in speaking out in the face of
opposition.

11
You've got to know when to keep your
mouth shut. The Senate's the cruelest judge

in the world. A man's a fool to talk to other
fellows about any subject unless he knows
more about that subject than they do.
LYNDON B. JOHNSON. (HENRY A. ZEIGER,
*Lyndon B. Johnson: Man and Presi-
dent*, p. 67)

12
You hesitate to stab me with a sword,
And know not Silence is the sharper sword.
ROBERT UNDERWOOD JOHNSON, *To One
Who Has Forgotten*.

13
Better to remain silent and be thought a fool
than to speak out and remove all doubt.
ABRAHAM LINCOLN. (*Golden Book*, Nov.,
1931)

14
What shall I say to you? What can I say
Better than silence is?
HENRY WADSWORTH LONGFELLOW, *Mori-
turi Salutamus*, l. 128.

15
Three Silences there are: the first of speech,
The second of desire, the third of thought.
HENRY WADSWORTH LONGFELLOW, *The
Three Silences of Molinos*.

16
I have known the silence of the stars and of
the sea,
And the silence of the city when it pauses,
And the silence of a man and a maid, . . .
And the silence for which music alone finds
the word.
EDGAR LEE MASTERS, *Silence*.

17
Why, know you not soul speaks to soul?
I say the use of words shall pass—
Words are but fragments of the glass,
But silence is the perfect whole.
JOAQUIN MILLER, *Why, Know You Not?*

18
Be silent and safe—silence never betrays
you.
JOHN BOYLE O'REILLY, *Rules of the Road*,
st. 2.

19
Love silence, even in the mind; for thoughts
are to that as words are to the body, troublesome: much speaking, as much thinking,
spends. True silence is the rest of the mind;
and it is to the spirit what sleep is to the
body, nourishment and refreshment.
WILLIAM PENN, *Advice to His Children*.

20
A wise old owl sat on an oak,
The more he saw the less he spoke;
The less he spoke the more he heard;
Why aren't we like that wise old bird?
EDWARD HERSEY RICHARDS, *A Wise Old
Owl*. This was quoted by John D. Rock-
efeller, Sr., and used by Calvin Coolidge
as a motto over the fireplace of his
home in Northampton, Mass.

1
The dark is at the end of every day,
And silence is the end of every song.
> EDWIN ARLINGTON ROBINSON, *Woman and the Wife.*

2
Of every noble work the silent part is best
Of all expression that which cannot be expressed.
> W. W. STORY, *The Unexpressed.*

3
It takes a man to make a room silent.
> HENRY D. THOREAU, *Journal*, 9 Feb., 1839.

4
I have been breaking silence these twenty-three years and have hardly made a rent in it. Silence has no end; speech is but the beginning of it.
> HENRY D. THOREAU, *Journal,* 9 Feb., 1841.

5
The sweet voice into silence went,
A silence which was almost pain.
> JOHN GREENLEAF WHITTIER, *The Grave by the Lake,* st. 45.

6
You ain't learnin' nothing when you're talking.
> UNKNOWN, Motto that hung in the office of Lyndon B. Johnson during his years in the U.S. Senate. (HENRY A. ZEIGER, *Lyndon B. Johnson: Man and President,* p. 67)

SIMPLICITY

7
Simplicity is the most deceitful mistress that ever betrayed man.
> HENRY ADAMS, *The Education of Henry Adams,* ch. 30.

8
Art, it seems to me, should simplify.
> WILLA CATHER, *On the Art of Fiction.*

9
Nothing is more simple than greatness; indeed, to be simple is to be great.
> EMERSON, *Nature, Addresses, and Lectures: Literary Ethics.*

10
There are some things which cannot be learned quickly, and time, which is all we have, must be paid heavily for their acquiring. They are the very simplest things and because it takes a man's life to know them the little new that each man gets from life is very costly and the only heritage he has to leave.
> ERNEST HEMINGWAY, *Death in the Afternoon,* ch. 16.

11
His words were simple words enough,
    And yet he used them so,
That what in other mouths was rough

In his seemed musical and low.
> JAMES RUSSELL LOWELL, *The Shepherd of King Admetus,* st. 5.

12
We have exchanged the Washingtonian dignity for the Jeffersonian simplicity, which was in truth only another name for the Jacksonian vulgarity.
> BISHOP HENRY C. POTTER, Address, Washington Centennial Service, New York City, 30 Apr., 1889.

13
No one has ever exhausted the potentialities of a Brownie.
> EDWARD STEICHEN, commenting on photography. (New York *Times,* 7 Jan., 1966, p. 58)

14
I have Bloomington to thank for the most important lesson I have learned: that in quiet places reason abounds, that in quiet people there is vision and purpose, that many things are revealed to the humble that are hidden from the great.
> ADLAI E. STEVENSON, commenting on his home town, Bloomington, Ill. (New York *Times,* 19 July, 1965, p. 13)

15
Simplicity, simplicity, simplicity! I say, let your affairs be as two or three, and not a hundred or a thousand. . . . Simplify, simplify.
> HENRY D. THOREAU, *Walden,* ch. 2.

16
The art of art, the glory of expression and the sunshine of the light of letters, is simplicity.
> WALT WHITMAN, *Leaves of Grass:* Preface.

SIN

See also Crime, Evil, Guilt, Vice

17
There is not any memory with less satisfaction than the memory of some temptation we resisted.
> JAMES BRANCH CABELL, *Jurgen,* p. 39.

18
It takes two bodies to make one seduction.
> GUY WETMORE CARRYL. (BEER, *The Mauve Decade,* p. 197)

19
Every sin is the result of a collaboration.
> STEPHEN CRANE.

20
Sinners, you are making a bee-line from time to eternity.
> LORENZO DOW, *Sermons,* vol. i, p. 215.

21
Sin makes its own hell, and goodness its own heaven.
> MARY BAKER EDDY, *Science and Health,* p. 196.

1
Sin kills the sinner and will continue to kill him as long as he sins.
> MARY BAKER EDDY, *Science and Health*, p. 203.

2
Sin brought death, and death will disappear with the disappearance of sin.
> MARY BAKER EDDY, *Science and Health*, p. 426.

3
That which we call sin in others is experiment for us.
> EMERSON, *Essays, Second Series: Experience*.

4
Sin is not hurtful because it is forbidden, but it is forbidden because it is hurtful. Nor is a duty beneficial because it is commanded, but it is commanded because it is beneficial.
> BENJAMIN FRANKLIN, *Poor Richard*, 1739.

5
How many po' sinners'll be kotched out late
En fin' no latch ter de golden gate?
No use fer ter wait twell ter-morrer,
De sun mus'n't set on yo' sorrer,—
Sin's ez sharp ez a bamboo-brier,—
O Lord! fetch de mo'ners up higher!
> JOEL CHANDLER HARRIS, *Uncle Remus: His Songs and His Sayings*.

6
Unto each man comes a day when his favorite sins all forsake him,
And he complacently thinks he has forsaken his sins.
> JOHN HAY, *Distichs*.

7
Through sin do men reach the light.
> ELBERT HUBBARD, *Epigrams*.

8
Men are punished by their sins, not for them.
> ELBERT HUBBARD, *The Philistine*, vol. xi, p. 7.

9
The world loves a spice of wickedness.
> HENRY WADSWORTH LONGFELLOW, *Hyperion*, ch. vii, bk. 1.

10
They enslave their children's children who make compromise with sin.
> JAMES RUSSELL LOWELL, *The Present Crisis*, st. 9.

11
Sin has always been an ugly word, but it has been made so in a new sense over the last half-century. It has been made not only ugly but passé. People are no longer sinful, they are only immature or underprivileged or frightened or, more particularly, sick.
> PHYLLIS MCGINLEY, *The Province of the Heart: In Defense of Sin*, p. 35.

12
The sins they sinned in Eden, boys,

Are bad enough for me.
> CHRISTOPHER MORLEY, *A Glee Upon Cider*.

13
My sin is the black spot which my bad act makes, seen against the disk of the Sun of Righteousness.
> C. H. PARKHURST, *Sermons: Pattern in the Mount*.

14
I hate the sin, but I love the sinner.
> THOMAS BUCHANAN READ, *What a Word May Do*, st. 1.

15
Miniver loved the Medici,
  Albeit he had never seen one;
He would have sinned incessantly
  Could he have been one.
> EDWIN ARLINGTON ROBINSON, *Miniver Cheevy*, st. 5.

16
For my part I believe in the forgiveness of sin and the redemption of ignorance.
> ADLAI E. STEVENSON, replying to a heckler during a United Nations Day speech delivered by Stevenson in Dallas, 24 Oct., 1963. After the speech Stevenson was struck with a placard and spat on by demonstrators.

17
'Cause I's wicked,—I is. I's mighty wicked, anyhow. I can't help it.
> HARRIET BEECHER STOWE, *Uncle Tom's Cabin*, ch. 20.

18
We cannot well do without our sins; they are the highway of our virtue.
> HENRY D. THOREAU, *Journal*, 22 Mar., 1842.

19
When one has broken the tenth commandment, the others are not of much account.
> MARK TWAIN, *Pudd'nhead Wilson's Calendar*.

20
Sin, every day, takes out a new patent for some new invention.
> E. P. WHIPPLE, *Essays: Romance of Rascality*.

21
But he who never sins can little boast
Compared to him who goes and sins no more!
The "sinful Mary" walks more white in heaven
Than some who never "sinn'd and were forgiven"!
> N. P. WILLIS, *The Lady Jane*, canto ii, st. 44.

22
But the sin forgiven by Christ in Heaven
By man is cursed alway!
> N. P. WILLIS, *Unseen Spirits*.

SINCERITY
See also Candor

1
Private sincerity is a public welfare.
C. A. Bartol, *Radical Problems: Individualism.*

2
Sincerity is the luxury allowed, like diadems and authority, only to the highest rank. . . . Every man alone is sincere.
Emerson, *Essays, First Series: Friendship.*

3
Never was a sincere word utterly lost.
Emerson, *Essays, First Series: Spiritual Laws.*

4
Profound sincerity is the only basis of talent as of character.
Emerson, *Essays: Natural History of Intellect.*

5
Every sincere man is right.
Emerson, *Essays: Natural History of Intellect.*

6
Wrought in sad sincerity.
Emerson, *The Problem.*

7
The honest man must keep faith with himself; his sheet anchor is sincerity.
Emerson, *Table Talk.*

8
At last be true; no gesture now let spring
But from supreme sincerity of art;
Let him who plays the monarch be a king,
Who plays the rogue, be perfect in his part.
John Erskine, *At the Front.*

9
Don't be "consistent," but be simply *true.*
Oliver Wendell Holmes, *The Professor at the Breakfast-Table,* ch. 2.

10
See, talk, and feel the people. But above all be yourself in any direction. Then you'll be what you are and represent America.
John F. Kennedy, Instruction to John Steinbeck when the novelist set out on a mission for the United States behind the Iron Curtain in 1963. Steinbeck quoted these words at a press conference in Vienna, 26 Nov., 1963, four days after the death of Kennedy.

11
The only conclusive evidence of a man's sincerity is that he gave *himself* for a principle.
James Russell Lowell, *Among My Books: Rousseau.*

12
Sincerity is impossible, unless it pervade the whole being, and the pretence of it saps the very foundation of character.
James Russell Lowell, *Essays: Pope.*

13
Then grow as God hath planted, grow
A lordly oak or daisy low,
As He hath set His garden; be
Just what thou art, or grass or tree.
Joaquin Miller, *With Love to You and Yours,* pt. ii, sec. 8.

14
I want to see you shoot the way you shout.
Theodore Roosevelt, Speech in New York City, Oct., 1917.

15
That my weak hand may equal my firm faith,
And my life practise more than my tongue saith.
Henry D. Thoreau, *My Prayer.*

SKY

16
The mountain at a given distance
In amber lies;
Approached, the amber flits a little,—
And that's the skies!
Emily Dickinson, *Poems,* Pt. i, No. 45.

17
I have need of the sky,
I have business with the grass.
Richard Hovey, *I Have Need of the Sky.*

18
The sky
is that beautiful old parchment
in which the sun and the moon
keep their diary.
Alfred Kremyborg, *Old Manuscript.*

19
The very clouds have wept and died
And only God is in the sky.
Joaquin Miller, *The Ship in the Desert.*

20
The skies they were ashen and sober.
Edgar Allan Poe, *Ulalume.*

21
If all the skies were sunshine,
Our faces would be fain
To feel once more upon them
The cooling plash of rain.
Henry van Dyke, *If All the Skies,* st. 1.

22
Over all the sky—the sky! far, far out of reach, studded, breaking out, the eternal stars.
Walt Whitman, *Bivouac on a Mountain Side.*

23
Green calm below, blue quietness above.
John Greenleaf Whittier, *The Pennsylvania Pilgrim.*

SLANDER
See also Scandal

1
Hear no ill of a friend, nor speak any of an enemy.

> BENJAMIN FRANKLIN, *Poor Richard,* 1739.

2
A Slander counts by Threes its victims, who Are Speaker, Spoken Of, and Spoken To.

> ARTHUR GUITERMAN, *A Poet's Proverbs,* p. 39.

3
There are two sides to a story,
Hear them both before you blame;
For a woman's crowning glory
Is a fair, unblemished name!
Heaven holds no gift that's grander,
So beware of idle slander;
There are two sides to a story—
Right and wrong!

> WILL A. HEELAN AND J. FRED HELF, *There Are Two Sides to a Story* (1900).

4
Defamation is becoming a necessity of life; insomuch that a dish of tea in the morning or evening cannot be digested without this stimulant.

> THOMAS JEFFERSON, *Writings,* vol. xi, p. 224.

5
Truth is generally the best vindication against slander.

> ABRAHAM LINCOLN, Letter to Edwin M. Stanton, 18 July, 1864.

6
To persevere in one's duty and be silent is the best answer to calumny.

> GEORGE WASHINGTON, *Moral Maxims.*

7
If for a tranquil mind you seek,
These things observe with care:
Of whom you speak, to whom you speak,
And how, and when, and where.

> UNKNOWN, *A Rule of Conduct.* Quoted by Edwin Booth.

SLAVERY

8
If those laws of the southern states by virtue of which slavery exists there and is what it is, are not wrong, nothing is wrong.

> LEONARD BACON, *Slavery Discussed:* Preface (1846).

If slavery is not wrong, nothing is wrong.

> ABRAHAM LINCOLN, Letter to A. G. Hodges, 4 Apr., 1864.

9
Running through the dark center of American history there is a vivid red thread of tragedy. Deep in the national subconscious lies the stain put there by the fact that through nearly half of its independent existence the nation had to live with an intolerable thing which could neither be rationally justified nor peacefully disposed of—the institution of human slavery.

> BRUCE CATTON, *Reading, Writing and History; American Heritage,* Oct., 1956, p. 98.

10
I do not see how a barbarous community and a civilized community can constitute a state. I think we must get rid of slavery or we must get rid of freedom.

> EMERSON, *The Assault upon Mr. Sumner's Speech,* 26 May, 1856.

11
Under the whip of the driver, the slave shall feel his equality with saints and heroes.

> EMERSON, *Conduct of Life: Worship.*

12
Slavery it is that makes slavery; freedom, freedom. The slavery of women happened when the men were slaves of kings.

> EMERSON, *Miscellanies: Women.*

13
Resolved: That the compact which exists between the North and the South is a covenant with death and an agreement with hell, involving both parties in atrocious criminality, and should be immediately annulled.

> WILLIAM LLOYD GARRISON, Resolution adopted by the Massachusetts Anti-Slavery Society, 27 Jan., 1843.

14
In all social systems there must be a class to do the mean duties. . . . It constitutes the very mudsills of society. . . . Fortunately for the South, she found a race adapted to that purpose. . . . We use them for that purpose and call them slaves.

> JAMES H. HAMMOND, Speech in U.S. Senate, Mar., 1858.

15
It is far better to be a mortal freeman than an immortal slave.

> ROBERT G. INGERSOLL, *Voltaire.*

16
Man's mind and not his master makes him slave.

> ROBERT U. JOHNSON, *To the Spirit of Byron.*

17
"A house divided against itself cannot stand." I believe this government cannot endure permanently half-slave and half-free. I do not expect the Union to be dissolved—I do not expect the house to fall—but I do expect it will cease to be divided. It will become all one thing, or all the other. Either the opponents of slavery will arrest the further spread of it, and place it where the public mind shall rest in the belief that it is in the course of ultimate extinction; or its advocates will push it forward, till it shall

become alike lawful in all the States, old as well as new—North as well as South.

> ABRAHAM LINCOLN, Speech at the Republican state convention, Springfield, Ill., 17 June, 1858. The opening sentence is a paraphrase of the *New Testament: Mark*, iii, 25.

1

I intend no modification of my oft-expressed wish that all men everywhere could be free.

> ABRAHAM LINCOLN, Letter to Horace Greeley, 22 Aug., 1862.

2

My paramount object in this struggle is to save the Union, and is not either to save or to destroy slavery. If I could save the Union without freeing any slave, I would do it; and if I could do it by freeing all the slaves, I would do it; and if I could save it by freeing some and leaving others alone, I would also do that.

> ABRAHAM LINCOLN, Letter to Horace Greeley, 22 Aug., 1862.

3

It is my last card, and I will play it and may win the trick.

> ABRAHAM LINCOLN, speaking of the Emancipation Proclamation. These words are quoted in the diary of Robert C. Winthrop of Sharon Springs, N.Y. Winthrop quoted Lincoln on the authority of Judge Edwards Pierrepont, who visited Lincoln shortly before the proclamation was issued in 1862; during this visit, Lincoln is reported to have made the statement.

4

In giving freedom to the slave we assure freedom to the free,—honorable alike in what we give and what we preserve.

> ABRAHAM LINCOLN, Second Annual Message to Congress, 1 Dec., 1862.

5

It may seem strange that any men should dare to ask a just God's assistance in wringing their bread from the sweat of other men's faces; but let us judge not, that we be not judged.

> ABRAHAM LINCOLN, Second Inaugural Address, 4 Mar., 1865.

6

Whenever I hear anyone arguing for slavery, I feel a strong impulse to see it tried on him personally.

> ABRAHAM LINCOLN, Address, 17 Mar., 1865.

7

Men! whose boast it is that ye
Come of fathers brave and free,
If there breathe on earth a slave,
Are ye truly free and brave?

> JAMES RUSSELL LOWELL, *Stanzas on Freedom*.

8

Free men set themselves free.

> JAMES OPPENHEIM, *The Slave*.

9

Slavery is a flagrant violation of the institutions of America—direct government—over all the people, by all the people, for all the people.

> THEODORE PARKER, Sermon, Music Hall, Boston, 4 July, 1858.

10

One of the tragedies of the "abolitionists" 100 years ago is that they spent all their energies on the legal abolition of slavery and did little to plan for the realities of victory. Ten years after the "integration" decision [outlawing segregation in public schools], the same ironical problem exists. The integrationists are winning, ever so slowly, but neither they, nor the country, nor the Negroes are prepared for the responsibilities of legal equality.

> JAMES RESTON, Washington Column, New York *Times*, 15 May, 1964.

11

The blow that liberates the slave
But sets the master free.

> JAMES JEFFREY ROCHE, *Gettysburg*.

12

An irrepressible struggle between opposing and enduring forces.

> W. H. SEWARD, Speech in Rochester, N.Y., 25 Oct., 1858.

13

This is a world of compensations, and he who would *be* no slave must consent to *have* no slave. Those who deny freedom to others deserve it not for themselves, and, under a just God, they cannot long retain it.

> CHARLES SUMNER, Letter, 6 Apr., 1859, declining an invitation to a festival in honor of the anniversary of Jefferson's birthday. This has been wrongly attributed to Lincoln, who probably quoted it.

14

By the Law of Slavery, man, created in the image of God, is divested of the human character, and declared to be a mere chattel.

> CHARLES SUMNER, Address in New York City, 9 May, 1859.

15

Where Slavery is, there Liberty cannot be; and where Liberty is, there Slavery cannot be.

> CHARLES SUMNER, Speech: *Slavery and the Rebellion*, before the New York Young Men's Republican Union, 5 Nov., 1864.

16

Under a government which imprisons any unjustly, the true place for a just man is also a prison, . . . the only house in a slave State in which a free man can abide with honor.

> HENRY D. THOREAU, *The Duty of Civil Disobedience.*

1

I never mean, unless some particular circumstances should compel me to do it, to possess another slave by purchase, it being among my first wishes to see some plan adopted by which slavery in this country may be abolished by law.

> GEORGE WASHINGTON, Letter to John Francis Mercer, 9 Sept., 1786. (*Writings*, vol. xxix, p. 5)

2

No person held to service or labour in one State, under the laws thereof, escaping into another, shall . . . be discharged from such service or labour, but shall be delivered up on claim of the party to whom such service or labour may be due.

> U.S. Constitution, art. iv, sec. 2 (1787).

3

There shall be neither slavery nor involuntary servitude in the said territory.

> NATHAN DANE, Article added to the Ordinance for the Government of the Northwest Territory, 1787.

4

No more slave States and no more slave territory.

> SALMON P. CHASE, Platform Resolutions, adopted by the Free-Soil national convention, 9 Aug., 1848.

5

The question is simply this: Can a Negro, whose ancestors were imported into this country, and sold as slaves, become a member of the political community formed and brought into existence by the Constitution and as such become entitled to all the rights, and privileges, and immunities, guaranteed by that instrument to the citizen? We think not.

> U.S. Supreme Court Decision in Scott vs. Sanford, 6 Mar., 1857—the Dred Scott case.

6

I do order and declare that all persons held as slaves within said designated States and parts of States are, and henceforward shall be, free.

> ABRAHAM LINCOLN, Emancipation Proclamation, proclaimed 22 Sept., 1862, to become effective 1 Jan., 1863. This abolished slavery in specified areas of the Confederate states. Complete emancipation of the slaves awaited passage of the Thirteenth Amendment to the U.S. Constitution in 1865.

7

Neither slavery nor involuntary servitude, except as a punishment for crime whereof the party shall have been duly convicted, shall exist within the United States, or any place subject to their jurisdiction.

> U.S. Constitution, Thirteenth Amendment, sec. 1, adopted 18 Dec., 1865.

SLEEP

8

If, my dear, you seek to slumber,
Count of stars an endless number;
If you still continue wakeful,
Count the drops that make a lakeful;
Then, if vigilance yet above you
Hover, count the times I love you;
And if slumber still repel you,
Count the times I did not tell you.

> FRANKLIN P. ADAMS, *Lullaby.*

9

Heaven trims our lamps while we sleep.

> AMOS BRONSON ALCOTT, *Table Talk: Sleep.*

10

We sleep, but the loom of life never stops and the pattern which was weaving when the sun went down is weaving when it comes up tomorrow.

> HENRY WARD BEECHER, *Life Thoughts,* p. 12.

11

Fly away, Kentucky Babe, fly away to rest,
Lay yo' kinky, woolly head on yo' mammy's breast,—
  Close yo' eyes in sleep.

> RICHARD HENRY BUCK, *Kentucky Babe* (1896).

12

No civilized person ever goes to bed the same day he gets up.

> RICHARD HARDING DAVIS, *Gallegher.*

13

Health is the first muse, and sleep is the condition to produce it.

> EMERSON, *Resources.*

14

Those only can sleep who do not care to sleep.

> EMERSON, *Society and Solitude: Works and Days.*

15

If thou wilt close thy drowsy eyes,
  My mulberry one, my golden son,
The rose shall sing thee lullabies,
  My pretty cosset lambkin!

> EUGENE FIELD, *Armenian Lullaby.*

16

The Rock-a-By Lady from Hushaby street
Comes stealing; comes creeping.

> EUGENE FIELD, *The Rock-a-By Lady,* st. 1.

17

Mother tells me "Happy dreams!" and takes away the light,
An' leaves me lyin' all alone an' seein' things at night.

> EUGENE FIELD, *Seein' Things,* st. 1.

1
Wynken, Blynken, and Nod one night
  Sailed off in a wooden shoe—
Sailed on a river of crystal light
  Into a sea of dew.
    EUGENE FIELD, *Wynken, Blynken, and
    Nod*, st. 1.

2
There will be sleeping enough in the grave.
    BENJAMIN FRANKLIN, *Poor Richard*,
    1758.

3
It is recorded of Methusalem, who, being the
longest liver, may be supposed to have best
preserved his health, that he slept always in
the open air; for, when he had lived five
hundred years, an angel said to him, "Arise,
Methusalem, and build thee an house, for
thou shalt live yet five hundred years longer." But Methusalem answered and said, "If
I am to live but five hundred years longer, it
is not worth while to build me an house; I
will sleep in the air, as I have been used to
do."
    BENJAMIN FRANKLIN, *Letter to Miss ---*.

4
Insomnia never comes to a man who has to
get up at exactly six o'clock. Insomnia troubles only those who can sleep any time.
    ELBERT HUBBARD, *The Philistine*, vol. xxv,
    p. 78.

5
I lay me down in peace and sleep,
For thou, dear Lord, my soul will keep.
And as I rest, this prayer I make:
To do thy will when I awake.
    GRENVILLE KLEISER, *Evening Prayer*.

6
Bed is the boon for me!
  It's well to bake and sweep,
But hear the word of old Lizette:
  It's better than all to sleep.
    AGNES LEE, *Old Lizette on Sleep*.

7
Dreams of the summer night!
  Tell her, her lover keeps
Watch! while in slumbers light
  She sleeps! My lady sleeps!
    HENRY WADSWORTH LONGFELLOW, *The
    Spanish Student*, act i, sc. 3.

8
Thou driftest gently down the tides of sleep.
    HENRY WADSWORTH LONGFELLOW, *To a
    Child*, l. 115.

9
Sleep, dear Sleep, sweet harlot of the senses,
Delilah of the spirit, you unnerve
The strong man's knees, depose his laughing
  brain,
And make him a mere mass of steady breath-
  ing.
    CHRISTOPHER MORLEY, *Sleep*.

10
I have forgotten how to sigh—

Remembered how to sleep.
    DOROTHY PARKER, *The Danger of Writing
    Defiant Verse*.

11
          Sleep, baby, sleep!
Thy father's watching the sheep,
Thy mother's shaking the dreamland tree,
And down drops a little dream for thee.
  Sleep, baby, sleep!
    ELIZABETH PRENTISS, *Cradle Song*.

12
He thought sleep was for children.
    JAMES RESTON, referring to Edward R.
    Murrow; Washington Column, New
    York *Times*, 22 Jan., 1964. Reston spe-
    cifically recalled Murrow's strenuous
    life as a reporter in World War II.

13
Maybe it's because I sleep slow.
    JACK TEAGARDEN, explaining why he liked
    to sleep for long periods. This was
    quoted in many articles about the fa-
    mous jazz trombonist, including the
    New York *Herald Tribune* obituary of
    him, 16 Jan., 1964.

14
Hush-a-bye, baby, on the tree-top,
When the wind blows, the cradle will rock;
When the bough breaks, the cradle will fall,
And down will come baby, cradle, and all.
    UNKNOWN. *The Book Lover* (Feb., 1904)
    calls it the first poem produced on
    American soil, by a youth who arrived
    on the Mayflower. It has also been
    credited to Charles Blake.

15
Now I lay me down to sleep,
I pray the Lord my soul to keep;
If I should die before I wake,
I pray the Lord my soul to take.
    UNKNOWN, *Prayer at Lying Down*. (*New
    England Primer*, 1737) In a few editions
    the wording is "I pray, Thee, Lord
    . . ."

Now I lay me down to sleep,
I pray Thee, Lord, my soul to keep;
When in the morning light I wake,
Lead Thou my feet, that I may take
The path of love for Thy dear sake.
    UNKNOWN, *Now I Lay Me: Revised*.

SMILE

16
There are smiles that make us happy,
  There are smiles that make us blue,
There are smiles that steal away the tear-
  drops
  As the sunbeams steal away the dew.
There are smiles that have a tender mean-
  ing,
  That the eyes of love alone may see,
But the smiles that fill my life with sun-
  shine

Are the smiles that you give to me.
    J. WILL CALLAHAN, *Smiles* (song, c. 1917,
        with music by Lee S. Roberts).

1
Give me your smile, the lovelight in your
    eyes,
Life could not hold a fairer paradise.
    LEONARD COOKE, *The Sunshine of Your
        Smile* (song, 1915).

2
Simple and faithless as a smile and shake of
    the hand.
    T. S. ELIOT, *La Figlia Che Piange.*

3
My smile falls heavily among the bric-à-
    brac.
    T. S. ELIOT, *Portrait of a Lady.*

4
He smiled a kind of sickly smile and curled
    up on the floor,
And the subsequent proceedings interested
    him no more.
    BRET HARTE, *The Society Upon the Stanis-
        laus.*

5
A stale article, if you dip it in a good, warm,
sunny smile, will go off better than a fresh
one that you've scowled upon.
    NATHANIEL HAWTHORNE, *The House of
        the Seven Gables,* ch. 4.

6
Make two grins grow where there was only a
grouch before.
    ELBERT HUBBARD, *Pig-Pen Pete.*

7
When Milly smiled it was a public event—
when she didn't it was a chapter of history.
    HENRY JAMES, *The Wings of the Dove,* p.
        132.

8
If the world's a vale of tears,
Smile, till rainbows span it!
    LUCY LARCOM, *Three Old Saws.*

9
All kin' o' smily round the lips,
An' teary round the lashes.
    JAMES RUSSELL LOWELL, *The Courtin'.*

10
He's a man way out there in the blue, riding
on a smile and a shoeshine. And when they
start not smiling back—that's an earthquake.
    ARTHUR MILLER, *Death of a Salesman:*
        requiem. Referring to a salesman—
        specifically to Willy Loman, the protag-
        onist of the play.

11
The smile that won't come off.
    JOSEPH W. STANDISH, Title and refrain of
        popular song (1903).

12
Wrinkles should merely indicate where
smiles have been.
    MARK TWAIN, *Pudd'nhead Wilson's New
        Calendar.*

13
'Tis easy enough to be pleasant,

When life flows along like a song;
But the man worth while is the one who will
    smile
When everything goes dead wrong;
For the test of the heart is trouble,
    And it always comes with the years,
But the smile that is worth the praise of
    earth
    Is the smile that comes through tears.
    ELLA WHEELER WILCOX, *Worth While.*

14
When you call me that, *smile!*
    OWEN WISTER, *The Virginian,* ch. 2, p.
        28.

SMOKING, see Tobacco
SNOB

15
Snobbery sometimes is thought to be a
prerogative of the rich. But no man is so
poverty-stricken he can't afford to be a
snob.
    HAL BOYLE, Column, Associated Press,
        datelined 27 Jan., 1966.

16
Don't be proud and turn up your nose
At poorer people in plainer clothes;
But learn, for the sake of your soul's repose,
That all proud flesh, where'er it grows,
    Is liable to irritation.
    SAMUEL S. COX, *Because You Flourish in
        Worldly Affairs.*

17
Snobbery is but a point in time. Let us have
patience with our inferiors. They are ourselves of yesterday.
    ISAAC GOLDBERG, *Tin Pan Alley.*

18
We are all snobs of the Infinite, parvenus of
the Eternal.
    JAMES GIBBONS HUNEKER, *Iconoclasts,* p.
        16.

19
Now she is dead she greets Christ with a
    nod,—
(He was a carpenter)—*but she knows God.*
    VIRGINIA McCORMICK, *The Snob.*

SNOW

20
Lo, what wonders the day hath brought,
Born of the soft and slumbrous snow!
    ELIZABETH AKERS ALLEN, *Snow.*

21
And out of the frozen mist the snow
In wavering flakes begins to glow;
    Flake after flake
They sink in the dark and silent lake.
    WILLIAM CULLEN BRYANT, *The Snow-
        Shower.*

22
The sky is low, the clouds are mean,
A travelling flake of snow

Across a barn or through a rut
Debates if it will go.
    EMILY DICKINSON, *Poems*, Pt. ii, No. 80.

1
Whenever a snowflake leaves the sky,
It turns and turns to say "Good-by!
Good-by, dear clouds, so cool and gray!"
Then lightly travels on its way.
    MARY MAPES DODGE, *Snowflakes*.

2
But when a snowflake, brave and meek,
Lights on a rosy maiden's cheek,
It starts—"How warm and soft the day!"
" 'Tis summer!" and it melts away.
    MARY MAPES DODGE, *Snowflakes*.

3
Announced by all the trumpets of the sky,
Arrives the snow, and, driving o'er the
    fields,
Seems nowhere to alight: the whited air
Hides hills and woods, the river, and the
    heaven,
And veils the farm-house at the garden's
    end.
The sled and traveller stopped, the courier's
    feet
Delayed, all friends shut out, the housemates
    sit
Around the radiant fireplace, enclosed
In a tumultuous privacy of storm.
    EMERSON, *The Snow-Storm*, l. 1.

4
Come, see the north wind's masonry.
Out of an unseen quarry evermore
Furnished with tile, the fierce artificer
Curves his white bastions with projected
    roof
Round every windward stake, or tree, or
    door.
    EMERSON, *The Snow-Storm*, l. 10.

5
The frolic architecture of the snow.
    EMERSON, *The Snow-Storm*, l. 28.

6
Like ghost of sleigh-bells in a ghost of snow.
    ROBERT FROST, *Hyla Brook*.

7
Whose woods these are I think I know.
His house is in the village though;
He will not see me stopping here
To watch his woods fill up with snow.
    ROBERT FROST, *Stopping by Woods on a
    Snowy Evening*, st. 1.

8
Where the snow-flakes fall thickest there's
    nothing can freeze!
    OLIVER WENDELL HOLMES, *The Boys*.

9
Out of the bosom of the Air,
    Out of the cloud-folds of her garments
    shaken,
Over the woodlands brown and bare,
    Over the harvest-fields forsaken,

Silent, and soft, and slow
Descends the snow.
    HENRY WADSWORTH LONGFELLOW, *Snow-
    Flakes*.

10
The pity of the snow, that hides all scars.
    EDWIN MARKHAM, *Lincoln, The Man of
    the People*.

11
Oh, the snow, the beautiful snow,
Filling the sky and the earth below; . . .
Beautiful snow, from the heavens above,
Pure as an angel and fickle as love.
    JOHN WHITAKER WATSON, *Beautiful
    Snow*.

SOCIETY

12
Who Killed Society?
    CLEVELAND AMORY, Title of book (1960).

13
The Hostess with the Mostes' on the Ball.
    IRVING BERLIN, Title of song from the
    musical comedy *Call Me Madam*
    (1950), sung by Ethel Merman.

14
American social fences have to be continually repaired; in England they are like wild
hedges; they grow if left alone.
    D. W. BROGAN, *The English People*.

15
Those families, you know, are our upper
crust, not upper ten thousand.
    JAMES FENIMORE COOPER, *Ways of the
    Hour*, ch. 6 (1850).

At present there is no distinction among the
upper ten thousand of the city.
    NATHANIEL P. WILLIS, *Necessity for a
    Promenade Drive* (1860).

There are only about four hundred people in
New York society.
    WARD MCALLISTER, at the Union Club, 1
    Feb., 1892, as he reduced the list of
    guests for a ball given by Mrs. William
    Astor. The expression "four hundred"
    has remained an enduring one.

16
the Cambridge ladies who live in furnished
    souls
are unbeautiful and have comfortable minds
    . . .
they believe in Christ and Longfellow, both
    dead.
    E. E. CUMMINGS, *Sonnets: Realities*.

17
Fine society is only a self-protection against
the vulgarities of the street and the tavern.
. . . 'Tis an exclusion and a precinct. . . .
It is an unprincipled decorum; an affair of
clean linen and coaches, of gloves, cards, and
elegance in trifles.
    EMERSON, *Conduct of Life: Considera-
    tions by the Way*.

1
Society is a masked ball, where every one hides his real character, and reveals it by hiding.

> EMERSON, *Conduct of Life: Worship.*

2
The thoughts of the best minds always become the last opinion of society.

> EMERSON, *Correspondence of Carlyle and Emerson,* vol. i, p. 29.

3
Society is a joint stock company, in which the members agree, for the better securing of his bread to each shareholder, to surrender the liberty and culture of the eater.

> EMERSON, *Essays, First Series: Self-Reliance.*

4
Society everywhere is in conspiracy against the manhood of every one of its members. . . . The virtue in most request is conformity. Self-reliance is its aversion. It loves not realities and creators, but names and customs.

> EMERSON, *Essays, First Series: Self-Reliance.*

5
Society never advances.

> EMERSON, *Essays, First Series: Self-Reliance.*

6
Society is frivolous, and shreds its day into scraps, its conversation into ceremonies and escapes.

> EMERSON, *Essays, Second Series: Character.*

7
Society will pardon much to genius and special gifts, but, being in its nature a convention, it loves what is conventional, or what belongs to coming together.

> EMERSON, *Essays, Second Series: Manners.*

8
Comme il faut, is the Frenchman's description of good society.

> EMERSON, *Essays, Second Series: Manners.*

9
Here is the use of society: it is so easy with the great to be great.

> EMERSON, *Essays: Society and Solitude.*

10
Solitude is impracticable, and society fatal.

> EMERSON, *Essays: Society and Solitude.*

11
The solitary worshipper knows the essence of the thought: the scholar in society sees only its fair face.

> EMERSON, *Journals,* 1864.

12
Society is a hospital of incurables.

> EMERSON, *New England Reformers.*

13
No society can ever be so large as one man.

> EMERSON, *New England Reformers.*

14
Of all the cordials known to us, the best, safest, and most exhilarating, with the least harm, is society.

> EMERSON, *Society and Solitude: Clubs.*

15
When a man meets his fitting mate society begins.

> EMERSON, *Social Aims.*

16
When there are repressions, or inhibitions, or fears, or timidities, or prudences, you can't have a good society.

> FELIX FRANKFURTER. (New York *Times,* 23 Feb., 1965, p. 27)

17
Many a heart is aching, if you could read them all,
Many the hopes that have vanished, after the ball.

> CHARLES K. HARRIS, *After the Ball* (song, 1892), first sung by J. Aldrich Libby, a well-known baritone, at a matinee of Charles Hoyt's *A Trip to Chinatown,* at the Bijou Theatre, Milwaukee.

18
Ermined and minked and Persian-lambed,
Be-puffed (be-painted, too, alas!)
Be-decked, be-diamonded—be-damned!
The Women of the Better Class.

> OLIVER HERFORD, *The Women of the Better Class.*

19
The Brahmin caste of New England. This is the harmless, inoffensive, untitled aristocracy referred to.

> OLIVER WENDELL HOLMES, *Elsie Venner,* ch. 1.

20
Without society, and a society to our taste, men are never contented.

> THOMAS JEFFERSON, *Writings,* vol. vi, p. 15.

21
It is rendering mutual service to men of virtue and understanding to make them acquainted with one another.

> THOMAS JEFFERSON, *Writings,* vol. vi, p. 424.

22
The great society is not a safe harbor . . . The great society is a place where men are more concerned with the quality of their goals than the quantity of their goods.

> LYNDON B. JOHNSON, Address at the University of Michigan, Ann Arbor, Mich., 22 May, 1964—the first use of "great society" with reference to his administration.

23
This nation, this generation, in this hour has man's first chance to build the Great Society—a place where the meaning of man's life matches the marvels of man's labor. We seek a nation where every man can seek

knowledge, and touch beauty, and rejoice in the closeness of family and community. We seek a nation where every man can, in the words of our oldest promise, follow the pursuit of happiness—not just security, but achievements and excellence and fulfillment of the spirit.

> LYNDON B. JOHNSON, Speech upon accepting the presidential nomination, Atlantic City, N.J., 27 Aug., 1964.

1

In general, American social life constitutes an evasion of talking to people. Most Americans don't, in any vital sense, get together; they only do things together.

> LOUIS KRONENBERGER, Company Manners, p. 148.

2

A really healthy society, so Thoreau once wrote, would be like a healthy body that functions perfectly without our being aware of it. We, on the other hand, are coming more and more to assume that the healthiest society is one in which all citizens devote so much of their time to arguing, weighing, investigating, propagandizing, and signing protests in a constant effort to keep a valetudinarian body politic functioning in some sort of pseudo-health that they have none of that margin for mere living that Thoreau thought important. It's no wonder that such a situation generated beatniks by way of a reaction.

> JOSEPH WOOD KRUTCH, Wilderness as a Tonic; The Saturday Review, 8 June, 1963, p. 16.

3

A town that boasts inhabitants like me
Can have no lack of good society!

> HENRY WADSWORTH LONGFELLOW, The Birds of Killingworth.

4

Solitude is as needful to the imagination as society is wholesome for the character.

> JAMES RUSSELL LOWELL, Among My Books: Dryden.

5

The Don Quixote of one generation may live to hear himself called the savior of society by the next.

> JAMES RUSSELL LOWELL, Essays: Don Quixote.

6

Society is like the air, necessary to breathe, but insufficient to live on.

> GEORGE SANTAYANA, Little Essays.

7

To say what you think will certainly damage you in society; but a free tongue is worth more than a thousand invitations.

> LOGAN PEARSALL SMITH, Afterthoughts.

8

The name of the subspecies, then, is Exurbanite; its habitat, the Exurbs. The exurb

is generally further from New York than the suburb on the same railway line. Its houses are more widely spaced and generally more various and more expensive. The town center tends to quaintness and class, rather than modernity and glass, and the further one lives from the station the better.

> A. C. SPECTORSKY, The Exurbanites.

9

Fire is the most tolerable third party.

> HENRY D. THOREAU, Journal. (EMERSON, Thoreau)

10

What men call social virtue, good fellowship, is commonly but the virtue of pigs in a litter, which lie close together to keep each other warm.

> HENRY D. THOREAU, Journal, 23 Oct., 1852.

11

I went to the woods because I wished to live deliberately, to front only the essential facts of life, and see if I could not learn what it had to teach, and not, when I came to die, discover that I had not lived.

> HENRY D. THOREAU, Walden: Where I Lived, and What I Lived For.

12

Society waits unform'd, and is for a while
    between things ended and things begun.

> WALT WHITMAN, Thoughts: Of These Years.

13

High society is for those who have stopped working and no longer have anything important to do.

> WOODROW WILSON, Address in Washington, D.C., 24 Feb., 1915.

SOLDIER

See also America; War

14

It were better to be a soldier's widow than a coward's wife.

> THOMAS BAILEY ALDRICH, Mercedes, act ii, sc. 2.

15

Lay him low, lay him low,
In the clover or the snow!
What cares he? he cannot know:
    Lay him low!

> GEORGE HENRY BOKER, Dirge for a Soldier.

16

Dear God, I raised my boy to be a soldier; I tried to make him strong of will and true.

> FLORENCE EARLE COATES, A Soldier. This was written in reply to a song, I Did Not Raise My Boy to Be a Soldier (1914), by ALBERT BRYAN. In 1917 Bryan composed It's Time for Ev'ry Boy to Be a Soldier, in tune with the times.

The man who has not raised himself to be a

soldier, and the woman who has not raised her boy to be a soldier for the right, neither one of them is entitled to citizenship in the Republic.

THEODORE ROOSEVELT, Speech to troops at Camp Upton, 1917.

1
She was accustomed to fast riding with our cavalry . . . she does not know how to treat a doughboy.

MRS. GEORGE CUSTER, Letter, Mar., 1867; an early recorded use of the term "doughboy." It was applied to infantry-men in the Civil War because, according to one theory, the infantrymen wore large brass buttons resembling dough. A contributor to *Life* (23 July, 1956) dated the term from the Battle of Mon-terey, 1846. Subsequently another con-tributor to the magazine (13 Aug., 1956) stated the term was used by British sol-diers at least as early as the start of the nineteenth century; according to that account, the British troops used pipe clay to whiten their uniforms, and rain sometimes gave the clay a doughy look.

2
Let me give you some advice, Lieutenant. Don't become a general. Don't ever become a general. If you become a general you just plain have too much to worry about.

GENERAL DWIGHT D. EISENHOWER, to Lieutenant Andrew Wnukowski of the Army Reserve, when the latter was in-troduced to Eisenhower at the New York World's Fair, 9 May, 1965.

3
Ye living soldiers of the mighty war,
Once more from roaring cannon and the drums,
And bugles blown at morn, the summons comes;
Forget the halting limb, each wound and scar:
  Once more your Captain calls to you;
  Come to his last review!

RICHARD WATSON GILDER, *The Burial of Grant.*

4
Over hill, over dale, we have hit the dusty trail
And those caissons go rolling along.
Countermarch! Right about! hear those wagon soldiers shout
While those caissons go rolling along.

EDMUND L. GRUBER, *The Caisson Song.*

5
He that stepped forward to follow the flag,
To ride with a saber or march with a Krag,
You'll find now, with thousands, shipped home in a bag,
  Just a little brass tag.

EDGAR A. GUEST, *A Little Brass Tag.*

6
Learning to suspend your imagination and live completely in the very second of the present with no before and no after is the greatest gift a soldier can acquire.

ERNEST HEMINGWAY, *Men at War:* Intro-duction.

7
He was a foe without hate, a friend without treachery, a soldier without cruelty, and a victim without murmuring.

BENJAMIN H. HILL, on Robert E. Lee. (T. N. PAGE, *Robert E. Lee*)

8
The only prize much cared for by the power-ful is power. The prize of the general is not a bigger tent, but command.

JUSTICE OLIVER WENDELL HOLMES, *Law and the Court.*

9
These heroes are dead. They died for liberty—they died for us. They are at rest. They sleep in the land they made free, under the flag they rendered stainless, under the solemn pines, the sad hemlocks, the tearful willows, the embracing vines. They sleep be-neath the shadows of the clouds, careless alike of sunshine or storm, each in the win-dowless palace of rest. Earth may run red with other wars—they are at peace. In the midst of battles, in the roar of conflict, they found the serenity of death.

ROBERT G. INGERSOLL, *Memorial Day Vi-sion.*

10
In a wood they call the Rouge Bouquet,
There is a new-made grave today,
Built by never a spade nor pick,
Yet covered with earth ten metres thick.
There lie many fighting men,
  Dead in their youthful prime.
Never to laugh nor love again
  Nor taste the Summertime.

JOYCE KILMER, *Rouge Bouquet.*

11
A man should have dinner with his friends, and the commanding general has no friends.

GENERAL CURTIS LEMAY, refusing a din-ner invitation from fellow officers. (*Look,* 2 Nov., 1965)

12
I have heard, in such a way as to believe it, of your recently saying that both the army and the government needed a dictator. . . . Only those generals who gain successes can set up dictators. What I ask of you now is military success, and I will risk the dictator-ship.

ABRAHAM LINCOLN, Letter to Major-General Joseph Hooker, in which Hooker received word of his appoint-ment as commander of the Army of the Potomac, 26 Jan., 1863.

1

We have met on a great battlefield of that war. We have come to dedicate a portion of that field as a final resting-place for those who here gave their lives that that nation might live. It is altogether fitting and proper that we should do this. But in a larger sense, we cannot dedicate, we cannot consecrate, we cannot hallow this ground. The brave men, living and dead, who struggled here, have consecrated it far above our poor power to add or detract. The world will little note, nor long remember, what we say here, but it can never forget what they did here.

ABRAHAM LINCOLN, Gettysburg Address, 19 Nov., 1863.

2

I am sorry it was not a general—I could make more of them.

ABRAHAM LINCOLN, Remark, upon hearing of the death of a private.

3

Get me the brand, and I'll send a barrel to my other generals.

ABRAHAM LINCOLN, Retort, upon being told that General Grant was drinking too much whiskey.

4

I personally wish Jacob Freese, of New Jersey, to be appointed colonel of a colored regiment, and this regardless of whether he can tell the exact shade of Julius Caesar's hair.

ABRAHAM LINCOLN, Letter to Secretary of War Stanton.

5

Ninepunce a day fer killin' folks comes kind o' low fer murder.

JAMES RUSSELL LOWELL, *The Biglow Papers*, Ser. i, No. 2.

6

An army all of captains, used to pray
And stiff in fight, but serious drill's despair,
Skilled to debate their orders, not obey.

JAMES RUSSELL LOWELL, *Under the Old Elm*. He was referring to the Continental army.

7

Old soldiers never die; they just fade away.

GENERAL DOUGLAS MACARTHUR, Address to joint session of U.S. Congress, 19 Apr., 1951. He was quoting an old army ballad.

8

Today marks my final roll call with you, but I want you to know that when I cross the river my last conscious thoughts will be of The Corps, and The Corps, and The Corps.

GENERAL DOUGLAS MACARTHUR, Address at U.S. Military Academy, West Point, N.Y., 12 May, 1962.

9

In my dreams I hear again the crash of guns, the rattle of musketry, the strange, mournful mutter of the battlefield. But in the evening of my memory, always I come back to West Point.

GENERAL DOUGLAS MACARTHUR, Address at U.S. Military Academy, West Point, N.Y., 12 May, 1962.

10

My estimate of him [the American man-at-arms] was formed on the battlefield many, many years ago, and has never changed. I regarded him then as I regard him now—as one of the world's noblest figures . . . His name and fame are the birthright of every American citizen.

GENERAL DOUGLAS MACARTHUR, Address at U.S. Military Academy, West Point, N.Y., 12 May, 1962.

11

Your mission remains fixed, determined, inviolable—it is to win our wars. Everything else in your professional career is but corollary to this vital dedication.

GENERAL DOUGLAS MACARTHUR, Address to cadets at U.S. Military Academy, West Point, N.Y., 12 May, 1962.

12

The soldier, above all other people, prays for peace, for he must suffer and bear the deepest wounds and scars of war.

GENERAL DOUGLAS MACARTHUR, Address at U.S. Military Academy, West Point, N.Y., 12 May, 1962.

13

High honors have come my way, but I shall believe the greatest honor was being a West Point cadet.

GENERAL DOUGLAS MACARTHUR, to a delegation of West Point cadets who visited him in New York City on his 84th birthday, 27 Jan., 1964.

14

My first recollection is that of a bugle call.

GENERAL DOUGLAS MACARTHUR. (New York *Herald Tribune*, 6 Apr., 1964, p. 12—obituary of MacArthur)

15

So came the Captain with the mighty heart.

EDWIN MARKHAM, *Lincoln, the Man of the People*, st. 4.

16

The little green tents where the soldiers sleep
and the sunbeams play and the women weep,
are covered with flowers today.

WALT MASON, *The Little Green Tents*.

17

The muffled drum's sad roll has beat
    The soldier's last tattoo;
No more on Life's parade shall meet
    The brave and fallen few.
On Fame's eternal camping-ground
    Their silent tents are spread,
And Glory guards, with solemn round,
    The bivouac of the dead.

THEODORE O'HARA, *The Bivouac of the Dead*.

1

Nor shall your story be forgot,
    While Fame her record keeps,
Or Honor points the hallowed spot
    Where Valor proudly sleeps.
        THEODORE O'HARA, *The Bivouac of the Dead.*

2

These are the times that try men's souls. The summer soldier and the sunshine patriot will, in this crisis, shrink from the service of their country; but he that stands it *now,* deserves the love and thanks of man and woman.
        THOMAS PAINE, *The Crisis:* introduction, Dec., 1776.

3

Sleep, soldiers! still in honored rest
    Your truth and valor wearing:
The bravest are the tenderest,—
    The loving are the daring.
        BAYARD TAYLOR, *The Song of the Camp.*

4

I heard the bullets whistle; and believe me, there is something charming in the sound.
        GEORGE WASHINGTON, Letter to his mother, written after his encounter with the French at Great Meadows, 3 May, 1754.

5

When we assumed the soldier, we did not lay aside the citizen.
        GEORGE WASHINGTON, Address to the provincial Congress of New York, 26 June, 1775. Inscribed on the memorial amphitheater in Arlington National Cemetery.

6

When I peruse the conquer'd fame of heroes and the victories of mighty generals, I do not envy the generals.
        WALT WHITMAN, *Leaves of Grass: When I Peruse the Conquer'd Fame.*

7

Let it be your pride, therefore, to show all men everywhere not only what good soldiers you are, but also what good men you are. . . . Let us set for ourselves a standard so high that it will be a glory to live up to it, and then let us live up to it and add a new laurel to the crown of America.
        WOODROW WILSON, Address to U.S. troops, 1917.

8

Here rests in honored glory an American soldier known but to God.
        Inscription on tomb of the Unknown Soldier, Arlington National Cemetery.

9

It ain't the guns or armament, or the money they can pay,
It's the close cooperation that makes them win the day;
It ain't the individual, nor the army as a whole,
But the everlastin' teamwork of every bloomin' soul.
        Cooperation, attributed to J. MASON KNOX, but also credited to other writers. It was claimed for Knox by his wife in a letter to the New York *Times,* 1 Aug., 1920.

SOLITUDE
See also Society

10

To mind my own business.
        BERNAND M. BARUCH, Reply, when asked the most important lesson he had learned during his life. (St. Louis *Post-Dispatch,* 21 June, 1965, p. 5A)

11

The right to be alone—the most comprehensive of rights, and the right most valued by civilized men.
        LOUIS D. BRANDEIS, Opinion in Olmstead vs. United States, U.S. Supreme Court, 1928.

12

The secret of solitude is that there is no solitude.
        JOSEPH COOK, *Boston Monday Lectures: Conscience.*

13

Solitude would ripen a plentiful crop of despots.
        EMERSON, *Essays, Second Series: Nominalist and Realist.*

14

There is one means of procuring solitude which to me, and I apprehend to all men, is effectual, and that is to go to the window and look at the stars.
        EMERSON, *Journals,* vol. iii, p. 263.

15

Inspiration makes solitude anywhere.
        EMERSON, *Nature, Addresses, and Lectures: Literary Ethics.*

16

Go cherish your soul; expel companions; set your habits to a life of solitude; then will the faculties rise fair and full within.
        EMERSON, *Nature, Addresses, and Lectures: Literary Ethics.*

17

One aged man—one man—can't fill a house.
        ROBERT FROST, *An Old Man's Winter Night.*

18

I want to be alone.
        Attributed to GRETA GARBO, but later disclaimed by her. The actress maintained that she really said, "I want to be let alone."

19

Let there be spaces in your togetherness.
        KAHLIL GIBRAN, *The Prophet: On Marriage.*

1

All by my own-alone self.

JOEL CHANDLER HARRIS, *Nights with Uncle Remus*, ch. 36.

2

Living in solitude till the fulness of time, I still kept the dew of my youth and the freshness of my heart.

NATHANIEL HAWTHORNE, Inscription beneath his bust in the Hall of Fame.

3

Such dirty business.

JUSTICE OLIVER WENDELL HOLMES, Opinion in Olmstead vs. United States, U.S. Supreme Court, 1928. This famous quotation refers to the use of wire-tap evidence in prosecuting those charged with crime (violation of the National Prohibition Act, in this case). Holmes and Louis D. Brandeis dissented from the majority opinion, which maintained that wire-tapping did not violate the Constitutional prohibition of unreasonable searches and seizures.

4

An age of publicity cannot but make privacy first difficult and at length undesirable: eventually people, if they can feel sure that everyone will know their address, will cheerfully live in glass houses.

LOUIS KRONENBERGER, *Company Manners*, p. 130.

5

Modern Americans are so exposed, peered at, inquired about, and spied upon as to be increasingly without privacy—members of a naked society and denizens of a goldfish bowl.

EDWARD V. LONG, Address before the Association of Federal Investigators, Washington, D.C., 25 Feb., 1965. Long, a U.S. Senator from Missouri, was then chairman of a Senate subcommittee investigating governmental surveillance including mail cover and electronic eavesdropping.

6

When writers come, I find I'm talking all the time, exchanging thoughts I haven't exchanged for some time. I get stupid in solitude.

MARY MCCARTHY. (*Lady with a Switchblade; Life*, 20 Sept., 1963, p. 62)

7

The human animal needs a freedom seldom mentioned, freedom from intrusion. He needs a little privacy quite as much as he wants understanding or vitamins or exercise or praise.

PHYLLIS MCGINLEY, *The Province of the Heart: A Lost Privilege*, p. 58.

8

I never found the companion that was so companionable as solitude.

HENRY D. THOREAU, *Walden: Solitude*.

9

Why should I feel lonely? is not our planet in the Milky Way?

HENRY D. THOREAU, *Walden: Solitude*.

10

Far from the clank of crowds.

WALT WHITMAN, *Starting from Paumanok*, sec. 1.

SON
See also Father

11

A lively and lasting sense of filial duty is more effectually impressed on the mind of a son or daughter by reading King Lear, than by all the dry volumes of ethics, and divinity, that ever were written.

THOMAS JEFFERSON, Letter to Robert Skipwith, 1771.

12

I have been shown in the files of the War Department a statement of the Adjutant-General of Massachusetts that you are the mother of five sons who have died gloriously on the field of battle. I feel how weak and fruitless must be any words of mine which should attempt to beguile you from the grief of a loss so overwhelming. But I cannot refrain from tendering to you the consolation that may be found in the thanks of the Republic they died to save. I pray that our heavenly Father may assuage the anguish of your bereavement, and leave you only the cherished memory of the loved and lost, and the solemn pride that must be yours to have laid so costly a sacrifice upon the altar of freedom.

ABRAHAM LINCOLN, Letter to a Mrs. Bixby, 21 Nov., 1864. Her five sons had been listed as killed in action during the Civil War.

13

The rich man's son inherits cares;
    The bank may break, the factory burn,
A breath may burst his bubble shares,
    And soft white hands could hardly earn
    A living that would serve his turn.
JAMES RUSSELL LOWELL, *The Heritage*.

14

Build me a son, O Lord, who will be strong enough to know when he is weak, and brave enough to face himself when he is afraid; one who will be proud and unbending in honest defeat, and humble and gentle in victory.

Build me a son whose wishes will not take the place of deeds; a son who will know Thee—and that to know himself is the foundation stone of knowledge.

Lead him, I pray, not in the path of ease

and comfort, but under the stress and spur of difficulties and challenge. Here let him learn to stand up in the storm; here let him learn compassion for those who fail.

Build me a son whose heart will be clear, whose goal will be high, a son who will master himself before he seeks to master other men, one who will reach into the future, yet never forget the past.

And after all these things are his, add, I pray, enough of a sense of humor, so that he may always be serious, yet never take himself too seriously. Give him humility, so that he may always remember the simplicity of true greatness, the open mind of true wisdom, and the meekness of true strength.

Then I, his father, will dare to whisper, "I have not lived in vain."

> GENERAL DOUGLAS MACARTHUR. This prayer, written in the Philippine Islands in the early days of the Pacific war, was left as a spiritual legacy to his son Arthur. It was made public shortly after the general's death in 1964.

1
The gulf of years and pathos which always must divide a father from his son.

> J. P. MARQUAND, *The Late George Apley*, ch. 10.

SONG

(Many individual songs will be found elsewhere in this book under headings appropriate to their content.)

2
Carry me back to old Virginny,
There's where the cotton and the corn and taters grow.

> JAMES A. BLAND, *Carry Me Back to Old Virginny*.

3
You call it a waste of time, this taste
For popular tunes, and yet
Good-bye to care when you whistle the air
Of the song that you can't forget.

> GUY WETMORE CARRYL, *The Organ Man*.

4
Invisible beauty has a word so brief
A flower can say it or a shaken leaf,
But few may ever snare it in a song.

> GRACE HAZARD CONKLING, *After Sunset*.

5
Sweet Adeline, My Adeline,
At night, dear heart, For you I pine.
In all my dreams, Your fair face beams;
You're the flower of my heart, Sweet Adeline.

> RICHARD H. GIRARD, *Sweet Adeline* (song, 1903, with music by Harry Armstrong).

6
So she poured out the liquid music of her voice to quench the thirst of his spirit.

> NATHANIEL HAWTHORNE, *Mosses from an Old Manse: The Birthmark*.

7
What is the voice of song, when the world lacks the ear of taste?

> NATHANIEL HAWTHORNE, *The Snow Image: Canterbury Pilgrims*

8
There'll be a hot time in the old town tonight.

> JOSEPH HAYDEN, Refrain of song (1896), set to music by Theodore Metz when the McIntyre and Heath Minstrels visited Old Town, La. The song was extremely popular with troops during the Spanish-American War.

9
Home, home on the range,
Where the deer and the antelope play;
Where seldom is heard a discouraging word,
And the skies are not cloudy all day.

> DR. BREWSTER HIGLEY, *The Western Home* (1873, music by Dan Kelly, Higley's neighbor in South Center, Kan.). The title later was changed to *Home on the Range*. There have been other claims of authorship, and other songs that closely resemble the Higley-Kelly composition.

10
A few can touch the magic string,
And noisy Fame is proud to win them:—
Alas for those that never sing,
But die with all their music in them!

> OLIVER WENDELL HOLMES, *The Voiceless*, st. 1.

11
And now we are aged and gray, Maggie,
The trials of life nearly done,
Let us sing of the days that are gone, Maggie,
When you and I were young.

> GEORGE W. JOHNSON, *When You and I Were Young* (song, 1866, with music by J. A. Butterfield).

12
While I yield to no one in my enjoyment of harmony—you can take that any way you like—I yield to anyone in my ability to carry a tune.

> LYNDON B. JOHNSON, Remark to members of a chorus from Bakersfield, Calif., who visited the White House, 4 Aug., 1965.

13
Because the road was steep and long
And through a dark and lonely land,
God set upon my lips a song
And put a lantern in my hand.

> JOYCE KILMER, *Love's Lantern*.

14
We're tenting tonight on the old campground,
Give us a song to cheer
Our weary hearts, a song of home

And friends we love so dear.
WALTER KITTREDGE, *Tenting on the Old Camp-Ground*, st. 1.

1
In the ink of our sweat we will find it yet,
The song that is fit for men!
F. L. KNOWLES, *The Song*.

2
As a singer you're a great dancer.
AMY LESLIE, to George Primrose. (MARKS, *They All Sang*, p. 67)

3
      The song on its mighty pinions,
Took every living soul, and lifted it gently to
  heaven.
HENRY WADSWORTH LONGFELLOW, *Children of the Lord's Supper*, l. 44.

4
Such songs have power to quiet
  The restless pulse of care,
And come like the benediction
  That follows after prayer.
HENRY WADSWORTH LONGFELLOW, *The Day Is Done*, st. 9.

5
I have a passion for ballads. . . . They are
the gypsy-children of song, born under green
hedgerows, in the leafy lanes and bypaths of
literature.
HENRY WADSWORTH LONGFELLOW, *Hyperion*, bk. ii, ch. 2.

6
I care not who writes the laws of a country
so long as I may listen to its songs.
GEORGE JEAN NATHAN, *The World in Falseface*: foreword.

7
K-K-Katy, beautiful Katy,
You're the only g-g-girl that I adore,
When the m-m-m-moon shines over the cow-
  shed,
I'll be waiting at the k-k-kitchen door.
GEOFFREY O'HARA, *K-K-Katy* (1918).

8
Somewhere, Somewhere, Beautiful Isle of
  Somewhere,
Land of the true, where we live anew,
Beautiful Isle of Somewhere!
JESSIE BROWN POUNDS, *Beautiful Isle of Somewhere* (1901).

9
Tin Pan Alley.
MONROE H. ROSENFELD, Title of an article
on the music business, published in a
New York newspaper about 1892. (See
GOLDBERG, *Tin Pan Alley*, p. 173.) The
phrase is also claimed by Robert H.
Duiree, who, just before he died in
1935, told the press that he had coined
it many years earlier as a name for West
28th Street in New York City, then the
home of many music publishing houses.
Duiree was not specific about the date,
but said he mentioned the phrase to

Epes W. Sargent of the New York
Morning Telegraph, who used in it that
newspaper.

10
A sweet Tuxedo girl you see,
Queen of swell society,
Fond of fun as fond can be,
When it's on the strict Q.T.
  Ta-ra-ra Boom-der-é [four times repeat-
    ed].
    HENRY J. SAYERS, *Ta-ra-ra Boom-der-é*
    (1891). Sometimes written *Ta-ra-ra*
    Boom-de-ay.

11
Song like a rose should be;
  Each rhyme a petal sweet;
For fragrance, melody,
  That when her lips repeat
The words, her heart may know
What secret makes them so.
  Love, only Love!
FRANK DEMPSTER SHERMAN, *Song*.

12
Meet me in St. Louis, Louis,
  Meet me at the fair,
Don't tell me the lights are shining
  Any place but there.
  ANDREW B. STERLING, *Meet Me in St. Louis, Louis* (1904).

13
Mister Jefferson Lord, play that barber shop
  chord,
That soothing harmony, it makes an awful,
  awful hit with me.
  WILLIAM TRACEY, *Play That Barber Shop Chord* (song, c. 1910, with music by
  Lewis Muir).

14
Old songs are best—how sweet to hear
The strains to home and memory dear!
CLARENCE URMY, *Old Songs Are Best*.

15
I can't sing. As a singist I am not a success. I
am saddest when I sing. So are those who
hear me. They are sadder even than I am.
ARTEMUS WARD, *Lecture*.

16
I hear America singing, the varied carols I
  hear.
WALT WHITMAN, *I Hear America Singing*.

17
No really great song can ever attain full purport till long after the death of its singer—
till it has accrued and incorporated the many
passions, many joys and sorrows, it has itself
aroused.
WALT WHITMAN, *November Boughs: The Bible As Poetry*.

18
Bring the good old bugle, boys! we'll sing
  another song—
Sing it with a spirit that will start the world
  along—

Sing it as we used to sing it, fifty thousand
   strong,
   While we were marching through Georgia.
   HENRY CLAY WORK, *Marching Through
   Georgia*.

1
I was seeing Nellie home,
I was seeing Nellie home;
And 'twas from Aunt Dinah's quilting party
I was seeing Nellie home.
   UNKNOWN, *The Quilting Party*.

2
I've been workin' on the railroad,
   All the live-long day,
I've been workin' on the railroad
   Just to pass the time away.
Don't you hear the whistle blowing,
   Rise up so early in the morn,
Don't you hear the captain shouting:
   Dinah, blow your horn.
   UNKNOWN, *I've Been Workin' on the
   Railroad*. The first known publication
   was in *Carmina Princetonia*, in 1894;
   the title was recorded as *Levee Song*
   then, and no author was given.

3
Frankie and Johnny were lovers, O Lordy,
   how they could love.
Swore to be true to each other, true as the
   stars above;
He was her man, but he done her wrong.
   UNKNOWN, *Frankie and Johnny*. There
   are many versions of this classic ballad.
   The original is said to be the one titled
   Frankie and Albert, and is based on the
   killing of Albert (or Allen) Britt by
   Frankie Baker in St. Louis, 15 Oct.,
   1899.

4
We're here because we're here,
Because we're here, because we're here;
Oh, here we are, and here we are,
And here we are again.
   UNKNOWN, first popular as a soldiers' song
   in World War I.

SORROW

See also Grief

5
I love the friendly faces of old sorrows;
I have no secrets that they do not know.
   KARLE WILSON BAKER, *I Love the Friend-
   ly Faces*.

6
Men die, but sorrow never dies;
   The crowding years divide in vain,
And the wide world is knit with ties
   Of common brotherhood in pain.
   SUSAN COOLIDGE, *The Cradle Tomb in
   Westminster Abbey*.

7
Who ne'er his bread in sorrow ate,
   Who ne'er the mournful midnight hours
Weeping upon his bed has sate,

He knows you not, ye Heavenly Powers.
   GOETHE, *Wilhelm Meister's Apprentice-
   ship*. LONGFELLOW used this as the
   motto for his *Hyperion*, bk. i.

8
For Sorrow's a woman a man may take
And know, till his heart and body break.
   SAMUEL HOFFENSTEIN, *Sorrow That Cries.*

9
The sorrow for the dead is the only sorrow
from which we refuse to be divorced. Every
other wound we seek to heal, every other
affliction to forget; but this wound we consider it a duty to keep open; this affliction
we cherish and brood over in solitude.
   WASHINGTON IRVING, *The Sketch-Book,
   Rural Funerals*.

10
Words are less needful to sorrow than to
joy.
   HELEN HUNT JACKSON, *Ramona*, ch. 17.

11
A lean sorrow is hardest to bear.
   SARAH ORNE JEWETT, *Life of Nancy*, p.
   278.

12
Sorrow is a form of self-pity . . . and we
have to go on.
   ROBERT F. KENNEDY, speaking from personal experience after the assassination
   of his brother, John F. Kennedy. (PE-
   TER LISAGOR, *Portrait of a Man Emerg-
   ing from Shadows; New York Times
   Magazine*, 19 July, 1964, p. 28)

13
Believe me, every man has his secret sorrows, which the world knows not; and oftentimes we call a man cold when he is only
sad.
   HENRY WADSWORTH LONGFELLOW, *Hyperion*, bk. iii, ch. 4.

14
Into each life some rain must fall,
Some days must be dark and dreary.
   HENRY WADSWORTH LONGFELLOW, *The
   Rainy Day*.

15
Sorrow, the great idealizer.
   JAMES RUSSELL LOWELL, *Among My
   Books: Spenser*.

16
I had a little Sorrow,
Born of a little Sin.
   EDNA ST. VINCENT MILLAY, *The Penitent.*

17
True sorrow makes a silence in the heart.
   ROBERT NATHAN, *A Cedar Box.*

18
There are few sorrows, however poignant, in
which a good income is of no avail.
   LOGAN PEARSALL SMITH, *Afterthoughts.*

1

The secret source of Humor is not joy but sorrow.

MARK TWAIN, *Pudd'nhead Wilson's New Calendar*, ch. 10.

SOUL

2

There's a quiet harbor somewhere
  For the poor a-weary soul.

H. H. BROWNELL, *The Burial of the Dane*.

3

A soul,—a spark of the never-dying flame that separates man from all the other beings of earth.

JAMES FENIMORE COOPER, *Afloat and Ashore*, ch. 12.

4

The soul selects her own society,
Then shuts the door;
On her divine majority
Obtrude no more.

EMILY DICKINSON, *Poems*, Pt. i, No. 13.

5

My mind is incapable of conceiving such a thing as a soul. I may be in error, and man may have a soul; but I simply do not believe it.

THOMAS A. EDISON, *Do We Live Again?*

6

The Supreme Critic on the errors of the past and the present, and the only prophet of that which must be, is that great nature in which we rest as the earth lies in the soft arms of the atmosphere; that Unity, that Over-Soul, within which every man's particular being is contained and made one with all other.

EMERSON, *Essays, First Series: The Over-Soul*.

7

The soul is lost by mimicking soul.

EMERSON, Lecture: *Table Talk*.

8

The one thing in the world, of value, is the active soul.

EMERSON, *Nature, Addresses, and Lectures: The American Scholar*.

9

Though a sound body cannot restore an unsound mind, yet a good soul can, by its virtue, render the body the best possible.

EMERSON, *Representative Men: Plato*.

10

Whether or not the philosophers care to admit that we have a soul, it seems obvious that we are equipped with something or other which generates dreams and ideals, and which sets up values.

JOHN ERSKINE. (DURANT, *On the Meaning of Life*, p. 39)

11

But it is the will of God and nature, that these mortal bodies be laid aside, when the soul is to enter into real life. . . . A man is not completely born until he be dead.

BENJAMIN FRANKLIN, Letter to Miss Hubbard, 23 Feb., 1756.

12

Build thee more stately mansions, O my soul,
  As the swift seasons roll!
  Leave thy low-vaulted past!
Let each new temple, nobler than the last,
Shut thee from heaven with a dome more vast,
  Till thou at length art free,
Leaving thine outgrown shell by life's unresting sea!

OLIVER WENDELL HOLMES, *The Chambered Nautilus*.

13

For every soul is a circus,
And every mind is a tent,
And every heart is a sawdust ring
Where the circling race is spent.

VACHEL LINDSAY, *Every Soul Is a Circus*.

14

Ah, the souls of those that die
Are but sunbeams lifted higher.

HENRY WADSWORTH LONGFELLOW, *The Golden Legend*, pt. iv: *The Cloisters*, l. 19.

15

Hands of invisible spirits touch the strings
Of that mysterious instrument, the soul,
And play the prelude of our fate. We hear
The voice prophetic, and are not alone.

HENRY WADSWORTH LONGFELLOW, *The Spanish Student*, act i, sc. 3, l. 111.

16

Give thanks, O heart, for the high souls
That point us to the deathless goals.

EDWIN MARKHAM, *Conscripts of the Dream*.

17

The dust's for crawling, heaven's for flying,
Wherefore, O Soul, whose wings are grown,
Soar upward to the sun!

EDGAR LEE MASTERS, *The Spoon River Anthology: Julian Scott*.

18

I count that soul exceeding small
That lives alone by book and creed,—
A soul that has not learned to read.

JOAQUIN MILLER, *The Larger College*.

19

I will hew great windows for my soul.

ANGELA MORGAN, *Room*.

20

I am the captain of my soul;
  I rule it with stern joy;
And yet I think I had more fun
  When I was cabin boy.

KEITH PRESTON, *An Awful Responsibility*.

21

The perfect body is itself the soul.

GEORGE SANTAYANA, *Before a Statue of Achilles*.

1

A mule can travel only in two directions: either right or left. He must be either a reactionary or a liberal. But because you have a soul there is another direction open to you, toward God for whom you were made.

FULTON J. SHEEN, Radio Address from Washington, D.C., 23 Mar., 1941.

2

Most people sell their souls and live with good conscience on the proceeds.

LOGAN PEARSALL SMITH, Afterthoughts.

3

My soul is a dark ploughed field
In the cold rain;
My soul is a broken field
Ploughed by pain.

SARA TEASDALE, The Broken Field.

4

I love a soul not all of wood,
Predestined to be good,
But true to the backbone
Unto itself alone
And false to none;
Born to its own affairs,
Its own joys and own cares;
By which the work that God begun
Is finished, and not undone.

HENRY D. THOREAU, Conscience.

5

The human soul is a silent harp in God's quire, whose strings need only to be swept by the divine breath to chime in with the harmonies of creation.

HENRY D. THOREAU, Journal, 10 Aug., 1838.

6

Our life is but the Soul made known by its fruits, the body. The whole duty of man may be expressed in one line: Make to yourself a perfect body.

HENRY D. THOREAU, Journal, 21 June, 1840.

7

Be careless in your dress if you must, but keep a tidy soul.

MARK TWAIN, Pudd'nhead Wilson's Calendar.

8

"Two things," the wise man said, "fill me with awe:
The starry heavens and the moral law."
Nay, add another wonder to thy roll,—
The living marvel of the human soul!

HENRY VAN DYKE, Stars and the Soul.
Kant is the "wise man" referred to.

9

Nobody knows how the idea of a soul or the supernatural started. It probably had its origin in the natural laziness of mankind.

JOHN B. WATSON, Behaviorism, p. 3.

10

What do you suppose will satisfy the soul,

except to walk free and own no superior?

WALT WHITMAN, Laws for Creations.

11

O my brave soul! O farther farther sail!
O daring joy, but safe! are they not all the seas of God?
O farther, farther, farther sail!

WALT WHITMAN, Passage to India, sec. 9.

12

The soul has that measureless pride which revolts from every lesson but its own.

WALT WHITMAN, Song of Prudence, l. 43.

SPEECH

See also Conversation, Orator and Oratory, Silence, Tongue

13

No one means all he says, and yet very few say all they mean, for words are slippery and thought is viscous.

HENRY ADAMS, The Education of Henry Adams, ch. 31.

14

We live in an age of words, of talk, of constant oral expression. Language is getting progressively looser. Oral expression is sometimes graphic, but it is often flabby. It is almost always repetitive. Nobody can speak quite as well as he can write, certainly as well as he ought to be able to write if he doesn't tie himself into knots of affectation.

ERWIN D. CANHAM, Introduction to Words on Paper, by ROY COPPERUD.

15

Happiness is speechless.

GEORGE WILLIAM CURTIS, Prue and I, ch. 4.

16

There is no inspiration in evil and . . . no man ever made a great speech on a mean subject.

EUGENE V. DEBS, Efficient Expression.

17

The music that can deepest reach,
And cure all ill, is cordial speech.

EMERSON, Conduct of Life: Considerations by the Way.

18

A man cannot speak but he judges himself.

EMERSON, Essays, First Series: Compensation.

19

Eloquence is the power to translate a truth into language perfectly intelligible to the person to whom you speak.

EMERSON, Letters and Social Aims: Eloquence.

20

Eloquence a hundred times has turned the scale of war and peace at will.

EMERSON, Letters and Social Aims: Progress of Culture.

1
When you've got a thing to say,
Say it! Don't take half a day.
When your tale's got little in it,
Crowd the whole thing in a minute!
>JOEL CHANDLER HARRIS, *Advice to Writers for the Daily Press.*

2
Speak clearly, if you speak at all;
Carve every word before you let it fall.
>OLIVER WENDELL HOLMES, *A Rhymed Lesson,* l. 408.

3
The flowering moments of the mind
Drop half their petals in our speech.
>OLIVER WENDELL HOLMES, *To My Readers,* st. 11.

4
No, never say nothin' without you're compelled tu,
An' then don't say nothin' thet you can be held tu.
>JAMES RUSSELL LOWELL, *The Biglow Papers,* Ser. ii, No. 5.

5
But as they hedn't no gret things to say,
An' sed 'em often, I come right away.
>JAMES RUSSELL LOWELL, *The Biglow Papers,* Ser. ii: *Mason and Slidell.*

6
In general those who nothing have to say
  Contrive to spend the longest time in doing it,
They turn and vary it in every way,
  Hashing it, stewing it, mincing it, *ragouting* it.
>JAMES RUSSELL LOWELL, *An Oriental Apologue,* st. 15.

7
To the man with an ear for verbal delicacies —the man who searches painfully for the perfect word, and puts the way of saying a thing above the thing said—there is in writing the constant joy of sudden discovery, of happy accident.
>H. L. MENCKEN, *A Book of Prefaces,* ch. 2.

8
He said enough, Enough said.
>GERTRUDE STEIN, *Enough Said.* The poem consists of these words, five times repeated.

Speech: Freedom of Speech

9
The United States is a land of free speech. Nowhere is speech freer—not even here where we sedulously cultivate it even in its most repulsive form.
>WINSTON CHURCHILL, Address in the House of Commons, 28 Sept., 1944.

10
This is the convention of free speech, and I have been given the floor. I have only a few words to say to you, but I shall say them if I stand here until tomorrow morning.
>GEORGE WILLIAM CURTIS, Address at the Republican national convention, 1860.

11
The right to be heard does not automatically include the right to be taken seriously. To be taken seriously depends entirely upon what is being said.
>HUBERT H. HUMPHREY, Address at the University of Wisconsin, Madison, Wis., 23 Aug., 1965. The statement, by implication, was a reply to student demonstrators demanding immediate American withdrawal from the war in Vietnam.

12
So let no citizen that is secure in his own liberty ever forget how precious it is, and how brave we must be if we are to keep it, how many generations of men have perished in order to guard its light, and how many scattered throughout the world are dying still to protect it.
>LYNDON B. JOHNSON, Commencement Address at National Cathedral School for Girls, Washington, D.C., 1 June, 1965.

13
Let no one ever think for a moment that national debate means national division.
>LYNDON B. JOHNSON, Commencement Address at National Cathedral School for Girls, Washington, D.C., 1 June, 1965.

14
And I honor the man who is willing to sink
Half his present repute for the freedom to think,
And, when he has thought, be his cause strong or weak,
Will risk t' other half for the freedom to speak.
>JAMES RUSSELL LOWELL, *A Fable for Critics,* l. 1067.

15
The first is freedom of speech and expression—everywhere in the world.
>FRANKLIN D. ROOSEVELT, Message to Congress, 6 Jan., 1941, defining the "four essential human freedoms," familiarly known as the "four freedoms."

16
The first principle of a free society is an untrammeled flow of words in an open forum.
>ADLAI E. STEVENSON. (New York *Times,* 19 Jan., 1962)

17
It is by the goodness of God that in our country we have those three unspeakably precious things: freedom of speech, freedom of conscience, and the prudence never to practise either of them.
>MARK TWAIN, *Pudd'nhead Wilson's New Calendar,* ch. 20.

1

If men are to be precluded from offering their sentiments on a matter, which may involve the most serious and alarming consequences that can invite the consideration of mankind, reason is of no use to us; the freedom of speech may be taken away, and dumb and silent we may be led, like sheep to the slaughter.

> GEORGE WASHINGTON, Address to Officers of the Revolutionary Army, 15 Mar., 1783.

2

Congress shall make no law . . . abridging the freedom of speech, or of the press.

> U.S. Constitution, First Amendment (1791).

SPIRIT

See also Soul

3

If matter mute and inanimate, though changed by the forces of Nature into a multitude of forms, can never die, will the spirit of man suffer annihilation when it has paid a brief visit, like a royal guest, to this tenement of clay?

> WILLIAM JENNINGS BRYAN, *The Prince of Peace.*

4

Spirit is the real and eternal; matter is the unreal and temporal.

> MARY BAKER EDDY, *Science and Health,* p. 468.

5

Every spirit makes its house, but afterwards the house confines the spirit.

> EMERSON, *Conduct of Life: Fate.*

6

Great men are they who see that spiritual is stronger than any material force.

> EMERSON, *Letters and Social Aims: Progress of Culture.*

7

More brightly must my spirit shine
Since grace of beauty is not mine.

> JANIE SCREVEN HEYWARD, *The Spirit's Grace.*

8

Grant to us life that though the man be gone
The promise of his spirit be fulfilled.

> JOHN MASEFIELD, *John Fitzgerald Kennedy,* a tribute published in London three days after Kennedy's death.

9

Bend low, O dusky Night,
　And give my spirit rest,
　Hold me to your deep breast,
And put old cares to flight.

> LOUISE CHANDLER MOULTON, *Tonight.*

10

Of my own spirit let me be
In sole though feeble mastery.

> SARA TEASDALE, *Mastery.*

11

A subtle spirit has my path attended,
In likeness not a lion but a pard;
And when the arrows flew like hail, and hard,
He licked my wounds, and all my wounds were mended.

> ELINOR HOYT WYLIE, *One Person,* sonnet 9.

SPORT

See also Horse, Horsemanship; Leisure

General

12

As I understand it, sport is hard work for which you do not get paid.

> IRVIN S. COBB, *Sports and Pastimes; The Saturday Evening Post,* 1912. (Reprinted in *Sport U.S.A.,* ed. by H. T. Paxton, p. 74)

13

Don't come home a failure.

> WILLIAM HERSCHEL COBB, to his son, Tyrus Raymond (Ty) Cobb, when the younger Cobb hesitantly broke the news that he was considering professional baseball as a career, instead of following his father's advice to try for an appointment to the U.S. Military Academy. (TY COBB, *My Life in Baseball,* p. 47)

14

Is not true leisure one with true toil?

> JOHN S. DWIGHT, *True Rest.*

15

The bigger they come the harder they fall.

> BOB FITZSIMMONS, just before he was beaten in a heavyweight boxing match by James J. Jeffries, 25 July, 1902.

16

Games played with the ball, and others of that nature, are too violent for the body and stamp no character on the mind.

> THOMAS JEFFERSON, *Writings,* vol. v, p. 83.

17

The strength of our democracy is no greater than the collective well-being of our people. The vigor of our country is no stronger than the vitality and will of all our countrymen. The level of physical, mental, moral and spiritual fitness of every American citizen must be our constant concern

> JOHN F. KENNEDY, Message to American schools on the physical fitness of youth, 1961.

18

Football today is far too much a sport for the few who can play it well; the rest of us, and too many of our children, get our exercise from climbing up the seats in stadiums, or from walking across the room to turn on our television sets. And this is true for one sport after another, all across the board.

> JOHN F. KENNEDY, Speech at the National Football Foundation dinner, 5 Dec., 1961. Kennedy, like Theodore Roosevelt, was an advocate of participant sports.

1

A couple of years ago they told me I was too young to be President and you were too old to be playing baseball. But we fooled them.

> JOHN F. KENNEDY, to Stan Musial, of the St. Louis Cardinals, at the 1962 All-Star game in Washington, D.C. Kennedy was forty-five at the time, and Musial was three years younger.

2

There are only two kinds of coaches—those who have been fired and those who will be fired.

> KEN LOEFFLER, a veteran and highly successful basketball coach who was referring to the hazards involved in coaching or managing in any sport—the consequence of failure. (BOB BROEG, "Sports Comment," St. Louis *Post-Dispatch*, 29 Dec., 1964, p. 4-B)

A successful coach is one who is still coaching.

> BEN SCHWARTZWALDER, himself a successful football coach, to a gathering of coaches in San Francisco, 19 Dec., 1963.

3

Avoid fried meats which angry up the blood. If your stomach disputes you, lie down and pacify it with cool thoughts. Keep the juices flowing by jangling around gently as you move. Go very light on the vices, such as carrying on in society. The social ramble ain't restful. Avoid running at all times. Don't look back. Someone might be gaining on you.

> LEROY (SATCHEL) PAIGE, the ageless baseball pitcher's prescription for staying young. (*Collier's*, 13 June, 1953)

4

For when the One Great Scorer comes to
    write against your name,
He marks—not that you won or lost—but
    how you played the game.

> GRANTLAND RICE, *Alumnus Football*.

Nice guys finish last.

> LEO DUROCHER.

Winning isn't everything, but wanting to win is.

> VINCE LOMBARDI. (ROBERT RIGER, *Pro Football's Bright New Breed; Esquire*, Nov., 1962)

I do not think winning is the most important thing. I think winning is the only thing.

> BILL VEECK. (*The Spirit of Sport; New York Times Magazine*, 18 Oct., 1964)

My riding career was fired with an ambition to be on the front end as often as possible.

> EDDIE ARCARO, Foreword, *The Fireside Book of Horce Racing*.

I do not believe in defeat.

> BILL HARTACK, the credo of a leading jockey. (Quoted by JACK MANN in the New York *Herald Tribune*, 11 Feb., 1964)

The champion, the record, the victory; that is the thing that interests the average citizen of the United States. Not how the game is played; but the result is what he cares most about. This demand for victory by the sporting public has been a big factor in the development of champions. It has also taken most of the fun out of competitive sport.

> JOHN R. TUNIS.

Men like to win; but women hate to lose. The difference can be summed up in one word: bridgemanship.

> CHARLES GOREN. (*McCall's*, Aug., 1961)

5

Oh! the old swimmin'-hole! When I last saw
    the place,
The scene was all changed, like the change in
    my face.

> JAMES WHITCOMB RILEY, *The Old Swimmin'-Hole*, st. 5.

6

I wish to preach, not the doctrine of ignoble ease, but the doctrine of the strenuous life.

> THEODORE ROOSEVELT, Speech to the Hamilton Club, Chicago, 10 Apr., 1899. In sports, too, Roosevelt pursued this philosophy.

7

In life as in a football game, the principle to follow is: Hit the line hard.

> THEODORE ROOSEVELT, *The Strenuous Life: The American Boy*.

8

I read the newspapers quickly and spent about half the time on the sports section, because there you find the truth. You don't read a sports story and then say to yourself, "Now, I must rush out and see what the Republicans or the Democrats have to say about it." Sports must be good reading, because normal people are involved as a rule. You don't see neurotics interested in sports.

> FULTON J. SHEEN. (*The Sporting News*, 23 June, 1962; quoted in column by DICK YOUNG)

1

Work consists of whatever a body is *obliged* to do . . . Play consists of whatever a body is not obliged to do.
> MARK TWAIN, *The Adventures of Tom Sawyer*, ch. 2.

2

This is a sport which makes the body's very liver curl with enjoyment.
> MARK TWAIN, *Life on the Mississippi*, referring to piloting.

3

Sports constantly make demands on the participant for top performance, and they develop integrity, self-reliance and initiative. They teach you a lot about working in groups, without being unduly submerged in the group.
> BYRON R. WHITE, an outstanding football player (known as "Whizzer" White) before being named to the Supreme Court. (ALFRED WRIGHT, *A Modest All-America Who Sits on the Highest Bench; Sports Illustrated,* 10 Dec., 1962)

4

Ivy League.
> STANLEY WOODWARD, coined when he was sports editor of the New York *Herald Tribune.*

5

Sittin' in the catbird seat.
> UNKNOWN, signifying a favorable position in general, but best known to baseball fans through its use by Red Barber, the broadcaster.

Baseball

6

These are the saddest of possible words:
"Tinker to Evers to Chance."
Trio of bear cubs, and fleeter than birds,
Tinker and Evers and Chance.
Ruthlessly pricking our gonfalon bubble,
Making a Giant hit into a double—
Words that are heavy with nothing but trouble:
"Tinker to Evers to Chance."
> FRANKLIN P. ADAMS, *Baseball's Sad Lexicon,* referring to the famed double-play combination of the Chicago Cubs in the early 1900's: Joe Tinker, Johnny Evers, and Frank Chance.

7

Whoever wants to know the heart and mind of America had better learn baseball, the rules and realities of the game—and do it by watching first some high school or small-town teams.
> JACQUES BARZUN, *God's Country and Mine.*

8

I want to thank everyone who made this day necessary.
> LAWRENCE PETER (YOGI) BERRA. One of

baseball's favorite pixies, Berra was also famous for his talent for malapropism. This was his way of publicly thanking some admirers who had paid tribute to him before a game—who "made this day possible," in other words.

9

If the people don't want to come out to the park, nobody's gonna stop em.
> YOGI BERRA, a familiar example of his malapropism. He was referring to lagging baseball attendance in Kansas City, and the impossibility of forcing fans to attend games.

10

Can't Anybody Here Play This Game?
> JIMMY BRESLIN, Title of book (1963).

11

Say this much for big league baseball—it is beyond any question the greatest conversation piece ever invented in America.
> BRUCE CATTON, *Book Week,* New York *Herald Tribune,* 12 Apr., 1964, p. 1.

12

He comes to play.
> LEO DUROCHER, on Eddie Stanky, whom Durocher managed and greatly admired for his spirit and devotion to baseball.

13

You don't save a pitcher for tomorrow. Tomorrow it may rain.
> LEO DUROCHER.

14

Baseball Is a Funny Game.
> JOE GARAGIOLA, Title of humorous book (1960).

15

He may not score, and yet he helps to Win
Who makes the Hit that brings the Runner in.
> ARTHUR GUITERMAN, *A Poet's Proverbs,* p. 17.

16

Knowin' all about baseball is just about as profitable as bein' a good whittler.
> KIN HUBBARD.

17

Why do I like baseball? The pay is good, it keeps you out in the fresh air and sunshine, and you can't beat them hours.
> TIM HURST. It should be pointed out that the veteran umpire's classic words applied to the early 1900's—an era of daytime baseball and rapid play.

18

We cheer for the [Washington] Senators, we pray for the Senators, and we hope that the Supreme Court doesn't declare that unconstitutional.
> LYNDON B. JOHNSON, Speech at a luncheon given in connection with the 1962 All-Star baseball game in Washington, D.C., 9 July, 1962.

1
I hit em where they ain't.
>WILLIAM HENRY (WILLIE) KEELER. A leading player between 1892 and 1909, Keeler was one of the great exponents of scientific batting before the home run became the rage in baseball.

Who can think and hit at the same time?
>LAWRENCE PETER (YOGI) BERRA.

2
Slide, Kelly, Slide!
>J. W. KELLY, title of song (1899), referring to the base-running feats of Michael Kelly, of the Chicago and Boston baseball teams during the last two decades of the century.

3
It ain't nothin' till I call it.
>BILL KLEM. One of the most famous of baseball umpires used this line effectively to cool the fire of rival players and managers who would charge up to him after close plays, demanding to know whether a ball was fair or foul, or whether a hit or an out was to be recorded.

4
Sure, I have muffed a few in my time. But I never called one wrong in my heart.
>BILL KLEM.

5
A sensational event was changing from the brown suit to the gray the contents of his pockets. He was earnest about these objects. They were of eternal importance, like baseball or the Republican Party.
>SINCLAIR LEWIS, *Babbitt,* ch. 1.

6
Good field, no hit.
>Attributed to both ADOLFO LUQUE and MIKE GONZALES, early Cuban Players whose command of English was limited. This was a famous scouting report dispatched to a big-league baseball team interested in a youthful player in the minors.

7
Take me out to the ball game,
Take me out with the crowd,
Buy me some peanuts and cracker-jack,
I don't care if I never get back.
Let me root, root, root for the home team,
If they don't win it's a shame,
For it's one, two, three strikes you're out,
At the old ball game.
>JACK NORWORTH, *Take Me Out to the Ball Game* (song, 1908, with music by Albert Von Tilzer).

8
You done splendid.
>CHARLES DILLON (CASEY) STENGEL. (FRANK GRAHAM, JR., *Casey Stengel: His Half-Century in Baseball*)

9
He lets the ball go too far.
>CASEY STENGEL, commenting on Jay Hook, one of his pitchers with the New York Mets during the team's first year of operation, 1962. Hook yielded many home runs.

10
Brooklyn—are they still in the league?
>BILL TERRY, manager of the New York Giants, before the start of the 1934 baseball season. Although Brooklyn is now no longer in the National League, this quotation remains the classic baseball version of the maxim about letting sleeping dogs lie. Terry's Giants had won the world championship in 1933. His taunt about Brooklyn was in reply to a sports writer's request for a prediction about 1934. On the final two days of the 1934 season, Brooklyn twice beat the Giants, costing them the pennant.

The Giants is dead.
>CHARLES (CHUCK) DRESSEN, manager of the Brooklyn Dodgers, midway in the 1951 baseball season. The aroused New York Giants eventually overtook Dressen's team and won the pennant.

11
There was ease in Casey's manner as he stept into his place,
There was pride in Casey's bearing and a smile on Casey's face,
And when responding to the cheers he lightly doft his hat,
No stranger in the crowd could doubt, 't was Casey at the bat.
>ERNEST LAWRENCE THAYER, *Casey at the Bat,* st. 6.

12
Oh, somewhere in this favored land the sun is shining bright;
The band is playing somewhere, and somewhere hearts are light,
And somewhere men are laughing, and little children shout;
But there is no joy in Mudville—mighty Casey has struck out.
>ERNEST LAWRENCE THAYER, *Casey at the Bat,* st. 13.

13
Say it ain't so, Joe.
>UNKNOWN, the plea of an unidentified small boy who ran up to "Shoeless Joe" Jackson, in 1920, when Jackson emerged from a courtroom after telling a grand jury about his part in the corrupt World Series of 1919. The investigation showed that members of the Chicago White Sox, Jackson's team, had sold out to gamblers during the Series. As a result, Jackson and seven of his teammates were barred

from baseball. Also quoted as "Say it
ain't true" and "Say it isn't so."

1
Baseball must be a great game to survive the
people who run it.

> UNKNOWN, quoted by ARTHUR DALEY in
> "Sports of the Times," New York
> *Times,* 10 Nov., 1964.

Football

2
Pro football is like nuclear warfare. There
are no winners, only survivors.

> FRANK GIFFORD. (*Sports Illustrated,* 4
> July, 1960)

3
Coach, some day when the going gets rough,
tell the boys to win one for the Gipper.

> GEORGE GIPP, on the authority of Knute
> Rockne, football coach at the University
> of Notre Dame. Gipp died in Dec.,
> 1920, two weeks after he had been
> named to the All-America team of that
> year. On his deathbed, according to
> Rockne, Gipp spoke these words to
> Rockne. Gipp's outstanding play and his
> inspirational message became legendary
> at Notre Dame. On several occasions
> Rockne used Gipp's words to fire up
> Notre Dame teams at half time, when
> the going was "rough."

4
I do not see the relationship of these highly
industrialized affairs on Saturday afternoons
to higher learning in America.

> ROBERT M. HUTCHINS, referring to college
> football.

I've had enough of a game that isn't a game
any more. I've had enough of trying to
stretch a blanket to cover all the strange
bedfellows of college football. I am no longer
interested in trying to please the public with
a professional show put on by semipros under amateur sponsorship.

> BLAIR CHERRY. This blast appeared origi-
> nally as a *Saturday Evening Post* arti-
> cle, "Why I Quit Coaching," in Sept.,
> 1951, a year after his resignation as
> football coach at the University of Tex-
> as. (*Sport U.S.A.,* ed. by H. T. Paxton,
> p. 405)

Football is not the be-all and end-all.

> CHARLES (BUD) WILKINSON, who com-
> piled a brilliant record as football coach
> at the University of Oklahoma, 1947–
> 63. (ARTHUR DALEY, "Sports of the
> Times," New York *Times,* 20 Jan.,
> 1964)

5
Some people try to find things in this game
or put things into it which don't exist. Football is two things. It's blocking and tackling.
I don't care anything about formations or
new offenses or tricks on defense. You block
and tackle better than the team you're playing, you win.

> VINCE LOMBARDI. (*Sports Illustrated,* 8
> Jan., 1962)

6
Run to Daylight.

> VINCE LOMBARDI AND W. C. HEINZ, Title
> of book on football (1963).

7
Dancing is a contact sport; football is a hitting sport.

> VINCE LOMBARDI. (New York *Times,* 3
> Jan., 1966)

8
Outlined against a blue-gray October sky, the
Four Horsemen rode again. In dramatic lore
they were known as Famine, Pestilence, De-
struction and Death. These are only aliases.
Their real names are [Harry] Stuhldreher,
[Don] Miller, [Jim] Crowley and [Elmer]
Layden.

> GRANTLAND RICE, writing of the Notre
> Dame-Army football game of 1924. The
> "Four Horsemen" made up the legend-
> ary Notre Dame backfield of that era.

9
In pro football you begin with the quarter-
back. If you have a good one, you're in business. If you don't, you're dead.

> AL SHERMAN, himself a quarterback be-
> fore becoming a successful coach in the
> professional sport. (*New York Times
> Magazine,* 10 Nov., 1963)

10
It was an ideal day for football—too cold for
the spectators and too cold for the players.

> RED SMITH, quoting a classic line and ap-
> plying it to the 1963 National Football
> League championship game between
> New York and Chicago, played in Chi-
> cago, 29 Dec., 1963.

11
A punt, a pass, and a prayer.

> FIELDING YOST, noted football coach at
> the University of Michigan during the
> 1920's, describing his style of play.

Boxing

12
This is the story about a man
With iron fists and a beautiful tan,
He talks a lot and boasts indeed
Of a powerful punch and blinding speed.

> CASSIUS CLAY, a fragment of his autobio-
> graphical verse.

13
I am the greatest.

> CASSIUS CLAY.

I just said I'm the greatest. I never said I
was the smartest.

> CASSIUS CLAY, upon being rejected for
> military service, 22 Mar., 1964.

1

It was sufficient to convince me that professional boxing is in need of an official and public fumigation.

    MICHAEL FEIGHAN, U.S. Representative from Ohio, suggesting a congressional investigation of boxing, 26 Feb., 1964, as an aftermath of the first Cassius Clay-Sonny Liston heavyweight title bout. The rematch a year later led to further demands for government control or abolition of boxing.

2

Boxing is definitely here to stay, no matter what the general attitude of those male grandmothers and young men of the nincompoop class who want to see its demise.

    NAT FLEISCHER, veteran boxing authority. (Interview, New York *Times*, 3 Jan., 1965)

3

I'll bet th' hardest thing about prize fightin' is pickin' up yer teeth with a boxin' glove on.

    KIN HUBBARD.

4

We was robbed!

    JOE JACOBS. The veteran boxing manager shouted this charge in the summer of 1932 when his fighter, Max Schmeling, lost a heavyweight title match to Jack Sharkey, on a decision. It became a classic in sports in general.

5

I should of stood in bed.

    JOE JACOBS, a widely quoted saying that applies to any exercise in frustration, though Jacobs, a boxing manager, coined it after an experience in baseball. He had been bedridden just prior to the 1935 World Series, and the only reward he got for journeying to the Series was picking the wrong team (Chicago) to back.

6

The Sweet Science.

    A. J. LIEBLING, Title of book (1956). This wryly humorous definition of the sport occasionally appeared in individual articles on boxing, written by Liebling for *The New Yorker* during the same period.

7

What is this, Jacobs Beach?

    DAMON RUNYON, upon passing the theatrical-sports ticket agency operated by the fight promoter Michael Strauss (Mike) Jacobs, in 1934, and seeing members of the boxing fraternity sitting in brightly colored bridge chairs. "Jacobs Beach" remained in the language for many years, identifying the area around Madison Square Garden in New York City—the mecca of all pugilists.

8

The old pitcher went to the well once too often, but I'm glad the championship remains in America.

    JOHN L. SULLIVAN, after his defeat by the heavyweight boxer James J. Corbett, 7 Sept., 1892.

Golf

9

Cow-pasture pool.

    O. K. BOVARD, his description of golf, when he was managing editor of the St. Louis *Post-Dispatch*.

10

I don't know what I would do without this game. I really love it.

    DWIGHT D. EISENHOWER, after a charity exhibition match in Ardmore, Pa., 26 May, 1964.

11

If you watch a game, it's fun. If you play it, it's recreation. If you work at it, it's golf.

    BOB HOPE. (*The Reader's Digest,* Oct., 1958)

12

Golf is essentially an exercise in masochism conducted out of doors; it affords opportunity for a certain swank, it induces a sense of kinship in its victims, and it forces them to breathe fresh and addictive rite calculated to breathe fresh air, but it is, at bottom, an elaborate and addictive rite calculated to drive them crazy for hours on end and send them straight to the whisky bottle after that.

    PAUL O'NEIL, *Palmer Tightens His Grip on Golf; Life,* 15 June, 1962, p. 103.

13

Golf is a plague, invented by the Calvinistic Scots as a punishment for man's sins . . . As General Eisenhower discovered, it is easier to end the cold war or stamp out poverty than to master this devilish pastime.

    JAMES RESTON, Washington Column, New York *Times,* 26 Apr., 1964.

Fishing

14

Modern fishing is as complicated as flying a B-58 to Tacoma. Several years of preliminary library and desk work are essential just to be able to buy equipment without humiliation.

    RUSSELL BAKER, "Observer" column, New York *Times,* 28 July, 1964.

15

Oh, you who've been a-fishing will endorse me when I say
That it always *is* the biggest fish you catch that gets away!

    EUGENE FIELD, *Our Biggest Fish.*

1

Inch for inch and pound for pound, the gamest fish that swims.

JAMES A. HENSHALL, *Book of the Black Bass*, p. 380.

2

There are only two occasions when Americans respect privacy, especially in Presidents. Those are prayer and fishing. So that some have taken to fishing.

HERBERT HOOVER, 1944.

3

All men are equal before fish.

HERBERT HOOVER, 1951.

4

Fishing is much more than fish; it is the vitalizing lure to outdoor life. It is the great occasion when we may return to the fine simplicity of our forefathers.

HERBERT HOOVER, 1963.

5

Of all the fish that swim or swish
  In ocean's deep autocracy,
There's none possess such haughtiness
  As the codfish aristocracy.

WALLACE IRWIN, *Codfish Aristocracy*.

6

Fishing is a delusion entirely surrounded by
  liars in old clothes.

DON MARQUIS.

7

Ye monsters of the bubbling deep,
  Your Maker's praises spout;
Up from the sands ye codlings peep,
  And wag your tails about.

COTTON MATHER, *Hymn*.

8

Only the gamefish swims upstream,
But the sensible fish swims down.

OGDEN NASH, *When You Say That, Smile*.

9

Where the puddle is shallow the weakfish
  stay
To drift along with the current's flow;
To take the tide as it moves each day
With the idle ripples that come and go.

GRANTLAND RICE, *Ballade of the Gamefish*.

10

Then come, my friend, forget your foes, and
  leave your fears behind.
And wander forth to try your luck, with
  cheerful, quiet mind.

HENRY VAN DYKE, *The Angler's Reveille*.

11

Two honest and good-natured anglers have never met each other by the way without crying out, "What luck?"

HENRY VAN DYKE, *Fisherman's Luck*.

Hunting

12

Hast thou named all the birds without a gun?

EMERSON, *Hymn: Forbearance*.

13

The woods are made for the hunters of
  dreams,
  The brooks for the fishers of song;
To the hunters who hunt for the gunless
  game
  The streams and the woods belong.

SAM WALTER FOSS, *Bloodless Sportsmen*.

14

Don't think to hunt two hares with one dog.

BENJAMIN FRANKLIN, *Poor Richard*, 1734.

15

A wild bear chase didst never see?
  Then thou hast lived in vain.
Thy richest bump of glorious glee
  Lies desert in thy brain.

ABRAHAM LINCOLN, *The Bear Hunt* (1844).

Horse Racing

16

There is no more thrilling place in the world than a race track unless it be the Mint, because there is so much money about. And in the Mint it lies in cold, austere, static, unapproachable piles. At the race track it is red hot, alive, pulsating, and constantly changing hands. You keep seeing it.

PAUL GALLICO, *Farewell to Sport: Come On—My Horse*.

17

The Totalisator is much more than a mere machine. It is an implacable electronic giant that compresses all the hopes, fears, prejudices and sentiments of a great racing crowd into relentless numbers flashed on the infield board. A mammoth kibitzer at the greatest game in sport, it is also a calculating tease silently winking out hints on which way the betting weather blows.

TOM O'REILEY, *The Iron Men*. (In *The Fireside Book of Horse Racing*)

18

A Handy Guy Like Sande.

DAMON RUNYON, Title of poem in tribute to Earl Sande, a leading jockey of the 1920's and early 1930's.

19

It is difference of opinion that makes horse-races.

MARK TWAIN, *Pudd'nhead Wilson's Calendar*.

20

All men are equal on and under the turf.

UNKNOWN, a familiar race-track maxim.

Other Sports

21

When I was forty, my doctor advised me that a man in his forties shouldn't play tennis. I heeded his advice carefully and could hardly wait until I reached fifty to start again.

> HUGO L. BLACK. (*Think*, Feb., 1963)

1

Nowhere are the dark forces that impel a man toward athletic self-destruction more clearly definable than in a hockey player.

> WILLIAM BARRY FURLONG, *They Call Him the Greatest on Ice; New York Times Magazine*, 23 Feb., 1964, p. 36.

2

Hockey players are like mules. They have no fear of punishment and no hope of reward.

> EMORY JONES, general manager of the St. Louis Arena. (BOB BROEG, "Sports Comment," St. Louis *Post-Dispatch*, 26 Dec., 1963)

3

Any man who has to ask about the annual upkeep of a yacht can't afford one.

> J. P. MORGAN, to a reporter who wanted to know the cost involved in yachting.

4

The art of running the mile consists, in essence, of reaching the threshold of unconsciousness at the instant of breasting the tape.

> PAUL O'NEIL, *Sports Illustrated*, 16 Aug., 1955.

SPRING

5

Spring beckons! All things to the call respond,
The trees are leaving and cashiers abscond.

> AMBROSE BIERCE, *The Devil's Dictionary*, p. 15.

6

She comes with gusts of laughter,—
    The music as of rills;
With tenderness and sweetness,
    The wisdom of the hills.

> BLISS CARMAN, *Over the Wintry Threshold*.

7

And the glad earth, caressed by murmuring showers,
Wakes like a bride, to deck herself with flowers!

> HENRY SYLVESTER CORNWELL, *May*.

8

If there comes a little thaw,
Still the air is chill and raw,
Here and there a patch of snow,
Dirtier than the ground below,
Dribbles down a marshy flood;
Ankle-deep you stick in mud
In the meadows while you sing,
    "This is Spring."

> C. P. CRANCH, *A Spring Growl*.

9

Men are the devil—they all bring woe.
In winter it's easy to say just "No."

Men are the devil, that's one sure thing,
But what are you going to do in spring?

> MARY CAROLYN DAVIES, *Men Are the Devil*.

10

A trap's a very useful thing:
Nature in our path sets Spring.
It is a trap to catch us two,
It is planned for me and you.

> MARY CAROLYN DAVIES, *Traps*.

11

All the veneration of Spring connects itself with love.

> EMERSON, *Journals*, vol. ix, p. 178.

12

Daughter of Heaven and Earth, coy Spring,
With sudden passion languishing,
Teaching barren moors to smile,
Painting pictures mile on mile,
Holds a cup of cowslip-wreaths,
Whence a smokeless incense breathes.

> EMERSON, *May-Day*.

13

When the trellised grapes their flowers unmask,
And the new-born tendrils twine,
The old wine darkling in the cask
Feels the bloom on the living vine,
And bursts the hoops at hint of spring.

> EMERSON, *May-Day*, l. 77.

14

Spring in the world!
And all things are made new!

> RICHARD HOVEY, *Spring*.

15

In the tassel-time of Spring.

> ROBERT U. JOHNSON, *Before the Blossom*.

16

Came the Spring with all its splendor,
All its birds and all its blossoms,
All its flowers, and leaves, and grasses.

> HENRY WADSWORTH LONGFELLOW, *Hiawatha*, pt. xxi, l. 109.

17

Then came the lovely spring with a rush of blossoms and music,
Flooding the earth with flowers, and the air with melodies vernal.

> HENRY WADSWORTH LONGFELLOW, *Tales of a Wayside Inn*: pt. III, *The Theologian's Tale*.

18

Wag the world how it will,
Leaves must be green in spring.

> HERMAN MELVILLE, *Malvern Hill*.

19

Spring rides no horses down the hill,
But comes on foot, a goose-girl still.
And all the loveliest things there be
Come simply so, it seems to me.

> EDNA ST. VINCENT MILLAY, *The Goose-Girl*.

20

Never yet was a springtime,
    Late though lingered the snow,

That the sap stirred not at the whisper
  Of the southwind, sweet and low;
Never yet was a springtime
  When the buds forgot to blow.
    MARGARET ELIZABETH SANGSTER, *Awakening*.

1
I sing the first green leaf upon the bough,
  The tiny kindling flame of emerald fire,
The stir amid the roots of reeds, and how
  The sap will flush the briar.
    CLINTON SCOLLARD, *Song in March*.

2
Spring, with that nameless pathos in the air
Which dwells in all things fair,
Spring, with her golden suns and silver rain,
Is with us once again.
    HENRY TIMROD, *Spring*.

3
Again the blackbirds sing; the streams
Wake, laughing, from their winter dreams,
And tremble in the April showers
The tassels of the maple flowers.
    JOHN GREENLEAF WHITTIER, *The Singer*,
    st. 20.

STAGE

See also Acting; Criticism
4
Playwriting seems to be the last stronghold,
in any craft, where a man or woman is penal-
ized for not seeing life from a tormented,
neurotic or decadent point of view. There
seems to be some sort of dividend on hope-
lessness and despair, but a well-constructed,
funny play, peopled with rich, full-bodied
characters is usually written off as a minor
piece of work because nobody died of a
dread disease, committed suicide, ended up
insane from sex, or ate three of his best
friends and his wife in full view of the audience, while waiting to be castrated.
    RONALD ALEXANDER, *It's Only Funny*;
    New York *Times* drama section, 30
    Aug., 1964.

5
The theatre is much older than the doctrine
of evolution, but its one faith, asseverated
again and again for every age and every
year, is a faith in evolution, in the reaching
and the climb of men toward distant goals,
glimpsed but never seen, perhaps never
achieved, or achieved only to be passed im-
patiently on the way to a more distant horizon.
    MAXWELL ANDERSON, *Off Broadway: The
    Essence of Tragedy*.

6
The Jukes family of journalism.
    MAXWELL ANDERSON, on critics. (*The Pas-
    sionate Playgoer*, ed. by George Oppen-
    heimer, p. 602)

7
If there is anything sacred in the theatre, it
is an occasional statement of the truth amid
the hubbub of the street. In the midst of
Broadway's usual brummagem a genuine coin
is discovered; that is time for rejoicing.
    BROOKS ATKINSON, Column, New York
    Times, 13 Mar., 1938.

8
Good plays drive bad playgoers crazy.
    BROOKS ATKINSON, Column, New York
    Times, 1956, on the perversity of the
    handful who wrote in to criticize such
    widely acclaimed shows as *My Fair
    Lady*.

9
There's No Business Like Show Business.
    IRVING BERLIN, Title of song from the
    musical comedy *Annie Get Your Gun*.

10
Dramatizations, as a rule, prove more like
sieves than containers for the virtues of a
book.
    JOHN MASON BROWN, Review of *Mister
    Roberts*; *The Saturday Review of Lit-
    erature*, 6 Mar., 1948. *Mister Roberts*
    was cited as a noteworthy exception to
    the rule.

11
A theater which depends entirely on the production of immediate smash hits is doomed.
. . . The theater, once a profession, ceases to
preserve that status as a business.
    HAROLD CLURMAN, *Where Are the New
    Playwrights? 'Waiting'*; New York
    Times Magazine, 7 June, 1964, p. 26.

12
When a society becomes conscious of itself
—its needs, aspirations, enthusiasms, beliefs
and hardships—the theater is born. That is
why the theater as an organized institution,
being a collective affair, usually develops
later than the other arts.
    HAROLD CLURMAN, *Where Are the New
    Playwrights? 'Waiting'*; New York
    Times Magazine, 7 June, 1964, p. 118.

13
To me it seems as if when God conceived the
world, that was Poetry; He formed it, and
that was Sculpture; He colored it, and that
was Painting; He peopled it with living beings, and that was the grand, divine, eternal
Drama.
    CHARLOTTE CUSHMAN. (Stebbins, *Char-
    lotte Cushman*)

14
Theater people are always pining and agonizing because they're afraid that they'll be forgotten. And in America they're quite right.
They will be.
    AGNES DE MILLE. (*The Grande Dame of
    Dance; Life*, 15 Nov., 1963)

15
Sing a lament for the plays that fail—
A dirge for the shows that fold.

A tear on the bier of the flops of the year
And the ticket that couldn't be sold.
> HOWARD DIETZ, *Lament for Failures.*

1
The Big Black Giant.
> OSCAR HAMMERSTEIN II, Title of song from the musical comedy *Me and Juliet* (1953). The title refers to the audience in the theater, as seen by the performers and all others connected with a production.

2
The Fabulous Invalid.
> MOSS HART AND GEORGE S. KAUFMAN, Title of play (1938). The term has become synonymous with the American theater in general.

3
Behind the curtain's mystic fold
The glowing future lies unrolled.
> BRET HARTE, Address, opening of the California Theatre, San Francisco, 19 Jan., 1870.

4
The world's a stage,—as Shakespeare said, one day;
The stage a world—was what he meant to say.
> OLIVER WENDELL HOLMES, *Prologue,* l. 9.

5
I would just as soon have the opinion of a stagehand as to the likelihood of a play's success as that of the drama's ablest observer.
> ARTHUR HOPKINS, *To a Lonely Boy.* Hopkins was a noted producer.

6
The anomalous fact is that the theatre, so called, can flourish in barbarism, but that any *drama* worth speaking of can develop but in the air of civilization.
> HENRY JAMES, Letter to C. E. Wheeler, 9 Apr., 1911.

7
The historian, essentially, wants more documents than he can really use; the dramatist only wants more liberties than he can really take.
> HENRY JAMES, *Prefaces: The Aspern Papers.*

8
The time-honored bread-sauce of the happy ending.
> HENRY JAMES, *Theatricals,* ser. ii.

9
The Torch Bearers.
> GEORGE KELLY, Title of play (1922) that satirizes the pretensions of amateur theatricals.

10
The most alarming thing about the contemporary American theater is the absolute regularity of its march toward extinction.
> WALTER KERR, *How Not to Write a Play* (1955): introduction, p. 1.

11
Nobody—but nobody—is willing to subject himself to any contemporary theatrical experience he can get out of. A rival medium has but to rear its head to draw off yet another portion of that public which had once been regarded as the theater's.
> WALTER KERR, *How Not to Write a Play,* introduction, p. 4.

12
The sort of play that gives failures a bad name.
> WALTER KERR, Review of *Hook 'n' Ladder,* a short-lived Broadway production of the 1950's, in the New York *Herald Tribune.*

13
True tragedy may be defined as a dramatic work in which the outward failure of the principal personage is compensated for by the dignity and greatness of his character.
> JOSEPH WOOD KRUTCH, Introduction to *Nine Plays by Eugene O'Neill.*

14
In all ages the drama, through its portrayal of the acting and suffering spirit of man, has been more closely allied than any other art to his deeper thoughts concerning his nature and his destiny.
> LUDWIG LEWISOHN, *The Modern Drama,* p. 1.

15
The theatre is the last free institution in the amusement world.
> RICHARD MANEY, *Fanfare,* p. 362.

16
The theatre is both the cliffhanger and the phoenix of the arts. Its swoons are deceptive. No gadget wired for sound, sight or ptomaine will ever subdue it.
> RICHARD MANEY, *Fanfare,* p. 362.

17
The theatre is no place for painful speculation; it is a place for diverting representation.
> H. L. MENCKEN, *Prejudices,* ser. i, p. 201.

18
I believe there is a confusion in many minds between Show Business and the Theatre. I belong to the Theatre, which happens at the moment to be in a bad way, but since this word, when capitalized, usually implies something uplifting and boring, I must add that the rarely seen but very real Theatre is the most engrossing theatre of all; and when it isn't it is nothing.
> ARTHUR MILLER, *The American Theatre; Holiday,* Jan., 1955, p. 91.

19
More than any other art, Theater asks for relevance. A play that convinces us that this is the way it is now can be excused many shortcomings. At any one moment there is a particular quality of feeling which dominates

in human intercourse, a tonality which marks the present from the past, and when this tone is struck on the stage, the theater seems necessary again, like self-knowledge.

> ARTHUR MILLER, *What Makes Plays Endure?;* New York *Times,* 15 Aug., 1965, p. 1-X.

1

So long as there is one pretty girl left on the stage, the professional undertakers may hold up their burial of the theatre.

> GEORGE JEAN NATHAN. (*Theatre Arts,* July, 1958)

2

Great drama is the reflection of a great doubt in the heart and mind of a great, sad, gay man.

> GEORGE JEAN NATHAN, *Materia Critica.*

3

Drama—what literature does at night.

> GEORGE JEAN NATHAN, *Testament of a Critic.*

4

I've never seen a play I didn't like.

> RICHARD M. NIXON, Interview with Peter Kihss in the New York *Times,* 29 Dec., 1963.

5

Most modern plays are concerned with the relation between man and man, but that does not interest me at all. I am interested only in the relation between man and God.

> EUGENE O'NEILL. (JOSEPH WOOD KRUTCH, Introduction to *Nine Plays by Eugene O'Neill,* 1932)

6

We want to create a "theater," not build one. Formal externals are not important. It is the activity within that counts.

> LEE STRASBERG, speaking as artistic director of the Actors Studio, New York City. (Interview with Paul Gardner, New York *Times,* 5 May, 1964)

7

It is the destiny of the theater nearly everywhere and in every period to struggle even when it is flourishing.

> HOWARD TAUBMAN, Article, New York *Times,* 4 Aug., 1964, p. 20.

8

One charge, and I suppose only one, can never be brought against the theater. It can't be accused of promoting an era of smug good feeling. Tempers are always soaring, and someone is constantly infuriated by something. Playwrights who have a light touch are assailed as hollowly frivolous and those with a somber vision of the world are denounced for their unhealthy lack of cheerfulness. Audiences are scolded for flocking to a production or for staying away. Let an author or actor be hailed as the new hero and some group will arise and insist he's a bum.

The most savage attacks are saved for the works that have been most praised.

> RICHARD WATTS, JR., Column, New York *Post,* 13 June, 1965.

9

The critic leaves at curtain fall
  To find, in starting to review it,
He scarcely saw the play at all
  For watching his reaction to it.

> E. B. WHITE, *Critic.*

10

The amateur at whose activity the theater manifests all the symptoms of chills and fever is the amateur playwright. And this, I think, is true, that men who would never think of attempting a novel or an ode or even a book of essays are not one whit abashed at the prospect of writing a four-act problem play.

> ALEXANDER WOOLLCOTT, *Shouts and Murmurs.*

STARS

11

The sad and solemn Night
Hath yet her multitude of cheerful fires;
The glorious host of light.

> WILLIAM CULLEN BRYANT, *Hymn to the North Star,* l. 1.

12

Teach me your mood, O patient stars!
  Who climb each night the ancient sky,
Leaving on space no shade, no scars,
  No trace of age, no fear to die.

> EMERSON, *The Poet.*

13

Hitch your wagon to a star.

> EMERSON, *Society and Solitude: Civilization.*

14

God be thanked for the Milky Way that runs across the sky.
That's the path that my feet would tread whenever I have to die.

Some folks call it a Silver Sword, and some a Pearly Crown.
But the only thing I think it is, is Main Street, Heaventown.

> JOYCE KILMER, *Main Street.*

15

Silently one by one, in the infinite meadows of heaven,
Blossomed the lovely stars, the forget-me-nots of the angels.

> HENRY WADSWORTH LONGFELLOW, *Evangeline,* pt. i, sec. 3.

16

Then stars arise, and the night is holy.

> HENRY WADSWORTH LONGFELLOW, *Hyperion,* bk. i, ch. 1.

17

There is no light in earth or heaven
  But the cold light of stars;

And the first watch of night is given
  To the red planet Mars.
  HENRY WADSWORTH LONGFELLOW, *The
  Light of Stars,* st. 2.

1
A wise man,
Watching the stars pass across the sky,
Remarked:
In the upper air the fireflies move more slow-
ly.
  AMY LOWELL, *Meditation.*

2
       Each separate star
Seems nothing, but a myriad scattered stars
Break up the Night, and make it beautiful.
  BAYARD TAYLOR, *Lars,* bk. iii, conclusion.

3
I was thinking the day most splendid till I
  saw what the not-day exhibited;
I was thinking this globe enough till there
  sprang out so noiseless around me myri-
  ads of other globes.
  WALT WHITMAN, *Night on the Prairies.*

4
We have loved the stars too fondly to be
  fearful of the night.
  UNKNOWN, Inscription on slab covering
  the ashes of John and Phoebe Brashear,
  in the crypt of the observatory at Alle-
  gheny, Pa., where they worked together
  many years.

STATESMAN

See also Government, Politics

5
A statesman cannot afford to be a moralist.
  WILL DURANT, *What Is Civilization?*

6
A statesman makes the occasion, but the oc-
  casion makes the politician.
  G. S. HILLARD, *Life and Services of Daniel
  Webster.*

7
A ginooine statesman should be on his
  guard,
Ef he *must hev* beliefs, not to b'lieve 'em tu
  hard.
  JAMES RUSSELL LOWELL, *The Biglow Papers,* Ser. ii, No. 5.

8
The statesman throws his shoulders back,
  and straightens out his tie,
And says, "My friends, unless it rains, the
  weather will be dry."
And when this thought into our brains has
  percolated through,
We common people nod our heads and loud-
  ly cry, "How true!"
  WALT MASON, *The Statesman.*

9
You can always get the truth from an American statesman after he has turned seventy,
or given up all hope of the Presidency.
  WENDELL PHILLIPS, Speech, 7 Nov.,
  1860.

10
A statesman is a successful politician who is
dead.
  THOMAS B. REED. (LODGE, *The Democracy of the Constitution,* p. 191) According to a magazine article by Senator
  Henry Cabot Lodge, the elder, an editor
  telegraphed Reed, "Why don't you die
  and become a statesman?" Reed replied,
  "No; fame is the last infirmity of a noble mind."

11
In statesmanship get the formalities right,
never mind about the moralities.
  MARK TWAIN, *Pudd'nhead Wilson's New
  Calendar.*

12
Why don't you show us a statesman who can
rise up to the Emergency, and cave in the
Emergency's head?
  ARTEMUS WARD, *Things in New York.*

13
Oft the statesman and the saint
Think they're doing good, but ain't.
  EUGENE FITCH WARE, *Aesop's Fables.*

14
Any statesman who stands for sanity and
democracy and liberal ideals risks being a
target for fanatics. The Stalins of the world
mostly die in their beds. It is the Lincolns
and the Kennedys who are shot down.
  UNKNOWN, Editorial, London *Daily Herald,* 23 Nov., 1963, the day after the
  death of John F. Kennedy.

STRENGTH

15
Strengthen me by sympathizing with my
strength, not my weakness.
  AMOS BRONSON ALCOTT, *Table-Talk:
  Sympathy.*

16
O, do not pray for easy lives. Pray to be
stronger men.
  PHILLIPS BROOKS, *Going Up to Jerusalem.
  (Visions and Tasks,* p. 330)

17
Our real problem is not our strength today;
it is the vital necessity of action today to
ensure our strength tomorrow.
  DWIGHT D. EISENHOWER, State of the Union message, 9 Jan., 1958.

18
We acquire the strength we have overcome.
  EMERSON, *Conduct of Life: Considera-
  tions by the Way.*

19
It is as easy for the strong man to be strong,
as it is for the weak to be weak.
  EMERSON, *Essays, First Series: Self-Reliance.*

1
Success to the strongest, who are always, at last, the wisest and best.
EMERSON, Lecture: *Public and Private Education.*

2
The superior man is the providence of the inferior. He is eyes for the blind, strength for the weak, and a shield for the defenseless. He stands erect by bending over the fallen. He rises by lifting others.
ROBERT G. INGERSOLL, *Liberty.*

3
The United States is a peaceful nation. And where our strength and determination are clear, our words need merely to convey conviction, not belligerence. If we are strong, our strength will speak for itself. If we are weak, words will be no help.
JOHN F. KENNEDY, Speech prepared for delivery in Dallas on 22 Nov., 1963, the day of his death.

4
I realize that this nation often tends to identify turning points in world affairs with the major addresses which preceded them. But it was not the Monroe Doctrine that kept all Europe away from this hemisphere—it was the strength of the British fleet and the width of the Atlantic Ocean. It was not General Marshall's speech at Harvard which kept Communism out of Western Europe—it was the strength and stability made possible by our military and economic assistance.
JOHN F. KENNEDY, Speech prepared for delivery in Dallas on 22 Nov., 1963, the day of his death.

5
But noble souls, through dust and heat,
Rise from disaster and defeat
    The stronger.
HENRY WADSWORTH LONGFELLOW, *The Sifting of Peter,* st. 7.

6
If we seek merely swollen, slothful ease and ignoble peace, if we shrink from the hard contests where men must win at the hazard of their lives and at the risk of all they hold dear, then bolder and stronger peoples will pass us by, and will win for themselves the domination of the world.
THEODORE ROOSEVELT, *The Strenuous Life.*

7
Government cannot be stronger or more tough-minded than its people. It cannot be more inflexibly committed to the task than they.
ADLAI E. STEVENSON, Speech in Chicago, 29 Sept., 1952, during the presidential campaign.

8
I would be strong, for there is much to suffer.
HOWARD ARNOLD WALTER, *My Creed.*

STUPIDITY
See also Fool

9
A thick head can do as much damage as a hard heart.
HAROLD WILLIS DODDS.

10
Nature delights in punishing stupid people.
EMERSON, *Journals,* vol. v, p. 238.

11
I don't know what a moron is,
    And I don't give a damn.
I'm thankful that I am not one—
    My God! Perhaps I am.
HENRY PRATT FAIRCHILD, *The Great Economic Paradox; Harper's Magazine,* May, 1932.

I want to be a moron
    And with the morons train;
A low, receding forehead,
    A silly, half-baked brain.
I want to be a moron,
    Because you see, gee whiz!
I like congenial spirits,
    I'm lonely as it is.
CAROLYN WELLS, *A Longing.*

12
It is occasionally possible to charge Hell with a bucket of water but against stupidity the gods themselves struggle in vain.
DORIS FLEESON, Syndicated Column, 17 Feb., 1964. The second clause is a paraphrase of Schiller's *The Maid of Orleans.*

13
Dreadful things are just as apt to happen when stupid people control a situation as when definitely ill-natured people are in charge.
DON MARQUIS, *Chapters for the Orthodox,* ch. 8.

14
It is the dull man who is always sure, and the sure man who is always dull.
H. L. MENCKEN, *Prejudices,* ser. ii, p. 101.

15
    The highest of renown
Are the surest stricken down;
But the stupid and the clown
They remain.
EUGENE FITCH WARE, *Paresis.*

STYLE
See also Words, Writing

16
A chaste and lucid style is indicative of the same personal traits in the author.
HOSEA BALLOU, *Sermons.*

17
A man's style is his mind's voice.
EMERSON, *Journals,* vol. x, p. 457.

1

The style's the man, so books avow;
The style's the woman, anyhow.
> OLIVER WENDELL HOLMES, *How the Old Horse Won the Bet.*

2

Clarity, the greatest of legislative and judicial virtues, like the sunshine, revealing and curative.
> CHARLES EVANS HUGHES, Address, Feb., 1931.

3

What is called style in writing or speaking is formed very early in life, while the imagination is warm and impressions are permanent.
> THOMAS JEFFERSON, *Writings*, vol. v, p. 185.

4

Master alike in speech and song
Of fame's great antiseptic—Style,
You with the classic few belong
Who tempered wisdom with a smile.
> JAMES RUSSELL LOWELL, *To Oliver Wendell Holmes on His Seventy-fifth Birthday*, st. 15.

5

In a style, to be sure, of remarkable fullness,
But which nobody reads on account of its dullness.
> JOHN G. SAXE, *Pyramus and Thisbe.*

6

As to the Adjective: when in doubt, strike it out.
> MARK TWAIN, *Pudd'nhead Wilson's Calendar.*

7

The whole purport of literature, which is the notation of the heart. Style is but the faintly contemptible vessel in which the bitter liquid is recommended to the world.
> THORNTON WILDER, *The Bridge of San Luis Rey.*

SUCCESS

8

Success is full of promise till men get it; and then it is a last-year's nest from which the birds have flown.
> HENRY WARD BEECHER, *Life Thoughts.*

9

The toughest thing about success is that you've got to keep on being a success.
> IRVING BERLIN. (Interview with Ward Morehouse, *Theatre Arts*, Feb., 1958)

10

It takes twenty years to make an overnight success.
> Attributed to EDDIE CANTOR. (*New York Times Magazine*, 20 Oct., 1963)

11

Have little care that Life is brief,
And less that Art is long.

Success is in the silences
Though Fame is in the song.
> BLISS CARMAN, *Songs from Vagabondia: Envoy.*

12

Some shall reap that never sow
And some shall toil and not attain.
> MADISON CAWEIN, *Success.*

13

Success is counted sweetest
By those who ne'er succeed.
> EMILY DICKINSON, *Poems*, Pt. i, No. 1.

14

One thing is forever good;
That one thing is Success.
> EMERSON, *Destiny*, l. 45.

15

Self-trust is the first secret of success.
> EMERSON, *Society and Solitude: Success.*

16

I git thar fustest with the mostest men.
> NATHAN BEDFORD FORREST, giving his formula for military success. Quoted by Winston Churchill at a press conference in Washington, D.C., 25 May, 1943.

17

Success has ruined many a man.
> BENJAMIN FRANKLIN, *Poor Richard*, 1752.

18

Be studious in your profession, and you will be learned. Be industrious and frugal, and you will be rich. Be sober and temperate, and you will be healthy. Be in general virtuous, and you will be happy. At least, you will, by such conduct, stand the best chance for such consequences.
> BENJAMIN FRANKLIN, Letter to John Alleyn.

19

The success of any great moral enterprise does not depend upon numbers.
> WILLIAM LLOYD GARRISON. (W. P. AND F. J. T. GARRISON, *William Lloyd Garrison*, vol. iii, p. 473)

20

He started to sing as he tackled the thing
That couldn't be done, and he did it.
> EDGAR A. GUEST, *It Couldn't Be Done.*

21

If you want to know whether you are destined to be a success or a failure in life, you can easily find out. The test is simple and it is infallible. Are you able to save money? If not, drop out. You will lose.
> JAMES J. HILL.

22

Failure is often that early morning hour of darkness which precedes the dawning of the day of success.
> LEIGH MITCHELL HODGES, *Success.*

23

Every man who can be a first-rate something—as every man can be who is a man at all—has no right to be a fifth-rate something; for a fifth-rate something is no better than a first-rate nothing.

Josiah G. Holland, *Plain Talks: Self-Help.*

1

The bitch-goddess, Success.

William James.

2

Like William James, he [Henry George] saw success as a bitch-goddess and simply did not like her company.

Gerald W. Johnson, *The Lunatic Fringe,* p. 111.

3

I wish him some margin of success.

John F. Kennedy, Speech in New York City, 8 Nov., 1963, referring humorously to the presidential aspirations of Nelson A. Rockefeller, who a short time earlier had announced his availability for the Republican nomination in the 1964 campaign.

4

Sweet Smell of Success.

Ernest Lehman, Title of novel and screen play (1956) for motion picture.

5

The talent of success is nothing more than doing what you can do well; and doing well whatever you do, without a thought of fame.

Henry Wadsworth Longfellow, *Hyperion,* bk. i, ch. 8.

6

Not in the clamor of the crowded street,
Not in the shouts and plaudits of the throng,
But in ourselves, are triumph and defeat.

Henry Wadsworth Longfellow, *The Poets.*

7

The incomputable perils of success.

James Russell Lowell, *Under the Old Elm.*

8

Nothing fails like success; nothing is so defeated as yesterday's triumphant Cause.

Phyllis McGinley, *The Province of the Heart: How to Get Along with Men,* p. 71.

9

There is only one success—to be able to spend your life in your own way.

Christopher Morley, *Where the Blue Begins,* p. 85.

10

To stand upon the ramparts and die for our principles is heroic, but to sally forth to battle and win for our principles is something more than heroic.

Franklin D. Roosevelt, Speech, nominating Alfred E. Smith for the presidency, Houston, June, 1928.

11

I don't feel like a gift from Providence, and I really don't believe I am. I feel very much like a corn-fed Illinois lawyer who has gotten into the big time unintentionally.

Adlai E. Stevenson, Speech in Denver, 1952.

12

Success to me is having ten honeydew melons and eating only the top half of each one.

Barbra Streisand. (*Life,* 20 Sept., 1963, p. 112)

13

Life lives only in success.

Bayard Taylor, *Amran's Wooing,* st 5.

14

Only he is successful in his business who makes that pursuit which affords him the highest pleasure sustain him.

Henry D. Thoreau, *Journal,* 10 Jan., 1851.

15

Not to the swift, the race:
Not to the strong, the fight:
Not to the righteous, perfect grace:
Not to the wise, the light.

But often faltering feet
Come surest to the goal;
And they who walk in darkness meet
The sunrise of the soul.

Henry van Dyke, *Reliance.*

SUFFERING

16

Even pain confers spiritual insight, a beauty of outlook, a philosophy of life, an understanding and forgiveness of humanity—in short, a quality of peace and serenity—that can scarcely be acquired when we are in good health. Suffering is a cleansing fire that chars away triviality and restlessness.

Louis E. Bisch, *Turn Your Sickness Into an Asset; The Reader's Digest,* Nov., 1937 (reprinted in Dec., 1963 issue).

17

Tragedy is in the eye of the observer, and not in the heart of the sufferer.

Emerson, *Natural History of Intellect: The Tragic.*

18

If you suffer, thank God!—it is a sure sign that you are alive.

Elbert Hubbard, *Epigrams.*

19

Know how sublime a thing it is
To suffer and be strong.

Henry Wadsworth Longfellow, *The Light of Stars,* l. 36.

20

Civilized mankind has of will ceased to torture, but in our process of being civilized we have won, I suspect, intensified capacity to suffer.

S. Weir Mitchell, *Characteristics,* ch. 1.

SUMMER

1
Ah, summer, what power you have to make
us suffer and like it.
> RUSSELL BAKER, "Observer" Column, New
> York *Times,* 27 June, 1965, p. 10E.

2
I question not if thrushes sing,
  If roses load the air;
Beyond my heart I need not reach
  When all is summer there.
> JOHN VANCE CHENEY, *Love's World.*

3
The Indian Summer, the dead Summer's
soul.
> MARY CLEMMER, *Presence,* l. 62.

4
Do what we can, summer will have its flies.
> EMERSON, *Essays, First Series: Prudence.*

5
The summer is the time for exploring: for
visiting our own country or one of its regions; for seeing a foreign land; for learning
more of nature; or, if we are tied to our
home, then for entering a new world of skill,
or art, or knowledge.
> GILBERT HIGHET, *Talents and Geniuses:*
> *Summer Reading,* p. 294.

6
The folks that on the first of May
  Wore winter coats and hose,
Began to say, the first of June,
  "Good Lord! how hot it grows!"
> OLIVER WENDELL HOLMES, *The Hot Sea-*
> *son.*

7
O for a lodge in a garden of cucumbers!
  O for an iceberg or two at control!
O for a vale that at midday the dew cum-
    bers!
  O for a pleasure trip up to the pole!
> ROSSITER JOHNSON, *Ninety-Nine in the*
> *Shade.*

8
O summer day beside the joyous sea!
O summer day so wonderful and white,
So full of gladness and so full of pain!
Forever and forever shalt thou be
To some the gravestone of a dead delight,
To some the landmark of a new domain.
> HENRY WADSWORTH LONGFELLOW, *A Sum-*
> *mer Day by the Sea.*

9
I only know that summer sang in me
A little while, that in me sings no more.
> EDNA ST. VINCENT MILLAY, *What Lips*
> *My Lips Have Kissed.*

10
Sound loves to revel in a summer night.
> EDGAR ALLAN POE, *Al Aaraaf,* pt. ii.

11
In the good old summer time,
In the good old summer time,
Strolling thro' the shady lanes,
With your baby mine;
You hold her hand and she holds yours,
And that's a very good sign
That she's your tootsey-wootsey
In the good old summer time.
> REN SHIELDS, *In the Good Old Summer*
> *Time* (song, 1902, with music by
> GEORGE EVANS). Sung by Blanche Ring
> in *The Defender.*

SUN

12
Pleasantly, between the pelting showers, the
  sunshine gushes down.
> WILLIAM CULLEN BRYANT, *The Cloud on*
> *the Way,* l. 18.

13
Oft did I wonder why the setting sun
  Should look upon us with a blushing face:
Is't not for shame of what he hath seen
    done,
  Whilst in our hemisphere he ran his race?
> LYMAN HEATH, *On the Setting Sun.*

14
The sun is a-wait at the ponderous gate of
  the West.
> SIDNEY LANIER, *The Marshes of Glynn.*

15
Down sank the great red sun, and in golden,
  glimmering vapors
Veiled the light of his face, like the Prophet
  descending from Sinai.
> HENRY WADSWORTH LONGFELLOW, *Evan-*
> *geline,* pt. i, sec. 4.

16
After a day of cloud and wind and rain
Sometimes the setting sun breaks out again,
  And, touching all the darksome woods
    with light,
Smiles on the fields, until they laugh and
    sing,
Then like a ruby from the horizon's ring,
  Drops down into the night.
> HENRY WADSWORTH LONGFELLOW, *Hang-*
> *ing of the Crane,* pt. vii.

17
That hour of the day when, face to face, the
rising moon beholds the setting sun.
> HENRY WADSWORTH LONGFELLOW, *Hype-*
> *rion,* bk. ii, ch. 10.

18
The sun is set; and in his latest beams
Yon little cloud of ashen gray and gold,
Slowly upon the amber air unrolled,
The falling mantle of the Prophet seems.
> HENRY WADSWORTH LONGFELLOW, *A Sum-*
> *mer Day by the Sea.*

19
Wait 'till the sun shines, Nellie,
  When the clouds go drifting by,
We will be happy, Nellie,
  Don't you sigh.
> ANDREW B. STERLING, *Wait 'Till the Sun*

Shines, Nellie (song, 1905, with music by HARRY VON TILZER).

1
And yonder fly his scattered golden arrows,
And smite the hills with day.
> BAYARD TAYLOR, *The Poet's Journal:*
> *Third Evening: Morning.*

2
Sad soul, take comfort, nor forget
That sunrise never failed us yet.
> CELIA THAXTER, *The Sunrise Never Failed*
> *Us Yet.*

3
It is true, I never assisted the sun materially
in his rising; but, doubt not, it was of the
last importance only to be present at it.
> HENRY D. THOREAU, *Walden,* ch. 1.

4
Give me the splendid silent sun with all his
beams full-dazzling!
> WALT WHITMAN, *Give Me the Splendid*
> *Silent Sun.*

5
The sunshine seemed to bless,
The air with a caress.
> JOHN GREENLEAF WHITTIER, *The Maids*
> *of Attitash,* st. 24.

6
Touched by a light that hath no name,
A glory never sung,
Aloft on sky and mountain wall
Are God's great pictures hung.
> JOHN GREENLEAF WHITTIER, *Sunset on*
> *the Bearcamp,* st. 3.

SUNDAY, see Sabbath
SWEARING
See also Anger

7
Take not God's name in vain; select
A time when it will have effect.
> AMBROSE BIERCE, *The Devil's Dictionary:*
> *The Decalogue Revised.*

8
Th' best thing about a little judicyous
swearin' is that it keeps th' temper. 'Twas
intinded as a compromise between runnin'
away an' fightin'.
> FINLEY PETER DUNNE, *Observations by*
> *Mr. Dooley: Swearing.*

9
I confess to some pleasure from the stinging
rhetoric or a rattling oath.
> EMERSON, *Journals,* 1840.

10
It's most enough to make a deacon swear.
> JAMES RUSSELL LOWELL, *The Biglow Pa-*
> *pers,* Ser. ii, No. 2.

11
I sent down to the rum mill on the corner
and hired an artist by the week to sit up
nights and curse that stranger.
> MARK TWAIN, *A Mysterious Visit.*

12
In certain trying circumstances, urgent circumstances, desperate circumstances, profan-
ity furnishes a relief denied even to prayer.
> MARK TWAIN, *Pudd'nhead Wilson's Cal-*
> *endar.*

SYMPATHY

13
Harmony of aim, not identity of conclusion,
is the secret of the sympathetic life.
> EMERSON, *Essays, First Series: Friend-*
> *ship.*

14
We sink as easily as we rise, through sympathy.
> EMERSON, *Essays: Society and Solitude.*

15
The perception of the comic is a tie of sympathy with other men.
> EMERSON, *Letters and Social Aims: The*
> *Comic.*

16
The secrets of life are not shown except to
sympathy and likeness.
> EMERSON, *Representative Men: Mon-*
> *taigne.*

17
Sensibility of mind is indeed the parent of
every virtue, but it is the parent of much
misery, too.
> THOMAS JEFFERSON, *Writings,* vol. xix, p.
> 46.

18
No one is so accursed by fate,
No one so utterly desolate
But some heart, though unknown,
Responds unto his own.
> HENRY WADSWORTH LONGFELLOW, *Endym-*
> *ion,* st. 8.

19
There is much satisfaction in work well
done; praise is sweet; but there can be no
happiness equal to the joy of finding a heart
that understands.
> VICTOR ROBINSON, *William Godwin; The*
> *Truth Seeker,* 6 Jan., 1906.

20
And nothing, not God, is greater to one than
one's self is,
And whoever walks a furlong without sympathy walks to his own funeral drest in his
shroud.
> WALT WHITMAN, *Song of Myself,* sec. 48.

T

TALENT

See also Genius

1
The difference between talents and character is adroitness to keep the old and trodden round, and power and courage to make a new road to new and better goals.
> EMERSON, *Essays, First Series: Circles.*

2
Each man has his own vocation. The talent is the call.
> EMERSON, *Essays, First Series: Spiritual Laws.*

3
Talent is habitual facility of execution.
> EMERSON, *Essays: Natural History of Intellect.*

4
Profound sincerity is the only basis of talent, as of character.
> EMERSON, *Essays: Natural History of Intellect.*

5
Each man has an aptitude born with him.
> EMERSON, *Society and Solitude: Success.*

6
Hide not your talents, they for use were made.
What's a Sun-dial in the Shade?
> BENJAMIN FRANKLIN, *Poor Richard,* 1750.

7
You cannot define talent. All you can do is build the greenhouse and see if it grows.
> WILLIAM P. STEVEN. (*Time,* 23 Aug., 1963, p. 36)

8
If a man has a talent and cannot use it, he has failed. If he has a talent and uses only half of it, he has partly failed. If he has a talent and learns somehow to use the whole of it, he has gloriously succeeded, and won a satisfaction and a triumph few men ever know.
> THOMAS WOLFE, *The Web and the Rock,* ch. 30.

TASTE

9
Every man carries his own inch-rule of taste, and amuses himself by applying it, triumphantly, wherever he travels.
> HENRY ADAMS, *The Education of Henry Adams,* p. 182.

10
Other virtues are in request in the field and workyard, but a certain degree of taste is not to be spared in those we sit with.
> EMERSON, *Essays, Second Series: Manners.*

11
Those who are esteemed umpires of taste are often persons who have acquired some knowledge of admired pictures or sculptures, and have an inclination for whatever is elegant; but if you inquire whether they are beautiful souls, and whether their own acts are like fair pictures, you learn that they are selfish and sensual.
> EMERSON, *Essays, Second Series: The Poet.*

12
Men lose their tempers in defending their taste.
> EMERSON, *Journals,* vol. ii, p. 147.

13
Love of beauty is Taste. . . . The creation of beauty is Art.
> EMERSON, *Nature, Addresses: Beauty.*

14
There is no accounting for tastes.
> HENRY JAMES, *The Portrait of a Lady,* ch. 12.

15
Well, for those who like that sort of thing I should think that is just about the sort of thing they would like.
> ABRAHAM LINCOLN, to Robert Dale Owen, the spiritualist, when the latter asked for Lincoln's opinion of a long article on spiritualism that Owen had just read. (GROSS, *Lincoln's Own Stories,* p. 96)

16
I've developed my taste. I know now what is really good wine, what is really good vodka, what is really good caviar. Thirty years ago I could be fooled. No more.
> ARTUR RUBINSTEIN. (*Rubinstein Speaking; New York Times Magazine,* 26 Jan., 1964)

TAXES

17
The marvel of all history is the patience with which men and women submit to burdens unnecessarily laid upon them by their governments.
> WILLIAM H. BORAH, Speech in U.S. Senate.

18
The income tax is just. It simply intends to put the burdens of government justly upon the backs of the people. I am in favor of an income tax. When I find a man who is not willing to bear his share of the burdens of the government which protects him, I find a man who is unworthy to enjoy the blessings of a government like ours.
> WILLIAM JENNINGS BRYAN, Speech at Democratic national convention in Chicago, 8 July, 1896.

1

We can trace the personal history of a man, and his successes and failures, just by looking at his tax returns from his first job to his retirement.

> CHARLES ALDEN CHURCH, Interview, New York *Times*, 10 Mar., 1964. He was then director of the Manhattan District, Internal Revenue Service.

2

The point to remember is that what the government gives it must first take away.

> JOHN S. COLEMAN, Address to the Detroit Chamber of Commerce. He was then president of that body.

3

Of all debts men are least willing to pay the taxes. What a satire is this on government! Everywhere they think they get their money's worth, except for these. Hence the less government we have the better—the fewer laws and the less confided power.

> EMERSON, *Essays, Second Series: Politics.*

4

Was it Bonaparte who said that he found vices very good patriots?—"he got five millions from the love of brandy, and he should be glad to know which of the virtues would pay him as much." Tobacco and opium have broad backs, and will cheerfully carry the load of armies.

> EMERSON, *Society and Solitude: Civilization.*

5

But in this world, nothing is certain but death and taxes. (*Mais dans ce monde, il n'y a rien d'assure que la mort et les impôts.*)

> BENJAMIN FRANKLIN, Letter to Leroy, 1789.

6

Taxation must not lead men into temptation, by requiring trivial oaths, by making it profitable to lie, to swear falsely, to bribe or to take bribes.

> HENRY GEORGE, *The Condition of Labor,* p. 11.

7

Taxation must not take from individuals what rightly belongs to individuals.

> HENRY GEORGE, *The Condition of Labor,* p. 11.

8

No one should be permitted to hold natural opportunities without a fair return to all for any special privilege thus accorded to him, and that value which the growth and improvement of a community attaches to land should be taken for the use of the community. . . . We are in favor of raising all public revenues by a single tax upon land values.

> HENRY GEORGE, *The Single Tax Theory.*

9

Where is the politician who has not promised to fight to the death for lower taxes—and who has not proceeded to vote for the very spending projects that make tax cuts impossible?

> BARRY M. GOLDWATER, Article, *The Reader's Digest,* Jan., 1961.

10

Unnecessary taxation is unjust taxation.

> ABRAM S. HEWITT, Democratic party platform, 1884.

11

Taxes are what we pay for civilized society.

> JUSTICE OLIVER WENDELL HOLMES, Opinion, Companie de Tobaccos v. Collector, 1904.

12

The purse of the people is the real seat of sensibility. Let it be drawn upon largely, and they will then listen to truths which could not excite them through any other organ.

> THOMAS JEFFERSON, *Writings,* vol. x, p. 59.

13

I want to be the President who helped to feed the hungry and to prepare them to be taxpayers instead of tax eaters.

> LYNDON B. JOHNSON, Address to joint session of Congress on voting rights for Negroes, 15 Mar., 1965.

14

Taxes milks dry, but, neighbor, you'll allow Thet havin' things onsettled kills the cow.

> JAMES RUSSELL LOWELL, *The Biglow Papers: Mason and Slidell.*

15

That the power to tax involves the power to destroy [is] not to be denied.

> CHIEF JUSTICE JOHN MARSHALL, Decision in McCulloch v. Maryland, 1819. Daniel Webster, in his argument in this case, similarly declared, "An unlimited power to tax involves, necessarily, the power to destroy."

The power to tax is not the power to destroy while this court sits.

> JUSTICE OLIVER WENDELL HOLMES, Dissenting Opinion, Panhandle Oil Co. v. Knox, 1928.

16

Taxation without representation is tyranny.

> JAMES OTIS, Argument on the illegality of the Writs of Assistance, before the Superior Court of Massachusetts, Feb., 1761. For a fuller discussion of this famous quotation, see America: Famous Historical Sayings.

17

Taxes are paid in the sweat of every man that labors.

> FRANKLIN D. ROOSEVELT, Speech in Pittsburgh, 19 Oct., 1932, during the presidential campaign.

TEACHING

See also Education

1
A teacher affects eternity; he can never tell where his influence stops.
> HENRY ADAMS, *The Education of Henry Adams*, ch. 20.

2
Nothing is more tiresome than a superannuated pedagogue.
> HENRY ADAMS, *The Education of Henry Adams*, ch. 23.

3
The true teacher defends his pupils against his own personal influence. He inspires self-distrust. He guides their eyes from himself to the spirit that quickens him.
> AMOS BRONSON ALCOTT, *The Teacher*.

4
Teaching is not a lost art, but the regard for it is a lost tradition.
> JACQUES BARZUN. (*Newsweek*, 5 Dec., 1955)

5
It is the supreme art of the teacher to awaken joy in creative expression and knowledge.
> ALBERT EINSTEIN, Motto for the astronomy building, Junior College, Pasadena, Calif.

6
There is no teaching until the pupil is brought into the same state or principle in which you are; a transfusion takes place; he is you and you are he; then is a teaching, and by no unfriendly chance or bad company can he ever quite lose the benefit.
> EMERSON, *Essays, First Series: Spiritual Laws*.

7
He teaches who gives and he learns who receives.
> EMERSON, *Essays, First Series: Spiritual Laws*.

8
The man who can make hard things easy is the educator.
> EMERSON, *Journals*, 1861.

9
The Spirit only can teach. Not any sensual, not any liar, not any slave can teach.
> EMERSON, *Nature, Addresses and Lectures: An Address Delivered before the Senior Class in Divinity College, Cambridge, 15 July, 1838*.

10
The greatest job of teachers is to cultivate talent until it ripens for the public to reap its bounty.
> JASCHA HEIFETZ, on teaching music. (*Newsweek*, 11 Feb., 1963, p. 58)

11
It is a luxury to learn; but the luxury of learning is not to be compared with the luxury of teaching.
> ROSWELL D. HITCHCOCK, *Eternal Atonement: Receiving and Giving*.

12
Our American professors like their literature clear and cold and pure and very dead.
> SINCLAIR LEWIS, Address in Stockholm, 12 Dec., 1930, upon receiving the Nobel Prize in literature.

13
For him the Teacher's chair became a throne.
> HENRY WADSWORTH LONGFELLOW, *Parker Cleaveland*.

14
The average schoolmaster is and always must be essentially an ass, for how can one imagine an intelligent man engaging in so puerile an avocation?
> H. L. MENCKEN, *Prejudices*, ser. iii, p. 244.

15
I'll learn him or kill him.
> MARK TWAIN, *Life on the Mississippi*, ch. 8. A veteran pilot thus expresses his philosophy of teaching.

16
Seven pupils in the class
Of Professor Callias,
Listen silent while he drawls,—
Three are benches, four are walls.
> HENRY VAN DYKE, *The Professor*.

TEARS

17
The soul would have no rainbow
Had the eyes no tears.
> JOHN VANCE CHENEY, *Tears*.

18
It's such a little thing to weep,
So short a thing to sigh;
And yet by trades the size of these
We men and women die!
> EMILY DICKINSON, *Poems*, Pt. i, No. 91.

19
Weep no more, my lady, oh! weep no more today!
> STEPHEN C. FOSTER, *My Old Kentucky Home*.

20
Onions can make even heirs and widows weep.
> BENJAMIN FRANKLIN, *Poor Richard*, 1734.

21
I crave the stain
Of tears, the aftermark
Of almost too much love,
The sweet of bitter bark
And burning clove.
> ROBERT FROST, *To Earthward*.

1

With hearts too full for utterance, with but a
silent tear.
J. S. GIBBONS, *We Are Coming, Father
Abraham,* referring to Lincoln.

2

Never a tear bedims the eye
That time and patience will not dry.
BRET HARTE, *The Lost Galleon,* l. 33.

3

She would have made a splendid wife, for
crying only made her eyes more bright and
tender.
O. HENRY, *Options.*

4

A flood of thoughts came o'er me
That filled my eyes with tears.
HENRY WADSWORTH LONGFELLOW, *The
Bridge,* st. 6.

5

Give other friends your lighted face,
The laughter of the years;
I come to crave a greater grace—
Bring me your tears.
EDWIN MARKHAM, *Your Tears.*

6

Some reckon their age by years,
Some measure their life by art;
But some tell their days by the flow of their
tears,
And their lives by the moans of their
heart.
ABRAM J. RYAN, *The Rosary of My Tears.*

7

The young man who has not wept is a savage, and the old man who will not laugh is a
fool.
GEORGE SANTAYANA, *Dialogues in Limbo.*

8

Of all the languages of earth in which the
human kind confer
The Master Speaker is the Tear: it is the
Great Interpreter.
FREDERIC RIDGELY TORRENCE, *The House
of a Hundred Lights.*

9

Why these weeps?
ARTEMUS WARD, *Artemus Ward's Lecture.*

10

Laugh and the world laughs with you,
Weep and you weep alone.
ELLA WHEELER WILCOX, *Solitude.*

Joy is a partnership,
Grief weeps alone.
F. L. KNOWLES, *Grief and Joy.*

TEMPERANCE

See also Drinking, Drunkenness,
Moderation

11

Health, longevity, beauty, are other names
for personal purity; and temperance is the
regimen for all.
AMOS BRONSON ALCOTT, *Table Talk: Habits.*

12

Let us become more cheerful and we will
become a more temperate people. . . . Men
cannot be driven into temperance.
WILLIAM ELLERY CHANNING, THE ELDER,
Works, p. 112.

13

Eat not to dullness; drink not to elevation.
BENJAMIN FRANKLIN, *Autobiography,* ch.
1.

14

There are two times when you can never tell
what is going to happen. One is when a man
takes his first drink; and the other is when a
woman takes her latest.
O. HENRY, *The Gentle Grafter.*

15

Of my merit
On thet pint you yourself may jedge;
All is, I never drink no sperit,
Nor I haint never signed no pledge.
JAMES RUSSELL LOWELL, *The Biglow Pa-
pers,* Ser. i, No. 7.

16

There are two things that will be believed of
any man whatsoever, and one of them is that
he has taken to drink.
BOOTH TARKINGTON, *Penrod,* ch. 10.

17

I prefer temperance hotels—although they
sell worse liquor than any other kind of hotels.
ARTEMUS WARD, *Temperance.*

TEMPTATION

18

Greater is he who is above temptation than
he who being tempted overcomes.
AMOS BRONSON ALCOTT, *Orphic Sayings:
xii.*

19

There is not any memory with less satisfaction than the memory of some temptation we
resisted.
JAMES BRANCH CABELL, *Jurgen,* p. 39.

20

The Woman tempted me—and tempts me
still!
Lord God, I pray You that she ever will!
EDMUND VANCE COOKE, *Adam.*

21

So you tell yourself you are pretty fine clay
To have tricked temptation and turned it
away,
But wait, my friend, for a different day;
Wait till you want to want to!
EDMUND VANCE COOKE, *Desire.*

22

As the Sandwich Islander believes that the
strength and valor of the enemy he kills
passes into himself, so we gain the strength
of the temptation we resist.
EMERSON, *Essays, First Series: Compensation.*

1

How much, preventing God, how much I
owe
To the defences thou hast round me set;
Example, custom, fear, occasion slow,—
These scornèd bondmen were my parapet.
I dare not peep over this parapet
To gauge with glance the roaring gulf be-
low,
The depth of sin to which I had descended,
Had not these me against myself defended.
    EMERSON, *Grace*.

2

For we're only poor weak mortals, after all,
Sons of apple-eating Adam, prone to fall.
    OTTO A. HARBACH, *Madam Sherry*, act iii.

3

There are temptations that require all of
one's strength to yield to.
    ELBERT HUBBARD, *The Philistine*, vol. xx,
        p. 86.

4

You may be lustrous as a star, with all the
virtues in you canned, but if you fool around
with tar you'll blacken up to beat the band.
    WALT MASON, *At the Theatre*.

5

Many men have too much will power. It's
won't power they lack.
    JOHN A. SHEDD, *Salt from My Attic*, p.
        16.

6

Hold the hand that is helpless and whisper,
    "They only the victory win
Who have fought the good fight and have
    vanquished the demon that tempts us
    within."
    WILLIAM WETMORE STORY, *He and She*.

7

There are several good protections against
temptations, but the surest is cowardice.
    MARK TWAIN, *Pudd'nhead Wilson's New
        Calendar*.

8

It is easier to stay out than get out.
    MARK TWAIN, *Pudd'nhead Wilson's New
        Calendar*.

9

Could'st thou boast, O child of weakness!
    O'er the sons of wrong and strife,
Were there strong temptations planted
    In thy path of life?
    JOHN GREENLEAF WHITTIER, *What the
        Voice Said*, st. 8.

THANKSGIVING DAY

10

Heap high the board with plenteous cheer,
    and gather to the feast,
And toast the sturdy Pilgrim band whose
    courage never ceased.
Give praise to that All-Gracious One by
    whom their steps were led,
And thanks unto the harvest's Lord who
    sends our "daily bread."
    ALICE WILLIAMS BROTHERTON, *The First
        Thanksgiving Day*.

11

Thanksgiving-day, I fear,
If one the solemn truth must touch,
Is celebrated, not so much
To thank the Lord for blessings o'er,
As for the sake of getting more!
    WILL CARLETON, *Captain Young's Thanks-
        giving*.

12

Over the river and through the wood,
Now grandmother's cap I spy!
    Hurrah for the fun!
    Is the pudding done?
Hurrah for the pumpkin pie!
    LYDIA MARIA CHILD, *Thanksgiving Day*.

13

So once in every year we throng
    Upon a day apart,
To praise the Lord with feast and song
    In thankfulness of heart.
    ARTHUR GUITERMAN, *The First Thanks-
        giving*.

14

Thanksgiving Day . . . the one day that is
purely American.
    O. HENRY, *The Trimmed Lamp: Two
        Thanksgiving Day Gentlemen*.

15

Over three centuries ago, our forefathers in
Virginia and in Massachusetts far from home
in a lonely wilderness set aside a time for
Thanksgiving.
    JOHN F. KENNEDY, Thanksgiving Procla-
        mation, 5 Nov., 1963. The significance
        of this was the recognition, by a man
        from Massachusetts, of Virginia's claim
        to having shared in the origin of
        Thanksgiving Day. Some Virginians, in
        fact, maintain that the day was first ob-
        served in their state, more than a year
        before the landing at Plymouth Rock.

16

Gather the gifts of Earth with equal hand;
Henceforth ye too may share the birthright
    soil,
The corn, the wine, and all the harvest-
    home.
    E. C. STEDMAN, *The Feast of Harvest*.

17

And let these altars, wreathed with flowers
    And piled with fruits, awake again
Thanksgivings for the golden hours,
    The early and the latter rain!
    JOHN GREENLEAF WHITTIER, *For an Au-
        tumn Festival*, st. 12.

18

Ah! on Thanksgiving day, when from East
    and from West,
From North and South, come the pilgrim
    and guest, . . .

What moistens the lip and what brightens
the eye?
What calls back the past, like the rich
Pumpkin pie?
JOHN GREENLEAF WHITTIER, *The Pump-
kin,* st. 3.

THEATER, see Stage
THIEVING

1
In labor as in life there can be no cheating.
The thief steals from himself.
EMERSON, *Essays, First Series: Compensa-
tion.*

2
In vain we call old notions fudge,
And bend our conscience to our dealing;
The Ten Commandments will not budge,
And stealing *will* continue stealing.
JAMES RUSSELL LOWELL, *International
Copyright.* Adopted as its motto by the
American Copyright League.

3
For de little stealin' dey gits you in jail soon
or late. For de big stealin' dey makes you
emperor and puts you in de Hall o' Fame
when you croaks.
EUGENE O'NEILL, *The Emperor Jones.*

4
If you give to a thief he cannot steal from
you, and he is then no longer a thief.
WILLIAM SAROYAN, *The Human Comedy,*
ch. 4.

5
They inwardly resolved that so long as they
remained in the business their piracies
should not again be sullied with the crime of
stealing.
MARK TWAIN, *Tom Sawyer,* ch. 13.

THOUGHT
See also Mind

6
We'd like to get people thinking, which television doesn't want people to do. It wants to
keep them down to a level of comfortable
euphoria.
GOODMAN ACE, Interview, St. Louis *Post-
Dispatch,* 19 Feb., 1965, p. 3-D.

7
During my eighty-seven years I have wit-
nessed a whole succession of technological
revolutions. But none of them has done away
with the need for character in the individual
or the ability to think.
BERNARD M. BARUCH, *Baruch: My Own
Story* (1957), ch. 22.

8
Nothing is too sacred to be thought about.
ERNEST CROSBY. (*Cosmopolitan,* Dec.,
1905)

9
Our thought is the key which unlocks the
doors of the world.
SAMUEL MCCHORD CROTHERS. (NEWTON,
My Idea of God, p. 211)

10
How do most people live without any
thoughts? There are many people in the
world,—you must have noticed them in the
street,—how do they live? How do they get
strength to put on their clothes in the morning?
EMILY DICKINSON, Letter to Thomas
Wentworth Higginson, Aug., 1870.

11
There is no expedient to which a man will
not go to avoid the real labor of thinking.
THOMAS A. EDISON, Motto, posted
throughout his laboratories.

12
So far as a man thinks, he is free.
EMERSON, *Conduct of Life: Fate.*

13
The revelation of Thought takes man out of
servitude into freedom.
EMERSON, *Conduct of Life: Fate.*

14
Concentration is the secret of strength in
politics, in war, in trade, in short, in all man-
agement of human affairs.
EMERSON, *Conduct of Life: Power.*

15
Beware when the great God lets loose a
thinker on this planet.
EMERSON, *Essays, First Series: Circles.*

16
What is the hardest task in the world? To
think.
EMERSON, *Essays, First Series: Intellect.*

Thinking is the hardest work there is, which
is the probable reason why so few engage in
it.
HENRY FORD, Interview, Feb., 1929.

17
The ancestor of every action is a thought.
EMERSON, *Essays, First Series: Spiritual
Laws.*

18
Thought is the seed of action.
EMERSON, *Society and Solitude: Art.*

19
Do not craze yourself with thinking, but go
about your business anywhere. Life is not
intellectual and critical, but sturdy.
EMERSON, *Essays, Second Series: Experience.*

20
Man carries the world in his head, the whole
astronomy and chemistry suspended in a
thought.
EMERSON, *Essays, Second Series: Nature.*

21
Every thought which genius and piety throw
into the world, alters the world.
EMERSON, *Essays, Second Series: Politics.*

1

Nothing in the universe so solid as a thought.

EMERSON, *Journals*, 1864.

2

It takes a great deal of elevation of thought to produce a very little elevation of life.

EMERSON, *Journals*, vol. iv, p. 441.

3

As certainly as water falls in rain on the tops of mountains and runs down into valleys, plains and pits, so does thought fall first on the best minds, and run down, from class to class, until it reaches the masses, and works revolutions.

EMERSON, *Lectures and Biographical Sketches: The Man of Letters.*

4

He chose, wisely no doubt for himself, to be the bachelor of thought and Nature.

EMERSON, *Lectures and Biographical Sketches: Thoreau*—referring to Henry D. Thoreau.

5

A rush of thoughts is the only conceivable prosperity that can come to us.

EMERSON, *Letters and Social Aims: Inspiration.*

6

The senses collect the surface facts of matter. . . . It was sensation; when memory came, it was experience; when mind acted, it was knowledge; when mind acted on it as knowledge, it was thought.

EMERSON, *Letters and Social Aims: Poetry and Imagination.*

7

Great men are they who see that spiritual is stronger than any material force, that thoughts rule the world.

EMERSON, *Letters and Social Aims: Progress of Culture.*

8

Thought is the property of him who can entertain it and of him who can adequately place it.

EMERSON, *Representative Men: Shakespeare.*

9

We must dare to think about "unthinkable things," because when things become "unthinkable," thinking stops and action becomes mindless.

J. WILLIAM FULBRIGHT, Address in U.S. Senate, 26 Mar., 1964.

10

You may give them your love but not your thoughts,
For they have their own thoughts.

KAHLIL GIBRAN, *The Prophet: On Children.*

11

Thought, the gaseous ashes of burned-out thinking, the excretion of mental respiration.

OLIVER WENDELL HOLMES, *The Professor at the Breakfast-Table*, ch. 1.

12

Why can't somebody give us a list of things that everybody thinks and nobody says, and another list of things that everybody says and nobody thinks?

OLIVER WENDELL HOLMES, *The Professor at the Breakfast-Table*, ch. 6.

13

If there is any principle of the Constitution that more imperatively calls for attachment than any other it is the principle of free thought—not free thought for those who agree with us but freedom for the thought that we hate.

JUSTICE OLIVER WENDELL HOLMES, Dissenting Opinion in U.S. vs. Schwimmer, 27 May, 1929. This was a Supreme Court case involving the denial of citizenship to an avowed pacifist, Rosika Schwimmer.

14

You have no right to erect your toll-gate upon the highways of thought.

ROBERT G. INGERSOLL, *The Ghosts.*

15

The glow of one warm thought is to me worth more than money.

THOMAS JEFFERSON, *Writings*, vol. iv, p. 23.

16

A thought often makes us hotter than a fire.

HENRY WADSWORTH LONGFELLOW, *Drift-Wood: Table-Talk.*

17

My own thoughts Are my companions.

HENRY WADSWORTH LONGFELLOW, *The Masque of Pandora*, pt. iii.

18

And what they dare to dream of, dare to do.

JAMES RUSSELL LOWELL, *Commemoration Ode*, st. 3.

19

And I honor the man who is willing to sink Half his present repute for the freedom to think.

JAMES RUSSELL LOWELL, *A Fable for Critics*, l. 1067.

20

All thoughts that mould the age begin Deep down within the primitive soul.

JAMES RUSSELL LOWELL, *An Incident in a Railroad Car.*

21

The Power of Positive Thinking.

NORMAN VINCENT PEALE, Title of book (1952).

22

He was the man of thought in an age of action.

JAMES RESTON, Article, New York *Times*,

15 July, 1965, p. 1. Referring to Adlai E. Stevenson.

1
Sell your clothes and keep your thoughts. God will see that you do not want society. If I were confined to a corner of a garret all my days, like a spider, the world would be just as large to me while I had my thoughts about me.

HENRY D. THOREAU, *Walden:* conclusion.

2
Human thought is the process by which human ends are ultimately answered.

DANIEL WEBSTER, Address, upon laying the cornerstone of Bunker Hill Monument.

THRIFT
See also Economy

3
A penny saved is two pence clear,
A pin a day's a groat a year.

BENJAMIN FRANKLIN, *Necessary Hints to Those That Would Be Rich.*

4
Get what you can, and what you get hold;
'Tis the stone that will turn all your lead into gold.

BENJAMIN FRANKLIN, *The Way to Wealth.*

5
Never ask of money spent
Where the spender thinks it went.
Nobody was ever meant
To remember or invent
What he did with every cent.

ROBERT FROST, *The Hardship of Accounting.*

6
That rule which I wish to see you governed by through your whole life, of never buying anything which you have not the money in your pocket to pay for. Be assured that it gives much more pain to the mind to be in debt, than to do without any article whatever which we may seem to want.

THOMAS JEFFERSON, Letter to his daughter Martha, 14 June, 1787. Martha had sought money with which to buy some dresses; she received it from Jefferson, together with this admonition.

7
Never spend your money before you have it.

THOMAS JEFFERSON, Letter to Thomas Jefferson Smith, 21 Feb., 1825.

Draw your salary before spending it.

GEORGE ADE, *Forty Modern Fables: The People's Choice.*

8
"I had" is a heartache, "I have" is a fountain,

You're worth what you saved, not the million you made.

JOHN BOYLE O'REILLY, *Rules of the Road.*

TIME

9
Alas! how swift the moments fly!
How flash the years along!
Scarce here, yet gone already by,
The burden of a song.
See childhood, youth, and manhood pass,
And age with furrowed brow;
Time was—Time shall be—drain the glass—
But where in Time is now?

JOHN QUINCY ADAMS, *The Hour Glass.*

10
Time is one's best friend, teaching best of all the wisdom of silence.

AMOS BRONSON ALCOTT, *Table Talk: Learning.*

11
Backward, turn backward, O time, in your flight,
Make me a child again just for to-night.

ELIZABETH AKERS ALLEN, *Rock Me to Sleep.*

12
Give me no changeless hours, for I know
Moments of earth are sweeter that they go.

HERVEY ALLEN, *Moments.*

13
The rust will find the sword of fame,
The dust will hide the crown;
Ay, none shall nail so high his name
Time will not tear it down.

JOHN VANCE CHENEY, *The Happiest Heart.*

14
Look back on time with kindly eyes,
He doubtless did his best;
How softly sinks his trembling sun
In human nature's west!

EMILY DICKINSON, *Poems*, Pt. iv, No. 8.

15
Time is a test of trouble,
But not a remedy.
If such it prove, it prove too
There was no malady.

EMILY DICKINSON, *Poems*, Pt. iv, No. 85.

16
When a man sits with a pretty girl for an hour, it seems like a minute. But let him sit on a hot stove for a minute, and it's longer than any hour. That's relativity.

ALBERT EINSTEIN.

17
Time dissipates to shining ether the solid angularity of facts.

EMERSON, *Essays, First Series: History.*

18
The surest poison is time.

EMERSON, *Society and Solitude: Old Age.*

1

Remember that time is money.
> BENJAMIN FRANKLIN, *Advice to a Young Tradesman.*

2

Time is an herb that cures all diseases.
> BENJAMIN FRANKLIN, *Poor Richard,* 1738.

3

Lost time is never found again.
> BENJAMIN FRANKLIN, *Poor Richard,* 1748.

4

Dost thou love life? Then do not squander time, for that's the stuff life is made of.
> BENJAMIN FRANKLIN, *Poor Richard,* 1758.

5

You may delay, but time will not.
> BENJAMIN FRANKLIN, *Poor Richard,* 1758.

6

Time flies over us, but leaves its shadow behind.
> NATHANIEL HAWTHORNE, *The Marble Faun,* ch. 24.

7

Old Time, in whose bank we deposit our notes,
Is a miser who always wants guineas for groats;
He keeps all his customers still in arrears
By lending them minutes and charging them years.
> OLIVER WENDELL HOLMES, *Our Banker,* st. 1.

8

Pick my left pocket of its silver dime,
But spare the right,—it holds my golden time!
> OLIVER WENDELL HOLMES, *A Rhymed Lesson,* l. 324.

9

No person will have occasion to complain of the want of time who never loses any.
> THOMAS JEFFERSON, Letter to his daughter, 5 May, 1787.

10

Time! what an empty vapor 'tis!
And days, how swift they are.
> ABRAHAM LINCOLN, *Time.*

11

     I recognize that face,
Though Time has touched it in his flight.
> HENRY WADSWORTH LONGFELLOW, *The Golden Legend,* pt. iv, l. 11.

12

Time has laid his hand
Upon my heart, gently, not smiting it,
But as a harper lays his open palm
Upon his harp, to deaden its vibrations.
> HENRY WADSWORTH LONGFELLOW, *The Golden Legend,* pt. iv, *The Cloisters,* l. 77.

13

What is time? The shadow on the dial, the striking of the clock, the running of the sand, day and night, summer and winter, months, years, centuries—these are but arbitrary and outward signs, the measure of Time, not Time itself. Time is the Life of the soul.
> HENRY WADSWORTH LONGFELLOW, *Hyperion,* bk. ii, ch. 6.

14

Lost, yesterday, somewhere between sunrise and sunset, two golden hours, each set with sixty diamond minutes. No reward is offered for they are gone forever.
> HORACE MANN, *Lost, Two Golden Hours.*

15

Time is a great legalizer, even in the field of morals.
> H. L. MENCKEN, *A Book of Prefaces,* ch. iv, sec. 6.

16

Time is a flowing river. Happy those who allow themselves to be carried, unresisting, with the current. They float through easy days. They live, unquestioning, in the moment.
> CHRISTOPHER MORLEY, *Where the Blue Begins,* p. 81.

17

Poets and kings are but the clerks of Time.
> EDWIN ARLINGTON ROBINSON, *The Clerks.*

18

The small intolerable drums
Of Time are like slow drops descending.
> EDWIN ARLINGTON ROBINSON, *The Poor Relation.*

19

Dollars cannot buy yesterday.
> ADMIRAL HAROLD R. STARK, commenting, as Chief of Naval Operations, about a $300,000,000 appropriation for improving the protection of U.S. warships. (*Time,* 16 Dec., 1940, p. 26)

20

Time is
Too Slow for those who Wait,
Too Swift for those who Fear,
Too Long for those who Grieve,
Too Short for those who Rejoice,
    But for those who Love
       Time is not.
> HENRY VAN DYKE, *For Katrina's Sun-Dial.*

21

Whether or not we admit it to ourselves, we are all haunted by a truly awful sense of impermanence. I have always had a particularly keen sense of this at New York cocktail parties, and perhaps that is why I drink the martinis almost as fast as I can snatch them from the tray.
> TENNESSEE WILLIAMS, *The Timeless World of a Play* (introduction to *Three Plays of Tennessee Williams*).

TOBACCO

1

Those who give up cigarette smoking aren't the heroes. The real heroes are the rest of us—who have to listen to them. Sometimes they make me feel so sad I have to light up a big, fat cigar to keep from breaking into tears.

> HAL BOYLE, Column, Associated Press, 21 Jan'., 1964.

2

Let us take the air, in a tobacco trance,
Admire the monuments,
Discuss the late events,
Correct our watches by the public clocks,
Then sit for half an hour and drink our
    bocks.

> T. S. ELIOT, *Portrait of a Lady.*

3

The scatterbrain, Tobacco. Yet a man of no conversation should smoke.

> EMERSON, *Journals,* 1866.

4

Nobody can be so revoltingly smug as the man who has just given up smoking.

> SYDNEY J. HARRIS, *Strictly Personal.*

5

Tobacco is a dirty weed: I like it.
It satisfies no normal need: I like it.
It makes you thin, it makes you lean,
It takes the hair right off your bean;
It's the worst darn stuff I've ever seen:
    I like it.

> GRAHAM HEMMINGER, *Tobacco;* Penn State *Froth,* Nov., 1915, p. 19.

6

Certain things are good for nothing until they have been kept a long while; and some are good for nothing until they have been long kept and *used.* Of the first, wine is the illustrious and immortal example. Of those which must be kept and used I will name three,—meerschaum pipes, violins, and poems. The meerschaum is but a poor affair until it has burned a thousand offerings to the cloud-compelling deities.

> OLIVER WENDELL HOLMES, *The Autocrat of the Breakfast-Table,* ch. 5.

7

The tobacco business is a conspiracy against womanhood and manhood. It owes its origin to that scoundrel, Sir Walter Raleigh, who was likewise the founder of American slavery.

> DR. JOHN HARVEY KELLOGG, *Tobacco.*

8

Noah an' Jonah an' Cap'n John Smith,
Mariners, travelers, magazines of myth,
Settin' up in Heaven, chewin' and a-chawin'
Eatin' their terbaccy, talkin' and a-jawin'.

> DON MARQUIS, *Noah an' Jonah an' Cap'n John Smith.*

9

What this country really needs is a good five-cent cigar.

> THOMAS R. MARSHALL, Remark, while presiding over the U.S. Senate.

10

The light ones may be killers,
    And the dark ones may be mild;
Not the wrappers, but the fillers,
    Make cigars or women wild.

> KEITH PRESTON, *Popular Fallacies.*

11

Yes, social friend, I love thee well,
    In learned doctors' spite;
Thy clouds all other clouds dispel,
    And lap me in delight.

> CHARLES SPRAGUE, *To My Cigar.*

12

I have a faint recollection of pleasure derived from smoking dried lily-stems, before I was a man. I have never smoked anything more noxious.

> HENRY D. THOREAU. (EMERSON, *Thoreau*)

13

To cease smoking is the easiest thing I ever did; I ought to know because I've done it a thousand times.

> MARK TWAIN.

14

More than one cigar at a time is excessive smoking.

> MARK TWAIN.

15

Cigarette smoking is a health hazard of sufficient importance in the United States to warrant appropriate remedial action.

> Advisory Committee to the Surgeon General of the U.S. Public Health Service, Report: *Smoking and Health,* released 11 Jan., 1964. The key statement of a lengthy report, and one of the most quoted passages of the 1960's.

16

The habit originates in a search for contentment.

> Advisory Committee to the Surgeon General of the U.S. Public Health Service, Report: *Smoking and Health,* 11 Jan., 1964.

17

On top of Old Smoking
A year has gone by,
But the smoke we're deploring
Still gets in our eye.

> UNKNOWN. This ditty was introduced as part of a satirical entertainment at the Christmas party of the U.S. Surgeon General's staff in 1964. It was quoted by Dr. Luther Terry, the Surgeon General, in Jan., 1965, when he made public a follow-up report on smoking and health.

TOLERANCE

1
I know not what record of sin awaits me in the other world, but this I know, that I was never mean enough to despise a man because he was ignorant, or because he was poor—or because he was black.
> JOHN ALBION ANDREW, Address at Martha's Vineyard, Mass., 10 Aug., 1862.

2
He preached upon "breadth" till it argued him narrow,—
The broad are too broad to define.
> EMILY DICKINSON, *Poems*, Pt. i, No. 64.

3
We do not know, nor can we know, with absolute certainty that those who disagree with us are wrong. We are human and therefore fallible, and being fallible, we cannot escape the *element of doubt* as to our own opinions and convictions.
> J. WILLIAM FULBRIGHT, Address in Washington, D.C., 5 Dec., 1963.

4
I have learned silence from the talkative, toleration from the intolerant, and kindness from the unkind; yet strange, I am ungrateful to those teachers.
> KAHLIL GIBRAN, *Sand and Foam.*

5
Give to every other human being every right that you claim for yourself.
> ROBERT G. INGERSOLL, *Limitations of Toleration.*

6
If we must disagree, let's disagree without being disagreeable.
> LYNDON B. JOHNSON, Remark, at the California State Democratic convention, Aug., 1963. He was seeking to assuage discord within the party. (*Time,* 23 Aug., 1963, p. 18)

7
Let us today renew our dedication to the ideals that are American. Let us pray for His divine wisdom in banishing from our land any injustice or intolerance or oppression to any of our fellow Americans, whatever their opinion, whatever the color of their skins, for God made all of us, not some of us, in His image. All of us, not just some of us, are His children.
> LYNDON B. JOHNSON, Thanksgiving Day message, 1963.

8
Our house is large, and it is open. It is open to all, those who agree and those who dissent.
> LYNDON B. JOHNSON, Speech to Democratic fund-raising dinners, Washington, D.C., 24 June, 1965. He was referring specifically to dissent over his foreign policy as it affected Vietnam.

9
The United States of America is opposed to discrimination and persecution on grounds of race and religion anywhere in the world, including our own nation. We are working to right the wrongs of our own nation.
> JOHN F. KENNEDY, Address to the United Nations General Assembly, 20 Sept., 1963.

10
Wise with the history of its own frail heart,
With reverence and sorrow, and with love,
Broad as the world for freedom and for man.
> JAMES RUSSELL LOWELL, *Prometheus,* l. 216.

11
The Military Academy taught me many things, some of them not within the covers of books written by any man. The first of these is tolerance—not to debase nor deprive those from whom you may differ because of character or custom, race or color or distinction.
> GENERAL DOUGLAS MACARTHUR, Statement, on receiving a visit from a delegation of West Point cadets on his 84th birthday, 26 Jan., 1964.

12
Americans are not by nature tolerant. They are more likely to be strong-minded on things, in line with American history in the past. We have been essentially intolerant of varied creeds especially.
> JAMES THOMSON SHOTWELL, Interview with Raymond Daniell, New York *Times,* 6 Aug., 1964.

13
In our own free society, we ask that all citizens participate as equals. We accept their views and interests as significant. We struggle for unforced consensus. We tolerate conflict and accept dissent. But we believe that because each citizen knows he is valued and has his chance for comment and influence, his final loyalty to the social order will be more deeply rooted and secure. As heirs to the tradition of free government, what else can we do?
> ADLAI E. STEVENSON, *Outline for a New American Policy; Look,* 24 Aug., 1965, p. 81.

TONGUE

14
He who has no hands
Perforce must use his tongue;
Foxes are so cunning
Because they are not strong.
> EMERSON, *Orator.*

15
If the tongue had not been framed for articulation, man would still be a beast in the forest.
> EMERSON, *Representative Men: Plato.*

1
When men and women die, as poets sung,
His heart's the last part moves,—her last, the
    tongue.
    BENJAMIN FRANKLIN, *Poor Richard*,
        1739.

2
A soft tongue may strike hard.
    BENJAMIN FRANKLIN, *Poor Richard*,
        1744.

3
The tongue is ever turning to the aching
tooth.
    BENJAMIN FRANKLIN, *Poor Richard*
        1746.

4
A Slip of the Foot you may soon recover,
But a Slip of the Tongue you may never get
    over.
    BENJAMIN FRANKLIN, *Poor Richard*,
        1747.

5
The tongue offends and the ears get the
cuffing.
    BENJAMIN FRANKLIN, *Poor Richard*,
        1757.

6
A tart temper never mellows with age, and a
sharp tongue is the only edged tool that
grows keener with constant use.
    WASHINGTON IRVING, *Rip Van Winkle*.

7
I should think your tongue had broken its
    chain!
    HENRY WADSWORTH LONGFELLOW, *The
        Golden Legend*, pt. iv.

8
How like an angel speaks the tongue of
    woman,
When pleading in another's cause her own!
    HENRY WADSWORTH LONGFELLOW, *The
        Spanish Student*, act iii, sc. 5.

TRADE, see Commerce
TRAVEL
See also Wanderlust

9
The traveled mind is the catholic mind educated from exclusiveness and egotism.
    AMOS BRONSON ALCOTT, *Table Talk:
        Travel*.

10
Traveling is no fool's errand to him who carries his eyes and itinerary along with him.
    AMOS BRONSON ALCOTT, *Table Talk:
        Travel*.

11
Travel is broadening, particularly where the
food and drink are good. But the journey
home is an exultant occasion.
    BROOKS ATKINSON, "Critic at Large" Col-
        umn, New York *Times*, 12 Mar., 1965.

12
In America there are two classes of travel—
first-class, and with children. Traveling with
children corresponds roughly to traveling
third class in Bulgaria. They tell me there is
nothing lower in the world than third-class
Bulgarian travel.
    ROBERT BENCHLEY, *Kiddie-Kar Travel*.

13
Virtue and vice, happiness and misery, are
much more equally distributed to nations
than those are permitted to suppose who
have never been from home, and who believe, like the Chinese, that their residence is
the center of the world, of light, of privilege,
and of enjoyment.
    AMASSA DELANO, *Narrative of Voyages*, p.
        256.

14
There are three wants which never can be
satisfied: that of the rich, who wants something more; that of the sick, who wants
something different; and that of the traveller, who says, "Anywhere but here."
    EMERSON, *Conduct of Life: Considera-
        tions by the Way*.

15
The world is his who has money to go over
it.
    EMERSON, *Conduct of Life: Wealth*.

16
        Why seek Italy,
Who cannot circumnavigate the sea
Of thoughts and things at home?
    EMERSON, *The Day's Ration*.

17
It is for want of self-culture that the superstition of Travelling, whose idols are Italy,
England, Egypt, retains its fascination for all
educated Americans. They who made England, Italy, or Greece venerable in the imagination, did so by sticking fast where they
were. . . . The soul is no traveller; the wise
man stays at home. . . . Travelling is a
fool's paradise.
    EMERSON, *Essays, First Series: Self-Reli-
        ance*.

18
I journeyed fur, I journeyed fas'; I glad I
    foun' de place at las'!
    JOEL CHANDLER HARRIS, *Nights with Un-
        cle Remus*, ch. 35.

19
I am like the Huma bird that never lights,
being always in the cars as he is always on
the wing.
    OLIVER WENDELL HOLMES, *The Autocrat
        of the Breakfast-Table*, ch. 1.

20
Travelling makes a man wiser, but less happy.
    THOMAS JEFFERSON, *Writings*, vol. vi, p.
        31.

21
How shall I know, unless I go
    To China and Cathay,
Whether or not this blessed spot

Is blest in every way?
EDNA ST. VINCENT MILLAY, *To the Not Impossible Him.*

1
My heart is warm with the friends I make,
And better friends I'll not be knowing;
Yet there isn't a train I wouldn't take,
No matter where it's going.
EDNA ST. VINCENT MILLAY, *Travel.*

2
Never a ship sails out of the bay
But carries my heart as a stowaway.
ROSELLE MERCIER MONTGOMERY, *The Stowaway.*

3
I like to get where the cabbage is cooking and catch the scents.
RED SMITH, explaining his travels in the course of covering major sports events. (*Newsweek,* 21 Apr., 1958)

4
The man who goes alone can start today; but he who travels with another must wait till that other is ready.
HENRY D. THOREAU, *Walden,* ch. 1.

5
The swiftest traveller is he that goes afoot.
HENRY D. THOREAU, *Walden,* ch. 1.

6
I have travelled a good deal in Concord.
HENRY D. THOREAU, *Walden,* ch. 1.

7
It is not worth while to go round the world to count the cats in Zanzibar.
HENRY D. THOREAU, *Walden:* conclusion.

TREASON

8
A traitor to his country commits equal treason against mankind.
JOHN A. ANDREW, Address in the Massachusetts legislature, 3 Jan., 1862.

9
I had rather take my chance that some traitors will escape detection than spread abroad a spirit of general suspicion and distrust, which accepts rumor and gossip in place of undismayed and unintimidated inquiry.
LEARNED HAND, Address, Oct., 1952.

10
Caesar had his Brutus; Charles the First, his Cromwell; and George the Third ["Treason!" cried the Speaker]—*may profit by their example.* If *this* be treason, make the most of it.
PATRICK HENRY, Speech, Virginia Convention, 29 May, 1765.

11
The unsuccessful strugglers against tyranny have been the chief martyrs of treason laws in all countries.
THOMAS JEFFERSON, *Writings,* vol. viii, p. 332.

12
No private individual has a private right to brand American citizens as traitors. That can be done only by due process of law, and to do it privately is libelous. The laws of libel do not permit the private assassination of private character.
WALTER LIPPMANN, Syndicated Column, 21 July, 1964.

13
I first drew in New England's air, and from her hardy breast
Sucked in the tyrant-hating milk that will not let me rest;
And if my words seem treason to the dullard and the tame,
'T is but my Bay-State dialect,—our fathers spake the same.
JAMES RUSSELL LOWELL, *On the Capture of Certain Fugitive Slaves Near Washington,* st. 2.

14
The traitor to Humanity is the traitor most accursed;
Man is more than Constitutions; better rot beneath the sod,
Than be true to Church and State while we are doubly false to God!
JAMES RUSSELL LOWELL, *On the Capture of Certain Fugitive Slaves Near Washington,* st. 5.

15
The issue between the Republicans and Democrats is clearly drawn. It has been deliberately drawn by those who have been in charge of twenty years of treason.
JOSEPH R. MCCARTHY, Speech in Charleston, W. Va., 4 Feb., 1954. "Twenty Years of Treason," a widely quoted phrase, was the title of a series of speeches Senator McCarthy delivered during this period on a tour arranged by the Republican National Committee.

16
I think lightly of what is called treason against government. That may be your duty today, or mine. But treason against the people, against mankind, against God, is a great sin not lightly to be spoken of.
THEODORE PARKER, Speech on the Mexican War, 1846.

17
Write on my gravestone: "Infidel, Traitor."
—infidel to every church that compromises with wrong; traitor to every government that oppresses the people.
WENDELL PHILLIPS.

18
We must fight traitors with laws. We already have the laws. We must fight falsehood and evil ideas with truth and better ideas. We have them in plenty. We must not confuse the two. Laws infringing our rights and intimidating unoffending persons without enlarging our security will neither catch sub-

versives nor win converts to our better ideas.

ADLAI E. STEVENSON, Speech upon accepting the presidential nomination, Democratic national convention, Chicago, July, 1952.

1

I personally believe [John Foster] Dulles to be a Communist agent who has had one clearly defined role to play; namely, always to say the right things and always to do the wrong ones.

ROBERT WELCH, *The Politician,* p. 223. The book was written between 1954 and 1958, for the most part, but published in 1963.

2

I defy *anybody,* who is not actually a Communist himself, to read all the known facts about his career and not decide that since at least sometime in the 1930's George Catlett Marshall has been a conscious, deliberate, dedicated agent of the Soviet conspiracy.

ROBERT WELCH, *The Politician,* p. 15.

3

For it is obvious that the Communist thinking and planning for Eisenhower's actions, and for the tenor of his public statements, are all done by others. He is only the shell through which the Communist mix of action and propaganda is extruded.

ROBERT WELCH, *The Politician,* p. 277.

4

For the Communists can now use all the power and prestige of the Presidency of the United States to implement their plans, just as fully and even openly as they dare. They have arrived at this point by three stages. In the first stage, Roosevelt thought he was *using* the Communists, to promote his personal ambitions and grandiose schemes. Of course, instead, the Communists were *using him* . . . In the second stage, Truman was passively *used* by the Communists, with his knowledge and acquiescence, as the price he consciously paid for their making him President. In the third stage the Communists have installed in the Presidency a man who, for whatever reasons, appears *intentionally* to be carrying forward Communist aims. . . . With regard to this third man, Eisenhower, it is difficult to avoid raising the question of deliberate treason.

ROBERT WELCH, *The Politician,* p. 278.

5

Treason against the United States shall consist only in levying war against them, or in adhering to their enemies, giving them aid and comfort. No person shall be convicted of treason unless on the testimony of two witnesses to the same overt act, or on confession in open court.

U.S. Constitution, art. iii, sec. 3.

TREE
See also Woods

6

What do we plant when we plant the tree?
We plant the ship that will cross the sea,
We plant the mast to carry the sails,
We plant the planks to withstand the gales—
The keel, the keelson, and beam and knee—
We plant the ship when we plant the tree.
HENRY ABBEY, *What Do We Plant?*

What do we plant when we plant the tree?
A thousand things that we daily see.
We plant the spire that out-towers the crag,
We plant the staff for our country's flag,
We plant the shade from the hot sun free;
We plant all these when we plant the tree.
HENRY ABBEY, *What Do We Plant?*

7

To-day I have grown taller from walking with the trees.
KARLE WILSON BAKER, *Good Company.*

8

I'll lie here and learn How, over their ground,
Trees make a long shadow And a light sound.
LOUISE BOGAN, *Knowledge.*

9

Come, let us plant the apple-tree.
Cleave the tough greensward with the spade;
Wide let its hollow bed be made;
There gently lay the roots, and there
Sift the dark mould with kindly care.
WILLIAM CULLEN BRYANT, *The Planting of the Apple-Tree.*

10

What does he plant who plants a tree?
He plants the friend of sun and sky;
He plants the flag of breezes free;
The shaft of beauty, towering high;
He plants a home to heaven anigh
For song and mother-croon of bird
In hushed and happy twilight heard—
The treble of heaven's harmony—
These things he plants who plants a tree.
HENRY C. BUNNER, *The Heart of the Tree.*

11

They say that trees were only practice work
When God made sure his hand
Before he passed to cows and men.
I cannot think that true,
Else there would surely sometimes be
An ugly tree.
AVIS D. CARLSON, *Trees.*

12

God wrote his loveliest poem on the day
He made the first tall silver poplar tree.
GRACE NOLL CROWELL, *Silver Poplars.*

1

The hemlock's nature thrives on cold;
The gnash of northern winds
Is sweetest nutriment to him,
His best Norwegian wines.
    EMILY DICKINSON, *Poems*, Pt. ii, No. 81.

2

He that betaketh him to a good tree hath
good shade.
    EMERSON, *Journals*, 1866.

3

I think that I shall never see
A poem lovely as a tree.

A tree whose hungry mouth is pressed
Against the earth's sweet flowing breast. . . .

Poems are made by fools like me,
But only God can make a tree.
    JOYCE KILMER, *Trees*.

4

He who plants a tree Plants a hope.
    LUCY LARCOM, *Plant a Tree*.

5

Sweet is the air with the budding haws, and
    the valley stretching for miles below
Is white with blossoming cherry-trees, as if
    just covered with lightest snow.
    HENRY WADSWORTH LONGFELLOW, *The
    Golden Legend*, pt. 4.

6

And the great elms o'erhead
Dark shadows wove on their aërial looms
Shot through with golden thread.
    HENRY WADSWORTH LONGFELLOW, *Haw-
    thorne*, st. 2.

7

The birch, most shy and ladylike of trees.
    JAMES RUSSELL LOWELL, *An Indian-Sum-
    mer Reverie*, st. 8.

8

The chestnuts, lavish of their long-hid gold,
To the faint Summer, beggared now and
    old,
Pour back the sunshine hoarded 'neath her
    favoring eye.
    JAMES RUSSELL LOWELL, *An Indian-Sum-
    mer Reverie*, st. 10.

9

Woodman, spare that tree!
    Touch not a single bough!
In youth it sheltered me,
    And I'll protect it now.
    GEORGE POPE MORRIS, *The Oak*. First pub-
    lished in the New York *Mirror*, 7 Jan.,
    1837.

10

My faith is all a doubtful thing,
    Wove on a doubtful loom,
Until there comes each showery Spring
    A cherry tree in bloom.
    DAVID MORTON, *Symbol*.

11

Any fool can destroy trees. . . . It took more
than three thousand years to make some of
the trees in these Western woods . . .
Through all the wonderful, eventful centuries since Christ's time—and long before
that—God has cared for these trees, saved
them from drought, disease, avalanches, and
a thousand straining, leveling tempests and
floods; but he cannot save them from fools,
—only Uncle Sam can do that.
    JOHN MUIR, *The American Forests; Atlan-
    tic Monthly*, vol. lxxx, p. 157.

12

No tree has so fair a bole and so handsome
an instep as the beech.
    HENRY D. THOREAU, *Journal*. (EMERSON,
    Thoreau)

13

He that planteth a tree is the servant of
    God,
He provideth a kindness for many genera-
    tions,
And faces that he hath not seen shall bless
    him.
    HENRY VAN DYKE, *The Friendly Trees*.

14

Many a tree is found in the wood,
And every tree for its use is good;
Some for the strength of the gnarled root,
Some for the sweetness of flower or fruit.
    HENRY VAN DYKE, *Salute the Trees*.

TRIFLES

15

Little drops of water, Little grains of sand,
Make the mighty ocean And the pleasant
    land.
So the little moments, Humble tho' they be,
Make the mighty ages Of Eternity!

So our little errors Lead the soul away
From the paths of virtue, Far in sin to
    stray.
Little deeds of kindness, Little words of
    love,
Help to make earth happy Like the Heaven
    above!
    JULIA FLETCHER CARNEY, *Little Things*.
    Often wrongly attributed to other writ-
    ers.

Little drops of water poured into the milk,
give the milkman's daughter lovely gowns of
silk. Little grains of sugar mingled with the
sand, make the grocer's assets swell to beat
the band.
    WALT MASON, *Little Things*.

16

He that despiseth small things will perish by
little and little.
    EMERSON, *Essays, First Series: Prudence*.

17

Large streams from little fountains flow,
Tall oaks from little acorns grow.
    DAVID EVERETT, *Lines Written for a
    School Declamation*.

1

Little strokes fell great Oaks.
BENJAMIN FRANKLIN, *Poor Richard*, 1750.

By conscientious indentation
The beaver bevels down the tree.
CHRISTOPHER MORLEY, *The Epigram*.

2

For the want of a nail the shoe was lost,
For the want of a shoe the horse was lost,
For the want of a horse the rider was lost,
For the want of a rider the battle was lost,
For the want of a battle the kingdom was
    lost—
And all for want of a horseshoe-nail.
BENJAMIN FRANKLIN, *Poor Richard*, 1758.

3

Many a little makes a mickle.
BENJAMIN FRANKLIN, *Poor Richard*, 1758.

4

The mighty are brought low by many a
    thing
Too small to name. Beneath the daisy's disk
Lies hid the pebble for the fatal sling.
HELEN HUNT JACKSON, *Danger*.

5

The massive gates of Circumstance
    Are turned upon the smallest hinge,
And thus some seeming pettiest chance
    Oft gives our life its after-tinge.

The trifles of our daily lives,
    The common things scarce worth recall,
Whereof no visible trace survives,
    These are the mainsprings, after all.
UNKNOWN, *Trifles; Harper's Weekly*, 30
    May, 1863.

TROUBLE

See also Adversity, Misfortune

6

Pack up your troubles in your old kit-bag,
And smile, smile, smile.
GEORGE ASAF, Title and refrain of song
    (1915).

7

I see not a step before me as I tread on
    another year;
But I've left the Past in God's keeping,
    —the Future His mercy shall clear;
And what looks dark in the distance may
    brighten as I draw near.
MARY GARDINER BRAINARD, *Not Knowing*.

8

Oh, a trouble's a ton, or a trouble's an
    ounce,
    Or a trouble is what you make it.
And it isn't the fact that you're hurt that
    counts,
    But only how did you take it?
EDMUND VANCE COOKE, *How Did You
    Die?*

9

I say the very things that make the greatest
    stir
An' the most interestin' things, are things
    that didn't occur.
SAM WALTER FOSS, *Things That Didn't
    Occur.*

10

Women like to sit down with trouble as if it
were knitting.
ELLEN GLASGOW, *The Sheltered Life*, p.
    213.

11

"Law, Brer Tarrypin," sez Brer Fox, sezee,
"you ain't see no trouble yit. Ef you wanter
see sho' nuff trouble, you des oughter go
'longer me; I'm de man w'at kin show yer
trouble," sezee.
JOEL CHANDLER HARRIS, *Nights with Un-
    cle Remus*, ch. 17.

12

If pleasures are greatest in anticipation, just
remember that this is also true of trouble.
ELBERT HUBBARD, *Epigrams*.

13

How much pain have cost us the evils which
have never happened.
THOMAS JEFFERSON, *Writings*, vol. xvi, p.
    111.

I have had many troubles in my life, but the
worst of them never came.
JAMES A. GARFIELD, Remark in conversa-
    tion.

Let us be of good cheer, however, remembering that the misfortunes hardest to bear are
those which never come.
JAMES RUSSELL LOWELL, *Democracy and
    Addresses*.

14

Better never trouble Trouble
    Until Trouble troubles you;
For you only make your trouble
    Double-trouble when you do;
And the trouble—like a bubble—
    That you're troubling about,
May be nothing but a cipher
    With its rim rubbed out.
DAVID KEPPEL, *Trouble*.

15

Don't cross the bridge till you come to it,
Is a proverb old, and of excellent wit.
HENRY WADSWORTH LONGFELLOW, *The
    Golden Legend*, pt. 6.

16

He saves me trouble, and that is a saving I
would rather buy dear than any other. Beyond meat and drink, it is the only use I
have ever discovered for money.
JAMES RUSSELL LOWELL, Letter, 1873,
    referring to an old servant.

17

The more complicated life becomes, the
more people are attracted by simple solu-

tions; the more irrational the world seems, the more they long for rational answers; and the more diverse everything is, the more they want it all reduced to identity.

> JAMES RESTON, Washington Column, New York *Times*, 22 July, 1964.

1
He can always be counted upon to make an impossible situation infinitely worse.

> BRANCH RICKEY, on Leo Durocher as a baseball manager.

2
Trouble has a trick of coming butt end first;
Viewed approaching, then you've seen it at its worst.
Once surmounted, straight it waxes ever small,
And it tapers till there's nothing left at all.
So, whene'er a difficulty may impend,
Just remember you are facing the butt end;
And that, looking back upon it, like as not,
You will marvel at beholding just a dot!

> EDWIN L. SABIN, *Trouble's Strong Front.*

3
When the going gets tough, the tough get going.

> UNKNOWN, Maxim adopted by Joseph P. Kennedy as a motto for his sons. (WILLIAM V. SHANNON, *The Emergence of Senator Kennedy; New York Times Magazine,* 22 Aug., 1965, p. 64)

TRUST

4
Grow wise, trust woman, doubt not man.

> THOMAS BAILEY ALDRICH, *Nourmadee,* st. 10.

5
Trust men and they will be true to you; treat them greatly, and they will show themselves great.

> EMERSON, *Essays, First Series: Prudence.*

The chief lesson I have learned in a long life is that the only way to make a man trustworthy is to trust him; and the surest way to make him untrustworthy is to distrust thim and show your distrust.

> HENRY L. STIMSON, *The Bomb and the Opportunity; Harper's Magazine,* Mar., 1946.

6
Trust thyself: every heart vibrates to that iron string.

> EMERSON, *Essays, First Series: Self-Reliance.*

7
And this be our motto, "In God is our trust."

> FRANCIS SCOTT KEY, *The Star-Spangled Banner.*

8
O holy trust! O endless sense of rest!
Like the beloved John

To lay his head upon the Saviour's breast,
And thus to journey on!

> HENRY WADSWORTH LONGFELLOW, *Hymn for My Brother's Ordination,* st. 5.

9
Distrust that man who tells you to distrust.

> ELLA WHEELER WILCOX, *Distrust.*

TRUTH

10
Truth is inclusive of all the virtues, is older than sects or schools, and, like charity, more ancient than mankind.

> AMOS BRONSON ALCOTT, *Table Talk: Discourse.*

11
Yet the deepest truths are best read between the lines, and, for the most part, refuse to be written.

> AMOS BRONSON ALCOTT, *Concord Days: June.*

12
The fewer the voices on the side of truth, the more distinct and strong must be your own.

> WILLIAM ELLERY CHANNING THE ELDER, *Charge on Ordination of Rev. J. S. Dwight.*

13
Whatever you do, tell the truth.

> GROVER CLEVELAND, to Charles W. Goodyear, when asked what should be done in replying to the charge, denied by Cleveland, that Cleveland was the father of an illegitimate child by Maria Halpin, of Buffalo, N.Y. This was a hot issue in the presidential campaign of 1884. (NEVINS, *Grover Cleveland,* p. 163)

14
Truth is such a rare thing, it is delightful to tell it.

> EMILY DICKINSON, Letter to Thomas Wentworth Higginson, Aug., 1870.

15
Truth, Life, and Love are a law of annihilation to everything unlike themselves, because they declare nothing but God.

> MARY BAKER EDDY, *Science and Health,* p. 243.

16
The highest compact we can make with our fellow is,—Let there be truth between us two forevermore.

> EMERSON, *Conduct of Life: Behavior.*

17
God offers to every mind its choice between truth and repose. Take which you please, —you can never have both.

> EMERSON, *Essays, First Series: Intellect.*

18
Truth is the summit of being; justice is the application of it to affairs.

> EMERSON, *Essays, Second Series: Character.*

1
Nothing shall warp me from the belief that every man is a lover of truth.
EMERSON, *Essays, Second Series: New England Reformers.*

2
Wherever truth is injured, defend it.
EMERSON, *Journals,* vol. iii, p. 269.

3
Truth is beautiful. Without doubt; and so are lies.
EMERSON, *Journals,* vol. iii, p. 437.

4
No man speaks the truth or lives a true life two minutes together.
EMERSON, *Journals,* vol. iii, p. 455.

5
When what should be the greatest truths flat out into shallow truisms, then we are all sick.
EMERSON, *Journals,* vol. iv, p. 30.

6
Reality, however, has a sliding floor.
EMERSON, *Journals,* vol. x, p. 365.

7
Truth, whose centre is everywhere and its circumference nowhere, whose existence we cannot disimagine; the soundness and health of things, against which no blow can be struck but it recoils on the striker.
EMERSON, *Letters and Social Aims: Progress of Culture.*

8
Half the truth is often a great lie.
BENJAMIN FRANKLIN, *Poor Richard,* 1758.

Some falsehood mingles with all truth.
HENRY WADSWORTH LONGFELLOW, *The Golden Legend,* pt. ii.

Half-truths to which men are accustomed are so much easier to pass than the golden mintage they rarely encounter!
CHRISTOPHER MORLEY, *Religio Journalistici,* p. 32.

9
The core of the democratic idea is the *element of doubt* as to the ability of any man or any movement to perceive ultimate truth. Accordingly, it has fostered societies in which the individual is left free to pursue truth and virtue as he imperfectly perceives them, with due regard for the right of every other individual to pursue a different, and quite possibly superior, set of values.
J. WILLIAM FULBRIGHT, Address in Washington, D.C., 5 Dec., 1963.

10
In proportion as we perceive and embrace the truth do we become just, heroic, magnanimous, divine.
WILLIAM LLOYD GARRISON, *Free Speech and Free Inquiry.*

11
He who sees the truth, let him proclaim it, without asking who is for it or who is against it.
HENRY GEORGE, *The Land Question,* ch. 3.

12
And fierce though the fiends may fight, and long though the angels hide,
I know that truth and right have the universe on their side.
WASHINGTON GLADDEN, *Ultima Veritas.*

13
In fact, there's nothing that keep its youth,
So far as I know, but a tree and truth.
OLIVER WENDELL HOLMES, *The Deacon's Masterpiece.*

14
Truth is for other worlds, and hope for this;
The cheating future lends the present's bliss.
OLIVER WENDELL HOLMES, *The Old Player.*

15
Truth is tough. It will not break, like a bubble, at a touch; nay, you may kick it about all day, like a foot-ball, and it will be round and full at evening.
OLIVER WENDELL HOLMES, *The Professor at the Breakfast-Table,* ch. 5.

The truth is the most robust and indestructible and formidable thing in the world.
WOODROW WILSON, Address in Tacoma, Wash., 13 Sept., 1919.

16
A lie travels by the Marconi route, while Truth goes by slow freight and is often ditched at the first water-tank.
ELBERT HUBBARD, *Epigrams.*

17
Truth is always at the bottom of a grave.
JAMES G. HUNEKER, *Iconoclasts,* p. 63.

18
The truth, naked and unashamed, is always unpleasant.
JAMES G. HUNEKER, *Iconoclasts,* p. 188.

19
The man who finds a truth lights a torch.
ROBERT G. INGERSOLL, *The Truth.*

20
For we believe that truth is stronger than error and that freedom is more enduring than coercion.
JOHN F. KENNEDY, Address to the United Nations General Assembly, 20 Sept., 1963.

21
In time of war, truth is always replaced by propaganda.
CHARLES A. LINDBERGH, Speech in New York City, 23 Apr., 1941.

The first casualty in every war is truth.
JAMES RESTON, Washington Column, New York *Times,* 29 Jan., 1964.

1

No power can die that ever wrought for
  Truth;
  Thereby a law of Nature it became,
And lives unwithered in its blithesome
  youth,
  When he who called it forth is but a
  name.
    JAMES RUSSELL LOWELL, *Elegy on the
    Death of Dr. Channing*. Inscription on
    Lowell's bust in the Hall of Fame.

2

Who speaks the truth stabs Falsehood to the
  heart,
And his mere word makes despots tremble
  more
Than ever Brutus with his dagger could.
    JAMES RUSSELL LOWELL, *L'Envoi*, l. 100.

3

Get but the truth once uttered, and 't is
  like
A star new-born, that drops into its place,
And which, once circling in its placid round,
Not all the tumult of the earth can shake.
    JAMES RUSSELL LOWELL, *A Glance Behind
    the Curtain*, l. 173.

4

I do not fear to follow out the truth,
Albeit along the precipice's edge.
    JAMES RUSSELL LOWELL, *A Glance Behind
    the Curtain*, l. 251.

5

Put golden padlocks on Truth's lips, be callous as ye will,
From soul to soul, o'er all the world, leaps
  one electric thrill.
    JAMES RUSSELL LOWELL, *On the Capture
    of Certain Fugitive Slaves Near Wash-
    ington.*

6

They must upward still, and onward, who
  would keep abreast of Truth.
    JAMES RUSSELL LOWELL, *The Present
    Crisis*, l. 87.

7

Once to every man and nation comes the
  moment to decide,
In the strife of Truth with Falsehood, for the
  good or evil side.
    JAMES RUSSELL LOWELL, *The Present Cri-
    sis*, st. 5.

8

Then to side with Truth is noble when we
  share her wretched crust,
Ere her cause bring fame and profit, an 't is
  prosperous to be just;
Then it is the brave man chooses, while the
  coward stands aside,
Doubting in his abject spirit, till his Lord is
  crucified.
    JAMES RUSSELL LOWELL, *The Present Cri-
    sis*, st. 11.

9

The smallest atom of truth represents some

man's bitter toil and agony; for every pon-
derable chunk of it there is a brave truth-
seeker's grave upon some lonely ash-dump
and a soul roasting in hell.
    H. L. MENCKEN, *Prejudices*, ser. iii, p.
    274.

10

Truth keeps the bottom of her well.
    JOAQUIN MILLER, *Song of the South*, sec.
    iii, pt. 2.

Truth, after all, wears a different face to
everybody, and it would be too tedious to
wait till all were agreed. She is said to lie at
the bottom of a well, for the very reason,
perhaps, that whoever looks down in search
of her sees his own image at the bottom, and
is persuaded not only that he has seen the
Goddess, but that she is far better-looking
than he had imagined.
    JAMES RUSSELL LOWELL, *Democracy.*

11

Truth is the strong compost in which beauty
may sometimes germinate.
    CHRISTOPHER MORLEY, *Inward Ho.*

12

Truth is not a diet But a condiment.
    CHRISTOPHER MORLEY, *Veritas vos Dam-
    nabit.*

13

Truth for authority, not authority for truth.
    LUCRETIA MOTT, Motto. (HIBBEN, *The
    Peerless Leader*, p. 100)

14

Truth stood on one side and Ease on the
other; it has often been so.
    THEODORE PARKER, *A Discourse of Mat-
    ters Pertaining to Religion.*

15

Truth never yet fell dead in the streets; it
has such affinity with the soul of man, the
seed however broadcast will catch somewhere
and produce its hundredfold.
    THEODORE PARKER, *A Discourse of Mat-
    ters Pertaining to Religion.*

16

Naked Truth needs no shift.
    WILLIAM PENN, Title of broadside (1674).

17

Truth often suffers more by the heat of its
defenders than from the arguments of its op-
posers.
    WILLIAM PENN, *Fruits of Solitude.*

18

Truth is a jewel which should not be painted
over; but it may be set to advantage and
shown in a good light.
    GEORGE SANTAYANA, *Life of Reason.*

19

You will find that the truth is often unpopular and the contest between agreeable fancy
and disagreeable fact is unequal. For, in the
vernacular, we Americans are suckers for
good news.
    ADLAI E. STEVENSON, Address at Michigan

State University, East Lansing, Mich., 8 June, 1958.

1

All fear of the world or consequence is swallowed up in a manly anxiety to do Truth justice.

> HENRY D. THOREAU, *Journal*, 13 Feb., 1838.

2

What everybody echoes . . . as true today, may turn out to be falsehood tomorrow, mere smoke of opinion.

> HENRY D. THOREAU, *Walden*, ch. 1.

3

It takes two to speak truth—one to speak and another to hear.

> HENRY D. THOREAU, *A Week on the Concord and Merrimack Rivers: Wednesday.*

4

There was things which he stretched, but mainly he told the truth.

> MARK TWAIN, *The Adventures of Huckleberry Finn*, ch. 1. Huck here vouches for Twain's veracity in *The Adventures of Tom Sawyer.*

5

Truth is the most valuable thing we have. Let us economize it.

> MARK TWAIN, *Pudd'nhead Wilson's Calendar.*

6

Truth is stranger than fiction—to some people, but I am measurably familiar with it.

> MARK TWAIN, *Pudd'nhead Wilson's New Calendar.*

7

When in doubt tell the truth.

> MARK TWAIN, *Pudd'nhead Wilson's New Calendar.*

8

Tell the truth or trump—but get the trick.

> MARK TWAIN, *Pudd'nhead Wilson's Calendar.*

9

Truth will ultimately prevail where there is pains taken to bring it to light.

> GEORGE WASHINGTON, *Maxims.*

10

There is nothing so powerful as truth, and often nothing so strange.

> DANIEL WEBSTER, Argument on the murder of Captain White.

TYRANNY

11

This hand, to tyrants ever sworn the foe,
For freedom only deals the deadly blow;
Then sheathes in calm response the vengeful blade
For gentle peace in Freedom's hallowed shade.

> JOHN QUINCY ADAMS. These lines, written in an album in 1842, are based on some earlier ones by Algernon Sidney.

12

The worst tyrants are those which establish themselves in our own breasts.

> WILLIAM ELLERY CHANNING THE ELDER, *Spiritual Freedom.*

13

With reasonable men, I will reason; with humane men I will plead; but to tyrants I will give no quarter, nor waste arguments where they will certainly be lost.

> WILLIAM LLOYD GARRISON. (W. P. AND F. J. T. GARRISON, *William Lloyd Garrison*, vol. i)

14

Every tyrant who has lived has believed in freedom—for himself.

> ELBERT HUBBARD, *The Philistine*, vol. xi, p. 61.

15

He who endeavors to control the mind by force is a tyrant, and he who submits is a slave.

> ROBERT G. INGERSOLL, *Some Mistakes of Moses.*

16

Resistance to tyrants is obedience to God.

> THOMAS JEFFERSON, Epigram, found among his papers.

17

I have sworn upon the altar of God eternal hostility against every form of tyranny over the mind of man.

> THOMAS JEFFERSON, Letter to Benjamin Rush, 23 Sept., 1800. Inscribed inside the Jefferson monument in Washington.

18

The time to guard against corruption and tyranny is before they shall have gotten hold of us. It is better to keep the wolf out of the fold than to trust to drawing his teeth and claws after he shall have entered.

> THOMAS JEFFERSON, *Writings*, vol. ii, p. 163.

19

Fear, that reigns with the tyrant.

> HENRY WADSWORTH LONGFELLOW, *Evangeline*, pt. i, l. 35.

20

there is bound to be a certain amount of trouble running any country
if you are president the trouble happens to you
but if you are a tyrant you can arrange things so
that most of the trouble happens to other people

> DON MARQUIS, *archy does his part: archy's newest deal.*

21

Tyranny, like hell, is not easily conquered.

> THOMAS PAINE, *The Crisis:* Introduction.

1

Oppression is but another name for irresponsible power.

WILLIAM PINKNEY, Speech, 15 Feb., 1820.

2

There is no tyranny so hateful as a vulgar and anonymous tyranny. . . . Such a headless people has the mind of a worm and the claws of a dragon.

GEORGE SANTAYANA, *The Life of Reason*, vol. ii, p. 127.

3

Sic semper tyrannis. (Thus always with tyrants, or Thus ever to tyrants.)

UNKNOWN. This Latin maxim is closely associated with America. It was adopted as the motto of Virginia, Oct., 1779, and it was the sentence uttered by John Wilkes Booth as he fired at Lincoln, 14 Apr., 1865.

U

UNITY

See also America: The Union

4

Yes, we must, indeed, all hang together, or, most assuredly, we shall all hang separately.

BENJAMIN FRANKLIN, to John Hancock, just before the signing of the Declaration of Independence. In his address to the Continental Congress, Hancock had just said, "It is too late to pull different ways; the members of the Continental Congress must hang together."

5

A mandate for unity.

LYNDON B. JOHNSON, Speech in Austin, Tex., 4 Nov., 1964, commenting on the landslide victory he had just scored in the presidential balloting.

6

There are no problems we cannot solve together, and very few we can solve by ourselves.

LYNDON B. JOHNSON, News Conference, Johnson City, Tex., 28 Nov., 1964. Referring to the NATO alliance, then strained by France.

7

We come to reason, not to dominate. We do not seek to have our way, but to find a common way.

LYNDON B. JOHNSON, Speech at Georgetown University, Washington, D.C., 3 Dec., 1964. Referring to the United States in its relation to NATO.

8

A house divided against itself cannot stand.

ABRAHAM LINCOLN, Address at the Republican state convention, Springfield, Ill., 16 June, 1858. A paraphrase of the *New Testament: Mark* iii, 25: "If a house be divided against itself, that house cannot stand."

9

All your strength is in your union, All your danger is in discord.

HENRY WADSWORTH LONGFELLOW, *The Song of Hiawatha*, bk. i, l. 113.

10

United we stand, divided we fall!

G. P. MORRIS, *The Flag of Our Union*, l. 3.

11

One nation, indivisible.

JAMES B. UPHAM AND FRANCIS BELLAMY, *Pledge to the Flag*.

12

Liberty and Union, now and forever, one and inseparable!

DANIEL WEBSTER, Speech on Foote's Resolution, 26 Jan., 1830.

13

One country, one constitution, one destiny.

DANIEL WEBSTER, Speech in New York City, 15 Mar., 1837.

UNIVERSE

14

A man said to the universe:
"Sir, I exist!"
"However," replied the universe,
"The fact has not created in me
A sense of obligation."

STEPHEN CRANE, *War Is Kind*, pt. 4.

15

The whole creation is made of hooks and eyes, of bitumen, of sticking-plaster . . . it coheres in a perfect ball.

EMERSON, *Conduct of Life: Worship*.

16

There is a crack in everything God has made.

EMERSON, *Essays, First Series: Compensation*.

17

The universe is not composed of newts only; it has its Newtons.

HARRY EMERSON FOSDICK, *Easter Sermon*.

18

The universe is not hostile, nor yet is it friendly. It is simply indifferent.

JOHN HAYNES HOLMES, *The Sensible Man's View of Religion*.

19

Think of our world as it looks from that rocket that's heading toward Mars. It is like a child's globe, hanging in space, the continents stuck to its side like colored maps. We are all fellow passengers on a dot of earth. And each of us, in the span of time, has really only a moment among our companions.

> LYNDON B. JOHNSON, *Inaugural Address,* 20 Jan., 1965.

1

Every mortal man of us holds stock in the only public debt that is absolutely sure of payment, and that is the debt of the Maker of this Universe to the Universe he has made.

> JAMES RUSSELL LOWELL, *On a Certain Condescension in Foreigners.*

2

A handful of sand is an anthology of the universe.

> DAVID McCORD, *Once and for All:* Introduction.

3

The universe, as far as we can observe it, is a wonderful and immense engine; its extent, its order, its beauty, its cruelty, make it alike impressive. If we dramatize its life and conceive its spirit, we are filled with wonder, terror, and amusement, so magnificent is that spirit, so prolific, inexorable, grammatical and dull.

> GEORGE SANTAYANA, *Little Essays,* p. 85.

4

Great is this organism of mud and fire, terrible this vast, painful, glorious experiment.

> GEORGE SANTAYANA, *Little Essays,* p. 86.

5

When I view the universe as a whole, I admit that it is a marvelous structure; and what is more, I insist that it is of what I may call an intelligent design. . . . There is really very little difference between my own thoughts about the matter and the thoughts of a Fundamentalist.

> W. F. G. SWANN, *The Architecture of the Universe.*

6

In Tune with the Infinite.

> RALPH WALDO TRINE, Title of book.

7

It is a harnessing of the basic power of the universe.

> HARRY S TRUMAN, Public Statement, 6 Aug., 1945. The first announcement of the atomic bomb.

8

The whole theory of the universe is directed unerringly to one single individual— namely to You.

> WALT WHITMAN, *By Blue Ontario's Shore,* sec. 15.

9

Let your soul stand cool and composed before a million universes.

> WALT WHITMAN, *Song of Myself,* sec. 48.

UNIVERSITY, see Colleges

USE

10

The richest of all Lords is Use.

> EMERSON, *Conduct of Life: Considerations by the Way.*

11

In all human action those faculties will be strong which are used.

> EMERSON, *Conduct of Life: Culture.*

12

The used key is always bright.

> BENJAMIN FRANKLIN, *The Way to Wealth.*

13

Nothing useless is, or low;
   Each thing in its place is best;
And what seems but idle show
   Strengthens and supports the rest.

> HENRY WADSWORTH LONGFELLOW, *The Builders,* st. 2.

14

Not what we have, but what we use;
Not what we see, but what we choose—
These are the things that mar or bless
The sum of human happiness.

> CLARENCE URMY, *The Things That Count.*

V

VAGABOND

See also Wanderlust

15

Are you not scared by seeing that the gypsies are more attractive to us than the Apostles?

> EMERSON, *Journals,* vol. vi, p. 184.

16

Brother, Can You Spare a Dime?

> E. Y. HARBURG, Title and refrain of song (1932).

17

Whose furthest footstep never strayed
Beyond the village of his birth,

Is but a lodger for the night
In this old wayside inn of earth.
To-morrow he shall take his pack,
And set out for the ways beyond,
On the old trail from star to star,
An alien and a vagabond.

> RICHARD HOVEY, *More Songs from Vagabondia: Envoy.*

18

A hobo is a man who builds palaces and lives in shacks,
He builds Pullmans and rides the rods, . . .

He reaps the harvest and stands in the bread line.
GODFREY IRWIN, *American Tramp and Underworld Slang.*

1
O the Raggedy Man! He works fer Pa;
An' he's the goodest man you ever saw!
JAMES WHITCOMB RILEY, *The Raggedy Man.*

2
I will sing, I will go, and never ask me why
I was born a rover and a passer-by.
RIDGELY TORRENCE, *Eye-Witness.*

3
Oh, why don't you work like other men do?
How the hell can I work when there's no work to do?
Hallelujah, I'm a bum, hallelujah, bum again,
Halleujah, give us a hand-out to revive us again.
UNKNOWN, *Hallelujah, I'm a Bum.*

This old song [*Hallelujah, I'm a Bum*], heard at the water tanks of railroads in Kansas in 1897 and from harvest hands who worked in the wheat fields of Pawnee County, was picked up later by the I.W.W.'s who made verses of their own for it and gave it wide fame.
CARL SANDBURG, *The American Songbag,* p. 184.

VALOR

See also Courage

4
There is always safety in valor.
EMERSON, *English Traits: The Times.*

5
Valor consists in the power of self-recovery.
EMERSON, *Essays, First Series: Circles.*

6
Valour, which knows itself only in war.
EMERSON, *Journal,* 1863. Quoted as from a Persian saying.

7
'Tis still observed those men most valiant are
Who are most modest ere they came to war.
EMERSON, *Society and Solitude: Courage.* Quoted.

8
There is no holier spot of ground
Than where defeated valor lies,
By mourning beauty crowned!
HENRY TIMROD, *Ode.* Referring to the graveyard of Confederate dead in Charleston, S.C.

VANITY

See also Conceit, Egotism, Self-Love

9
Why does the blind man's wife paint herself?
BENJAMIN FRANKLIN, *Poor Richard,* 1736.

10
Tilling the fertile soil of man's vanity.
ELLEN GLASGOW, *A Certain Measure.*

11
Vain? Let it be so! Nature was her teacher.
What if a lovely and unsistered creature
Loved her own harmless gift of pleasing feature?
OLIVER WENDELL HOLMES, *Iris, Her Book.*

12
No vain man matures, he makes too much new wood;
His blooms are too thick for the fruit to be good;
'Tis the modest man ripens, 't is he that achieves,
Just what's needed of sunshine and shade he receives.
JAMES RUSSELL LOWELL, *A Fable for Critics,* l. 978.

13
The highest form of vanity is love of fame.
GEORGE SANTAYANA, *Little Essays,* p. 22.

14
The meaning of the word vanity never crosses the vulgar heart.
GEORGE SANTAYANA, *Little Essays,* p. 82.

15
She keeps on being queenly in her own room with the door shut.
EDITH WHARTON, *The House of Mirth,* p. 302.

16
Vanity as an impulse has without doubt been of far more benefit to civilization than modesty has ever been.
WILLIAM E. WOODWARD, *George Washington,* ch. 5.

VICE

See also Sin

17
Vice never yields the fruits of virtue.
WILLIAM ELLERY CHANNING THE ELDER, *The Working Classes.*

18
There is no man who is not at some time indebted to his vices, as no plant that is not fed from manures.
EMERSON, *Conduct of Life: Considerations by the Way.*

19
As crabs, goats, scorpions, the balance and the waterpot, lose all their meanness when hung as signs in the zodiac, so I can see my own vices without heat in the distant persons of Solomon, Alcibiades, and Catiline.
EMERSON, *Essays, First Series: History.*

20
Our faith comes in moments; our vice is habitual.
EMERSON, *Essays, First Series: The Over-Soul.*

21
Men imagine that they communicate their

virtue or vice only by overt actions, and do not see that virtue or vice emit a breath every moment.
> EMERSON, *Essays, First Series: Self-Reliance.*

1

Men wish to be saved from the mischiefs of their vices, but not from their vices.
> EMERSON, *Essays, Second Series: Experience.*

2

Search others for their virtues, thyself for thy vices.
> BENJAMIN FRANKLIN, *Poor Richard,* 1738.

3

Let thy vices die before thee.
> BENJAMIN FRANKLIN, *Poor Richard,* 1738.

4

What maintains one vice would bring up two children.
> BENJAMIN FRANKLIN, *Poor Richard,* 1758.

5

Men do not vary much in virtue: their vices only are different.
> ELBERT HUBBARD, *Epigrams.*

6

Saint Augustine! well hast thou said,
  That of our vices we can frame
A ladder, if we will but tread
  Beneath our feet each deed of shame!
> HENRY WADSWORTH LONGFELLOW, *The Ladder of St. Augustine.*

7

Vice should not correct sin.
> WILLIAM PENN, *Fruits of Solitude,* No. 45.

8

We are double-edged blades, and every time we whet our virtue the return stroke straps our vice.
> HENRY D. THOREAU, *Journal,* 8 Feb., 1841.

VICTORY

See also Sport, Success, War

9

A great victor, in defeat as great,
No more, no less, always himself in both.
> STEPHEN VINCENT BENÉT, *John Brown's Body,* bk. 4.

10

The ground they gained; but we The victory.
> GEORGE HENRY CALVERT, *Bunker Hill.*

11

Not one of all the purple host
Who took the flag to-day
Can tell the definition
So clear, of victory,
As he, defeated, dying,
On whose forbidden ear
The distant strains of triumph

Break, agonized and clear.
> EMILY DICKINSON, *Poems,* Pt. i, No. 1.

12

Let the victory fall where it will, we are on that side.
> EMERSON, *Essays, Second Series: Nature.*

13

The victor belongs to the spoils.
> F. SCOTT FITZGERALD, *The Beautiful and the Damned.* For the famous quotation of which this is a paraphrase, see under Politics.

14

Why Not Victory?
> BARRY M. GOLDWATER, Title of book (1962), advocating a strongly nationalistic foreign policy.

15

Victory and defeat are each of the same price.
> THOMAS JEFFERSON.

16

Victory is no longer a truth. It is only a word to describe who is left alive in the ruins.
> LYNDON B. JOHNSON, Speech in New York City, 6 Feb., 1964.

17

I don't want to hear of any of you men getting into any fights with the British. But if you do, you'd better not get whipped.
> CURTIS E. LEMAY, to his Air Force officers during World War II, while he was stationed in England. (New York *Times,* 8 Dec., 1964, p. 14)

18

Beware of rashness, but with energy and sleepless vigilance go forward and give us victories.
> ABRAHAM LINCOLN, Letter to Major General Joseph Hooker, 25 Jan., 1863.

19

In war there is no substitute for victory.
> GENERAL DOUGLAS MACARTHUR, Address to a joint session of Congress, 19 Apr., 1951.

20

It is fatal to enter any war without the will to win it.
> GENERAL DOUGLAS MACARTHUR, Speech at the Republican national convention, 7 July, 1952.

No-win policy.
> UNKNOWN, the description of U.S. foreign policy during the Korean War and thereafter, as viewed by advocates of a more militant policy.

21

Be ashamed to die until you have won some victory for humanity.
> HORACE MANN, Commencement Address at Antioch College, 1859.

22

Shout "Victory, victory, victory ho!"
  I say, 'tis not always with the hosts that win!

I say that the victory, high or low,
　Is given the hero who grapples with sin,
Or legion or single; just asking to know
When duty fronts death in his Alamo.
　　JOAQUIN MILLER, *The Defense of the Alamo.*

1
Let this be your motto,—Rely on yourself!
For, whether the prize be a ribbon or
　　throne,
The victor is he who can go it alone!
　　JOHN G. SAXE, *The Game of Life,* st. 7.

2
With the development of modern technology,
"victory" in war has become a mockery.
What victory—victory for what or for
whom?
　　ADLAI E. STEVENSON, *The Hard Kind of
　　　Patriotism; Harper's Magazine,* July,
　　　1963.

3
Speak, History! who are Life's victors? Unroll thy long annals and say,
Are they those whom the world called the
　　victors,—who won the success of a
　　day?
The martyrs, or Nero? The Spartans, who
　　fell at Thermopylae's tryst,
Or the Persians and Xerxes? His judges, or
　　Socrates? Pilate, or Christ?
　　WILLIAM WETMORE STORY, *Io Victis.*

4
　　They only the victory win
Who have fought the good fight and have
　　vanquished the demon that tempts us
　　within;
Who have held to their faith unseduced by
　　the prize that the world holds on high;
Who have dared for a high cause to suffer,
　　resist, fight—if need be, to die.
　　WILLIAM WETMORE STORY, *Io Victis.*

5
Win without boasting. Lose without excuse.
　　ALBERT PAYSON TERHUNE, *More About
　　　Dog Shows.*

VIRTUE

See also Goodness, Vice

6
One's outlook is a part of his virtue.
　　AMOS BRONSON ALCOTT, *Concord Days:
　　　April Outlook.*

7
Virtue has always been conceived of as victorious resistance to one's vital desire to do
this, that or the other.
　　JAMES BRANCH CABELL, *Beyond Life,* p.
　　　114.

8
The highest virtue is always against the law.
　　EMERSON, *Conduct of Life: Worship.*

9
There is no virtue which is final; all are

initial. The virtues of society are the vices of
the saint.
　　EMERSON, *Essays, First Series: Circles.*

10
The only reward of virtue is virtue.
　　EMERSON, *Essays, First Series: Friendship.*

11
Speak to his heart, and the man becomes
suddenly virtuous.
　　EMERSON, *Essays, First Series: The Over-
　　　Soul.*

12
Virtues are, in the popular estimate, rather
the exception than the rule. There is the man
and his virtues.
　　EMERSON, *Essays, First Series: Self-Reliance.*

13
We fancy it rhetoric when we speak of eminent virtue. We do not yet see that virtue is
Height.
　　EMERSON, *Essays, First Series: Self-Reliance.*

14
Virtue is the adherence in action to the nature of things, and the nature of things
makes it prevalent. It consists in a perpetual
substitution of being for seeming, and with
sublime propriety God is described as saying,
I AM.
　　EMERSON, *Essays, First Series: Spiritual
　　　Laws.*

15
All the devils respect virtue.
　　EMERSON, *Essays, First Series: Spiritual
　　　Laws.*

16
Be in general virtuous, and you will be happy.
　　BENJAMIN FRANKLIN, *On Early Marriages.*

Virtue and Happiness are Mother and
Daughter.
　　BENJAMIN FRANKLIN, *Poor Richard,*
　　　1746.

17
He is ill clothed who is bare of virtue.
　　BENJAMIN FRANKLIN, *Poor Richard,*
　　　1733.

18
Hast thou virtue? acquire also the graces and
beauties of virtue.
　　BENJAMIN FRANKLIN, *Poor Richard,*
　　　1733.

19
Sell not virtue to purchase wealth, nor liberty to purchase power.
　　BENJAMIN FRANKLIN, *Poor Richard,*
　　　1738.

20
You may be more happy than princes, if you
will be more virtuous.
　　BENJAMIN FRANKLIN, *Poor Richard,*
　　　1738.

1

And if the Wise be the happy man, as these sages say, he must be virtuous too; for without virtue happiness cannot be.

> THOMAS JEFFERSON, *Writings*, vol. xiv, p. 405.

2

Though men may falter, it is Virtue's strength
To be indelible: our smallest good
By our worst evil cannot be undone.

> ROBERT U. JOHNSON, *The Voice of Webster*.

3

Wisdom is knowing what to do next; virtue is doing it.

> DAVID STARR JORDAN, *The Philosophy of Despair*, p. 37.

4

Virtue treads paths that end not in the grave.

> JAMES RUSSELL LOWELL, *Commemoration Ode*.

5

Virtue is an angel, but she is a blind one, and must ask of Knowledge to show her the pathway that leads to her goal.

> HORACE MANN, *A Few Thoughts for a Young Man*.

6

When we are planning for posterity, we ought to remember that virtue is not hereditary.

> THOMAS PAINE, *Common Sense*, ch. 4.

7

If there be no nobility of descent, all the more indispensable is it that there should be nobility of ascent—a character in them that bear rule, so fine and high and pure, that as men come within the circle of its influence they involuntarily pay homage to that which is the one pre-eminent distinction, the Royalty of Virtue.

> HENRY CODMAN POTTER, Address, 30 Apr., 1889.

8

Be good and you will be lonesome.

> MARK TWAIN, *Following the Equator:* caption for author's photograph, which is used as a frontispiece.

9

Be virtuous and you will be eccentric.

> MARK TWAIN, *Mental Photographs*.

10

Be virtuous & you'll be happy!

> ARTEMUS WARD, *Fourth of July Oration*.

11

It is easy enough to be prudent,
   When nothing tempts you to stray;
When without or within no voice of sin
   Is luring your soul away;
But it's only a negative virtue
   Until it is tried by fire,
And the life that is worth the honor of earth,

Is the one that resists desire.

> ELLA WHEELER WILCOX, *Worth While*.

VOICE

12

A man's style is his mind's voice. Wooden minds, wooden voices.

> EMERSON, *Journals*, 1872.

13

At some glad moment was it nature's choice
To dower a scrap of sunset with a voice?

> EDGAR FAWCETT, *To an Oriole*.

14

I love to hear thine earnest voice,
Wherever thou art hid.

> OLIVER WENDELL HOLMES, *To an Insect*.

15

Then read from the treasured volume
   The poem of thy choice,
And lend to the rhyme of the poet
   The beauty of thy voice.

> HENRY WADSWORTH LONGFELLOW, *The Day Is Done*, st. 10.

16

Oh, there is something in that voice that reaches
The innermost recesses of my spirit!

> HENRY WADSWORTH LONGFELLOW, *The Divine Tragedy: The First Passover*, pt. 6.

17

Thy voice Is a celestial melody.

> HENRY WADSWORTH LONGFELLOW, *The Masque of Pandora*, pt. v, l. 2.

18

A voice in the darkness, a knock at the door,
And a word that shall echo forevermore!

> HENRY WADSWORTH LONGFELLOW, *Paul Revere's Ride*, st. 14.

19

    Her silver voice
Is the rich music of a summer bird,
Heard in the still night, with its passionate cadence.

> HENRY WADSWORTH LONGFELLOW, *The Spirit of Poetry*, l. 55.

20

I know a Jew fish crier down on Maxwell
   Street with a voice like a north wind
   blowing over corn stubble in January.

> CARL SANDBURG, *Fish Crier*.

21

A soft Kentucky strain was in his voice,
And the Ohio's deeper bloom was there,
With some wild accents of old Wabash days,
And winds of Illinois;
And when he spoke he took us unaware,
With his high courage and unselfish ways.

> MAURICE THOMPSON, *At Lincoln's Grave*.

22

Vocal velvet.

> RICHARD GRANT WHITE, referring to the

voice of Pauline Markham. (MARKS, *They All Sang,* p. 53)

1
For it stirs the blood in an old man's heart,
And makes his pulses fly,
To catch the thrill of a happy voice,
And the light of a pleasant eye.
N. P. WILLIS, *Saturday Afternoon.*

2
Love takes my voice away.
GEORGE E. WOODBERRY, *Song.*

VOTE AND VOTING
See also Government, Politics

3
Where annual elections end, there slavery begins.
JOHN ADAMS, *Thoughts on Government.*

4
I consider biennial elections as a security that the sober, second thought of the people shall be law.
FISHER AMES, Speech, Jan., 1788.

5
While it may not be possible to draw Congressional districts with mathematical precision, that is no excuse for ignoring our Constitution's plain objective of making equal representation for equal numbers of people the fundamental goal for the House of Representatives.
HUGO L. BLACK, Majority Opinion in Wesberry v. Sanders, U.S. Supreme Court, 17 Feb., 1964. According to this historic decision, the Constitution requires that Congressional districts within each state be substantially equal in population. The court in this case found the existing apportionment of Congressional districts in Georgia unfair to city voters. The case climaxed a growing controversy over alleged discrimination against urban areas in the apportionment of seats in the national and state legislatures.

One man, one vote.
UNKNOWN. A popular paraphrase of Justice Hugo L. Black's opinion in Wesberry v. Sanders, "equal representation for equal numbers," and of the 1964 Supreme Court ruling that both houses of state legislatures be apportioned on the basis of population only.

6
Your every voter, as surely as your chief magistrate, under the same high sanction, though in a different sphere, exercises a public trust.
GROVER CLEVELAND, Inaugural Address, 4 Mar., 1885.

7
A vote on th' tallysheet is worth two in the box.
FINLEY PETER DUNNE, *Mr. Dooley's Philosophy.*

8
A straw vote only shows which way the hot air blows.
O. HENRY. (*New American Literature,* p. 170)

9
The freeman casting, with unpurchased hand,
The vote that shakes the turrets of the land.
OLIVER WENDELL HOLMES, *Poetry, A Metrical Essay,* l. 83.

10
This right to vote is the basic right without which all others are meaningless. It gives people—people as individuals—control over their own destinies.
LYNDON B. JOHNSON, Speech, in 1957, in support of the voting-rights bill of that year. He was then Senate majority leader.

11
There no longer can be anyone too poor to vote.
LYNDON B. JOHNSON, upon signing the twenty-fourth amendment to the Constitution, 4 Feb., 1964. The amendment, officially certified on that date, bans the poll tax in federal elections.

12
We preach the virtues of democracy abroad. We must practice its duties here at home. Voting is the first duty of democracy.
LYNDON B. JOHNSON, Address in Washington, D. C., 11 Aug., 1964, urging voter registration for the presidential election of that year.

13
The mandate of November's election must be by vote of the people—not by default of the people.
LYNDON B. JOHNSON, Address in Washington, D.C., 11 Aug., 1964, urging voter registration.

14
We cannot have government for all the people until we first make certain it is government of and by all the people.
LYNDON B. JOHNSON, Message to Congress, 15 Mar., 1965. This was a call for new and broad legislation to guarantee voting rights in all elections—specifically, to strike down existing bars to Negro voting.

15
We have been awakened to justice by the sound of songs and sermons, speeches and peaceful demonstrations. But the noiseless,

secret vote will thunder forth a hundred times more loudly.

> LYNDON B. JOHNSON, Public Statement, 10 July, 1965, congratulating the House of Representatives on its passage of the voting-rights bill of that year.

1

The vote is the most powerful instrument ever devised by man for breaking down injustice and destroying the terrible walls which imprison men because they are different from other men.

> LYNDON B. JOHNSON, Address, 6 Aug., 1965, upon signing the voting-rights bill of 1965.

2

Among free men there can be no successful appeal from the ballot to the bullet.

> ABRAHAM LINCOLN. (E. J. YOUNG, The Lesson of the Hour; Magazine of History, No. 43)

3

I go for all sharing the privileges of the government who assist in bearing its burdens. Consequently I go for admitting all whites to the right of suffrage who pay taxes or bear arms, by no means excluding females.

> ABRAHAM LINCOLN, Letter, 1836.

4

In ordinary circumstances voters cannot be expected to transcend their particular, localized and self-regarding opinions. As well expect men laboring in the valley to see the land as from a mountain top. In their circumstances, which as private persons they cannot readily surmount, the voters are most likely to suppose that whatever seems obviously good to them must be good for the country, and good in the sight of God.

> WALTER LIPPMANN, The Public Philosophy, bk. i, ch. 4.

5

The Gallup polls are reports of what people are thinking. But that a plurality of the people sampled in the poll think one way has no bearing upon whether it is sound public policy. . . . It is, rather, the beginning of the argument. In that argument their opinions need to be confronted by the views of the executive, defending and promoting the public interest. In the accommodation reached between the two views lies practical public policy.

> WALTER LIPPMANN, The Public Philosophy, bk. i, ch. 4.

6

"Vote early and vote often," the advice openly displayed on the election banners in one of our northern cities.

> W. P. MILES, of South Carolina, Speech in the U.S. House of Representatives, 31 Mar., 1858.

7

They have such refined and delicate palates
That they can discover no one worthy of their ballots,
And then when someone terrible gets elected
They say, There, that's just what I expected!

> OGDEN NASH, Election Day Is a Holiday.

8

A weapon that comes down as still
As snowflakes fall upon the sod;
But executes a freeman's will,
As lightning does the will of God;
And from its force, nor doors nor locks
Can shield you; 'tis the ballot-box.

> JOHN PIERPONT, A Word from a Petitioner.

9

The secret ballot in America is the most sacred heritage which we have and that I have stood by. Even my wife doesn't know how I voted.

> NELSON A. ROCKEFELLER, Reply to a reporter who asked how Rockefeller had voted in the 1964 presidential election, shortly after the balloting. Before the nomination of the Republican candidate in that election, Barry M. Goldwater, Rockefeller had bitterly opposed Goldwater.

10

More men have been elected between Sundown and Sunup, than ever were elected between Sunup and Sundown.

> WILL ROGERS, The Illiterate Digest, p. 152.

11

All forward-looking minds know that, sooner or later, the chief public question in this country will be woman's claim to the ballot.

> THEODORE TILTON. (Independent, 18 Jan., 1866)

12

As long as I count the votes, what are you going to do about it?

> WILLIAM MARCY TWEED, of elections in New York City, Nov., 1871.

13

Your telegram received. I would feel deeply mortified to have you or anyone like you vote for me. Since you have access to many disloyal citizens and I have not, I will ask you to convey this message to them.

> WOODROW WILSON, Reply to a telegram from Jeremiah O'Leary, in the campaign of 1916, threatening Wilson with the loss of votes of those sympathetic to the German cause.

14

Slavery is but half abolished, emancipation is but half completed, while millions of freemen with votes in their hands are left without education.

> ROBERT C. WINTHROP, Yorktown Oration.

W

WALKING

1

The palms of your hands will thicken,
  The skin of your cheek will tan,
You'll go ragged and weary and swarthy,
  But you'll walk like a man!
    HAMLIN GARLAND, *Do You Fear the Wind?*

2

I'd rather see a sermon than hear one any
    day;
I'd rather one should walk with me than
    merely tell the way.
    EDGAR A. GUEST, *Sermons We See.*

3

Walking is the best possible exercise. Habituate yourself to walk very far. The Europeans value themselves on having subdued the horse to the uses of man; but I doubt whether we have not lost more than we have gained, by the use of this animal.
    THOMAS JEFFERSON, *Writings*, vol. v, p. 84.

4

Here where the wind is always north-north-east
And children learn to walk on frozen toes.
    EDWIN ARLINGTON ROBINSON, *New England.*

5

Every walk is a sort of crusade, preached by some Peter the Hermit in us, to go forth and reconquer this Holy Land from the hands of the Infidels.
    HENRY D. THOREAU, *Walking.* Here he explains the fanciful derivation of "saunter" from *à la Sainte Terre.*

6

Take a two-mile walk every morning before breakfast.
    HARRY S TRUMAN, Advice, on how to reach the age of eighty. This was part of a prescription for long life, given by him on his eightieth birthday, 5 May, 1964.

7

The age is dull and mean. Men creep,
Not walk.
    JOHN GREENLEAF WHITTIER, *Lines Inscribed to Friends under Arrest for Treason Against the Slave Power.*

WANDERLUST

See also Travel, Vagabond

8

The ships are lying in the bay,
  The gulls are swinging round their spars;
My soul as eagerly as they
  Desires the margin of the stars.
    ZOË AKINS, *The Wanderer.*

9

Again let us dream where the land lies sunny
And live, like the bees, on our hearts' old honey.
Away from the world that slaves for money—
  Come, journey the way with me.
    MADISON CAWEIN, *Song of the Road.*

10

I am fretful with the bay,
For the wander-thirst is on me
And my soul is in Cathay.
    RICHARD HOVEY, *The Sea Gypsy.*

11

Drop anchor anywhere and the anchor will drag—that is, if your soul is a limitless, fathomless sea, and not a dogpound.
    ELBERT HUBBARD, *Epigrams.*

12

Upon the road to Romany
  It 's stay, friend, stay!
There 's lots o' love and lots o' time
  To linger on the way;
Poppies for the twilight,
  Roses for the noon,
It 's happy goes as lucky goes,
  To Romany in June.
    WALLACE IRWIN, *From Romany to Rome.*

13

I'm the ramblin' son with the nervous feet
That never was made for a steady beat.
I had many a job—for a little while;
I've been on the bum, and I've lived in style,
But there was the road windin' mile after mile,
  And nothing to do but go.
    H. H. KNIBBS, *Nothing to Do But Go.*

14

It's little I know what's in my heart,
What's in my mind it's little I know,
But there's that in me must up and start,
And it's little I care where my feet go.
    EDNA ST. VINCENT MILLAY, *Departure.*

15

Better sit still where born, I say,
  Wed one sweet woman and love her well,
Love and be loved in the old East way,
  Drink sweet waters, and dream in a spell,
Than to wander in search of the Blessed Isles,
And to sail the thousands of watery miles
In search of love, and find you at last
On the edge of the world, and a curs'd outcast.
    JOAQUIN MILLER, *Pace Implora.*

16

When I was very young and the urge to be someplace else was on me, I was assured by mature people that maturity would cure this itch. When years described me as mature, the remedy prescribed was middle age. In middle age I was assured that greater age would calm my fever, and now that I am fifty-eight perhaps senility will do the job.

JOHN STEINBECK, *Travels with Charley.*

1

I looked in his eyes and I read the news;
His heart was having the railroad blues.
Oh, the railroad blues will cost you dear,
Keeps you moving on for something that you
    don't see here.

RIDGELY TORRENCE, *Eye-Witness.*

2

So let the way wind up the hill or down,
O'er rough or smooth, the journey will be
    joy,
Still seeking what I sought when but a boy.

HENRY VAN DYKE, *Three Best Things.*

3

Afoot and light-hearted I take to the open
    road,
Healthy, free, the world before me,
The long brown path before me leading
    wherever I choose.
Henceforth I ask not good-fortune, I myself
    am good-fortune,
Henceforth I whimper no more, postpone no
    more, need nothing,
Done with indoor complaints, libraries, quer-
    ulous criticisms,
Strong and content I travel the open road.

WALT WHITMAN, *Song of the Open Road.*

WANT, WANTS

4

"Man wants but little here below
    Nor wants that little long,"
'Tis not with me exactly so;
    But 'tis so in the song.

My wants are many, and, if told,
    Would muster many a score;
And were each wish a mint of gold,
    I still should long for more.

JOHN QUINCY ADAMS, *The Wants of Man.*
The quoted lines are from Goldsmith's
Vicar of Wakefield.

5

Much wanting makes many a maid a wanton.

MAXWELL ANDERSON, *Elizabeth the Queen,*
act 1.

6

I want what I want when I want it.

HENRY BLOSSOM, Title and refrain of song
from the musical play Mlle. Modiste
(1905).

7

Men called the doctor's son the Great Dis-
senter. The title was misleading. *To want
something fiercely and want it all the time—*
this is not dissent but affirmation. The things

Holmes wanted were great things, never to
be realized.

CATHERINE DRINKER BOWEN, *Yankee
from Olympus,* p. 419. Referring to Justice Oliver Wendell Holmes.

8

Want is a growing giant whom the coat of
Have was never large enough to cover.

EMERSON, *Conduct of Life: Wealth.*

9

If a man could have half his wishes he would
double his Troubles.

BENJAMIN FRANKLIN, *Poor Richard,*
1752.

10

What a woman wants is what you're out of.

O. HENRY, *Heart of the West: Cupid à la
Carte.*

11

Little I ask; my wants are few;
    I only wish a hut of stone,
(A *very plain* brown stone will do,)
    That I may call my own;—
And close at hand is such a one,
In yonder street that fronts the sun.

OLIVER WENDELL HOLMES, *Contentment,*
st. 1.

12

I care not much for gold or land;—
    Give me a mortgage here and there,—
Some good bank-stock, some note of hand,
    Or trifling railroad share,—
I only ask that Fortune send
A *little* more than I shall spend.

OLIVER WENDELL HOLMES, *Contentment,*
st. 3.

13

Man wants but little drink below,
But wants that little strong.

OLIVER WENDELL HOLMES, *A Song of Other Days.*

14

A rational man acting in the real world may
be defined as one who decides where he will
strike a balance between what he desires and
what can be done. It is only in imaginary
worlds that we can do whatever we wish. In
the real world there are always equations
which have to be adjusted between the possible and the desired.

WALTER LIPPMANN, *The Public Philosophy,* bk. i, ch. 4.

15

The things that I can't have I want,
    And what I have seems second-rate,
The things I want to do I can't,
    And what I have to do I hate.

DON MARQUIS, *Frustration.*

16

Waste not, want not is a law of nature.

JOHN PLATT, *Economy,* p. 22.

17

I'd rather be handsome than homely;
    I'd rather be youthful than old;
If I can't have a bushel of silver

I'll do with a barrel of gold.
JAMES JEFFREY ROCHE, *Contentment.*

1
There are two things to aim at in life: first, to get what you want, and, after that, to enjoy it. Only the wisest of mankind achieve the second.
LOGAN PEARSALL SMITH, *Afterthoughts.*

WAR

See also America: Famous Historical Sayings; Peace; Preparedness; Soldier; Victory

2
Every modern war, however fortunate its outcome for us, has changed the world by subtracting from it abidingly. Every modern war has had to represent, in order to be won, a temporary abdication of ethical and humane standards. Every modern war has, in other words, demanded a certain retreat even of its victors and meant that they have lost in the very process of winning.
JOHN MASON BROWN, *Seeing Things; The Saturday Review,* 12 Aug., 1950.

3
To be at war openly and to the full is one thing; to be at peace, real peace, another. To be at both is disquieting (to put it mildly) if for. no other reason than that it is confusing.
JOHN MASON BROWN, *Seeing Things; The Saturday Review,* 12 Aug., 1950. This was written shortly after the outbreak of hostilities in Korea, and refers to the limited nature of the war.

4
If democracy loses its touch, then no great war will be needed to overwhelm it. If it keeps and enhances its strength, no great war need come again.
VANNEVAR BUSH, *Modern Arms and Free Men.*

5
War will never yield but to the principles of universal justice and love, and these have no sure root but in the religion of Jesus Christ.
WILLIAM ELLERY CHANNING THE ELDER, Lecture on war.

6
Mother whose heart hung humble as a button
On the bright splendid shroud of your son,
Do not weep.
War is kind.
STEPHEN CRANE, *War Is Kind.*

7
For justice guides the warrior's steel,
And vengeance strikes the blow.
JOSEPH RODMAN DRAKE, *To the Defenders of New Orleans.*

8
Local defense must be reinforced by the further deterrent of massive retaliatory power.
JOHN FOSTER DULLES, Speech to the Council of Foreign Relations, 12 Jan., 1954. In the Apr., 1954 issue of *Foreign Affairs* and in subsequent speeches, Dulles elaborated on this policy of "massive retaliation" (a much quoted phrase) as a means of deterring aggressors.

One of the great advances of our time is recognition that one of the ways to prevent war is to deter it by having the will and the capacity to use force to punish the aggressor.
JOHN FOSTER DULLES, Address at Williams College, Williamstown, Mass., 6 Oct., 1956.

9
As long as there are sovereign nations possessing great power, war is inevitable.
ALBERT EINSTEIN. (*Einstein on the Atomic Bomb; The Atlantic Monthly,* Nov., 1945)

10
I do not believe that civilization will be wiped out in a war fought with the atomic bomb. Perhaps two thirds of the people of the earth might be killed, but enough men capable of thinking, and enough books, would be left to start again, and civilization could be restored.
ALBERT EINSTEIN. (*Einstein on the Atomic Bomb; The Atlantic Monthly,* Nov., 1945)

11
I feel impelled to speak today in a language that in a sense is new—one which I, who have spent so much of my life in the military profession, would have preferred never to use. That new language is the language of atomic warfare.
DWIGHT D. EISENHOWER, Address to the United Nations General Assembly, 8 Dec., 1953.

12
We must use our skills and knowledge and, at times, our substance, to help others rise from misery, however far the scene of suffering may be from our shores. For wherever in the world a people knows desperate want, there must appear at least the spark of hope. the hope of progress—or there will surely rise at last the flames of conflict.
DWIGHT D. EISENHOWER, Second Inaugural Address, 21 Jan., 1957.

13
War gratifies, or used to gratify, the combative instinct of mankind, but it gratifies also the love of plunder, destruction, cruel discipline, and arbitrary power.
CHARLES W. ELIOT, *Five American Contributions to Civilization.*

1

But the real and lasting victories are those of
peace, and not of war.
> EMERSON, *Conduct of Life: Worship.*

2

By the rude bridge that arched the flood,
  Their flag to April's breeze unfurled,
Here once the embattled farmers stood,
  And fired the shot heard round the world.
> EMERSON, *Hymn: Sung at the Completion
> of the Concord Monument, April 19,
> 1836.*

3

The cannon will not suffer any other sound
to be heard for miles and for years around
it.
> EMERSON, *Journals,* 1864.

4

War, to sane men at the present day, begins
to look like an epidemic insanity, breaking
out here and there like the cholera or influ-
enza, infecting men's brains instead of their
bowels.
> EMERSON, *Miscellanies: War.*

5

War educates the senses, calls into action the
will, perfects the physical constitution,
brings men into such swift and close collision
in critical moments that man measures man.
> EMERSON, *Miscellanies: War.*

6

We're ready for a fight or a frolic.
> REAR ADMIRAL ROBLEY D. EVANS, Re-
> mark, 16 Dec., 1907, as the fleet under
> his command began a cruise around the
> world, with the purpose of impressing
> Japan.

7

There never was a good war or a bad peace.
> BENJAMIN FRANKLIN, Letter to Josiah
> Quincy, 11 Sept., 1773.

8

Nothing is harder, in the midst of war, than
to look beyond the immediate struggle to the
problems and hopes of the long future.
> MAX FREEDMAN, Syndicated Column, 25
> May, 1965.

9

A dangerous exercise in complete and total
futility.
> BARRY M. GOLDWATER, Speech at the
> Wings Club, New York City, 12 Nov.,
> 1962. Referring to disarmament.

10

The atomic bomb is not an inhuman weapon.
I think our best answer to anyone who
doubts this is that we did not start the war,
and if they don't like the way we ended it, to
remember who started it.
> MAJOR GENERAL LESLIE R. GROVES, of the
> Manhattan Project, Public Statement,
> Aug., 1945.

11

Hit hard, hit fast, and hit often.
> ADMIRAL WILLIAM F. (BULL) HALSEY,
> Motto.

12

Even to observe neutrality you must have a
strong government.
> ALEXANDER HAMILTON, Address in the
> Constitutional Convention, 29 June,
> 1787.

13

Hark! I hear the tramp of thousands,
  And of armèd men the hum;
Lo! a nation's hosts have gathered
  Round the quick alarming drum,—
Saying, "Come, Freemen, come!
Ere your heritage be wasted," said the quick
  alarming drum.
> BRET HARTE, *Reveillé,* st. 1.

14

Let the only walls the foe shall scale
  Be ramparts of the dead.
> PAUL HAMILTON HAYNE, *Vicksburg.*

15

The battle, sir, is not to the strong alone; it
is to the vigilant, the active, the brave.
> PATRICK HENRY, Speech to the Virginia
> convention of delegates to the Continen-
> tal Congress, 23 Mar., 1775.

16

The life of humanity upon this planet may
yet come to an end, and a very terrible end.
But I would have you notice that this end is
threatened in our time not by anything that
the universe may do to us, but only by what
man may do to himself.
> JOHN HAYNES HOLMES, *The Sensible
> Man's View of Religion.*

17

Older men declare war. But it is youth that
must fight and die.
> HERBERT HOOVER, Speech at the Republi-
> can national convention, Chicago, 27
> June, 1944.

18

An association of men who will not quarrel
with one another is a thing which never yet
existed, from the greatest confederacy of nations down to a town-meeting or a vestry.
> THOMAS JEFFERSON, Letter to John Tay-
> lor, 1798.

19

Their seducers have wished war . . . for the
loaves and fishes which arise out of war ex-
penses.
> THOMAS JEFFERSON, *Writings,* vol. iv, p.
> 300. A paraphrase of *John,* vi, 26.

20

Establish the eternal truth that acquiescence
under insult is not the way to escape war.
> THOMAS JEFFERSON, *Writings,* vol. ix, p.
> 308.

21

You have not been mistaken in supposing
my views and feelings to be in favor of the
abolition of war. . . . I hope it is practicable, by improving the mind and morals of

society, to lessen the disposition to war; but of its abolition I despair.

> THOMAS JEFFERSON, *Writings*, vol. xviii, p. 298.

1

We must meet our duty and convince the world that we are just friends and brave enemies.

> THOMAS JEFFERSON, *Writings*, vol. xix, p. 156. Referring to preparedness.

2

The first casualty when war comes is truth.

> HIRAM JOHNSON, Speech in U.S. Senate.

3

Once upon a time even large-scale wars could be waged without risking the end of civilization. But what was once upon a time is no longer so, because general war is impossible.

> LYNDON B. JOHNSON, Address in Washington, D.C., 24 Mar., 1964.

4

Make no mistake. There is no such thing as a conventional nuclear weapon.

> LYNDON B. JOHNSON, Speech in Detroit, 7 Sept., 1964.

5

The world remembers—the world must never forget—that aggression unchallenged is aggression unleashed.

> LYNDON B. JOHNSON, Speech in Syracuse, N.Y., 5 Aug., 1964.

6

Get the bombs on the targets.

> GENERAL CURTIS E. LeMAY, his definition of his job as a ranking Air Force officer during World War II.

7

Military glory—that attractive rainbow that rises in showers of blood, that serpent's eye that charms to destroy.

> ABRAHAM LINCOLN, Speech against the war with Mexico, U.S. House of Representatives, 12 Jan., 1848.

8

It is more important to know that we are on God's side.

> ABRAHAM LINCOLN, Reply to a delegation of Southerners during the Civil War, after their spokesman had remarked, "We trust, sir, that God is on our side."

9

Ez fer war, I call it murder,—
  There you hev it plain an' flat;
I don't want to go no furder
  Than my Testyment fer that;
God hez sed so plump an' fairly,
  It 's ez long ez it is broad,
An' you've gut to git up airly
  Ef you want to take in God.

> JAMES RUSSELL LOWELL, *The Biglow Papers,* Ser. i, No. 1.

10

We kind o' thought Christ went agin war an' pillage.

> JAMES RUSSELL LOWELL, *The Biglow Papers,* Ser. i, No. 3.

11

Not but wut abstract war is horrid,
  I sign to thet with all my heart,—
But civilysation *doos* git forrid
  Sometimes upon a powder-cart.

> JAMES RUSSELL LOWELL, *The Biglow Papers*, Ser. i, No. 7.

12

War's very object is victory, not prolonged indecision. In war there is no substitute for victory.

> GENERAL DOUGLAS MACARTHUR, Address to a joint session of Congress, 19 Apr., 1951, following his dismissal as commander of United Nations forces in Korea.

13

Nuclear war is not an acceptable instrument of national policy.

> JOHN J. McCLOY, Public Statement, as chairman of the General Advisory Committee on Disarmament, Jan., 1964.

14

Look at an infantryman's eyes and you can tell how much war he has seen.

> BILL MAULDIN, *Up Front.*

15

I suppose one of the fringe benefits of getting through an old-fashioned war is the opportunity to read about it later and find out what really did happen.

> BILL MAULDIN, *Book Week;* New York *Herald Tribune*, 12 Apr., 1964, p. 3.

16

War is the only sport that is genuinely amusing. And it is the only sport that has any intelligible use.

> H. L. MENCKEN, *Prejudices*, ser. v, p. 28.

17

When the guns boom, the arts die and this law of life is far stronger than any law man may devise.

> ARTHUR MILLER, Telegram to the White House, 25 Sept., 1965, rejecting an invitation to witness the signing of the Arts and Humanities Act of that year by President Lyndon B. Johnson. His refusal was in protest to U.S. military action in Vietnam at that time.

18

Invincible in peace and invisible in war.

> E. F. NOYES, referring to James G. Blaine, Simon Cameron, and Roscoe Conkling, during Rutherford B. Hayes's campaign for the presidency. (NEVINS, *Grover Cleveland,* p. 176)

19

In planning any operation, it is vital to remember, and constantly repeat to oneself, two things: "In war nothing is impossible, provided you use audacity," and "Do not take counsel of your fears." If these two principles are adhered to, with American troops victory is certain.

> GENERAL GEORGE S. PATTON, JR., *War As I Knew It.*

1

Stand! the ground's your own, my braves!
Will ye give it up to slaves?
JOHN PIERPONT, *Warren's Address.*

2

Leaden rain and iron hail
Let their welcome be!
JOHN PIERPONT, *Warren's Address.*

3

From the Rio Grande's waters to the icy
    lakes of Maine,
Let all exult, for we have met the enemy
    again.
Beneath their stern old mountains we have
    met them in their pride,
And rolled from Buena Vista back the bat-
    tle's bloody tide.
GENERAL ALBERT PIKE, *Battle of Buena
    Vista.*

4

Lies are the stuff from which armies built
morale.
DANIEL V. POLING.

5

The bird of war is not the eagle but the
stork.
CHARLES FRANCIS POTTER, at a Senate
    hearing on a proposed birth-control bill,
    1931.

6

The terrible rumble, grumble and roar
Telling the battle was on once more—
    And Sheridan twenty miles away!
THOMAS BUCHANAN READ, *Sheridan's
    Ride.*

7

The first casualty in every shooting war is
common sense, and the second is free and
open discussion.
JAMES RESTON, Washington Column, New
    York *Times,* 12 Feb., 1965.

8

I have seen war. I hate war.
FRANKLIN D. ROOSEVELT, Speech, 14 Aug.,
    1936.

9

War is a contagion.
FRANKLIN D. ROOSEVELT, Speech in Chi-
    cago, 5 Oct., 1937.

10

A really great people, proud and high-spirit-
ed, would face all the disasters of war rather
than purchase that base prosperity which is
bought at the price of national honor.
THEODORE ROOSEVELT, Speech at Harvard
    University, 23 Feb., 1907.

11

Dictatorship underestimates democracy's
willingness to do what it has to do.
DEAN RUSK, on resistance to aggression.
    (HENRY F. GRAFF, *How Johnson Makes
    Foreign Policy; New York Times Mag-
    azine,* 4 July, 1965, p. 16)

12

We shall not find it possible to learn from

World War III because there would not be
enough left.
DEAN RUSK, Address to American Legion
    convention, Portland, Ore., 24 Aug.,
    1965.

13

There is many a boy here today who looks
on war as all glory, but, boys, it is all hell.
You can bear this warning voice to generations yet to come. I look upon war with
horror.
WILLIAM T. SHERMAN, Address to a
    G.A.R. convention, Columbus, Ohio, 11
    Aug., 1880. This extempore speech is al-
    most surely the basis of the epigram
    "War is hell," which Sherman could not
    remember having uttered in precisely
    that form. Some sources attribute the
    epigram to Sherman on the not very
    convincing evidence supplied by those
    who claim to have heard him say it in
    the course of other speeches. Another
    version of the epigram is: "War is hell
    when you're getting licked."

14

You cannot qualify war in harsher terms
than I will. War is cruelty, and you cannot
refine it.
WILLIAM T. SHERMAN, *Memoirs,* ii, 126.

15

Man's tragedy has all too often been that he
has grown weary in the search for an honorable alternative to war, and, in desperate impatience, has turned to violence.
ADLAI E. STEVENSON, Speech in Ham-
    tramck, Mich., 1952.

16

War under modern conditions is bereft of
even that dubious logic it may have had in
the past.
ADLAI E. STEVENSON, *The Hard Kind of
    Patriotism; Harper's Magazine,* July,
    1963.

17

This Korean War is a Truman war.
ROBERT A. TAFT, Speech in Milwaukee, 9
    June, 1951.

18

We have spent two billion dollars on the
greatest scientific gamble in history—and
won.
HARRY S TRUMAN, Public Statement, on
    the first use of the atomic bomb, 6 Aug.,
    1945.

19

Three Nations of French Indians had taken
up the hatchet.
GEORGE WASHINGTON, *Journal,* vol. i, p.
    21.

20

Away with themes of war! Away with war
    itself!
Hence from my shuddering sight to never

more return that show of blacken'd, mutilated corpses!

That hell unpent and raid of blood, fit for wild tigers or for lop-tongued wolves, not reasoning men.

WALT WHITMAN, *Song of the Exposition,* pt. 7.

1

Peace hath higher tests of manhood
    Than battle ever knew.

JOHN GREENLEAF WHITTIER, *The Hero,* st. 19.

2

War is a natural phenomenon at deeper than political or nationalistic levels. The aggressive instinct has been of value and can still be educable for man's service. Civilization in itself is a long hard *fight* to maintain and advance.

THORNTON WILDER. (FLORA LEWIS, *Thornton Wilder at 65; New York Times Magazine,* 15 Apr., 1962, p. 28)

3

Militarism does not consist in the existence of any army, nor even in the existence of a very great army. Militarism is a spirit. It is a point of view. It is a system. It is a purpose. The purpose of militarism is to use armies for aggression.

WOODROW WILSON, Speech at West Point, 13 June, 1916.

4

It is not an army that we must train for war; it is a nation.

WOODROW WILSON, Speech, 12 May, 1917.

5

Mr. Madison's War.

UNKNOWN, referring to President James Madison and the War of 1812.

WASHINGTON, GEORGE

6

These are high times when a British general is to take counsel of a Virginia buckskin.

GENERAL EDWARD BRADDOCK, Comment in 1755, upon rejecting advice from Washington.

7

        Washington,
Whose every battle-field is holy ground,
Which breathes of nations saved, not worlds undone.

BYRON, *Don Juan,* canto viii, st. 5.

8

Where may the wearied eye repose
    When gazing on the great;
Where neither guilty glory glows,
    Nor despicable state?
Yes—one—the first—the last—the best—
The Cincinnatus of the West,
    Whom envy dared not hate,
Bequeathed the name of Washington,

To make man blush there was but one!

BYRON, *Ode to Napoleon Bonaparte,* st. 19.

9

No gilded dome swells from the lowly roof to catch the morning or evening beam; but the love and gratitude of united America settle upon it in one eternal sunshine. While it stands, the latest generations of the grateful children of America will make this pilgrimage to it as to a shrine; and when it shall fall, if fall it must, the memory and the name of Washington shall shed an eternal glory on the spot.

EDWARD EVERETT, *Oration on the Character of Washington.* Referring to Mount Vernon.

10

The character, the counsels, and example of our Washington . . . will guide us through the doubts and difficulties that beset us; they will guide our children and our children's children in the paths of prosperity and peace, while America shall hold her place in the family of nations.

EDWARD EVERETT, *Speech: Washington Abroad and at Home,* 5 July, 1858.

11

Here you would know, and enjoy, what posterity will say of Washington. For a thousand leagues have nearly the same effect with a thousand years.

BENJAMIN FRANKLIN, Letter to Washington, 5 Mar,, 1780, during Franklin's stay in France.

12

He comes!—the Genius of these lands—
Fame's thousand tongues his worth confess,
Who conquered with his suffering bands,
    And grew immortal by distress.

PHILIP FRENEAU, *Occasioned by General Washington's Arrival at Philadelphia.*

13

It was not very long before I discovered that he was neither remarkable for delicacy or good temper.

ALEXANDER HAMILTON, Letter to Philip Schuyler, 18 Feb., 1781.

14

If virtue can secure happiness in another world, he is happy.

ALEXANDER HAMILTON, Letter to Tobias Lear, 2 Jan., 1800.

15

He errs as other men do, but errs with integrity.

THOMAS JEFFERSON, Letter to W. B. Giles, 1795.

16

His character was, in its mass, perfect.

THOMAS JEFFERSON, Letter to Dr. Walter Jones, 2 Jan., 1814.

1

His mind was great and powerful, without being of the very first order, . . . and as far as he saw, no judgment was ever sounder. . . . He was incapable of fear, meeting personal dangers with the calmest unconcern. His integrity was most pure, his justice the most inflexible I have ever known. . . . He was, indeed, in every sense of the words, a wise, a good, and a great man.

> THOMAS JEFFERSON, Letter to Dr. Walter Jones, 2 Jan., 1814.

2

It may truly be said that never did nature and fortune combine more perfectly to make a man great, and to place him in the same constellation with whatever worthies have merited from men an everlasting remembrance.

> THOMAS JEFFERSON, Letter to Dr. Walter Jones, 2 Jan., 1814.

3

Few men lived whose opinions were more unbiased and correct. Not that it is pretended he never felt bias. His passions were naturally strong, but his reason, generally, stronger. . . . He possessed the love, veneration, and confidence of all.

> THOMAS JEFFERSON, *The Anas*, 4 Feb., 1818.

4

Were an energetic and judicious system to be proposed with your signature it would be a circumstance highly honorable to your fame . . . and doubly entitle you to the glorious republican epithet, The Father of your Country.

> HENRY KNOX, Letter to Washington, 19 Mar., 1787. But the phrase "Father of His Country" was probably first applied to Washington on a German calendar— as *Des Landes Vater*—which was published in 1779 in Lancaster, Pa., by the printer Francis Baily.

The Father of his Country—We celebrate Washington!

> UNKNOWN, Editorial, *Pennsylvania Packet*, 9 July, 1789.

5

A citizen, first in war, first in peace, and first in the hearts of his countrymen.

> COLONEL HENRY (LIGHT-HORSE HARRY) LEE, Resolution, adopted by Congress on the death of Washington, 19 Dec., 1799. John Marshall, who introduced the resolution in the House of Representatives, is sometimes wrongly credited for these words. In his *Life of Washington* (vol. v, p. 765), Marshall misquotes the resolution, in part, as "first in the hearts of his fellow citizens."

6

Washington is the mightiest name on earth

—long since mightiest in the cause of civil liberty, still mightiest in moral reformation. On that name no eulogy is expected. It cannot be. To add brightness to the sun or glory to the name of Washington is alike impossible. Let none attempt it. In solemn awe pronounce the name, and in its naked deathless splendor leave it shining on.

> ABRAHAM LINCOLN, Address in Springfield, Ill., 22 Feb., 1842.

7

Firmly erect, he towered above them all,
The incarnate discipline that was to free
With iron curb that armed democracy.

> JAMES RUSSELL LOWELL, *Under the Old Elm*, pt. iii, sec. 1.

8

Soldier and statesman, rarest unison.

> JAMES RUSSELL LOWELL, *Under the Old Elm*, pt. v, sec. 3.

9

Oh, Washington! thou hero, patriot sage,
Friend of all climes, and pride of every age!

> THOMAS PAINE, *Washington*.

10

Sit down, Mr. Washington; your modesty is equal to your valor, and that surpasses the power of any language that I possess.

> JOHN ROBINSON, Speaker of the Virginia House of Burgesses, to Washington in 1759, when the latter sought to reply to the thanks of that assembly but was unable to say a word.

11

The prevailin' weakness of most public men is to Slop Over! . . . G. Washington never slopt over.

> ARTEMUS WARD, *Fourth of July Oration*.

12

As to pay, sir, I beg leave to assure the Congress that as no pecuniary consideration could have tempted me to accept this arduous employment at the expense of my domestic ease and happiness, I do not wish to make any profit from it.

> GEORGE WASHINGTON, Statement to Congress on his appointment as Commander-in-Chief, 16 June, 1775.

13

Washington is in the clear upper sky.

> DANIEL WEBSTER, Eulogy on Adams and Jefferson, 2 Aug., 1826.

14

"George," said his father, "do you know who killed that beautiful little cherry tree yonder in the garden?" . . . Looking at his father with the sweet face of youth brightened with the inexpressible charm of all-conquering truth, he bravely cried out, "I can't tell a lie, Pa; you know I can't tell a lie. I did cut it with my hatchet."

> MASON LOCKE WEEMS, *The Life and Memorable Actions of George Washington*, ch. 1. Often quoted, "with my little

hatchet." Though the story is not grounded in fact, it is deeply embedded in American tradition.

The crude commercialism of America, its materialising spirit . . . are entirely due to the country having adopted for its national hero a man who was incapable of telling a lie.

> OSCAR WILDE, *The Decay of Lying.*

WASHINGTON, D.C.

1
There are a number of things wrong with Washington. One of them is that everyone has been too long away from home.

> DWIGHT D. EISENHOWER, Statement at presidential press conference, 11 May, 1955.

2
Washington is a city of Southern efficiency and Northern charm.

> JOHN F. KENNEDY.

3
City of magnificent vistas.

> PIERRE CHARLES L'ENFANT, the architect-engineer who planned the city and began its building. Afterwards corrupted to "City of magnificent distances."

4
This city is at once the most gentle and brutal of the Western capitals. Its parks are now full of white and scarlet tulips, its trees clothed in the gentle green of spring, but its main industry is politics, and this is a savage business. Those who succeed here have almost more power than they can use, those who fail almost more regrets than they can bear.

> JAMES RESTON, Washington Column, New York *Times,* 6 May, 1964.

5
No matter what anybody says or thinks about Washington, it is us inescapably.

> JOEL SAYRE.

6
The tendency to make the capital a catch-all for a variety of monuments to honor the immortals, the not-so-immortals, the greats, the near-greats, and the not-so-greats must stop. We must be on our guard lest the nation's capital come to resemble an unplanned cemetery.

> HUGH SCOTT, commenting as U.S. Senator from Pennsylvania, 10 Sept., 1960.

7
First in war, first in peace, and last in the American League.

> UNKNOWN, a paraphrase of Colonel Henry Lee's tribute to George Washington, plus a comment on the low (at times) estate of baseball in the city.

WEALTH, see Riches
WEATHER

8
I was born with a chronic anxiety about the weather.

> JOHN BURROUGHS, *Is It Going to Rain?*

9
> All sorts of things and weather
> Must be taken in together,
> To make up a year
> And a Sphere.
>> EMERSON. *Fable, The Mountain and the Squirrel.*

10
> Oh, what a blamed uncertain thing
>> This pesky weather is!
> It blew and snew and then it thew
>> And now, by jing, it's friz!
>> PHILANDER JOHNSON, *Shooting Stars.*

11
This is Methodist weather—sprinkling. We Baptists prefer total immersion.

> ADAM CLAYTON POWELL, JR., Comment, before the start of a parade in Harlem, New York City, staged in honor of him, 19 Sept., 1964. (New York *Times,* 21 Sept., 1964)

12
> It hain't no use to grumble and complane,
>> It's jest as easy to rejoice;
> When God sorts out the weather and sends rain,
>> Why rain's my choice.
>> JAMES WHITCOMB RILEY, *Wet-Weather Talk.*

13
Weather is a literary specialty, and no untrained hand can turn out a good article on it.

> MARK TWAIN, *The American Claimant.*

14
There is a sumptuous variety about New England weather that compels the stranger's admiration—and regret. . . . In the Spring I have counted one hundred and thirty-six different kinds of weather inside of twenty-four hours.

> MARK TWAIN, *New England Weather:* speech at a dinner of the New England Society, New York City, 22 Dec., 1876.

The most serious charge which can be brought against New England is not Puritanism but February.

> JOSEPH WOOD KRUTCH, *The Twelve Seasons.*

15
Everybody talks about the weather, but nobody does anything about it.

> CHARLES DUDLEY WARNER, Editorial, Hartford *Courant* (c. 1890). This is often wrongly credited to Mark Twain.

I guess it's no use; they still believe Mark

Twain said it, despite all my assurances that it was Warner.
> CHARLES HOPKINS CLARK, editor of the Hartford *Courant*.

1
A sunshiny shower
Won't last half an hour.

Rain before seven,
Fair by eleven.

The South wind brings wet weather,
The North wind wet and cold together;
The West wind always brings us rain,
The East wind blows it back again.

March winds and April showers
Bring forth May flowers.

Rainbow at night is the sailor's delight;
Rainbow at morning, sailors, take warning.
> UNKNOWN, *Old Nursery Rhymes*.

WEEPING, see Tears
WELCOME, see Hospitality
WIFE
See also Husband, Marriage

2
I want (who does not want?) a wife,
 Affectionate and fair,
To solace all the woes of life,
 And all its joys to share;
Of temper sweet, of yielding will,
 Of firm yet placid mind,
With all my faults to love me still,
 With sentiment refin'd.
> JOHN QUINCY ADAMS, *Man Wants But Little*.

3
Earning a living for a wife, a fellow finds out, is one of the easier things about marriage. It takes only about eight hours a day. This leaves a man sixteen full hours for wife-waiting and other such essential chores as sleeping, shaving, eating, walking the dog and obeying his children.
> HAL BOYLE, Column, Associated Press, 16 June, 1964.

4
His wife not only edited his works but edited him.
> VAN WYCK BROOKS, *The Ordeal of Mark Twain*, ch. 5.

5
When singleness is bliss, it's folly to be wives.
> BILL COUNSELMAN, *Ella Cinders*.

6
I want a girl just like the girl that married dear old dad.
> WILLIAM DILLON, Title and refrain of song (1911), with music by Harry von Tilzer.

7
To Mamie, for never-failing help since 1916—in calm and in stress, in dark days and in bright.
> DWIGHT D. EISENHOWER, Inscription on a medallion presented to Mrs. Eisenhower, 25 Dec., 1955.

8
The luckiest thing that ever happened to me was the girl I married.
> DWIGHT D. EISENHOWER, Interview with Felix Belair, Jr., New York *Times*, 11 Oct., 1965.

9
Behind every man with pull is a woman with push.
> DEAN ROBERT H. FELIX, Address at a seminar of Metropolitan College, St. Louis University. (St. Louis *Post-Dispatch*, 23 Nov., 1965, p. 4-D)

10
Ill thrives that hapless family that shows
A cock that's silent, and a hen that crows:
I know not which live more unnatural lives,
Obeying husbands, or commanding wives.
> BENJAMIN FRANKLIN, *Poor Richard*, 1734.

11
He that takes a wife takes care.
> BENJAMIN FRANKLIN, *Poor Richard*, 1736.

12
A widow of doubtful age will marry almost any sort of a white man.
> HORACE GREELEY, Letter to Dr. Rufus Griswold.

13
Such a wife as I want . . . must be young, handsome (I lay most stress upon a good shape), sensible (a little learning will do), well bred, chaste, and tender. . . . As to religion a moderate stock will satisfy me. She must believe in God and hate a saint.
> ALEXANDER HAMILTON, Letter to John Laurens, Dec., 1779.

14
You can't appreciate home till you've left it, money till it's spent, your wife till she's joined a woman's club, nor Old Glory till you see it hanging on a broomstick on the shanty of a consul in a foreign town.
> O. HENRY, *Roads of Destiny*.

15
His wife "ruled the roast," and in governing the governor, governed the province, which might thus be said to be under petticoat government.
> WASHINGTON IRVING, *Knickerbocker's History of New York*, bk. iv, ch. 4.

16
I will try to be a balm, sustainer and sometimes critic for my husband; to help my children look at this job with all the reverence due it; to get from it the knowledge their unique vantage point gives them, and to retain the lightheartedness to which every

teen-ager is entitled. For my own self, my role must emerge in deeds, not words.

    CLAUDIA TAYLOR (MRS. LYNDON B.) JOHNSON, *Statement*, 7 Dec., 1963, the day on which the Johnsons moved into the White House.

1

I have learned that only two things are necessary to keep one's wife happy. First, let her think she's having her way. And second, let her have it.

    LYNDON B. JOHNSON, to Lord Snowdon of Great Britain at a White House reception for Princess Margaret and Snowdon (her husband), 17 Nov., 1965.

2

No angel she; she hath no budding wings;
  No mystic halo circles her bright hair;
But lo! the infinite grace of little things,
  Wrought for dear love's sake, makes her very fair.

    JAMES B. KENYON, *A Wife*.

3

For of all wise words of tongue or pen
The wisest are these: "Leave pants to men."

    SAMUEL E. KISER, *Maud Muller A-Wheel*.

4

Sail forth into the sea of life,
O gentle, loving, trusting wife,
And safe from all adversity
Upon the bosom of that sea
Thy comings and thy goings be!
For gentleness and love and trust
Prevail o'er angry wave and gust;
And in the wreck of noble lives
Something immortal still survives!

    HENRY WADSWORTH LONGFELLOW, *The Building of the Ship*, l. 368.

5

But thou dost make the very night itself
Brighter than day.

    HENRY WADSWORTH LONGFELLOW, *The Divine Tragedy: The First Passover*, pt. iii, l. 133.

6

And I'd rather be bride to a lad gone down
Than widow to one safe home.

    EDNA ST. VINCENT MILLAY, *Keen*.

7

A modernist married a fundamentalist wife,
And she led him a catechism and dogma life.

    KEITH PRESTON, *Marital Tragedy*.

8

Marilla W. Ricker has often told us that widows are divided into two classes—the bereaved and relieved. She forgot the deceived —the grass widows.

    VICTOR ROBINSON, *William Godwin; The Truth Seeker*, 6 Jan., 1906.

9

An ideal wife is any woman who has an ideal husband.

    BOOTH TARKINGTON, *Looking Forward*, p. 97.

10

My wife is one of the best wimin on this continent, altho' she isn't always gentle as a lamb, with mint sauce.

    ARTEMUS WARD, *A War Meeting*.

11

My wife's gone to the country,
  Hurrah! Hurrah!
She thought it best; I need a rest,
  That's why she went away.

    GEORGE WHITING AND IRVING BERLIN, *My Wife's Gone to the Country* (song, 1909).

12

The world well tried—the sweetest thing in life
Is the unclouded welcome of a wife.

    N. P. WILLIS, *The Lady Jane*, canto ii, st. 11.

WILL

13

A breath of will blows eternally though the universe of souls in the direction of the Right and Necessary.

    EMERSON, *Conduct of Life: Fate*.

14

Unless to Thought is added Will,
Apollo is an imbecile.

    EMERSON, *Fragments on the Poetic Gift*.

15

The education of the will is the object of our existence.

    EMERSON, *Society and Solitude: Courage*.

16

Peggy has a whim of iron.

    OLIVER HERFORD, referring to his wife—a remark prompted by one of her hats of which he strongly disapproved.

17

Nothing is troublesome that we do willingly.

    THOMAS JEFFERSON, *Writings*, vol. xvi, p. 111.

18

A tender heart; a will inflexible.

    HENRY WADSWORTH LONGFELLOW, *John Endicott*, act iii, sc. 2.

19

The star of the unconquered will,
  He rises in my breast,
Serene, and resolute, and still,
  And calm, and self-possessed.

    HENRY WADSWORTH LONGFELLOW, *The Light of Stars*, st. 7.

WIND

1

The wind
Sweeps the broad forest in its summer
    prime,
As when some master-hand exulting sweeps
The keys of some great organ.
    WILLIAM CULLEN BRYANT, *Among the
    Trees*, l. 63.

2

The faint old man shall lean his silver head
To feel thee; thou shalt kiss the child
    asleep.
    WILLIAM CULLEN BRYANT, *Evening Wind*,
    st. 4.

3

Where hast thou wandered, gentle gale, to
    find
The perfumes thou dost bring?
    WILLIAM CULLEN BRYANT, *May Evening*,
    st. 4.

4

Wind of the sunny south! oh, still delay
    In the gay woods and in the golden air,
    Like to a good old age released from care,
Journeying, in long serenity, away.
    WILLIAM CULLEN BRYANT, *October*, l. 5.

5

A breeze came wandering from the sky,
    Light as the whispers of a dream;
He put the o'erhanging grasses by,
    And softly stooped to kiss the stream,
The pretty stream, the flattered stream,
The shy, yet unreluctant stream.
    WILLIAM CULLEN BRYANT, *The Wind and
    Stream*, st. 2.

6

There paused to shut the door
A fellow called the Wind,
With mystery before,
    And reticence behind.
    BLISS CARMAN, *At the Granite Gate*.

7

The wind is awake, pretty leaves, pretty
    leaves,
Heed not what he says, he deceives, he de-
    ceives;
    Over and over To the lowly clover
He has lisped the same love (and forgotten
    it, too),
He'll be lisping and pledging to you.
    JOHN VANCE CHENEY, *The Way of It*.

8

Have you heard the wind go "Yo-o-o-o"?
'Tis a pitiful sound to hear.
    EUGENE FIELD, *The Night Wind*.

9

I hear the wind among the trees
Playing celestial symphonies;
I see the branches downward bent,
Like keys of some great instrument.
    HENRY WADSWORTH LONGFELLOW, *A Day
    of Sunshine*, st. 3.

10

Chill airs and wintry winds! my ear
    Has grown familiar with your song;
I hear it in the opening year,
    I listen, and it cheers me long.
    HENRY WADSWORTH LONGFELLOW, *Woods
    in Winter*, st. 7.

11

And the South Wind—he was dressed
With a ribbon round his breast
That floated, flapped, and fluttered
    In a riotous unrest,
And a drapery of mist
From the shoulder to the wrist
Floating backward with the motion of the
    waving hand he kissed.
    JAMES WHITCOMB RILEY, *The South Wind
    and the Sun*.

12

The gypsy wind goes down the night;
    I hear him lilt his wander-call,
And to the old divine delight
    Am I athrall.
    CLINTON SCOLLARD, *The Gypsy Wind*.

WINE

See also Drinking, Drunkenness

13

In the order named these are the hardest to
control: Wine, Women and Song.
    FRANKLIN P. ADAMS, *The Ancient Three*.

One of the oldest and quietest roads to contentment lies through the conventional trini-
ty of wine, woman and song.
    REXFORD GUY TUGWELL, Address to the
    Woman's National Democratic Club,
    Washington, D.C., May, 1934.

14

Well, my dear fellow, what did you expect
—champagne?
    GROVER CLEVELAND, to John Finley, who
    had complained that there was water in
    the cellar of a house he had rented from
    Cleveland. (FINLEY, *Cleveland; Scrib-
    ner's Magazine*, Apr., 1927)

15

Wine which Music is,—
Music and wine are one.
    EMERSON, *Bacchus*, st. 6.

16

A man will be eloquent if you give him good
wine.
    EMERSON, *Representative Men: Mon-
    taigne*.

17

Take counsel in wine, but resolve afterwards
in water.
    BENJAMIN FRANKLIN, *Poor Richard*,
    1733.

18

Fill every beaker up, my men, pour forth the
    cheering wine:

There's life and strength in every drop,—
    thanksgiving to the vine!
    ALBERT GORTON GREENE, *Baron's Last
    Banquet.*

1
Wine is like rain: when it falls on the mire it
    but makes it the fouler,
But when it strikes the good soil wakes it to
    beauty and bloom.
    JOHN HAY, *Distichs.*

2
God made the Vine,
    Was it a sin
That Man made Wine
    To drown trouble in?
    OLIVER HERFORD, *A Plea.*

3
Can name his claret—if he sees the cork.
    OLIVER WENDELL HOLMES, *The Banker's
    Secret.*

4
No nation is drunken where wine is cheap;
and none sober where the dearness of wine
substitutes ardent spirits as the common
beverage.
    THOMAS JEFFERSON, *Writings*, vol. xv, p.
    179.

5
Wine's a traitor not to trust.
    ROBERT U. JOHNSON, *Hearth-Song*, st. 2.

6
When you ask one friend to dine,
Give him your best wine!
When you ask two,
The second best will do!
    HENRY WADSWORTH LONGFELLOW. (BRAND-
    ER MATTHEWS, *Recreations of an An-
    thologist*, p. 117)

7
    This song of mine
    Is a Song of the Vine
To be sung by the glowing embers
    Of wayside inns,
    When the rain begins
To darken the drear Novembers.
    HENRY WADSWORTH LONGFELLOW, *Cataw-
    ba Wine*, st. 1.

8
The unearned increment of my grandfather's
Madeira.
    JAMES RUSSELL LOWELL, to Judge Hoar,
    in sympathizing with him on his suffer-
    ing from gout.

9
I drank at every vine.
    The last was like the first.
I came upon no wine
    So wonderful as thirst.
    EDNA ST. VINCENT MILLAY, *Feast.*

WINTER

10
The tendinous part of the mind, so to speak,
is more developed in winter; the fleshy, in
summer. I should say winter had given the
bone and sinew to literature, summer the tissues and the blood.
    JOHN BURROUGHS, *The Snow-Walkers.*

11
Winter lies too long in country towns; hangs
on until it is stale and shabby, old and sullen.
    WILLA CATHER, *My Ántonia*, bk. ii, ch.
    7.

12
There's a certain slant of light,
On winter afternoons,
That oppresses, like the weight
Of cathedral tunes.
    EMILY DICKINSON, *Poems*, Pt. ii, No. 82.

13
Oh, every year hath its winter,
    And every year hath its rain—
But a day is always coming
    When the birds go north again.
    ELLA HIGGINSON, *When the Birds Go
    North Again.*

14
Oh the long and dreary Winter!
Oh the cold and cruel Winter!
    HENRY WADSWORTH LONGFELLOW, *The
    Song of Hiawatha*, pt. 20.

15
Winter lingered so long in the lap of Spring,
that it occasioned a great deal of talk.
    BILL NYE, *Spring.*

16
Now there is frost upon the hill
And no leaf stirring in the wood;
The little streams are cold and still;
Never so still has winter stood.
    GEORGE O'NEIL, *Where It Is Winter.*

17
Such a winter eve. Now for a mellow fire,
some old poet's page, or else serene philosophy.
    HENRY D. THOREAU, *Journal.*

18
Despite March's windy reputation, winter
isn't really blown away; it is washed away.
It flows down all the hills, goes swirling
down the valleys and spills out to sea. Like
so many of this earth's elements, winter itself is soluble in water.
    Editorial, New York *Times*, 17 Mar.,
    1964.

WISDOM

See also Knowledge

19
If a man had half as much foresight as he
has twice as much hindsight, he'd be a lot
better off.
    ROBERT J. BURDETTE, *Hawkeyes*. Some-
    times paraphrased: "If our foresight
    were as good as our hindsight, we'd be
    better off a damn sight."

1

Some people are suffering from lack of work, some from lack of water, many more from lack of wisdom.

CALVIN COOLIDGE, 1931.

2

Before God we are all equally wise—equally foolish.

ALBERT EINSTEIN, *Cosmic Religion*, p. 105.

3

We are wiser than we know.

EMERSON, *Essays, First Series: The Over-Soul.*

4

To finish the moment, to find the journey's end in every step of the road, to live the greatest number of good hours, is wisdom.

EMERSON, *Essays, Second Series: Experience.*

5

The invariable mark of wisdom is to see the miraculous in the common.

EMERSON, *Nature, Addresses, and Lectures: Prospects.*

6

Raphael paints wisdom, Handel sings it, Phidias carves it, Shakespeare writes it, Wren builds it, Columbus sails it, Luther preaches it, Washington arms it, Watt mechanizes it.

EMERSON, *Society and Solitude: Art.*

7

Go where he will, the wise man is at home.

EMERSON, *Woodnotes*, pt. iii.

8

The wise know too well their weakness to assume infallibility; and he who knows most, knows best how little he knows

THOMAS JEFFERSON, *Writings,* vol. xviii, p. 129.

9

Wisdom is the child of experience.

JOHN F. KENNEDY, Address to the National Academy of Sciences, Washington, D.C., 22 Oct., 1963.

10

His form was ponderous, and his step was slow;
There never was so wise a man before;
He seemed the incarnate, "Well, I told you so!"

HENRY WADSWORTH LONGFELLOW, *The Birds of Killingworth*, st. 9.

11

Ripe in wisdom was he, but patient and simple and childlike.

HENRY WADSWORTH LONGFELLOW, *Evangeline*, pt. i, sec. 3, l. 11.

12

For only by unlearning Wisdom comes.

JAMES RUSSELL LOWELL, *The Parting of the Ways*, st. 8.

13

Nine-tenths of wisdom is being wise in time.

THEODORE ROOSEVELT, Speech in Lincoln, Neb., 14 June, 1917.

14

O world, thou choosest not the better part!
It is not wisdom to be only wise,
And on the inward vision close the eyes,
But it is wisdom to believe the heart.

GEORGE SANTAYANA, *O World.*

15

By Wisdom wealth is won;
But riches purchased wisdom yet for none.

BAYARD TAYLOR, *The Wisdom of Ali.*

16

Whatever of past or present wisdom has published itself to the world, is palpable falsehood till it come and utter itself by my side.

HENRY D. THOREAU, *Journal,* 4 Aug., 1838.

17

A man is wise with the wisdom of his time only, and ignorant with its ignorance.

HENRY D. THOREAU, *Journal,* 31 Jan., 1853.

18

One may almost doubt if the wisest man has learned anything of absolute value by living.

HENRY D. THOREAU, *Walden,* ch. 1.

19

The wisest man preaches no doctrines; he has no scheme; he sees no rafter, not even a cobweb, against the heavens. It is clear sky.

HENRY D. THOREAU, *A Week on the Concord and Merrimack Rivers,* p. 60.

20

Wisdom is not finally tested in the schools,
Wisdom cannot be pass'd from one having it
    to another not having it,
Wisdom is of the soul, is not susceptible of
    proof, is its own proof.

WALT WHITMAN, *Song of the Open Road,* sec. 6.

21

Oh, thriftlessness of dream and guess!
Oh, wisdom which is foolishness!
Why idly seek from outward things
The answer inward silence brings?

JOHN GREENLEAF WHITTIER, *Questions of Life.*

WIT

See also Humor, Laughter

22

Wit makes its own welcome, and levels all distinctions. No dignity, no learning, no force of character, can make any stand against good wit.

EMERSON, *Letters and Social Aims: The Comic.*

1
True wit never made us laugh.
EMERSON, *Letters and Social Aims: Social Aims.*

2
Of all wit's uses the main one
Is to live well with who has none.
EMERSON, *Life.*

3
And leave thy peacock wit behind.
EMERSON, *Woodnotes*, pt. ii.

4
There is nothing breaks so many friendships as a difference of opinion as to what constitutes wit.
ELBERT HUBBARD, *Epigrams.*

5
Wit, at its best, consists in the terse intrusion into an atmosphere of serene mental habit of some uncompromising truth.
PHILANDER JOHNSON, *Colyumists' Confessional; Everybody's Magazine*, May, 1920.

6
Endow me, if Thou grant me wit,
Likewise with sense to mellow it.
DON MARQUIS, *Prayer.*

7
Wit is the only wall
Between us and the dark.
MARK VAN DOREN, *Wit.*

WOMAN

See also Man

8
Women have, commonly, a very positive moral sense; that which they will, is right; that which they reject, is wrong; and their will, in most cases, ends by settling the moral.
HENRY ADAMS, *The Education of Henry Adams*, ch. 6.

9
The woman who is known only through a man is known wrong.
HENRY ADAMS, *The Education of Henry Adams*, ch. 23.

10
Where women are, the better things are implied if not spoken.
AMOS BRONSON ALCOTT, *Table Talk: Conversation.*

11
There is nothing enduring in life for a woman except what she builds in a man's heart.
JUDITH ANDERSON, Newspaper Interview, 8 Mar., 1931.

12
Women love the lie that saves their pride, but never an unflattering truth.
GERTRUDE ATHERTON, *The Conqueror*, bk. iii, ch. 6.

13
The perfect friendship of two men is the deepest and highest sentiment of which the finite mind is capable; women miss the best in life.
GERTRUDE ATHERTON, *The Conqueror*, bk. iii, ch. 12.

14
A woman who is loved always has success.
VICKI BAUM, *Grand Hotel*, p. 132.

15
Here's to woman! Would that we could fall into her arms without falling into her hands.
AMBROSE BIERCE, Toast—said to be his favorite toast. (GRATTAN, *Bitter Bierce*, p. 55)

16
To men a man is but a mind. Who cares
What face he carries or what form he wears?
But woman's body is the woman.
AMBROSE BIERCE, *The Devil's Dictionary.*

17
More bitter than death the woman
(Beside me still she stands)
Whose heart is snares and nets,
And whose hands are bands.
MORRIS BISHOP, *Ecclesiastes.* ("And I find more bitter than death the woman, whose heart is snares and nets, and her hands as bands."—*Ecclesiastes*, vii, 26)

18
Women have no wilderness in them,
They are provident instead,
Content in the tight hot cell of their hearts
To eat dusty bread.
LOUISE BOGAN, *Women.*

19
The world is full of women, and the women full of wile.
GELETT BURGESS, *Willy and the Lady.*

20
A woman's honor is concerned with one thing only, and it is a thing with which the honor of a man is not concerned at all.
JAMES BRANCH CABELL, *Jurgen*, p. 63.

21
And every century
Spawn divers queens who die with Antony
But live a great while first with Julius.
JAMES BRANCH CABELL, *Retractions.*

22
No lady is ever a gentleman.
JAMES BRANCH CABELL, *Something About Eve*, p. 25.

A lady is one who never shows her underwear unintentionally.
LILLIAN DAY, *Kiss and Tell.*

One man's lady is another man's woman; sometimes, one man's lady is another man's wife. Definitions overlap but they almost never coincide.
RUSSELL LYNES, *Is There a Lady in the House?; Look*, 22 July, 1958.

Edie was a lady.
DOROTHY PARKER, Caption of a review of Edith Wharton's autobiography.

1

Cécile: Do you think it wrong for a girl to know Latin?

Pierre: Not if she can cook a hare or a partridge as well as Mademoiselle Auclaire! She may read all the Latin she pleases.

    WILLA CATHER, *Shadows on the Rock.*

2

Her best and safest club is the home. . . . Sensible and responsible women do not want to vote. The relative positions to be assumed by man and woman in the working out of our civilization were assigned long ago by a higher intelligence than ours

    GROVER CLEVELAND. (*Ladies' Home Journal*, Apr. and Oct., 1905)

I believe a woman's place not only is in the home, but in the House and Senate and throughout the government. One thing we are insisting on is that we not have this stag government.

    LYNDON B. JOHNSON, Speech in Washington, D.C., 3 Mar., 1964, commending career women in government service.

I want to make a policy statement. I am unabashedly in favor of women.

    LYNDON B. JOHNSON, Comment, 4 Mar., 1964, upon announcing the appointment of several women to high governmental posts.

To conclude that women are unfitted to the task of our historic society seems to me the equivalent of closing male eyes to female facts.

    LYNDON B. JOHNSON, Speech at the White House, 13 Apr., 1964.

It is a good time to be a woman because your country, more now than at any time in its history, is utilizing your abilities and intelligence.

    CLAUDIA TAYLOR (MRS. LYNDON B.) JOHNSON, Remark, 31 Mar., 1964, upon receiving an honorary degree from Texas Woman's University, Denton, Tex.

3

The Woman tempted me—and tempts me still!

Lord God, I pray You that she ever will!

    EDMUND VANCE COOKE, *Book of Extenuations: Adam.*

4

Women are door-mats and have been,—
    The years those mats applaud,—
They keep their men from going in
    With muddy feet to God.

    MARY CAROLYN DAVIES, *Door-Mats.*

5

What soft, cherubic creatures
    These gentlewomen are!
One would as soon assault a plush
    Or violate a star.

Such dimity convictions.

    EMILY DICKINSON, *Poems*, Pt. i, No. 130.

6

Because when Women cease to be handsome, they study to be good. To maintain their Influence over Man, they supply the Diminution of Beauty by an Augmentation of Utility. . . . And hence there is hardly such a thing to be found as an old Woman who is not a good Woman.

    BENJAMIN FRANKLIN, Letter to an unidentified young man, 25 June, 1745. This was Franklin's second stated reason for preferring older women.

7

Love well, whip well.

    BENJAMIN FRANKLIN, *Poor Richard*, 1733.

8

Are women books? says Hodge, then would
    mine were
An Almanack, to change her every year.

    BENJAMIN FRANKLIN, *Poor Richard*, 1737.

9

Dally not with other folks' women or money.

    BENJAMIN FRANKLIN, *Poor Richard*, 1757.

10

If men knew how women pass the time when they are alone, they'd never marry.

    O. HENRY, *The Four Million: Memoirs of a Yellow Dog.*

11

The hydrogen derivatives.

    O. HENRY, *Man About Town*, referring to women.

12

History is bright and fiction dull with homely men who have charmed women.

    O. HENRY, *Roads of Destiny: "Next to Reading Matter."*

13

A Woman Is a Sometime Thing.

    DUBOSE HEYWARD AND IRA GERSHWIN, Title and refrain of song from *Porgy and Bess* (1935), with music by George Gershwin.

14

Women may be whole oceans deeper than we are, but they are also a whole paradise better. She may have got us out of Eden, but as a compensation she makes the earth very pleasant.

    JOHN OLIVER HOBBES, *Ambassador*, act 3.

15

The most precious possession that ever comes to a man in this world is a woman's heart.

    JOSIAH G. HOLLAND, *Lessons in Life: Perverseness.*

1
Man has his will—but woman has her way!
OLIVER WENDELL HOLMES, Prologue: *The
Autocrat of the Breakfast-Table*, ch. 2.

2
Nature is in earnest when she makes a
woman.
OLIVER WENDELL HOLMES, *The Autocrat
of the Breakfast-Table*, ch. 12.

3
A woman never forgets her sex. She would
rather talk with a man than an angel, any
day.
OLIVER WENDELL HOLMES, *The Poet at
the Breakfast-Table*, ch. 4.

4
The brain-women never interest us like the
heart-women; white roses please less than
red.
OLIVER WENDELL HOLMES, *The Professor
at the Breakfast-Table*, ch. 6.

5
"I love you" is all the secret that many, nay,
most women have to tell. When that is said,
they are like China-crackers on the morning
of the fifth of July.
OLIVER WENDELL HOLMES, *The Professor
at the Breakfast-Table*, ch. 8.

6
When Darby saw the setting sun
He swung his scythe, and home he run,
Sat down, drank off his quart and said,
"My work is done, I'll go to bed."
"My work is done!" retorted Joan,
"My work is done! Your constant tone,
But hapless woman ne'er can say
'My work is done' till judgment day."
ST. JOHN HONEYWOOD, *Darby and Joan*.
The lines recall one of the *Roxburghe
Ballads:* "Man's work lasts till set of
sun;/Woman's work is never done."

7
They were Americans, and they knew how to
worship a woman.
WILLIAM DEAN HOWELLS, *The Lady of
the Aroostook*.

8
A man is as good as he has to be, and a
woman as bad as she dares.
ELBERT HUBBARD, *Epigrams*.

9
When rewards are distributed, the woman
gets one half the pay that a man does, and if
disgrace is given out she bears it all.
ELBERT HUBBARD, *The Philistine*, vol. iv,
p. 179.

10
When a woman writes her confession she is
never further from the truth.
JAMES G. HUNEKER, *Pathos of Distance*,
p. 58.

11
I had rather live with the woman I love in a
world full of trouble, than to live in heaven
with nobody but men.
ROBERT G. INGERSOLL, *Liberty of Man,
Woman and Child*.

12
There is in every true woman's heart a spark
of heavenly fire, which lies dormant in the
broad daylight of prosperity; but which kin-
dles up, and beams and blazes in the dark
hour of adversity.
WASHINGTON IRVING, *Sketch-Book: The
Wife*.

13
"Sayin' nothin'," says the goldsmith, "is a
woman's rarest skill."
"Birds should sing," remarked the Doctor,
"but a woman should be still."
WALLACE IRWIN, *The Chamber of Tranquillity*.

14
What is cunning in the kitten may be cruel
in the cat.
ROBERT U. JOHNSON, *Daphne*.

15
The woman was not taken
From Adam's head, we know,
To show she must not rule him—
'Tis evidently so.
The woman she was taken
From under Adam's arm,
So she must be protected
From injuries and harm.
ABRAHAM LINCOLN, *Adam and Eve's
Wedding Song*. Written for Sarah Hag-
gard on her marriage to Aaron Grigsby.

16
The life of woman is full of woe,
Toiling on and on and on,
With breaking heart, and tearful eyes,
And silent lips, and in the soul
The secret longings that arise,
Which this world never satisfies!
Some more, some less, but of the whole
Not one quite happy, no, not one!
HENRY WADSWORTH LONGFELLOW, *The
Golden Legend*, pt. ii.

17
A Lady with a Lamp shall stand
In the great history of the land,
A noble type of good,
Heroic womanhood.
HENRY WADSWORTH LONGFELLOW, *Santa
Filomena*, st. 10.

18
To say why gals act so or so,
Or don't, 'ould be persumin';
Mebby to mean *yes* an' say *no*
Comes nateral to women.
JAMES RUSSELL LOWELL, *The Courtin'*.

19
Earth's noblest thing, a Woman perfected.
JAMES RUSSELL LOWELL, *Irene*, l. 62.

20
Although the story goes that woman was

contrived from Adam's rib, I have a different theory. In her public sense, she sprang full-panoplied out of his imagination.
> PHYLLIS MCGINLEY, *The Province of the Heart: Some of My Best Friends . . . ,* p. 103.

1

Women like other women fine. The more feminine she is, the more comfortable a woman feels with her own sex. It is only the occasional and therefore noticeable adventuress who refuses to make friends with us.
> PHYLLIS MCGINLEY, *The Province of the Heart: Some of My Best Friends . . . ,* p. 103.

Women are always rather pleased when one of them gets away with something. This is contrary to popular belief that women gang up on other women. It's a rather nice quality. You wouldn't find it among men because men don't regard themselves as a separate group.
> MARY MCCARTHY. (*Lady with a Switchblade; Life,* 20 Sept., 1963, p. 64)

2

When you educate a man you educate an individual; when you educate a woman you educate a whole family.
> DR. CHARLES D. MCIVER, Address at North Carolina College for Women.

3

Nowadays, any woman who wants the approval of men might do well to modify her brilliance and rein her wit: in short, to avoid collision, she should dim her headlights.
> MARYA MANNES. (*New Bites by a Girl Gadfly; Life,* 12 June, 1964, p. 59)

4

Nobody objects to a woman being a good writer or sculptor or geneticist as long as she manages also to be a good wife, mother, good-looking, good-tempered, well-dressed, well-groomed, unaggressive.
> MARYA MANNES. (*New Bites by a Girl Gadfly; Life,* 12 June, 1964, p. 62)

5

the females of all species are most dangerous when they appear to retreat
> DON MARQUIS, *archy does his part: farewell.*

6

Love is the delusion that one woman differs from another.
> H. L. MENCKEN, *A Mencken Chrestomathy.*

7

Women hate revolutions and revolutionists. They like men who are docile, and well-regarded at the bank, and never late at meals.
> H. L. MENCKEN, *Prejudices,* ser. iv, p. 252.

8

O woman, born first to believe us;

Yea, also born first to forget;
Born first to betray and deceive us,
　Yet first to repent and regret!
> JOAQUIN MILLER, *Charity,* st. 11.

9

Never Take No for an Answer.
> J. F. MITCHELL, Title and refrain of popular song (1886).

10

Oh, there are many things that women know,
That no one tells them, no one needs to tell;
And that they know, their dearest never guess.
> ROSELLE MERCIER MONTGOMERY, *Ulysses Returns: Penelope Speaks.*

11

　Women all
Raiment themselves most brightly for the dark
Which is, on information and belief,
Their true dominion.
> CHRISTOPHER MORLEY, *Toulemonde.*

12

Women would rather be right than reasonable.
> OGDEN NASH, *Frailty, Thy Name Is a Misnomer.*

13

Women are ethereal beings, subsisting entirely on chocolate marshmallow nut sundaes and cantaloupe,
But they open up a package of cigarettes like a lioness opening up an antelope.
> OGDEN NASH, *Thoughts Thought After a Bridge Party.*

14

Prince, a precept I'd leave for you,
　Coined in Eden, existing yet;
Skirt the parlor, and shun the zoo—
　Women and elephants never forget.
> DOROTHY PARKER, *Ballade of Unfortunate Mammals.*

15

Patience makes women beautiful in middle age.
> ELLIOT PAUL, *The Life and Death of a Spanish Town,* ch. 2.

16

I fill this cup to one made up
　Of loveliness alone,
A woman, of her gentle sex
　The seeming paragon;
To whom the better elements
　And kindly stars have given
A form so fair, that, like the air,
　'Tis less of earth than heaven.
> EDWARD COOTE PINKNEY, *A Health.*

17

Any woman who has a career and a family automatically develops something in the way of two personalities, like two sides of a dollar bill, each different in design. But one can complement the other to make a valuable

whole. Her problem is to keep one from draining the life from the other.
> Ivy Baker Priest, *Green Grows Ivy*.

1
For when a woman is left too much alone,
Sooner or later she begins to think;
And no man knows what then she may discover.
> Edwin Arlington Robinson, *Tristram*, pt. 7.

2
Parasite women.
> Theodore Roosevelt. (*Metropolitan Magazine*, May, 1916)

3
When loving woman wants her way,
God hesitates to say her nay.
> Arthur William Ryder, *When Woman Wills*.

4
Men, dying, make their wills, but wives
 Escape a task so sad;
Why should they make what all their lives
 The gentle dames have had?
> John G. Saxe, *Woman's Will*.

5
Woman's virtue is man's greatest invention.
> Cornelia Otis Skinner, *Paris '90*.

6
Complacencies of the peignoir, and late
Coffee and oranges in a sunny chair.
> Wallace Stevens, *Sunday Morning*.

7
Never believe her love is blind,
All his faults are locked securely
In a closet of her mind.
> Sara Teasdale, *Appraisal*.

8
In the East, women religiously conceal that they have faces; in the West, that they have legs. In both cases they make it evident that they have but little brains.
> Henry D. Thoreau, *Journal*, 31 Jan., 1852.

9
If I were asked . . . to what the singular prosperity and growing strength of that people ought mainly to be attributed, I should reply: To the superiority of their women.
> Alexis de Tocqueville, *Democracy in America*, pt. ii, bk. iii, ch. 12.

10
She was born to make hash of men's buzzums.
> Artemus Ward, *Piccolomini*.

11
The female woman is one of the greatest institooshuns of which this land can boste.
> Artemus Ward, *Woman's Rights*.

12
"N-O," Dan Cupid wrote with glee,
 And smiled at his success:

"Ah, child," said Venus, laughing low,
"We women do not spell it so,
 We spell it Y-E-S."
> Carolyn Wells, *The Spelling Lesson*.

13
But Woman is rare beyond compare,
 The poets tell us so;
How little they know of Woman
 Who only women know!
> Carolyn Wells, *Woman*.

14
If woman lost us Eden, such
As she alone restore it.
> John Greenleaf Whittier, *Among the Hills*.

15
He owns her logic of the heart,
And wisdom of unreason.
> John Greenleaf Whittier, *Among the Hills*.

16
Oh, woman wronged can cherish hate
More deep and dark than manhood may!
> John Greenleaf Whittier, *Mogg Megone*, pt. i, st. 21.

17
A woman tropical, intense,
In thought and act, in soul and sense,
She blended in a like degree
The vixen and the devotee.
> John Greenleaf Whittier, *Snow-Bound*, l. 531. Referring to Harriet Livermore.

18
It ever has been since time began,
 And ever will be, till time lose breath,
That love is a mood—no more—to man,
 And love to woman is life or death.
> Ella Wheeler Wilcox, *Blind*.

19
Reason and religion teach us that we too are primary existences, that it is for us to move in the orbit of our duty around the holy center of perfection, the companions not the satellites of men.
> Emma Willard, Inscription beneath her bust in the Hall of Fame.

20
Sex is the tabasco sauce which an adolescent national palate sprinkles on every course in the menu.
> Mary Day Winn, *Adam's Rib*, p. 8.

21
In the argot of the sub-deb, "U.S.A." has long ago lost its patriotic meaning. It now stands for "Universal Sex Appeal."
> Mary Day Winn, *Adam's Rib*, p. 17.

22
I was, being human, born alone;
I am, being woman, hard beset;
I live by squeezing from a stone
The only nourishment I get.
> Elinor Wylie, *Let No Charitable Hope*.

WOODS

1
The groves were God's first temples.
WILLIAM CULLEN BRYANT, *A Forest Hymn.*

2
This forest looks the way
Nightingales sound.
GRACE HAZARD CONKLING, *Frost on a Window.*

3
At the gates of the forest, the surprised man of the world is forced to leave his city estimates of great and small, wise and foolish. The knapsack of custom falls off his back.
EMERSON, *Essays, Second Series: Nature.*

4
This is the forest primeval.
HENRY WADSWORTH LONGFELLOW, *Evangeline,* l. 1.

5
The forests of America, however slighted by man, must have been a great delight to God; for they were the best he ever planted.
JOHN MUIR, *The American Forests; Atlantic Monthly,* vol. lxxx, p. 145.

6
       The Woods appear
With crimson blotches deeply dashed and crossed,—
Sign of the fatal pestilence of Frost.
BAYARD TAYLOR, *Mon-da-Min,* st. 38.

7
The woods are full of them.
ALEXANDER WILSON, *American Ornithology* (1808): preface. Quoting the story of a boy who returned from gathering wild flowers.

WORDS

See also Deeds, Language, Speech

8
No one means all he says, and yet very few say all they mean, for words are slippery and thought is viscous.
HENRY ADAMS, *The Education of Henry Adams,* ch. 31.

9
All words are pegs to hang ideas on.
HENRY WARD BEECHER, *Proverbs from Plymouth Pulpit: Human Mind.*

10
Slang has no country, it owns the world . . . It is the voice of the god that dwells in the people.
RALCY HUSTED BELL, *The Mystery of Words.*

11
"Correct my manners or my waggeries,
But though my accent's not the berries,
Spare my pronunciation's vagaries . . ."
   To that she merely said, "Vagaries!"
MORRIS BISHOP, *Why and How I Killed My Wife.*

12
God wove a web of loveliness,
   Of clouds and stars and birds,
But made not any thing at all
   So beautiful as words.
ANNA HEMPSTEAD BRANCH, *Her Words.*

13
The power-seeking despots of the world, the propagandists, have long known the power of words. They have been trying to steal the finest and dearest words that free society has inherited, in order to subvert them to the purposes of tyranny. The word "peace" is the best example. "Democracy" is used lavishly by those who would destroy it. "The people" are enshrined in the formal titles of nations which deny the rights of people.
ERWIN D. CANHAM, Introduction to *Words on Paper,* by ROY H. COPPERUD.

14
Weasel words are words that suck all the life out of the words next to them, just as a weasel sucks an egg and leaves the shell.
STEWART CHAPLIN, *The Stained-Glass Political Platform; Century Magazine,* June, 1900, p. 305.

One of our defects as a nation is a tendency to use what have been called "weasel words." When a weasel sucks an egg, the meat is sucked out of the egg; and if you use a "weasel word" after another there is nothing left of the other.
THEODORE ROOSEVELT, Speech in St. Louis, 31 May, 1916.

15
The little *and,* the tiny *if,*
   The ardent *ahs* and *ohs,*
They haunt the lanes of poesy,
   The boulevards of prose.
NATHALIA CRANE, *Alliances.*

16
A word that is not spoken never does any mischief.
CHARLES A. DANA, *The Making of a Newspaper Man,* maxim 4.

17
A word is dead
When it is said,
   Some say.
I say it just
Begins to live
   That day.
EMILY DICKINSON, *Poems,* Pt. i, No. 89.

18
She dealt her pretty words like blades,
As glittering they shone,
And every one unbared a nerve
Or wantoned with a bone.
EMILY DICKINSON, *Poems,* Pt. v, No. 29.

19
There is no choice of words for him who clearly sees the truth. . . . Any word, every word in language, every circumstance, be-

comes poetic in the hands of a higher thought.

> EMERSON, *Letters and Social Aims: Poetry and Imagination*.

1

Poetry teaches the enormous force of a few words, and, in proportion to the inspiration, checks loquacity.

> EMERSON, *Parnassus:* preface.

2

Americans have enriched our vocabulary enormously, whether we like it or not.

> ERNEST GOWERS, Press Conference in London, 5 May, 1965. Gowers had recently completed the job of editing and revising the second edition of H. W. FOWLER's famous *Dictionary of Modern English Usage*.

3

Brief words, when actions wait, are well.

> BRET HARTE, Address at the opening of the California Theatre, San Francisco, 19 Jan., 1870.

4

Articulate words are a harsh clamor and dissonance. When man arrives at his highest perfection, he will again be dumb!

> NATHANIEL HAWTHORNE, *American Note-Books*, Apr., 1841.

5

All our words from loose using have lost their edge.

> ERNEST HEMINGWAY, *Death in the Afternoon*, ch. 7.

6

Life and language are alike sacred. Homicide and *verbicide*—that is, violent treatment of a word with fatal results to its legitimate meaning, which is its life—are alike forbidden.

> OLIVER WENDELL HOLMES, *The Autocrat of the Breakfast-Table*, ch. 1.

7

Words lead to things; a scale is more precise,—
Coarse speech, bad grammar, swearing, drinking, vice.

> OLIVER WENDELL HOLMES, *A Rhymed Lesson*, l. 374.

8

A word is not a crystal, transparent and unchanging, it is the skin of a living thought and may vary greatly in color and content according to the circumstances and time in which it is used.

> JUSTICE OLIVER WENDELL HOLMES, Decision, Towne v. Eisner. (245 U.S. 418)

9

He can compress the most words into the smallest ideas of any man I ever met.

> ABRAHAM LINCOLN, speaking of a fellow lawyer. (GROSS, *Lincoln's Own Stories*, p. 36)

10

Speaking words of endearment where words of comfort availed not.

> HENRY WADSWORTH LONGFELLOW, *Evangeline*, pt. i, sec. 5, l. 43.

11

My words are little jars
For you to take and put upon a shelf.
Their shapes are quaint and beautiful,
And they have many pleasant colours and lustres
To recommend them.
Also the scent from them fills the room
With sweetness of flowers and crushed grasses.

> AMY LOWELL, *A Gift*.

12

There comes Emerson first, whose rich words, every one,
Are like gold nails in temples to hang trophies on.

> JAMES RUSSELL LOWELL, *A Fable for Critics*, l. 527.

13

His words were simple words enough,
    And yet he used them so,
That what in other mouths was rough
    In his seemed musical and low.

> JAMES RUSSELL LOWELL, *The Shepherd of King Admetus*.

14

To the man with an ear for verbal delicacies —the man who searches painfully for the perfect word, and puts the way of saying a thing above—the thing said—there is in writing the constant joy of sudden discovery, of happy accident.

> H L. MENCKEN, *A Book of Prefaces*, ch. 2.

15

I almost had forgotten
    That words were meant for rhyme:
And yet how well I knew it—
    Once upon a time!

> CHRISTOPHER MORLEY, *I Almost Had Forgotten*.

16

Such little, puny things are words in rhyme:
Poor feeble loops and strokes as frail as hairs;
You see them printed here, and mark their chime,
And turn to your more durable affairs.
Yet on such petty tools the poet dares
To run his race with mortar, bricks and lime,
And draws his frail stick to the point, and stares
To aim his arrow at the heart of Time.

> CHRISTOPHER MORLEY, *Quickening*.

17

Each of us . . . is the possessor of not one vocabulary but three. The largest of your three vocabularies is your recognition vocabulary—the words whose meanings you recognize when you see them in print or hear them spoken. The next smaller vocabulary —usually about two-thirds the size of the recognition vocabulary—is your writing vocabulary. These are the words you not only can recognize but know thoroughly enough so that you can command them to use in your own writing. The smallest of your vocabularies—about sixty per cent of your recognition vocabulary—is your speaking vocabulary. That's because you—like all the rest of us—will often hesitate to say a word aloud because of fear that you may mispronounce it.

WILLIAM MORRIS, *It's Easy to Increase Your Vocabulary*, p. 4.

1

Look out how you use proud words.
When you let proud words go, it is not easy to call them back.
CARL SANDBURG, *Primer Lesson*.

2

Kind words are benedictions.
FREDERICK SAUNDERS, *Stray Leaves: Smiles and Tears*.

3

It is the man determines what is said, not the words.
HENRY D. THOREAU, *Journal*, 11 July, 1840.

4

A powerful agent is the right word.
MARK TWAIN, *Essays on William Dean Howells*.

5

Some of his words were not Sunday-school words. . . . Some of those old American words do have a kind of a bully swing to them.
MARK TWAIN, *A Tramp Abroad*, ch. 20.

6

Briticism.
RICHARD GRANT WHITE, *Galaxy*, Mar., 1868.

7

On wings of deeds the soul must mount!
When we are summoned from afar,
Ourselves, and not our words, will count—
Not what we said, but what we are!
WILLIAM WINTER, *George Fawcett Rowe*.

8

The word Americanism, which I have coined, . . . is exactly similar in its formation and signification to the word Scotticism.
JOHN WITHERSPOON, *The Druid*, No. 5 (1781).

It was Witherspoon who coined the word Americanism, and at once the English guardians of the sacred vessels began employing it

as a general synonym for vulgarism and barbarism.
H. L. MENCKEN, *The American Language*, p. 49.

9

I love smooth words, like gold-enameled fish
Which circle slowly with a silken swish,
And tender ones, like downy-feathered birds:
Words shy and dappled, deep-eyed deer in herds.
ELINOR HOYT WYLIE, *Pretty Words*.

10

Honied words like bees,
Gilded and sticky, with a little sting.
ELINOR HOYT WYLIE, *Pretty Words*.

WORK

See also Labor

11

A wife is afraid of having her husband enjoy his work too much; she doesn't mind if he suffers at it—for her sake.
HAL BOYLE, Column, Associated Press, 21 Oct., 1964.

12

Don't worry and fret, faint-hearted,
  The chances have just begun,
For the best jobs haven't been started,
  The best work hasn't been done.
BERTON BRALEY, *No Chance*.

13

The dictionary is the only place where success comes before work.
ARTHUR BRISBANE, as quoted by Bennett Cerf.

14

I hold that a man had better be dead
  Than alive when his work is done.
ALICE CARY, *Work*.

15

Honor lies in honest toil.
GROVER CLEVELAND, Letter, in which he accepted nomination for the presidency, 18 Aug., 1884.

16

When a great many people are unable to find work, unemployment results.
CALVIN COOLIDGE, Syndicated Column. (STANLEY WALKER, *City Editor*, p. 131)

17

Work thou for pleasure! Sing or paint or carve
The thing thou lovest, though the body starve.
Who works for glory misses oft the goal;
Who works for money coins his very soul.
Work for the work's sake, then, and it may be
That these things shall be added unto thee.
KENYON COX, *The Gospel of Art; Century Magazine*, Feb., 1895.

1

There's only one way to work—like hell.
BETTE DAVIS. (*Look,* 9 Mar., 1965, p. 23)

2

Work and thou wilt bless the day
Ere the toil be done;
They that work not, can not pray,
Can not feel the sun.
God is living, working still,
All things work and move;
Work, or lose the power to will,
Lose the power to love.
J. S. DWIGHT, *Working.*

3

There is no substitute for hard work.
THOMAS A. EDISON. (*Golden Book,* Apr., 1931)

4

As a cure for worrying, work is better than whiskey.
THOMAS A. EDISON, Interview, on prohibition.

5

The high prize of life, the crowning fortune of a man, is to be born with a bias to some pursuit which finds him in employment and happiness.
EMERSON, *Conduct of Life: Considerations by the Way.*

6

Our chief want in life is, somebody who shall make us do what we can.
EMERSON, *Conduct of Life: Considerations by the Way.*

7

I look on that man as happy, who, when there is question of success, looks into his work for a reply.
EMERSON, *Conduct of Life: Worship.*

8

That which each can do best, none but his Maker can teach him.
EMERSON, *Essays, First Series: Self-Reliance.*

9

The legs of the throne are the plough and the oar, the anvil and the sewing-machine.
EMERSON, *Journals,* 1857.

10

Serve and thou shalt be served. If you love and serve men, you cannot, by any hiding or stratagem, escape the remuneration.
EMERSON, *Lectures and Biographical Studies: The Sovereignty of Ethics.*

11

[Thoreau's] father was a manufacturer of lead-pencils, and Henry applied himself for a time to this craft, believing he could make a better pencil than was then in use. After completing his experiments, he exhibited his work to chemists and artists in Boston, and having obtained their certificates to its excellence and to its equality with the best London manufacture, he returned home contented. His friends congratulated him that he had now opened his way to fortune. But he replied that he should never make another pencil. "Why should I? I would not do again what I have done once."
EMERSON, *Lectures and Biographical Studies: Thoreau.*

12

On bravely through the sunshine and the showers,
Time hath his work to do, and we have ours.
EMERSON, *The Man of Letters: Motto.*

13

Too busy with the crowded hour to fear to live or die.
EMERSON, *Quatrains: Nature.*

14

The sum of wisdom is, that the time is never lost that is devoted to work.
EMERSON, *Society and Solitude: Success.*

15

The body of Benjamin Franklin, Printer, (like the cover of an old book, its contents torn out and stripped of its lettering and gilding), lies here, food for worms; but the work shall not be lost, for it will (as he believed) appear once more in a new and more elegant edition, revised and corrected by the Author.
BENJAMIN FRANKLIN, Epitaph on himself, written in 1728 when he was twenty-two.

16

Work is love made visible. And if you cannot work with love but only with distaste, it is better that you should leave your work and sit at the gate of the temple and take alms of those who work with joy.
KAHLIL GIBRAN, *The Prophet: On Work.*

17

Run, if you like, but try to keep your breath;
Work like a man, but don't be worked to death.
OLIVER WENDELL HOLMES, *A Rhymed Lesson,* l. 300.

18

The riders in a race do not stop short when they reach the goal. There is a little finishing canter before coming to a standstill. There is time to hear the kind voices of friends and to say to one's self: "The work is done." But just as one says that, the answer comes: "The race is over, but the work never is done while the power to work remains." The canter that brings you to a standstill need not be only coming to rest. It cannot be while you still live. For to live is to function. That is all there is in living.
JUSTICE OLIVER WENDELL HOLMES, Public Statement on his ninetieth birthday, 8 Mar., 1931. (CATHERINE DRINKER BOWEN, *Yankee from Olympus,* p. 409)

1

If you work for a man, in heaven's name work for him! If he pays you wages that supply you your bread and butter, work for him—speak well of him, think well of him, stand by him and stand by the institution he represents.

ELBERT HUBBARD, *Get Out or Get in Line.*

2

Give us this day our daily work.

ELBERT HUBBARD, *The Philistine,* vol. xxv, p. 51.

3

Every child should be taught that useful work is worship and that intelligent labor is the highest form of prayer.

ROBERT G. INGERSOLL, *How to Reform Mankind.*

4

Father, I scarcely dare to pray,
    So clear I see, now it is done,
How I have wasted half my day,
    And left my work but just begun.

HELEN HUNT JACKSON, *A Last Prayer.*

5

All week long the Americans have been doing what Americans do best—working together.

LYNDON B. JOHNSON, News Conference, Johnson City, Tex., 8 Aug., 1964.

6

With a good conscience our only sure reward, with history the final judge of our deeds, let us go forth to lead the land we love, asking His blessing and His help, but knowing that here on earth God's work must truly be our own.

JOHN F. KENNEDY, Inaugural Address, 20 Jan., 1961. The concluding sentence.

7

The lady bearer of this says she has two sons who want to work. Set them at it if possible. Wanting to work is so rare a merit that it should be encouraged.

ABRAHAM LINCOLN, Letter to Major Ramsay.

8

Each morning sees some task begin,
    Each evening sees it close;
Something attempted, something done,
    Has earned a night's repose.

HENRY WADSWORTH LONGFELLOW, *The Village Blacksmith.*

9

Bad work follers ye ez long's ye live.

JAMES RUSSELL LOWELL, *The Biglow Papers,* Ser. ii, No. 2.

10

No man is born into the world whose work
Is not born with him; there is always work,
And tools to work withal, for those who will.

JAMES RUSSELL LOWELL, *A Glance Behind the Curtain,* l. 202.

11

Isn't it nice that no one cares which twenty-three hours of the day I work?

THURGOOD MARSHALL, during his years (1938–61) as special counsel for the National Association for the Advancement of Colored People. (SIDNEY E. ZION, *Thurgood Marshall Takes a New 'Tush-Tush' Job; New York Times Magazine,* 22 Aug., 1965, p. 11)

12

I go on working for the same reason that a hen goes on laying eggs.

H. L. MENCKEN. (DURANT, *On the Meaning of Life,* p. 30)

13

A man who gets his board and lodging on this ball in an ignominious way is inevitably an ignominious man.

H. L. MENCKEN, *Prejudices,* ser. iv, p. 200.

14

Work, it seemed to me even at the threshold of life, is an activity reserved for the dullard. It is the very opposite of creation, which is play, and which just because it has no raison d'être other than itself is the supreme motivating power in life. Has any one ever said that God created the universe in order to provide work for Himself?

HENRY MILLER, *The Creative Life.* (*Essays of Our Time,* ed. by Leo Hamalian and Edmond L. Volpe, 1960; p. 187)

15

Work!
Thank God for the swing of it,
For the clamoring, hammering ring of it,
Passion of labor daily hurled
On the mighty anvils of the world.

ANGELA MORGAN, *Work: A Song of Triumph.*

16

    Work is the least o' my idees
When the green, you know, gits back in the trees!

JAMES WHITCOMB RILEY, *When the Green Gits Back in the Trees.*

17

I feel that the greatest reward for doing is the opportunity to do more.

JONAS SALK, Speech of acceptance upon receiving a medal from President Eisenhower, 26 Jan., 1956. This was granted for his development of anti-polio vaccine.

18

The head of the most successful employment agency in America.

ADLAI E. STEVENSON, referring to Mrs. Joseph P. Kennedy, mother of the late President. (*Mother of a Dynasty;* New York *Times,* 15 Feb., 1965, p. 16)

19

Good for the body is the work of the body,

good for the soul the work of the soul, and good for either the work of the other.

> HENRY D. THOREAU, *Journal,* 23 Jan., 1841.

1
As for work, we haven't any of consequence. We have the Saint Vitus' dance, and cannot possibly keep our heads still.

> HENRY D. THOREAU, *Walden,* ch. 2.

2
Give me simple laboring folk,
Who love their work,
Whose virtue is a song
To cheer God along.

> HENRY D. THOREAU, *A Week on the Concord and Merrimack Rivers.*

3
The law of work does seem utterly unfair, but there it is, and nothing can change it: the higher the pay in enjoyment the worker gets out of it, the higher shall be his pay in cash also.

> MARK TWAIN, *A Connecticut Yankee at King Arthur's Court,* p. 269.

4
Let us be grateful to Adam, our benefactor. He cut us out of the "blessing" of idleness and won for us the "curse" of labor.

> MARK TWAIN, *Pudd'nhead Wilson's Calendar.*

5
This is my work; my blessing, not my doom;
Of all who live, I am the one by whom
This work can best be done in the right way.

> HENRY VAN DYKE, *The Three Best Things: Work.*

6
Work brings its own relief;
He who most idle is
Has most of grief.

> EUGENE FITCH WARE, *Today.*

7
Commuter—one who spends his life
In riding to and from his wife;
A man who shaves and takes a train,
And then rides back to shave again.

> E. B. WHITE, *The Commuter.*

8
There is no trade or employment but the young man following it may become a hero.

> WALT WHITMAN, *Song of Myself.*

WORLD

See also Earth

9
I am convinced that the world is not a mere bog in which men and women trample themselves in the mire and die. Something magnificent is taking place here amid the cruelties and tragedies, and the supreme challenge to intelligence is that of making the noblest and best in our curious heritage prevail.

> CHARLES A. BEARD. (DURANT, *On the Meaning of Life,* p. 43)

10
The optimist proclaims that we live in the best of all possible worlds; and the pessimist fears this is true.

> JAMES BRANCH CABELL, *The Silver Stallion,* ch. 26.

11
This is the way the world ends
Not with a bang but a whimper.

> T. S. ELIOT, *The Hollow Men.*

12
We must see that the world is rough and surly.

> EMERSON, *Conduct of Life: Fate.*

13
For the world is not painted or adorned, but is from the beginning beautiful; and God has not made some beautiful things, but Beauty is the creator of the universe.

> EMERSON, *Essays, Second Series: The Poet.*

14
Good-bye, proud world! I'm going home.
I am going to my own hearth-stone,
Bosomed in yon green hills alone,— . . .
A spot that is sacred to thought and God.

> EMERSON, *Good-Bye.*

15
Our Copernican globe is a great factory or shop of power, with its rotating constellations, times, and tides.

> EMERSON, *Letters and Social Aims: Resources.*

16
The existing world is not a dream, and cannot with impunity be treated as a dream; neither is it a disease; but it is the ground on which you stand, it is the mother of whom you were born.

> EMERSON, *Nature, Addresses, and Lectures: The Conservative.*

17
The world is a divine dream, from which we may presently awake to the glories and certainties of day.

> EMERSON, *Nature, Addresses, and Lectures: Spirit.*

18
The world is always equal to itself.

> EMERSON, *Social Aims: Progress of Culture.*

19
The world is a proud place, peopled with men of positive quality, with heroes and demigods standing around us, who will not let us sleep.

> EMERSON, *Society and Solitude: Books.*

20
Some say the world will end in fire,
Some say in ice.
From what I've tasted of desire

I hold with those who favor fire.
ROBERT FROST, *Fire and Ice.*

1

And were an epitaph to be my story
I'd have a short one ready for my own.
I would have written of me on my stone:
I had a lover's quarrel with the world.
ROBERT FROST, *The Lesson for Today.*

2

I can't change the world; I'll leave that to
the young men—the men who can get angry
every day the way I used to. When you come
down to it, the world has to change itself. I
suppose human nature is better now than it
was eighty years ago, but it's got a long way
to go, and I can't wait for it.
RUBE GOLDBERG. (Interview with R. W.
Apple, Jr., New York *Times,* 24 Apr.,
1964) The cartoonist was eighty-one at
the time.

3

I do not share in the apprehension held by
many as to the danger of governments becoming weakened and destroyed by reason of
their extension of territory . . . Rather do I
believe that our Great Maker is preparing
the world, in His own good time, to become
one nation, speaking one language, and when
armies and navies will no longer be required.
U. S. GRANT, Second Inaugural Address, 4
Mar., 1873.

4

The world is a fine place and worth fighting
for.
ERNEST HEMINGWAY, *For Whom the Bell
Tolls.*

5

The visible world is but man turned inside
out that he may be revealed to himself.
HENRY JAMES THE ELDER. (J. A. KELLOG,
*Digest of the Philosophy of Henry
James*)

6

If the world seems cold to you,
Kindle fires to warm it!
LUCY LARCOM, *Three Old Saws.*

7

If all the world must see the world
As the world the world hath seen,
Then it were better for the world
That the world had never been.
C. G. LELAND, *The World and the World.*

8

Oh, what a glory doth this world put on
For him who, with a fervent heart, goes
forth
Under the bright and glorious sky, and
looks
On duties well performed, and days well
spent!
HENRY WADSWORTH LONGFELLOW, *Autumn,* l. 30.

9

Truly, this world can go on without us, if we
would but think so.
HENRY WADSWORTH LONGFELLOW, *Hyperion,* bk. i, ch. 5.

10

Glorious indeed is the world of God around
us, but more glorious the world of God within us. There lies the Land of Song; there lies
the poet's native land.
HENRY WADSWORTH LONGFELLOW, *Hyperion,* bk. i, ch. 8.

11

In vain we build the world, unless
The builder also grows.
EDWIN MARKHAM, *Man-Making.*

12

O world, I cannot hold these close enough!
EDNA ST. VINCENT MILLAY, *God's World.*

13

The world stands out on either side
No wider than the heart is wide;
Above the world is stretched the sky,—
No higher than the soul is high.
EDNA ST. VINCENT MILLAY, *Renascence.*

14

My country is the world.
THOMAS PAINE, *Rights of Man,* pt. ii, ch.
5.

My country is the world; my countrymen
are mankind.
WILLIAM LLOYD GARRISON, *The Liberator:*
prospectus.

15

Yes, Heaven is thine; but this
Is a world of sweets and sours;
Our flowers are merely—flowers,
And the shadow of thy perfect bliss
Is the sunshine of ours.
EDGAR ALLAN POE, *Israfel.*

16

Fer the world is full of roses, and the roses
full of dew,
And the dew is full of heavenly love that
drips fer me and you.
JAMES WHITCOMB RILEY, *Thoughts fer
the Discuraged Farmer.*

17

The world is . . . a kind of spiritual kinder-
garten where millions of bewildered infants
are trying to spell God with the wrong
blocks.
EDWIN ARLINGTON ROBINSON, Letter to
The Bookman, Mar., 1897, p. 7.

18

One real world is enough.
GEORGE SANTAYANA, *Little Essays,* p. 31.

19

The world is not respectable; it is mortal,
tormented, confused, deluded for ever; but is
shot through with beauty, with love, with
glints of courage and laughter; and in these

the spirit blooms timidly, and struggles to the light among the thorns.

> GEORGE SANTAYANA, *Platonism and the Spiritual Life.*

1

The world is a perpetual caricature of itself; at every moment it is the mockery and the contradiction of what it is pretending to be.

> GEORGE SANTAYANA, *Soliloquies in England: Dickens.*

2

Gyrate, old Top, and let who will be clever;
    The mess we're in is much too deep to solve.
Me for a quiet life while you, as ever,
    Continue to revolve.

> BERT LESTON TAYLOR, *To a Well-Known Globe.*

3

The world was never less beautiful though viewed through a chink or knothole.

> HENRY D. THOREAU, *Journal,* 16 Jan., 1838.

4

One world at a time.

> HENRY D. THOREAU, Remark, shortly before his death in 1862, to a visitor intent on talking about the next world. According to F. B. Sanborn (in *Henry D. Thoreau*), the visitor was Parker Pillsbury, an antislavery orator; BROOKS ATKINSON (*Walden and Other Writings of Thoreau*) says it was William Ellery Channing, Thoreau's "closest friend."

5

The responsibility of the great states is to serve and not to dominate the world.

> HARRY S TRUMAN, Message to Congress, 16 Apr., 1945, four days after he became President.

6

I have had the good fortune to live through an era of increasingly menacing crises and disasters until the very recent moment when I could sense that, at long last, a turn had come in the fortunes of mankind. If I were to die tomorrow, I would feel that the world was nearer to becoming what I had hoped it would be when I was a young man than it has been at any time during my lifetime.

> JAMES P. WARBURG, *The Long Road Home* (1964).

7

Long and long has the grass been growing,
Long and long has the rain been falling,
Long has the globe been rolling round.

> WALT WHITMAN, *Song of the Exposition,* pt. i.

8

I swear the earth shall surely be complete to
    him or her who shall be complete,
The earth remains jagged and broken only to

him or her who remains jagged and broken.

> WALT WHITMAN, *Song of the Rolling Earth,* pt. 3.

9

The splendid discontent of God
With Chaos, made the world.

> ELLA WHEELER WILCOX, *Discontent.*

10

One World.

> WENDELL L. WILLKIE, Title of book (1943), written following his extensive travels abroad, and containing a call for international co-operation as a key to a peaceful world.

One world or none, say the atomic scientists. Has it occurred to them that if their one world turned out to be totalitarian and obscurantist, we might better have no world at all?

> ELMER DAVIS, *No World, If Necessary; The Saturday Review of Literature,* 30 Mar., 1946.

WORRY

See also Care, Trouble

11

There are two days in the week about which and upon which I never worry. . . . One of these days is Yesterday. . . . And the other day I do not worry about is Tomorrow.

> ROBERT JONES BURDETTE, *The Golden Day.*

12

Hurried and worried until we're buried, and
    there's no curtain call,
Life's a very funny proposition, after all.

> GEORGE M. COHAN, *Life's a Funny Proposition* (song, 1907).

13

Don't fight with the pillow, but lay down
    your head
And kick every worriment out of the bed.

> EDMUND VANCE COOKE, *Don't Take Your Troubles to Bed.*

14

The world is wide
In time and tide,
And God is guide,
    Then—do not hurry.
That man is blest
Who does his best
And leaves the rest,
    Then—do not worry.

> CHARLES F. DEEMS, *Epigram,* composed on his seventieth birthday.

15

As a cure for worrying, work is better than whiskey.

> THOMAS A. EDISON, Interview, on prohibition.

1
"Worry" is a word that I don't allow myself to use.

> DWIGHT D. EISENHOWER, News Conference, 12 Sept., 1956.

2
Worry, the interest paid by those who borrow trouble.

> GEORGE W. LYON. (*Judge,* 1 Mar., 1924, p. 6; *New York Times Book Review,* 23 Oct., 1932, p. 27)

3
This was a great year for preventive worrying. Seldom in recent history have so many people worried about so many things that didn't happen in the end.

> JAMES RESTON, Washington Column, New York *Times,* 30 Dec., 1964, p. 24.

WORTH
See also Price

4
He is rich or poor according to what he *is,* not according to what he *has.*

> HENRY WARD BEECHER, *Proverbs from Plymouth Pulpit.*

5
A man passes for that he is worth. What he is engraves itself on his face in letters of light.

> EMERSON, *Essays, First Series: Spiritual Laws.*

6
He has paid dear, very dear, for his whistle.
> BENJAMIN FRANKLIN, *The Whistle.*

7
It is better to deserve without receiving, than to receive without deserving.

> ROBERT G. INGERSOLL, *The Children of the Stage.*

8
I succeed him; no one could replace him.

> THOMAS JEFFERSON, Reply to the Comte de Vergennes, when the latter said, "You replace Mr. [Benjamin] Franklin" (as envoy to France).

9
Life is continually weighing us in very sensitive scales, and telling every one of us precisely what his real weight is to the last grain of dust.

> JAMES RUSSELL LOWELL, *On a Certain Condescension in Foreigners.*

10
In life's small things be resolute and great
To keep thy muscle trained: know'st thou when Fate
Thy measure takes, or when she'll say to thee,
"I find thee worthy; do this deed for me"?
> JAMES RUSSELL LOWELL, *Sayings.*

11
I never knew the worth of him Until he died.

> EDWIN ARLINGTON ROBINSON, *An Old Story.*

12
All good things are cheap: all bad are very dear.

> HENRY D. THOREAU, *Journal,* 3 Mar., 1841.

WRITING
See also Art and Artists, Books, Fiction, Literature, Plagiarism, Poetry, Poets, Style, Words

13
He dipped his pen into the tears of the human race, and with celestial clearness wrote down what he conceived to be eternal truths.

> JOHN P. ALTGELD, *In Memoriam, Henry George.*

14
My father said I was the ugliest child he had ever seen. He told me that all his life, and I believed him. And I'd accepted that nobody would ever love me. But do you know, nobody cares what a writer looks like. I could write to be eighty and be as grotesque as a dwarf and that wouldn't matter. For me, writing was an act of love. It was an attempt not to get the world's attention, it was an attempt to be loved.

> JAMES BALDWIN, Television Narrative based on his childhood, WNEW-TV, New York City, 1 June, 1964.

15
Art thou a pen, whose task shall be
  To drown in ink What writers think?
  Oh, wisely write, that pages white
Be not the worse for ink and thee!
> ETHEL LYNN BEERS, *The Gold Nugget.*

16
There is probably no hell for authors in the next world—they suffer so much from critics and publishers in this.

> C. N. BOVEE, *Summaries of Thought: Authors.*

17
Thoreau's quality is very penetrating and contagious; reading him is like eating onions—one must look out or the flavor will reach his own page.

> JOHN BURROUGHS, *Journal,* 1878.

18
I dip my pen in the blackest ink, because I am not afraid of falling into my inkpot.

> EMERSON, *Conduct of Life: Worship.*

19
He that writes to himself writes to an eternal public.

> EMERSON, *Essays, First Series: Spiritual Laws.*

1
All writing comes by the grace of God.
> EMERSON, *Essays, Second Series: Experience.*

2
No man can write anything who does not think that what he writes is, for the time, the history of the world.
> EMERSON, *Essays, Second Series: Nature.*

3
People do not deserve to have good writing, they are so pleased with bad.
> EMERSON, *Journals,* vol. vi, p. 132.

4
Good writing is a kind of skating which carries off the performer where he would not go.
> EMERSON, *Journals,* vol. vii, p. 334.

5
It is very hard to go beyond your public. If they are satisfied with your poor performance, you will not easily make it better.
> EMERSON, *Journals,* vol. ix, p. 304.

6
The nobler the truth or sentiment, the less imports the question of authorship.
> EMERSON, *Letters and Social Aims: Quotation and Originality.*

7
All great men have written proudly, nor cared to explain. They knew that the intelligent reader would come at last, and would thank them.
> EMERSON, *Natural History of Intellect: Thoughts on Modern Literature.*

8
The writer, like the priest, must be exempted from secular labor. His work needs a frolic health; he must be at the top of his condition.
> EMERSON, *Poetry and Imagination: Creation.*

9
Talent alone cannot make a writer. There must be a man behind the book.
> EMERSON, *Representative Men: Goethe.*

10
The lover of letters loves power too.
> EMERSON, *Society and Solitude: Clubs.*

11
I know I must write. If I don't write, I'll die. There is a history of long life in my family, and I expect to live a long time and do a lot more writing.
> JAMES T. FARRELL, interview with Arnold De Wease of United Press International, datelined 17 Nov., 1964.

12
He must teach himself that the basest of all things is to be afraid; and, teaching himself that, forget it forever, leaving no room in his workshop for anything but the old verities and truths of the heart, the old universal truths lacking which any story is ephemeral and doomed—love and honor and pity and pride and compassion and sacrifice.
> WILLIAM FAULKNER, Address in Stockholm, 10 Dec., 1950, when he received the Nobel Prize in literature. A statement of the writer's creed.

13
By my rambling digressions I perceive myself to be grown old. I used to write more methodically. But one does not dress for private company as for a public ball.
> BENJAMIN FRANKLIN, *Autobiography,* ch. 1.

14
Write with the learned, pronounce with the vulgar.
> BENJAMIN FRANKLIN, *Poor Richard,* 1738.

15
If you would not be forgotten, as soon as you are dead and rotten, either write things worth reading, or do things worth the writing.
> BENJAMIN FRANKLIN, *Poor Richard,* 1738.

16
Nothing gives an author so much pleasure as to find his works respectfully quoted by other learned authors.
> BENJAMIN FRANKLIN, *Poor Richard,* 1758.

17
Whatever an author puts between the two covers of his book is public property; whatever of himself he does not put there is his private property, as much as if he had never written a word.
> GAIL HAMILTON, *Country Living and Country Thinking:* preface.

18
I don't want to be a doctor, and live by men's diseases; nor a minister to live by their sins; nor a lawyer to live by their quarrels. So I don't see there's anything left for me but to be an author.
> NATHANIEL HAWTHORNE, Remark to his mother.

19
Decision by democratic majority vote is a fine form of government, but it's a stinking way to create.
> LILLIAN HELLMAN, Interview, New York *Times,* 27 Feb., 1966, p. 5X. She was referring to screenwriting collaboration.

20
A writer must write what he has to say, not speak it.
> ERNEST HEMINGWAY, Address, prepared for his acceptance of the 1954 Nobel Prize in literature.

21
Writing, at its best, is a lonely life. Organizations for writers palliate the writer's loneliness, but I doubt if they improve his writing.

He grows in public stature as he sheds his loneliness and after his work deteriorates.

ERNEST HEMINGWAY, Address prepared for his acceptance of the 1954 Nobel Prize in literature.

1

Easy writing makes hard reading.

ERNEST HEMINGWAY. (SAMUEL PUTNAM, *Paris Was Our Mistress*)

2

The first and most important thing of all, . . . is to strip language clean, to lay it bare down to the bone.

ERNEST HEMINGWAY. (SAMUEL PUTNAM, *Paris Was Our Mistress*)

3

A serious writer is not to be confused with a solemn writer. A serious writer may be a hawk or a buzzard or even a popinjay, but a solemn writer is always a bloody owl.

ERNEST HEMINGWAY, *Death in the Afternoon*, ch. 16.

4

I never saw an author in my life, saving perhaps one, that did not purr as audibly as a full-grown domestic cat on having his fur smoothed the right way by a skilful hand.

OLIVER WENDELL HOLMES, *The Autocrat of the Breakfast-Table*, ch. 3.

5

If all the trees in all the woods were men,
And each and every blade of grass a pen;
If every leaf on every shrub and tree
Turned to a sheet of foolscap; every sea
Were changed to ink, and all the earth's
    living tribes
Had nothing else to do but act as scribes,
And for ten thousand ages, day and night,
The human race should write, and write, and
    write,
Till all the pens and paper were used up,
And the huge inkstand was an empty cup,
Still would the scribblers clustered round its
    brink
Call for more pens, more paper, and more
    ink.

OLIVER WENDELL HOLMES, *Cacoëthes Scribendi.*

6

And since, I never dare to write
As funny as I can.

OLIVER WENDELL HOLMES, *The Height of the Ridiculous.*

7

The only happy author in this world is he who is below the care of reputation.

WASHINGTON IRVING, *Tales of a Traveller: Poor-Devil Author.*

8

Great writers leave us not just their works, but a way of looking at things.

ELIZABETH JANEWAY, *New York Times Book Review,* 31 Jan., 1965, p. 1.

9

I get up in the morning, torture a typewriter until it screams, then stop.

CLARENCE BUDINGTON KELLAND. (New York *Herald Tribune* obituary of Kelland, 20 Feb., 1964)

10

O thou sculptor, painter, poet!
    Take this lesson to thy heart:
That is best which lieth nearest;
    Shape from that thy work of art.

HENRY WADSWORTH LONGFELLOW, *Gaspar Becerra*, st. 7.

11

If you once understand an author's character, the comprehension of his writings becomes easy.

HENRY WADSWORTH LONGFELLOW, *Hyperion*, bk. i, ch. 5.

12

Perhaps the greatest lesson which the lives of literary men teach us is told in a single word: Wait!

HENRY WADSWORTH LONGFELLOW, *Hyperion*, bk. i, ch. 8.

13

The pen became a clarion.

HENRY WADSWORTH LONGFELLOW, *Monte Cassino*, st. 13.

14

Whatever hath been written shall remain,
Nor be erased nor written o'er again;
The unwritten only still belongs to thee:
Take heed, and ponder well what that shall
    be.

HENRY WADSWORTH LONGFELLOW, *Morituri Salutamus*, l. 168.

15

Look, then, into thine heart and write.

HENRY WADSWORTH LONGFELLOW, *Voices of the Night:* prelude, st. 19.

16

What boots all your grist? It can never be ground
Till a breeze makes the arms of the windmill go round.

JAMES RUSSELL LOWELL, *A Fable for Critics,* l. 83.

17

In creating, the only hard thing's to begin;
A grass-blade 's no easier to make than an oak;
If you've once found the way, you've achieved the grand stroke.

JAMES RUSSELL LOWELL, *A Fable for Critics,* l. 534.

18

Nature fits all her children with something to do,
He who would write and can't write, can surely review.

JAMES RUSSELL LOWELL, *A Fable for Critics,* l. 1784.

1

It may be glorious to write
Thoughts that will glad the two or three
High souls, like those far stars that come in
    sight
    Once in a century;—
But better far it is to speak
    One simple word, which now and then
Shall waken their free natures in the weak
    And friendless sons of men.
    JAMES RUSSELL LOWELL, *An Incident in a
        Railroad Car*, st. 19.

2

If the works of the great poets teach anything, it is to hold mere invention somewhat
cheap. It is not the finding of a thing, but
the making something out of it after it is
found, that is of consequence.
    JAMES RUSSELL LOWELL, *My Study Win-
        dows: Chaucer*.

3

Dead or alive, the playwright is the theatre's
only indispensable.
    RICHARD MANEY, *Fanfare*, p. 313.

4

I can't write what I feel: I'm coarse, when
    terse.
    DON MARQUIS, *Savage Portraits*.

5

The impulse to create beauty is rather rare
in literary men. . . . Far ahead of it comes
the yearning to make money. And after the
yearning to make money comes the yearning
to make a noise.
    H. L. MENCKEN, *Prejudices*, ser. v, p.
        189.

6

Years ago, to say you were a writer was not
the highest recommendation to your landlord. Today, he at least hesitates before he
refuses to rent you the apartment—for all he
knows you may be rich.
    ARTHUR MILLER, Address to a congress of
        P.E.N., the international association of
        writers, in Bled, Yugoslavia, 5 July,
        1965. (New York *Times*, 6 July, 1965)

7

There is no such thing as a dirty theme.
There are only dirty writers.
    GEORGE JEAN NATHAN, *Testament of a
        Critic*, p. 179.

8

There can be nothing so gratifying to an author as to arouse the respect and esteem of
the reader. Make him laugh and he will
think you a trivial fellow, but bore him in
the right way and your reputation is assured.
    WILLIAM LYON PHELPS.

9

God have mercy on the sinner
Who must write with no dinner,
No gravy and no grub,
No pewter and no pub,

No belly and no bowels,
Only consonants and vowels.
    JOHN CROWE RANSOM, *Survey of Litera-
        ture*.

10

When the going is good a writer knows very
little, if any, loneliness. When it is bad he
believes he knows nothing else.
    WILLIAM SAROYAN, *The Saturday Review*,
        25 Feb., 1961.

11

Pretty women swarm around everybody but
writers. Plain, intelligent women *somewhat*
swarm around writers.
    WILLIAM SAROYAN, *A Writer's Declara-
        tion*.

12

A best-seller is the gilded tomb of a mediocre
talent.
    LOGAN PEARSALL SMITH, *Afterthoughts*.

13

What I like in a good author is not what he
says but what he whispers.
    LOGAN PEARSALL SMITH, *Afterthoughts*.

14

The profession of book-writing makes horse
racing seem like a solid, stable business.
    JOHN STEINBECK, Address, upon accepting
        the 1962 Nobel Prize in literature.

15

Failure is very difficult for a writer to bear,
but very few can manage the shock of early
success.
    MAURICE VALENCY, *New York Times
        Book Review*, 23 May, 1965, p. 5.

16

The first writers are first and the rest, in the
long run, nowhere but in anthologies.
    CARL VAN DOREN, *What Is American Lit-
        erature?*

17

If the writing is honest it cannot be separated from the man who wrote it. It isn't so
much his mirror as it is the distillation, the
essence, or what is strongest and purest in his
nature, whether that be gentleness or anger,
serenity or torment, light or dark. This
makes it deeper than the surface likeness of
a mirror and that much more truthful.
    TENNESSEE WILLIAMS, *The Writing Is
        Honest*. (Introduction to *The Dark at
        the Top of the Stairs*, by WILLIAM
        INGE)

18

Nobody but a writer knows how exhausting
it is to write. Nobody except perhaps a writer's wife. She knows what hell he goes
through and how little he is paid for his
efforts. I can write only three or four hours a
day. After that I'm emotionally worn out.
    TENNESSEE WILLIAMS, Interview with Bob
        Thomas of Associated Press, datelined 1
        Nov., 1963.

WRONGS

1
You cannot do wrong without suffering wrong.

EMERSON, *Essays, First Series: Compensation.*

2
His heart was as great as the world, but there was no room in it to hold the memory of a wrong.

EMERSON, *Letters and Social Aims: Greatness.* Referring to Abraham Lincoln.

3
For every social wrong there must be a remedy. But the remedy can be nothing less than the abolition of the wrong.

HENRY GEORGE, *Social Problems,* ch. 9.

4
Wrong rules the land and waiting Justice sleeps.

JOSIAH G. HOLLAND, *Wanted.*

5
Not the wrongs done to us harm us, only those we do to others.

HENRY WADSWORTH LONGFELLOW. (BRADFORD, *Biography and the Human Heart,* p. 42)

6
Truth forever on the scaffold, Wrong forever on the throne.

JAMES RUSSELL LOWELL, *The Present Crisis,* st. 8.

7
The fact that man knows right from wrong proves his *intellectual* superiority to the other creatures; but the fact that he can *do* wrong proves his *moral* inferiority to any creature that *cannot.*

MARK TWAIN, *What Is Man?,* ch. 6.

Y

YEAR

See also Time

8
   Years have hardier tasks
Than listening to a whisper or a sigh.

STEPHEN VINCENT BENÉT, *The Golden Corpse.*

9
Lament who will, in fruitless tears,
  The speed with which our moments fly;
I sigh not over vanished years,
  But watch the years that hasten by.

WILLIAM CULLEN BRYANT, *The Lapse of Time.*

10
The years teach much which the days never know.

EMERSON, *Essays, Second Series: Experience.*

11
All sorts of things and weather
Must be taken in together,
To make up a year.

EMERSON, *Fable.*

12
The specious panorama of a year
But multiplies the image of a day.

EMERSON, *Xenophanes.*

13
I will not let the years run over me like a Juggernaut car.

HENRY D. THOREAU, *Journal,* 25 June, 1840.

14
In masks outrageous and austere
The years go by in single file;
But none has merited my fear,
And none has quite escaped my smile.

ELINOR WYLIE, *Let No Charitable Hope.*

II—New Year

15
Even while we sing, he smiles his last,
  And leaves our sphere behind.
The good Old Year is with the past,
  O be the New as kind!

WILLIAM CULLEN BRYANT, *A Song for New-Year's Eve.*

16
A song for the Old, while its knell is tolled,
  And its parting moments fly!
But a song and a cheer for the glad New Year,
  While we watch the Old Year die!
Oh! its grief and pain ne'er can come again,
  And its care lies buried deep;
But what joy untold doth the New Year hold,
  And what hopes within it sleep!

GEORGE COOPER, *The New Year.*

17
Then sing, young hearts that are full of cheer,
  With never a thought of sorrow;
The old goes out, but the glad young year
  Comes merrily in to-morrow.

EMILY HUNTINGTON MILLER, *New Year Song.*

YOUTH

See also Age; Boy, Boyhood; Girl

18
All lovely things will have an ending,
  All lovely things will fade and die,
And youth, that's now so bravely spending,
  Will beg a penny by and by.

CONRAD AIKEN, *All Lovely Things Will Have an Ending.*

1

Sociologists agree that one of the worst things that can happen to an American child nowadays is youth.

> RUSSELL BAKER, "Observer" Column, New York *Times*, 27 Feb., 1966.

2

Young blood! Youth will be served.

> STEPHEN VINCENT BENÉT, *Young Blood*.

3

One may return to the place of his birth,
He cannot go back to his youth.

> JOHN BURROUGHS, *The Return*, st. 3.

4

Hobbledehoy, neither man nor boy,
With a burden of pain and a purpose of joy,
With a heart and a hunger of human alloy,
He's a lad whom the jungle and heaven decoy.
There's a god and a devil in Hobbledehoy!

> WITTER BYNNER, *Hobbledehoy*.

5

"And youth is cruel, and has no remorse
And smiles at situations which it cannot see."
I smile, of course,
And go on drinking tea.

> T. S. ELIOT, *Portrait of a Lady*.

6

Say, was it never heard
That wisdom might in youth be gotten,
Or wit be ripe before 'twas rotten?

> EMERSON, *Fame*.

7

Shuffle-Shoon and Amber-Locks
Sit together, building blocks;
Shuffle-Shoon is old and gray,
Amber-Locks a little child,
But together at their play
Age and Youth are reconciled.

> EUGENE FIELD, *Shuffle-Shoon and Amber-Locks*.

8

I think it is fair to describe yours as a generation of unusually genuine and intense concern with social justice and intellectual freedom.

> ROBERT F. KENNEDY, Commencement Address, Marquette University, 7 June, 1964. Several editorial writers and commentators subsequently paraphrased his words as "the concerned generation."

9

Youth comes but once in a lifetime.

> HENRY WADSWORTH LONGFELLOW, *Hyperion*, bk. ii, ch. 10.

10

How beautiful is youth! how bright it gleams
With its illusions, aspirations, dreams!
Book of Beginnings, Story without End,
Each maid a heroine, and each man a friend!

> HENRY WADSWORTH LONGFELLOW, *Morituri Salutamus*, l. 66.

11

Youth condemns; maturity condones.

> AMY LOWELL, *Tendencies in Modern American Poetry*, p. 60.

12

If youth be a defect, it is one that we outgrow only too soon.

> JAMES RUSSELL LOWELL, Address in Cambridge, Mass., 8 Nov., 1886.

13

The elbowing self-conceit of youth.

> JAMES RUSSELL LOWELL, *A Good Word for Winter*.

14

Youth sees too far to see how near it is
To seeing farther.

> EDWIN ARLINGTON ROBINSON, *Tristram*.

15

I confess to pride in this coming generation. You are working out your own salvation; you are more in love with life; you play with fire openly, where we did in secret, and few of you are burned!

> FRANKLIN D. ROOSEVELT, Address: *Whither Bound?*, at Milton Academy, May, 1926.

16

Our youth is like a rustic at the play
That cries aloud in simple-hearted fear,
Curses the villain, shudders at the fray,
And weeps before the maiden's wreathèd bier.

> GEORGE SANTAYANA, *The Rustic at the Play*.

17

The youth gets together his materials to build a bridge to the moon, or, perchance, a palace or temple on the earth, and, at length, the middle-aged man concludes to build a woodshed with them.

> HENRY D. THOREAU, *Journal*, 14 July, 1852.

18

It is better to be a young June-bug than an old bird of paradise.

> MARK TWAIN, *Pudd'nhead Wilson's Calendar*.

19

Youth is a silly, vapid state.

> CAROLYN WELLS, *My Boon*.

Z

ZEAL
See also Enthusiasm

1
A single zealot may commence persecutor,
and better men be his victims.

> THOMAS JEFFERSON, *Notes on the State of
> Virginia*, Query 17.

2
Our Hero, whose homeopathic sagacity
With an ocean of zeal mixed his drop of
    capacity.

> JAMES RUSSELL LOWELL, *A Fable for Crit-
> ics*, l. 370.

3
Press bravely onward! not in vain
    Your generous trust in human-kind;
The good which bloodshed could not gain
    Your peaceful zeal shall find.

> JOHN GREENLEAF WHITTIER, *To the Re-
> formers of England*, st. 13.

4
Zaccheus, he
Did climb the tree,
His Lord to see.

> UNKNOWN, *The New England Primer*.

INDEX AND CONCORDANCE

Boston, *continued*
in B. they ask 289: 4
is state of mind 67: 4
man, east wind made flesh .66:12
sea took B. in arms 66:15
solid man of B. 67: 5
solid men of B. 67: 5
State-house, the hub 67: 2
thinking center 66:19
Botany is Latin names 354:12
Bottle: I prefer b. 128:19
large cold b. 132: 4
Bough where I cling 10:12
Bought: politician stay b. .303: 7
Bowery 270: 5
Boxing in need of fumiga-
  tion 391: 1
is here to stay 391: 2
Boy 67
barefoot b. 68: 1
dreamy b., untaught 67:12
had Aladdin's lamp 67:13
has two jobs 67:10
one of best things to be ...67:14
rather laugh, a b., than
  reign, a king 67: 9
Boy's heart, roamer 68: 3
will is wind's will 67:11
Boyhood: here's to b. 67: 8
Boyhood's time of June ...68: 2
Boys: bless little b. 67: 6
old b. have playthings ...10:10
old fellow mixed with b. .67: 7
your b. not going to be sent
  into foreign wars 34: 4
Brahmin caste 374:19
Brain: full belly, dull b. .58: 8
trust 311: 2
whatever comes from b. .192: 7
Brains: beauty better than b. 53:19
heads, but no b. 285:16
made of gingerbread 252:17
reflect crown of hat 253:18
seventy-year clocks 253:11
women have but little b. .449: 8
Brandy: how b. lies 128: 6
Brave: home of b. and free .13: 6
home of the b. 13: 9
man [in] thickest of fight .99: 2
men, b. men 98:16
world in conspiracy against
  b. 98:12
Bread 68
in sorrow ate 382: 7
live for b. N 54: 8
morning b., smooth 68: 6
not live by b. alone 68: 4
will it bake b. 68: 5
wringing b. from sweat of
  other men's faces 369: 5
Break: never give sucker ..172: 7
Breakfast of champions 7:18
Breath: last b. 110: 7
Breathing: keep b. 234:20
Breeding consists in conceal-
  ing 247:16
Breeze came wandering 442: 5
Bribed: public not to be b. .68:13
Bridge: don't cross b. ...418:15
on b. at midnight 272: 1
Brief as water falling ...68: 8
condition of being inspired 68:11
Bring me men to match ...14:11
Brink: walked to b. (of war) 8: 1
Brinkmanship 38: 1
Briticism 452: 6
Broadway: give my regards
  to 269:14
Bromide: are you a b. 331: 8
Bronx, no thonx 270:16
Brooklyn: still in the league 389:10
Brother 68
can you spare dime 33:10
consult B. Jonathan 28: 4
fold to thy heart 292: 5
is a comfort 170:23
little brown b. 69:12

Brother, *continued*
thy b. every man below 13:10
whom someone must save ..69:13
Brotherhood 68
crest of all good 69: 7
crown thy good with b. ..13: 5
of all men before law 267: 9
under fatherhood of God ..69: 9
world neighborhood before b. 69: 4
Brothers: destiny makes us b. 69: 8
learn to live as b. 69:11
must live together as b. ..69: 6
Brow of labor 308:11
wet with honest sweat ...222: 3
Brown, John 69
body lies a-mouldering ...70: 1
died for slave 70: 3
may trouble you more than
  ever 70: 4
of Ossawatomie 70: 5
Washington slaying Spartacus 70: 2
Buck: the b. stops here ...113: 7
Bucket: drop your b. 275: 2
Buckets: let down your b. ..275: 2
Bugle: first recollection, a b.
  call 377:14
good old b., boys 381:18
Build better mouse-trap ..151: 8
me straight 362:14
to b., noblest art 44: 5
Builders wrought with care 44: 7
Built heart into stones ..44: 6
house of sticks and mud ..62:10
Bull bears Europa upon back 140:16
stand behind b. 333: 2
Bulldog: with b. grip 287:11
Bull moose 313
Bum: hallelujah, I'm b. ...425: 3
Buncombe: talking for B. .308: 8
Bundle of aches 63: 3
Bunkum: talking to B. ...308: 8
Burden 70
of world on his back 70:10
rather have big b. 70: 9
soldier's pack not so heavy .70: 7
Burdens heavier than heart
  can bear 70: 6
Buried: do not intend to be b. 39: 2
revisionists will be b. ..39: 2
where he b. hatchet 139: 9
Bury: intend to b. no one ..39: 2
room enough to b. dead ...29: 5
we will b. you 39: 2
Business 70
big b. give square deal ...72: 1
dinners never interferred
  with b. 131:18
dirty b. 379: 3
drive thy b. 71: 4
getting people to believe he
  has something they want 71:11
haven't done anything for b. 71: 7
is business 70:12
keeping the mind steady ..71:12
lone God of Congress 72: 6
make b. a pleasure 292:16
make money in honorable
  manner 71: 1
mind my own b. 378:10
never fear want of b. 71: 6
no b. like show b. 394: 9
of America is b. 70:15
persuading crowds 71:10
Businessmen all sons-of-
  bitches 71: 8
don't elect Presidents ...72: 4
no President could please all 71: 9
Busts: we are b. 152:14
Busy: Americans too b. to be
  thoughtful 23: 7
my b. day 107:10
Butter-and-egg man 331:14
Buttercups: yellow japanned 164:14
Buttered no parsnips 149: 5
Buy new book 65:10
what is cheap 326:13

Buy new books, *continued*
minding my own b. 309: 8
Buys: Morgan b. partners ..70:13

C

Cabinet: kitchen c. 314: 8
nine salesmen, one credit
  manager 133:11
took Panama without con-
  sulting 32: 2
Cabots can't see Kabotschniks 66:13
talk only to God 66:13
Caesar had his Brutus 26: 2
Cafeteria: God's jolly c. ..100: 2
Caissons go rolling 376: 4
Call for Philip Morris 7: 9
Calling: office of profit ..221: 8
Calumny: best answer to ..368: 6
Cambridge ladies 373:16
Camel: black c. 72: 8
lumpy, bumpy, humpy ...72: 9
never question about di-
  gestion 72:10
only asks a thorn 72: 7
Candle 72
better to light one c. 72:13
burns at both ends 72:12
fills a mile with rays ...72:11
rather light c. 72:13
Candor 73
come not to play with me ..73: 3
Candy is dandy 128:13
Can't take it with you ...256: 7
Canoe: paddle your own c. ..208:10
Cant: king of c. 203:12
Canvas: great picture, small
  ....49: 2
Capital: fruit of labor ...221:14
labor, in connection with .221:14
labor, independent of c. ..221:14
let your c. be simplicity ..161: 5
Capitalism is worn-out old
  mare 39: 2
will give way to socialism .39: 2
would be buried 39: 2
Captain: O C., my C. 237: 1
with mighty heart 377:15
Car in every garage 317: 1
Card: it is my last c. 369: 3
Care 73
first cat killed by C. 92:12
has mortgage on estate ...73:11
nobody will c. for him who
  cares for nobody 4:10
rarely sits behind rider ..73:10
Career: caress better than c. 239:17
Careful: be c., if can't be
  good 179:17
Cares: multiplies riches, c. 346: 5
silently steal away 73: 9
Caress: better than career .239:17
Carload: not a cough in c. ..7: 8
Carriage: body, not private c. 40: 5
Carry: American people
  never c. umbrella 18: 2
big stick 313: 6
forests on my back 186:10
me back to old Virginny ..380: 2
message to Garcia 1:11
Casey at the bat 389:11
would waltz 106: 4
Castles: gayest c. in air ..73:12
in air, foundations under .73:14
in Spain 73:13
Cat 73
by solemnly sneezing 73:16
differences between c., lie .231: 1
first c. killed by Care ...92:12
in gloves catches no mice .73:15
on hot stove-lid 74: 1
that wears silk mittens ..73:15
which way c. jumping 326: 5
Catbird: in the c. seat ...388: 5
Catharsis: art, form of c. ..48:10
Cathedral blossoming in stone 44: 2

Duty, *continued*
when d. comes a-knocking 130: 9
where d. seemed to call ...281:15
which nobody need listen to 130:11
whispers, Thou must 129:18

E

E Pluribus Unum 20: 4
Each: all for e. 21: 3
Eagle: Europe looks to see .25: 8
long as E. harms no dove 13:10
on back iv dollar 124: 5
Ear: hearing e., speaking
tongue 130:17
listening e. of night 131: 1
only true writer, reader ...130:18
Early to bed 191: 9
to rise, to bed 349: 7
Earned night's repose 114: 8
Earnest: I am in e. 29: 1
Earth **131**
all e. thy dwelling-place ..13: 8
complete to him 457: 8
cultivation of e. 154:18
echo of voice of God 131: 2
in this broad e. 131:10
is given as common stock 154:12
laughs in flowers 164:12
maternal e. which rocks ..131: 4
receive my lance in rest ..50: 2
right place for love 56:12
sends incense up 131:11
that is sufficient 131: 9
this is last of e. 111: 3
Easter **131**
Christ will rise on 131:12
'twas E. Sunday 131:13
Easy: dying man can do
nothing e. 111: 8
to industry 205: 3
Eat: bad to e. apples 3:14
more you e., more you want 6:18
not for good of living 132: 1
not to dullness 406:13
to live, not live to e. 132: 5
to please thyself 126:22
will not work, shall not e. .18: 3
young e. anything 132:16
Eaten: never repent of having e. too little 132:17
Eating **131**
do all e., none of work ...221:16
hundred thousand die of ..132:10
that's believing 133: 3
those who do not enjoy e. 131:19
Eating's: for e. sake 131:17
Eccentricity not proof of
genius 175: 2
Echo: a choice, not an e. ..310: 3
Economic power important
only as put to human
use 134: 9
royalists 135: 2
Economy **133**
fuel of magnificence 134: 6
in art is beauty 47: 6
"producer's e." 5: 7
so long as e. remains strong 134: 8
what we all think, do 134: 5
wisdom expended on pri-
vate e. 134: 6
Edie was a lady 445:22
Educate a woman 448: 2
Educated beyond intelli-
gence 137:11
only e. men are self-e. ...137: 7
so stupid as e. man 137:14
Education **135**
abandon moral neutrality .135:10
able to do what you've
never done before 137:12
answer for all problems ..136:15
better part, he gives himself 137: 7
conduct us to enjoyment 137: 9
desire time when [it] shall
become more general ..137: 4

Education, *continued*
discredit hard work 136: 5
get along without intelligence 138: 2
higher e., a necessity 135: 7
in making common, com-
pulsory 137: 6
makes ditch of brook 137:18
makes for inequality 137:15
no nation borrowed for e. 136: 8
no such thing without 136: 7
only interest worthy 137:13
respecting the pupil 136: 2
self-e. fine when 137: 7
slavery half abolished without e. 138: 4
soap and e., more deadly .138: 1
sometimes a curse 137:16
system of despair 136: 1
value as tool, not experience 136: 4
[vital to] freedom, justice 136:10
with universal cheap e. ...136: 3
wonder, that it does not
ruin 135: 5
Educator: make hard things
easy 405: 8
Educators: observation, experience 135: 6
Effect: behind coarse e. ...74:11
cause and e. cannot be severed 74:12
cause and e., two sides of
one fact 74:11
Effigies: light of my 309:12
Egg: goodness of a good e. 138: 5
mightier than the pen 138: 7
Wall Street lays e. 33: 9
Eggheads, unite 254: 1
Eggs **138**
can you unscramble e. 138: 8
put all in one basket 138: 9
Egoism: intolerance is e. ..138:14
Egotist: the e. dread 138:12
Egotists pest of society ...138:10
Elected between sundown
and sunup 430:10
not serve if e. 314: 1
someone terrible gets e. ..430: 7
Elections as a security 429: 4
emphasize the worst 299:12
where annual e. end 429: 3
Elephant: got e. by hind leg 333: 4
Elephants: call them e. ...160: 3
Eloquence has turned scale 384:20
translate a truth 384:19
Embarrassing moments 6: 4
Emerald: May birthstone ...61: 7
Emotion: heart so full of .157:20
sentiment is intellectual-
ized e. 157:21
Empire: westward the
course of e. 14: 1
Empires: men with e. in
purpose 14:11
Employment: never fails of
e. 71: 6
Empty stomach 202:18
Emulation: propensity for 361: 2
Enchantment: distance lends
e. 1: 1
End: beauty exactly answers 54: 3
fall of first Adam, e. of
beginning 3:13
Ending: greater is art of e. 56:13
Ends I aim at 18:12
means, e. cannot be sev-
ered 74:12
Endurance **138**
is crowning quality 139: 2
patient e. is godlike 139: 1
victory of e. born 138:17
Enemies: civilized man has
no e. 139: 4
deserved e., [not] friends 139:17
have no trouble with e. ..171: 1
if we could read history
of our e. 139:11

Enemies, *continued*
just friends and brave e. ..23:15
love e.; they tell faults ...139: 7
love him for e. he made ..139: 3
man who has no e. 139:13
we must not be e. 8: 6
Enemy **139**
and friend, hurt you 139:15
be e. to none 56:21
do good to e., gain him ..139: 6
greatness measured by e. 139:14
hardly a warm e. left 139:16
lend money to e. 66: 6
pray, give us good e. 139: 5
we have met e. 28: 6
Enemy's: the e. country ...309: 1
Energy: American charac-
teristic 18: 6
Enforce: let him e. [deci-
sion] 310:12
Engagement binding on you 99:10
Engagements: play star e.
above 3: 3
Engineer: lunatic for an e. 242:10
Engineer's high privilege .354:17
Engineering: doing well
with $1 ....356: 4
England **139**
is my wife 140: 7
no higher worship than
Fate 140: 5
stability is security 140: 4
England's oaken-hearted
mood 141: 3
English **139**
[America] of E. blood 25: 5
are not inventive 139:19
government unprincipled ..140:13
mentioned in the Bible ...141: 4
metropolitan E. speech ...222:19
wut's good's all E. 140:15
Englishman: American never
imitates E. 22:10
faults smack of good 140:11
has firm manners 140: 6
is an island himself 140: 3
is like stout ship 140:10
natural, holding tongue ..140:12
stands firmest in shoes ..140: 2
Englishmen not polishable 140: 8
our brothers 141: 6
Enjoy: who saves should e. 317:13
Ennui: sign of intelligence 212:15
Enough said 385: 8
Ensign: tear tattered e.
down 162: 5
Entangle: never e. ourselves
in Europe 24: 1
why e. in toils of Europe .25: 7
Enterprise: free e. 134: 7
free private e. 135: 4
ounce of e. is worth 141:13
Enthusiasm **141**
great moment, triumph of e. 141:10
is leaping lightning 141: 9
nothing great without e. .141: 8
Entrances more dramatic ..103: 4
Envy **141**
hate most what e. most ..141:17
is for the dead 141:18
is ignorance 141:15
vice of republics 117: 4
Equal and exact justice ...15: 8
as men 117:10
both e. in the earth 185: 2
calling that which is just, e. 142: 3
man e. to every other man 142: 2
men e. before fish 392: 3
protection of laws 225:14
representation for e. numbers 20: 2
separate but e. 268: 9
talked long enough about e.
rights 142: 7
that all men created
e. 142:6, 209: 7
Equality **141**
beats inequality 142:-10